Revised Second Edition

Masterplots

1,801 Plot Stories and Critical Evaluations
of the World's Finest Literature

Revised Second Edition

Volume 6
Icl – Los
3111 – 3732

Edited by
FRANK N. MAGILL

Story Editor, Revised Edition
DAYTON KOHLER

Consulting Editor, Revised Second Edition
LAURENCE W. MAZZENO

SALEM PRESS

Pasadena, California   Englewood Cliffs, New Jersey

Editor in Chief: Dawn P. Dawson
Consulting Editor: Laurence W. Mazzeno   *Managing Editor:* Christina J. Moose
Project Editors: Eric Howard   *Research Supervisor:* Jeffry Jensen
Juliane Brand   *Research:* Irene McDermott
Acquisitions Editor: Mark Rehn   *Proofreading Supervisor:* Yasmine A. Cordoba
Production Editor: Cynthia Breslin Beres   *Layout:* William Zimmerman

Library of Congress Cataloging-in-Publication Data
Masterplots / edited by Frank N. Magill; consulting editor, Laurence W. Mazzeno. —
Rev. 2nd ed.
    p.   cm.
Expanded and updated version of the 1976 rev. ed.
Includes bibliographical references and indexes.
1. Literature—Stories, plots, etc. 2. Literature—History and criticism. I. Magill,
Frank Northen, 1907-   . II. Mazzeno, Laurence W.
PN44.M33   1996
809—dc20   96-23382
ISBN 0-89356-084-7 (set)   CIP
ISBN 0-89356-090-1 (volume 6)

Revised Second Edition
First Printing

PRINTED IN THE UNITED STATES OF AMERICA

LIST OF TITLES IN VOLUME 6

 page

I, Claudius—*Robert Graves* 3111
I Know Why the Caged Bird Sings—*Maya Angelou* 3116
The Iceman Cometh—*Eugene O'Neill* 3120
The Idiot—*Fyodor Dostoevski* 3124
Idylls—*Theocritus* 3128
Idylls of the King—*Alfred, Lord Tennyson* 3131
If Not Now, When?—*Primo Levi* 3136
Ignes de Castro—*Antonio Ferreira* 3140
The Iliad—*Homer* 3144
Imaginary Conversations of Literary Men and Statesmen—
   Walter Savage Landor 3149
The Imitation of Christ—*Thomas à Kempis* 3152
Immensee—*Theodor Storm* 3155
The Importance of Being Earnest—*Oscar Wilde* 3158
In Cold Blood—*Truman Capote* 3162
In Dubious Battle—*John Steinbeck* 3166
In Memoriam—*Alfred, Lord Tennyson* 3170
In the Heart of the Seas—*Shmuel Yosef Agnon* 3174
In the Wilderness—*Sigrid Undset* 3178
Independent People—*Halldór Laxness* 3182
Indian Summer—*William Dean Howells* 3187
Indiana—*George Sand* 3191
The Informer—*Liam O'Flaherty* 3195
The Inheritors—*William Golding* 3199
The Inspector General—*Nikolai Gogol* 3203
The Interpretation of Dreams—*Sigmund Freud* 3208
The Intruder—*Maurice Maeterlinck* 3212
Intruder in the Dust—*William Faulkner* 3217
Inundación castálida—*Sor Juana Inés de la Cruz* 3221
Invisible Man—*Ralph Ellison* 3224
The Invisible Man—*H. G. Wells* 3228
Iolanthe—*W. S. Gilbert* 3233
Ion—*Euripides* 3236
Iphigenia in Aulis—*Euripides* 3240

page

Iphigenia in Tauris—*Euripides* 3244
Irish Melodies—*Thomas Moore* 3248
Israel Potter—*Herman Melville* 3252
The Italian—*Ann Radcliffe* 3256
The Itching Parrot—*José Joaquín Fernández de Lizardi* 3263
Ivanhoe—*Sir Walter Scott* 3267

J. B.—*Archibald MacLeish* 3272
Jack of Newbery—*Thomas Deloney* 3276
Jack Sheppard—*William Harrison Ainsworth* 3281
Jacques the Fatalist and His Master—*Denis Diderot* 3286
Jane Eyre—*Charlotte Brontë* 3290
Jason and the Golden Fleece—*Unknown* 3295
Jealousy—*Alain Robbe-Grillet* 3299
Jennie Gerhardt—*Theodore Dreiser* 3303
Jerusalem Delivered—*Torquato Tasso* 3308
The Jew of Malta—*Christopher Marlowe* 3313
John Brown's Body—*Stephen Vincent Benét* 3317
John Halifax, Gentleman—*Dinah Maria Mulock* 3321
Jonathan Wild—*Henry Fielding* 3325
Jorrocks' Jaunts and Jollities—*Robert Smith Surtees* 3329
Joseph Andrews—*Henry Fielding* 3333
The Journal of a Tour to the Hebrides with Samuel Johnson, LL.D.—
   James Boswell 3338
A Journal of the Plague Year—*Daniel Defoe* 3341
Journal to Eliza—*Laurence Sterne* 3344
Journey to the End of the Night—*Louis-Ferdinand Céline* 3347
The Journey to the West—*Wu Ch'eng-en* 3351
The Joy Luck Club—*Amy Tan* 3355
Jude the Obscure—*Thomas Hardy* 3359
Julius Caesar—*William Shakespeare* 3364
July's People—*Nadine Gordimer* 3369
The Jungle—*Upton Sinclair* 3373
The Jungle Books—*Rudyard Kipling* 3377
Juno and the Paycock—*Sean O'Casey* 3382
Jurgen—*James Branch Cabell* 3387

Kalevala—*Elias Lönnrot* 3391
Das Kapital—*Karl Marx* 3396
Kenilworth—*Sir Walter Scott* 3399
Kidnapped—*Robert Louis Stevenson* 3403
Kim—*Rudyard Kipling* 3406

page

Kinflicks—*Lisa Alther* 3410
A King and No King—*Francis Beaumont* and *John Fletcher* 3414
King Horn—*Unknown* 3418
King Johan—*John Bale* 3422
King John—*William Shakespeare* 3426
King Lear—*William Shakespeare* 3430
King Solomon's Mines—*H. Rider Haggard* 3435
The King, the Greatest Alcalde—*Lope de Vega Carpio* 3440
Kiss of the Spider Woman—*Manuel Puig* 3445
The Knight of the Burning Pestle—*Francis Beaumont* 3449
The Knights—*Aristophanes* 3453
Krapp's Last Tape—*Samuel Beckett* 3457
The Kreutzer Sonata—*Leo Tolstoy* 3461
Kristin Lavransdatter—*Sigrid Undset* 3465

The Labyrinth of Solitude—*Octavio Paz* 3470
Lady Chatterley's Lover—*D. H. Lawrence* 3473
The Lady from the Sea—*Henrik Ibsen* 3477
The Lady of the Lake—*Sir Walter Scott* 3481
Lady Windermere's Fan—*Oscar Wilde* 3485
The Lady's Not for Burning—*Christopher Fry* 3489
The Lais of Marie de France—*Marie de France* 3493
Lalla Rookh—*Thomas Moore* 3500
Lancelot—*Chrétien de Troyes* 3505
Largo Desolato—*Václav Havel* 3509
The Last Chronicle of Barset—*Anthony Trollope* 3513
The Last Days of Pompeii—*Edward Bulwer-Lytton* 3517
The Last of the Mohicans—*James Fenimore Cooper* 3521
The Last of the Wine—*Mary Renault* 3526
The Last Puritan—*George Santayana* 3529
The Last Temptation of Christ—*Nikos Kazantzakis* 3533
The Last Tycoon—*F. Scott Fitzgerald* 3537
The Late George Apley—*John Phillips Marquand* 3540
Laughter—*Henri Bergson* 3545
Lavengro—*George Henry Borrow* 3548
The Lay of Igor's Campaign—*Unknown* 3552
The Lay of the Last Minstrel—*Sir Walter Scott* 3555
Lazarillo de Tormes—*Unknown* 3560
Leaves of Grass—*Walt Whitman* 3565
The Left Hand of Darkness—*Ursula K. Le Guin* 3569
The Legend of Good Women—*Geoffrey Chaucer* 3573
The Legend of Sleepy Hollow—*Washington Irving* 3576

page

The Leopard—*Giuseppe Tomasi di Lampedusa* 3580
Let Us Now Praise Famous Men—*James Agee* 3584
Letters from an American Farmer—*J. Hector St. John* 3587
Letters from the Underworld—*Fyodor Dostoevski* 3591
Letters to His Son—*Lord Chesterfield* 3596
Leviathan—*Thomas Hobbes* 3598
The Liar—*Pierre Corneille* 3602
Liber Amoris—*William Hazlitt* 3606
Lie Down in Darkness—*William Styron* 3609
The Life and Opinions of Tristram Shandy, Gent.—*Laurence Sterne* 3613
Life Is a Dream—*Pedro Calderón de la Barca* 3618
The Life of Marianne—*Marivaux* 3623
The Life of Samuel Johnson, LL.D.—*James Boswell* 3627
Life on the Mississippi—*Mark Twain* 3630
Ligeia—*Edgar Allan Poe* 3634
Light in August—*William Faulkner* 3638
Lightning—*Santō Kyōden* 3643
Liliom—*Ferenc Molnár* 3647
The Little Clay Cart—*Unknown* 3651
Little Dorrit—*Charles Dickens* 3655
The Little Foxes—*Lillian Hellman* 3659
Little Women—*Louisa May Alcott* 3662
Lives of the Poets—*Samuel Johnson* 3666
Lolita—*Vladimir Nabokov* 3669
A Long and Happy Life—*Reynolds Price* 3673
Long Day's Journey into Night—*Eugene O'Neill* 3677
The Long Journey—*Johannes V. Jensen* 3681
The Longest Journey—*E. M. Forster* 3687
A Longing for the Light—*Vicente Aleixandre* 3691
Look Back in Anger—*John Osborne* 3695
Look Homeward, Angel—*Thomas Wolfe* 3699
Looking Backward—*Edward Bellamy* 3703
Lord Jim—*Joseph Conrad* 3707
Lord of the Flies—*William Golding* 3711
Lorna Doone—*R. D. Blackmore* 3715
Lost Horizon—*James Hilton* 3719
Lost Illusions—*Honoré de Balzac* 3724
A Lost Lady—*Willa Cather* 3729

Revised Second Edition

I, CLAUDIUS

Type of work: Novel
Author: Robert Graves (1895-1985)
Type of plot: Historical
Time of plot: 10 B.C.E.-41 C.E.
Locale: Rome
First published: 1934

Principal characters:

TIBERIUS CLAUDIUS DRUSUS NERO GERMANICUS, the emperor of Rome
 after Caligula
AUGUSTUS CAESAR, the first emperor of Rome
LIVIA, his wife and Claudius' grandmother
JULIA, the daughter of Livia and Augustus
TIBERIUS, Claudius' uncle and successor to Augustus
GERMANICUS, Claudius' brother
CALIGULA, Germanicus' son and successor to Tiberius
URGULANILLA, Claudius' detested wife
POSTUMUS, Augustus' banished son
AGRIPPINA, Germanicus' wife
SEJANUS, a friend of Tiberius
AELIA, Sejanus' sister by adoption and Claudius' second wife
MACRO, the commander of the guards
MESSALINA, Claudius' third wife
CALPURNIA, Claudius' only true friend

The Story:

Claudius, the emperor of Rome, was held in little esteem because he was lame and he stammered. He was, moreover, a scholar in a nation that worshiped soldiering. He had compiled state histories, but he realized that they were dull, sententious drivel. At last, he decided to tell the true story of his own life. As the source of his inspiration, he cited the Cumaean sibyl whom he had visited in her inner cavern. She had said that eventually he would speak clearly.

From the beginning, the Claudian family felt ashamed of young Claudius, who seemed unlikely to carry on the family tradition of power. For that reason, he developed into a scholarly person interested in the lives of others. His teachers told him stories about famous people, and as he matured he picked up stray scraps of knowledge about them from various sources.

He was greatly interested in his grandmother, the Empress Livia. Bored with her husband, she had secured a divorce, arranged her own marriage with the Emperor Augustus, and poisoned thereafter anyone who interfered with her plans. Power was her sole delight. Another of the infamous people about him was Tiberius, who was for years the official successor of Augustus. Son of Livia by an early marriage, he married the wanton Julia, daughter of Livia and Augustus. Tiberius had offended Augustus and was banished. Livia then insisted that Julia be banished as well. Tired of his banishment, Tiberius promised that if Livia would secure his return he would agree with her every wish thereafter. About that time, the two sons of Julia and Tiberius died mysteriously.

Between Claudius' ninth and sixteenth years, he occupied himself with the affairs of his older relatives. He was married early to a girl named Urgulanilla, who detested him as much as he detested her. Claudius' first love had been mysteriously poisoned, and Claudius suspected Livia, who had later forced him to marry Urgulanilla. Claudius' scholarship and stability eventually brought him into the good graces of Augustus and Livia. They made him a priest of Mars and showed, by public displays of interest in him, that he was an accepted member of the imperial family.

A grain shortage caused rioting accompanied by arson. Augustus distributed grain according to the usual custom, banished such people as did not hold property in Rome, and rationed what food was available. Livia staged a sword fight in the arena to restore the goodwill of the populace. Because Claudius fainted publicly when witnessing the brutal sports, Livia decided that never again might he show his face in public. Soon afterward, the last of Augustus' sons was banished for life. Tiberius was proclaimed the adopted son and successor of Augustus.

Tiberius and young Germanicus, brother of Claudius, campaigned against the barbarians, but Tiberius was unpopular in spite of his victories with the army. Augustus suffered stomach disorders and died. Claudius knew that about a month before his death he had decided to restore his banished son, Postumus, grant money and honor to Claudius, and replace Tiberius. Claudius suspected Livia of the emperor's death.

Postumus was reported killed by a captain of the guard that had been placed around him. Livia slowly starved Julia to death. Because Germanicus was too honorable to seize the empire from Tiberius, there remained only the proof that Postumus was really dead to make Tiberius safe upon the throne. When Postumus returned to disprove reports of his death, Tiberius had him tortured and killed.

Germanicus continued his successful campaign against the Germans. Tiberius was jealous and insisted that Germanicus return to Rome for his triumph. By that time, Livia suspected Claudius and Germanicus of plotting against Tiberius. She sent Claudius to Carthage to dedicate a temple to Augustus, who had been deified by the Roman Senate. Germanicus was next dispatched to the east to command the armies there, but Livia and Tiberius began to fear that Germanicus would win favor in the east as he had already done in the west. Germanicus was finally poisoned. His wife, Agrippina, sought protection from Claudius.

Claudius promised his thirteen-year-old son in marriage to the daughter of Sejanus, the friend of Tiberius. A few days later, his son was found dead. He again suspected Livia. Shortly afterward, a divorce was arranged for Claudius by Sejanus, who was anxious to have Claudius marry Aelia, his sister by adoption. Claudius knew better than to oppose the wills of those in power, and he accepted his new wife with little concern.

Tiberius set Livia aside. She was now growing old, and he no longer had great reason to fear her. Bitter at the removal of her power, she began to make plans for his successor. She determined that Caligula, the son of Germanicus, should succeed him. She called in Claudius to declare a truce on the condition that he would have her declared a goddess after her death. In return, she told him most of her state secrets; she said that all the murders she had planned were committed solely for the good of the state.

Tiberius was sixty-seven years old and seemed destined to die soon. He was living on Capri with a court of scholars, doctors, confidants, and entertainers; Sejanus had been left in Rome with authority to rule for him. When Livia finally died at the age of eighty-six, Tiberius refused to return to Rome even for her funeral. He then began a reign of terror against all members of Livia's faction. When Sejanus attempted to rebel against the emperor's cruel decrees, Tiberius ordered his execution. His children were also put to death. Claudius was ordered to divorce Aelia.

At last, the mad Tiberius lay dying at Misenum. Macro, commander of the guards, and Caligula, next in line for the throne, planned to take over the country. Caligula, already infamous among people who knew him, was still popular with the Romans. They took command of the army in too great a hurry. Then, learning that Tiberius was still alive, they smothered him.

In order to establish himself, Caligula pretended sympathy and generosity, but Claudius wrote in his history that Caligula held the record for infamy among the princes up to that time. He began by spending the money Tiberius and Livia had hoarded for so long. Then he fell ill. When he began to recover, he announced to Claudius that he had been transformed into a god, in fulfillment of the many prophecies that a god was soon to be given to the earth.

Caligula celebrated his godhood by wholesale assassination. Claudius' mother committed suicide because of Caligula's infamies. Soon Macro was forced to kill himself. At last, the people began to turn against Caligula because of levies forced on the populace and of the indescribable depravities of the palace brothel. Caligula decided to become a general and led an expedition into Germany. On his return, he forced Claudius to marry his cousin Messalina. Calpurnia, Claudius' only true friend, was banished. The Romans were now plotting, almost openly, the assassination of Caligula. Before long he was murdered, and Claudius, the retiring scholar, was named the emperor of Rome.

Critical Evaluation:

Throughout his long career, Robert Graves considered himself first and foremost a poet. He published more than seventy volumes of poetry. He seems equally likely, however, to be remembered as a historical novelist, particularly as the author of *I, Claudius*. In a way, Graves resembles Sir Arthur Conan Doyle, who wanted to be recognized as an author of serious novels but whose memory survives primarily because he created the immortal Sherlock Holmes.

I, Claudius was a financial success when it was published in 1934 and has continued to be popular ever since. It was translated into seventeen languages and brought to the attention of additional millions of people around the world after being made into a television drama by the British Broadcasting Corporation (BBC) in 1976. Graves tells his story in the first person, using the ingenious fiction that the novel is a printed translation of the Emperor Claudius' actual "lost autobiography," which has been miraculously rediscovered in 1934 after having been thought to have been destroyed by war, accident, or natural disaster like so many other priceless artifacts of the ancient world.

Claudius has strong republican sympathies which he takes great pains to conceal, since he is well aware that many prominent citizens, including a number of his own friends and relatives, have lost their lives for being insufficiently supportive of the imperial system instituted by Augustus and his sinister wife Livia. Claudius' observations of the degeneration of Rome under three increasingly dangerous despots only confirm his belief that authoritarian rule spreads corruption. The thesis of *I, Claudius* might be summarized in an often-quoted statement by the British historian Lord Acton: "Power tends to corrupt, and absolute power corrupts absolutely." When, after Caligula's well-merited assassination, Claudius is forced to become emperor, he does so with the hope of finding a means of restoring a regenerative republican form of government. As a student of history, Claudius is one of the few surviving Romans who really understands what the republic was like before the dynasty of the Caesars.

It should be noted that, although Claudius is intelligent and well educated, Graves characterizes him as a child of his times who believes in the Greek and Roman gods, magic, conjuring, augury, omens, and prophecies. The modern reader can identify with Claudius while at the same time feeling somewhat superior. The reader can understand how the pagan view of the ancient Romans explains their odd combination of civilization and barbarity. By analogy, the modern reader can also see that contemporary society might be comparably benighted without people being able to realize that what they regard as the height of modernism might be just another primitive stage in humanity's upward struggle to attain true civilization, true justice, and true enlightenment.

In addition to dramatizing Roman history by fictionalizing it with a single-viewpoint character, Graves focuses and dramatizes his material by providing that character, Claudius, with a single guiding motivation which is the one consistent thread running through the long story of Rome under Augustus, Tiberius, and Caligula. Depicting a central character driven by a single dominant motivation gives history the quality of a story which traditional historical accounts rarely have. *I, Claudius* can be studied as a model historical novel.

Graves continues to humanize and dramatize his novel by projecting himself—his own tastes, opinions, problems, prejudices, and idiosyncracies—into his characters. One striking example is his depiction of the odd asexual relationship between Augustus and his wife Livia. Another is Claudius himself, who, according to Graves's depiction, had essentially passive, asexual relationships with all of his wives. Graves has been described as "incurably uxorious," the kind of man who is unusually submissive to his wife. Graves was married twice and had a long-term relationship with a third woman, the domineering Laura Riding, whose indelible influence on his writing has been the subject of much scholarly attention. It is largely because Graves put so much personal feeling into his historical novel that it evokes much stronger emotional interest than the ordinary history book.

I, Claudius has been called both a "Cinderella story" and an "ugly duckling story." Claudius' resilient, resourceful character was formed, according to Graves, by his physical sufferings and the mental sufferings inflicted by people who despised him for his handicaps. He acquired an unsentimental view of human nature which helped him survive in his perilous environment. He found solace in reading and on his own initiative became one of the most learned men of his time. Again, Claudius resembles Graves himself, who was despised, ridiculed, and tormented at school because his intelligence and poetic sensitivity made him conspicuously different from the other boys in his boarding school. Graves, who knew both Greek and Latin, also buried himself in reading and was able to write about the ancient Mediterranean world with ease and authority when he decided to create his most famous novel.

Reading *I, Claudius* provides not only an opportunity to travel back in time to the ancient Roman world but also an opportunity to share in the wisdom and sensibilities of Robert Graves, poet, novelist, historian, and one of the best educated and most gifted authors of the twentieth century. *I, Claudius* makes readers aware of the reality of history—that Augustus, Livia, Tiberius, Caligula, and all the others were not mere names in books but real people who, like ourselves, believed they were living in "modern times" and who loved and hated and experienced all the emotions that every human being experiences.

I, Claudius continues to inspire readers with a desire to look deeper into ancient history, while it continues to inspire others to learn more about Robert Graves's long and interesting life. His autobiographical work *Goodbye to All That* (1929) is a fascinating book which tells about his unhappiness at school, his struggles to become a writer, and his harrowing experiences in World War I. He knew many of the most important writers of his time and has had a lasting influence on English and American literature.

"Critical Evaluation" by Bill Delaney

Bibliography:

Bloom, Harold, ed. *Robert Graves*. New York: Chelsea House, 1987. Bloom gathers what he calls the most useful available criticism of Graves. Entries most pertinent to the study of *I, Claudius* are "Autobiography, Historical Novels, and Some Poems," by J. M. Cohen, and "Claudius," by Martin Seymour-Smith.

Canary, Robert H. *Robert Graves*. Boston: G. K. Hall, 1980. Contains a biography and a thorough discussion of Graves as poet and prose writer, with one section devoted to *I, Claudius* and its sequel, *Claudius the God and His Wife Messalina*.

Graves, Robert. *Claudius the God and His Wife Messalina*. New York: Smith and Haas, 1935. Readers who enjoy *I, Claudius* will want to continue Claudius' story with this sequel, which takes up exactly where *I, Claudius* ends. It covers Claudius' successful reign as emperor and his death by murder.

Seymour-Smith, Martin. *Robert Graves: His Life and Work*. New York: Holt, Rinehart and Winston, 1982. A full-length, definitive biography by a friend who knew Graves for more than forty years. Discusses Graves's interest in ancient history and contains much information about the creation of *I, Claudius*. Good photographic illustrations.

Suetonius. *The Twelve Caesars*. Translated by Robert Graves. London: Penguin, 1957. Graves, who achieved distinction as a translator, drew on the Roman historian Gaius Suetonius Tranquillus (69-122) for information fictionalized in *I, Claudius* and its sequel. Since *I, Claudius* is a popular introduction to Roman history, Suetonius himself is an easy next step for further exploration.

I KNOW WHY THE CAGED BIRD SINGS

Type of work: Novel
Author: Maya Angelou (Marguerite Johnson, 1928-   )
Type of plot: Social realism
Time of plot: 1930's-1940's
Locale: Arkansas, Missouri, and California
First published: 1970

> *Principal characters:*
> MARGUERITE (MAYA) JOHNSON
> BAILEY JOHNSON, JR., her brother
> ANNIE HENDERSON (MOMMA), her paternal grandmother
> UNCLE WILLIE, her paternal uncle
> VIVIAN BAXTER JOHNSON, her mother
> BAILEY JOHNSON, SR., her father

The Story:

Marguerite and Bailey, Jr. were sent by their newly divorced parents to Stamps, Arkansas, when they were three and four, respectively, to live with their grandmother, Momma. Momma, a staid Christian woman, owned the William Johnson General Merchandise Store that made a solid living for her and her crippled son, Willie. She set, in her no-nonsense way, about raising her grandchildren to use their minds, mind their manners, and survive in the Depression-era South.

Marguerite and Bailey were bright children. They soon took pleasure in learning to read and do their numbers. They also learned while still quite small to deal very carefully with white people. On more than one occasion the family faced a very real danger of a Ku Klux Klan atrocity. It was a given that black people were generally powerless against white people.

Marguerite watched her proud stoic grandmother deal with the "powhitetrash" children who sometimes came around the store, trying to goad Momma into some kind of undignified reaction. A group of poor white girls cavorted for several minutes one time in front of Momma, who stood at the door of her store, softly humming a hymn. One girl, wearing no underwear, did a revealing handstand right in front of Momma, who did not miss a beat in her humming. When the girls finally tired of the game and went off, saying "'Bye, Annie," Momma, with her dignity intact, said good-bye to each one of them by name.

When Marguerite was six, her father came to Stamps to visit and to take her and Bailey to St. Louis to stay with their mother. Both children were stunned to discover that the parents they had assumed were dead were in fact alive. Bailey, Jr. fell in love at first sight with his beautiful, vivacious mother. Marguerite, more reserved, held back her feeling until she was sure that the beautiful creature truly accepted her smart but very plain daughter.

In St. Louis, Marguerite and Bailey met Grandmother and Grandfather Baxter and learned what it meant to live almost like a white family. Grandmother Baxter was a precinct captain in St. Louis politics and had considerable clout. Her three strapping sons who were, according to Angelou, mean as snakes were as menacing as Grandmother Baxter's political power. This brought the family a wary and widespread respect unfamiliar to Marguerite.

While in St. Louis, Marguerite, at age eight, was raped by her mother's lover, Mr. Freeman. When her mother found out—Marguerite tried to hide it because Mr. Freeman had threatened to kill Bailey, Jr. if she told—Mr. Freeman was arrested and tried. Although convicted and sentenced to a year and a day, he was released on the same day. Later that same day, he was "found dead on the lot behind the slaughterhouse." Marguerite's reaction to his killing was to believe that her talking to and about others was dangerous, so she decided not to speak to anyone except Bailey, for fear that whomever she talked to or about would die. Her continued silence over a period of time finally so exasperated her family that she and Bailey were sent back to Stamps.

Back in Stamps, Marguerite's continued silence was eventually breached by Miss Bertha Flowers, an acquaintance of Momma's. She enticed Marguerite to read literary works aloud and to memorize and recite poetry. Marguerite eventually regained her self-esteem. She was able to put her St. Louis experience in perspective: She was not the bad and dangerous person she had thought she was.

By the time Marguerite was graduated from the eighth grade, she had acquired her first real friend, Louise Kendricks. Bailey had had his first sexual relationship with an older girl, who taught him to steal from Momma's store and who ultimately ran off to marry a railroad man.

Momma decided that Marguerite and Bailey, now in their teens, should go to live with their parents, who both lived in California. World War II had started, and black folks were moving into California neighborhoods recently vacated by interned Japanese Americans. Marguerite and Bailey adapted well to their new life. She spent a summer in Southern California with her father. He took her on an overnight trip to Mexico, which caused a fight between Marguerite and his fiancée. Marguerite ran away and for a month lived in a junkyard with other homeless children. She finally returned to her mother's home, none the worse for her experiences.

Bailey, Jr. had become so "mannish" that his mother ordered him to leave her house. When he did, Marguerite began to feel the need to be more independent. She got a job, becoming the first African American conductorette on a San Francisco streetcar. School had lost much of its charm, but she recognized the need to finish high school.

Also at this time, Marguerite began to worry about her femininity. Her body had few of the contours of a sixteen-year-old. She began to think she might be a lesbian. To prove to herself that she was not, she seduced a neighbor boy and got pregnant. No one was aware, though, even as she was graduated from high school with only about a month before the baby was due. She finally told her mother about the impending birth. Her family rallied around her and she gave birth to a son.

Critical Evaluation:

I Know Why the Caged Bird Sings has been called autobiography by some and a novel by others. Organized episodically, it moves chronologically from the early 1930's through the early 1940's. It begins when Marguerite and Bailey are three and four and ends just after V-Day and her high school graduation. In describing what happened to the main character, Marguerite Johnson, it shows what happened in the black communities of Stamps, Arkansas; St. Louis; and parts of wartime California.

Autobiographical elements include what happened to Marguerite and her family and how she felt, as an adult, about the people and events. The novelistic elements include her graphic and detailed reconstruction of long-past events and conversations. The resulting work creates a character in Marguerite Johnson who is intelligent, curious, perceptive, and fascinated by all kinds of things. What she endured, the events and people who touched her life, all are blended into a mélange of appealing stories.

Nearly every episode seems to have at least one of two aims—to give a picture of what it was like to be an African American during the Great Depression and World War II, and to show how one very determined black girl faced obstacles, overcame them, and triumphed. The dangers of being black in the days before the civil rights struggle is illustrated in the episode in which crippled Uncle Willie must hide all night in a hidden compartment of the store's potato bin because the Ku Klux Klan is on the rampage. Another episode shows Marguerite working as a maid in a white household and being called "Mary" because the white mistress of the house decides "Marguerite" is too much name for her to have to say. When the entire black community of Stamps gathers around the store's radio to hear the Joe Louis-Primo Carnera fight, Angelou re-creates the pride blacks felt in their hero. When it seemed that Louis might lose, she said, "my race groaned. It was our people falling. . . . A Black boy whipped and maimed . . . hounds on the trail of a man . . . a white woman slapping her maid. . . . We didn't breathe. We didn't hope. We waited." Then when Louis knocked out his white opponent and was announced "still heavyweight champion of the world," the black people of Stamps, clearly representative of black people all over America, celebrated. Another time when Marguerite had a bad toothache, her grandmother took her to the only dentist in Stamps, a white man to whom Momma had lent money during the Depression. He utterly refused to help, saying, "I'd rather stick my hand in a dog's mouth" than in the mouth of any black person. Angelou's reaction was to fantasize that her grandmother got revenge by humiliating the dentist and putting him out of business. These and other episodes depict many other aspects of the black experience, enhancing what is conveyed blandly, if at all, in history books.

Maya Angelou's affinity for poetry is evident in her writing style, full of poetic imagery and unusual phraseology. She mixes African American sayings and idioms to achieve her own inimitable mode of expression. The book begins with the African American rhyme, "What you looking at me for?/ I didn't come to stay./ I just came to tell you,/ it's Easter Day." She describes "the kissing sounds of the tires" on her father's car as they drive to St. Louis. A summer afternoon is recalled as "sweetmilk fresh in [her] memory." Vomiting is described as "My lunch was in my mouth a second time."

Some figures of speech are not successful. They sometimes require rereading to grasp the intent. For example, Angelou describes a set of false teeth as "looking empty—and at the same time appearing to contain all the emptiness in the world." For the most part, however, the language of the narration and the dialogue is fresh, vivid, and characteristic of twentieth century African American expression.

Angelou's kind of black family is not often the subject of literature. Her grandparents on both sides are not only hard-working but successful. Hard work has often been shown as the lot of black people, particularly before the 1960's. Almost always, the result of their labor was minimal subsistence. The Johnsons and the Baxters not only made a good living, they were also in a position to help others. They are seen as realizing to a great extent the American Dream, and Angelou shows herself and her brother Bailey as growing up with the American Dream of being educated and successful.

I Know Why the Caged Bird Sings does for the Southern rural black experience what James Baldwin's *Go Tell It on the Mountain* (1953) does for the Northern urban black experience. Its historical commentary is instructive about the Depression in the South. The portrayal of a young woman's search for identity is unforgettable.

Jane Lee Ball

Bibliography:

Demetrakopoulos, Stephanie A. "The Metamorphosis of Matrilinearism in Women's Autobiography." In *Women's Autobiography*, edited by Estelle C. Jelinek. Bloomington: Indiana University Press, 1980. *I Know Why the Caged Bird Sings* is one of four modern women's autobiographies analyzed.

Fox-Genovese, Elizabeth. "Myth and History: Discourse of Origins in Zora Neale Hurston and Maya Angelou." *Black American Literature Forum* 24 (Summer, 1990): 221-235. Discusses plot and themes of *I Know Why the Caged Bird Sings* along with Hurston's *Dust Tracks on a Road* (1942).

Graham, Joyce. "Making Language Sing: An Interview with Maya Angelou." *Journal of Reading* 34 (February, 1991): 406-410. Angelou discusses her technique writing *I Know Why the Caged Bird Sings* and what she tried to achieve artistically.

Lupton, Mary Jane. "Singing the Black Mother: Maya Angelou and Autobiographical Continuity." *Black American Literature Forum* 24 (Summer, 1990): 257-276. Shows how Angelou achieves continuity from one autobiographical volume to the next. Analyzes her autobiographical series with particular emphasis on *I Know Why the Caged Bird Sings* and the theme of motherhood.

McPherson, Dolly A. *Order Out of Chaos: The Autobiographical Works of Maya Angelou*. New York: Peter Lang, 1990. Examines the organization of Angelou's autobiographical works around certain recurring themes. An addendum contains an insightful and illuminating interview with Angelou that throws new light on *I Know Why the Caged Bird Sings*.

Washington, Carla. "Maya Angelou's Angelic Aura." *The Christian Century* 105 (November 16, 1988): 1031-1032. Proposes that Angelou's work, especially *I Know Why the Caged Bird Sings*, has a quality of spirituality. Focuses on the religious events and spiritual concerns of the novel.

THE ICEMAN COMETH

Type of work: Drama
Author: Eugene O'Neill (1888-1953)
Type of plot: Tragedy
Time of plot: 1912
Locale: Harry Hope's Saloon, New York City
First performed: 1946; first published, 1946

Principal characters:

HARRY HOPE, the proprietor of a saloon and rooming house
LARRY SLADE, a former Syndicalist-Anarchist
THEODORE "HICKEY" HICKMAN, a hardware salesman
DON PARRITT, the newest and youngest roomer

The Story:

It was early morning in the summer of 1912. In the back room and a section of the bar of Harry Hope's saloon, with tables and chairs squeezed closely together, nine men were seated, mostly dozing, at the tables, including sixty-year-old host Harry Hope and Larry Slade, about the same age. Larry's expression of tired tolerance gave his face "the quality of a pitying but weary old priest's." These men were alcoholics who frequented the saloon. With the exception of the black Joe Mott, they were also roomers who lived on the upstairs floors. All were eagerly awaiting the arrival of the salesman Hickey, due to join them to celebrate Hope's birthday the next day. Larry, contemplating his friends' and his addiction to alcohol, commented in an early speech, "The lie of a pipe dream is what gives life to the whole misbegotten mad lot of us."

Don Parritt, an eighteen-year-old, good-looking but unpleasant fellow who had rented one of Hope's rooms the previous night, engaged Larry in an intense conversation. Don was the only son of Rosa Parritt, an anarchist leader arrested and imprisoned for a bombing on the West Coast. Larry speculated that some member of the movement had betrayed Rosa Parritt to the police and hoped that the informer's soul would rot in hell. He had left the movement eleven years ago, having come to regard humanity as too base for its idealism. Parritt described his mother as an independent, fierce-willed woman who had taken and abandoned many men, including Larry. Sardonically, Larry told Parritt not to expect any intimacy from him, because he had none left to give and only wished to be left alone.

Willie Oban, a dropout from Harvard Law School, hoped that "Hickey or Death would come!" Two streetwalkers, Margie and Pearl, returned from their night's work and turned their earnings over to Rocky, the night bartender, who deeply resented being called a pimp, just as they insisted that they were tarts, not whores. The day bartender, Chuck, a tough but amiable Italian American, entered with his girlfriend Cora, a thin blonde several years older than Pearl and Margie. Cora was also a prostitute.

Toward the end of Act I Hickey finally arrived, a roly-poly man of fifty, with a salesman's affable, hearty personality. Warmly welcomed, he shocked his friends by announcing his abstention from alcohol and his evangelical program for these derelicts: He would rescue them from the illusions of their "pipe dreams," would force them to confront themselves honestly and realistically; then they would find the peace that he now had.

In Act II the regulars assembled toward midnight for Harry Hope's long-awaited birthday party. They were anxious and irritable: Hickey had spoken to many of them in their rooms, urging them to discard their delusions. The women, for example, should admit to themselves that they were whores and that the bartenders were pimps. Larry should befriend Parritt and help him punish himself for having betrayed his mother to the police. Mosher should return to the circus; and Harry Hope should leave his saloon and reacquaint himself with the neighborhood. As for Hickey, he announced, as a climax to the birthday celebration, that Evelyn had died and that he felt no grief for his "dearly beloved" mate. She had found her peace at last, released from his faithless and drunken ways.

Act III took place in the middle of the next morning. The sobered residents of the saloon turned in their room keys, resigned to risking life in the outside world. Their mood was bellicose. Chuck and Cora, then Chuck and Rocky, quarreled. Joe was subjected to racial taunts and in turn threatened others with his knife. Piet, a former Boer commando, and Cecil, a former British officer, refought the Boer War. Larry blamed Hickey for everyone's bad humor: "Didn't I tell you he'd brought death with him?"

As the roomers hesitated to step outside the building, Harry Hope and Jimmy entered the bar, followed by Hickey, who goaded them to leave the premises. Harry was particularly hesitant to stroll outdoors. He finally did so, only to lurch back into the bar after a few minutes, complaining of the heavy automobile traffic and desperate for a drink. Larry angrily confronted Hickey, demanding a clear accounting of his wife's death. Hickey responded, to everyone's shock, that Evelyn had been shot to death.

The last act occurred at 1:30 A.M. the following day. All the habitués had returned by now to the saloon, their expectations of self-improvement shattered. The room's atmosphere was one of "oppressive stagnation." Parritt pleaded with Larry to advise him what to do, now that his mother had been convicted. Larry refused to be Parritt's "executioner." Then Hickey returned, having made a phone call, but his manner was no longer confident.

In a long monologue, occasionally interrupted by one of the regulars, Hickey revealed that he had murdered his wife. He recalled his early life in a small town, where he had drunk and whored in rebellion against his strict father. He and Evelyn had loved each other from an early age, and she would always forgive him after he had confessed his alcoholic binges and infidelities. Her pardoning him for his sins and her persistent yet ineffectual efforts to reform him only succeeded in making him feel worthless. "There's a limit," he told his listeners, "to the guilt you can feel and the forgiveness and pity you can take!" Finally, Hickey decided he could no longer bear his humiliation, that he needed to free Evelyn from her—and his—misery in loving him. So he had shot her in her sleep.

Hickey's confession caused Parritt to unburden himself in parallel fashion regarding his feelings toward his mother. He admitted to Larry that he had betrayed his mother because he hated her, causing Larry to shout at him to "get the hell out of life." Parritt thanked Larry for his judgment, went up to his room, and threw himself off the balcony to his death. Two policemen arrived to arrest Hickey for murder. Before they led him away, Hickey called himself "insane" for having expressed hatred for Evelyn. Harry Hope and the other derelicts eagerly seized upon Hickey's last remarks. They decided that he had been insane and that his exhortations to them that they should abandon their pipe dreams had been "nutty." They resumed their heavy drinking. After Hickey had been arrested and Parritt had committed suicide, Larry expressed the wish that he himself would die soon, concluding, "Be God, I'm the only real convert to death Hickey made here."

Critical Evaluation:

The Iceman Cometh is a memory play, with Eugene O'Neill's homeless outcasts drawn from people he had known, a generation earlier, during his vagabond period. Harry Hope's saloon is primarily derived from a New York waterfront dive, Jimmy the Priest's, where O'Neill had often stayed in 1911 and 1912, subsisting on free lunches and cheap beer between jobs as a seaman. He also drew on characters he had met during a time in the Hell Hole, a Greenwich Village barroom-hotel, and the taproom of the Garden Hotel, located across the street from Madison Square Garden. The prototype for Harry Hope, for example, was Tom Wallace, proprietor of the Hell Hole.

The Iceman Cometh is commonly regarded, along with O'Neill's *Long Day's Journey into Night* (1956), as among the most impressive dramatic achievements of the twentieth century. Its theme, that most human beings cannot live without illusions, parallels that of Henrik Ibsen's *The Wild Duck* (1884), while its seedy, dissipated characters and gloomy setting resemble Maxim Gorky's *The Lower Depths* (1902).

O'Neill assembles fifteen illusionists, all of whom live on alcohol and the pipe dream that they have been or some day will be happy and respectable. The large cast results in an extremely long play, and since each character restates his or her single obsession, the work can also be faulted for being boringly repetitious. O'Neill indulges in his restatements with full awareness of their effect, seeking to achieve a lyric, incantatory effect. The sum of his many characters' self-deluded dreams is intended to represent no less than the total content of human illusion.

Political illusions are illustrated by Hugo's will to power through his pretended love of the proletariat. Racial illusions are brought to light by Joe's insistence on his equality with whites. Domestic illusions are maintained by Chuck and Cora's fantasy of marriage and a farm. Status illusions are manifested by the prostitutes' refusal to recognize their whoredom or the bartenders' refusal to admit their pimp status. Psychological illusions belong to Parritt's recital of false motives for having betrayed his mother. Intellectual illusions belong to Willie for citing excuses to explain his failure to finish law school. Philosophical illusions are held by Larry Slade as he parades his detachment from all issues and problems. Religious illusions are harbored by Hickey when he professes to have discovered peace and salvation. Together, these outcasts constitute a family of humanity, each able to discern the lie of the other but not his or her own. Before Hickey's arrival and evangelism, the people exist in relative harmony and toleration by adhering to a vague anticipation of tomorrow, that day when they will confront their feelings and surmount them.

Against this escapism into tomorrow, Hickey insists on interposing his doctrine of today, thereby forcing the unhappy derelicts to live their lives without illusions. Hickey's antagonist is Larry Slade. Larry is often doomed to passivity by his penchant for seeing both sides of an issue. He is, however, instinctively kind and compassionate and tries to protect his friends, as well as himself, from Hickey's drive to destroy all their pipe dreams. Whereas Hickey is certain that only the truth will bring people peace, Larry knows that their survival, uncertain as it is, requires self-deception and mutual deception.

In this play O'Neill rejects any superhuman providence, affirming only humaneness, pity, and friendship. Beneath the text's realistic surface, he develops an ironic Christian parable. Hickey's long-delayed entrance has supernatural implications: "Would that Hickey or Death would come," groans one character. Hickey is identified not only with death—he is, after all, a killer—but also with the iceman, whose coming is a parody of the savior's arrival. Hickey turns out to be the false messiah, and Parritt is like Judas Iscariot, having betrayed his mother for money. Larry, admitting at the end that he has developed into the only convert to Hickey's religion of death, assumes the role of Peter, the rock on which Hickey builds his false church.

Hickey escapes tragic dimensions by pleading insanity, so he can escape the grim realization that he hated his forgiving wife. He joins the other derelicts by embracing his own delusion. Larry Slade, however, is too truthful to lie and too cowardly to take his life, as Parritt does. He stares grimly into the abyss as the play ends.

Gerhard Brand

Bibliography:
Bogard, Travis. *Contour in Time: The Plays of Eugene O'Neill.* New York: Oxford University Press, 1972. Unites theatrical understanding with textual insights. Emphasizes the resemblance of *The Iceman Cometh*, in its use of the chorus, to Greek tragedy.
Cargill, Oscar, N. Bryllion Fagin, and W. J. Fisher, eds. *O'Neill and His Plays.* New York: New York University Press, 1961. A collection of reviews and articles, including Helen Muchnic's important essay comparing *The Iceman Cometh* to Maxim Gorky's *The Lower Depths.*
Falk, Doris V. *Eugene O'Neill and the Tragic Tension.* New Brunswick, N.J.: Rutgers University Press, 1958. Brilliant and short interpretive study, astute in analyzing Larry Slade.
Floyd, Virginia. *The Plays of Eugene O'Neill: A New Assessment.* New York: Frederick Ungar, 1987. Reviews the plot of the play in detail.
Raleigh, John Henry. *The Plays of Eugene O'Neill.* Carbondale: Southern Illinois University Press, 1965. Stresses the autobiographical and sociological elements in *The Iceman Cometh*. Argues that the characters form a hierarchy, not a democracy.

THE IDIOT

Type of work: Novel
Author: Fyodor Dostoevski (1821-1881)
Type of plot: Psychological realism
Time of plot: Mid-nineteenth century
Locale: St. Petersburg, Russia
First published: Idiot, 1868-1869 (English translation, 1887)

> Principal characters:
> PRINCE LEF NICOLAIEVITCH MYSHKIN
> PARFEN ROGOZHIN, a friend of the prince
> MADAME EPANCHIN, a friend and relative of the prince
> AGLAYA EPANCHIN, her daughter
> NATASYA FILIPOVNA, Aglaya's rival
> GANYA ARDALIONOVITCH, the secretary to General Epanchin

The Story:

After four years spent in Switzerland, where he was treated for epilepsy at a sanatorium, Prince Myshkin returned to St. Petersburg. On the train, the threadbare shabbiness of his clothing attracted the attention of the other passengers. One of these, Parfen Rogozhin, began to question him. By the time they reached St. Petersburg, the prince and Rogozhin were well informed about each other, and Rogozhin offered to take the prince to his home and to give him money.

Myshkin, however, first wanted to introduce himself to General Epanchin, whose wife was distantly related to him. At the Epanchin home, he met the general and his secretary, Ganya, who invited him to become one of his mother's boarders. The prince interested the general, who gave him some money, and fascinated the general's wife and three daughters. His lack of sophistication, his naïveté, and his frankness charmed and amused the family. Soon they began to call him "the idiot," half in jest, half in earnest, but he remained on good terms with them.

Ganya, a selfish young man given to all kinds of scheming, wanted to marry the beautiful Aglaya Epanchin, chiefly for her money. At the time, he was also involved in an affair with the notorious Natasya, an attractive young woman who lived under the protection of a man she did not love. Extremely emotional and neurotic, Natasya was really innocent of the sins with which she was charged. Myshkin realized her helplessness and pitied her. At a drinking party one night soon after his arrival, he asked her to marry him, saying that he had received an unexpected inheritance. She refused, declaring that she had no desire to cause his ruin. Instead she went with Rogozhin, who had brought her a hundred thousand rubles. More than ever, Natasya became the object of spirited controversy among the Epanchins and their circle. Myshkin alone remained unembittered and always kindhearted. Ganya and Rogozhin poured out their troubles to him, bared the sordidness and shamelessness of their lives, and swore undying friendship to him. They nevertheless distrusted Myshkin and plotted against him. When Natasya left Rogozhin, he swore that he would kill "the idiot" because he was sure that Natasya had fled from him because she really loved Myshkin.

Myshkin then became the victim of an extortion attempt. During a violent, repugnant scene, at which the Epanchins were present, he successfully refuted the charge that he had deprived Rogozhin's supposed illegitimate son of his rightful inheritance. Having proved that the individual who sought the money was not the illegitimate son, he then offered to give money to the extortionist and to become his friend. This action disgusted Madame Epanchin, who considered the prince more of an idiot than ever.

Meanwhile, Aglaya Epanchin fell in love with Myshkin, but she continued to treat him scornfully and at first refused to admit that she was in love with him. When her true feelings at last became apparent, Madame Epanchin gave reluctant consent to their betrothal and planned an evening party to introduce Myshkin to St. Petersburg society. Worried lest he should commit some social blunder, she and her daughter advised him to sit quietly and to say nothing during the evening. At the party, however, Madame Epanchin herself drew out the prince, so that he was soon launched on one of his wild and peculiar conversations. The staid, conservative guests were astounded. In the midst of the discussion, he knocked over a huge and priceless vase, then stared at the debris like "an idiot." A few minutes later, he fell into an epileptic fit and had to be carried to his home. For several days, the Epanchins were cold to him, but Madame Epanchin finally relented and invited him to their home once more.

In the meantime, Aglaya had been corresponding with Natasya, and a friendship had strangely developed between them. One evening Aglaya asked Myshkin to go with her to see Natasya. In Natasya's apartment a hectic and turbulent argument developed, so that the two women showed their anger and bitterness against each other. For the first time Aglaya revealed fully her love for Myshkin. During the argument, Natasya fainted. When Myshkin rushed to her aid, Aglaya considered herself rejected and angrily left the house. The scene between the two women became a scandal, and the Epanchins barred their home to Myshkin. Natasya agreed to marry him and made preparations for the wedding, but on the day of the wedding, while Myshkin waited at the church, Natasya fled with Rogozhin, still haunted by her own helplessness and his terrible possessiveness.

Myshkin received the news calmly. Although there were many who laughed at "the idiot," there were some who were sorry for him when he attempted to discover Natasya's whereabouts. He left the village where the ceremony was to have been performed and went to the city. There he inquired among Natasya's acquaintances, but nobody knew where she was. Finally he went to Rogozhin's apartment and learned from a porter that Rogozhin had slept there the previous night. Myshkin continued his search, convinced that Rogozhin would kill him if he could. Rogozhin himself, however, stopped him on the street and took him to the apartment where Myshkin found Natasya lying on the bed. Rogozhin had killed her.

Filled with compassion for the miserable Rogozhin, Myshkin spent that night with the body of Natasya and her murderer. At daybreak Natasya's worried friends and the police broke into the apartment. Rogozhin confessed to the murder. Myshkin was questioned by the police, but he was not implicated in the crime. He was sent back to the sanatorium in Switzerland where he was visited, from time to time, by the Epanchin family and other friends. There was little hope that he would ever recover from his epilepsy.

Critical Evaluation:

The Idiot has been faulted for technical imperfections as a novel. Such imperfections do indeed exist. The novel begins well—in fact shows outstanding promise—but as it progresses, the author's control over his material seems to deteriorate. Consequently, the latter part of the novel, despite occasional flashes of brilliance, appears ill-conceived and sloppily written. In all fairness, however, consideration must be given to the circumstances under which Fyodor Mikhailovich Dostoevski was working when he wrote *The Idiot*. He was living abroad with his second wife (the first had died in 1864), moving too frequently to put down roots in any one place. During this period, he suffered severe attacks of epilepsy. His first child was born and died three months after birth. He gambled compulsively, was constantly in debt to his publisher for advances on the novel, and felt intermittent guilt about subjecting his wife and child to privation because of his gambling. Shortly after the death of the first child, whom Dostoevski mourned excessively, his wife became pregnant again, adding more worries and responsibilities to Dostoevski's already heavy burden. Under these conditions and demands, Dostoevski wrote *The Idiot*.

The Idiot has also been blamed for obscurity. Without a doubt, it has languished in the shadow of its two more renowned siblings, *Crime and Punishment* (1866) and *The Brothers Karamazov* (1879-1880). That kind of obscurity, however, is an equivocation of the term. The obscurity charge leveled at *The Idiot* is really one of impenetrability, the inability of the reader to grasp what is happening in the novel. Much of this confusion is simply a failure not of the novel but of the Western mind to apprehend the essence of the Russian soul, for *The Idiot* is a quintessentially Russian novel. Its uniqueness—and hence its so-called obscurity—derives from the distinctive qualities of the Russian psyche unfamiliar to Western readers. At least seven such qualities can be identified.

First is the concept of Russian brotherhood. It is illustrated, among other places, in Myshkin's return from Switzerland when he is befriended en route by Rogozhin, a complete stranger, and on arrival by the Epanchins. The concept, however, is not thus limited. Myshkin's enduring reputation as "the idiot" with the Epanchins and others throughout the novel evidences an affectionate alliance or brotherhood often underappreciated in the West.

Another trait is an unmethodical approach to life. Western people tend to place high value on social ritual and punctuality; however, Russians express themselves spontaneously and observe time schedules only when the schedules do not interfere with the more important business of living. Such a tendency leads to a rather irrational attitude toward handling the necessary trivialities as well as the serious aspects of everyday life. Hence, against all logic and reason, Myshkin proposed marriage to Natasya. Myshkin does not calculate advantages and disadvantages; he simply responds automatically to what each situation requires. His impulsive behavior, like the impulsive behavior of many others in the novel, is typically Russian.

Russian people are also compassionate and humble. The Epanchins, with affectionate compassion, refer to Myshkin as "the idiot." Myshkin's own compassion is demonstrated in his impulsive proposal of marriage to Natasya. In fact, Myshkin, throughout the novel, remains kindhearted and compassionate. Likewise, he is humble, just as are—ultimately—Natasya, Rogozhin, Ganya, and the Epanchins.

Religiosity is yet another Russian characteristic manifested in *The Idiot*. This quality is particularly demonstrated in Myshkin's peculiar diatribe at Madame Epanchin's party when he launches upon a recollection of four conversations which he had concerning the matter of faith. It is evidence of the Russians' unquestioning devotion to Eastern Orthodox Christianity. In fact, Dostoevski even goes so far as to allege that Roman Catholicism and socialism are working conjointly toward imposing authoritarian goals and standards, whereas Eastern Orthodoxy encourages individuality—albeit within a set standard of ethics. This logic can be understood only within the framework of the faithful believer.

The belief in the messianic destiny of Russia adds still another dimension to Dostoevski's view of the Russian soul in *The Idiot*. This belief manifests itself as a sense of honor, which is best displayed when Myshkin goes to Rogozhin's apartment only to find the dead body of Natasya. Myshkin spends the night with Rogozhin, the murderer, and Natasya's corpse—performing his honorable duty. The next morning, Rogozhin confesses to the police that he murdered Natasya. These dutiful observances of honorable behavior are, in the context of the novel, attributed to proper Russian conduct. As such, they are individual contributions to Russia's manifest destiny in fulfillment of her obligation to save the world from perdition.

Closely allied to this Russian mission to save the world is the practice of public confession. This practice, too, is intimately connected with the difference between Roman Catholicism and Eastern Orthodoxy. The former requires whispered revelations to a closeted priest; the latter mandates publicly spoken admission of wrongdoing to the full congregation. Consonantly, Ganya and Rogozhin make "confessions" of misdeeds early in the novel. Other characters as well confess transgressions—as Rogozhin confesses murder to Myshkin—throughout the novel. Everyone, it seems, has some dirty little secret hidden away and, finally, can hide it no longer, "confessing" it to someone else. Such purgation is but another typical Russian trait.

The last essential Russian quality in *The Idiot* is the warping effect of the conflict between humility and pride. On the most literal level, this trait is demonstrated by Rogozhin's vow to kill "the idiot" because Rogozhin is sure that Natasya left him for Myshkin, while, as a consequence, Myshkin becomes an extortion victim for being deluded by the same misapprehensions. On a more sophisticated level, all the characters in the novel are warped by the conflict between pride and humility. They are, in effect, the double personalities so typical in Dostoevski's novels. Myshkin, for example, is Dostoevski's penultimate Christ figure as well as the idiot savant of folklore. Natasya is a sadomasochist, reveling in her exploitation while she avenges it. Other characters follow suit.

These factors make *The Idiot* a uniquely Russian novel—dense, complex, and at times too Russian for the non-Russian reader. It can be appreciated best from the Russian point of view—native or trained.

"Critical Evaluation" by Joanne G. Kashdan

Bibliography:

Curle, Richard. *Characters of Dostoevsky: Studies from Four Novels.* London: Heinemann, 1950. A fine look at the most important Dostoevski characters of several novels, including *The Idiot.* Extensive quotations are followed by explanations.

Dalton, Elizabeth. *Unconscious Structure in "The Idiot": A Study in Literature and Psychoanalysis.* Princeton, N.J.: Princeton University Press, 1979. Contains two sections. One is on theories of psychoanalytic method in the study of literature, and the other is a demonstration of that method applied to *The Idiot.* Very worthwhile and interesting insights.

Jones, Malcolm V. *Dostoyevsky: The Novel of Discord.* London: Elek Books, 1976. Gives an overview of the complexity, chaos, and discord that are to be expected in Dostoyevski. From *The Idiot,* Dostoyevski's use of psychological illness versus the ideal is explored. This serious study of Dostoyevski contains extensive notes from the text, a bibliography, and an index.

Leatherbarrow, William J. *Fedor Dostoevsky.* Boston: Twayne, 1981. Includes a chronology and a biographical sketch of Dostoevski. Designed for the beginner, this is an excellent guide to Dostoevski with commentary on his early work and four major novels, including *The Idiot.*

Miller, Robin Feuer. *Dostoevsky and "The Idiot": Author, Narrator, and Reader.* Cambridge, Mass.: Harvard University Press, 1981. Includes references from Dostoevsky's notebooks for *The Idiot* and a general synopsis on the writing process as *The Idiot* took shape. A very thorough guide to *The Idiot.*

IDYLLS

Type of work: Poetry
Author: Theocritus (c. 308 B.C.E.-c. 260 B.C.E.)
First transcribed: c. 270 B.C.E.?; first published, 1566 (English translation, 1684)

Theocritus is perhaps the originator of the literary genre of pastoral poetry. The *Idylls* has, therefore, exerted tremendous influence on European literature. The *Idylls* is a collection of thirty short poems that were ascribed to Theocritus in antiquity, perhaps incorrectly. Taking its basic inspiration from the yearnings and concerns of Greek shepherds and simple country folk, pastoral poetry is potentially a confining genre. Readers of Theocritus will acknowledge, however, that his poems explore an astonishingly wide variety of themes—love, death, the meaning of art, the joys of life in the country, the nuisances of the city, the mysteries of myth and magic. Part of the explanation for this great diversity of theme and subject matter in the *Idylls* is to be found in the special character of ancient poetry collections, which frequently included any and all works that might possibly be attributed to a famous name. In fact, some of the poems that are contained in the *Idylls* are almost certainly the work of imitators of Theocritus.

Little is known about Theocritus beyond occasional hints in his poetry. The dates of his birth and death are not preserved, but he was certainly active in the first quarter of the third century B.C.E. From subtle references in his poetry a tentative biography can be reconstructed. Born in Syracuse, he apparently emigrated from Sicily and spent time in southern Italy, on the Aegean island of Cos, and at the court of Ptolemy Philadelphus in the bustling, cosmopolitan city of Alexandria, Egypt. His poetry seems to suggest connections with all of these places. The pastoral poems are filled with characteristic details of the environs of southern Italy, Sicily, and Cos; those with an urban setting depict life in two great metropolitan centers of the ancient world, Syracuse and Alexandria. Thus, familiarity with very different aspects of life in the ancient Mediterranean world provided Theocritus with rich material for his poetry. This poet's particular genius is his ability to synthesize these polarities of human existence in a satisfying artistic whole.

"Thyrsis" (idyll 1) clearly illustrates Theocritus' brilliant ability to combine high art with an atmosphere of rustic charm. The dramatic situation of the poem is a meeting between a shepherd named Thyrsis and an unnamed goatherd. The goatherd urges Thyrsis to sing a song about the legendary Daphnis, for which Thyrsis is widely admired. In return for the song, the goatherd promises a splendid, carved wooden cup, which the goatherd describes in detail. Up to this point, the dramatic circumstances of the poem do not especially tax the credulity of the reader. The image of lonely herdsmen singing songs to pass the time has elements of realism. As the cup is described by the goatherd, the pastoral illusion becomes more fragile. Intricate scenes are depicted on this marvelous drinking cup, and the descriptions invite a symbolic interpretation. Thus, the scene of the woman who is flanked by two suitors may be seen to represent the important role of love and competition in pastoral poetry. Similarly, the boy who weaves a cricket cage while a fox attempts to steal his lunch seems to suggest how artistic creation makes one oblivious of practical considerations. Thyrsis accepts the offer and sings the song of Daphnis, a legendary herdsman who wasted away because of some mysterious unrequited love. Like the scenes on the cup, Daphnis is a symbol for the artistic experience.

"Pharmaceutria" (idyll 2) presents a strong contrast to the circumstances of the first poem. Theocritus offers an urban scene, a dramatic monologue in which a young woman employs magic to regain the affection of her former lover. In the course of her monologue, Simaetha reveals the details of her seduction and abandonment by Delphis. Gradually the reader understands that Simaetha is familiar with magic. As she speaks she is also weaving a spell to make her lover return or, failing that, perhaps punish him for his faithlessness.

Idylls 3 through 6 present variations on a number of bucolic staples: unrequited love, the healing power of art, rural singing contests, the earthy vulgarity of much of rural life. "Serenade" (idyll 3) is another monologue, but this time it is a serenade delivered by a distraught lover at the entrance to a cave where the beautiful Amaryllis lives. Argument, mythological examples, even threats of suicide are invoked to persuade Amaryllis to return his love. In the end no answer is heard from the cave. The singing contests of idylls 4, 5, and 6 may well represent something that Theocritus actually experienced; however, each contest is highly stylized, employing different structures and different personalities (for example, the hostile competitors in idyll 5 standing in comparison to the friendly pair in idyll 6). It should be noted that, in depicting his rustic herdsmen, Theocritus is less interested in realism than in the learning and wit his characters can display in these artistic competitions.

"The Harvest-Home" (idyll 7) occupies a special place in the collection, not only because of its excellence, but also on account of suggestions that Theocritus himself may be identified with Smichidas, the narrator. Smichidas tells the story of a poet's journey to a harvest festival. Along the way he and his companions encounter the goatherd-poet Lycidas, with whom the narrator engages in a friendly singing contest to pass the time. The circumstances of this poem have suggested the possibility of further identifications of the characters with some lesser-known members of a poet's club once located on the island of Cos. When Lycidas presents his staff to Smichidas as a token of friendship and then says good-bye to the group, one is inclined to interpret this as a symbolic handing down of a poetic tradition. This beautiful poem ends with a few lines describing the friends' arrival at their destination and enjoyment of the harvest festival.

Some scholars have argued that the first seven poems of *Idylls* form an independent unit, a kind of poetry book, complete with intricate internal correspondences and a consistent tone. Later poems were supposedly added to this collection as the poet's output and fame grew. As if to confirm this conclusion, the next two poems in the collection, idylls 8 and 9, are not by Theocritus. Their attempt to mimic the art of Theocritus shows the difference between a master's skill and the student's attempt to imitate. "The Reapers" (idyll 10), while almost certainly authentic, shows a slightly different focus from the earlier poems. The scene is agricultural, not pastoral. A worker finds that his heart is not in the task at hand, and his friendly encounter with his foreman leads to an amusing variation on a singing contest with the object of curing him of his lovesickness and getting him back to work. This poem and the next underscore another important theme in Theocritus: art as a cure for unrequited love. The medical metaphor is explicit in "Cyclops" (idyll 11), which is actually addressed to a doctor named Nicias. As proof of the healing power of art, Theocritus cites the experience of the Cyclops Polyphemus, who—in this mythological variant—fell hopelessly in love with the beautiful nymph Galatea. Although his love is not returned, the monster soon realizes that the love song he has sung has acted as a palliative for the pain of unrequited love.

Of the remaining poems in the collection, only a few can be singled out for special mention. "Hylas" (idyll 13) tells of Hercules' loss of Hylas on the voyage of the Argonauts and his desperate search to find his young companion. Similarly, in "Hymn to the Dioscouri" (idyll 22) Theocritus tells a little-known story from the adventures of the brothers Castor and Polydeuces. In "The Young Heracles" (idyll 24) and "Heracles the Lion-Slayer" (idyll 25), peculiar exploits of the Greek hero form the basis of Theocritus' narrative. Although the authenticity of some of these works has been doubted, it is clear that poems about mythological tales were a favorite art form of Theocritus and his contemporaries, perhaps because this genre provides a way to introduce mythological subjects on a smaller scale than that of the great heroic epics. A mythological tale of a different sort is the "Wedding Song for Helen" (idyll 18), in which the marriage of young Helen to Menelaus is celebrated in song by the young women of Sparta. Here also there is an attempt to create a work of art that touches only indirectly on the great stories of Greek legend.

Despite these forays into mythological topics, Theocritus excels in those poems that deal with love and the common experiences of ordinary people. "Aeschines and Thyonichus" (idyll 14) treats the theme of unhappy love in a new way by depicting a conversation between two men of the world, one of whom is frustrated in his passion. In a brilliant touch of realism, Thyonichus simply listens to his friend's vivid story and, with a bland comment, changes the subject. Thyonichus knows from experience how such matters develop and will offer only practical advice should Aeschines wish to terminate the liaison. Realistic depiction of the frustrations of city life seems to be at least one object of "The Women at the Festival of Adonis" (idyll 15). Gorgo and Praxinoa, two women of Alexandria, make preparations to visit the palace of Ptolemy for a celebration of the festival of Adonis. Theocritus depicts their gossip, their frustration as they make their way through a throng of celebrants, and—when they finally arrive—their genuine admiration for the works of art that adorn the palace. In a brief dramatic skit Theocritus beautifully captures the essence of this event in the lives of these two ordinary women.

Theocritus' ability to make high art out of a moment of ordinary life is the essence of his genius. His primary legacy to later writers was the idea of a pastoral genre. His most brilliant follower was certainly the Roman poet Vergil. Vergil's pastoral poetry, with its political background and even deeper appreciation of nature, also represents a transformation in the Greek poet's original concept. Primarily through Vergil, rather than directly from Theocritus, the pastoral genre became the common property of European literature.

John M. Lawless

Bibliography:
Halperin, D. M. *Before Pastoral: Theocritus and the Ancient Tradition of Bucolic Poetry.* New Haven, Conn.: Yale University Press, 1983. Discussion of the possible antecedents and followers of Theocritus. Useful for understanding the development of the genre in its earliest form.
Lawall, Gilbert. *Theocritus' Coan Pastorals: A Poetry Book.* Cambridge, Mass.: Center for Hellenic Studies, 1967. Presents a persuasive argument for viewing of idylls 1 through 7 as a self-contained poetry book, intended as such by Theocritus. The study also offers valuable insights into structural and thematic interconnections among these poems.
Rosenmeyer, Thomas G. *The Green Cabinet: Theocritus and the European Pastoral Lyric.* Berkeley: University of California Press, 1969. Traces the evolution of the pastoral genre in later European literature. Valuable discussion of the concept of pastoral poetry and its later manifestations.
Segal, Charles. *Poetry and Myth in Ancient Pastoral.* Princeton, N.J.: Princeton University Press, 1981. A collection of interpretive essays that shed light on the poetic qualities of Greek and Roman pastoral poetry. Discussion of some individual poems is invaluable.
Walker, S. F. *Theocritus.* Boston: Twayne, 1980. Treats the entire collection of Theocritus' poetry. Highly recommended for the reader interested in a basic introduction to Theocritus.

IDYLLS OF THE KING

Type of work: Poetry
Author: Alfred, Lord Tennyson (1809-1892)
Type of plot: Arthurian romance
Time of plot: Fifth century
Locale: England
First published: 1859-1885

> *Principal characters:*
> KING ARTHUR
> QUEEN GUINEVERE
> SIR LANCELOT,
> GARETH,
> GERAINT,
> BALIN,
> BALAN,
> GAWAIN,
> SIR GALAHAD,
> SIR BORS,
> SIR PELLEAS,
> SIR PERCIVALE,
> SIR MODRED,
> SIR TRISTRAM, and
> SIR BEDIVERE, Knights of the Round Table
> MERLIN, a magician
> LYNETTE, who married Gareth
> ENID, who married Geraint
> VIVIEN, an enchantress
> ELAINE, the lily maid of Astolat
> ETTARRE, loved by Pelleas and Gawain
> ISOLT, of the white hands, Tristram's wife

The Story:

The Coming of Arthur. Gorlois and Ygerne had borne one daughter, Bellicent. King Uther overcame Gorlois in battle and forced the widow to marry him immediately. Shortly afterward King Uther died. Ygerne's son, Arthur, was born at a time when he could have been the son of Gorlois or the son of Uther. The birth of Arthur was shrouded in great mystery. Merlin the magician reared the prince until it was time for him to take over Uther's kingdom and to receive from the Lady of the Lake the magic sword, Excalibur. After the marriage of Arthur and Guinevere, the king and his loyal members of the Round Table, in twelve battles, drove the enemy out of the kingdom.

Gareth and Lynette. Bellicent, Arthur's sister, allowed her youngest son to join his two brothers in King Arthur's court on the condition that Gareth serve as a kitchen knave under the surly directions of Sir Kay the seneschal. When the young boy presented himself to King Arthur, Gareth made the king promise to give him the first quest which came along. One day

Lynette came to the court asking for Sir Lancelot to save her sister from wicked knights who held her captive. King Arthur sent Gareth with Lynette, who grumbled disdainfully at the kitchen knave ordered to serve her.

The first knight Gareth overcame was the Morning Star. Lynette still sneered at the knave. After Gareth had defeated another knight, Lynette began to relent. When he conquered a third strong knight, she allowed him to ride at her side. Next Gareth encountered a terrible knight, Death, who proved to be a mere boy forced by his brothers to assume a fierce appearance. Gareth returned to the Round Table victorious and married Lynette.

The Marriage of Geraint and Enid. Geraint, on a quest for Guinevere, came to the impoverished castle of Earl Yniol and his daughter Enid, a woman whose faded brocades spoke of former wealth and family pride. There Geraint learned that the rejected suitor of Enid had caused the ruin of Yniol. The earl gave Geraint Enid for his wife.

Geraint, fearing that the sin of the queen's love for Lancelot would taint Enid's love, went to his own castle and there idled away the hours in company with his wife until neighbors began to gossip that Geraint had lost his courage. Enid feared to tell her lord about the gossip, and Geraint, observing her strange attitude, decided that she had fallen in love with some knight of the Round Table. One morning, bidding Enid to don her faded brocade gown, Geraint set out with his wife after ordering her not to speak to him. Riding ahead of Geraint, Enid encountered men who would attack her husband, and each time she broke his command by warning him of his danger. After a while Enid was able to prove her love to her suspicious husband. They returned to Camelot, where Guinevere warmly welcomed Enid to the court.

Balin and Balan. Balan left Balin, his mad brother, and went on a mission to quell King Pellam, who had refused to pay his yearly tribute to King Arthur. With his brother gone, Balin was left alone in his gloomy moods. He worshiped the purity of Lancelot and the faithfulness of Guinevere until one day he saw his two idols speaking familiarly in the garden. Disillusioned, Balin fled to the woods. There he met Vivien, a wanton woman of the court, who poisoned his mind against Lancelot and Guinevere. He left hanging on a tree the shield Guinevere had given him years before. Hearing Balin's mad shrieks among the trees, Balan rushed out to seek Balin. In the ensuing struggle Balin killed Balan and then was crushed by his own horse.

Merlin and Vivien. Vain and coquettish Vivien set out to ensnare the most chivalric man in all the kingdom, King Arthur, but her wiles failed to win the attention of a king whose mind could harbor no evil thoughts. Vivien then turned to Merlin, who she knew possessed a magic spell. She tried to charm the magician with her beauty, pretending to love the ancient, bearded man, but he knew that she was not to be trusted. When she asked him to teach her the spell, he refused. Vivien was not to be denied. At last, tricked by her beauty, Merlin taught her his magic powers. She enchanted him and caused him to disappear forever, a prisoner in a hollow tree.

Lancelot and Elaine. Lancelot in disguise went to Astolat, where he left his shield with Elaine and rode off with her brother Lavaine to the tournaments. Lancelot won the jousts: then, wounded, he fled before anyone could discover who he was. King Arthur sent Gawain to search for the winner of the tournament. Gawain rode to Astolat, where he lingered because he had fallen in love with Elaine. She told him that she loved the knight who had left his shield with her. When Gawain saw the shield, he identified it as that of Lancelot.

Elaine nursed Lancelot back to health in the hope that he would return her love. Recovered, he sadly told her that he could never marry any woman. After he had gone, Elaine became ill and finally died in her grief. Her dying wish was to be put into a boat and sent to Camelot, in her hand a letter to Lancelot.

In Camelot Guinevere coldly rejected Lancelot, for Gawain had told of the affair between Lancelot and Elaine. When the body of Elaine floated to Camelot, King Arthur and Lancelot found the beautiful maiden in her boat, the letter in her hand. Lancelot authorized a fitting burial for the lily maid. He unhappily lamented his hopeless love for the queen.

The Holy Grail. One day while Sir Galahad, the youngest and purest of all the knights, sat in Merlin's chair, the Holy Grail descended upon the Round Table in a flash and then was gone. When the knights swore to go on a quest for the Holy Grail, King Arthur gloomily predicted that the search would end in disaster for many of his knights because none was pure enough, save Galahad or Percivale, to see the holy vessel.

To Galahad the Grail appeared in all its splendor. Percivale, who followed him, also saw the holy sign. Sir Bors returned to King Arthur to report that he had viewed the Grail; but Lancelot had seen only a sign of it. Some of the other knights never returned to the Round Table from their perilous quest.

Pelleas and Ettarre. Pelleas had given Ettarre a trophy he had won in a tournament, but she, scorning the young knight, barred him from her court. Gawain, meeting Pelleas in his despair, offered to help him. After telling the knight to hide in the forest, Gawain went to Ettarre and told her he had killed Pelleas. As the days passed, Pelleas became impatient. One night, stealing into the castle, he found Gawain and Ettarre sleeping together and placed his naked sword across the throats of the sleeping lovers. Then in a mad rage he rode through the forest until he met Percivale, who accidentally revealed to Pelleas the scandal about Lancelot and Guinevere. Disillusioned, the young knight returned to the Round Table, where his rude manner to the queen foreshadowed evil to Lancelot and Guinevere. Sir Modred saw that the ruin of the Round Table was near at hand.

The Last Tournament. To a tournament at Camelot came Tristram, who had left his bride, Isolt of the white hands. Her name was the same as that of his beloved, Isolt, the wife of King Mark of Cornwall. Lancelot, laboring under the guilt of his sinful love for Guinevere, decided to fight with the similarly guilty Tristram, who won the tournament. Tristram then went to Isolt of Cornwall. King Mark was away on a hunting trip. He returned unexpectedly, found the lovers together, and killed Tristram.

In the north a knight rebelled against King Arthur's rule and charged that the Round Table was a thing of falseness and guilt where harlots and adulterers lived disguised as ladies and knights. King Arthur rode to quell the revolt and the guilty man was killed; but King Arthur was heavy in heart when he returned to Camelot.

Guinevere. Fearing exposure of her love for Lancelot, Guinevere asked him to leave Camelot. On the night of their farewell Modred trapped the lovers together, and Guinevere, feeling that she was shamed forever, went to Almesbury and took refuge in a nunnery. There she recalled how Lancelot had brought her from her father's home to marry Arthur, how she had thought Arthur cold and had fallen in love with the courtly, outgoing Lancelot.

King Arthur went to Almesbury. To Guinevere he spoke of his pride in the marvelous ideals that the Round Table had upheld and that Guinevere had inspired. Now all was lost, but he forgave Guinevere before he went off to fight against Modred and his traitor knights.

Filled with remorse, Guinevere asked the nuns to accept her in their order. There she gave her services until they made her abbess. After three years in that rank she died.

The Passing of Arthur. In Modred's revolt King Arthur was mortally wounded. As he lay dying he told Sir Bedivere to cast the sword Excalibur into the lake. When Bedivere finally brought to King Arthur the tale that amid flashing and strange sights an arm reached out from the lake to receive the sword, King Arthur knew that Bedivere had truly sent Excalibur back to

3133

the Lady of the Lake. Next King Arthur told Bedivere to carry him to the shore. There three maidens came in a barge to take King Arthur away. As Bedivere stood weeping, King Arthur assured him that the old order of the Round Table must pass to give way to something new.

So King Arthur passed, in the manner of his legendary beginning, back across the waters to Avalon, but many men believed that some day he would return to his people in their need. Bedivere watched on the shore until the wintry dawn broke bringing a new year.

Critical Evaluation:

The Arthurian legends fascinated Alfred, Lord Tennyson throughout his life. The main source for *Idylls of the King* is *Le Morte d'Arthur* (1485) by Sir Thomas Malory, but Tennyson also studied other versions. The composition of the various parts of the poem took place over a period of four decades. Tennyson began in 1833 with the drafting of a poem inspired by an event that had a fundamental impact on Tennyson's work, the death of his beloved friend, Arthur Hallam. The poem was ultimately developed into "The Passing of Arthur," the last section of *Idylls of the King*.

The title itself, *Idylls of the King*, suggests that the component poems are separate. The narrative is not continuous but rather consists of a number of individual stories. There are, however, several unifying elements that bind the poem into a cohesive structure. The overall movement of the narrative traces the reign of the king, including discussion of his ancestry, the building of the society of the Round Table, its existence, its disintegration, and ultimately the mysterious passing of Arthur. There is also a similar movement in time. *Idylls of the King* is generally considered an epic poem. It consists of twelve parts, or books, the pattern established by Vergil's epic poem *The Aeneid* (c. 29-19 B.C.E.) and there are other shared characteristics. As Vergil does, Tennyson writes about heroism, conflict, the supernatural, all in relationship to a nation, with the intention of considering such matters as nobility and human achievement.

The individual idylls focus on different characters, but certain characters receive steady attention. For example, Sir Modred is briefly mentioned and characterized as "sullen" early on, foreshadowing his later importance. Gawain is seen in several idylls, becoming progressively more cynical. Lancelot and Guinevere and their disloyal love are frequently referred to as being a part of the consciousness of most of the other characters. Readers observe the increasing self-destructiveness of their guilt throughout the idylls. Characters are sometimes linked by shared attributes such as the mysterious parentage of Arthur, Lancelot, and Galahad. Sometimes, characters are shown in sharp contrast, for example in the image of the treacherous Vivien sitting on Merlin's knee, combing his long gray beard with her fingers, and the steadfast Elaine likewise sitting on her father's knee playing with his beard. Both women are being coquettish in an attempt to get what they want, but Vivien's purpose is evil, whereas Elaine's is good. Most important, the serene presence of Arthur pervades the lives of all the characters, and is always in the background of the narrative.

Tennyson's poem is concerned with much more than the events it narrates. It is also an exploration of humanity's inner nature, and paints a picture of virtues and spirituality constantly battling with baser instincts. There is a clear expression of this theme in the story of Balin, who struggles with his melancholia, attempting in vain to suppress his potential for violence that is always threatening to reemerge. A similar dual nature is found in Lancelot. Lancelot seems to be particularly blessed with virtues and is consequently held in the greatest esteem, not only for his valor but also for his attractive personality. He, too, however, has an inner conflict between his sinful love for the queen and his virtuous love for the king. Elaine sees the legacy of his guilt in his "marr'd" face.

Arthur embodies virtues such as piety, purity, justice, and valor. He is wise in all areas except one: the conduct of his marriage. He seems almost willfully blind in his refusal to address the relationship between Lancelot and Guinevere, of which everyone else is aware. Guinevere fell in love with Lancelot because she found Arthur to be cold and colorless. She recoils from his perfection: "He is all fault who hath no fault at all." Indeed, Tennyson's Arthur does seem dull and flat. He is more easily understood in symbolic rather than psychological terms.

Tennyson himself resisted a strictly allegorical reading of *Idylls of the King*. Although he may not have intended his readers to assign a system of consistent symbolic meanings to his characters, institutions, and landscapes, the poem is rich in a symbolism that conveys meaning. In simplified terms, Arthur represents the soul, and he symbolizes humanity's highest aspirations of spirituality, faith, and grace. He is the founder, leader, and harmonizing element of the Round Table, which represents humankind's other capacities. Guinevere is the body or the senses, and is unable to keep faith with the soul. Ultimately, the soul is deserted by all other elements, which are unwilling or unable to live up to its perfection. The wasteland that is the world outside of Camelot is largely unknown and potentially evil. Tennyson's symbolic meanings tend to be broad, not allegorical, and are inclusive of a range of suggestions.

Very popular when first published, *Idylls of the King* has in many cases not been acclaimed by critics. It has been suggested that the moral message is heavy-handed and that it is unacceptably anachronistic to apply Victorian values, as it seems the poem does, to Arthur's time. These Victorian values are often unappealing to twentieth century critics. Other critics, however, find the poem to be an important work, the mature flowering of the poetic genius of a major poet.

"Critical Evaluation" by Susan Henthorne

Bibliography:
Kissane, James. *Alfred Tennyson*. New York: Twayne, 1970. Introduces Tennyson's work. Discusses symbolic meanings and moral themes in *Idylls of the King*. Bibliography.
Priestley, F. E. L. "Tennyson's Idylls." In *Critical Essays on the Poetry of Tennyson*, edited by John Killham. New York: Barnes & Noble Books, 1960. Helps the student begin to evaluate Tennyson's stature. Stresses Tennyson's serious purpose in *Idylls of the King* in asserting the primacy of idealism and spiritual values over materialism.
Reed, John R. *Perception and Design in Tennyson's "Idylls of the King."* Athens: Ohio University Press, 1969. Analyzes individual idylls in depth to trace the artistic strategy and moral design of the poem. Emphasis on the tension between the physical and the spiritual.
Rosenberg, John D. *The Fall of Camelot: A Study of Tennyson's "Idylls of the King."* Cambridge, Mass.: Harvard University Press, 1973. Defends the poem against negative criticism, claiming that in the poem Tennyson invents a new form, the originality of which has caused critics to misunderstand it. Emphasis on symbolism of poem.
Ryalls, Clyde de L. *From the Great Deep: Essays on "Idylls of the King."* Athens: Ohio University Press, 1967. Asserts that *Idylls of the King* is a philosophical poem concerned with the nature of human existence. Contains useful sections about the publication history of individual idylls.

IF NOT NOW, WHEN?

Type of work: Novel
Author: Primo Levi (1919-1987)
Type of plot: Adventure
Time of plot: 1943-1945
Locale: Russia, Poland, and Italy
First published: Se non ora, quando?, 1982 (English translation, 1985)

> *Principal characters:*
> MENDEL, a Jewish partisan
> GEDALEH, the leader of a Jewish partisan band
> DOV,
> LEONID, and
> PAVEL, partisan men
> LINE,
> WHITE ROKHELE, and
> BLACK ROKHELE, partisan women
> ISIDOR, a young Jewish survivor, not yet seventeen years old

The Story:
Mendel, a village watchmaker, was one of the hundreds of thousands of stragglers missing from the Red Army. He met Leonid, another Russian Jew, behind the German lines. Together, they hid from the Germans and the peasants. From another straggler, Mendel and Leonid learned of the bands of partisans hidden in the woods. Mendel, tired of being a missing person living like a wolf, decided to join a band. The pair made their way to Novoselki, a village of armed Jews in the midst of the Polessia marshes.

Despite its members' being weak and poorly armed, the hidden settlement was the safest place for Jews who had escaped from ghettos and German labor camps. The camp leader, Dov, an older man, did his best to keep the camp fed and guarded while carrying on acts of sabotage. In Novoselki, Mendel met a passionate Zionist woman named Line and a clever and strong former actor named Pavel.

During the harsh winter, Dov, who by now considered Mendel his lieutenant, received a message from the legendary Jewish partisan leader Gedaleh, who belonged to a strong and well-organized band. He invited Dov's participation in a mission, and, feeling it was important to show the Russians that the Jews would fight the Germans, Dov agreed. The engagement wasnot a success, and German reprisal with machine guns and tanks wiped out most of the Novoselki band.

Dov, Mendel, Leonid, Line, and Pavel set off to locate Ulybin, the chief of Gedaleh's band, to continue to fight their partisan war. In Ulybin's prosperous, well-organized camp, Mendel learned more about Gedaleh, who was away on a mission. Gedaleh's life had been saved by his violin, which had stopped a bullet. It appeared that there had been a quarrel between Ulybin and Gedaleh over accepting Jews in the band.

While they waited for orders in the camp, they experienced great hunger and homesickness. For the Russians, the longing for home was not unreasonable, for their homes still existed, but for the Jews, regret for their destroyed villages and dead families was complete despair, and they wondered for what future they were fighting.

Because of an old knee wound, Dov was taken by plane to a hospital in Russia. The others continued to wait. Then a ragged band appeared, led by Gedaleh, with Dov among them. They brought the news that the Germans were weakened and retreating. It would be possible to head west into Poland.

The band split up. Mendel and the other Jews went with Gedaleh and Dov to harass the German rear lines. They made their way west, in relative safety. It was a period of rest. Gedaleh played the violin and sang the anthem of the Jewish partisans: "If I'm not for myself, who will be for me? If not this way, how? If not now, when?"

After the rest period, the band hijacked a freight train. Upon learning that the Germans were losing ground in Russia, that German cities were being bombed, and that the Allies were gaining in Italy, they left their life of hiding in the marshes and entered the inhabited world of Poland. Their purpose was to continue to sabotage and harass the German army and to liberate camps of war prisoners and Jews.

They found that Poland had been devastated by German reprisals. The partisans helped the starving local peasants with the harvest. Gedaleh and the band formulated their determination to fight until the end of the war and then go to Palestine to start over.

The band found a small labor camp, in which 120 Jewish prisoners were being guarded by only a few Germans. The retreating Germans had already killed most of the Jews, but the guards remained. The band raided the camp that night, killing the guards and freeing the few remaining prisoners. Leonid was killed in the attack.

The band passed the winter with a group of Polish partisans. During this time, White Rokhele became pregnant by young Isidor, and they were married. Now Gedaleh's band was more than ever resolved to head for Palestine, carrying new life. They planned to go through Italy, from where as they had heard ships were leaving for Palestine.

The Russians arrived, liberating Poland from the Germans but leaving the Jews in an undefined, uneasy situation. Not recognized as partisans, they became men and women without papers. Dov returned to his home in Siberia. The others realized that as Jews they were no safer with the Russians than they had been with the Germans. They continued on their way in a stolen truck. They were delayed by the Russians and lost the truck, but by the spring of 1945 the Gedalist band resumed their trek, traveling through defeated Germany. They continued to encounter hatred from German refugees, and while looking for food in a German town, Black Rokhele was shot. The band took revenge by killing the town mayor.

Once the war was over, they continued westward during the late days of Rokhele's pregnancy. They commandeered a passenger car, set off across the Alps by train, and made their way to an assistance center for refugees in Milan. Here they were introduced to Italian Jews who were to help them find a boat to Palestine. In Milan, Isidor and White Rokhele's child, the child of them all, was born. There was hope for a new life.

Critical Evaluation:

Primo Levi, who was born in Turin in 1919 and trained as a chemist, was deported to Auschwitz in 1944. His experiences in the Nazi death camp are the subject of several of his memoirs, *Survival in Auschwitz* (1947), *The Reawakening* (1963), *The Periodic Table* (1975), and *The Drowned and the Saved* (1989). As an Italian Jew, he holds an unusual place among Holocaust writers. Jews in Italy had not been subject to the same degree of hatred and prejudice as had Eastern European Jews. In general, they were thoroughly assimilated in Italian society until the 1938 race laws of fascist Italy officially adopted Nazi racial theories. As a result, Jewish tradition had become attenuated in Italy. Even at Auschwitz,

Levi writes, there were Jews who were suspicious of the Italians because they did not speak Yiddish.

Language, its use and power, is an important theme in Levi's work. In his books about the concentration camps, Levi explores how language reflects relationships between inmates and between inmates and guards. His novel *If Not Now, When?* is an attempt to understand and explore Eastern European culture and the Yiddish language, which was unfamiliar to Levi himself, and to present Eastern European Jews to his Italian audience, who also knew little of them.

Levi's own voice is noted for restraint. The precision and economy of his style, and the acuteness of his observation, have been attributed to his training as a scientist. He writes of the horrors of the death camps with a quiet understatement that is immensely effective. Although *If Not Now, When?* is outwardly an adventure story, it is also a quiet and rather private tale. The narrator, Mendel, is as reflective as Levi himself is when he narrates the story of his experience. The inner dynamics of the partisan group are as much a part of the story as are their acts of sabotage. Levi contrasts Mendel, for example, who is always careful and thoughtful, with Line, who is bold and outspoken.

One of Levi's purposes in writing *If Not Now, When?* is to disprove the misconception that Jews could not or would not fight and that they were led to the death camps like sheep to the slaughter. The tale of a Jewish partisan band is based on a true story told to Levi by a friend who worked at an Italian assistance center at the end of the war and encountered a band like the one in the novel. A central irony of the novel is the image of guns in the hands of the children of tailors and rabbis. Mendel learns to kill, yet remains a philosopher and a watchmender. These Jews have fought and killed without losing their deep repugnance at having to take up arms.

In the course of the novel, the war ends and the band of wandering Jews shift their purpose from harassing the Germans to making their way to a new home in Palestine. At this point, the novel becomes the description of an odyssey, a series of adventures and mishaps as the partisans make their way home from the war. Mendel is a gentle survivor, a blend of Ulysses returning from Troy and Levi himself returning home after Auschwitz. The novel ends on a rather stereotypical note of hope when a child is born. Isidor and White Rokhele's child has been sheltered and awaited as a child of them all. He is born in Italy, on the shore of their departure for Palestine. A new life is beginning.

If Not Now, When? won prestigious prizes in Italy, yet it is qualified as an artistic success. Irving Howe writes that Levi stakes everything on his capacity to imagine experiences that are alien to him. Because Levi has had to base his novel on research into Eastern European Jewish culture and language, the novel lacks the immediacy of his memoirs. Yet Howe finds that Levi's literary gift for narrative movement reaches full play in this adventure story.

Fernanda Eberstadt, on the other hand, concludes that *If Not Now, When?* must be judged an artistic failure. Although she credits Levi with having chosen an important and engrossing subject, she finds the plot at once stiffly schematic and unsettlingly random and the conversation leaden.

Primo Levi is acclaimed for his concentration camp memoirs, in which detailed observation and the impact of his understated, restrained, economical style are juxtaposed with the horror of his material. The novel *If Not Now, When?* has a place in his total work, because here he seeks to understand and explain an aspect of the war that was alien to his own experience. He explores the culture of the Eastern European Jews that was unfamiliar to his own Italian Jewish culture, and he places Jews in the role of fighters. His style in the novel is as understated and ironic as in the memoirs. Artistically, the picaresque adventures of the partisan band allow him a freer imaginative rein than his own memoirs, at the same time that he continues to explore the place of language in relationships and cultures.

Susan Butterworth

Bibliography:
Eberstadt, Fernanda. "Reading Primo Levi." *Commentary* 80 (October, 1985): 41-47. Discusses Levi's style, precision, irony, wit, and understatement. Eberstadt pronounces *If Not Now, When?* an artistic failure in spite of its important and engrossing subject.
Howe, Irving. "Primo Levi: An Appreciation." In *If Not Now, When?*, by Primo Levi. New York: Penguin Books, 1986. Discusses Levi's use of imagination and adventure in the novel.
Hughes, H. Stuart. *Prisoners of Hope: The Silver Age of the Italian Jews 1924-1974.* Cambridge, Mass.: Harvard University Press, 1983. Discussion of six prose writers. Places Levi's work in the context of his background as an Italian Jew.
Roth, Philip. "Afterword: A Conversation with Primo Levi." In *Survival in Auschwitz*, by Primo Levi, translated by Stuart Woolf. New York: Collier Books, 1993. Offers Levi's statements about what motivated him to write *If Not Now, When?*
Tager, Michael. "Primo Levi and the Language of Witness." *Criticism* 35, no. 2 (Spring, 1993): 265-288. A thoroughly researched and documented discussion of Levi's use of language. The theme of language as identity is found throughout the dramatic action of *If Not Now, When?*

IGNES DE CASTRO

Type of work: Drama
Author: Antonio Ferreira (1528-1569)
Type of plot: Tragedy
Time of plot: 1354-1360
Locale: Portugal
First performed: c. 1553-1556; first published, 1587 as *A Castro* (English translation, 1825)

> *Principal characters:*
> ALFONSO IV, King of Portugal
> PRINCE PEDRO, his son
> IGNES DE CASTRO, secretly married to Pedro
> SECRETARY TO THE PRINCE
> DIOGO LOPES PACHECO,
> PEDRO COELHO, and
> GONZALVES, King Alfonso's advisers

The Story:

On a lovely spring day in the middle of the fourteenth century, Ignes de Castro felt especially happy as she walked in her garden in Portugal. Although she was an illegitimate daughter of a famous Galician noble, she had won the love of Prince Pedro, son of Alfonso IV of Portugal; at last she felt sure the world was about to learn that he loved her too. Theirs had been a star-crossed love. Pedro's father, trying his best to destroy his son's love for a woman unsuitable to rule Portugal, had compelled his heir to marry the Princess Constanza of Castile. Ignes confided to her nurse, however, that fate had been on the side of true love. The birth of Constanza's son, heir to the crown of Portugal, had cost his mother her life. At last Pedro was free. He had carried out his father's command. He had ensured a continuation of the dynasty, and now he was coming back to the woman he really loved. Surely King Alfonso would now relent. The beauty of the day seemed an omen, and Ignes was weeping with joy as she waited for her lover to appear.

The old nurse was less sure, however, that her mistress' tears were an omen of joy; they might be a foreboding of tragedy. She begged Ignes not to count on happiness until everything was settled. Ignes, hearing Pedro approaching, would listen to no warnings.

The prince greeted her with an assurance that all would go well. To himself, however, he wondered why he was not loved by the common people of Portugal and why his father had been so incensed by his sincere love for Ignes. Nevertheless, he was confident, like Ignes, that their four children would move the stern old king to pity. Pedro hoped for the royal acceptance of the love between them and a state wedding to show King Alfonso's recognition of his grandchildren.

Pedro's secretary tried to disillusion him. In spite of the nobility of her famous father, the irregularity of Ignes' birth was cause enough for King Alfonso's repeated orders that Pedro must put her out of his mind. The secretary begged Pedro, for the good of the state, to let reason conquer desire and to give up the passion that enslaved him and made him disobedient to the royal will. The prince refused. He had obeyed his father in marrying Constanza. Events had proved that Ignes was fated to be his real wife.

King Alfonso, meanwhile, was pacing his throne room. His three advisers, Diogo Lopes Pacheco, Pedro Coelho, and Gonzalves, were deaf to his complaints that a king had more woes than pleasures. They preached the obligation of power, pointing out that an officially sanctioned marriage between Pedro and Ignes, whose children were older than the recently born son of Constanza, might jeopardize the succession of the young child. One of the advisers, the dominating Pacheco, argued that the removal of Ignes would solve all difficulties. In spite of King Alfonso's basic agreement with the suggestion, much argument was needed before the king finally gave the trio orders to kill his son's mistress.

That night Ignes had a dream in which she was about to die. She interpreted it as proof that Pedro was dead; otherwise he would have been quick to defend her. Before she could discover what truth there was in her dream, the king arrived with a sentence of death. He was accompanied by Pacheco, who intended to block any appeals for royal mercy. Ignes pleaded so touchingly, however, insisting on her innocence and the helplessness of her four children related through Pedro to King Alfonso, that the king, reminded of his love for his own child, finally agreed to spare her.

The reprieve did not last long. Once more the king's advisers worked on the king, determined that Constanza's child should inherit, without difficulty, the throne. They could not get his consent to the death of Ignes, but King Alfonso did not actually forbid it. Twisting his less-than-unmistakable statements into permission, the evil trio hurried away to murder the innocent Ignes de Castro.

In the meantime Pedro, hurrying eagerly to join her and confident that the king would consider his son's happiness and permit their official marriage, was met by a messenger who told the prince that the three advisers had sought out Ignes and killed her. Out of his mind with grief, Pedro swore to have revenge on all concerned, including his father. He would cast him from the throne and then hunt down and torture the three evil murderers, and he would not only see to it that a child of Ignes should be named his successor, but when he was crowned he would also have Ignes' corpse exhumed and seated on the throne beside him to receive the honors of a royal coronation.

Critical Evaluation:
Ignes de Castro (also known as *Inês de Castro*) has the distinction of being the first tragedy written in Portuguese modeled on the works of classical dramatists. In composing the play, Antonio Ferreira consciously set out to adapt materials from the history of his homeland to the rigid formulas of Greek and Roman drama. His contemporaries would have been quite familiar with the story of the star-crossed lovers Ignes and Pedro, since their tale had been the subject of earlier literary works; however, the form of the drama used by the playwright was one not seen before on the Portuguese stage. While a university student, Ferreira became captivated by the theories of literature emerging from Italy; the work of writers such as Giraldi Cinthio influenced his concept of the drama. Numerous critics have concentrated on his borrowings from the Greek stage, frequently to the exclusion of any discussion of the playwright's originality in producing a drama that transcends its models and presents a fresh look at the central moral and political issues that Ferreira discovered in the story of Pedro and his mistress. No mere slave to his classical models, Ferreira worked hard to use his native history and his vernacular language within the classical models he adopted. While the result is not wholly successful, his accomplishments are nevertheless noteworthy.

The central conflict in the drama is a familiar one: personal passion versus duty to society. The dilemma faced by Pedro and his father is not a simple one, however. The prince is deeply in love with Ignes, and it is clear that, before the action of the play begins, he has obeyed his father's wishes regarding the question of succession to the throne by taking a wife acceptable to the king and the nobility. Her death has freed him once again to pursue a union with the woman he has loved for years. Having fathered a legitimate son to inherit the throne when he dies, Pedro believes he should be free to marry Ignes, the mother of his four illegitimate children. The king sees the situation differently, of course. The possibility exists that the children of Pedro and Ignes (some of whom are older than Pedro's legitimate son) might lay claim to the throne, casting the country into a bloody civil conflict. Hence, the king must make his difficult choice. The choice, and the bloody results that follow it, is common to classical drama.

Ferreira makes good use of the classical format and of a number of other dramatic techniques. Particularly noteworthy is his handling of the minor characters in the play, especially Alfonso's counselors. When the king seems to vacillate, one or another of them stands ready to remind him that it is his duty as head of state to eliminate all threats to the body politic. Seeing Ignes as a danger, they remain insistent that only her death can secure peace in the kingdom. Although their assessment may seem cruel and their motives questionable, as representatives of the forces of society their attitude is understandable if not completely laudable. Their insistence that the king must do something if he is to prevent a civil war highlights the complexity of the central conflict. They become useful, too, as tools for carrying out the assassination while allowing the king to remain distanced from the execution. Ferreira also uses his chorus exceptionally well, in the fashion of Greek playwrights: The group offers commentary on the action while providing the audience emotional relief from the strong passions exhibited by the chief actors in the drama.

Ignes de Castro is not without its faults, however. Ferreira gives Pedro little opportunity to display his love for Ignes, relying on statement rather than on drama to convince audiences that the prince is sincere in wanting to defy his father's wishes and marry his mistress. Many of the scenes are merely long monologues, speeches in which one character or another stakes out a political or philosophical position rather than engaging others in conversation. As a result, at times the play seems to move slowly or not at all; audiences and readers may get the sense that they are witnessing a debate rather than a drama. Nevertheless, it may be useful to remember that Ferreira was working with no contemporary dramatic models for his play; he had only the work of the theorists and the texts of classical dramas as his guides. When viewed in this light, his tragedy seems a remarkable accomplishment. Certainly his contemporaries and successors in Portugal found it to be so.

This tragedy has flaws. The lengthy exposition by Ignes in blank verse is hardly inspiring, and the simple plot allows little onstage action. In spite of these defects, moments of dramatic brilliance and scenes of suspense, emotion, and moving poetry give the drama other reasons for permanence besides its status as a pioneer effort.

This is one of history's most famous love stories, describing "the love that endured beyond the grave." The story is based on fact. Ignes is still remembered by the maidens of the university town of Coimbra, where the murder occurred, tradition having it that their tears formed a fountain of love around Pedro's statue there.

Maddened by sorrow, the historical Pedro took the throne in 1357. He exercised ferocious revenge on Ignes' killers, staking them out on stone slabs and cutting out their hearts. He then declared that he had been legally married to Ignes. Tradition has it that he exhumed her body from the grave, brought it to the palace in Alcobaca, and had her crowned with sumptuous ceremony, obliging the highest nobles of the kingdom to kiss the hand of "the Queen after death." Pedro and Ignes are buried in marble tombs in Alcobaca, foot to foot, so that, upon arising on Judgment Day, they will see each other immediately. This tragedy has long been a favorite theme, not only of Portuguese playwrights but also of the playwrights of other literatures.

"Critical Evaluation" updated by Laurence W. Mazzeno

Bibliography:

Bell, Aubrey F. G. *Portuguese Literature*. Oxford, England: Clarendon Press, 1922. *Ignes de Castro* is discussed in the context of sixteenth century Portuguese plays imitative of classical drama. Describes Ferreira as a competent craftsman but not at his best as a dramatist; his poetry receives greater praise in another section of the study.

Earle, T. F. *The Muse Reborn: The Poetry of Antonio Ferreira*. Oxford, England: Clarendon Press, 1988. A book-length study of Ferreira's literary art. Offers brief remarks on *Ignes de Castro*, highlighting Ferreira's debt to classical sources; the analysis of Ferreira's techniques of imitation in his poetry offer insight into similar methodology in his drama.

Friederich, Werner. *Outline of Comparative Literature from Dante Alighieri to Eugene O'Neill*. Chapel Hill: University of North Carolina Press, 1954. Places Ferreira in the context of Portuguese and European writers of the sixteenth century. Discusses his version of *Ignes de Castro* as one of several works that retell the story of the legendary heroine.

Sismondi, Simonde de. *Historical View of the Literature of the South of Europe*. Translated by Thomas Roscoe. London: Henry Bohn, 1846. Considers Ferreira a greater dramatist than poet. Careful, detailed analysis of *Ignes de Castro*, focusing on Ferreira's development of his heroine and examining his adherence to the classical unities.

THE ILIAD

Type of work: Poetry
Author: Homer (c. ninth century B.C.E.)
Type of plot: Epic
Time of plot: Antiquity
Locale: Troy
First transcribed: c. 800 B.C.E. (English translation, 1611)

Principal characters:
PRIAM, the king of Troy
HECTOR, a Trojan warrior, Priam's son
HELEN OF TROY
PARIS, Hector's brother and Helen's lover
MENELAUS, Helen's husband
AGAMEMNON, Menelaus' brother
ACHILLES, a Greek warrior
PATROCLUS, Achilles' friend

The Story:

The Greeks were camped outside the walls of Troy, in the tenth year of their siege on that city. Agamemnon, king of the Achaians, wanted the maid, Briseis, for his own, but she was possessed by Achilles, a mortal son of Zeus, king of the gods. When Achilles was forced to give up the maid, he withdrew angrily from the battle and returned to his ship. He won from Zeus the promise that the wrong that he had suffered would be revenged on Agamemnon.

That evening Zeus sent a messenger to the Greek king to convey to him in a dream an order to rise and marshal his Achaian forces against the walls of Troy. When the king awoke, he called all his warriors to him and ordered them to prepare for battle. All night long the men armed themselves in battle array, making ready their horses and their ships. The gods appeared on earth in the disguise of warriors, some siding with the Greeks, some hastening to warn the Trojans. With the army mustered, Agamemnon began the march from the camp to the walls of the city, while all the country around was set on fire. Only Achilles and his men remained behind, determined not to fight on the side of Agamemnon.

The Trojan army came from the gates of the city ready to combat the Greeks. Then Paris, son of King Priam and Helen's lover, stood out from the ranks and suggested that he and Menelaus settle the battle in a fight between them, the winner to take Helen and all her possessions, and friendship to be declared between the warring nations. Menelaus agreed to these words of his rival, and before the warriors of both sides, and under the eyes of Helen, who had been summoned to witness the scene from the walls of Troy, he and Paris began to fight. Menelaus was the mightier warrior. As he was about to pierce his enemy, the goddess Aphrodite, who loved Paris, swooped down from the air and carried him off to his chamber. She summoned Helen there to minister to her wounded lord. Then the victory was declared for Menelaus.

In the heavens the gods who favored the Trojans were much disturbed by this intervention. Athena appeared on earth to Trojan Pandarus and told him to seek out Menelaus and kill him. He shot an arrow at the unsuspecting king, but the goddess watching over Menelaus deflected the arrow so that it only wounded him. When Agamemnon saw that treacherous deed (the armies were in agreement at that moment not to fight), he revoked his vows of peace and exhorted the Greeks once more to battle. Many Trojans and many Greeks lost their lives that day, because of the foolhardiness of Pandarus.

Meanwhile Hector, son of King Priam, had returned to the city to bid farewell to Andromache, his wife, and to his child, for he feared he might not return from that day's battle. He rebuked Paris for remaining in his chambers with Helen when his countrymen were dying because of his misdeeds. While Paris made ready for battle, Hector said good-bye to Andromache, prophesying that Troy would be defeated, himself killed, and Andromache taken captive. Then Paris joined him and they went together into the battle.

When evening came the Greeks and the Trojans retired to their camps. Agamemnon instructed his men to build a huge bulwark around the camp and in front of the ships, for fear the enemy would press their attack too close. Zeus then remembered his promise to Achilles to avenge the wrong done to him by Agamemnon. He summoned all the gods and forbade them to take part in the war. The victory, Zeus said, was to go to the Trojans; thus would the insult to Zeus's son be avenged.

The next day, Hector and the Trojans swept through the fields slaughtering the Greeks. Hera, the wife of Zeus, and many of the other goddesses could not be content to watch the defeat of their mortal friends. When the goddesses attempted to intervene, Zeus sent down his messengers to warn them to desist. Fearing his armies would be destroyed before Achilles would relent, Agamemnon sent Odysseus to Achilles. Odysseus begged the hero to accept gifts and be pacified. Achilles, still wrathful, threatened to sail for home at the break of day. Agamemnon was troubled by the proud refusal of Achilles. That night he stole to the camp of the wise man, Nestor, to ask his help in a plan to defeat the Trojans. Nestor told him to awaken all the great warriors and summon them to a council. It was decided that two warriors should steal into the Trojan camp to determine its strength and numbers. Diomedes and Odysseus volunteered. As they crept toward the camp, they captured and killed a Trojan spy. Then they themselves stole into the camp of the enemy, spied upon it, and as they left, took with them the horses of one of the kings.

The next day the Trojans pressed hard upon the Greeks with great slaughter. Diomedes and Odysseus were wounded and many warriors killed. Achilles watched the battle from his ship but made no move to take part in it. He sent his friend Patroclus to Nestor to learn how many had been wounded. The old man sent back a despairing answer, pleading that Achilles give up his anger and help his fellow Greeks. At last the Trojans broke through the bulwark that the Greeks had built, and Hector was foremost in an attack upon the ships.

Meanwhile, many of the gods plotted to aid the Greeks. Hera lulled Zeus to sleep, and Poseidon urged Agamemnon to resist the onrush of the Trojans. In the battle that day Hector was wounded by Aias, but as the Greeks were about to seize him and bear his body away the bravest of the Trojans surrounded their hero and covered him with their shields until he could be carried to safety. When Zeus awakened and saw what had happened, his wrath was terrible, and he ordered Apollo to restore Hector to health. Once again the walls were breached and the Trojans stormed toward the ships, eager to set fire to them. Zeus inspired the Trojans with courage and weakened the Greeks with fear. He determined that after the ships were set afire he would no longer aid the Trojans but would allow the Greeks to have the final victory.

Patroclus went to his friend Achilles and again pleaded with him to return to the fight. Achilles, still angry, refused. Then Patroclus begged that he be allowed to wear the armor of Achilles so that the Greeks would believe their hero fought with them, and Achilles consented. Patroclus charged into the fight and fought bravely at the gates of the city. Hector mortally wounded Patroclus and stripped from his body the armor of Achilles.

All that day the battle raged over the body of Patroclus. Then a messenger carried to Achilles word of his friend's death. His sorrow was terrible, but he could not go unarmed into the fray to rescue the body of Patroclus.

The next morning his goddess mother, Thetis, brought him a new suit of armor from the forge of Hephaestus. Then Achilles decked himself in the glittering armor that the lame god of fire had prepared for him and strode forth to the beach. There he and Agamemnon were reconciled before the assembly of the Greeks, and he went out to battle with them. The whole plain was filled with men and horses, battling one another. Achilles in his vengeance pushed back the enemy to the banks of the River Xanthus, and so many were the bodies of the Trojans choking the river that at length the god of the river spoke to Achilles, ordering him to cease throwing their bodies into his waters. Proud Achilles mocked him and sprang into the river to fight with the god. Feeling himself overpowered, he struggled out upon the banks, but still the wrathful god pursued him. Achilles then called on his mother to help him, and Thetis, with the aid of Hephaestus, quickly subdued the angry river god.

As Achilles drew near the walls of Troy, Hector girded on his armor. Amid the wailing of all the Trojan women he came from the gates to meet the Greek warrior, who was understood to be completely invincible. Not standing to meet Achilles in combat, he fled three times around the city walls before he turned to face Achilles' fatal spear. Then Achilles bound Hector's body to his chariot and dragged it to the ships, a prey for dogs and vultures.

In the Trojan city there was great grief for the dead hero and rage at the treatment of his body. The aged King Priam resolved to drive in a chariot to the camp of Achilles and beg that the body of his son Hector be returned to him. The gods, too, asked Achilles to curb his wrath and restore the Trojan warrior to his own people, and so Achilles received King Priam with respect, granted his request, and agreed to a twelve-day truce that both sides might properly bury and mourn their dead. Achilles mourned for Patroclus as the body of his friend was laid upon the blazing funeral pyre. In the city the body of mighty Hector was also burned and his bones were buried beneath a great mound in the stricken city.

Critical Evaluation:

Homer has been hailed as the father of all poetry, and the *Iliad* has survived as a masterpiece for all time. The *Iliad*, within a three-day period of the Trojan War, tells the story of the wrath of Achilles against King Agamemnon. The battle episodes reveal the characters of the warriors, their strength and their weaknesses. These figures step out of unrecorded history as human beings, not of one era, but of all eras and for all time. The earliest extant work of European literature, the *Iliad* is also one of the most enduring creations of Western culture. Of the author, or possibly authors, nothing is known for certain. Tradition says that Homer was a Greek of Asia Minor. Herodotus surmised that Homer lived in the ninth century B.C.E., which seems reasonable in the light of modern scholarship and archaeology. The poet drew on a large body of legend about the siege of Troy, material with which his audience was familiar, and which was part of an oral tradition. Homer himself may not have transcribed the two epics attributed to him, but it is probable that he gave the poems their present shape.

The *Iliad* was originally intended to be recited or chanted, rather than read. Its poetic style is vivid, taut, simple, direct, full of repeated epithets and elaborate visual similes. The treatment is serious and dignified throughout, and the total effect is one of grandeur. Homer's greatness also reveals itself in the action of the *Iliad*, in which, within the scope of a few weeks in the tenth year of the siege of Troy, Homer gives the impression of covering the whole war by a few deft incidents. The appearance of Helen on the walls of Troy reminds the reader that she was the cause of the war. The catalog of ships and warriors calls to mind the first arrival of the Greek army at Troy. The duel between Paris and Menelaus would properly have come in the first years of the war, but its placement in the poem suggests the breakdown of diplomacy that lead to the bloodbath of fighting. Hector's forebodings of his own death and of the fall of Troy as he talks to his wife, not to mention his dying prediction of the supposedly invincible Achilles' death, all point to the future of the war and its conclusion. Homer thus gives the rather narrow scope of the poem's events much greater breadth.

The *Iliad* is not a mere chronicle of events in the Trojan War. It deals with one specific, and crucial, set of sequences of the war: the quarrel of Achilles with his commander, Agamemnon; Achilles' withdrawal from the war; the fighting in his absence; Agamemnon's futile attempt to conciliate Achilles; the Trojan victories; Patroclus' intervention and death at Hector's hands; Achilles' reentry to the war to avenge his friend's murder; the death of Hector; and Priam's ransom of Hector's body from Achilles. The poem has a classical structure, with a beginning, middle, and end.

This sequence is important in its effect on the war as a whole for two reasons. Without Achilles, the ablest fighter, the Greeks are demoralized, even though they have many powerful warriors. It is foretold that Achilles will die before Troy is taken, so the Greeks will have to capture Troy by other means than force. The second reason is that the climax of the poem, the killing of Hector, prefigures the fall of Troy, for as long as Hector remained alive the Greeks were unable to make much headway against the Trojans.

Achilles is the precursor of the tragic hero according to Aristotle's definition. Young, handsome, noble, courageous, eloquent, generous, and of unsurpassed prowess, his tragic flaw lies in the savage intensity of his emotions. He knows he will die young. In fact, he has chosen to die at Troy, and thereby win a lasting reputation, rather than to grow old peacefully. It is precisely his pride, his supreme skill in warfare, and his lust for future glory that makes him so ferocious when he is crossed. He has a hard time restraining himself from killing Agamemnon, and a harder time bearing Agamemnon's insult. He puts pride before loyalty when his Greek comrades are being overrun. Only when the war touches him personally, after his friend Patroclus enters the combat and is slain, does he come to terms with Agamemnon. Then his rage against the Trojans and Hector consumes him, and he is merciless in his vengeance, slaughtering Trojans by scores, gloating over Hector's corpse and abusing it, and sacrificing twelve Trojan nobles on Patroclus' funeral pyre. His humanity is restored in the end when, at Zeus's command, he allows old King Priam to ransom Hector's body. Trembling with emotion, he feels pity for the old man and reaches out his hand to him. It is the most moving moment in the epic.

Achilles lives by a rigid code of personal honor and fights to win a lasting reputation, so he has nothing to lose by dying. Life is worthless to him except insofar as it allows him to prove his own value. Yet, paradoxically, this very ethic makes his life more intense and tragic than it might have been. Hector, by contrast, is fighting on the defensive for a city he knows is doomed, and his responsibilities as a leader tend to burden him. He has others to think about, even though he foresees their fate, and all of this hinders his becoming a truly effective warrior like Achilles. Whereas Achilles' life seems tragic, Hector's life is one of pathos, but the pathos of a man fighting heroically against overwhelming odds.

The gods play a prominent part in the *Iliad*, and they are thoroughly humanized, having human shapes, sexes, and passions. Although they have superhuman powers, they behave in an all-too-human fashion—feasting, battling, fornicating, lying, cheating, changing their minds, protecting their favorites from harm. Just as the Greek army is a loose confederation under Agamemnon, so the gods are subject to Zeus. As the gods behave like humans, so the link

---

between god and human is surprisingly direct; superhuman and human forces interact constantly. Divinity penetrates human action through oracles, dreams, visions, inspiration; it shows itself in inspired warfare where a hero seems invincible, and in miraculous interventions where a wounded hero is spirited away and healed. Moreover, the gods are not omnipotent. Even Zeus can merely delay the death of a person, but in the end must bow to Fate. Further, men have free will; they are not mere puppets. Achilles has deliberately chosen his destiny. Humans, finally, have more dignity than the gods because they choose their actions in the face of death, while the gods have no such necessity, being immortal. It is death that gives human decisions their meaning, for death is final and irrevocable. The *Iliad* is a powerful statement of what it means to be human in the middle of vast and senseless bloodshed.

"Critical Evaluation" by James Weigel, Jr.

Bibliography:
Mueller, Martin. *The Iliad*. Winchester, Mass.: Allen & Unwin, 1984. A comprehensive introduction to critical study of the *Iliad*. The information is clearly presented and detailed. Contains particularly informative sections on principles of Homeric fighting, the Homeric simile, and the Greek gods.
Schein, Seth L. *The Mortal Hero: An Introduction to Homer's "Iliad."* Berkeley: University of California Press, 1984. Addressed primarily to the general reader, this book provides background to the *Iliad*. Discusses the function of the gods in the poem, outlines the fall of Troy and the death of Hector, and examines the heroic characterization of Achilles.
Silk, Michael S. *Homer, "The Iliad."* Cambridge, England: Cambridge University Press, 1987. Presents information on the religious understanding of Homeric society and summarizes the main events narrated in the poem. Discusses Achilles' place in the center of a balanced plot structure.
Vivante, Paolo. *"The Iliad": Action as Poetry*. Boston: Twayne, 1990. An excellent source of background material, organized for quick reference. Includes chapters on the historical context of Homer and the *Iliad*, plot structure, family relationships within the poem, and characterization; and the poetic roles of fate, the gods, time, and nature. The final chapter compares the *Iliad* to other epics.
Wright, John, ed. *Essays on "The Iliad": Selected Modern Criticism*. Bloomington: Indiana University Press, 1978. Eight essays on various aspects of the poem.

IMAGINARY CONVERSATIONS OF LITERARY MEN AND STATESMEN

Type of work: Philosophy
Author: Walter Savage Landor (1775-1864)
First published: 1824-1829 (five volumes)

Landor once said, "Poetry was always my amusement, prose my study and business." When he was forty-five years of age, after having devoted many years to poetic composition, he began what became *Imaginary Conversations of Literary Men and Statesmen*, in which he found the form best suited to the peculiar aim and direction of his art. Although some of his poetry attains a gemlike perfection, it suffers by comparison with the work of his more famous contemporaries. While the major Romantic writers, with their emphasis on imagination, were bringing new life to poetry, Landor chose not to go beyond ideas that could be clearly grasped. His poetry thus lacks the emotional appeal necessary to the highest attainment in this form. In prose writing, however, where clarity and restraint are more to be desired, Landor deserves consideration with the best of his age.

By the nature of his character, Landor was drawn for guidance and inspiration to the classical tradition. One side of his personality admired balance, moderation, and precision, qualities admirably displayed in his writing. The other side was irascible, impractical, and impulsive; these traits are revealed in some of his personal relationships. Like Wolfgang Amadeus Mozart, Landor appears to have found in his restrained and faultless art a counterpoise to his external world of turbulence.

Landor was a true classicist, not a belated adherent of neoclassicism with its emphasis on rules over substance. He was rigorously trained in youth and continued his scholarly pursuits throughout his adult life. His knowledge was no mere surface phenomenon; he was so immersed in the ancients that he took on their characteristic habits of thought. Thus these five volumes not only make use of events and characters from the Greco-Roman civilization, but also are infused with classical ideals of clarity and precision in style and tough intellectualism in content.

The "conversations" in *Imaginary Conversations of Literary Men and Statesmen*, are grouped into classical dialogues, dialogues of sovereigns and statesmen, dialogues of literary men, dialogues of famous women, and miscellaneous dialogues. The conversations, usually between two people, cover many centuries, ranging from the time of the Trojan War to Landor's own period, and they include people from many geographical areas. Many of the scenes are based on suggestions from history or mythology, but the actual remarks of the individuals are never used. Landor did not attempt to re-create a sense of the past by use of artificial or archaic language. He did, however, endeavor to represent faithfully the spirit of the age and the essential nature of the personage presented.

Landor is, above all, concerned with interpretation of character. Although he displays brilliant insights into human nature, he does not aim toward fully developed characters, but abstract idealizations. They are not products of observation directly reported but of observation, especially that gained from reading, filtered through a long process of reflection. Never are the predilections of the author—his sympathies and his aversions—far from the surface.

Many of the dialogues depict a manly, heroic character; two examples of this type are found in "Marcellus and Hannibal." History records the death of Marcellus in the Second Punic War and the respect paid him by Hannibal. Landor creates a scene in which Marcellus survives long enough to converse with the Carthaginian leader. When the wounded Marcellus is brought to the camp, Hannibal makes every effort to save his life and to make him comfortable. A contrast to Hannibal's chivalric behavior is provided by that of his ally, a Gallic chief who thinks only of revenge and of glory to Gaul. Marcellus welcomes death as an escape from capture and politely declines Hannibal's request that Rome agree to a peace treaty. Although under great suffering, he avoids any outward expression of pain. In return for Hannibal's kindness, Marcellus presents him with a ring that might benefit him with the Romans, if his fortunes change. As Marcellus is dying, the two men are more closely united by their common nobility and respect for nobility in others than were they divided by the exigencies of war.

Women of praiseworthy character are depicted in several of the conversations. In "Lady Lisle and Elizabeth Gaunt," Landor portrays the remarkable idealism of two women who are condemned to death for sheltering fugitives. They act through simple Christian charity: Confronted with a choice between the law of the king and the commandment of Jesus, they embrace the latter. Lady Lisle has no blame for the jury that, under duress, had convicted her. Elizabeth, serene about her own fate, feels sorrow for her companion. Betrayed by the very man she had concealed, she feels no anger toward him, but pities him for his having to suffer a guilty conscience. Both view execution as the avenue to eternal bliss and wish that others might have their perfect serenity.

A more complex character study is found in "Oliver Cromwell and Walter Noble." Cromwell is controlled by conflicting emotions—ambition, pride, compassion, vindictiveness, humility, fear. In response to the practically irrefutable arguments of Noble against regicide, Cromwell constantly shifts position and even contradicts himself. As a last refuge, he justifies his proposed action as the carrying out of God's will.

Although Landor sometimes uses crucial situations as settings for his conversations, he seldom reveals character in truly dramatic fashion. His dialogues, unlike Robert Browning's monologues, do not have a close causal relationship between the stresses of the moment and the disclosures of the speaker. Nor do Landor's speakers often reveal their inner natures unwittingly. While Browning's works are subtle and require reading between the lines, Landor's are direct and leave little to implication. In the treatment of characters with whom he is unsympathetic, Landor uses an irony that is unmistakable, even too obvious at times.

In some of the dialogues, especially the long discursive ones, the characters are not important in themselves, but serve as vehicles for the ideas of the author. Neither a systematic philosopher nor a highly original thinker, Landor was alive to the whole range of humankind's thought, past and present. A wise and judicious man, he expresses his opinions felicitously.

Love of freedom is a leading theme in *Imaginary Conversations of Literary Men and Statesmen*. Fighters for liberty, such as George Washington and Thaddeus Kosciusko, who combined modesty with valor, evoke Landor's highest admiration. Equally fervid is his detestation of tyrants, as expressed, for example, in "Peter the Great and Alexis," a dialogue in which Peter, having failed to make his son as brutal as he, callously orders the boy's execution.

Landor believed in a republican form of government and opposed pure democracy because of the corruption, intemperance, and anti-intellectualism that such a system fostered. His expression of political ideas seldom went beyond a statement of general principles.

Landor is often critical of religious leaders, and he shows his antipathy to fanaticism in such dialogues as "Mahomet and Sergius" and "Melanchthon and Calvin." Hypocrisy is attacked in other dialogues, such as "Fra Filippo Lippi and Pope Eugenius IV," which is, in part, a satire on the pope, who makes an outward show of piety and displays great zeal in maintaining the forms of religion, but who is essentially a worldly and sensual man. Also, in this conversation, the Christian-spirited barbarians of Tunisia are, with heavy irony, contrasted with the barbaric Christians of Rome. Landor favors a simple religion that stays close to its basic tenets. Believing in the limitation of human reason in such matters, he dislikes dogmatism and theological quibbling.

His philosophy was influenced by Epicurus and by the Stoics. He believes in meditation, detachment, and freedom from the ambition and envy of the world. These sentiments are expressed in "Epicurus, Leontion, and Ternissa." Feeling that man's happiness depends on his use of reason to overcome doubts and worries, in many of his character portrayals Landor reveals his belief in self-control, fortitude, sympathy, and humanitarianism.

A significant part of *Imaginary Conversations of Literary Men and Statesmen* is devoted to literary criticism. Classical standards were Landor's guide. He disapproves of unnecessary ornamentation in writing. "Never try to say things admirably, try only to say them plainly." "Whatever is rightly said, sounds rightly." Landor was not a narrow classicist in his tastes; he admired a variety of authors, his favorites being John Milton, Francis Bacon, William Shakespeare, Dante Alighieri, and Pindar. Among his contemporaries, he most respected William Wordsworth and Robert Southey.

Landor predicted that only a small, select group of people would prize his writings. He was correct. One reason for the failure of his major work to attract a large audience is the fact that the dialogues lack direction and cohesive development. The absence of dramatic motivation and the presence of disconcerting gaps and shifts in argument create difficulties for the reader.

This weakness, which is a considerable one, has prevented the high merits of the *Imaginary Conversations of Literary Men and Statesmen* from being widely appreciated. The aphorisms scattered throughout the work are among the best in the language. The range of Landor's thought is impressive. His prose style is unexcelled in vigor and purity.

Bibliography:

Dilworth, Ernest. *Walter Savage Landor.* New York: Twayne, 1971. Introductory survey of Landor's works and his achievements as a writer. Contains numerous insights into the writer's unusual method for creating *Imaginary Conversations of Literary Men and Statesmen,* and comments on the technical merits of these sketches.

Elwin, Malcolm. *Savage Landor.* New York: Macmillan, 1941. Full-length biography aimed at rescuing Landor from the poor reputation he had earned from nineteenth century critics. Comments on *Imaginary Conversations of Literary Men and Statesmen* are interspersed throughout the narrative; discusses possible motives for choosing individual figures as subjects for these dialogues.

Hanley, Keith. Introduction to *Walter Savage Landor: Selected Poetry and Prose.* Manchester, England: Carcanet Press, 1981. Discusses the dramatic qualities of the various individual segments of *Imaginary Conversations of Literary Men and Statesmen.* Faults Landor for the liberties he takes with the historical record, but praises him for his ability to vivify the personalities he chooses as subjects.

Proudfit, Charles, ed. Introduction to *Selected Imaginary Conversations of Literary Men and Statesmen,* by Walter Savage Landor. Lincoln: University of Nebraska Press, 1969. Links Landor with the Romantics rather than the Victorians. Discusses the genesis of the project, and comments on the reception of these writings by Landor's contemporaries and succeeding generations.

Super, R. H. *Walter Savage Landor: A Biography.* New York: New York University Press, 1954. Comprehensive scholarly biography and critical study of Landor's works. Discusses individual "conversations" in the context of Landor's career; explains the writer's interest in the figures he chose as subjects for his work.

THE IMITATION OF CHRIST

Type of work: Religious
Author: Thomas à Kempis (Thomas Hemerken, 1379-1471)
First transcribed: Imitatio Christi, c. 1427 (English translation, c. 1460-1530)

Although arguments have been brought forward through the centuries in an effort to show that Thomas à Kempis did not really write *The Imitation of Christ*, evidence to the contrary has never been widely accepted, and Thomas à Kempis is usually regarded as the author of the famous work. Aside from the Bible, *The Imitation of Christ* is undoubtedly the most famous religious work of the Christian world, having been translated into more than fifty languages and printed in more than six thousand editions. Widely known in manuscript, it was being circulated as early as 1420. Its first publication in English was in 1696. The original language of *The Imitation of Christ* is Latin, not the classical Latin of Rome, but medieval Latin. Many later writers have praised it. John Wesley thought so highly of it that he published an English translation. Matthew Arnold thought that it was, next to the Bible, the most eloquent expression of the Christian spirit ever penned.

The substance of *The Imitation of Christ* is that God is all and humanity is nothing, that from God flows the eternal truth that humanity must seek, and that by imitating the spirit and actions of Christ one may be helped to achieve a state of grace with God. As many writers have pointed out, the greatness of Thomas à Kempis' book does not lie in any originality; there is little that is new in the matter of the work. It is the expression of a spirit that makes *The Imitation of Christ* a piece of great religious literature. Traceable are most of the strands of Christian philosophy and theology of the time, including those that Christians adapted, at least in part, from the great pagan thinkers of Greece and Rome. The book has sometimes been described as a mosaic of matter and ideas taken from the early and medieval Christian mystics, the Bible, and writings of the Church fathers. Borrowings from St. Bernard, St. Gregory, St. Ambrose, St. Thomas Aquinas, Plato, Aristotle, Seneca, and even Ovid can be found within the pages of *The Imitation of Christ*, each contributing in a way to the spirit of Christian example. No reader can miss, even within a few pages, the eloquence and sincerity of the author. The religious feeling is expressed so ardently that it is unmistakably a call to the reader to heed the call of Christ.

Although he calls the reader to a Christian, hence otherworldly, life, Thomas à Kempis is eminently practical in his insights into human beings, their motivations, and their psychology. More than once the author points out that virtue is only to be claimed by those who have been tempted and have proved themselves equal to the challenge of denying worldly vanities and other snares of the devil. One must have experienced temptation in order to remain in act, thought, and spirit a follower of Christ's doctrines and example. Thomas à Kempis also acknowledges that established custom is not easily relinquished by the individual or the community and is thus always a means of keeping one from a Christian life. Relativism and Christianity do not go hand in hand in his philosophy. Although strict in his admonitions that there is no worldly good nor any human love that can be sufficient reason for doing evil, he admits that for the sake of the suffering, or for a better work, a good work might sometimes be postponed.

The palpable faith of Thomas in philosophical idealism is constantly before the reader. There may be doubt, however, as to whether this idealism is entirely Christian or whether there is an influence of Plato or of the later neo-Platonists of Alexandria. The author's faith in the ideal of God is a mystic belief, intuitive in nature, with little of the rational core of thought behind it, upon which Plato insisted. Thomas à Kempis believed, as did Plato, that the real world, the world of ideality, is the only true world. In Thomas' case the method by which truth is achieved is not through reason; rather, the immediate source is grace acquired through the sacraments of the Church, and through revelation acquired by abstinence from worldly matters, the application of prayer, and the use of contemplation. In answer to his own rhetorical question as to how the Christian saints became perfect, Thomas points out that their perfection lay in their contemplation of divinity. The greatness of the saints, he adds, comes from the fact that they steadfastly sought to abstain from all worldly considerations and to cling with their whole hearts to God. The power of God is, for Thomas à Kempis, in divine love, a good above all others that makes every burden light and equalizes all opportunity. He wrote:

> Love is swift, sincere, pious, pleasant, gentle, strong, patient, faithful, prudent, long-suffering, manly, and never seeking her own; for wheresoever a man seeketh his own, there he falleth from love. Love is circumspect, humble, and upright; not weak, not fickle, nor intent on vain things; sober, chaste, steadfast, quiet, and guarded in all senses. Love is subject and obedient to all that are in authority, vile and lowly in its own sight, devout and grateful towards God, faithful and always trusting in Him even when God hideth His face, for without sorrow we cannot live in love.

The pious author suggests in *The Imitation of Christ* that there were four rules for the accomplishment of peace and true liberty: that we should try to do another's will rather than our own, that we should seek always to have less than more, that we should seek the lowest place, and that we should wish and pray always to fulfill the will of God.

The Imitation of Christ is arranged in four parts. Book 1 deals with "Admonitions Profitable for the Spiritual Life"; book 2, "Admonitions Concerning the Inward Life"; book 3, "On Inward Consolation"; book 4, "Of the Sacrament of the Altar." The last, a kind of manual for the devout, gives instruction, advice, and guidance on preparing for the sacrament of communion. In the third book are many prayers noted for their eloquence and sincerity of devotion. The last paragraph of a prayer for the spirit of devotion is one of the best examples:

> How can I bear this miserable life unless Thy mercy and grace strengthen me? Turn not away Thy face from me, delay not Thy visitation. Withdraw not Thou Thy comfort from me, lest my soul 'gasp after Thee as a thirsty land.' Lord, teach me to do Thy will, teach me to walk humbly and uprightly before Thee, for Thou are my wisdom, who knowest me in truth, and knewest me before the world was made and before I was born into the world.

Although a monk, devoted to his order, his vocation, and to God's service through most of his life, Thomas à Kempis was gifted with a keen insight into the world. He inculcated submission to divine will and recognized at the same time that most people would have difficulty in making such submission. He advocates an ascetic, otherworldly life and point of view, and yet he also recognizes the worth of practical goodness. The rules and suggestions he writes in *The Imitation of Christ* are clearsighted; the analysis is keen; the tone is humane. The seriousness of its message, the sincerity of its tone, and the humility and compassion of its author make understandable the place that this great devotional work has held in people's hearts for generations.

Bibliography:
Bryan, G. McLeod. *In His Likeness: Forty Selections on the Imitation of Christ*. London: S.P.C.K., 1961. Provides a historical review of meditative responses and devotional application of the book. Bibliography.

Giles, Constable. *Three Studies in Medieval Religious and Social Thought*. Cambridge, England: Cambridge University Press, 1995. Valuable for those interested in exploring the historical and social context of Christianity. Bibliographical references and an index.

Hyma, Albert. *The Brethren of the Common Life*. Grand Rapids, Mich.: Wm. B. Eerdmans, 1950. Somewhat dated, but copies can be found in libraries. Gives a perspective of how the imitation of Christ concept is applicable in the context of Christian communities.

Taylor, Jerome, and Alan H. Nelson, eds. *Medieval English Drama: Essays Critical and Contextual*. Chicago: University of Chicago Press, 1972. Contains critical essays concerning the religious and social world view from which *The Imitation of Christ* comes. The message of the work is discussed in relation to various liturgical and stylistic essays.

IMMENSEE

Type of work: Novella
Author: Theodor Storm (1817-1888)
Type of plot: Pastoral
Time of plot: Mid-nineteenth century
Locale: Germany
First published: 1850; final version, 1851 (English translation, 1863)

> *Principal characters:*
> REINHARD WERNER, a student
> MRS. WERNER, his mother
> ELISABETH, the young woman whom Reinhard loves
> ELISABETH'S MOTHER
> ERICH, the owner of Immensee and a friend of Reinhard

The Story:

Reinhard Werner, an old man, returned from his walk at dusk and entered his home. He climbed the stairs and sat in his usual place in his study. His housekeeper had not yet turned on the lights for the evening. As it became darker, a ray of moonlight entered the room and fell on a woman's portrait. Whispering the name "Elisabeth!" Reinhard recollected his youth.

As children, Reinhard and Elisabeth had been inseparable. When she was five and he was ten, he told her stories. Once he asked her if she would go to India with him, and she said that her mother would have to come with them. She was upset when he said that her mother would be too old to come by then, but she finally agreed to go with him. He was afraid, however, that Elisabeth would not be brave enough.

As the two grew older, they were always together; Reinhard wrote stories and poems about Elisabeth. When Reinhard was an adolescent, he had to go away to school. As a final celebration before his departure, the village families held a picnic in the woods. The children were told to gather strawberries for dinner, and Elizabeth and Reinhard went off together to look for them. They got lost and did not find any strawberries, although the other children did. Reinhard's love for Elisabeth was intensified by the experience, and he wrote a poem about that day in the woods.

While Reinhard was away at school, during Christmas student festivities when the students were drinking and joking at the Ratskeller, a popular student bar, he was interrupted by a friend who told him that Santa had visited Reinhard's rooms. Elisabeth had sent him a package and a letter in which she told him that Erich, an old friend of his, was doing her portrait and that she would give the portrait to Reinhard's mother. Elisabeth complained that Reinhard had not kept his promise to send her stories. Homesick, he was unable to go back to the Ratskeller crowd but instead gave the presents to a poor child and wrote letters to his mother and Elisabeth.

A visit home showed him that Elisabeth had grown into a beautiful young woman. Erich was often in the house, however; the linnet that Reinhard had given Elisabeth had died and been replaced by Erich's gift, a canary. Elisabeth's mother was cold to Reinhard; she was unhappy to have him there. Erich had taken over his father's estate, Immensee, and, from the mother's point of view, he had become the more desirable candidate for her daughter's hand. Reinhard showed Elisabeth the poems he had written to her; she returned the book with a leaf in it. Upon his return to school, Reinhard took up his studies and did not correspond with Elisabeth. Two years later, Reinhard received a letter from his mother telling him that Elisabeth had agreed to marry Erich.

Some years afterward, Reinhard paid the couple a visit at Immensee, where Elisabeth's mother also lived. Erich had prospered, and the estate was well kept. Elisabeth was subdued, but she appeared to be contented with her marriage. Reinhard wondered about her. One evening, the family was discussing and singing yodeling songs. One song, however, caused Elisabeth to go outside. The song contained the lines, "My mother wished it so,/ Yet it was not my will/ That I should leave the love I had,/ Surrender to another lad,/ And bid my heart be still." When Elisabeth fled, Reinhard realized that she still loved him and that she had agreed to marry Erich only because her mother had wished it.

Later that night, Reinhard jumped into the lake and tried to swim to a beautiful water lily he saw in the distance. However, he was unable to reach it, for when he drew close to the flower, it seemed as if he were being dragged down by the vegetation in the lake; he panicked and swam back to shore.

Erich and Elisabeth's mother made a short business trip the following day. Reinhard and Elisabeth were able to take a walk alone around Immensee. He asked her if she would like to look for strawberries, as they had done so long ago, but she refused. Later, as he rowed her back to the house, her hand betrayed the emotional turmoil she felt. When she arrived at the house, she gave all the money in her purse to a beggar girl at the gate, burst into tears, and rushed into the house.

That night, Reinhard left a note and prepared to depart. Elisabeth came up as he was leaving. She stood in front of him in a state of great agitation, unable to speak. Finally, she told Reinhard that he must not come back, and he agreed.

He never returned to Immensee. As an old man, he recalled those events with wistful sadness. In his study in the dark, he imagined that he once again saw the distant, solitary water lily he had failed to reach that night at Immensee. When the housekeeper came in with the evening lamp, however, he turned again to his books and his scholarship.

Critical Evaluation:

Theodor Storm was both a lyric poet and a writer of fiction. *Immensee*, one of his earliest and perhaps best-known stories, is similar to his poetry in its lyricism and its poetic language.

Storm's poetry and his early stories tend to express nostalgia for a happier world, often a world of youth. Nature is a looming presence. The individuals are simplified almost to the point of being allegorical figures. There are usually only a few characters in each story, and there is such an intense concentration on the main character that the other characters sometimes seem shadowy. Symbols are obvious yet effective. Characters do not seem to be clearly located in time and place, although the northern Germany of Storm's homeland is the presumed backdrop. After *Immensee*, the reality in Storm's narratives increased, but he never fully lost the poetic language and Romantic imagery that had first gained him his reputation.

The two lovers in *Immensee* seem helpless before fate. The young poet Reinhard is strangely reluctant to make direct contact with his beloved after he goes away to school. Elisabeth, a less clearly defined character, is apparently too timid to make her desires known, yet she writes very clearly and decisively in her letter to Reinhard. Even the character who displays determination, the mother, who separates the lovers because she wants Elisabeth to marry a practical, prosperous man, does not come to life. The story nevertheless has a strong appeal because it is a timeless fable of love and loss. Its few symbols recur repeatedly as motifs, gaining more intensity with each recurrence.

Most of the symbols are from nature, in the tradition of the Romantic writers, and they serve as commentary on the turmoil of the central characters. The water lily, which represents remote and unattainable beauty, stands not only for Elisabeth but also for the ideal love that Reinhard can never experience. The birds too have symbolic significance, as when Reinhard's poetic linnet is replaced in Elisabeth's home by Erich's more mundane canary. The hunt for wild strawberries at the celebration outing suggests the young couple's search for full communion with nature and with each other. Enjoying wild strawberries together might have suggested a happy conclusion to Elisabeth and Reinhard's love, but they do not find the strawberries. When, after Elisabeth is married, Reinhard asks her if she will look for strawberries with him, her refusal seems to indicate that she will be faithful to her husband and that Reinhard's offer comes too late.

The choices in Storm's tale are simple and unshadowed by cosmic implications. No one dies; there is no major power of evil. Erich is a cheerful, practical man who is unaware of his wife's secret grief. Even Elisabeth's mother is pragmatic and insensitive rather than evil. The tale also concerns the conflict between the real and the ideal, between practicality and poetry. The promise of young love and the feeling of missed fulfillment are reflected in the images of nature. While Reinhard, as an old man, reminisces, the images of his present reality—his books, the room, and the house—dissolve into the more vivid images of Immensee and scenes from Reinhard's youth. The distance between his youth and his age is underscored by the contrast between the images of enclosure and limit and the past images of vital, expansive nature. With this contrast, the story acquires the power of legend.

The themes of loss and exile—Reinhard is, in a sense, exiled from Immensee—are frequent in Storm's work. His lyrical poetry, like this novella, re-creates images of a magical nature that reflect the emotions of those whose lives are entwined with it. In later stories, written after Theodor Storm had spent fourteen years in exile because of the Danish occupation of his home province of Schleswig, the element of realism in his work increases, and his prose acquires harsher edges. For many readers, the earlier, more nostalgic works, such as *Immensee* and much of the poetry, retain the stronger appeal.

Janet McCann

Bibliography:
Alt, Arthur Tilo. *Theodor Storm.* New York: Twayne, 1973. The most helpful source for the English-speaking student of Storm. Discusses Storm's life and character and analyzes all his major works, including *Immensee.* An annotated bibliography.
Bernd, Clifford A. *Theodor Storm's Craft of Fiction.* 2d rev. ed. Chapel Hill: University of North Carolina Press, 1966. A reading of two of Storm's novellas. Outlines a methodology that casts light on *Immensee,* although it contains no extended discussion of the book. Bibliography covers everything written on Storm until 1965.
Jackson, David A. *Theodor Storm: The Life and Works of a Democratic Humanitarian.* New York: Berg/St. Martin's Press, 1992. Emphasizes social and political perspectives in integrating Storm's life and work. Provides a new context for such works as *Immensee.*
McHaffie, M. A., and J. M. Ritchie. "Bee's Lake: Or, The Curse of Silence. A Study of Theodor Storm's *Immensee.*" *German Life and Letters* 16, no. 1 (October, 1962): 36-45. A close reading of *Immensee.* Compares the novella with Thomas Mann's *Tonio Kröger* (1903).
Mare, Margaret Laura. *Theodor Storm and His World.* Cambridge, England: Cambridge Aids to Learning Limited, 1970. Overview of Storm's work. Places his work in the context of his time.

THE IMPORTANCE OF BEING EARNEST
A Trivial Comedy for Serious People

Type of work: Drama
Author: Oscar Wilde (1854-1900)
Type of plot: Comedy of manners
Time of plot: Late nineteenth century
Locale: London and Hertfordshire
First performed: 1895; first published, 1899

Principal characters:

ALGERNON MONCRIEFF (ALGY), a man about town
LADY AUGUSTA BRACKNELL, his aunt
GWENDOLEN FAIRFAX, her daughter
JACK WORTHING, Algernon's friend, who is in love with Gwendolen
CECILY CARDEW, his ward
MISS LETITIA PRISM, Cecily's governess
THE REVEREND CANON CHASUBLE, D.D.

The Story:

Algernon Moncrieff, nephew of the aristocratic Lady Bracknell, was compelled by necessity to live a more or less double life to avoid being completely at the mercy of his Aunt Augusta. To escape from her dull dinner parties, he had invented a wholly fictitious friend named Bunbury, whose precarious state of health required Algernon's absence from London whenever his aunt summoned him to attendance.

Algernon's friend, Jack Worthing, was forced into a similar subterfuge for quite a different reason. He had under his care a young ward named Cecily Cardew, who lived at Jack's country estate in Hertfordshire under the care of a stern governess, Miss Prism. Jack thought it necessary to preserve a high moral tone in the presence of Cecily and her governess. To escape from this restraint, he invented an imaginary brother named Ernest, who was supposed to be quite a reprobate and whose name and general mode of behavior Jack assumed during his frequent trips to London.

To complicate matters, Jack had fallen in love with Gwendolen Fairfax, the daughter of Algernon's aunt, Lady Bracknell. Gwendolen returned his love, but she had in particular fallen in love with his name, Ernest, of which she was very fond. When Lady Bracknell learned of his intentions toward Gwendolen, she naturally wanted to know something of his family history, but he could supply nothing more definite than the fact that he had been found in a leather bag at the Victoria Railway Station, and that he had been raised by a benefactor. Given that his parentage was unknown, Lady Bracknell refused to consider his marriage to her daughter.

Jack realized that the time had come to put an end to Ernest. He even went so far as to appear at the manor house in Hertfordshire in deep mourning for his brother Ernest. His friend Algernon, "Bunburying" as usual, had preceded him, however, posing as Ernest. Cecily took an immediate interest in this supposed brother of her guardian. When Jack and Algernon came face to face, Jack promptly announced that his brother Ernest had been unexpectedly called back to London and was leaving at once. Algernon, however, having fallen in love with Cecily, refused to leave. Cecily, in turn, confessed that it had always been her dream to love someone named Ernest.

Algernon, realizing that his hopes of marrying Cecily depended on his name, decided to have himself rechristened Ernest. For that purpose, he called on the local clergyman, the Reverend Canon Chasuble, but Jack had preceded him with a like request. Dr. Chasuble thus had an engagement for two christenings at five-thirty that afternoon.

Gwendolen arrived at the manor house in search of Jack. Because both Gwendolen and Cecily believed that they were in love with the same man, the nonexistent Ernest, their initial politeness to each other soon gave way to open warfare. When Jack and Algernon appeared together, the real identities of the two pretenders were established. Both girls were furious. At first Jack and Algernon upbraided each other for their mutual duplicity, but they finally settled down to tea and consoled themselves with muffins. Cecily and Gwendolen at last decided to forgive their suitors, after Algernon had admitted that the purpose of his deception was to meet Cecily, and Jack maintained that his imaginary brother was his excuse to go to London to see Gwendolen. Both girls agreed that in matters of grave importance—such as marriage—style and not sincerity was the vital thing.

Lady Bracknell, arriving in search of her daughter, discovered her nephew engaged to Cecily. Afraid that the girl, like her guardian, might possibly have only railway station antecedents, Lady Bracknell demanded to know Cecily's origin. She was informed that Cecily was the granddaughter of a very wealthy man and the heiress to one hundred and thirty thousand pounds. When she willingly gave her consent to the marriage, Jack refused to allow the match, pointing out that Cecily could not marry without his consent until she came of age, and that, according to her grandfather's will, was when she turned thirty-five. However, he said he would give his consent the moment Lady Bracknell approved of his marriage to Gwendolen.

Lady Bracknell's objections to Jack as a suitable husband for Gwendolen remained, but the mystery was cleared up to Lady Bracknell's satisfaction when it was revealed that Miss Letitia Prism, Cecily's governess, was the nurse who had left Lord Bracknell's house with a perambulator containing a male infant which she had placed in a leather handbag and left in the cloakroom of the Victoria Station. The infant was the son of Lady Bracknell's sister, a circumstance that made Jack, Algernon's older brother. Jack's Christian name turned out to be Ernest. The Reverend Chasuble was relieved of his two christenings that afternoon, and Gwendolen was happy that she was actually going to marry a man named Ernest.

Critical Evaluation:

Oscar Wilde, the literary representative of the so-called Yellow Nineties, stood at the end of the nineteenth century and jeered at the Victorian age. He ridiculed Victorian values most particularly in *The Importance of Being Earnest*, which became probably his most popular work. Turning on the play of words in the title, the drama also satirizes the very idea of earnestness, a virtue to which the Victorians attached the utmost significance. To work hard, to be sincere, frank, and open, and to live life earnestly was the Victorian ideal. Wilde not only satirized hypocrisy and sham virtue, he also mocked its authentic presence.

Wilde mocked the high society of his time, and he paid a high price for it. Within weeks of the first production of *The Importance of Being Earnest*, Wilde's career came to a scandalous and tragic end brought on by himself. Although Wilde was married and the father of two children, he, like many apparently heterosexual men, also practiced homosexuality, a not unusual situation in late-nineteenth century England. Wilde's mistake was to flaunt his behavior. When the marquis of Queensbury accused him in public of being a sodomite because of Wilde's homosexual affair with the marquis' son, Lord Alfred Douglas, the playwright had brought a suit of slander against the marquis. The case was dismissed after it was established in civil court that the marquis' allegations were a matter of fact. However, because British law held homosexual acts to be criminal, once Wilde lost his suit alleging slander the door was open for criminal proceedings against him. The first trial ended in a hung jury, but Wilde was immediately tried again, found guilty, and sentenced to two years at hard labor. After serving the full sentence, he went at once to France. He did not set foot again on English soil and died in Paris two years later, a broken man.

These biographical details are closely connected with the art of Oscar Wilde and with *The Importance of Being Earnest*, a play in which a number of the characters lead double lives. The play's characters too let truths slip out while pretending to be engaged in social chitchat. They are adroit at saying and doing two opposing things at once, and they are virtuosic in their use of language. Nearly all the humor in the play depends on these devices.

At times, it is not quite clear that characters actually did intend to imply another, usually hidden (because socially dangerous) meaning, and then they can appear quite unconscious and even inept. This shimmer between intention and its opposite is constant throughout the play, making the play a parade of cognitive dissonance. Reading or watching the play is to observe the unconscious of the society of Wilde's day. Indeed, Wilde's popularity stemmed from the fact that his society loved the experience of watching its own unconscious on display. *The Importance of Being Earnest*, in particular, was immensely popular, its run only cut short by the real-life scandal that overtook the playwright. The man who exposed secrets so subtly in his writing had exposed his own altogether too crudely.

The four young characters of the play have an engaging insouciance about them; they are defiant in their frankness and loveable for their vulnerability. At the same time, they represent a very distinct character type. Algernon, Jack, Gwendolen, and Cecily show intelligence, wit, and taste, but they also reveal the shallowness, frivolity, and hypocrisy of their kind. Indeed, they can strike an audience as downright idiotic at times, a reminder of the author's final joke: a marriage pending between first cousins, the kind of union that society condemns for its possible consequences. The jibe at the inbred nature of polite society remains implicit, but it is all the funnier for being so.

An intellectual glow emanates equally from all the characters. The formidable and overbearing Lady Bracknell is given such wonderful lines that the audience grows fond even of her. The plain, uptight Miss Prism and her pompous lover, Canon Chasuble, would have been two-dimensional characters in anyone's treatment but Wilde's. Yet he gives them things to say that are every bit as puzzling and funny as what the wittier characters say. Wilde's humor is so often puzzling because it is not clear whether what is said is meant to suggest all that it does suggest. It is the kind of humor that often requires a double take.

The plot of *The Importance of Being Earnest* hinges on mistaken identity, as many plots do, though not many do so to such comic effect. What is funny about the play is that the audience realizes that the characters could easily be someone quite other than who they seem. It is no wonder that audiences continue to love the play: Its humor is intoxicating, its critique of society breathtaking.

"Critical Evaluation" by David Bromige

Bibliography:
Ellmann, Richard. *Oscar Wilde*. New York: Alfred A. Knopf, 1988. A study that focuses on Wilde's recklessness, which provides background for *The Importance of Being Earnest*. Includes detailed references to the play's creation, variant editions and versions, and amendations. Full of comical, lurid stories that add fodder to the Wilde legend.

Ericksen, Donald H. *Oscar Wilde*. Boston: Twayne, 1977. Regards *The Importance of Being Earnest* as the culmination of Wilde's dramatic creativity. In this play, he integrates his aesthetic principles well despite the contrived language, plot, and characters. Ericksen demonstrates that the play is a satire on the priggishness and hypocrisy often associated with late Victorian high society.

Ganz, Arthur. *Realms of the Self: Variations on a Theme in Modern Literature*. New York: New York University Press, 1980. Includes two excellent essays on *The Importance of Being Earnest*, as well as many allusions to it. Discusses the play as a conduit for self-discovery for all ages and lifestyles. Ganz exhibits a firm understanding of theatrical ploys and gimmicks.

Paglia, Camille. "The English Epicene: Wilde's *The Importance of Being Earnest*." In *Sexual Personae: Art and Decadence from Nefertiti to Emily Dickinson*. New Haven, Conn.: Yale University Press, 1990. A scintillating, provocative study of Wilde's marketing of the 1890's lifestyle. Discusses the extroverted, audience-pleasing aspects of Wilde's play.

Powell, Kerry. *Oscar Wilde and the Theatre of the 1890's*. Cambridge, England: Cambridge University Press, 1990. Provides extensive discussion of the London stage, with many behind-the-scenes glimpses. Discusses the various actors who performed in the play and analyzes the typical ingredients of Victorian farce. Includes an appendix of one hundred names and biographical information for each.

IN COLD BLOOD

Type of work: Novel
Author: Truman Capote (Truman Streckfus Persons, 1924-1984)
Type of plot: Detective and mystery
Time of plot: 1959
Locale: Kansas
First published: 1966

Principal characters:
PERRY SMITH
DICK HICKOCK
THE FOUR CLUTTER VICTIMS, father, mother, daughter, and son
ALVIN DEWEY, Special Agent of the Kansas Bureau of Investigation

The Story:

Near the western border of Kansas, among wheat fields and dusty roads, lay Holcomb, a small community of farmers and ranchers. On the morning of November 14, 1959, Herb Clutter strolled across the grounds of River Valley Farm, heading toward a grove of trees that he had nursed to life with the same care and purpose that he had used to raise four children and build one of the largest, most prosperous spreads in Finney County. An educated, widely respected wheat farmer, Mr. Clutter had little to worry about that Saturday morning. A lingering illness had left his wife, Bonnie, a semi-invalid, but recent medical tests had encouraged the family to think that her medical problem was improving. Daughter Nancy, sixteen, the town sweetheart, helped with the household chores. She and her brother, Kenyon, fifteen, were outstanding students in the local high school. Two older daughters lived out of town.

On that same morning, nearly four hundred miles east, in Olathe, Kansas, Perry Smith sat in a café waiting for his friend, Dick Hickock. They planned to drive to Holcomb, rob Herb Clutter, kill everyone in the house, and flee to Mexico, where they would buy a boat and hunt for undersea treasure. Recently paroled from Kansas State Penitentiary and ordered to stay out of the state, Perry had been persuaded to return to Kansas when Dick, also paroled, wrote him of his plan to rob Herb Clutter. According to Dick's last cellmate, a former hired hand of Clutter's, Herb Clutter kept as much as ten thousand dollars in his house.

Arriving at the Clutter farm near midnight, Perry and Dick entered through an unlocked door, awakened the victims, tied them up and put them in separate rooms in the house. The killers found no wall safe stuffed with thousands of dollars; instead, they found only Herb Clutter's wallet, containing about forty dollars. Still determined to leave no witnesses, the killers cut Mr. Clutter's throat, then shot him in the head at close range with a shot gun; the other three victims were shot in similar fashion, one by one.

When the bodies were discovered the next morning, neighbors, friends, and relatives were all electrified by the shocking crime. Alvin Dewey and his team of three investigators from the Kansas Bureau of Investigation in nearby Garden City interviewed anyone remotely connected to the Clutters or River Valley Farm. Nothing developed from these efforts, not even a firm theory as to whether the Clutters had been killed by one person or two, and none of the investigators was sure why the four had been killed. Robbery was a possible motive, but the few clues left by the killers confirmed none of these theories.

Back in Olathe, Perry and Dick continued with their plans to go to Mexico, despite their failure in Holcomb. On November 21, Dick began passing bad checks to finance their Mexican venture. Mexico, however, proved grimly disappointing. After a week in Mexico City and a trip to Acapulco, they had used up most of their money, and the pawned merchandise was all but gone as well. A wealthy German financed a few days on a fishing boat, but plans of diving for treasure were scuttled by the obvious: Neither took well to water, and money was as elusive as the buried treasure of Perry's dream. Back in Mexico City, their car sold and their finances rapidly dwindling, they decided to return to the United States. A bus took them to Barstow, California, where they set about hitchhiking toward Kansas, harboring a plan to rob and kill a motorist. That plan was foiled when the prospective victim, a salesman who had given them a ride, stopped for another hitchhiker.

Al Dewey's investigation took an upward turn when Hickock's former prison cellmate told the warden of Hickock's plan to rob and kill the Clutters. That lead proved most promising. The agents began hunting Smith and Hickock, but the killers eluded capture as they drove through Kansas in a stolen car. They passed bad checks to finance a trip to Miami, where they spent Christmas. Once again without money, they turned toward home, redeeming empty bottles found along the highway. Their journey ended in Las Vegas with their arrest in front of the post office; they had stopped to pick up the package containing the boots worn during the Clutter murders. Perry had mailed the package from Mexico. Al Dewey and his team hurried to Las Vegas, where, under the pressure of interrogation, Dick confessed to the crime. On the car ride back to Garden City, Perry recounted the details of the crime in full.

Housed in the county jail, the pair spent three months awaiting trial. The prosecution had a strong case, based on the murder weapons, the boots worn by the killers during the murders, the testimony of Dick's former cellmate, and the killers' confessions. The defense attorneys had no case. A psychiatric examination failed to justify a plea of insanity, and a few character witnesses did not sway the jury in favor of the two defendants. Both were convicted of all four murders and sentenced to hang.

Sent to the state penitentiary in Lansing in April, 1960, Perry and Dick spent the next five years on Death Row. Through a narrow window they could see across an empty lot the door that led to the gallows. Three execution dates came, and when their last appeal was denied, they were hanged on April 14, 1965.

Critical Evaluation:

Although not the first writer to use actual events as a basis for a novel—Theodore Dreiser based the plot of *An American Tragedy* (1925) on an actual murder case, for example—Truman Capote treats actual events in *In Cold Blood* (1966) in undisguised documentary style. He was first to tout such a work a "nonfiction novel," calling attention to the relationship between real-life events and the literary techniques used to convey them. Chief among the techniques is the arrangement of events in an order that contrasts the Clutter world with the world of their killers. Capote emphasizes the contrast between these two worlds by alternating between the two, giving the reader scenes and dialogue in a brief section (or session), then shifting to the other world.

The novel's mystery is not who committed the murders, for with the introduction of Perry Smith and Dick Hickock, the reader knows who the killers are and whom they kill. The mystery is reflected, instead, in the inability of anyone, including the team of investigators, to discover the identity and motive of the murderers. One of Capote's impressive achievements is to sustain the reader's interest in the events, although the crime, its victims, and its perpetrators have been known from the very beginning. Capote does so by continuing to contrast the world of Dick and Perry with that of the Clutters, implying by doing so that in an orderly universe these two realms should not intertwine. Harmony between humanity and nature, reflected in the autumn setting at the beginning of the book, is disrupted by the murders. The community is perplexed and frightened; its sense of order having been shaken by the inexplicable nature of the crime.

Another of Capote's achievements is to maintain a degree of independence from the material as he lays it before the reader, thereby creating the illusion of the omniscient narrator. Critics have noted that Capote is more interested in Perry than in Dick. Perry's interior life is given much more attention. Readers learn of Perry's fantasies of being "Perry O'Parsons," a singer in the limelight at a Las Vegas showplace. Readers are told of his dreams in which he is swallowed by a huge snake, rescued at the last moment by a big yellow bird, a Christ-figure, that wafts him to heaven. His "artistic" and "sensitive" side is showcased in letters from a prison friend, and Capote gives extensive attention to the years of Perry's troubled childhood and youth, including his difficulties with his father and the motorcycle accident that left him with crippled legs. By comparison, Dick's character and background are given scant attention, amounting to little more than his passion for "blond chicken" and his conviction that he is "a normal."

This apparent imbalance in characterization is part of Capote's thematic control of his material, however, because Perry is the one who cuts Herb Clutter's throat and shoots each member of the family. Focusing on Perry's fantasy world and his background addresses the mystery at the heart of the novel: how four members of a family like the Clutters could have been murdered in cold blood. Who would want to commit such a horrible crime? What could the killer's motivation be? Capote develops a portrait of the murderer as the product of the murderer's upbringing, suggesting that bad circumstances can produce bad people.

Citing the opinion of a psychologist who examines Perry, Capote explains that the murders happened because of the relationship between Perry and Dick. Without the other, neither would have murdered. Chance teamed Dick with a cellmate who happened to have worked for the Clutters, yet the novel connects events and people in a way that suggests that the Clutter murders were, if not predictable, somehow inevitable. The investigators solve the murder mystery halfway through the novel, but Capote keeps in the reader's mind from beginning to end the mystery of how, in a larger sense, such evil intrudes into the Clutter world, a world of control, self-discipline, religious faith, and dedication to hard work. The world that Dick and Perry have created for themselves subjects them to the authority of others. Feeling victimized, they take revenge by victimizing others. Their only power is violence, and the only order they know is disorder.

Another of the novel's fictional characteristics is the arrangement of the material so that the murders take on a universal significance. In the Clutter world, one must believe in and adhere to the principles of justice and humanity. One is responsible for one's actions. God and nature are both just and predictable. The murders seem senseless in this world; one learns that an evil can strike down anyone at any time, and no one can fathom the justice of it all. Capote ends his novel with an image of Al Dewey leaving the graveyard where the Clutters are buried. Behind him is "the whisper of wind voices in the wind-bent wheat." Behind him is the mystery that the voices do not explain.

Bernard E. Morris

Bibliography:
Garson, Helen S. *Truman Capote*. New York: Frederick Ungar, 1980. Chiefly valuable as a survey, almost a paraphrase, of Capote's literary works, including *In Cold Blood*, prefaced by a brief look at Capote's life.

Malin, Irving, ed. *Truman Capote's "In Cold Blood": A Critical Handbook*. Belmont, Calif.: Wadsworth, 1968. A compendium of articles that focuses on *In Cold Blood* and critical reaction to the novel. Includes articles that place *In Cold Blood* in the context of Capote's other works. Of special interest is George Plimpton's interview with Capote; the interview gives excellent perspective to Capote's novel and literary intent, his relationship to the events and people in the book, and how he worked the material into what he calls a "nonfiction novel."

Nance, William L. *The Worlds of Truman Capote*. Briarcliff Manor, N.Y.: Stein and Day, 1970. Two chapters are devoted to *In Cold Blood*, the first chapter placing the novel in Capote's career, the second chapter offering a critical study of the novel.

Reed, Kenneth T. *Truman Capote*. Boston: Twayne, 1981. Surveys Capote's short fiction, novels, and efforts at reportage, which include work on *In Cold Blood*. Reed ends with a study of Capote's style, his themes, and the influences on his writing.

Stanton, Robert J. *Truman Capote: A Primary and Secondary Bibliography*. Boston: G. K. Hall, 1980. Very helpful annotations accompany the lists of works about Capote and his writings. Extremely thorough.

IN DUBIOUS BATTLE

Type of work: Novel
Author: John Steinbeck (1902-1968)
Type of plot: Social realism
Time of plot: 1930's
Locale: California
First published: 1936

> *Principal characters:*
> MAC, a Communist labor organizer
> JIM NOLAN, his assistant and friend
> LONDON, the leader of the fruit pickers
> DOC BURTON, a friend of the strikers
> AL TOWNSEND, a man sympathetic to the strikers

The Story:

Jim Nolan's father was a working man brought to his death by the blows of police clubs and pistol butts. As a youngster, Jim witnessed both his father's courage and his despair. Jim saw his mother lose even her religious faith as poverty and starvation overwhelmed the family. Older, but still keenly remembering his youth, with the scars of brutality and starvation deeply embedded in his heart, Jim Nolan became a member of the Communist Party. He was assigned to work with Mac, an able, experienced organizer. Together, they became fruit pickers, at a time when the fruit growers had cut wages lower than the workers had thought possible. A strike was brewing, and Mac and Jim determined to hurry it along and to direct its course.

Luck was with them. Shortly after their arrival at the camp of the workers, Mac, giving the impression that he was a doctor, helped London's thirteen-year-old daughter-in-law Lisa give birth. Word of Mac's accomplishment spread throughout the area. After Mac and Jim became friendly with London, leader of the camp, and the other workers, they persuaded the fruit pickers to organize and to strike for higher wages and better living conditions. This was not easy to do. As usual, the orchard owners had made effective use of Communism as a bogey. Furthermore, the vigilantes were a constant menace, not to mention deputies, troops, and strikebreakers, all hirelings of the fruit growers. In addition, the authorities could always close down the camp by maintaining that it violated the sanitation laws and was a menace to public health. There was also the problem of money and food; the poor migrant workers desperately needed work to supply their daily necessities.

Despite these difficulties, a strike at last was called. On the night that the strikers were to sneak out to meet the strikebreakers called in by the owners, Mac and Jim were ambushed by vigilantes. They succeeded in escaping, but Jim was shot in the arm. Word of their plan for the next morning had leaked out, and they suspected that a stool pigeon was in their midst. Nevertheless, the next day they marched out to meet the strikebreakers at the railroad station and to implore them not to fight against their fellow workers. Although the police had assembled in force, they seemed afraid of the strikers. During the encounter, Joy, an old and crippled comrade, was shot and killed. The strikers carried the body back to the camp, and over the body of their comrade, Mac delivered a fiery and eloquent speech, exhorting the strikers to carry on and to fight to the finish. This action proved to be the best of all possible

3166

spurs to bring the workers together, and the strikers were aroused to carry on the struggle even more fiercely.

Luck was with them in other ways. They had persuaded the father of Al Townsend, who owned a lunch cart and gave handouts to Party members, to allow them to camp on his farm, after they promised him that his crop would be picked and that his property would be protected. Doc Burton, a philosopher and skeptic, took charge of the sanitation, thus protecting the camp against the health inspectors. Dick, a handsome comrade, used his charms on women in order to get money and food for the strikers. Meanwhile, the owners tried everything to break up the strike. They attempted to intimidate the workers, to divide them, to bribe London, but all their efforts failed. Then another problem arose. The owners had an article published in which it was stated that the county was feeding the strikers. The report was not true, but those who sympathized with the strikers believed it and stopped helping them altogether. Dick was getting far fewer results from his endeavors, and the situation became desperate.

Mac was often on the point of losing his head, of letting his anger get the best of him, so that the strategy of the strike was sometimes imperiled. By contrast, Jim grew more able, more hardened. He ignored the women of the camp who sought to lure him into their tents and did not allow his feelings for Lisa to become anything more than a casual, friendly relationship. Thus, he provided a sort of balance for his more emotional comrades. Conditions grew worse. The strikers had practically no money and no food. Dick finally managed to get a cow and some beans, but the food sufficed for only a few days. Meanwhile, Doc Burton had vanished. Without his help, the sick and the wounded could not be attended to, and the sanitation of the camp grew progressively worse. One night, someone managed to outwit the guards and set a barn afire. The barn and an adjacent kennel housing some favorite pointers were totally destroyed. The next day the owner called in the sheriff to evict the strikers.

The strike seemed lost. The spirits of the men were at a very low ebb, and they gave signs of yielding. On the following night, a boy came and told Jim and Mac that Doc Burton was lying wounded in a field. They rushed out, only to realize, when they were fired upon, that they had fallen into a trap. Mac called out a word of warning and fell to the ground. When he got up, after the firing had stopped, he called out to Jim. He got no answer. Jim was dead. By that time, the shots had aroused the others, and they came forward. Over the body of his comrade and friend, Mac made a strong and rousing speech, urging the workers to stick together, to fight on, and to win the strike.

Critical Evaluation:

Critic Tetsumaro Hayashi has termed 1936 to 1939 the great years of John Steinbeck's career. The novel that culminated this period of greatness, *The Grapes of Wrath* (1939), won the American Book Award and the Pulitzer Prize. Years later, in 1962, the work of this period contributed to Steinbeck's winning the Nobel Prize in Literature. Although *In Dubious Battle* is a less important book than *The Grapes of Wrath*, most critics see it as a thematic precursor to the greater work. Steinbeck's first full-length novel, *In Dubious Battle* narrates a fictional part of the epic struggle of poverty against wealth and worker against boss. Borrowing his title from book 1, line 104, of John Milton's *Paradise Lost* (1667), Steinbeck recalls the epic struggle in Heaven between good and evil.

Two important themes in the novel are the idea of waking "sleepers" to social action and the function of the "group man." Sleepers are people who go through life without trying to improve living and working conditions for themselves or others. Henry David Thoreau used a similar metaphor in his essay "Civil Disobedience" (1849). The story opens with the "sleepwalking" young Jim Nolan joining the Party. Jim has no family of his own (both parents are dead); the Party becomes his new family. In this sense, Jim is like many other Party members in the novel—Mac, Dick, and Joy—who have no families. Other characters who consider joining also have minimal families: Al Anderson has only his father (who has practically disowned him), and London has only his son Joey, Lisa, and a grandchild. Dakin, on the other hand, is slower to join the strike because he has much to lose: a wife, two children, a light truck, and comfortable portable furnishings (when vigilantes later destroy the truck, Dakin withdraws from the group).

Mac's first objective in organizing the fruit pickers' strike is to awaken the people to their exploitation by the orchard owners. Mac himself seldom sleeps in the novel. Individuals awakened from their "sleep" join the Party, submit to the will of the majority, and come together to function as "group man," a concept explained by Doc Burton: "A man in a group isn't himself at all, he's a cell in an organism." The group acts or retreats as a whole, and Mac realizes that some cells (individuals) must be sacrificed for the organism to survive. When an "infection," such as poor wages, threatens the organism, the group must rebel as a whole to save itself. Some individuals must die in the workers' struggle to gain fair profit from their labor, and even Party members—first Joy and later Jim Nolan—are expendable for the good of the group. The "group man" phenomenon makes the striking fruit workers react in predictable ways. When roused, usually by bloodshed, to fight, they move together as an unstoppable force. However, without an immediate goal, the organism relaxes and weaker members shed away, so the organism must be "fed" repeatedly to prevent the movement's failure. Damage (loss or injury of an individual) can be repaired as long as the remaining cells work together toward a common goal. In pursuit of the goal, members take advantage of every opportunity, from delivering a baby and gaining the workers' trust to using the body of a slain comrade to boost morale with a ritual funeral. In "group man's" moral vision, objects and people can and should be used as a means to an end— the ultimate good of the Party. In a larger sense, the striking fruit pickers of *In Dubious Battle* are being sacrificed for the success of future Party efforts. Mac never truly believes the strike will get the workers the fair wages they demand, yet he proceeds with his plans, knowing that workers will be blacklisted, go hungry, and perhaps even die because of the strike. The Party justifies its often brutal practices by arguing that the fruit pickers will benefit from their current troubles when, in the future, farmers will be less likely to lower wages for fear of another strike.

Steinbeck's realistic fiction suggests that it is factual history. Readers should note, however, that although loosely based on historic people and events, the novel is not always historically accurate. Critics have noted the absence of women and Mexican workers among the fruit pickers. London's thirteen-year-old daughter-in-law Lisa is the only developed female character. Moreover, she is first seen in labor, and never thereafter appears without her infant son. Although a minor character, her presence in the book allows the reader to see a human side to Jim, Mac, and other characters through the interest they take in Lisa and her baby. What Steinbeck seems to suggest with her constant breastfeeding and confessed enjoyment of the act is that while a masculine revolution fights for better conditions for "group man," an underlying femininity will nurture the group and replenish its humanity. Lisa's character foreshadows Rose of Sharon in *The Grapes of Wrath*, who after the death of her newborn infant offers her breast milk to a starving adult man, a stranger.

How groups of people react in struggles against society or nature is a common theme throughout Steinbeck's works. Readers may note, for example, his observation of antisegregation demonstrators outside a New Orleans public school in *Travels with Charley* (1962). *In Dubious Battle* fits well in context with other social protest fiction such as Harriet Beecher

Stowe's *Uncle Tom's Cabin* (1851), Upton Sinclair's *The Jungle* (1906), Richard Wright's *Native Son* (1940), and Steinbeck's own *The Grapes of Wrath*.

"Critical Evaluation" by Geralyn Strecker

Bibliography:

Benson, Jackson J. *The True Adventures of John Steinbeck, Writer.* New York: Viking Press, 1984. Definitive biography considers *In Dubious Battle* in context with the author's life and works.

Benson, Jackson J., and Anne Loftis. "John Steinbeck and Farm Labor Unionization: The Background of *In Dubious Battle.*" *American Literature* 52, no. 2 (May, 1980): 194-223. Situates Steinbeck's novel within the social conditions from which it emerged. Just as intriguing as the similarities between fact and fiction are the instances in which Steinbeck altered facts, notably his omission of women from the labor movement and Mexicans from the migrant community.

French, Warren. *John Steinbeck.* 2d rev. ed. Boston: Twayne, 1975. Illustrates Steinbeck's use of Arthurian legend.

Hayashi, Tetsumaro, ed. *John Steinbeck: The Years of Greatness, 1936-1939.* Tuscaloosa: University of Alabama Press, 1993. Collection of essays on Steinbeck's life and literary achievements during the late 1930's. Several articles are pertinent to *In Dubious Battle.*

Pressman, Richard S. "Individualists or Collectivists? Steinbeck's *In Dubious Battle* and Hemingway's *To Have and Have Not.*" *Steinbeck Quarterly* 25, nos. 3/4 (Summer/Fall, 1992): 119-132. Discusses Steinbeck's representation and occasional misrepresentation of American communism.

IN MEMORIAM

Type of work: Poetry
Author: Alfred, Lord Tennyson (1809-1892)
First published: 1850

In Memoriam A.H.H., Obiit. MDCCCXXXIII, unquestionably one of the four greatest elegies of English literature, records the intellectual, emotional, religious, and aesthetic changes Alfred, Lord Tennyson underwent in the sixteen-year period following the early and tragic death of his closest friend, Arthur Henry Hallam, in Vienna, on September 15, 1833. The year *In Memoriam* was first published, 1850, was also the year Tennyson married Emily Sellwood and succeeded William Wordsworth as poet laureate.

In Memoriam, the poem for which Tennyson is most remembered, is organized structurally around the three Christmas lyrics strategically placed within the sequence. It bears resemblances not only to the classical elegies and their English counterparts, most notably John Milton's *Lycidas* (1638) and Percy Bysshe Shelley's *Adonais* (1821), but also to the common thematic pattern used to describe the Victorian crisis of faith so aptly characterized in Thomas Carlyle's *Sartor Resartus* (1833-1834): the movement from despair (Carlyle's "Everlasting No") through a period of questioning and doubt ("The Center of Indifference") to a final affirmation of the sense of human existence ("The Everlasting Yea") reached when one is convinced that there is an ultimate purpose to life, even if that purpose is veiled from humankind.

The similarities of Tennyson's poem to *Sartor Resartus* occur not only in structure but in imagery: the poet repeatedly uses "the veil" to suggest a separation between his own world and his dead friend's, and between himself and God. Another common image appearing throughout the poem is the hand of his dead friend, metaphorically reaching out toward the despairing narrator to touch him and reassure him that his suffering is not in vain.

The poem is not, however, simply an expression of personal grief. Although the "I" of *In Memoriam* is sometimes clearly to be associated with the poet, Tennyson himself said that it is frequently intended to represent "the voice of the human race speaking thro' him." The poet's personal grief and doubt becomes a microcosm for the suffering being endured by nineteenth century men and women who were losing faith in received religion, because the advances in science were leading to the conclusion that there was no divine hand guiding existence. The speaker suffers from his loss, but eventually accepts the notion that, despite the outward signs of chaos, the world is really evolving into something better; his friend Hallam comes to be seen as a harbinger of a "higher race" that will lead humankind to God.

Thus, *In Memoriam* represents the chief Victorian conflict of science and faith as truly as any work of its era; Tennyson's attempt to reconcile the religious doubts arising from his personal sorrow and the effects of pre-Darwinian theories of evolution was hailed by thinkers of his time as an intellectual landmark. The cyclic change, the turn from private grief and despair to the larger public vision and concern for wider, social issues, that can be found in this poem reflects Tennyson's growing acceptance of and reconciliation with the problems of his age.

It appears that Tennyson did not think of publishing the 131 lyrics of *In Memoriam* until late in the 1840's, when he brought them together as one poem, arranged so the three-year time scheme of the poem would reflect the sixteen-year period of his life that they actually represent. These lyrics were written over a long time span, and they vary considerably in the tone and mood of reaction to Hallam's death, thus dramatizing lyrically Tennyson's psychological condition. Although many organizational schemes have been offered, the most generally accepted views the poem as illustrating a movement from initial grief (1-27); to philosophic doubt and despair (28-77); to rising hope (78-103); to affirmation of faith (104-131). The actual growth is more subtle than this and requires close attention to repeated images, such as the two yew-tree poems or the two visits to Hallam's house.

The "Prologue," dated 1849, and addressed to "Strong Son of God, immortal Love," expresses the poet's conviction that faith, not knowledge, leads to a harmonious union of the intellectual and the spiritual. The first section relates the poet's nearly complete self-absorption in grief, but even here a change is evident, for example, in the difference between "I held it truth" (1) to "I hold it true" (27). Although Love provides a "higher life" for man hereafter, few can find immediate comfort for present loss in this promise of future tranquility. Nevertheless, the poet affirms his belief that "'Tis better to have loved and lost/ Than never to have loved at all." This acceptance of his experience, despite its accompanying sorrow, comes only after intervening poems reveal the true depth of his despair; his identification, for instance, with the yew tree, a symbol of death, shows the poet's marked conviction that he, like the yew tree that is not subject to seasonal changes, is imprisoned in grief and can merely endure in "stubborn hardihood."

This fellowship with "Sorrow" (3) induces an intellectual despair and alienates him from comforting Love.

> "The stars," she whispers, "blindly run;
> A web is woven across the sky;
> From out waste places comes a cry,
> And murmurs from the dying sun."

In one sense, this conception of the universe as a blindly run mechanism is the central intellectual conflict of the poem. In his deep melancholy, Tennyson questions not only the justice of Hallam's tragic death, but also the justice of the entire creation.

Tennyson moves alternately from numbed despair to self-awareness (4) and finds composing poetry an anodyne for pain (5). Poems 9 through 17 constitute a group unified by the poet's meditation upon the return of Hallam's body from Italy by ship. A calmer grief now pervades his heart (11). The pain of grief "slowly forms the firmer mind" (18), but the deeper sorrows that words cannot relieve remain locked in his heart (20). He writes not to parade his emotions publicly, but because he must (21).

The second section commences with the first Christmas celebration some three months after Hallam's death. The poet hears the bells' message of peace and goodwill, but almost wishes never to hear them again. Yet even in his despondency, the bells recall his happy youth, and, touching pain with joy, ease his misery. In the renewal of "old pastimes in the hall" they make a vain pretense (30), but one can find consolation in the thought of an afterlife for the dead, although what that afterlife may be remains unrevealed (31).

The second yew tree poem illustrates a lightening of his burden, for he now sees the tree with "fruitful cloud," subject to change, as is his grief. The group of poems from 11 to 58 represents Tennyson's attempt to resolve the question of an afterlife and also the possibility of a reunion with Hallam. These speculations are not meant to solve the problems, he tells us (48), but were "Short swallow-flights of song" that soothed his mind.

In 54, Tennyson expresses the vague "trust that somehow good/ Will be the final goal of ill." The two following poems call in doubt this qualified optimism, so that all he can permit himself is to "faintly trust the larger hope" (55). In his agitated state of mind, the poet sees nature as "red in tooth and claw" (56). The rest of this section deals with the poet's former relationship with Hallam.

The third section opens with the second Christmas and finds the poet with the sense of the abiding presence of his friend. His subdued grief allows him to treasure their friendship, "Which masters Time indeed, and is Eternal, separate from fears."

Tennyson contemplates the possibility of a visitation by Hallam and experiences a mystic trance in 95, when "The dead man touch'd" him "from the past." The third section concludes with a four-poem series relating to the Tennyson family's removal from Somersby, with its pleasant and sorrowful associations.

With the fourth and final section, the poet turns from the past and his personal grief to the future of humankind; this change is signaled by the famous lyric "Ring out, wild bells" (106). Tennyson resolves not to allow sorrow to alienate him from society (108). Hallam's qualities emerge clearly for the first time; in a series of poems, Tennyson praises his friend, particularly for his attributes of leadership and dedication to social good.

Tennyson draws an important distinction in poem 114 of the difference between knowledge and wisdom; with wisdom, man does not fear death since wisdom is of the soul, but knowledge must learn to submit to wisdom and know its place. Acknowledging Love as his lord and king, Tennyson proclaims that all is well (127). His optimism is buttressed by his knowledge that Hallam "O'erlook'st the tumult from afar,/ And smilest, knowing all is well."

As the elegy draws to a close, the poet more strongly feels the certainty of cosmic design: "That all, as in some piece of art,/ Is toil cooperant to an end" (128). He feels more confident of Hallam's omnipresence: "Thy voice is on the rolling air;/ I hear thee where the waters run" (130). His love, although founded on their previous earthly relationship, is "vaster passion" now that Hallam's presence is spiritual and diffused through God and nature. The elegy concludes with the poet's self-confident assertion of the permanence of the living will that purifies humanity's deeds and of the faith in truths that will not be proved until after death.

In the epilogue, Tennyson celebrates the marriage of his friend, Edward Lushington, to the poet's sister. The wedding ceremony is a most appropriate subject for the epilogue: It symbolizes the continuation of life and an affirmation in human nature.

Although the work ends on an affirmative note, many critics have found the strengths of *In Memoriam* to lie principally in its portrayal of doubt. In that sense, it shares affinities with many twentieth century poems. In addition, its fragmented structure suggests something of the modern condition. In these respects, *In Memoriam* is a precursor to other examinations of contemporary life, such as T. S. Eliot's *The Waste Land* (1922), among others.

Bibliography:
Beetz, Kirk H. *Tennyson: A Bibliography, 1827-1982.* Metuchen, N.J.: Scarecrow Press, 1984. An introduction explains the organization of the work. Multiple references to *In Memoriam* and Arthur Henry Hallam are provided in the lengthy subject index.
Bradley, A. C. *A Commentary on Tennyson's "In Memoriam."* 3d ed. Hamden, Conn.: Arachon Books, 1966. Provides a close study of the poem, showing the relation of each section to others. Confronts difficulties in interpretation. Traces origin, composition, and structure of the eulogy, with other discussion, prior to commentary. Chart of changes in the text, appendix.
Buckley, Jerome Hamilton. *Tennyson: The Growth of a Poet.* Cambridge, Mass.: Harvard University Press, 1960. Chapter 6 is devoted to *In Memoriam* and provides biographical

background to—and explication of—the work. Relates critical response to it. Sees Tennyson as a major poet, whose work must be understood by familiarity with the imagination that produced it.

Chesterton, G. K., and Dr. Richard Garnett. *Tennyson*. London: Hodder and Stoughton, 1903. This reprint of a classic is important for researchers. Numerous illustrations; long biographical note on Tennyson.

Lang, Cecil Y., and Edgar F. Shannon, Jr. *The Letters of Alfred Lord Tennyson*. 2 vols. Cambridge, Mass.: The Belknap Press of Harvard University Press, 1981. Volume 1 contains 32 separate references to *In Memoriam*. The synthesis of primary sources (letters) with secondary sources (books about Tennyson's *In Memoriam*) strengthens good research.

Pinion, F. B. *A Tennyson Companion: Life and Works*. New York: St. Martin's Press, 1984. Illustrated, indexed, chronology, notes, and appendices. Provides a brief coverage of the poet's life and long coverage of the poet's writings, including a chapter about *In Memoriam*.

IN THE HEART OF THE SEAS
A Story of a Journey to the Land of Israel

Type of work: Novel
Author: Shmuel Yosef Agnon (Shmuel Yosef Czaczkes, 1888-1970)
Type of plot: Folklore
Time of plot: Eighteenth century
Locale: Buczacz, in the Austro-Hungarian Empire; the Land of Israel; and places in between
First published: Bi-levav yamim: Sipur agadah, 1935 (English translation, 1947)

> *Principal characters:*
> HANANIAH, a wonder-working stranger
> RABBI SHMUEL YOSEF, a teller of pious legends
> ZUSHA, a robber chief
> HIS ABANDONED WIFE

The Story:

Before a group of men and women started on their journey to settle in the Land of Israel, a stranger named Hananiah entered their town of Buczacz, entreating them to allow him to accompany them. The man, barefoot and in rags, carried all his worldly goods tied up in a kerchief. With some prompting, he recounted his adventures, full of perils and narrow escapes. He stayed for a time with robbers who had been forced by their oppressors into a life of crime. Asking why the robber chief put on phylacteries, Hananiah learned of the death of Zusha, the band's former leader, whom the present one imitates by this action. Ashamed to have to decline the chief's offer to lead him through a certain cave to the Land of Israel, Hananiah left the band to resume his travels.

The group was delighted to have Hananiah join them, for he would complete the quorum of ten men required for communal prayer. Among the men were Rabbi Shmuel Yosef, well versed in legends of the Holy Land, and Rabbi Yosef Meir, who had divorced his wife because she refused to go to the Land of Israel. Among the women were Milka, who had married a man on condition they would immigrate to Israel, only then to have him insist on staying and divorce her, and the wives of four of the men.

Hananiah rejected the group's offer of boots, swearing that his feet must remain bear because, while in a country that never celebrated the Sabbath or festivals, he lost track of the time and failed to honor the Day of Atonement. He proceeded to polish the lamps and other implements in the House of Study, to repair torn books, to make trunks for the pilgrims, and to fashion a Holy Ark for the Torah Scroll accompanying them to the Land of Israel.

All the town gathered to speed them on their journey, except Buczacz's rabbi, who believed that settlement in the Land of Israel must await the coming of the Messiah. The group had hired and outfitted two large wagons, the men and women to ride separately; the wagoner drove one and Hananiah, though denying he was a wagoner, expertly guided the other. Everywhere they stopped, people, even rival townsfolk and gentiles, showed them respect upon learning of their destination.

As they approached Lashkovitz, which boasted a grand fair, Satan stood in their path and began coaxing them to turn aside and indulge in the splendors of the fair. Coming to himself, one of the group urged the wagoner to direct the horses quickly on the road to the next stop. Passing a horde of cripples carrying waxen models of limbs, the pilgrims realized that they had escaped temptation.

Joining the company along the way was a woman whose husband, Zusha, had disappeared. Rumors arose that he had become a robber chief and been hanged. According to Jewish law, the woman could not remarry because her husband's death remained unproved. Refusing to despair, the woman continued to search for Zusha.

Once the women of the company saw the sea, on which their journey must continue, they began to fear for their lives and cried for divorces. When these had been obtained, the women remembered the pains those buried outside the Land of Israel must endure to reach it. They then entreated their former husbands to remarry them, which the men did.

On board ship, when the men gathered for prayer, they discovered they lacked a quorum and realized that Hananiah had been left behind. Miserable, they blamed themselves for this loss. As the dawn brightened, they stared in wonder at a man sitting on his kerchief and floating by them on the sea.

Arriving at Istanbul, a city of splendor and squalor, the comrades awaited the ship hired annually by Istanbul's congregation for pilgrims to the Land of Israel. Boarding the ship with the Buczacz company were Jews and gentiles of all nationalities. After three peaceful weeks, a storm threatened to sink the ship. Once the danger was past, the passengers found themselves back at Istanbul. A second departure was successful, and all arrived safely in the Holy Land. All along the way, Rabbi Shmuel Yosef had heartened the company with legends extolling the land.

Immediately, however, the group encountered the reality of its fierce heat. Upon reaching Jerusalem, the men went to pray at the Western Wall, or the remains of the Holy Temple, adding a special prayer for Hananiah. At the synagogue, during the Sabbath service, they were reunited with him—grown taller and wearing shoes. It was Hananiah who had sailed alongside their boat on his kerchief. He also had met the robber chief who had imitated the holy actions of his predecessor. Hananiah had brought this man to the widow searching for her lost husband, thereby resolving the matter of Zusha's fate.

While all eventually were reduced to living on charity, only Leibush the butcher left in bitterness. Two of the women died violently, and Rabbi Yosef Meir's divorced wife arrived and they remarried. Hananiah lived past the age of one hundred, accruing strength with each year.

Critical Evaluation:

The image Shmuel Yosef Agnon projected in public as well as in his narrating persona was that of a simple, pious man. Certainly a practicing Jew, immersed from childhood in an Orthodox religious tradition, Agnon was also well read in German, Russian, French and Scandinavian literature. The writer with whom Agnon is most often compared is Franz Kafka, who also evokes, perhaps more vividly, an unsettling world where ordinary laws of time, space, and logic do not apply. While some critics derive this quality directly from the telescoping of time and place that marks Jewish homiletic literature, others trace it to a resurgence of the romantic spirit in Europe in the late nineteenth century, which, admittedly, was influenced by folklore and spirituality. In any case, characteristic of Romantic writing is the impression made on the reader of the subjective nature of the narrative.

Nightmare and irony result when a character attempts and, inevitably, fails to internalize and comprehend the outside world. Readers may miss the cosmic and bleak comedy in Agnon and Kafka; catastrophes, especially those of modern history, also are likely to influence readers' understandings of works written before the Holocaust. The choice of Agnon as recipient of the 1966 Nobel Prize in Literature not only recognized his prodigious body of work but also— along with that of cowinner Nelly Sachs, a poet of the Holocaust—acknowledged the shocking fate of European Jewry in the twentieth century. Agnon's saturation of his fiction with Jewish folklore and religious tradition can be argued to have fulfilled a historical role, as it preserves, in the pages of books and the minds of readers, a world that faced annihilation.

In the Heart of the Seas clearly reflects Agnon's creative use of folk styles and motifs. A folk device Agnon employs, for example, is that of the story within a story. When a new character is introduced, the main plot line is abandoned while the character's history is related, so that the new character's story is interwoven with the frame story. An often playful narrative personality presides. Agnon slyly projects himself into the novel in the character of Rabbi Shmuel Yosef the storyteller, whose tales of Zion inspire the pilgrims. The style of the novel is that of a pious folktale, its ostensible purpose articulated in a colophon reminiscent of those found in medieval manuscripts: "There are those who shall read my book like a man reading books of legends, and there are those who shall read and derive some benefit for themselves."

In a period marked by the rise of fascism and mass emigration to Palestine, in which secular Zionism dominated Hebrew writing, Agnon revived a romantic, deeply spiritual yearning for Zion. As is demonstrated by *In the Heart of the Seas*, the typical subject of Agnon's fiction is the dispossessed. While this choice of subject is far from unique, Agnon's treatment is distinguished by how he connects dispossession and homelessness to the complex of symbols expressing the concept of exile in Jewish tradition. Agnon is able to draw upon a storehouse of language and imagery to represent the state of rootlessness. Folklore is also a way to interpret the phenomena, endowing his fiction with a remarkable coherence.

In the Heart of the Seas throws the traditional antithesis of exile and Israel into relief. The movement from Buczacz to Jerusalem forms the plot of the novel. The renewal for which one hopes upon entering the Holy Land is exemplified by Hananiah, who appears to grow younger and stronger with each year spent there. Hananiah is an agent of *tikun*, or reparation of the broken and alienated things of the world in exile. He fixes and restores holy objects and also helps to solve the problem of Zusha's widow. The reuniting of Rabbi Yosef Meir and his wife in Israel signifies this power of *tikun*.

Characteristic of the ambivalence that pervades Agnon's writing, however, violence and poverty prey on the pilgrims in Israel, as violence and poverty preyed on them in exile. Another area of ambivalence is toward the miraculous and pietistic. The reader does not always know whether miracles are intended to be accepted at face value or not.

Agnon's conscious incorporation of Jewish folklore in his novels and stories follows a major trend in Hebrew and Yiddish literature since the 1870's. In this tradition, a playful, ironic tone and structural elements betray works of fiction as something other than the naïve work of simple piety. Instead of answers to how one can resolve contradictions between past and present, between practical nation building and spiritual yearning, between vision and reality, Agnon, imaginative writer that he is, gives only wondrous and perplexing stories.

Amy Adelstein

Bibliography:
Alter, Robert. "S. Y. Agnon: The Alphabet of Holiness." In *After the Tradition: Essays on Modern Jewish Writing*. New York: Dutton, 1969. Insightful evaluation of themes and motifs that have preoccupied Agnon. Traces much of the originality of Agnon's art to his painstaking care with words.
Band, Arnold J. *Nostalgia and Nightmare: A Study in the Fiction of S. Y. Agnon*. Berkeley: University of California Press, 1968. A detailed, chronological study of Agnon that illumi-

nates the context and content of his work. Analysis of *In the Heart of the Seas* emphasizes its humor and fantastical qualities.

Fisch, Harold. *S. Y. Agnon*. New York: Frederick Ungar, 1975. A brief introduction to Agnon. Argues that Agnon, an endlessly inventive storyteller, attempts to comprehend Jewish history.

Hochman, Baruch. *The Fiction of S. Y. Agnon*. Ithaca, N.Y.: Cornell University Press, 1970. Positing Agnon's gift as more lyrical than novelistic, Hochman determines yearning to be the dominant mode of Agnon's fiction. Describes the ambivalence in Agnon's work.

Ribalow, Menachem. "Samuel Joseph Agnon, Major Novelist of Yesterday and Today." In *The Flowering of Modern Hebrew Literature: A Volume of Literary Evaluation*, edited and translated by Judah Nadich. New York: Twayne, 1959. A sympathetic look at Agnon's achievement by a leader of the Hebrew movement in America. Identifies the influences in Agnon's work.

IN THE WILDERNESS

Type of work: Novel
Author: Sigrid Undset (1882-1949)
Type of plot: Historical
Time of plot: Early fourteenth century
Locale: Norway
First published: Olav Audunssøn i Hestviken and *Olav Audunssøn og hans børn,* 1925-1927
  (*The Master of Hestviken,* 1928-1930; volume 3, *In the Wilderness,* 1929)

Principal characters:

OLAV AUDUNSSØN, the master of Hestviken
EIRIK, his heir
CECILIA, Olav's daughter
BOTHILD ASGARSDATTER, Olav's foster daughter
LADY MÆRTA, Bothild's grandmother
TORHILD BJÖRNSDATTER, the mother of Olav's son Björn
SIRA HALLBJÖRN, a priest

The Story:

Olav Audunssøn had little desire to stay on at Hestviken through the summer following his wife's death. When the sons of the English armorer in Oslo asked him to be shipmaster of their boat on a trading voyage to London, it was plain that the idea pleased him. Eirik, Ingunn's son by the Icelander, also wanted to go on the trip, but Olav told him nay—he must remain at Hestviken and be companion to little Cecilia, the daughter Ingunn had borne in her last years.

In England, two adventures befell Olav. At evensong in the Dominican's church, he saw a woman so much like dead Ingunn that for a moment his breath failed him. So like she was, and yet young enough to be his daughter. With her was a blind man, apparently her husband. Olav saw her again, at mass and evensong, and after a time they began to exchange glances and smiles. One night, her serving woman stopped him after the service and led him to a great house outside the walls. The strange woman was in the garden, her only dress a thin silk shift. For a moment Olav felt that he was about to clasp Ingunn again. Then he realized that she was only a wanton wife seeking sport with a stranger. Thrusting her from him, he ran away.

At another time he went with his shipmates to a famous shrine north of London. Separated from his companions, he wandered in the woods until he encountered some men beside a brook. That night they attacked him for his rich dress and jewels. While Olav fought with the robbers in the dark, he felt the battle surge he had known in his outlawed youth. Later it seemed to him that he had been tempted by pleasures of the flesh and of violence, sent to lead him from the path of redemption he must follow to atone for the secret slaying of Teit, Eirik's father.

When Olav sailed home in late summer, he found Eirik grown taller and strong for his age and Cecilia fairer than ever, with promise of great beauty. Resolving that Liv, the slatternly serving woman, was unfit to train the daughter of Hestviken, he wed Liv to Arnketil, his housecarl, and sent the pair to live at Rundmyr, the farm he carried on for Torhild Bjørnsdatter, who had borne him a son out of wedlock two years before. One day he went across the fjord to Auken, where Torhild was living, to discuss his arrangement. Seeing his son and Torhild again, he thought of asking the woman to return and keep his house, but he sadly put the thought out of his mind.

After Liv and Arnketil moved to Rundmyr, the place began to have a bad reputation because of the dicing, wenching, and worse that went on there. At last Sira Hallbjörn, the priest, warned Olav to keep Eirik away from that thieves' den. For years Olav had been of two minds about Eirik. He wanted to like the boy whom he had claimed as his heir, yet he could not abide Eirik's insolence and boasting. He realized that he should give more time to his training but shrank from that duty because of the old clash of wills between them. Urged to marry again, he wanted no other wife beside him at table and bed.

His problem was solved in part when Asger Magnusson, an old friend, died in Tunsberg after asking Olav to foster his daughter Bothild and provide for his mother-in-law, Mærta Birgers-datter. Lady Mærta was grim and gaunt but capable. Never had Hestviken been better kept than it was under her charge. Cecilia and Bothild, close in age, lived as sisters. Lady Mærta dressed them well, and people said that in the whole southland there were no fairer maids than those at Hestviken.

Eirik set himself against Lady Mærta from the first, and Olav was always angry when he was drawn into their rows and forced to rebuke the boy. In the winter of Eirik's sixteenth year, they quarreled after Olav found him in rude sport with a serving girl. That night Eirik left Hestviken without farewell. There was no report of him at Rundmyr or among Olav's distant kin, but at last word came that he was in Oslo, among the men-at-arms who served Sir Ragnvald Torvaldsson. Knowing Sir Ragnvald a gentle knight from whom Eirik would learn the skills of weapons and courtly ways, Olav was satisfied. He went to Oslo and gave the runaway money and a squire's gear. There was much kindness between them when they parted, Olav almost in envy for Eirik's youth.

Three years passed more quietly than any Olav had known since boyhood. Cecilia was his great delight, with little in her nature to recall her weak-willed, sickly mother. One night some men from another parish came to Hestviken. After drinking in the hall, one of the men tried to seize Bothild and Cecilia. Bothild was terrified, but Cecilia drew her knife and slashed at the man until the blade was red. Olav felt that she should have been the boy of the house.

Olav, beginning to grow restless, was often in the company of Sira Hallbjörn, a priestly lover of falconry and hunting. One night, while they supped at a wedding feast, Olav's ancient Viking ax, Kin-fetch, rang. For a moment they saw in each other's eyes old pagan stirrings that neither could have spoken aloud. Riding home later that night, Olav went into the graveyard and called to Ingunn to arise. On another day he went to Auken, where he found Torhild married to Ketil, a young man on the farm. Olav asked her to send Björn, their son, to live with him. She refused.

The snows lay deep that December when Duke Eirik crossed the border from Sweden to lead his troops against his father-in-law, King Haakon. Torhild brought word of the invasion to Hestviken one frosty dawn. After sending Cecilia, Bothild, and Lady Mærta to Auken for safety, Olav rode off to warn his neighbors. When the franklins tried to ambush the Swedes, they were routed by the mailed horsemen. Olav and Sira Hallbjörn were among the few who made their way to the manor at Sundrheim and spent the Yule there. Meanwhile, the Swedes occupied Oslo and besieged Akershus, the royal fortress. Olav was in that great fight at Aker church and at Frysja bridge, where there was hard fighting to keep Duke Eirik from taking the castle. Sira Hallbjörn was killed at the bridge, and in the press a crossbow bolt shattered Olav's jaw.

Olav lay in fever for days. After Duke Eirik withdrew from the siege, a merchant took Olav into Oslo and cared for him there. One day he looked at himself in a mirror. His cheek was furrowed and scarred, and his hair was gray. When he went back to Hestviken in the spring, Olav felt that he had become an old man.

Critical Evaluation:

The third volume in the Master of Hestviken tetralogy, *In the Wilderness* is set in the Middle Ages, a period whose significance in the development of Western thought and values had achieved great importance in scholarly circles when Sigrid Undset began writing her novels. More than other works in the series, *In the Wilderness* depends for its action on the large historical movements of the time; the protagonist's journeys and his service in actual historical conflicts link the novel more closely to other examples of historical fiction, especially since Olav's viewpoint—that of the rank and file soldier—on these events is one not likely to be represented in the actual chronicles of the period. The colorful details of war and trade are in fact merely the background for a concentrated examination of the protagonist's character and spiritual condition.

The central theme of *In the Wilderness* is Olav Audunssøn's confrontation with his selfish pride. With the death of his wife Ingunn, recorded in the final pages of *The Snake Pit*, Olav expects to be able to abandon the lie in which he has lived for so long. Instead, he finds himself more closely bound to it than before, for he must continue his silence about his act of murder and about the licentiousness of his wife for the sake of his daughter Cecilia and his wife's son Eirik. The tensions created by his inability to articulate his guilt lead him to behave miserably toward Eirik, whom he accepts intellectually as his son and heir but who still brings up in Olav strong feelings of revulsion when he remembers that Eirik is the product of Ingunn's liaison with Teit, the man Olav murdered. Away from Hestviken, he hopes to escape the torments of conscience by immersing himself in travel, trade, and warfare. When the struggles of his conscience come to a head at the church for pilgrims near London, however, he decides to resolve the problem by going on pilgrimage to Jerusalem without returning to Hestviken first. He changes his mind when he realizes that his resolution is prompted as much by his desire to avoid the vexed situation at home as by a wish to humble himself before God and be cleansed of his old sin.

In taking up his old life as a cross to be borne for his children's sake, Olav acts out the Christian precept that sin is its own punishment; his decision not to take Torhild into his house again carries out the penitential theme. Nevertheless, in consciously giving up his soul that his children might thrive, he regresses, in effect, into a pre-Christian state of being. The last part of the novel shows him immersing himself in thoughtless paganism: attempting to call Ingunn from her grave, applauding Cecilia's spirited use of a knife, and glorying in the panoply and comradeship in war. In a way, he comes full circle, experiencing again the emotions of his youth and his early manhood.

This sense of returning to his youth gives only temporary and false hope, however, since Olav is unable to shake free from the feelings of emptiness and despair that continue to plague him. He knows he must do something to atone for his transgressions, but he is not yet ready to engage in the final act of abnegation that will bring forgiveness from God. His journey toward self-knowledge and acceptance of Christianity is not yet complete. At the end of the novel he is forced to recognize that his body has deteriorated, and that he has become old. As a result, the link with his early life as Ingunn's husband dissolves, making way for the renewal of the conflict between Christian and pagan values that characterize the final novel of the series, *The Son Avenger.*

When Sigrid Undset was awarded the Nobel Prize in Literature in 1928, that award was made, according to the citation, "principally with regard to her powerful pictures of Northern life in medieval times." No one who has read *Kristin Lavransdatter* (1920-1922) or *The Master of Hestviken* will deny the justice of that statement. Those not familiar with her novels must be prepared to find a writer who, while true to the life and spirit of a past age, pays little attention to great personages and big historical events. Undset's stories of medieval life are so rich in detail that there is little need in her books for a parade of names and dates. *In the Wilderness* is the one exception to her usual practice, however, in that the closing episode of this novel deals with a traceable historical event, the invasion of Norway by Duke Eirik of Sweden in 1308.

"Critical Evaluation" by Laurence W. Mazzeno

Bibliography:
Allen, W. Gore. *Renaissance in the North.* New York: Sheed & Ward, 1946. Notes strong Catholic underpinning of Undset's works. Claims Undset approaches her medieval material with no preconceptions, and portrays her hero as living in a golden age when religious values guided people's lives.
Bayerschmidt, Carl. *Sigrid Undset.* New York: Twayne, 1970. General study for nonspecialists; provides overview of Undset's life and major works. Commentary on *In the Wilderness* is included in a chapter discussing Undset's novels of the Middle Ages. Concentrates on the moral development of the hero.
Gustafson, Alrik. *Six Scandinavian Novelists.* Minneapolis: University of Minnesota Press, 1971. Analysis of the four novels that make up the chronicle titled *The Master of Hestviken.* Considers Undset's portrait of the hero of *In the Wilderness* as gloomy; highlights her concern for the perennial battle between flesh and spirit.
Whitehouse, J. C. "Sigrid Undset." In *Vertical Man: The Human Being in the Catholic Novels of Graham Greene, Sigrid Undset, and Georges Bernanos.* New York: Garland, 1990. Analysis of Undset's view of human nature seen in her novels and stories. Discussion of *In the Wilderness* is included in a discussion of Undset's vision of humanity. Calls Undset a great moralist whose characters reveal her optimism for the future of the human race.
Winsnes, A. H. *Sigrid Undset: A Study in Christian Realism.* Translated by P. G. Foote. New York: Sheed & Ward, 1953. A biography of the novelist that traces the strong strand of Christian belief that undergirds all of her fiction. Discusses the characters in the multivolume saga of which *In the Wilderness* is a part.

INDEPENDENT PEOPLE

Type of work: Novel
Author: Halldór Laxness (Halldór Kiljan Guðjónsson, 1902-   )
Type of plot: Social
Time of plot: Twentieth century
Locale: Iceland
First published: Sjálfstætt fólk, 1934-1935 (English translation, 1946)

> *Principal characters:*
> BJARTUR, a crofter
> ROSA, his first wife
> FINNA, his second wife
> ASTA SOLLILJA, Rosa's daughter
> GVENDUR, Bjartur's son
> NONNI, Bjartur's younger son
> INGOLFUR ARNARSON, Asta's father

The Story:

After working for eighteen years for Bailiff Jon, Bjartur was at last able to buy, with a heavy mortgage, the croft (small farm) called Winterhouses. Proud of his new status as a landowner and fiercely independent, Bjartur promptly renamed the place Summerhouses. It was a poor place, fit only for sheep grazing. The house, which Bjartur rebuilt, consisted of one room over the stable. The walls were of sod, and the roof was made of a few sheets of corrugated iron covered with turf. Nevertheless, it was his own place, and Bjartur was determined to be a hired workman for no one and to put his trust in sheep. For his wife he chose the twenty-six-year-old Rosa, a small sturdy woman with a cast in one eye, who had also been in service to the bailiff. Rosa was disappointed in her house, and Bjartur was disappointed in Rosa. He soon found that she was already pregnant. He suspected, and was sure much later, that the man was the bailiff's son, Ingolfur.

After a few months of marriage, Bjartur left on a cold winter day to look for his sheep. Seeing a buck reindeer in the woods, he jumped on the animal's back and attempted to subdue it. The reindeer, however, was too strong and took off in mad flight for the river. With Bjartur still holding on, the animal swam downstream and finally landed on the other shore. Bjartur, nearly frozen to death, stayed to recuperate at a nearby croft.

He returned home after several days to find his wife dead from childbirth and a baby daughter still alive. Disregarding the parentage of the girl, he proudly named her Asta Sollilja. The bailiff's wife sent the pauper Finna and her mother to look after Bjartur and the baby. Finna was nearly forty years old but strong and well preserved. To settle the problem of the child's care, Bjartur married her.

Each year Finna had another child, usually stillborn. After some years, however, there were Helgi, Gvendur, and Nonni, and their half-sister Asta. The croft was crowded, and the beds were all dirty and filled with vermin, but the land was clear of debt.

A southerner came to the croft one day to ask permission to camp and hunt. The stranger delighted Asta, who was awkward and uncouth but bursting with love. The stranger hardly noticed her, however, and each night he was gone most of the night. The reason for his visit came out later, when the bailiff's daughter left the country in great haste.

After little Helgi was lost on the moor, the tie between Asta and Bjartur became closer. When Finna died from poor diet and childbearing, the father tried his best to make life easier for the girl. He refused to let Asta go to school, but he did teach her much of the old Icelandic poetry. Bjartur took Asta on his yearly trip to town, where, after doing the shopping, they stayed overnight in a lodging house for country folk. To save money, father and daughter both slept in the same bed. Asta was unhappy. The townspeople had laughed at her homely clothes, and the snores of the drunken farmers in the nearby beds were terrifying. She snuggled closer to her father and kissed him. He put his arms around her, but to his horror he found that she was kissing him repeatedly. Bjartur abruptly got up and went out for their horse. Father and daughter left for home in the rainy night.

Then a series of misfortunes, which the Icelanders attributed to a witch buried near Summerhouses, greatly reduced Bjartur's flock of sheep, and he went to town to work. Trying to meet his obligations to his children, Bjartur sent a schoolmaster to instruct Asta, Gvendur, and Nonni during the winter; but Bjartur's choice of teacher was unfortunate. After getting drunk one night, the schoolmaster took Asta. When Bjartur came home in the spring, Asta was pregnant. In his rage Bjartur cast out his daughter, who went gladly, full of romantic notions of her lover. She walked to his fine town house, which turned out to be a shack. There she learned that he had many children and that his wife was again pregnant.

Just before World War II, Nonni went to America to join his uncle. Only Gvendur and Bjartur were left, as well as the old mother-in-law. The war boom raised the price of lambs, and Bjartur prospered. He had two cows and three horses. At the same time, a cooperative movement, with Ingolfur at its head, was organized. In the parish, only Bjartur held out; he remained loyal to the merchants who had been gouging him for years.

Nonni sent two hundred dollars from America to pay for Gvendur's passage. In spite of his father's objections, Gvendur, who was seventeen years old and big and strong for his age, decided to emigrate. He put on his best clothes and went to town to take the coastal steamer. There he was admired because he was going to America. During the day and night as Gvendur waited before his ship sailed, he met the bailiff's granddaughter. She took him riding on the moor, where they spent the night together. Hoping to win her love, Gvendur renounced his emigration and went back to Summerhouses.

In spite of the depression following the war, Bjartur resolved to build his new house. He went deeply into debt to buy great supplies of stone and timber. That year he got the walls and roof completed, but there were no doors and windows. Before he could finish the house, the mortgage was foreclosed, and Summerhouses passed into the hands of the bank. The only place left for the family was the mother-in-law's old croft, long since abandoned. During the moving, Bjartur met Asta and was reconciled to her. Asta had a second child by another man, and she was carrying a third. The family was complete again, except for Nonni.

Asta, like Bjartur, was independent. Ingolfur, now rich and a member of Parliament, had revealed to her that he was her father. His offer of support had been soundly rejected. Bjartur fell in with some strikers who had struck against the government's low wages. For a while he was sympathetic with the men, who were, in a way, Communist led. Gvendur was even more sympathetic, but they both rejected in principle the idea of collective action. They were independent farmers and herders.

They moved to the wretched hovel far to the north, with only Blesi, their twenty-five-year-old horse, to do the hauling. By hard work, they could continue their old way of life. They would have one room in a turf-covered hut. Their diet would be refuse fish. With luck they would be only a little less comfortable than savages in a jungle.

Critical Evaluation:

Independent People is one of the few novels to give a faithful and artistic picture of some essentially unrewarding lives in bleak, small Iceland. In addition to the background, Halldór Laxness has written in a style and with a scope approaching the epic. The reader gets some of the feeling of the traditions of the Vikings and sees the old give way to the new. Only the hard, barren life of the crofter is unchanging, for the Icelander in the remoter sections of his country lives on about the plane of the primitive savage.

Laxness' work is an excellent example of the naturalistic novel, for it demonstrates the thesis that people have no connection with a religious or spiritual world and that people are subject to the natural forces of heredity and environment. According to the tenets of naturalism, one's life is largely determined by the social and economic forces of one's background, which are usually presented by an author of this school with elaborate and minute documentation. The characters usually show strong animal drives, but they are helpless in their fight against sociological pressures. All of these characteristics fit *Independent People*. In it, Laxness starkly presents all the grim details of the life of Bjartur, the "independent man," who fights to rise above his environment, becomes successful for a period, and then sinks back into the miserable life he had worked so hard to escape.

Except for occasional references to automobiles and electricity, one would not know that the novel is set in the twentieth century, for the lifestyle of the crofters is no better than that of peasants in medieval times. The poverty of the crofters is almost unbelievable. They live in small, one-room hovels above the stables and are plagued by the smoke of peat-stoked fires, the dampness of spring, and the bitter cold of winter, when snow may cover the entire house. In an environment where humans live little better than beasts, it is almost unavoidable that they become animalistic and lose compassion and emotion. In *Independent People*, there is no communication or understanding among the characters, and any attempt at communication is viewed with suspicion.

The role of women in such circumstances is particularly hard. This is shown in the grotesque death of Rosa, who is found dead on the croft floor in a pool of blood. Her infant is kept alive by the warmth of the dog that lies upon it until Bjartur returns. The harshness of a woman's life is also seen in the yearly pregnancies of Finna and in the miserable life Asta is forced to live after Bjartur drives her from the house.

Even more interesting, however, is the perverted responses that one is conditioned into making by the hard life one lives. For example, Bjartur mourns for neither of his wives. When looking for a housekeeper to care for the infant Asta, he admits that he talks more about animals than about human beings. He dismisses Rosa's death by telling the minister that she just died from loss of blood. No effort to care for her seems to have entered his mind.

There are several prominent themes running through the novel; politics, economics, social reform, and the clash between religion and ancient superstitions are all dealt with in some detail. For years Laxness had searched for a sustaining religious and political ideology, and in *Independent People*, the restless energy generated by that search found its first powerful outlet in his bitter attack on materialism. He held the greed and oppression inherent in the materialistic philosophy was responsible for the sordidness and suffering that filled the lives of his countrymen in rural Iceland. In exposing the cruelties of rural conditions with all the merciless determination of the naturalist school, the author enraged many Icelanders—who resented having such a brutal picture of their emerging nation published abroad—and impressed liberals all over Europe and America. For all Laxness' revolutionary vigor, hatred of power and authority, scorn for bourgeois morality, and anger and grim satire, he still is able to express his artist's love of beauty. Alongside scenes of coarseness and themes marked by their bitterness, Laxness displays throughout *Independent People* a great compassion and sensitivity, a capacity for tenderness and concern, and a burning devotion to the spirit of individualism and idealism.

The center of interest, however, is always the character Bjartur. At times, his seeming indifference is nothing more than an attempt to cope with life's harshness. In the spring following Helgi's disappearance, for example, Bjartur, looking for a lost ewe, finds the decayed body of a young boy, which no longer looks like a human being. Bjartur touches it once or twice with his stick, takes a good pinch of snuff, and leaves. Bjartur reveals, at times, that affection is possible in his life. Although he knows Asta is not his child, she is his favorite. He calls her his "little flower" and is horrified when he finds his fingers undoing the fastenings of her undergarment in the bed they share. He also has a poetic side, for he continually composes complicated verses and teaches the ancient poems of Iceland to Asta. Yet poetry is the only fancy he allows himself; all else is harsh reality. To Bjartur, the sheep and the land are the most important things in the world, for after years of debt his only desire is to be considered an independent man. When he brings his bride, Rosa, to Summerhouses, he says that independence is the most important thing in life. He intends to maintain his independence. This is the great irony of the book, for his independence is false; he is completely at the mercy of his environ-ment. His stubbornness and pride lead him to disaster when he refuses to take the advice of wiser men and falls into bankruptcy when he borrows money to build a "real" house, which he hopes will rival the Bailiff's mansion. Bjartur defies everything and everyone. He refuses to believe in either the Christian religion or in the ancient superstitions of the country. In a show of bravado, he defies the spirit of Gunnvor, the witch buried upon his land, who was supposed to have killed most of her children and to have drunk the blood of those who survived. Everyone else in the district adds a rock to her grave when they pass, but this Bjartur refuses to do. Instead, he purchases a headstone for her grave marked "To Gunnvor from Bjartur." It is after this act of defiance that his financial troubles begin.

Laxness was reared in the country and is able to give an intimate picture of the starkness of Icelandic life on the frontier. This great attention to detail makes the book approach epic proportions. There are, however, some flaws in the author's style. He often makes authorial intrusions, commenting upon politics, economics, or human nature. The style is also uneven. At times, it is smooth and poetic, but at others it is extremely awkward. On the whole, however, the book is valuable as a social document and as the story of Bjartur, the independent man, who, struggling against impossible odds, is never defeated psychologically, even when he loses all he has worked so hard for. Without remorse, he plans to begin again at the wretched, abandoned croft of his mother-in-law.

"Critical Evaluation" by Vina Nickels Oldach

Bibliography:
Einarsson, Stefán. *A History of Icelandic Literature.* Baltimore: The Johns Hopkins University Press, 1957. Sketches the writer's career and comments on major publications. Claims that in *Independent People* and other novels, Laxness deals sensitively with contemporary themes. The poor farmer in the novel emerges as a symbol of his class and a hero of great stature.
Hallberg, Peter. *Halldór Laxness.* Translated by Rory McTurk. New York: Twayne, 1971. Chapter devoted to *Independent People* compares the novel with the work of Knut Hamsun and discusses Laxness' infatuation with socialism. Extensive commentary on the protagonist and his children.

Hallmundsson, Hallbe. *Georgia Review* 49, no. 1 (Spring, 1995): 39-63. Collection of essays on the novelist's achievements. Includes a critical essay on the ways the novelist is able to use regional materials to describe universal traits of human character. Reprints Laxness' 1955 Nobel Prize acceptance speech.

Leithauser, Brad. "The Book of My Life: Halldór Laxness' *Independent People*." In *Penchants and Places*. New York: Alfred A. Knopf, 1995. Personal commentary on a book that Leithauser claims has great power to evoke sympathetic responses in readers, especially those whose experiences parallel the novelist and his characters.

Rossel, Sven H. *A History of Scandinavian Literature 1870-1980*. Translated by Anne C. Ulmer. Minneapolis: University of Minnesota Press, 1982. Provides a biographical sketch and a summary of Laxness' literary achievements. Places *Independent People* in the context of the author's canon, examining ways the novel shows Laxness' faith in socialism as an antidote to capitalism.

INDIAN SUMMER

Type of work: Novel
Author: William Dean Howells (1837-1920)
Type of plot: Domestic realism
Time of plot: Shortly after the American Civil War
Locale: Florence, Italy
First published: 1886

Principal characters:
  THEODORE COLVILLE, a middle-aged bachelor
  MRS. LINA BOWEN, a middle-aged friend of Colville
  IMOGENE GRAHAM, a girl chaperoned by Mrs. Bowen
  EFFIE BOWEN, Mrs. Bowen's thirteen-year-old daughter
  MR. MORTON, an admirer of Imogene Graham

The Story:

Theodore Colville studied architecture as a young man and continued his professional education by spending some months in Italy. While there, he went about with two young women. He fell in love with one of them, but the girl rejected his suit. Soon afterward, he went back to the United States at the request of his older brother, who had recently purchased a newspaper. Colville became the editor of his brother's paper and eventually purchased it. He entered politics in his fortieth year. After being defeated, he left his home in Indiana and went again to Italy.

He tried to resume the study of architecture but was diverted after meeting Mrs. Bowen, who had been the companion he had not fallen in love with in Italy years before. Mrs. Bowen, now a widow, invited Colville to visit at her home. Colville met Mrs. Bowen's thirteen-year-old daughter Effie, who quickly became fond of him, as well as Imogene Graham, a twenty-year-old American woman whom Mrs. Bowen was chaperoning.

Colville spent many pleasant days and evenings with Mrs. Bowen, Imogene Graham, and Effie Bowen. At first, Imogene regarded him as an old man, since he was twice her age, but she soon realized that she enjoyed his company much more than that of many men her own age. In an effort to be companionable with her, Colville danced and went about socially as he had not done for many years. Mrs. Bowen also enjoyed Colville's company.

Mrs. Bowen chose carefully the places where she and her charges went. During the carnival season, she permitted Colville to take them all to a masked ball. At the ball, little Effie became ill and had to be taken home unexpectedly. As a result, Imogene and Colville spent much of the evening together unchaperoned. They began to realize their affection for each other.

Mrs. Bowen was quick to realize that a love affair was developing between them. She tactfully pointed out to Imogene the differences between her and the much older man. When she said, rather less tactfully, that she thought Colville had only been trying to be amusing, the girl reported the conversation to Colville. Hurt, he went to Mrs. Bowen and talked with her, finally agreeing to her suggestion that for propriety's sake he leave Florence. Because it was a weekend and Colville had insufficient funds to settle his hotel bill, he was forced to wait until the following Monday. By that time, Imogene had decided that it was unfair to make him leave the city because of her. When she asked him to stay, he agreed to do so.

A few days later, Colville and Imogene met accidentally in a public park. They decided that they loved each other and went back to Mrs. Bowen's residence to tell her that they had decided to be married. Mrs. Bowen, as Imogene's chaperon, told them she would be forced to write immediately to the girl's parents to inform them of this recent development. The lovers agreed to her plan and promised to say nothing about an official engagement until they heard from Imogene's parents. Imogene warned her chaperon, however, that she would marry Colville even without her parents' consent.

While they were awaiting word from America, a young minister named Morton, who was also in love with Imogene, returned to Florence. Both Colville and Mrs. Bowen wished to tell the young man the state of affairs, but the girl refused to permit it. Finally, word came from Imogene's parents. Her mother had decided to sail for Europe, to see Colville for herself before giving her decision.

During the intervening days before Mrs. Graham's arrival, the four—Mrs. Bowen, Mr. Morton, Imogene, and Colville—went on an excursion to see the Etruscan ruins in Fiesole. At one point, Colville and the young minister walked a short distance beside the carriage. A peasant driving a band of sheep came over the brow of a hill, frightening the horses, who began to back the carriage dangerously close to a precipitous drop at the side of the road. The two men rescued the women from the carriage. While Mr. Morton was taking Imogene from the vehicle, Colville ran to the horses' heads to try to hold them. When his hand caught in the curb strap, he was dragged with the team when the carriage plunged over the edge of the road.

For two weeks, Colville lay very ill. When he was finally able to have visitors, Imogene's mother came to see him and told him she was taking her daughter back to America immediately. She felt that Colville had acted like a gentleman but she told him that her daughter was not really in love with him although she thought too much of him to break the engagement. Colville was stricken but perceived that Imogene's departure was the only answer to the situation. After her mother left, Imogene herself came into the sickroom and bade Colville a hasty good-bye.

Some time later, Mrs. Bowen and Colville talked over the affair. During the conversation, they admitted that they loved each other, but Mrs. Bowen refused to marry Colville because of the embarrassing position in which she had been placed during his affair with Imogene. She had hated herself the whole time she tried to prevent the affair because, although she hoped she could see the situation objectively, she had always feared that her actions and thinking had been colored by her feeling for Colville.

Little Effie Bowen, having formed a very strong attachment for Colville, refused to hear of his departure. Within a few months, under the influence of their mutual love and Effie's attitude toward her mother's suitor, Mrs. Bowen was reconciled to a marriage. They were married quietly and then moved to Rome, where no one who knew them could spread gossip about the affair with Imogene. Not long after their marriage, they heard that Mr. Morton, who had been deeply in love with Imogene, had been appointed to a church in a community near Buffalo, where the Grahams lived. Both Mr. and Mrs. Colville hoped that he and Imogene Graham would make a match of their own.

Critical Evaluation:

Indian Summer reflects an American realist's interest in the phenomenon of the surge of Americans who traveled abroad after the Civil War. Both of the two other major novelists with whom William Dean Howells is usually bracketed had already explored this theme, Mark Twain hilariously in *The Innocents Abroad* (1869), and Henry James with great sophistication in a series of novels and tales beginning with *The American* (1877).

In many ways Howells, who was one of the first American critics to recognize the genius of Twain and James, occupies a position between them. *Indian Summer*, like *The Innocents Abroad*, although in a much less satirical and pointed way, registers the humorous aspects of American tourists' and expatriates' experiences in Europe. Howells' naïve young Americans face dangers that they realize only dimly, if at all, but, unlike their Jamesian equivalents, they usually manage to avoid catastrophes. Indeed, Imogene Graham's main danger in Florence is the possibility of her marrying another American—the well-intentioned but plainly inappropriate Colville.

Howells uses the Italian setting to provide a backdrop for his novel, but he is less interested in the cultural collisions between American innocents and European predators than in the uneasy relationship between two Americans—a man in his Indian summer and a woman in the early spring of her adulthood—and a man's slowly developing relationship with a woman near his age. This second relationship is complicated by the conflict between her love for him and her obligations as Imogene Graham's chaperon. Imogene is always referred to, not unjustifiably, as a "girl." She is only slightly more mature than James's Daisy Miller. It is because she is a beauty living in the city where Colville had fallen in love seventeen years earlier that she becomes the object of his romantic yearnings. The reader soon recognizes Colville's folly in pursuing her and not Lina Bowen, a mature and still beautiful woman much better suited to Colville at this stage of his life.

Though Howells' hero is foolish, he is basically a gentleman, courtly in a lighthearted way and eager to please not only Imogene but Mrs. Bowen and her daughter Effie, who is an eminently pleasable child. He is witty, self-effacing, kind, and attentive to them all but of course most attentive to Imogene. He has reached the dangerous age of forty-one and looks even older. Never having been a handsome man, he is now bordering on corpulence. Though painfully conscious of his physical defects in the eyes of one as young as Imogene, he dares to hope that she may prefer him to the young men who inevitably flock about her. Thus Howells makes Colville a character study in affable, civilized, well-meaning illusion.

The author guards against the possibility that the reader (and for that matter Colville himself) might take him too seriously. Colville is described as having spent years as editor of a newspaper in a midwestern town called Des Vaches (the cows). The name of the paper, *Democrat Republican*, suggests a comic political irresoluteness. Colville, who trained to be an architect, jokes sarcastically about his limited success in journalism and in life to date.

Colville converses with Mrs. Bowen on such topics as "American girlhood," a subject that Howells lightly implies had by that time became an old literary standby, especially among Americans abroad who have the opportunity to compare it to the more socially constrained European variety of girlhood. At one point, Colville and an acquaintance compare themselves with characters in a novel, "one of Mr. James's," Colville offers; the woman counters by mentioning Howells as more appropriate, though in his novels "nothing happens." In such ways Howells sets a light tone that advises the reader that the plot, built around a sophisticated middle-aged man pursuing an unformed twenty-year-old woman, will, though it is serious, not end tragically like James's *Daisy Miller* (1878) in which an older man tries unavailingly to protect the young female from unsuspected peril abroad.

Imogene naturally considers Colville old, but she is romantic enough to be touched by his attention to her and eventually to persuade herself to accept him as a fiancé. As a dedicated foe of the romantic outlook, which in his opinion had spoiled most fiction after the time of Jane Austen, Howells tried to reveal the folly of the planned match. He accomplishes this by contradicting his own insistence that in his fiction "nothing happens," by which he meant an avoidance of spectacular and purely adventitious incidents. The sight of the injured Colville after he had attempted to perform heroically jolts Imogene into an awareness that not love but pity had led her to accept his proposal. She also has a guilty feeling that she has somehow seduced an essentially honorable man and is now ready to value the attentions of Mr. Morton, a suitor much closer to her own age.

Howells' fictional worlds are marked neither by Jamesian tragedy nor by Mark Twain's kind of broad comedy; *Indian Summer* is, rather, an ironic comedy of manners in which the characters embroil themselves in troublesome social situations that require them to perceive and work out morally satisfactory solutions. Not only Colville and Imogene but also Mrs. Bowen must struggle to determine the decent way out of the posited dilemma. Although *Indian Summer* does not possess the larger social significance of Howells' earlier *The Rise of Silas Lapham* (1885) or his later *A Hazard of New Fortunes* (1889), it is one of his most finely wrought studies of moral responsibility in the personal lives of deftly delineated central characters.

"Critical Evaluation" by Robert P. Ellis

Bibliography:
Eble, Kenneth. *William Dean Howells.* 2d ed. Boston: Twayne, 1982. A chronological assessment of Howells' fiction. In the chapter focusing on *Indian Summer* and the 1888 novel *April Hopes*, Eble ranks the former among Howells' most successful dramatizations of the folly of a romantic-sentimental outlook.

Howells, William Dean. *Indian Summer.* Vol. 11 in *A Selected Edition of William Dean Howells.* Bloomington: Indiana University Press, 1971. The standard edition of the novel with introduction and notes by Scott Bennett, who counters the often-express view of *Indian Summer* as an exercise in nostalgia and argues that the novel reflects Howells' full artistic maturity.

Wagenknecht, Edward. *William Dean Howells: The Friendly Eye.* New York: Oxford University Press, 1969. No sustained discussion of *Indian Summer* but shrewd observations on the novel in many references. Wagenknecht notes, for example, that the novel contradicts Howells' critical disapproval of violence in fiction by resolving the hero's love affair through the medium of a carriage accident.

Woodress, James J., Jr. *Howells and Italy.* New York: Greenwood Press, 1952. Assesses *Indian Summer* as a neatly plotted minor masterpiece, though unrepresentative of Howells' work generally. Woodress emphasizes the correlation between the author's fiction and his own Italian experiences, as well as his skill at evoking the Italian setting in *Indian Summer*.

Wright, Nathalia. *American Novelists in Italy: The Discoverers—Allston to James.* Philadelphia: University of Pennsylvania Press, 1965. Discusses a succession of nineteenth century novelists and gives considerable attention to Howells' Italian novels. Views *Indian Summer* as reflecting his tendency to emphasize that Europe exerted a more pernicious influence on American men than on American women.

INDIANA

Type of work: Novel
Author: George Sand (Amandine-Aurore-Lucile Dupin, Baronne Dudevant, 1804-1876)
Type of plot: Sentimental
Time of plot: Early nineteenth century
Locale: France
First published: 1832 (English translation, 1833)

> *Principal characters:*
> INDIANA, a young Creole
> MONSIEUR DELMARE, her husband
> NOUN, her foster sister and maid
> RODOLPHE BROWN or SIR RALPH, Indiana's cousin
> RAYMON DE RAMIÈRE, her lover

The Story:

Indiana was married to pompous, quick-tempered Monsieur Delmare, a retired army officer no longer young. Loyal to her suspicious and jealous husband, Indiana had lived a discontented, uneventful life. Her cousin, Sir Ralph Brown, himself unhappy and frustrated, was her only companion. Although Monsieur Delmare kept a watchful eye over the young couple, there was nothing improper in the relationship between them. As a matter of fact, Sir Ralph had secured the good graces of Monsieur Delmare, and he was accepted as one of the household. If not an intimate friend, he was at least a close companion. Indiana was as reserved in her behavior toward Sir Ralph as she was toward her husband, but to a close observer it was apparent that in a friendly, inarticulate manner, Sir Ralph was fond of Indiana.

The submerged tensions of the household erupted one evening when someone was discovered scaling the garden wall and entering the grounds of the estate. Monsieur Delmare rushed out and fired in the darkness at the intruder. When the wounded prowler was brought into the house, he revealed himself as Raymon de Ramière, a young man who, he maintained, wished to see Monsieur Delmare regarding the latter's manufacturing enterprise. De Ramière further explained that his brother had a similar business in another part of the country, and that he would profit by Delmare's information.

Delmare's suspicions were dissolved. He had not noticed the behavior of Noun, Indiana's friend and maid. Noun had become extremely agitated at the entrance of de Ramière, a fact that nobody noticed in the excitement. She knew that de Ramière had come to the estate not to see Delmare on business but to keep a rendezvous with her. Noun had been his mistress for some time. Once in the house, however, he was immediately attracted to Indiana, especially because he was already tiring of Noun.

De Ramière systematically began his suit for Indiana's affections, and to that end, he enlisted the aid of both his mother and Indiana's aunt. Before long, Indiana began to reciprocate his attentions, and the affair became the subject of much discussion in Parisian salons. Delmare remained ignorant of the gossip. Despite de Ramière's urgent avowals and protestations, however, Indiana refused to yield herself to him because she preferred a pure and spiritual love. Upset by her refusals, de Ramière contracted a fever that kept him confined to his bed for several days. Indiana was strongly affected as well and experienced several spells of swooning.

One night, impatient to achieve his desire, de Ramière impetuously entered the Delmare house. Indiana was away, but Noun was there awaiting the return of her mistress. The two met in Indiana's room, and Noun, as passionate as ever, enticed the young man's surrender. When Indiana returned, Noun escaped, leaving de Ramière to face her mistress alone. Indiana, disturbed to find her suitor in her room, ordered him to leave before his presence was discovered.

A short time later, Noun's body was discovered floating in a nearby stream. Pregnant, she had taken her life because of de Ramière's refusal to marry her or even continue their relationship. Indiana was brokenhearted at the death of her maid, and de Ramière himself was greatly perturbed. By that time, he had tired of his pursuit of Indiana and had determined to forget her. One night, Indiana, having decided at last to become his mistress, went to his rooms. Learning that he was not at home, she waited until he returned at dawn. Then she offered herself to him. Unfortunately, while they were talking, dawn broke. Compromised by her presence in de Ramière's rooms at that hour, Indiana returned to her home, where Delmare, agitated by the discovery of her absence, received her with cold suspicion.

Soon afterward, Delmare suffered business reverses and faced complete ruin. Indiana contritely went with him to the Isle of Bourbon, where he hoped to make another fortune. Unhappy in her new home, she lived only for the letters de Ramière wrote her. At last, she decided to leave Delmare and arranged for her secret passage back to France. On her arrival in Paris, she learned that fickle de Ramière had recently married.

For weeks, she lived a miserable existence. Penniless and starving, she decided to die. When she and Sir Ralph, who had followed her to Paris, were strangely reunited, they agreed to commit suicide by drowning. At the last minute, however, they changed their minds. Moved by Sir Ralph's devotion, Indiana realized that he was the man she truly loved. Together they forsook civilization and lived as recluses, away from all people and society, but satisfied and happy at last.

Critical Evaluation:

George Sand's *Indiana* presents the story of a woman fighting against the oppressions of her society, a woman challenging, as Sand called it in her 1842 preface to the novel, "the false relationship between the sexes." Through this theme, Sand explores a spectrum of issues touched by this struggle—individualism, duty, honor, love, jealousy, fear, falsehood, truth.

When the public was first introduced to the novel in 1832, it provoked controversy over Sand's criticism of the strictures of traditional roles of men and women, particularly those of husbands and wives. That controversy earned Sand instant fame. She was praised and condemned for her commentary on society's injustices. Some called the novel treacherous for threatening the stability of traditional institutions; others marveled at its capacity to dramatize the struggle and eventual triumph of a single soul fighting against the arbitrary whims of an oppressive husband and the glaring hypocrisies of an unjust society. Sand herself noted that she, as "a young author—a mere neophyte in the world of social ideas, one whose literary and philosophical equipment consisted of a little imagination, a bit of courage, and a love of truth—was thus endowed with a weighty role."

Sand's own personal rebellions—her decision to flee her husband to live a bohemian life in Paris, her preference for men's clothing, her active participation in renowned literary circles, and her liberated sexual attitudes—became as noted as her novels. She was an active member of the literary community in Paris and a close friend to such influential figures as Honoré de Balzac, Alfred de Musset, Eugene Delacroix, Frédéric Chopin, Franz Liszt, and Gustave Flaubert.

Indiana is a quest for the happiness that is possible only through liberty and equality, an assertion of the primacy of the individual over the demands of society. Contrary to the novel's crusade for equality among the sexes, however, is its presentation of women; Sand's depiction of women as nurturers bound by a duty to love and serve is inconsistent with the ideal of true independence. Her pleas for equality are irreconcilable with her views on the course a woman's life must necessarily take. Sand asserts that women have a fundamentally different temperament than men and that this feminine temperament predisposes them to certain roles. The capacity for boundless love and devotion are, to Sand, distinguishing aspects of what makes a woman noble. A woman's outlet for such nobility is, of course, as mother, wife, nurse, companion—roles in which a woman's life is conceptualized primarily in terms of her relationship to men.

At the heart of Indiana's struggle is the search for truth. In order for Indiana to develop the spirit of individualism necessary to cast aside the forces that chain her, she must first confront society's values and identify its failings. Indiana refuses to withstand the continued oppression of her married life and leaves her husband. Believing in the integrity of de Ramière's professions of love, despite evidence to the contrary, she runs to him. She realizes her error when she is confronted with the indisputable fact that his words of love were but momentary fancies, created as much to flatter his own vanity as to win her favor. In the preface to the 1832 edition of *Indiana*, Sand observed that "[de Ramière] is the false reason, the false morality, by which society is governed; the world considers him an honorable man because the world does not examine things closely enough to see them clearly."

Each of the three main male characters represents a prevailing political force at the time of the novel's publication. Delmare clings fiercely to his Napoleonic heritage; Sir Ralph supports a democratic society where all are equal under the law; and de Ramière upholds the supremacy of post-Napoleonic aristocracy. Sand's endorsement of a democratic society is evident throughout the novel. As her career as a writer progressed, the importance of politics in her work increased.

As with many of the novels of the early nineteenth century Romantics, the characters' motivations are grounded in psychology. Indiana's desperate urge to liberate herself from the oppressions of her position, Sir Ralph's self-imposed loneliness, Delmare's excessive violence, and de Ramière's compulsive need for romantic conquest illustrate how the culminating forces of social classes, gender roles, personal experiences, and individual judgments influence each character's fundamental beliefs. The parallels between Indiana and Noun, her maid and foster sister, recount the conflict-ridden evolution of Indiana's own character. Sand's use of double characters enabled her to examine a duality common to Western culture; Indiana, high-born, chaste, and spiritual contrasts with the low-born, sensual, and earthly Noun. As Indiana begins her journey toward self-fulfillment, Noun dies, and Indiana begins to integrate the paralleled characteristics. Noun's death after being betrayed by de Ramière, the man who teaches Indiana a harsh lesson in love, portends the tumultuous passage that Indiana must make before she gains the independence, sexual confidence, and clarity of judgment that will enable her to achieve the happiness she seeks.

The conclusion of the novel reaffirms the individual's responsibility for his or her life and happiness. Indiana realizes that she must make her own decisions if she is to be truly happy and liberates herself from her abusive husband to join de Ramière. De Ramière's ambivalence toward her devotion leads her to recognize the cruel façade with which society has replaced honor. Those lessons lead Indiana and Sir Ralph to flee to a remote cottage to live out their days in peaceful happiness. As *Indiana* closes, Sir Ralph concludes that "society has no right to demand anything from the person who demands nothing from it" and advises one to "respect [society's] laws if they protect you, accept its judgments if they seem fair—but if someday society slanders and spurns you, have enough self-respect and pride to do without it."

"Critical Evaluation" by Heidi Aubrey

Bibliography:

Crecelius, Kathryn J. *Family Romances: George Sand's Early Novels*. Bloomington: Indiana University Press, 1987. Chronicles the early period of Sand's literary career, when her thematic focus was directed toward rebellion against the oppression of traditional marriage. Offers criticism and interpretation of *Indiana*; considers the work in the context of other novels from this period in Sand's career.

Dickenson, Donna. *George Sand: A Brave Man, the Most Womanly Woman*. New York: St. Martin's Press, 1988. Offers insight into Sand's work, her life as an author, and her struggle as a woman attaining literary success in a primarily male field. Examines her open rejection of women's roles and discusses her noted rebellions and successes.

Sand, George. *Story of My Life: The Autobiography of George Sand: A Group Translation*. Edited and translated by Thelma Jurgrau. Albany: State University of New York Press, 1991. Offers a wealth of insight into the author's life and work. A critical introduction by Thelma Jurgrau and a historical introduction by Walter D. Gray provide insightful commentaries that set the context of Sand's autobiography.

Schor, Naomi. *George Sand and Idealism*. New York: Columbia University Press, 1993. An examination of feminism and idealism in Sand's novels. Explores Sand's Romanticism; considers the influence of society and politics on her work.

Thomson, Patricia. *George Sand and the Victorians: Her Influence and Reputation in Nineteenth-Century England*. New York: Columbia University Press, 1977. Employs historical and literary evidence to determine the cultural and literary influence of George Sand's work on the Victorian period.

THE INFORMER

Type of work: Novel
Author: Liam O'Flaherty (1896-1984)
Type of plot: Psychological realism
Time of plot: 1920's
Locale: Dublin
First published: 1925

Principal characters:
> FRANCIS JOSEPH MCPHILLIP, a political murderer
> GYPO NOLAN, the informer
> DAN GALLAGHER, a revolutionist
> KATIE FOX, a prostitute

The Story:

Francis McPhillip came to the door of the public lodging house. He was unobtrusively and shabbily dressed. With the caution born of necessity, he waited in the doorway until he was sure he was not followed, keeping his hand inside his raincoat to feel the reassuring butt of his pistol. For six months, he had been a hunted man, hiding out in the wild mountains.

In October, he had killed the secretary of the Farmers' Union. His orders from the revolutionary organization had been to use his gun only if necessary; after the killing, the organization had disavowed his act and expelled him. Since then, he had been a lone fugitive, but now he was back in Dublin to see his family.

He searched among the public rooms crowded with Dublin's poor. In the dining room, he found the man he had come to see: Gypo Nolan. Gypo was eating from a huge plate of cabbage and bacon he had stolen from a locker. Francis sat down and inquired hoarsely of Gypo if the police were still watching his parents' house. At first, Gypo only grunted in response, then he said he thought the coast was clear. After eating voraciously from Gypo's plate, Francis slipped away.

Gypo thought stolidly of his former companion in the organization. Then he reflected bitterly on his empty pockets and on the fact that he could not buy a bed that night. He tried to link up the two facts, but Gypo thought only with great difficulty. He had been Francis' companion at the time of the murder, and the organization had expelled him too. Without Francis and his agile brain, Gypo was unable to make plans. Now, finally, an idea came to him. He went to the police station and told the officers where they could find Francis. He received twenty pounds for his information. Shortly afterward, when police officers surrounded his father's house, Francis shot himself.

In a public house, Gypo met Katie Fox, a prostitute who took care of him occasionally when he was destitute. He bought her a few glasses of gin and told her he had no need of her bed that night. She was suspicious because he had money and accused him of robbing a church. During the quarrel, she accidentally let drop the word "informer." Gypo was startled. He was glad to leave her and go out in the night.

To keep up appearances, Gypo went to the McPhillip house. He quarreled with Francis' father, who blamed him for the wild life his son had led, but Francis' mother and his sister, Mary, praised Gypo for his visit of sympathy. As he left, he gave Mrs. McPhillip four silver coins.

3195

Bartly, an organization member sent out to bring Gypo in, followed him. When he made a taunting reference to the coins Gypo had given Francis' mother, Gypo choked Bartly, who was saved only by the arrival of a friend who was armed. By dint of threats and persuasion, Gypo was led to the organization headquarters, where he met Dan Gallagher, the revolutionists' feared and respected leader.

Because of his stupidity and his great strength, Gypo had no fear of men or guns, but Dan was intelligent and soon overcame Gypo's hostility. If Gypo could give them a lead on the person who had informed the police of Francis' return, he would be taken back into the organization. Dan brought out a bottle and gave Gypo several drinks. Under the influence of the liquor, Gypo concocted a story that Rat Mulligan had a grudge against Francis for betraying his sister and that he had seen Rat following Francis away from the lodging house. Dan was skeptical but sent for Rat and ordered Gypo to appear for the hearing that night at one-thirty.

Followed by Bartly, his shadow, Gypo went out confidently. In a street fight, he knocked out a policeman from sheer exuberance. Trailed by an admiring rabble, he went to a lunch stand and bought food for all of his admirers. In the confusion, he slipped away from Bartly.

Gypo was elated. He had money, he was safe, and he would be back in the organization. He went to a superior brothel and spent money recklessly. A well-dressed woman with a scar on her face held aloof. She refused Gypo's advances, saying she was the wife of an army officer and wanted to get back to London. Gypo gave her what she needed for the fare and accepted the companionship of another girl, Maggie. Bartly found him with her and reminded him of the inquiry. Gypo gave Maggie a pound to take to Katie and followed Bartly willingly.

Dan had been at the McPhillip house to take the family's statements. He had briefly made love to Mary and induced her to accompany him to the inquiry, a kangaroo court held in the wine cellar of a ruined house. Dan acted as prosecutor, and three of his men were judges.

When Rat Mulligan was questioned, it became clear that he could not possibly have been the informer. When Gypo was brought in, Dan made a convincing case that Gypo had known where Francis was going, had left the lodging house at the right time, and had been squandering money all night. At last, Gypo broke down and confessed. Dan ordered him imprisoned in a cellar room with armed guards at the door.

Much earlier, Francis had discussed with Gypo how to get out of the cell. In the ceiling there was a trapdoor covered with dirt. Exerting his great strength, Gypo seized the iron ring with his hands and with his legs forced up both the trapdoor and the earth covering it. The alerted guards shot at him as he scrambled out, but he escaped. Dan was terrified that Gypo might go to the police and that the organization would be broken up. Mary was astonished to see how weak Dan was. When he pulled himself together, however, he sent agents to cover the roads leading out of the area, and Gypo was trapped.

Every time Gypo tried to leave the slum district, he found waiting guards. His only refuge was Katie's room. She let him stay, and he thankfully fell into brutish sleep. Somehow, Katie began to think of her own lost and vicious life, and she identified her misery with Gypo's. With a notion that she would be canonized, she crept off to inform the organization of Gypo's hiding place.

As four armed men closed in on him, Gypo awoke just in time to fight them off. He crippled two of them in a struggle on the stairs, but he was wounded several times as he ran to escape execution.

Gypo became weaker as he fled. Dan saw him but shrugged as he turned away. He knew the informer was done for. In growing confusion, Gypo went into a church where early mass was being celebrated. With dimming vision, he made out the figure of Mrs. McPhillip. He fell in front of her seat and confessed his treachery. When she forgave him, Gypo stood up and in a loud voice called to Francis that his mother had forgiven him. With a gurgle, he fell forward and shivered as blood gushed from his mouth.

Critical Evaluation:

This novel is set in Ireland during the 1920's in a period when the Irish Republican Army (IRA) was dormant after its civil conflict with the Free State. Several isolated bands of rebels—units of the IRA and communists—still waged a quasi-war. Gypo Nolan had belonged to one of these communist groups, but this is not a story about Irish politics or about the way rebels deal with informers. Liam O'Flaherty keeps Gypo Nolan's politics vague partly because Gypo himself understands them so vaguely and partly because the author wishes to focus his attention, and the reader's, on the fact of Gypo's abandonment. The novel focuses on the nature and progress of Gypo's torment.

O'Flaherty is recognized as one of the central figures of the literary movement called the Irish Renaissance. Seán O'Faoláin believed that O'Flaherty shared center stage in this period with James Joyce. One of his claims to this honor is *The Informer*, which some critics consider the most universal and least provincial of O'Flaherty's novels. More than any other of his works, it is a novel about humanity and the human condition.

O'Flaherty focuses on the condition of anxiety. The fact that Gypo Nolan is an informer is less important than the fact that he is cut off from human society, which O'Flaherty considers to be the state of all people to a greater or lesser degree. In this novel, he explores the pain of this condition and describes it from the point of view of an observer, one outside the soul. The same existential loneliness is described internally, as it were from inside the soul, in one of O'Flaherty's earlier novels, *The Black Soul* (1924), which is the most autobiographical of all his works. He put a great deal of his own loneliness and suffering into the characterizations of that work, to which *The Informer* can best be understood as a companion piece. The two novels explore the same problem in different ways.

O'Flaherty skillfully describes things to create atmosphere, and he deepens the reader's understanding of loneliness by showing the misery of Gypo's surroundings. With deft strokes, O'Flaherty paints the environment in which Gypo Nolan, Gallagher, and the other characters operate. He is able to make settings, rooms, household objects, trolley tracks, and paper packages speak volumes. His use of words is vivid. Not only does he conjure up the scenes in the mind's eye of the reader, he also uses the same scenes to illuminate the lives, thoughts, and very souls of the characters. It has been said that O'Flaherty writes more for the eye than for the ear. This criticism is all the more appropriate in view of the stunning artistic success of the film version of the novel. In the motion picture, as in the book, inanimate objects and scenes of action serve to intensify and illuminate the spiritual lives of the main characters. That Gypo is a miserable man becomes clearer when he is shown moving in his miserable world, a world O'Flaherty brings alive for the reader.

One of the underlying themes in the book, which operates on several levels, is that of parallels with the New Testament. Gypo Nolan can be understood in these terms as both an Everyman and a Judas figure. The parallel with the New Testament is most explicit in the final scene, when Gypo, dying, asks Francis McPhillip's mother to forgive him. She does so because he did not know what he was doing. Gypo turns in his friend to the authorities for a sum of money, and like Judas, he learns that this betrayal cuts him off from human society. The betrayal is unable to bring any sort of happiness: both Gypo and Judas throw the money away and die.

O'Flaherty implies that no one can find happiness when cut off from humanity. This is the tragedy of Gypo Nolan, Judas Iscariot, and everyone. Gypo manages to do some good with the money, but in the end he has wasted it all and is left with only the loneliness that is his only birthright.

Gypo's lack of intelligence is the immediate cause of his downfall, although on a deeper level it is his humanity that makes him an outcast from human society. In an amazing example of literary skill, O'Flaherty is able to create sympathy for his informer in the course of the novel by gradually allowing the reader to understand that Gypo is only a child. He also creates sympathy by showing that Gypo Nolan is only incidentally a traitor. He is primarily Everyman, and O'Flaherty ultimately makes this clear by depicting Gypo in his humanity. This achievement is one of the great strengths of O'Flaherty's art.

"Critical Evaluation" by Glenn M. Edwards

Bibliography:
Donoghue, Denis. Preface to *The Informer*, by Liam O'Flaherty. New York: Harcourt Brace Jovanovich, 1980. In this scholarly introduction to *The Informer*, the leading Irish literary critic of his generation discusses the historical and cultural conditions from which the novel emerged, as well as its place in the O'Flaherty canon. Also refers to O'Flaherty's sense of language and to the novel's genre.

Doyle, Paul A. *Liam O'Flaherty*. New York: Twayne, 1971. An introductory survey of the wide range of O'Flaherty's writings. In the chapter devoted to *The Informer*, Doyle notes the novel's methods of representing the atmosphere of a newly independent Ireland. Critical discussion focuses mainly on the novel's characterization. Contains a bibliography of primary and secondary sources.

O'Brien, James H. *Liam O'Flaherty*. Lewisburg, Pa.: Bucknell University Press, 1973. A brief introductory survey that concentrates on O'Flaherty's fiction, particularly his novels. Provides a biographical sketch, as well as a chronology and bibliography. Discussion of *The Informer* is included in a chapter devoted to O'Flaherty's war novels and focuses on the work's preoccupation with its protagonist.

Sheeran, Patrick F. *The Novels of Liam O'Flaherty: A Study in Romantic Realism*. Dublin: Wolfhound Press, 1976. Contains valuable information about O'Flaherty's cultural and personal background and its relevance to his major works. Also includes a detailed account of the genesis of *The Informer* and an analysis of its cinematic dimension.

Zneimer, John. *The Literary Vision of Liam O'Flaherty*. Syracuse, N.Y.: Syracuse University Press, 1970. Remains the most systematic overview of O'Flaherty's work. Focuses throughout on the darker side of O'Flaherty's imagination and provides information on the complicated genesis of *The Informer* and on the author's attitude to the novel. Critical analysis is largely devoted to the work's psychological and spiritual dimensions.

THE INHERITORS

Type of work: Novel
Author: William Golding (1911-1993)
Type of plot: Allegory
Time of plot: Paleolithic period
Locale: A mountainous, wooded countryside not far from the sea
First published: 1955

Principal characters:
THE PEOPLE:
MAL, the old leader
THE OLD WOMAN
HA, the wisest of the younger people
NIL, a young mother
THE NEW ONE, Nil's baby
LOK, the People's clown
FA, a young woman
LIKU, a child
THE NEW PEOPLE:
MARLAN, the leader, called "the old man"
TUAMI, his successor
VIVANI, Marlan's woman, called "the fat woman"
TANAKIL, a child
TWAL, Tanakil's mother, a servant

The Story:

Each spring, Mal led his small tribe, the last of their kind, from their winter quarters by the sea to a terrace and overhang above a waterfall, which was their summer home. The way to their summer homeland led over a river that divided around a rocky island. The people feared water and had never considered going to the island. When they discovered that the log by which they had always crossed the river had disappeared, they were confused until Mal imagined, in the form of a picture, a past time when wise members of the group had taken the original log and had used it to bridge the water. These pictures of the imagination were an embryonic thought process: They served as memories and ideas. The pictures were rarely consecutive and faded as soon as the need for them passed because they were an instinctual and not a rational function. The people could share their pictures without words or express them in simple sentences.

The people had retained the strong senses of animals, but they had also developed their own human rituals concerned with food, fire, and burial. The old woman always carried the fire from the winter to the summer home. When women arrived and the smell of smoke came to Lok from the island, he was bemused and, tricked by his senses into following the familiar scent, he almost fell into the river. The rest of the people had not caught the faint scent, so Lok could not communicate his picture. This second indication that something had changed was forgotten in the people's eager journey to the security of the overhang. Lok almost recaptured his experience while guarding the people that night, but the picture faded before he could fully recapture it.

The people's failure to retain ideas not relevant to day-to-day life made their survival impossible when faced with the challenge of the others. Their lack of the knowledge of evil also made them powerless to combat it. This is one of the main themes of the novel. When Ha disappeared, although the people could tell by the scent that he had encountered another, their emotions were grief at the loss rather than abiding fear. What happened next revealed Golding's grim assertion that the meek do not inherit the earth.

After Mal's death and Ha's disappearance, Lok was the only surviving adult male; it was his task to seek out the others. These others were true *Homo sapiens*, with the power of reason. Their senses were weaker and their artifacts far more sophisticated than the people's. They used animal skins for covering, had bows and arrows, canoes, and crude alcohol. They also knew sexual jealousy. They were near famine because they could not eat the bulbs, slugs, and fungi that sustained the people (who never killed for food) and because hunting had been poor.

When the others captured Liku and the New One on the people's side of the river, Lok heard Liku's screams and tried to reach her. He thus exposed himself to the others' arrows. These weapons merely interested him, although he sensed danger when he smelled the poison on the barbed heads. Lok's apprehensions of danger were lulled at various times by the others' obvious hunger and by his sympathy for them.

Finally, only Lok and Fa remained; the old woman was drowned and Nil slain. Lok rejected Fa's suggestion that they escape and survive. Lok insisted on trying to rescue Liku and the New One. The others moved their camp from the island to the people's side of the river to hunt for deer. The new camp was made by a hollow tree, where Lok and Fa hid from the others. From this tree, the two Neanderthals witnessed an incomprehensible day of ritual and night of debauchery that included, while Lok slept, the killing of Liku. The only communication between the people and the others had been Liku's growing friendship with Tanakil, a girl of her own age. They had been able to exchange names, and Liku had fed Tanakil fungus when Tanakil was hungry. This deed, together with the others' need for a sacrifice to make their hunting successful, caused them to kill her.

In an attempt to snatch the New One from the camp, Lok became separated from Fa and, believing that she was dead, he mourned for her. Although he believed that he was the last of his people, his hope was still sustained by the presence of the others, and at that moment he reached his furthest point of comprehension, which he did not have the power to retain. Fa found Lok again, but during a last effort to recover the New One before the others could take him upstream with them, she was stunned and swept away in the falls. After the final disappearance of Fa and the departure of the others, Lok was alone; his humanity left him.

Solitary, Lok reverted to an anthropoid state. In a coda passage before the reversal of viewpoint in the last chapter, the first complete physical description of one of the people partly explains the others' destructive terror. The only human aspect remaining to Lok was the tears on his face as he lay down to die on Mal's grave.

In the final chapter, in a reversal of point of view, the others are named. Tuami was the younger leader. The old man was Marlan; the most important woman, who suckled the New One, was Vivani. As Tuami steered the boat toward the open plains, away from "the devils," he and all the others were overcome by grief and bitterness. Tuami cried out to ask what else they could have done. The people were quite human and understandable, their murderous actions against the Neanderthals having been dictated by the twin evils of fear and ignorance. Some grace, however, had gone out of their lives forever; their slow-moving boat was a point of darkness between the light of the sky and the water as they fled what they perceived to be devil-infected mountains.

Critical Evaluation:

Like *Lord of the Flies* (1954), *The Two Deaths of Christopher Martin* (1956), and *The Spire*

(1964), *The Inheritors* has a setting remote from a reader's own life and civilization. In these isolated settings, William Golding explores humanity's struggle for survival: the struggle with fellow human beings, with the physical environment, and with oneself. Such preoccupations are, in themselves, common to many novels, but one of the distinctive features of Golding's work is that at the opening of each novel his characters are already at their hour of reckoning. The success of Golding's approach is achieved by an exercise of great imaginative power and the ability to create an environment of great believability, so that what has gone before is apparent through implication in the way the characters react to present circumstance. To the Neanderthal people of *The Inheritors*, the natural, physical world of tree, mountain, river, and rock is the prime reality; when forces alien to their world intrude, Golding begins their story.

In many of his novels, Golding structures the thematic material around specific subtexts, with which his text engages in argument. In this novel, one chief subtext is H. G. Wells's *The Outline of History: Being a Plain History of Life and Mankind* (1920), a book that reflects the social evolutionism theories of the early twentieth century. Wells's book espouses a fairly uncritical belief in progress and in the inferiority of earlier life-forms and cultures. Golding uses a quotation from the book as an epigraph. Golding, in opposition to the sanguine view of progress and of humanity in Wells's book, questions in what way *Homo sapiens* may be considered an improvement on *Homo neanderthalis*. A skeptical reading of the novel might suggest that in no way at all may humanity be considered an improvement on its forbearers. The Neanderthals, in Golding's view, appear innocent, with a deep reverence for life, respectful to each other, and unafraid. By contrast, the new people kill, kidnap, are cannibalistic, and plot assassinations, as well as indulge in crude drunken rituals.

There are other subtexts, however, that bring further resonances to the novel. For example, Golding reverses a Wells short story in which Neanderthals kidnap a human baby. The two most significant subtexts after Wells's are John Milton's *Paradise Lost* (1667) and Joseph Conrad's *Heart of Darkness* (1902). Like Milton, Golding explores the concept of a fall from innocence, and what this fall might be like. In *The Inheritors*, Lok and Fa discover the remains of the new people's mead (fermented honey) and get drunk on it. In *Paradise Lost*, Adam and Eve's fall is marked by a similar drunken state. The new people fall too as they experience fear and panic, which destroys their previous confidence in themselves and gives outward reality to the evil that readers, godlike perhaps, have already perceived within them. Conrad's famous novella is echoed in the closing chapter, in which the motif of darkness closing in on the new people, as they sail across a wide expanse of water, appears.

Golding's novels contain theological dimensions. The Fall in general is one such. More specifically in *The Inheritors*, the gentle and numinous female religion of the Neanderthals is contrasted to the masculine, ritualistic, and brutal religion of the new people. The difference is seen more as an effect than a cause of the two peoples' differences. The cause is never described, but part of it must lie in the new people's technical achievements: They can construct boats, thus losing their fear of water; build huts; and make bows and arrows. The new people have also lost an intimate association with nature, and other living things are seen as hostile, including the Neanderthals. From this hostility springs fear. The new people project their inner fears onto the Neanderthals, and in this way construct devil figures out of them. This is a typical Golding theme, that evil lies within, not without, but people have to deal with it by inventing beasts, as in *Lord of the Flies*.

The way in which Fa refuses to let Lok understand that Liku has been cannibalized reflects her horror of the taboo against taking any form of life. Secrecy is thus one response to evil, but a wrong one, since it causes Lok to risk their lives in a continued effort to regain the girl.

Golding also explores primitive psychology, especially the relationship between thought, imagination, and language. Lok is shown discovering the power of similitudes (similes), moving from pictures (mental images) to the beginnings of literary creation (figurative language). Tuami, on the other hand, finds it difficult, in his fear, to keep conscious logical thought and imagination focused: confusion quickly intrudes. The new people's self-awareness is of a much higher mental order. The Neanderthals' body parts, on the other hand, often move independently of brain control.

Golding's style in *The Inheritors* is marked by self-imposed limitations. He tries to confine himself to the consciousness of his two male protagonists. This is especially noticeable where Lok observes the new people's behavior, most of which is incomprehensible to him. As readers, we are left to guess what is really happening. The language Golding allows himself to use is modern literary language, and a tension is set up between primitive perception and sophisticated vocabulary. Readers see with Lok's eyes and yet read with their own.

Golding has set himself fascinating technical problems. His shifts of perspective are dramatically sudden. One example occurs when Golding moves away from Lok, and readers suddenly see Lok as the new people do, basically an animal. There is a short transition passage in which Golding as narrator keeps his own perspective. Readers have become, however, so deeply sympathetic to the Neanderthals that the final chapter is far too short a space to develop any sympathies for the new people. Indeed, readers are not meant to: Readers are meant, as in satire, to stay alienated from their own species. Other shifts of perspective stem from the Neanderthals' lack of integration; their disconnections jerk readers back to a consciousness of the continuity of the narrative line.

In the last two chapters, the color symbolism becomes noticeable. The redness of the Neanderthals reflects the setting sun and suggestions of fire as symbol of violent and final destruction. This is contrasted to the color blue, which represents sky, a new day, and therefore hope. Blue also, however, represents the deepening night and the shadows that now surround and threaten the life of the new people. They have truly discovered "the darkness of the world."

"Critical Evaluation" by David Barratt

Bibliography:

Dick, Bernard F. *William Golding*. Rev. ed. Boston: Twayne, 1987. The chapter on *The Inheritors* views it mainly in the light of Golding's recurring theme of the Fall. Selected bibliography and index.

Gindin, James. *William Golding*. New York: Macmillan, 1988. Contains an excellent introduction and a full yet economic reading of *The Inheritors*. Gindin sees the novel achieving something of myth, but ultimately having a unique status of its own. Selected bibliography and index.

Kinkead-Weekes, Mark, and Ian Gregor. *William Golding: A Critical Study*. Rev. ed. Winchester, Mass.: Faber & Faber, 1984. Contains an early essay on the novel (1967) that is one of the most perceptive. Discusses the technical problems facing Golding.

Oldsey, Berard S., and Stanley Weintraub. *The Art of William Golding*. New York: Harcourt, Brace & World, 1965. Another early introductory study on Golding, with a chapter on each of the early novels. In the chapter on *The Inheritors*, the concept of evolution is the focus.

Redpath, Philip. *William Golding: A Structural Reading of His Fiction*. New York: Barnes & Noble Books, 1986. Takes a structural approach to *The Inheritors*, seeing the novel's structure as circular, moving away from any simplistic good-bad antithesis.

THE INSPECTOR GENERAL

Type of work: Drama
Author: Nikolai Gogol (1809-1852)
Type of plot: Satire
Time of plot: Early nineteenth century
Locale: Russia
First performed: Revizor, 1836 (English translation, 1890)

Principal characters:

ANTON ANTONOVICH SKVOZNIK-DMUKHANOVSKY, mayor of
    a small provincial town
ANNA, his wife
MARIA, his daughter
IVAN ALEXANDROVICH KHLESTAKOV, a traveler
OSIP, Ivan's servant

The Story:

The mayor of the town, Anton Antonovich, had received a disquieting letter. A friend wrote that an inspector was coming to visit the province and particularly his district. The inspector would probably travel incognito. The friend advised the mayor to clean up the town and hide evidence of any bribes that might discredit him. The mayor in haste called a meeting of the local dignitaries and instructed them how to make a good impression on the official from the capital.

Zemlyanika, the hospital manager, was advised to put clean nightcaps on the patients and take away their strong tobacco for a time. The manager was thoughtful; he had always proceeded on the theory that if a patient were going to die, he would die anyway. He decided, however, to clean up both the patients and the hospital and to put up a sign in Latin over each bed to tell the patient's malady.

Lyapkin-Tyapkin, the judge, spent most of his time hunting. He kept a whip and other sporting equipment in his courtroom, and in the vestibule the porter kept a flock of geese. His assessor always smelled of liquor. Ammos protested that the assessor was injured as a baby and had smelled of brandy ever since. Anton suggested that he be made to eat garlic to cover the smell. Hlopov, the head of the school, was advised to cover up the more obvious foibles of his teachers. The one with a fat face, for instance, always made horrible grimaces when a visitor came and pulled his beard under his necktie, and the history teacher jumped on his desk when he described the Macedonian wars.

Piqued by a recital of their weaknesses, the others turned on the mayor and reminded him that he took monetary bribes and only recently had had the wife of a noncommissioned officer flogged. During the wrangle the postmaster came in to see if they had any news of the inspector's arrival. The mayor advised the postmaster to open all letters in an attempt to discover who the inspector might be and when he would arrive. The advice was superfluous, for the postmaster always read all the letters anyway.

Two squires of the town, Bobchinsky and Dobchinsky, rushed in with exciting news. A mysterious stranger, obviously a high-born gentleman, was at that moment lodging in the local inn, and had been there a fortnight. His servant had let it out that his master was from St. Petersburg. Sure that the stranger was the inspector, the company trembled to think what he might already have learned. They scattered to repair any damage they could.

At the inn Osip was lying on his master's bed and ruminating on the queerness of gentlefolk. His gentleman was always gambling, always broke, always selling his clothes to get funds. They were stuck in this wretched inn because there was no money to pay their bill. At this point, Ivan Alexandrovich burst in, loudly calling for supper.

When the waiter was summoned, he insolently refused to serve Khlestakov until the guest had paid his bill. After a long argument, some watery soup and a tough hen were brought, and perforce Khlestakov dined poorly. As the dishes were being removed amidst a tussle between Osip and the waiter for the remains of the supper, visitors were announced.

Nervous and apologetic, the mayor stood before Khlestakov's august person. Khlestakov thought, however, that he was to be put in jail. For a time the conversation was at cross purposes, but Khlestakov had the nimbler wit and allowed the mayor to do most of the talking. When he began to suspect what the mayor was trying to say, he coolly accepted two hundred roubles to pay his bill, an invitation to stay at the mayor's house, and a nomination as the guest of honor at an official dinner at the hospital.

Anna and Maria were arguing about clothes, as usual, when Dobchinsky rushed in to announce the arrival of the inspector and his fine condescension in coming to stay at their house. Dobchinsky thought that he was being honest when he assured them their guest was a general. Thrilled at the idea of entertaining a general, the two ladies began to primp and preen. When the men came in, the mayor tried to impress Khlestakov, thought to be the inspector, by saying that he never played cards. Khlestakov, playing his role, approved; he especially abhorred gambling. Osip snickered at his master's remark, but fortunately he was not noticed. To impress the household Khlestakov then informed them that he was an author; besides writing for the papers he composed poetry and novels. When he referred casually to his high political connections, his hearers were agog, particularly the ladies. Meanwhile Khlestakov was steadily drinking wine. At last he fell into a drunken sleep in his chair.

With Osip remaining conscious, the mayor tried to pump the servant as to his master's habits and tastes, while the ladies tried to find out something about Khlestakov's love life. Since Anton kept giving him money, Osip obliged by telling many details of his master's place in high society.

Khlestakov was put to bed to sleep off the wine. When he awoke, the dignitaries of the town waited on him one by one. Lyapkin-Tyapkin, the judge, introduced himself and asked for the inspector's orders. Khlestakov carelessly promised to speak well of the judge to his friends, and just as carelessly borrowed money from his suppliant. The postmaster was impressed with Khlestakov's friendliness and was glad to lend him three hundred roubles. Luka and Artemy were glad to lend the inspector three or four hundred roubles, but Bobchinsky and Dobchinsky together could raise only sixty-five roubles.

When the petitioners left, Osip begged his master to leave while the pickings were still good. Khlestakov, agreeing that immediate departure might be prudent, sent the servant to make arrangements. Osip wangled the best coach the town could offer. In the meantime several shopkeepers also came in to protest against the mayor, who was making them pay tribute. From them Khlestakov borrowed five hundred roubles.

When Maria came in, Khlestakov was so elated at his successes that he spoke lovingly to her and finally kissed her on the shoulder. The daughter scurried away as her mother came in, and Khlestakov ogled the older lady too. The daughter came back, full of curiosity, and in his confusion Khlestakov proposed marriage to Maria, who accepted him graciously. After writing a letter to a friend, in which he detailed his humorous adventures, Khlestakov left town. He promised, however, to return the next day.

In the morning the mayor and his wife received the envious congratulations of friends. The ladies, green with envy, assured Maria that she would be a belle in St. Petersburg society. The parents, much taken with the idea, decided that their new son-in-law would insist on taking the whole family to live in the capital. The mayor was sure that he would be made a general at least. At that moment the postmaster arrived with Khlestakov's letter. When he read the frank description of the pretended inspector's love-making and his franker opinion of the muddle-headed town officials, the fact of the hoax gradually dawned on the company. As the crestfallen crowd was counting up the losses, a gendarme came in with an official announcement. An inspector from St. Petersburg had just arrived and desired them all to wait upon him immediately. He was staying at the inn.

Critical Evaluation:

This comedy, a high point of Nikolai Gogol's work, represents an effective protest against the fumbling, venal bureaucracy of Russia's small towns. The situation, which is credibly presented, makes this comedy work. The Inspector General builds almost entirely on the simple device of the mistaken identity of its hero. Khlestakov is not a typical hero. Like many of Gogol's characters, he lacks positive qualities and is instead defined by his absence of intellectual and spiritual traits. He appears a mixture of fool and rogue, hero and villain. Throughout the play, he remains passive, guided primarily by vulgar epicureanism and the imagination of town officials. As a social being, Khlestakov is not exceptional. He is a minor civil servant from a landowning family of modest means. The comedy, however, hinges precisely on his status as a non entity. As an inert, indeterminate character, rather than a confidence man, he participates in the collective fantasy of the town and shares their fear of being unmasked.

Gogol never tries to convince the town members or the audience that Khlestakov could be the inspector; he instead flaunts the incongruity of Khlestakov's demeanor and the interpretation of the town. The comedy concentrates on the town as a collective persona. The town officials, who originate and confirm the rumor of the inspector's arrival, are terrified of being exposed. The mayor heads the group and establishes relations between Khlestakov and the provincial officials. The impression of solidarity created by the collective of officials and gentry is reinforced by their static function. Gogol originally considered the play as a parody of Judgment Day, with Khlestakov representing the deceiving conscience and the townspeople representing the passions, but the play emerged as a satirical commentary on contemporary society. The play presents a social microcosm, specifically in the sphere of public law, based on a hierarchy of rights that sanctions swindling, tyrannizing, and coercing. Gogol portrays officialdom as a tangled web of misunderstandings caused by self-satisfied philistines occupying positions for which they are ill-suited.

The theme of identity is a key to the play. The civil servants in the town are very conscious of rank—their own and Khlestakov's. The comic treatment of character often relies on identity; in this case, Khlestakov's ambiguous persona elicits the hidden identities of the officials, while his own identity is only partially revealed. The mayor, who invariably praises his own virtues, reveals himself as a petty dictator. Zemlyanika, the manager of charitable institutions, is not at all charitable but rather the comic embodiment of the informer. Lyapkin-Tyapkin, reputedly liberal and whose name means "a bungler," acts with military precision. Bobchinsky and Dobchinsky, a slapstick pair, physically realize the duality of the identity and the external persona found in the other characters.

The common human desires to please, impress, and assert authority are wed to the lunatic fantasy of the townspeople. Khlestakov participates in the delusions of the mayor and his associates mainly out of complaisant idiocy. The extraordinary lies he tells about his position as the czar's right-hand man are misplaced poetic inspiration rather than calculation. For Khlestakov, the boundaries between the real and the imaginary are tenuous; therefore, he plays an unwitting role in the confusion. Social satire is frequently overwhelmed by poetry when characters embrace their own fictions. Life in St. Petersburg, as described by Khlestakov, is pure fantasy. The image of St. Petersburg as a symbol of banal glory competes with the sinister character of the city as the center of hypocrisy. The fantasy world unravels after Khlestakov, laden with gifts and betrothed to the mayor's daughter, gallops off. When the officials of the town finally learn of the arrival of the real inspector, they freeze in terror and leave the audience to contemplate the possible ramifications. This sudden draining of comic animation is a hallmark of Gogol. The whole play is, in a manifestation of absurdity, an accidental usurpation of the real drama anticipated in the opening lines of the play, namely, the arrival of the inspector general.

The structure is concentrated in time and space, the action unified by the initial announcement of the inspector's visit and his arrival in the final moments. Gogol also reaches beyond the confines of the stage: Minor characters are mentioned but never appear, action is heard offstage, and actors address the audience directly. Gogol also eliminates common moralizing features of comedy, such as the virtuous lovers, wise elders, and servant-confidants. His treatment of the love interest veers toward parody, with Khlestakov's crude advances toward mother and daughter and their deflating responses. The contrasting esthetic categories of satire and light comedy are unified within *The Inspector General*. Slips of the tongue, misspoken clichés, and banalities comprise much of the comedy. Typical of Gogol's work, the trivial is endowed with extreme importance, so there is a wealth of bizarre and improbable detail, whether from Khlestakov's fantasy of life in St. Petersburg or the other character's assessment of provincial life.

The two planes of action allow the audience to perceive the "true" plot while the "false" plot is elaborated. The first act of the play creates the false point of view; the second builds on it; the third and fourth acts consolidate the false plot. The false plot is concerned primarily with the characterization of Khlestakov, out of which the characters of the officials are developed. Although the officials seem to triumph near the end of the play, from the audience's point of view, Khlestakov's engagement and departure are a culmination of the misunderstandings and deflation of the town officials. In the final moment of the play, the true and false plots have these points of unity.

Few contemporary critics saw the play's novelty—namely, its lack of positive characters, love intrigue, and stage resolution—and the audience mistook it for a crude vaudeville. Despite Gogol's careful direction and animated readings, the play's depiction of the bureaucrats and merchants outraged the audience. As time has passed, the appreciation for *The Inspector General* has grown. The clever structure of the play and the insightful evaluation of the instability of identity remain powerful, while his depiction of bureaucracy still rings true.

"Critical Evaluation" by Pamela Pavliscak

Bibliography:
Brown, Nigel. *Notes on Nikolai Gogol's "The Government Inspector."* Nairobi, Kenya: Heinemann Educational Books, 1974. The only book devoted entirely to a discussion of *The Inspector General*. Provides a broad overview of previous criticism and offers detailed consideration of characters, with particular attention devoted to Khlestakov.

Fanger, Donald. *The Creation of Nikolai Gogol*. Cambridge, Mass.: Harvard University Press, 1979. Considers the relationship between Gogol and his audience. Evaluates Gogol's comic theory and his efforts at staging and self-interpretation.

Gippius, V. V. *Gogol*. Translated by Robert Maguire. Durham, N.C.: Duke University Press, 1989. Classic treatment of Gogol's life and works. The chapter on *The Inspector General* analyzes the play's structure and presents Gogol's play as the beginning of social comedy with a serious purpose in Russia.

Nabokov, Vladimir. *Nikolai Gogol*. New York: New Directions, 1944. The clever tone of Nabokov's book mirrors that of Gogol's prose. The stylistic analysis is brilliant. Focuses on the theme of banality, with Khlestakov as one of its primary representatives. Points out Gogol's genius in his attention to the absurd in everyday life.

Peace, Richard. *The Enigma of Gogol: An Examination of the Writings of N. V. Gogol and Their Place in the Russian Literary Tradition*. Cambridge, England: Cambridge University Press, 1981. Evaluates the plot, characters, and structure of the play within the larger framework of the Russian tradition. Develops the theme of individual and social identity.

THE INTERPRETATION OF DREAMS

Type of work: Psychology
Author: Sigmund Freud (1856-1939)
First published: Die Traumdeutung, 1900 (English translation, 1913)

In March, 1931, in a foreword to the third English edition of *The Interpretation of Dreams*, Sigmund Freud expressed the opinion that the volume contained the most valuable of all the discoveries he had been fortunate enough to make. The author's estimation of his work concurs with that of most students and critics. The ideas that dreams are wish-fulfillments, that the dream disguises the wishes of the unconscious, that dreams are always important, always significant, and that they express infantile wishes—particularly for the death of the parent of the same sex as that of the dreamer—all appear in this masterpiece of psychological interpretation. In this work, the Oedipus complex is first named and explained, and the method of psychoanalysis is given impetus and credibility by its application to the analysis of dreams.

It is a common criticism of Freud to say that the father of psychoanalysis, although inspired in this and other works, went too far in his generalizations concerning the basic drives of the unconscious. Freud is charged with regarding every latent wish as having a sexual object, and he is criticized for supposing that dreams can be understood as complexes of such universally significant symbols as umbrellas and boxes.

Although Freud argues that repressed wishes that show themselves in disguised form in dreams generally have something to do with the unsatisfied sexual cravings of childhood—for dreams are important and concern themselves only with matters that one cannot resolve by conscious deliberation and action—he allows for the dream satisfaction of other wishes that reality has frustrated. These desires include the desire for the continued existence of a loved one already dead, the desire for sleep as a continuation of the escape from reality, the desire for a return to childhood, the desire for revenge when revenge is impossible.

As for the charge that Freud regarded dreams as complexes of symbols having the same significance for all dreamers, this is clearly unwarranted. Freud explicitly states that "only the context can furnish the correct meaning" of a dream symbol. He rejects as wholly inadequate the use of any such simple key as a dream book of symbols. All dreamers utilize the material of their own experience in their own way, and only by a careful analytical study of associations—obscured by the manifest content of the dream—is it possible to get at the particular use of symbols in an individual's dream. It is worth noting, Freud admits, that many symbols recur with much the same intent in many dreams of different persons; this knowledge, however, must be used judiciously. The agreement in the use of symbols is only partly a matter of cultural tendencies; it is largely attributable to limitations of the imagination imposed by the material itself. "To use long, stiff objects and weapons as symbols of the female genitals, or hollow objects (chests, boxes, etc.) as symbols of the male genitals, is certainly not permitted by the imagination."

It is not surprising that most of the symbols discussed by Freud, either as typical symbols or as symbols in individual cases, are sexually significant. Although Freud did not regard all dreams as the wish-fulfillments of repressed sexual desires, he did suppose that a greater number of dreams have a sexual connotation: "The more one is occupied with the solution of dreams, the readier one becomes to acknowledge that the majority of the dreams of adults deal with sexual material and give expression to erotic wishes." Freud adds, "In dream-interpretation this importance of the sexual complexes must never be forgotten, though one must not, of course, exaggerate it to the exclusion of all other factors."

The technique of dream-interpretation is certainly not exhausted, according to Freud, by the technique of symbol interpretation. Dreams involve the use of the images dreamed, the manifest dream-content, as a way of disguising the unconscious "dream-thoughts" or latent dream-content. The significance of a dream may be revealed only after one has understood the dramatic use of the symbolism of the dream. To interpret dreams, one needs to understand the condensation of the material, the displacement of the conventional meaning of a symbol or utterance, or even a displacement of the "center" of the dream-thoughts. The manifest dream may center about a matter removed from the central concern of the dream. As Freud explains the problems of dream-interpretation, making numerous references to dream examples, it becomes clear that dream interpretation must be at least as ingenious as dreaming—and there is nothing more ingenious.

Freud begins *The Interpretation of Dreams* with a history of the scientific literature of dream problems from ancient times to 1900. He then proceeds to make his basic claim: that dreams are interpretable as wish-fulfillments. To illustrate his point, he begins with an involved dream of his own, justifying his procedure by arguing that self-analysis is possible and, even when faulty, illustrative.

A problem arises with the consideration of painful dreams. If dreams are wish-fulfillments, why are some dreams nightmares? Who wishes to be terrified? Freud's answer is that the problem arises from a confusion between the manifest and the latent dream. What is painful, considered as manifest, may, because of its disguised significance, be regarded as satisfactory to the unconscious. When one realizes, in addition, that many suppressed wishes are desires for punishment, the painful dream presents itself as a fulfillment of such wishes. To understand the possibility of painful dreams, it is necessary to consider Freud's amended formula: "The dream is the (disguised) fulfillment of a (suppressed, repressed) wish."

In describing the method most useful in enabling people to recall their dreams both by facilitating memory and by inhibiting the censorship tendency of the person recounting the dream, Freud presents what has become familiar as the psychoanalytic method of free association. He suggests that patients be put into a restful position with the eyes closed, that patients be told not to criticize their thoughts or to withhold the expression of them, and that they continue to be impartial about their ideas. This problem of eliminating censorship while recounting the dream is merely an extension of the problem of dealing with the censorship imposed by the dreamer while dreaming. Dreamers do not want to acknowledge their desires; for one reason or another they have repressed them. The fulfillment of the suppressed desire can be tolerated by dreamers only if they leave out anything that would be understandable to the waking mind. Consequently, only a laborious process of undoing (or understanding) the dream can result in some understanding of the meaning that the censor tries to hide.

Among the interesting corollaries of Freud's theory is the idea that the dream-stimulus is always to be found among the experiences of the hours prior to sleeping. Some incident from the day becomes the material of the dream, its provocative image. Although the dream-stimulus is from the day preceding sleep, the repressed wish which the dream expresses and fulfills is from childhood, at least, in the majority of cases: "The deeper we go into the analysis of dreams, the more often are we put on to the track of childish experiences which play the part of dream-sources in the latent dream-content." To explain the difficulty of getting at the experiences in childhood which provide the latent dream-content, Freud argues for a conception of dreams as stratified: in the dream, layers of meaning are involved, and it is only at the lowest stratum that the source in some experience of childhood may be discovered.

Among the typical dreams mentioned by Freud are the embarrassment dream of nakedness, interpreted as an exhibition dream, fulfilling a wish to return to childhood (the time when one ran about naked without upsetting anyone); the death-wish dream in which one dreams of the death of a beloved person, interpreted as a dream showing repressed hostility toward brother or sister, father or mother; and the examination dream in which one dreams of the disgrace of flunking an examination, interpreted as reflecting the ineradicable memories of punishments in childhood.

Of these typical dreams, the death-wish dream directed to the father (by the son) or to the mother (by the daughter) is explained in terms of the drama of *Oedipus* by Sophocles. In the old Greek play, Oedipus unwittingly murders his own father and marries his mother. When he discovers his deeds, he blinds himself and exiles himself from Thebes. The appeal of the drama is explained by Freud as resulting from its role as a wish-fulfillment. The play reveals the inner self, the self which directed its first sexual impulses toward (in the case of a male) the mother and its first jealous hatred toward the father. These feelings have been repressed during the course of developing maturity, but they remain latent, ready to manifest themselves only in dreams somewhat more obscure than the Oedipus drama itself. Freud mentions *Hamlet* as another play in which the same wish is shown, although in *Hamlet* the fulfillment is not achieved. Freud accounts for Hamlet's reluctance to complete the task of revenge by pointing out that Hamlet cannot bring himself to kill a man who accomplished what he himself wishes he had accomplished: the murder of his father and marriage to his mother.

In his discussion of the psychology of the dream process, Freud calls attention to the fact that dreams are quickly forgotten—a natural consequence, if his theory is correct. This fact creates problems for the analyst who wishes to interpret dreams in order to discover the root of neurotic disturbances. The self that forgets the dream, however, is the same self that dreamed, and it is possible by following the implications of even superficial associations to get back to the substance of the dream.

Realizing that many would be offended by his ideas, Freud attempts to forestall criticism by insisting on the universal application of his theory and by claiming that dreams themselves—since they are not acts—are morally innocent, whatever their content.

There seems little question but that Freud's contribution to psychology in *The Interpretation of Dreams* will remain one of the great discoveries of the human mind. Whatever its excesses, particularly in the hands of enthusiastic followers, Freud's central idea gains further confirmation constantly in the experiences of dreamers and analysts alike.

Bibliography:
Frieden, Ken. *Freud's Dream of Interpretation.* SUNY Series in Modern Jewish Literature and Culture. Albany: State University of New York Press, 1990. Asserts Freud was influenced by biblical and rabbinical modes of dream interpretation, which, ironically, he denied. Convincingly argues that, because interpretation is never a neutral act, Freud failed to acknowledge the prophetic aspect of his dream work.
Hyman, Stanley Edgar. "*The Interpretation of Dreams.*" In *The Tangled Bank: Darwin, Marx, Frazer, and Freud as Imaginative Writers.* New York: Atheneum, 1962. Contends that the power of Freud's ideas owes a great deal to his ability as an imaginative writer. As literary criticism, examines the tone, imaginative organization, and thematic metaphors of the work.
Isbister, J. N. *Freud: An Introduction to His Life and Work.* Cambridge, England: Polity Press, 1985. Evaluates Freud's ideas in a biographical and philosophical context and finds them wanting. Criticizes Freudian psychology as reductive and nihilistic. Calls for a revision of psychoanalytic dream theory in light of more recent studies on sleep.

Rand, Nicholas, and Maria Torok. "Questions to Freudian Psychoanalysis: Dream Interpretation, Reality, Fantasy." Translated by Nicholas Rand. *Critical Inquiry* 19 (Spring, 1993): 567-594. Demonstrates how fundamental methodological discrepancies develop with successive editions of the work. The authors focus on the impact of theory on practice.

Soule, George. "Freud and *The Interpretation of Dreams*." In *Books That Changed Our Minds*, edited by Malcolm Cowley and Bernard Smith. New York: Kelmscott, 1939. Traces widespread influence of Freud's ideas on art, language, culture, and the study of history. Attempts to distinguish psychoanalytic theory from popular misconceptions.

THE INTRUDER

Type of work: Drama
Author: Maurice Maeterlinck (1862-1949)
Type of plot: Tragedy
Time of plot: Early twentieth century
Locale: A dark room in an old château
First published: L'Intruse, 1890 (English translation, 1891); first performed, 1891

Principal characters:
    THE GRANDFATHER, who is blind
    THE FATHER, who is weary
    THE UNCLE, who is rationalistic
    THE THREE DAUGHTERS, who are obedient
    THE SISTER OF CHARITY, a nurse
    THE MAIDSERVANT, who is defensive

The Story:

Six characters felt enormous tension one Saturday evening between shortly after nine o'clock and midnight in a somber sitting room of an old château surrounded by gardens and a lake. Together with their father, uncle, and grandfather, three young women hopefully awaited the visit of the father's and the uncle's eldest sister, a nun who was the mother superior of her convent, and of the doctor who was to check on their sickly mother in the room on the left and the silent baby in the room on the right.

The family entered the sitting room, disagreeing. The father and the daughters wanted to sit outside while the uncle, because it had rained for one week, preferred to remain inside. The grandfather resolved the dispute by saying that it was better to stay in since one never knew what might happen. The father declared that his wife, who had been sick for several weeks, was out of danger from her illness. The grandfather disagreed, since he had heard her voice. The uncle supported his brother and recommended that all should relax and enjoy the first pleasant evening they had had in a long time.

The uncle remarked that sickness was like a stranger in the family, and the father noted that one could count only on family members, not outsiders, for help. The men asked Ursula, the eldest daughter, if she could see anyone in the avenue. She saw no one yet, but reported that the avenue was moonlit and the weather fine, that the nightingales could be heard, and that the trees stirred a little in the wind.

The mood changed when the grandfather announced that he no longer heard the nightingales. Ursula believed that someone had entered the garden, although she saw no one. The men disbelieved her, but she persisted, since the nightingales had suddenly fallen silent and the swans had become frightened. The father agreed that "there is a stillness of death," but the mood changed again when the uncle asked disgustedly if they were going to discuss nightingales all night.

The conversation turned to the cold room. Ursula and her sisters tried to obey their father by shutting the door, but it would not close entirely. The father promised to have the carpenter fix it the next day. The family was then disturbed by the sound of the sharpening of a scythe outside, although the gardener should not have been working on a Saturday evening. Ursula again tried to soothe fears by suggesting that perhaps the gardener was occupied in the shadow of the house.

Everyone's attention turned to the lamp, which was not burning very well that evening, although its oil had been filled that same morning. One daughter noted that, after not sleeping for three nights, the grandfather had finally dozed off. While he slept, the father and the uncle discussed his blindness and his irrationality. When the clock struck ten, the grandfather woke up, saying someone was standing by the glass door leading to the terrace. Although Ursula reassured him that she saw no one, he thought someone had been waiting there. When he asked the father and the uncle if their sister had arrived, the uncle peevishly remarked that it was now too late for her to come and that it was not very nice of her.

Everyone heard a noise as if someone were entering the house, and they believed it was finally the long-awaited nun. After the father summoned the maidservant, the grandfather noted twice that she was not alone. When the father asked the maidservant who had entered the house, she replied that no one had come in. The father accused her of pushing open the door to the sitting room, although she was standing three steps from it. Although blind, the grandfather announced that suddenly everything seemed to be dark in the room. The maidservant's exit was marked by eleven strokes of the old clock.

The grandfather thought the maidservant had entered their room and was now sitting at their table. His anxiety grew, and he begged Ursula to tell him the truth. He urged his children to tell him who was sitting beside him, who had entered the room, and what was happening around him. He was amazed that they saw no one besides the six of them. He announced that he probably would not live much longer and that he wished he were at home. The father protested that he already was at home. The grandfather wished to be with his daughter because he wanted to know the truth. He reassured the daughters that he knew they would have told him the truth if they had not been deceived by the men.

Finally, the father invited the grandfather to enter his daughter's room, but the old man refused; the uncle remarked that he was not being reasonable. Suddenly the lamp went out completely, and the men decided to remain in the dark rather than enter the sick woman's room. Now the clock seemed very loud. Ursula was asked to open the window a bit. All noticed that there was no sound outside. The silence inside and out was extraordinary. The uncle began to pace in the darkness, after declaring that he did not like the country. The grandfather asked Ursula to shut the window.

Suddenly an odd ray of moonlight penetrated the room's darkness. The clock struck midnight; someone unidentified seemed to rise from the table, the uncle called for the lamp to be lit, the baby wailed in terror, and heavy steps were heard in the mother's room. Then all fell silent. The door to the sick woman's chamber opened. There stood the sister of charity, dressed in black. Her bow and the sign of the cross announced silently that the mother had died. All entered the bedroom except the grandfather, who was left alone to grope about the table in confusion.

Critical Evaluation:

In *The Intruder*, Maurice Maeterlinck superbly evokes feelings of fearful suspense and anxiety through the simple repetition of phrases, the device of light diminishing into darkness, and invocation of nature's response to the unseen intruder when the birds, swans, and dogs are suddenly hushed for no apparent reason. Maeterlinck admired Edgar Allen Poe's ability to create a haunting atmosphere that leads up to tragic consequences. In *The Intruder*, a similar haunted atmosphere evolves as the family converses banally. While the intruder, death, stalks the premises, the six relatives argue about the weather, sounds they hear, the opening and shutting of doors and windows, and the arrival of the long-awaited nun.

Although the play is set in the twentieth century, it resembles a medieval allegory. None of the characters is given a proper name, and the invisible figure of death is really the star of the show. The intruder hovering about the gardens and the château is sensed only by the blind grandfather who alarms the younger members of his family as he persistently asks who is present or whose footsteps are on the stairs. Like a blind prophet, the grandfather intuitively feels the macabre presence, but he is not understood by his family, who even call him demented. His premonitions are justified at the conclusion of the play when the sister of charity silently, by making the sign of the cross, announces the ill mother's death. The father's and uncle's sister never arrives.

The mother has been suffering ever since giving birth to an infant who, since it has not yet made a single sound, resembles a wax effigy. The grandfather fears that it may be deaf and mute because his daughter has married her cousin. Maeterlinck thus suggests an underlying theme of incest in this very enclosed family; the newborn baby, the new life remaining after the mother's death, seems to be already cursed.

Influenced by medieval mysticism, Maeterlinck suggestively portrays the realm of the irrational, uncontrollable, and unspeakable through contrasting light and darkness, sound and silence, outside and inside, female and male, youth and age, health and illness, and ultimately, life and death. He does not want his brief drama to be fully understood but merely to be felt by the reader or spectator, who silently enters the family's privacy, participates in its anxiety, and understands that nothing and no one can keep death away when it approaches.

It is significant that the grandfather, who can still see bright light, feels that all light has gone out even when the dim lamp still burns. He is probably intuitively sensing death approaching his daughter in the next room. His anguish about this inner darkness is echoed by the others when their lamp actually extinguishes itself and they are left talking quietly in total darkness. Rays of moonlight at the conclusion of the play suggest that a strange light from outside the family and their home can still penetrate their personal and physical darkness.

The grandfather is also out of tune with the other family members when he hears the foot-steps on the stairs not made by the maidservant and the sounds of someone other than his loved ones by him at the table. The others hear none of this and wish that he would be "reasonable." They do, however, hear with him the strange silences that also occasionally invade the premises.

The grandfather's inner world contrasts with the outer world of the others and with the even broader world that lies beyond their enclosed sitting room in the bedrooms of the sick mother and the mute infant and outside in the gardens. The father and the uncle long for their sister's arrival since they distrust persons outside the family. Just as they are enclosed in their sitting room, so are they, despite their external façade of confidence, immured in their fears and prejudices. The three daughters are torn between trying to please their intuitive grandfather and wishing to accommodate their father and uncle. The trust the grandfather places in Ursula, the eldest daughter, suggests that she too is intuitive, sensitive, and truthful, but her efforts are often stifled by the patriarchal heads of her family, her father and uncle. They resent her answering the grandfather's questions sincerely since this seems, from their point of view, only to add to his dementia. Thus the women in this strange household are not only as physically enclosed as the men but also psychologically enclosed by the guardians of reason.

There are equal numbers of females and males in the play, with the three daughters balanced by the grandfather, the father, and the uncle; the ill mother rests in the room on the left while her infant son lies in the room on the right. This balance is upset by the three supporting characters, the maidservant who remains outside on the landing of the steps, the sister of charity who stays in the doorway of the mother's bedroom, and the expected sister of the father and the uncle, who never arrives. Yet Maeterlinck does not suggest that all the women are intuitive and all the men rational. The grandfather is misunderstood by all because of his intuitive feelings and premonitions, and at times the daughters try to reason with him much as do the father and the uncle. The dramatist seems to indicate that it is age and blindness rather than gender that confers prophetic power.

The daughters are strongly shaped by the patriarchs of their family. An extreme of feminine passivity is shown by the silent mother's slow death. All of the characters are focused on her but choose not to be with her, since they believe that she needs solitary rest; only the sister of charity accompanies her on her last journey. Although the grandfather senses that she is dying, he refuses to enter her room when given the opportunity. Perhaps he fears the time when he, too, will meet death. Thus age recoils from extinction but the recently born infant finally, after weeks of silence, howls at the moment of the mother's death. Three generations are represented in this play. Although age seems to bestow wisdom, youth appears to embody courage. The three daughters are the first to enter their dead mother's chambers, while the grandfather gropes around the table in confusion.

The Intruder, Maeterlinck's second play, breaks with traditional, realistic drama. Fascinated by both death and symbolism, the playwright experiments with arousing emotions of uncertainty, anxiety, and horror. He does not fully develop his characters as did the authors of many naturalistic plays of his era. Rather, the family members are only superficially drawn; the focus is on the way they fall prey to the frightening atmosphere around them, which they cannot understand.

All of the characters wish for the good health of the mother, yet illness invades their domain like an unwelcome stranger who cannot be ignored and, despite the doctors' predictions of renewed health, death claims the mother. Illness and death are not "reasonable," and the strong desires and arguments of the father and the uncle are useless against its irrational force. Maeterlinck seems to be communicating that somehow human beings at their best—those always seeking both intuitive and rational truths—must embrace the paradoxical awareness that life and death occur simultaneously.

Carole J. Lambert

Bibliography:
Bass, Ruth. "Backstage at the Guggenheim." Review of *The Intruder*, by Maurice Maeterlinck. *Art News* 85, no. 6 (Summer, 1986): 16, 18. In this review of Hanne Tierney's staging of Maeterlinck's play with puppetlike figures at the Guggenheim Museum in New York in January, 1986, Bass shows how the play lends itself to creative revival and aesthetic innovation. Tierney designed her expressionistic figures, controled them at a keyboard by invisible fishing lines, and spoke all of their parts in a monotone.
Block, Haskell M. *Mallarmé and the Symbolist Drama*. Detroit: Wayne State University Press, 1963. Block provides a broad view of symbolist drama and discusses in depth the aesthetic theory of its precursor, Mallarmé, and its masters, of whom Maeterlinck was the most outstanding. Block includes a discussion of *The Intruder*.
Daniels, May. *The French Drama of the Unspoken*. Edinburgh: University Press, 1953. After discussing the positivistic mind-set of the end of the nineteenth century, Daniels devotes two chapters to Maeterlinck's plays, all of which are a strong reaction to naturalistic theater. Analyzes the nature of spectator response to Maeterlinck's theater of the unexpressed in *The Intruder* and *Pelléas and Mélisande* (1892).

Finney, Gail. "Dramatic Pointillism: The Examples of Holz and Schlaf's *Die Familie Selicke* and Maeterlinck's *L'Intruse*." *Comparative Literature Studies* 30, no. 1 (1993): 1-15. Finney describes George Seurat's pointillistic neo-impressionistic painting style and shows how "temporal or linguistic pointillism" occurs in Johannes Schlaf's *Die Familie Selicke* (1890) and Maeterlinck's *The Intruder*. She indicates that many of the dramatic techniques found in Maeterlinck's play are used by such later twentieth century playwrights as Tennessee Williams, Arthur Miller, Eugene O'Neill, Samual Beckett, and Harold Pinter.

Heller, Otto. *Prophets of Dissent: Essays on Maeterlinck, Strindberg, Nietzsche and Tolstoy.* New York: Alfred A. Knopf, 1918. Includes one essay devoted to Maeterlinck. Heller in 1918 already understood that the dramatist's secular mysticism represented a retreat into the "central ego" and an effort to express the unknown internal forces that motivate individuals. Maeterlinck's theater communicates humankind's frustration before the invisible, uncontrollable forces, both internal and external, that no longer fall under the old categories of fate and religion.

INTRUDER IN THE DUST

Type of work: Novel
Author: William Faulkner (1897-1962)
Type of plot: Detective and mystery
Time of plot: Early 1930's
Locale: Jefferson, Mississippi
First published: 1948

Principal characters:
> CHARLES "CHICK" MALLISON, a sixteen-year-old boy
> GAVIN STEVENS, his uncle and a lawyer
> LUCAS BEAUCHAMP, an old black man
> ALECK SANDER, Chick's young black friend
> MISS HABERSHAM, an old woman
> HOPE HAMPTON, the sheriff

The Story:

On a cold afternoon in November, Chick Mallison, twelve years old, accompanied by two black boys, went rabbit hunting on Carothers Edmonds' place. When he fell through the ice into a creek, an old black man, Lucas Beauchamp, appeared and watched while the boy clambered awkwardly ashore. Then Lucas took the white boy and his companions to his home. There, Chick dried out in front of the fire and ate Lucas' food. Later, when Chick tried to pay the old man for his hospitality, Lucas spurned his money. Chick threw it down, but Lucas made one of the other boys pick it up and return it. Chick brooded over the incident, ashamed to be indebted to a black man, especially one as arrogant as Lucas Beauchamp. Again trying to repay the old man, he sent Lucas' wife a mail-order dress bought with money he had saved; again refusing to acknowledge payment and thus admit his inferiority, Lucas sent Chick a bucket of sorghum sweetening.

Some four years later when Lucas was accused of shooting Vinson Gowrie in the back, Chick still had not forgotten his unpaid debt to the man. Realizing that Vinson's poor white family and friends were sure to lynch Lucas, Chick wanted to leave town. Yet, when Sheriff Hope Hampton brought Lucas to the jail in Jefferson, Chick, unable to suppress his sense of obligation, was standing on the street where the old man could see him. Lucas asked Chick to bring his uncle, Gavin Stevens, to the jail.

At the jail, Lucas refused to tell Stevens what happened at the shooting, whereupon the lawyer left in disgust; but Lucas did tell Chick that Vinson Gowrie had not been shot with his gun—a forty-one Colt—and he asked the boy to verify this fact by digging up the corpse. Although the body was buried nine miles from town and the Gowries would be sure to shoot a grave robber, Chick agreed to the request; he knew that Lucas would undoubtedly be lynched if someone did not help him. Barbershop and poolroom loafers had already gathered while waiting for the pine-hill country Gowries to arrive.

Stevens laughed at the story, so Chick's only help came from a black boy—Aleck Sander—and Miss Habersham, an old woman of good family who had grown up with Lucas' wife, now dead. So the task of digging up a white man's grave in order to save a haughty, intractable, but innocent black man was left to two adolescents and a seventy-year-old woman who felt it her obligation to protect those more helpless than she. The three succeeded in opening the grave without incident. In the coffin, they found not Vinson Gowrie but Jake Montgomery, whose skull had been bashed in. They filled the grave, returned to town, wakened Stevens, and went to the sheriff with their story.

This group, joined by old man Gowrie and two of his sons, reopened the grave. When they lifted the lid, the coffin was found to be empty. A search disclosed Montgomery's body hastily buried nearby and Vinson's sunk in quicksand. When the sheriff took Montgomery's body into town, the huge crowd that had gathered in anticipation of the lynching of Lucas Beauchamp soon scattered.

Questioning of Lucas revealed that Crawford Gowrie had murdered his brother, Vinson. Crawford, according to the old man, had been cheating his brother in a lumber deal. Jake Montgomery, to whom Crawford had sold the stolen lumber, knew that Crawford was the murderer and had dug up Vinson's grave to prove it. Crawford murdered Montgomery at the grave and put him in Vinson's coffin. When he saw Chick and his friends open the grave, he was forced to remove Vinson's body too. Sheriff Hampton soon captured Crawford, who killed himself in his cell to avoid a trial.

At last, Chick thought, he had freed himself of his debt to the old black man. A short time later, however, Lucas appeared at Stevens' office and insisted on paying for services rendered. Stevens refused payment for both himself and Chick but accepted two dollars for "expenses." Proud, unhumbled to the end, Lucas Beauchamp demanded a receipt.

Critical Evaluation:

Intruder in the Dust is an excellent introduction to William Faulkner's numerous and complex novels of the Deep South. Set in Faulkner's mythical Yoknapatawpha County, his standard fictional location, *Intruder in the Dust* also includes such familiar inhabitants as attorney Gavin Stevens and farmer Carothers Edmonds. This novel, however, includes only a few examples of such famous Faulknerian stylistic devices as elongated, periodic sentences, disconnected narratives, multiple narrative perspectives, psychological time, and stream of consciousness. While the very substance of *The Sound and the Fury* (1929), *Absalom, Absalom!* (1936), *Light in August* (1932), and *As I Lay Dying* (1930) consists of these variations in style or form, *Intruder in the Dust* (except for Chick Mallison's meditations and flashbacks) is a relatively straightforward narration. Faulkner novels typically use parable and folklore as a basis for forming a vision of life as a neurotic and involved psychological process. *Intruder in the Dust*, however, blends folklore and parable with a formula mystery story and strikes a much simpler note than most of Faulkner's work.

Aspects of folklore permeate *Intruder in the Dust*. Faulkner's panorama of rural local color includes a generous sampling of cracker-barrel philosophers, bigoted rednecks, mischievous and shoeless youngsters, and fading ladies of breeding long past their prime. The plot crackles with anecdotes, bits of country wisdom, humor, and superstition. It is thematically enriched by Gavin Stevens' philosophical speeches. After Chick, Aleck, and Miss Habersham discover that Vinson Gowrie's grave contains the body of Jake Montgomery, *Intruder in the Dust* becomes a highly suspenseful mystery story with Sheriff Hampton and Lawyer Stevens solving the crime in barely enough time to prevent Lucas Beauchamp from being lynched by a mob far more interested in violence than justice.

The novel also contains several parables, one of which is a Southern version of the biblical Cain and Abel story. The brothers Vinson and Crawford Gowrie have joined forces in several business ventures, including timber dealing. Crawford, increasingly greedy for his own profits, steals timber from his brother and sells it to the shady Jake Montgomery. When Lucas

Beauchamp sees Crawford stealing the timber and threatens to expose him, Crawford kills his brother in a way to make Lucas appear as the murderer. Crawford relies on the townspeople's readiness to blame a black man for the murder of a white man. Much like Mink Snopes in Faulkner's *The Hamlet* (1931), Crawford learns too late that violence, instead of eradicating problems, creates more violence, and eventually one's downfall. Truth simply will not stay buried, Faulkner seems to be saying. In a hair-raising midnight scene combining the best of Edgar Allan Poe and Raymond Chandler, plus his own inimitable sense of place and wry humor, the author has three very frightened individuals uncover the truth that frees Lucas.

Beyond the Cain and Abel story, Gavin Stevens' speeches expand *Intruder in the Dust* into a parable about the people's right to govern themselves. Critics have frequently condemned Stevens' rhetoric as the propaganda of an unfeeling and aristocratic bigot. While this interpretation holds some validity, Stevens is not a mouthpiece for Faulkner's views; nor should Stevens' pleadings, however prolix, be discounted. In the filibuster tradition of Southern oratory, he articulates a code of noninterference, following Candide's words of "till your own garden." The intruder of the title may refer not only to those who open Vinson Gowrie's grave, but also to "outlanders" who would dictate moral action to these people. With their own sense of justice, the Southerners close this incident in their own way. They come to realize that Beauchamp could have little to do with what is fundamentally a family feud. As a result of his cruel victimization, Lucas in the future will be shown, or will suffer, innumerable courtesies by white people. He has suffered, and he is wise. Lucas will endure. The true villains here are the poor whites, those who have perverted the opportunities of their position.

The elderly spinster Eunice Habersham supports Beauchamp enough to rob a grave to prove his innocence. Had Miss Habersham been less sentimental and more skeptical, Crawford Gowrie, guilty and white, would have escaped. On the other hand, Hope Hampton, sheriff of Yoknapatawpha County, is highly skeptical and totally unsentimental. Hampton seeks justice, not conviction; evidence, not the will of the voters, persuades him to act. He is a diametric opposite to the familiar stereotype of the rural Southern sheriff, a big-bellied hunter and political animal. The villains of *Intruder in the Dust* behave in predictably stereotyped and evil ways, while the figures in power—Hampton, the prosecutor; Stevens, the defender; and Eunice Habersham, the moral sentiment—are humane, rounded characters.

As a story of initiation, the novel is an unqualified success. Young Chick Mallison must unlearn old values as well as learn new ones. In attempting to pay Lucas for his act of kindness, Chick denies the old black man his humanity. What others often interpret as arrogance is really Lucas' unyielding demand that he be treated as a human being, worthy of respect. Gradually, Chick comes to realize the moral rightness in the demand Lucas makes. After the death of Mrs. Beauchamp, Chick sees Lucas and understands that grief can come to a black man as well as to a white. By the time Lucas has been accused of committing murder, Chick knows that he must act with the same humanity Lucas showed him. Through Lucas, Chick also learns to accept Aleck as an equal. Thus, through the initiation of Chick Mallison, Faulkner makes a powerful, positive statement about race relations as fundamentally an encounter between one human being and another.

Intruder in the Dust, because it includes Gavin Stevens' philosophical discourses on the South's ability to handle its own problems after the action has essentially been resolved, is too often dismissed as a distasteful polemic, a lapse in Faulkner's series of brilliant novels. Yet, *Intruder in the Dust* is not so much inferior to such works as *The Sound and the Fury* or *Absalom, Absalom!* as it is different in its approach. Always the experimenter and innovator, Faulkner here turns with considerable success to establishing his vision in genre—namely, detective—fiction, as he did earlier with *Sanctuary* (1931), an even more gothic murder mystery, and *Pylon* (1935), an adventure story about flying.

"Critical Evaluation" by Patrick Morrow

Bibliography:
Bassett, John, ed. *William Faulkner: The Critical Heritage.* London: Routledge & Kegan Paul, 1975. Ninety-four critical reviews and essays on Faulkner, including six on *Intruder in the Dust.* Bibliography.
Brooks, Cleanth. *William Faulkner: The Yoknapatawpha Country.* New Haven, Conn.: Yale University Press, 1963. Contains a chapter on *Intruder in the Dust.* Description of plot and comparisons of the characters and the subtexts of the works. One of the most helpful and accessible books for information on Faulkner.
Howe, Irving. *William Faulkner: A Critical Study.* New York: Vintage Books, 1962. Focuses on the Southern myth and memory. Finds *Intruder in the Dust* to be the novel in which Faulkner frees himself from the Southern tradition of racism and stereotypes that are normally inherent to Southern life.
Jehlen, Myra. *Class and Character in Faulkner's South.* New York: Columbia University Press, 1976. Finds class distinctions to be the central theme in Faulkner's novels, including *Intruder in the Dust.* Considers treatment of characters relative to their classes.
Powers, Lyall H. *Faulkner's Yoknapatawpha Comedy.* Ann Arbor: University of Michigan Press, 1980. Emphasizes Faulkner's vision of good versus evil and his dark optimism. Draws a comparison between *Go Down, Moses* and *Intruder in the Dust,* using the character Chick Mallison.

INUNDACIÓN CASTÁLIDA

Type of work: Poetry and prose
Author: Sor Juana Inés de la Cruz (Juana Inés de Asbaje y Ramírez de Santillana, 1648-1695)
First published: 1689

Sor Juana Inés de la Cruz is the most significant poet and writer of the colonial period in the Americas. Born of a poor but honorable family in the village of San Miguel de Nepantla near a town called Amecameca, not far from Mexico City, she learned to read at the age of three, and the pursuit of knowledge subsequently became her true passion. Barred from attending the University in Mexico City because she was a woman, her plan to attend classes dressed as a man failed. Sor Juana's intellectual precocity attracted the interest of Viceroy Marquis de la Laguna, and for a time she served in his palace. During this period (1680-1686) she became a very good friend of the Viceroy's wife, Vicereine Luisa Gonzaga Manrique de Lara, Countess of Paredes, Marchioness de la Laguna. In 1669, Sor Juana took vows as a nun and entered the Convent of San Jerónimo in Mexico City; at this point she adopted the name Sor Juana Inés de la Cruz, by which she is conventionally known. While there, Sor Juana wrote plays, poetry, and prose. Her life of intellectual pleasure was ruined, however, with the publication of her *Respuesta de la Poetisa a la muy ilustre Sor Filotea de la Cruz* (reply to Sister Philotea), written in response to the Bishop of Puebla's recommendation that she turn her mind to spiritual rather than mundane, literary matters. The authorities silenced her; she sold her library and distributed the profits to the poor. She died while tending the sick in Mexico City. Just before her death, in a bout of deep contrition, she signed her name in blood with the words "I, Sister Juana Inés de la Cruz, the worst in the world."

Inundación castálida (the Castilian flood of the unique poetess), published in Spain in 1689, was dedicated to Vicereine de la Laguna, who was so impressed by its contents that she took it upon herself to take the manuscript to Madrid in order to have it printed. Its publication was funded by Don Juan Camacho Gayna, a gentleman of the Order of Santiago and then governor of the city of Puerto de Santa María, as the frontispiece of *Inundación castálida* states. While in the Convent of San Jerónimo, Sor Juana continued to write, her fame spread, and she became known as the Tenth Muse of Mexico. When *Inundación castálida* was published, it was a great success and was reprinted a total of nine times (a very high number for a time when the printing of a book was a major financial enterprise and when books rarely went beyond a first edition). It was intended to be the first of the three volumes of her complete works. After the publication of *Inundación castálida*, Sor Juana's confessor, Father Núñez de Miranda, perhaps through jealousy, put pressure on Sor Juana to give up writing poetry in order to concentrate on her religious duties.

The works collected in *Inundación castálida* are not grouped either thematically or chronologically in the original 1689 edition. This may seem strange to the modern reader who expects more order in the edition of a work of literature. It is important to recall, however, that *Inundación castálida* is a compilation and therefore brings together separate pieces of creative writing. It would not have been unusual for parts of this book to have been copied down by readers and then circulated to others. The poems in *Inundación castálida* can, however, be divided into four groups: *loas*, *villancicos*, the extended poem *Neptuno*, and personal lyrics.

The *loas*, *villancicos*, and *Neptuno* in *Inundación castálida* are all circumstantial poems; that is, they were commissioned by a third party, normally to commemorate an important historical or ritual event. The *loa* is an introit, or miniplay, that acts as a preface to a play about to be performed. One of the best examples of the *loa* in *Inundación castálida* is dedicated to Charles II and was performed on November 6, 1681 or 1682, in the viceroy's palace before the performance of Pedro Calderón de la Barca's play *En esta vida todo es verdad y todo es mentira* (in this life everything is true and everything is lies). It has five speaking parts: La Vida (life), La Majestad (majesty), La Plebe (the people), La Naturaleza (nature), and La Lealtad (loyalty), and is accompanied by two choirs. The *loa* begins by praising the king, Carlos II, passes to a discussion of the meaning of majesty (which is presented in positive terms), and then briefly describes the contents of Calderón's play, which is about to begin.

The second type of work in the *Inundación castálida* is the *villancico*, which, like the *loa*, is circumstantial. The *villancico* is a popular poetic composition with a refrain based on a religious theme and normally sung in church at Christmas or at other religious holidays. One of the best set of *villancicos* in this work was originally sung in 1865 in the Cathedral of Mexico in honor of the Virgin Mary to celebrate her Assumption, and then printed in the *Inundación castálida*. It has various prayers to the Virgin Mary asking for her protection, choral parts, a refrain that is repeated, and even different linguistic styles and languages; one section is in Latin, another in black Spanish, and another in Basque.

The third element in the *Inundación castálida*, the *Neptuno*, is an allegorical description of the triumphal arch which was built for the viceroys de la Laguna on their arrival in Mexico City in 1680. This poem mixes actual description of the arch with references to classical mythology and other sources which delve into the symbolic meaning of the arch. It has three main parts: the dedication to the viceroy; the "Razón de la fábrica," in which the building process is described; and the "Explicación del Arco," in which the allegorical meaning of the building is drawn out for the audience.

The three elements described thus far are all circumstantial poems, written at the behest of a third party, whether it be the church, the king, or the viceroy. For this reason, they are sometimes seen by modern readers as not authentic literature. It is important to recall, however, that in the seventeenth century the writer was often backed by a wealthy patron. Later, and particularly during the nineteenth century, when Romanticism was at its height, readers began to demand and expect creative writing that focused on the private sphere of the emotions. In the process, the more practical view of literature fell out of fashion. It is important, however, to remember that Sor Juana's work was produced in an era in which it was normal for a work of literature to be commissioned by the church or the king or the viceroy.

It is on the fourth group of poems, the personal poems, that Sor Juana's international fame is based. These poems have the most varied types of poetic composition, ranging from sonnets (poems that have fourteen eleven-syllable lines) to *décimas* (poems that have ten eight-syllable lines), from *redondillas* (a metrical combination of four eight-syllable lines) to *liras* (a five-line metrical sequence combining lines of seven and eleven syllables). The most common form in this group of poems is the sonnet, a poetic form that denotes seriousness. Like the other three groups, this group of poems has a circumstantial dimension; thus, some poems were written for special circumstances, such as the vicereine's birthday. What differentiates these poems, however, is that the circumstantial aspect becomes the springboard for something more profound. A poem that begins as the description of a portrait painting becomes a philosophical inquiry into the meaning of life: "Este, que ves, engaño colorido" (this that you gaze on, colorful deceit). There are a number of common themes in these poems, such as the conflict between appearance and essence, between the natural and the artificial, the brevity of human life, the delusion of love, and baroque disillusionment. The style of these poems is baroque, that is, characterized by a complex and elaborate form, ambiguous imagery, and dynamic intellectual oppositions and contrasts.

The better of the personal poems deal with philosophy and with love. Her philosophical poem "Rosa divina que en gentil cultura" (divine rose which in gentle culture), for example, deliberately chooses one of the most beautiful creations of the natural world (the rose) in order, ironically, to expose its frailty. The last line of the poem stresses the contrast between appearance and essence: "viviendo engañas y muriendo enseñas" (in living you deceive and in dying you teach). The most intellectually brilliant poems within this group are the poems dedicated to love. Some of these poems, written, it must be assumed, before she took her vows, expose her as caught in an unbearable love triangle. She loves a man who does not love her, and is loved by another man whom she does not love. The first stanza of "Al que ingrato me deja, busco amante" is a fine example of baroque conceit. It begins: "To the one who leaves me ungratefully, I seek as a lover;/ to the one who pursues me for love, I ungratefully leave;/ I constantly adore the one who mistreats my love;/ and I mistreat him who constantly desires my love." Sor Juana's most celebrated poem, "Hombres necios," looks at the same dilemma but presents it from a universal rather than a subjective point of view. In this poem there is a clear example of Sor Juana's feminist ideology. With devastating irony she criticizes men for attempting to find in women something they themselves are lacking. The first stanza encapsulates the argument of the whole poem. It reads: "Misguided men who will chastize/ a woman when no blame is due/ oblivious that it is you/ who prompted what you criticize." The various examples that Sor Juana then uses are all designed to flesh out the abstraction of this argument. The sixth stanza, for example, refers to the irony of the man who breathes on a mirror (takes a woman's virginity) and then complains he cannot see his own reflection (complains she is not chaste).

Stephen M. Hart

Bibliography:
Bergmann, Emilie L. "Sor Juana Inés de la Cruz: Dreaming in a Double Voice." In *Women, Culture, and Politics in Latin America/Seminar on Feminism and Culture in Latin America*, edited by Emilie Bergmann et al. Berkeley: University of California Press, 1990. Argues that Sor Juana's imagination is "gendered"; discusses the love poems as well as the "*Hombres necios*" poem mentioned above.

Daniel, Lee A. *The Loa of Sor Juana Inés de la Cruz.* Fredericton, New Brunswick, Canada: York, 1994. Contains a general overview of the *loa* in Sor Juana's work. Looks specifically at the echo effect and the distancing effect that the *loa* creates with respect to the main play.

Franco, Jean. *Plotting Women: Gender and Representation in Mexico.* New York: Columbia University Press, 1989. A suggestive reading of Sor Juana's work, in which the author shows that the Mexican nun was able to create a new space for her identity in a patriarchal world through the written word.

Leonard, Irving. "A Baroque Poetess." In *Baroque Times in Old Mexico.* Ann Arbor: University of Michigan Press, 1959. An excellent overview of Sor Juana's work, with discussion of the paradoxes in the love sonnets.

Merrim, Stephanie, ed. *Feminist Perspectives on Sor Juana Inés de la Cruz.* Detroit: Wayne State University Press, 1991. An indispensable collection of essays that put the case convincingly for seeing Sor Juana's work in feminist terms. Separate essays deal with the essays, plays, and also the poetry first published in *Inundación castálida*.

INVISIBLE MAN

Type of work: Novel
Author: Ralph Ellison (1914-1994)
Type of plot: Social realism
Time of plot: Late 1930's and early 1940's
Locale: The South and New York City
First published: 1952

> *Principal characters:*
> THE NARRATOR, an innocent young man
> GRANDFATHER, whose deathbed instruction made the narrator rethink his
>   relationship with society
> MR. NORTON, a white Northern philanthropist
> DR. A. HERBERT BLEDSOE, the president of an all-black college
> BROTHER JACK, the head of the Brotherhood
> TOD CLIFTON, an idealist
> RINEHART, a person who had many identities
> RAS, THE DESTROYER, a radical

The Story:

The narrator and protagonist in the novel was nameless. An innocent teenager, he was born and grew up in the South of the United States. He was used to the social patterns of the region. With maturity, the narrator gradually recognized the chaotic understructure of "orderly" society. The demarcation line between the "two" societies was blurred in his mind for the first time when he heard his grandfather's deathbed instruction to his father. Although the old man had seemed to be "obedient" and "obsequious" all his life, he told his son and grandchildren that he had "been a traitor all his born days, a spy in the enemy's country" and advised them to overcome their enemies "with yeses, undermine 'em with grins, agree 'em to death and destruction, let 'em swoller you till they vomit or bust wide open."

Later the narrator witnessed a formal social function which was attended by all "big shots" of the town. The party degenerated into a nightmare of barbarity, vulgarity, and bestial desire. At the battle royal, black students were asked to fight each other for white people's entertainment. The black students were forced to watch a naked white woman dance; they were also urged by the audience to pick up coins on electrified rugs (the coins later turned out to be advertisement souvenirs). As a reward for his Booker-T.-Washington kind of valedictory speech, the narrator received a calfskin briefcase. That night, the narrator dreamed of meeting his grandfather, who told him to read a note in the briefcase. The note said: "To Whom It May Concern: Keep This Nigger-Boy Running."

As part of the prize for his speech, the narrator also received a scholarship to go to college. What he learned there, however, only further confused him: A white philanthropist and a black sharecropper shared the same kind of incestuous desire for their daughters. A black minister who gave a wonderful speech about the importance of education turned out to be blind. The president of the college confessed that he used both black and white people to advance his own career. It was also from Dr. Bledsoe, the president of the all-black college, that the narrator heard for the first time in his life that he was a "nobody," someone who, in a sense, did not exist at all. The narrator was finally expelled from the college for showing Mr. Norton, the white trustee of the college, the "seamy" side of the campus.

3224

Equipped with Dr. Bledsoe's recommendation letter, which the narrator later learned was full of insulting remarks about him, he moved to the North. The road to the North, in a traditional sense, meant freedom to African Americans. What the narrator found there was alienation and disillusionment. While working in a paint factory, whose slogan was Keep America Pure with Liberty Paints, he was caught in the conflict between a skilled black worker and white unionists. After a boiler room accident, the narrator was sent to the factory hospital, where he received electric shock treatment. After the doctors had made sure he had forgotten his name and family background, the narrator was declared cured and released from the hospital.

Then one day, as he was helping people who were being evicted from an apartment building in New York City, the narrator's oratorical talent was discovered by the Brotherhood, a group meant to represent the poor and downtrodden. Brother Jack, the leader of the Brotherhood, asked the narrator to join the group. Inside the Brotherhood, the narrator not only was confronted again with the paradox of organization and disorder but also completely lost his personal identity: He was given a new name and place to live, expected to become the next Booker T. Washington, and told he was "hired to talk," but not "to think." The narrator's association with the Brotherhood, nevertheless, introduced him to all kinds of people: the white men who, for their own political gains, unscrupulously used blacks; a young black idealist who was killed for his idealism; Rinehart, the man who had multiple identities; and Ras, the Destroyer, a black radical, who lashed out indiscriminately and ended up in utter isolation.

The narrator finally realized that the Brotherhood was just as chaotic, manipulative, and power-hungry as all the other groups of people he met in both the South and the North. He left the Brotherhood feeling thoroughly disillusioned. Walking away from the Brotherhood, he chanced upon a riot, where he was mistaken for another person. Suddenly the narrator saw the truth: When a person was associated with either an ethnic group or a social organization, he became a person with no identity and, therefore, invisible. He started to understand the significance of his grandfather's last words. At the end of the novel, the narrator crept into a dark empty cellar to indulge in his reflections.

Critical Evaluation:

In modern American letters, the development of African American literature has followed a zigzag course. The literary movement of the Harlem Renaissance in the 1920's saw the flourishing of black writing, but the Great Depression dealt it a serious blow. The popularity and success of Richard Wright's *Native Son* (1940) and *Black Boy: A Record of Childhood and Youth* (1945) resurrected African American literature in the 1940's. The emergence of Ralph Ellison and James Baldwin in the 1950's helped push the development of African American literature to a new height. *Invisible Man*, the only novel that Ellison published, won the National Book Award for fiction in 1953. In a *Book Week* poll of two hundred critics and writers in 1965, the book was voted the "most distinguished single work" published between 1945 and 1965 in the United States.

Besides drawing inspiration from Wright's works, Ellison was also influenced by T. S. Eliot's insistence upon the importance of tradition. Wright's use of lengthy sentences, rapid flow of consciousness conveyed by a string of participles, and long lists of abstract nouns joined together by overworked conjunctions in *Invisible Man* reminds the reader of William Faulkner's writing style. Ellison's originality, however, lies in his skillful depiction and enthusiastic celebration of African American culture. Ellison believed that black vernacular, black folklore, and black music were highly developed cultural forms that had helped shape the mainstream culture in America. African American writers who either looked down upon or ignored their own cultural heritage in their writings were often trapped in using stereotypes to portray African American experience; a conscious study and celebration of African American culture could release them from the bondage of stereotypes.

In *Invisible Man*, Ellison took pains to exploit African American culture to the full. His portrayal of Rinehart, for example, follows the trickster tradition in African American literature. Rinehart has several identities: He is a lover, a number runner, a preacher, and a con man. Meeting Rinehart helps the narrator understand why his grandfather had two identities: a public one (false) and a private one (real). It also makes him realize that the relationship between having an identity and not having an identity is dialectical: A person's invisibility also gives that person an opportunity to create and adopt whichever identity he or she would like to have.

Ellison's use of black-oriented humor in *Invisible Man* produces an effect similar to that of the blues. According to Ellison, blues is an impulse to keep the painful details and episodes of a brutal experience alive in one's aching consciousness, "to finger its jagged grain, and to transcend it, not by the consolation of philosophy but by squeezing from it a near-tragic, near-comic lyricism." Ellison revealed that several of the book's themes and motifs were inspired by jokes that circulated among African Americans. The theme of invisibility, for instance, was developed from the joke that some blacks were so black they could not be seen in the dark. The paint factory's slogan If It's Optic White, It's the Right White originated from another joke: "If you're black, stay back; if you're brown, stick around; if you're white, you're right."

Invisible Man reverberates with the lyrical, musical, and rhythmic cadence of black English. Ellison borrowed phrases freely from different sources and used them effectively to accentuate his thematic concerns. *Invisible Man* abounds with phrases and sentences such as "I'll verse you but I won't curse you—," "I yam what I am!" and "Stephen's problem, like ours, was not actually one of creating the uncreated conscience of his race, but of creating the uncreated features of his face." The first part of the last sentence is taken from James Joyce's *A Portrait of the Artist as a Young Man* (1916) and the second part is added by the author with a bearing on the theme of the book.

The tone of *Invisible Man* is bitter, ironic, and sometimes pessimistic. The style is vivid and flexible. When commenting on the style of the book, Ellison said: "In the South, where he (the protagonist) was trying to fit into a traditional pattern and where his sense of certainty had not yet been challenged, I felt a more naturalistic treatment was adequate."

As the hero passes from the South to the North, from the relatively stable to the swiftly changing, "his sense of certainty is lost and the style becomes expressionistic." Later on, "during his fall from grace in the Brotherhood it becomes somewhat surrealistic." Surrealism permits itself to develop nonlogically in order to reveal the operation of the subconscious mind. Ellison's use of incongruous images in *Invisible Man* works well with his thematic accentuation of the protagonist's phantasmal state of mind and the chaotic state of society.

Even though *Invisible Man* is about African American experience, the novel illuminates the common plight of people who are in earnest search for their true identity. Ellison's thematic treatment of the conflict between dream and reality, between individual and society, and between innocence and experience appeals to both black and white readers. This thematic concern is highlighted by the fact that the book opens with the narrator's claiming that his invisibility is not "exactly a matter of a biochemical accident to" his "epidermis" and it ends with the narrator's making a foreboding declaration to the reader: "Who knows but that, on the lower frequencies, I speak for you?"

Qun Wang

Bibliography:
Bone, Robert A. *The Negro Novel in America.* Rev. ed. New Haven, Conn.: Yale University Press, 1965. Takes a historical look at the development of the African American novel. Has a section on Ralph Ellison and *Invisible Man.*
Gottesman, Ronald. *The Merrill Studies in "Invisible Man."* Westerville, Ohio: Charles E. Merrill, 1971. A collection of essays focuses on Ellison's thematic concerns, narrative point of view, style, and use of language in *Invisible Man.*
Hersey, John, ed. *Ralph Ellison: A Collection of Critical Essays.* Englewood Cliffs, N.J.: Prentice-Hall, 1974. A collection of essays on different aspects of Ellison's work. Provides a panoramic view on Ralph Ellison as an artist, a musician, and a writer. The book also includes John Hersey and James McPherson's interview with Ellison.
O'Meally, Robert G. *The Craft of Ralph Ellison.* Cambridge, Mass.: Harvard University Press, 1980. An excellent study of Ellison's work. Contains biographical information about the author, a bibliography, and key references on Ellison and *Invisible Man.*
Reilly, John M., ed. *Twentieth-Century Interpretations of "Invisible Man."* Englewood Cliffs, N.J.: Prentice-Hall, 1970. Ten interpretations of the novel and five excerpted "viewpoints," several of which criticize Ellison as insufficiently militant.

THE INVISIBLE MAN
A Grotesque Romance

Type of work: Novel
Author: H. G. Wells (1866-1946)
Type of plot: Science fiction
Time of plot: Late nineteenth century
Locale: England
First published: 1897

Principal characters:
GRIFFIN, the Invisible Man
MR. HALL, the landlord of the Coach and Horses Inn
MRS. HALL, his wife
DR. KEMP, a physician in the town of Burdock
COLONEL ADYE, the chief of the Burdock police
MARVEL, a tramp

The Story:

The stranger arrived at Bramblehurst railway station on a cold, snowy day in February. Carrying a valise, he trudged through driving snow to Iping, where he stumbled into the Coach and Horses Inn and asked Mrs. Hall, the hostess, for a room and a fire. The stranger's face was hidden by dark blue spectacles and bushy sideburns.

He had dinner in his room. When Mrs. Hall took a mustard jar up to him, she saw that the stranger's head was completely bandaged. While she was in his room, he covered his mouth and chin with a napkin.

His baggage arrived the next day, consisting of several trunks and boxes of books and a crate of bottles packed in straw. The drayman's dog attacked the stranger, tearing his glove and ripping his trousers. Mr. Hall, landlord of the inn, ran upstairs to see if the stranger had been hurt and entered his room without knocking. He was immediately struck on the chest and pushed from the room. When Mrs. Hall took up the lodger's supper, she saw that he had unpacked his trunks and boxes and set up some strange apparatus. The lodger was not wearing his glasses; his eyes looked sunken and hollow.

In the weeks that followed, the villagers made many conjectures as to the stranger's identity. Some thought he suffered from a strange disease that had left his skin spotted. Unusual happenings also mystified the village. One night, the vicar and his wife were awakened by a noise in the vicar's study and the clinking of money. Upon investigation, they saw no one, although a candle was burning and they heard a sneeze.

In the meantime, Mr. Hall found clothing and bandages scattered about the lodger's room; the stranger had disappeared. The landlord went downstairs to call his wife. They heard the front door open and shut, but no one came into the inn. While they stood wondering what to do, their lodger came down the stairs. Where he had been and how he had returned to his room unnoticed were mysteries that he made no attempt to explain.

A short time later, the stranger's bill being overdue, Mrs. Hall refused to serve him. When the stranger became abusive, Mr. Hall swore out a warrant against him. The constable, the landlord, and a curious neighbor went upstairs to arrest the lodger. After a struggle, the man agreed to unmask. The men were struck with horror; the stranger was invisible to their view. In the confusion, the Invisible Man, as the newspapers were soon to call him, fled from the inn.

The next person to encounter the Invisible Man was a tramp named Marvel. The Invisible Man frightened Marvel into accompanying him to the Coach and Horses Inn to get his clothing and three books. They arrived at the inn while the vicar and the village doctor were reading the stranger's diary. They beat the two men, snatched up the clothes and books, and left the inn.

Newspapers continued to print stories of unnatural thefts. Money had been taken and carried away; the thief was invisible while the money was in plain view. Marvel always seemed to be well-supplied with funds.

One day Marvel, carrying three books, came running into the Jolly Cricketers Inn. He said that the Invisible Man was after him. A barman, a policeman, and a cabman awaited the Invisible Man's arrival after hiding Marvel; the Invisible Man found Marvel, however, dragged him into the inn kitchen, and tried to force him through the door. The three men struggled with the unseen creature while Marvel crawled into the bar. When the voice of the Invisible Man was heard in the inn yard, a villager fired five shots in the direction of the sound, but searchers found no body in the yard.

Meanwhile, Dr. Kemp worked late in his study in Burdock. Preparing to retire, he noticed drops of drying blood on the stairs. He found the doorknob of his room smeared with blood and red stains on his bed. While he stared in amazement at a bandage that was apparently wrapping itself about nothing in midair, a voice called him by name. The Invisible Man had taken refuge in Kemp's rooms. He identified himself as Griffin, a young scientist whom Kemp had met at the university where both had studied. Griffin asked for whiskey and food. He said that except for short naps he had not slept for three days and nights.

That night, Kemp sat up to read all the newspaper accounts of the activities of the Invisible Man. At last, after much thought, he wrote a letter to Colonel Adye, chief of the Burdock police.

In the morning, Griffin told his story to Kemp. He explained that for three years he had experimented with refractions of light on the theory that a human body would become invisible if the cells could be made transparent. He had needed money for his work and had robbed his father of money belonging to someone else; his father had shot himself. At last, his experiments were successful. After setting fire to his room in order to destroy the evidence of his research, he had begun his strange adventures. He had terrorized Oxford Street, where passersby had seen only his footprints. He discovered that in his invisible state he was compelled to fast, for all unassimilated food or drink was grotesquely visible. At last, prowling London streets and made desperate by his plight, he had gone to a shop selling theatrical supplies. There he had stolen the dark glasses, the sideburns, and the clothes he wore on his arrival in Iping.

Griffin planned to use Kemp's house as a headquarters while terrorizing the neighborhood. Kemp, believing that Griffin was insane, attempted to restrain him, but the Invisible Man escaped. Shortly thereafter, a man called Mr. Wicksteed was found murdered, and a manhunt began.

The next morning, Kemp received a note announcing that the reign of terror had begun; one person would be executed daily. Kemp himself was to be the first victim. He was to die at noon; nothing could protect him. Kemp sent at once for Colonel Adye. While they were discussing possible precautions, stones were hurled through the windows. The colonel left to return to the police station for some bloodhounds to set on Griffin's trail, but Griffin snatched a revolver from Adye's pocket and wounded the police officer. When Griffin began to smash Kemp's kitchen door with an ax, the doctor climbed through a window and ran to a neighbor's house. He was refused admittance. He ran to the inn. The door was barred. Suddenly, his invisible assailant seized him. While they struggled, some men came to the doctor's rescue. Kemp got hold of Griffin's arms. A constable seized his legs. Someone struck through the air with a spade. The writhing unseen figure sagged to the ground. Kemp announced that he could not hear Griffin's heartbeats. While the crowd gathered, Griffin's body slowly materialized, naked, dead. A sheet was brought from the inn, and the body was carried away. The reign of terror was ended.

Critical Evaluation:

The Invisible Man has an honored place as one of the first works of modern science fiction. H. G. Wells, a science student and teacher, was keenly interested in how the twentieth century would develop its technical knowledge. He was equally concerned with the morality of the scientific experimenter. Griffin is one type of scientist, aloof, aggressive, and contemptuous of his fellow humans. Ordinary people irritate him. They seem petty compared to his lofty concern with the mechanisms of nature. His knowledge has isolated him; he thinks only of his discovery and the power that his special knowledge gives him. Consequently, he becomes a menace to society.

Wells does not reveal the full implications of Griffin's threat to order until the last pages of the novel. At first, Griffin is a mysterious stranger seeking seclusion. His gruff manner is partly excusable because he is fending off the prying questions of his landlady and other villagers. After his plight as an invisible man is revealed, the narrative shifts to an absorbing, intricate account of how he tries to remain at large. The moral implications of his discovery are not considered while society is still mobilizing to cope with this new phenomenon.

Only when Griffin feels cornered and takes refuge in Kemp's home does Wells fully reveal Griffin's mind and character. For the first time, Griffin has a scientific colleague to whom he can unburden himself. Griffin believes that Kemp will understand the scientific details and share his commitment to terrorizing and remaking society. So Griffin reasons, because he has completely lost contact with his fellow man. He sees society only as material that he can manipulate.

Griffin is so absorbed in his own views that he does not detect the revulsion Kemp feels for his murderous plans. Griffin means to use science as an instrument of terror; the scientist will become a dictator, deciding who shall live and who shall die. In the process, the scientist himself becomes a monster, oblivious of humanity.

In a sense, Wells has rewritten Mary Shelley's classic *Frankenstein* (1818). In that novel, Victor Frankenstein tries to improve humanity by using parts of human bodies to create a perfect being. Frankenstein also isolates himself from his community, allows his enthusiasm for scientific discovery to outweigh moral considerations, and consequently produces a monster. Frankenstein, however, reacts to his terrible invention with horror and contrition, realizing that he has separated himself from humanity. Griffin, on the other hand, is the model of the disinterested scientist. He is solely concerned with his experiments. He will destroy anything that impedes his scientific progress. He is the modern professional, cool and self-contained. He has no emotional involvement with anything but his experiments.

That Kemp should triumph over Griffin suggests that there are natural limitations to the damage a scientist like Griffin can inflict on society. Griffin fails to gain Kemp as a collaborator precisely because Griffin does not recognize Kemp's humanity. Because Griffin is himself the monster, he guarantees his own doom. Society will have to crush him just as he has planned to crush it.

There is something heroic in Griffin's dedication to science, but his quest has become perverted. Science offers the possibility of specialized knowledge, of improving the human condition, and of learning more about nature. The scientist, however, must realize that he is a part of what he studies and that he cannot set himself apart from it. Victor Frankenstein cannot make a perfect human being because he himself is imperfect and the human body parts he uses to make his monster are flawed as well. Similarly, Wells shows that Griffin becomes a criminal as soon as he becomes invisible because of his defective nature. Invisibility merely increases his sense of isolation from society and intensifies his sense of uniqueness and superiority; invisibility does not contribute to Griffin's understanding of nature.

Griffin's cruelty is a striking feature of his characterization. It is painful to witness his torturing of the poor tramp, Marvel. Like the other characters in *The Invisible Man*, Marvel is a vivid, colorful creation. He is given a distinct voice. He may seem pathetic, an easy target for Griffin's jeers, but his individuality and his right to his own life are precious values that Griffin would deny him. In Griffin's hands, science becomes a tool of tyranny, a way of denying all individuality, a way of blending all of humanity into the mad scientist's vision of carefully controlled experiments. People become test subjects.

Because Griffin's explanation of his experiments and of his scornful view of humanity are withheld until nearly the end of the novel, Wells is able to maintain extraordinary tension and suspense. How has Griffin made himself invisible? Why has he done so? How has his invisibility affected him? The answers to these questions are held until the denouement of the novel, until the narrative has worked through several exciting scenes of pursuit and violence. Not until the unbearability of Griffin's isolation is complete is he given an opportunity to explain himself.

These final scenes constitute Griffin's confession, defense, and defiance of society's conventions. He acts as though his invention entitles him to violate morality, even to murder. At this point, he sounds demented, a man overtaken by intellectual passions, in the grip of ideas that have shriven him of his humanity.

Although Griffin's cruelty would seem to deprive the reader of any sense of sympathy for him, the novel ends with a touching image of him, "naked and pitiful on the ground, the bruised and broken body of a young man about thirty." The scene suggests that Griffin is also a victim, hardly yet mature, deluded, fragile, and misled, a representative of erring humanity, vulnerable and tragic.

"Critical Evaluation" by Carl Rollyson

Bibliography:
Costa, Richard Hauer. *H. G. Wells*. Boston: Twayne, 1967. Explains the influence of science on the novel, compares the novel to Wells's earlier science fiction, and explores the struggle of the characters to cope with new scientific attitudes.
Hammond, J. R. *An H. G. Wells Companion: A Guide to the Novels, Romances, and Short Stories*. Totowa, N.J.: Barnes & Noble Books, 1979. Describes the sense of excitement that greeted the first publication of the novel, its circumstantial and realistic setting, the sharp observation of social details, and the economical and dramatic structure of the narrative.
McConnell, Frank. *The Science Fiction of H. G. Wells*. New York: Oxford University Press, 1981. Emphasizes the novel's grim realism and considers nineteenth century works that may have influenced Wells's unique sense of the apocalyptic and his powerful descriptions of society in disorder. Analyzes Griffin's character and his proneness to violence, Wells's depiction of middle-class society and how it organizes itself to capture Griffin, and the role of Marvel as a comic character and victim.

Mackenzie, Norman, and Jeanne Mackenzie. *The Time Traveller: The Life of H. G. Wells.* Rev. ed. London: Hogarth Press, 1987. Compares Griffin to Wells's other mad scientists and discusses Wells's ambivalence about science, his choice of characters, and the place of the characters in his thinking about science and nature.

Williamson, Jack. *H. G. Wells: Critic of Progress.* Baltimore: Mirage Press, 1973. Discusses Griffin's inhuman qualities and the role of the intellect as a theme in the novel. Explores the precise evocation of setting, Wells's handling of point of view, and his tendency to overlook inconsistencies in order to build his narrative.

IOLANTHE
Or, The Peer and the Peri

Type of work: Drama
Author: W. S. Gilbert (1836-1911)
Type of plot: Operetta
Time of plot: Nineteenth century
Locale: England
First performed: 1882; first published, 1882

Principal characters:
THE LORD CHANCELLOR
STREPHON, an Arcadian shepherd
QUEEN OF THE FAIRIES
IOLANTHE, Strephon's fairy mother
PHYLLIS, a shepherdess and ward in Chancery
THE EARL OF MOUNTARARAT and
EARL TOLLOLLER, her suitors
PRIVATE WILLIS, a palace guard

The Story:

The Fairy Queen had banished Iolanthe because Iolanthe had married a mortal. Normally the punishment for such an act was death, but the queen so loved Iolanthe that she had been unable to enforce the penalty. Iolanthe had been sentenced to penal servitude for life, on the condition that she never see her mortal husband again. At last the other fairies begged the queen to relent, to set aside even this punishment. Iolanthe had served twenty-five years of her sentence by standing on her head at the bottom of a stream.

The queen, unable to resist their pleas, summoned the penitent Iolanthe and pardoned her. Iolanthe explained that she had stayed in the stream to be near her son Strephon, an Arcadian shepherd who was a fairy to his waist and a human from the waist down. While they spoke, Strephon entered, announcing that he was to be married that day to Phyllis, a ward of Chancery. The Lord Chancellor had not given his permission, but Strephon was determined to marry his Phyllis anyway. He was delighted when he learned that his mother had been pardoned, but he begged her and all the fairies not to tell Phyllis that he was half fairy. He feared that she would not understand.

The queen determined to make Strephon a member of Parliament, but Strephon said that he would be no good in that august body, for the top of him was a Tory, the bottom a Radical. The queen solved that problem by making him a Liberal-Unionist and taking his mortal legs under her particular care. Phyllis talked with Strephon and warned him that to marry her without the Lord Chancellor's permission would mean lifelong penal servitude for him. Strephon could not wait the two years until she was of age. He feared that the Lord Chancellor himself or one of the peers of the House of Lords would marry her before that time had passed.

Strephon's fears were well founded; the Lord Chancellor did want to marry his ward. Fearing that he would have to punish himself for marrying her without his permission, however, he decided to give her instead to one of the peers of the House of Lords. Two were at last selected, the Earl of Mountararat and Earl Tolloller, but there was no agreement as to the final choice. Phyllis did not wish to accept either, since she loved only Strephon. Then she saw Strephon talking with Iolanthe, who, being immortal, looked like a young and beautiful woman, although she was Strephon's mother. Phyllis was filled with jealousy, augmented by the laughter of the peers when Strephon, in desperation, confessed that Iolanthe was his mother. Weeping that he had betrayed her, Phyllis left Strephon. No one had ever heard of a son who looked older than his mother.

The Fairy Queen told the Lord Chancellor and the peers that they would rue their laughter over Iolanthe and her son. To punish them, Strephon would change all existing laws in the House of Lords. He would abolish the rights of peers and give titles to worthy commoners. Worst of all, from then on peers would be chosen by competitive examinations. Strephon would be a foe they would not soon forget.

The queen's prediction came true. Strephon completely ruled the House of Lords. Every bill he proposed was passed, the fairies making the other members vote for Strephon even when they wanted to vote against him. The peers appealed to the fairies, but although the fairies admired the peers, the fairies could not be swayed against Strephon. The Earl of Mountararat and Earl Tolloller tried to decide who should have Phyllis. Each wanted the other to sacrifice himself by giving up all rights to her. Both had a family tradition that they must fight anyone who took their sweethearts, and since a fight meant that one of them would die and the survivor would be left without his friend, each wanted to make the sacrifice of losing his friend. At last the two decided that friendship was more important than love. Both renounced Phyllis.

Strephon and Phyllis met again, and at last he convinced her that Iolanthe was really his mother. Phyllis still could not believe that Strephon looked like a fairy, and she could not quite understand that his grandmother and all his aunts looked as young as his mother. She was sensible, however, and promised that whenever she saw Strephon kissing a very young woman she would know the woman was an elderly relative. There was still the Lord Chancellor to contend with. When they went to Iolanthe and begged her to persuade him to consent to their marriage, Iolanthe told them that the Lord Chancellor was her mortal husband. He believed her dead and himself childless, and if she looked on him the queen would carry out the penalty of instant death.

Iolanthe could not resist the pleas of the young lovers. As she told the Lord Chancellor that she was his lost wife, the queen entered and prepared to carry out the sentence of death against Iolanthe. Before she could act, however, the other fairies entered and confessed that they too had married peers in the House of Lords. The queen grieved, but the law was clear. Whoever married a mortal must die. The Lord Chancellor's great knowledge of the law saved the day. The law would now read that whoever did not marry a mortal must die. Thinking that a wonderful solution, the queen took one of the palace guards, Private Willis, for her husband. Knowing that from now on the House of Lords would be recruited from persons of intelligence, because of Strephon's law, the current peers could see that they were of little use. Sprouting wings, they all flew away to Fairyland.

Critical Evaluation:

While *Patience* was still enjoying a long run at the Savoy Theatre, William Schwenck Gilbert prepared for his musical collaborator, Arthur Seymour Sullivan, the libretto for a new comic opera. Sullivan, as usual, was not wholly satisfied with the preliminary draft of the book, and at his urging Gilbert rewrote the first act. Gilbert had trouble with the title. His last three successful D'Oyly Carte productions had begun with the letter *P*—*Pinafore* (1878), *The Pirates of Penzance* (1880), and *Patience* (1881)—Gilbert thrashed about for another title beginning with the "lucky" initial. He considered and then rejected "Perola," "Phyllis," and "Princess Pearl" before he chose *Iolanthe*, with the acceptable subtitle *The Peer and the Peri*. This last matter settled, Gilbert and Sullivan's "entirely new and original fairy opera" opened at the Savoy on the evening of November 25, 1882, and continued to hold the stage for a year and two months.

No doubt Gilbert wished to emphasize the "fairy" elements of *Iolanthe* in order to soften any possible criticism of his spoof upon the House of Lords. In the course of Parliamentary debates in Victorian England, the House of Lords—a privileged and largely hereditary body lacking any democratic representation—was under constant fire as antiquated, unresponsive to the people, and ultraconservative. Almost every one of the era's reform bills widened the franchise and diminished the powers of the Lords, who eventually lost most of their real authority to the House of Commons. Gilbert, clearly on the side of the liberals, wished to satirize the absurdity of the Peers, but not so directly as to excite political controversy. For the framework of his plot, he reworked an old idea from one of his Bab Ballads concerning a hero who is half fairy and half human. Not even a crusty Tory could complain that the adventures of Strephon could possibly insult the dignities of a modern Lord. At the conclusion of *Iolanthe*, all the Peers marry the fairies, and the doughtiest Lord in Parliament would have to acquiesce in pleasure to Gilbert's romantic jest.

Behind the jest, Gilbert's satire applies not only to the House of Lords but also to the notion of a privileged class. The Peers announce their arrival ("Loudly Let the Trumpets Bray") with the contemptuous salutation: "Bow, bow, ye lower middle classes . . . ye tradesmen, bow ye masses!" The powerful Lord Chancellor, who argues that the law is the "true embodiment of everything that's excellent," cynically changes the law to suit himself and ensure that every fairy shall die who does not marry a mortal. In "Spurn Not the Nobly Born," Lord Tolloller insists that high rank "involves no shame," so women should never withhold affection from "Blue Bloods." Finally, Lord Mountararat, in "When Britain Really Ruled the Waves," looks backward to the good old days of Queen Bess, when the House of Peers "made no pretence to intellectual eminence or scholarship sublime." By their own merry words, the Peers indict themselves as a class of drones, bores, and fools. Gilbert, not disposed to press the point, permits the Lords to grow wings to fly off to a fairyland blessedly distant from the responsibilities of office.

Bibliography:

Bailey, Leslie. *Gilbert and Sullivan and Their World.* New York: Thames and Hudson, 1973. Examines the original production of *Iolanthe* and notes its allusions to Wagnerian opera. Photographs and sketches of early productions.

Dark, Sidney, and Rowland Grey. *W. S. Gilbert: His Life and Letters.* Ann Arbor, Mich.: Gryphon Books, 1971. Shows *Iolanthe*'s indebtedness to *The Bab Ballads* (1869) and considers the development of the patter song in the Lord Chancellor's songs. Examines the role of the chorus in relation to other Gilbert and Sullivan works.

Dunn, George E. *A Gilbert and Sullivan Directory.* New York: Da Capo Press, 1971. A comprehensive dictionary that includes references to Gilbert's many allusions. Shows correlations among various Gilbert and Sullivan works.

Heylar, James, ed. *Gilbert and Sullivan: Papers Presented at the International Conference Held at the University of Kansas in May, 1970.* Lawrence: University of Kansas Library, 1971. Examines the considerable abridgments made to *Iolanthe* over the years and the reasons for these changes. Connects the operetta to similar works.

Moore, Frank Ledlie. *Handbook of Gilbert and Sullivan.* New York: Schocken Books, 1975. Gives an overview of *Iolanthe*. Places the opera in the pastoral tradition and considers its many allusions to the operas of Richard Wagner.

ION

Type of work: Drama
Author: Euripides (c. 485-406 B.C.E.)
Type of plot: Tragicomedy
Time of plot: Antiquity
Locale: The temple of Apollo at Delphi
First performed: Iōn, c. 411 B.C.E. (English translation, 1781)

Principal characters:
> HERMES, the speaker of the prologue
> ION, the son of Apollo and Creusa
> CREUSA, the daughter of Erechtheus, King of Athens
> XUTHUS, Creusa's husband
> AGED SLAVE TO CREUSA
> A PRIESTESS OF APOLLO
> PALLAS ATHENA, goddess of wisdom
> CHORUS OF CREUSA'S HANDMAIDENS

The Story:

Years before, Phoebus Apollo had ravished Creusa, daughter of King Erechtheus, who subsequently and in secret gave birth to a son. By Apollo's command she hid the infant in a cave, where Hermes was sent to carry him to the temple of Apollo. There he was reared as a temple ministrant. Meanwhile, Creusa had married Xuthus as a reward for his aid in the Athenian war against the Euboeans, but the marriage remained without issue. After years of frustration, Xuthus and Creusa decided to make a pilgrimage to Delphi and ask the god for aid in getting a son.

At dawn Ion emerged from the temple of Apollo to sweep the floors, chase away the birds, set out the laurel boughs, and make the usual morning sacrifice. Creusa's handmaidens came to admire the temple built upon the navel of the world and to announce the imminent arrival of their mistress. At the meeting of Creusa and Ion, Creusa confirmed the story that her father had been drawn from the earth by Athena and was swallowed up by the earth at the end of his life. The credulous Ion explained that his own birth, too, was shrouded in mystery, for he had appeared out of nowhere at the temple and had been reared by the priestess of Apollo. The greatest sorrow of his life, he said, was not knowing who his mother was. Creusa sympathized and cautiously revealed that she had a friend with a similar problem, a woman who had borne a son to Apollo, only to have the infant disappear and to suffer childlessness for the rest of her life.

Ion, shocked and outraged at the insult to his god, demanded that Creusa end her accusation of Apollo in his own temple, but the anguished woman assailed the god with fresh charges of injustice, breaking off only at the arrival of her husband. Xuthus eagerly took his wife into the temple, for he had just been assured by the prophet Trophonius that they would not return childless to Athens. The perplexed Ion was left alone to meditate on the lawlessness of gods who seemed to put pleasure before wisdom.

Xuthus, emerging from the temple, fell upon the startled Ion and attempted to kiss and embrace him. He shouted joyfully that Ion must be his son, for the oracle had said that the first person he would see upon leaving the temple would be his son by birth. Stunned and unconvinced, Ion demanded to know who his mother was, but Xuthus could only conjecture that possibly she was one of the Delphian women he had encountered at a Bacchanal before his marriage. Ion, reluctantly conceding that Xuthus must be his father if Apollo so decreed, begged to remain an attendant in the temple rather than become the unwelcome and suspicious heir to the throne of Athens—for Creusa would surely resent a son she had not borne. Xuthus understood his anxiety and agreed to hide his identity; however, he insisted that Ion accompany him to Athens, even if only in the role of distinguished guest. He then gave orders for a banquet of thanksgiving and commanded that the handmaidens to Creusa keep their silence on pain of death. As they departed to prepare the feast, Ion expressed the hopes that his mother might still be found and that she might be an Athenian.

Accompanied by the aged slave of her father, Creusa reappeared before the temple and demanded from her handmaidens an account of the revelation Xuthus had received from Apollo. Only under relentless cross-examination did the fearful servants reveal what had passed between Xuthus and Ion. Overcome by a sense of betrayal, Creusa cursed Apollo for his cruelty but dared not act upon the old slave's suggestion that she burn the temple or murder the husband who had, after all, been kind to her.

Murder of the usurper, Ion, however, was another matter. After some deliberation Creusa decided upon a safe and secret method of eliminating the rival of her lost son. From a phial of the Gorgon's blood which Athena had given to Creusa's grandfather and which had been passed down to her, the old slave was to pour a drop into Ion's wineglass at the celebration feast. Eager to serve his master's daughter, the slave departed, and the chorus chanted their hope for success.

Some time later a messenger came running to warn Creusa that the authorities were about to seize her and submit her to death by stoning, for her plot had been discovered. He described how at the feast a flock of doves had dipped down to drink from Ion's cup and had died in horrible convulsions and how Ion had tortured a confession out of the old slave. The court of Delphi had then sentenced Creusa to death for attempting murder of a consecrated person within the sacred precincts of the temple of Apollo. The chorus urged Creusa to fling herself upon the altar and remain there in sanctuary.

A short time later Ion arrived at the head of an infuriated crowd, and he and Creusa began to hurl angry charges and counter-charges at each other. Suddenly the priestess of the temple appeared, bearing the cradle and the tokens with which the infant Ion had been found years before. Slowly and painfully the truth emerged: Ion was the lost son of Creusa and Apollo. Creusa was seized with a frenzy of joy, but the astounded Ion remained incredulous. As he was about to enter the temple to demand an explanation from Apollo himself, the goddess Athena appeared in mid-air and confirmed the revelation. She urged that Xuthus not be told the truth so that he might enjoy the delusion that his own son was to be his heir, while Creusa and Ion could share their genuine happiness. Creusa renounced all her curses against Apollo and blessed him for his ultimate wisdom. As she and Ion departed for Athens the chorus called upon everyone to reverence the gods and take courage.

Critical Evaluation:

Two issues dominate criticism of *Ion*: what genre it belongs to, and who Ion's father is. The answer to the first issue can only be that it is neither comedy nor tragedy; it is simple melodrama. After confusion and misunderstandings, the characters work out their differences and are happily reconciled. In this regard, the play is comic. The anger that the characters feel throughout so much of the play, however, establishes a mood that distracts from a comic, festive finale. For example, how can an audience desire a happy ending for Creusa after she has plotted to poison Ion? Her intention reveals a cruel nature that alienates an audience.

When the flock of doves dies in convulsions after sipping from the cup meant for Ion, the old slave confesses under duress, and Creusa is sentenced to die. Here again, although Ion has cause to beat the old slave in order to obtain the truth, acts of torture coarsen the tone of the play, and they work against the lighthearted tone expected in comedy.

The deception that the characters engage in also detracts from any sympathy felt for them. When Xuthus thinks that he is Ion's father, he accepts Ion's wish to keep their relationship secret from Creusa, even though Xuthus insists that Ion come with him to Athens. When Xuthus organizes a banquet to celebrate his honored guest—the role that Ion agrees to play—he threatens Creusa's servants with death if they reveal the truth. Creusa does learn the truth and curses Apollo, although she does not dare to burn Apollo's temple or to kill her husband.

The second major deception occurs at the end when the priestess materializes and asserts that Ion is, indeed, the lost son of Creusa and Apollo. To make this public knowledge, however, would rob Xuthus of his conviction that he is the biological father of Ion, and so Athena urges Creusa and Ion to enjoy their knowledge in secret. Creusa then retracts all her blasphemies against Apollo, and she thanks him for his superior wisdom. The play ends with a happiness structured upon falsehoods, and the gods and praised for this solution.

The second question asks who is Ion's father, Apollo or Xuthus? Greeks of Euripides' day would answer this question according to how they felt about the gods. The pious answer would be that Apollo was truly the father and that Ion was raised just as Hermes explains in the prologue. This is not a difficult story to accept, given the history and reputation of the gods.

The other answer, rational and obvious to anyone skeptical of religious explanations, says that Xuthus—or some other young man—fathered the boy. For a young woman to have had an illegitimate child whom she leaves in a cave to die—the same cave, perhaps, where the child was fathered—must have been possible. Apollo's reasoning in the conclusion, then, could be interpreted this way: Creusa has suffered enough for abandoning her bastard child. What would make everyone happy? Let us convince her that this child is really hers, as he apparently is, and let her believe that I am his father if that rationalization helps her; then, let us also allow Xuthus to keep on thinking that the child is his.

In this way, youthful folly is repaired, Ion and his mother find each other, and Xuthus has the son that fulfills his aspirations. This interpretation attributes genuine benevolence to the gods; however, all three characters remain deceived: Ion and Creusa believe that Apollo is the father, and Xuthus thinks that he is Ion's father by some nameless Delphian woman he encountered at a Bacchic festival. What does this say about the gods? Are they mere cynics about the value of truth, or is it their wisdom about human affairs that makes them truly gods. Whatever answer prevails, this melodrama clearly intends to raise questions about the gods' role, and even their existence, and this becomes one of the important themes of *Ion*.

Another theme that deserves comment centers on Ion's historical destiny. Hermes announces at the beginning of the story that Ion will become the leader of the Ionic communities to the East, and at the end, Athena instructs Creusa to raise Ion as royalty so that he and his four sons will be famous. Ion's grandsons will themselves colonize the Asian side of the strait, and the people there will be called Ionians. The practical effect of all this manipulation is to bestow on Ion a supernatural lineage that will provide grandeur for his historic role. Contemporary readers of *Ion* will hardly be very alert to this patriotic theme, but it was not overlooked by Euripides' contemporaries.

Despite its problems of interpretation, *Ion* benefits from Euripides' craftsmanship. Ion grows and matures as the bewildering reversals and revelations overtake him. It is difficult to accept Creusa when she plots to poison Ion, but the scheme does build dramatic interest as it leads up to the crisis that culminates in the priestess' arrival, when she announces that Ion is the lost son of Apollo and Creusa. The cradle and the tokens are effective stage props, and Athena's late appearance is a well-contrived *deus ex machina*. Except for the selfish and vengeful behavior of its main characters, *Ion* is effective in its melodramatic effects.

"Critical Evaluation" by Frank Day

Bibliography:

Burnett, Anne Pippin. *Catastrophe Survived: Euripides' Plays of Mixed Reversals.* Oxford, England: Clarendon Press, 1971. Distinguishes *Ion* from Euripides' other plays because its multiple actions play out simultaneously. Creusa dominates a revenge plot with "catastrophe interrupted," and Ion illustrates the theme of a return to wealth and power.

Conacher, D. J. *Euripidean Drama: Myth, Theme and Structure.* Toronto: University of Toronto Press, 1967. Classifies *Ion* as "romantic tragedy" and praises its technical virtuosity and characterizations. Identifies irony as the dominant tone and the key to the play's interpretation. Situates Ion and Xuthus in the political context of the day.

Decharme, Paul. *Euripides and the Spirit of His Dramas.* New York: Macmillan, 1906. Divided into a section on Euripides' critical spirit and another on his art. Analyzes the artistry, the religious traditions, and the philosophical views in the plays. Discusses the recognition scene in *Ion*.

Euripides. *"The Bacchae" and Other Plays.* Translated by Philip Vellacott. Rev. ed. New York: Penguin Books, 1973. Paperback edition with Vellacott's excellent introduction. Argues that Ion is "the son of some visitor to the Bacchic mysteries" and defends Euripides against the common charge that he was a misogynist.

Grube, G. M. A. *The Drama of Euripides.* N.Y.: Barnes & Noble Books, 1941. Judges *Ion* a delightful play that at some points achieves genuine tragic effects. Calls the old retainer more comic than tragic. Finds Xuthus to be "slightly ridiculous" and assumes that the secret of Ion's birth will be kept from Xuthus.

IPHIGENIA IN AULIS

Type of work: Drama
Author: Euripides (c. 485-406 B.C.E.)
Type of plot: Tragedy
Time of plot: Beginning of the Trojan War
Locale: Aulis, on the west coast of Euboea
First performed: Iphigeneia ē en Aulidi, 405 B.C.E. (English translation, 1782)

Principal characters:
AGAMEMNON, King of Mycenae
CLYTEMNESTRA, his wife
IPHIGENIA, their daughter
ACHILLES, a Greek warrior
MENELAUS, King of Sparta

The Story:

At Aulis, on the west coast of Euboea, part of Greece, the Greek host had assembled for the invasion of Ilium. The war had been declared to rescue Helen, wife of King Menelaus, after her abduction by Paris, a prince of Troy. Lack of wind, however, prevented the sailing of the great fleet.

While the ships lay becalmed, Agamemnon, commander of the Greek forces, consulted Calchas, a seer. The oracle prophesied that all would go well if Iphigenia, Agamemnon's oldest daughter, were sacrificed to the goddess Artemis. At first, Agamemnon was reluctant to see his daughter so destroyed, but Menelaus, his brother, persuaded him that nothing else would move the weatherbound fleet. Agamemnon wrote to Clytemnestra, his queen, and asked her to conduct Iphigenia to Aulis, his pretext being that Achilles, the outstanding warrior among the Greeks, would not embark unless he were given Iphigenia in marriage.

After dispatching the letter, Agamemnon had a change of heart; he felt that his continued popularity as coleader of the Greeks was a poor exchange for the life of his beloved daughter. In haste, he dispatched a second letter countermanding the first, but Menelaus, suspicious of his brother, intercepted the messenger and struggled with him for possession of the letter. When Agamemnon came upon the scene, he and Menelaus exchanged bitter words. Menelaus accused his brother of being weak and foolish, and Agamemnon accused Menelaus of supreme selfishness in urging the sacrifice of Iphigenia.

During this exchange of charge and countercharge, a messenger announced the arrival of Clytemnestra and Iphigenia in Aulis. The news plunged Agamemnon into despair; weeping, he regretted his kingship and its responsibilities. Even Menelaus was so affected that he suggested disbanding the army. Agamemnon thanked Menelaus but declared that it was too late to turn back from the course they had elected to follow. Actually, Agamemnon was afraid of Calchas and Odysseus, and he believed that widespread disaffection and violence would break out in the Greek army if the sacrifice were not made. Some Chalcian women who had come to see the fleet lamented that the love of Paris for Helen had brought such chaos and misery instead of happiness.

When Clytemnestra arrived, accompanied by her young son, Orestes, and Iphigenia, she expressed pride and joy over the approaching nuptials of her daughter and Achilles. Agamemnon greeted his family tenderly; touching irony was displayed in the conversation between

Agamemnon, who knew that Iphigenia was doomed to die, and Iphigenia, who thought her father's ambiguous words had a bearing only on her approaching marriage. Clytemnestra inquired in motherly fashion about Achilles' family and background. She was scandalized when the heartbroken Agamemnon asked her to return to Argos, on the excuse that he could arrange the marriage details. When Clytemnestra refused to leave the camp, Agamemnon sought the advice of Calchas. Meanwhile the Chalcian women forecast the sequence of events of the Trojan War and hinted in their prophecy that death was certain for Iphigenia.

Achilles and his Myrmidons were impatient with the delay and anxious to get on with the invasion of Ilium. Clytemnestra met Achilles and mentioned the impending marriage. Achilles was mystified and professed to know nothing of his proposed marriage to Iphigenia. The messenger then confessed Agamemnon's plans to the shocked Clytemnestra and Achilles. He also mentioned the second letter and cast some part of the guilt upon Menelaus. Clytemnestra, grief-stricken, prevailed upon Achilles to help her in saving Iphigenia from death by sacrifice.

Clytemnestra then confronted her husband, who was completely unnerved when he realized that Clytemnestra at last knew the dreadful truth. She rebuked him fiercely, saying that she had never really loved him because he had slain her beloved first husband and her first child. Iphigenia, on her knees, implored her father to save her and asked Orestes, in his childish innocence, to add his pleas to his mother's and her own. Although Agamemnon was not heartless, he knew that the sacrifice must be made. He argued that Iphigenia would die for Greece, a country and a cause greater than them all.

Achilles spoke to the army on behalf of Iphigenia, but he admitted his failure when even his own Myrmidons threatened to stone him if he persisted in his attempt to stop the sacrifice. At last, he mustered enough loyal followers to defend the girl against Odysseus and the entire Greek host. Iphigenia refused his aid, however, saying that she had decided to offer herself as a sacrifice for Greece. Achilles, in admiration, offered to place his men about the sacrificial altar so that she might be snatched to safety at the last moment.

Iphigenia, resigned to certain death, asked her mother not to mourn for her. Then she marched bravely to her death in the field of Artemis. Clytemnestra was left prostrate in her tent. Iphigenia, at the altar, said farewell to all that she held dear and submitted herself to the sacrifice.

The Chalcian women, onlookers at the sacrifice, invoked Artemis to fill the Greek sails now with wind so that the ships might carry the army to Troy to achieve eternal glory for Greece.

Critical Evaluation:

This play is a mass of contradictions, a fact that accounts, in part at least, for its rather lukewarm reception until modern times. It is not a tragedy in the Aristotelian sense in its characters, its plot, or its theme, nor is it easily categorized with respect to any of these criteria. *Iphigenia in Aulis* has been described as the tragedy of Agamemnon, who must make the horrible decision of whether to sacrifice his daughter or abandon the war effort he has made a solemn pledge to advance. Although Agamemnon's grief is no doubt real, there is no real suspense as to what his ultimate decision will be. For example, he sends a second messenger to Clytemnestra, urging her to ignore his earlier summons, but only after he must know that it is too late to prevent the trip. Menelaus cares little for the fate of his niece; his only interest is in retrieving Helen, and more for the sake of his own honor than for any tender feelings for his wife. Clytemnestra berates Agamemnon, but the principal impetus for her tirade is her own welfare, not that of Iphigenia. Achilles is more concerned with the fact that Agamemnon had used his name without his permission than with the slaughter of an innocent. Achilles claims he will fight to the last to protect Iphigenia, but his speech sounds hollow, and the chorus immediately follows with an ode lamenting Iphigenia's imminent sacrifice. Iphigenia is to be killed despite her unquestioned innocence, and the resolve she appears to show at the end of the play ironically underscores the hypocrisy of the Greek cause: She is either more courageous than any of the soldiers or, at the very least, willing to pretend to be the willing victim of the sacrifice (a good omen) in order that the Greeks might retrieve Helen, who appears to have gone to Troy as a result of promiscuity rather than kidnapping.

Even the terms of the plot can be called into question. Whereas in earlier versions of the myth, the Greek fleet must put up at Aulis because of rough water and unfavorable winds, Euripides makes it clear that it is calm seas that force the layover. Greek warships, however, were powered principally by oars, not by sails, and would hardly have been affected adversely by calm seas. The final moments of the play suggest that Iphigenia has not been sacrificed, but was transported off the island by Artemis, who had demanded the sacrifice in the first place. The audience, however, must be aware that even seemingly objective narration carries with it a point of view. The messenger, after all, is a specially selected soldier in Agamemnon's army, sent to tell the news of the sacrifice to Clytemnestra, whose wrath might possibly be at least partially assuaged by the thought that her daughter is indeed still alive. Some critics argue that the ending of the play as it now exists was written by someone other than Euripides, perhaps by his son, several years after the original production. Nothing is necessarily what it seems to be.

Euripides almost certainly wrote *Iphigenia in Aulis* in Macedon, while in self-imposed exile from Athens. The play was presented posthumously, along with *The Bacchae* and the lost *Alcmaeon in Corinth*, at the Dionysian festival in 405 B.C.E.. Athens had been fighting the Peloponnesian Wars for more than a generation, and it was becoming increasingly clear not only that Athens would probably lose (as indeed it did the year after the play was produced), but also that imperialist overreaching would be a contributing cause to any loss. Athenian politics had been factionalized for several years, with coups and countercoups of oligarchs and radical democrats both contributing to the ferment. Euripides was a pacifist and a political conservative; it should come as no surprise either that the Trojan War is portrayed in *Iphigenia in Aulis* as senseless carnage precipitated by egocentricity, or that one of the greatest dangers the play describes is the chaos resulting from the inability of Agamemnon, Menelaus, and Achilles to control their respective armies. Democracy, to Euripides, was never far from mob rule. Euripides was also an agnostic if not an atheist; not surprisingly, the most bloodthirsty figure in the play may be the high priest, Calchas, who never appears, but whose pronouncements incite the action.

In many senses, *Iphigenia in Aulis* is one of the most modern of ancient plays: The characters are complex, flawed human beings, not merely one-dimensional heroes, and the thematic material intertwines in complex and sometimes topical ways. It is easy, perhaps, to criticize the play for not adhering more rigorously to tragic norms, for taking its iconoclasm too far, or for relatively frequently lapsing into melodrama. Still, the play is admirably constructed (and in conformity with the so-called three-actor rule of Greek tragedy). The movement from Agamemnon's first letter to Clytemnestra (well before the beginning of the play) to the sacrifice itself is inexorable, and the forces of reason and compassion consistently, but inevitably, fall short of derailing the killing. All of the major characters, except perhaps Menelaus, are given speeches of exceptional eloquence, and the final messenger's speech may be the most evocative of all. The play is rather static in theatrical terms: Agamemnon, Iphigenia, and, to a lesser extent, Clytemnestra and Achilles all engage in fairly lengthy internal debates, and the principal physical actions of the play take place off-stage.

The ambiguities of *Iphigenia in Aulis* make it particularly receptive to readings employing particular critical methodologies. Accordingly, the play has experienced a resurgence of interest from modern critics who analyze it through the lenses of Freudian psychology, power dynamics, and, especially, gender roles. Ultimately, however, it is probably the ambiguities themselves, not critical responses to them, that will serve as the play's most enduring legacy.

"Critical Evaluation" by Richard Jones

Bibliography:
Conacher, D. J. *Euripidean Drama: Myth, Theme, and Structure.* Toronto: University of Toronto Press, 1967. Excellent introduction to Euripides in general, with a particularly good discussion of *Iphigenia in Aulis.* Especially useful for providing mythological and literary background.
Foley, Helene P. "Marriage and Sacrifice in Euripides' *Iphigeneia in Aulis.*" *Arethusa* 15 (1982): 159-180. Concentrates on the similarities of marriage and sacrifice rituals, which are merged in this play. Discusses the implications of the play in terms of the politics of Panhellenism.
Rabinowitz, Nancy Sorkin. *Anxiety Veiled: Euripides and the Traffic in Women.* Ithaca, N.Y.: Cornell University Press, 1993. Discusses Iphigenia as a voluntary sacrifice, with particular attention to the gender implications of her action.
Smith, Wesley D. "Iphigenia in Love." In *Arktouros: Hellenic Studies Presented to Bernard M. W. Knox on the Occasion of His Sixty-fifth Birthday,* edited by Glen W. Bowersock, Walter Burkert, and Michael C. J. Putnam. New York: Walter de Gruyter, 1979. Argues that Iphigenia's acceptance of her fate is founded on a desire to protect Achilles. Also claims the extant ending to the play is corrupt.
Snell, Bruno. "From Tragedy to Philosophy: *Iphigenia in Aulis.*" In *Oxford Readings in Greek Tragedy,* edited by Erich Segal. Oxford, England: Oxford University Press, 1983. Places the play in historical context, with special emphasis on the concepts of knowing and doing. Claims the play is indicative of Euripides' tendency to begin plays with confusion and end them with heroism, the reverse of Sophocles' technique.

IPHIGENIA IN TAURIS

Type of work: Drama
Author: Euripides (c. 485-406 B.C.E.)
Type of plot: Melodrama
Time of plot: Several years after the Trojan War
Locale: Tauris, in the present-day Crimea
First performed: Iphigeneia ē en Taurois, c. 414 B.C.E. (English translation, 1782)

Principal characters:

IPHIGENIA, a priestess of Artemis
ORESTES, her brother
PYLADES, Orestes' friend
THOAS, the king of Tauris
ATHENA, goddess of the hunt

The Story:

When the Greek invasion force, destined for Ilium, was unable to sail from Aulis because of a lack of wind, Agamemnon, the Greek commander, appealed to Calchas, a Greek seer, for aid. Calchas said that unless Agamemnon gave Iphigenia, his oldest daughter, as a sacrifice to Artemis, the Greek fleet would never sail. By trickery Agamemnon succeeded in bringing Clytemnestra, his queen, and Iphigenia to Aulis, where the maiden was offered up to propitiate the goddess. At the last moment, however, Artemis substituted a calf in Iphigenia's place and spirited the maiden off to the barbaric land of Tauris, where she was doomed to spend the rest of her life as a priestess of Artemis. One of Iphigenia's duties was to prepare Greek captives— any Greek who was apprehended in Tauris was by law condemned to die—for sacrifice in the temple of the goddess.

Iphigenia had been a priestess in Tauris for many years when, one night, she had a dream which she interpreted to mean that her brother Orestes had met his death; now there could be no future for her family, Orestes having been the only son.

Orestes, however, was alive; in fact, he was actually in Tauris. After he and his sister Electra had murdered their mother to avenge their father's death at her hands, the Furies had pursued Orestes relentlessly. Seeking relief, Orestes was told by the Oracle of Delphi that he must procure a statue of Artemis that stood in the temple of the goddess in Tauris and take it to Athens. Orestes would then be free of the Furies.

Orestes and his friend Pylades reached the temple and were appalled at the sight of the earthly remains of the many Greeks who had lost their lives in the temple. They resolved, however, to carry out their mission of stealing the statue of Artemis.

Meanwhile Iphigenia, disturbed by her dream, aroused her sister priestesses and asked their help in mourning the loss of her brother. In her loneliness she remembered Argos and her carefree childhood. A messenger interrupted her reverie with the report that one of two young Greeks on the shore had in a frenzy slaughtered Taurian cattle which had been led to the sea to bathe. The slayer was Orestes, under the influence of the Furies. In the fight which followed, Orestes and Pylades held off great numbers of Taurian peasants, but at last the peasants succeeded in capturing the two youths. The Greeks were brought to Thoas, the king of Tauris.

Iphigenia, as a priestess of Artemis, directed that the strangers be brought before her. Heretofore she had always been gentle with the doomed Greeks and had never participated in the bloody ritual of sacrifice. Now, depressed by her dream, she was determined to be cruel.

Orestes and Pylades, bound, were brought before Iphigenia. Thinking of her own sorrow, she asked them if they had sisters who would be saddened by their deaths. Orestes refused to give her any details about himself, but he answered her inquiries about Greece and about the fate of the prominent Greeks in the Trojan War. She learned to her distress that her father was dead by her mother's treachery and that Orestes was still alive, a wanderer.

Deeply moved, Iphigenia offered to spare Orestes if he would deliver a letter for her in Argos. Orestes magnanimously gave the mission to Pylades; he himself would remain to be sacrificed. When he learned that Iphigenia would prepare him for the ritual, he wished for the presence of his sister to cover his body after he was dead. Iphigenia, out of pity, promised to do this for him. She went to bring the letter. Orestes and Pylades were convinced that she was a Greek. Pylades then declared that he would stay and die with his friend. Orestes, saying that he was doomed to die anyway for the murder of his mother, advised Pylades to return to Greece, marry Electra, and build a temple in his honor.

Iphigenia, returning with the letter, told Pylades that it must be delivered to one Orestes, a Greek prince. The letter urged Orestes to come to Tauris to take Iphigenia back to her beloved Argos; it explained how she had been saved at Aulis and spirited by Artemis to Tauris. Pylades, saying that he had fulfilled the mission, handed the letter to Orestes. Iphigenia, doubtful, was finally convinced of Orestes' identity when he recalled familiar details of their home in Argos. While she pondered escape for the three of them, Orestes explained that first it was necessary for him to take the statue of Artemis, in order to avoid destruction. He asked Iphigenia's aid.

Having received a promise of secrecy from the priestesses who were present, Iphigenia carried out her plan of escape. As Thoas, curious about the progress of the sacrifice, entered the temple, Iphigenia appeared with the statue in her arms. She explained to the mystified Thoas that the statue had miraculously turned away from the Greek youths because their hands were stained by domestic murder. She declared to King Thoas that it was necessary for her secretly to cleanse the statue and the two young men in sea water. She commanded the people of Tauris to stay in their houses lest they too be tainted.

When Orestes and Pylades were led from the temple in chains, Thoas and his retinue covered their eyes so that they would not be contaminated by evil. Iphigenia joined the procession and marched solemnly to the beach. There she ordered the king's guards to turn their backs on the secret cleansing rites. Fearful for Iphigenia's safety, the guards looked on. When they beheld the three Greeks entering a ship, they rushed down to the vessel and held it back. The Greeks beat off the Taurians and set sail. The ship, however, was caught by tidal currents and forced back into the harbor.

Thoas, angry, urged all Taurians to spare no effort in capturing the Greek ship. Then the goddess Athena appeared to Thoas and directed him not to go against the will of Apollo, whose Oracle of Delphi had sent Orestes to Tauris to get the statue of Artemis. Thoas complied. Iphigenia, Orestes, and Pylades returned to Greece, where Orestes, having set up the image of the Taurian Artemis in Attica, was at last freed from the wrath of the Furies. Iphigenia continued, in a new temple, to be a priestess of Artemis.

Critical Evaluation:

Iphigenia in Tauris is not, strictly speaking, a tragedy but a melodrama. Iphigenia, after years in a barbaric land, may at first still have hatred for her kin, the Greeks, who were willing to kill her to fight a pointless war, but her sentimental longing to return to Argos, her birthplace and the scene of her happy childhood, is intense. She describes her feelings most touchingly. The play abounds in breathtaking situations of danger and in sentimental passages of reminiscence.

The recognition scene is perhaps the most thrilling, if not the most protracted in the classic Greek drama.

Like William Shakespeare, Euripides turned to the melodrama, or romance, in his later years to convey a more optimistic view of the world. In fact, he invented this new dramatic form. *Iphigenia in Tauris* is one of the few surviving examples. As a play, *Iphigenia in Tauris* is masterly. It is carefully plotted, full of suspense, and genuinely moving. The setting is distant, dangerous, romantic. A wistful love for Greece illuminates the action, especially in the beautiful choral odes. The characters are realistically drawn, and their reactions at tense moments are both unexpected and credible. The mixture of accurate psychology and miraculous occurrences is typical of Euripides. Further, the long recognition scene between Iphigenia and Orestes is thrilling in its execution. It would be hard to find a better piece of pure theater in the repertoire of classical drama. This play also has the penetrating depth of Euripides' finest works, in addition to being high entertainment.

Euripides seems to have been fascinated by the legend of the House of Atreus. From the final years of his life five plays on the subject have survived. *Iphigenia in Tauris, Electra* (413 B.C.E.), *Helen* (412 B.C.E.), *Orestes* (408 B.C.E.), and *Iphigenia in Aulis* (405 B.C.E.) treat this story in different ways. Sometimes the depiction of a character varies from play to play, particularly in the cases of Orestes and Helen. Of these works *Iphigenia in Tauris* comes closest to *Helen* in mood and plot. Both are romances in which a woman has been supernaturally transported to a remote, barbaric land and there held in chaste captivity. Iphigenia and Helen long for one deliverer whom they believe to be dead. Promptly they meet the man and a recognition scene follows. Then they plot a means of escape, trick the king, and return home by divine intervention. The similarities are remarkable and suggest that one of these plays attempts to repeat the success of the other, although Euripides may have written more plays along these lines.

The plot of *Iphigenia in Tauris* has two major climaxes and can be divided into two parts. The first part begins with Iphigenia believing her brother, Orestes, to be dead and ends with her accepting the captive Orestes. The second part begins with the two of them planning the escape and ends as they overcome all obstacles with Athena's aid.

Euripides uses an interesting technique. Often a character will state a principle by which he or she intends to act and then immediately betray the principle. Thus, in lines 350-353, Iphigenia states her intention of being harsh to the Greek captives because of her own misery and melts on hearing news of her homeland, offering to spare Orestes. In this case the technique points up her intense homesickness for Greece and Argos, a passion that animates not only her, but the chorus of Greek maidens, Orestes, and Pylades as well.

With Orestes, Euripides varies the technique in relation to a major theme. When Orestes appears before Iphigenia as a prisoner he says he disdains self-pity; a few lines after, when Iphigenia asks his name, he replies sullenly, "Call me unfortunate." The method indicates his misery. It also underscores his nobility of character later when he insists on being sacrificed to free his friend, Pylades. Disinterested love is always a sign of redemption in Euripides.

The barbarian king, Thoas, claims no barbarian would murder his mother, as the Greek, Orestes, had done. Yet he has no compunction about ordering a massacre of all Greeks, including the temple virgins. Euripides uses Thoas as a gullible, vengeful foil to the clever Greeks.

However, the most important theme of the play has to do with divine injustice and human suffering. Iphigenia is in thrall to the goddess Artemis, a victim who has been offered up herself for sacrifice, transported far away from home, and then set to aid in the sacrifices of all strangers and Greeks, a task she loathes. Artemis has been the perpetrator of the whole sequence.

Artemis' twin, Apollo, has visited similar suffering on Orestes, causing him to kill his mother, be pursued and driven mad by Furies, and sent to Colchis (not Tauris), where he is captured for sacrifice. At first glance the gods Apollo and Artemis appear to be arch-villains ruthlessly dealing out anguish.

There is another perspective, however, that mitigates this view. Orestes is working out his redemption and must face death before he can free himself of the guilt of matricide. He is offered a chance to live, but he chooses to save Pylades. Presumably Apollo sent him to Colchis for that very purpose, to act as a free man rather than an embittered victim. Once this choice occurs, things begin falling into harmony. Iphigenia accepts him as her brother and contrives an escape. Orestes repays the favor by saving her life as they board the ship. Then in the moment of greatest danger the goddess Athena arrives to rescue the Greeks, showing that the gods give help to those who help others.

Euripides is showing that as long as a people regard themselves as victims they can only suffer. Only when they act freely and unselfishly does their suffering cease and the gods come to help. Through disinterested love, divine injustice is transmuted to true justice.

"Critical Evaluation" by James Weigel, Jr.

Bibliography:
Burnett, Anne Pippin. *Catastrophe Survival: Euripides' Plays of Mixed Reversal.* Oxford, England: Clarendon Press, 1971. Examines how the surprising and redemptive plot in the play operates to upset expectations inherent in the tragic genre. Also sensitive to the mythic overtones of the play, developing them in contrast and parallel to the play's drama.
Caldwell, Richard. "Tragedy Romanticized." *Classical Journal* 70 (1974): 23-40. Examines how the reappearance of the presumed-dead Iphigenia provides a cosmic atonement for the cruelty of her father's putative sacrifice of her. Shows how the play turns from tragedy to romance through the emphasis on miracle and recognition.
Hartigan, Karelisa. *Ambiguity and Self-Deception.* Frankfurt, Germany: Peter Lang, 1991. Emphasizes the unsettling effect of the play's recognition scenes. Shows how the characteristic Euripidean device of the *deus ex machina* stresses the artificiality and aestheticism of the play.
Powell, Anton, ed. *Euripides, Women, and Sexuality.* London: Routledge & Kegan Paul, 1990. This collection of essays influenced by gender studies emphasizes Iphigenia as one of Euripides' major female characters, as well as the only one seen in both tragic and romantic contexts. Examines how Iphigenia is at once a victim and a redeemer of her male-dominated society.
Rabinowitz, Nancy Sorkin. *Anxiety Veiled: The Traffic in Women in Euripides.* Ithaca, N.Y.: Cornell University Press, 1993. This major feminist study of Euripidean drama is also the best available introduction to *Iphigenia in Tauris.* Although Rabinowitz recognizes the more positive role played by women in Euripides' plays as opposed to previous Greek drama, she demonstrates that Euripides tends to use women as tokens of exchange to underscore men's continuing hold over social and economic relations.

IRISH MELODIES

Type of work: Poetry
Author: Thomas Moore (1779-1852)
First published: 1807-1834, 1835

Few men of letters have been able to write on Thomas Moore without disparaging the financial and social success of his life or the great mass of his work, mostly verse, from which so little of any worth is still remembered except *Irish Melodies.* The quantity of his work and the ready charm that contributed to his success in London society are largely attributable to the fact that Moore, like many other aspirants from the provinces, had to get on as best he could. Starvation in a garret may be the mark of genius but only posterity can decide between the respective merits of Thomas Chatterton and William Blake. Moore took no chances; he stuck by the Whigs, forswore his early Republicanism, and modulated his Irishness into its most acceptable form in the London drawing room, the real source of political power and hence patronage in Regency England. He also sang Irish songs, thereby gaining practically the only claim he has on the memory and affections of later times. The rest of his work fills up that yawning gulf of trivia that kept the London publishers prosperous, their readers contented, the popular authors wealthy, and the best of contemporary English writers—among them Percy Bysshe Shelley, John Keats, and Blake—out of sight.

Yet Moore was in his way a pioneer. He always claimed to have originated modern Irish poetry, enjoying a personal application of the song that takes its title from the opening words:

> Dear Harp of my Country! in darkness I found thee,
> The cold chain of silence hung o'er thee long,
> When proudly, my own Island Harp! I unbound thee,
> And gave all thy chords to light, freedom and song!

In the rest of the lyric Moore sums up his subjects—death, love, mirth, and patriotism—and specifies his technique as being "wild sweetness." The revolutionary effect of this combination in London when he began the composition of *Irish Melodies* in 1806 (seven years after his arrival there from Dublin) was more noticeable because of the stolidity of both the serious and the popular light verse of the time, to both of which Moore had contributed enough to acquire a lucrative government post in the Bermudas. He left London in 1803 to take up the post, but soon returned and set to work on his *Irish Melodies,* exile from London having apparently sharpened his love for Ireland. This new style of drawing room entertainment, which Moore, being an accomplished musician, often provided in person, was soon earning him five hundred pounds a year. The lyric was restored to popularity in English literature not by William Wordsworth's and Samuel Coleridge's *Lyrical Ballads,* by Robert Burns, or by Blake, all of whom preceded him, but by Moore's *Irish Melodies.*

Moore had given a sample of his ability to write lyrics to folk tunes in the "Canadian Boat Song" of his feebly satirical *Poems Relating to America* (1806); he had heard his "voyageurs" sing the song as they rowed down the St. Lawrence from Kingston to Montreal. Both words and music had been published in ten parts between 1807 and 1834, with editions of the words alone appearing from 1820 on. Time has established the concert repertoire selected from the songs: "The Harp That Once Thro' Tara's Halls," "Believe Me if All Those Endearing Young Charms," "She Is Far from the Land," "'Tis the Last Rose of Summer," "The Minstrel Boy,"

"Sweet Inishfallen, Fare Thee Well," to which may be added the "Canadian Boat Song" and two later songs, the "Vesper Hymn" and "Oft in the Stilly Night" from *National Airs*, lyrics and arrangements of folk songs from most European countries.

Only one of the lyrics remained in the repertory as a poem apart from its setting. "The Time I've Lost in Wooing" shows Moore's abilities to advantage: The rhymes are feminine in the longer lines and in triples (wooing . . . pursuing . . . undoing); the shorter lines (none is long) end in masculine rhyme; the alternations give a pleasing variation to the run of the poem, and the poem in three stanzas reaches a witty conclusion that echoes the Caroline poets. In the conflict between Wisdom and Beauty the poet's time has been wasted in pursuit of the latter; he knows this but still cannot cease his pursuit:

> Poor Wisdom's chance
> Against a glance
> Is now as weak as ever.

Of the language of the lyrics, English poet and man of letters Edmund Gosse observed that "words of a commonplace character are so strung together as to form poetry easily grasped and enjoyed by the ear." The secret of Moore's original and continuing popularity lies in his having provided acceptable poetry for the ear, not for the eye. Because the gift so enjoyed by Elizabethans has become lost, it is little wonder that later audiences needed to be assisted by folk tunes.

In the collected editions of Moore's works, the *Irish Melodies* number one hundred twenty-five, beginning with "Go Where Glory Waits Thee" and ending with "Silence Is in Our Festal Halls," Moore's elegy for Sir John Stevenson, who wrote the arrangements for the parts. Most of the parts as they were issued contained Moore's dedications to his patrons as well as advertisements from his publisher, Power, to the general public, in which it was insisted that there were plenty more "airs" in the treasury of Irish folk song for future parts. A certain amount of national feeling is evident in both advertisements and dedications, especially in that to the first part, which includes a letter from Moore referring to the Irish reputation for song as "the only talent for which our English neighbors ever deigned to allow us any credit." A more important preface is that to the third part. As well as dealing with the age of Irish songs, their resemblance to Scottish song, and the harmonic peculiarities of Irish music, Moore refers to three aspects that in their way sum up much of the melodies: their national feeling, their peculiar mixture of defiance and despondency, and their being not poems but lyrics to songs.

On the last point, he begs exemption from "the rigors of literary criticism" because he can "answer for their sound with somewhat more confidence than for their sense." This statement is admirable but makes it difficult to discuss the *Irish Melodies* as if they were poems. If Moore's guiding principle was to make them singable, only a singer can argue in their behalf. Moreover, many a trite phrase and conventional rhyme can be excused on this ground. Moore's other two remarks point to two obvious features in the lyrics. They often begin strongly and fade into resignation with a parting, death, the passage of time, or the decay of good customs. Where the poems reach a strong conclusion, they do so generally by appealing to the divine or to Ireland. The endings to two patriotic poems illustrate the difference: "Let Erin Remember the Days of Old" declines into "Thus, sighing, look through the waves of time/ For the long-faded glories they cover." By contrast, "Sublime Was the Warning" challenges Irish national aspirations by appealing to the success of Spanish independence after the Napoleonic wars and concludes with "The young spirit of Freedom shall shelter their grave/ Beneath shamrocks of Erin and olives of Spain."

The Irish quality of the poems is most apparent in their subjects. Some are taken from Irish history, others contain references to Irish legends and customs, but the thread that runs through the volume is "Erin." Much of the reference to Ireland is a prophecy of longed-for independence, a purely poetic exercise Moore's contemporaries in London must have thought it, but history has realized Moore's longing, and it would be an interesting point to settle how much his songs had to do with maintaining Irish nationalism during the struggles of the nineteenth century—such songs as "Where Is the Slave?" "Erin, Oh Erin," "Oh the Shamrock," and the better-known "Minstrel Boy" and "The Harp That Once Thro' Tara's Halls." The most curious of these is "As Vanquished Erin," which describes how the Fiend of Discord persists in sending "his shafts of desolation . . . through all her maddening nation." When Erin asks the "Powers of Good" when this will end, the Demon answers "Never." This is possibly the truest statement Moore made about Ireland.

The phrase that sums up the quality of the lyrics in the *Irish Melodies* is Moore's "wild sweetness," an unusual and romantic combination of opposites, its Irishness, one may say. Yet the sweetness of the verses is obtained by both technical dexterity (Moore maintains, as he must, the rhythm of the melody in a variety of meters) and a neatness of phrasing that might be called Irish wit were it not that, except in a few light pieces of which "The Time I've Lost in Wooing" is the best, this gift is usually spent on general topics and does not show to advantage: "Love, nursed among pleasures, is faithless as they,/ But the love born of Sorrow, like Sorrow, is true." Much of the wild note comes from the subjects of war, chains, and heroic death, but also from the ecstasy of the love poems, tinged as they generally are with sadness. Oddly enough it is probably the romantic combination Moore achieved that was responsible for the gradual disfavor into which the *Irish Melodies* fell about the turn of the century, though they are still referred to in James Joyce and Sean O'Casey. When the Gaelic Revival and the independence of Eire finally arrived, a more genuine folk song with real Irish lyrics seems to have lessened Moore's popularity and reduced it to the proportions of the man himself, whom Sir Walter Scott once called "a little, very little man."

Bibliography:
Davis, Leith. "Irish Bards and English Consumers." *Ariel* 24, no. 2 (April, 1993): 7-25. An analysis of *Irish Melodies* as the cultural products of a colonized country. Takes into account the various factors influencing their conception, dissemination, and reception. Concludes that the work promoted Ireland's cause by reflecting romantic images of Irish defeat and subordination.
Deane, Seamus. "Thomas Moore (1779-1852)." In *The Field Day Anthology of Irish Writing*, edited by Seamus Deane. 3 vols. New York: W. W. Norton, 1991. Points out that *Irish Melodies* made the Gaelic tradition acceptable to the dominant taste of the reading public in England of the time and made Irish rebelliousness aesthetic. Provides a representative selection, annotated, with bibliography.
Jones, Howard Mumford. *The Harp That Once—*. 1937. Reprint. New York: Russell & Russell, 1970. Despite its date, still the authoritative biography of Thomas Moore, which depicts him as the embodiment of Romanticism. Places him in his cultural and historical milieu. Balances criticism and appreciation of his character and work with exemplary judgment and elegance.
Tessier, Theresa. *The Bard of Erin: A Study of Thomas Moore's "Irish Melodies" (1808-1834)*. Salzburg, Austria: Institut für Anglistik und Amerikanistik, 1981. A comprehensive and detailed study centered on Moore's composite art: the fusion of poetry and music. Refers to the "musical prosody" of *Irish Melodies*. Valuable appendices and bibliography.

Welch, Robert. *Irish Poetry from Moore to Yeats*. Gerrard Cross, England: Smythe, 1980. Points out that Moore's *Irish Melodies* wove lovely verbal patterns around Irish airs and political sentiments and that they were the starting point for later Anglo-Irish poetry. Declares that in their fabricated Hibernicism, they are similar to Macpherson's Ossianic fragments.

ISRAEL POTTER
His Fifty Years of Exile

Type of work: Novel
Author: Herman Melville (1819-1891)
Type of plot: Historical
Time of plot: 1774-1826
Locale: Vermont, Massachusetts, England, France, and the Atlantic Ocean
First published: 1855

> *Principal characters:*
> ISRAEL POTTER, a wanderer
> ISRAEL'S FATHER
> KING GEORGE III
> BENJAMIN FRANKLIN
> JOHN PAUL JONES
> ETHAN ALLEN
> SQUIRE WOODCOCK, an American agent
> THE EARL OF SELKIRK

The Story:

Born among the rugged stones of the New England hills, in the Housatonic Valley, Israel Potter grew up with all the virtues of the hard, principled, new land. After an argument with his father over a girl whom his stern parent did not think a suitable match, Israel decided to run away from home while his family was attending church. He wandered about the countryside, hunting deer, farming land, becoming a trapper, and dealing in furs. During his wanderings, he learned that most men were unscrupulous. He also hunted whales from Nantucket to the coast of Africa.

In 1775, Israel joined the American forces and took part in the Battle of Bunker Hill. He fought bravely, but the battle, as he saw it, was simply disorganized carnage. Wounded, Israel enlisted aboard an American ship after his recovery. Once at sea, the ship was captured by the British. Israel was taken prisoner and conveyed to England on a British ship, but on his arrival in London, he managed to make his escape.

Wandering about London, Israel met various Englishmen who mocked his American accent. Some of the English were kind and helpful to him. Others cuffed him about and berated the scurrilous Yankee rebels. He found various odd jobs, including one as a gardener working for a cruel employer. He escaped from this job and found one as a gardener on the king's staff at Kew Gardens. One day, Israel met King George III. The king, completely mad, realized that Israel was an American and was ineffectually kind to him. Eventually, in a slack season, Israel was discharged. He then worked for a farmer, but when other farmers in the area discovered that he was an American, Israel was forced to run away.

Israel met Squire Woodcock, a wealthy and secret friend of America, who sent him on a secret mission to Benjamin Franklin in Paris. Israel carried a message in the false heel of his new boots. On his arrival in Paris, while he was looking for Benjamin Franklin, a poor man tried to shine his boots on the Pont Neuf. Israel, in fright, kicked the man and ran off. At last, he found Benjamin Franklin, who took the message and then insisted that Israel return and pay damages to the bootblack.

In this fashion, Israel, under the tutelage of Franklin, learned his first lesson in European politeness and consideration. From this incident, Franklin proceeded to instruct Israel in the ways of proper behavior. Israel, still innocent, absorbed the teaching carefully, although none of it ever applied to his later experiences. Franklin promised that Israel would be sent back to America, if he would first return to England with a message. While still in Paris, Israel met the stormy and ferocious Captain John Paul Jones, who also visited Franklin. John Paul Jones found Israel a bright young man.

Israel made his way back across the Channel and went to Squire Woodcock. The Squire urged him to hide in the dungeon cell for three days, since their plot was in danger of discovery. When Israel emerged from the cell, he recognized that the good Squire must have been killed for his activities in the American cause.

Having appropriated some of the Squire's clothes, Israel masqueraded as Squire Woodcock's ghost and escaped from a house filled with his enemies. He then traded clothes with a farmer, wandered to Portsmouth, and signed on as a foretopman on a British ship bound for the East Indies. In the Channel, his ship met another ship whose captain had authority to impress some of the men; Israel was among those taken. That same night, the ship was captured by an American ship under the command of John Paul Jones. Having revealed himself to his old friend, Israel soon became the quartermaster of the *Ranger.* With John Paul Jones, Israel engaged in piracy, capturing and looting ships.

In Scotland, they called on the Earl of Selkirk in order to rob him, but the nobleman was not at home. John Paul Jones impressed the earl's wife with his Parisian manners, drank tea with her, and assured her that he and Israel did not intend to do the lady any harm. The crew, however, insisted that plunder was a part of piracy, and so Israel and John Paul Jones were forced to allow the men to take the family silver and other valuables. Jones promised to restore all articles of value, and when he received a large sum of money from another exploit, he bought back all the earl's articles from the men and returned them to the Selkirk family.

Other adventures did not end so cheerfully. The sea fight between the *Bon Homme Richard* and the *Serapis* was a violent and bloody battle, fought along national lines and devoid of all the amenities of piracy. Both ships were lost, and Israel and John Paul Jones, still hoping to get to America, sailed on the *Ariel.* The *Ariel* engaged a British vessel, which pretended to surrender. The Americans got ready to board, but only Israel boarded before the vessel sailed away. No one on the vessel knew where Israel came from. He pretended to have been on the vessel all along and thus ended up once again in the British navy. By feigning madness to hide his Yankee origins, he got back to England safely.

In England, Israel met Ethan Allen, a strong, heroic, Samsonlike figure, held prisoner by the English. Israel tried to help Allen escape but was unsuccessful. Disguised as a beggar, he went to London, where he remained for more than forty years. During that time, he worked as a brick-maker and laborer, always hoping to save enough money to return to America but never finding the economic situation in London stable enough to permit saving. A wanderer in an alien land, he became part of the grime and poverty of London. During those years, he married a shopgirl who bore him a son. Finally, in 1826, he secured some credit and, with the help of the American consul, sailed for America with his son.

Israel arrived in Boston on July 4, during a public celebration of the Battle of Bunker Hill. No one recognized him or acknowledged his right to be there. Instead, people laughed at him and thought he was mad. He returned to his father's farm, but the homestead had long since disappeared. Old Israel, his wanderings ended, found no peace, comfort, or friendship in his old age. Although heroes of the Revolution were publicly venerated, the aged man could not even get a small pension.

Critical Evaluation:
  Israel Potter is called Herman Melville's one piece of historical fiction. In it, Melville pretends to be writing literal biography. In form, it is close to *Typee: A Peep at Polynesian Life* (1846), *Omoo: A Narrative of Adventures in the South Seas* (1847), *Redburn, His First Voyage* (1849), and *White Jacket: Or, The World in a Man-of-War* (1850). *Israel Potter* is basically an unadorned narrative rather than the kind of highly digressive, philosophical novel associated with Melville's later years.

  Melville wrote *Israel Potter*, according to his biographers, to make up for the financial and critical failure of *Pierre: Or, The Ambiguities* (1852), and by far the majority of contemporary reviews were favorable. He received an initial $421.50. At first, the book sold fairly well. It quickly went into a third printing, but Melville's royalties were small, ranging between $190 and $240. The money gave Melville what at the time was a fairly good income but only for a short while.

  Melville's main source for *Israel Potter* is *Life and Remarkable Adventures of Israel R. Potter, (A Native of Cranston, Rhode Island.) Who Was a Soldier in the American Revolution* (1824), by Henry Trumbull, a first-person narrative of the life of what Trumbull calls "one of the few survivors who fought and bled for American independence." The narrative is a supposedly true account of the life of the real Israel Potter, who fought at Bunker Hill, served in the navy, and ironically led most of his adult life in exile in England. Melville also used as sources biographies of and narratives by Benjamin Franklin, Ethan Allen, and John Paul Jones.

  Toward the end of the novel, Melville writes: "The gloomiest and truthfulest dramatist seldom chooses for his theme the calamities, however extraordinary, of inferior and private persons; least of all, the pauper's," for "few feel enticed to the shanty, where, like a pealed knucklebone, grins the unupholstered corpse of the beggar." Yet it is precisely such a life that Melville recounts in *Israel Potter*. During the Revolutionary War, Potter worked with Benjamin Franklin and John Paul Jones and saw Ethan Allen while Allen was in captivity in England. As Melville depicts him, Potter was a true patriot, a fierce fighter, and may even have been the one most responsible for the defeat of the *Serapis* by the *Bon Homme Richard*, one of the most famous naval engagements in United States history. It was during this battle that John Paul Jones uttered his famous words: "I have not yet begun to fight." Yet through various twists of fate, Israel Potter was forgotten even during his own lifetime, while Franklin, Allen, and Jones won the admiration of all their countrymen and lasting fame.

  Potter, however, ended his days in poverty working at extremely unpleasant jobs for very little reward. Melville describes Potter's later life, especially his forty years in exile in England, in hellish terms. Before he entered the city of London, he worked in a brickyard, a period that Melville refers to as Potter's time in Egypt. Then, he entered London, a city Melville describes using Dantesque terms.

  When Israel's son finally managed to get passage for his father and himself back to America, Israel was in his eighties. When he entered Boston on the Fourth of July, he was almost run over by "a patriotic triumphal car" inscribed with the words, "Bunker Hill/1775/Glory to the heroes that fought!" The irony is clear: History forgets the modest man, so it often overlooks true heroes. The irony is extended when the reader learns that Potter could not even get a pension from the nation to which he gave so much.

  One of the main things that distinguished Melville's Potter from his more famous contemporaries was his modesty. Melville describes Franklin as a confidence man, always promoting his maxims, writings, and way of life. Melville treats John Paul Jones as an accomplished naval officer with tremendous energy but also as an incredible braggart absolutely sure of his extraordinary abilities. Melville's Ethan Allen is a magnificent figure in captivity, but he also constantly brags and exaggerates. Jones and Allen exaggerate their accomplishments and abilities in the tall tale tradition. Melville's Potter, on the other hand, is content to let others take the glory while he does the kind of hard work that ultimately resulted in America's independence from England. Unlike Melville's Jones, who can be incredibly irresponsible, Melville's Potter constantly tries to act responsibly toward others, so much so that he stays in England for forty years after the Revolution ends not only because of economic conditions but also out of loyalty to his wife and son.

Potter's life as Melville recounts it also illustrates the fickleness of fate. As John Paul Jones and Potter sail back to America on the *Ariel*, they engaged an English frigate class ship. The ship strikes its colors, and Potter boards it. Immediately, with Potter on board, the frigate sails away so that no one else can board it and with no one but Potter knowing how he got there. As a result, he begins his years in exile.

An additional theme Melville treats is the brutality that lies beneath the surface of civilization. He wonders whether humankind has made any progress, and his descriptions of battles, especially naval battles, indicate that it has not. He also comments that the French Revolution showed that in humankind "primeval savageness . . . slumbers."

Israel Potter has been classified as one of Melville's minor works. Still, critics praise it for its humor, its sympathy shown for the downtrodden, and its unusual view of some of the heroes of the American Revolution.

"Critical Evaluation" by Richard Tuerk

Bibliography:
Dillingham, William B. *Melville's Later Novels*. Athens: University of Georgia Press, 1986. Focuses on poverty and liberty in the novel. Sees Potter as a kind of Christ figure, a "sacrificial victim," with whom Melville identifies.
Hillway, Tyrus. *Herman Melville*. Rev. ed. Boston: Twayne, 1979. Briefly treats the work as an example of Melville's awareness of "man's ingratitude to man," of "tragic inconsistencies" "in human conduct," and of the "emptiness of worldly fame."
Karcher, Carolyn L. *Shadow over the Promised Land: Slavery, Race, and Violence in Melville's America*. Baton Rouge: Louisiana State University Press, 1980. Calls the novel a reconstruction of the American Revolution as seen by what she calls "the forgotten common man." Demonstrates that the book shows Melville's sympathy for the oppressed.
Melville, Herman. *Israel Potter: His Fifty Years of Exile*. Edited by Harrison Hayford, Hershel Parker, and G. Thomas Tanselle. The Writings of Herman Melville 8. Evanston: Northwestern University Press, 1982. In addition to containing the authoritative text of the novel, this volume has the full text of Henry Trumbull's book, an excellent introduction, useful notes, and an excellent historical essay about the writing and publication of the book.
Samson, John. *White Lies: Melville's Narratives of Facts*. Ithaca, N.Y.: Cornell University Press, 1989. Treats Melville's novel as an ironic narrative of the American Revolution that "breaks narrative conventions" and "frustrates audience expectations."

THE ITALIAN
Or, The Confessional of the Black Penitents

Type of work: Novel
Author: Ann Radcliffe (1764-1823)
Type of plot: Gothic
Time of plot: 1758
Locale: Italy
First published: 1797

Principal characters:
      VINCENTIO DI VIVALDI, a young nobleman of Naples
      ELLENA DI ROSALBA, Vincentio's beloved
      THE MARCHESE and MARCHESA DI VIVALDI, Vincentio's parents
      SCHEDONI, the marchesa's confessor and formerly the count di Bruno
      SIGNORA BIANCHI, Ellena's aunt
      SISTER OLIVIA, formerly the countess di Bruno
      PAULO MENDRICO, Vincentio's faithful servant

The Story:

Vincentio di Vivaldi saw Ellena di Rosalba for the first time at the Church of San Lorenzo in Naples. He was so impressed by the sweetness of her voice and the grace of her person that at the end of the service he followed the girl and her elderly companion in the hope of catching a glimpse of her features. When the elderly woman stumbled and fell, Vivaldi seized the opportunity to offer her his arm, a gallant gesture that gave him the excuse to accompany the two women to the Villa Altieri, their modest home on an eminence overlooking the Bay of Naples.

The next day, he returned to inquire about the health of the older woman, Signora Bianchi, who received her guest courteously. Ellena did not appear. Despondent at her absence, he inquired of his acquaintances into the girl's family but learned only that she was an orphan, the niece and ward of her aged relative.

That night, resolved to see Ellena again, he left a reception his mother was giving and returned to the Villa Altieri. The hour was late, and only one window was lighted. Through a lattice, he saw Ellena playing on her lute and singing a midnight hymn to the Virgin Mary. Entranced, he drew near the lattice and heard her pronounce his name; but when he revealed himself, the girl hastily closed the lattice and left the room. Vivaldi lingered in the garden for some time before returning to Naples. Lost in reverie, he was passing under a shattered archway extending over the road when a shadowy figure in a monk's robe glided across his path and in a ghostly whisper warned him to beware of future visits to the villa.

Thinking that the warning had been given by a rival, he returned the next night in the company of his friend Bonorma. Again, the dark figure appeared and uttered a sepulchral warning. Later, as the two young men were passing under the arch, the figure showed itself once more. Vivaldi and Bonorma drew their swords and entered the ancient fortress in search of the mysterious visitant. They found no trace of anyone lurking in the ruins.

Still believing that these visitations were those of a rival, Vivaldi decided to end his suspense by making a declaration for Ellena's hand. Signora Bianchi listened to his proposal and then reminded him that a family as old and illustrious as his own would object to an alliance with a girl of Ellena's humble station. Vivaldi realized that she spoke wisely, but with all the fervor of a young man in love, he argued his suit so eloquently that at last Signora Bianchi withdrew her refusal. After Vivaldi had made repeated visits to the villa, a night came when the aged woman placed Ellena's hand in his and gave them her blessing. To Vivaldi's great joy, it was decided that the marriage would be solemnized during the coming week.

The marchese and marchesa di Vivaldi had not remained ignorant of their son's frequent visits at the Villa Altieri. On several occasions, the marchese, a man of great family pride and strict principles, had remonstrated with his son and assured him that marriage to one so far below him in station was impossible. Vivaldi answered by declaring that his affections and intentions were irrevocable. His mother, a haughty and vindictive woman, was likewise determined to end what she regarded as her son's foolish infatuation. Realizing that the young man could not be moved by persuasion or threats, she summoned her confessor and secret adviser, the monk Schedoni, and consulted him on measures to separate Ellena and Vivaldi.

Schedoni, a monk at the Convent of the Santo Spirito, was a man of unknown family and origins. His spirit appeared haughty and disordered, and his appearance conveyed an effect of gloom that corresponded to his severe and solitary disposition. Because of his austere manners, brooding nature, and sinister appearance, he was loved by none, hated by many, and feared by most. Vivaldi disliked the monk and avoided him, even though he had no presentiment of the fate Schedoni was preparing for him and Ellena.

On the morning after his acceptance as Ellena's suitor, Vivaldi hastened to the villa. In the darkened archway, the ghostly figure again appeared and told him that death was in the house. Vivaldi was deeply disturbed and hurried on. Upon his arrival, he learned that Signora Bianchi had died suddenly during the night. When Beatrice, the old servant, confided her suspicions that her mistress had been poisoned, Vivaldi grew even more concerned. His own suspicions fell on Schedoni, and he confronted the monk in the marchesa's apartment on his return to Venice, but the confessor cleverly parried all the questions Vivaldi put to him. Vivaldi, apologizing for his conduct and accusing speech, failed to realize that he had made an enemy of Schedoni and that the monk was already planning his revenge.

It was decided that Ellena was to find a sanctuary in the Convent of Santa Maria della Pieta after her aunt's funeral, and Vivaldi was in agreement with her desire to withdraw to that shelter during her period of mourning. Ellena was packing in preparation for her departure the next day, when she heard Beatrice scream in another room. At the same moment, three masked men seized Ellena and carried her from the house. Thrust into a closed carriage, she was driven throughout the night and most of the next day into the mountainous region of Abruzzo. There her captors conducted her to a strange religious establishment where she was turned over to the care of the nuns. Almost distracted, the girl was led to a cell where she gave way to her terror and grief.

Knowing nothing of these events, Vivaldi had decided that same night to explore the ruined fortress and to discover, if possible, the secret of the strange visitant he had encountered there. Paulo Mendrico, his faithful servant, went with him. When they were within the archway, the figure of the monk suddenly materialized, this time telling Vivaldi that Ellena had departed an hour before. Paulo fired his pistol, but the figure eluded them. Following drops of blood, Vivaldi and Paulo came at last to a chamber into which the figure had disappeared. As they entered, the great door shut behind them. In the chamber, they found only a discarded, bloody robe. During the night they spent as prisoners in the gloomy room, Paulo told his master of a muffled penitent who had appeared at the Church of Santa Maria del Pianto and made a confession apparently so strange and horrible that Ansaldo di Rovalli, the grand penitentiary, had been thrown into convulsions. During this recital, they were startled by hearing groans close by, but they saw no one. In the morning, the door of the chamber stood open, and Vivaldi and Paulo made their escape.

Alarmed for Ellena's safety, Vivaldi went at once to the villa. There he found Beatrice tied to a pillar and learned from her that her mistress had been abducted. Convinced that the strange events of the night were part of a plot to prevent his intended marriage, he again confronted Schedoni at the Convent of the Santo Spirito and would have assaulted the monk if others had not seized the distraught young man and restrained him. That night, Vivaldi accidentally heard from a fisherman that early in the day a closed carriage had been seen driving through Bracelli. Hoping to trace the carriage and find Ellena, he set off in pursuit, accompanied by the faithful Paulo.

On the fourth day of her imprisonment, Ellena was conducted to the parlor of the abbess, who informed her that she must choose between taking the veil or marrying the person whom the marchesa di Vivaldi had selected as her husband. When Ellena refused both offers, she was taken back to her cell. Each evening, she was allowed to attend vespers and there her attention was attracted to Sister Olivia, a nun who tried to reconcile her to the hardships of her confinement. For this reason, perhaps, Sister Olivia was the nun chosen by the abbess to inform Ellena that if she persisted in refusing a husband proper to her station, she must take holy orders immediately.

Meanwhile, Vivaldi was continuing his search for Ellena. On the evening of the seventh day, he and Paulo fell in with a company of pilgrims on their way to worship at the shrine of a convent about a league and a half distant. Traveling with this company, Vivaldi arrived at the convent in time to witness the service at which Ellena was to be made a novitiate. Hearing her voice raised in protest, he rushed to the altar and caught her as she fainted. Unable to secure Ellena's freedom, Vivaldi left the convent to try another plan to set her free. Although he did not know it, there was need of haste; the abbess had decided to punish Ellena by confining her in a chamber from which none had ever returned alive. Alarmed for the girl's life, Sister Olivia promised to help her escape from the convent that night.

Dressed in the nun's veil, Ellena attended a program of music given in honor of several distinguished strangers who were visiting the convent. There Vivaldi, disguised as a pilgrim, passed her a note in which he told her to meet him at the gate of the nuns' garden. Guided by Sister Olivia, Ellena went to the gate where Vivaldi was waiting with Brother Jeronimo, a monk whom he had bribed to lead them from the convent by a secret path. Brother Jeronimo tried to betray them, however, and Ellena would have been recaptured if an aged monk whom they disturbed at his solitary prayers had not pitied them and unlocked the last door standing between the lovers and freedom.

Once in the open air, Vivaldi and Ellena descended the mountains to the place where Paulo waited with the horses for their escape. Instead of taking the road toward Naples, the fugitives turned westward toward Aquila. They were resting at a shepherd's cabin that day, when Paulo brought word that they were being pursued by two Carmelite friars. Eluding their pursuers, they rode toward Lake Celano, where Ellena took refuge for the night in the Ursuline convent and Vivaldi stayed in an establishment of Benedictines.

While these events were taking place, the marchese, who knew nothing of his wife's scheming with Schedoni, was suffering great anxiety over his son's whereabouts and welfare. The marchesa, on the other hand, was apprehensive only that Ellena would be found and her plans undone. When Schedoni suggested in his sly, indirect fashion that Ellena be put out of the way for good, she was at first horrified by his suggestion. Later, she reconsidered, and eventually she and the sinister monk came to agree that Ellena was to die. Schedoni, who had spies everywhere, was not long in locating the fugitives. As Vivaldi and Ellena were about to be married in the chapel of San Sebastian at Celano, armed men broke into the church and arrested the two under a warrant of the Holy Inquisition. Ellena was charged with having broken her nun's vows and Vivaldi with having aided her escape. Vivaldi, though wounded in his struggle to prevent arrest, was carried to Rome and after a short hearing before the Inquisitor was imprisoned to await future trial and possibly torture to extort a confession. Paulo was also confined.

After the agents of the Inquisition had taken Vivaldi and Paulo away, Ellena's guards put her on a waiting horse and set out on a road that led toward the Adriatic. After traveling with little interruption for two nights and two days, they came to a lonely house on the seashore. There she was turned over to a villainous-looking man whom the guards called Spalatro and locked in a room in which the only furnishing was a tattered mattress on the floor. Exhausted, she fell asleep. Spalatro came to her room twice during the next day, looking at her with a gaze that was a mixture of impatience and guilt. On one occasion, he took her to walk on the beach, where she met Schedoni, whose face was hidden by his cowl. When he spoke to her, Ellena realized that this monk was neither a friend nor a protector but an enemy, and she fainted. She was revived and returned to her room.

Schedoni was determined that Ellena should die that night. When Spalatro confessed pity for the girl and refused to be the executioner, Schedoni swore to do the deed himself. He went to the room where the girl was sleeping and stood over her, dagger in hand. Suddenly, he bent to look closely at a miniature she wore about her neck. Agitated, he awoke Ellena and asked her if she knew whose portrait she wore. When she answered that it was the miniature of her father, Schedoni was even more shaken. He was convinced that he had discovered his lost daughter.

Overcome by remorse for his persecution of Ellena and the accusation that had exposed Vivaldi to the tortures of the Inquisition, Schedoni tried to make amends. He and Ellena traveled as quickly as possible to Naples. After leaving her at the Villa Altieri, the monk hastened to the Vivaldis' palace and in an interview with the marchesa begged, without disclosing his connection with Ellena, that objections to Vivaldi's suit be withdrawn. When the marchesa proved inattentive, he determined to solemnize the nuptials of Vivaldi and Ellena without her consent.

Called a second time before the tribunal of the Inquisition, Vivaldi heard again among those present at the trial the voice that had warned him on earlier occasions against his visits to the Villa Altieri. That night, a strange monk visited him in his cell and asked how long he had known Schedoni. The monk instructed Vivaldi to reveal to the Inquisition that Schedoni was actually Count Fernando di Bruno, who had lived fifteen years in the disguise of a Dominican monk. He was also to ask that Ansaldo di Rovalli, the grand penitentiary of the Black Penitents, be called to testify to a confession he had heard in 1752. When Vivaldi was again brought before the Inquisition, he did as he had been told; Schedoni was arrested on his way to Rome to intercede for Vivaldi's freedom.

At Schedoni's trial, the mystery that linked the sinister father confessor and the two lovers became clear. Years before, Schedoni, then a spendthrift younger son known as the count di Marinella, had schemed to possess himself of his brother's title, his unencumbered estate, and his beautiful wife. He had arranged to have his brother, the count di Bruno, assassinated by Spalatro and had contrived the story that the count had perished while returning from a journey to Greece. After a proper season of mourning, he had solicited the hand of his brother's widow. When she rejected him, he had carried her off by force. Although the lady's honor had been secured by marriage, she looked on her new husband with disdain; in his jealousy, he became convinced that she was unfaithful. One day, returning unexpectedly, he found a visitor with his wife. Drawing his stiletto with the intention of attacking the guest, he struck and killed his wife instead. This was the confession that had so agitated the grand penitentiary, for he himself had been the guest and for him an innocent woman had died.

Further proof was Spalatro's dying confession, whose death had been caused by a wound inflicted by Schedoni. Condemned to die for plotting his brother's death, Schedoni still persisted in his declaration that Ellena was his daughter. The mystery was cleared up by Sister Olivia, who had returned to the Convent of Santa Maria della Pieta; she was the unfortunate countess di Bruno, the sister of Signora Bianchi. Her wound had not been mortal, but the report of her death had been given out to protect her from her vengeful husband. Wishing to withdraw from the world, she had entrusted her daughter by the first count di Bruno and an infant daughter by the second to Signora Bianchi. The infant had died within a year.

Ellena, who knew nothing of this story, had been mistaken in her belief that the miniature was that of her father, and it was on her word that Schedoni had claimed her as his daughter. It was also revealed that Father Nicola, who had collected the evidence against Schedoni, had been the mysterious monk whose ghostly warnings Vivaldi heard under the arch of the old fortress. Appalled by the father confessor's villainy, he had turned against him after being wounded by Paulo's pistol on the night of the midnight search.

Schedoni had his final revenge. In some manner, he administered a fatal dose of poison to Father Nicola and then died of the same mysterious drug. In his last moments, he boasted that he was escaping an ignominious death at the hands of the Inquisition.

Because of Schedoni's dying confession, Vivaldi was immediately set free. During his imprisonment, the marchesa had died repentant of the harm she had plotted against Ellena. Now the marchese, overjoyed to be reunited with his son, withdrew all objections to Vivaldi's suit. With all doubts of Ellena's birth and goodness removed, he went in person to the Convent of Santa Maria della Pieta and asked Sister Olivia for her daughter's hand in the name of his son. Vivaldi and Ellena were married in the convent church in the presence of the marchese and Sister Olivia. As a mark of special favor, Paulo was allowed to be present when his master and Ellena were married. If it had not been for the holy precincts and the solemnity of the occasion, the faithful fellow would have thrown his cap into the air and shouted that this was indeed a happy day.

Critical Evaluation:

In *A Journey Made in the Summer of 1794 Through Holland and the Western Frontier of Germany* (1795), an account of a trip through Holland and Germany with her husband in 1794, Ann Radcliffe told of her trip up the Rhine River, where she encountered two Capuchins "as they walked along the shore, beneath the dark cliffs of Boppart, wrapt in the long black drapery of their order, and their heads shrouded in cowls, that half concealed their faces." She saw them as "interesting figures in a picture, always gloomily sublime." This vision is commonly believed to have inspired the character of Schedoni, the most sinister villain in the genre of the gothic novel. As in her other books, *The Italian* mingles the wild or idyllic beauty of nature with scenes of nightmare and terror.

The Italian is one of the most skillful and successful examples of the gothic novel, a literary genre whose aim is to astound, terrify, and thrill its readers. More controlled and convincing than her earlier *The Mysteries of Udolpho* (1794), Radcliffe's novel is filled with such conventional gothic qualities as a highly melodramatic (and unlikely) plot set in the remote past, a minimal degree of character development, and a painstakingly developed setting and atmosphere.

The plot is a familiar one to readers of the gothic: A mysterious and black-hearted villain, Schedoni, plots against a beautiful damsel, Ellena, who spends most of the novel either imprisoned or in imminent danger of death, while her chivalrous and faithful lover, Vivaldi, struggles against incredible odds to rescue her. The character delineation is crude, and, predictably, the villainous monk Schedoni is much more fascinating than the somewhat vapid hero and heroine. The air of mystery and terror in the monk is strikingly described: "A habitual gloom and severity prevailed over the deep lines of his countenance; and his eyes were so piercing that they seemed to penetrate, at a single glance, into the hearts of men, and to read their most secret thoughts."

Setting is crucial to *The Italian*. Here are gloomy monasteries, the dank dungeons of the Inquisition, and the dizzying precipices and crags of Abruzzo. There are also scenes of quiet but spine-tingling terror, as the one between Ellena and Schedoni on the deserted beach. Just as the evil characters are made even more menacing by their contrast to the good characters, the wild landscapes and brooding interiors are made more threatening by their contrast to the descriptions of Naples' beauty at the beginning and end of the novel.

The excesses and improbabilities of the lurid plot are tempered in a number of ways. Despite the manifold mysteries and hints of ghostly or demoniac forces pervading the work, nothing supernatural or magical actually does occur; unlike the events in *The Castle of Otranto*, for instance, there is ultimately a rational explanation for everything. Further, Radcliffe's handling of suspense, mystery, dramatic pacing, and realistic detail and description is expert and gripping throughout. The author also shows a serious concern for the main gothic theme of man's inhumanity to man, as seen, for instance, in Vivaldi's outburst against the brutalities of the Inquisition: "Can this be in human nature!—Can such horrible perversion of right be permitted! Can man, who calls himself endowed with reason, and immeasurably superior to every other created being, argue himself into the commission of such horrible folly, such inveterate cruelty, as exceeds all the acts of the most irrational and ferocious brute. . . !"

Such novels as *The Italian* were adroitly satirized by Jane Austen in *Northanger Abbey* (1818). Radcliffe's novel, however, is significant not only for its literary qualities but for the influence it had on such later writers as Sir Walter Scott, Charlotte Brontë, Samuel Taylor Coleridge, John Keats, and Edgar Allan Poe, all of whom drew on mysterious, threatening gothic settings and atmospheres in many of their own works.

Bibliography:
Hennelly, Mark M., Jr. "The Slow Torture of Delay: Reading *The Italian*." *Studies in Humanities* 14, no. 1 (June, 1987): 1-17. Explores Radcliffe's technique of suspense in the Inquisition segment of the novel.
Howells, Coral Ann. "The Pleasure of the Woman's Text: Ann Radcliffe's Subtle Transgressions in *The Mysteries of Udolpho* and *The Italian*." In *Gothic Fictions: Prohibition/Transgression*, edited by Kenneth W. Graham. New York: AMS Press, 1939. Concludes that Radcliffe's interest lies in the subtle disruptions of the conventions of sentimental novels.
Murray, E. B. *Ann Radcliffe*. New York: Twayne, 1972. Connects Radcliffe's works with the literary tradition of sensibility. The chapter on *The Italian* focuses on ethics.
Ronald, Ann. "Terror-Gothic: Nightmare and Dream in Ann Radcliffe and Charlotte Brontë." In *The Female Gothic*, edited by Juliann E. Fleenor. Montreal: Eden Press, 1983. Discusses archetypal images in works of Radcliffe and Brontë.
Ruff, William. "Ann Radcliffe: Or, The Hand of Taste." In *The Age of Johnson: Essays Presented to Chauncey Brewster Tinker*, edited by F. W. Hilles. New Haven, Conn.: Yale

University Press, 1949. Discusses *The Italian*, the "novel of taste," as Radcliffe's most significant contribution to English letters.

Todd, Janet. "Posture and Imposture: The Gothic Manservant in Ann Radcliffe's *The Italian*." In *Men by Woman*, edited by Janet Todd. New York: Holmes and Meier, 1981. Analyzes the character of Paolo and shows how Radcliffe created him to embody ideal qualities of a manservant.

Varma, Devendra P. *The Gothic Flame, Being a History of the Gothic Novel in England.* London: Arthur Barker, 1957. In the section on Radcliffe, Varma observes the structure of Radcliffe's novels, her explanations of the supernatural occurrences, and her ability to create suspense.

THE ITCHING PARROT

Type of work: Novel
Author: José Joaquín Fernández de Lizardi (1776-1827)
Type of plot: Picaresque
Time of plot: 1770's to 1820's
Locale: Mexico
First published: El periquillo sarniento, 1816 (English translation, 1942)

Principal characters:
PEDRO SARMIENTO, the Itching Parrot, or Periquillo, or Poll,
  a young Mexican
DON ANTONIO, Poll's prison mate and benefactor
JANUARIO, Poll's schoolmate
AN ARMY COLONEL, Poll's superior and benefactor

The Story:

Pedro Sarmiento was born to upper-middle-class parents in Mexico City between 1771 and 1773; of the actual date, he was not sure. As a child he was willful, and his mother's excessive devotion only made him worse. He became such a scamp that at last his father sent him off to school. At school, he was nicknamed Parrot. A little later, when he contracted the itch, his schoolmates nicknamed him the Itching Parrot, or Poll for short, and the name stuck to him through most of his life.

In addition to his nickname, Poll acquired many vicious habits from his schoolfellows. Poll's father resolved to put Poll out as an apprentice in a trade, but Poll's mother, not wishing her son to disgrace her family by becoming a vulgar tradesman, insisted that the boy be sent to college. Against his better judgment, the father agreed, and so Poll was sent off to study for a college degree. After learning some Latin, some Aristotle, some logic, and a little physics, Poll was awarded a baccalaureate degree by the College of San Ildefonso. Shortly after receiving his degree, Poll went into the countryside to visit a hacienda owned by the father of a former schoolmate. At the hacienda, he earned the hatred of his schoolmate, Januario, by making advances to the latter's cousin, with whom Januario was infatuated. Januario took his revenge by tempting Poll into a bullfight. Poll, who lost both the fight and his trousers, became the laughingstock of the hacienda. Still unsatisfied, Januario tricked Poll into trying to sleep with the girl cousin. Through Januario, the girl's mother discovered the attempt, beat Poll with her shoe, and sent him back to Mexico City in disgrace.

Upon his return to the city, Poll was told by his father that he had to find some means of earning a livelihood. Poll, searching for the easiest way, decided he would study theology and enter the church. Theology quickly proved uninteresting, and Poll gave up that idea. Trying to escape his father's insistence that he learn a trade, Poll then decided to enter a Franciscan monastery. There he soon found that he could not stand the life of a monk; he was glad when his father's death gave him an excuse to leave the monastery. After a short period of mourning, Poll rapidly exhausted his small inheritance through his fondness for gambling, parties, and women. The sorrow he caused his mother sent her, also, to an early death. After his mother died, Poll was left alone. None of his relatives, who knew him for a rogue, would have anything to do with him.

In his despair, Poll fell in with another schoolmate, who supported himself by gambling and trickery. Poll took up a similar career in his schoolmate's company. A man Poll gulled discovered his treachery and beat him severely. After his release from the hospital, Poll went back to his gambling partner, and they decided to turn thieves. On their first attempt, however, they were unsuccessful. Poll was caught and thrown into prison.

Poll had no family or friends to call upon, so he languished in jail for several months. He made one friend in jail who helped him; that friend was Don Antonio, a man of good reputation who had been unjustly imprisoned. Don Antonio tried to keep Poll away from bad company but was not entirely successful. When Don Antonio was freed, Poll fell in with a mulatto who got him into all kinds of scrapes. By chance, Poll was taken up by a scrivener who was in need of an apprentice and was pleased with Poll's handwriting. The scrivener had Poll released from prison to become his apprentice. Poll's career as a scrivener's apprentice was short, for he made love to the man's mistress, was discovered, and was driven from the house. The next step in Poll's adventures was service as a barber's apprentice. He then left that work to become a clerk in a pharmacy. After getting into trouble by carelessly mixing a prescription, Poll left the pharmacy for the employ of a doctor.

Having picked up some jargon and a few cures from his doctor-employer, Poll set out to be a physician. Everything went well until he caused a number of deaths and was forced to leave the profession.

Trying to recoup his fortunes once more, Poll returned to gambling. In a game, he won a lottery ticket which, in its turn, won for him a small fortune. For a time, Poll lived well: He even married a woman who thought he had a great deal of money. The life the couple led soon exhausted the lottery money, however, and they were almost penniless again. After his wife died in childbirth, Poll set out once again in search of his fortune. His work as a sacristan ended when he robbed a corpse. Poll then joined a group of beggars. Finding that they were fakes, he reported them to the authorities. One of the officials, pleased with Poll, secured him a place in government service. For a time all went well, but Poll, who was left in charge of the district when his superior was absent, abused his authority so much that he was arrested and sent in chains to Mexico City. There he was tried, found guilty of many crimes, and sent to the army for eight years.

Through his good conduct and pleasing appearance, Poll was made clerk to the colonel of the regiment. The colonel placed a great deal of trust in Poll. When the regiment went to Manila, the colonel saw to it that Poll was given an opportunity to do some trading and save up a small fortune. Poll completed his sentence and prepared to return to Mexico as a fairly rich man. All his dreams and fortune vanished, however, when the ship sank and he was cast away upon an island. On the island, he made friends with a Chinese chieftan, in whose company Poll, pretending all the while to be a nobleman, returned to Mexico. When they reached Mexico, the lie was discovered, but the Chinese man continued to be Poll's friend and patron.

Poll stayed with the Chinese man for some time, but he finally left in disgrace after having introduced prostitutes into the house. Leaving Mexico City, Poll met the mulatto who had been his companion in jail. Along with the mulatto and some other men, Poll turned highwayman but barely escaped with his life from their first holdup. Frightened, Poll went into retreat at a church, where he discovered his confessor to be a boy he had known years before in school. The kind confessor found honest employment for Poll as an agent for a rich man. Poll became an honest, hardworking citizen, even being known as Don Pedro rather than Poll. Years passed quickly. Then one day, Don Pedro, befriending some destitute people, found one to be his old benefactor of prison days, Don Antonio. The others were Don Antonio's wife and daughter. Don Pedro married the daughter, thus completing his respectability. He lived out the rest of his days in honesty, industry, and respect.

Critical Evaluation:

The Itching Parrot is Fernández de Lizardi's masterpiece and has been canonized as the first Spanish American novel. It is a picaresque novel, describing the misadventures of a young man driven by hunger and poverty to make his way in the world, in which he must, he says, cheat to survive. The book also has a liberal amount of slapstick humor (good examples of which occur during Poll's spell as a doctor's assistant and the episode in which he attempts to steal jewelry from a corpse). Like the protagonist of *Lazarillo de Tormes* (1553), Poll experiences a series of apprenticeships (in a ranch, a monastery, a barber's shop, a pharmacy), learning a variety of trades, which range from the socially prestigious (doctor's assistant, sacristan's assistant) to the dubious (croupier, cardsman) to the illegal (thief). The important part of these learning experiences is that all the occupations are based on deception. Those elements that *The Itching Parrot* shares with the great Spanish classic are effective. Unlike *Lazarillo de Tormes*, however, Fernández de Lizardi's novel inserts long, moralizing passages that describe the moral meaning of events in the plot and, for the modern reader at least, reduce their impact.

The society that *The Itching Parrot* describes is in flux. In the second half of the eighteenth century, Spain's colonies saw a displacement of power from the hands of the church, the monarchy, and the landowning elite to a new, professional class of doctors, lawyers, and merchants. *The Itching Parrot* is sensitive to this social change and gives a vivid picture of a society that gradually was becoming more politically independent from Spain. An indication of this change of ambience is evident in the opening pages of the novel. The novel's prologue describes an imaginary conversation between the author and a friend, who advises the author against dedicating his work to a wealthy patron, instead saying that the author should dedicate the book to his readers, since they are "the ones who will pay for the printing." It is not by chance that the first Spanish American novel should refer to a new mode of production (capital-based book production) and, by implication, to the new class from which it sprang.

Most critics agree that the main aim of *The Itching Parrot* is to identify the abuse of power in the professions in colonial New Spain. In Spanish America, as elsewhere, the growth of the new professional classes, including doctors, lawyers, merchants, suppliers, and printers, was accompanied by the growth of a parasitic group of unqualified and dishonest professionals; it is these latter that *The Itching Parrot* sets out to satirize. The protagonist is used not so much as a means whereby the hypocrisy and corruption of others is exposed; rather, he becomes himself the object of scorn and ridicule. In part 1, chapter 1, for example, Poll takes great pains to list the circumstances of his upbringing as a way of explaining his wayward ways. He can assign blame to his parents' lack of education, their lack of concern for his upbringing and, in particular, their frequent recourse to wet nurses. The irony underlying these details becomes clear when the narrator refers to the way in which old wives' tales affected him as a young child, and the narrative begins to creak under its self-imposed burden of moralism. It could be argued that the moralistic intention of this passage (which is typical of many others) is too transparent, and that Pedro's credibility as a narrator is diminished as a result.

The rationale behind the many episodes of Pedro's life emerges at the end of the novel. In book 3, chapter 3, the narrator is shipwrecked on an unidentified island in the Pacific Ocean. He finds himself obliged to justify the laws and customs of his native land to a skeptical Chinese chieftain (who may be Fernández de Lizardi's spokesman). In describing his society's customs (such as the idea that nobles cannot work, work being beneath them), Pedro manages to make the customs sound absurd. Pedro's stupidity is revealed when, in the same chapter, he not only fails to recognize a plant but diagnoses its medicinal function in precisely the wrong way. Events finally run against Pedro, and he is humiliated by the Chinese chieftain. When readers ask the question At what or whom is the satire being directed? the answer must surely be Spanish American society.

There are some scenes in the novel that show Fernández de Lizardi's consummate skill in allowing irony to emerge from events rather than from commentary. A good example is the frequently anthologized scene in part 2, chapter 6, in which Poll decides to become a doctor, takes on André as his assistant and, with the luck of the devil, manages to revive a tax collector who is on his deathbed. Poll's use of Latin to hoodwink his audience and hide his ignorance, when faced with medical symptoms, is effectively done. In this vignette Fernández de Lizardi offers a convincing picture of a society in which half-learned Latin tags are used to confound the populace and fleece the poor.

"Critical Evaluation" by Stephen M. Hart

Bibliography:
Bell, Steven M. "Mexico." In *Handbook of Latin American Literature*, edited by David William Foster. 2d ed. New York: Garland, 1992. The section on *The Itching Parrot* shows that Fernández de Lizardi did not seek to entertain the colonial nobility in his novel but instead to enlighten the masses.

Cros, Edmond. "The Values of Liberalism in *El Periquillo Sarniento*." *Sociocriticism* 2 (December, 1985): 85-109. Studies the relationship between the Spanish colony of New Spain and its metropolis through the relationship between father and son, which the first-person novel relies upon as a guiding theme.

Franco, Jean. *An Introduction to Spanish-American Literature*. Cambridge, England: Cambridge University Press, 1969. The section on *El periquillo sarniento* argues that Fernández de Lizardi represents a new type of Spanish American, one for whom the newspaper served as a weapon, and contends that Poll is too passive a hero to be sympathetic to the modern reader.

González, Aníbal. *Journalism and the Development of Spanish American Narrative*. Cambridge, England: Cambridge University Press, 1993. The section on *El periquillo sarniento* argues that the main character is an allegory of the journalist and of the duplicitous nature of writing.

Vogeley, Nancy. "Defining the 'Colonial Reader.'" *PMLA* 102, no. 5 (1987): 784-800. Argues that Fernández de Lizardi's aim in writing the novel was to challenge readers' expectations that a literary work should follow European standards and have an elevated style. Argues that Fernández de Lizardi created a new genre and a new readership.

IVANHOE
A Romance

Type of work: Novel
Author: Sir Walter Scott (1771-1832)
Type of plot: Romance
Time of plot: 1194
Locale: England
First published: 1819

> *Principal characters:*
> CEDRIC THE SAXON, the owner of Rotherwood Grange
> WILFRED OF IVANHOE, his disinherited son
> THE LADY ROWENA, his ward and Ivanhoe's beloved
> ISAAC OF YORK, a Jewish moneylender
> REBECCA, his daughter
> SIR BRIAN DE BOIS-GUILBERT, a Norman Knight Templar
> KING RICHARD I, a king returned from the Third Crusade
> ROBIN HOOD, an outlaw

The Story:

Night was drawing near when Prior Aymer of Jorvaux and the haughty Templar Brian de Bois-Guilbert overtook a swineherd and a fool by the roadside and asked directions to Rotherwood, the dwelling of Cedric the Saxon. The answers of these serfs so confused the Templar and the prior that they would have gone far afield had it not been for a pilgrim from the Holy Land whom they encountered shortly afterward. The pilgrim was also traveling to Rotherwood, and he brought them safely to Cedric's hall, where they claimed lodging for the night. It was the custom of those rude days to afford hospitality to all travelers, so Cedric gave a grudging welcome to the Norman lords.

There was a feast at Rotherwood that night. On the dais beside Cedric the Saxon sat his ward, the lovely Lady Rowena, descendant of the ancient Saxon princes. It was the old man's ambition to wed her to Athelstane of Coningsburgh, who came from the line of King Alfred. Because his son, Wilfred of Ivanhoe, had fallen in love with Rowena, Cedric had banished him, and the young knight had gone with King Richard to Palestine. None in the banquet hall that night suspected that the pilgrim was Ivanhoe himself.

Another traveler who had claimed shelter at Rotherwood that night was an aged Jew, Isaac of York. Hearing some orders the Templar muttered to his servants at the feast's end, Ivanhoe warned the Jew that Bois-Guilbert had designs on his moneybag or his person. Without taking leave of their host the next morning, the disguised pilgrim and Isaac of York left Rotherwood together and continued on to the nearby town of Ashby de la Zouche.

Many other travelers were on their way to the town, for a great tournament was to be held there. Prince John, the regent of England in King Richard's absence, was to preside. The winner of the tournament would be allowed to name the Queen of Love and Beauty and receive the prize of the passage of arms from her hands.

Ivanhoe attended the tournament with the word Disinherited written on his shield. Entering the lists, he struck the shield of Bois-Guilbert with the point of his lance and challenged the knight to mortal combat. In the first passage, both knights splintered their lances, but neither was unhorsed. At the second passage, Ivanhoe's lance struck Bois-Guilbert's helmet and upset him. Then, one by one, Ivanhoe vanquished five knights who had agreed to take on all comers. When the heralds declared the Disinherited Knight victor of the tourney, Ivanhoe named Rowena the Queen of Love and Beauty.

In the tournament on the following day, Ivanhoe was pressed hard by three antagonists, but he received unexpected help from a knight in black, whom the spectators had called the Black Sluggard because of his previous inactivity. Because of his earlier triumphs during the day, Ivanhoe was again named champion of the tournament. To receive the gift from Lady Rowena, Ivanhoe had to remove his helmet, and when he did so, he was recognized. He received the chaplet, his prize, kissed the hand of Lady Rowena, and then fainted from loss of blood. Isaac of York and his daughter, Rebecca, were sitting nearby, and Rebecca suggested to her father that they nurse Ivanhoe until he was well. Isaac and his daughter started for their home with the wounded knight being carried in a horse litter. On the way, they joined the train of Cedric the Saxon, who was still ignorant of the Disinherited Knight's identity.

Before the travelers had gone far, however, they were set upon and captured by a party led by three Norman knights, Bois-Guilbert, Maurice de Bracy, and Reginald Front de Boeuf. They were imprisoned in Front de Boeuf's castle of Torquilstone. De Bracy had designs on Lady Rowena because she was an heiress of royal lineage. The Templar desired to possess Rebecca. Front de Boeuf hoped to extort a large sum of money from the aged Jew. Cedric was held for ransom. The wounded knight was put into the charge of an ancient hag named Ulrica.

Isaac and his daughter were placed in separate rooms. Bois-Guilbert went to Rebecca in her tower prison and asked her to adopt Christianity so that they might be married. The plot of the Norman nobles against their prisoners was thwarted by an assault on the castle by Richard the Lion-Hearted, the knight known as The Black Sluggard at the Ashby tournament, in company with Robin Hood and his outlaws. Ulrica aided the besiegers by starting a fire within the castle walls. Robin Hood and his men took the prisoners to the forest along with the Norman nobles. In the confusion, however, Bois-Guilbert escaped with Rebecca, and Isaac prepared to ransom her from the Templar. De Bracy was set free, and he hurried to inform Prince John that he had seen and talked with Richard. John plotted to make Richard his prisoner.

Isaac went to the establishment of the Knights Templar and begged to see Bois-Guilbert. Lucas de Beaumanoir, the grand master of the Templars, ordered Isaac admitted to his presence. Isaac was frightened when the grand master asked him his business with the Templar. When he told his story, the grand master learned that Bois-Guilbert had abducted Rebecca. It was suggested that Rebecca had cast a spell on Bois-Guilbert. Condemned as a witch, she was sentenced to be burned at the stake. In desperation, she demanded, as was her right, a champion to defend her against the charge. Lucas de Beaumanoir agreed and named Bois-Guilbert to face that champion.

The day arrived for Rebecca's execution. A pile of wood had been laid around the stake. Seated in a black chair, Rebecca awaited the arrival of her defender. Three times the heralds called on a champion to appear. At the third call, a strange knight rode into the lists and announced himself as Rebecca's champion. When Bois-Guilbert realized that the stranger was Ivanhoe, he at first refused combat because Ivanhoe's wounds were not completely healed. Nevertheless, the grand master gave orders for the contest to begin. As everyone expected, the tired horse of Ivanhoe and its exhausted rider went down at the first blow, so that Ivanhoe's lance merely touched the shield of the Templar. To the astonishment of all, however, Bois-Guilbert reeled in his saddle and fell to the ground. Ivanhoe arose and drew his sword. Placing his foot on the breast of the fallen knight, he called on Bois-Guilbert to yield himself or die on the spot. There was no answer from Bois-Guilbert; he was dead, a victim of the violence of his own passions. The grand master declared that Rebecca was acquitted of the charge against her. At that moment, the Black Knight appeared, followed by a band of knights and men-at-arms. It was King Richard, who had come to arrest Rebecca's accusers on a charge of treason. The grand master saw the flag of the Temple hauled down and the royal standard raised in its place.

King Richard had returned in secret to reclaim his throne. Robin Hood became his true follower. Athelstane let go his claims to Lady Rowena's hand so that she and Ivanhoe could be married. Reconciled at last with his son, Cedric the Saxon gave his consent, and Richard himself graced their wedding. Isaac and Rebecca left England for Granada, hoping to find in that foreign land greater happiness than could ever be theirs in England.

Critical Evaluation:

Since publication, *Ivanhoe* has retained its charm for readers as the epitome of chivalric novels. It has among its characters two of the most popular of English heroes, Richard the Lion-Hearted and Robin Hood, and it tells a powerful story of romance in addition to offering action and color. Although *Ivanhoe* may not be Sir Walter Scott's greatest novel, it is without doubt his most popular.

Scott himself wrote that he left the Scottish scenes of his previous novels and turned to the Middle Ages in *Ivanhoe* because he feared the reading public was growing weary of the repetition of Scottish themes in his books. He was fascinated with history all his life, and it was logical that he should turn to the past for subject matter. Many faults have been found with the historical facts of *Ivanhoe*; Robin Hood, if he had lived at all, would have lived in a later century than that represented in the novel, for example, and by the time of Richard I, the distinction between Saxons and Normans had faded. Nevertheless, whatever liberties Scott took with history, the thrilling drama continues to grip readers.

Scott's four great chivalric novels all possess similar structures. They all focus on a moment of crisis between two great individuals, a moment that determines the survival of one and destruction of the other. In *Ivanhoe*, the contrast is between Richard the Lion-Hearted and his brother John. The struggle reflects one of the principal themes of the novel: the decadence of chivalry. For generations of juvenile readers, *Ivanhoe* represented the glory of chivalric adventure, but Scott actually entertained serious doubts about the tradition. At several strategic points in Ivanhoe, he unequivocally damns the reckless inhumanity of romantic chivalry.

The novel is symmetrically designed in three parts, each reaching its climax in a great military spectacle. The first part ends with the Ashby tournament, the second with the liberation from the castle of Front de Boeuf, and the third with the trial by combat for Rebecca. The beginning chapters draw together all of the character groups for the tournament, though Ivanhoe is present only as the mysterious palmer. The problem of seating at the tournament provides a sketch of the cultural animosities that divided the world of the novel.

Richard is the moral and political center of the book and, therefore, the proper object of Ivanhoe's fidelity. The captive king does not appear until he fights the mysterious Black Knight during the second day of the tournament. He saves Ivanhoe and then disappears until the scene of his midnight feast with Friar Tuck, who regards him as a man of "prudence and of counsel." Richard possesses a native humanity and a love of life, as well as the traditional heroic chivalric qualities, and he is always ready to act as a protector of others.

By contrast, John is an ineffectual ruler whose own followers despise him. His forces quickly disintegrate, and his followers abandon him for their own selfish ends. He is a petulant, stupid man, incapable of inspiring loyalty. It is inevitable that the historical climax of the novel should be the confrontation between Richard and John. The chivalric code has become completely corrupt in the England left to John's care. Both the narrator and the characters make clear that chivalry is no more than a mixture of "heroic folly and dangerous imprudence."

Rebecca speaks against chivalry, asking during the bloody siege of the castle if possession by a "demon of vainglory" brings "sufficient rewards for the sacrifice of every kindly affection, for a life spent miserably that yet may make others miserable." (Rebecca is antichivalric, yet she is the most romantic character in the book, suggesting the traditional chivalric attitude toward women.) The narrator speaks most sharply against the chivalric code at the end of the tournament:

> This ended the memorable field of Ashby-de-la-Zouche, one of the most gallantly contested tournaments of that age; for although only four knights, including one who was smothered by the heat of his armour, had died upon the field, yet upwards of thirty were desperately wounded, four or five of whom never recovered. Several more were disabled for life; and those who escaped best carried the marks of the conflict to the grave with them. Hence it is always mentioned in the old records as the "gentle and joyous passage of arms at Ashby."

An argument has been made that Scott's historical novels, such as *Ivanhoe*, are inferior to his earlier novels based on his direct, personal knowledge of the Scottish customs, characters, and land. Even in the historical novels, however, Scott's characters are colorful, full of vitality, and realized with amazing verisimilitude. Scott's knowledge of the past about which he was writing was so deep that he could draw upon it at will to clothe out his fictions. He did not find it necessary to research a novel such as *Ivanhoe* in order to write it; the historical lore was already part of him. Years before, at the time when he was beginning the Waverley series, he had written a study about chivalry. His prolific writing did not seem to exhaust his resources.

Scott was one of the most prolific writers in the history of British fiction; only Trollope approached his record. Scott's novels were originally published anonymously, although their authorship came to be an open secret. Scott's friends found it difficult to believe that he was the author of the novels, for he lived the life of a county magistrate and landowner and spent long hours in these occupations as well as entertaining lavishly and writing poetry and nonfiction works. He managed to accomplish so much because he habitually rose early and completed all novel-writing before breakfast. In time, his compulsive working injured his health. While writing *Ivanhoe*, he was tortured by a cramp of the stomach and suffered such pain that he could not hold the pen but was forced to dictate much of the story.

Like many great novels, *Ivanhoe* betrays its author's complex attitude. In tandem with Scott's severe view of the code of chivalry is his attraction to the Romantic traditions of the period. Although Richard's personality is not romantic, it is this character whom Scott gives the chivalric virtues. Scott dramatized his more ambivalent feelings about chivalry in the characters of Rebecca and Rowena, Ivanhoe and Richard. The tension created through these mixed feelings, coupled with the dramatic (if historically inaccurate) story and the vast accumulation of detail as to costume and social customs and historical anecdotes, combine to create a novel that has remained popular ever since it was first published.

"Critical Evaluation" by Bruce D. Reeves

Bibliography:
Hayden, John O., ed. *Scott: The Critical Heritage*. New York: Barnes & Noble Books, 1970.
    A collection of reviews of many of Scott's novels, including *Ivanhoe*. Also includes an

extended essay on Scott by Samuel Taylor Coleridge and anonymous letters written to Scott about the novel.

Hillhouse, James T. *The Waverley Novels and Their Critics.* New York: Octagon Books, 1970. A history of the critical reception Scott received. The first part offers early reviews from *The Edinburgh, The Quarterly, Blackwood's,* and other periodicals, and the second part provides critical interpretations from the fifty years following his death.

Johnson, Edgar. *Sir Walter Scott: The Great Unknown.* New York: Macmillan, 1970. An immense two-volume set that includes a synopsis and historical explanation of the characters and setting of *Ivanhoe.* Considers the differing treatments of Jews and Christians, and explains aspects of Scott's views on the Catholic church, morality, and nobility.

Lauber, John. *Sir Walter Scott.* Rev. ed. Boston: Twayne, 1989. Compares *Ivanhoe* with the other Scott novels and places it in the context of Scott's entire oeuvre. Explains the stereotypes and the concept of chivalry.

J. B.
A Play in Verse

Type of work: Drama
Author: Archibald MacLeish (1892-1982)
Type of plot: Symbolism
Time of plot: The 1940's to the 1950's
Locale: A large American city
First performed: 1958; first published, 1958

> *Principal characters:*
> MR. ZUSS, a bombastic, run-down actor who represents God
> NICKLES, a sardonic clown who acts as Satan
> J. B., the Job figure, a businessman
> SARAH, J. B.'s wife

The Story:

Two broken-down actors who had fallen on bad days were ready for their parts in the ensuing drama. Zuss was a large, red-faced, and dignified man, and Nickles was sarcastic and gaunt to the point of grotesqueness. As outsiders, they would control the ensuing action, but they would also be drawn into the drama. The Book of Job is the Old Testament story of a good man who was punished so that God could prove to Satan, his adversary, that there are good people who love God despite their hardships. Unlike Satan in the Book of Job, Nickles seemed to sympathize with humanity and denounce God for torturing innocent people. It would be Job's demand for reasons, for justice, that would force him to confront God.

In a bedraggled circus sideshow, Zuss (whose attitude reinforced his self-image of what God would be like) and Nickles (who was disillusioned and bitter because this play had been done over and over throughout the centuries, with the same actions and ending) argued over Heaven and Hell as they watched modern Job (J. B.) and his happy family. Nickles mocked Zuss's sincerity, and Zuss declared that God had reasons for testing Job (who represented humanity). Nickles tended to see himself as Job as he claimed that God was jealous because Job had a soul and intellect that allowed him to question God's actions. As Nickles chanted, "If God is God He is not good, If God is good He is not God."

Zuss recalled World War II and its horrors to reveal that someone was always playing Job, punished "for walking round the world in the wrong skin." Modern Jobs were no longer perfect, as Job was described; rather, they were average people trying to survive in an unfriendly universe. Hell was not only suffering, however. According to Nickles, Hell was Job's consciousness of consciousness—knowing that he would continue to love God even though he was destroyed and had lost his wealth, his children, and everything else.

J. B. was a complacent, successful New Englander in his thirties, with children appropriately named David (age thirteen), Mary (age twelve), Jonathan (age ten), Ruth (age eight), and Rebecca (age six). His wife, Sarah, warned Job not to trust in their "luck" or success. It was Sarah who was devoted to God and Sarah who insisted that they give proper thanks to God. She said that justice demanded that God punish as well as reward, but J. B. refused to listen. He trusted that God's gift, symbolized in the greening of the leaves, would never be removed. Nickles and Zuss plotted his destruction.

In succession, two messengers in the roles of soldiers, newspapermen, and police officers met with Job and Sarah to announce the horrifying deaths of their children: first David, shot by

3272

his own men after the war ended; then Mary and Jonathan, slammed into a brick wall in a car wreck; Rebecca, raped and killed by a nineteen year old; and finally Ruth, crushed beneath a falling wall in their bombed-out city. In every case, the second messenger declared, like his biblical counterpart, "I only am escaped alone to tell thee." This messenger also suggested that some are doomed to witness the destruction and the losses of other people—witnesses, too, suffer.

After every revelation, Sarah wept and withdrew, while Job continued to believe in God and his goodness. He also called out to the silence as he sought an answer to humanity's eternal question—why does God permit the suffering of innocent people? Meanwhile, as J. B. and Sarah sat in the rubble of their home, Nickles sarcastically mocked Zuss for his bad aim—he had destroyed an entire city to "blister one man's skin."

For J. B., the meaninglessness of his children's suffering was worse than the curses inflicted upon them. In their despair at losing all of their children, the couple split up rather than holding on to each other. J. B. tried to pray while Sarah rocked and wept. Nickles was disgusted at Job's acceptance of "God's will"; it was not decent to still love a God who took those children. Finally, Sarah left Job because he insisted that he or their children must have been guilty of something for which they were being punished. To her, this was a lie calculated to save God's image of goodness. Sarah said that she would not love Job any more if he bought God's goodness in exchange for their children.

Like biblical Job, J. B. was visited by his three "comforters." In the 1950's world, they were a fat priest, a psychiatrist, and a communist. Eliphaz the psychiatrist argued that guilt was an illusion or disease, and Zophar the priest exploded with the cry that guilt was the only reality. The communist also was not much help.

Finally, Job heard the Distant Voice from the Whirlwind, and he matched his silence with God's earlier refusals to speak with Job. Nickles was angry that Job knuckled under to God's grandeur, but it seemed that J. B. actually forgave God, as if Job's suffering were justified by his acceptance of God's will.

As Zuss attempted to restore J. B.'s family and wealth, Nickles tried to convince J. B. to renounce God's creation by committing suicide. What saved J. B. was the return of his wife Sarah. As she had wandered through the rubble of their bombed-out city, also contemplating suicide, Sarah had found a forsythia blooming in the debris of ashes and death. This silent promise of life brought J. B. and Sarah back together as she declared that there was no justice in the world, a concept Job had believed throughout their ordeal. The only thing left was love. They trusted now in each other's love, not in God's justice.

Critical Evaluation:

Awarded three Pulitzer Prizes (one for *J. B.*) and enjoying an illustrious career as a poet, Librarian of Congress, and playwright, Archibald MacLeish relied upon myth and symbolism, particularly biblical symbols, to focus and inform his work. Like T. S. Eliot, MacLeish allowed past and present to intertwine as he sought to create a recurring image of fertility (as in *The Pot of Earth*, 1925) or a determined rationality (as in *Nobodaddy*, 1926) that reinforced the notion of humanity's domination of nature.

J. B. is MacLeish's response to the wanton slaughter of innocent people in World War II. In this play, modern Job is a typical American businessman who takes his good fortune for granted, as somehow "deserved." This humanistic drama elevates humanity while lessening the importance of God, perhaps explaining the negative critical response the play suffered when presented on Broadway in 1958.

Unlike other versions of the Job story, *J. B.* gives Job's wife Sarah (who has the same name as Abraham's wife, who created the Hebrew "dynasty" in the Old Testament) as much a part in the suffering as Job has. Sarah is the one who recognizes that it is God who is killing their children, and it is Sarah's love, not God's, that brings the couple back together and renews their faith in life.

The broken-down actor who plays God is aptly named Zuss, to reinforce his image—Zeus was the king of the ancient Greek gods. That he is a has-been, a failure, adds dimension to the story. Nickles is not only a nickel-plated clown or a phony; he is also the "Old Nick"—the deceiver, Satan himself. The children all have biblical names to reinforce MacLeish's frame of reference. Zuss represents the traditional, theistic (believing in God) view, and Nickles presents a more humanistic interpretation of innocent suffering.

To MacLeish, it is the poet's duty to use his or her experience of life to bring a "human focus" and understanding. This can be seen clearly in his political writings as well. For him, it is humanity's love of life and the urge to endure that is the miracle of existence. *J. B.* reveals that answers come not from a distant or nonexistent God but from humanity itself. MacLeish believed that the answers to the mystery of life must come not from without, but from within each person. To deal with the tragic meaninglessness of World War II, MacLeish needed Job as a symbol for those who died senselessly, needlessly, because they were "in the wrong skin" or because the moonlight shone on the water, making an easy bombing target. Although Job is an appropriate myth for humanity's attempt to confront an unjust universe, this play is also a "supreme affirmation of the love of life." That love, MacLeish says, is where "God exists and triumphs."

Some critics derided J. B. (Job) as shallow and self-righteous, but that is the poet's point—humans are no longer the Promethean heroes of the past. (Prometheus stole fire from the gods to help humanity and was tortured by Zeus for this outrage.) People are ordinary, with faults, doubts, and failings.

Nickles insists on humanity's spiritual independence from God, but Zuss reiterates the Distant Voice from the Whirlwind that silences Job. At times, the actors hear another Voice intoning the words from the Bible's Book of Job, and their masks seem to have lives of their own. The audience begins to suspect that there still is a Voice beyond the mask—God may be distant, but He still controls the good and the evil that humanity must confront and defeat.

If Job is complacent at first and bitter after his catastrophes, Sarah is a better wife than he deserves. Like William Blake (English Romantic poet of the eighteenth and nineteenth centuries) and Robert Frost (twentieth century American poet and author of *A Masque of Reason*, 1945, a verse play about modern Job), MacLeish insists on Sarah's equal participation in the suffering as well as in the renewal of life following the test. She knows before Job that it is God who is torturing them. It is also Sarah who returns with the greening forsythia to rekindle her love of Job and of life.

The suffering, though, is shared by the second messenger, who witnessed each act of terror and so is doomed as well. His repeated line of "I only am escaped alone to tell thee" is key to his character. People of the twentieth century are witnesses to the most heinous crimes imaginable, yet we seem to share the guilt of the victimizers.

J. B. denies Sarah the right to suffer as much as he in the deaths of their children. He makes the deaths a contest between himself and God and ignores the fact that Sarah is as guilty or as innocent as he. She leaves him because of his seeming lack of emotion, his lack of anger and despair at the horrifying details of their children's deaths.

MacLeish must separate J. B. and Sarah so that they face the final crisis alone. Job thus confronts his false comforters and rejects the cliché that he has been spouting—"The Lord giveth, the Lord taketh away." It is not the pain they have suffered so much as the meaninglessness of it all that grieves him.

According to MacLeish, modern humanity's comforters—psychiatrists and religious and political leaders—deny people their individual right to guilt and individual responsibility for the sins of the world. Without individual guilt, there can be no identity, no innocence or humanity.

When God speaks out of the Whirlwind, He silences Job without answering his complaints. Job bows and forgives God. Like Satan, Nickles thinks incorrectly that Job will reject his newly reconstituted life. The play's ending, in which Job and Sarah are reconciled, has been controversial since the play's publication. Critics who deride the playwright do so because *J. B.* does not focus the Job story on God and His majesty. Instead, MacLeish gives humanity center stage and insists in this humanistic drama that Job and Sarah's choice of life comes from within, where God is.

Linda L. Labin

Bibliography:

Campbell, Shannon O. "The Book of Job and MacLeish's *J. B.*: A Cultural Comparison." *English Journal* 61 (May, 1972): 653-657. Clarifies the connections between the Old Testament story and the poet's unique approach to it.

Falk, Signi Lenea. *Archibald MacLeish*. New York: Twayne, 1965. A thorough analysis of the poet's major contributions to poetry and drama. Focuses on suggesting connections between MacLeish and other twentieth century poets.

Roston, Murray. "MacLeish's *J. B.*" In *Biblical Images in Literature*, edited by Roland Bartel. Nashville: Abingdon Press, 1975. Analyzes the supernatural elements in *J. B.* in contrast to the ordinary modern scene of horror.

Sanders, Paul S., ed. *Twentieth Century Interpretations of the Book of Job: A Collection of Critical Essays*. Englewood Cliffs, N.J.: Prentice-Hall, 1968. An excellent collection of critical articles on the Old Testament Book of Job, including one by Richard B. Sewall, who calls Job the symbol of undeserved suffering.

JACK OF NEWBERY

Type of work: Novel
Author: Thomas Deloney (1543?-1600)
Type of plot: Picaresque
Time of plot: Reign (1509-1547) of Henry VIII
Locale: England
*First published: The Pleasant History of John Winchcomb, in His Younger Days Called
  Jack of Newbery,* 1597

> *Principal characters:*
> JACK WINCHCOMB, a weaver
> JACK'S MASTER'S WIDOW
> JACK'S SECOND WIFE
> HENRY VIII, the king of England
> QUEEN CATHERINE, his wife
> CARDINAL WOLSEY, the lord chancellor of England

The Story:

In the days of King Henry VIII, there lived in the English town of Newbery a young weaver named Jack Winchcomb. As a young man he was something of a prodigal, spending as much as he made and having a reputation as a merry young fellow; he was known in all the county of Berkshire as Jack of Newbery. After his master died, however, Jack changed his ways. His mistress, who had acquired a fondness for the young man, entrusted to him the entirety of her husband's business. Jack became a careful man, both with his mistress' affairs and with his own, and he soon lost his reputation for prodigality. In its place, he acquired a reputation as an honest, hardworking, and intelligent businessman.

His mistress thought so highly of Jack that she even made him an adviser in affairs of the heart. His advice was of little value to her, however, for she had already made up her mind, despite the difference in their years, to marry Jack himself. She tricked him into agreeing to further her marriage with an unknown suitor. When they arrived at the church, Jack found that he was to be the bridegroom; thus Jack became her husband and the master of her house and business.

The marriage went none too smoothly at first; despite her love for Jack, the woman did not like to be ordered about by the man who had once been her servant. At last, however, they came to an understanding and lived happily for several years, after which interval the good woman died, leaving Jack master of the business and rich in the world's goods.

Not long after his first wife died, Jack remarried, this time to a young woman. The wife was a poor choice, although he had the pick of the wealthy women of his class in the county. Not many months passed after the marriage, which had been a costly one, before James, the king of Scotland, invaded England while King Henry was in France. The justices of the county called upon Jack to furnish six men-at-arms to join the army raised by Queen Catherine. Jack chose to raise a company of a hundred and fifty foot and horse, which he armed and dressed at his own expense in distinctive liveries. Jack rode at the head of his men. Queen Catherine was greatly pleased and thanked Jack Winchcomb personally for his efforts, although his men were not needed to achieve the English victory at Flodden Field. In reward for his services, Jack received a chain of gold from the hands of the queen herself.

In the tenth year of his reign, King Henry made a trip through Berkshire. Jack Winchcomb introduced himself in a witty way to the king as the Prince of the Ants, who was at war with the Butterflies, a sally against Cardinal Wolsey. The king was vastly pleased and betook himself to Newbery, along with his train, where all were entertained by Jack at a fabulous banquet. After the banquet, the king viewed the weaving rooms and warehouses Jack owned. Upon his departure, the king wished to make Jack a knight, but the weaver refused the honor, saying he would rather be a common man and die, as he had lived, a clothier.

In his house, Jack of Newbery had a series of fifteen paintings, all denoting great men whose fathers had been tradesmen of one kind or another, including a portrait of Marcus Aurelius, who had been a clothier's son. Jack kept the pictures and showed them to his friends and workmen in an effort to encourage one and all to seek fame and dignity in spite of their humble offices in life.

Because of the many wars in Europe during King Henry's reign, trade in general was depleted. The lot of the clothiers and weavers was particularly bad; they joined together and sent leaders to London to appeal to the government on their behalf. One of the envoys they sent was Jack Winchcomb of Newbery. The king remembered Jack and in private audience assured him that measures would be taken to alleviate the hardships of the clothiers. Another man who had not forgotten Jack was the lord chancellor, Cardinal Wolsey. In an attempt to circumvent the king's promise, he had Jack and the other envoys thrown into prison for a few days. Finally, the duke of Somerset intervened and convinced the cardinal that the clothiers meant no harm.

Some time later, an Italian merchant named Benedick came to the house of Jack of Newbery to trade. While there, he fell in love with one of Jack's workers, a pretty young woman named Joan. She, however, paid no attention whatever to Benedick and asked a kinsman to tell the Italian not to bother her. When the kinsman did as he was asked, he angered the Italian, who vowed to make a cuckold of the kinsman for his pains. With gifts and fair speech, the Italian finally had his way with the weaver's wife, although the woman was immediately sorry. She told her husband, who had his revenge on the Italian by pretending that he would see to it that the Italian was permitted to go to bed with Joan. The Italian fell in with the scheme and found himself put to bed with a pig, whereupon all the Englishmen laughed at him so heartily that he left Newbery in shame.

Jack's second wife was a good young woman, but she sometimes erred in paying too much attention to her gossipy friends. At one time, a friend told her that she was wasting money by feeding the workmen so well. She cut down on the quantity and the quality of the food she served to the workers, but Jack, who remembered only too well the days when he had been an apprentice and journeyman forced to eat whatever was placed in front of him, became very angry and made her change her ways again. His workers were gratified when he said that his wife's friend was never to set foot in his house again.

At another time, Jack of Newbery went to London, where he found a draper who owed him five hundred pounds working as a porter. Learning that the man, through no fault of his own, had become a bankrupt, Jack showed his confidence in the man by setting him up in business again. Friends warned him that he was sending good money after bad, but Jack's judgment proved correct. The man paid back every cent and later became an alderman of London.

Jack was always proud of his workers. One time a knight, Sir George Rigley, seduced a pretty and intelligent young woman who worked for Jack. Jack vowed that he would make it right for her. He sent the woman, disguised as a rich widow, to London. Not knowing who she was, Sir George fell in love with her and married her. The knight was angry at first, but he soon saw the justice of the case and was very well pleased with the hundred pounds Jack gave the woman as a dower. Still knowing their places in life, Jack and his wife gave precedence to Sir George and his new lady, even in their own house.

Critical Evaluation:

Very little is known about the pamphleteer and balladeer Thomas Deloney, the English writer whose works became precursors of the English novel. By trade a silk weaver, probably of Norwich, Deloney wrote topical ballads and, through his pamphlets, took part in the religious controversies of the day. Even the date of his birth is not certain. Nevertheless, it seems certain that Deloney died early in 1600 after producing at least three "novels" (that is, episodic narratives) in a short but crowded life. He seems to have had more education than most weavers of the time would have had, and he translated from Latin into his uniquely vigorous English. The ballads of the day were the newspapers of the period, and Deloney's apprenticeship, like that of so many novelists, might be said to have been in journalism. That was probably how he learned to write concisely and how to choose popular subjects. He wrote broadside ballads on such subjects as the defeat of the Spanish Armada, great fires, the execution of traitors, and domestic tragedies, but current events were not Deloney's only ballad subjects. Using Holinshed and other sources, he drew on English history for subject matter. A collection of Deloney's ballads entitled *The Garland of Good Will* appeared in 1631, and earlier editions, like those of his prose fictions, were probably read out of existence. More than once, Deloney's pamphlets and more than fifty ballads put him in trouble with the authorities, even sending him for a time to Newgate Prison. One ballad in particular, which showed disrespect for the queen, caused him serious difficulties.

Though widely read, Deloney's novels were scorned by the university-educated writers of the day as mere plebeian romances from the pen of a balladmaker, and it was not until the twentieth century that his merits as a writer were recognized. His three novels, all approximately the same length, appeared between 1597 and 1600. *Jack of Newbery* was probably the first one to be written and published. Each novel was in praise of a trade: *Jack of Newbery* of weaving, *The Gentle Craft* of shoemaking, and *Thomas of Reading* of the clothiers' trade.

Deloney's stories contain excellent pictures of contemporary middle-class London life, and they introduce a variety of quaint characters. The realism of the novels, however, is only in matters of setting and dialogue; probability is disregarded and wish-fulfillment fantasy prevails, for members of the hardworking trade class are inevitably rewarded for their diligence with large fortunes. The tales are rich with humor and told in a straightforward manner, with the exception of "ornamental" language used in some romantic passages.

Deloney may have been commissioned by the cloth merchants to compose a life of one of their order. Jack of Newbery was a real person who lived in Newbery under Henry VIII, but his history is merely traditional. Deloney, however, knew the town and had a gift for elaborating a tale with circumstantial facts and humorous episodes.

Despite its popularity in its own day, Deloney's fiction probably had little real effect on the subsequent development of English prose fiction, which had to wait a hundred years and more for the geniuses of Daniel Defoe and Samuel Richardson to get it off the ground. Yet *Jack of Newbery* may be considered the first really dramatic novel in English. The fictions of Thomas Nash and Robert Greene are witty and satirical, but they do not have the dramatic plots of Deloney's work. Sir Philip Sidney's *Arcadia* (1581) and John Lyly's *Euphues* (1578-1580) were only minor influences, if any, on Deloney, who seems to have been more impressed by the Elizabethan stage than anything else (the widow and the other characters display a sense of rhetoric in their dialogue reminiscent of the stage). Deloney's view of life was essentially dramatic, and the people he wrote about in *Jack of Newbery* and his other novels are people of action, people who set out to accomplish material things.

Deloney's focus is on the details of everyday life. Love and marriage and money and food are the main topics of conversation. Materialist to his heart, he is fascinated by business and household matters. Like Charles Dickens, Deloney plunges into scenes that summarize dramatically an entire situation, painting a picture of an entire culture along the way. There are few irrelevant incidents in *Jack of Newbery*. The story of the middle-aged widow who falls in love with her young apprentice and of his subsequent adventures (including that concerning the king) is told with great enthusiasm. The widow is portrayed as a lusty, self-sufficient female, a woman who knows what she wants and goes after it. Jack is apparently as virtuous and industrious an apprentice as Ben Franklin, but he is not as innocent as he pretends and soon moves up in the world.

The tradesmen heroes such as Jack are idealized characters. Jack rises less from his own efforts than from those of the people around him. It almost seems that he is above certain efforts, resembling in this the king himself. The women in *Jack of Newbery* are the book's finest characterizations. In creating the gallery of female portraits, Deloney leaves behind him all of his rivals in the prose fiction of the time and approaches the best of Elizabethan stage comedy. Queen Catherine, the first Mistress Winchcomb, and other women in the story are colorful figures, alive with natural vitality. As the plots develop, the women remain in the midst of the action. Perhaps it is a man's world, but the wife seems to be responsible for her husband's success. Deloney knew and understood middle-class women and recorded their foibles and unique characteristics with a sharp eye and a precise pen. For the author, the good wife was one who was never idle but knew her place and did not "gad about." Thus Jack and his first wife made no headway at all until she decided to stay at home and manage the household.

The minor characters are well drawn, especially Randoll Pert. Recently out of debtor's prison, Pert becomes a porter to support his family. His description is delightful, and his antics add both comic and pathetic touches to the novel. The meeting of Jack and Pert at the Spread Eagle in London is superbly handled. The whole episode, including the part where Jack agrees not to collect five hundred pounds until Pert is sheriff of London, is excellent comedy.

Although the novel is episodic, it forms a coherent and dramatic whole and is filled with humorous scenes and witty dialogue. *Jack of Newbery* stands as a fine novel in its own right as well as the first example of its kind in English literature.

"Critical Evaluation" by Bruce D. Reeves

Bibliography:
Jusserand, J. J. *The English Novel in the Time of Shakespeare.* Translated by Elizabeth Lee. London: T. Fisher Unwin, 1890. The classic study of early narrative tradition in English. Establishes an invaluable context for understanding the traditions Deloney inherited, including those of medieval romance, travel literature, euphuism, and pastoral. Also discusses picaresque and realistic fiction and carries the study into the seventeenth century with the historical romance.
Lawlis, Merritt E. *Apology for the Middle Class: The Dramatic Novels of Thomas Deloney.* Bloomington: Indiana University Press, 1960. Discusses *Jack of Newbery* in light of its dialogue. Concludes that the novel is replete with realistic detail, but that realism combines with confessional, satirical, and humorous modes. Deloney also employed euphuistic and jestbook styles, but he prepared the way for later realist writers.

_____, ed. Introduction to *The Novels of Thomas Deloney*. Westport, Conn.: Greenwood Press, 1978. Places Deloney in his literary context, comparing his works to those by Ben Jonson, John Webster, and William Shakespeare. Deloney was the first in English prose fiction to employ dialect and malapropism. Includes an excellent index to all Deloney's novels.

Linton, Joan Pong. "*Jack of Newbery* and Drake in California: Narratives of English Cloth and Manhood." *ELH* 59, no. 1 (Spring, 1992): 23-51. Discusses the rise of the cloth trade in England as reflecting the transition from household economics to capitalism. Investigates Deloney's portrayal of the bourgeois hero, showing that it was not simply a nostalgic appropriation of the feudal model. Examines new ways in which Deloney defines manhood, showing that the novel participated in reshaping discourses of the self.

Wright, Eugene P. *Thomas Deloney*. Boston: Twayne, 1981. Includes an excellent introduction to *Jack of Newbery*, tracing its sources and plot and analyzing major themes. Contends that the novel is a cosmic apologia for workers in the cloth trade. Examines the relation of the novel to the contemporary social scene. Includes some discussion of narrative structure, character development, and imagery.

JACK SHEPPARD

Type of work: Novel
Author: William Harrison Ainsworth (1805-1882)
Type of plot: Picaresque
Time of plot: 1702-1724
Locale: London and environs
First published: 1839

> *Principal characters:*
> JACK SHEPPARD, a housebreaker and popular jailbreaker
> JOAN SHEPPARD, his mother
> OWEN WOOD, a London carpenter
> MRS. WOOD, his wife
> WINIFRED, their daughter
> SIR ROWLAND TRENCHARD, an aristocrat
> THAMES DARRELL, Sir Rowland's nephew and foster son of Owen Wood
> JONATHAN WILD, a thief-taker
> BLUESKIN, the devoted henchman of Jack Sheppard

The Story:

When Owen Wood went to offer his condolence to Joan, the widow of Tom Sheppard, who had been executed for stealing from Wood, he found the woman living in misery near the Old Mint, a haven for mendicants, thieves, and debtors. Joan told Wood that Van Galgebrok, a Dutch seaman and conjurer, had prophesied that her baby, Jack, would be executed as his father had been. The prophecy was based on the presence of a mole behind Jack's ear. Wood offered to take the infant out of the sordid environment in order to avert fulfillment of the prophecy, but the mother refused to part with her child.

Left alone with the infant while Joan went to the attic to get a key that her deceased husband had ordered given to Wood, the carpenter was accosted by a mob led by Sir Rowland Trenchard, in pursuit of a young man named Darrell. In the confusion, Jonathan Wild, a thief-taker, picked up the key that Joan was to return to Wood.

While a great storm raged, Darrell, the fugitive, with a baby in his arms, was again pursued by Sir Rowland. The chase continued to the flooded Thames, where Darrell was drowned after a struggle with Sir Rowland. On his way home, Wood rescued the baby from drowning. Some falling bricks saved him and the baby from Sir Rowland's wrath. Understanding little of the night's strange events, Wood took the child home with him. He named the boy Thames Darrell.

Twelve years later, Wood had taken Jack Sheppard as an apprentice in his carpenter shop, but he found the boy indifferent and listless in his work. Thames Darrell, reared by the Woods, was a model apprentice. A third child in the household was Winifred, Wood's daughter, a charming, beautiful girl. The three twelve-year-olds were very fond of one another.

Mrs. Wood, a termagant, had long berated her husband for his kindness to Jack and to Joan Sheppard, who lived modestly and respectably in Willesden. Following an episode in which Thames was injured while trying to prevent injury to Jack, Mrs. Wood reprimanded Jack and predicted that he would come to the same end that his father had met. Her chastisement was strong enough to arouse a spirit of criminality in Jack.

Jonathan Wild, who had hanged Tom Sheppard, boasted that he would hang the son as well. A resolute and subtle plotter, he worked slyly to bring about the boy's ruin. One day, he gave

Jack the key that he had found on the floor of the Mint twelve years before. It was Wood's master key; his hope was that Jack would rob the carpenter. Investigating Thames's parentage, Wild learned also that Thames was the child of Sir Rowland Trenchard's sister, Lady Alvira, whose husband Sir Rowland had drowned and whose child he had tried to destroy on the night of the great storm. Later, Lady Alvira had been forced to marry her cousin, Sir Cecil Trafford. Lady Trafford was dying, in which event the estates would revert to her brother if she left no other heir. Wild promised Sir Rowland that he would remove Thames in order that Sir Rowland could inherit the entire estate. As a hold over the nobleman, he told him also that he knew the whereabouts of Sir Rowland's other sister, Constance, carelessly lost in childhood to a gypsy.

Wild and Sir Rowland trapped Thames and Jack in Sir Rowland's house and accused them of robbery. Imprisoned, Jack and Thames made a jailbreak from Old Giles's Roundhouse, the first of innumerable and difficult escapes for Jack, and the last for Thames, who was sent off to sea to be disposed of by Van Galgebrok, the Dutch seaman and conjurer.

Jack was soon fraternizing with the patrons of the Mint, much to the pleasure of the derelicts, prostitutes, and gamblers who gathered there. It was in this environment that Joan saw Jack as the criminal he had become. When she went there to admonish her son to live a life of righteousness, she was answered by the taunts and sneers of the patrons, who reminded her that she had at one time enjoyed the life of the Mint. Jack, egged on by two prostitutes, spurned her pleas. Joan returned to her little home in Willesden to pray for Jack.

Jonathan Wild had rid himself of Thames, an obstacle in his scheme to get control of the fortune of Sir Montacute Trenchard, Thames's grandfather. He now set about to remove Sir Rowland as well. Plotting against the aristocrat, Wild had him arrested for treason in connection with a proposed Jacobite uprising against the crown.

Jack Sheppard used the key given to him by Wild to rob Wood's house. Caught and jailed in the Cage at Willesden as he was going to visit his mother, he soon escaped from the supposedly escape-proof structure. At his mother's house, Jack declared his undying love for her but announced that he could not return to honest living. Questioned by Joan as to how long he would wait to execute his threat against Jack, Wild, who had followed Jack to Willesden, answered boldly and confidently, "Nine."

Nine years later in 1742, Jack had become the most daring criminal and jailbreaker of the day. By that time, the Woods were affluent citizens living in Willesden. Joan Sheppard went insane because of worry over Jack and had been committed to Bedlam, a squalid, filthy asylum. Sir Rowland had been released from prison. Thames Darrell, thrown overboard by Van Galgebrok, had been picked up by a French fishing boat and carried to France, where he was employed by and subsequently commissioned by Philip of Orleans. Wild had continued in his pleasures of execution and in collecting keepsakes of his grisly profession.

Jack Sheppard and Blueskin, one of Wild's henchmen, quarreled with Wild because he would not help Thames Darrell get his rightful share of the estate that Sir Rowland had confiscated, and Blueskin became Jack's loyal henchman. The two robbed the Wood home again, Blueskin slashing Mrs. Wood's throat as she attempted to detain him.

Jack went to see his mother, a haggard, demented object of human wreckage, in chains and on a bed of straw. Wild followed Jack to the asylum. During a brawl, Wild struck Joan, and the blow restored the poor woman's senses. After her release from Bedlam, Wild divulged to Sir Rowland Trenchard the fact that Joan was his long-lost sister and an heir to the Trenchard estates.

Wild disposed of Sir Rowland by bludgeoning him and throwing him into a secret well. Sir Rowland, almost dead from the beating, attempted to save himself by catching hold of the floor around the opening of the well, but Wild trampled his fingers until the nobleman dropped to his watery grave. The thief-taker, still plotting to secure the Trenchard wealth, took Joan captive, but she killed herself rather than be forced into a marriage with the villain. At her funeral, Jack was apprehended after a jailbreak that required passage through six bolted and barred doors and the removal of innumerable stones and bricks from the prison walls.

In the meantime, Thames Darrell had returned from France to visit in the Wood household. Through information contained in a packet of letters that reached him in circuitous fashion, he learned that his father, the fugitive known only as Darrell, had been the French Marquis de Chatillon. His paternity proved, he inherited the Trenchard estates as well. He then married Winifred Wood.

After his seizure at his mother's funeral, Jack Sheppard was executed at Tyburn. As his body swung at the end of the rope, Blueskin cut him down in an attempt to save his life. A bullet from Wild's gun passed through Jack's heart. The body was buried beside Joan Sheppard in Willesden cemetery; in later years, the Marquis de Chatillon and his wife tended the grave and its simple wooden monument. Jonathan Wild eventually paid for his crimes; he was hanged on the same gallows to which he had sent Jack Sheppard and his father.

Critical Evaluation:

William Harrison Ainsworth began creative writing as a youth in Manchester and published poetry, short stories, and a novel while he was studying to be a lawyer. After abortive careers in publishing and law, success came to him in 1834 with *Rookwood,* a best-seller that made his name and that catapulted him to the top of London's literary scene. He followed this with *Crichton* (1837), which had respectable, although not large, sales.

Jack Sheppard, Ainsworth's third mature novel, was a spectacular success, eclipsing his first two novels in sales. The novel has its roots in the eighteenth century picaresque style of Tobias Smollett and Henry Fielding. This style moves the story along by recounting the adventures that a rogue has while traveling. The novel also follows in the tradition of the Newgate novel; its hero and namesake is a lowborn criminal. Finally, Ainsworth sets his novel in the past, rather than telling a story about his contemporary society.

These three novelistic elements had proven their popularity with the early Victorian reading public when Ainsworth set out to write. Edward Bulwer-Lytton, already an established author, added to his popularity with the novels *Paul Clifford* (1830) and *Eugene Aram* (1832), which featured sensitive and intelligent heroes driven by circumstances to a criminal life. Ainsworth's *Rockwood* uses the Newgate theme of a glamorous criminal hero as well as the gothic features of sensationalism and mystery. When the sales of *Crichton,* a historical romance set in the sixteenth century French court, failed to match those of *Rookwood,* Ainsworth returned to the more popular Newgate formula. Crime stories continued to be read in the late 1830's: Charles Dickens' *Oliver Twist* (1837-1839), for example, began appearing before *Jack Sheppard,* and for four months the two novels were serialized together in *Bentley's Miscellany.*

Jack Sheppard's chief strength lies in its tight plotting. Ainsworth devoted considerable effort to planning the structure of his early novels, and this effort resulted in works that are coherent and fast-paced, and in which all the loose ends of the story line are tied up. In the case of *Jack Sheppard,* Ainsworth faced the problem of how to tell a story spanning twenty-two years without turning it into an increasingly monotonous recitation of adventure after adventure. He solved the problem by focusing on three periods in his hero's life, which he calls epochs. There is a short prologue, occurring in 1703, which introduces the main characters; then a few weeks in 1715, during which Jack turns to a life of crime; and finally six months in 1724, when the most exciting action takes place. The epochs are tied together with linking narratives, and an epilogue resolves the fates of the surviving characters. This strategy is effective in maintaining the reader's interest, but it is a modification of the picaresque tradition's episodic nature.

Ainsworth took pains to research thoroughly the historical background of his novels. As a result, his books have a strong sense of setting; the descriptions of buildings, clothing and surroundings are vivid. His pages are populated with clearly drawn and believable historical figures. *Jack Shepherd* has all of these characteristics. Ainsworth was prepared, however, to change the past for the sake of his story. In this novel, for example, he turns the real Jonathan Wild, a historical figure of ambiguity, into an unmitigated villain.

Ainsworth shared with many of his contemporaries the belief that the characters in his works should be judged by the omniscient narrator. Using simple, black-and-white criteria, Ainsworth judges his characters as loyal or disloyal, brave or cowardly, noble or ignoble. Sometimes the author uses description to tell his readers what they should think of a character; sometimes he provides summary judgments. The author's voice is rarely unheard in Ainsworth's novels, whether as moral judge or as guide pointing out scenes. *Jack Sheppard* is no exception.

Ainsworth also wrote melodramatic episodes that were popular with his early nineteenth century audience. (*Jack Sheppard* was adapted for the stage in eight pirated versions— a measure of the novel's popularity.) He depicts the scene in which Wild throws Sir Rowland Trenchard into the well in especially lurid colors. Ainsworth fills his pages with examples of cruelty, violence, brutality, and murder. Sometimes this is effective and appropriate to the subject matter, but at other times it becomes an artistic flaw. Ainsworth focuses so closely on the details of Jonathan Wild's cruelty (a depth of cruelty unusual by Victorian standards) that he fails to explain why the character is so malevolent. His failure to explain makes the character seem less real. (Several of Ainsworth's later novels also include characters whose villainy has no motives.)

Jack Sheppard reflects the concerns and interests of the society that produced it. Its historical approach was attractive at a time when the study of history was very popular. Its concern with urban violence and criminality came at a time when worries about maintaining public order in the streets were at the forefront of public debate. Its melodramatic passages were to the taste of a generation that liked terror and the exaggerated display of emotions.

At the height of his popularity, Ainsworth earned the princely sum of £1,500 a novel from his publishers, in addition to his handsome income from editing *Bentley's Magazine* and *Ainsworth's Magazine*. Later generations of readers came to dislike Ainsworth's melodrama; after the mid-1850's, his novels ceased to sell and his career went into decline. Ainsworth knew that the tastes of his audience were changing, but he was unable to change with them. Instead, he continued to produce novels in the Newgate and picaresque traditions. When he at last began to write novels set in the nineteenth century, he was too late to regain his readership. By the end of his career, he was lucky to get as much as £50 for a novel.

"Critical Evaluation" by D. G. Paz

Bibliography:
Chandler, Frank W. *The Literature of Roguery*. Boston: Houghton Mifflin, 1907. Provides a very detailed overview of *Jack Sheppard*.
Hollingsworth, Keith. *The Newgate Novel, 1830-1847: Bulwer, Ainsworth, Dickens, and Thackeray*. Detroit: Wayne State University Press, 1963. The best study of the tradition of

stories about criminals. Places *Jack Sheppard* in that tradition, showing how Ainsworth is indebted to eighteenth century picaresque writers for many of his themes, images, and techniques. Contrasts that novel with Dickens' *Oliver Twist*.

Sanders, Andrew. *The Victorian Historical Novel, 1840-1880*. New York: St. Martin's Press, 1979. The best recent study of the historical novel in the nineteenth century. Explains the literary techniques that made *Jack Sheppard* Ainsworth's best novel.

Sutherland, J. A. *Victorian Novelists and Publishers*. Chicago: University of Chicago Press, 1976. Includes Ainsworth's literary output as a major example in his well-written, thoughtful, and detailed examination of how business relationships between novelists and publishers affected the novels. He shows how *Jack Sheppard* propelled Ainsworth's career.

Worth, George J. *William Harrison Ainsworth*. New York: Twayne, 1972. The only book-length critical study of Ainsworth's career. Describes the ways in which *Jack Sheppard* set the pattern of Ainsworth's writing style for the rest of his career.

JACQUES THE FATALIST AND HIS MASTER

Type of work: Novel
Author: Denis Diderot (1713-1784)
Type of plot: Picaresque
Time of plot: Mid-eighteenth century
Locale: Rural France
First published: Jacques le fataliste et son maître, 1796 (English translation, 1797)

Principal characters:
JACQUES, a servant and former soldier
THE MASTER (unnamed), Jacques' employer
THE NARRATOR, the ostensible author of the novel
THE CAPTAIN, Jacques' military commander, who influenced his fatalism
THE HOSTESS, the talkative wife of the innkeeper of the Great Stag
MME DE LA POMMERAYE, an aristocratic widow jilted by her lover
MARQUIS DES ARCIS, the unfaithful lover of Mme de la Pommeraye
DENISE, Jacques' most important love

The Story:

Jacques and his master were on a journey whose purpose and destination were unknown to the narrator. The latter even scolded the inquisitive reader for wanting to know such irrelevant information as how the travelers had met, what their names were, where they had come from, or where they were going. Instead, the narrator merely informed the reader that, as the novel opened, the master was not saying anything, and that Jacques was repeating, for his master's benefit, the fatalist creed he had learned from his captain. Everything that happens to us on earth, good or bad, Jacques explained, is foreordained, written on the great scroll "up above." As an appropriate example, his captain would always add that every bullet shot in battle had someone's name on it.

Jacques illustrated the truth of the captain's doctrine by noting the interconnected chain of events in his own life: He had joined the army as the result of a quarrel with his father; soon after, in his first battle, he received "his" bullet, which shattered his knee; and had it not been for that bullet, he would probably never have fallen in love. That remark aroused the master's curiosity, and he asked his servant to tell him the story of his loves to make their journey more interesting.

The telling of that story, like the recurrent discussions of the doctrine of fatalism, constitutes a running theme throughout the novel. During the entire eight days of travel recounted in the novel, Jacques kept trying to advance his story, but he was constantly interrupted and ultimately prevented from finishing it. The narrator provided a third running theme, periodically interrupting the narrative, as he did at the very outset, to engage the reader in discussions about storytelling in general and about the truth and morality of each story or interpolated tale that came up during the journey.

The narrator's account of the journey was frequently interrupted by unexpected events, by digressions in dialogue between Jacques and his master and between the narrator and the reader, and by the telling of apparently unrelated tales volunteered by individuals they encountered on their journey. Some of the tales were brief but bizarre, such as the account of the relationship between Jacques' captain and his best friend, a relationship based on their mutual passion for fighting duels with each other whenever possible. Others were more elaborate and often comical, such as the story of a Monsieur Gousse who, wishing to live with his mistress unimpeded by his wife, devised a scheme by which he brought suit against himself to force the release of his furniture from his own home; he lost the suit and ended in jail. Still other tales depicted the corruption in public morals, as in the tale of Father Hudson, a priest in charge of a monastery, who was considered by everyone in that town an excellent administrator of his institution but who successfully and in secret conducted a life of debauchery involving many women of the town.

The longest tale was told by the hostess of the Inn of the Great Stag, where Jacques and his master were obliged to stay for two nights because of inclement weather. The hostess, who was of peasant origin and exceptionally skillful as a storyteller, described her tale as that of a "strange marriage." The marriage was brought about by an elaborate plot of vengeance, patiently worked out by a widow, Mme de la Pommeraye, against the man who had jilted her, the Marquis des Arcis. Mme de la Pommeraye bribed a woman and her attractive daughter, whose circumstances had forced them both into a life of prostitution, to appear under assumed names in respectable company, where the Marquis des Arcis would be sure to make their acquaintance. The widow so maneuvered events that the smitten Marquis eagerly agreed to marry the daughter. Thereupon, Mme de la Pommeraye took her vengeance by informing the Marquis of the true background of the woman he had married. Though shocked and angry at first, the Marquis decided that he could be happy with his new wife. That decision left Mme de la Pommeraye feeling cheated of her revenge.

During the last two days of the eight-day journey, Jacques made rapid progress in the story of his loves, including the ribald tale of how he lost his virginity. He finally told of his encounter with Denise, who nursed him after his knee surgery and with whom he fell in love. During those two days, the master told Jacques the sad story of his one great love, whom he had lost to a rival. At last they came to a village, where the master wished to visit the son of the woman he had once wooed and lost. As the master dismounted from his horse, he fell to the ground. Jacques admitted that he had purposely loosened the strap, causing his master to fall. The incident led to the final debate between Jacques and his master on the question of fatalism and free will. In an unexpected outburst of violence, the master's victorious rival emerged from the house where his son was living and abruptly challenged the master to a duel. The rival was killed, the master fled, and Jacques was taken to jail as a material witness. Jacques' final reflections, in jail, were about the prospect of marrying his beloved Denise, followed by uneasy speculation as to whether he could escape the likely fate of all husbands; that of becoming a cuckold. Jacques then fell asleep, reminding himself of the futility of such speculation, since whatever befell him would have been written "up above."

Critical Evaluation:

Denis Diderot, a prominent member of the group of leading thinkers and writers in eighteenth century France known as The Philosophers, expressed so many radical and controversial ideas about society and human nature in his novels, plays, and philosophical dialogues, that he did not dare publish most of them out of fear of the stringent government censorship. Instead, he circulated his works in manuscript among his trusted friends. Long after his death in 1784, those friends arranged for publication of his works.

Jacques the Fatalist and His Master was composed during the 1770's, when Diderot was over sixty. It was an experimental work in which Diderot tried to fuse together his most controversial views about the writing of fiction, his boldest speculations about fatalism as a philosophy of life, and his opinions about the hypocritical conduct occasioned by the rigid moral values demanded by society. The experiment seemed designed to sum up his nearly forty years of reflection about life and literature. When it was finally published, in 1796, it was met with bewildered incomprehension at best and angry outrage at worst, for the text seemed almost perverse to its early readers in systematically thwarting their expectations of how a novel should be constructed and how characters should be shown to comport themselves. They were puzzled by the constant interruptions to the narrative thread that allowed no coherent story to emerge.

It was only in the last half of the twentieth century that readers both in France and elsewhere discovered and began to appreciate what it was that Diderot had attempted in this culminating composition of his career. The narrator's interruptive discussions with the reader were now read as Diderot's declaration that fiction must avoid facile invention of heroic adventures in the interests of truth, a principle requiring him to shatter conventions of the novel. By deliberately presenting his novel's characters as inconsistent, neither wholly good nor wholly evil, neither purely rational nor purely irrational, Diderot was attempting to indict conventional novels for their oversimplified, one-dimensional characters that lacked true humanity. As for the endless chain of digressions, diversions, and changing scenes that prevent the main narrative from moving forward, they were Diderot's means, borrowed from Laurence Sterne's *Tristram Shandy* (1759-1767), of reminding readers that no life unfolds logically and coherently, free of interruptions or diversions, and that society is too complex, varied, and unpredictable to conform to preconceived patterns, whether attributable to God or to novelists. In Diderot's view, a novel must display the chaotic and unpredictable procession of events, behaviors, and motivations that characterize real life. Finally, since his unorthodox narrative techniques evoke the reader's laughter, Diderot seems to be arguing that the spectacle of life's chaotic unpredictability is best seen as an occasion for joyous delight in the vastness of human diversity.

This theme of chaotic unpredictability is announced by the title, which places the servant first and the master last and gives the servant a name and the master none. By calling Jacques a fatalist, the title also hints at his possible superiority of intellect over the master, since Jacques has at least reflected about the meaning of existence. This intellectual superiority of Jacques' naturally produces moments of tension between the two, but the master's attempts to put Jacques "in his place" during these quarrels are always vehemently resisted, and each quarrel leads both back to the abiding truth that they need each other. This equality of mutual dependency was daring social doctrine for the times and is one of the ways in which this unusual novel can be seen as a forerunner of the French Revolution.

Unconventional moral themes are freely evoked in this novel, including the wide discrepancy in the sexual behavior of men and women; the moral teachings of the Catholic Church; the randomness with which sinful behavior is sometimes punished and sometimes rewarded; and the equally capricious consequence of virtue, which can produce suffering as often as it produces a clear conscience. The novel mocks Jacques' fatalism by demonstrating how it distorts reality and by pointing out that Jacques himself often contradicts its tenets. Yet the novel also shows that fatalism has the power to console Jacques and enable him to accept evils he cannot prevent.

The interpolated tales in this novel exemplify the chaotic disorder of everyday life and illustrate concretely the novel's running themes. Indeed, careful analysis of the most celebrated tale in *Jacques the Fatalist and His Master*, that of Mme de la Pommeraye and her unfaithful lover, the Marquis des Arcis, reveals that it touches directly on every major theme of the entire novel: the problematical relations between the sexes; the morally perverse consequences of sin and virtue; and the comical unpredictability of human motivation, among others. This astonishing single tale embodies, for the thoughtful reader, the essence of what Diderot hoped to achieve with his farewell novel, a joyous celebration of the variety of human nature and the stunning but delightful unpredictability of human conduct.

Murray Sachs

Bibliography:

Fellows, Otis. *Diderot*. Boston: Twayne, 1989. In this updated edition, the author was able to incorporate the latest research on Diderot in general and on *Jacques the Fatalist and His Master*, which is discussed in the penultimate chapter, in particular.

Furbank, P. N. *Diderot: A Critical Biography*. New York: Alfred A. Knopf, 1992. Fine biographical study, which includes critical analyses of Diderot's writings. The study of *Jacques the Fatalist and His Master* in chapter 24 offers astute treatment of the philosophical issues and of the theories about fiction.

Loy, J. Robert. *Diderot's Determined Fatalist*. New York: King's Crown Press, 1950. The pioneering study that first opened up Diderot's experimental novel to intelligent critical evaluation of its qualities as a work of art and as a profound philosophical discussion of the nature of human existence.

Vartanian, Aram. "*Jacques the Fatalist*: A Journey into the Ramifications of a Dilemma." In *Essays on Diderot and the Enlightenment in Honor of Otis Fellows*. Geneva: E. Droz, 1974. Exceptionally clear and elegant essay on Diderot's uncomfortable awareness of the contradictions in fatalism and determinism as philosophical systems.

Wilson, Arthur M. *Diderot*. New York: Oxford University Press, 1972. A thorough and scholarly critical study of Diderot's life and works. Chapter 46 has a fine discussion of *Jacques the Fatalist and His Master* as an exposition of Diderot's views on determinism and humanism.

JANE EYRE
An Autobiography

Type of work: Novel
Author: Charlotte Brontë (1816-1855)
Type of plot: Domestic realism
Time of plot: 1800
Locale: Northern England
First published: 1847

Principal characters:
  JANE EYRE, an orphan
  MRS. REED, the mistress of Gateshead Hall
  BESSIE LEAVEN, a nurse
  EDWARD ROCHESTER, the owner of Thornfield
  ST. JOHN RIVERS, a young clergyman
  MARY and
  DIANA RIVERS, his sisters

The Story:

Jane Eyre was an orphan whose parents had died when she was a baby, at which time she had passed into the care of Mrs. Reed of Gateshead Hall. Mrs. Reed's husband, now dead, had been the brother of Jane Eyre's mother; on his deathbed, he had directed his wife to look after the orphan as after her own three children. At Gateshead Hall, Jane knew ten years of neglect and abuse. One day, a cousin knocked her to the floor. When she fought back, Mrs. Reed punished her by sending her to the gloomy room where Mr. Reed had died. There Jane lost consciousness, and the experience caused a dangerous illness from which she was nursed slowly back to health by sympathetic Bessie Leaven, the Gateshead Hall nurse.

No longer wishing to keep her unwanted charge in the house, Mrs. Reed made arrangements for Jane's admission to Lowood School. Early one morning, Jane left Gateshead Hall without farewells and was driven fifty miles by stage to Lowood, her humble possessions in a trunk beside her.

At Lowood, Jane was a diligent student and well-liked by her superiors, especially by Miss Temple, one of the teachers, who had refused to accept without proof Mrs. Reed's low estimate of Jane's character. During the period of Jane's schooldays at Lowood, an epidemic of fever that caused many deaths among the girls led to an investigation, after which there were improvements at the institution. At the end of her studies, Jane was retained as a teacher but she grew weary of her life at Lowood and advertised for a position as a governess. She was engaged by Mrs. Fairfax, housekeeper at Thornfield, near Millcote.

At Thornfield, the new governess had only one pupil, Adele Varens, a ward of Jane's employer, Mr. Edward Rochester. From Mrs. Fairfax, Jane learned that Mr. Rochester traveled much and seldom came to Thornfield. Jane was pleased with the quiet country life, with the beautiful old house and gardens, the book-filled library, and her own comfortable room.

While she was out walking one afternoon, Jane met Mr. Rochester for the first time, going to his aid after his horse had thrown him. She found her employer a somber, moody man, quick to change in his manner and brusque in his speech. He commended her work with Adele, however, and confided that the girl was the daughter of a French dancer who had deceived him and deserted her daughter. Jane felt that this experience alone could not account for Mr. Rochester's moody nature.

Mysterious happenings at Thornfield puzzled Jane. Alarmed by a strange noise one night, she found Mr. Rochester's door open and his bed on fire. When she attempted to arouse the household, he commanded her to keep quiet about the whole affair. She learned that Thornfield had a strange tenant, a woman who laughed like a maniac and stayed in rooms on the third floor of the house. Jane believed that this woman was Grace Poole, a seamstress employed by Mr. Rochester.

Mr. Rochester attended many parties in the neighborhood, where he was obviously paying court to Blanche Ingram, daughter of Lady Ingram. One day, the inhabitants of Thornfield were informed that Mr. Rochester was bringing a party of houseguests home with him. The fashionable Miss Ingram was among the party guests. During the house party, Mr. Rochester called Jane to the drawing room, where the guests treated her with the disdain they thought her humble position deserved. To herself, Jane had already confessed her interest in her employer, but it seemed to her that he was interested only in Blanche Ingram. One evening, while Mr. Rochester was away from home, the guests played charades. At the conclusion of the game, a Gypsy fortune-teller appeared to read the palms of the lady guests. During her interview with the Gypsy, Jane discovered that the so-called fortune-teller was Mr. Rochester in disguise. While the guests were still at Thornfield, a stranger named Mason arrived to see Mr. Rochester on business. That night, Mason was mysteriously wounded by the inhabitant of the third floor. The injured man was taken away secretly before daylight.

One day, Robert Leaven came from Gateshead to tell Jane that Mrs. Reed, now on her deathbed, had asked to see her former ward. Jane returned to her aunt's home. The dying woman gave Jane a letter, dated three years earlier, from John Eyre in Madeira, who had asked that his niece be sent to him for adoption. Mrs. Reed confessed that she had written back informing him that Jane had died in the epidemic at Lowood. The sin of keeping the news of her relatives from Jane—news that would have meant relatives, adoption, and an inheritance—had become a burden on the conscience of the dying woman.

Jane went back to Thornfield, which she now looked on as her home. One night in the garden, Edward Rochester embraced her and proposed marriage. Jane accepted and made plans for a quiet ceremony in the village church. She also wrote to her uncle in Madeira, explaining Mrs. Reed's deception and telling him she was to marry Mr. Rochester. Shortly before the date set for the wedding, Jane had a harrowing experience, awakening to find a strange, repulsive-looking woman in her room. The intruder tried on Jane's wedding veil and then ripped it to shreds. Mr. Rochester tried to persuade Jane that the whole incident was her imagination, but in the morning she found the torn veil in her room. When she and Mr. Rochester were saying their vows at the church, a stranger spoke up and declared the existence of an impediment to the marriage. He presented a document, signed by the Mr. Mason who had been wounded during his visit to Thornfield, which stated that Edward Fairfax Rochester had married Bertha Mason, Mr. Mason's sister, in Spanish Town, Jamaica, fifteen years earlier. Mr. Rochester admitted the fact, and then conducted the party to the third-story chamber at Thornfield. There they found the attendant Grace Poole and her charge, Bertha Rochester, a raving maniac. Bertha Rochester was the woman Jane had seen in her room.

Jane felt that she must leave Thornfield at once. She notified Mr. Rochester and left early the next morning, using all of her small store of money for the coach fare. Two days later, she was set down on the north midland moors. Starving, she actually had to beg for food. Finally, she was befriended by the Reverend St. John Rivers and his sisters, Mary and Diana, who took Jane in and nursed her back to health. Assuming the name of Jane Elliot, she refused to divulge any of her history except her connection with the Lowood institution. St. John Rivers eventually found a place for her as mistress in a girls' school.

Shortly afterward, St. John Rivers received word from his family solicitor that John Eyre had died in Madeira, leaving Jane Eyre a fortune of twenty thousand pounds. Because Jane had disappeared under mysterious circumstances, the lawyer was trying to locate her through the next of kin, St. John Rivers. Jane's identity was revealed through her connection with Lowood School, and she learned, to her surprise, that St. John and his sisters were really her cousins. She insisted on sharing her inheritance with them.

When St. John decided to go to India as a missionary, he asked Jane to go with him as his wife—not because he loved her, as he frankly admitted, but because he admired her and wanted her services as his assistant. Jane felt indebted to him for his kindness and aid, but she hesitated and asked for time to reflect.

One night, while St. John was awaiting her decision, she dreamed that Mr. Rochester was calling her name. The next day, she returned to Thornfield by coach. She found the mansion gutted—a burned and blackened ruin. Neighbors told her that the fire had broken out one stormy night, set by the madwoman, who died while Mr. Rochester was trying to rescue her from the roof of the blazing house. Mr. Rochester had been blinded during the fire and now lived at Ferndean, a lonely farm some miles away. Jane Eyre went to him at once and shortly after married him. Two years later, Mr. Rochester regained the sight of one eye, so that he was able to see his first child when it was placed in his arms.

Critical Evaluation:

Charlotte Brontë was always concerned that her work be judged on its own merits and not because of her sex. She continued to use her pseudonym even after her authorship was revealed and in her letters often referred to herself as Currer Bell. *Jane Eyre*, her first published novel, has been called feminine because of the Romanticism and deeply felt emotions of the heroine-narrator. It would probably be more correct to point to the feminist qualities of the novel, as reflected in a heroine who refuses to be placed in the traditional female position of subservience and who disagrees with her superiors, stands up for her rights, and ventures creative thoughts. More important, Jane Eyre is a narrator who comments on the role of women in society and the greater constraint imposed on them. Those feminine emotions often ascribed to in the character of Jane are found as well in Rochester, and the continued popularity of this work must suggest the enduring human quality of these emotions.

Brontë often discussed the lack of passion in her contemporaries' work and especially in that of Jane Austen, about whom she said, "Her business is not half so much with the human heart as with the human eyes, mouth, hands and feet." Coldness, detachment, excessive analysis, and critical distance were not valued by Brontë. The artist must be involved in her subject, she believed, and must have a degree of inspiration not to be rationally explained. Such a theory of art is similar to that of the Romantic poets, an attitude no longer entirely popular by the mid-nineteenth century.

In *Jane Eyre*, Brontë chose the point of view of a first-person narrator, which suited both her subject matter and her artistic theory, The story is told entirely through the eyes of the heroine, a technique that enabled Brontë to deliver the events with an intensity that involved the reader in the passions, feelings, and thoughts of the heroine. A passionate directness characterizes Jane's narration: Conversations are rendered in direct dialogue, and actions are given just as they occurred, with little analysis of event or character. In a half dozen key scenes, Brontë shifts to present tense instead of the immediate past, so that Jane Eyre narrates the event as if it were happening at the very moment. After Jane flees Thornfield and Rochester, when the coachman puts her out at Whitcross where her fare runs out, she narrates to the moment: "I am alone . . . I am absolutely destitute." After a long description of the scene around her and her analysis of her situation, also narrated in the present tense, she reverts to the more usual past tense in the next paragraph: "I struck straight into the heath." Such a technique adds to the immediacy of the novel and further draws the reader into the situation.

Like all of Brontë's heroines, Jane Eyre has no parents and no family that accepts or is aware of her. She, like Lucy Snowe in *Villette* (1853) and Caroline Helstone in *Shirley* (1849), leads a life cut off from society, since family was the means for a woman to participate in society and community. Lacking such support, Jane had to face her problems alone. Whenever she forms a close friendship (Bessie at Gateshead, Helen Burns and Miss Temple at Lowood, Mrs. Fairfax at Thornfield), she discovers that nonkinship ties can be broken easily by higher authority, death, or marriage. Cutting her heroines off so radically from family and community gave Brontë the opportunity to make her women independent and to explore the Romantic ideal of individualism.

Jane Eyre is a moral tale, akin to a folk or fairy tale, with hardly any ambiguities of society, character, or situation. Almost all of Jane's choices are morally straightforward, and her character—though she grows and matures—does not change significantly. Her one difficult choice is to refuse to become Rochester's mistress and leave Thornfield. That choice was difficult precisely because she had no family or friends to influence her with their disapproval. No one would have been hurt if she had consented; that is, no one but Jane herself, and it is her own self-love that helps her to refuse.

Like a fairy tale, *Jane Eyre* is full of myth and superstition. Rochester often calls Jane his "elf," "changeling," or "witch"; there are mysterious happenings at Thornfield; Jane is inclined to believe the gypsy fortune-teller (until Rochester reveals himself) and often thinks of the superstitions she has heard; and the weather often presages mysterious or disastrous events. Most important, at the climax of the story, when Jane is about to consent to be the unloved wife of St. John Rivers, she hears Rochester calling her—at precisely the time, readers learn later, that he had in fact called to her. This event is never explained rationally and readers must accept Jane's judgment that it was a supernatural intervention.

Many symbolic elements pervade the novel. Often something in nature symbolizes an event or person in Jane's life. The most obvious example is the chestnut tree, which is split in two by lightning on the night that Jane accepts Rochester's marriage proposal, signifying the rupture of their relationship. The two parts of the tree, however, remain bound, as do Jane and Rochester despite their physical separation.

The novel is also full of character foils and parallel situations. Aunt Reed at Gateshead is contrasted with Miss Temple at Lowood; the Reed sisters at the beginning are contrasted with the Rivers sisters—cousins all—at the end; Rochester's impassioned proposal and love is followed by St. John's pragmatic proposition. Foreshadowing is everywhere in the book, so that seemingly chance happenings gain added significance as the novel unfolds, and previous events are echoed in those that follow. Because of the novel's artful structure and carefully chosen point of view, as well as the strong and fascinating character of Jane herself, *Jane Eyre*, if not a typical Victorian novel, remains a classic among English novels.

"Critical Evaluation" by Margaret McFadden-Gerber

Bibliography:
Gilbert, Sandra, and Susan Gubar. "Dialogue of Self and Soul in Charlotte Brontë's *Jane Eyre*." In *The Madwoman in the Attic: The Woman Writer in the Nineteenth Century Literary Imagination*. New Haven, Conn.: Yale University Press, 1979. A seminal text that examines Jane's self-construction as a visionary and an intellectual in a period when women's roles were limited to those of wife, mother, daughter, and governess.

Imlay, Elizabeth. *Charlotte Brontë and the Mysteries of Love: Myth and Allegory in "Jane Eyre."* New York: St. Martin's Press, 1989. Discusses the relationships in the novel, focusing particularly on that between Jane and Rochester. Looks at uses of myth and symbol in Brontë's depiction of relationships.

Kadish, Doris Y. *The Literature of Images: The Narrative Landscape from "Julie" to "Jane Eyre."* New Brunswick, N.J.: Rutgers University Press, 1987. Discusses the web of image and metaphor that governs *Jane Eyre* and transforms this realist novel.

London, Bette. "The Pleasures of Submission: *Jane Eyre* and the Production of the Text." *English Literary History* 58, no. 1 (Spring, 1991): 195-214. A look at the historical period when the novel was written. Specifically addresses the portrayals of women in nineteenth century fiction by women writers.

Nestor, Pauline. *Charlotte Brontë's "Jane Eyre."* New York: St. Martin's Press, 1992. A full-length study of historical, political, and formal aspects of the novel.

Peters, Joan D. "Finding a Voice: Toward a Woman's Discourse of Dialogue in the Narration of *Jane Eyre*." *Studies in the Novel* 23, no. 2 (Summer, 1991): 217-236. Discusses the instabilities, difficulties, and resistances of the narrative voice in the novel.

JASON AND THE GOLDEN FLEECE

Type of work: Folklore
Author: Unknown
Type of plot: Adventure
Time of plot: Antiquity
Locale: Greece
First published: Unknown

> *Principal characters:*
> JASON, the prince of Iolcus
> KING PELIAS, his uncle
> CHIRON, the centaur who reared Jason
> ÆETES, the king of Colchis
> MEDEA, his daughter

The Story:

In ancient Greece there lived a prince named Jason, son of a king who had been driven from his throne by a wicked brother named Pelias. To protect the boy from his cruel uncle, Jason's father took him to a remote mountaintop where he was raised by Chiron the Centaur, who many say was half man and half horse. When Jason had grown to young manhood, Chiron the Centaur told him that Pelias had seized his father's crown. Jason was instructed to go and win back his father's kingdom.

Pelias had been warned to beware of a stranger who came with one foot sandaled and the other bare. It happened that Jason had lost one sandal in a river he crossed as he came to Iolcus, where Pelias ruled. When Pelias saw the lad, he was afraid and plotted to kill him; but he pretended to welcome Jason. At a great feast he told Jason the story of the golden fleece.

In days past, a Greek king called Athamus banished his wife and took another, a beautiful but wicked woman who persuaded Athamus to kill his own children. A golden ram swooped down from the skies, however, and carried the children away. The girl slipped from his back and fell into the sea, but the boy came safely to the country of Colchis. There the boy let the king of Colchis slaughter the ram for its golden fleece. The gods were angered by these happenings and placed a curse on Athamus and all of his family until the golden fleece should be returned from Colchis.

As Pelias told Jason the story, he could see that the young prince was stirred, and he was not surprised when Jason vowed that he would bring back the golden fleece. Pelias promised to give Jason his rightful throne when he returned from his quest, and Jason trusted Pelias and agreed to the terms. He gathered about him many great heroes of Greece: Hercules, the strongest and bravest of all heroes; Orpheus, whose music soothed savage beasts; Argus, who with the help of Juno built the beautiful ship *Argo*; Zetes and Calais, sons of the North Wind, and many other brave men.

They encountered great dangers on their journey. One of the heroes was drawn under the sea by a nymph and was never seen again by his comrades. They visited Salmydessa, where the blind King Phineus was surrounded by harpies, loathsome creatures, with the faces of women and the bodies of vultures. Zetes and Calais chased the creatures across the skies, and when the heroes left they had restored peace to the old king.

Phineus had warned the heroes about the clashing rocks through which they must pass. As they approached the rocks, they were filled with fear, but Juno held the rocks back and they sailed past the peril. They rowed along the shore until they came to the land of Colchis.

Æetes, the king of Colchis, swore never to give up the treasure, but Jason vowed that he and his comrades would do battle with Æetes. Then Æetes consented to yield the treasure if Jason would yoke to the plow two wild, fire-breathing bulls and sow a field with dragon's teeth. When a giant warrior sprang from each tooth, Jason had to slay each one. Jason agreed to the trial.

Æetes had a beautiful daughter Medea, who had fallen in love with the handsome Jason, and she brewed a magic potion that gave Jason godlike strength; thus it was that he was able to tame the wild bulls and slay the warriors. Æetes promised to bring forth the fleece the next day, but Jason saw the wickedness in the king's heart and warned his comrades to have the *Argo* ready to sail.

In the night, Medea secured the seven golden keys that unlocked the seven doors to the cave where the golden fleece hung, and she led Jason to the place. Behind the seven doors, he found a hideous dragon guarding the treasure. Medea's magic caused the dragon to fall asleep, and Jason seized the fleece. It was so bright that it turned night into day.

Fearing for her life, Medea sailed away from her father's house with Jason and the other heroes. After many months, they reached their homeland, where Jason placed the treasure at the feet of Pelias. The fleece, however, was no longer golden. Pelias was wrathful and swore not to give up his kingdom, but in the night the false king died. Afterward, Jason wore the crown, and the enchantress Medea reigned by his side.

Critical Evaluation:

The journey of the Argonauts may well be one of the oldest of Greek adventure myths. Homer alludes to it, and it is placed in the generation preceding the Trojan War; the roster of heroes includes Telamon, the father of Ajax, and Peleus, the father of Achilles. No doubt its folk tale theme of a sea journey to inhospitable lands in quest of a valuable prize was the model for the adventures of Odysseus, Hercules, Theseus, and others. There are strong resemblances between this tale and such elements in later stories as the dragon-guarded golden apples of the Hesperides in the eleventh labor of Hercules; the beautiful young princess who aids her father's enemy and is eventually cast aside, as was Ariadne by Theseus; Odysseus' journey to Aeaea, the island of Circe; a kingdom usurped, as was that of Hercules, and regained with a vengeance, as that of Odysseus. Typical of such tales is the accomplishment of an impossible task and the confrontation with death and the fantastically inhuman, all to prove nobility of birth and the right to reign. The retrieval of the fleece is therefore not the subject of this myth but the occasion; it is a device by which the hero becomes involved with the heroic. Furthermore, the entire expedition would not have come about were it not for Hera, whom Pelias had refused to honor. Her tortuous plan was to have Jason sent off to Colchis so that he would bring back with him the sorceress Medea, who would kill Pelias; Medea did just that, by convincing the old king's daughters to kill him so that she might rejuvenate him.

Despite the age of this myth, the earliest extensive literary account is found in Pindar's *Pythian Ode 4* (462 B.C.E.), and it was not until the third century B.C.E. that the myth received formal expanded treatment by Apollonius Rhodius, who revived the epic genre. His romantic effort, the *Argonautica*, was not only the model for other versions of the quest but also greatly influenced Roman epic poets, notably Vergil.

Apollonius' work, despite its obvious stylistic and structural inferiority to Homer's poems, nevertheless contains some very charming descriptions and characterizations. The first two books are devoted to the voyage from Thessaly to Colchis. Among the more prominent episodes are the Argonauts' landfall at Lemnos, where they are entertained for a year by the women who, having once been plagued with a malodor, killed their men because they had taken Thracian brides. Reaching the Asian mainland, they soon were forced to fight six-armed giants and were involved in two other battles before rescuing the prophet-king Phineus. Book 3 contains the arrival at Colchis and Medea's falling in love with Jason. Unlike the *Iliad* (c. 800 B.C.E.), in which Hera and Athena are at odds with Aphrodite, the *Argonautica* portrays them as allies who instigate the mischievous Eros, or Cupid, to fire a shaft into the princess Medea. Torn between filial loyalty and her uncontrollable passion, she soon yields to love. Her escape with Jason and their eventual arrival at Iolchus in book 4, include the murder of Medea's brother Absyrtus and the necessary expiation on Circe's island, Aeaea. Apollonius had Jason kill Absyrtus through Medea's treachery; in the earlier version, Medea herself murders her brother and scatters the butchered remains over the sea in order to delay the pursuing Colchians, who must gather the pieces for burial.

The exact return route supposedly taken by the Argonauts was disputed in ancient times. Doubtless the various versions were based on the trade routes begun in the Mycenaean age. Apollonius takes the Argonauts from the mouth of the river Phasis on the Black Sea to the Ister (Danube), overland to the Adriatic, where they are confronted by Absyrtus; then to the Eridanus (possibly the Po) and the Rhone, to the Tyrrhenian Sea and Circe's island. Other accounts include a return using the same route by which they came; sailing east up the Phasis to the world-encircling river Ocean, then southwest to Africa and overland to the Mediterranean (Pindar's version); and sailing up the Phasis, through Russia, and over northern sea routes past Britain and through the Pillars of Hercules. Apollonius includes in the journey the perils of the sirens, Scylla and Charybdis, and the Wandering Rocks; Medea and Jason, like Odysseus, are given refuge in hospitable Phaeacia on the west coast of Greece, but only after the young lovers marry to void Æetes' claim to his daughter.

The myth receives brief attention in Ovid's *Metamorphoses* (c. 8) and would have been retold at length in the Latin hexameters of the first century Valerius Flaccus, but his *Argonautica* is incomplete. Jason's adventure, nevertheless, is included in Apollodorus' *The Library*, the invaluable second century Greek collection of myths. Like most myths, the search for the fleece was subject to the rationalizing minds of classical writers; the geographer Strabo theorized, for example, that the Argonauts were an expedition in search of alluvial gold. Whatever the origins of the myth, it stands out as a magnificent prototype of the perilous search for the marvelous prize. In a sense, this search is also the theme of the Trojan cycle, in which the greatest figures of a distant glorious age attempt to retrieve the most beautiful mortal woman. The voyage of the *Argo*, however, like the wanderings of Odysseus, belongs to that entertaining genre, that attends to the unnatural, the exotic, the romantic. Jason-like heroes are not only seen in the many local legends of ancient Greece but also in history, as in Alexander's oriental conquests, which were subsequently romanticized. Comparisons may be drawn between Jason and Celtic heroes, and between the fleece and the grail. In 1867, William Morris revived the original myth with a seven-thousand-line Victorian epic entitled *The Life and Death of Jason*, and in 1944 Robert Graves wrote a novel about the search for the fleece, *Hercules, My Shipmate*.

Classical authors seemed to be more concerned with Medea than with Jason. Euripides' masterpiece tragedy *Medea* (431 B.C.E.) deals with Jason's cruel rejection of the woman who sacrificed all—even murdered—for him. Her vengeance, to deprive Jason of the things he loves most, requires that she kill not only the girl he intends to marry but also Jason and Medea's sons. Her refuge in Athens as the wife of the aging King Aegeus is brief; she escapes to Colchis after an unsuccessful attempt to poison Theseus. Nothing is known of her death. Jason, however, overcome with grief, loneliness, and shame, returned to the rotting hulk of the *Argo*, which he had beached at Corinth. There he died after being struck by a falling beam.

"Critical Evaluation" by E. N. Genovese

Bibliography:
Bacon, Janet Ruth. *The Voyage of the Argonauts*. Boston: Small, Maynard, 1925. Excellent study of the story of Jason and the golden fleece. Follows the Argonauts through their extended history with literary evidence and illustrations. Excellent interpretations of the myth, including maps of voyage and art illustrations.
Deforest, Mary Margolies. *Apollonius' "Argonautica."* Leiden, The Netherlands: E. J. Brill, 1994. Extensive bibliography and detailed index. Examines the significance of the Golden Fleece in the myth of Jason as well as relationships between the characters. Symbolic comparison of Medea to the golden fleece.
Graves, Robert. *Greek Myths*. Rev. ed. 2 vols. London: Penguin Books, 1973. Cites the sources and various interpretations of the themes involved in the myth. Excellent companion to the historical study of the myth through literature. Details most of the major Greek myths and identifies the history and relationships of the gods and heros.
Pinsent, John. *Greek Mythology*. New York: Peter Bedrick Books, 198. Includes a number of Greek art illustrations and interprets the meaning of the myth through the symbols found in literature and art.
Severin, Tim. *The Jason Voyage*. New York: Simon & Schuster, 1985. Follows the voyage of the Argonauts with a twentieth century crew. Captures the atmosphere and time of Jason's voyage. Provides excellent archeological details, evidence, and explanation of the origins of the myth. Final chapter examines the reasons behind the timelessness of the legend of the golden fleece.

JEALOUSY

Type of work: Novel
Author: Alain Robbe-Grillet (1922-   )
Type of plot: Antistory
Time of plot: Probably the early 1950's
Locale: Indeterminate
First published: La Jalousie, 1957 (English translation, 1959)

> *Principal characters:*
> THE UNNAMED NARRATOR, the owner of a banana plantation
> A . . . ., the narrator's wife
> FRANCK, the owner of a neighboring plantation

The Story:

In the usual understanding of the term, there is no story in this novel. The author's method of narration is deliberately designed to challenge conventional reader expectations. Events in the novel do not follow in a straight line from beginning to end; the pattern is more a convolution of episodes repeated again and again with minor variations, out of which there emerges a partially realized story.

The narrator suspected his wife, A . . . ., of infidelity with their neighbor Franck. The narrator and Franck owned banana plantations; they and their wives formed a little enclave of French colonialism in the tropics, with common concerns about crops, the weather, and the unreliability of native workers. Most important, they shared emotions of boredom and loneliness. For Franck and A . . . ., the consequence was an affair—at least, so it seemed. For the narrator, the consequence was the intense jealousy produced by his suspicions.

Franck and his wife, Christiane, had been frequent dinner guests of the narrator and his wife in the past. Christiane seemed not to get along well with A . . . .; that, together with her child's reported illness and her own vague ailments, kept her away, although her husband continued to visit. At one of these dinners, Franck mentioned that he had to go to town the next week to see about various business matters, principally getting a new truck. The subject of motor trouble had come up in earlier conversations, along with the difficulty of obtaining adequate repair and the unreliability of native drivers. Franck suggested that A . . . . might like to accompany him for a day of shopping. She gladly accepted; they agreed to leave at 6:30 in the morning and be back by night.

Franck and A . . . . left at the agreed time, but did not return by nightfall. Instead, they showed up the next day, saying that car trouble had forced them to spend the night in town while waiting for a repair. This excuse seemed untrue because of the glances the two exchanged, Franck's suspiciously casual manner, the absence of purchases by A . . . ., and their double-entendres (for example, Franck asked A . . . . to forgive him for being a "bad mechanic," with the implication that their sexual encounter was not as thrilling as expected).

The narrator spied on his wife's behavior several times. Once he observed her from the veranda, through the bedroom window secretly writing a letter—presumably to Franck. Other times he watched her comb her hair, get into Franck's car to go to town, and get out of the car upon returning with a suggestive lingering at the car window. He also watched the work of a gang of laborers repairing a small bridge, and observed his property, including the rows of banana trees.

The narrator's observations were embedded within his constant role as voyeur—a not-entirely-objective observer, a roving camera eye whose meticulously objective impressions carried an emotional subtext that charged inconsequential events with latent meanings. The most pointed of these was the killing of a nasty-looking, poisonous centipede. At one of Franck's dinner visits, the centipede was noticed crawling up a wall; A . . . . was horrified by it, and Franck immediately killed it with a rolled-up napkin, leaving an oddly-shaped stain on the wall. This story was told several times with minor variations—in one of which, it occurs not in the narrator's house, but in the hotel room where A . . . . and Franck spent the night. It is still from the jealous husband's subjective point of view that this version of the episode is related in the form of a fantasy. The narrator has not proved his suspicions of his wife's adultery. The novel ends very much as it began, with nothing really resolved.

Critical Evaluation:

A synopsis of *Jealousy* tends to sound strange, with good reason. The type of novel exemplified by *Jealousy*, and of which Alain Robbe-Grillet has been both the principal theorist and practitioner, is termed "new novel" or "antinovel." Even considering the innovations in the novel by major twentieth century novelists such as James Joyce, Franz Kafka, and William Faulkner, the new novel is, in many ways, without precedent. From the 1950's through the 1970's especially, it represented an extremely provocative, internationally influential approach to the craft of fiction by French writers such as Michel Butor, Natalie Sarraute, Claude Simon, and Robbe-Grillet.

Born in 1922, Robbe-Grillet came to intellectual maturity in a mid-twentieth century France divided by vicious political antagonisms and shattered by war, but also animated by tremendous artistic and intellectual creative activity, such as the Theater of the Absurd, abstract expressionist painting, and existentialist philosophy—especially the latter. Existentialism's main assertions—that the human is a radically free agent; the universe has no meaning; "meaning" itself is a perceptual construct validated only by action—became articles of faith for the French intellectual Left during the 1940's and 1950's. Many writers derived themes of alienation or despair from such premises, but for Robbe-Grillet, the meaninglessness of life is simply a neutral fact. Meaning is the pattern imposed by consciousness upon experience; reality cannot be understood apart from our perceptions of it, which are always subjective no matter how objective they may seem. For Robbe-Grillet, the role of the novelist is not to seek out truths on such subjects as life, character, or morals, but to challenge the reader's uncritical acceptance of such myths. The meaning of a Robbe-Grillet novel is to be sought in the techniques by which he subverts the very notion of meaning while creating an intriguing fictional structure that shimmers like a mirage with enigmatic significance.

The most basic and profound of these techniques is the fragmentation of linear time-sequence. This is a central feature of all his fiction, and is especially noticeable in *Jealousy*. Narrated entirely in present tense, the action consists of a repetitive pattern of the narrator's principal impressions: A . . . .'s brushing her hair and writing a letter; several possibly flirtatious interactions between her and Franck at dinner and lunch; her departure and return; and the killing of the centipede, among the more important. Repeated in the manner of a fugue, with small but noticeable variations, they describe a circle, or better a Moebius strip, in which the events of the beginning, middle, and end are parts of a constantly unfolding present.

Complementing the absence of a linear plot is the foregrounding of minor incidents and details. Among the many examples, the killing of the centipede is the most significant: Trivial though it is, this is the most dramatic and memorable event in the novel—the one outbreak of intuitive action, or impropriety, or violence. The narrator's consciousness records, with camera-like objectivity, the minute details of A . . . .'s and Franck's gestures; the comings and goings of servants; the stain left by the centipede; various other stains and surface blemishes, such as a bit of peeling paint on the veranda rail; the exact layout, row by row, of the banana trees; and the shadow cast by the southwest corner column of the veranda, which, by its variations, marks the passage of time. The detailed, geometric precision of such descriptions is the most arresting feature of the novel—so much so that it may seem that Robbe-Grillet is concerned more with objects then with people. His early critics in France were inclined to praise him for just such an objectivism.

To an extent, his preoccupation with objective description grows out of his radical critique of fictional form. He has no use for the conventions by which character is made to seem convincing, events real, and the story true. For him, the form and purpose of a novel begins and ends with structure. The intricate pattern of such descriptions, with their repetitions and serial permutations, thus constitutes a kind of meaning, in the manner of a modernist musical composition or an abstract painting. Much of Robbe-Grillet's critical acclaim, for this novel and others, reflects the extent to which he has apparently succeeded in displacing humanist concerns with purely formalist ones.

Although *Jealousy* is not exactly a slice of life, it nevertheless creates a memorable disturbing impression of human psychology. The title in the original French, *La Jalousie*, is a pun that links the narrator's psychology to the mode of narration. The tropical plantation house does not have glass windows, but blinds, or "jalousies," to keep out the sun while allowing the circulation of air; it is through the slats of these blinds that the narrator spies on his wife. The ingenuity of Robbe-Grillet's formal designs partly explains their artistic power, but not entirely. Filtered through the narrator's consciousness, they carry its imprint. The reader cannot be objectively sure that any impropriety occurred: The narrator's descriptions are cool and detached, but also obsessive—the objective correlatives of a mind given to fantasy, infinite regression, and paranoid suspicion. Thus, without anything remotely resembling characterization, a kind of silhouette image of a morbidly jealous man emerges from the text by tone and implication.

Robbe-Grillet has said of his narrators that they generally are men engaged "in an emotional adventure of the most obsessive kind, to the point of often distorting their vision." Much of his power as a novelist lies in just this ability to create unsettling psychological portraits out of ostensibly neutral, objective material—perhaps not camera images so much as images projected by a magic lantern from the unconscious, and framed ironically by the most lucid, elegant prose.

Charles Freeman Duncan

Bibliography:
Barthes, Roland. "Objective Literature: Alain Robbe-Grillet." In *Two Novels by Robbe-Grillet: "Jealousy" and "In the Labyrinth,"* translated by Richard Howard, New York: Grove Press, 1965. Important introductory essay to the standard English language edition of *Jealousy* by the leading French structuralist critic and proponent of objective literature.
Fletcher, John. *Alain Robbe-Grillet.* New York: Methuen, 1983. Good monographic overview of Robbe-Grillet's fiction and critical theory. Section on *Jealousy* emphasizes the psychological aspects of the narrator's consciousness rather than the structural patterns of his descriptions.

Leki, Ilona. *Alain Robbe-Grillet*. Boston: Twayne, 1983. A thorough, readable survey of the author's life and works. Chapter on *Jealousy* suggests that the narrator's paranoid psychology is produced by a generalized fear of dispossession and loss of control, not only of his wife, but also of his house and property.

Morrissette, Bruce. *Alain Robbe-Grillet*. New York: Columbia University Press, 1965. Short but excellent monograph by Robbe-Grillet's premier critic. Extremely perceptive commentary on *Jealousy*, with a nice balance between formalist and humanist interpretative reading.

Stoltzfus, Ben. *Alain Robbe-Grillet and the New French Novel*. Carbondale: Southern Illinois University Press, 1964. Although to an extent superseded by Stoltzfus' later work on Robbe-Grillet, still a very useful introductory study. Sees in *Jealousy* the fusion of two narrative centers: the selective omniscience of the jealous husband with the hidden editorial omniscience of the author.

JENNIE GERHARDT

Type of work: Novel
Author: Theodore Dreiser (1871-1945)
Type of plot: Naturalism
Time of plot: Last two decades of the nineteenth century
Locale: Chicago, Columbus, Cleveland, and Cincinnati
First published: 1911

Principal characters:
JENNIE GERHARDT
WILLIAM GERHARDT, her father
MRS. GERHARDT, her mother
SEBASTIAN GERHARDT, her brother
SENATOR BRANDER, Jennie's first lover
VESTA, Jennie's daughter
MRS. BRACEBRIDGE, Jennie's employer in Cleveland
LESTER KANE, a carriage manufacturer and Jennie's second lover
ROBERT KANE, Lester's brother
MRS. LETTY PACE GERALD, a widow, Lester's childhood sweetheart, and
later his wife

The Story:

Jennie Gerhardt, a beautiful and virtuous eighteen-year-old, was one of six children of a poor, hard-working German family in Columbus, Ohio, in 1880. Her father, a glassblower, was ill, and Jennie and her mother were forced to work at a local hotel in order to provide for the younger children in the family. Jennie did the laundry for the kind and handsome Senator Brander (he was fifty-two at the time) and attracted his eye. Senator Brander was kind to Jennie and her family. When he was able to keep Jennie's brother Sebastian out of jail for stealing some needed coal from the railroad, Jennie, full of gratitude, allowed him to sleep with her. Senator Brander, struck by Jennie's beauty, charm, and goodness, promised to marry her. He died suddenly, however, while on a trip to Washington.

Left alone, Jennie discovered that she was pregnant. Her father, a stern Lutheran, insisted that she leave the house, but her more understanding mother allowed her to return when her father, once in better health, left to find work in Youngstown. Jennie's child was a daughter, whom she named Vesta. At Sebastian's suggestion, the family moved to Cleveland to find work. While her mother looked after Vesta, Jennie found a job as a maid in the home of Mrs. Bracebridge. One of Mrs. Bracebridge's guests, Lester Kane, the son of a rich carriage manufacturer, found Jennie temptingly attractive. When he tried to seduce Jennie, the girl, though greatly attracted to him, managed to put off his advances.

Mr. Gerhardt was injured in a glassblowing accident and lost the use of both of his hands. Again, the family needed money badly, and Jennie decided to accept Lester's offer of aid for her family. The price was that she become his mistress, go on a trip to New York with him, and then allow him to establish her in an apartment in Chicago. Although Jennie loved Lester, she knew that he did not intend to marry her because his family would be horrified at such an alliance, but once again, she sacrificed her virtue because she felt that her family needed the offered aid. After Jennie had become Lester's mistress, he gave her family money for a house. Jennie was afraid, however, to tell Lester about the existence of her daughter Vesta.

Jennie and Lester moved to Chicago and lived there. Her family began to suspect that, contrary to what Jennie had told them, she and Lester were not married. When Mrs. Gerhardt died several years later, Jennie moved Vesta to Chicago and boarded the child in another woman's house. One night, Jennie was called because Vesta was seriously ill, and Lester discovered Vesta's existence. Although upset at first, when Jennie told him the story, Lester understood and agreed to allow Vesta to live with them. Some time later, while Lester was staying at the apartment to recover from an illness, his sister Louise visited and discovered the relationship, which she reported to the Kane family upon her return to Cincinnati. Lester and Jennie soon moved to a house in Hyde Park, a middle-class residential district in Chicago. Mr. Gerhardt, now old and ill and willing to accept the situation between Jennie and Lester, also came to live with them and to tend the furnace and the lawn.

Although they were constantly aware of the increasing disapproval of Lester's family, Jennie and Lester lived happily for a time. Lester's father, violently opposed to the relationship with Jennie, whom he had never met, threatened to disinherit Lester if he did not leave her. Lester's brother Robert urged his father on and attempted to persuade Lester to abandon Jennie. Nevertheless, Lester felt that he owed his allegiance, as well as his love, to her, and he remained with her in spite of the fact that they were snubbed by most of Lester's society connections.

When Lester's father died, still believing that his son's relationship with Jennie demonstrated irresponsibility, he left Lester's share of the estate in trust with Robert. Lester was given three alternatives: He could leave Jennie and receive all his money; he could marry Jennie and receive only $10,000 a year for life; or he could continue his present arrangement with the knowledge that if he did not either abandon or marry Jennie within three years, he would lose his share of the money. Characteristically, Lester hesitated. He resigned from his managerial position in the family business and took Jennie to Europe, where they met Mrs. Letty Pace Gerald, a beautiful and accomplished widow who had been Lester's childhood sweetheart and who was still fond of him. In the meantime, Robert had expanded the carriage business into a monopoly and eased Lester into a subordinate position. When Lester returned to Chicago, he decided to attempt to make an independent future for himself and Jennie. He put a good deal of money into a real estate deal and lost it. Mrs. Gerald also moved to Chicago in pursuit of Lester.

After old Mr. Gerhardt died, Jennie found herself in a difficult situation. Lester, out of the family business because of her, was finding it more difficult to earn a living. Mrs. Gerald and Robert's lawyers kept pressing her to release him, claiming this suggestion was for his own economic and social good. Jennie, always altruistic, began to influence Lester to leave her. Before long, both were convinced that separation was the only solution so that Lester could return to the family business. Finally, Lester left Jennie, setting up a house and an income for her and Vesta in a cottage an hour or so from the center of Chicago.

Once more established in the family business, Lester married Mrs. Gerald. Six months after Lester had left Jennie, Vesta, a fourteen-year-old girl already showing a good deal of sensitivity and talent, died of typhoid fever.

Jennie, calling herself Mrs. Stover, moved to the city and adopted two orphan children. Five years passed. Jennie, although still in love with Lester, accepted her quiet life. At last, she was able to cope with experience in whatever terms it presented itself to her, even though she had never been able to impose her will on experience in any meaningful way. One night while in Chicago on business, Lester was stricken by severe cardiovascular illness and sent for Jennie; his wife was in Europe and could not reach Chicago for three weeks. Jennie tended Lester throughout his last illness. One day he confessed that he had always loved her and that he had made a mistake ever to permit the forces of business and family pressure to make him leave her.

Jennie felt that his final confession, his statement that he should never have left her, indicated a kind of spiritual union and left her with something that she could value for the rest of her life. Lester died. Jennie realized that she would now be forced to live through many years that could promise no salvation, no new excitement—that would simply impose themselves upon her as had the years in the past. She was resolved to accept her loneliness because she knew there was nothing else for her to do.

Jennie went to see Lester's coffin loaded on the train. She realized then, even more clearly, that the individual was simply a figure, moved about by circumstance. Virtue, beauty, moral worth could not save anyone, nor could evil or degeneracy. One simply yielded and managed the best one could under the circumstances of one's nature, one's society, and one's economic situation.

Critical Evaluation:

Theodore Dreiser began writing his second novel *Jennie Gerhardt* in 1901, soon after the publication of *Sister Carrie* (1900). As in the earlier work, Dreiser's main theme is the individual's struggle to find happiness in an uncaring, often cruel world. In this struggle, all is chance. One might have a slight advantage if born into a wealthy family (as Lester Kane is), but this does not guarantee success. On the other hand, a person born without material advantages must struggle to make up for the lack.

From the beginning, Jennie faces obstacles that her brother Sebastian does not. The wages she receives from helping her mother as a scrubwoman in a fashionable hotel in downtown Columbus, Ohio, were much less than men received for comparable work. She and her mother took in laundry to supplement their income. At the time, few honest jobs allowed women to earn a living wage. This put Jennie at a great risk because she had to enter Senator Brander's hotel room to pick up and deliver his laundry. The beautiful eighteen-year-old Jennie was vulnerable to Brander not only because of her age and social class, but also because of her gender. During the last half of the nineteenth century, women engaged in domestic work, whether in hotels or private homes, were often targeted by men with less than honorable intentions. Jennie soon learned that her sexuality had value and could be exchanged for trinkets, clothes, and finally, money.

By exchanging her virginity for Sebastian's bail, Jennie not only becomes pregnant but also is caught in a trap from which she never escapes. The possibility of marriage and a happy life with someone of her own class made impossible, she struggles as best she can. Given her situation, Jennie succeeds amazingly well. She lives comfortably in Chicago for several years with the man she loves, traveling extensively in America and Europe and enjoying the material comforts of wealth. Even after her separation from Lester, her basic needs are guaranteed by a trust fund he has set up for her. She has a nice house, food (she grows "stout"), and her daughter's companionship. Fate rears its ugly head, and Vesta is taken away by typhoid fever. Still unwilling to surrender to despair, Jennie takes in two foster children.

Jennie's constant struggle for survival makes this novel perhaps an even better example of literary naturalism than its predecessor, *Sister Carrie*, but Jennie's is not the only struggle in the novel. Lester tries to find his place in life, balanced between his own happiness and the dictates of his family's social position. Even when he seems successful (wealth, marriage to Letty Pace), his happiness is not guaranteed. In fact, his material success brings the cause of his demise. Lester's rich lifestyle includes the finest foods and drinks. He becomes very obese and unhealthy. Symbolically, his material success overfills his physical body, stretching his form and clogging his arteries. Fate is unpredictable and can attack the individual in many ways.

Lester dies not in a gutter, but in a luxurious Chicago hotel, smothered to death by his own good fortune. Lester's fondness for gambling during his marriage to Letty symbolizes fate's role in life. His favorite game was roulette—spinning the wheel of fortune.

Dreiser uses a different set of images for Jennie, whom he describes as "a pale gentle flower," "a rare flower," or "like a rudderless boat on an endless sea." Flower and boat metaphors are common in literary naturalism and echo Stephen Crane's description of the title character in *Maggie: A Girl of the Streets* (1893, a girl who "blossomed in a mud puddle") and the "rudderless" boat in his sixth poem from *The Black Riders* (1895). Dreiser also refers to Jennie several times as a "wayfarer," an image Crane uses in the poem "The Wayfarer" in *War Is Kind* (1899) to suggest that people have no control over their destinies and that even a seemingly inconsequential decision can have disastrous results. Dreiser foreshadowed Jennie's unluckiness in life by giving the Gerhardt family address as 13th Street in Columbus and 1314 Lorrie Street in Cleveland.

In Dreiser's naturalistic vision, nature has no concern for an individual's happiness, and those who look to religion for assistance get no relief. Jennie's father was a devout Lutheran, but still his family was torn apart by harsh social and economic conditions. Dreiser's original title for *Jennie Gerhardt* was *The Transgressor*. Against whom or what did Jennie transgress— God, society, nature? Dreiser asks the reader to question Jennie's sins, but in the end the reader can not condemn her choices. "How could the poor girl, amid such unfortunate circumstances, do otherwise than she did." Dreiser's statement implies no favorable alternatives.

Jennie Gerhardt has not enjoyed a high place in literary history and is usually put aside for *Sister Carrie* and Dreiser's later novel with working-class themes, *An American Tragedy* (1925). Perhaps this is the result of social attitudes toward events in the book. Readers want to sympathize with Jennie, but society tells them that the sins she falls into—sleeping with Brander and Lester—are wrong. During the great wave of social "improvement" in the first decade of the twentieth century, this issue caused Dreiser difficulty in publishing the work, and he had to soften its message considerably before the book was printed in 1911. Changes made for that edition have allowed critics to find weaknesses (such as Jennie's lack of psychological development) that were less telling in Dreiser's original manuscripts. Fortunately, the original text (now referred to as the Pennsylvania edition) has been restored and published, but readers should be aware that criticism written before the original text's publication in 1992 might be distorted by reliance on the bowdlerized version.

Jennie Gerhardt fits thematically with other works in which women are forced to go against Christianity's teachings to survive, including Daniel Defoe's *Moll Flanders* (1722), Crane's *Maggie: A Girl of the Streets*, Upton Sinclair's *The Jungle* (1906), and Dreiser's own *Sister Carrie* and *An American Tragedy*.

"Critical Evaluation" by Geralyn Strecker

Bibliography:
Dreiser, Theodore. *Jennie Gerhardt*. Edited by James L. W. West III. Philadelphia: University of Pennsylvania Press, 1992. Reclaims Dreiser's original intentions for the novel. Includes informative introduction, explanatory notes, a map, illustrations of pages from Dreiser's manuscript, and other useful materials.
Hapke, Laura. "Dreiser and the Tradition of the American Working Girl Novel." *Dreiser Studies* 22, no. 2 (Fall, 1991): 2-19. Uses social history to discuss the situation Jennie Gerhardt and her five million historical contemporaries faced struggling to survive in low-paying jobs.

Lingeman, Richard. *Theodore Dreiser: At the Gates of the City, 1871-1907* and *Theodore Dreiser: An American Journey, 1908-1945.* New York: G. P. Putnam's Sons, 1986, 1990. The standard biography offers information on the writing and biographical context of *Jennie Gerhardt* in volume 1 and information on its revision, publication, and critical reception in volume 2.

Pizer, Donald. *The Novels of Theodore Dreiser: A Critical Study.* Minneapolis: University of Minnesota Press, 1976. The section on *Jennie Gerhardt* establishes information about the novel's sources and composition. Gives biographical details suggesting that Jennie was modeled after Dreiser's sister Mame. Valuable discussion of structure, characterization, and themes.

West, James L. W., III, ed. *Dreiser's "Jennie Gerhardt": New Essays on the Restored Text.* Philadelphia: University of Pennsylvania Press, 1994. A collection giving historical background and new interpretations of the novel in its restored version.

JERUSALEM DELIVERED

Type of work: Poetry
Author: Torquato Tasso (1544-1595)
Type of plot: Epic
Time of plot: Middle Ages
Locale: The Holy Land
First published: Gerusalemme liberata, 1581 (English translation, 1600)

Principal characters:
GODFREY DE BOUILLON, leader of the Crusaders
CLORINDA, a female warrior
ARGANTES, a pagan knight
ERMINIA, princess of Antioch
ARMIDA, an enchantress
RINALDO, an Italian knight
TANCRED, a Frankish knight

The Story:

For six years the Crusaders had remained in the Holy Land, meeting with success. Tripoli, Antioch, and Acre were in their hands, and a large force of Christian knights occupied Palestine. Yet there was a lassitude among the nobles; they were tired and satiated with fighting. They could not generate enough warlike spirit to continue to the real objective of their Crusade, the capture of Jerusalem. In the spring of the seventh year, God sent the Archangel Gabriel to Godfrey de Bouillon, ordering him to assemble all his knights and encouraging him to begin the march on Jerusalem. Obeying the Lord's command, Godfrey called a council of the great nobles and reminded them stirringly of their vows. When Peter the Hermit added his exhortations, the Crusaders accepted their charge, and all preparations were made to attack the Holy City.

Within the walls of Jerusalem the wicked King Aladine heard of the projected attack. At the urging of Ismeno the sorcerer, he sent soldiers to steal the statue of the Virgin Mary, hoping to make the Christian symbol a Palladium for Jerusalem. The next morning, the statue had disappeared. Enraged when he could not find the culprit who had spirited away the statue, Aladine ordered a general massacre of all his Christian subjects. To save her co-religionists, the beautiful and pure Sophronia confessed to the theft. Aladine had her bound to the stake. As her guards were about to light the fire, Olindo, who had long loved Sophronia in vain, attempted to save her by confessing that he himself had stolen the statue.

Aladine ordered them both burned. While they were at the stake, Sophronia admitted her love for Olindo. They were saved from burning, however, by the arrival of Clorinda, a beautiful woman warrior who knew that both were admitting the theft to save the other Christians from death. Released, Sophronia and Olindo fled the city. Clorinda was a great warrior who scorned female dress. On a previous campaign she had met Tancred, a mighty Christian noble. Tancred had fallen in love with her; but she rejected his love. On the other hand, Erminia of Antioch had become enamored of Tancred when he had taken her city, but Tancred felt only friendship for her.

The Christians came within sight of Jerusalem. A foraging party encountered first a small force under Clorinda. She was so valorous that she defeated them. The king of Egypt, whose army was advancing to the aid of Jerusalem, sent Argantes to parley with Godfrey. The Crusader chief haughtily rejected the overtures of the Egyptians, and Argantes angrily joined the infidel defenders of the Holy City. Although the Crusaders met with some initial successes, Argantes was always a formidable opponent.

Satan was annoyed at the prospect of the fall of Jerusalem. He induced Armida, an enchantress, to visit the Christian camp and tell a false story of persecution. Many of the knights succumbed to her wiles and eagerly sought permission to redress her wrongs. Godfrey was suspicious of her, but he allowed ten knights chosen by lot to accompany her. In the night forty others slipped away to join her, and she led the fifty to her castle, where she changed them into fishes. Their loss was a great blow to Godfrey because the pagans were slaying many of his men.

Rinaldo, one of the Italian knights among the Crusaders, sought the captaincy of a band of Norwegian adventurers. Gernando, who sought the same post, quarreled with him, and in a joust Gernando was killed. For this breach of discipline Rinaldo was banished.

When Argantes challenged to personal combat any champion in the Crusaders' camp, Tancred was chosen to meet him. On the way to the fight, Tancred saw Clorinda and stopped to admire her. Otho, his companion, took advantage of his bemusement and rushed in ahead to the battle. Otho was defeated by Argantes and taken prisoner. Then Tancred, realizing what had happened, advanced to meet the pagan knight. Both men were wounded in the mighty, day-long duel. They retired to recuperate, agreeing to meet again in six days.

When Erminia heard of Tancred's wounds, she put on Clorinda's armor and went to his camp to attend him. He heard of her coming and waited impatiently, thinking his beloved Clorinda was approaching. Erminia was surprised by the sentries, and in her maidenly timidity she ran away to take refuge with a shepherd. When the supposed Clorinda did not arrive, Tancred went in search of her and came to the castle of Armida, where he was cast into a dungeon. Godfrey received word that Sweno, prince of Denmark, who had been occupying Palestine, had been surprised by pagan knights and killed with all his followers. The messenger announced that he had been divinely appointed to deliver Sweno's sword to Rinaldo. Although Rinaldo was still absent, Godfrey set out to avenge the Palestine garrison.

Godfrey and his army fought valiantly, but Argantes and Clorinda were fighters too powerful for the shaken Christians to overcome. Then Tancred and the fifty knights, who had been freed from Armida's enchantment, arrived to rout the pagans. Godfrey learned that the missing men had been liberated by Rinaldo. Peter the Hermit was then divinely inspired to foretell the glorious future of Rinaldo.

In preparation for the attack on Jerusalem, the Christians celebrated a solemn mass on the Mount of Olives before they began the assault. Wounded by one of Clorinda's arrows, Godfrey retired from the battle while an angel healed his wound. The Christians set up rams and towers to break the defense of the city.

At night Clorinda came out of the city walls and set fire to the great tower by which the Christians were preparing to scale the wall. She was seen, however, by the Crusaders, and Tancred engaged her in combat. After he had run his sword through her breast, he discovered to his sorrow that he had killed his love. He had time to ask her pardon and baptize her before her death.

Godfrey was taken in a vision to heaven where he talked with Hugh, the former commander of the French forces. Hugh bade him recall Rinaldo, and Godfrey sent two knights to find the banished Italian. On the Fortunate Islands the messengers discovered the Palace of Armida where Rinaldo, having fallen in love with the enchantress, was dallying with his lady love. The sight of the two knights quickly reminded him of his duty. Leaving his love, he joined the besieging forces of Godfrey.

With the arrival of Rinaldo, the Christians were greatly heartened. Then the Archangel Michael appeared to Godfrey and showed him the souls of all the Christians who had died in the Crusades. With this inspiration, the Crusaders redoubled their efforts to capture Jerusalem. The walls of the city were breached. Tancred met Argantes and killed him in single combat. Finally the victorious invaders stormed through the streets and sacked the Holy City. When the Egyptians arrived to help the pagan defenders of Jerusalem, they too were beaten and their king was slain by Godfrey. Armida, all hope gone, surrendered herself to Rinaldo, who had been the most valorous of the conquerors. After the fighting was over, Godfrey and all his army worshiped at the Holy Sepulchre.

Critical Evaluation:

Torquato Tasso had two objectives in writing *Jerusalem Delivered*: one religious, to exhort the Christian peoples of Europe to crusade against the heathen; the other, literary, to write a new epic fusing the heroic epic and chivalric romance, conforming to classical theory. Different forces operated within him. He was a devout Catholic, product of the Counter-Reformation and education by the Jesuits. He was also the product of court life at Ferrara, a center of chivalry and romantic tradition. Moreover, he was part of literary circles in Ferrara and Paris which were committed to the rules of pre-Christian writers.

Jerusalem Delivered is a Christian epic in its subject matter (the First Crusade), sentiment, and plot. Its poetic focus, however, is on the love stories. It is a new kind of epic, in the classical tradition but replacing pagan mythology with Christian figures and pagan magic with Christian miracle. It intermingles sober fact with invention, imposing classical majesty on chivalric and romantic material. Under the influence of Dante, it is an epic in the vernacular.

The main characters (except for Rinaldo) and events are historically authentic, but Tasso adds imaginary episodes in which his imagination can find free expression, especially in the love scenes and battle and single combat scenes. He adds supernatural forces, divine and evil, intervening on behalf of the Christians and pagans.

The miraculous had a special appeal for Tasso, which he found in close relation to real experience. He held the traditional view of magic as the work of devils, but he did not confine it to them. He gave it a new interpretation, linking it to unintelligible human fears and dreads.

The importance of love appears early in the epic in the willingness of Sofronia and Olindo to die for each other. Love, capable of transcending human limitation, gives rise to complex situations: Pagan Erminia is frustrated by her love for the Christian Tancred; Christian Tancred falls in love with another pagan, the Amazon Clorinda. The pagan witch Armida is in love with the Christian Rinaldo, who finally succumbs to her seductions, then renounces her, only to be reconciled as she converts to Christianity.

Tasso's characters are complex. They are convincing human beings but also stern and mighty warriors. They have shortcomings and are differentiated. The ideal lies not in any one character (although Godfrey, with his talents as leader and with his common sense and control, is the closest to the ideal Christian warrior). Godfrey is the one chosen to receive divine help. Tancred is the ideal courtier—courteous, free from envy, patient, a good swordsman, reflective but able to act. Rinaldo is the proud adventurer and romantic. He is restless, quick-tempered, formidable in battle, and with a high sense of honor. He is finally disciplined to the Christian cause. The pagans are different from those in romances; they are not evil but mostly honorable men and worthy warriors. They are, however, pagan and misguided.

The debate over allegory in *Jerusalem Delivered* began almost as soon as it appeared in public. Tasso almost immediately began to comment on his work. In 1579, with *Allegoria dei poema*, he says that there is allegory in the poem but that the literal might be enough. He later adds that readers may make multiple readings. He also says that he did not think about any allegory at first but that thinking about it later, realized it was there, but that not all details have allegorical meaning.

The principal allegory relates to the body politic. In the disintegration of the Christian forces in the first half of the epic, and the subsequent taking of control by Godfrey, with divine help (a reflection of Tasso's authoritarian convictions), the allegory is clear. The wood where Tancred and Erminia are lost, the Enchanted Forest produced by the evil Ismeno, protected by demons and exorcised by Rinaldo, are symbols of intellectual error and confusion. The wanderings of the characters and the circuitous reasons of Ismeno reinforce this meaning. Significantly, many episodes take place at night or in darkness. Tancred represents incontinent love, like the historical Tancred that was Tasso's source. He pursues wrong love—Erminia in Clorinda's armor. His wanderings represent false goals.

The Crusade is essentially a war between Good, watched over and aided by God, and Evil, watched over and aided by Satan. The providence of God is displayed by his periodic interventions: He brings about Godfrey's selection as commander of the Christian forces and sends Michael to him with instructions for beginning the Crusade. Periodically He sends one of the angels to advise and even to help in repelling the demons. His agent, Peter the Hermit, plays a key role too in inspiring and counseling the Christians. On the other side, Satan sends his demons to aid the pagan army, and employs the services of the magician Ismeno and the enchantress Armida to confuse the Christians.

A main theme is regeneration and redemption by the miracle of grace. Much of the first half of the epic dwells on the disintegration of the Christian forces, their revitalization beginning with the assumption of command by Godfrey. Subsequently the Christians make their arduous way through dangers, fears, and seductions on their way to victory. Individuals are redeemed. Clorinda, born of Christian parents but a zealous pagan, on dying learns of her Christian roots and is baptized a Christian. Rinaldo, after seduction by Armida, awakens anew to the crusading vision. Even the pagan seductress, Armida, released from her hatred and finding a higher love, is converted and baptized.

Jerusalem Delivered is generally recognized as one of the best Christian epics, and Tasso is generally recognized as the greatest Italian poet of the late Renaissance. The poem is testimony to Tasso's goals, as a part of the Counter-Reformation, of expressing his religious ideas and, as a poet, of composing a poem in the epic form. His reformed idea of Christian heroism is colored by his love of passionate personalities and a pleasure in varied and vivid action—combining seriousness and love of life.

"Critical Evaluation" by Thomas Amherst Perry

Bibliography:
Bowra, C. M. "Tasso and the Romance of Christian Chivalry." In *From Virgil to Milton.* New York: Macmillan, 1961. Analyzes the plot elements that show how Tasso integrated romance with Christian sentiment. Finds it the product both of the Counter-Reformation and a court life steeped in chivalric tradition.
Fichter, Andrew. "Tasso: Romance, Epic, and Christian Epic." In *Poets Historical, Dynastic Epic in the Renaissance.* New Haven, Conn.: Yale University Press, 1982. Suggests that Tasso's purpose was to construct a true Christian epic with the formal properties of the classical epic. The theme of regeneration provides the required unity.

Giametti, A. Bartlett. "Tasso." In *The Earthly Paradise and the Renaissance Epic*. Princeton, N.J.: Princeton University Press, 1966. Summarizes the plot, with special attention to Tasso's sensuous treatment of the lovers. Argues that Tasso attempts to incorporate classical and romantic materials into a Christian point of view.

Greene, Thomas M. "The Counter-Reformation: Tasso." In *The Descent from Heaven*. New Haven, Conn.: Yale University Press, 1963. With frequent quotations from *Jerusalem Delivered*, suggests that this poem is composed of several elements: a framework of history, echoes of earlier poets, lyricism, a feeling for sensuous beauty, the flavor of court life, a formal self-consciousness, the moral climate of the Counter-Reformation, and Platonism.

Roditi, Edouard. "Torquato Tasso: The Transition from Baroque to Neo-Classicism." *The Journal of Aesthetics and Art Criticism* 6 (1947-1948): 235-245. Suggests that Tasso strives to move away from baroque license toward classical restraint, carefully placing the Christian marvels above magic and enchantment. His classicism is also evident in his careful attention to stanza form.

THE JEW OF MALTA

Type of work: Drama
Author: Christopher Marlowe (1564-1593)
Type of plot: Tragedy
Time of plot: Fifteenth century
Locale: Malta
First performed: c. 1589; first published, 1633

Principal characters:
BARABAS, a Jewish merchant
ABIGAIL, his daughter
ITHAMORE, a slave
FERNEZE, the Governor of Malta

The Story:

Barabas, a Christian-hating merchant of Malta, received in his countinghouse a party of merchants who reported the arrival of several vessels laden with wealth from the East. At the same time three Jews arrived to announce an important meeting at the senate. The import of the meeting was that the Turkish masters of Malta had demanded tribute long overdue. The Turkish Grand Seignior had purposely let the payment lapse over a period of years so that the Maltese would find it impossible to raise the sum demanded. The Maltese had a choice of payment or surrender. The Christian governor of the island, attempting to collect the tribute within a month, decreed that the Jews would have to give over half of their estates or become Christians. All of the Jewish community except Barabas submitted to the decree of the governor. The governor seized all of Barabas' wealth as punishment and had the Jew's house turned into a Christian convent.

Barabas, to avoid complete ruin, purposely failed to report part of his treasure hidden in the foundation of his house. Then he persuaded his daughter, Abigail, to pretend that she had been converted to Christianity so that she might enter the convent and recover the treasure. Abigail dutifully entered the nunnery as a convert and subsequently threw the bags of money out of the window at night to her waiting father.

Martin Del Bosco, vice-admiral of Spain, sailed into the harbor of Malta for the purpose of selling some Turkish slaves he had aboard his ship. The governor was reluctant to allow the sale because of the difficulties he was having with the Grand Seignior. Del Bosco, by promising military aid from Spain, persuaded the governor to defy the Turks and to permit the sale.

Barabas bought one of the slaves, an Arabian named Ithamore. During the sale, Barabas fawned upon Don Lodowick, the governor's son, and Don Mathias. He invited the two young men to his house and ordered Abigail, now returned from the convent, to show favor to both. In his desire for revenge, Barabas arranged with each young man, separately, to marry his daughter. He then sent forged letters to Don Lodowick and Don Mathias, and provoked a duel in which the young men were killed. Meanwhile Barabas trained his slave, Ithamore, to be his aide in his plot against the governor and the Christians of Malta.

As a result of her father's evil intentions, Abigail returned to the convent. Barabas, enraged, sent poisoned porridge to the convent as his gesture of thanks on the Eve of St. Jacques, the patron saint of Malta. All in the convent were poisoned, and Abigail, before she died, confessed to Friar Jacomo, disclosing to him all that Barabas had done and all that he planned to do.

When the Turks returned to Malta to collect the tribute, the governor defied them and prepared for a siege of the island.

Meanwhile the friars, in violation of canon law, revealed the information they had gained from Abigail's confession. Barabas, again threatened, pretended a desire to become a convert and promised all of his worldly wealth to the friars who would receive him into the Christian faith. The greediness of the friars caused differences to arise among them; Barabas took advantage of this situation and with the help of Ithamore strangled a friar named Bernardine. He then propped up Bernardine's body in such a way that Friar Jacomo knocked it down. Observed in this act, Friar Jacomo was accused of the murder of one of his clerical brothers.

Ithamore met a strumpet, Bellamira, who, playing upon the slave's pride and viciousness, persuaded him to extort money from his master by threatening to expose Barabas. His master, alarmed by threats of blackmail, disguised himself as a French musician, went to the strumpet's house, and poisoned Bellamira and Ithamore with a bouquet of flowers. Before their deaths, they managed to communicate all they knew to the governor, who, despite his preoccupation with the fortifications of Malta, threw Barabas into prison. By drinking poppy essence and cold mandrake juice, Barabas faked death. His body was placed outside the city. Reviving, he joined the Turks and led them into the city. As a reward for his betraying Malta, Barabas was made governor. He now turned to the conquered Maltese, offering to put the Turks into their hands for a substantial price. The Maltese accepted the deal.

Under the direction of Barabas, explosives were set beneath the barracks of the Turkish troops. Then Barabas invited the Turkish leaders to a banquet in the governor's palace, after arranging to have them fall through a false floor into cauldrons of boiling liquid beneath. The Turkish troops were blown sky-high, but the Christian governor, who preferred to seize the Turkish leaders alive, exposed Barabas' scheme. The Jew of Malta perished in the trap he had set for the Turks.

Critical Evaluation:

Barabas dominates *The Jew of Malta*; the other characters are merely sketched. The plot of the play seems to have come wholly from the fertile mind of Christopher Marlowe, whose exotic plots and romantic heroes set a pattern which was followed by subsequent Elizabethan playwrights, including William Shakespeare. *The Jew of Malta* begins well, but it degenerates into an orgy of blood after the second act. Although Marlowe may have found his initial inspiration for the story and its hero in the person of Juan Michesius, recorded in Philippus Lonicerus' *Chronicorum Turcicorum* (1578) and in Sebastian Munster's *La Cosmographie Universelle* (1575), it is clear from a comparison with the aforementioned works that the character of Barabas owes at least as much to the tradition of Italian revenge tragedy, to the English morality plays, and to Marlowe's own preferences in characterization as demonstrated in *Doctor Faustus* (1588), in *Tamburlaine the Great, Part I* (1587), and in *Tamburlaine the Great, Part II* (1587). Considered the most important English dramatist before Shakespeare, Marlowe was of a social background similar to that of his illustrious successor, although Marlowe's formal schooling was more extensive than Shakespeare's. Marlowe's theatrical career, however, was unfortunately much briefer. Marlowe constructed his greatest plays around characters obsessed with one thing or another; for them, the obsession itself is all-important, not particularly its object. Marlowe has been given credit for raising the formerly stilted and academic English theater to the level of both serious and entertaining art.

Although *The Jew of Malta* is written in Marlowe's most masterful and fully developed style, it remains an enigmatic and difficult play because of the unevenness of its structural impact and emotional effect. Perhaps this is inevitable in the very combination of the morality drama with the drama of personality; it is hard to maintain Barabas as both a typical figure of evil and a sympathetic, understandable person in his own right. T. S. Eliot considered it a farce, characterized by "terribly serious even savage comic humor." What is certain is its thematic resemblance to Marlowe's other great plays. Marlowe's plays share a concern with exploring the limits of human power. In *The Jew of Malta*, a self-made hero rises to power from lowly origins and brings about his own end by an obsessive passion. The play is unified by this hero's personality alone. Moreover *The Jew of Malta* is Marlowe's first Machiavellian play, the first in which the word "policy" appears. As he speaks at the play's opening, Machiavelli embodies in general and final fashion the vices that Barabas' history will reenact: unbounded greed, accompanied by a complete absence of conscience or moral scruples. In many senses, a major theme of the play is amorality rather than immorality—the amorality displayed by the governor as a representative of the political realm, or by the friars as representative Catholics, as well as by Barabas himself as a type of the commercial sphere.

The Jew of Malta is critically difficult because of its apparent structural disjunction, as it moves from an emphasis on Barabas' mind and motivations in the first part to a concentration solely upon his evil actions in the second. In the first part, familiar Marlovian themes are presented. Barabas' Machiavellian egocentrism is apparently justified by the hypocrisy of his Christian enemies; the splendor of his wealth is delineated in appropriate mercantile detail. The scene between Barabas and the governor develops the satirical tone, as it seems to contrast the hypocrisy of the Maltese Christians with the Jew's overt wickedness, their greed with his—an extension of the quarrel between Christians and infidels in *Tamburlaine the Great, Part II*. Barabas nearly captures the sympathies of the audience by making the audience believe that he will suffer from Ferneze's decree; that decree is manifestly unjust.

In the second part, as the play moves from what the noted critic M. C. Bradbrook calls the "technique of verse" to the "technique of action," the audience sees Barabas' subterfuge more clearly; he appears as a completely villainous Machiavellian. Marlowe therefore no longer presents introspective revelations of Barabas' mental and emotional processes but turns instead to concentrate on verbal and narrative reversals in the last three acts. The primary interest becomes clever stage situations and adroit manipulation of the narrative, as, for example, when Barabas constantly reverses his overt meaning by his tagged-on asides. The entrapment of Lodowick and Mathias, of the two friars, of Ithamore and Bellamira, and the final series of double-crosses between Ferneze, Calymath, and Barabas, are obviously influenced by the revenge tragedy tradition. The plot of *The Jew of Malta*, then, is largely episodic, constructed through the "symmetrical pairing" of a series of figures around that of Barabas: the three Jews at the beginning, the abbess and the nun, Mathias and Lodowick, Friar Bernardine and Friar Jacomo, Bellamira and Pilia-Borsa, the Calymath and Del Bosco.

The focus of the play is Barabas' own character. He is at one and the same time, according to the critic David M. Bevington, the "lifelike Jewish merchant caught in a political feud," an "embodiment of moral vice," and the "unrepenting protagonist in [a] homiletic 'tragedy.'" Once the audience's initial sympathies for Barabas have vanished, the audience sees him only as a heinous culprit who unintentionally fashions his own downfall. The complications of his evil schemes and his ultimate inability to control those around him who, in their own lesser ways, are also evil schemers, are what bring about his downfall. It would be, clearly, a mistake to consider Barabas as an epitome of a race persecuted by prejudice; he shows, at the very beginning, that he himself has no more respect for Jews than he does for Christians or Turks. Abigail, before entering the convent for the second time, this time in earnest, makes this point when she says, "But I perceive there is no love on earth,/ Pity in Jews, nor piety in Turks." Barabas, instead, proclaims himself "a sound Machiavell," as the prologue predicts, when he instructs Ithamore in the ways of evil: "First, be thou void of these affections,/ Compassion, love, vain hope, and heartless fear." It is supremely ironic that he calls Ithamore his "second self," since in the end Barabas murders the slave, figuratively revealing the self-destructive bent of his evil. On a larger scale, the same irony pervading the entire play is proclaimed in the absurdly righteous closing words of Ferneze: "So, march away; and let due praise be given/ Neither to Fate nor Fortune, but to Heaven." Heaven has had little hand in this story; instead, the hand of the pessimistic atheist Marlowe leaves its prints everywhere.

"Critical Evaluation" by Kenneth John Atchity

Bibliography:
Bartels, Emily C. "Malta, the Jew, and the Fictions of Difference: Colonialist Discourse in Marlowe's *The Jew of Malta.*" *English Literary Renaissance* 20 (1990): 1-16. An excellent Marxist reading of the text that posits imperialism as the controlling discourse and Malta as the object of the colonizer's lust.
Bowers, Fredson Thayer. *Elizabethan Revenge Tragedy: 1587-1642.* Gloucester, Mass.: P. Smith, 1959. Asserts that Barabas fails as a tragic hero because he avenges a material wrong with murder, because his motives are petty and treacherous, and because his demise is unconnected to his revenge.
Danson, Lawrence. "Christopher Marlowe: The Questioner." *English Literary Renaissance* 12 (1982): 3-29. Argues that the play is written in an interrogative mode. Characters ask questions without pausing for answers. These rhetorical questions draw the audience into the answering process.
Deats, Sara Munson, and Lisa S. Starks. "'So neatly plotted, and so well perform'd': Villain as Playwright in Marlowe's *The Jew of Malta.*" *Theatre Journal* 44, no. 3 (October, 1992): 375-389. Examines the significance of the play's metadramatic elements, its ambivalent attitude toward the theater and toward role-playing, arguing that these elements are a reflection of the violent debate raging in Shakespeare's time about the moral worth of the theater, and that they shed new light on Barabas' motives.
Rothstein, Eric. "Structure as Meaning in *The Jew of Malta.*" *Journal of English and Germanic Philology* 65 (1966): 260-273. Views the play as ironic parody and demonstrates this reading through an analysis of language and action. The play parodies the Bible, the pastoral, the code of friendship, and Catholicism, using Barabas to expose the weaknesses of other characters.

JOHN BROWN'S BODY

Type of work: Poetry
Author: Stephen Vincent Benét (1898-1943)
Type of plot: Epic
Time of plot: 1859-1865
Locale: United States
First published: 1928

> *Principal characters:*
> JACK ELLYAT, a soldier from Connecticut
> CLAY WINGATE, a soldier from Georgia
> LUKE BRECKINRIDGE, a Southern mountaineer
> MELORA VILAS, Jack Ellyat's beloved
> SALLY DUPRÉ, Clay Wingate's fiancée
> LUCY WEATHERBY, Sally's rival
> SHIPPY, a Union spy
> SOPHY, a Richmond hotel employee

The Story:

Jack Ellyat, a Connecticut youth, had premonitions of trouble as he walked with his dog in the mellow New England Indian summer. He and his family were abolitionists, in favor of making slavery illegal in the United States. The influence of Ralph Waldo Emerson and Henry David Thoreau was felt in Concord, where they talked about an ideal state. In Boston, Minister Higginson and Dr. Howe waited for reports of a project planned for Harpers Ferry. In Georgia, young Clay Wingate also received a premonition of impending disaster and great change.

John Brown, a fanatic, believing that he was chosen by God to free slaves, led his troop of raiders to seize the United States arsenal at Harpers Ferry, Virginia. The first man killed in the fracas was Shepherd Heyward, a free African American. The South was alarmed. Federal troops under Robert E. Lee subdued the Brown party in fifteen minutes; all was ended but the slow, smoldering hatred and the deaths to come.

At Wingate Hall in Georgia, all was peaceful. Sally Dupré and Clay Wingate were expected to marry. When Cudjo, the majordomo of the Wingate plantation, heard of the Harpers Ferry raid and John Brown, he opined that the business of African Americans was not the business of the white Americans. In Connecticut, Mrs. Ellyat prayed for John Brown.

Brown was tried at Charles Town, Virginia. During the trial, he denied the complicity of anyone but himself and his followers in the raid. He insisted that he had done what he thought was right. A legend grew around his name and mushroomed after he was hanged. John Brown's body rested in its grave, but his spirit haunted the consciences of North and South alike.

Fort Sumter surrendered, and the Confederate States of America elected gaunt, tired Jefferson Davis as president. Lank, sad-faced Abraham Lincoln, the frontier wit and small-time politician, was president of the United States. He ordered conscription of fighting men. Clay Wingate, loyal to the South, joined the Black Horse Troop and rode to the war. Jack Ellyat marched off with the Connecticut volunteers.

Raw soldiers of North and South met at Bull Run under the direction of Generals McDowell, Johnston, and Beauregard. Congressmen and their ladies drove out from Washington to watch the Union victory. While they watched, the Union lines broke and retreated in panic. A movement to negotiate with the Confederacy for peace got underway in the North. Lincoln was alarmed, but he remained steadfast.

Jack Ellyat was discharged from service after Bull Run. Later he joined the Illinois volunteers in Chicago and became known as "Bull Run Jack." Near Pittsburg Landing, in Tennessee, he lost his head and ran during a surprise attack. He was captured but escaped again during a night march. Hungry and weary, Jack arrived at the Vilas farm, where he stayed in hiding and fell in love with Melora Vilas. At last he left the farm to seek the courage he had lost near Pittsburg Landing, but not before he had made Melora pregnant. He was recaptured soon afterward.

Meanwhile Clay Wingate returned to Georgia on leave. At Wingate Hall, the war seemed far away, for the successful running of the Union blockade of Southern ports made luxuries still available. Lucy Weatherby, a Virginian whose sweetheart had been killed at Bull Run, attended a dance at Wingate Hall and replaced Sally Dupré in Clay's affections. Spade, a slave on the nearby Zachary plantation, escaped that same night.

New Orleans was captured. Davis and Lincoln began to bow under the burdens of the war. McClellan began his Peninsular campaign. Lee inflicted defeat after defeat on the Army of the Potomac. Jack Ellyat was sent to a prison in the deep South. The fortunes of the Union were at their lowest ebb after the Confederate victory at the Second Battle of Manassas, and the spirit of John Brown was generally invoked by editors and preachers. Lincoln issued the Emancipation Proclamation. In the meantime, Spade made his way north and swam across a river to freedom, but when he arrived in the land of the free he was railroaded into a labor gang. McClellan was relieved by Burnside, who, in turn, was relieved by Hooker, as commander of the Army of the Potomac. Jack Ellyat, sick, was returned to the North in an exchange of prisoners of war.

Slowly the Confederacy began to feel the effects of the blockade and the terrible costs of war. Clay Wingate thought of his next leave—and of Lucy Weatherby. Jack Ellyat spent the dark winter of 1862-1863 convalescing at his home in the cold Connecticut hills. He had been assigned to the Army of the Potomac as soon as his recovery was complete. In Tennessee, Melora Vilas gave birth to a baby boy.

Grant and Sherman led the Union forces to victory in the West; Vicksburg was surrounded. Hunger and anti-inflation riots broke out in Richmond. America, meanwhile, was expanding. New industries sprang up in the North, and the West was being developed. In Richmond, Shippy, a Union spy posing as a peddler, promised Sophy, a servant at the Pollard Hotel, that he would bring her some perfume from the North. Sophy knew that Clay Wingate and Lucy Weatherby had stayed together in the hotel. Luke Breckinridge, Sophy's rebel suitor, was a member of a patrol that stopped Shippy to search him. When they found incriminating papers in his boots, Luke gloated, for he was jealous of Shippy.

Stonewall Jackson was killed by his own pickets, and Lee, desperate for provisions, invaded the North. Jack Ellyat was in the Union army that converged on Gettysburg and was wounded during a battle there. After three days of bloody fighting at Gettysburg, Lee fell back to Virginia. Then Vicksburg surrendered. Nearly defeated, the South continued to fight doggedly. Sheridan marched through the Shenandoah Valley and left it bare and burned. Petersburg was besieged. Luke, along with thousands of other rebel troops, deserted the Confederate Army, and, when he headed back toward his home in the mountains, took Sophy with him. Melora and her father, John Vilas, traveled from place to place in search of Jack Ellyat; they became a legend in both armies. General Sherman captured Atlanta and marched on to the sea. During Sherman's march,

Wingate Hall caught fire accidentally and burned to the ground. Clay Wingate was wounded in a rearguard action in Virginia. The war came to an end when Lee surrendered to Grant at Appomattox.

Spade, who had gone from the labor gang into the Union Army and had been wounded at the Petersburg crater, hired out as a farm laborer in Cumberland County, Pennsylvania. Clay Wingate returned to his ruined home in Georgia, where Sally Dupré was waiting. In Connecticut, Jack Ellyat heard stories of strange gypsy travelers who were going from town to town looking for a soldier who was the father of the child of the woman who drove the creaking cart. One day he was standing beneath the crossroads elms when he saw a cart come slowly up the hill. He waited. The woman driving was Melora.

Critical Evaluation:

Stephen Vincent Benét's poem *John Brown's Body* is one of the few American poetic works which reach epic proportions; its length of nearly fifteen thousand lines qualifies it as an epic in the classical sense, and ranks it, in form and purpose at least, with the great epics of Western literature. Although the poem as a whole is traditional in its classic structure, it is distinctly and uniquely American in its atmosphere, imagery, style, and symbolism. In his invocation, Benét calls upon the American Muse to aid him, providing inspiration for what he humbly acknowledges to be an almost impossible task because of the magnitude of its scope. The poet's Muse becomes a symbol of America, his elusive subject: She is beautiful and strong, colorful and diverse, a unique, mysterious offspring of European and native parentage. Within the poem (line 311), Benét describes his work as a "cyclorama," a series of large pictures of America spread around the reader, who views them from the center.

The major unifying element in this cyclorama is the spirit of John Brown. Based on the historical figure of the man who raided the arsenal at Harpers Ferry, Benét's hero becomes the focal symbol of the epic; although he is condemned and hanged early in the work, his memory grows into the legend that gives hope and inspiration during the dark days of the Civil War. The second unifying thread throughout the loosely woven eight books is provided in the characters of Northerner Jack Ellyat and Southerner Clay Wingate. Other minor characters help round out the scheme whereby all the regions and social groups of a huge nation are represented: Melora Vilas and her father typify the border states and the expanding West; Lucy Weatherby is the Southern coquette; Luke Breckinridge, the independent mountaineer; Jake Diefer, the settled farmer; Spade, the runaway slave; Cudjo, the loyal slave; and Shippy, the Northern spy. By tracing the fortunes of such diverse people, Benét dramatizes not only how the war affects their lives but also how their lives shape the nation.

While Benét does not fully explore the complexities of the Northern family and their way of life, one of the greatest achievements of *John Brown's Body* is his accurate and balanced picture of Southern life. With realism and insight, he probes the character of John Brown and of his legend. Judging the raid as foolish, he sees Brown as a murderer and a fanatic, a man so caught in his zealous dream that he remains coldly unmoved by his son's horrible death. Brown the man was a failure; but dead, he became a crucial legend and symbol. Likewise, the Southern slaves are portrayed in all the complexity, ambiguity, and irony of their situation, and the Wingates embody the dilemma of the genteel Southern aristocratic family.

Bibliography:

Capps, Jack L., and C. Robert Kemble. Introduction to *John Brown's Body*, by Stephen Vincent Benét. New York: Holt, Rinehart and Winston, 1968. The editors identify Benét's sources, mark recurring motifs in the poem, and identify and annotate the names of persons, names of places, and literary quotations and allusions in the text.

Fenton, Charles A. *Stephen Vincent Benét: The Life and Times of an American Man of Letters, 1898-1943*. New Haven, Conn.: Yale University Press, 1958. Discusses Benét's sources for *John Brown's Body*, his writing habits, and the contemporary critical and popular responses to the poem.

Gregory, Horace, and Mary Zaturenska. *A History of American Poetry, 1900-1940*. New York: Harcourt, Brace, 1946. In this survey, the authors devote a few pages to Benét. They identify the virtues of *John Brown's Body*—clarity, vividness, occasional humor, easy rhythms, and patriotic purposes—and then its defects—stereotypical characters and shallow treatment of griefs and delights.

Monroe, Harriet. "A Cinema Epic." *Poetry: A Magazine of Verse* 33 (November, 1928): 91-96. A laudatory contemporary review of *John Brown's Body*, stressing its several movielike aspects.

Stroud, Perry. *Stephen Vincent Benét*. New York: Twayne, 1962. Contains a long chapter praising *John Brown's Body* as an epic poem of historical and philosophical significance. Discusses its clusters of imagery, notably those involving Phaeton and his chariot, stones, and seeds, its contrasting realistic depiction of war and romantic conception of love, and its varied meters—blank verse, versatile long line, and poetic prose.

JOHN HALIFAX, GENTLEMAN

Type of work: Novel
Author: Dinah Maria Mulock (Mrs. George Craik, 1826-1887)
Type of plot: Domestic realism
Time of plot: 1795-1834
Locale: Rural England
First published: 1856

> *Principal characters:*
> JOHN HALIFAX, one of nature's gentlemen
> URSULA, his wife
> MURIEL JOY,
> GUY,
> EDWIN,
> WALTER, and
> MAUD, their five children
> ABEL FLETCHER, John's benefactor
> PHINEAS FLETCHER, his invalid son and the narrator
> LORD RAVENEL, a landowner

The Story:

When Phineas Fletcher and his father, Abel, first saw John Halifax, they were immediately struck with his honest face and behavior; although the boy was only fourteen years old and an orphan, he would accept help from no one. Instead, he preferred to make his own way, even though it meant that he was always half-starved. Phineas was only sixteen years old and an invalid; he would have enjoyed having John for a companion, but Abel Fletcher, a wealthy Quaker, put the boy to work in his tannery. Although Abel was a Christian and wanted to help others, he knew that the boy would be better off if he helped himself. Then, too, there was a class distinction between Phineas and John that even Abel could not entirely overlook.

Phineas and John became good friends; the orphan was the only friend Phineas had ever loved as a brother. John rose rapidly in the tannery because of his honesty and his willingness to work at any job. He also had the ability to handle men, an ability ably proved when a hungry mob tried to burn down the Fletcher home and the mill that the Quaker owned. John arranged to have the workers get wheat for their families, and from then on, they were loyal to him through any crisis.

When they were in their early twenties, Phineas and John took a cottage in the country so that Phineas might have the advantage of the country air. While there, they met a lovely girl, Ursula March, who had taken her dying father to the same spot. John was attracted to the modest girl from the beginning, but since she was a lady, he felt that he could not tell her of his feelings. After the death of her father, it was learned that she was an heiress. She was therefore even more unattainable for John. When Ursula was told of John's feelings for her, however, she, knowing his true character, was happy to marry him. Everyone was shocked but Phineas, and Ursula's kinsman, a dissolute nobleman, refused to give her her fortune. John would not go to court to claim the fortune as would have been his legal right as Ursula's husband.

After the death of Abel Fletcher, Phineas lived with John and Ursula and their children, the oldest of whom, Muriel, was a lovely blind girl. Abel had made John a partner in the tannery, but because John did not like the tanyard and it was losing money, he sold it and put the money into the operation of the mill. Times were often hard during the next few years, but eventually, for political reasons, Ursula's kinsman released her fortune. After settling a large amount on his wife and children, John used the rest to lease a new mill and expand his business interests. His hobby was a steam engine to turn the mill, and before long, he began to be successful. The family moved to a new home in the country and lived many long years there in peace and happiness. John became influential in politics, especially in connection with the Reform Bill and the abolition of slavery. He made powerful enemies, too, but his concern was always for what was right. He became a wealthy man during this time, and his family moved to a more opulent home.

The steam engine, built and put into operation, gave John new advantages. Nevertheless, he provided generously for his workmen so that they would not suffer because of the machine. Then tragedy struck the family. Shortly after the birth of Maud, their last child, Muriel died. It was a sorrow from which John never completely recovered. The years brought other troubles. When two of his sons both fell in love with the governess of their little sister, they quarreled bitterly and the loser, Guy, left home and went abroad. After two or three years, they learned that Guy had nearly killed a man in Paris and had fled to America. From that time on, Ursula aged, for Guy was her favorite son.

Shortly afterward, Lord William Ravenel revealed to John that he was in love with Maud. Not only was Lord Ravenel the son of a worldly family, he had also led a useless and sometimes Byronic life. John would not listen to the man's pleas, and Lord Ravenel, agreeing that he was unworthy of Maud, left without telling her of his love. John revised his opinion of the man somewhat when, after the death of his father, Lord Ravenel gave up his inherited fortune to pay his father's debts. After this incident, Lord Ravenel was not heard from for many years. Maud did not marry. Her parents knew that she had never lost her affection for Lord Ravenel, although she did not know that he had returned her feelings.

Years passed. The married children gave John and Ursula grandchildren. John could have had a seat in Parliament, but he rejected it in favor of others. He continued to do good with his money and power, even when suffering temporary losses. He always longed for his lost blind child, just as Ursula longed for her missing oldest son. Their own love grew even deeper as they reached their twilight years. John often suffered attacks that left him gasping in pain and breathless, but in order to spare his family any unnecessary worry, he kept this information from all but Phineas.

Then came the wonderful news that Guy was coming home. All the family rejoiced, Ursula more than any other. They had six anxious months when his ship seemed to have been lost at sea, but at last Guy arrived. He had been shipwrecked but had eventually made his way home. With him was Lord Ravenel. Both men had done well in America but had lost everything in the shipwreck. This seemed of little importance in the happy reunion. John now realized that Lord William Ravenel had proved himself worthy of Maud, and the two lovers were at last allowed to express their love for each other. Guy, too, began to show interest in a childhood friend, and another wedding in the family seemed likely.

John felt that his life was now complete, his peace and happiness being broken only by longing for his dead child. He was soon to join her. One day he sat down to rest, and his family found him in the peaceful sleep of death. That night, as she sat by her husband's body, Ursula must have felt that she could not live without him, for the children and Phineas found her lying dead beside her husband. They were buried side by side in the country churchyard.

Critical Evaluation:

Of the more than twenty novels that Dinah Mulock wrote, *John Halifax, Gentleman*, was by far the most popular, not only during her own lifetime, but well into the twentieth century. Toward the end of that century, critical interest turned to those among her novels that deal with gender issues from a woman's point of view, among them *Olive* (1850) and *Agatha's Husband* (1853), and to some of her nonfictional work, such as *A Woman's Thoughts about Women* (1858). Mulock herself married late, in 1865; for a period in her early life she was responsible for supporting her family financially after her father, a nonconformist preacher, had been committed as insane.

Some of this personal experience of successful independence permeates *John Halifax, Gentleman*. It was, however, also a period when the British Victorian dream was closest to the American Dream, when people believed that anyone could make it to the top through sheer hard work and good character. Samuel Smiles's best-seller, *Self-Help*, appeared a few years after Mulock's novel, in 1859. Both works owe a great deal to Thomas Carlyle, who posited the idea of new meritocracy in the form of a sort of neofeudal industrialism.

The breakdown of the old English class structures is clearly portrayed in *John Halifax, Gentlemen*. Central to this account is the figure of John Halifax himself, who is orphaned and destitute at the beginning of the novel. His belief that he is already a gentleman never wavers, nor does his life's ambition to manifest this to the world. He first convinces Abel Fletcher, who as a Quaker is already committed to a more democratic worldview. Then he convinces Ursula March, who loved him before she knew he was an apprentice tanner. Her guardian, Richard Brithwood, is never convinced, but he is shown to be part of a degenerate upperclass whose claims to being the ruling class are morally bankrupt. His wife, Lady Caroline, is more sympathetic but equally morally bankrupt, and Mulock shows her to be literally destitute at the end. John also stands up to Lord Luxmore, Lady Caroline's father, during a corrupt election. In this episode, Mulock demonstrates her ability to describe both character clashes and socioeconomic ones. William Ravenel's renunciation of his title and estate is a sign of his moral worthiness to become part of the new Halifax family.

The debate on what constitutes a gentleman was conducted in a number of contemporary novels, the one chronologically nearest to Mulock's book being *North and South* (1855) by Elizabeth Gaskell, one of her acquaintances. Gaskell's novel deals with a woman learning to accept a self-made man as an equal. Mulock manages to explicate the man's mind. Charles Dickens deals with the same issue in *Great Expectations* (1861) but in a much less straightforward fashion. Mulock hints in the character of Guy that inherited wealth (or the promise of it) can be corrupting, but she allows him to redeem himself. Dickens portrays much more openly the corruption of wealth not earned through hard work, and in *Hard Times* (1854), he actually parodies the self-made Josiah Bounderby. In fact, it has been argued that since John Halifax's only record of ancestry is that his father was a gentleman, he is merely retrieving a lost rank.

Mulock, like Gaskell and Dickens, defines the term "gentleman" as a Christian man, within the context of a largely undogmatic, uninstitutionalized Christianity. This puts the norm well outside the traditional Church of England squirearchy.

The case of the rise of a new middle-class meritocracy illustrates well Mulock's very straightforward views and their portrayal. As illustrated by the Reform Act and the emancipation of slaves, progress is coming. Mulock never portrays the evils of industrialism, keeping the setting determinedly pastoral. In fact, one of the stated subtexts to the novel is Phineas Fletcher's own ancestor of the same name, a Caroline poet whose *The Purple Island* (1633) is quoted as the epitome of pastoral idyll. John Halifax seeks to capture that idyll at his first rural dwelling, Longfield. As his status in life rises, however, he feels, despite Ursula's objections, that he should move to a grander house.

Mulock never resolves the apparent paradox of the impossibility of the pastoral in a life of increasing wealth, since it is her firm Roman philosophy that wealth brings public duty, and duty comes even before love, let alone pastoral seclusion. That is her moral platform.

John, for no clear reason, refuses political office, in much the same way as Mulock, unlike Mrs. Gaskell, refused political debate. By setting the story one generation back from her own, she is dealing, in fact, with issues that had largely been settled. Her preference is to concentrate on domestic issues, and it is in this that her enduring attraction as a writer lies. Although certain plot sequences are stereotyped and predictable, among them the blind daughter, the child's death, the mother's boy who errs, and the brothers' quarrel, there is nevertheless real observation, resulting in a convincing study of family relationships. The absence of any sort of united family in Mulock's own life may have created a desire in her for a fictional one, but she is realistic enough to know that changelessness, the pastoral dream of *otiosa*, is ultimately impossible. Suffering and unrest always lie lurking, whether for the poor or for the rich.

Indeed, as a result of the narrative viewpoint, that of Phineas, the novel constantly reminds the reader of sickness. Although in his adult years Phineas' poor health is never alluded to, he has vowed never to marry so as not to pass on his genetic disease, and this androgynous stance comments ironically at times on the sexual passions that touch the other characters. Phineas is a man of peace, without pretension, and he mediates Mulock's admiration for strength, action, and heroism, above all in his friend and brother John Halifax. He thereby ensures a totally sympathetic narrative account of this ideal Victorian.

"Critical Evaluation" by David Barratt

Bibliography:
Altick, Richard D. *The Presence of the Present: Topics of the Day in the Victorian Novel.* Columbus: Ohio State University, 1991. Covers a large number of Victorian novelists, showing how they used everyday materials and experiences to satisfy readers' interest in the contemporary scene and ordinary social life. Specific discussions of *John Halifax, Gentlemen.*

Brantlinger, Patrick. *The Spirit of Reform: British Literature and Politics, 1832-1867.* Cambridge, Mass.: Harvard University Press, 1977. An excellent discussion of the novel in chapter 5, "The Entrepreneurial Ideal," identifies the strengths and weaknesses of Mulock's social idealism. Index.

Gilmour, Robin. "Dickens and the Self-Help Idea." In *The Victorians and Social Protest*, edited by John Butt and I. F. Clarke. Newton Abbot, England: David and Charles, 1973. Much of the chapter is a detailed comparison between *Great Expectations* and *John Halifax, Gentleman.* Bibliography and index.

_____. *The Idea of the Gentleman in the Victorian Novel.* London: Allen & Unwin, 1981. Gilmour sees *John Halifax, Gentleman* as "the classic novel of self-help . . . in its purest, least critical form." Notes the idea of retrieval of status and the way that John's self-culture is colored by sexual desire and social ambition. Index.

Mitchell, Sally. *Dinah Mulock Craik.* Boston: Twayne, 1983. A useful life-and-works study, with a good section on *John Halifax, Gentleman.* Bibliography and index.

JONATHAN WILD

Type of work: Novel
Author: Henry Fielding (1707-1754)
Type of plot: Social satire
Time of plot: Late seventeenth century
Locale: England
First published: The History of the Life of the Late Mr. Jonathan Wild the Great, 1743

> *Principal characters:*
> JONATHAN WILD, a "great man"
> LAETITIA, his wife
> COUNT LA RUSE, a rogue
> THOMAS HEARTFREE, a good man
> MRS. HEARTFREE, his good wife

The Story:

Jonathan Wild was prepared by nature to be a "great man." His ancestors were all men of greatness, many of them hanged for thievery or treason. Those who escaped were simply shrewder and more fortunate than the others. Jonathan, however, was to be so "great" as to put his forefathers to shame.

As a boy, he read about the great villains of history. He learned little at school; his best field of study was picking the pockets of his tutors and fellow students. When he was seventeen years old, his father moved to town, where Jonathan was to put his talents to even better use. There he met the Count La Ruse, a knave destined to be one of the lesser "greats." La Ruse was in prison for debt, but Jonathan's skill soon secured his friend's freedom. Together they had many profitable ventures, picking the pockets of their friends and of each other. Neither became angry when the other stole from him, for each respected the other's abilities.

For unknown reasons, Jonathan traveled in America for seven or eight years. Returning to England, he continued his life of villainy. Since he was to be a truly "great" man, he could not soil his own hands with too much thievery because there was always the danger of the gallows if he should be apprehended. He gathered about him a handful of lesser thieves who took the risks while he collected most of the booty. La Ruse joined him in many of his schemes, and the two friends continued to steal from each other. This ability to cheat friends showed true "greatness."

Jonathan admired Laetitia Snap, a woman with qualities of "greatness" similar to his own. She was the daughter of his father's friend, and she too was skilled in picking pockets and cheating at cards. In addition, she was a lady of wonderfully loose morals. No matter how hard he tried, Jonathan could not get Laetitia to respond to his passion. The poor fellow did not at first know that each time he approached her, she was hiding another lover in the closet. Had he known, his admiration would have been even greater.

Jonathan's true "greatness" did not appear until he renewed his acquaintance with Mr. Heartfree, a former schoolmate. Heartfree would never be a "great" man because he was a good man. He cheated no one, held no grudges, and loved his wife and children. These qualities made him the sort of person Jonathan liked to cheat. Heartfree was a jeweler; he had become moderately prosperous through hard work and honest practices. With the help of La Ruse, Jonathan was able to bring Heartfree to ruin. They stole his jewels and his money and hired thugs to beat him unmercifully, all the time convincing the good man that they were his friends.

La Ruse approached the greatness of Jonathan by leaving the country after stealing most of their booty. Poor Heartfree was locked up for debt after the two scoundrels had ruined him. Then Jonathan performed his greatest act. He also had a strong passion for Mrs. Heartfree, a good and virtuous woman, and he persuaded her that her husband had asked him to take her and some remaining jewels to Holland until her husband could obtain his release. He talked so cleverly that the woman did not even tell her husband good-bye, although she loved him dearly. Instead, she put her children in the hands of a faithful servant and accompanied the rogue on a ship leaving England immediately.

When a severe storm arose, Jonathan was sure that death was near. Throwing caution aside, he attacked Mrs. Heartfree. Her screams brought help from the captain. After the storm subsided, the captain put Jonathan adrift in a small boat. The captain did not know that Jonathan was a "great" man, not destined to die in an ignoble fashion. After a while, he was rescued. He returned to England with tall tales of his adventure, none of which were the least bit true.

In the meantime, Heartfree had begun to suspect his friend of duplicity. When Jonathan returned, he was for a time able to persuade Heartfree that he had done everything possible to help the jeweler. He told just enough of the truth to make his story acceptable; for "in greatness," the lie must always contain some truth. Jonathan, however, went too far. He urged Heartfree to attempt an escape from prison by murdering a few guards. Heartfree saw his supposed friend as the rogue he was and denounced Jonathan in ringing tones. From that time on, Jonathan lived only to bring Heartfree to complete destruction.

While Jonathan was plotting Heartfree's trip to the gallows, Laetitia's father finally gave his consent to his daughter's marriage to the rogue. It took only two weeks, however, for his passion to be satisfied; then the couple began to fight and cheat each other constantly.

After his marriage, Jonathan continued in all kinds of knavery. His most earnest efforts were directed toward sending Heartfree to the gallows. At last, he hit upon a perfect plan. He convinced the authorities that Heartfree had plotted to have his wife take the jewels out of the country in order to cheat his creditors. Mrs. Heartfree had not returned to England. Although Jonathan hoped she was dead, he thought it better to have her husband hanged at once in case she should somehow return. Before Heartfree's sentence was carried out, however, Jonathan was arrested and put in jail. He was surprised by a visit from Laetitia. She came only to revile him. She had been caught picking pockets, and was also a prisoner. Her only wish was that she could have the pleasure of seeing Jonathan hanged before her turn came to die on the gallows.

On the day that Heartfree was to be hanged, his wife returned. After many adventures and travel in many lands, she came back in time to tell her story and to save her husband from hanging. She had brought with her a precious jewel that had been given to her by a savage chief she had met on her travels. Heartfree was released, and his family was restored to prosperity. It was otherwise with Jonathan, whose former friends hastened to hurry him to the gallows. On the appointed day he was hanged, leaving this world with a curse for all humanity. His wife and all his friends were hanged, save one. La Ruse was captured in France and broken on the wheel. Jonathan Wild was a "great" man because he was a complete villain.

Critical Evaluation:

Jonathan Wild appeared almost two decades after the real master criminal of that name had been hanged and a year after the fall from power of the corrupt British prime minister Robert Walpole, who had frequently been likened to Wild. Henry Fielding did not intend to write another biography of Wild, who was no longer at the forefront of public interest, nor was there any point in reiterating the points of similarity between Wild and Walpole, which had been pointed out by so many others, most unforgettably by Fielding's friend and fellow Tory John Gay in *The Beggar's Opera* (1728). It is true that shortly before his death Fielding revised his novel, removing a number of references to Walpole. However, even in its original form, *Jonathan Wild* was not primarily an attack on Walpole or on his Whig party, which remained in power after his departure from the government. Instead, Fielding's book is philosophical in nature, an examination of two ways of life, which may be contrasted through the use of one familiar character from the annals of crime and a whole set of characters from the author's imagination. Fielding wanted to show his readers that, whatever their circumstances, they had the power to choose between being "great," and ending in misery, and being "good," which would lead them to happiness, or at least to inner peace.

As the full title of the book indicates, Jonathan Wild represents the first alternative. His hero is Alexander the Great, and he sets himself to become "great." His purpose in life is not just to obtain power over as many people as possible, but to prove to himself that he is superior to everyone else. Thus he cheats the wily Count and betrays the members of his gang not merely to enrich himself or even to inspire fear in others, but, more important, to give himself an excuse for admiring his own intelligence.

On the other hand, in keeping with his name, Thomas Heartfree is generous to a fault, giving and forgiving. Honest himself, he expects others to be the same. As a result, as Fielding says, he seems to be the natural victim of "great" men like Wild, who consider "goodness" to be just another name for "silliness." It is not surprising that Wild and his confederates take advantage of Heartfree. What at first seems more puzzling is Wild's determination to annihilate the inoffensive Heartfree, who on the face of it is a far less worthy opponent than a clever crook like the Count.

However, given the polarity on which Fielding has based his novel, Wild's need to destroy Heartfree is understandable. If indeed human beings are inherently selfish, then Wild is right in his view of the world, and Heartfree is insignificant. However, Wild is threatened by the possibility that another view is correct, that represented by Heartfree. Like many other eighteenth century thinkers, Fielding was an adherent of Anthony Ashley Cooper, the Third Earl of Shaftesbury, who in his *Characteristicks of Men, Manners, Opinions, Times* (1711) argued not only that it is natural for human beings to have "affections" for others, but also that people are born with a "moral sense," which enables them to distinguish between right and wrong. Following Shaftesbury, Fielding presents Heartfree as a "natural" man and Wild as an "unnatural" representative of the human species whose interpretation of life is fatally flawed.

Wild's obsession with getting rid of Heartfree, then, is motivated by his need to prove himself "natural," and his own world view correct. Surely, Wild wants to believe, he will someday find happiness. What he does not realize, however, is that, like Alexander the Great regretting that there were no more worlds to conquer, Wild is enslaved by his own will. Nothing satisfies him. Every trick calls for another, even cleverer; every betrayal accomplished demands the next; and every sexual conquest is fast forgotten in the need for the next. In fact, in his relationships with women, Wild admits his weakness. As he himself is tricked and cheated by the likes of Molly Straddle, he feels more like a slave to his own desires than the master he has willed himself to be.

As the novel progresses, it becomes increasingly apparent that even in the public arena, where he seems so successful, Wild is not truly free. He may be able to wrest control over the criminal world from another "great" man, but he cannot overcome the foolish desire to adorn himself, thus alienating his followers. As a result, when society decides that Wild is no longer of more value outside of prison than in, there is no shortage of people to betray him. In fact, however, Wild has already been betrayed, both by his own weakness and by his misreading of the world.

Fielding's statement about the antipathy of great men toward "liberty" is thus revealed as doubly ironic. While on one level it reminds readers that Walpole used censorship to drive Fielding and his plays from the stage, the comment has a broader application. While the "great" believe themselves at liberty to do whatever they wish, they do not have the moral independence that Heartfree and his wife experience, even in their darkest hours. Fielding has already proven his point about virtue and happiness, even before he works out a providential happy ending for the Heartfrees and their family.

Admittedly, one can hardly expect total consistency from a writer whose own philosophy was so peculiar a compound of Deism, Christianity, and Platonism, and whose own habit of mind was so playfully ironic. Fielding's disquisitions on Fortune, for example, contradict each other. Similarly, it is not clear whether he expects those who are neither villains nor saints, but only half-hearted and easily swayed, to suffer like Wild or to be pardoned by a divinity as generous as Heartfree. What is clear, however, is that in this novel Fielding has taken up the weapon that "great" men employ to deceive the world, and instead has used language as "good" men do, in the service of virtue and truth.

"Critical Evaluation" by Rosemary M. Canfield Reisman

Bibliography:
Battestin, Martin C., with Ruthe R. Battestin. *Henry Fielding: A Life.* London: Routledge & Kegan Paul, 1989. A standard biography, detailed but highly readable. Includes a chronological bibliography of Fielding's works and letters.
Dircks, Richard J. *Henry Fielding.* Boston: Twayne, 1983. Argues that Fielding's target was not Robert Walpole himself, but what he represented. Includes chronology, notes, and annotated bibliography.
Irwin, William Robert. *The Making of Jonathan Wild: A Study in the Literary Method of Henry Fielding.* Hamden, Conn.: Archon Books, 1966. The first book-length study of the novel, still an important source. Discusses biographical and historical background, ethical import, and genre.
Nokes, David. *"Jonathan Wild."* In *Henry Fielding,* edited by Harold Bloom. New York: Chelsea House, 1987. Comparing the novel to some modern works, Nokes points out subtleties that he feels other critics have overlooked. Interesting introductory comments place the novel in its historical context.
Shesgreen, Sean. *Literary Portraits in the Novels of Henry Fielding.* DeKalb: Northern Illinois University Press, 1972. Believes that Fielding reveals character as much through description, both physiological and psychological, as through action and dialogue. Unlike the fully developed characters in his later works, those in *Jonathan Wild* are types, representing extremes in what is intended to be a moral allegory.

JORROCKS' JAUNTS AND JOLLITIES

Type of work: Novel
Author: Robert Smith Surtees (1803-1864)
Type of plot: Wit and humor
Time of plot: 1830's
Locale: England and France
First published: 1838

Principal characters:
    JORROCKS, a grocer and sportsman
    MR. STUBBS, a Yorkshireman
    THE COUNTESS BENVOLIO

The Story:

When they went out to hunt, the members of Jorrocks' Surrey fox hunt did not always keep their minds on the sport. As they gathered, their talk included shouts to the dogs, quotations on the price of cotton, advice on horses, and warnings of bank policies. While waiting for the dogs to run the fox closer, they all eagerly pulled out bread and meat from their roomy pockets.

One morning, a new man joined the veteran Surrey hunters. He was plainly an aristocrat. The others were paunchy and stooped, but he was thin and straight. His handsome mount contrasted sharply with their skinny nags. They all watched him enviously. He was evidently new in Surrey, for he drove his horse at a fast clip through the bottomlands, heedless of the numerous flints. The riders were glad when he had to retire from the chase with a lame horse.

As he left, Jorrocks rushed up with the news that the stranger was no less a personage than a Russian diplomat. The whole hunt joined in heartily wishing him back in Russia for good.

In town, Jorrocks ran into agreeable Mr. Stubbs, a footloose Yorkshireman. He invited Stubbs to go to the hunt on Saturday morning. So long as Jorrocks paid the bills, the Yorkshireman was glad for any entertainment. On the appointed foggy morning, Jorrocks was on time. He was riding his own bony nag and leading a sorry dray horse for his guest. The fog was so thick that they bumped into carriages and sidewalk stands right and left. The Yorkshireman would have waited for the fog to lift, but doughty Jorrocks would tolerate no delay. Mrs. Jorrocks had a fine quarter of lamb for supper, and her husband had been sternly ordered to be back at five-thirty sharp. Jorrocks was never late for a meal.

On the way, Jorrocks' horse was nearly speared by a carriage pole. The resourceful hunter promptly dismounted and chattered a bit with a coach driver. When he remounted, he had a great coach lamp tied around his middle. Thus lighted, the two horsemen got safely out of town.

The hunt that day held an unexpected surprise for both of them. Jorrocks put his horse at a weak spot in a fence to show off a little for his younger friend. He wanted to sail over in good time and continue after the fox. Instead, he landed in a cesspool. His bright red coat was covered with slime and mud for the rest of the day. The Yorkshireman, however, noted that Jorrocks carried on until the end of the hunt and got home in time for his lamb dinner.

As usual, Jorrocks went hunting in Surrey on a Saturday. When his horse went lame, he stopped at the smith's shop for repairs, and his five-minute delay made him lose sight of the pack. Consequently, he lost out on a day's sport. As he sat brooding in a local inn and threatening to withdraw his subscription to the Surrey hunt, Nosey Browne entered. Jorrocks was delighted to see his old friend and willingly accepted an invitation to a day's shooting on Browne's estate.

A few days later, he collected the Yorkshireman and set out eagerly for the shooting. He was saddened to find that Nosey's big estate was little more than a cramped spot of ground covered with sheds and other outbuildings. Squire Cheatum, learning that Nosey was bankrupt, had forbidden his neighbor to hunt in his woods; Jorrocks, therefore, was forced to hunt in the yard behind the sheds. Soon he saw a rabbit. In his excitement, he took a step forward and shot the animal. As he was about to pick up his prize, a gamekeeper arrived and accused him of trespassing. After an extended argument, it was shown that Jorrocks' toe had, at the moment of shooting, been over the line on Squire Cheatum's land, and so the wrathful Jorrocks was fined more than one pound.

Jorrocks would not accept calmly a fine that was so obviously unfair. He hired a lawyer and appealed the case to the county court. On the day of the trial, Jorrocks beamed as his attorney pictured him as a substantial citizen with a reputation for good works. He squirmed as the squire's lawyer described him as a cockney grocer who was infringing on the rights of countryfolk. At the end, the judges woke up and sustained the fine.

After the fox hunting season ended, Jorrocks accepted an invitation to a stag hunt. The Yorkshireman came to breakfast with him on the appointed morning. Jorrocks led him down into the kitchen, where the maid had set out the usual fare. There were a whole ham, a loaf of bread, and a huge sausage. There were muffins, nine eggs, a pork pie, and kidneys on a spit. Betsy was stationed at the stove, where she deftly laid mutton chops on the gridiron.

As the two friends ate, Mrs. Jorrocks came in with an ominous look on her face. She held up a card, which was inscribed with a woman's name and address, that she had found in her spouse's pocket. Jorrocks seized the card, threw it into the fire, and declared that it was an application for a deaf and dumb institute.

The men set out for the hunt in Jorrocks' converted fire wagon. Ahead of them was a van carrying a drowsy doe. They were shocked to learn on arriving that their "stag" was that same tame deer imported for the day. She had to be chased to make her stop grazing on the common. Jorrocks' disappointment was complete when he learned that he had been invited only for his contribution to the club fund.

Abandoning the hunt for a while, Jorrocks took a boat trip to Margate with the Yorkshireman. The expedition was also a failure, for he left his clothes on the beach when he went for a swim and the tide engulfed them. The unhappy grocer was forced to go back to London in hand-me-downs.

Jorrocks, seeing numerous books for sale at fancy prices, determined to write a four-volume work on France that would sell for thirty pounds. With little more ado, he collected the Yorkshireman and set out for Dover. He was charmed with Boulogne because the French were merry and the weather was sunny. On the coach to Paris, Jorrocks met the Countess Benvolio, as he called her in cockney fashion. The countess was quite receptive to the rich grocer. She seemed to be a beautiful, youthful woman, until she went to sleep in the coach and her teeth dropped down. Once in Paris, Jorrocks was snugly installed as the favored guest in her apartment. He began to collect information for his book.

The countess was avid for presents, and before long, Jorrocks began to run short of money. He tried to recoup at the races, but the Frenchmen were too shrewd for him. Finally, he offered to race fifty yards on foot with the Yorkshireman perched on his shoulders, against a fleet French baron who was to run a hundred yards. Jorrocks took a number of wagers and gave them to the countess to hold. He won the race easily. When he regained his breath and looked about for the countess, she had disappeared.

With little money and being unable to speak French, the Englishmen took quite some time to return to the countess' apartment. By the time they arrived, a gross Dutchman was installed as her favorite. When Jorrocks tried to collect his wagers, she presented him with a detailed board bill. Pooling his last funds with the Yorkshireman's hoard, he was barely able to pay the bill. Chastened by his sojourn among the French, Jorrocks returned to England.

Critical Evaluation:

Immensely popular with its first readers, *Jorrocks' Jaunts and Jollities* remains a minor classic of British fiction, although overshadowed by the early work of Robert Smith Surtees' more famous contemporary, Charles Dickens. Many critics have noted the similarities between Surtees' sporting novel and Dickens' first masterpiece, *Pickwick Papers* (1836-1837). Unfortunately for Surtees, his younger contemporary went on to become the most celebrated novelist of his day, moving beyond the picaresque tradition that informs these two early works and taking with him a reading public that could not get enough of Dickens' blend of social realism and Victorian sentimentalism. Although he continued to write for several decades after *Jorrocks' Jaunts and Jollities* appeared in 1838, Surtees never again achieved the popular following he enjoyed for this delightful look at the adventures of a goodhearted grocer whose penchant for sport leads him across Britain and to the Continent in search of adventure.

Much of the strength, and many of the weaknesses, associated with *Jorrocks' Jaunts and Jollities* can be traced to the form of its initial publication in *New Sporting* magazine. Forced to relate his tale in a series of vignettes that could stand alone for readers of the periodical, Surtees sometimes sacrifices unity of plotting for the sense of completeness in individual scenes. When the individual stories are read as parts of a single novel, readers find themselves wondering at times about the causal relationships between parts; the sense of the well-plotted novel, central to later works of the nineteenth century (for example, the complexities of publications by Dickens or Thomas Hardy) is noticeably absent. Instead, Surtees is forced to rely on readers' engagement with Jorrocks as the bait that will lure them from one chapter to the next. Fortunately for the author, his sporting hero does have many endearing qualities, and succeeding generations have found his adventures humorous and engaging, thus ensuring a continued readership for the work.

The initial publication as a serial work also leads Surtees to repeat incidents, if not verbatim, then certainly by type. Because of the time lapse between the appearance of individual installments, what was funny to readers in one issue could be counted on to appeal to their sense of mirth several months later, and one should not fault the novelist for relying on stock situations for his humor. Reading *Jorrocks' Jaunts and Jollities* as a novel, in a much shorter time than the two years it took to publish the tale in serial form, highlights the weaknesses of plotting and the sense of indirection created by the episodic nature of the story.

The choice of *New Sporting* as the place of publication also had an impact on the story. Readers of that magazine were drawn to it by their love of the sporting life, and Surtees does all he can to fulfill their expectations for fiction that will satisfy their interest and teach them something about sport and travel in a leisurely, genial fashion. Many of the episodes are set within a day's ride of London, and Surtees' descriptions of the various locales in which Jorrocks has his adventures are meticulous. Readers not only could get a good laugh at the exploits of the good-natured grocer-turned-sportsman, but also could learn about potential sites for their own sporting exploits.

Jorrocks' Jaunts and Jollities is no mere travelogue or sporting digest, however; despite the limitations placed on him by the form of publication, Surtees uses his story as a means of social commentary. The novel is a gentle satire on topics of special interest to the British public: the sham and duplicity of people who pretend to be something other than what they are; the evils of small-minded populaces such as the one at Newmarket, which receives especially odious treatment by the author; and the inferiority of French life and culture, a topic often held up for ridicule to a reading public already prejudiced against their neighbors across the English Channel.

Surtees' models for *Jorrocks' Jaunts and Jollities* are the great masters of eighteenth century fiction: Henry Fielding, Tobias Smollett, and Laurence Sterne. Like Fielding and Sterne, Surtees is more interested in creating character types whose adventures are emblematic of larger, universal patterns of behavior. Like them, too, he has a comic view of humanity, seeing humankind as essentially good, but susceptible to corruption in a society where excess of any kind may lead one into danger. Like all three of his predecessors, Surtees relies on the importance of incident and the loose episodic structure made popular in picaresque fiction to capture and maintain readers' interest. Although Jorrocks is no rogue, he shares affinities with those rapscallions who move from one adventure to another, escaping through good fortune only to fall victim to another snare from which they will be rescued only through ingenuity or grace. Perhaps the closest parallel exists between *Jorrocks' Jaunts and Jollities* and Sterne's *A Sentimental Journey Through England and France* (1768); in that novel, as in Surtees' work, the hero wanders, apparently without aim, through the countryside of his native land and the country across the English Channel, falling victim to men and women intent on drawing personal gain from his misfortune. Like Sterne, Surtees uses the journey motif as a means of calling attention to the evils and follies of people from various walks of life. Through Jorrocks, his opinionated yet lovable mouthpiece, Surtees provides a commentary on the humbugs and hypocrites who stand in the way of happiness for the person of good will.

"Critical Evaluation" updated by Laurence W. Mazzeno

Bibliography:
Cooper, Leonard. *R. S. Surtees*. London: Arthur Baker, 1952. Biographical study of the novelist. Comments on *Jorrocks' Jaunts and Jollities* are interspersed throughout the narrative of Surtees' career; explains the composition process and the relationship of fictional characters and situations to the author's life.
Gash, Norman. *Robert Surtees and Early Victorian Society*. Oxford, England: Clarendon Press, 1993. General study of the novelist's ability to dramatize and comment on social situations in the early decades of the nineteenth century. Relates details of *Jorrocks' Jaunts and Jollities* to larger social issues that interested the novelist throughout his career.
Hamilton, Alex. Introduction to *Jorrocks' Jaunts and Jollities*, by Robert Smith Surtees. London: Cassell, 1968. Excellent commentary on the significance of the novel in Surtees' career; also explains how it served as the stimulus for later, similar productions, especially those by Dickens and Anthony Trollope.
Neumann, Bonnie Rayford. *Robert Smith Surtees*. Boston: Twayne, 1978. General introduction to the novelist's career. Includes a scholarly examination of *Jorrocks' Jaunts and Jollities*, focusing on Surtees' development of his title character as a spokesperson for the author's views about society and its values; describes ways in which Surtees distinguishes genuine emotions from hypocrisy and sham.
Welcome, John. *The Sporting World of R. S. Surtees*. New York: Oxford University Press, 1982. General survey of Surtees' career. Comments on the development of characters in *Jorrocks' Jaunts and Jollities* and on the novel's publication history.

JOSEPH ANDREWS

Type of work: Novel
Author: Henry Fielding (1707-1754)
Type of plot: Social realism
Time of plot: Early eighteenth century
Locale: England
First published: The History of the Adventures of Joseph Andrews, and of His Friend Mr. Abraham Adams, 1742

>   *Principal characters:*
>   JOSEPH ANDREWS, a footman to Lady Booby
>   PAMELA ANDREWS, his sister, and the wife of Squire Booby
>   LADY BOOBY, Squire Booby's aunt
>   FANNY, Joseph's sweetheart
>   MRS. SLIPSLOP, Lady Booby's maid
>   PARSON ADAMS, the parson of Booby parish and a friend of Joseph
>   Andrews

The Story:

For ten or eleven years, Joseph Andrews had been in the service of Sir Thomas Booby, the uncle of the Squire Booby who was married to the virtuous Pamela, Joseph's sister. When Lord Booby died, Joseph at first remained in the employ of Lady Booby as her footman. This lady, much older than her twenty-one-year-old servant and apparently little disturbed by her husband's death, was attracted to the pleasant-mannered, handsome young man. Joseph, however, was as virtuous as his famous sister, and when Lady Booby's advances became such that even his innocence could no longer overlook their true nature, he was as firm in resisting her as Pamela had been in restraining Squire Booby. The lady was insulted and discharged Joseph on the spot, despite the protests of Mrs. Slipslop, her maid, who was herself attracted to the young man.

With very little money and even fewer prospects, Joseph set out from London to Somersetshire to see his sweetheart, Fanny, for whose sake he had held firm against Lady Booby's advances. On the first night of his journey, Joseph was attacked by robbers, who stole his money, beat him soundly, and left him lying naked and half dead in a ditch. A passing coach stopped when the passengers heard his cries, and he was taken to a nearby inn.

Joseph was well cared for until the innkeeper's wife discovered that he was penniless. He was recognized, however, by a visitor at the inn, his old tutor and preceptor, Parson Adams, who was on his way to London to sell a collection of his sermons. He paid Joseph's bill out of his own meager savings; then, discovering that in his absentmindedness he had forgotten to bring the sermons with him, he decided to accompany Joseph back to Somersetshire.

They started out, alternately on foot and on the parson's horse. Fortunately, Mrs. Slipslop overtook them in a coach on her way to Lady Booby's country place. She accommodated the parson in the coach while Joseph rode the horse. The inn at which they stopped next had an innkeeper who gauged his courtesy according to the appearance of his guests. When he insulted Joseph, Parson Adams, despite his clerical cassock, challenged the host, and a fistfight followed that extended to a tussle between the hostess and Mrs. Slipslop. When the battle finally ended,

Parson Adams came off looking the bloodiest, since in her excitement the hostess had doused him with a pail of hog's blood.

The journey continued, this time with Joseph in the coach and the parson on foot, for with typical forgetfulness the good man had left his horse behind. Nevertheless, because he walked rapidly and the coach moved slowly, he easily outdistanced his friends. While he was resting on his journey, he heard the shrieks of a woman. Running to her rescue, he discovered a young woman being cruelly attacked by a burly fellow. The parson belabored the attacker with such violence that he felled him to the ground. As a group of fox hunters rode up, the ruffian rose from the ground and accused Parson Adams and the woman of being conspirators in an attempt to rob him. The parson and the woman were quickly taken prisoners and led off to the sheriff. On the way, the parson discovered that the young woman whom he had aided was Fanny. Having heard of Joseph's unhappy dismissal from Lady Booby's service, she had been on her way to London to help him when she had been so cruelly molested.

After some uncomfortable moments before the judge, the parson was recognized by an onlooker, and both he and Fanny were released. Upon going to the inn where Mrs. Slipslop and Joseph were staying, Joseph and Fanny were overjoyed to see each other. Mrs. Slipslop was displeased to see Joseph's display of affection for another woman and drove off in the coach, leaving Parson Adams and the young lovers behind.

None of the three had any money to pay their bill at the inn. With indomitable optimism, Parson Adams went to visit the clergyman of the parish to borrow the money, but he was unsuccessful. Finally, a poor peddler at the inn gave them every penny he had, which was just enough to cover the bill. They continued their trip on foot, stopping at another inn where the host was more courteous than any they had met and more understanding about their financial difficulties. Still farther on their journey, they came across a secluded house at which they were asked to stop and rest. Mr. and Mrs. Wilson were a charming couple who gave their guests a warm welcome. Mr. Wilson entertained the parson with the story of his life, telling them that in his youth he had been attracted by the vanity of London life, had squandered his money on foppish clothes, gambling, and drinking, and had eventually been imprisoned for debt. He was rescued from this situation by the kindly cousin whom he later married. The two had retired from London to this quiet country home. They had two lovely children and their only sorrow, but that a deep one, was that a third child, a boy with a strawberry mark on his shoulder, had been stolen by gypsies and had never been heard of since.

After a pleasant visit with the kindly family, the travelers set out again. Their adventures were far from over. Parson Adams suddenly found himself caught in the middle of a hare hunt, with the hounds inclined to mistake him for the hare. Their master goaded on the dogs, but Joseph and the parson were victorious in the battle. They found themselves face-to-face with an angry squire and his followers; but when the squire caught sight of the lovely Fanny, his anger softened, and he invited the three to dine.

Supper was a trying affair for the parson, who was made the butt of many practical jokes. Finally, the three travelers left the house in great anger and went to an inn. In the middle of the night, some of the squire's men arrived, overcame Joseph and the parson, and abducted Fanny. An old acquaintance of Fanny, Peter Pounce, met the party of kidnappers, however, and rescued Fanny.

The rest of the journey was relatively uneventful, but when they arrived home further difficulties arose. Joseph and Fanny stayed at the parsonage and waited eagerly for their wedding banns to be published. Lady Booby had also arrived in the parish, the seat of her summer home. Still in love with Joseph, she exerted every pressure of position and wealth to prevent the marriage. She even had Fanny and Joseph arrested. At this point, however, Squire Booby and his wife Pamela arrived. Booby insisted on accepting his wife's relatives as his own, even though they were of a lower station, and Joseph and Fanny were quickly released from custody.

All manner of arguments were presented by Pamela, her husband, and Lady Booby in their attempts to turn Joseph aside from his intention of marrying Fanny. Her lowly birth made a difference to their minds, now that Pamela had made a good match and Joseph had been received by the Boobys. Further complications arose when a traveling peddler revealed that Fanny, whose parentage until then had been unknown, was the sister of Pamela. Mr. and Mrs. Andrews were summoned at this disclosure, and Mrs. Andrews described how, while Fanny was still a baby, gypsies had stolen the child and left behind them a sickly little boy she had brought up as her own. Now it appeared that Joseph was the foundling. A strawberry mark on Joseph's chest, however, soon established his identity. He was the son of the kindly Wilsons. Both lovers being now secure in their social positions, nothing further could prevent their marriage, which took place soon afterward to the happiness of all concerned.

Critical Evaluation:

Joseph Andrews has been called the first realistic novel of English literature. Henry Fielding turned aside from the episodic sentimental writing of the age to give an honest picture of the manners and customs of his time and to satirize the foibles and vanities of human nature. In particular, he ridiculed affectation, whether it stemmed from hypocrisy or vanity. Although the structure of the novel is loose and rambling, the realistic settings and the vivid portrayal of English life in the eighteenth century more than compensate for this weakness.

Joseph Andrews is many things: a parody of Samuel Richardson's *Pamela* (1740-1741), a sentimental tale of virtue rewarded; a realistic portrayal of the English road in the eighteenth century; a resetting of the values of comic epic poetry in prose that resulted in what Fielding calls a "comic epic romance," by which he had in mind the model of Miguel de Cervantes' *Don Quixote de la Mancha* (1605/1616); and an experiment in social satire. Fielding blended all these characteristics masterfully.

Fielding, along with Richardson, is sometimes called the father of the English novel because he ventilated the concept of narrative itself; his brilliant plotting in *Tom Jones* (1749) and the desultory Odyssean travels of Joseph Andrews are contrasting patterns for realizing a broadly imagined action rich in human nature. *Joseph Andrews* is one of the earliest examples of literature's successful extension of mimetic possibilities beyond the models of classical antiquity and folklore. The novel is a mixed genre, being composed of tale, parable, ballad, and epic. The mixture, however, becomes a whole greater than its parts with true innovators such as Fielding.

What holds Fielding's novel together is its cosmic exposure of appearance. Wherever Joseph and Parson Adams go, their naïveté and innocence make them inadvertent exposers of affectation, that most ridiculous form of "appearance" among human beings. Affectation invites derision and must be exposed: The effect is morally healthy but, even more to the point, mimetically revealing. Behind appearance lie the "true springs of human action." The essence of individuals is often better than their appearance, although their vanity may commit them to affectation. Parson Adams is a lovable character mainly because a heart of gold beats under his pedantries and vanities. His naïve trust in human goodness and his unshakable belief in practiced Christianity define the true man: The real Adams is better than his affectations. Similarly, when Joseph is robbed, beaten, and stripped of his clothes, Fielding takes the opportunity to demonstrate the fact that true human charity may emanate from a person whose appearance and life history would seem to mark him incapable of any kindness: "The postilion (a lad who has since been transported for robbing a hen-roost) . . . voluntarily stripped off a greatcoat, his only garment; at the same time swearing a great oath, for which he was rebuked by the passengers, that he would rather ride in his shirt all his life, than suffer a fellow passenger to lie in so miserable a condition."

Fielding trusts in his satiric method—the exposure of affectation and the questioning of appearance—because he senses that it will not ground his comic vision in despair or cynicism. He avoids the satiric manner of Jonathan Swift, whose contempt for human imperfections of character and principle drove him to contempt for human beings in general. Fielding maintains a love of life itself, an essential state of mind for an artist who presumes to epic achievements in the imaginative grasp of social reality. Swift could never have written Fielding's great comic novel *The History of Tom Jones, a Foundling*, with its tolerant but objective picture of human nature. *Joseph Andrews* is a preface, in theme and style, to that more carefully plotted masterpiece.

As tolerant as Fielding is of human nature, he is also capable of making biting judgments. As the critic Walter Allen pointed out, Fielding is not a misanthrope like Swift, but he is a tough-minded moralist who will pass harsh judgment when it is called for. He was, after all, a court judge in real life. Parson Trulliber is a case in point. Fielding has Parson Adams fall into the mud with Trulliber's pigs, but this embarrassment is typical of the many other physical beatings and discomforts that the good parson suffers throughout the novel. They are emblematic of Fielding's mild judgment of Adams' clerical vanity. Once the mud is washed off, the naïve but true Christian in Parson Adams is all the more shiningly revealed. Things are exactly the opposite with Trulliber. His Christianity is completely superficial; Parson Adams' innocent request for fourteen shillings of charity is met by cries of thief. Once Trulliber's false Christianity is exposed, he is all hogs' mud underneath. This is established from the beginning of his encounter with Parson Adams, whom he mistakes for a hog merchant. Trulliber sees and feels with the eyes and temperament of a hog. He is stingy with food as well as money and quick to belligerence like his angry pigs. The only way he can defend himself against Parson Adams' accusation that he is not a good Christian is by clenching his fist. The most telling irony is Trulliber's contempt for Parson Adams' appearance. Because Trulliber's Christianity is all surface, it is he, not Parson Adams, who is dripping in hogs' mud from first to last.

Through the stripping away of affectation and appearance, Fielding pursues the essential humanity in his characters and is so successful that, by the end of the novel, he can indulge in burlesque without dehumanizing. Two chapters from the end, Parson Adams, thinking he is about to rescue Fanny from rape, finds himself wrestling with Slipslop, whom he mistakes for the rapist. Aroused to his mistake by Slipslop's huge bosom and Lady Booby's entrance, he staggers back to what he mistakenly thinks is his own room and lies down beside Fanny. In the morning, Joseph discovers them lying together. Everything is explained, and everyone is appeased. Even Slipslop seems to have enjoyed the "attention" of both the rapist (Beau Didapper) and her attacker, the parson. All of this is pure farce, a broad joke to usher in the warmly comic conclusion of the novel. It is a measure of Fielding's fictive power that he can people a story with characters rich enough to shift from burlesque to comedy without compromising their credibility. In fact, both plot and character seem to benefit from the author's comic exuberance.

"Critical Evaluation" by Peter A. Brier

Bibliography:

Battestin, Martin C. *The Moral Basis of Fielding's Art: A Study of "Joseph Andrews."* Middletown, Conn.: Wesleyan University Press, 1959. Battestin examines the corrective nature of satire in the novel. A particularly useful chapter examines the quest theme in relationship to the novel's structure.

Dircks, Richard J. *Henry Fielding.* Boston: Twayne, 1983. Offers a general introduction to the author's life and work. The third chapter, "Experiments in Prose Fiction," includes a detailed discussion of themes, characterization, and structure in *Joseph Andrews.*

Mack, Maynard. "*Joseph Andrews* and *Pamela.*" In *Fielding: A Collection of Critical Essays*, edited by Ronald Paulson. Englewood Cliffs, N.J.: Prentice-Hall, 1962. Mack examines Fielding's use of Richardson's novel *Pamela*, which inspired *Joseph Andrews*, noting ways in which Fielding uses the comic mode and his training as a dramatist to create a novel that is far more than a mere parody of *Pamela.*

Spilka, Mark. "Comic Resolution in *Joseph Andrews.*" In *Henry Fielding: Modern Critical Views*, edited by Harold Bloom. New York: Chelsea House, 1987. Spilka shows how Fielding ties the farcical events at Booby Hall to his themes of vanity and hypocrisy to create an artistic whole.

Wright, Andrew. *Henry Fielding: Mask and Feast.* Berkeley: University of California Press, 1966. In three chapters, Wright discusses Fielding's conscious artistry in the narrative of *Joseph Andrews*, the novel's relationship to the epic, and Fielding's use of characterization.

THE JOURNAL OF A TOUR TO THE HEBRIDES WITH SAMUEL JOHNSON, LL.D.

Type of work: Diary
Author: James Boswell (1740-1795)
First published: 1785

Principal personages:
> JAMES BOSWELL, the author, a young Scottish lawyer
> SAMUEL JOHNSON, his aging friend, the great essayist, biographer, poet, and critic
> LORD AUCHINLECK, Boswell's father, a noted Scottish judge

In August, 1773, James Boswell finally succeeded in persuading his distinguished friend Samuel Johnson to accompany him on a tour of his native Scotland, a country for which the learned Dr. Johnson's scorn was legendary. Boswell kept a detailed journal for most of their journey together, and he published it, in a version edited and revised with the help of the Shakespearian scholar, Edmund Malone, in 1785, as a companion volume to Johnson's own account, the *Journey to the Western Islands of Scotland*, that had appeared in 1775. Boswell's original journal was discovered with many of his other private papers in this century, and the modern reader has the opportunity to peruse a considerably franker account than the one that was first issued to the public.

The Journal of a Tour to the Hebrides is a fascinating travelogue, an unusually full record of life in the Scottish highlands and on the remote islands of the Hebrides, a character sketch of Johnson, and, like Boswell's other diaries, a mirror of his personal idiosyncrasies. Boswell seems especially anxious to show the respect and deference with which his friend was greeted by his countrymen; he wanted to prove to Johnson and to the world that the Scots were indeed capable of being scholars and gentlemen, closely in touch with the world of learning, and, being a Scot himself, he naturally felt pride in having the privilege of introducing so great a figure to the professors and noblemen of his homeland.

Perhaps the greatest appeal of Boswell's account lies in the absolute naturalness of style and content. Discussion of the quality of the food and the beds at every inn along the way is interspersed with Johnson's comments on whatever volumes of prayers, sermons, or poems he was able to procure and with accounts of long conversations between the scholar and many of his hosts on religion, philosophy, politics, and literature. As the trip went on, Boswell tended to fall farther and farther behind in his account, and throughout the journal he casually tossed in collections of Johnsoniana after having forgotten the specific occasions of many of the doctor's comments. He chose, too, to stop his narrative at intervals to give geographical and historical details.

Boswell is brutally frank, in his unpublished account, about the character of some of their hosts. He is relatively sympathetic when treating the weakness of Donald MacLeod, a young kinsman of the chief of the MacLeod clan of Dunvegan, on the Isle of Skye, who took their money to town to have it changed and squandered a portion of it on his own refreshment, much to his later chagrin and shame. The arrogance and lack of hospitality of Sir Alexander Macdonald, whose manners seemed to Boswell entirely out of keeping with his station in life, are treated much more harshly. Boswell gives a particularly amusing account of their visit to the duke and duchess of Argyll at Inverary. The duchess refused so much as to acknowledge his presence, because he had opposed her in a celebrated lawsuit, but she and her husband welcomed Johnson cordially.

Johnson appears throughout the journal as a man remarkably willing to adapt to circumstances, however uncomfortable they might be; it was Boswell, many years his junior, who was most disturbed by the lack of clean bedding and who was almost overcome by fright when they ran into a storm as they traveled from one island to another in a small boat. Dr. Johnson teased the young daughters of his hosts, flattered and complimented the elderly ladies, and, for the most part, restrained himself from severely attacking those with whose views he differed violently, especially on such questions as the once burning issue of the authenticity of James MacPherson's Ossian poems, published, Johnson thought fraudulently, as translations from the Gaelic.

One of the most delightful episodes in the journal is Boswell's description of Johnson's meeting with Boswell's father, Lord Auchinleck, a staunch Whig and Presbyterian. Johnson was an equally dogmatic Tory, whose sympathies with the Jacobite cause led him to inquire with great interest about the activities of "Bonny Prince Charlie" when he escaped to Skye after the disastrous battle of Culloden; he was so loyal a member of the Church of England that he read his own prayers throughout most of his trip rather than participate in Presbyterian services. Boswell cautioned Johnson to avoid the controversial topics of politics and religion whenever possible, and the encounter of the two men the young lawyer revered most was, for a time, smooth. However, the "collision," as Boswell calls it, finally came. A medal with Oliver Cromwell's portrait on it was the cause, introducing the subject of Charles I and the Tories, with the inevitable results. Boswell discreetly withholds the details of the argument, but he does mention that afterwards his father dubbed Johnson "Ursa Major," the great bear. In spite of their altercation, however, the two aging gentlemen apparently parted on terms of mutual respect, if not of friendship, and Boswell appears well-satisfied at having brought them together.

Boswell's portrait of himself in this account is less revealing than that in *Boswell's London Journal 1762-1763* (1950); age had apparently curtailed some of his frankness and unself-consciousness, but even here, in the original diary, although not in the published version, he describes in some detail his spiritual experiences in several of the old ruins he visited, and he records with chagrin how quickly his resolutions for increased temperance and self-control were overcome by the offer of a fresh bowl of punch. His concern for his wife, whom he had left at home in Edinburgh, runs throughout his pages, and he had what proved to be false premonitions of disasters befalling her and their children. His uxoriousness did not, however, curtail his roving eye for the various young ladies he and Johnson met on their travels.

Among the most interesting sections of the book for the modern reader are those that describe in detail the daily life of the heads of the various clans that inhabited the western islands. The civilized manners of the MacLeods of Raasay had made their daughters welcome at fashionable gatherings in Edinburgh and London, yet the lords and their young heirs were acquainted with the most menial tasks involved with the running of their estates. The wide reading of many of the Highlanders, especially of the clergymen, and the education of the young people also surprised the travelers, and Johnson on one occasion presented an arithmetic book to a bright young girl with whose family he had lodged. However, the primitiveness of many of the tenants of the great landholders is presented in sharp contrast to the sophistication of their masters.

The Journal of a Tour to the Hebrides, like Boswell's other biographical and autobiographical writings, has had and will continue to have great appeal for readers, primarily for the spirit of life that infuses every page. Servants, obscure clergymen, elderly Scotswomen, and youthful lords come to life vividly as do Boswell and Johnson themselves, and the naturalness of Boswell's style makes his work contemporary and fascinating throughout.

Bibliography:
Bate, W. Jackson. *Samuel Johnson*. New York: Harcourt Brace Jovanovich, 1975. Offers an insightful comparison between Johnson's travel account and Boswell's journal. Explains how Boswell's writings constitute a biographical memoir and record of conversation rather than a straightforward narration of events.
Brady, Frank. *James Boswell, the Later Years: 1769-1795*. New York: McGraw-Hill, 1984. Brady's coverage of Boswell's journal is annotated, indexed, thoroughly researched, and enthusiastically written. Examines Boswell's moral and psychological character, with fascinating accounts of his morbid curiosity.
Bronson, B. H. "Johnson, Traveling Companion, in Fancy and Fact." In *Johnson and His Age*, edited by James Engell. Cambridge, Mass.: Harvard University Press, 1984. Reviews the differences between the published version and the actual journal that Boswell kept, which appeared in 1936. Underscores Boswell's efforts to use the journal as a rehearsal for *The Life of Samuel Johnson, LL.D.*, which was published in 1791.
LaScelles, Mary. *Notions and Facts: Johnson and Boswell on Their Travels*. Oxford, England: Clarendon Press, 1972. Re-creates Boswell's attempts to capture Johnson's response to unaccustomed circumstances. Reviews the circle of friends and contacts who arranged the tour.
Turnbull, Gordon. "Generous Attachment: The Politics of Biography in the *Tour of the Hebrides*." In *Modern Critical Views: Dr. Samuel Johnson and James Boswell*, edited by Harold Bloom. New York: Chelsea House, 1986. Examines the political risks that Boswell took in exposing Scotland to Samuel Johnson and in exposing Samuel Johnson to Scotland. A unique contribution.

A JOURNAL OF THE PLAGUE YEAR

Type of work: Novel
Author: Daniel Defoe (1660-1731)
First published: A Journal of the Plague Year: Being Observations or Memorials of the Most Remarkable Occurrences, as Well Publick as Private, Which Happened in London, During the Last Great Visitation in 1655, 1722

Unlike Daniel Defoe's other books and novels, *A Journal of the Plague Year* is rarely read as a whole, although a number of writers, such as Virginia Woolf, testify to its impact. It is more likely than Defoe's novels, however, to be anthologized in college anthologies of English literature, where its presence is justified as appropriate for reprinting in extracts by its episodic construction and by its historical significance. Both grounds indicate the nature and worth of the whole work. On every page, the book shows more clearly than *Moll Flanders* (1722), or any of the other episodic novels posing as true accounts, the intricate and slow development of the English novel. As the English novel developed, writers moved away from sermons, romances, and polemics and established a formal tradition developed thereafter for some two centuries. Defoe's reputation as the founder of the English novel rests as much on *A Journal of the Plague Year* as it does on *Robinson Crusoe* (1719) or *Roxana* (1724).

The first problem in the development of the novel was to establish a working relationship between fact and fiction. The traditional novel still uses realistic narration to assist readers in the willing suspension of disbelief. Defoe's invention was to use statistics. Tabulated on the pages of *A Journal of the Plague Year* are the weekly death bills or returns from the ninety-seven parishes in the city of London and the sixteen or so in Southwark and outside the city limits. The tables are disposed artfully throughout the work, instead of appearing as appendices, and they are surrounded by further realistic particulars. In a very short time, the reader is in a region of rumor that Defoe first solemnly reports, then rationally dismisses or qualifies. Rumor is the middle ground between statistics and the imagination, and Defoe is careful to allow readers to believe it or not as they wish. Readers accept such folklore at face value, perhaps, because gossip is more entertaining than truth. The first sentence of *A Journal of the Plague Year*, for example, specifies September, 1664, as the date the narrator first heard the rumor that the plague had come to Holland for the second year running. The first paragraph then expands with rumors about its place of origin: "they say . . . some said . . . others . . . all agreed."

The full title of *A Journal of the Plague Year* contains a bland lie that indicates the second way Defoe encouraged the reader's imagination to work. "Observations or Memorials" sufficiently confuses the distinction between what was recorded at the time and what was remembered later. Defoe's sources, beyond the death bills, were not extensive, and his memories were secondhand. His imagination, however, was fertile. He carefully controlled and encouraged the imagination by the threefold organization of his work. Contrary to the word "journal" in the title, the book is not a daily record. Time references shift from September to August and over the whole summer of the plague. Instead of daily entries, Defoe uses time references, from September, 1664, to December, 1665, as ways of beginning and concluding his narrative, ending with the doggerel quatrain that celebrates the narrator's deliverance. Within the work, he preserves a gradual movement of the plague from the western to the eastern parts of the city, ending with a central holocaust, and scattered throughout the work readers find his tables of statistics. Neither the geographical, the chronological, nor the numerical progress of the plague is consistently followed. The jumps in geography and time make one want to restore logical order to the work and thereby turn it into a literal "journal," at the same time risking loss of its imaginative qualities. Much about the plague's effects and progress is left to the imagination, as the author intends.

Defoe's imagination proceeds mechanically but energetically by considering a general topic and its related topics one at a time. Therefore, readers get several pages of increasingly horrific detail about the practices of nurses, then a catalog of various kinds of quacks, fortune-tellers, prophets, and necromancers who flourished during that awful summer. The section on women in childbirth, for example, coolly divides their tragedies into those who died in childbirth with and without the plague, and the former are further subdivided into those who died before giving birth, or in the middle of giving birth, or before the cord was cut. Defoe's narrator could see little of these matters for himself, but "they say" and "I heard" fill up the paragraphs one after another until all possible contingencies have been covered.

Defoe's imagination works with three classes of corroborative detail: the quick summary, the brief anecdote, and the extended story. The summary paragraph often introduces a series of brief anecdotes but sometimes stands alone, as in his brief recital of the killing of forty thousand dogs and two hundred thousand cats as a precaution against the spread of the plague. There are many brief anecdotes, such as the frequently anthologized account of purifying a purse, that exhibit at once the commonsense caution Defoe admires, the honesty of the Londoner, and the belief that the plague was spread by contaminated air. The longest of the stories, filling about one-tenth of *A Journal of the Plague Year*, is that of the three men and their company who spent the summer camping in Epping Forest. Defoe tells the story at length to show what happened to Londoners who left the city and retired to places where his narrator could not follow them.

Defoe's subject was epic in scope: A great metropolis is slowly strangled by a hidden enemy. The size of his subject gives ample scope for the inclusion of all sorts of material, but his handling of it is typically original. Instead of a heroic poem, readers are presented with the sober account of an average Londoner. The Londoners who stayed in London are the heroes of Defoe's book—those from Lord Mayor to beggar who did not abandon their city. The narrator is simply identified by the subscription of "H. F." throughout the novel (possibly an allusion to Defoe's uncle, Henry Foe) and is described as a saddler engaged in the American trade. This, like all trade and manufacturing, ended with the onslaught of the plague in June, 1665, and left his narrator free to observe the reactions of his townsfolk.

Defoe's choice of narrator serves to control his material. Presenting the terrible soberly, the narrator offers views on the prevention of the plague. For example, the narrator is critical of shutting up the living with the sick when one plague victim is found in the house. The opinions of the narrator, however, seem contradictory in two respects. The first is purely technical; the saddler recommends shutting up one's house at the beginning of the plague but acknowledges that supplies have to be brought by servants and thus the plague spreads. He shuts up his house and servants but wanders through the streets even to the death pits (he observes that one in his parish of Aldgate holds eleven hundred and fourteen corpses when full); he must wander in order to write his journal. Except for a period of three weeks when he is conscripted as an examiner, he remains an observer and thus uncharacteristic of London's energetic and resourceful citizens. The populace's organization is practical, and the narrator lauds the Londoners' community spirit during the plague and bewails its passage as the plague diminishes.

In a second respect, the ambivalence of the narrator is more striking. He lauds common sense and courage where he finds it but looks for the salvation of the city in divine providence during the despair most felt at the end of September, when deaths numbered over ten thousand weekly. Then, suddenly, the weekly bills showed a dramatic decrease. To whom should go the praise?

Defoe is equivocal, in much the same way that he solemnly introduces the scandalous history of Moll Flanders as a moral tract. This ambivalence may be called the true foundation of the English novel, a recital of fictions that rings true.

Bibliography:

Backscheider, Paula R. *Daniel Defoe: His Life*. Baltimore: The Johns Hopkins University Press, 1989. Scholarly and well-written, this biography is remarkably detailed in every aspect of Defoe's life and career. This refreshing cache of information is a work of history with few forays into literary criticism.

Defoe, Daniel. *A Journal of the Plague Year*. Edited by Paula Backscheider. New York: W. W. Norton, 1992. This is the definitive modern edition of Defoe's novel.

Flanders, W. Austin. "Defoe's *Journal of the Plague Year* and the Modern Urban Experience." In *Daniel Defoe: A Collection of Critical Essays*, edited by Max Byrd. Englewood Cliffs, N.J.: Prentice-Hall, 1976. Investigates Defoe's concern with the moral challenges that confront the urban dweller. Discusses Defoe's imaginative exploration of those challenges.

Nicholson, Watson. *The Historical Sources of Defoe's "Journal of the Plague Year."* Boston: Stratford, 1919. Illustrated by extracts from the original documents in the Burney collection and the manuscript room in the British Museum. Of particular importance are the excerpts from the original sources, which are included. The comparisons of the novel with actual events and the careful examination of the errors found in Defoe's work offer an opportunity to scrutinize aspects of the novel that are often ignored by literary critics.

Richetti, John J. *Daniel Defoe*. Boston: Twayne, 1987. An excellent introduction to Defoe's life and works. Bibliography.

Zimmerman, Everett. *Defoe and the Novel*. Berkeley: University of California Press, 1975. Chapter 5, "*A Journal of the Plague Year*: Fact and Fiction," is a study of the evolution of Defoe's style and in particular his reaction to the demands entailed in fictionalizing a recent historical event.

JOURNAL TO ELIZA

Type of work: Diary
Author: Laurence Sterne (1713-1768)
First published: 1904

> *Principal personages:*
> YORICK, Sterne's alter ego, the writer of the journal
> ELIZA DRAPER, the object of his sentimental passion

Laurence Sterne's *Journal to Eliza* has been considered by unsuspecting readers as conclusive evidence that its author was a lachrymose sentimentalist. Yet anyone familiar with *Tristram Shandy* (1759-1767) and *A Sentimental Journey Through France and Italy* (1768) will recognize touches of that humorous view of eighteenth century sentimentalism that makes Sterne's novels so appealing.

Sterne was neither a parodist nor a satirist in the usual sense. He seems, in fact, to have enjoyed dramatizing his emotions on numerous occasions, and he could not have created some of his finest fictional scenes without real sensitivity to nuances of feeling. Nevertheless, an ironic humorist always occupied one corner of his mind, ready to appear at any moment to undercut the effect of a particularly touching episode. He was always aware of the ridiculous aspects of human behavior, and he appropriately adopted the name of one of literature's most famous jesters for his alter ego. It is as Parson Yorick that he sheds copious tears over the departure of his beloved Eliza and, in *A Sentimental Journey*, invokes her name to protect him from the amorous intrigues that awaited him at every coach station.

The *Journal to Eliza* is not an easy work to analyze; numerous readers have puzzled over its tone. Is it to be considered as an autobiographical document, as a purely literary creation, or as something between the two? Sterne met Eliza Draper, the wife of an employee of the East India Company, in 1767, the year before his death. Extant letters suggest that he fancied himself in love with her, while she regarded him as a friend, but no more. It was not out of character for Sterne to indulge himself in a literary romance that existed primarily in his imagination. Some of the letters he wrote his wife before their marriage are almost identical to the effusions of his journal, and he later addressed other ladies who struck his fancy in similar terms. Whatever his feelings may have been, Sterne was the same man who was composing the brilliantly witty *A Sentimental Journey* during the last months of his life, and it is difficult to believe that he did not perceive the essential absurdity of some of his outpourings of emotion in the *Journal to Eliza*.

Yorick's diary, which is really an extended letter, begins just after Eliza has left for India with her husband. He has promised his "Bramine" that he will record his activities and his feelings every day, and he begins with extravagant protestations of grief at her departure. Few external events find a place in the journal; Yorick visits friends, travels from London to his country home, and, in the latter part of the book, anticipates a visit from his estranged wife and their daughter, but most of the pages are filled with accounts of the parson's illness and the torments of his sorrowing soul.

His laments over a solitary dinner are typical of the ludicrous sentimentality of the work:

> I have just been eating my Chicking, sitting over my repast upon it with Tears—a bitter Sause— Eliza! but I could eat it with no other—when Molly spread the Table Cloath, my heart fainted within me—one solitary plate—one knife—one Glass! O Eliza; 'twas painfully distressing. . . .

The disjointed phrases, the apostrophes to the absent lady, the potent emotional effects of everyday objects characterize the style of the entire journal. The work abounds in tears. Yorick weeps over his dinner, over Eliza's picture, over dreams of her; he joins their friend Mrs. James in lamenting his pale, wan countenance, and he sobs with his maid, Molly, who comments emotively on how much Mrs. Draper is missed. Sterne is a master of the language of overwrought emotions, and it is not surprising that some readers have taken him completely seriously.

There are, however, clues along the way which suggest that Yorick's laments are not quite what they seem. It is typical that the writer who filled *Tristram Shandy* with bawdy double entendres should make much of the fact that Yorick's illness, brought on by grief at Eliza's leaving, has been diagnosed as venereal disease. He protests vehemently "'tis impossible, at least to be that, replied I—for I have had no commerce whatever with the Sex—not even with my wife, added I, these 15 years." This is not the kind of comment one expects to find in a truly "sentimental" work. Yorick's apology for bringing up the subject simply enhances the humor of the situation: "'Tis needless to tell Eliza, that nothing but the purest consciousness of Virtue, could have tempted Eliza's friend to have told her this Story—Thou are too good my Eliza to love aught but Virtue—and too discerning not to distinguish the open character, which bears it, from the artful and double one which affects it." Immediately after this statement, Sterne the novelist comes to the fore: "This, by the way, would make no bad anecdote in T. Shandy's Life." Other references to his writing later in the journal provide reassuring intervals of everyday life in the morass of sentiment.

Yorick began his journal in April, and the entries for that month are long and impassioned. Sterne evidently became less interested in his romance in May; the daily comments are briefer and more perfunctory, although there is an occasional burst of emotion: "Laid sleepless all the night, with thinking of the many dangers and sufferings, my dear Girl! that thou art exposed to—." At the end of the month, Yorick records his journey from London to his country cottage, where he nurses himself, fancies Eliza beside him in every picturesque spot in his garden, and daydreams of a sequence of events that would allow them to marry.

The entries for early June initiate a new autobiographical episode that is the chief focus of the rest of the journal. Yorick receives a letter from his daughter Lydia announcing that she and her mother, who is throughout the book referred to as Mrs. Sterne, will visit him to discuss financial arrangements to enable them to retire to France permanently. The monetary details, discussed at length, are probably fairly accurate, as is the resentment with which Yorick predicts that the ladies will carry off all his household possessions: "In short I shall be pluck'd bare—all but of your Portrait and Snuff Box and your other dear Presents." It is, perhaps, significant of Sterne's state of mind that the entries for the month after the receipt of Lydia's letter are much longer and more emotional than those which preceded it. There is considerable discussion concerning the happy expression of concern about the forthcoming visit, and one is tempted to speculate that Sterne is using the journal less as a literary game and more as a means of putting his mind at ease. In any case, he seems finally to have grown tired of the project toward the end of the summer. The July entries are fond, but increasingly less frequent, and, on August 4, Yorick writes that his family is soon to arrive and that their presence will put an end to his diary. A single paragraph, dated November 1, concludes the work. Mrs. Sterne is to retire to France with an annuity of 300 guineas a year, and Yorick is free to think again of Eliza:

But What can I say,—What can I write—But the Yearnings of heart wasted with looking and wishing for thy Return—Return—Return! my dear Eliza! May heaven smooth the Way for thee to send thee safely to us, and joy for Ever.

The *Journal to Eliza* has attracted considerable attention as a biographical document, though it is one of somewhat dubious value, and as a work illustrating eighteenth century sentimental writing. It falls far below *Tristram Shandy* and *A Sentimental Journey*, however, in literary interest; the unceasing protestations of love, grief, and despair inevitably become monotonous, as Sterne himself seems to have discovered. Readers will, however, continue to turn to the journal for the insights it gives into the author's peculiar genius.

Bibliography:
Anderson, Howard. "Sterne's Letters: Consciousness and Sympathy." In *The Familiar Letter in the Eighteenth Century*, edited by Howard Anderson, Philip B. Daghlian, and Irvin Ehrenpreis. Lawrence: University of Kansas Press, 1966. While this study focuses primarily on Sterne's letters, Anderson also considers the *Journal to Eliza*, analyzing Sterne's literary style.
Cash, Arthur H. "Eliza: 1766-1767." In *Laurence Sterne: The Later Years*, by Arthur H. Cash. London: Methuen, 1986. A critical biography, here describing Sterne's love for the married Eliza Draper, and interpreting his motives for writing the journal. Contains several passages from the work, with biographical details explaining them.
Madoff, Mark S. "'They Caught Fire at Each Other': Laurence Sterne's Journal on the Pulse of Sensibility." In *Sensibility in Transformation: Creative Resistance to Sentiment from the Augustans to the Romantics*, edited by Syndy McMillen Conger. Rutherford: Fairleigh Dickinson University Press, 1990. Examines Sterne's treatment of the eighteenth century idea of sensibility.
Thomson, David. *Wild Excursions: The Life and Fiction of Laurence Sterne*. New York: McGraw-Hill, 1972. Examines how Sterne's life and his relationship with Eliza Draper, evidenced by the *Journal to Eliza*, show Sterne to be a modern figure struggling with good nature, animal appetite, and intellectual detachment. Illustrated.
Van Leewen, Eva C. *Sterne's "Journal to Eliza": A Semiological and Linguistic Approach to the Text*. Tübingen: G. Narr, 1981. The only full-length study of the *Journal to Eliza*. Although some of the material is for specialists, there is much for the general reader, and the thorough table of contents makes it easy to select interesting and useful sections, such as those on genre.

JOURNEY TO THE END OF THE NIGHT

Type of work: Novel
Author: Louis-Ferdinand Céline (Louis-Ferdinand Destouches 1894-1961)
Type of plot: Naturalism
Time of plot: World War I and after
Locale: France, Africa, and the United States
First published: Voyage au bout de la nuit, 1932 (English translation, 1934)

> *Principal characters:*
> FERDINAND BARDAMU, a rogue
> LÉON, his friend
> MADELON, a woman engaged to Léon

The Story:

Ferdinand, an indifferent student of medicine in Paris, was emphatically pacifistic, and anarchistic in his reaction to authority. Immediately prior to World War I, he was expounding his cynical disregard for nationalistic pride in a café. Down the street came a colonel at the head of a military band. The music and the uniforms captured Ferdinand's fancy, and in spite of his declarations he rushed off to enlist. During the fighting he was a runner, constantly exposed to scenes of savage brutality and to great danger on his errands. On one mission he met Léon.

When Ferdinand suffered a slight wound in his arm, he was given convalescent leave in Paris. There he met Lola, an American Red Cross worker who idolized the French. She romanticized his wound, became his temporary mistress, and filled him with stories of the United States. When she came to think of Ferdinand as a coward and a cynic, she left him.

The thought of losing Lola was more than Ferdinand could bear. When his mind gave way, he was sent to a variety of mental hospitals, where he quickly learned to ingratiate himself with the psychiatrists by agreeing with everything they said. His tactics at last procured his release as cured but unfit for active duty.

In Paris, he led a precarious life, but he bettered his existence by acting as a go-between for Musyne, a dancer who was greatly sought after by rich Argentine meat dealers. The thought of all that beef to be sold at high prices was too much for Ferdinand, and after some months with Musyne, he left for colonial Africa. During the voyage, he became the scapegoat of the passengers, but flattered them shamelessly to avoid being flung overboard.

In French West Africa, he was assigned to a trading post far in the interior. He made the ten-day trip by canoe into the hot, lush jungle, where his trading post turned out to be a shack anchored by two big rocks. The mysterious trader he had come to relieve was, frankly, a thief, who told Ferdinand that he had no goods left to trade, very little rubber, and only canned stew for provisions. The rascal gave Ferdinand three hundred francs, saying it was all he had, and left in the direction of a Spanish colony. Only after he had gone did Ferdinand realize that his predecessor had been Léon.

After several weeks of fever and canned stew, Ferdinand left the trading post, which he had accidentally burned, and his only baggage was the three hundred francs and some canned stew. His overland safari was a nightmare. His fever rose dangerously high, and during much of the trip he was delirious. His porters stole his money and left him with a Spanish priest in a seaport. The priest, for a fee, delivered him to a captain of easy scruples. Ferdinand, still sick, was shanghaied on a ship bound for the United States.

When he attempted to jump ship in New York, he was caught by the immigration authorities. Pretending to be an expert on flea classification, he was put to work in a quarantine station catching and sorting fleas for the Port of New York. After gaining the confidence of his chief, he got himself sent into the city to deliver a report, although technically he was still under detention. In New York, he looked up Lola, now older but still attractive, who gave him a hundred dollars to get rid of him. With the money he took a train to Detroit. Soon he was employed by the Ford Motor Company.

In Dearborn he fell in love with Molly, who lived in a brothel. Each day, he escorted her to the bordello in the early evening. Then he rode streetcars until she was through for the night. On one of his nightly trips, he met Léon again. Léon was unhappy in America because he could not learn enough English to get along. He had to be content with a janitor's job. Ferdinand learned that Léon also wished to return to France.

Although he loved Molly very much, Ferdinand left her and Detroit to go back to Paris. Completing his medical course, he was certified as a doctor, and he settled down to practice in a poor neighborhood. His patients rarely paid him. Mostly he was called for abortion cases.

One day, the Henrouilles summoned him to attend the old grandmother who lived in a hut behind their house. They hated to spend the money necessary to feed the old woman, and Madame Henrouille offered Ferdinand a thousand francs if he would certify that the grandmother was insane. Through conscience or fear, Ferdinand refused. Then Léon was called on the same case. He agreed to set a bomb next to the old woman's hut so that she would kill herself when she opened the door. Clumsy Léon bungled the job; he accidentally detonated the bomb and lost his sight.

With the help of the Abbé Protiste, the family worked out a scheme to get rid of the old woman and Léon. They proposed to send the two to Toulouse, where there was a display of mummies. Léon would be a ticket seller and old Madame Henrouille would be the guide. For persuading Léon to accept the proposition, Ferdinand received a thousand francs.

Ferdinand's practice grew smaller. At last, he went to the Montmartre section of Paris, where for a time he was pleased with his job as supernumerary in a music hall. The Abbé Protiste looked him up after some months and offered to pay his expenses to Toulouse, where Ferdinand was to see if Léon was likely to make trouble for the Henrouilles on the score of attempted murder.

In Toulouse, Ferdinand learned that Léon was regaining his sight. He had also become engaged to Madelon. The old lady was a vigorous and successful guide. Ferdinand dallied a little with the complaisant Madelon but decided to leave before their intimacy was discovered. Old Madame Henrouille fell, or was tripped, on the stairs and was killed in the fall. It was a good time for Ferdinand to leave—hurriedly.

Dr. Baryton ran a genteel madhouse. By great good luck Ferdinand was hired on his staff. He ingratiated himself with his employer by giving him English lessons. Dr. Baryton read Thomas Macaulay's *History of England* (1849-1855) and became so enamored of English things that he departed for foreign lands and left Ferdinand in charge. Shortly afterward, Léon showed up, broke and jobless. He had run away from Madelon. Ferdinand took him in and gave him a job.

Madelon came looking for Léon and haunted the hospital gate. Hoping to appease her, Ferdinand arranged a Sunday party to visit a carnival. In the party were Léon, Madelon, Ferdinand, and Sophie, Ferdinand's favorite nurse. After a hectic day they took a taxi home. On the way Léon declared he no longer loved Madelon. The spurned woman took out her revolver and killed him. Ferdinand knew that the time had arrived for him to move on once more.

Critical Evaluation:

"His real self as you saw it in a war," says the narrator and antihero of this novel, of another of its characters. This phrase is central to a long, rambling, and rather improbable account of one man's life during and after World War I. The narrator, Ferdinand Bardamu, has a life out of a picaresque novel. He goes from one scrape to another, his narrow escapes as often as not taking him from the frying pan into the fire. By the same token, by using his wits, he sometimes is blessed with good luck. Chance and luck rule this novel and, by implication, the world.

Bardamu may often be confused and stunned in the many crises of his life, but in the telling of them, he is never at a loss. He is a man who has reflected intensely upon his experiences, and has come to these conclusions regarding them. Readers may not like these conclusions— Bardamu is an incurable cynic—but readers can recognize, enjoy, and even honor them. Actually, Bardamu is less cynic than misanthrope, and one recalls the provocative definition of a misanthrope as someone who thinks too well of people. Bardamu has been deeply wounded in his idealism. One day, he is marching off to glory, awash in patriotic fervor; the next, he finds himself in the thick of horrendous war. What makes this betrayal all the more bitter is that he knew better even before he joined up. Having found that his sardonic armor has not protected him from a passing fit of patriotism, Bardamu has two choices: to allow emotions to deafen one to the voice of calculation, or to redouble his efforts to guard against unpleasant surprises. The novel shows Bardamu, in the second mode, surrounded by people rendered dangerous by the first. The presence of one lone fleck of humanity in a sea of madness is not without its comic aspect.

In the slaughter of World War I, many notions of proper conduct perished. Céline was among the first to announce this staggering change of heart, and he found a generation ready to listen to it. This novel's immediate success testifies to its currency, and its continuing appeal speaks of Céline's genius. Bardamu is crippled, emotionally and spiritually, by the war, but the resolution and alacrity with which he continues to show what he has learned about survival, inspire as well as entertain. He lies, he cheats, he steals, but there is an inevitability about his every act. No one else is any better; he was not born rich; and he was of military age when the war broke out. To Céline, the blame needs to be placed squarely where it belongs: on society, or humanity as a species, but certainly not upon the shoulders of an individual.

Bardamu has a way of interspersing his narrative with lectures upon the meaning of the latest episode. He seems to be telling his story in order to help readers wise up to the way things really are. There is no way out, no exit from the insanity. It is appropriate that Bardamu finds employment in a mental hospital. His journey may take him to the end of night, but it cannot carry him beyond. Metaphorically, night is always falling, and nightmare always looms. There is no dawn for humanity that is not false. Bardamu's only light is the light of the truth, always present even as one or another character is lying.

While being absolutely in tune with its times, *Journey to the End of the Night* also has a place in tradition. Literature has many other works of war and bitter disillusionment. Unfriendly critics of Céline object to the hatefulness of his characters and the narrowness of his vision, but within the limitations he set himself, he works as a master.

"Critical Evaluation" by David Bromige

Bibliography:
Knapp, Bettina. *Céline, Man of Hate.* Tuscaloosa: University of Alabama Press, 1974. Dis-

cusses hate in Céline's works. Presents a fuller and more complex Céline than one might guess from the title.

Ostrovaky, Erika. *Céline and His Vision*. New York: New York University Press, 1967. Uses Céline's pronouncements and speculations on the art of the novel to elucidate his work. Attempts to pull his various books together into a unified reading. Explores Céline's treatment of death in *Journey to the End of the Night*, noting how death is disparaged, but also that the author distinguishes among kinds of dying.

Richard, Jean-Paul. *La Nausée de Céline*. Paris: Scolies Fata Morgana, 1973. Concentrates on *Journey to the End of the Night*.

Thiher, A. *Céline: The Novel as Delirium*. New Brunswick, N.J.: Rutgers University Press, 1972. Points out how often people suffer from fevers in Céline's works, and the feverish nature of the prose. Discusses the sense of matter disintegrating that pervades *Journey to the End of the Night*.

Thomas, Merlin. *Louis-Ferdinand Céline*. New York: New Directions, 1980. Places Céline in his historical period and discusses his books in relation to his life. Speaks of *Journey to the End of the Night* as concerning not only death but also survival.

THE JOURNEY TO THE WEST

Type of work: Novel
Author: Wu Ch'eng-en (c. 1500-c. 1582)
Type of plot: Fantasy
Time of plot: Seventh century
Locale: China, India, and various mythical regions
First published: Hsi-yu chi, 1592 (abridged English translation, *Monkey,* 1943; English translation, 1977-1983)

> *Principal characters:*
> MONKEY, a monster with miraculous powers
> BUDDHA, the founder of Buddhism and Lord of the Western Paradise
> KUAN-YIN, a Bodhisattva (commonly known as the Goddess of Mercy)
> HSÜAN TSANG or TRIPITAKA, a Chinese Buddhist priest
> T'AI TSUNG, the great Chinese emperor of the T'ang Dynasty
> PIGSY and
> SANDY, monsters and Tripitaka's disciples

The Story:

In the beginning there was a rock. The rock gave birth to a stone egg, and the egg developed into the shape of a monkey. The monkey became alive and played with other monkeys. He was made their king.

One day, troubled by the thought of death, he bade farewell to the monkey tribe and set out on a journey to seek immortality. He became a pupil of the Patriarch Subodhi, from whom he learned seventy-two transformations and the cloud trapeze. When he showed off his newly learned magic of transformation by changing into a pine tree, this public display of magic enraged his master, who disowned him. Monkey went back to his cave, but now he did not have to travel over mountains and rivers. One leap carried him head over heels a hundred and eight thousand leagues.

He killed the demon who had molested his "little ones" during his absence. He got the magic iron staff from the Sea Treasury of the Dragon King. The weapon could shrink, at his will, to the size of an embroidery needle. Despite all of these powers, however, his allotted life span of 342 years had come to an end. In a dream he was taken to the Land of Darkness. Furiously, he crossed out his name in the Registers of Death, together with whatever names of other monkeys he could find.

His meddling at the Palace of the Dragon King and the Court of Death had been reported to the Jade Emperor. Monkey was summoned to Heaven so that he could be constantly watched. At first he was happy to have an appointment from the emperor, but upon learning how humble his position as groom in the heavenly stables really was, he returned to his monkeys.

As a rebel, he called himself "Great Sage, Equal of Heaven," and he defeated the heavenly hosts sent off to arrest him. The Jade Emperor consented to appoint him to the rank he wished. Then he crashed the Peach Banquet, to which he was not invited. By the joint effort of the gods he was caught and imprisoned in the crucible of Lao Tzu, where for forty-nine days he was burned with alchemical fire before he escaped. It seemed that nothing could stop him until Buddha came to help the heavenly powers. Monkey was placed under a five-peaked mountain, originally the five fingers of Buddha's hand, where he was to serve his penance.

Buddha wished that some believer from sinful China would come to the Western Continent to fetch the True Scriptures. Kuan-yin volunteered to help someone accomplish this. The someone was Hsüan Tsang. His father, a young scholar, had been murdered while on his way to take up his duties as governor of Chiang-chou. The murderer, a ferryman, assumed the dead man's name and took his wife and office. The wife would have committed suicide if it were not for her unborn child. Immediately after the boy was born, she tied him to a plank with a letter written in blood tucked to his breast and pushed the plank into the river. The child was picked up by the abbot of a temple, who learned the tragic story of the boy's birth from the blood letter.

Hsüan Tsang was brought up as a monk. He did not know of his parentage until he was eighteen years old; then he met his mother and made plans to avenge his father. The false governor was executed, on the spot where he had committed his evil deed. Suddenly a body came floating up through the water. It was Hsüan Tsang's father, whom everyone had thought dead, but who had been saved by the Dragon King of the River. Thus the family was reunited. Hsüan Tsang chose to remain a monk.

The Emperor T'ai Tsung of T'ang made a visit to the World of Darkness. He had promised to celebrate a great mass for the salvation of the hungry ghosts, and Hsüan Tsang was chosen to preside over the ceremonies. Kuan-yin, appearing in the disguise of a ragged priest, interrupted the service by pointing out that there were Three Baskets (or Tripitaka) of Mahayana scriptures for a pilgrim to bring from India. Then she revealed herself in her glory and vanished. Hsüan Tsang volunteered to undertake the quest in spite of the length and perils of the journey. His request was granted, and he was given a new name, Tripitaka.

He had passed several dangers before he arrived at the mountain where Monkey had been imprisoned for five hundred years, waiting for the man who, according to Kuan-yin, would release him and whom he was to follow, protect, and obey as his master. When Tripitaka said a prayer, the seal of the prison was lifted into the air, and Monkey was freed.

Three other monsters had received similar instructions from Kuan-yin to wait for the priest of T'ang at three different places. They did not know what the man looked like, so they had to be defeated in battle before they could be convinced to join the pilgrimage. A young dragon devoured Tripitaka's horse, but, learning his mistake, he allowed himself to be changed into a horse to serve the priest. Pigsy, a banished marshal of the heavenly hosts, now reincarnated in the shape of a pig, had to be driven away from his human wife and father-in-law. The last to join was Sandy, a man-eating monster with red hair and a blue face, also a banished heavenly marshal.

Monkey and Pigsy sometimes created trouble. Pigsy was cowardly, lazy, self-indulgent, clumsily shrewd, and jealous of the much more powerful Monkey. Nevertheless, he seemed to be Tripitaka's favorite. The brilliant Monkey could not be a paragon of obedience, and on several occasions, he quarreled with his master. The priest, however, needed only to say a certain spell, and the fillet on the monkey's head began to hurt him by becoming tighter. He had been tricked into wearing the cap with the fillet, and now he could not take it off. This was the only control Tripitaka, with Kuan-yin's help, held over the unruly Monkey.

The travelers passed the kingdom of Crow-cock, where a Lion Demon had murdered the king and, disguised as the monarch, usurped the throne. The ghost of the dead king asked help from Tripitaka. After the king had been fished up from a well and miraculously revived, the usurper was forced to flee. He turned out to be the gelded lion in the service of the Bodhisattva Manjusri. The travelers also came to Cart-slow Kingdom, where Taoists were the privileged class and Buddhists were persecuted. Monkey challenged three Taoist magicians, who had won the full confidence of the king, to a contest of miracles. The first magician could not recover his head, chopped off in the contest, and he fell dead, leaving the corpse of a headless tiger. The second magician was found to be only a white deer, now dead, since he was not able to close his ripped-open belly. The third was fried to death in boiling oil, leaving in the cauldron the bones of a ram. Monkey survived every one of the ordeals.

Monkey and Pigsy changed into a boy and a girl for the Great King of Miracles, who demanded annual human sacrifice. Although the monster proved no match for Tripitaka's disciples, he captured the priest and brought him down to the River That Leads to Heaven. There the monster, caught at last in Kuan-Yin's basket, turned out to be a golden fish. A big turtle carried Tripitaka across the river. The turtle had been perfecting himself for more than one thousand years, but he was worried because he could not yet achieve human form. Tripitaka promised to ask Buddha about the turtle's wish.

The travelers finally arrived in the Blessed Region of Buddha, found the scriptures, and began to carry them to China. Tripitaka, however, had forgotten to ask about the turtle's prospects. Annoyed, the turtle made a dive, leaving the pilgrims, who had been riding on his back to recross the river, and the scriptures in the water. The pilgrims were all saved, but a part of the scriptures was lost. This was the "eighty-first calamity."

Carried back to paradise after completing their mission, Tripitaka and Monkey were both made Buddhas, and Pigsy was promoted to be Cleanser of the Altar. Sandy, Golden-Bodied Arhat, and the white horse, who had also aided Tripitaka, were set among the eight senior Heavenly Dragons. Buddhism prospered in China.

Critical Evaluation:

The Journey to the West was inspired by the pilgrimage of the Chinese priest Hsüan Tsang to India in the seventh century. Except for the priest and a few other historical personages, the novel is fantastic, with the whole mythical universe as its background. It is interpreted as a satire, with the rebellious monkey against the bureaucratic heavenly government, and as an allegory, what Westerners might consider a Buddhist version of John Bunyan's Christian adventure tale, *Pilgrim's Progress* (1678). For centuries, however, the Chinese—adults and children alike—have loved this absurd story of monsters simply because of its imagination, humor, and delightful nonsense. Arthur Waley has translated thirty out of the original one hundred chapters, omitting many of the calamities the pilgrim and his disciples encounter. The story before the start of the pilgrimage is preserved almost in its entirety, and this alone makes interesting reading.

Wu Ch'eng-en was a sixteenth century magistrate as well as a novelist. Starting his hundred-chapter novel with Monkey's birth in the creation myth, Wu Ch'eng-en has made him a divine hero on an unflinching quest for immortality, to which the subsequent pilgrimage is but the final chapter. Waley used *Monkey* as the title of his partial yet witty translation of the book. The novel represents the "dual modes of myth and comedy." Most fully developed myths in the novel have some relation to the story of Monkey, and these include the creation, the quest for immortality, the journey to the underworld, the fall from grace, the divine mercy, the mission, the redeeming pilgrimage, and the apotheosis.

Nevertheless, Monkey is not the only hero in the pilgrimage. He and Pigsy are a pair of complementary characters. When Monkey is alone, his adventures are not so interesting as those in which Pigsy joins him. In addition, the five pilgrims almost achieve a harmony of personalities among themselves after reaching the Crow-cock Kingdom. On their way they are transformed from isolated victims of fate into united victors in faith. In the Cart-slow Kingdom, they not only help themselves but they also become the destined saviors of suffering people.

This harmony of personalities among the pilgrims is vitally related not only to character development but also to the union of the dual modes of myth and comedy in the novel. The characters of Monkey and Pigsy, for example, gradually balance each other, while in the plot, Pigsy often provides a comic relief to temper Monkey's mythic adventures. The pilgrims' quest in the physical world is also a quest within their personalities. As the quest continues, the relations among them become more and more harmonious. It is chiefly through the harmony of their personalities that they at last attain their goal.

In Monkey's fearless quest for immortality, his determination almost becomes a kind of destiny. In his heroic striving, he reaches a height of spiritual awareness at which time stands still. In most journey themes in world literature, the end revisits the beginning. The quest of Monkey also goes in a cycle, in which the perpetual process can be identified with the final goal. Buddha himself tells the pilgrims that even the Mahayana scriptures ought to be left behind in a quest for enlightenment. The plot of the quest, therefore, is like a circle which has no end; the important part of the pilgrimage is the pilgrimage, not so much the recovery of the scriptures.

Myth and comedy are further related by the author's lyrical vision of life and the lyrical style of his narrative. Nature is charged with human feeling in the story, which uses some of the lively conventions of the oral traditions, such as the recurring exclamation, "Dear Monkey!" Humor and myth are joined, for example, in the pilgrims' last calamity on the river; the author uses an old Chinese folk motif to reach the mythic number of eighty-one. This is also a joke at the expense of storytellers, who tend to miscount their calamities during their oral performances.

Bibliography:
Bantly, Francisca-Cho. "Buddhist Allegory in the *Journey to the West*." *Journal of Asian Studies* 48, no. 3 (1989): 512-524. Analyzes and explains Buddhist allegorical elements interwoven into this novel.
Ch'en, Shou-yi. *Chinese Literature: A Historical Introduction.* New York: Ronald Press, 1961. Discusses the structure of the work and traces the literary development of the presumed author.
Hsia, C. T. *The Classic Chinese Novel.* New York: Columbia University Press, 1968. Critical analysis of six major classical Chinese works includes *Journey to the West.* Gives historical background and traces similarities to and divergences from the epic pilgrimage of Hsüan Tsang to India, which provides its historical basis.
Hsia, C. T., and T. A. Hsia. "New Perspectives on Two Ming Novels: *Hsi Yu Chi* and *Hsi Yu Pu.*" In *Wen-lin: Studies in the Chinese Humanities*, edited by Chow, Tse-tsung. Madison: University of Wisconsin Press, 1968. Provides historical background in its comparison of *The Journey to the West* to another novel of the era.
Liu, Wu-chi. *An Introduction to Chinese Literature.* Bloomington: Indiana University Press, 1966. Chapter 16 discusses *Journey to the West* as a supernatural novel that is as much a product of folk tradition as of the author's creative imagination. Discusses the structure of the novel and concludes that it is a good-natured satire of human foibles and bureaucratic stupidity.
So, Francis K. H. "Some Rhetorical Conventions of the Verse Sections of *Hsi-yu-chi*." In *China and the West: Comparative Literature Studies*, edited by William Tay et al. Hong Kong: Chinese University Press, 1980. Analyzes the verse sections, which use all the major genres of verse in Chinese literature, in *Journey to the West.*

THE JOY LUCK CLUB

Type of work: Novel
Author: Amy Tan (1952-   )
Type of plot: Social realism
Time of plot: Twentieth century
Locale: China and San Francisco
First published: 1989

> *Principal characters:*
> JING-MEI (JUNE) WOO, the protagonist
> SUYUAN WOO, Jing-mei's mother
> ROSE HSU JORDAN, a homemaker
> AN-MEI HSU, Rose's mother
> WAVERLY JONG, a businesswoman
> LINDO JONG, Waverly's mother
> LENA ST. CLAIR, an architect
> YING-YING ST. CLAIR, Lena's mother

The Story:

After Suyuan Woo passed away, her daughter, Jing-mei, was asked by her mother's friends to take her mother's place as a member of their Joy Luck Club, a group of friends who played Mah-Jongg together. At first, Jing-mei was reluctant to join the club. She was not very good at Mah-Jongg and not particularly interested in hearing her "aunties" talk about the past. Once she accepted, however, she began to learn more about her mother's past and about the twin daughters her mother had left in China. She also learned about her aunties' lives and about their daughters.

The aunties described their childhood experience in China and their journey to the United States. An-mei Hsu recalled how her mother had been mistreated by her husband's family after his death, and how she was disowned by Popo, her mother, for marrying Wu Tsing, who already had a wife and two concubines. When Popo became very sick, An-mei's mother nevertheless returned home to take care of her. An-mei later learned from a servant, Yan Chang, that her mother had been raped by Wu Tsing and tricked into the marriage, and that she was physically abused and emotionally tortured by Wu Tsing's wife and concubines.

Lindo Jong had been a child bride. Her husband, Tyan-yu, was several years younger than she and even more immature. When Huang Taitai, Tyan-yu's mother, became angry with Lindo for not bearing the family a son, Lindo told her that from a meeting she had had with the ghosts of the family's ancestors she had been warned to leave the family to prevent calamity from descending on them. That trick enabled Lindo to leave Huang Taitai's house without disgracing her own family. The money Huang Taitai gave her was enough for her to go to America.

Ying-ying St. Clair had been born to a well-to-do family, and she had been brought up with strict rules about how to behave properly. Both her mother and Amah, the maid, believed that a "girl can never ask, only listen"; while a "boy can run and chase dragonflies, because that is his nature . . . a girl should stand still." In the legendary figure Chang-o, the Moon Lady, Ying-ying found a companion and someone she could trust, but after Ying-ying made a secret wish to Chang-o while watching a play, she was shocked to find out that the person who played Chang-o was a man.

3355

The aunties' daughters also told their stories about the cultural conflicts they experienced growing up in America. Waverly Jong was Chinatown's chess champion when she was a child, but because she did not like the way her mother bragged about her achievement, she had stopped playing. Lately, Waverly had been fighting her mother over the way she was treating her boyfriend, Rich Shields; it seemed that her mother considered neither Rich nor Waverly's former Chinese husband good enough.

Lena St. Clair was tired of hearing her mother talk about how her marriage with Harold Livotny was unbalanced. She eventually came to think that her mother had been right all along and that she and her husband did not have an equal relationship. Lena was as important as Harold in the architectural firm Livotny and Associates but was not paid accordingly; yet they split the household bills and expenses evenly in half.

In the story "Half and Half," Rose Hsu Jordan saw a parallel between what had happened to her brother Bing and what was happening to her marriage. When Rose was a teenager, she was once given the responsibility to take care of her younger brothers while the family was vacationing on a beach. A misunderstanding between Rose and her father resulted in Bing's disappearance. From that incident, Rose learned that fate was shaped "half by expectation, half by inattention." Just as she knew now that she had never expected to find Bing, Rose now also knew she would not find a way to save her marriage to Ted Jordan, who not only did not respect her being a housewife but also had an affair with another woman.

Jing-mei Woo was the spokesperson for both her and her mother. When Jing-mei was a child, Suyuan believed that her daughter was a prodigy and hired a piano teacher for her. Jing-mei had not been very excited about playing piano, however, and did not practice hard. After a disastrous appearance on a talent show, Jing-mei had a big altercation with her mother, after which she never touched the piano again. After her mother died, Jing-mei had developed a sentimental attachment to the piano, and one day she played Robert Schumann's piano pieces "Pleading Child" and "Perfectly Contented" a few times and discovered that they were actually "two halves of the same song."

When the aunties gave Jing-mei an envelope with $1,200 and told her to go to China to meet her twin sisters, she started to understand the ontological significance of having taken her mother's place at the Mah-Jongg table—on the East, where things began. In the last story of the book, "A Pair of Tickets," Jing-mei Woo described her trip to China in search of her "lost" twin sisters. When she finally met them, Jing-mei could see that together they looked just like their mother.

Critical Evaluation:

The development of Asian American literature can be divided into two periods. The first period was marked by the writers' interest in using an autobiographical approach to identify their relationship with the mainstream American culture and their increased awareness of their own cultural heritage. The second period in the development of Asian American literature began with the publication of Amy Tan's *The Joy Luck Club* in 1989, which heralded the emergence of a large group of Asian American writers who were interested in experimenting with various literary genres and styles in search of a medium that could reflect and depict their experience accurately. Besides rekindling hope for many Asian American writers, the success of *The Joy Luck Club* also pushed publishers' doors a bit wider. The book was succeeded in 1991 by Tan's second successful novel, *The Kitchen God's Wife*, and, that same year, by Gish Jen's *Typical American*, David Wong Louie's collection of short stories *Pangs of Love*, (which won the *Los Angeles Times* 1991 book prize for first fiction), Frank Chin's

Donald Duk, and Gus Lee's autobiographical novel *China Boy*.

In *The Joy Luck Club*, Tan intermingles the thematic treatment of intercultural conflict with that of intergenerational conflict. The mothers who immigrated to the United States from China and still have very strong cultural ties to their old home want to raise their children in the traditional Chinese way. Their Chinese American daughters, however, feel that they are trapped in the conflict between traditional Chinese culture and mainstream American society, between their aspirations for individual freedom and their sense of familial and social obligations, and between their false and their true identities. Paradoxically, the conflict is both frustrating and constructive. The daughters are eventually led to conclude that they must embrace what they cannot culturally reject, and that they are as American as they are Chinese.

Tan has spoken of her constant search "to find a harmony between the self and the world." Tan's thematic preoccupation with balance and harmony in *The Joy Luck Club* is not only revealed by chapter titles such as "Half and Half," "Two Kinds," "Four Directions," "Without Wood," "Best Quality," "Double Face," and "A Pair of Tickets" but also accentuated by her skillful use of structure. The book begins with the mothers' stories about their experiences in China and emigrating to the United States, and it ends with their conclusion that, much as they would like to believe they are still completely Chinese, they too now have two faces, a Chinese face and an American one. The daughters, on the other hand, come to the realization that "Once you are born Chinese, you cannot help but feel and think Chinese."

Jing-mei Woo is first reluctant to join the Joy Luck Club, and she only halfheartedly accepts her Chinese name, though she mentions that it is "becoming fashionable for American-born Chinese to use their Chinese names." She was not aware, however, that it was impossible for her to find her true identity without reclaiming her relationship with her ethnic cultural heritage. Only after joining the Joy Luck Club, could Jing-mei begin to understand her mother. The trip to China finally enabled her to see that, together with her sisters, they looked just like their mother: her "same eyes, her same mouth, open in surprise to see, at last, her long-cherished wish."

Tan's use of ancient Chinese myths and legends in *The Joy Luck Club* works well with her thematic concerns. In the story "The Moon Lady," for example, Ying-ying St. Clair, who was told that woman is "yin, the darkness within where untempered passions" lie and that man is "yang, bright truth lighting our minds," found a friend in Chang-o, the Moon Lady. According to the legend, Chang-o took medicine that belonged to her husband and was sent to the moon as punishment. Tan uses both Ying-ying's story and the story within the story to lament the way women were treated in a feudalist society and to suggest that that way should be rejected in traditional Chinese culture.

Qun Wang

Bibliography:

Chin, Frank. "Come All Ye Asian American Writers of the Real and the Fake." In *The Big Aiiieeeee! An Anthology of Chinese American and Japanese American Literature*, edited by Jeffery Paul Chan et al. New York: Meridian, 1991. The article discusses Maxine Hong Kingston, Amy Tan, and David Henry Hwang's use of ancient Chinese myths and legends in their works.

Ling, Amy. *Between Worlds: Women Writers of Chinese Ancestry*. New York: Pergamon Press, 1990. The book takes a feminist look at Asian American women writers' contribution to the development of Asian American literature. Includes a section on *The Joy Luck Club*.

Souris, Stephen. " 'Only Two Kinds of Daughters': Inter-Monologue Dialogicity in *The Joy Luck Club*." *Melus* 19, no. 2 (1994): 99-123. Souris uses Wolfgang Iser's reader-response theory in discussing how the novel requires the reader's active involvement to create the meaning.

Tan, Amy. Interview by Angels Carabi. *Belles Lettres* (Summer, 1991): 16-19. Tan discusses her thoughts on being a creative writer and the popular success she achieved with *The Joy Luck Club*.

Wong, Sau-ling Cynthia. *Reading Asian American Literature: From Necessity to Extravagance*. Princeton, N.J.: Princeton University Press, 1993. The book takes a thematic approach to the study of contemporary Asian American literature. There are several places where the writer discusses Amy Tan and *The Joy Luck Club*'s significance in the history of Asian American literature.

JUDE THE OBSCURE

Type of work: Novel
Author: Thomas Hardy (1840-1928)
Type of plot: Philosophical realism
Time of plot: Nineteenth century
Locale: Wessex, England
First published: 1895

Principal characters:
JUDE FAWLEY, a stonemason
ARABELLA DONN, a vulgar country girl
SUE BRIDEHEAD, Jude's cousin and a freethinker
LITTLE FATHER TIME, Jude's son by Arabella
RICHARD PHILLOTSON, a schoolmaster
DRUSILLA FAWLEY, Jude's great-grandaunt

The Story:

When he was eleven years old, Jude Fawley said good-bye to his schoolmaster, Richard Phillotson, who was leaving the small English village of Marygreen for Christminster to study for a degree. Young Jude was hungry for learning and yearned to go to Christminster too, but he had to help his great-grandaunt, Drusilla Fawley, in her bakery. At Christminster, Phillotson did not forget his former pupil. He sent Jude some classical grammars, which the boy studied eagerly.

Anticipating a career as a religious scholar, Jude apprenticed himself at the age of nineteen to a stonemason engaged in the restoration of medieval churches in a nearby town. Returning to Marygreen one evening, he met three young girls who were washing pigs' chitterlings by a stream bank. One of the girls, Arabella Donn, caught Jude's fancy, and he arranged to meet her later. The young man was swept off his feet and tricked into marriage, but he soon realized that he had married a vulgar country girl with whom he had nothing in common. Embittered, he tried unsuccessfully to commit suicide; when he began to drink, Arabella left him.

Once he was free again, Jude decided to carry out his original intention. He went to Christminster, where he took work as a stonemason. He had heard that his cousin, Sue Bridehead, lived in Christminster, but he did not seek her out because his aunt had warned him against her and because he was already a married man. Eventually, he met her and was charmed. She was an artist employed in an ecclesiastical warehouse. Jude met Phillotson, who was again a simple schoolteacher. At Jude's suggestion, Sue became Phillotson's assistant. The teacher soon lost his heart to his bright and intellectually independent young helper, and Jude was hurt by evidence of intimacy between the two. Disappointed in love and ambition, he turned to drink and was dismissed by his employer. He went back to Marygreen.

At Marygreen, Jude was persuaded by a minister to enter the church as a licentiate. Sue, meanwhile, had won a scholarship to a teachers' college at Melchester; she wrote Jude and asked him to visit her. Jude worked at stonemasonry in Melchester to be near Sue, even though she told him she had promised to marry Phillotson after completing her schooling. Dismissed from college after an innocent escapade with Jude, Sue influenced him away from the church with her unorthodox beliefs. Shortly afterward, she married Phillotson. Jude was despondent and returned to Christminster, where he came upon Arabella working in a bar. Jude heard that

Sue's married life was unbearable. He continued his studies for the ministry and thought a great deal about Sue.

Succumbing completely to his passion for Sue, Jude at last forsook the ministry. His Aunt Drusilla died, and at the funeral, Jude and Sue realized that they could not remain separated. Sympathizing with the lovers, Phillotson released Sue, who now lived apart from her husband. The lovers went to Aldbrickham, a large city where they would not be recognized. Phillotson gave Sue a divorce and subsequently lost his teaching position. Jude gave Arabella a divorce so that she might marry again.

Sue and Jude now contemplated marriage, but they were unwilling to be joined by a church ceremony because of Sue's dislike for any binding contract. The pair lived together happily, and Jude continued his simple stonework. One day, Arabella appeared and told Jude that her marriage had not materialized. Sue was jealous and promised Jude that she would marry him. Arabella's problem was solved by eventual marriage, but out of fear of her new husband, she sent her young child by Jude to live with him and Sue. This pathetic boy, nicknamed Little Father Time, joined the unconventional Fawley household.

Jude's business began to decline, and he lost a contract to restore a rural church when the vestry discovered that he and Sue were unmarried. Forced to move on, they traveled from place to place and from job to job. At the end of two and a half years of this itinerant life, the pair had two children of their own and a third on the way. Jude, in failing health, became a baker; Sue sold cakes in the shape of Gothic ornaments at a fair in a village near Christminster. At the fair, Sue met Arabella, who was now a widow. Arabella reported Sue's poverty to Phillotson, who was once more the village teacher in Marygreen.

Jude took his family to Christminster, where the celebration of Remembrance Week was underway. Utterly defeated by failure, Jude still loved the atmosphere of learning that pervaded the city.

The family had difficulty finding lodgings and was forced to separate. Sue's landlady, learning that Sue was an unmarried mother and fearful that she might have the trouble of childbirth in her rooming house, told Sue to find other lodgings. Sue became bitter, and she told Little Father Time that children should not be brought into the world. When she returned from a meal with Jude, she found that the boy had hanged the two babies and himself. She collapsed and gave premature birth to a dead baby.

Her experience brought about a change in Sue's point of view. Believing she had sinned and wishing now to conform, she asked Jude to live apart from her. She also expressed the desire to return to Phillotson, whom she believed, in her misery, to be still her husband. She returned to Phillotson, and the two remarried. Jude was utterly lost and began drinking heavily. In a drunken stupor, he was again tricked by Arabella into marriage. His lungs failed; it was evident that he would die soon. Arabella would not communicate with Sue, whom Jude desired to see once more, and so Jude traveled in the rain to see her. The lovers had a last meeting. She then made complete atonement for her past mistakes by becoming Phillotson's wife completely. This development was reported to Jude, who died in desperate misery of mind and body. Fate had grown tired of its sport with a luckless man.

Critical Evaluation:

An extraordinary transitional figure who straddled the Victorian and twentieth century literary worlds, Thomas Hardy was initially an undistinguished architect whose novels and poems became his chief profession. Although his rustic characters and some of his poems exhibit a humorous touch, most of his creations are permeated by a brooding irony reflecting life's disappointments and a pessimistic belief that human beings are victims of an impersonal force that darkly rules the universe. Hardy divided his novels into three groups: novels of ingenuity, such as *Desperate Remedies* (1871); romances and fantasies, such as *A Pair of Blue Eyes* (1872-1873); and novels of character and environment. This class includes his best and most famous works, *Tess of the D'Urbervilles* (1891), *The Return of the Native* (1878), *Far from the Madding Crowd* (1874), *The Mayor of Casterbridge* (1886), and *Jude the Obscure*.

First published in a modified form as an 1894 serial in *Harper's*, *Jude the Obscure* came to be considered by many critics to be Hardy's best novel. It was the outraged initial reception accorded *Jude the Obscure* that turned Hardy from the novel to concentrating on his poetry. Reception had ranged from moral outrage to indignation that the book was not as spectacularly evil as touted, and Hardy's disgust with the public was bitter and enduring.

The best explanation of the book was stated by Hardy himself in his preface, where he declared that the work was intended "to tell, without a mincing of words, of a deadly war waged between flesh and spirit; and to point the tragedy of unfulfilled aims." To these could be added two other important themes: an attack on convention and society and an examination of human beings' essential loneliness.

Exhibiting the flesh-spirit division is, of course, Jude's conflicting nature. His relationship with Arabella represents his strong sexual propensities, while his attraction to intellectual pursuits and his high principles reveal his spiritual side. His obsession with Sue is a reflection of both sides of his personality; for while he is compelled by her mind and emotion, he is also drawn to her physically. At the crucial moments of his life, Jude's fleshly desires are strong enough temporarily to overwhelm his other hopes. His two major goals are checked by this flaw, for his initial attempt at a university career is halted when he succumbs to Arabella and his plans for the ministry end when he kisses Sue and decides that as long as he loves another man's wife he cannot be a soldier and servant of a religion that is so suspicious of sexual love.

"The tragedy of unfilled aims" is forcefully present in both Jude and Sue. For years Jude, in a truly dedicated and scholarly fashion, devotes himself to preparing to enter Christminster (Hardy's name for Oxford). Even after he frees himself from the sexual entanglement with Arabella, his hopes for an education are doomed, for the master of the college who bothers to reply advises him to "remain in your own sphere." Through no fault of his own and despite his seeming ability, he is continually denied what he so desperately seeks. The fact of his birth as a poor person is unchangeable, and Jude must accept its results. His second great desire, a spiritual (as well as sexual) union with Sue, is also doomed. When Jude first sees Sue's picture, he thinks of her as a saint, and he eventually derives many of his maturing intellectual concepts from her. His passion for Sue is true and full; yet Sue's deeply flawed character necessitates her self-destruction as well as Jude's destruction. She drains Jude while simultaneously serving as a source of his growth, for she is irresponsible, cold, and cruel. She is an imperfect being, afraid not only of her physical side but of her very ideas. She tells Jude that she does not have the courage of her convictions, and when he adopts her iconoclastic stance, she abandons it and demonstrates how conventional she really is. Her pagan shouts, her free thought, her brave spirit prove as much a sham as Christminster's promises. Her tragedy, the gap between what she is and what she might have been, is not hers alone but is shared by Jude and becomes his.

As an attack on convention and society, *Jude the Obscure* focuses on three major areas: the British university system, marriage, and religion. Jude's exclusion from Christminster is an indictment of the structure of an institution that allegedly symbolizes the noble part of the human mind yet actually stands only for a closed, tightly knit club. In its criticism of marriage, a union that Hardy said should be dissolvable by either side if it became a burden, the novel reveals how false is the view of marriage as a sacred contract. Marriage, as in Jude's merger with Arabella, is often the fruit of a temporary urge, but its harvest can be lifelong and ruinous. Sue's fear of marriage also suggests that the bond can be one of suffocation.

Perhaps most important are the novel's charges against Christianity. The fundamental hollowness and hypocrisy of Christianity, Hardy asserts, damn it. A farmer thrashes Jude for lovingly letting the birds feed, and the sounds of the beating echo from the church tower that the same farmer had helped finance. Hardy's scorn for such inconsistencies abounds throughout the book, and he proposes that the only valuable part of Christianity is its idea that love makes life more bearable.

Mirroring the development of these themes is the final impression that the book is also a cry of loneliness. Jude's hopelessness is in the final analysis a result of his alienation not only from Arabella and Sue but from his environment. Used in connection with Jude, the word "obscure," in addition to conveying his association with darkness, his lack of distinction in the eyes of the world, and his humble station, suggests also that he is not understood and that he is hidden from others and only faintly perceptible. In Hardy's world, the happiest people are those who are most in touch with their environment, a condition that usually occurs in the least reflective characters. Jude, however, is always grasping for the ideal and ignoring the unpleasantness around him as much as he can; this inevitably leads to isolation. Hardy hints that such is the price human beings must pay for the refusal unquestionably to accept their status.

All the ills that Hardy ascribes to this world are, he feels, merely a reflection of the ills of the universe. Human beings ruin society because they are imperfect and caught in the grip of a fatal and deterministic movement of the stars. In defense of his dark outlook, Hardy writes: "If a way to the better there be, it demands a full look at the worst." In a philosophy that he termed evolutionary meliorism, Hardy further amplifies this concept in both a brighter and a more disastrous vein. That philosophy proposes that not only may human beings improve but they must find the way to that better condition if they are to survive.

"Critical Evaluation" by Judith Bolch

Bibliography:
Butler, Lance St. John. *Thomas Hardy*. Cambridge, England: Cambridge University Press, 1978. A short introductory study that deals with the issue of flesh versus spirit in *Jude the Obscure*. The quality of the novel, Butler claims, lies in its plotting.

Gatrell, Simon. *Thomas Hardy and the Proper Study of Mankind*. Charlottesville: University Press of Virginia, 1993. Discusses the way Hardy treats the theme of the conflict between the sexes and notes that Hardy believes sexual union to be the essence of marriage.

Hardy, Thomas. *"Jude the Obscure": An Authoritative Text, Backgrounds and Sources, Criticism*. Edited by Norman Page. New York: W. W. Norton, 1978. Contains, in addition to the text of the novel, six contemporary reviews, comments from Hardy's letters, and ten twentieth century critical essays. These deal with *Jude the Obscure* as a distinctively progressive novel and as tragedy; the authors discuss the novel's poetic power, its pessimism and meliorism, its imagery and symbolism, and Hardy's portrait of Sue Bridehead.

Hawkins, Desmond. *Hardy: Novelist and Poet*. New York: Barnes & Noble Books, 1976. In this bio-critical study, Hawkins maintains that the significance of the changing partnerships in *Jude the Obscure* is the fact that the two lesser characters, Arabella and Phillotson, represent the more conventional, tolerant, conformist elements in society, while Jude and Sue are unconventional, rebellious, and critical of the social order.

Vigar, Penelope. *The Novels of Thomas Hardy: Illusion and Reality.* London: Athlone Press, 1974. Emphasizes that *Jude the Obscure* achieves its intense psychological verisimilitude from its many short scenes and episodes in which the abstractions of feeling are transcribed into observable actions and events.

JULIUS CAESAR

Type of work: Drama
Author: William Shakespeare (1564-1616)
Type of plot: Tragedy
Time of plot: 44 B.C.E.
Locale: Rome
First performed: c. 1599-1600; first published, 1601

Principal characters:
> JULIUS CAESAR, dictator of Rome
> MARCUS ANTONIUS, his friend
> MARCUS BRUTUS, a conspirator against Caesar
> CAIUS CASSIUS, another conspirator against Caesar
> PORTIA, wife of Brutus and Cassius' sister
> CALPURNIA, Caesar's wife

The Story:

At the feast of Lupercalia all Rome rejoiced, for the latest military triumphs of Julius Caesar were being celebrated during that holiday. Yet tempers flared and jealousies seethed beneath the public gaiety. Flavius and Marallus, two tribunes, coming upon a group of citizens gathered to praise Caesar, tore down their trophies and ordered the people to go home and remember Pompey's fate at the hands of Caesar.

Other dissatisfied noblemen discussed with concern Caesar's growing power and his incurable ambition. A soothsayer, following Caesar in his triumphal procession, warned him to beware the Ides of March. Cassius, one of the most violent of Caesar's critics, spoke at length to Brutus of the dictator's unworthiness to rule the state. Why, he demanded, should the name of Caesar have become synonymous with that of Rome when there were so many other worthy men in the city?

While Cassius and Brutus were speaking, they heard a tremendous shouting from the crowd. From aristocratic Casca they learned that before the mob Marcus Antonius had three times offered a crown to Caesar and three times the dictator had refused it. Thus did the wily Antonius and Caesar catch and hold the devotion of the multitude. Fully aware of Caesar's methods and the potential danger that he embodied, Cassius and Brutus, disturbed by the new turn of events, agreed to meet again to discuss the affairs of Rome. As they parted, Caesar arrived in time to see them, and suspicion of Cassius entered his mind. Cassius did not look contented; he was too lean and nervous to be satisfied with life. Caesar much preferred to have fat, jolly men about him.

Cassius' plan was to enlist Brutus in a plot to overthrow Caesar. Brutus himself was one of the most respected and beloved citizens of Rome; if he were in league against Caesar, the dictator's power could be curbed easily. It would, however, be difficult to turn Brutus completely against Caesar, for Brutus was an honorable man and not given to treason, so that only the most drastic circumstances would override his loyalty. Cassius plotted to have Brutus receive false papers that implied widespread public alarm over Caesar's rapidly growing power. Hoping that Brutus might put Rome's interests above his own personal feelings, Cassius had the papers secretly laid at Brutus' door one night. The conflict within Brutus was great. His wife Portia complained that he had not slept at all during the night and that she had found him wandering, restless and unhappy, about the house. At last he reached a decision. Remembering Tarquin, the tyrant whom his ancestors had banished from Rome, Brutus agreed to join Cassius and his conspirators in their attempt to save Rome from Caesar. He refused, however, to sanction the murder of Antonius, which was being planned for the same time—the following morning, March 15—as the assassination of Caesar.

On the night of March 14, all nature seemed to misbehave. Strange lights appeared in the sky, graves yawned, ghosts walked, and an atmosphere of terror pervaded the city. Caesar's wife, Calpurnia, dreamed she saw her husband's statue with a hundred wounds spouting blood. In the morning, she told him of the dream and pleaded with him not to go to the Senate that morning. When she had almost convinced him to remain at home, one of the conspirators arrived and persuaded the dictator that Calpurnia was unduly nervous and that the dream was actually an omen of Caesar's tremendous popularity in Rome, the bleeding wounds a symbol of Caesar's power extending out to all Romans. The other conspirators arrived to allay any suspicions Caesar might have of them and to make sure that he attended the Senate that day.

As Caesar made his way through the city, more omens of evil appeared to him. A paper detailing the plot against him was thrust into his hands, but he neglected to read it. When the soothsayer again cried out against the Ides of March, Caesar paid no attention to the warning.

In the Senate chamber, Antonius was drawn to one side. Then the conspirators crowded about Caesar as if to second a petition for the repealing of an order banishing Publius Cimber. When he refused the petition, the conspirators attacked him, and he fell dead of twenty-three knife wounds.

Craftily pretending to side with the conspirators, Antonius was able to reinstate himself in their good graces. In spite of Cassius' warning, he was granted permission to speak at Caesar's funeral after Brutus delivered his oration. Before the populace, Brutus frankly and honestly explained his part in Caesar's murder, declaring that his love for Rome had prompted him to turn against his friend. The mob cheered him and agreed that Caesar had been a tyrant who deserved death. Then Antonius rose to speak. Cleverly and forcefully, he turned the temper of the crowd against the conspirators by explaining that even when Caesar was most tyrannical, everything he did was for the people's welfare. The mob became so enraged over the assassination that the conspirators were forced to flee from Rome.

The people's temper gradually changed and they split into two camps. One group supported the new triumvirate of Marcus Antonius, Octavius Caesar, and Aemilius Lepidus. The other group followed Brutus and Cassius to their military camp at Sardis.

At Sardis, Brutus and Cassius quarreled constantly over various small matters. In the course of one violent disagreement, Brutus told Cassius that Portia, despondent over the outcome of the civil war, had killed herself. Cassius, shocked by this news of his sister's death, allowed himself to be persuaded to leave the safety of the camp at Sardis and meet the enemy on the plains of Philippi. The night before the battle, Caesar's ghost appeared to Brutus in his tent and announced that they would meet at Philippi.

At first, Brutus' forces were successful against those of Octavius. Cassius, however, was driven back by Antonius. One morning, Cassius sent one of his followers, Titinius, to learn if approaching troops were the enemy or Brutus' soldiers. When Cassius saw Titinius unseated from his horse by the strangers, he assumed that everything was lost and ordered his servant Pindarus to kill him. Actually, the troops had been sent by Brutus; rejoicing over the defeat of Octavius, they were having rude sport with Titinius. When they returned to Cassius and found him dead, Titinius also killed himself. In the last charge against Antonius, Brutus' soldiers, tired and discouraged by events, were defeated. Brutus, heartbroken, asked his friends to kill him.

When they refused, he commanded his servant to hold his sword and turn his face away. Then Brutus fell upon his sword and died.

Critical Evaluation:

The first of William Shakespeare's so-called Roman plays—which include *Coriolanus* (c. 1607-1608) and *Antony and Cleopatra* (c. 1606-1607)—*Julius Caesar* also heralds the great period of his tragedies. The sharply dramatic and delicately portrayed character of Brutus is a clear predecessor of Hamlet and Othello. With *Titus Andronicus* (1594) and *Romeo and Juliet* (c. 1595-1596), *Julius Caesar* is one of the three tragedies written before the beginning of the sixteenth century. It is, however, more historical than Shakespeare's four great tragedies—*Hamlet* (c. 1600-1601), *Othello* (1604), *Macbeth* (1606), and *King Lear* (c. 1605-1606)—being drawn in large part from Sir Thomas North's wonderfully idiomatic translation of Plutarch's *Lives of the Noble Grecians and Romans* (1579). A comparison of the Shakespearean text with the passages from North's chapters on Caesar, Brutus, and Antony reveals the remarkable truth of T. S. Eliot's statement: "Immature poets borrow; mature poets steal." In instance after instance, Shakespeare did little more than rephrase the words of North's exuberant prose to fit the rhythm of his own blank verse. The thievery is brilliant.

Shakespeare's originality, found in all his historical plays, is similar to that of the great classical Greek playwrights Aeschylus, Sophocles, and Euripides. They too faced a dramatic challenge very unlike that of later writers, who came to be judged by their sheer inventiveness. Just as the Greek audience came to the play with full knowledge of the particular myth involved in the tragedy to be presented, the Elizabethan audience knew the particulars of events such as the assassination of Julius Caesar. Shakespeare, like his classical predecessors, had to work his dramatic art within the restrictions of known history. He accomplished this by writing "between the lines" of Plutarch, offering insights into the mind of the characters that Plutarch does not mention and which become, on the stage, dramatic motivations. An example is Caesar's revealing hesitation about going to the Senate because of Calpurnia's dream, and the way he is swayed by Decius into going after all. This scene shows the weakness of Caesar's character in a way not found in a literal reading of Plutarch. A second major "adaptation" by Shakespeare is a daring, dramatically effective telescoping of historical time. The historical events associated with the death of Caesar and the defeat of the conspirators actually took three years; Shakespeare condenses them into three tense days, following the unity of time (though not of place).

Although prose is used in the play by comic and less important characters or in purely informative speeches or documents, the general mode of expression is Shakespeare's characteristic blank verse, which consists of five stressed syllables, generally unrhymed. The iambic pentameter, a rhythm natural to English speech, has the effect of making more memorable lines such as Flavius' comment about the commoners, "They vanish tongue-tied in their guiltiness," or Brutus' observation, "Men at some time are masters of their fates." As in most of his tragedies, Shakespeare follows a five-part dramatic structure, consisting of the exposition (to Act 1, scene ii), complication (Act I, scene ii, to Act II, scene iv), climax (Act III, scene i), consequence (Act III, scene i, to Act V, scene ii), and denouement (Act V, scenes iii to v).

The main theme of *Julius Caesar* combines the political with the personal. The first deals with the question of justifiable revolutions and reveals with the effectiveness of concentrated action the transition from a republic of equals to an empire dominated by great individuals such as Antony, influenced by the example of Caesar himself, and Octavius, who comes into his own at the end of the play. The personal complication is the tragedy of a noble spirit involved in matters it does not comprehend. Despite the title, Brutus, not Caesar, is the hero of this play. It is true that Caesar's influence motivates Marcus Antonius' (also called Mark Antony), straightforward and ultimately victorious actions throughout the play and accounts for his transformation from an apparently secondary figure into one of stature. It is, however, Brutus as he gradually learns to distinguish ideals from reality who captures the sympathy of the audience. Around his gentle character, praised at last even by Antonius, Shakespeare weaves the recurrent motifs of honor and honesty, freedom and fortune, ambition and pride. Honor as it interacts with ambition is the theme of Brutus' speech to the crowd in the forum: "As Caesar loved me, I weep for him; as he was fortunate, I rejoice at it; as he was valiant, I honour him, but, as he was ambitious, I slew him." After the deed, Brutus comments, "Ambition's debt is paid." One of the great, dramatically successful ironies of the play is that Antonius' forum speech juxtaposes the same two themes: "Yet Brutus says he was ambitious/ And Brutus is an honourable man." By the time Antonius is finished, the term "honour" has been twisted by his accelerating sarcasm until it has become a curse, moving the fickle crowd to call for death for the conspirators.

The conjunction of Brutus and Antonius in this scene reveals the telling difference between their dramatic characterizations. Whereas Caesar may have had too much ambition, Brutus has too little; Brutus is a man of ideals and words, and therefore he cannot succeed in the arenas of power. Cassius and Antonius, in contrast, are not concerned with idealistic concepts or words such as honor and ambition; yet there is a distinction even between them. Cassius is a pure doer, a man of action, almost entirely devoid of sentiment or principle; Antonius is both a doer of deeds and a speaker of words—and therefore prevails over all in the end, following in the footsteps of his model, Caesar. To underline the relationships among these characters and the themes that dominate their actions, Shakespeare weaves a complicated net of striking images: the monetary image, which creates tension between Brutus and Cassius; the tide image ("Thou are the ruins of the noblest man/ That ever lived in the tide of times") connected with the theme of fortune; the star image (Caesar compares himself, like Marlowe's Tamburlaine, to a fixed star while Cassius says, "The fault, dear Brutus, is not in our stars,/ But in ourselves, that we are underlings"); and the image of wood and stones used to describe the common people by those who would move them to their own will.

In yet another way, *Julius Caesar* marks the advance of Shakespeare's artistry in its use of dramatic irony. In this play, the Shakespearean audience itself almost becomes a character in the drama, as it is made privy to knowledge and sympathies not yet shared by all the characters on the stage. This pattern occurs most notably in Decius' speech interpreting Calpurnia's dream, showing the ability of an actor to move men to action by well-managed duplicity. The pattern is also evident when Cinna mistakes Cassius for Metellus Cimber, foreshadowing the mistaken identity scene that ends in his own death; when Cassius, on two occasions, gives in to Brutus' refusal to do away with Antonius; and, most effectively of all, in the two forum speeches when Antonius addresses two audiences, the one in the theater (who know his true intentions), and the other the Roman crowd whose ironic whimsicality is marked by its startling shift of sentiment. The effect of the irony is to suggest the close connection between functional politics and the art of acting. Antonius, in the end, defeats Brutus—as Bolingbroke defeats Richard II—because he can put on a more compelling act.

"Critical Evaluation" by Kenneth John Atchity

Bibliography:
Bloom, Harold, ed. *William Shakespeare's "Julius Caesar."* New York: Chelsea House, 1988.
   Nine essays on various aspects of the play by distinguished Shakespeare critics of the 1970's

and 1980's, Marjorie Garber's essay on the significance of dreams and Michael Long's on the social order are particularly worthwhile.

Bonjour, Adrien. *The Structure of "Julius Caesar."* Liverpool, England: Liverpool University Press, 1958. Sensitive, illuminating monographic study that sees *Julius Caesar* as a drama of divided sympathies. Brutus and Caesar are both heroic, both wrong; opposing motives and antithetical themes from the texture of the play as well as a balanced inner structure.

Dean, Leonard F., ed. *Twentieth Century Interpretations of "Julius Caesar."* Englewood Cliffs, N.J.: Prentice-Hall, 1968. Informative collection of short articles by leading mid-twentieth century Shakespeare critics. Dean's introduction gives an overview of earlier criticism. Various articles provide character studies, analyze language, and supply literary-historical background.

Thomas, Vivian. *"Julius Caesar."* London: Harvester Wheatsheaf, 1992. Concise study of *Julius Caesar* that reflects various postmodernist approaches to Shakespeare while also providing a thorough analysis of the play's stage history, style, and relationship to its principal source, Plutarch's *Lives of the Noble Grecians and Romans*. Includes an extensive bibliography.

Traversi, Derek. *Shakespeare: The Roman Plays*. Stanford, Calif.: Stanford University Press, 1963. Chapter two of this classic study focuses on the moral and political themes of *Julius Caesar*. Following the text closely and in detail, Traversi probes the interplay of contrasting personalities and motives that generated a political tragedy with universal significance.

JULY'S PEOPLE

Type of work: Novel
Author: Nadine Gordimer (1923-   )
Type of plot: Psychological realism
Time of plot: Soon after 1980
Locale: A small settlement in rural South Africa
First published: 1981

> *Principal characters:*
> MAUREEN SMALES, Johannesburg wife and mother, a political liberal
> BAMFORD "BAM" SMALES, her husband, an architect, also a liberal
> JULY, their male servant

The Story:

July, incongruously both servant and host, brought morning tea to Maureen and Bamford Smales where they were sleeping with their three children in a one-room mud hut with only a piece of sack cloth for a door. A small truck, bought for hunting holidays for Bam's fortieth birthday, had brought the Smales family six hundred kilometers across the veld in a journey that took three days and nights. The revolutionary forces trying to wrest power from the whites in South Africa had caused the family to flee Johanesburg with their servant July to his rural settlement, which was populated only by his relatives. Maureen and Bam's feelings about the revolution were mixed. It brought danger to them as privileged whites, but on the other hand it represented a possible end to the racist system they did not endorse.

Noticing one of the huts contained mining artifacts, Maureen thought about her childhood as the daughter of a shift boss for the mines. A photographer had once snapped a picture of Maureen and Lydia, her family's servant. Years later she saw the photograph in a book. The photograph captured their social relationship, one that Maureen had been too young at the time to discern herself: the black servant carrying the white girl's school bag.

One day, without asking, July rode off in the truck, with his friend Daniel driving. Upset, not knowing where July had gone or why, Maureen and Bam began bickering about why they had failed to flee South Africa while there was still time, about whether their attitude toward the politics of South Africa had been realistic, and about each other's character. That night, after the children and Bam fell asleep, Maureen went outside in the dark to shower in the rain. Before returning to the hut, she noticed the lights of the truck returning. July returned with supplies and reports of shortages at the store and fighting at the mines not far from the settlement. Daniel taught July to drive the truck, and July explained its presence to people in nearby villages by saying he had taken it from his Johannesburg employers. There was no longer any white authority in the area to worry July.

Maureen and July argued about who should keep the truck's keys, but the argument revealed deeper conflicts. July made it clear he had always been their "boy," and Maureen, angered at his representation of their fifteen-year relationship, struck back by asking how he could have left Ellen, the woman he lived with in Johannesburg, in the midst of the fighting. The reversal of roles between July and the Smales family was complete. July walked away, with the keys, "his head moved from side to side like a foreman's inspecting his workshop or a farmer's noting work to be done on the lands." July had the power to make the Smales family leave the settlement or to allow them to stay.

Bamford helped July mend farm tools and installed a water tank for the settlement, whose water supply had been the river. He shot warthogs and fished to help supply his and July's family with food. Maureen and Bamford were dependent, however, on July for nearly everything. They were able to pay with the notes they had brought from the bank. During their stay, they listened to a radio, hearing reports of martial law, fighting, and closed airports. Maureen and Bam's children got along fine with the other children of the village, playing with them, picking up their habits and some of their language.

After they had been living in the settlement for more than three weeks, a representative from the chief told July to bring the Smales family to see him. The chief asked about the fighting in the cities and wanted Bam to show him how to use his gun and to help him fight any who came to take over the surrounding villages. Bam responded that the chief should not fight against the black revolutionaries. One day the Smales family joined the rest of July's relatives as a music box was set up for entertainment; when they returned to the hut, Bam's gun and ammunition were missing. Bam was devastated by the loss of the second of his two possessions—first the truck, then the gun. Maureen went to July to tell him to get the gun back. July told her Daniel might have taken the gun because he had gone off to join the revolutionaries. One afternoon, when Bam and the children were fishing at the river, Maureen heard a helicopter land nearby; she ran toward it, leaving behind the sounds of her husband and children.

Critical Evaluation:

Awarded the Nobel Prize in Literature in 1991, Nadine Gordimer has published nonfiction, more than two hundred short stories, and eleven novels. Born in South Africa, Gordimer has set most of her fiction in that country and as a consequence deals with apartheid, the racist system of government that lasted until 1991. Her eighth novel, *July's People*, deals with the possibility of a successful black revolution against the white power structure. The revolution is the background of the novel, not the central focus. As with her other novels, *July's People* concentrates on individual lives, not the broad politics. Gordimer centers her attention on Maureen Smales, a twenty-nine-year-old Johannesburg wife and mother. As the novel opens, a revolution is in progress and the Smales family has taken refuge with July, their male servant, in a rural settlement. The novel traces the sudden role reversal between Maureen, who for fifteen years has employed July, and July, who suddenly has taken control not only of his life but also of the Smales family too. The role reversals of Maureen and July serve as the microcosm for the supposed effects of the revolution. The title of the novel is deliberately ambiguous: the phrase "July's people" appears twice in the novel, the first time referring to the Smales family and the second time to July's extended family in the settlement. Once in the novel the narrator refers to "July's white people," distinguishing them from his relatives.

Although the novel lets the reader understand July's position, Maureen is who is central. A privileged citizen in South Africa, she deplores apartheid and feels her treatment of July as a servant for fifteen years is beyond reproach. Maureen and Bam pay him for his services, give him living quarters in their yard, send home presents to his family, start a special bank account for him with a hundred rands in honor of ten years of service, and never question his relationship with Ellen, the woman who lives with him in Johannesburg. The novel reveals that July feels he has not been treated with dignity. Maureen gives him their cast-offs, orders him about, and is seemingly oblivious to some of his hardships. He has every Wednesday and every second Sunday off, but has leave to visit his wife and children in the rural area only every other year.

Once Maureen lives in his home, she realizes what it is like to be dependent, not to have status. For example, she can not walk far for fear of being seen by someone who might report the presence of whites in the area. (July, as a black South African, for years had to follow very strict laws governing where he was permitted to live, work, and travel.) Necessities—food and shelter—come mainly from July's willingness to supply them, and his willingness could end at a moment's notice, just as a new white farm owner in South Africa had the power to tell black farmworkers born on the farm to leave.

Maureen's whole life begins to fall apart. Her children do not seem to need her care. She feeds them from the supplies July brings, but otherwise they take care of themselves, spending time with the other children of the village. She does not recognize her husband as the same man she lived with in Johannesburg, and she bickers with him, pointing out his character flaws. She herself changes. When her civilized life is stripped to the primitive, she sees her past as a pose. She is not content with her present either. She finds life in the rural area degrading; she has no function there.

In his home area, when July realizes power has passed from Maureen to him, his language becomes more assertive. In fact, during the last conversation he has in the novel with Maureen, July uses his own language, a language Maureen can not understand. That language, in the settlement, is the language of power. Maureen thought that she and July communicated well, understood each other. Maureen has been mistaken for fifteen years; the agreeableness of July has been the response of one who knew his position in South Africa. He never forgot he was the servant who could stay in the city only as long as Maureen signed his pass book each month.

Although the broader story of *July's People* may be the revolution in South Africa, the central story is the discovery by one woman of how deluded she has been about her own life, about her treatment of July, and about her liberal stance regarding South African politics. *July's People* is Gordimer's first novel to center all the action on the home ground of the blacks in South Africa. Although Maureen is the protagonist, she can only be understood through an understanding of July. Gordimer tells Maureen's story and in doing so reveals July's.

The closing of the novel does not clarify Maureen's future. Will she be successful in gaining access to the helicopter? Who is in the helicopter? Americans who come to rescue their countrymen from the revolution? Cubans who come to aid the revolutionaries? The ending does make clear that Maureen wants to abandon her past life in Johannesburg and her present life in July's settlement. That her running can lead to a better life is suspect, but it does suggest she realizes the failure of her past.

Marion Boyle Petrillo

Bibliography:
Bodenheimer, Rosemarie. "The Interregnum of Ownership in *July's People*." *The Later Fiction of Nadine Gordimer*. Edited by Bruce King. New York: St. Martin's Press, 1993. Sees the novel as revealing the hollowness of a materialistic life. Removed from their privileged society, detached from their material possessions, Bamford and Maureen lose their selfhood.
Clingman, Stephen. *The Novels of Nadine Gordimer: History from the Inside*. Winchester, Mass.: Allen & Unwin, 1986. Places Gordimer's first eight novels in the context of South African society and politics; sees major themes of *July's People* as racial and class revolution and also a revolution in language and sexual roles.
Dojka, Stephanie. "*July's People*: She Knew No Word." *Joinings and Disjoinings: The Significance of Marital Status in Literature*, edited by JoAnna Stephens Mink and Janet Doubler Ward. Bowling Green, Ohio: Bowling Green State University Popular Press, 1991. Sees the deterioration of the marriage of the Smales as an indication that white institutions based on

exploitation must be dismantled; the marriage is successful at July's expense.

Neill, Michael. "Translating the Present: Language, Knowledge, and Identity in Nadine Gordimer's *July's People*." *Journal of Commonwealth Literature* 25, no. 1 (1990): 71-97. Sees the novel as being not so much about the revolutionary future as about the difficulties of the South Africa of the novel's present. Analyzes how language, knowledge, and identity break down with a change of culture.

Smith, Roland, "Masters and Servants: Nadine Gordimer's *July's People* and the Themes of Her Fiction." In *Critical Essays on Nadine Gordimer*, edited by Roland Smith. Boston: G. K. Hall, 1990. Centers on Maureen's recognition of the flaws of her liberalism. Sees a main theme of the novel as the inability of whites and blacks to communicate.

THE JUNGLE

Type of work: Novel
Author: Upton Sinclair (1878-1968)
Type of plot: Social realism
Time of plot: Early twentieth century
Locale: Chicago
First published: 1906

Principal characters:
JURGIS RUDKUS, a stockyards worker
DEDE ANTANAS, Jurgis' father
ONA, Jurgis' wife
LITTLE ANTANAS, child of Jurgis and Ona
ELZBIETA, Ona's stepmother
JONAS, Elzbieta's brother
MARIJA, Ona's orphan cousin

The Story:

While he was still a peasant boy in Lithuania, Jurgis Rudkus had fallen in love with a gentle girl named Ona. When Ona's father died, Jurgis, planning to marry her as soon as he had enough money, came to America with her family. Besides the young lovers, the emigrant party was composed of Dede Antanas, Jurgis' father; Elzbieta, Ona's stepmother; Jonas, Elzbieta's brother; Marija, Ona's orphan cousin; and Elzbieta's six children. By the time the family arrived in Chicago, they had very little money. Jonas, Marija, and Jurgis at once got work in the stockyards. Dede Antanas tried to find work, but he was too old.

They all decided that it would be cheaper to buy a house on installments than to rent. A crooked agent sold them a ramshackle house that had a fresh coat of paint and told his ignorant customers that it was new. Jurgis found his job exhausting, but he thought himself lucky to be making forty-five dollars a month. At last, Dede Antanas also found work at the plant, but he had to give part of his wages to the foreman in order to secure his job.

Jurgis and Ona saved enough money for their wedding feast and were married. Then the family found that they needed more money. Elzbieta lied about the age of her oldest son, Stanislovas, and he too got a job at the plant. Ona had already begun to work. Dede Antanas worked in a moist, cold room, where he developed consumption. When he died, the family had scarcely enough money to bury him. Winter came, and everyone suffered in the flimsy house. When Marija lost her job, the family income diminished. Jurgis joined a union and became an active member. He went to night school to learn to read and speak English.

At last, summer came with its hordes of flies and oppressive heat. Marija found work as a beef trimmer, but at that job the danger of blood poisoning was very great. Ona had her baby, a fine boy, whom they called Antanas after his grandfather. Winter came again, and Jurgis pulled a tendon in his ankle while attempting to avoid a rampaging steer at the plant. Compelled to stay at home for months, he became moody. Two more of Elzbieta's children left school to sell papers. When Jurgis was well enough to look for work again, he could find none, because he was no longer the strong man he had been. Finally, he got a job in a fertilizer plant, a last resort, for men lasted only a few years at that work.

One of Elzbieta's daughters was now old enough to care for the rest of the children, and Elzbieta also went to work. Jurgis began to drink. Ona, pregnant again, developed a consumptive cough and was often seized with spells of hysteria. Hoping to save her job, she allowed herself to be seduced by her boss, Connor. When Jurgis learned what she had done, he attacked Connor and was sentenced to thirty days in jail. Having time to think in jail, Jurgis saw how unjustly he had been treated by society. No longer would he try to be kind, except to his own family. From now on, he would recognize society as an enemy rather than a friend.

After he had served his sentence, Jurgis went to look for his family. He found that they had lost the house because they could not meet the payments and had moved. He found them at last in a rooming house. Ona was in labor with her second child, and Jurgis frantically searched for a midwife. By the time he found one, Ona and the child were past saving. Now he had only little Antanas to live for. He tried to find work. Blacklisted in the stockyards for his attack on Connor, he finally found a job in a harvesting machine factory. Soon after, he was discharged when his department closed down for a lack of orders.

Next he went to work in the steel mills. In order to save money, he moved near the mills and came home only on weekends. One weekend he came home to find that little Antanas had drowned in the street in front of the house. In order to flee his inner demons, his remorse, and his grief, he hopped a freight train and rode away from Chicago. He became one of the thousands of hobos and workers; his old strength came back in healthful, rural surroundings.

In the fall, Jurgis returned to Chicago. He got a job digging tunnels under the streets. Then a shoulder injury made him spend weeks in a hospital. Discharged with his arm still in a sling, he became a beggar. By luck he obtained a hundred-dollar bill from a drunken son of a packing owner. When he went to a saloon to get it changed, however, the barkeeper tried to cheat him out of his money. In a rage, Jurgis attacked the man. He was arrested and sent to jail again. There he became acquainted with a dapper safecracker, Jack Duane, whom he had met during his last incarceration. After their release, Jurgis joined Duane in several muggings and became acquainted with Chicago's underworld. At last, he was making money.

Jurgis became a political worker. About that time, the packing plant workers began to demand more rights through their unions. When packinghouse operators would not listen to union demands, there was a general strike. Jurgis went to work in the plant as a scab and was given a managerial position. One night, however, he met Connor and attacked him again. After getting out on bond and learning that Connor was well connected, Jurgis fled from the district to avoid a penitentiary sentence. On the verge of starvation, he found Marija working as a prostitute. Jurgis was ashamed to think how low he and Marija had fallen since they had come to Chicago.

Jurgis left, despondent, but happened upon a Socialist meeting. He experienced something like a religious transformation. At last, he knew how the workers could find self-respect. He found a job in a hotel where the manager was a Socialist. It was the beginning of a new life for Jurgis, the rebirth of hope and faith.

Critical Evaluation:

The Jungle is indisputably Upton Sinclair's best and most influential book. He was, nevertheless, never entirely happy with its reception. While it contributed to the passage of the Pure Food and Drug Act in 1906 and other consumer protection legislation, his intent was to lay bare the capitalist system and demonstrate the need for democratic socialism. This message was largely ignored.

The Jungle's critique of capitalism is unrelenting. Sinclair depicts a world that is dominated, as his title suggests, by might rather than right, a world that pits everyone against everyone else and metes out rewards on the basis of clout rather than merit. People are lured to the cities in droves and then discarded when they no longer serve the purposes of the powerful. They are maimed, forced to work in unsafe and unsavory conditions, and pushed, psychologically and physically, well past their breaking points.

Even as Sinclair describes the wedding feast in the opening chapter, he intermixes images of gaiety and trays of piping-hot food with vignettes that chronicle the hardships of those forced to work as canners, picklers, beef boners, and general laborers. These workers' tales are tragic, yet the workers refuse to admit defeat.

Jurgis personifies their defiance, constantly vowing to work harder and refusing to accept the systemic causes of his sufferings. He has dedicated himself to achieving the American Dream and is convinced that through his own resolve and determination he can provide for his family and loved ones and rise through the system.

Characterizing Jurgis as a strict individualist who believes that anyone can succeed, Sinclair makes a direct appeal to his nonsocialist readers. The characters in *The Jungle* are not slackers; they are working men and women with simple dreams and expectations who are more than willing to contribute their fair share.

To bring his point home, Sinclair depicts a family more than willing to make sacrifices in order to become full-fledged members of the larger social order. Even Jurgis' father, who is clearly too old to endure the ruthless conditions of the factory, pours his energies into securing employment so the family can afford the basic necessities and provide the youngsters a proper education.

From the beginning, it is clear to the readers that Jurgis and his family are fighting against the odds. Each new detail makes it abundantly clear that the system tempts people with unrealistic dreams and then erects insurmountable barriers to prevent the attainment of those dreams. Instead of a promised land, the family has found a land where greed and exploitation rule. It is not only the greed of the factory owners that the family encounters but also that of the owners' lackeys who sell repossessed tract homes as new, the judges and politicians who have long since abandoned any moral scruples, and the slumlords who live in splendor while their tenants are surrounded by filth and disease. Added to this mix are the churches and the missions that are callously indifferent to the conditions the poor endure, and, quite often, contribute to their suffering.

For the first two-thirds of the book, however, Jurgis is ill-equipped to comprehend the realities that surround him. Until the time of little Antanas' death, he clings to a vague belief that, despite their setbacks, he and the remaining family members will somehow be able to save enough money to allow them a comfortable life and to revive "their habits of decency and kindness."

Once he loses his son, however, he loses the last vestige of hope. He steels himself against emotions and heads for the country. He recovers his health there but finds that even those farmers who are willing to help him (and many are not) treat their work animals better than they do their hired hands. Jurgis resorts to guile and thievery as a way to make ends meet. He cannot, however, silence his conscience, and after coming to terms with the painful losses that he has already endured, returns to the city and resumes his search for a better life.

Although the most memorable and horrifying scenes in the book are those that center on the meatpacking industry, Sinclair goes to great lengths to demonstrate that conditions in other industries are no better. Whether Jurgis is working at Packingtown, the Harvester Works, the steel mills, or in the city's underground tunnels, he is treated with indifference and contempt and, when supply exceeds demand, summarily discharged, "turned out to starve for doing his duty too well." The brutalization is underscored by Sinclair's use of numerous analogies that compare the individuals to wild and hunted animals and parallels the fate of the innocent livestock to the fate of the common working person. The factory life is variously compared to an inferno, a bubbling cauldron, and a medieval torture chamber where it is considered good sport to extract the last ounce of flesh from the hapless workers. The factory, however, is only a reflection of society's disregard for democratic values and its indifference to truth and justice.

This, not the vile conditions and practices of the meat packers, was Sinclair's primary message. It was not, however, the message that the majority of his readers received. Coming as it did on the heels of the embalmed beef scandal exposed by William Randolph Hearst in 1899, the book merely added to the clamor for stricter regulation of the meatpacking industry and Sinclair's larger purpose was ignored.

In part, the fault was Sinclair's. Rather than integrating his call for democratic socialism into the fiber of the novel, he tacks it on almost like an addendum; it lacks authenticity. In describing Jurgis' conversion, he somehow loses sight of Jurgis, reducing him to spectator status, and does not fill the void that this creates with any memorable presence. Sinclair was aware of the flaws that weakened the last third of the novel and, at one point, even suggested ending the novel with little Antanas' death and then publishing a sequel. One cannot but wish that his publisher had agreed. It would have strengthened *The Jungle* and allowed Sinclair the time to develop his critique of the role the political and judicial system plays in the disempowerment of the average citizen. Whether it would have made his socialist appeal any more compelling, however, is a moot point.

"Critical Evaluation" by C. Lynn Munro

Bibliography:
Bloodworth, William A., Jr. *Upton Sinclair.* Boston: Twayne, 1977. Portrays Sinclair as a literary rebel who weds art and ideology and sacrifices the last four chapters of *The Jungle* in his attempt to introduce hope into an otherwise dismal world. Analyzes the novel as a contemporary tragedy, paying attention to the conservative biases inherent in the message.
Harris, Leon. *Upton Sinclair: American Rebel.* New York: Thomas Y. Crowell, 1975. Depicts Sinclair as the most influential (but not the best) writer in the United States because he changed the way Americans viewed themselves, their rights, and their expectations. Bibliography.
Mookerjee, R. N. *Art for Social Justice: The Major Novels of Upton Sinclair.* Metuchen, N.J.: The Scarecrow Press, 1988. Argues that Sinclair's novels must be assessed as an extension of his social activism and desire to communicate with the masses. Examines Sinclair's use of a documentary style and defends Sinclair's characterization, noting that in addition to Jurgis, Sinclair manages to give heroic status to both Marija and Elzbieta.
Rideout, Walter B. *The Radical Novel in the United States: 1900-1954.* New York: Hill & Wang, 1956. After distinguishing between radical fiction and social protest fiction, examines the two major strains of the radical novel. Provides a useful discussion of Sinclair's place within the radical movement, an analysis of the strengths and weaknesses of his fiction, and useful comparisons to the works of Charles Dickens.
Yoder, Jon A. *Upton Sinclair.* New York: Frederick Ungar, 1975. Analyzes the reasons Sinclair's works have been neglected and why Sinclair deemed *The Jungle* a failure. Explains the underpinnings of Sinclair's vision of democratic socialism.

THE JUNGLE BOOKS

Type of work: Short fiction
Author: Rudyard Kipling (1865-1936)
Type of plot: Fables
Time of plot: Nineteenth century
Locale: India
First published: The Jungle Book, 1894; *The Second Jungle Book,* 1895

Principal characters:
MOWGLI, an Indian boy
FATHER WOLF
MOTHER WOLF
SHERE KHAN, the tiger
AKELA, the leader of the wolf pack
BAGHEERA, the black panther
BALOO, the bear
KAA, the rock python
THE BANDAR-LOG, the monkey people
HATHI, the elephant
MESSUA, a woman who adopted Mowgli for a time
MESSUA'S HUSBAND
BULDEO, a village hunter
GRAY BROTHER, a young wolf

The Story:

Shere Khan, the tiger, pursued a small Indian boy who had strayed from his native village, but Shere Khan was lame and missed his leap upon the child. When Father Wolf took the boy home with him to show to Mother Wolf, Shere Khan followed and demanded the child as his quarry. Mother Wolf refused. The tiger retired in anger. Mowgli, the frog, for such he was named, was reared by Mother Wolf along with her own cubs.

Father Wolf took Mowgli to the Council Rock to be recognized by the wolves. Bagheera, the panther, and Baloo, the bear, spoke for Mowgli's acceptance into the Seeonee wolf pack. Therefore, Mowgli became a wolf. Baloo became Mowgli's teacher and instructed him in the lore of the jungle. Mowgli learned to speak the languages of all the jungle people. Throughout his early life, the threat of Shere Khan hung over him, but Mowgli was certain of his place in the pack and of his friends' protection; someday when Akela, the leader of the wolves, would miss his kill, the pack would turn on him and Mowgli. Bagheera told Mowgli to get the Red Flower, or fire, from the village to protect himself. When Akela missed his quarry one night and was about to be deposed and killed, Mowgli attacked all of the mutual enemies with his fire sticks and threatened to destroy anyone who molested Akela. That night, Mowgli realized that the jungle was no place for him, and that someday he would go to live with men. That time, however, was still far off.

One day, Mowgli climbed a tree and made friends with the Bandar-Log, the monkey tribe, who because of their stupidity and vanity were despised by the other jungle people. When the Bandar-Log carried off Mowgli, Bagheera and Baloo went in pursuit, taking along Kaa, the

3377

rock python, who loved to eat monkeys. Mowgli was rescued at the old ruined city of the Cold Lairs by the three pursuers, and Kaa feasted royally upon monkey meat.

One year during a severe drought in the jungle, Hathi the elephant proclaimed the water truce; all animals were allowed to drink at the water hole unmolested. Shere Khan announced to the animals gathered there one day that he had killed a man, not for food but from choice. The other animals were shocked. Hathi allowed the tiger to drink and then told him to be off. Then Hathi told the story of how fear came to the jungle and why the tiger was striped. It was the tiger who first killed man and earned the human tribe's unrelenting enmity; for his deed, the tiger was condemned to wear stripes. For one day a year, the tiger was not afraid of man and could kill him. This day was called, among jungle people, the Night of the Tiger.

One day, Mowgli wandered close to a native village, where he was adopted by Messua, a woman who had lost her son some years before. Mowgli became a watcher of the village herds; from time to time, he met Gray Wolf, his brother, and heard the news of the jungle. Learning that Shere Khan intended to kill him, he laid plans with Akela and Gray Brother to kill the tiger. They lured Shere Khan into a gully and then stampeded the herd. Exiled by stoning from the village because he was believed to be a sorcerer who spoke to the animals, Mowgli returned to the jungle, resolved to hunt with the wolves for the rest of his life.

Buldeo, the village hunter, followed the trail of Mowgli, Gray Brother, and Akela. Mowgli overheard Buldeo say that Messua and her husband were imprisoned in their house and would be burned at the stake. Messua's husband had saved some money, and he had one of the finest herds of buffaloes in the village. Knowing that the imprisonment of Messua and her husband was a scheme for the villagers to get their property, Mowgli laid plans to help his friends. Entering the village, he led Messua and her husband beyond the gates in the darkness. Then the jungle people began to destroy, little by little, the farms, the orchards, and the cattle, but no villager was harmed because Mowgli did not desire the death of any human. Finally, just before the rains, Hathi and his three sons moved into the village and tore down the houses. The people left, and thus the jungle was let into the village.

Kaa took Mowgli to Cold Lairs to meet the guardian of the king's treasure, an old white cobra who had expressed a desire to see Mowgli. The old cobra showed them all the treasure; when he left, Mowgli took a jeweled elephant goad, a king's ankus, with him, even though the cobra had said it brought death to the person who possessed it.

Back in the jungle, Mowgli threw the ankus away. Later that day, he went with Bagheera to retrieve the ankus and discovered that it was gone. They followed the trail of the man who had picked it up and found that altogether six men who had had possession of the ankus had died. Believing it to be cursed, Mowgli returned the ankus to the treasure room in the Cold Lairs.

Sometimes fierce red dogs called dholes traveled in large packs, destroying everything in their paths. Warned of the approach of the dholes, Mowgli led the marauders, by insults and taunts, toward the lairs of the Little People, the bees. Then he excited the bees to attack the dholes. The destruction of the red dogs that escaped the fury of the bees was completed by the wolves lying in ambush a little farther down the river, which flowed under the cliffs where the Little People lived; it was the last battle of old Akela, the leader of the pack when Mowgli was a little boy. He crawled out slowly from under a pile of carcasses to bid Mowgli goodbye and to sing his death song.

The second year after the death of Akela, Mowgli was about seventeen years old. In the spring of that year, Mowgli knew that he was unhappy, but none of his friends could tell him what was wrong. Mowgli left his own jungle to travel to another, and on the way he met Messua. Her husband had died and had left her with a child. Messua told Mowgli that she believed he was her own son lost in the jungle years before and that her baby must be his brother. Mowgli did not know what to make of the child and the unhappiness he felt. When Gray Brother came to Messua's hut, Mowgli decided to return to the jungle. On the outskirts of the village, however, he met a girl coming down the path. Mowgli melted into the jungle and watched the girl. He knew at last that the jungle was no longer a place for him and that he had returned to the man-pack to stay.

Critical Evaluation:

Although originally published separately, *The Jungle Books* are usually combined into one volume. For most readers, *The Jungle Books* tell the story of Mowgli, the boy raised by wolves to become ruler of the jungle, only to have to return to the human world as an adult. Mowgli's adventures in fact take up only eight of the fifteen stories that make up *The Jungle Books*, but those eight stories captivate the reader's imagination in a way that the others do not. Mowgli's story is essentially a reworking of an ancient folklore theme, the child raised by animals. In most versions of this motif, human society remains the frame of reference; the child's animal existence is simply a prelude to his or her reintegration into humanity. In contrast, Kipling places Mowgli in the context of a complete jungle society, which appears more attractive than the few glimpses of the human world allowed into the stories. Although Mowgli's return to the outside world is predicted in the first of the stories, it is his development within the animal world that interests the author. Kipling wrote one story about Mowgli as an adult in the human world, but did not choose to include it in *The Jungle Books*.

The animal world in the Mowgli stories has been described as a post-Darwinian Eden, with Mowgli as Adam given dominion over the animals. Animal existence is rough, with survival dependent on the individual's strength and cunning, and even the revered leader of the wolf pack, Akela, must constantly demonstrate his fitness. That a helpless human child in such an environment could survive infancy, let alone grow to dominate all other jungle creatures, seems an impossible fantasy. Kipling makes it more plausible by reversing expectations. It is the savage jungle that is governed by order and law, while the "civilized" humans are bound by no law and little morality. Humans attack their own out of superstitious fear of witchcraft, or out of greedy desire for gold. To Mowgli, gold seems useless—it cannot be eaten and is too soft to use as a tool or weapon.

In contrast, each animal has its place under the law of the jungle. All know what is required and what is prohibited, both for themselves and for others. With the singular exception of Shere Khan, each animal obeys the law with scrupulous care. The law, with its prohibition on killing humans, protects the infant Mowgli. His eventual mastery of the law in all its nuances grants him authority over the jungle animals.

Kipling's jungle law is in many ways little more than a codification of (carnivorous) animal instincts, which accounts for its universal applicability. As various critics have written, the insistence on law and order reflects late-nineteenth century concepts about the formation of stable societies and the legal basis of imperial rule.

Born to English parents in India, learning Hindi before he learned his mother tongue, Kipling found himself as child and adult without a stable place in either Indian or British society. At the age of six, he was sent away from his family to be schooled in England, where he lived with an abusive caretaker. Later, he endured life in an English boarding school designed to prepare boys for military life, for which he was personally unfitted. As a young man, he returned to India as a newspaperman, reporting on the Anglo-Indian community.

To Kipling, personal experience and professional observation demonstrated the vulnerability of the individual in an unregulated, chaotic world. The law, with its strictures on behavior and social relationship, offered a means to offset the precarious condition of life as he knew it, and incidentally provided a place for everyone regardless of background.

Mowgli is accepted by the animal world, but he can never completely become part of it. In the final Mowgli story, the python Kaa cites the law: "Man goes to man at the last, though the jungle does not cast him out." Mowgli, caught between two worlds, is an extension of the author into his work. Kipling's own childhood was less than idyllic; Mowgli's life would compensate. In the jungle, Mowgli experiences a world of freedom made possible, ironically, by the strictness of a law that grants even an in-between child protection. Moreover, Mowgli's position as an outsider enables him to learn as much as the jungle can teach; he masters far more of the jungle law than any animal.

The Anglo-Indian community into which Kipling was born and which he chronicled as a journalist also had reason to feel its position precarious. On behalf of the crown, a comparative handful of British soldiers, bureaucrats, and ordinary citizens ruled millions of Indians. Just how tenuous that rule could be was demonstrated by the Indian Mutiny of 1857-1858, an event that continued to reverberate forty years later. Kipling alludes to the Indian Mutiny in "The Undertakers," one of *The Jungle Books'* non-Mowgli stories.

Only by a strict adherence to imperial law, and by the subject peoples' recognition of the laws, could order prevail in such a colonial empire. Kipling's jungle law serves as a model for effective colonial administration, just as Mowgli's complete immersion in and knowledge of the culture of those he will later rule is Kipling's model for the ideal colonial education. The other stories in *The Jungle Books* elaborate the vision of a hierarchical world, one in which harmony prevails when socially ordained boundaries are respected. Still essentially beast fables, these stories are more realistic in depicting animal protagonists without the ability to communicate with humans. While several, such as "Rikki-Takki-Tavi," are interesting in their own right, they function in the context of *The Jungle Books* primarily as foils to Mowgli's experiences.

"Critical Evaluation" by A. Waller Hastings

Bibliography:
Blount, Margaret. *Animal Land: The Creatures of Children's Fiction.* New York: William Morrow, 1975. Analyses the Mowgli stories as variants on the school story. Discusses the inversion of moral order between the animal and human worlds.
Frey, Charles, and John Griffith. *The Literary Heritage of Childhood: An Appraisal of Children's Classics in the Western Tradition.*Westport, Conn.: Greenwood Press, 1987. Analyzes Mowgli as a character situated between two cultures, unable to fit into either fully, and connects Mowgli's situation to Kipling's position in regard to Indian and English society.
McBratney, John. "Imperial Subjects, Imperial Space in Kipling's *Jungle Book.*" *Victorian Studies* 35, No. 3 (Spring, 1992): 277-293. Detailed examination of Mowgli stories in relation to contemporary categories of race and ethnicity. Argues that the stories are an attempt to create in fiction a society in which distinctions of caste and race do not operate. Kipling is a "quiet rebel" against prevailing racial ideas.
McClure, John A. *Kipling and Conrad: The Colonial Fiction.* Cambridge, Mass.: Harvard University Press, 1981. Examines *The Jungle Books* in relation to the politics of imperialism. Mowgli stories offer Kipling's conception of the ideal education for imperial rule. The beast fable structure obscures the flaws in his concept.

Murray, John. "The Law of *The Jungle Books*." *Children's Literature* 20 (1992): 1-14. Provides a good summary of earlier writings on Kipling's concept of law and argues that this concept must be understood in the context of group survival against inimical forces, rather than as natural or ethical law.

JUNO AND THE PAYCOCK

Type of work: Drama
Author: Sean O'Casey (John Casey, 1880-1964)
Type of plot: Satire
Time of plot: 1922
Locale: Dublin
First performed: 1924; first published, 1925

>   *Principal characters:*
>   "CAPTAIN" JACK BOYLE, a ne'er-do-well
>   JUNO BOYLE, his wife
>   JOHNNY BOYLE, their son
>   MARY BOYLE, their daughter
>   "JOXER" DALY, the Captain's pal
>   JERRY DEVINE, Mary's suitor
>   CHARLIE BENTHAM, a schoolteacher
>   MRS. MAISIE MADIGAN, a neighbor
>   "NEEDLE" NUGENT, a tailor

The Story:

Waiting for Captain Boyle to come in from his morning visit to the pub, Mary Boyle and her mother, Juno, discussed the newspaper account of the murder of Robbie Tancred, a fanatic Irish Republican. Johnny Boyle, who had been shot in the hip and had lost an arm fighting against the Free State, left the living room after denouncing the two women for their morbid insensitivity. Juno scolded Mary for participating in the Trades Union Strike, especially at a time when the family was in debt for food but Mary defended her activities, and her brother's as well, as matters of principle.

When Jerry Devine rushed in with a message from Father Farrell, who had found a job for Boyle, Juno sent Jerry to look for her husband at his favorite bar. Soon afterward she heard her husband and his crony, Joxer Daly, singing on the stairs. She hid behind the bed curtains so as to catch them talking about her. Disclosing herself, she frightened Joxer away and berated her husband for his laziness and malingering. Jerry returned and delivered his message to Boyle, who immediately developed a case of stabbing pains in his legs. Juno, not deceived, ordered him to change into his working clothes. She then left for her own job.

Jerry accosted Mary, complained of her unfriendliness, and once again proposed to her. Although Jerry offered her love and security, Mary refused him, and both left in a huff.

Ignoring his wife's instructions to apply for the job, Boyle, leisurely proceeding to get his breakfast, was rejoined by Joxer. Absorbed in their talk, they refused to acknowledge a loud knocking at the street door, though the continuance of it seemed to upset young Johnny Boyle. Their rambling discourse on family life, the clergy, literature, and the sea was interrupted by Juno and Mary, who had returned with Charlie Bentham, a schoolteacher and amateur lawyer, to announce that a cousin had bequeathed £2,000 to Boyle. Boyle declared that he was through with Joxer and the like, whereupon Joxer, who had been hiding outside the window, reappeared, expressed his indignation, and left.

Two days later the two cronies had been reconciled, Joxer having served as Boyle's agent for loans based on expectations of the inheritance. The entrance of Juno and Mary with a new gramophone was followed by that of Bentham, now Mary's fiancé. Over family tea, Bentham explained his belief in theosophy and ghosts. Johnny, visibly upset by this conversation about death, left the room but quickly returned, twitching and trembling. He was convinced that he had seen the bloody ghost of Robbie Tancred kneeling before the statue of the Virgin.

The arrival of Joxer with Mrs. Madigan, a garrulously reminiscing neighbor, smoothed over the incident. A party featuring whiskey and song ensued. The revelry was interrupted by Mrs. Tancred and some neighbors, on their way to Robbie Tancred's funeral. Soon thereafter the merriment was again dispelled, this time by the funeral procession in the street. A young man, an Irregular Mobilizer, came looking for Johnny, whom he reproached for not attending the funeral. He ordered Johnny to appear at a meeting called for the purpose of inquiring into Tancred's death.

Two months later, Juno insisted on taking Mary to the doctor, for the young woman seemed to be pining away over Bentham, who had disappeared.

After the women had left, Joxer and Nugent, a tailor, slipped into the apartment. Having learned that Boyle would not receive the inheritance, Nugent had come to get the suit which he had sold to Boyle on credit. Taking the suit from a chair, Nugent scoffed at Boyle's promise to pay and his order for a new topcoat as well. Joxer, who had sneaked out unseen, returned, hypocrite that he was, to commiserate with Boyle. Mrs. Madigan, who had also heard that Boyle would not receive his inheritance, arrived to collect the three pounds she had lent him. Rebuffed, she appropriated the gramophone and left, followed by Joxer.

News of Boyle's misadventure spread rapidly; two men arrived to remove the new, but unpaid-for, furniture. Mrs. Boyle ran out to find her husband. Mary having returned, Jerry Devine came to see her. Again he proposed. Although he was willing to forget that Mary had jilted him for Bentham, he recoiled at her admission that she was pregnant.

Left alone with the two moving men, Johnny imagined that he felt a bullet wound in his chest. At that moment two armed Irish Irregulars entered the apartment and accused Johnny of informing on Robbie Tancred to the gang that had murdered him. Ignoring Johnny's protestations of innocence and loyalty, the men dragged him out. A little later, Mrs. Madigan notified Mary and Juno that the police were waiting below, requesting that Juno identify a body. Juno and Mary left, vowing never to return to the worthless Boyle.

Soon Boyle and Joxer stumbled into the abandoned apartment, both very drunk and unaware of Johnny's death or Juno and Mary's desertion. Joxer stretched out on the bed; Boyle slumped on the floor. With thick tongues they stammered out their patriotic devotion to Ireland, and Boyle deplored the miserable state of the world.

Critical Evaluation:

Sean O'Casey's plays mark the culmination, in drama, of the Irish Renaissance. Drama of the Irish Renaissance had begun as a part of the European movement toward realistic theater in opposition to the French romantic drama, but diverged from the dramaturgic techniques of Henrik Ibsen and George Bernard Shaw. Believing that Continental and English dramas were too intellectualized, O'Casey, along with his compatriots William Butler Yeats and John Millington Synge, tried to make Irish drama individualistic and realistic by adding heavy doses of Irish local color. Formlessness—ignoring formal dramatic technique to reflect the vigor and vitality of life—was O'Casey's unique contribution to the Irish movement. In *Juno and the Paycock* he reached a new peak of realism. He dispensed with an elaborate plot, ideas, and consistency of character, content merely to show Irish characters in action.

Captain Jack Boyle is such a character. "The whole worl's in a state of chassis!" (chaos) he says; he is the "paycock" (peacock) of the play. The background of "chassis"—in particular the turbulence of the civil wars that wracked Ireland during the first quarter of the twentieth century—is in O'Casey's great trilogy of realistic plays about violence and strife in Dublin. The plays are *The Shadow of a Gunman* (1923), *Juno and the Paycock*, and *The Plough and the Stars* (1926).

Civic disorder provides the atmosphere of general bitterness and tension, as well as determining the fate of the son, Johnny, in *Juno and the Paycock*, the most domestic of the three plays. What happens to the Boyle family is largely the product of their own actions, but, because they embody personal qualities that are common to the Irish, the Boyles are representative. Their actions illuminate the follies, evils, and strengths of the national character in a time of turmoil.

Twice, in the early moments of the play, Mary tells her mother that "a principle's a principle," once in reference to her own support of a fellow striker and once in regard to her crippled brother's nationalistic activities. A short time later Johnny repeats the same slogan to Juno, but this time she answers it emphatically: "Ah, you lost your best principle, me boy, when you lost your arm; them's the only sort o' principles that's any good to a workin' man." That exchange sets up the thematic dichotomy of the play—abstract moral principles, based on generalized causes such as nationalism, Marxism, or religion, versus a practical morality based on human loyalties, needs, and sympathies. The abstractions are used either as justifications for violence or as rationalizations for no action at all.

Captain Boyle is a veritable catalog of Irish weaknesses. His capacity for strong drink is exceeded only by his capacity for self-deception and pompous moralizing. Most of his time is spent in idle chatter and drinking with his equally irresponsible crony, Joxer Daly. If offered honest work, Boyle has a sudden attack of leg pains. He continually complains about the moral state of the world ("is there any morality left anywhere?" he asks Joxer), but he refuses any involvement with the problems of others ("We've nothing to do with these things, one way or t'other"). Boyle is nevertheless charming; he sings, he recites poetry, and, when not in a drunken stupor, he speaks with style and vigor. He has opinions on every current political, social, and religious subject and, although they are trite, they are not stupid. If he is never exactly lovable, he is at least likable at the beginning of the play; these defects do not seem too harmful and, most important, he is very funny. His early scenes with Joxer are masterpieces of comic repartee.

The audience's attitude toward Boyle changes during the course of the play. As the action progresses it becomes clear that his buffoonery has serious implications. When his daughter's unsanctified pregnancy is revealed, he rises to heights of moral indignation as though she did it as a personal insult to him ("when I'm done with her she'll be a sorry girl!"). He continues to squander money on credit even after he learns that it has been lost, in spite of the serious damage that it will do to the household. So when, at the end of the play, he and Joxer come in very drunk and do a repeat of their earlier routine, what was previously funny becomes grotesque. The consequences of his braggadocio are too real and serious to laugh at a second time. Dramatically this mixture of tragedy and farce is most powerful. Thematically O'Casey is suggesting that many of those "lovable" Irish failings, so celebrated in popular myth and song, may, on closer inspection, prove to be dangerous and destructive.

Although Boyle's faults may be the most blatant, the kind of self-righteousness he exhibits infects others in the play. Jerry Devine's abstract pieties prevent him from marrying Mary because she is a "fallen woman." It is strongly hinted that the death of Tancred was the inevitable result of his politics. The men who take Johnny make sure that he "has his beads" so that the proper religious proprieties will not be missing from his murder. All of the men in the play cling to their narrow patterns of thought and rigid moral postures, and they fail in every situation that requires practical, humane responses. Thus, instead of "freedom," their ideas produce confusion, violence, and pain.

The men are a damning influence, and the women in *Juno and the Paycock* are a redeeming one—although, even for them, there are important lessons to be learned. The difference is that they are capable of learning and growing because they react to personal needs and sorrows, not abstractions. At the play's beginning, Mary chides her mother about the need for "principles," but by the end of it, having been impregnated and deserted by Charlie Bentham and rejected by Jerry Devine, she has come to understand and accept human weakness without bitterness. As she says to Jerry: "I don't blame you . . . your humanity is as narrow as the humanity of the others."

Juno Boyle is the supreme embodiment of compassionate action. Throughout the play it is evident that it has been her strength which has kept the Boyle household intact. Juno has nevertheless been tainted by the atmosphere of the times and the prospect of easy money. She is casual about the Captain's defects, intolerant of her children's feelings and opinions, and somewhat callous toward those outside the family. She feels no special sympathy for her bereaved neighbor, Mrs. Tancred, and even plays her new phonograph while the rituals of mourning are going on nearby. After Juno faces the loss of the money, her husband's betrayal, Mary's pregnancy, and Johnny's execution, she gains a new insight into her fellow man and a deeper, more sympathetic humanity. She overcomes her grief for Johnny, casts aside her political and moral prejudices ("Why didn't I remember that when he wasn't a Diehard or a Stater, but only a poor dead son!"), leaves Boyle, accepts the burden of Mary and her unborn child, and hopefully assumes the "biggest part o' the trouble."

Whether or not the strength evidenced by Juno is enough to overcome the weaknesses, follies, and evils the men exhibit is not answered in the play. In the end it depends upon whether or not it is possible to give a positive response to Juno's final, plaintive prayer: "Sacred Heart o' Jesus, take away our hearts o' stone, and give us hearts o' flesh! Take away this murdherin' hate, and give us Thine own eternal love!"

"Critical Evaluation" by Keith Neilson

Bibliography:
Ayling, Ronald. *Sean O'Casey*. Nashville, Tenn.: Aurora Press, 1970. Selection from O'Casey criticism includes valuable comments on *Juno and the Paycock*. Considerations of O'Casey's poetic gifts, his use of symbols, his socialism, and his place in the Irish dramatic movement.

Hogan, Robert. *The Experiments of Sean O'Casey*. New York: St. Martin's Press, 1960. A synthesis of dramatic theory and theatrical technique. Argues that in his Dublin trilogy, O'Casey is continually expanding his technical capacities and that *Juno and the Paycock* is a stage in his continuing experimentation.

Kilroy, Thomas, ed. *Sean O'Casey: A Collection of Essays*. Englewood Cliffs, N.J.: Prentice-Hall, 1975. An excellent selection from leading Irish, British, and American O'Casey critics: his politics, dramatic technique, and development. Representing disagreements about O'Casey's achievement as a political dramatist.

Krause, David. *Sean O'Casey: The Man and His Work*. New York: Macmillan, 1975. One of the best studies of O'Casey's dramatic genius and the complex engagement between this milieu and his dramatic work. Describes the economic, political, and religious tensions in Dublin in his time, his involvement with Irish revolutionary movements, the Gaelic League, and the Irish Labor Movement.

Owens, Cóilín, D., and Joan N. Radner, eds. *Irish Drama: 1900-1980*. Washington, D.C.: Catholic University of America Press, 1990. Places *Juno and the Paycock* in the context of the Irish dramatic movement, provides a clear general introduction to the critical issues in the play, a bibliography, and comprehensive annotations to the text.

JURGEN
A Comedy of Justice

Type of work: Novel
Author: James Branch Cabell (1879-1958)
Type of plot: Fantasy
Time of plot: Middle Ages
Locale: Poictesme, a mythical land
First published: 1919

> *Principal characters:*
> JURGEN, a middle-aged pawnbroker
> DAME LISA, his wife
> DOROTHY LA DÉSIRÉE, his childhood sweetheart
> QUEEN GUENEVERE
> DAME ANAÏTIS
> CHLORIS, a Hamadryad
> QUEEN HELEN OF TROY
> MOTHER SEREDA
> KOSHCHEI, the maker of things as they are

The Story:

Once in the old days, a middle-aged pawnbroker named Jurgen said a good word for the Prince of Darkness. In gratitude, the Prince of Darkness removed from the earth Dame Lisa, Jurgen's shrewish wife. Some time later, Jurgen heard that his wife had returned to wander on Amneran Heath; consequently, the only manly thing for him to do was to look for her.

It was Walpurgis Night when Jurgen met Dame Lisa on the heath. She led him to a cave, but when he followed her inside, she disappeared and Jurgen found a centaur instead. Jurgen inquired for his wife. The centaur replied that only Koshchei the Deathless, the maker of things as they are, could help Jurgen in his quest. The centaur gave Jurgen a beautiful new shirt and started off with him to the Garden between Dawn and Sunrise, the first stopping place of Jurgen's journey to find Koshchei.

In the garden, Jurgen found Dorothy la Désirée, who had been his first sweetheart and who retained all the beauty he had praised in his youthful poetry. She no longer knew him, for she was in love only with Jurgen as he had been in youth, and he could not make her understand that in the real world she too had become middle-aged and commonplace. Sadly he parted from her and found himself suddenly back in his native country.

His friend the centaur had now become an ordinary horse. Jurgen mounted and rode through a forest until he came to the house of Mother Sereda, the goddess who controlled Wednesdays and whose job it was to bleach the color out of everything in the world. By flattery, Jurgen persuaded her to let him live over a certain Wednesday in his youth with Dorothy la Désirée. When the magic Wednesday ended, however, Dorothy la Désirée turned into the old woman she really was, and Jurgen quickly departed.

He wandered again to Amneran Heath and entered the cave to look for Koshchei and Dame Lisa. There he found a beautiful girl who said that she was Guenevere, the daughter of King Gogyrvan of Glathion. Jurgen offered to conduct her back to her home. When they arrived at the court of King Gogyrvan, Jurgen, pretending to be the duke of Logreus, asked for the hand of Guenevere as a reward for her safe return, but she had already been promised to King Arthur.

Jurgen stayed on at court. He had made the discovery that he still looked like a young man; the only trouble was that his shadow was not his shadow; it was the shadow of Mother Sereda.

King Arthur's envoys, Dame Anaïtis and Merlin, had arrived to take Guenevere to London. Jurgen watched her depart for London without feeling any sorrow because of a magic token Merlin had given him. Dame Anaïtis invited Jurgen to visit her palace in Cockaigne, the country where time stood still. There Jurgen participated with her in a ceremony called the Breaking of the Veil, to learn afterward that it had been a marriage ceremony and that Dame Anaïtis was now his wife. Dame Anaïtis, a myth woman of lunar legend, instructed Jurgen in every variety of strange pleasures she knew.

Jurgen visited a philologist, who told him that he too had become a legend; consequently, he could not remain long in Cockaigne. When the time came for him to leave the country, Jurgen chose to go to Leuke, the kingdom where Queen Helen and Achilles ruled. Jurgen's reason for wishing to go there was that Queen Helen resembled Dorothy la Désirée.

In Leuke, Jurgen met Chloris, a Hamadryad, and married her. He was still curious about Queen Helen, however, and one evening he entered her castle and went to her bedchamber. The sleeping queen was Dorothy la Désirée, but he dared not touch her. Her beauty, created from the dreams of his youth, was unattainable. He left the castle and returned to Chloris.

Shortly afterward, the Philistines invaded Leuke and condemned all its mythical inhabitants to limbo. Jurgen protested because he was flesh and blood, and he offered to prove his claim by mathematics. Queen Dolores of the Philistines agreed with him after he had demonstrated his proof to her by means of a concrete example. However, he was condemned by the great tumblebug of the Philistines for being a poet.

After Chloris had been condemned to limbo, Jurgen went on to the hell of his fathers. There he visited Satan and learned that Koshchei had created hell to humor the pride of Jurgen's forefathers. Then he remembered that he was supposed to be looking for Dame Lisa. Learning that she was not in hell, he decided to look for her in heaven. Mistaken for a pope by means of the philologist's charm, he managed to gain entrance to heaven, but Dame Lisa was not there. St. Peter returned him to Amneran Heath.

On the heath, he again met Mother Sereda, who took away his youth and returned him to his middle-aged body. Actually, it was a relief to Jurgen to be old again. Then for the third time, he entered the cave in search of Dame Lisa. Inside he found the Prince of Darkness who had taken her away. The Prince was really Koshchei; Jurgen was near the end of his quest. He asked Koshchei to return Dame Lisa to him.

Koshchei again showed him Guenevere, Dame Anaïtis, and Dorothy la Désirée, but Jurgen would not have them. He had had his youth to live over, and he had committed the same follies. He was content now to be Jurgen the pawnbroker. Koshchei agreed to return Jurgen to his former life, but he asked for the centaur's shirt in return. Jurgen gladly gave up the shirt. Koshchei walked with him from the heath into town. As they walked, Jurgen noticed that the moon was sinking in the east. Time was turning backward. It was as if the past year had never been. He approached his house and saw through the window that the table was set for supper. Inside, Dame Lisa sat sewing and looking quite as if nothing had ever happened.

Critical Evaluation:

The famous 1922 obscenity trial over *Jurgen* has probably drawn too much attention away from literary issues of the novel's style and organization, but the attempted censorship does provide a clue to the book's continuing importance. Like James Joyce's *Ulysses* (1922), published only three years after *Jurgen* and also the subject of an obscenity case, *Jurgen* dares to lampoon all the sacred beliefs of Anglo-American ideology. It mocks human beings' belief in their own importance, romantic notions of male-female relationships, belief in an afterlife, faith in cosmic justice, idealistic ideas of human motives, and the well-meaning idea of literary censorship. It mocks, however, in an upbeat, comic, and sometimes wistful tone. Cabell's "Gallantry" is the most lighthearted form of cynicism ever conceived.

Cabell agreed with his critics that he opposed the prevalent naturalism of his time. It is true that Cabell diligently avoids realistic detail in his narrative, yet in one respect—his cynical treatment of human motives—he is in fact naturalistic. The novel is characterized by psychological realism while maintaining a veneer of romanticism in its incidents and motifs, which are drawn mostly from myth, folklore, and medieval romances. Because Cabell refuses to lie about the human heart, *Jurgen*, again like *Ulysses*, remains contemporary. Cabell's honesty ensures that it does not appear dated.

The gaily disillusioned and cynical tone of the book is mainly a result of Cabell's view of the sordidness of human motives. Because Jurgen is portrayed lying to himself about his own character and motives, Cabell's irony and satire apply as much to the title character himself as they do to the characters he dupes and uses.

The ironic tone is also a constant reminder that this is a satirical farce, an artifice of words, and that Cabell in no sense believes in the world he has created. In this respect, he contrasts with those fantasy writers who maintain a serious tone and, by pretending to believe in their creations, lay claim to a transcendent importance that Cabell calls into question. His skeptical modernism is the opposite of Christian Neoplatonism.

The author's tone should not divert attention from his staggering inventiveness and his ability to adapt and develop characters and motifs from myth, legend, and folklore. Cabell, who was familiar with a wide range of sources, was surely one of America's most learned authors.

A first-time reader, even if familiar with some of Cabell's source material, is apt to become confused because of the multitude of the characters, settings, and incidents in *Jurgen*. The allegorical point of the rather episodic plot is simple, however. Jurgen learns to abandon his regrets because his forays into his past reveal that his youthful ideals, especially about people, were all illusions and his dreams therefore impossible to fulfill, even when he was given a second chance with the advantage of foreknowledge.

The plot revolves around three excursions Jurgen makes into a cave in search of his lost wife. In the second excursion, he relives a year of his youth, which he spends mainly in three realms: Glathion, Cockaigne, and Leuke. Glathion is modeled on Arthurian romance, Cockaigne on medieval legends of a land of plenty, and Leuke on Greek mythology. Because medieval romance often served as a vehicle for religious allegory, Guenevere, the woman he seduces in Glathion, becomes a symbol for the beauty of simple religious faith. When Jurgen loses Guenevere, he seeks solace in the arms of another woman of Arthurian legend, Anaïtis, the Lady of the Lake, who is symbolic of passion and with whom he journeys to the land of sensual delight. Continuous sexual overstimulation soon becomes cloying, however, and he tricks Anaïtis into sending him to Leuke, where he hopes to come face to face with the ideal of perfection, symbolized by Helen of Troy.

In the central chapter—entitled "Economics of King Jurgen"—Cabell suggests a metaphor through which the governing principle of the novel can be understood. Just as Helen is within his grasp, Jurgen refrains from attempting to possess her, because he now understands that perfection (and, by implication, fulfillment) is an illusion created by temporal and physical distance from the object of desire. Rather than risk disillusionment, he withdraws, preferring to remain in the comfort of his unattainable dreams.

In deliberately declining to face truth, Jurgen necessarily chooses a kind of double-think, clinging to beliefs that at the deepest level he knows to be false. Disturbingly, Cabell seems to be suggesting that this is the nature of all cherished human beliefs about a universe that ultimately refuses to be explained coherently by any philosophy or model. Cabell presents Jurgen's double-think as a compromise between reality and the comforting illusions used to maintain sanity. Compromise is the basis of Gallantry. Jurgen proceeds through an allegorical series of dissatisfactions. He seeks to replace his lost faith with sensual pleasure; when that proves cloying, he seeks after ideal beauty, but eventually abandons that quest, too.

Like most allegories, *Jurgen* is heavily laden with symbolic objects. The phallic symbols of Jurgen's sword, lance, and scepter were the offensive elements that occasioned the obscenity trial—though only a sophisticated reader already attuned to such possibilities would actually notice them. In other words, people already had to be "corrupt," by the censors' definition, in order to be "corrupted" by the material. The earthiness of the novel is less interesting and less profound than the two central objects that reinforce Cabell's philosophy: the shirt of Nessus and the shadow of Mother Sereda, both of which Jurgen wears for the duration of his one year excursion into the past, and both of which he loses when his odyssey ends. The shirt, which in the classical myth of Hercules was supposed to ensure Hercules' devotion to his wife but which turned out to be poisonous, represents the youthful charm Jurgen uses to deceive and seduce women. The ominous shadow, which prevents Jurgen from entering wholeheartedly into any of his enterprises, seems to represent his awareness of the impossibility of recovering the past or reaching fulfillment, effectively summing up the novel's theme.

"Critical Evaluation" by James David Schiavoni

Bibliography:
Attebery, Brian. *The Fantasy Tradition in American Literature: From Irving to Le Guin.* Bloomington: Indiana University Press, 1980. Places Cabell in the larger context of American literature, comparing and contrasting him specifically with science fiction writer Edgar Rice Burroughs. A perceptive and ground-breaking study.
Carter, Lin. *Imaginary Worlds: The Art of Fantasy.* New York: Ballantine Books, 1973. Discusses Cabell and *Jurgen* in relation to a tradition extending from the ancient epics to literature of the early 1970's. An appreciation rather than a rigorous analysis.
Davis, Joe Lee. *James Branch Cabell.* New York: Twayne Publishers, 1962. Treats *Jurgen* as a volume in Cabell's series "The Biography of the Life of Manuel" and ranks him with such internationally known writers as George Bernard Shaw and André Gide. The obvious starting point for anyone interested in Cabell.
Fiedler, Leslie A. "The Return of James Branch Cabell: Or, The Cream of the Cream of the Jest." In *James Branch Cabell: Centennial Essays,* edited by M. Thomas Inge and Edgar E. MacDonald. Baton Rouge: Louisiana State University Press, 1983. An informal essay praising Cabell for writing what Fiedler ironically labels "juvenile trash" (as opposed to "high art"). *Jurgen* is also discussed in many of the other essays in this collection.
Riemer, James D. *From Satire to Subversion: The Fantasies of James Branch Cabell.* New York: Greenwood Press, 1989. Evaluates a handful of Cabell's best fantasies, including *Jurgen*, and concludes that he successfully merges satire and subversion. Useful secondary bibliography.

KALEVALA

Type of work: Poetry
Author: Elias Lönnrot (1802-1884)
Type of plot: Saga
Time of plot: Mythological times
Locale: Finland and Lapland
First published: 1835 (English translation, 1888)

Principal characters:
> VÄINÄMÖINEN, the Son of the Wind and the Virgin of the Air,
>   the singer-hero
> ILMARINEN, the smith-hero
> LEMMINKÄINEN, the warrior-hero
> LOUHI, ruler of Pohjola, the North Country
> AINO, a young Lapp maiden
> JOUKAHÄINEN, a Laplander, Aino's brother
> KULLERVO, an evil, sullen, and very powerful slave
> THE DAUGHTER OF LOUHI, Ilmarinen's wife
> MARJATTA, a holy woman

The Story:

After his mother had created the land, the sun, and the moon out of sea duck eggs, Väinämöinen was born, and with the help of Sampsa Pellervoinen he made the barren land fruitful, sowing seeds and planting trees. By the time Väinämöinen was an old man, he had gained great fame as a singer and charmer. When a brash young man named Joukahäinen challenged him to a duel of magic songs, Väinämöinen won easily and forced the young man to give him his sister Aino for a wife. Aino was greatly saddened, however, at having to marry an old man and so she drowned herself, to Väinämöinen's sorrow. He looked all over the sea for her and found her at last in the form of a salmon, but in that form she escaped him forever.

In time he heard of the beautiful daughters of Louhi in the far North Country and he decided to seek them out. On the way to Pohjola, the land of Louhi, his horse was killed by the bold young man whom he had defeated in the duel of songs, and Väinämöinen was forced to swim to Pohjola. Louhi, the witch, found him on the beach, restored his health, told him that he would have to forge a magic Sampo (a mill that ground out riches) in order to win a daughter, and then sent him on his way.

Väinämöinen found one of Louhi's daughters seated on a rainbow and asked her to become his wife. She gave him three tasks to do. After completing two, he was wounded in the knee while trying to complete the third. The wound, which bled profusely, was healed by a magic ointment prepared under the directions of an old man skilled in leechcraft. Väinämöinen went home and raised a great wind to carry Ilmarinen, the mighty smith who had forged the sky, into the North Country to make the Sampo for Louhi. Ilmarinen forged the Sampo, but still Louhi's daughter refused to marry and leave her homeland. Ilmarinen, who was also in love with the maiden, went sadly home.

A gallant youth, Lemminkäinen, was famous for winning the love of women. Having heard of Kyllikki, the flower of Saari, he was determined to win her for his wife. When he arrived in Esthonia she refused him, and he abducted her. They lived happily together until one day she disobeyed him. In retaliation he went north to seek one of Louhi's daughters as his wife. In Pohjola, Lemminkäinen charmed everyone except an evil herdsman whom he scorned. Like Väinämöinen, he was given three tasks and performed the first two without much difficulty; but while trying to complete the third he was slain by the evil herdsman. Alarmed by his long absence, his mother went searching for him, found him in pieces at the bottom of a river, and restored him finally to his original shape.

Meanwhile, Väinämöinen was busy building a ship by means of magic, his third task for Louhi's daughter; suddenly he found that he had forgotten the three magic words needed to complete the work. He searched everywhere for them and was almost trapped in Tuonela, the kingdom of death. Then he heard that the giant Vipunen might know them. When they met, Vipunen swallowed him, but Väinämöinen caused the giant so much pain that the creature was forced to release him and reveal the magic charm. With the charm Väinämöinen completed his ship and again set sail for Pohjola.

Ilmarinen, learning of Väinämöinen's departure, started after him on horseback. When they met they agreed to abide by the maiden's choice. On their arrival at Pohjola, Louhi gave Ilmarinen three tasks to perform: to plow a field of snakes, to capture a bear and a wolf, and to catch a great pike. Ilmarinen performed these tasks. Since Väinämöinen was old, Louhi's daughter chose Ilmarinen for her husband. There was great rejoicing at the marriage. Väinämöinen sang for the bridal couple. A gigantic ox was slain and mead was brewed, and the bride and groom were both instructed in the duties of marriage. At last Ilmarinen took his new bride to his home in the south.

Lemminkäinen had not been invited to the festivities because of his quarrelsome nature, and he was therefore angry. Although his mother warned him of the dangers he would have to face on the journey and of Louhi's treachery, he insisted on going to Pohjola. With his magic charms he was able to overcome all dangers along the way. In Pohjola, Louhi tried to kill him with snake-poisoned ale, but Lemminkäinen saw through the trick. Then he and Louhi's husband engaged in a duel of magic which ended in a tie. Finally they fought with swords and Lemminkäinen slew Louhi's husband. Lemminkäinen then turned into an eagle and flew home. In fear of retribution he took his mother's advice and went to live for several years on an obscure island where the only inhabitants were women whose warrior husbands were away from home.

Forced to flee when the time came for the husbands to return, Lemminkäinen set out for his own land in a boat. The craft turned over and he was forced to swim to shore. Upon arriving home, he found the country desolate and his mother missing. At last he found her hiding in the forest. Swearing to avenge himself on the warriors of Pohjola who had desolated the land, he set sail with Tiera, a warrior companion, but Louhi sent the frost to destroy him. Although Lemminkäinen managed to charm the frost, he and his companion were shipwrecked and were forced to retreat.

The wife of Kalervo had been carried off by her brother-in-law, Untamoinen, who then laid waste to Kalervo's land. In the cradle, Kullervo, born to Kalervo's wife, swore to be avenged on his uncle. Kullervo grew up strong, but so stupid and clumsy that he broke or ruined everything he touched. He tried to kill his uncle and his uncle tried to kill him. Finally, the uncle gave him to Ilmarinen. Ilmarinen's wife immediately disliked the boy and gave him a loaf of bread with a stone in it. In return, while Ilmarinen was away from home, Kullervo had her killed by wild beasts. He then fled into the forest, where he found his parents and lived with them for a long time. He performed all his chores badly. After a time he set out on a journey. Two women having refused him, he ravished a third, only to learn that she was his sister. In anguish, she killed herself, and Kullervo returned home in sorrow. When his family rejected him, he set off to attack Untamöinen. After killing his uncle he returned to find his family dead and the countryside desolate. He wandered off into the forest and killed himself by falling on his sword. Ilmarinen, after weeping for his dead wife, made up his mind to make another in his forge. He fashioned a woman out of gold and silver, but she remained cold and lifeless; so Ilmarinen went north again to Pohjola. When Louhi refused to give him a wife, he abducted one of her daughters. This wife soon proved unfaithful, and in anger he turned her into a seagull.

Väinämöinen had been thinking about the Sampo, that magic mill. Determined to steal it from Louhi, he built a ship and Ilmarinen forged a sword for him, and the two heroes started for Pohjola. On the way Lemminkäinen called to them from the shore and asked to accompany them. They took him along. During the voyage the boat struck a giant pike. Väinämöinen killed the great fish and from its bones fashioned a harp with which he sang everyone in Pohjola to sleep. With the help of an ox the three heroes took the Sampo and sailed for home. When Louhi awoke, she sent fog and wind after the heroes. During the storm Väinämöinen's harp fell overboard.

Louhi and her men followed in a warboat. The two boats met in a great battle. Although Väinämöinen was victorious, Louhi dragged the Sampo from his boat into the lake. There it broke into pieces, most of which sank to the bottom. Only a few smaller pieces floated to shore. After making violent threats against Kalevala, Louhi returned home with only a small and useless fragment of the Sampo. Väinämöinen collected the pieces on the shore and planted them for good luck; the land became more fruitful. Having searched in vain for his lost harp, Väinämöinen made another of birchwood, and his songs to its music gave joy to everyone.

Vexed because her land was barren after the loss of the Sampo, Louhi sent a terrible pestilence to Kalevala, but Väinämöinen healed the people by magic and salves. Next Louhi sent a great bear to ravish the herds, but Väinämöinen killed the savage beast. Then Louhi stole the moon and the sun, which had come down to earth to hear Väinämöinen play and sing. She also stole the fire from all the hearths of Kalevala. When Ukko, the supreme god, kindled a new fire for the sun and the moon, some of it fell to earth and was swallowed by a fish in a large lake. Väinämöinen and Ilmarinen finally found the fish, and Ilmarinen was badly burned. The fire escaped and burned a great area of country until it was at last captured and returned to the hearths of Kalevala. Ilmarinen, recovered from his burns, prepared great chains for Louhi and frightened her into restoring the sun and the moon to the heavens.

Marjatta, a holy woman and a virgin, swallowed a cranberry, whereupon a son was born to her in a stable. The child was baptized as the king of Carelia, despite Väinämöinen's claim that such an ill-omened child should be put to death. Angered because the child proved wiser than he, Väinämöinen sailed away to a land between the earth and the sky, leaving behind him, for the pleasure of his people, his harp and his songs.

Critical Evaluation:

The stories contained in the *Kalevala* stem from Finnish folktales that are many centuries old. However, it is important to remember that the *Kalevala* that now exists took shape only in 1835. This was when Elias Lönnrot published a compilation of folktales he had spent years gathering and arranging. Lönnrot did not invent any of the stories in the *Kalevala*, but he did codify and edit them so that they would flow into each other in a smoother narrative that would make up a unified aesthetic whole. Lönnrot was no doubt influenced in his compilation of the *Kalevala* by the Finnish nationalism of his day (Finland was ruled by Russia until 1917). Finland was one of many European countries that experienced a nationalistic revival in the nineteenth century, and throughout Europe folk legends were an important part of this revival.

The *Kalevala* is a cohesive story, but it contains dozens of individual tales within the central narrative. The stories are legends, not historical fact. The adventures of Väinämöinen, Ilmarinen, and Kullervo are fantastic and mythical. Nevertheless, the epic chronicles a development through time that can be termed historical. Like the Hindu epic the *Mahabharata* (c. 400 B.C.E.-200 C.E.) and the Babylonian creation story *Enuma elish*, the *Kalevala* starts at the beginning of time, with the creation of the cosmos itself, and then tells the story of the Adam-like Väinämöinen, who is many ways epitomizes basic human strivings and yearnings. As further generations are born and the epic's list of characters lengthens, the narrative moves on in a historical progression to more complex strivings and conflicts, ending with the birth of Marjatta's child who heralds a new order of being. The *Kalevala* is the ontogenesis of humankind.

Väinämöinen has to be accounted the major character of the *Kalevala*, yet he is in many ways an enigmatic and unfulfilled figure. Like the biblical Adam and Greek hero Prometheus, he is the first to do many things, but he never finds earthly happiness, particularly with regard to women. He repeatedly meets younger men, among them Joukahäinen and Ilmarinen, who do better with the opposite sex and also represent more active, vitalistic forces than Väinämöinen does, whatever his intelligence and ingenuity. Väinämöinen's practical failure, though, is compensated by his musical gifts, which have to do not only with performance and entertainment but also with a kind of fundamental shaping of the universe through beauty. Väinämöinen's sorrow is transfigured into aesthetic power.

Kullervo, like Väinämöinen and, indeed, many of the *Kalevala*'s heroes, is not a conventionally sympathetic protagonist. This epic is different from many others, however, in that its protagonists are not so much paragons of humanity as they are people suffering ordinary human misfortune in extraordinary ways. Kullervo's short and savage life is doomed to tragedy, yet he clearly desires alleviation for his sense of being ill at ease in the world. Kullervo's combination of bravery and stupidity is reminiscent of the biblical Samson or the Greek Hercules; like these heroes, his martial prowess finally falls victim to a kind of earthly luck that even the most pugnacious of men cannot control.

Ilmarinen represents another archetypal kind of hero. He is the smith whose ability to forge human beings out of inanimate material can be read as a metaphor for a kind of creative force. Like Väinämöinen's poignant melodies, Ilmarinen's smithy exemplifies the attempt to order an often chaotic and random world. Ilmarinen's failure to forge a wife for himself is a parable of the limited human ability to exercise a full creative power in the cosmos. Ilmarinen's great achievement, the Sampo, is an interesting feature of the *Kalevala*. The Sampo is a talisman, a token of great deeds, a symbol of wealth and glory, and a proof of heroic achievement. Yet it is more than merely an inanimate object, for it produces wealth and can bring prosperity and happiness. The Sampo is practical as well as symbolic, and it may well reflect the harsh realities of a tribal society in a cold climate where there was little time for leisure and little role for mere ornaments.

One of the salient features of the *Kalevala* is its lyrical evocation of the Finnish landscape, which is, however, not portrayed romantically or sentimentally. In comparison with many other so-called primary epics that are compiled largely out of oral tales, the *Kalevala* avoids easy idealizations and gratifying closures. The landscape, vast and desolate yet starkly beautiful, is always surrounded with an air of remoteness and mournful if majestic pathos. The *Kalevala* does not concern only deeds of war or brute strength; its heroes are for the most part intellectuals and craftsmen, and the poem has a spiritual depth that transcends its apparently "primitive" atmosphere.

The ending of the *Kalevala* expresses this spirituality in an even more recognizable fashion. The birth of the child to the virgin Marjatta is clearly meant to parallel the birth of Christ to the Virgin Mary, and it also takes place in a stable. The final acknowledgment of defeat by Väinämöinen in his confrontation with the newly born child is an allegory of the replacement of the mythic world of the *Kalevala* with the world of redemption and hope represented by Christ. In this world, though, the legends and folktales compiled by Lönnrot will always have a special significance for the Finnish nation. Lönnrot's efforts gave the world a work that is a national epic yet, at the same time, one of the most considerable repositories of mythic spirituality available.

"Critical Evaluation" by Nicholas Birns

Bibliography:
Ahokas, Jaakko. *A History of Finnish Literature*. Bloomington: Indiana University Press, 1973. Demonstrates the importance of Lönnrot's compilation of traditional Finnish folktales in giving the impetus for the formation of a Finnish literary tradition.
Honko, Lauri. *Religion, Myth, and Folklore in the World's Epics: "The Kalevala" and Its Predecessors*. Berlin: Mouton de Gruyter, 1990. Collection of scholarly essays that takes a comparative and analytical focus. Occasionally difficult, but worthwhile for its illumination of how much intellectual reflection and debate the *Kalevala* is capable of inspiring among scholars.
Jones, Michael Owen. *The World of the "Kalevala": Essays in Celebration of the 150 Year Jubilee of the Finnish National Epic*. Los Angeles: UCLA Folklore and Myth Publications, 1987. By far the best general book on the *Kalevala*. Provides a clear and cogent description of the story of the epic, as well as of its significance in Finnish literary history and cultural life.
Sawin, Patricia G. "Lönnrot's Brainchildren: The Representation of Women in Finland's *Kalevala*." *Journal of Folklore Research* 25, no. 3 (1988): 187-217. A feminist exsmination of the epic. Examines such characters in the story as Aino, the daughter of Louhi, and Marjatta, and discusses the way they express and epitomize gender roles. Despite the overall domination of the epic by a patriarchal vision, Sawin isolates many occasions where women are able to assert themselves.
Vikis-Freiberg, Vaira. "The Lyrical and the Epical in Latvian and Finnish Folk Poetry." *Journal of Baltic Studies*, Summer, 1986, 98-107. Examines how the formulaic techniques of the oral epic present an engrossing narrative interspersed with individual lyric moments.

DAS KAPITAL

Type of work: Political
Author: Karl Marx (1818-1883)
First published: volume 1, 1867; volumes 2 and 3, edited by Friedrich Engels, 1885-1894
   (English translation, 1886, 1907, 1909)

According to Karl Marx, the Russian Revolution was as inevitable as the subsequent worldwide growth of communism as a dynamic political force. It may be, however, that communism would not have emerged had it not been for Marx's having written *Das Kapital.* Even if economic unbalance had resulted in a revolutionary uprising of the proletariat some- where, it might not have taken the form it did or occurred when it did without the immense influence of this book.

Many of Marx's revolutionary ideas had already been expressed in his *Communist Manifesto* (1848), which he wrote together with Friedrich Engels. *Das Kapital* was, however, more than another call to arms; it was an attempt to base communism on a theory of political economy that was scientifically and dialectically defensible. Whereas the *Communist Manifesto* is a passionate document, an outline of a political philosophy, and something of a prophecy, *Das Kapital* is a scholar's treatise, the product of years of research and reflection, and a work of economic theory that continues to challenge professional economists. This contrast is illumi- nating, for the Communist movement has always been characterized by contrast: the intellectual leads the laborers; the reasoned defense is supplemented by violence and murder; and the scholar's program comes alive in revolution and the threat of war.

In the *Communist Manifesto*, Marx and Engels argue that the history of all societies has been a history of class struggles and that the struggle had become one between the bourgeois class and the proletariat. They state that because all the injustices of society result from the economic advantage the bourgeoisie have over the proletariat, the proletariat would finally rebel and take over the means of production, forming a classless society and a dictatorship of the proletariat. In *Das Kapital*, Marx uses a dialectic method that was inspired by Georg Wilhelm Friedrich Hegel, though it is put to a different use. Marx claimed that his dialectic method was the "direct opposite" of Hegel's, that with Hegel the dialectic "is standing on its head" and "must be turned right side up again, if you would discover the rational kernel within the mystical shell." The method is not mysterious; it involves attending to the conflicting aspects of matters under consideration in order to be able to attain a better idea of the whole. Thus Marx describes his "rational" dialectic as including "in its comprehension and affirmative recognition of the existing state of things, at the same time, also, the recognition of the negation of that state, of its inevitable breaking up." He goes on to maintain that his account regarded "every historically developed social form to be in fluid movement, and therefore takes into account its transient nature not less than its momentary existence." Marx's dialectic method led to what became known as dialectical materialism, the theory that history is the record of class struggles and the conflict of economic opposites.

Das Kapital begins with a study of commodities and money. Marx distinguishes between use value and value, the latter being understood in terms of exchange value but involving essentially the amount of labor that went into the production of the commodity; "that which determines the magnitude of the value of any article is the amount of labour socially necessary, or the labour-time socially necessary for its production."

Money results from the use of some special commodity as a means of exchange to equate different products of labor. Money serves as "a universal measure of value." According to Marx, it is not money that makes commodities commensurable; rather, it is the fact that commodities are commensurable in terms of human labor that makes money possible as a measure of value. Money begets money through the circulation of commodities: This is Marx's general formula for capital. Money is the first form in which capital appears, precisely because it is the end product of a circulatory process that begins with the use of money to purchase commodities for sale at higher than the purchase price.

Capital would not be possible without a change of value. If money were used to purchase a commodity sold at the initial price, no profit would be made, no capital made possible. To explain the surplus value that emerges in the process, Marx reminds the reader that the capitalist buys labor power and uses it. The material of production belongs to the capitalists; therefore the product of the productive process also belongs to them. The product has a use value, but capitalists do not intend to use the product; their interest is in selling it for a price greater than the sum of the costs of its production, including the cost of labor. The realization of surplus value is possible, finally, only by some sort of exploitation of the laborer: The capitalists must manage to make the cost of labor less than the value of labor.

One way of increasing surplus value is by increasing the productiveness of labor without decreasing the work day. The problem that then arises is the problem of keeping the price of commodities up. One solution takes the form of using large numbers of laborers and dividing them for special tasks. Capitalists take advantage of lower prices of commodities by paying labor less and purchasing materials more cheaply. At the same time, through a division of labor, they achieve greater productiveness without a corresponding rise in labor cost. In other words, capitalists hire individuals and put them to work in cooperation with others; they pay for the labor power of those individuals, but they gain the value that comes from using that power cooperatively.

Marx rejects the idea that machinery is introduced to make work easier. He argues that "like every other increase in the productiveness of labour, machinery is intended to cheapen commodities, and, by shortening that portion of the working day, in which the labourer works for himself, to lengthen the other portion that he gives, without an equivalent, to the capitalist. In short, it is a means for producing surplus value." Marx concluded that the possibility of the growth of capital depended on using labor in such a way as to free the capitalist from the need to pay for the use of labor power. He decided that capital is "the command over unpaid labour. All surplus value . . . is in substance the materialisation of unpaid labour."

Capitalist production, according to Marx, "reproduces and perpetuates the condition for exploiting the labourer. It incessantly forces labourers to sell their labour-power in order to live, and enables the capitalist to purchase labour-power in order that he may enrich himself." Accordingly, the division between people described in terms of classes is inevitable in a capitalistic society.

Marx explains the self-destruction of the capitalistic society by arguing that from the exploitation of laborers the capitalists, if they have the economic power, pass to the exploitation of other capitalists and, finally, to their expropriation. "One capitalist always kills many." When, therefore, the monopolistic tendencies of capitalists begin to hinder the modes of production and the mass exploitation of workers reaches a peak of misery and oppression, an uprising of the proletariat will destroy the capitalist state. "Capitalist production begets, with the inexorability of a law of Nature, its own negation." The transformation into the socialized state is much quicker and easier than the transformation of the private property of the workers into capitalist private property, for it is easier for the mass of workers to expropriate the property of a few capitalists than for the capitalists to expropriate the property of the laborers.

Das Kapital has often been criticized as an economic study written in the style of German metaphysics. It is generally regarded, particularly by those who have never read it, as an extremely difficult book, both in content and style. By its nature it is a complex, scholarly work, but it clearly and directly expounds Marx's ideas, and its theory is lightened by many hypothetical cases with which Marx vividly illustrates his points. In considering the work of other scholars, he is respectful if not acquiescent. Perhaps the primary fault of this momentous work is not that it is too difficult but that it is too simple. To argue that capital is made possible by exploitation of labor may be to ignore the ways in which profit can be realized and labor paid to the satisfaction of both the capitalist and the laborer. Yet impartial criticism of such a thesis is impossible. Whether a capitalist economic system gives cause for revolution is something that can only be shown by history.

Bibliography:
Carver, Terrell, ed. *The Cambridge Companion to Marx*. New York: Cambridge University Press, 1991. The essays in this volume focus on Marx the philosopher and attempt to draw a distinction between Marxism and Soviet Communism.
Gouverneur, Jacques. *Contemporary Capitalism and Marxist Economics*. Translated by Richard LeFanu. Totowa, N.J.: Barnes & Noble Books, 1983. Provides a nonmathematical account of the socioeconomic bases of Marxist theory. The first part focuses on the Marxist concepts of value and surplus value, and the second consists of a Marxist analysis of Western European capitalism.
Kernig, Claus D., ed. *Marxism, Communism, and Western Society: A Comparative Encyclopedia*. 8 vols. New York: Herder and Herder, 1972. The stated purpose of this comprehensive work was to provide a compatible system of thought to enhance communications between the capitalist West and the then Communist East. Provides a snapshot of Marxist thought at a time when the Communist world appeared to be at the height of its powers.
Sowell, Thomas. *Marxism: Philosophy and Economics*. New York: Morrow, 1985. An excellent jargon-free introduction to the foundations of *Das Kapital*. Ideal for the general reader who has had no prior exposure to Marxism.
Suchting, Wallis A. *Marx: An Introduction*. New York: New York University Press, 1983. Places the complicated philosophical and economic questions raised in *Das Kapital* against the background of the Revolution of 1848, the First International, the uprising of the Paris Commune, and other major historical events.

KENILWORTH
A Romance

Type of work: Novel
Author: Sir Walter Scott (1771-1832)
Type of plot: Romance
Time of plot: 1575
Locale: England
First published: 1821

Principal characters:
>DUDLEY, the earl of Leicester
>RICHARD VARNEY, his master of horse
>AMY ROBSART, Dudley's wife
>EDMUND TRESSILIAN, a Cornish gentleman and a friend of Amy Robsart
>WAYLAND SMITH, his servant
>THE EARL OF SUSSEX
>QUEEN ELIZABETH
>SIR WALTER RALEIGH
>MICHAEL LAMBOURNE, the nephew of Giles Gosling and an innkeeper
>DOCTOR DOBOOBIE, alias Alasco, an astrologer and alchemist
>DICKIE SLUDGE, alias Flibbertigibbet, a bright child and a friend of
>Wayland Smith

The Story:

Michael Lambourne, a ne'er-do-well in his early youth, had just returned from his travels. While drinking and boasting in Giles Gosling's inn, he wagered that he could gain admittance to Cumnor Place, a large manor where an old friend was now steward. It was rumored in the village that Tony Foster was keeping a beautiful young woman prisoner at the manor. Edmund Tressilian, another guest at the inn, went with Michael to Cumnor Place. As Tressilian had suspected, he found the woman there to be his former sweetheart, Amy Robsart, apparently a willing prisoner. He also encountered Richard Varney, her supposed seducer, and the two men engaged in a sword fight. Michael Lambourne, who had decided to ally himself with his old friend, Tony Foster, intervened.

Contrary to Tressilian's suspicion, Amy was not Varney's mistress but the wife of Varney's master, the earl of Leicester. Varney had only served as the go-between and accomplice in Amy's elopement. Leicester, who was competing for Queen Elizabeth's favor with the earl of Sussex, feared that the news of his marriage to Amy would displease the queen; he therefore had convinced Amy that their marriage must be kept secret.

Tressilian returned to Lidcote Hall to obtain Hugh Robsart's permission to bring Varney to justice on a charge of seduction. On his way, he employed Wayland Smith as his manservant. Smith had formerly served as an assistant to Dr. Doboobie, an alchemist and astrologer. Tressilian later visited the earl of Sussex, through whom he hoped to petition either the queen or the earl of Leicester in Amy's behalf. During that visit, Wayland Smith saved Sussex's life after the earl had been poisoned.

When the earl heard Tressilian's story, he presented the petition directly to the queen. Confronted by Elizabeth, Varney swore that Amy was his lawful wife, and Leicester, who was standing by, confirmed the lie. Elizabeth then ordered Varney to present Amy to her when she visited Kenilworth the following week.

Leicester sent a letter to Amy asking her to appear at Kenilworth as Varney's wife. She refused. In order to have an excuse for disobeying Elizabeth's orders regarding Amy's presence at Kenilworth, Varney had Alasco, the former Dr. Doboobie, mix a potion that would make Amy ill without killing her. This plan was thwarted, however, by Wayland Smith, who had been sent by Tressilian to help her. She escaped from Cumnor Place and with the assistance of Wayland Smith made her way to Kenilworth to see Leicester.

When she arrived at Kenilworth, the place was bustling in preparation for Elizabeth's arrival that afternoon. Wayland Smith took Amy to Tressilian's quarters, where she wrote Leicester a letter telling him of her escape from Cumnor Place and asking his aid. Wayland Smith lost the letter, and through a misunderstanding, he was ejected from the castle. Disappointed that Leicester did not come to her, Amy left her apartment and went into the garden. There she was discovered by the queen, who, judging Amy to be insane because of her contradictory statements, returned her to the custody of Varney, her supposed husband.

Leicester decided to confess the true story to the queen, but Varney was afraid for his own fortunes if Leicester fell from favor; he convinced the earl that Amy had been unfaithful to him and that Tressilian was her lover. Leicester, acting on Varney's lies, decided that death would be just punishment for Amy and her lover. Varney took Amy back to Cumnor Place and plotted her death. When Leicester relented and sent Michael Lambourne to tell Varney that Amy must not die, Varney killed Lambourne so that he might go through with Amy's murder. Leicester and Tressilian fought a duel; but before either could harm the other, they were interrupted by Dickie Sludge, the child who had stolen Amy's letter. Leicester read the letter and realized that Amy had been faithful to him and that the complications of the affair had been caused by Varney's machinations.

Leicester immediately went to the queen and confessed the whole story. Elizabeth was angry, but she sent Tressilian and Sir Walter Raleigh to bring Amy to Kenilworth. They arrived too late to save her. She had fallen through a rigged trapdoor and plunged to her death.

Tressilian and Sir Walter Raleigh seized Varney and brought him to prison. There Varney committed suicide. Elizabeth permitted the grief-stricken Leicester to retire from her court for several years but later recalled him to her favor. Much later in life, he remarried, and he eventually met his death as a result of poison he had intended for someone else.

Critical Evaluation:

To a historical novelist like Sir Walter Scott, vivid and accurate settings were invaluable tools for summoning a past age. Nowhere in his novels is his masterful use of setting more central to theme and meaning than in *Kenilworth*. In this novel of love and intrigue in Elizabethan England, the moral statements dramatized by the story are strengthened by their association with either of the two places where all the major action occurs—Cumnor Place and Kenilworth. Both places are described in highly charged images and richly symbolic language. Cumnor Place is like a gilded prison. Lavishly decorated, its rooms sumptuously comfortable and filled with expensive finery, it is nevertheless designed as a place of detainment and hiding. In one vivid, eerie passage, Scott describes its specially designed oaken shutters and thick drapes, which allow the rooms to be ablaze with light without the slightest flicker showing to an observer on the outside. Leicester uses this strictly private place as the hiding place for his wife and as a place of escape from court life for himself. He travels to Cumnor Place in disguise, and while there he sheds the finery that identifies and validates him at court.

By contrast, Kenilworth is a public manor house. With the entire court and nobility preparing for the royal entertainments, it exhibits all the pomp and splendor of a regal palace; it is literally exploding with feverish activity. The atmosphere at Kenilworth is one of unreality; in his initial picture of the place, Scott describes a row of guards along the battlements who are intended to represent King Arthur's knights—but uncannily, some are real men, some mere pasteboard figures, and it is impossible to distinguish from a distance which are which. A more sinister and frightening instance of the confusion between illusion and reality occurs when Elizabeth encounters Amy in the garden; unable to understand her replies given her supposed understanding of the situation, the queen assumes that Amy is one of the wandering actresses planted throughout the grounds to pay her homage, who has forgotten her lines in embarrassment or fright.

The two major characters—Leicester and Amy—are torn between these two places, and close beside each of them throughout their trials are their personal servants, whose relationships with them point up a major theme in the novel, that of the moral connection or interdependency between masters and their servants; a master, being responsible for his choice of servants, may be judged to a large extent by their attitudes and behavior. Therefore, when Varney interviews Michael Lambourne as a prospective employee for himself—and ultimately for Leicester—he is very pleased with Lambourne's list of desirable qualities in a courtier's servant, which includes "a close mouth" and "a blunt conscience." These are Varney's qualifications exactly, to which are added cunning, greed, and consuming ambition. The proper scheme of things is turned topsy-turvy early in the story in the symbolically prefigurative scene in which Varney persuades his master to disguise himself as a servant, while he impersonates the master. Leicester's moral guilt is clear when he recognizes his servant's true nature yet keeps him in service; he calls Varney a devil, but he is a devil indispensable to the earl's ambitious plans. In contrast to Leicester's and Varney's standards of a good servant are those of the admirable Tressilian, who warns Wayland Smith against knavery, pointing out that transgression committed "by one attending on me diminishes my honour." In addition to Wayland, Amy's maidservant offers another example of a loyal servant who reflects her mistress' worth; Janet Foster is totally devoted, even to the dangerous extreme of aiding her lady's escape from Cumnor Place in defiance of her father, Amy's jailer.

Scott said once that the sight of a ruined castle or relic of the medieval period made him wish to construct the life and times represented by the ruin. In *Kenilworth*, he demonstrates his imaginative powers in setting a vivid scene and creating compelling characters that bring the past to life.

Bibliography:
Hayden, John O., ed. *Scott: The Critical Heritage.* New York: Barnes & Noble Books, 1970. Provides information on the original reception of *Kenilworth*, presenting reviews ranging from 1805 to an 1883 selection written on Scott by Mark Twain. A thorough guide to the critical and literary treatment of Scott in later times as well.
Hillhouse, James T. *The Waverley Novels and Their Critics.* New York: Octagon Books, 1970. A collection of critical reviews, including criticism by Scott himself and reviews of *Kenilworth* after its publication. Also includes critical interpretations of Scott and *Kenilworth* in the fifty years following his death.
Johnson, Edgar. *Sir Walter Scott: The Great Unknown.* 2 vols. New York: Macmillan, 1970. Considers the historical significance of *Kenilworth*, with particular emphasis on Scott's treatment of royalty. Concludes that the subject matter and the setting are perfectly matched.

Macintosh, W. *Scott and Goethe: German Influence on the Writings of Sir Walter Scott.* Port Washington, N.Y.: Kennikat Press, 1970. Compares *Kenilworth* with William Shakespeare's *Othello* and Johann Wolfgang Goethe's *Egmont.* Also summarizes Goethe's opinion of Scott's writing.

Pearson, Hesketh. *Sir Walter Scott: His Life and Personality.* New York: Harper & Row, 1954. An account of the reception of *Kenilworth* in England and the period of Scott's life in which it was written. Some criticism of the characters and the setting of that novel. Also includes an extended bibliography and index.

KIDNAPPED
Being Memoirs of the Adventures of David Balfour in the Year 1751

Type of work: Novel
Author: Robert Louis Stevenson (1850-1894)
Type of plot: Adventure
Time of plot: 1751
Locale: Scotland
First published: 1886

Principal characters:
DAVID BALFOUR, a young man
EBENEZER BALFOUR OF SHAWS, his uncle
MR. RANKEILLOR, a lawyer
ALAN BRECK STEWART, a Jacobite adventurer

The Story:

When David Balfour's father died, the only inheritance he left his son was a letter to Ebenezer Balfour of Shaws, who was his brother and David's uncle. Mr. Campbell, the minister of Essendean, delivered the letter to David and told him that if things did not go well between David and his uncle he was to return to Essendean, where his friends would help him. David set off in high spirits. The house of Shaw was a great one in the Lowlands of Scotland, and David was eager to take his rightful place in the family from which his father had, for some unknown reason, separated himself.

As he approached the great house, he began to grow apprehensive. Everyone of whom he asked the way had a curse for the name Shaws and warned him against his uncle. When he arrived at the place, he found not a great house but a ruin with one wing unfinished and many windows without glass. No friendly smoke came from the chimneys, and the closed door was studded with heavy nails.

David found his Uncle Ebenezer even more forbidding than the house, and he began to suspect that his uncle had cheated his father out of his rightful inheritance. When his uncle tried to kill him, he was convinced of Ebenezer's villainy. His uncle promised to take David to Mr. Rankeillor, the family lawyer, to get the true story of David's inheritance, and they set out for Queen's Ferry. Before they reached the lawyer's office, David was tricked by Ebenezer and Captain Hoseason into boarding the *Covenant*, and the ship sailed away with David a prisoner, bound for slavery in the American colonies.

At first, he lived in filth and starvation in the bottom of the ship. The only person who befriended him was Mr. Riach, the second officer. Later, he found even some of the roughest seamen to be kind at times. Mr. Riach was kind when he was drunk but mean when sober, whereas Mr. Shuan, the first officer, was gentle except when he was drinking. It was while he was drunk that Mr. Shuan beat Ransome, the cabin boy, to death because the boy had displeased him. After Ransome's murder, David became the cabin boy, and for a time his life on the *Covenant* was a little better.

One night, the *Covenant* ran down a small boat and cut her in two. Only one man was saved, Alan Breck Stewart, a Scottish Highlander and Jacobite with a price on his head. Alan demanded that Captain Hoseason set him ashore among his own people, and the captain agreed.

When David overheard the captain and Mr. Riach planning to seize Alan, he warned Alan of the plot. Together, the two of them held the ship's crew at bay, killing Mr. Shuan and three others and wounding many more, including Captain Hoseason. Alan and David became fast friends and remained so during the rest of their adventures. Alan told David of his part in the rebellion against King George and of the way he was hunted by the king's men, particularly by Colin of Glenure, known as the Red Fox. David was loyal to the monarch, yet out of mutual respect, he and Alan swore to help each other in time of trouble.

It was not long before they had occasion to prove their loyalty. The ship broke apart on a reef. David and Alan, separated at first, soon found themselves together again, deep in the part of the Highlands controlled by Alan's enemies. When Colin of Glenure was murdered, the blame fell on Alan. If they were caught, they would both hang. They began to work their way to the Lowlands to find Mr. Rankeillor, their only chance for help. They hid by day and traveled by night. Often they went for several days without food. They were in danger, not only from the king's soldiers but also from Alan's own people, for there was always the danger that a trusted friend would betray them for the reward offered. Yet David was able to learn the meaning of loyalty. Many of Alan's clan endangered themselves to help the hunted pair.

When David was too weak to go on and wanted to give up, Alan offered to carry him. They finally reached Queen's Ferry and Mr. Rankeillor. At first, Mr. Rankeillor was skeptical when he heard David's story, but it began to check so well with what he had heard from others that he became convinced; he told David that his father and his Uncle Ebenezer had both loved the same woman, whom David's father had won. Because he was a kind man and because Ebenezer had taken to his bed over the loss of the woman, David's father had given up his inheritance as the oldest son in favor of Ebenezer. The story helped David realize why his uncle had tried to get rid of him. Ebenezer knew that his dealings with David's father would not stand up in the courts, and he had been afraid that David had come for his inheritance.

With the help of Alan and Mr. Rankeillor, David was able to frighten his uncle into offering him two-thirds of the yearly income from the land. David did not want to submit his family name to public scandal in the courts, and he knew he could better help Alan if the story of their escape were kept quiet, so he agreed to the settlement. In this way, he was able to help Alan reach safety and pay his debt to his friend.

Critical Evaluation:

Robert Louis Stevenson directed many of his works to young readers in deference to nineteenth century Romanticism's idealization of the innocence of childhood and the fecundity of children's imaginations. He believed strongly that youngsters were an important segment of the reading public. *Kidnapped* was originally published as a serial in a boys' magazine, and Stevenson first won fame as a novelist with the children's adventure story *Treasure Island* (1883). *A Child's Garden of Verses* (1885) also falls in this category.

A large part of the popular appeal of *Kidnapped* lies with the historical-romantic nature of the plot. The novel revolves around an actual historical incident, the murder of Colin Campbell, the Red Fox of Glenure, and other historical figures appear, among them King George. Thus the nonhistorical but pivotal events of the plot—David Balfour's trials and Alan Stewart's escapades, which constitute the largest part of the novel—are tied to actual history. This intertwining of history and fantasy has the effect of personalizing history and making fantasy credible.

Another factor that enhances the verisimilitude of *Kidnapped* is Stevenson's narrative technique. David Balfour tells his story in the first person. As a consequence, the reader develops a close rapport with the narrator and sympathizes with his plight. Most important, the first-person narrative makes the story highly plausible.

To some extent, Stevenson emphasized plot over characterization; his goal was above all to entertain, to transport the reader from mundane, daily existence to a believable world of excitement and adventure. To create this effect, Stevenson combined the extraordinary with the commonplace. David's kidnapping, Alan's rescue, and the shipwreck are combined with such more commonplace occurrences as family hostilities, the life of sailors, and Scottish feuds. This combination produces an exceptionally convincing tale.

Stevenson does not ignore the impact of character development, however. By juxtaposing David, the canny Lowlander, with Alan, the proud Highlander, he brings two opposing value systems together into a compatible relationship. David and Alan have contradictory points of view and antithetical sociopolitical commitments; yet they work together and form a lasting bond on the basis of friendship and loyalty that transcend their differences. Here Stevenson the novelist is at his best, forsaking dogma and ideology in favor of humanistic values.

Stevenson was a master storyteller. He wove this tale around the great and the small, the rich and the poor, virtuous men and scoundrels, and each character was truly drawn. A stolen inheritance, a kidnapping, a battle at sea, several murders—these are only a few of the adventures that befell the hero. It is easily understood why *Kidnapped* is a favorite with all who read it.

Bibliography:
Calder, Jenni. *Robert Louis Stevenson: A Life Study.* New York: Oxford University Press, 1980. Claims that Stevenson could not have written *Kidnapped* or *Treasure Island* if he had not had the life experiences he had. Discusses the characters of David Balfour and Alan Breck Stewart and concludes that the novel's success rests on the credibility of Balfour's character.

_____, ed. *Stevenson and Victorian Scotland.* Edinburgh: Edinburgh University Press, 1981. Includes a number of articles that refer to *Kidnapped*. Christopher Harvie's "The Politics of Stevenson" examines settings in Stevenson's novels and his development of a rich Scottish dialogue, as well as the role that Scottish politics play in *Kidnapped*. W. W. Robson, in "On *Kidnapped*," analyzes the way the vernacular and character interaction are affected by the intersection of time and place.

Stewart, Ralph. "The Unity of *Kidnapped*." *Victorian Newsletter* 64 (Fall, 1983): 30-31. Discusses how the setting in the Scottish Highlands advances the adventure plot and examines historic sources that inspired Stevenson.

Zharen, W. M. von. "*Kidnapped*: Improved Hodgepodge?" In *Children's Novels and the Movies*, edited by Douglas Street. New York: Frederick Ungar, 1983. Compares *Kidnapped* to motion picture productions of the novel and considers the reason behind changes made to the story. Discusses the reasons for the novel's appeal to children.

KIM

Type of work: Novel
Author: Rudyard Kipling (1865-1936)
Type of plot: Adventure
Time of plot: Late nineteenth century
Locale: British India
First published: 1901

Principal characters:
  KIMBALL O'HARA (KIM), a street boy
  A TIBETAN LAMA, Kim's teacher
  MAHBUB ALI, a horse trader
  COLONEL CREIGHTON, the director of the British Secret Service
  HURREE CHUNDER MOOKERJEE, a babu

The Story:

Kim grew up on the streets of Lahore. His Irish mother had died when he was born, and his father, a former color-sergeant of an Irish regiment called the Mavericks, died eventually of drugs and drink. He left his son in the care of a half-caste woman. Young Kimball O'Hara thereupon became Kim, and under the hot Indian sun, his skin grew so dark that one could not tell he was a white boy.

One day, a Tibetan lama, in search of the holy River of the Arrow that would wash away all sin, came to Lahore. Struck by the possibility of exciting adventure, Kim attached himself to the lama as his chela. That night, at the edge of Lahore, Mahbub Ali, a horse trader, gave Kim a cryptic message to deliver to a British officer in Umballa. Kim did not know that Mahbub was a member of the British Secret Service. He delivered the message as directed and then lay in the grass and watched and listened until he learned that his message meant that eight thousand men would go to war.

Out on the big road, the lama and Kim encountered many people of all sorts. Conversation was easy. Kim was particularly interested in one group, an old lady traveling in a family bullock cart attended by a retinue of eight men. Kim and the lama attached themselves to her party. Toward evening, they saw a group of soldiers making camp. It was the Maverick regiment. Kim, whose horoscope said that his life would be changed at the sign of a red bull in a field of green, was fascinated by the regimental flag, which was just that, a red bull against a background of bright green.

Caught by a chaplain, the Reverend Arthur Bennett, Kim accidentally jerked loose the amulet he carried around his neck. Mr. Bennett opened the amulet and discovered three papers folded inside, including Kim's baptismal certificate and a note from his father asking that the boy be taken care of. Father Victor arrived in time to see the papers. When Kim had told his story, he was informed that he would be sent away to school. Though he parted sadly from the lama, Kim was sure that he would soon escape. The lama asked that Father Victor's name and address and the costs of schooling Kim be written down and given to him. Then he disappeared. Kim, pretending to prophesy, told the priests and soldiers what he had heard at Umballa. They laughed at him, but the next day his prophecy came true, and eight thousand soldiers were sent to put down an uprising in the north. Kim remained in camp.

One day, a letter arrived from the lama. He enclosed enough money for Kim's first year at school and promised to provide the same amount yearly. He requested that the boy be sent to

St. Xavier's for his education. The drummer who had been ordered to keep an eye on Kim was cruel to his charge. When Mahbub Ali came upon the two boys, he gave the drummer a beating and began talking to Kim. While they were thus engaged, Colonel Creighton came up and learned from Mahbub Ali, in an indirect way, that once he was educated Kim would be a valuable member of the secret service.

On his way to St. Xavier's, Kim spied the lama, who had been waiting a day and a half to see him. They agreed to see each other often. Kim was an apt pupil, but he disliked being shut up in classrooms and dormitories. When vacation time came, he went to Umballa and persuaded Mahbub Ali to let him return to the road until school reopened.

Traveling with Mahbub Ali, he played the part of a horse boy and saved the trader's life when he overheard two men plotting to kill the horse dealer. At Simla, Kim stayed with Mr. Lurgan, who taught him a great many subtle tricks and games and the art of make-up and disguise. Just as Mahbub Ali had said, he was now learning the great game, as the work of the secret service was called. At the end of the summer, Kim returned to his studies at St. Xavier's, where he stayed for three years.

At the end of that time, Mahbub Ali advised Mr. Lurgan and Colonel Creighton that Kim be permitted to go out on the road with his lama again. Kim's skin was stained dark, and he resumed the dress of a street boy. Given the password by Hurree Chunder Mookerjee, a babu who was another member of the secret service, Kim set out with his lama.

Still seeking his river, the lama moved up and down India with Kim as his disciple. The two of them once more encountered the old woman they had met on the road three years before. A little later, Kim was surprised to see the babu, who told him that two of the five kings of the north had been bribed and that the Russians had sent spies down into India through the passes that the kings had agreed to guard. Two men, a Russian and a Frenchman, were to be apprehended, and the babu asked Kim's aid. Kim suggested to the lama a journey into the foothills of the Himalayas, and so he was able to follow the babu on his mission.

During a storm, the babu came upon the two foreigners. Discovering that one of their baskets contained valuable letters including a message from one of the traitorous kings, he offered to be their guide; in two days, he had led them to the spot where Kim and the lama were camped. When the foreigners tore almost in two a holy drawing made by the lama, the babu created a disturbance in which the coolies, according to plan, carried off the men's luggage. The lama conducted Kim to the village of Shamlegh. There, Kim examined all the baggage that the coolies had brought. He threw everything except letters and notebooks over an unscalable cliff. He hid the documents on his person.

In a few days, Kim and the lama set out again. At last, they came to the house of the old woman who had befriended them twice before. When she saw Kim's emaciated condition, she put him to bed, where he slept many days. Before he went to sleep, he asked that a strongbox be brought to him. He deposited his papers in it, locked the box, and hid it under his bed. When he woke up, he heard that the babu had arrived, and Kim delivered the papers to him. The babu told him that Mahbub Ali was also in the vicinity. They assured Kim that he had played his part well in the great game. The old lama knew nothing of these matters. He was happy because Kim had brought him to his river at last, a brook on the old lady's estate.

Critical Evaluation:

Rudyard Kipling won the Nobel Prize in Literature in 1907 and received honorary degrees from both Harvard and Oxford, but he was an extremely controversial writer, not only during his lifetime but also after it. Kipling was admired by such literary giants as Henry James, Mark

Twain, and T. S. Eliot. Many critics however who praised Kipling felt the need to preface their comments with an explanation or an apology; Ernest Hemingway commented that he liked "the good Kipling." The "bad" Kipling is seen as the defender of British imperialism who supported oppressors against native populations, espoused the idea of racial superiority, and remained casually unaware of the value of the cultures the British empire dismissed and dominated. Remarkably, Kipling manages to inspire great intensity of feeling long after that empire faded. Although *Kim* is not the most controversial of his works, it received widely disparate evaluations, both when it was first published in 1901 and in later criticism. It is perceived by some as a paternalistic, stereotypical, and unrealistic picture of India, whereas others find it a rich, sympathetic portrayal.

Kim is a complex book. It has elements of a boy's novel of adventure, a spy story, and a picaresque tale. Kipling himself once called *Kim* plotless. On a more serious level, it can be seen as a tale of initiation, a search for being and belonging, a quest. Because Kipling spent his first five years in Bombay, a time of great happiness for him, followed by six years of misery in England, where he was placed in a rigid, abusive household that he later described as the House of Desolation, *Kim* also has been viewed as a personal fantasy and a creation of a lost childhood idyll.

Setting is extremely important in *Kim*. The India that Kipling portrays stretches from Benares in the middle of the Indian peninsula to the Punjab and the Himalayas in the north. The story begins in Lahore with Kim sitting on the Zam-Zammah, the great gun that controls the north. The opening paragraphs introduce both India and the realities of the British presence there. In spite of the fact that Kim "consorted on terms of perfect equality with the street boys of the bazaar," he felt free to kick one of his companions off the gun "since the English held the Punjab and Kim was English." This opening may imply a belief in the superiority of the British, but as the novel moves to describe the bazaar in detail, it becomes obvious that Kim and Kipling relish life on the Indian streets. After Kim meets the lama, they travel through India following the path of the railroad, the Grand Trunk Road. In chapters 3 and 4 particularly, Kipling presents vivid portraits of people from different castes and backgrounds; the reader is introduced to the sights, sounds, and smells of many different places and peoples on the road. This rich variety has caused some critics to call India itself the main character of the novel.

Kim does more than present a fascinating, exotic picture of India; it also is a story about a boy's search for identity. Kim, an Irish orphan, has taken on the characteristics of the Indian street boy. He seems an ideal hero for a boy's adventure tale—clever, brave, able to overcome all odds, a perfect blend of Oliver Twist and the Artful Dodger. He becomes more than just an adventure hero, however, because he faces not only physical and emotional challenges but also spiritual ones. His search begins after he meets the lama, a truly holy man, who desires to free himself completely from the evils and bonds of this world. Kipling represents the novel's theme of the quest, the lama seeks salvation. When Kim decides to join him on this adventure, he too decides that he must have a goal. Since his father had said before he died that Kim's future would be secure when he found a red bull on a green field, Kim chooses to search for this bull; the quest that begins as a boy's adventure eventually becomes a quest for himself.

His search is complicated by the different, seemingly contradictory, directions that are pointed out to him by the individuals he meets. The lama leads Kim, his chela or disciple, in one direction, on the search for the river, to a life of religion, spiritualism, asceticism. One part of Kim embraces this life as he follows the lama, whom he truly loves. His other guides prepare him to follow the great game, the network of British spies operating in India, and the boy is also fascinated with the intrigue and excitement of this world. Kim is caught between these two worlds, often wondering just who he is. On several occasions he restates a variation of the question, "Who is Kim?"

Kipling uses powerful symbols to represent the opposing ways and the paths that will lead Kim to them. Repeatedly, Kipling refers to the River, the Road, the Wheel, the Way, the Game. Animal imagery recurs frequently as well. The white stallion represents the British empire, the bull his father's regiment, and Kim is often referred to as a pony. Colors, too, have symbolism. For the lama, red—the color of the bull—is the color of deceit.

Deeply involved in both worlds, Kim struggles to find his identity. On the one hand, he has England, adventure, and the life of a spy and a sahib; on the other lies India, the life of the spirit, and the search for salvation. The novel's end provides no clear answer for Kim or for the reader. Although in the last chapter Kim tells the lama, "I am not a Sahib, I am thy chela," it seems obvious the great game has not released Kim.

"Critical Evaluation" by Mary Mahony

Bibliography:
Bloom, Harold, ed. *Rudyard Kipling's "Kim."* New York: Chelsea House, 1987. An excellent introductory source gathering a cross section of essays providing extremely useful criticism. Analyzes character and theme, discusses Kipling's views on India, presents revisions from an earlier draft, and compares Kipling's views on the British empire with those of E. M. Forster and George Orwell.
Page, Norman. *A Kipling Companion.* London: Macmillan, 1984. Helpful introductory source providing a brief biography, chronology, and discussion of Kipling's world. Identifies historical figures and gives clear, insightful analyses of the novels, short stories, and verse. Helpful annotated bibliography.
Rao, K. Bhaskara. *Rudyard Kipling's India.* Norman: University of Oklahoma Press, 1967. Evaluates Kipling's place as a writer about India and compares with other British writers. Provides historical background and analyzes theme, setting, and character in *Kim.*
Shahane, Vasant. *Rudyard Kipling: Activist and Artist.* Carbondale: Southern Illinois University Press, 1973. Excellent introductory source. Provides chapter-by-chapter summary illustrating the novel's thematic unity and charting Kim's inner growth as he deals with his two separate worlds. Helpful in following the complex action in the novel. Clear analysis of major symbols, setting, and character.
Sullivan, Zohreh. *Narratives of Empire: The Fictions of Rudyard Kipling.* Cambridge, England: Cambridge University Press, 1993. A detailed analysis that stresses the quest of the lama and Kim, discusses theme and symbol, and provides detailed character analysis. Clear explanation of religious background.

KINFLICKS

Type of work: Novel
Author: Lisa Alther (1944-   )
Type of plot: Bildungsroman
Time of plot: 1960's, early 1970's
Locale: Tennessee, Boston, and Vermont
First published: 1975

> *Principal characters:*
> VIRGINIA "GINNY" BABCOCK BLISS, a young woman
> MRS. BABCOCK, Ginny's dying mother
> JOE BOB SPARKS, Ginny's football star boyfriend
> CLEM CLOYD, Ginny's motorcycle-riding boyfriend
> EDNA (EDDIE) HOLZER, Ginny's lover
> IRA BLISS, Ginny's husband
> WENDY BLISS, Ginny and Ira's daughter
> HAWK, an Army deserter whom Ginny befriends

The Story:

Ginny Babcock Bliss's mother was dying of a blood-clotting disorder, and Ginny had come back to Hullsport, Tennessee, to stay with her. Ginny had left her husband, Ira Bliss, behind in Vermont, with their two-year-old daughter, Wendy. In fact, Ira had made Ginny leave their home after finding her with another man. Ginny thought back on the steps of her life leading up to where she was at the time. Some of her memories were like the home movies from which the novel gets its name. She occasionally thought about growing up with her two brothers, but she was more concerned with the past twelve years, from her first serious boyfriend through the few years of her marriage.

Her first boyfriend was Joe Bob Sparks, a football star with very little intelligence. Their times together were happier for him than for her; she dated him primarily because he was popular and dating was what everyone did. Ginny's next boyfriend was Clem Cloyd, a motorcycle hoodlum whom she had known since childhood. Her parents strongly disapproved of her relationship with Clem and looked for a way to break them up. Again, Ginny was not in love with Clem; instead, he was someone with whom she experimented sexually and whom she used to rebel against her parents. Their relationship ended when Ginny was seriously injured in a fall from Clem's motorcycle.

After the accident, Ginny's parents decided to get her away from Hullsport by sending her to Worthley, a highly reputable women's college in Boston. Ginny objected to this move, but she went anyway, probably because she had no compelling reason to stay in Tennessee and because protesting took too much energy. At Worthley, Ginny met Miss Helena Head, a philosophy professor who became her mentor. Under Miss Head's tutelage, Ginny became increasingly interested in philosophy and cultural events. She threw herself into her studies and pondered the questions of the great philosophers. She abandoned her emotional life for a mental one, as Miss Head had done, and thought about everything with detachment.

Another woman who lived in Ginny's dormitory challenged Ginny during this cerebral stage. Eddie Holzer, an earthy, rebellious student, began discussing with Ginny the ideas of philosophers, arguing that denying the world of emotion was just as limiting as denying the world of the mind. Their friendship became even stronger when another woman on their hall tried to commit suicide and Ginny did not know what to do. Eddie took control of the situation and comforted Ginny. Eventually, Ginny and Eddie fell in love. When Ginny told Miss Head about their affair, then tried again to approach the world philosophically, Ginny became so distraught that Eddie decided they should both leave Worthley.

The two women lived for a time in an apartment in Boston, using money Ginny received from a trust fund. The trust fund was a problem, however, because the factory that Ginny's family owned made ammunition, and Eddie and Ginny opposed the Vietnam War. They finally calculated the proportion of the money earned from making defense materials and sent that amount to charity, living on the rest.

Eddie and Ginny later moved to Vermont and planned to live off the land. Eddie's relaxed attitude was not conducive to farm work, so the two struggled until friends moved in and helped them. Unfortunately, the four women began to have trouble with local people who wanted to hunt on their property. When the women protested, the locals killed their cow. The women strung barbed wire to try to keep the hunters, who used snowmobiles, off their land. One night as the locals partied on the women's lake, Eddie jumped on a snowmobile and drove toward them. She was decapitated when she ran into the barbed wire.

After grieving for a period of time, Ginny married a man from town, a man she had known before Eddie's death. She said that she needed some order in her life. As had been the case with her earlier relationships with men, her marriage to Ira Bliss was anything but blissful. He wanted a stereotypical wife and an extremely ordered life. Ginny had lived as a rebel and a bohemian. The two had a daughter, Wendy, whom Ginny loved.

One day as Wendy napped indoors and Ginny sat by the pool, a bearded man came up. Ginny learned that he was called Hawk and that he was an Army deserter. Their friendship developed, and Hawk tried to teach Ginny about meditation. Their rituals became increasingly bizarre, and one night Ira came back from a meeting and caught them asleep together in what appeared to be a sexual position. He ran Ginny off, telling her never to return. Ginny's memories of these events alternated throughout the book with visits to her mother's hospital bed, with trying unsuccessfully to save some baby birds, and with visits to Joe Bob Sparks and Clem Cloyd, both currently married. Mrs. Babcock too was exploring the past, especially her marriage to her late husband and the rearing of their children.

Two other patients at the hospital where Ginny's mother was being treated, a nun and a Jewish immigrant from Europe, often discussed the meaning of suffering and the existence of God. Their arguments contributed to Ginny's confusion.

Ginny gave her mother blood transfusions, but Ginny's blood could not save Mrs. Babcock. After her mother's death, Ginny tried to commit suicide by tying a rock to her leg and jumping off a pier, but she landed on a boat. She finally decided not to kill herself. In the end, she left the cabin on her parents' property, with no idea where she was going.

Critical Evaluation:

Lisa Alther's first published novel, *Kinflicks*, functions on three levels. First, it is a cultural history of America from the 1960's to the 1970's. Second, it is a maturation novel of a young American woman during that time. Third, it is a philosophical novel that explores the value of life and questions whether suffering, death, and life have meaning.

As a cultural history, *Kinflicks* looks at the effect the war in Vietnam had on the United States. As Ginny becomes more aware of the war, she loses her innocence. She moves from flag-twirling teenager who dates a gum-chewing football star to lesbian, vegetarian war protester who joins the revolution against the establishment. Like America, she can no longer conform to traditional patriotic and family values, such as settling down to be a housewife and mother; even after she marries and has a child, she becomes intimate with an army deserter. The Vietnam War changed America forever.

As a maturation novel, *Kinflicks* examines Ginny's search for an identity. This search is symbolized by her hairstyles, which always reflect someone else. For example, while dating the football player, she wears a ponytail. She teases her hair when she dates the biker, then puts it in a bun to imitate Miss Head. Eddie takes down the bun and braids Ginny's hair like her own. In short, Ginny always takes on the identity of the person she is with.

It is worth noting that Ginny is trying to find her way in a patriarchy, but she finds meaning only in her relationships with other women and girls—her mother, Miss Head, Eddie, and Wendy. Her relationships with men always seem to be disrupted by sex and sexual problems.

One of Ginny's fears is that she will take on her mother's personality and her burdens. She needs to escape her mother's influence to avoid such a fate. In the end Ginny comes full circle, returning to her home after marrying and becoming a mother. Ginny, however, does not resign herself to that life, and the way that she got there ensures that she is not following in her mother's footsteps. In the end, she is not sure who she is because she has no referent by which to define herself.

Finally, *Kinflicks* explores deeper questions. With Ginny, the reader considers conformity, then nonconformity, then conformity again. The novel moves between a false order and an unsatisfying rebellion against order. Ginny cannot decide whether to give in to passion, as she does with Eddie, or to remain unmoved, as she does under the influence of Miss Head. The arguments between the nun, who believes that God makes the noble suffer to ready them for heaven, and the Jewish man, who protests that no decent God could have let the Holocaust happen, could almost be the arguments in Ginny's own mind. She wonders whether her mother's suffering has any meaning. When Ginny contemplates suicide, she wonders whether life has meaning. Alther does not resolve these issues for the reader. She raises the questions in an intelligent and thought-provoking manner.

Early reactions to *Kinflicks* were mixed. Most scholars who have discussed the book see it as feminist. A problem with the novel is that readers may consider it dated. As an examination of the United States during the time of the Vietnam War, it is valuable. It also explores universal themes: maturation, the meaning of life, death, and suffering, and human relationships.

Kinflicks is also a witty and entertaining novel. Its episodic, almost picaresque qualities remind one of such classics as *Tom Jones* (1749) and *Adventures of Huckleberry Finn* (1884). Certainly some of Alther's material is autobiographical. More important, the novel is a biography of America as it moved from the innocence of the 1960's to the attempt to regain order after the Vietnam War.

M. Katherine Grimes

Bibliography:
Braendlin, Bonnie Hoover. "New Directions in the Contemporary *Bildungsroman:* Lisa Alther's *Kinflicks.*" *Women and Literature* 1 (1980): 160-171. Asserts that Alther's book is a new type of maturation novel because it emphasizes the woman rather than the man. She says the book alternates between the picaresque and the confessional modes, the first being patriarchal and the second matriarchal, as Ginny struggles between freedom and security.
Ferguson, Mary Anne. "The Female Novel of Development and the Myth of Psyche." *Denver*

Quarterly 17 (Winter, 1983): 58-74. Discusses the myth of Psyche and Cupid in *Kinflicks* and works by Eudora Welty and Erica Jong. She discusses Ginny's relationship with her mother as it parallels Ginny's development as heroine.

_____. "Lisa Alther: The Irony of Return?" *Southern Quarterly* 21 (Summer, 1983): 103-115. Ferguson discusses Ginny's relationship with her mother, including Ginny's attempt to imitate her mother by following her into death. She also focuses on Ginny's rebellion against the South and her return to it.

Hall, Joan Lord. "Symbiosis and Separation in Lisa Alther's *Kinflicks.*" *Arizona Quarterly* 38 (Winter, 1982): 336-346. Hall examines Ginny's behavior as symbolically related to her mother's blood: As Mrs. Babcock's blood cells turn upon themselves, Ginny wonders whether she is like a cell functioning in a larger organism. Hall asserts that Ginny can find freedom only when she becomes part of a larger community.

Leonard, John. Review of *Kinflicks*, by Lisa Alther. *The New York Times Book Review*, March 14, 1976. Compares Alther to Doris Lessing. Discusses *Kinflicks* as a comic maturation novel, putting Ginny Babcock in company with Holden Caulfield, Augie March, and Huck Finn.

A KING AND NO KING

Type of work: Drama
Authors: Francis Beaumont (c. 1584-1616) and John Fletcher (1579-1625)
Type of plot: Tragicomedy
Time of plot: Indeterminate
Locale: Armenia and Iberia
First performed: 1611; first published, 1619

> *Principal characters:*
> ARBACES, King of Iberia
> TIGRANES, King of Armenia
> GOBRIAS, Lord-Protector of Iberia and Arbaces' father
> BACURIUS, an Iberian nobleman
> MARDONIUS, an honest old captain in Arbaces' army
> BESSUS, a cowardly braggart
> LYGONES, an Armenian courtier, Spaconia's father
> ARANE, Queen-Mother of Iberia
> PANTHEA, her daughter
> SPACONIA, an Armenian lady, Tigranes' sweetheart

The Story:

Arbaces, the valiant young king of Iberia, had just ended a long war against Armenia by defeating in single combat Tigranes, the king of that country. Arbaces, although a hero in war, was also an intensely passionate man; honest and outspoken Mardonius commented that he was capable of the wildest extremities of emotion and that he could move through the entire emotional range with the greatest speed. Inflamed by his victory, Arbaces illustrated the qualities Mardonius ascribed to him. In a series of blustering speeches he showed himself to be inordinately proud. When Mardonius took him to task for boasting, he became, after a few gusts of ranting, temporarily contrite and amiable, and he resolved to give his beautiful, virtuous sister Panthea, whom he had not seen since her childhood, in marriage to the defeated but valorous Tigranes. Tigranes protested because he had already plighted his troth to Spaconia, a lady of his own land.

Messages arrived from Gobrias, in whose care the government of Iberia had been left, telling that a slave sent by Arane to poison Arbaces had been taken and executed. Instead of flying into a rage, Arbaces, in a burst of magnanimity and pity, forgave the queen mother's unnatural act. Thus he swung from the objectionable boastfulness of moments before to the opposite emotional pole.

Meanwhile, Tigranes, who was to accompany Arbaces home as a prisoner, arranged with Bessus, a fatuous and cowardly captain in the Iberian army, for him to convey Spaconia to Iberia and secure for her a place as one of Panthea's ladies-in-waiting. There, according to Tigranes' plan, it was to be Spaconia's task to set the princess' heart against a match with him.

In Iberia, where Arane had been put under guard for her attempt on Arbaces' life, Panthea was deeply torn between her love for her mother on the one hand and her loyalty and devotion to the king, her brother, on the other. Although the reason for Arane's crime was unexplained, her conversation with Gobrias revealed that there were secrets between them having an important bearing on her relationship with Arbaces. Bessus, accompanied by Spaconia, arrived with messages from the king, including a pardon for Arane. Importuned by the courtiers, the braggart gave an amusing account of the duel between Arbaces and Tigranes, contriving to make himself the central figure. Panthea, interrupting Bessus' tale frequently, revealed agonized concern for her brother's safety. Even though she had not yet seen him, she nevertheless felt a powerful attraction to him. Spaconia then revealed to Panthea her reason for coming to Iberia, and the virtuous princess vowed to reject the proposed match with Tigranes.

After a triumphal passage through the city, Arbaces and his company arrived at the court. When Panthea presented herself to her brother, Arbaces, overwhelmed by her beauty, realized that at first sight he had fallen hopelessly in love with her. Frantically he tried to convince himself that she was not really his sister but a lady of the court; however, he was unable to escape the guilty feeling that he had become the victim of an incestuous love.

At last, succumbing to his passion, he kissed her; then, overcome with guilt and shame, he violently ordered the weeping Panthea imprisoned. As time passed, however, his love for Panthea increased, and at last he begged Mardonius to act as his bawd. When Mardonius indignantly rejected Arbaces' plea, the king turned to Bessus, whom he found more willing to undertake such a task. Revolted by Bessus' ready acquiescence, and probably also by the image of himself that he saw in the minion, Arbaces swore to keep his sin within his own breast in spite of the torture his desire inflicted upon him.

Bessus, meanwhile, discovered that the reputation for bravery he had created for himself had serious drawbacks. Now that he was worthy of challenge, he was being called to account by all of the gentlemen he had insulted before leaving for the wars. He was dismissing the second of his two hundred and thirteenth challenger when Bacurius appeared, demanding satisfaction for a past wrong. Bessus, attempting to put him off, pleaded a lame leg; but Bacurius, recognizing the braggart's cowardice, browbeat him unmercifully and took away his sword. Bessus, after enlisting the aid of two professional swordsmen who were in reality as absurd and as cowardly as he, allowed himself to be convinced by a very peculiar exercise in logic that he was, after all, a valiant man. He was on the way to deliver this news to Bacurius when he encountered Lygones, who had journeyed from Armenia in search of his daughter Spaconia. Believing him to be Spaconia's seducer, Lygones gave Bessus a drubbing before the braggart could explain. Parting from Lygones, bruised Bessus located Bacurius, who, over Bessus' loud protests that he was no coward, mocked his logic and cudgeled his two hired companions. During this time Lygones had located Spaconia and Tigranes in prison; and he learned joyfully that his daughter, whom he had thought guilty of a disgraceful alliance with Bessus, was actually to be married to Tigranes and thus was to become the queen of Armenia.

Indirectly urged on by Gobrias and nearly mad with desire, Arbaces visited Panthea in her prison and at once begged her to yield and not to yield herself to his lust. Although she rejected his proposal, she confessed that she too had felt unsisterly desire for him. After they parted, Arbaces attempted to govern himself but finally concluded wildly that he could bear the situation no longer. He resolved to murder Mardonius, ravish Panthea, and then kill himself. At that moment, however, Gobrias and Arane revealed their secret: Arbaces was really the son of Gobrias. As an infant he had been adopted for political reasons by the barren Arane, who later conceived and bore Panthea. He was thus no king. Gobrias, however, who had protected his son against Arane's attempts to dispose of him so that Panthea could rule and who had subtly encouraged Arbaces' love for Panthea, found his complicated plan a success. Arbaces, now totally without pride of majesty, was overjoyed to learn that he was actually an impostor. His and Panthea's passion now became legitimate, and by marrying her he would once more assume the crown. Thus a happy ending was brought about, and to fill the moment completely Tigranes and Spaconia were released from prison and reunited.

Critical Evaluation:

This Francis Beaumont and John Fletcher play is richer in texture and plot than *The Maid's Tragedy*, which is less ambitious and tends to satisfy itself with a simple tragic plot. In *A King and No King*, however, the matter is somewhat more complicated by parallelisms between the major theme and the conduct of lesser figures. Like many of the Jacobean tragicomedies, the play is set in a foreign land, at the highest levels of aristocratic power, and one of the major figures, as in *The Maid's Tragedy*, has just successfully defended his country from the enemy. In this case, the contest came down to single combat between Arbaces, the king of Iberia, and Tigranes, the king of Armenia. Arbaces wins, but intends to act magnanimously by wedding his sister Panthea to the conquered king. There are obvious signs, however, that Arbaces is not an entirely stable character, and he is given to public declamations of his political and military prowess, which are comically echoed in the conduct of one of his lieutenants, Mardonius, a cowardly, loud-mouthed fool. Mardonius, a wiser, courageous soldier, chastises both men and seems to be able to talk some sense into the king, but there is always a feeling that the king is inclined to wild swings of mood and conduct, which culminate in his sudden infatuation with his sister, who returns his ardor. Their passion throws the two of them into a desperate indecision which is only resolved by the revelation that they are not, in fact, related to each other. This revelation comes just in time to forestall a bloodbath of considerable proportion.

Thus the play satisfies its description as a tragicomedy. The play begins with all the potential for serious damage, and flirts with the possibility of carnage until very late, when it turns both in structure and narrative into a comedy when the king learns that he is, in fact, not by birth the king, and, more happily, discovers that the woman with whom he is dangerously infatuated is not his sister and therefore can be his wife. They can live happily ever after, not only as lovers but also as rulers, since she is of royal birth. Played against this agonizing extravaganza of uncontrolled and menacing arbitrariness is the parallel, proper love affair of Tigranes, the defeated king and his loved one, Spaconia, which provides opportunity for the lyric expression of legitimate love, ironically echoing the immorality of the royal pair.

Royal lunacy is only barely balanced by the good sense of Mardonius, by the quiet patience and courage of the defeated Tigranes, and by Spaconia. On the other hand, the posturings of Bessus are something of a comic parallel to the repetitive boasting of his king. It all looks a bit silly, and a close look reveals a kind of contrived madness, closer to fantasy than to real life, but Jacobean tragicomedy is often inclined to excess. The romantic expostulations of Arbaces and Panthea, taken on the inflated level of high drama, allow for a rich manipulation of poetic language, made all the more credible by the fact that both parties, tempted as they are to consummate their love, are torn deeply by the awareness of the forbidden nature of their love. What somewhat undermines this power is the revelation of their real situation, with its rather dubious implicit suggestion that unconsciously they knew all along that their love was proper.

Quite as successful, if not more so, is the tale of Bessus, bluntly realistic in its exposure of a braggart who has gone too far too often and still has enough gall to attempt to talk his way out of the beating he deserves. On a more serious level, he is used to prick the conscience of the king, when he eagerly agrees to facilitate any incestuous affair that the king may have in mind, and, in so doing, reveals to the monarch how morally low he has sunk. The comic aspect of his story, however, is a good example of how these playwrights were able to relieve the afflatus of high declamatory language with blunt simplicities, and, in so doing, give the tragic matter a credibility in a world of common conduct.

For a modern reader, the ridiculous nature of the plot and the excessive conduct of the characters, especially the king, may blind one to the great success of the language. It is easiest appreciated in the Bessus material, with its quick, realistic ironies and insults, and it may be that this work is, in the main, the contribution of Fletcher. Harder to appreciate are the poetic intensities of the passages of deep feeling expressed by the king and his putative sister, both in tandem and in soliloquy. Here, the material has considerable power, if attention is paid, and it is sometimes suggested that it occasionally reaches the quality of William Shakespeare's work. It is usually presumed that Beaumont is responsible for this poetic material. This matter of authorship is of lesser concern; the real question is how well these two men used the rather ludicrous motifs of Jacobean drama to make reasonably good theater, and sometimes glorious language.

The seemingly vicious, and sometimes ridiculous excess of this typical Jacobean play should not, however, be dismissed out of hand as a simple example of bad theatrical taste. Many critics see the enthusiasm for violent, arbitrary conduct, for gratuitous cruelty, the disdain for the lower orders, for women, and for the older generation, and the exercise of irresponsible power by the rulers of the day as not very far from the truth of the times. The pessimism flaunted in a play like this may be, in part, simply an artistic expression of the prevailing social, political, and moral sensibility. Significantly, this form of tragicomedy had an influence on the drama that followed it.

"Critical Evaluation" by Charles Pullen

Bibliography:

Frost, David L. *The School of Shakespeare*. Cambridge, England: Cambridge University Press, 1968. A discussion of the various ways in which playwrights who knew Shakespeare and admired him, made use of his work. There is a chapter on his effect on Beaumont and Fletcher.

Misener, Arthur. "The High Design of *A King and No King*." *Modern Philology* 38 (November, 1940): 123-154. Questions how morally serious these playwrights were, or if they were simply interested in providing sensational scenes.

Oliphant, E. H. C. *The Plays of Beaumont and Fletcher*. New Haven, Conn.: Yale University Press, 1927. Standard, dependable discussion of the canon, with some detailed discussion of *A King and No King*.

Ornstein, Robert. *The Moral Vision of Jacobean Tragedy*. Madison: University of Wisconsin Press, 1965. Such frightful things—physical, moral, and political—happen in this sort of play that it is difficult for a contemporary reader to understand the context, and this book attempts to put the problem in perspective.

Sprague, Arthur Colby. *Beaumont and Fletcher on the Restoration Stage*. New York: Benjamin Blom, 1965. One of the best ways to understand a work of art is to examine how another historical period interprets and uses the material. These playwrights were not only an influence on Restoration drama, but were also very popular, in their own right, on the Restoration stage.

KING HORN

Type of work: Poetry
Author: Unknown
Type of plot: Romance
Time of plot: Sixth century
Locale: England and Ireland
First transcribed: c. 1225

Principal characters:
> HORN, a chivalrous young prince dispossessed of his kingdom
> QUEEN GODHILD, his mother
> ATHULF, his brother
> FIKENHILD, his treacherous friend
> AYLMAR, king of Westernesse
> RYMENHILD, his daughter, in love with Horn
> MODI, king of Reynes, Horn's enemy and another suitor for Rymenhild's hand
> THURSTON, an Irish king
> BERILD and
> HARILD, his sons
> REYNILD, his daughter
> ATHELBRUS, steward to King Aylmar

The Story:

Horn, the fairest youth ever born, was bright as glass and white as a flower; his color was rose-red, and he had no equal in any kingdom. When Horn was fifteen years old, his father, King Murry of Suddene Isle of Man, was killed by invading Saracens. His mother, Queen Godhild, found refuge under a rock, where she prayed for Horn's safety. Because of Horn's fairness, the Saracens spared him, setting him adrift with twelve companions, among them his brother Athulf and the wicked Fikenhild, on a ship that they expected would sink. The youths landed safely on the shore of Westernesse, where good King Aylmar received them kindly and took a special liking to Horn. Aylmar's daughter, Rymenhild, was also attracted to Horn and asked the steward, Athelbrus, who had been given charge of Horn's instruction, to bring him to her room. Disturbed at this command, Athelbrus brought Athulf instead. Mistaking him for Horn, Rymenhild told Athulf that she loved him. When she discovered that Athelbrus had tricked her, she threatened to have him hanged, whereupon Athelbrus brought Horn to her. Rymenhild asked him to marry her, but Horn refused, saying that he was a foundling and unworthy. At this rebuff, Rymenhild fell in a swoon. Horn took her in his arms, kissed her, and asked her to have her father make him a knight so that he might marry her.

King Aylmar knighted Horn and permitted him to knight his companions. As soon as Horn was knighted, Rymenhild wanted him to marry her; but Horn said that he must first prove his merit as a knight. Rymenhild gave him a ring engraved with her name and told him that if he looked at the ring and thought of her, he would overcome all enemies. On a handsome black steed, Horn set forth on his quest. He quickly found and slew at least one hundred Saracens. The next day, Rymenhild told him that she had dreamed that a great fish had escaped from her net. The significance of her distressing dream was clear when Fikenhild, envious of Horn, told King Aylmar that Horn was planning to kill him and marry Rymenhild. He said that Horn was at the moment in bed with Rymenhild. Aylmar, rushing into his daughter's chamber, found Horn embracing Rymenhild. The king ordered Horn to leave the castle. Before departing, Horn instructed Athulf to guard Rymenhild. He told Rymenhild that he expected to be back in seven years; if he had not returned by that time, she was to take another husband.

Horn went to Ireland, where he met two princes, Harild and Berild. He told them that his name was Cutberd, and they took him to their father, King Thurston. The time was Christmas. Soon a giant came from heathendom to offer a challenge from paynims who had arrived in the land. One of them offered to fight any three of the Irish knights. The king appointed his sons, Harild and Berild, as well as Cutberd. Cutberd offered to take on the challenger alone. Having fought with Cutberd, the champion said that he had encountered only one man who was his equal, King Murry of Suddene. Shuddering, Horn realized that he was facing his father's murderer. He looked on his ring, thought of Rymenhild, and smote the champion through the heart. The paynims turned to run to the boat, but Horn and his companions followed and killed them all. Harild and Berild were killed in the fighting. Thurston offered his daughter Reynild in marriage to Horn and planned to make the young knight heir to the throne. Horn replied that he would serve the king for seven years. At the end of that time, if he wanted his reward, including the princess for his wife, he would ask for it.

Back in Westernesse, Rymenhild heard nothing of Horn. King Modi of Reynes (Turness in northern Lancashire), Horn's enemy, wanted to marry her. She sent a messenger to find Horn. The messenger succeeded in his mission, but on his return he was drowned and washed up at Rymenhild's door. Horn, meanwhile, asked King Thurston to help him regain Rymenhild. In return, he promised his brother Athulf as husband for Reynild. Thurston gave him a ship, but when Horn arrived in Westernesse he found Rymenhild's wedding to King Modi in progress. A palmer told him that the bride had wept. Horn changed clothes with the palmer, disguised his features with dirt, and went to the wedding feast, where he asked the bride for wine. Rymenhild gave him wine in a bowl as if he were a thirsty beggar. Horn refused, saying he was a fisherman who had come to see if the net he set seven years ago had taken a fish. He said that he wanted to drink to Horn from horn. Rymenhild gave him wine in a drinking horn, and Horn dropped in it the ring that Rymenhild had given him. Rymenhild saw the ring and asked if Horn were dead. Horn replied that he died aboard ship after asking him to tell her of his death. Rymenhild threw herself on her bed and prepared to kill herself with the knife she had hidden there to kill both Modi and herself that night. Horn wiped the dirt from his face and told her that he was Horn, her true lover. Rymenhild ran to tell Athulf, who jumped for joy. Returning to the wedding party with his Irish warriors, Horn killed King Modi and his followers. After convincing King Aylmar that Fikenhild had slandered him, Horn told the king that he would return to Suddene and regain his kingdom, then marry Rymenhild. Horn recovered his kingdom from the Saracens and found that his mother was still alive.

While Horn was gone, Fikenhild, through bribery and by intimidating the king, was able to carry Rymenhild off to his castle. Warned of this in a dream, Horn returned to Westernesse, only to hear that Fikenhild had married Rymenhild. Disguised as harpers, Horn and his men gained access to Fikenhild's castle, where he killed Fikenhild, hacked him to pieces, and rescued Rymenhild. He made Athelbrus, the good steward, king of Reynes in place of Modi, and he took Athulf to Ireland to marry Reynild. Then he took Rymenhild to Suddene and there made her his queen.

Critical Evaluation:

King Horn represents a literary genre, the romance, that had its inception in France during the second half of the twelfth century. This new genre immediately spread to England and remained popular in both countries for about a century. While it never achieved the status of serious literature, it afforded light entertainment for the rural gentry and, possibly, for small numbers of the nobility and the merchant class. Medieval romances can be classified into three types: the hero-alone type, which *King Horn* represents; the family-based pattern; and the epic romance. *King Horn* also belongs to the subgenre that deals with the child exile—a type especially provocative of sympathy from the audience.

The romance developed from the *chanson de geste*, which had, in turn, grown from the Germanic epic. While the romance bears traces of its immediate and remote predecessors, however, it differs in its emphasis. That is, while the epic and *chanson de geste* primarily focused on military feats, the romance centered on the search of individuals for their place in society. When Horn asks King Aylmar of Westernesse to knight him, for example, he is asking for an authentic place in this foreign kingdom. Moreover, Horn is not content to be a knight in name only but must prove the validity of his position by his deeds. He exhibits great prowess in slaying the Saracens, but his prime motive in so doing is to win Rymenhild's hand by establishing himself as a proven defender in her land. Conversely, his use of an alias while in Ireland indicates that he does not desire permanent affiliation with that country.

By twentieth century standards, the medieval romance is neither stylistically, thematically, nor structurally sophisticated. Its meter is crude, its characters flat, and its plot predictable. It contains few, if any, symbols, and offers no insight for further reflection. Its very simplicity, however, served a purpose for its original audience. Members of the country gentry, who were beneath the nobles on the social ladder, and members of the rising merchant class may have felt somewhat insecure regarding their power and position in society. This was probably especially true of the women—who constituted most of the romance's audience—who had little genuine power or position in any class. By representing extremes of good and evil, rather than simulating realistic persons with complex personalities, romance characters and their actions offered clear-cut examples of how to behave in an ordered society. The kingdom of Aylmar, for example, is one of order and propriety. Aylmar graciously opens his home to the children from Suddene, but when Finkenhild falsely accuses Horn of sleeping with Rymenhild, the king has no choice but to banish the latter, whom he sees as a threat to a society where every activity has its prescribed time and circumstance. Although Horn has been wrongly treated, he obediently leaves Westernesse, with no apparent intention of vindicating himself or seeking revenge. His obedience to authority is rewarded by his eventual marriage to Rymenhild, whereas Finken-hild's deceit is punished by his loss of the princess.

To ensure the specific nature of the audience's reactions, romance poets made it clear at the outset whether a given character was good or bad. The poet of *King Horn* states as early as line 14 that Horn is "bright as the glass/ white as the flower." Since these similes describe the Virgin Mary in some lyrics of the same period, it is made obvious that Horn is pure and virtuous. All of his actions, including the murder of Modi, are meritorious. Finkenhild, on the other hand, is referred to in line 28 as "the worst," and everything he does is evil.

The romance not only provided paradigms of desirable conduct but also sought to inculcate in the audience accepted societal values. To this end, they were structured around predictable plots whose repetition reinforced values the audience had already accepted, whether con-sciously or unconsciously. The typical plot was one in which a good king dies and leaves a son, whose responsibility it becomes to save his father's kingdom from external or internal enemies. A beautiful heroine functions as the son's motive and reward for virtuous and heroic behavior. Finally, the son's marriage to the heroine results in the restoration of the late father's land, bringing full closure to the story. In *King Horn*, the enemies are Scandinavians, whom, possibly to give the poem a flavor of the crusading era, the poet calls Saracens. Throughout his sojourn in Ireland, Horn's valor is inspired by his love for Rymenhild, and their marriage reestablishes his father's line in Suddene. The action of the poem thus extols the values of order, fidelity, bravery, and lineage, all of which were previously honored but are now strengthened.

Because they were frequently sung or recited as well as read, it was imperative for romances to be memorable and pleasing. *King Horn*'s rhyming couplets give it a lyrical quality, and the presence of synecdoches (the use of a whole to represent a part or a part to represent the whole) make it vivid and retainable. Line 112, for example, conveys the agony of the banished children through the phrase "wringinde here honde" (wringing their hands). Similarly, the poet expresses all of Godhild's loss and despair when he says that "Under a roche [rock] of stone/ Ther heo [she] livede alone."

Although the writers of medieval romance did not achieve the wit of Chaucer or the perception of the Pearl Poet, they provided entertainment and escape for those who read or listened to their works. Like later authors of romances, they did not strive to offer novel ideas but sought only to reinforce conventional, widely accepted values and behaviors.

"Critical Evaluation" by Rebecca Stingley Hinton

Bibliography:
Barnes, Geraldine. *Counsel and Strategy in Middle English Romance.* Cambridge, England: D. S. Brewer, 1993. Discusses the nature and functions of kingdoms and advisory bodies described in romances. Barnes also includes recent research on the audiences of the romance.
Knight, Stephen. "The Social Function of the Middle English Romances." *Medieval Literature: Criticism, Ideology, & History,* edited by David Aers. New York: St. Martin's Press, 1986. Divides the medieval romance into three subgenres and describes each in detail.
Ramsey, Lee C. *Chivalric Romances: Popular Literature in Medieval England.* Bloomington: Indiana University Press, 1983. Provides background on the history and development of the medieval romance. Ramsey discusses elements common to all romances and includes information on the genre's audience.
Spearing, A. C. *Readings in Medieval Poetry.* New York: Cambridge University Press, 1987. Begins by discussing the relationship between self-perception and modes of language, then applies this material to various works, including *King Horn.* Spearing compares the medieval romance to twentieth century film.
Zesmer, David M. *Guide to English Literature from "Beowulf" Through Chaucer and Medieval Drama.* New York: Barnes & Noble Books, 1961. Includes a brief analysis of the romance and identifies the geography in *King Horn.*

KING JOHAN

Type of work: Drama
Author: John Bale (1495-1563)
Type of plot: Historical
Time of plot: Early thirteenth century
Locale: England
First published: 1538; first performed, 1539?

Principal characters:
    ENGLAND, a widow
    KING JOHAN
    NOBILITY,
    CLERGY,
    CIVIL ORDER, and
    COMMONALTY, betrayers of King Johan
    SEDITION
    DISSIMULATION
    PRIVATE WEALTH
    USURPED POWER
    THE POPE, INNOCENT III
    TREASON
    VERITY
    IMPERIAL MAJESTY
    STEPHEN LANGTON, a churchman and statesman
    CARDINAL PANDULPHUS

The Story:

England complained to King Johan that she had been stripped of her rights and her wealth by the rapacious clergy who had driven her husband, God, from the realm. King Johan promised to right her wrongs but was mocked by Sedition, the comic vice, and the foremost agent of the Church. Sedition, demonstrating the way in which he and the Church subverted the government of kings, introduced Dissimulation, his right-hand man. Dissimulation worked with Private Wealth and Usurped Power. Private Wealth was the darling of the religious orders; he gave strength to Usurped Power, who sustained the arrogance of popes.

King Johan defied Sedition and his cohorts. He called Nobility, Clergy, and Civil Order to him and prevailed on them for their support. Nobility and Civil Order gave theirs willingly, but Clergy was reluctant. King Johan had been too harsh on him. When the king reminded him of the temporal rights of rulers as outlined in the Gospel, Clergy, still reluctant, consented.

The allegiance of the three was short-lived, however, for Sedition and his minions had little trouble convincing them that the actual power of Rome was stronger than any abstract claim based on the Gospel. Besides, the Church had the sole right of interpreting the Gospel. Nobility, Clergy, and Civil Order were forsworn.

King Johan, now bereft of his three strongest allies, placed all of his hopes on Commonalty, his one sure support. Commonalty, the true child of England, was brought to King Johan by his mother, and the king was dismayed to learn that he was both impoverished and blind. He was impoverished, his mother explained, because the Church had stolen all his goods; his blindness symbolized his spiritual ignorance, an ignorance in which he was kept by the conspiracy of Clergy who was supposed to open his eyes. For all his failings, Commonalty still was faithful to the king who had always seen to his welfare. He willingly reasserted his faith.

In the end, however, he was no more staunch than his more exalted brothers. Clergy had too strong a hold on him, and he too became a victim of Sedition's plottings.

King Johan now stood alone in his attempt to save the widow England. Assured now of the king's vulnerability, the pope sent his agents to bring the king to his knees. King Johan's old enemy, Stephen Langton, the archbishop of Canterbury, returned. The interdict was proclaimed with bell, book, and candle, and the vindictive Cardinal Pandulphus arrived to enforce it.

King Johan stood firm, defying the pope to do his worst. Claiming that he would not betray England, he turned to history and the scriptures to defend his rights; he pointed out the ways in which the Church perverted the true faith and he cited the corruptions of the holy orders. Sedition mocked him and promised that his defiance would end.

End it did, for the pope gathered a strong alliance and threatened to invade England. Rather than see his country devastated and his people killed, King Johan submitted. He surrendered his crown to the pope and received it back as a fief of the Holy See. When England protested, she was reviled by Sedition and his aides.

King Johan ruled for a number of years as the vassal of the pope. If he tried to assert his power, Sedition and his agents were on hand to thwart it. Treason ran through the land with impunity, and when the king tried to punish him, he pleaded benefit of clergy and was released. Nevertheless, King Johan was determined to hang him.

Cardinal Pandulphus and Sedition conceived a plan to curb King Johan's power. Cardinal Pandulphus would not release England from the interdict until King Johan had handed over to the papacy a third of his lands as a dowry for the bride of Richard, his late brother. Although King Johan protested, Cardinal Pandulphus insisted on these harsh terms. Providentially, the king was released when it was announced that Julyane, the lady in question, was dead.

The forces of the Church were now determined to get rid of King Johan completely. Dissimulation, in the guise of Simon of Swinsett, a monk, concocted a poison cup from the sweat of a toad. When he offered Johan the draught, the king forced the monk to drink first and then drained the cup. Both died in agony.

Upon the death of King Johan, Verity appeared and proclaimed that all the evils that had been attributed to King Johan were false, the lies of slandering monks. He listed all of the good things the king had done for the benefit of the common people and asserted that, for three hundred years, that good had been undone by the corrupt Church. Now, he announced, Imperial Majesty had arrived to crush the Church and save the widow England.

Imperial Majesty confronted Nobility, Clergy, and Civil Order. Verity pointed out to them the error of their ways, and, contrite, they swore their eternal allegiance to Imperial Majesty. England was safe from the evils of Rome.

Critical Evaluation:

John Bale, Bishop of Ossory, one of the most outspoken champions of the English Reformation, claimed to have written some forty plays in his lifetime. Of these, five are extant; of these five, the allegorical *King Johan* is the most important. Although far too long and tedious for dramatic effectiveness, being in structure two plays or one play in two parts, it is interesting as a scathing and uncompromising attack on the Church of Rome and as a version of history different from that usually accepted. Challenging those historians—Polydore Virgil in particular—who made King Johan a knave, Bale depicts the king as a virtuous protector of the realm, who was betrayed by the covetousness and viciousness of the Church. History may be altered and revised to suit Bale's cause, but the fact that he used it at all is of concern, for *King Johan* announces the beginning of the great tradition of the English history play. It shows the transition from the old to the new—an allegorical play using the techniques of the medieval morality (Sedition, for instance, is an example of the morality "vice"), but using them to dramatize historical events.

King Johan well illustrates Bale's position as a follower of the so-called "New Learning" as it was espoused by Cambridge reformers during the reign of Henry VIII. Two of these reformers particularly link Bale to that group. William Tyndale's book on Christian obedience (1528) sets out the theme that Bale followed. To both Tyndale and Bale, King Johan was a king who was prevented from the exercise of his royal duty by the usurping power of an anti-Christian papacy. Thomas Cranmer, another member of the Cambridge Protestant circle, gave this play its first performance, in his house on January 2, 1539.

Reformation in England consisted of dissolving many monasteries and religious houses of England, and removal of the pope as the Church's recognized head. In matters of doctrine, Henry VIII was conservative. He retained the Mass and sacraments, and, although he permitted the Bible to be translated into English and allowed the vernacular liturgy, he tended to reject many of the Lutheran doctrines and those of the more radical reformers in Switzerland. Of all the Protestant sects, Bale attacks only the quasi-anarchical Anabaptists. He attacks monks strongly, as would be expected in Henry's England, but goes on to rail against the Mass, sacraments, relics, bells, vestments, and other "papist" accouterments retained by Henry. All this fits in well with the more radical reformation that reached England after Henry's death. Led by Cranmer and others, the Protestants of the old Cambridge school were riding high during the reign of Edward VI. The beliefs of Edward's time were presaged by Bale's play, but it is surprising to see such sentiments expressed so strongly when Henry VIII was alive and vigorous. This play, then, gives the reader a full picture of one part of religious belief during the reign of Henry VIII, a belief that was later to come powerfully into its own.

Bale also expresses in *King Johan* a significant idea that usually is called "Erastianism" after Thomas Erastus, but is more correctly ascribed to Marsiglio of Padua. Marsiglio held that the church was not an equal of the state, but instead was subject to civil authority as an arm of the state, like the army or any bureaucracy. Tied up in this concept is the idea of empire. England was an empire rather than a kingdom, and that the concept that England was autonomous is at the heart of both Bale's *King Johan* and Henry VIII's Reformation. It was Henry who first declared that England owed no allegiance to any other organization, and the reign of his daughter Elizabeth can partly be understood as an attempt to make Henry's dream of Imperial Majesty into a reality.

Bibliography:
Adams, Barry B., ed. Introduction to *King Johan*, by John Bale. San Marino, Calif.: Huntington Library, 1969. Comments on the manuscripts and early editions of the play; reviews sources Bale used in composing his drama; discusses the theatrics and versification, and the play's relationship to sixteenth century drama.
Blatt, Thora B. *The Plays of John Bale: A Study of Ideas, Technique, and Style.* Copenhagen: G. E. C. Gad, 1968. Provides information on extant manuscript sources; comments on structure and style; reviews history of productions. Attributes the play's popularity to the fact that it was the first English drama to "introduce characters from national history on the stage."

Happé, Peter, ed. *The Complete Plays of John Bale*. Vol. 1. Cambridge, Mass.: D. S. Brewer, 1985. Introduction provides useful information about Bale's career, gives details of production and printing, and analyzes sources and analogues. Comments on the language and versification and gives background about the religious controversy that inspired this drama.

Pafford, J. H. P., ed. Introduction to *King Johan*, by John Bale. New York: Oxford University Press, 1931. Modern edition of the play; includes an introduction providing extensive details about the manuscript, sources, text, and language. Most useful for specialists, but informative for general readers.

Walker, Greg. *Plays of Persuasion*. Cambridge, England: Cambridge University Press, 1991. A lengthy chapter on *King Johan* discusses the history of performances during the Renaissance, the political dimensions of the drama, and Bale's use of polemical language. Examines the play as a tool for influencing Henry VIII.

KING JOHN

Type of work: Drama
Author: William Shakespeare (1564-1616)
Type of plot: Historical
Time of plot: Early thirteenth century
Locale: England and France
First performed: c. 1596-1597; first published, 1623

Principal characters:
    JOHN, the king of England
    PRINCE HENRY, his son
    ARTHUR OF BRETAGNE, the king's nephew
    WILLIAM MARESHALL, the Earl of Pembroke
    GEFFREY FITZ-PETER, the Earl of Essex
    WILLIAM LONGSWORD, the Earl of Salisbury
    HUBERT DE BURGH, the Chamberlain to the king
    ROBERT FAULCONBRIDGE, an English baron
    PHILIP FAULCONBRIDGE, his half brother, the natural son
        of King Richard I
    CARDINAL PANDULPH, the papal legate
    LEWIS, the Dauphin of France
    ELINOR, King John's mother
    CONSTANCE, Arthur's mother
    BLANCH OF CASTILE, King John's niece

The Story:

King John sat on the throne of England without right, for the succession should have passed to Arthur of Bretagne, the fourteen-year-old son of King John's older brother. John and Elinor, his mother, prepared to defend England against the forces of Austria and France, after Constance of Bretagne had enlisted the aid of those countries to gain the throne for her son Arthur.

As John and Elinor made ready for battle, Philip Faulconbridge, the natural son of Richard the Lion-Hearted by Lady Faulconbridge, was recruited by Elinor to serve John's cause in the war. Faulconbridge, weary of his half brother's slights regarding his illegitimacy, willingly accepted the offer and was knighted by King John.

The French, Austrian, and British armies met at Angiers in France, but the battle was fought with words, not swords. To John's statement that England was ready for war or peace, King Philip of France answered that, for the sake of justice, France would fight for Arthur's place on the throne. When Elinor accused Constance of self-aggrandizement in seeking the throne for her son, Constance accused her mother-in-law of adultery. Faulconbridge and the Archduke of Austria resorted to a verbal volley.

Lewis, the Dauphin of France, halted the prattle by stating Arthur's specific claims, which John refused to grant. The citizens of Angiers announced that they were barring the gates of the city to all until they had proof as to the actual kingship. The leaders prepared for a battle.

After excursions by the three armies, heralds of the various forces appeared to announce their victories to the citizens of Angiers, but the burghers persisted in their demands for more definite proof. At last, Faulconbridge suggested that they destroy the city walls and continue to fight until one side or the other was conquered. Arrangements for the battle brought on more talk, for the citizens suggested a peace settlement among the forces and promised entrance to the city if Blanch of Castile were affianced to the Dauphin of France.

John gladly offered certain provinces as Blanch's dowry, and it was agreed that the vows should be solemnized. Faulconbridge analyzed John's obvious motive: It was better to part with some parcels of land and keep the throne than to lose his kingdom in battle.

Constance, displaying the persistence and tenacity of a mother who wished to see justice done to her child, doubted that the proposed alliance would succeed; she wished to have the issue settled in battle. Her hopes rose when Cardinal Pandulph appeared to announce John's excommunication because of his abuse of the Archbishop of Canterbury. John, unperturbed by the decree of excommunication, denounced the pope. The alliance between France and England, the outgrowth of Lewis and Blanch's marriage, could not stand, according to Pandulph, if France hoped also to avoid excommunication. King Philip wisely decided that it would be better to have England as an enemy than to be at odds with Rome.

His change of mind made war necessary. The battle ended with the English victorious. Faulconbridge beheaded the Archduke of Austria. Arthur was taken prisoner. When Hubert de Burgh pledged his unswerving support to the king, John told him of his hatred for Arthur. He asked that the boy be murdered. Grieved by her separation from Arthur, Constance lamented that she would never see her son again. Even in heaven, she said, she would be denied this blessing because Arthur's treatment at the hands of the English would change him from the gracious creature he had been. Pandulph, unwilling to let John have easy victory, persuaded Lewis to march against the English forces. The cardinal explained that with Arthur's death—and news of French aggression would undoubtedly mean his death—Louis, as Blanch's husband, could claim Arthur's lands.

In England, Hubert de Burgh had been ordered to burn out Arthur's eyes with hot irons. Although Hubert professed loyalty to John, he had become attached to Arthur while the boy was in his charge. Touched by Arthur's pleas, he refused to carry out King John's orders. After hiding Arthur in another part of the castle, he went to tell John of his decision. On his arrival at the palace, however, he found Pembroke and Salisbury, in conference with the king, pleading for Arthur's life. The people, they reported, were enraged because of John's dastardly action; they threatened to withdraw their fealty to the cruel king. John's sorrow was increased by the information that a large French army had landed in England and that Elinor was dead. Faulconbridge, who had been collecting tribute from monks, appeared with Peter of Pomfret, a prophet. When Peter prophesied that John would lose his crown at noon on Ascension Day, John had Peter jailed and ordered his execution if the prophecy were not fulfilled.

Told of Hubert de Burgh's refusal to torture Arthur, the king, overjoyed, sent his chamberlain in pursuit of Pembroke and Salisbury to tell them the good news. Arthur, however, fearful for his welfare, had attempted escape from the castle. In jumping from the wall, he fell on the stones and was killed. When Hubert overtook the lords and blurted his tidings, he was confronted by information and proof that Arthur was dead. Pembroke and Salisbury sent word to John that they could be found with the French.

Harried at every turn—deserted by his nobles, disowned by his subjects, attacked by his former ally—John, on Ascension Day, surrendered his crown to Cardinal Pandulph, thus fulfilling Peter's prophecy. He received it back only after he had acknowledged his vassalage to the pope. In return, Pandulph was to order the French to withdraw their forces. Opposed to such arbitration, however, Faulconbridge secured John's permission to engage the French. Lewis, now the king of France, rejected Pandulph's suit for peace. His claim was that officious

Rome, having sent neither arms, men, nor money for France's cause in opposing John's hereticism and deviltry, should remain neutral.

Under the direction of Faulconbridge, the English made a strong stand against the French. The defaulting barons, advised by Melun, a dying French lord, that Lewis planned their execution if France won the victory, returned to the king and received his pardon for their disloyalty. John's graciousness to his barons and his new alliance with Rome, however, brought him only momentary happiness. He was poisoned at Swinstead Abbey and died after intense suffering.

After his death, Cardinal Pandulph was able to arrange a truce between the English and French. Prince Henry was named king of England. King Lewis returned home to France. Faulconbridge, brave, dashing, vainglorious, swore his allegiance to the new king. His and England's pride was expressed in his words that England had never been and would never be at a conqueror's feet, except when such a position might lead to future victories.

Critical Evaluation:

An uneven product of William Shakespeare's early period and one of his first history plays, *King John* is neither as good as it might have been nor as bad as it has been considered. Written entirely in verse, the play sometimes fails to distinguish among the various characters in its portrayal of their speech—almost homogeneously filled with conceits and wordplays that, only in the case of Faulconbridge, fit the personality who speaks them. Its themes include the relationship between fortune and the individual's nature, the powerful finality of a king's words, the corrupt and conniving influence of the Church, and the degree of individual responsibility in the face of a leader's folly. This last is studied in Act IV, when John upbraids Hubert for taking him at his word in killing young Arthur; he tells Hubert that a king, too, has moods and his followers must protect him from his rash emotions. In general, as the brief abdication scene in the first part of Act V demonstrates, *King John* is generically a part of the *de casibus virorum illustrium* ("the fall of illustrious men") motif popular in medieval and Renaissance literature.

The play suffers from structural deficiencies that suggest Shakespeare had not yet mastered that peculiarly difficult combination of historical verisimilitude and artistic inspiration, that is, giving psychologically convincing motivation to actions that are "givens" of historical record. When Blanch and Lewis fall in love to order when Pandulph enters as a *deus ex machina* to alter the course of events dramatically and unpredictably, when Faulconbridge carries Austria's head across the stage, when young Arthur whimsically decides to escape and kills himself, and when Lewis' rebuff to Pandulph goes unanswered, we suspect that Shakespeare nods. Yet Arthur's speech on his sadness, Hubert's mercy, Faulconbridge's touching pardon of his mother's folly, his saucy exchange with Austria, and Constance's speech about the fears of a queen, a woman, and a mother all contain the fertile seeds that would blossom into the full flower of Shakespeare's imagination.

Bibliography:

Barroll, J. Leeds, ed. *Shakespeare Studies.* Vol. 1. Cincinnati, Ohio: University of Cincinnati, 1965. The first in a series of anthologies of Shakespearean criticism. "Shakespeare and the Double Image in *King John,*" by John R. Elliot, is principally concerned with the historical and literary sources of the play.

Honigmann, E. A. J., ed. *The Arden Shakespeare: King John.* Cambridge, Mass.: Harvard University Press, 1962. In addition to the text of the play itself, this volume contains more than seventy pages of introductory material. The sources, the production history, and the text itself are considered. There are also appendices dealing with the sources and problems with the text.

Lloyd Evans, Gareth. *The Upstart Crow: An Introduction to Shakespeare's Plays.* London: J. M. Dent and Sons, 1982. A comprehensive discussion of the dramatic works of William Shakespeare. While the major emphasis is on critical reviews of the plays, there are also discussions of sources as well as material on the circumstances which surrounded the writing of the plays.

Pierce, Robert B. *Shakespeare's History Plays: The Family and the State.* Columbus: Ohio State University Press, 1971. A general discussion of Shakespeare's history plays. *King John* is considered as a transitional play between the early history plays and the later plays on Henry IV and V, which Pierce considers to be far greater works.

Ribner, Irving. *The English History Play in the Age of Shakespeare.* London: Methuen, 1965. A revised edition of the 1957 work first published in the United States by Princeton University Press. A discussion of history plays in the Elizabethan era of English drama, including a discussion of Shakespeare's contributions in the field. The development of the form through the period is discussed, and its sources are considered.

KING LEAR

Type of work: Drama
Author: William Shakespeare (1564-1616)
Type of plot: Tragedy
Time of plot: First century B.C.E.
Locale: Britain
First performed: c. 1605-1606; first published, 1608

> *Principal characters:*
> KING LEAR OF BRITAIN
> KING OF FRANCE
> DUKE OF CORNWALL
> DUKE OF ALBANY
> EARL OF KENT
> EARL OF GLOUCESTER
> EDGAR, Gloucester's legitimate son
> EDMUND, Gloucester's illegitimate son
> GONERIL,
> REGAN, and
> CORDELIA, Lear's daughters

The Story:

King Lear, in foolish fondness for his children, decided to divide his kingdom among his three daughters. Grown senile, he scoffed at the foresight of his advisers and declared that each girl's statement of her love for him would determine the portion of the kingdom she received as her dowry. Goneril, his oldest daughter and the duchess of Albany, spoke first. She said that she loved her father more than eyesight, space, liberty, or life itself. Regan, the duchess of Cornwall, announced that the sentiment of her love had been expressed by Goneril, but that Goneril had stopped short of the statement of Regan's love. Cordelia, who had secretly confided that her love was more ponderous than her tongue, told her father that because her love was in her heart, not in her mouth, she was willing to sacrifice eloquence for truth. Lear angrily told her that truth alone should be her dowry and ordered that her part of the kingdom be divided between Goneril and Regan. Lear's disappointment in Cordelia's statement grew into a rage against the earl of Kent, who tried to plead for Cordelia with the foolish king. Because of Kent's blunt speech, he was given ten days to leave the country. Loving his sovereign, he risked death by disguising himself and remaining in Britain to care for Lear in his infirmity.

When Burgundy and France came as suitors to ask Cordelia's hand in marriage, Burgundy, learning of her dowerless fate, rejected her. France, honoring Cordelia for her virtues, took her as his wife, but Lear dismissed Cordelia and France without his benediction. Goneril and Regan, wary of their father's vacillation in his weakened mental state, set about to establish their kingdoms against change.

Lear was not long in learning what Goneril's and Regan's claims of love for him really meant. Their caustic comments about the old man's mental and physical feebleness, furnished Lear's fool with many points for philosophical recriminations against the king. Realizing that his charity to his daughters had made him homeless, Lear cried in anguish against his fate. His prayers went unanswered, and his daughters' abuse hastened his derangement.

The earl of Gloucester, like Lear, was fond of his two children. Edmund, a bastard, afraid that his illegitimacy would deprive him of his share of Gloucester's estate, forged a letter over Edgar's signature, stating that the sons should not have to wait for their fortunes until they were too old to enjoy them. Gloucester, refusing to believe that Edgar desired his father's death, was told by Edmund to wait in hiding and hear Edgar make assertions that could easily be misinterpreted against him. Edmund, furthering his scheme, told Edgar that villainy was afoot and that Edgar should not go unarmed at any time.

To complete his evil design, he later advised Edgar to flee for his own safety. After cutting his arm, he then told his father that he had been wounded while he and Edgar fought over Gloucester's honor. Gloucester, swearing that Edgar would not escape justice, had his son's description circulated so that he might be apprehended.

Edmund, meanwhile, allied himself with the dukes of Cornwall and Albany to defend Britain against the French army mobilized by Cordelia and her husband to avenge Lear's cruel treatment. Edmund won Regan and Goneril completely by his personal attentions to them and set the sisters against each other by arousing their jealousy.

Lear, wandering as an outcast on the stormy heath, was aided by Kent, disguised as a peasant. Seeking protection from the storm, they found a hut where Edgar, pretending to be a madman, had already taken refuge. Gloucester, searching for the king, found them there and urged them to hurry to Dover, where Cordelia and her husband would protect Lear from the wrath of his unnatural daughters.

Because he had attempted to give succor and condolence to the outcast Lear, Gloucester was blinded when Cornwall, acting on information furnished by Edmund, gouged out his eyes. While he was at his grisly work, a servant, rebelling against the cruel deed, wounded Cornwall. Regan killed the servant, but Cornwall died later as the result of his wound. Edgar, still playing the part of a madman, found his father wandering the fields with an old retainer. Edgar, who refrained from revealing his identity, promised to guide his father to Dover, where Gloucester planned to die by throwing himself from the high cliffs.

Goneril became bitterly jealous when widowed Regan was able to receive Edmund's full attention, who had been made earl of Gloucester. She declared that she would rather lose the battle to France than lose Edmund to Regan. Goneril's hatred became more venomous when Albany, whom she detested because of his kindliness toward Lear and his pity for Gloucester, announced that he would try to right the wrongs done by Goneril, Regan, and Edmund.

Cordelia, informed by messenger of her father's fate, was in the French camp near Dover. When the mad old king was brought to her by the faithful Kent, she cared for her father tenderly and put him in the care of a doctor skilled in curing many kinds of ills. When he regained his reason, Lear recognized Cordelia, but the joy of their reunion was clouded by his repentance for having misunderstood and mistreated his only loyal daughter.

Edgar, protecting Gloucester, was accosted by Oswald, Goneril's steward, on his way to deliver a note to Edmund. In the fight that ensued, Edgar killed Oswald; he then delivered the letter to Albany, in which Goneril declared her love for Edmund and asked that he kill her husband. Gloucester died, feeble and broken-hearted after Edgar revealed himself to his father. Edmund, who commanded the British forces, took Lear and Cordelia prisoners. When they were taken off to prison, he sent along written instructions for how they were to be treated.

Albany, who was aware of Edmund's ambition for personal glory, arrested him on a charge of high treason. Regan interceded for her lover but was rebuffed by Goneril. Regan was suddenly taken ill and carried to Albany's tent. When Edmund, as was his right, demanded a trial by combat, Albany agreed. Edgar, still in disguise, appeared and in the fight mortally wounded his false brother. Goneril, learning from Albany that he knew of her plot against his life, was desperate. She went to their tent, poisoned Regan, and killed herself.

Edmund, dying, revealed that he and Goneril had ordered Cordelia to be hanged and her death to be announced as suicide because of her despondency over her father's plight. Edmund, fiendish and diabolical always, was also vain. As he lay dying, he looked upon the bodies of Goneril and Regan and expressed pleasure that two women were dead because of their jealous love for him.

Albany dispatched Edgar to prevent Cordelia's death, but he arrived too late. Lear refused all assistance when he appeared carrying her dead body in his arms. After asking forgiveness of heartbroken Kent, whom he recognized at last, Lear, a broken, confused old man, died in anguish. Edgar and Albany alone were left to rebuild a country ravaged by bloodshed and war.

Critical Evaluation:

Despite the three-hundred-year-old debate regarding the lack of unity in the plot of *King Lear*, it is one of the most readable and gripping of William Shakespeare's dramas. The theme of filial ingratitude is presented clearly in the depiction of two families, whom circumstances eventually bring together as the two narrative lines converge. *King Lear* is not only an absorbing drama but a disturbing one as well. The beauty of diction and the overwhelming pathos of the treatment given to innocence and goodness add to the poignancy of the emotional play. Like all great tragic dramas, the story of Lear and his folly purges the emotions by terror and pity.

King Lear's first entrance in Act I is replete with ritual and ceremony. He is full of antiquity, authority, and assurance as he makes his regal way through the ordered court. When he reveals his intention to divide his kingdom into three parts for his daughters, he exudes the confidence generated by his long reign. The crispness and directness of his language suggest a power, if not imperiousness, that, far from senility, demonstrates the stability and certainty of long, unchallenged rule. From that point on, the play acts out the destruction of that fixed order and the emergence of a new, tentative balance.

In the opening scene, Lear speaks as king and father. The absolute ruler has decided to apportion his kingdom to his three heirs as a gift rather than bequest. In performing this act, which superficially seems both reasonable and generous, Lear sets in motion a chain of events that expose his vulnerabilities not only as a king and a father but also as a man. Shakespeare shows that it is foolish to divest oneself of power and responsibility and yet expect to retain the trappings of authority. This is exactly what Lear does when he relies with ill-placed confidence on the love of his daughters. He asks too much and he acts too precipitously, but he is punished by an inexorable universe out of all proportion to his errors in judgment.

When he asks his daughters for a declaration of love, as a prerequisite for a share of the kingdom, he is as self-assured a parent as he is an overbearing monarch. He credits the facile protestations of love by Goneril and Regan because they are what he wants to hear and because they conform to the ceremonial necessities of the occasion. Cordelia's honest response, born of a greater love, are out of keeping with the occasion. Lear has not looked beneath the surface. He has let the ritual appearances replace the internal reality, in fact, he has refused to distinguish between the two.

The asseverations of Goneril and Regan soon emerge as the cynical conceits they really are, but by then Lear has banished Cordelia and the loyal Kent, who saw through the sham. Lear is successively and ruthlessly divested of all the accoutrements of kingship by his villainous daughters, who eventually reduce him to the condition of a ragged, homeless madman. Paradoxically, it is in this extremity on the heath with Edgar and the fool, that Lear comes to a knowledge of himself and his community with humanity that he had never achieved while enjoying the glories of power. Buffeted by the natural fury of the storm, which is symbolic of the chaos and danger that come with the passing of the old order, Lear through his madness sees the common bond that connects him to the rest of humanity.

The experience of Lear is, on a more manageable, human level, mirrored in the Gloucester subplot. Gloucester too suffers filial ingratitude but not one raised to a cosmic level. He too mistakes appearance for reality in trusting the duplicitous Edmund and disinheriting the honest Edgar, but his behavior is more clearly the outgrowth of an existing moral confusion, which is reflected in his ambivalent and unrepentant affection for his illegitimate son. His moral blindness leads to physical blindness when his faulty judgment makes him vulnerable to the villains. In his blindness, he finally sees the truth of his situation, but his experience remains that of a father and a man.

Lear's experience parallels Gloucester's in that his figurative madness leads to a real madness in which he finally recognizes what he has lacked. He sees in the naked Edgar, himself a victim of Gloucester's moral blindness, the natural state of man, stripped of all external decoration, and he realizes that he has ignored the basic realities of the human condition. His experience finally transcends Gloucester's, however, because he is a king, preeminent among men. He not only represents the hazards of kingship but also the broadly human disposition to prefer pleasant appearances to troubling realities. Yet because of his position, Lear's failure brings the whole political and social order down with him.

Lear has violated nature by a culpable ignorance of it. The result is familial rupture, physical suffering, and existential confusion. Brought low, Lear begins to fashion a new salutary view of himself, human love, and human nature. In his insanity, Lear assembles a bizarre court of mad king, beggar, and fool that reasserts the common bonds of all men. Once he has achieved these realizations, the play's evil characters, so carefully balanced against the good in Shakespeare's precarious world, begin to kill each other off and succumb to the vengeance of regenerated justice.

It is however a mark of Shakespeare's uncompromising view of reality that there is no simple application of poetic justice to reward the good and punish the wicked. The good die too. Edgar finishes off his brother in a trial by combat, and the machinations of Goneril and Regan result in the destruction of both, but the redeemed Lear and Cordelia, the perfection of selfless love, also die. That Lear should die is perhaps no surprise. The suffering he has endured in his confrontation with the primal elements does not allow an optimistic return to normal life and prosperity. He has looked into the eye of nature and there is nothing left for him but to die.

The death of Cordelia is more troublesome because she is the perfectly innocent victim of the evil and madness that surround her. She dies gratuitously, not because of any internal necessity of the plot, but because the message to save her arrives too late. The dramatist has created his own inevitability to represent the ruthless consequences of the evil and chaos that have been loosed. When Lear enters with the dead Cordelia, he accomplishes the final expiation of his unknowing.

Out of these sufferings and recognitions comes a new moral stasis. Yet the purged world does not inspire great confidence that it will attain stability in the future. When Kent, who is old, refuses kingship, Edgar assumes authority but despite his rectitude there is an unsettling doubt that he has the force or stature to maintain the new order in this volatile world where evil and chaos always exist beneath the surface.

"Critical Evaluation" by Edward E. Foster

Bibliography:

Booth, Stephen. *"King Lear," "Macbeth," Indefinition, and Tragedy*. New Haven, Conn.: Yale University Press, 1983. In part 1, "On the Greatness of *King Lear*," much of the discussion focuses on the repeated false endings of the play. Booth also has an important appendix on the doubling of roles in Shakespeare's plays, especially in *King Lear.*

Halio, Jay L. *Critical Essays on "King Lear."* New York: Twayne, 1995. Contains a selection of the best essays on *King Lear*, including several on the "two-text hypothesis," the play in performance, and interpretation. The introduction surveys recent trends in criticism.

Leggatt, Alexander. *King Lear*. Harvester New Critical Introductions. Hemel Hempstead, Hertfordshire, England: Harvester-Wheatsheaf, 1988. Includes a brief discussion of the stage history and critical reception, as well as a thorough discussion of the play's dramatic idiom and characters.

Mack, Maynard. *"King Lear" in Our Time*. Berkeley: University of California Press, 1965. Surveys the play's historical background, sources, and aspects of its staging. Also provides many perceptive critical comments on the action and its significance.

Rosenberg, Marvin. *The Masks of King Lear*. 1972. Reprint. Newark: University of Delaware Press, 1993. Rosenberg examines the significance of each scene and the "polyphony" of the characters, with extensive reference to the history of *King Lear* on the stage as of the earliest recorded performances. Also discusses the so-called Lear myth.

KING SOLOMON'S MINES

Type of work: Novel
Author: H. Rider Haggard (1856-1925)
Type of plot: Adventure
Time of plot: Nineteenth century
Locale: Africa
First published: 1885

> *Principal characters:*
> ALLAN QUATERMAIN, an English explorer
> SIR HENRY CURTIS, his friend
> CAPTAIN JOHN GOOD, Curtis' friend
> UMBOPA, a Zulu, in reality Ignosi, hereditary chieftain of the Kukuanas
> TWALA, the ruler of the Kukuanas
> GAGOOL, a native sorceress

The Story:

Returning to his home in Natal after an unsuccessful elephant hunt, Allan Quatermain met Sir Henry Curtis and his friend, retired Captain John Good, aboard ship. Sir Henry inquired whether Quatermain had met a man named Neville in Bamangwato. Learning that he had, Sir Henry explained that Neville was his younger brother, George, with whom he had quarreled. When Sir Henry inherited his parents' estate, George had taken the name Neville and had gone to Africa to seek his fortune. He had not been heard from since.

Quatermain said that Neville was reported to have headed for King Solomon's Mines, diamond mines reputed to lie far in the interior. Ten years before, he himself had met a Portuguese man, José Silvestre, who had tried unsuccessfully to cross the desert to the mines and had dragged himself into his camp to die. Before he died, José had given him a map showing the location of the treasure. It was written on a piece of a shirt that had belonged to his relative, another José Da Silvestre, three hundred years before. Silvestre had seen the mines but had died in the mountains while trying to return. His servant had brought the map back to his family, and it had been passed down through succeeding generations of the Silvestre family. By the time the ship reached Natal, Quatermain had agreed to help Sir Henry Curtis find his brother.

In Natal, Quatermain got their equipment together, and the trio chose the five men who were to accompany them. Besides the driver and the leader for the oxen that were to pull their cart, they hired three servants: a Hottentot named Ventvogel and two Zulus, Khiva and Umbopa. Umbopa explained that his tribe lived far to the north in the direction in which they were traveling and that he was willing to serve for nothing if he might go with the party. Quatermain was suspicious of the native's offer, but Sir Henry agreed to take Umbopa as his servant.

On the journey from Durban, they lost Khiva when, trying to save Captain Good from attack by a wounded bull elephant, the native was torn in two by the animal. At Sitandra's Kraal at the edge of the desert, the men left all the equipment they could not carry on their backs. Quatermain's plan was to travel at night to avoid the heat of the sun and to sleep during the day. On the third day out, however, the men could find no shelter from the heat. They decided that trekking was more comfortable than trying to rest. They were out of water by the fourth day, but on the following day, Ventvogel discovered a spring. Refreshing themselves, they started off again that night. At the end of the next night, they reached the lower slope of a mountain marked on the map as Sheba's left breast. On the other side of the mountain lay King Solomon's road, which was supposed to lead to the diamond mines.

The climb up the mountain was not an easy one. The higher they ascended, the colder it grew. At the top of the ridge, they found a cave and climbed into it to spend the night. Ventvogel froze to death before morning. Ventvogel was not the only dead man in the cave. When it grew light the next morning, one of the party saw the body of a white man in its rocky recesses. Quatermain decided that it was the body of the first José Silvestre, preserved by the cold.

Leaving the bodies in the cave, the remaining men started down the mountain slope. As the mist cleared, they could distinguish fertile lands and woods below them. Reaching King Solomon's road, they followed it into the valley. The road was a magnificent engineering feat that crossed a ravine and even tunneled through a ridge. In the tunnel, the walls were decorated with figures driving in chariots. Sir Henry declared that the pictures had been painted by ancient Egyptians.

When Quatermain and his party had descended to the valley, they stopped to eat and rest beside a stream. Captain Good undressed to shave and bathe. Suddenly, Quatermain realized that they were being observed by a party of natives. As the leader of the band, an old man, stepped up to speak to them, Quatermain saw that he greatly resembled Umbopa.

If it had not been for Captain Good's peculiarities, the four men would surely have been killed. Luckily, Captain Good's false teeth, bare legs, half-shaven face, and monocle fascinated the savages so that they were willing to believe Quatermain's story that he and his friends had descended from the stars. To make the story more credible, he shot an antelope with what he declared was his magic tube. At Quatermain's insistence, the old man, whose name was Infadoos, agreed to lead the men to Twala, king of the Kukuanas. After a three-day journey, Quatermain and his party reached Loo, where Twala was holding his summer festival. The white men were introduced to the hideous one-eyed giant before an assemblage of eight thousand of his soldiers.

Before Twala's annual witch-hunt began that evening, the four travelers had a conference with Infadoos. They learned from him that Twala and his son, Scragga, were hated for their cruelty. Umbopa then revealed that he was, in reality, Ignosi, son of the rightful king, whom Twala had murdered. On the death of her husband, his mother had fled across the mountains and desert with her child. As proof of his claim, Ignosi displayed a snake that was tattooed around his middle. The snake was the sign of Kukuana kingship.

All the men, including Infadoos, agreed that they would help him overcome Twala and gain the throne. Infadoos declared that he would speak to some of the chiefs after the witch-hunt and win them to Ignosi's cause. He was certain that they could have twenty thousand men in their ranks by the next morning.

That night, Gagool and her sister sorceresses helped Twala search out more than a hundred of his men charged with evil thoughts or plots against their sovereign. When, in their wild dances, one of them stopped before any one of the twenty thousand soldiers who were drawn up in review, the victim was immediately stabbed to death. In her blood thirst, Gagool did not hesitate to stop in front of Ignosi. Quatermain and his friends fired their guns to impress Twala and persuade him that Ignosi's life should be spared.

Infadoos was true to his word. He brought all the chiefs he could muster, and Ignosi again exhibited the tattooing around his waist. The men feared he might be an impostor, however, and asked for a further sign. Captain Good, who knew from his almanac that an eclipse of the sun was due, swore that they would darken the sun the following day.

King Twala continued his festival and had his maidens dance before him the next afternoon.

When they had finished, he asked Quatermain to choose the most beautiful; his custom was to have the loveliest of the dancers slain each year. Foulata was selected, but before she could be killed, the white men interfered on her behalf. As they did so, the sun began to darken. Scragga was mad with fear and threw his spear at Sir Henry, but the Englishman was luckily wearing a mail shirt, a present from Twala. Seizing the weapon, he hurled it back at Scragga and killed him.

Quatermain and his friends, including Infadoos and the girl, took advantage of the eclipse to flee from the town with the chiefs who had rallied to them. Approximately twenty thousand men prepared for battle on a hill about two miles from Loo. Twala's regiments, some thirty thousand soldiers, attacked the next day. They were driven back and then set upon by their enemies who, driving at them from three directions, surrounded and slaughtered many of the Kukuanas. The vanquished Twala was slain in a contest with Sir Henry, who lopped off his head with a battle-ax.

In return for the help that his white friends had given him, the new king, Ignosi, ordered Gagool to lead them to King Solomon's mines, which lay in the mountains at the other end of the great road. Deep into the hills they went, past three enormous figures carved in the rock, images that Quatermain believed might be the three false gods for whom Solomon had gone astray. To reach the treasure room, they had to pass through a cave that Gagool called the Place of Death. There, seated around a table, were all the dead kings of the Kukuanas, petrified by siliceous water dripping upon them.

While the men stood dumbfounded by the sight, Gagool, unobserved, moved a lever that caused a massive stone to rise. On the other side of it were boxes full of diamonds, gold coins, and ivory. As the men stood gloating over the treasure, Gagool crept away. She released a lever to bring down the door, but Foulata caught her before she could escape. Gagool stabbed the girl fatally, but before she could pass under the door, it dropped and crushed her.

For several hours, Quatermain and his friends believed that they were buried alive, for they had no idea where to find the secret of the door. At last, in the dark, they found a lever that disclosed a subterranean passage. Through it, they found their way once more to the outside and to Infadoos, who was waiting for them.

A few weeks later, some of Ignosi's men guided them out of Kukuanaland, across the mountains, and on the first stage of their trip back across the desert. The only treasure they had with them was a handful of diamonds Quatermain had stuffed into his pockets before they found a way out of the treasure room.

Their guides, who knew of a better trail than that by which the travelers had come, led them to an oasis from which they could pass on to other green spots along their way. On their return trip they found a small hut near the bank of a stream. Sir Henry's lost brother, George, was in it. He had been badly injured by a boulder two years before, and had not been able to travel since that time. Quatermain and his friends supported George across the desert to Sitandra's Kraal, and then on to Quatermain's home. According to their agreement before setting out on the expedition, the diamonds were divided. Quatermain and Captain Good each kept a third, and they gave the rest of the stones to George, Sir Henry's brother.

Critical Evaluation:

This story of the search for King Solomon's legendary lost treasure, hidden in the land of the Kukuanas, provides absorbing reading for children and adults alike. The slaughter provoked by the cruelty of King Twala and the character of the ancient sorceress, Gagool, makes *King Solomon's Mines* a book that is not soon forgotten. This, the first great African adventure novel, set the pattern for a host of jungle stories to follow, from Edgar Rice Burroughs' *Tarzan* epics (the first of which was published in 1914) to serious novels such as Joseph Conrad's *Heart of Darkness* (1902) and Saul Bellow's *Henderson the Rain King* (1959).

H. Rider Haggard chooses his heroes for maximum dramatic effect. Allan Quatermain, the narrator, is the thorough professional. He is a moderate, practical, cost-conscious man, courageous when he has to be but quite willing to avoid danger if given the option; he is a firm believer in brain over brawn. Sir Henry Curtis is the more typical hero. Where Quatermain is rational and careful, Curtis is emotional and extravagant. Quatermain is the mechanical expert, especially with guns, but Curtis is most at home with primitive weapons and becomes fearsome in hand-to-hand combat. In short, Curtis is the natural warrior; it is he who kills the one-eyed villain, King Twala.

Captain John Good, the former naval officer, is the one hero who seems out of place in the depths of Africa. He is fastidious and fussy. His personal quirks and unusual accessories, such as his monocle, his false teeth that "snap" into place, his formal attire, and his delicate white legs, provide the necessary comic relief. Late in the novel, however, these humorous details become crucial plot elements when Good's half-shaved face and bare legs are taken as signs of divinity by the hostile natives. Although the characterizations are neither deep nor complex, they are vivid and thoroughly convincing.

Haggard also keeps the plot simple and the language plain, as Quatermain states in offering his "apologies for my blunt way of writing . . . simple things are always the most impressive, and books are easier to understand when they are written in plain language." The plot is organized around the most basic adventure formula—the treasure hunt—and has all the necessary ingredients: a mysterious map; an exotic, even mythic, destination; an unknown, dangerous terrain; and a pair of grotesque, diabolical villains. Haggard carefully develops his story by subjecting his heroes to a series of crises that become progressively more dangerous, more extreme, and more fantastic.

No matter how exotic these adventures become, the author keeps them believable with his matter-of-fact language and his careful, realistic use of detail. Calling upon his own youthful experiences in Africa, Haggard supports every incident with relevant particulars. Quatermain is a thoroughly seasoned professional. He uses the best equipment, detailed accurately, and demonstrates his expertise in dozens of small ways: handling animals, negotiating with natives, organizing and directing their hunts, and supervising the day-to-day safari routine. As the men encounter more unusual environments, Haggard continues to reinforce his narrative with concrete details. The natives' equipment, social and military organizations, tribal customs, and religious rituals are described with precision. Even the most fantastic sequences in the novel— the exploration of Solomon's mines, the discovery of the giant figures and the Place of Death, the search through the treasure room, and the escape through the underground tunnel—are explained minutely and logically by historical speculation, biblical references, and native folklore. Since the novel takes place in an area which was, at the time, as yet unexplored, the book seems "authentic," and many of its first readers even thought that the story was true.

As one of the first and best of the popular modern adventure novelists, Haggard understood the basic rule of escapist fiction: if the imaginative adventure is to succeed, the world the reader escapes to must be as real as the one he lives in, however improbable the particular events may be.

Bibliography:
Butts, Dennis. Introduction and notes to *King Solomon's Mines*, by H. Rider Haggard. New

York: Oxford University Press, 1989. Butts's introduction to the historical background and literary reception of the novel is concise and informative. Notes the novel's familiar structure as a folktale. Bibliography.

Cohen, Morton. *Rider Haggard: His Life and Works*. London: Hutchinson University Library, 1960. Scrupulously documented and judiciously restrained in its appreciation of Haggard as a writer. Provides rich historical context for the composition of *King Solomon's Mines*.

Higgins, D. S. *Rider Haggard: The Great Storyteller*. London: Cassell, 1981. Excellent, accessible biography, with limited literary analysis and thorough historical context and publishing history.

Katz, Wendy R. *Rider Haggard and the Fiction of Empire: A Critical Study of British Imperial Fiction*. Cambridge, England: Cambridge University Press, 1987. Suggests Haggard's considerable cultural significance as an imperial propagandist. Discusses his philosophy of life and commitment to empire through an analysis of *King Solomon's Mines* and other works.

Sandison, Alan. *The Wheel of Empire: A Study of the Imperial Idea in Some Late Nineteenth and Early Twentieth-Century Writers*. London: Macmillan, 1967. A provocative chapter on the intellectual foundations laid down by Charles Darwin, Georg Wilhelm Friedrich Hegel, and Karl Marx, leads to the assertion that Haggard adapted to modern thought more readily than did Rudyard Kipling, Joseph Conrad, or John Buchan. Thus he escaped the vice of racial prejudice so prevalent among writers on empire.

THE KING, THE GREATEST ALCALDE

Type of work: Drama
Author: Lope de Vega Carpio (1562-1635)
Type of plot: Tragicomedy
Time of plot: Sixteenth century
Locale: Spain
First published: El mejor alcalde, el rey, 1635 (English translation, 1918)

> *Principal characters:*
> SANCHO, a poor laborer
> NUNO, a farmer
> ELVIRA, his daughter
> DON TELLO DE NEIRA, a nobleman
> FELICIANA, his sister
> PELAYO, a swineherd
> DON ALFONSO VII, the king of Leon and Castile

The Story:

Sancho, a poor peasant, was in love with an equally poor girl, Elvira, the daughter of a farmer named Nuno. When the old man gave Sancho permission to wed his daughter, he insisted that Sancho also secure the consent of Don Tello, master of all the surrounding lands, and of Don Tello's sister, Feliciana. In obedience to Nuno, Sancho went with Pelayo, a swineherd, to the castle to ask his lord's approval of the marriage. Both Don Tello and his sister Feliciana readily gave their consent and their blessing, and they declared that they themselves would attend the wedding.

When Don Tello saw the beautiful Elvira, however, he was filled with such passion for her that he decided to postpone the wedding and take Elvira to satisfy his own lust before giving her to Sancho for his wife. Dismissing the priest, he told the assembled guests that the wedding must wait until the next day. Sancho and Elvira felt themselves already married, however, since the priest had heard them declare their true love for each other, and Sancho planned to go to Elvira's room that night. When Elvira opened her door, she confronted not her lover but Don Tello and his attendants, all masked, who carried her off to the castle.

Sancho and Nuno, learning of this betrayal, were ready to die. Nuno cautioned Sancho not to despair, however, for he knew his daughter would die rather than lose her honor. Nuno knew his daughter well. Although Don Tello pleaded with her and threatened her, she would not give herself to him. Feliciana begged him to remember his good name and his honor and not to force the girl.

Sancho and Nuno, going to Don Tello, pretended that they had heard but could not believe that he had stolen Elvira away. Don Tello pretended also that he was outraged at such a story and would have whipped those who told such lies to defame his honor. Yet when Elvira entered the room, Don Tello flew into a rage and ordered Sancho and Nuno beaten to death. They fled for their lives. Don Tello vowed that he would force Elvira to submit to him or be killed. Again Sancho wanted to die, but once more Nuno persuaded him that there was still hope. He sent Sancho and Pelayo to the court of Alfonso, the king of Castile, for the king was a good man and well known for his justice in dealing with high and low alike.

When the king heard Sancho's story, he immediately wrote a letter to Don Tello, ordering him to release Elvira at once. Don Tello ignored the letter and declared that on his own land his people would do only his will. Pelayo assured Sancho that Don Tello had not yet possessed Elvira, for he would have obeyed the king had his lust been satisfied. Sancho and Pelayo went again to the king, to tell him that Don Tello had not obeyed his orders. The king promised to go in person to Don Tello and force him to return Elvira to her father and husband-to-be. He intended to go in disguise, taking with him only two attendants.

Don Tello, filled with wild rage and passion at Elvira's refusal to accept him, swore that he would take her by force. Nuno spoke with her through the bars of the room where she was confined and told her that Sancho had gone for help, and she promised again to die rather than lose her virtue. When Sancho and Pelayo returned with word that the king was sending help, Nuno was not much encouraged, for he knew that Don Tello kept his castle well guarded and could not be overcome by only three men. What Nuno did not know was that the king himself was coming, though Pelayo was hard put to it to keep the secret.

When King Alfonso arrived, he questioned Nuno's servants and was convinced that Sancho and Nuno told the truth. Then he went in disguise to Don Tello's castle. There he was rudely received by that haughty nobleman. At last the king revealed himself and ordered Elvira brought before him. Elvira told the king of her pure love for Sancho, of having obtained her father's and Don Tello's permission, of her seizure by Don Tello and his men, and, finally, of her lost honor. Don Tello had carried out his vow. He had ordered her taken into a wood and there, even though she fought until she was weak, he had ravished her. She declared that she could never know joy again, for her honor was lost forever.

The king ordered Don Tello beheaded, both for his treatment of the innocent girl and for his failure to obey the king's command sent in his earlier letter. Although Feliciana pleaded for her brother, the king refused to be moved by her tears. Don Tello confessed that he deserved the penalty, for he had sinned twice, against his own honor and against the king. Then the king pronounced his final sentence. He would wed Elvira to Don Tello, then execute him. As his widow Elvira would inherit half his lands and gold. These would be her dowry when she married Sancho. Feliciana he would take to court, to wait on the queen until a noble husband could be secured for her. The peasants blessed the king's wisdom and actions for he had righted their wrongs as far as was humanly possibly.

Critical Evaluation:

The King, the Greatest Alcalde, which Lope de Vega Carpio wrote in 1620-1623, belongs, along with the earlier *Fuenteovejuna*, written 1611-1618, to the best work of one of the most remarkable literary men of all time. Like Samuel Johnson, Lord Byron, and the composer Franz Liszt, Vega Carpio is as much of a "personality" as he is an artist. Born of humble parents, he became a soldier, a sailor in the Spanish Armada (taking part in the ill-fated expedition of 1588), a duelist, an exile, a lover of innumerable ladies and the husband of two, a priest of passionate if temporary convictions, an arbiter of the theater, and reputedly the writer of about eighteen hundred plays and other dramatic works, less than a third of which have survived. A contemporary of William Shakespeare, he has often been compared to the English bard for his breadth of vision, his vitality, his role in the creation of a national theater, and the similar innyard-type theater (the *corral*) for which he wrote. As was perhaps inevitable for such a prolific dramatist, however, his artistry falls short of Shakespeare's. It cannot be said of his role in Spanish dramaturgy, as Johnson said of John Dryden's influence on English poetry, that he found it brick and left it marble; perhaps, however, it can be said that he found it sand and left it brick.

Vega Carpio wrote with a disdain for classical precedent and an open appeal for popular approval. "When I set out to write a play," he observed, "I lock up all the rules under ten keys, and banish Plautus and Terence from my study. . . . For I write in the style of those who seek the applause of the public, whom it is but just to humor in their folly, since it is they who pay for it." The Spaniards called him "monstruo de la naturaleza" or "the freak of nature," for his plays have the vices of their virtues: Bubbling with inventiveness, energy, and variety, they are also often careless in their construction, shallow in their characterization, and uneven in their poetic power.

The King, the Greatest Alcalde exhibits both the virtues and the vices and exemplifies Vega Carpio's dramatic outlook. The play, a tragicomedy, is a mixture of love story and realism. Sancho and Elvira are closely related to the Corydons and the Phyllises of pastoral tales in their rustic, idealized love for each other and in the miseries they must endure before they are finally reunited. They are, however, observed with a realism, as well as a pessimism, that takes due note of the branding power of evil in the world. "There is no interest beneath the sun by which an honest woman may be won," Feliciana assures Don Tello, underestimating the savage determination of her brother. In the standard pastoral tale, the honest woman would remain chaste to the end, despite all temptations and menaces, but Vega Carpio realizes that life is not like that, and Elvira is raped before the king can restore her to Sancho. The primary interest of the play, however, is Vega Carpio's treatment of social forces, especially the interaction among the peasants, the feudal lord Don Tello, and the king.

In *The King, the Greatest Alcalde*, Vega Carpio reveals an unalloyed admiration for the peasant class unlike that in any other dramas of the time, including Shakespeare's. In the twentieth century, Marxist critics seized on such plays as this one and *Fuenteovejuna* as examples of Vega Carpio's "proletariat" theater, which portrays an oppressed and hearty peasantry struggling against a corrupt and depraved aristocracy. There certainly is a discernible tendency toward idealization of the peasants. Sancho's opening paean to nature, and his elevated sentiments throughout mark him as a noble character indeed, far more noble, certainly, than the outwardly refined Don Tello. Sancho himself feels that "in the passion of the heart" he is a lord, and the king is highly impressed with Sancho's eloquence. Just as important, the king is taken with the honest and open nature of the peasants whom he questions about Don Tello's villainy: "The guilelessness of these folk is the most convincing proof," he remarks.

Lords like Don Tello were intermediate in the social structure between the peasants and the king (Vega Carpio gives virtually no hints of a middle class). Spain, in this period, was still in transition between a feudal and a national governmental structure, and Don Tello makes a fatal miscalculation as to how much power he retains in the new structure. Traditionally, the peasants living within the province of a lord were subject to his absolute authority in all matters of daily life (such as marriage). "You serve Don Tello in his flocks, who rears his powers over these lands, and is supreme through all Galicia," Nuno tells Sancho. Apparently, Don Tello's permission to marry is no longer strictly required, though Nuno strongly advises his future son-in-law to ask for permission anyway in the hope of receiving a generous gift. Don Tello can indeed be generous when he is in the mood, but he is also arrogantly proud of his undisputed authority. Living quite distant from the king, he accepts no remote challenges to his authority. Even when presented with a direct order in writing from the king he asserts his independence: "I reign here and here I do my will as the king does his in Castille. My forebears never owed land to him—they won it from the Moors." Only when the king personally appears before Don Tello does the once haughty lord crumble and acknowledge his higher authority.

The king himself is presented as the only recourse, this side of God, for the injustices heaped on the peasants. From the outset, he is their special friend. As one of Don Tello's courtiers warns him, "Alfonso was reared in Galicia . . . and for that reason they say he will never close his door to any Gallegan, though never so humble his birth." Indeed, the first view of the king reveals him asking his own courtiers whether there are any suppliants waiting with appeals to him; as he confesses, he is unable to resist the poor. As an indication of his lack of pretentiousness, Alfonso (unlike Don Tello) is unostentatiously dressed; when Sancho is first admitted he must ask a lord which person is the king. Yet this unpretentiousness does not in the least diminish the king's real importance and power, for he is nothing less than God's regent on earth. His face, Sancho declares to him, is the "Image of God," and "you reflect his glory!" Later, a humbled Don Tello admits that he has "offended God—God and the King!"

The motif of the king in disguise is a fairly common theatrical and literary device with high dramatic potential (Sir Walter Scott uses a disguised Richard the Lion-Hearted in his 1819 novel *Ivanhoe* to great effect, for example). Vega Carpio uses it not only for its suspense value but also as an emblem of his attitude toward the king. When Alfonso tells Sancho that he intends to intervene personally in the matter, disguised as an alcalde, or justice of the peace, the youth fears that the king is humbling himself by concerning himself so much with a peasant's honor, and he urges instead that the king simply dispatch an alcalde to the scene. Alfonso, however, conscious of his judicial as well as his executive role, replies, "The King, the greatest Alcalde!"

It must be noted that this play is not free from the flaws that mar the playwright's other, less important work. The poetry often sags, and the lyrical passages, apart from the fact that they sound faintly incongruous in the mouths of Sancho and Elvira, often become artificial and declamatory. There are, moreover, inconsistencies of characterization. Don Tello's passionate desire for Elvira is condemned by her as mere lust, yet at the opening of the play Sancho tells us repeatedly that his own love for Elvira is based entirely on her physical beauty and is, in fact, in direct proportion to it: "May your beauty grow, so that in me may grow the love I bear!" Vega Carpio's hasty writing also betrays itself in careless construction, as when Elvira, in the final scene of the play, declares that she has been taken out to a wood "a fourth league removed" and raped; yet only one scene earlier she was still untouched and still fleeing from Don Tello.

These flaws may be among the reasons why the plays of Vega Carpio are seldom performed outside his own country. Without question, however, he is an important and influential play-wright. The dramatic vitality and skillful inventiveness of his plays, despite their frequent lapses, make for exciting reading and playing. He was to influence such other, more highly regarded dramatists as Jean Racine and Molière, as is seen in the kingly intervention in *Tartuffe* (1664). Vega Carpio's concern with the social importance and dignity of the peasant, who had been conventionally represented in drama as a fool or a clown (such as Pelayo), marks his plays, thematically, as far ahead of their time.

"Critical Evaluation" by Laurence Behrens

Bibliography:
Chandler, Richard E., and Kessel Schwartz. *A New History of Spanish Literature.* Baton Rouge: Louisiana State University Press, 1961. An excellent survey of the development of Spanish drama. Provides a helpful explanation of Vega Carpio's art.
Hays, Francis C. *Lope de Vega.* New York: Twayne, 1967. Acquaints English-speaking readers with the life, career, and the new dramatic art of Vega Carpio's comedies. Contains an effective formula for comprehending the elements of Vega Carpio's comedies.
Northup, George Tyler. *An Introduction to Spanish Literature.* 3d rev. ed. Chicago: University of Chicago Press, 1960. A helpful presentation of the Spanish *comedia.* Includes a chapter devoted to Vega Carpio and his dramatic school.

Peers, Edgar Allison. *Spanish Golden Age Poetry and Drama*. Liverpool: Institute of Hispanic Studies, 1946. Chapter 2 discusses the role of the Spanish peasant in Vega Carpio's *The King, the Greatest Alcalde*.

Vega Carpio, Lope de. *Four Plays by Lope de Vega*. Translated by John Garrett Underhill. Westport, Conn.: Hyperion Press, 1978. Contains an English translation of *The King, the Greatest Alcalde* that is mainly in verse. The volume has an introduction and critical essay by Jacinto Benavente.

KISS OF THE SPIDER WOMAN

Type of work: Novel
Author: Manuel Puig (1932-1990)
Type of plot: Social realism
Time of plot: 1975
Locale: Argentina
First published: El beso de la mujer araña, 1976 (English translation, 1979)

>   *Principal characters:*
>   MOLINA (LUIS ALBERTO MOLINO), a gay prisoner
>   VALENTÍN ARREGUI PAZ, a political prisoner
>   MARTA, Valentín's girlfriend

The Story:

Molina, an effeminate gay windowdresser in Argentina, was growing discontented with the frivolous life he was leading with his friends; he wanted a lifelong partner. He became friends with a heterosexual waiter named Gabriel, who was married, but he knew the relationship would not lead to a romantic attachment. When he was arrested on charges of corrupting a minor, he was sentenced to eight years in prison without the possibility of parole.

Valentín was a journalism student who was in love with Marta, a beautiful and well-educated member of the upper class in Argentina. He was also secretly a member of the underground movement that sought to overthrow the corrupt and oppressive military regime of the country. When he told Marta of his involvement, she forced him to choose between her and the movement. Even though he loved Marta, he felt he had a responsibility to stand up to injustice and left her. In the movement, he had another girlfriend, named Lidia.

Valentín was never as deeply involved as were many in the political rebellion, but he did agree to help Dr. Americo escape the country by giving him his own passport. Americo was one of the oldest living members of an earlier movement for true democracy. At the airport after making the exchange, Valentín was arrested. He was put in Molina's cell.

At first, Valentín despised Molina. He thought his effeminacy was a disgusting display of irresponsibility in the face of the sacrifices his friends in the movement were willing to make. Nevertheless, he did find Molina at least entertaining. Molina's great talent was in telling stories, especially the tales he remembered from romantic films.

The film that Molina liked the most was a story set in Paris during World War II. Leni, a French chanteuse, learned that Michelle, the cigarette girl in her club, although a member of the French underground movement against the Germans, had fallen in love with a German soldier, by whom she was pregnant. Perhaps to help Michelle, or perhaps because of her own growing interest, Leni decided to accept the offer of Werner, the German officer in charge of counterintelligence, and visited his chateau. Meanwhile, thugs in the French underground learned of Michelle's betrayal and killed her. Then they sought to coerce Leni to take Michelle's place and to obtain the map to the German arsenal. When Leni learned of the German atrocities, she agreed to help. However, Werner convinced her that the Germans were really seeking to release the masses from the control of the elite in society, and she ended up killing the head of the French underground. She was then shot and died in Werner's arms, singing.

Though he was entertained, Valentín denounced the film as Nazi propaganda. Molina protested that life itself was painful and must be filled with dreams. When Valentín insisted, over his protests, that Molina take the larger helping of food, Molina became ill and went to the infirmary. When he returned, he continued telling film stories, and the two men became closer. They continued to argue over what it meant to be a man and over the possibilities for change in the world.

Molina recounted another film, this time a horror film with romantic overtones. People were becoming zombies. The beautiful heroine learned that her husband's first wife, who was now trying to help her escape, was a zombie, too. Molina's telling of the story was confused, and he mixed up many details.

Molina was called to see the warden, who reminded him that Molina's mother was quite ill and that he would be released sooner if he got Valentín to reveal secrets about the revolutionaries. Molina went back to the cell with several bags of wonderful food, supposedly a gift from his mother. Next it was Valentín's turn to become sick from the prison food, which had been poisoned both times, and he got terrible diarrhea. He was mortified and amazed when Molina cleaned him without complaint.

A new prisoner was brought into the cell across from them, and Valentín revealed that the new inmate was the Dr. Americo he had tried to help. The warden complained that Molina was not getting enough information, so Molina suggested that he be released in the hope that Valentín, who by now liked him, would suddenly reveal more. The warden agreed.

That evening Molina told a new story about a beautiful woman on a tropical island who was ensnared in a web that grew from her own body. She nursed back to health a shipwrecked man, who then saw a tear streaming down her face. The two men had an important conversation in which Molina revealed that he had fallen in love with Valentín. Valentín, in turn, showed that he had grown to respect Molina and to recognize his kindness. On this last evening of Molina's confinement, they had sexual relations.

The next morning, Valentín told Molina how to contact his revolutionary friends and asked him to pass along a message. Molina was frightened, but he decided to take this bold step. On the outside, he was reunited with his friends, who called him Luisa, and with his long-suffering mother. After a few days, he contacted Lidia and a meeting was arranged. Molina was followed by the police, however, and the revolutionaries killed him when they thought he had betrayed them.

In prison, Valentín was once again tortured, this time so severely that he was taken to the infirmary. A sympathetic nurse gave him a large shot of morphine, and Valentín slipped into a dream that combined his own memories of Marta with Molina's memories of romantic movies.

Critical Evaluation:

Made into a stage play, a Hollywood feature film, and a very successful Broadway musical, this novel is Manuel Puig's most famous. Some would say that it is also his most accomplished, using all his characteristic techniques in a way that remains accessible to the ordinary reader and coupling them with themes that are the closest to the author's heart.

Manuel Puig was born in rural Argentina in 1932 and attended the University of Buenos Aires and film school. In 1956, he moved to London and then Rome, where he worked as an assistant film director. He returned to Buenos Aires and worked as a director for a year but then moved to New York, where he took up permanent residence. His novels reflect his early life in the rural countryside, where he spent most of his time watching films made during the 1930's and 1940's. His experience with the simple people with whom he matured shaped the sorts of characters he includes in his novels. His studies and his travels, however, prepared him for the sophisticated techniques and daring themes that make his writing stand out in contemporary literature.

Kiss of the Spider Woman is a story without a narrator, and much of it reads like a movie script without definite indications of who is speaking. The variety of types of discourse is part of Puig's charm as a writer, and *Kiss of the Spider Woman* includes dream sequences, remembrances of film clips, official police reports, snatches of letters, interviews, and, most strangely, interminable footnotes. The effect is to force the reader to become involved in the act of creation, as if Molina were there recounting a story for the reader to visualize. In reading the novel, one is actually having an experience similar to that of the characters; one is lifted out of the chair and taken to many imaginary places. Using such metafictional techniques, Puig thus calls attention to the book as a product, as something put together by a real person.

Of more importance, however, are the novel's themes, which were so disturbing to the Argentine government that the book was banned until the military government was overthrown. Puig himself had more hope for influencing relations between individuals than for changing society itself, but in this novel he makes an attempt to marry the two. Molina, as a gay male in Argentina, has always been an outcast in society. To compensate for that exclusion from the world of significance, he and his friends have lived their lives in romantic illusion. Valentín, on the other hand, has dedicated himself to the Marxist ideal of a classless society. In pursuit of that goal, the needs of any one individual are seen as less important than those of the larger, anonymous group. In their cell, the two men must find some accommodation for these two conflicting approaches to life. Valentín comes to accept a broader definition of masculinity, and Molina learns that he can assume responsibility for changing an unjust society.

Although Puig's treatment of this topic is unique, especially within South American literature, he has been criticized by members of the homosexual community for choosing a stereotypically effeminate spokesperson for the gay male. He has also been criticized by various feminists for the stereotypical, and practically invisible, role that women play in the novel. However, Puig includes much information that educates the reader on the challenges faced by the homosexual community. As a gay man himself, Puig has said that he included the controversial footnotes, which offer an abbreviated history of psychoanalytic interpretations of the meaning of homosexuality, to bring the information to the attention of a large reading public that might not otherwise have given it much consideration. By concluding that supposed history with an unknown psychiatrist, Puig more or less puts himself in the picture and speaks through that "character." Significantly, this last speaker seems to lay the groundwork for the sort of political action that Molina ultimately decides to undertake.

On the structural level, the scientific footnotes distance the reader from the story and offer a reminder that the entertainment being provided, much like the films that Molina recounts, will ultimately dissolve into thin air. The problems that the story depicts, however, will not. The reader is also reminded that there are different types of truth, just as there are the various types of discourse embodied in the book. There is the supposedly objective truth of science and the more inclusive truth that can be adequately explored only in art.

John C. Hawley

Bibliography:
Boccia, Michael. "Versions (Con-, In-, and Per-) in Manuel Puig's and Hector Babenco's *Kiss of the Spider Woman*, Novel and Film." *Modern Fiction Studies* 32, no. 3 (1986): 417-426. Discusses Puig's fascination with film and the history of the novel's development as it went from book to screen. Notes how the plot turns on an inversion of the relationship of the two men.

Echavarrén, Roberto. "Manuel Puig: Beyond Identity." *World Literature Today* 65, no. 4 (1991): 581-585. Discusses the novel as Puig's most radical effort at gay liberation. Surrounded by other fascinating articles celebrating the author's life and works.

Rice-Sayre, Laura. "Domination and Desire: A Feminist-Materialist Reading of Manuel Puig's *Kiss of the Spider Woman*." In *Textual Analysis: Some Readers Reading*, edited by Mary Ann Caws. New York: Modern Language Association of America, 1986. Demonstrates how the novel explores the connections among emotion, politics, and sexuality. Notes how Puig condemns society as based upon aggression and humiliation, and proposes a respect for difference.

Stavans, Ilan, ed. "Manuel Puig." *Review of Contemporary Fiction* 11, no. 3 (1991): 159-259. This special edition of the journal, on the occasion of the novelist's early death, contains interesting tributes from other writers and provocative articles that describe this novel as unique among prison literature.

Tittler, Jonathan. *Manuel Puig*. New York: Twayne, 1993. Provides an excellent account of the writing of the novel, summarizes its plot, and discusses critical responses to it. Situates the book among the novelist's other works and describes it as his most complete, addressing his principal issues in the most satisfying way.

THE KNIGHT OF THE BURNING PESTLE

Type of work: Drama
Author: Francis Beaumont (c. 1584-1616)
Type of plot: Comedy
Time of plot: Early seventeenth century
Locale: England and Moldavia
First performed: 1607; first published, 1613

> Principal characters:
> GEORGE, a London greengrocer
> NELL, his wife
> RALPH, an apprentice to George
> VENTUREWELL, a London merchant
> JASPER MERRYTHOUGHT, his apprentice
> MASTER HUMPHREY, a slow-witted youth
> LUCE, Venturewell's daughter
> MERRYTHOUGHT, a carefree old gentleman

The Story:

A production in a London theater was abruptly interrupted when George, a greengrocer, declared that he wanted to see a new kind of play, one in which the common man of London was glorified. Sitting beside him in the audience, George's wife, Nell, further suggested that there be a grocer in the play and that he kill a lion with a pestle. The indulgent speaker of the prologue agreed to these demands after George had offered his own apprentice, Ralph, to play the part of the commoner-hero. So the play began.

For presuming to love Luce Venturewell, the daughter of his master, apprentice Jasper Merrythought was discharged. Old Venturewell had chosen Master Humphrey, a foolish young citizen, for his daughter, but Luce, in league with Jasper, told the gullible Humphrey that to win her love he must abduct her and take her to Waltham Forest, where she planned to meet Jasper. In the audience, Nell, the grocer's wife, commented that Humphrey was a fine young man.

In a grocer's shop, Ralph read a chivalric romance and, yearning for the olden times, determined himself to become a knight-errant. He enlisted his two apprentices, Tim and George, to be his foils: the one, his squire, the other, his dwarf. Dubbing himself The Knight of the Burning Pestle, Ralph explained the rules of knight-errantry to his amused followers. Nell, pleased with Ralph's first appearance on the stage, clamored for his immediate return.

Jasper went home and collected his patrimony—all of ten shillings—from his indigent but carefree father, old Merrythought. Mrs. Merrythought, sick of hard times, packed her few valuables into a small chest and, with her younger son, Michael, left home to seek a better fortune. In the pit, George and Nell grew impatient for the reappearance of Ralph, their prodigious apprentice. Simple-minded Humphrey told old Venturewell of Luce's whimsical conditions for their marriage, and the old man consented to the plan. Mrs. Merrythought and Michael, traveling afoot, arrived in Waltham Forest. While resting, they grew frightened and ran away when Ralph, as the Knight of the Burning Pestle, appeared with his retainers. George and Nell, from their places at the edge of the stage, shouted a welcome to Ralph. Ralph, assuming that Mrs. Merrythought had fled from some evil knight, followed her in order to rescue her from her distress. Jasper, arriving in the forest to meet Luce, picked up the casket containing Mrs. Merrythought's valuables. Nell, scandalized, declared that she would tell Ralph what Jasper had done. When Mrs. Merrythought reported her loss to Ralph, he, in extravagantly courteous language, promised to assist her in regaining her valuables. George and Nell commended themselves for having trained such a polite and virtuous apprentice.

Humphrey and Luce came also to the forest, where they found Jasper waiting. Jasper, after thrashing Humphrey soundly, departed with Luce. George and Nell, sorry for Humphrey, offered to call back Ralph to fight Jasper. The protests of the theater boy notwithstanding, the grocer and his wife wanted to change the plot to see Jasper properly punished. Ralph immediately abandoned his search for Mrs. Merrythought's valuables and set out after the runaways. Overtaking them, he challenged Jasper in the language of knight-errantry. Nell, at this juncture, exhorted Ralph to break Jasper's head. Jasper, taking Ralph's pestle from him, knocked down the Knight of the Burning Pestle. George tried to explain Ralph's defeat by saying that Jasper was endowed with magical powers.

Ralph, his retainers, Mrs. Merrythought, and Michael put up for the night at the Bell Inn in Waltham. When they mistook the inn for a castle, the innkeeper indulgently joined them in their make believe. Humphrey, meanwhile, had returned to old Venturewell, to whom he complained of his treatment at the hands of Jasper. Irate, Venturewell went to old Merrythought and threatened to kill Jasper. George and Nell at this point were so taken with the plot of the play that they believed it to be real. Old Merrythought, carefree as usual, paid no heed to Venturewell's vengeful threats. That night, while Luce was asleep in Waltham Forest, Jasper decided to test her love for him. Drawing his sword, he aroused the girl with threats that he intended to kill her because her father had discharged him. Nell excitedly urged George to raise the London watch, to prevent what appeared to her to be certain violence. As Luce trustingly submitted to Jasper's threats, Venturewell, Humphrey, and their men appeared and rescued her. Jasper, hopeful that he might somehow explain his behavior to Luce, followed them.

Next morning, at the Bell Inn, Ralph, unable to pay the reckoning, was threatened by the landlord. George gave Ralph twelve shillings so that he could pay. Mrs. Merrythought and Michael, disenchanted, went home. Ralph, still in search of romantic adventure, was directed by the innkeeper to a barbershop in the town, where, he said, a giant named Barbaroso committed enormities every day. At this point Mrs. Merrythought returned to the stage, only to be dragged off by George and Nell, who could not wait to see Ralph's fight with the barber.

Ralph, after challenging the barber to mortal combat, knocked him down. While he begged for mercy, Ralph directed his retainers to liberate the barber's victims. One was a knight whose face was covered with lather. Another was a man on whom the barber had done minor surgery. As other victims appeared, the barber was spared on the condition that he no longer subject humans to such indignities. George and Nell beamed with pride at Ralph's conquest of the giant Barbaroso, and Nell allowed Mrs. Merrythought and Michael to appear on the stage.

Mrs. Merrythought despaired because she was unable to get old Merrythought to have a serious thought. Nell, furious at the old man's carefree indifference, ordered a beer to calm her temper. Then the action of the play became somewhat too pedestrian for the tastes of George and Nell. The couple next requested that Ralph be involved in a truly exotic adventure. Ralph suddenly found himself an honored guest at the court of Moldavia. Courteously rejecting Princess Pompiana's favors, he declared that he was promised to Susan, the daughter of a cobbler in London. George gave Ralph a handful of small coins to distribute as largess to the royal household. Nell commended Ralph's loyalty and patriotism in preferring a London girl to a princess of a foreign land.

Luce, meanwhile, was confined to her room with the prospect of marriage to Humphrey in three days' time. Mrs. Merrythought sought aid, unsuccessfully, from old Venturewell. Venturewell received a letter of repentance from Jasper, allegedly written by the youth as he lay dying of a broken heart, with the request that his body be conveyed to Luce. Hard upon the letter came a coffin, which was carried to Luce's room. Jasper, quite alive, sprang from the coffin, made explanations to Luce, placed her in the coffin, and had it removed from the room. He hid in the closet. Venturewell, still vengeful, ordered the coffin to be delivered to old Merrythought, who by that time was penniless, although still merry. George, no respecter of plot, demanded that Ralph appear again. Ralph, in the guise of Maylord, presented the month of May to the city of London.

Jasper, meanwhile, covered his face with flour and, appearing as a ghost, told old Venturewell that he would never see his daughter again. Thoroughly frightened and repentant of his past actions, the old man thrashed Humphrey, who had come to see Luce, and sent him away. George and Nell, their interest flagging, demanded diversion in which Ralph would be the center of attention. Ralph appeared as a highly efficient captain leading a parade of London volunteers.

The coffin containing Luce was delivered to old Merrythought, who continued to be indifferent. When Jasper appeared and revealed Luce's presence, the young people prevailed upon old Merrythought to take back Mrs. Merrythought and Michael. Venturewell, still mindful of Jasper's ghost, told old Merrythought that he forgave all Jasper's transgressions. Jasper and Luce then confronted Venturewell, who offered them his blessings. George and Nell, unaware of dramatic proprieties, asked for the stage death of Ralph so that the play could end properly. Ralph, with a forked arrow through his head, delivered an absurd speech about Princess Pompiana and Susan. Highly pleased with the sad ending, Nell invited the audience to partake of tobacco and wine at her house.

Critical Evaluation:

Francis Beaumont, the son of a knight, could well have been cruel in a dramatic treatment of the ordinary citizens of London, but in *The Knight of the Burning Pestle*, he reveals, beneath the hilarious burlesque of the plot, a warm sympathy for and a large understanding of the London lower middle classes, as represented by George, the greengrocer, his wife Nell, and Ralph, their apprentice. An outstanding feature of the play is the farcical audience participation. This device, a startling innovation in 1607, survives to the present day in semidramatic situations of broad humor. *The Knight of the Burning Pestle* was probably written under the influence of the keen interest taken by the literate of James I's time in Spanish prose fiction; surely Beaumont had heard of, if he had not read, Miguel de Cervantes' *Don Quixote de la Mancha* (1605), echoes of which mark the play.

The prologue to the 1635 Beaumont and Fletcher Folio reprint of *The Knight of the Burning Pestle* makes clear that Beaumont's comedy was innovative when it was first presented about 1607. At that time the theatergoers' rage was all for satires full of "invective . . . touching some particular persons." So the mock-heroic play, with its parody of romantic bombast and its war treatment of the London lower middle class enjoyed little success until it was revived about 1635; then the aristocratic court audience delighted in its wordplay, wit, and ingenious construction. *The Knight of the Burning Pestle* has really three plots cleverly unified in one: a frame-story concerning George the grocer, his outspoken wife Nell, and his cloddish apprentice Ralph; a mock-romantic play, *The London Merchant*, which parodies stock conventions and concerns Jasper Merrythought, the witty apprentice who loves Luce, Venturewell's comely daughter; and finally a parody of chivalric romances, featuring the apprentice Ralph, now cast as "the right courteous and valiant knight," whose actions travesty the heroic traditions.

As Knight of the Burning Pestle, Ralph utters archaic, confused, hyperbolic language as he goes about his business of knight-errantry. Instead of performing brave, wonderful deeds, he confronts a monster who is in reality a barber; instead of being a noble warrior, he is in reality a grocer's boy who is faithful to his profession; instead of marrying a beautiful princess, he remains faithful to his cobbler's maid, Susan. Finally, instead of succeeding in the end, he dies; indeed, he does not even die on stage, but walks off with a forked arrow through his head.

Thus the play successfully parodies the whole gamut of romantic and heroic conventions. In addition to Ralph's misadventures, other stock elements of the theater are employed in satirical jest. Jasper and Humphrey are the traditional "rival wooers"; Jasper and Michael are the "double sons." George and Nell consistently support the wrong lover, as they display their lack of artistic sense. Venturewell, the rich London merchant, portrays the typical protective father-figure, just as Luce is the typical independent-minded daughter. Yet Beaumont's parody of stock theatrical situations and personalities never descends to the level of insult. His intent is to "move inward delight, not outward lightness . . . soft smiling, not loud laughing." Despite this modest disclaimer, *The Knight of the Burning Pestle* is Beaumont's most amusing, inventive comedy.

Bibliography:
Appleton, William E. *Beaumont and Fletcher: A Critical Study*. Winchester, Mass.: Allen & Unwin, 1956. Discusses the play as a brilliant burlesque whose humaneness makes it unique. Attributes its initial failure on the stage to Beaumont's misjudging his audience.
Beaumont, Francis. *The Knight of the Burning Pestle*. Edited by Sheldon P. Zitner. Manchester, England: Manchester University Press, 1984. A scholarly edition whose lengthy introduction includes a detailed commentary and a review of the play's stage history. Discusses the play's antecedents and innovations.
Bradbrook, Muriel C. *The Growth and Structure of Elizabethan Comedy*. London: Chatto & Windus, 1962. A classic study of comic drama from its beginnings at mid-century to 1616, when William Shakespeare died. Many references to Beaumont place his works in the thematic and structural context of the period.
Doebler, John. "Beaumont's *The Knight of the Burning Pestle* and the Prodigal Son Plays." *Studies in English Literature, 1500-1990* 5 (1965): 333-344. An analysis of a key element in the play, showing how Beaumont includes most traditional prodigal son characteristics but not in the same way that his predecessors did.
Greenfield, Thelma N. *The Induction in Elizabethan Drama*. Eugene: University of Oregon Books, 1969. A study of the frame, or play within a play, device in drama of the period. Believes that in *The Knight of the Burning Pestle* Beaumont demonstrates the most success-ful use of the technique, particularly as a means of character development.

THE KNIGHTS

Type of work: Drama
Author: Aristophanes (c. 450-c. 385 B.C.E.)
Type of plot: Satire
Time of plot: Fifth century B.C.E.
Locale: Athens
First performed: Hippēs, 424 B.C.E. (English translation, 1812)

> *Principal characters:*
> DEMUS, a slave master, a personification of the Athenian people
> DEMOSTHENES, slave of Demus
> NICIAS, another slave
> CLEON THE PAPHLAGONIAN, a favorite slave and a personification
>   of the Athenian tyrant Cleon
> A SAUSAGE SELLER, later called Agoracritus

The Story:

Demus, a selfish and irritable old man, a tyrant to his slaves, had purchased a tanner, who was nicknamed the Paphlagonian. This slave, a fawning, foxy fellow, quickly ingratiated himself with his new master, to the dismay of all the other slaves in Demus' household, Demosthenes and Nicias in particular. As a result of the Paphlagonian's lies, Demosthenes and Nicias received many floggings. The two at one time considered running away, but decided against this course because of the terrible punishment they would receive if caught and returned to their owner. They also considered suicide, but in the end they decided to forget their troubles by tippling. Going for the wine, Nicias found the Paphlagonian asleep in a drunken stupor.

While the drunken man slept, Nicias stole the writings of the sacred oracle that the Paphlagonian guarded carefully. In the prophecies of the oracle, Demosthenes and Nicias read that an oakum seller should first manage the state's affairs; he should be followed by a sheep seller, and he in turn should be followed by a tanner. At last the tanner would be overthrown by a sausage seller.

As they were about to set out in search of a sausage seller, a slave of that butcher's trade came to the house of Demus to sell his wares. Nicias and Demosthenes soon won him over to their cause, flattering him out of all reason and assuring him that his stupidity and ignorance fitted him admirably for public life. When the Paphlagonian awoke, he loudly demanded the return of the oracle's writings. The sausage seller, however, was able to fight him with success. Spectators became involved. Some of the citizens protested against the Paphlagonian's unjust accusations of the sausage seller. Others claimed that the state was falling into ruin while this shameless name-calling continued. Others accused the Paphlagonian of deafening all Athens with his din. The sausage seller accused the Paphlagonian of cheating everybody. A few citizens gloated that someone even more arrogant and dishonest than the Paphlagonian had been found in the person of the sausage seller. Others feared that this new demagogue would destroy all hope of defending Athens from her enemies.

While the citizens clamored, the sausage seller and the Paphlagonian continued to out-boast, out-shout, and out-orate each other. The sausage seller said that he would make meatballs out of the Paphlagonian. Demus' pampered slave threatened to twitch the lashes off both the sausage seller's eyes. Demosthenes broke in to suggest that the sausage seller inspect the Paphlagonian as he would a hog before butchering it.

At last both began to clamor for Demus, asking him to come out of his house and decide the merits of their claims. When he answered their calls, both boasted of a greater love to do him service. Convinced by the assurances of the sausage seller, Demus decided to dismiss the Paphlagonian and demanded that his former favorite return his seal of office. The two continued their efforts to bribe Demus for his favor. At last the rivals ran to consult the oracles, to prove to Demus the right of their contentions.

Each brought back a load of prophetic writings and insisted upon reading them aloud to Demus. In their prophecies they continued to insult one another, at the same time flattering Demus. The sausage seller related a dream in which Athena had come down from Olympus to pour ambrosia upon Demus and the sourest of pickles upon the Paphlagonian.

Demus sent them off on another foolish errand, laughing meanwhile because he had duped both of them into serving him. At last the sausage seller convinced the Paphlagonian that he had the right of stewardship by the word of an ancient oracle in whom both believed. Having won his victory, the sausage seller, now calling himself Agoracritus, began to browbeat his new master and to accuse him of stupidity and avarice. He boasted that he would now grow wealthy on bribes the Paphlagonian had formerly pocketed. To show his power, he ordered Cleon the Paphlagonian to turn sausage seller and peddle tripe in the streets.

Critical Evaluation:

The Knights satirizes Athenian politics in the form of an allegory. Although not named in the play, the two slaves in the opening scene are recognizable as representing the Athenian generals Demosthenes and Nicias. These were prominent figures in the Peloponnesian War (431-404 B.C.E.) between Athens and Sparta. The two generals were upstaged and humiliated by the demagogue Cleon. A particular incident that is mentioned frequently in the play is Cleon's intervention at a late stage in the battle for Spartan-controlled Sphacteria. Later, Cleon arrogantly took full credit for the Athenian victory. Aristophanes depicts these three political figures as slaves of a fickle and gullible master Demus (from the Greek world *demos*, "people"). The political rivalries among these figures from Athenian history are thus depicted—in a comic reduction—as a kind of domestic squabble with which most Athenians could identify.

Cleon dominated Athenian politics after Pericles died of the plague in 429 B.C.E. Although there is evidence that he was a capable leader, Aristophanes and many contemporaries saw Cleon as little more than a political manipulator who directed the will of the people in the assembly, which decided on all matters of policy, by appealing to the people's basest instincts. Accordingly, to secure the favor of his master Demus, the Paphlagonian tanner (Cleon operated a leather industry) uses bribes and shamelessly manipulates oracles. Not surprisingly, in late fifth century Athens there were countless charges among leaders of bribery and abuse of authority, including the fabrication of forged oracles to support one political program or another.

The Peloponnesian War and the proposals for winning or ending the conflict form the dramatic backdrop for *The Knights*, but the play is not simply a critique of contemporary politics. The focus is on the personality of Cleon, who is represented as a foreign-born slave. In fact, the name of Cleon is used only once in the play, in a remark by the chorus, but from various clues the audience certainly knew who was the object of Aristophanes' ridicule. Two years before *The Knights* was produced, Cleon was offended by Aristophanes' unrelenting criticism (in his *Babylonians*, a play now lost) and threatened the poet with a lawsuit. Cleon's object was to silence the comic poet. Very soon afterward, by way of answer, *The Knights* appeared, filled with vicious, personal criticism of Cleon's character. The Paphlagonian is a vulgar, loud, unscrupulous, and totally obnoxious character. These traits, along with the depiction of Cleon as a calculating and ruthless politician, suggest that *The Knights* reveals more about the poet's personal loathing of Cleon than about the political debates of the time.

The dramatic structure of the play depends on a fantastic contest in which the Paphlagonian experiences a humiliating fall from grace in the eyes of his master. In order to rid themselves of the obnoxious Cleon-figure, who has won the favor of Demus with lies and trickery (and, significantly, by claiming credit for the work of others), his fellow slaves concoct a plan. Most of Aristophanes' plays depend for their central plot on some such plan, termed a great idea, by means of which an unpleasant situation is to be remedied. In this play the great idea is suggested by an oracle, stolen from the Paphlagonian, revealing that he will ultimately be supplanted in the city by a sausage seller. The content of the oracle may seem somewhat inconsistent with the allegory that Aristophanes has constructed, since the sausage seller will presumably be a free man and not one of the household slaves. The outstanding qualification of the sausage seller, who happens to appear, is that he is even more shameless and calculating than the slave he is supposed to overthrow. He is also of bad family, virtually illiterate, and otherwise disreputable. Aristophanes could certainly have chosen a worthier alternative to Cleon. It suits his comic message, however, that the sausage seller, precisely because he is so vile, is the perfect person to remove the Paphlagonian from his master's affections and take charge of Demus.

Once the sausage seller is examined and approved, much of the rest of the play is concerned with the contest. The chorus of dashing knights, who provide the title for the play, represent a class in Athenian society that might ordinarily support the program of Cleon. Despite flattery and threats from the Paphlagonian, these knights stoutly support Demosthenes, Nicias, and the sausage seller in their struggle to win the favor of Demus. The first part of the contest is little more than a war of shouted boasts, in which the sausage seller seems almost at a loss, and yet he is victorious. The rivals soon turn their attention to winning over the Council. The sausage seller outdoes the Paphlagonian in utter shamelessness and bribery. The final part of the competition is the direct appeal to Demus. As befits the allegory, all of the methods used to flatter Demus are thinly veiled representations of techniques used by politicians to manipulate the Athenian people.

With the final victory of the sausage seller, Aristophanes offers a surprise for his audience. The allegory of a disreputable contest between slaves for the attention of their master gives way to an open political message. The sausage seller, now bombastically named Agoracritus (the people's choice), transforms Demus and extracts a promise from him that from now on he will be more sensible and less gullible to the manipulative influence of politicians like Cleon. The paradoxical result, that the depraved protagonist manages to reform Demus, is an inconsistency. *The Knights* moves with ease, however, between humble household allegory and weightier political satire, suggesting a larger message that proper management of the household resembles the proper governance of a city.

"Critical Evaluation" by John M. Lawless

Bibliography:
Aristophanes. *Knights*. Edited and translated by Alan H. Sommerstein. Warminster, Wiltshire, England: Aris & Phillips, 1981. Provides scholarly introduction, bibliography, Greek text, facing English translation, and commentary keyed to the translation. Sommerstein's translation supersedes most earlier versions.
Dover, K. J. *Aristophanic Comedy*. Berkeley: University of California Press, 1972. Useful and authoritative study of the plays of Aristophanes. Chapter 7 provides a synopsis of the play,

discussion of the use of allegory, notes on theatrical production, and important comments on political themes in the play. An absolutely essential starting point for study of the plays.

Murray, Gilbert. *Aristophanes: A Study*. Oxford, England: Oxford University Press, 1933. Contains valuable insights into the plays. Chapter 2 discusses the figure of Cleon as he is represented in *The Knights* and other plays of Aristophanes.

Spatz, Lois. *Aristophanes*. Boston: Twayne, 1978. A reliable introduction to Aristophanes for the general reader. Chapter 5 discusses the problems of the play and comments on characterization and the figure of Cleon.

Whitman, Cedric. *Aristophanes and the Comic Hero*. Cambridge, Mass.: Harvard University Press, 1964. A standard work on the Aristophanic protagonist. Chapter 3, "City and Individual," offers a valuable study of the play.

KRAPP'S LAST TAPE

Type of work: Drama
Author: Samuel Beckett (1906-1989)
Type of plot: Absurdist
Time of plot: An evening
Locale: Krapp's den
First performed: 1958; first published, 1958

Principal character:
KRAPP, a sixty-nine-year-old man

The Story:
In a circle of light surrounded by darkness, Krapp sat at a table in his den. Pale and clownlike in appearance, he had a bulbous purple nose and wore old black trousers, a dirty white shirt with a black vest, and oddly oversized dirty white boots. His gray hair was messy and he needed a shave. It was his sixty-ninth birthday. Krapp fumbled in his pocket, withdrew an envelope, and took out a small bunch of keys. He went to his desk where he unlocked a drawer and removed a recording tape. After peering at the tape he put it back and unlocked the second drawer, taking out a banana. Krapp stroked the banana, peeled it, and put the end in his mouth, meanwhile staring into space. Finally he ate the banana and dropped the peeling. In gestures suggesting a clown's comic pantomime, he paced back and forth, slipped on the peeling, then nudged the banana peel off stage with his toe. He took out another banana, fondled it suggestively, peeled it, tossed the peeling, and put it in his mouth. Then he thought of something. Krapp stuck the banana in his pocket and left the scene. A few moments later he returned with a ledger.

Scanning the ledger, for the first time Krapp spoke aloud. "Box . . . three . . . spool . . . five." He studied the ledger in which he had recorded the contents of tapes he made each year on his birthday and searched through his boxes of tapes. The one he was looking for was from his thirty-ninth birthday. A ledger note referred to his mother's death, an unexplained black ball, "the dark nurse," bowel problems, and a "memorable equinox." It ended, "Farewell to love." Krapp played the tape and heard his younger self, describe a birthday spent drinking, then returning to his room to write and eat bananas. This younger voice seemed self-satisfied and expressed the smug belief that, at thirty-nine, he was at the height of his powers. The voice of Krapp at thirty-nine went on to talk about listening to a still earlier tape of himself from ten or twelve years before. Krapp in his twenties had been living with someone named Bianca. Krapp at thirty-nine sneered at his younger self and called these sentimental memories "gruesome." He laughed at the lofty aspirations of his younger self, and Krapp at sixty-nine joined in the derisive laughter. Other events noted were his father's death and the end of an affair.

Krapp switched off the tape. He seemed disturbed. Abruptly he walked out. This time three corks popped. When he returned he began to sing drunkenly until he started coughing. When Krapp resumed listening to the tape he heard himself describing his mother's death. At the word "viduity" he stopped the tape and looked puzzled. He could no longer remember the meaning of this word he had once used. He went searching for a dictionary and brought it back to the table. He looked up the meaning of the word and found that it meant "widowhood." It also referred to a black bird. This seemed to amuse him. He continued listening. His younger voice told of sitting outside by a canal while his mother was dying and said he wished it were over. He was eyeing an attractive nursemaid when he noticed the window blind go down on his mother's window, a sign she had died. As he sat in the park along the canal, he had been throwing a small black ball for a stray dog. Now he paused. The dog pawed his hand and he let it take the ball. Krapp said he would never forget the feeling of the dog's mouth gently taking the ball from his hand moments after his mother's death.

At this point Krapp heard himself at thirty-nine beginning to tell of some revelation or meaningful insight. Impatiently he switched off the tape, fast-forwarded it, turned it on briefly, then switched it off and fast-forwarded again. He did this three times until a particular passage caught his attention. The voice spoke of an erotic past moment. Krapp listened, paused, and rewound the tape in order to hear it again. The voice described his being with a woman in a small boat on a lake. They had been swimming. Now she lay on the bottom of the boat, her eyes closed against the bright sun. He noticed small details: a scratch on her leg from picking gooseberries, the way she barely opened her eyes to look at him. Wild iris growing in the water bent before the movements of the boat and made a sighing sound. He lay down with her. The boat rocked gently.

When the voice resumed after a short pause, Krapp switched off the tape. Once more he went out of sight. This time there was a sound of whisky being poured into a glass. When he returned, Krapp walked somewhat unsteadily, but he took out a clean reel of tape and prepared to make a recording to mark his sixty-ninth birthday. He began by deriding his younger self. Then he fell into a reverie, forgot to speak, shut off the tape, began to speak and realized he had forgotten to turn it on again. He seemed distracted. In his mutterings Krapp referred to a publication, "Seventeen copies sold," a book he had written. His associations moved to women, Effie Briest, a figure in a German novel he had read, and someone named Fanny, an old prostitute, who had visited him a couple of times and flattered his failing virility. He derided this most recent sexual encounter as better than being kicked in the crotch.

Krapp turned again to the past. He spoke of going to vespers as a boy where he dozed and fell off the church pew, of gathering holly in the country in the west of Ireland, and hiking with his dog in the mountains. Momentarily doubts about his life assailed him but he chided himself for dwelling on the past, which he referred to as "All that old misery." Still, the memory of the woman in the boat haunted him. He removed the new tape and reinserted the one from his thirty-ninth birthday. He replayed the scene in the boat. This time, however, he did not turn it off. Then the voice stopped and the tape ran on in silence as Krapp stared at nothing.

Critical Evaluation:

One of the principal authors of the theater of the absurd, Samuel Beckett was born and grew up in Ireland, where he studied languages at Trinity College. As a young man he traveled to the Continent and eventually settled in Paris. Although *Krapp's Last Tape* was originally written in English, he wrote most of his works first in French and translated them into English. Besides plays, Beckett wrote and published novels, shorter fiction, and poetry. During World War II he served as a member of the French resistance and had to go into hiding to survive. He was awarded the Nobel Prize in Literature in 1969.

In *Krapp's Last Tape*, an older man reviews his life and confronts his isolation and inability to love. Krapp's failures as a human being are glaringly evident, but the audience may also identify with him. Like a mime or a circus clown, Krapp wrings his audience out with contrary emotions. He is laughable and pathetic, grotesque and human. Within the small framework of a one-act monologue, in the soiled comedic figure of Krapp, Beckett creates a complex reality. Describing *Krapp's Last Tape* as absurdist theater is subject to interpretation. Unlike more extremely absurdist Beckett plays such as *Waiting for Godot* (1952) or *Endgame* (1957), the play is fairly realistic. Krapp's comic appearance and the way it contrasts with his sad life is, however, absurdist. Here is an ordinary human being who has aspired to be a writer but with slight success, has suffered the death of parents, and has failed in love. He has wrestled (not too vigorously) with alcoholism. He is experiencing a lonely old age and, to judge by the title of the play, will soon experience death. The circle of light in which he operates is a symbol of his existence, a tiny spot in a vast darkness. Beckett chooses to picture Krapp as a down-at-heels clown. As a clown Krapp is absurd rather than tragic. The human condition, projected from Krapp's example, is absurd. Through Krapp the audience sees the individual as a posturing little spark in time, soon extinguished. Krapp himself is uneasy and disgusted with this role. When he listens to his younger voice on tape speaking of a visionary night on a jetty, he becomes impatient and switches off the tape. Other than his drinking, only the fact that he replays the section of the tape dealing with the scene in the boat implies that Krapp is touched by a sense of loss. The audience never knows for sure what Krapp is feeling. To create the illusion of meaning Krapp begins his annual ritual of making a birthday tape, but this time he fails to find value in the exercise. He has nothing to add, for in the end his life has come to nothing. The "memorable equinox" turns out to have been the beginning of the end. Beckett uses the stark setting and the contrast between the spotlight in which Krapp moves and the darkness beyond to give a concrete representation of Krapp's situation. The repetition of threes gives Krapp's actions a ritualistic character. For example, he goes offstage three times to drink, and he looks at his watch three times. The audience is presented with Krapp at three different times in his life.

The play is set during "a late evening in the future." It has been suggested that this is to avoid the anachronism of recording tape being available at an earlier date. Setting the play in the future also serves as an omen, imbuing the play with a mood of dark presentiment.

Krapp's ceremonial recording of his own life, as if for some posterity never realized, is in some ways a parody of the writer's life, but his life work has turned out to be the taped version of his life and he is both author and audience, a narcissistic circle. No wonder the play ends in silence as the blank portion of the tape winds on. The ending of the play is bleak but it also has a cleansing stoicism. Krapp is a moving human figure.

Barbara Drake

Bibliography:

Gontarski, S. E. *The Intent of Undoing in Samuel Beckett's Dramatic Texts.* Bloomington: Indiana University Press, 1985. Covers Beckett's plays. A chapter on *Krapp's Last Tape* connects the revision process to evolving interpretation of the play. Selected bibliography.

_____, ed. *On Beckett: Essays and Criticism.* New York: Grove Press, 1986. Essays by various scholars, including Ruby Cohn's "Beckett Directs: *Endgame* and *Krapp's Last Tape*," which discusses Beckett's adeptness at staging.

Kenner, Hugh. *Samuel Beckett: A Critical Study.* New ed. Berkeley: University of California Press, 1973. Important study of Beckett. Kenner consulted with Beckett in writing it. Does not focus on *Krapp's Last Tape* but the preface provides valuable insight into Beckett's attitude toward his work.

MacMillan, Dougald, and Martha Fehsenfeld. *From "Waiting for Godot" to "Krapp's Last Tape."* Vol. 1 in *Beckett in the Theatre.* New York: Riverrun Press, 1988. Devotes a chapter to *Krapp's Last Tape.* Discusses changes Beckett made from early to later drafts. Extensive interpretation of the play in relation to production.

Reid, Alec. *All I Can Manage, More than I Could: An Approach to the Plays of Samuel Beckett.* Dublin: The Dolmen Press, 1968. Accessible and valuable source on plays with publication, first production information, and synopses. Introductory essays on Beckett and his innovative work in broadening the scope of modern drama.

THE KREUTZER SONATA

Type of work: Novel
Author: Leo Tolstoy (1828-1910)
Type of plot: Social realism
Time of plot: Late nineteenth century
Locale: Russia
First published: Kreytserova sonata, 1889 (English translation, 1890)

Principal characters:
 VASYLA POZDNISHEF, a Russian aristocrat
 MADAME POZDNISHEF, his wife
 TRUKHASHEVSKY, the lover of Madame Pozdnishef

The Story:

One spring night a railway train was speeding across Russia. In one of the cars a sprightly conversation about the place of women, both in public and in the home, was in progress among a group of aristocrats. One of the listeners finally broke into the conversation with the statement that Russians married only for sexual reasons and that marriage was a hell for most of them unless they, like himself, secured release by killing the other party to the marriage. With that remark he left the group and retired to his own seat in the car. Later on, he told his story to his seat companion.

His name was Pozdnishef, and he was a landed proprietor. As a young man, he had learned many vices, but he had always kept his relationships with women on a monetary basis, so that he would have no moral responsibility for the unfortunates with whom he came in contact. His early life had taught him that people of his class did not respect sex. The men viewed women only in terms of pleasure. The women sanctioned such thoughts by openly marrying men who had become libertines; the older people by allowing their daughters to be married to men whose habits were known to be of a shameful nature.

At the age of thirty, Pozdnishef fell in love with a beautiful woman of his own class, the daughter of an impoverished landowner in Penza. During his engagement he was disturbed because she and he had so little about which to converse when they were left alone. They would say one sentence to each other and then become silent. Not knowing what should come next, they would fall to eating bonbons. The honeymoon was a failure, shameful and tiresome at the beginning, painfully oppressive at the end. Three or four days after the wedding they quarreled, and both realized that in a short time they had grown to hate each other. As the months of marriage passed, their quarrels grew more frequent and violent. Pozdnishef became persuaded in his own mind that love was something low and swinish.

The idea of marriage and sex became an obsession with him. When his wife secured a wet nurse for their children, he felt that she was shirking a moral duty by not nursing her offspring. Worse, Pozdnishef was jealous of every man who came into his wife's presence, who was received in his home, or who received a smile from his wife. He began to suspect that his wife had taken a lover.

The children born to Pozdnishef and his wife were a great trouble to him in other ways as well. They were continually bothering him with real or fancied illnesses, and they broke up the regular habits of life to which he was accustomed. They were new subjects over which he and his wife could quarrel.

In the fourth year of their marriage, the couple had reached a state of complete disagreement.

They ceased to talk over anything to the end. They were almost silent when they were alone, much as they had been during their engagement. Finally the doctors told the woman she could have no more children with safety. Pozdnishef felt that without children to justify their relations, the only reason for their life together was the other children who had been born and who held them like a chain fastening two convicts.

In the next two years, the young woman filled out and bloomed in health, after the burden of bearing children was taken from her. She became more attractive in the eyes of other men, and her husband's jealousy sharply increased.

Madame Pozdnishef had always been interested in music, and she played the piano rather well. Through her musical interest, she met a young aristocrat who had turned professional musician when his family fortune had dwindled away. His name was Trukhashevsky. When he appeared on the scene, the Pozdnishefs had passed through several crises in their marriage. The husband had at times considered suicide, and the wife had tried to poison herself. One evening, after a violent scene in which Pozdnishef had told his wife he would like to see her dead, she had rushed to her room and swallowed an opium compound. Quick action on the part of the husband and a doctor had saved her life, but neither could forget her desperate attempt.

One evening Trukhashevsky came to Pozdnishef's home in Moscow. He and Madame Pozdnishef played during the evening for a number of guests. The first piece they played together was Beethoven's *Kreutzer* Sonata. The first movement, a rapid allegro, worked upon the highly strung emotions of the husband until he began to imagine that there was already an understanding between the musician and his wife. The idea obsessed him so that he could hardly wait until the other man was out of the house. Never in his life had music affected Pozdnishef in that manner. Between it and his jealousy, he was almost violently insane.

Two days later, Pozdnishef left Moscow to attend a meeting. He went away fearful of what might happen while he was gone. On the second day of his absence, Pozdnishef received a letter from his wife saying that the musician had called at the house.

Jealousy immediately seized the husband. He rushed back to Moscow as fast as carriage and trains could carry him. He arrived at his home after midnight. Lights were burning in his wife's apartment. Taking off his shoes, he prowled about the house. He soon discovered the musician's overcoat. He went to the nursery and the children's rooms but found everyone there asleep. Returning to his study, he seized a dagger and made his way to his wife's apartment. There he found his wife and the musician seated at a table, eating. He rushed at the man, who escaped by ducking under the piano and then out the door. Pozdnishef, beside himself with anger and jealousy, seized his wife and stabbed her. When she dropped to the floor, he ran from the room and went to his study. There he fell asleep on a sofa.

A few hours later his sister-in-law awakened him and took him to see his dying wife. Shortly afterward the authorities carried Pozdnishef away to prison. He went under police escort to his wife's funeral. It was only after he had looked at the waxen face of the corpse that he realized he had committed a murder. Then, at his trial, Pozdnishef was found innocent because he had murdered while in the heat of anger at finding his wife unfaithful to him.

Now judged insane, Pozdnishef declared that if he had it to do over, he would never marry. Marriage, he insisted, was not for true Christians with strong sensibilities and weak moral restraints.

Critical Evaluation:

One of the strangest of Leo Tolstoy's works, *The Kreutzer Sonata* is almost entirely a raving monologue concerning sex and marriage. The sources for Tolstoy's *Kreutzer Sonata*, first published in 1889 in lithograph, are said to be autobiographical. An idea for the short novel initially came from a friend of Tolstoy, who told him about meeting a stranger on a train who, during the course of a long journey, related an account of his wife's infidelity. The story intrigued Tolstoy, who began working the idea into a story he was writing on the complexities arising out of the conflict between chastity and sexual love. About a year after he had begun this project, Tolstoy happened to go to a musical. Among the pieces performed that evening was the *Kreutzer* Sonata (1803). This piece deeply affected Tolstoy, and he was inspired to incorporate it into his novel.

The autobiographical aspects of the novel center on the dilemma Tolstoy experienced after his conversion in his later years to a life of asceticism and chastity. He was revolted by his former life, which he now saw as one of indulgence, greed, and lust. In trying to change his nature, he became obsessed by his desires, in particular, his sexual desires and the spiritual unrest arising from them. His obsession included his wife, Sonya; consequently, their final years together were, for the most part, miserable. On his deathbed, Tolstoy refused to see her, and although no one could claim that he, like the protagonist in *The Kreutzer Sonata*, murdered his wife, her heart was broken.

Since the publication of *The Kreutzer Sonata*, critics, in their assessment of the novel, have run the gamut from praise to disgust. Anton Chekhov wrote that "it is hardly possible to find anything of equal importance in conception and beauty of execution." Others have read it as a diatribe against sexuality rather than a work of fiction. Tolstoy himself once called it a negative, malicious work, and his wife complained, during the period Tolstoy was writing it, that he no longer was doing creative work.

Today, the critical scales might be balanced by reading the novel not only as a diatribe against lust, but also as a mesmerizing, gothic portrayal of a husband ravaged with jealousy. The short novel takes place on a train and, for the most part, inside a carriage in which the narrator and another passenger, Vasyla Pozdnishef, sit throughout the long night drinking glasses of strong tea, smoking, and talking—that is, Pozdnishef talks and the narrator listens. Earlier, a woman, a lawyer, a tradesman, and a clerk had entered the carriage and, in desultory fashion, begun talking about subjects that later become the center of the novel—sexual love, infidelity, jealousy, chastity, and marriage.

Outside Pozdnishef's monologue, there is little action. At one point, before dawn, the conductor comes by to remove a burned candle. Tea is made and drunk. They smoke. They change their positions—cross a leg, lean forward. The effect of little or no action outside the monologue is similar to being locked into the same, confining space as the characters. One is on the train, so to speak, and unable to get off. Listening to a deranged, although intelligent, man's obsessive tale is not everyone's idea of a pleasant journey. In a manner of speaking, Tolstoy imprisons the reader with the narrator in a situation in which there is no alternative but to listen if one wants to find out what happened and why.

Pozdnishef's monologue works on several levels. It is both a classic case of jealousy, dramatically and inextricably leading to murder, and also a polemic on sexual mores. The novel suffers from the latter—Pozdnishef's doctrinaire digressions on sexual mores. His bitter, impersonal view of marital love is chilling. He attributes falling in love to an excess of rich foods and to dressmakers' skills. Although he is not a misogynist (he claims that man has corrupted woman with his filthy passions), he claims that women enslave men through their sexuality.

What rescues the novel from didacticism, however, is the riveting drama, interwoven among the monologues, of the jealous husband caught in a tapestry of his own weaving. Pozdnishef introduces the violinist, Trukhashevsky, to Madame Pozdnishef. He encourages him to come to their home and participate in musicals with her, as she is an enthusiastic pianist. Thus he sets into motion sexual jealousy, a passion flaming out of his control to its tragic end. In this characterization, Tolstoy's skill is superb. Listening to his attractive wife and the young violinist play the *Kreutzer* Sonata, Pozdnishef imagines a pulsating, romantic, liaison between them, and his rage mounts.

Tolstoy's character, Pozdnishef, is equal to the best of a long list of nervous neurotics teetering on the edge of psychotic behavior. In *The Kreutzer Sonata*, Pozdnishef is portrayed as continually horrified, exasperated, painfully struck, or ashamed. He calls himself swinish, depraved, malicious, and evil. In telling his story, Pozdnishef is agitated, tense, and irritable. His eyes glitter and his movements are abrupt; he emits strange sounds, not quite human. He talks obsessively.

He is a type familiar to nineteenth century readers from writers such as E. T. A. Hoffmann and Edgar Allan Poe, who excelled in the psychological horror story. In these macabre tales, the character's body and soul or mental and instinctive drives are dissected, the rift or schism between body and spirit is exposed, and the personality is revealed to be founded on fear, cruelty, and madness. Pozdnishef is such a personality and, in portraying him, Tolstoy's skill is unsurpassed.

Although Tolstoy has created a remarkable character, his jeremiads on sexual mores weaken the plot. His didacticism threatens to overwhelm his narrative skills. The result is a flawed novel, but one of strange and compelling interest.

"Critical Evaluation" by Alice L. Swensen

Bibliography:

Bayley, John. "What Is Art?" In *Leo Tolstoy*, edited by Harold Bloom. Edgemont, Pa.: Chelsea House, 1986. Discusses Tolstoy's ideas about the function and moral purpose of art, with special reference to *The Kreutzer Sonata*. Contains many other excellent essays pertinent to understanding Tolstoy's ideas about art, love, and sex.

Maude, Almyer. *The Life of Tolstoy*. New York: Oxford University Press, 1953. Maude, Tolstoy's English friend and translator, produced the most tasteful and accurate English translations of Tolstoy's writings. This biography is outstanding because of Maude's close association with the Russian author and his opportunities to consult Tolstoy in person. Many references to *The Kreutzer Sonata*.

Shirer, William L. *Love and Hatred: The Troubled Marriage of Leo and Sonya Tolstoy*. New York: Simon & Schuster, 1994. Devotes an entire chapter to *The Kreutzer Sonata*, analyzing how it reflects the real-life marital relationship of the Tolstoys, and how its publication created further marital friction. Contains many excellent rare photographs.

Smoluchowski, Louise. *Lev and Sonya: The Story of the Tolstoy Marriage*. New York: G. P. Putnam's Sons, 1987. A revealing study of the tempestuous marriage of the Tolstoys, which lasted from 1862 to 1910. Discusses the marriage's powerful influence on the Russian author's ideas about love and marriage, as reflected in such works as *Anna Karenina* (1875-1877) and *The Kreutzer Sonata*.

Tolstoy, Leo. *What Is Art?* Translated by Almyer Maude. Indianapolis: Bobbs-Merrill, 1960. Originally published in Russian in 1896, this great, neglected work was the fruit of decades of intensive thought and study. Tolstoy condemned art designed to entertain the idle upper classes, a belief he dramatized in *The Kreutzer Sonata*.

KRISTIN LAVRANSDATTER

Type of work: Novel
Author: Sigrid Undset (1882-1949)
Type of plot: Historical realism
Time of plot: Fourteenth century
Locale: Norway
First published: 1920-1922 (English translation, 1923-1927): *Kransen,* 1920 (*The Bridal Wreath,* 1923); *Husfrue,* 1921 (*The Mistress of Husaby,* 1925); *Korset,* 1922 (*The Cross,* 1927)

Principal characters:
KRISTIN LAVRANSDATTER
LAVRANS BJÖRGULFSÖN, Kristin's father and the owner of Jörundgaard
RAGNFRID IVARSDATTER, Kristin's mother
ULVHILD and
RAMBORG, Kristin's sisters
ERLEND NIKULAUSSÖN, the owner of Husaby
SIMON ANDRESSON, the son of a neighboring landowner
LADY AASHILD, Erlend's aunt
NIKULAUS (NAAKVE),
BJÖRGULF,
GAUTE,
SKULE,
IVAR,
LAVRANS,
MUNAN, and
ERLEND, the sons of Erlend and Kristin

The Story:

Lavrans Björgulfsön and his wife Ragnfrid Ivarsdatter were descended from powerful landowners. Although Kristin had been born at her father's manor Skog, she spent most of her childhood at Jörundgaard, which fell to Lavrans and Ragnfrid upon the death of Ragnfrid's father. Kristin's childhood was exceedingly happy.

A second daughter, Ulvhild, was crippled at the age of three. Lady Aashild, a declared witch-wife, was sent for to help the child. Kristin became well acquainted with Lady Aashild that summer.

When she was fifteen years old, Kristin's father betrothed her to Simon Andresson of Dyfrin. One evening, Kristin slipped away to bid good-bye to a childhood playmate, Arne Gyrdson. On her way home, Bentein, Sira Eirik's grandson, accosted her. She escaped after a fight with him, physically unharmed but mentally tortured. Later that year, Arne was brought home dead after having fought with Bentein over Bentein's sly insinuations regarding Kristin. Kristin persuaded her father to put off the betrothal feast and permit her to spend a year in a convent at Oslo.

Soon after entering the Convent of Nonneseter, Kristin and her bed partner, Ingebjorg Filippusdatter, went into Oslo to shop, accompanied by an old servant. When they became separated from the old man, they were rescued by a group of men riding through the woods. In that manner Kristin met Erlend Nikulaussön, the nephew of Lady Aashild. In July, Kristin and Erlend met once more at the St. Margaret's Festival and that night vowed to love each other. The following morning, Kristin learned from Ingebjorg of Eline Ormsdatter, whom Erlend had stolen from her husband, and by whom Erlend had had two children. Later that summer, while visiting her uncle at Skog, Kristin and Erlend met secretly, and Kristin surrendered to Erlend. During the following winter, Kristin and Erlend managed to meet frequently. In the spring, Kristin told Simon of her love for Erlend and her desire to end their betrothal. He agreed, much against his will. Lavrans and Ragnfrid unwillingly accepted Kristin's and Simon's decision.

When Erlend's kinsmen brought suit for Kristin's hand in marriage, Lavrans refused. During the winter Erlend and Kristin planned to elope to Sweden. While they were making their plans at Lady Aashild's home, Eline Ormsdatter overtook them. Discovered by Erlend when she was trying to give poison to Kristin, she stabbed herself. Erlend and Sir Bjorn, Lady Aashild's husband, put her on a sled and took her south to be buried. Kristin returned home.

The following spring Erlend's relatives again made a bid for Kristin's hand, and worn out with suffering—Ulvhild's death and Kristin's unhappiness—Lavrans agreed to the betrothal. During Erlend's visit at Whitsuntide, Kristin became pregnant. On the night of the wedding, Lavrans realized that Kristin already belonged to Erlend. He had given to Erlend what Erlend had already possessed.

After her marriage Kristin moved to Erlend's estate at Husaby. She was quick to notice the neglect everywhere evident. In the next fifteen years she bore Erlend seven sons—Nikulaus, Björgulf, Gaute, the twins Ivar and Skule, Lavrans, and Munan. At the same time she struggled to save her sons' inheritance by better management of Husaby. Erlend, however, was intent on becoming a great man; he sold land to pay his expenses and granted tenants free rent in exchange for supplies for his military musters.

Simon Andresson lived at Formo with his sister Sigrid and his illegitimate daughter, Arngjerd. Simon made suit to Lavrans for Kristin's youngest sister, Ramborg. The following year Lavrans died, followed two years later by Ragnfrid. Kristin's part of the inheritance was Jörundgaard.

There was much unrest in the country at that time. A boy, Magnus VII, had been named king of both Sweden and Norway, and during his childhood, Erling Vidkunsson was made regent of Norway. When Magnus reached the age of sixteen, Sir Erling resigned, and soon Norway had little law or order. During those years of unrest, Erlend conspired to put another claimant on the throne of Norway. Arrested, he was tried for treason by a king's-men's court. Erlend survived, but he had to forfeit all of his lands.

Erlend went with Kristin and his sons to Jörundgaard to live; but he cared little for farming or for the people of the dale, and the neighbors avoided Jörundgaard. As the children grew to manhood, Kristin became more fearful for their future. In her desire to further their fortunes, she and Erlend came to harsh words, and she told him he was not a fit lord of Jörundgaard. He left her and went to Haugen, the farm where Lady Aashild had spent her last days. Although she longed to have Erlend back, Kristin felt that she had been in the right and struggled along with the help of Ulf, a servant, to make Jörundgaard produce.

The following winter her brother-in-law Simon died as a result of a cut on the arm, sustained while separating two drunken fighters. Before he died, he asked Kristin to go to Erlend and settle their quarrel. Kristin promised to do so. Ramborg gave birth to her son six weeks early and, upon Simon's death, named the child Simon Simonsson.

Kristin kept her promise and went to Haugen to ask Erlend to return to Jörundgaard, but he refused. She stayed at Haugen that summer and then returned home to her sons. Finding herself pregnant again, she sent her sons to tell her husband. When the child was born, Erlend still did not come to her. The child died before it was three months old. Soon thereafter, when Bishop Halvard came to the parish, Jardtrud, Ulf's wife, went to him and charged Ulf with adultery with Kristin. Lavrans, unknown to the rest of the family, rode to Haugen to get his father. Erlend returned immediately with his son, but in a scuffle in the courtyard, he was wounded and died. The same year Munan died of a sickness which went around the parish. Thus Kristin was left with six sons, each of whom must make his way in the world.

Ivar and Skule, the twins, took service with a distant kinsman. Ivar married Singe Gamalsdatter, a wealthy young widow. Nikulaus and Björgulf entered the brotherhood at Tautra. Gaute fell in love with Jofrid Helgesdatter, heiress of a rich landowner. The two young people eloped and were not married until the summer after the birth of their child, Erlend. During that winter, they lived at Jörundgaard, and after their marriage, Kristin relinquished the keys of the manor to Jofrid. Lavrans took service with the Bishop of Skaalholt and sailed to Iceland.

Kristin felt out of place in her old home after she was no longer mistress there. She decided to go to Nidaros and enter a convent. In the year 1349, after Kristin had been in the cloister for about two years, her son Skule went to see her. From him she received the first news of the Black Plague. The disease soon engulfed the whole city, carried off her two sons in the convent, Nikulaus and Björgulf, and finally caused Kristin's own death.

Critical Evaluation:

Sigrid Undset was one of many European writers in the twentieth century who felt a strong attraction to traditional Catholicism. Undset differed, though, from writers such as T. S. Eliot, G. K. Chesterton, and Charles Maurras, who supported reactionary political regimes and were opposed to the personal autonomy characteristic of the modern era. Undset was not opposed to twentieth century liberalism and individualism. She saw personal autonomy as expressing a human dignity consonant with Christian conception of the potentially exalted character of humanity that, though inevitably sinful, had been redeemed by the sacrificial love of Jesus Christ.

This delight in individualism can be seen in Undset's portrayal of the character of Kristin Lavransdatter. Kristin is no plaster saint. She has human desires, human passions, and human failings. She also is a pious Christian throughout the course of the work, although her religious dedication only reaches its full consummation in the last portion of the trilogy, *The Cross*, when she formally enters a convent. Undset indulges in no melodramatic contrast between pagan sin and Christian devotion. She recognizes that, in a society as totally Christian as medieval Norway, Christianity had to have tended to embrace the full range of human attributes and behaviors, even if it could not have officially condoned them all. Kristin's drives and passions may be gently chided by the clerical authorities in the book, but they are not constrained. Indeed, the defiance of social norms that Kristin displays at the beginning of the book (for instance, in her premarital relationship with Erlend Nikulaussön) is also displayed at the end of the book, when her passionate spirit diverges from the social norm in another direction (selfless devotion to the Church).

The significance of the character of Erlend is often missed by critics. Erlend's inadequacies as a man and as a husband are evident. Before he marries Kristin, he sires an illegitimate child by another woman. After their marriage, he has numerous affairs. He mismanages and mortgages his property to advance his unrealistic personal interests. At first, the reader infers that Kristin has made a disastrous match and that her religious devotion is a repudiation of Erlend's wayward secular morality. The truth, on consideration, is more complicated. Erlend, like Kristin, will not tolerate the limits placed upon him by stolid, unimaginative, run-of-the-mill people. Erlend's appetite can lead to ignoble and disagreeable behavior, but it also possesses a kind of zeal that has much akin to Kristin's own spiritual fire. If anything, Kristin's clear moral superiority to Erlend can be seen less as a religiously motivated gesture on the part of the author than as a feminist critique of male adventurism and self-serving charisma. It is in the middle section of the trilogy, *The Mistress of Husaby*, that the ambiguities of Erlend's character are most fruitfully displayed. Erlend agitates to replace the Swedish hegemony over Norway with rule by a native Norwegian noble. This conspiracy fails in worldly terms and is judged by Kristin to be a distraction from the truly primary spiritual goals of human life. Kristin's perspective is reminiscent of Beatrice's view of Dante Alighieri's political intrigues in Florence in Dante's *Paradiso* (c. 1320; English translation, 1802). The conspiracy does reflect a praiseworthy desire on the part of Erlend to make life better for his people and to strive for the general good. Erlend's Norwegian nationalism was hardly unattractive to Undset, who was twenty-three years old when Norway finally gained independence from Sweden in 1905. Kristin might have had a less tragedy-filled life had she married a more placid and dutiful man, such as her devoted suitor Simon Darre (who always remains constant to Kristin even after she has married another man), but her passions and ambitions would have been less fulfilled.

Erlend's house, Husaby, also plays an important role in the book, especially in contrast and comparison with Jörundgaard, the house of Kristin's father, Lavrans Björgulfsön. Put simply, Jörundgaard is more of a homestead, and Husaby more of a manor. Jörundgaard represents the simplicities of childhood, Husaby the challenges, rewards, and sorrows of being a mature adult. Much attention is paid to how Kristin renovates Husaby and restores it to its proper rank and station in the region. Yet when Kristin is old and widowed, it is to Jörundgaard that she returns, finding in its raw and windswept reaches a proper haven for her battered spirit.

It is neither the characters nor the houses of the novel, however, with which the reader must first relate. It is the setting of the book itself: medieval Norway. Almost incalculably remote to most English-speaking readers, Undset's setting threatens to dwarf the human protagonists of the book in a wealth of exotic detail. It is Undset's great achievement that this does not occur. Undset's fidelity to historical detail far exceeds that of the garden-variety historical novelist, yet the book is never wooden or fusty in its depiction of the past. Although the reader develops an interest in medieval Norway for its own sake Undset's character portraits are so powerful that eventually the reader takes the setting in stride and evaluates the characters within their given context much as he or she would do when reading a novel concerning contemporary life. Undset's objective historical accuracy is far greater than that of nineteenth century romantic historical writers (such as Sir Walter Scott). She is far less interested than they, however, in bringing the heroic spirit of the past to bear upon the perceived mediocrities of her time. Undset believes, rather, that people should value the past for its own sake but realize that the same conflicts that ensnare and beset contemporaries also have afflicted their predecessors. In her broad-mindedness in acknowledging the range of brilliance and shortsightedness, generosity and evil, of which women and men are capable, Undset succeeds in animating the distant past.

"Critical Evaluation" by Nicholas Birns

Bibliography:
Bayerschmidt, Carl. *Sigrid Undset*. Boston: Twayne, 1970. Contains excellent close readings, providing analysis and interpretation as well as plot summary. Especially good on Kristin's spiritual evolution and the ambiguities of Erlend's character.

Brunsdale, Mitzi. *Sigrid Undset: Chronicler of Norway*. Oxford, England: Berg, 1988. A comprehensive and wholly contemporary revaluation of Undset's canon, placing her firmly within a Norwegian historical and cultural context. Especially informative on the often neglected minor characters in the novel.

Gustafson, Alrik. "Christian Ethics in a Pagan World: Sigrid Undset." In *Six Scandinavian Novelists*. Minneapolis: University of Minnesota Press, 1968. Places Undset within the context of European and Scandinavian modernism. Shows how her Christianity differentiated her from other modernist authors but also suggests that the spiritual dilemmas faced by the characters in *Kristin Lavransdatter* have their counterparts in the modern age.

Lytle, Andrew. *Kristin*. Columbia: University of Missouri Press, 1992. This loving tribute to Undset's masterwork summarizes the plot and testifies to the book's moral values and its enduring emotional core. Filled with a tender affection for the book's central character. The most passionate criticism in English Undset has stimulated.

Winsnes, A. H. *Sigrid Undset: A Study in Christian Realism*. New York: Sheed and Ward, 1953. Demonstrates Undset's religious values. Explores how she embeds those values in the historical tableaux of her fictions. Shows how the history of Norway directs Undset's Christianity into a democratic, antireactionary channel.

THE LABYRINTH OF SOLITUDE
Life and Thought in Mexico

Type of work: Social criticism
Author: Octavio Paz (1914-   )
First published: El laberinto de la soledad: Vida y pensamiento de México, 1950; revised
and enlarged, 1959 (English translation, 1961)

Widely acknowledged as the greatest poet of his time in Mexico, Octavio Paz has led a life that in many ways is typical of the Mexican intelligentsia he describes in *The Labyrinth of Solitude*. He has published ten books of poetry, fought with the Loyalists in Spain, and served his country as a diplomat. Deeply involved in the future of the Mexican land, he has fitted himself out for defining it to the world by a career that includes the experiences of intense action and intense contemplation.

The Labyrinth of Solitude was first published in 1950 by Jesus Silva Herzog's famous and influential magazine, *Cuadernos Americanos*. The version that comes to North Americans through Lysander Kemp's translation is based upon a second edition, revised and expanded, published by the Fondo de Cultura Economica in 1959. This book is in effect the result of labors that span a decade, labors that show themselves best in Paz's understanding of his own implications: The labyrinth he describes is the modern world.

Paz begins with an analysis of the phenomenon of the *pachucos*, those youths of Latin descent who during the 1940's and 1950's alarmed the cities of the Southwest with their "antisocial" behavior, their peculiar dress, and their hostile acts and attitudes. He sees the *pachuco* as standing between Mexican culture and U.S. culture, in a limbo, unable to accept the values of either, equally alienated from both. Moreover, says Paz, the *pachuco* has, without understanding them, reasons for his attitude. Both cultures have cut themselves off from the flux of life, have failed in their separate ways to reconcile the individual and the universe. Unable to partake of communion, both the Mexican and the North American have thus become spiritual orphans, imprisoned in the sterility of solitude. If the Mexican seclusion is similar to stagnant water, Paz says, North America is similar to a mirror. Neither contains life any more.

The forces that confine the North American are summarized in the three sets of laws to which Paz pays due attention: the seventeenth century religious code of Calvin, the eighteenth century political code of the Founders, and the nineteenth century moral code of the American Victorians. Caged by these sets of laws, the North American has let himself become a cipher, handling the universe easily by simply denying any part of it that might conflict with these codes. The North American, therefore, lives in a wholly artificial world, creating psychological mothers and fathers out of the delusions of Panglossism (Pangloss is the fictional philosopher who states that this is the best of all possible worlds). The Mexicans, on the other hand, have no such delusions, but see themselves more or less clearly in their orphanhood, without a mother and without a father.

For a Mexican, life is a combat in which the role of an isolated individual can only be defensive. The Mexican's interior turbulence is a torture, and his or her exterior defensiveness destroys even the possibility of the communion that might bring happiness. Hence the Mexican's world is hollow, self-consuming, masochistic, and more or less devoid of love, for what love a Mexican knows is merely a form of narcissism. Paz says that the Mexicans refuse to progress beyond themselves, to free themselves, to expose themselves to the outside world. If

North American happiness exists only in illusions, Mexican happiness exists only in remotest theory.

Relief comes to a certain extent with the fiesta, a uniquely Mexican plunge into chaos from which the group emerges purified and strengthened, a drunken rapture during which people briefly confront themselves. The fiesta, however, cannot wholly offset the lack of communion; it is too impermanent, short-lived, and unstable. The Mexicans oscillate between intimacy and withdrawal, shouting and silence, fiesta and wake, without ever surrendering to anything but themselves. Despite fiestas, Mexicans never really transcend their solitude.

Paz sees this solitude in Mexico as largely the result of the reform movement, which, following so many years after independence, finally disrupted both the Aztec and Colonial traditions. The new Spanish American nations are not new, he claims. Instead, he views them as static or decadent societies, remnants of older, more integrated cultures. Reform was thus an attempt at social reanimation. Its method, however, was based not upon indigenous realities but rather upon abstract and geometrical reasoning imported from Europe. The profoundest effect of the liberal Constitution of 1857 was therefore the creation of a split between the individual Mexican and the native past. Mexicans became inevitably, at the moment of that split, orphaned from themselves.

The revolution that came after reform may be seen as a movement meant to overcome this orphanhood, to reconquer the past, to assimilate it, and to make it live in the present. Paz finds particular significance in the Zapatistas, whose program to reinstitute the ancient systems of land tenure epitomized the revolution on its ideological side. The revolution was above all, however, a "fiesta of bullets," the orgiastic celebration of a total Mexico daring at length to be, and to be in communion with itself.

Mexico's success in maintaining this communion after the shooting stopped has been, for various historical reasons, sharply limited. The essential solitude that Paz describes in his earlier chapters still stands, of course, as tragic as ever, with its accompanying problems. These problems are not merely Mexican; they are universal. In his view the crisis of time is not the opposition of two great and different cultures but an inward struggle of one civilization that, unrivaled, is shaping the future of the whole world. Each person's fate involves all of humanity. Thus, Mexicans cannot solve their problems as Mexicans, for they are involved in matters that are universal, not merely national.

The existence of "underdeveloped" countries and of totalitarian "socialist" regimes in the twentieth century Paz regards as equally anomalous, equally scandalous, equally symptomatic of the social chaos that is the outward and visible sign of the labyrinth of solitude. Too often, an undeveloped country attempting to emerge from its economic prison becomes merely another victim of totalitarianism. The real cure for chaos and sterility, says Paz, must therefore lie in an outgrowing and a rejection of those false divinities that rule the modern world: endless, infinite work and fixed, finite, chronometric time.

People today pretend they are always wide awake when they are thinking, but this is not true; usually thinking leads one into the nightmare of reason. After the nightmare is over one may realize that one was dreaming, not wide awake, and that dreams of reason are unbearable. With this in mind one may then close one's eyes to dream again. The only alternatives to the continuing frustration of labyrinthine solitude are suicide or some new kind of creative involvement and participation, the exercise of loving imagination in communion with the rest of the world.

The Labyrinth of Solitude is a wise book. Years spent in Paris did not seduce Octavio Paz into succumbing to the pathetic charms held out by existentialism. He avoids the promulgation of a doctrine, achieving instead the kind of essential statement that one should expect from a poet. Not only should the book prove stimulating to anyone who thinks about the world in which people live and what that world does to people; it should also provide perhaps the best gloss yet available on Paz's poetic work.

Bibliography:
Alves, Abel A. "History, Mexico, the United States, and Humanity in the Writings of Octavio Paz." *CLIO: A Journal of Literature, History, and the Philosophy of History* 20, no. 1 (Fall, 1990): 53-63. Surveys the main themes of the essay (gender roles, Mexico's history, and so on). Shows how Paz believes that the Mexicans can achieve an understanding of the present through an examination of the past.

Bell, Steven. "Contexts of Critical Reception in *El laberinto de la soledad*: The Contingencies of Value and the Discourse of Power." *Siglo XX/20th Century* 20, nos. 2-3 (1992): 101-124. Examines the changing critical reception that Paz's essay has received over the years. Studies Paz's view of power as male-centered.

Katra, William H. "Ideology and Society in *El laberinto de la soledad*, by Octavio Paz." *Chasqui* 15, nos. 2-3 (1986): 3-13. A fairly harsh reading of Paz's essay. Argues that the essay gives rise to some misconceptions about Mexican society and the roles of men and women in that society.

Klein, Leonard S., ed. *Latin American Literature in the Twentieth Century: A Guide*. New York: Frederick Ungar, 1986. A section on *El laberinto de la soledad* discusses how Paz identifies concealment, the use of a mask, as a symptom of the identity crisis suffered by modern Mexicans.

Wilson, Jason. *Octavio Paz*. Boston: Twayne, 1986. Section on *The Labyrinth of Solitude* shows how Paz universalized his personal experiences of alienation to create a theory of the noncenteredness of modern Mexicans. Following the inspiration of the Surrealists, Paz saw love as the only escape from the prison of the modern world.

LADY CHATTERLEY'S LOVER

Type of work: Novel
Author: D. H. Lawrence (1885-1930)
Type of plot: Psychological realism
Time of plot: 1910-1920
Locale: English Midlands, Venice, and London
First published: 1928

Principal characters:

LADY CONSTANCE CHATTERLEY, a young woman of intelligence and latent sensuality

SIR CLIFFORD CHATTERLEY, her husband, a baronet, paralyzed in World War I

OLIVER MELLORS, Sir Clifford's gamekeeper, an ex-soldier, former blacksmith, embittered idealist

BERTHA COUTTS, Mellor's wife, a vicious harridan

IVY BOLTON, a widow and nurse, Sir Clifford's personal care-giver

MALCOLM REID, Constance's father, a member of the royal academy of artists

MICHAELIS, an Irish playwright, briefly Connie's lover

TOMMY DUKES, old army friend of Sir Clifford's

The Story:

Constance (Connie) Chatterley felt that her life was empty and pointless. A well-educated young woman in her mid-twenties, she had married Sir Clifford Chatterley in 1917 when he was on leave and then had tried to remain cheerful and encouraging during the two years he spent recovering from severe wounds suffered when he returned to battle in France. Now that Clifford was paralyzed from the waist down, Connie's life with him was primarily restricted to Wragby, the Chatterley family estate in the English midlands, where she assisted him with the short fiction he was producing with the aim of satisfying "a lame instinct for publicity." She found the life of a baronet's wife to be stultifying in spite of her wish to be of support to her husband. She found the grimy coal towns soulless and ugly and feared her separation from sensual experience was leading toward a very premature numbing of her still embryonic passionate nature.

Aside from a brief interlude in Germany when she was eighteen, and her contact with Sir Clifford before his injury, Connie had no opportunity to develop a sense of real sexual intimacy. Her growing restlessness and feeling of futility combined with her distaste for many of the obligations of a landed aristocrat's wife rendered her susceptible to the invitation of an Irish playwright, Michaelis, to begin an affair, but his "small boy's frail nakedness" and his calculated, commercial approach to art disheartened Connie. She tried to find something positive in her relationships with Sir Clifford and with "Mick," but felt that there must be more to a life with a man. As a means of making some kind of connection to a more vital aspect of life and in revulsion from the mechanized, money-mad world she moved in, she began to spend time in the woods around Wragby, where she came upon the cottage of Oliver Mellors, Sir Clifford's gamekeeper, on a walk in the wilderness.

Mellors was almost forty, very much at home in the wild, a scholarship student and former soldier who had grown up in Tevershall, a nearby coal town. He was separated from his wife, Bertha Coutts, and had a daughter who lived with his mother. Connie gradually began to appreciate Mellor's sensitivity and intelligence, and although their early contact was frequently contentious, Mellors grew steadily more sympathetic about Connie's unhappiness and in the course of comforting her, they became involved sexually. Both of them recognized the terrible consequences of an affair, but the passionate attraction they shared continued to draw them together as they discovered that there was much more than just an erotic bond between them. Meanwhile, Ivy Bolton, a widow and nurse, was hired to help Sir Clifford with the basic tasks of his life, and this further enabled Connie and Mellors to spend time together.

As Connie and Mellors became more deeply involved, Connie resolved to spend an entire night with the keeper in his cottage in the woods. In a symbolic sense, this marked a turning point in Connie's life. She began to consider the possibility of having a child, of leaving Clifford, and of beginning a new life with Mellors, who remained very much aware of the obstacles they faced. Connie's sister Hilda arrived in preparation for a visit to the Continent that the women were making with their father, and Mellors, blunt and direct as always, immediately alienated Hilda. Connie took the side of Mellors, and in doing this, she realized that she was no longer really dependent on the opinion of either the men or women who had previously ordered her life. Neither London nor Paris especially engaged Connie, since she was preoccupied with the possibilities of joining Mellors, and Venice, their holiday destination, seemed frivolous and shallow. Back in England, Mellors had to deal with the return of his estranged wife who, apparently not entirely mentally stable, was trying to reclaim a place in his life, since they had not been officially divorced after she had deserted him.

In Venice, Connie told her father that she was pregnant, and a plan was proposed in which Connie would tell Sir Clifford that Duncan Forbes, an artist, was the child's father. Forbes was willing to cooperate if necessary. In London, Connie's father had a jovial meeting with Mellors, but then Mellors savaged Forbes's paintings, speaking with characteristic candor and insight, an indication of the absurdity of the entire scheme. Connie attempted to carry out the deception, but in the course of her discussion with Sir Clifford when she returned to Wragby, her displeasure with all of the demands of a "proper" society, one that required that one maintain appearances regardless of the human cost, drove her to a complete disclosure of her relationship with Mellors. Sir Clifford was both enraged and distraught, and obstinately refused to grant Connie a divorce. Connie left Wragby to stay with her sister Hilda in Scotland, and Mellors found work on a farm where he hoped to accumulate some savings while he and Connie waited for his divorce from Bertha to become official, for his and Connie's child to be born, and for the possibility that Sir Clifford might decide to grant Connie a divorce. Mellor's letter to Connie from the farm where he felt comfortable and among friends expressed his hope that in spite of their problems, the intensity of their love, which brought "a flame into being," could sustain them until they achieved a more permanent union in the future.

Critical Evaluation:

Lady Chatterley's Lover, a novel that D. H. Lawrence completed two years before his death, when he was already quite ill, might not be the culmination of his career as a writer, but it is a drawing together of the essential themes of his work. Between October, 1926 and January, 1928, Lawrence wrote three versions of the manuscript, polishing and revising the structure and language of the book in an attempt to convey his social, political, and artistic concerns as precisely and powerfully as he could. He realized that he would not be able to find a conventional publisher in England to issue the book since he was determined to write about the erotic experiences of Connie Chatterley and Oliver Mellors using every word and image that the subject required, so he printed the first edition privately with the Italian firm of Giuseppe Orioli. Appearing six years after James Joyce's *Ulysses* (1922) and six years before Henry Miller's *Tropic of Cancer* (1934), *Lady Chatterley's Lover* was subject to the same vilification as those other two milestones of twentieth century literature. *Lady Chatterley's Lover* was not legally sold in Great Britain in an unexpurgated edition until 1960.

Throughout his earlier work, Lawrence portrayed various male characters who tended toward either an emphasis on the physical nature of their being or their cerebral agility—either a man of the earth, rooted in elemental forces but limited in terms of linguistic dexterity, or a man of the air, whose mental facility was not adequate compensation for an absence of what Lawrence called "blood consciousness." In the short story "The Shades of Spring," Lawrence describes a gamekeeper who has a very vigorous physical presence and an intuitive understanding of the natural world but who can not articulate the splendor of his realm for the woman he lives with. In "The Blind Man" Lawrence delineates a brilliant, sophisticated barrister who was a sexual neuter and whose fragile veneer was crushed by a physical overture of friendship. These men, and many others in his writing, were Lawrence's expression of the defects of character inherent in men of the modern age, who had been damaged or stunted by what he regarded as an overly mechanized, relentlessly pecuniary and dreadfully classist society. In creating Oliver Mellors, Lawrence attempted to combine the strengths of a man who was at home in the natural world and who had awareness of his own body and pleasure in its capacity for sensual response with one who had eloquence in discussing it. Mellors has the style, education, manners and confidence of a member of the upper class, but despises the effects of class consciousness and division. The necessary complexity, as well as the unavoidable contradictions, of Mellors's character have made him an object of critical controversy since the novel was published.

Now that hysterical reaction to Lawrence's vividly explicit descriptions of sexual activity has subsided, it is the divergent strains of Mellors's personality, and of Connie Chatterley's, that compel critical attention. There is a poignance in the urgency with which Lawrence invested Mellors with many of his own ideas about art and life, frequently permitting Mellors to become engulfed by a passionate declaration that mocks the reserve and restraint of more circumspect novelists. Lawrence gave Mellors his own origins in coal mining country, his own fluency with the Derby vernacular which Mellors uses as a shield and a weapon, his own love for the English landscape which Mellors sees with the image-making power of Lawrence's poetry, his own considerable erudition, and his own highly questionable beliefs about the instinctual truth of the skin and senses. Similarly, his depiction of Connie Chatterley as a woman awakened by her sexual experiences with Mellors, but also as a woman with "an immense respect for thought" who steadily grows toward an independence of outlook, opinion, and personal resolution has been the subject of considerable critical controversy, particularly in the light of some recent feminist scholarship, which sees Mellors as a crude projection of phallic deity, and Connie Chatterley as a kind of male power fantasy of a compliant, easily aroused, grateful woman.

As indicated by the continuing divergence in commentaries on *Lady Chatterley's Lover*, the relationship at its center remains engrossing. Lawrence was a master at creating the tone and inflection of conversation, and Connie and Mellors emerge as psychologically plausible, their behavior convincing, as much through their talk as through their erotic involvement. Their relationship resonates with the authenticity of vividly drawn, substantial human beings who achieve an intensity of existence unavailable to either one singly, or by implication, with anyone else. It is not perfection that Lawrence is reaching for with them, but possibility. As Lawrence, speaking with authorial conviction, but from within the sphere of Connie's thoughts, writes:

And here lies the vast importance of the novel, properly handled. It can inform and lead into new places the flow of our Sympathetic consciousness, and it can lead our sympathy away from things gone dead. Therefore, the novel, properly handled, can reveal the most secret places of life.

Leon Lewis

Bibliography:
Balbert, Peter. *D. H. Lawrence and the Phallic Imagination.* New York: St. Martin's Press, 1989. A group of essays on "sexual identity and feminist misreading," including an extensive examination of feminist critiques of the novel.
Britton, Derek. *Lady Chatterley: The Making of the Novel.* Winchester, Mass.: Unwin Hyman, 1988. Traces Lawrence's life from 1925 until the completion of the novel. Much detailed data.
Holbrook, David. *Where D. H. Lawrence Was Wrong About Woman.* Cranbury, N.J.: Bucknell University Press, 1992. Discusses Lawrence's depictions of women characters in the major fiction, with a long, concluding chapter that argues that Lawrence fails in his attempt to portray Connie Chatterley as a free woman.
Squires, Michael. *The Creation of "Lady Chatterley's Lover."* Baltimore: The Johns Hopkins University Press, 1983. Very detailed discussion of the development of the novel through the three versions that Lawrence wrote.
Squires, Michael, and Dennis Jackson, eds. *D. H. Lawrence's "Lady": A New Look at "Lady Chatterley's Lover."* Athens: University of Georgia Press, 1985. Twelve essays covering the social and intellectual significance, the artistic techniques, the historical context, and the relationship to other works by the author of *Lady Chatterley's Lover.*

THE LADY FROM THE SEA

Type of work: Drama
Author: Henrik Ibsen (1828-1906)
Type of plot: Psychological realism
Time of plot: Nineteenth century
Locale: A small town in northern Norway
First published: Fruen fra havet, 1888 (English translation, 1890); first performed, 1889

Principal characters:
    DOCTOR WANGEL, a physician
    ELLIDA, his second wife
    BOLETTA and
    HILDA, his daughters by his first marriage
    ARNHOLM, a schoolmaster
    LYNGSTRAND, a sculptor
    A STRANGER

The Story:

There was no real affection between Ellida Wangel and her two stepdaughters, Boletta and Hilda. She had married their father, Doctor Wangel, several years before, soon after the death of his first wife and after meeting him in the seacoast town that was her home, which she loved because it was near the sea. In fact, the sea had always dominated her whole life, and she felt stifled in her new home, which was surrounded by mountains.

Arnholm, Boletta's former tutor, paid a visit to the Wangel home. He had known and loved Ellida before her marriage to Doctor Wangel, but she had refused his suit because she was already betrothed to another. As the two former friends talked, a traveling sculptor, Lyngstrand, stopped to tell them of a group he hoped to model. Lyngstrand had been at sea, where he had met a sailor who told him a strange story. The sailor had married a woman who had promised to wait for him, but three years earlier he had read that his wife had married another man. The sailor had told Lyngstrand that his wife was still his, that he would have her even though she had broken her vows.

This strange tale moved Ellida, seemed even to frighten her. She was moody after that, which made her husband think she was unhappy because she was away from the sea. He offered to move his family to the seashore so that Ellida could regain her peace of mind, but Ellida knew that a move would not bring her happiness, whereas it certainly would make him and the girls unhappy to leave their home. She told him the real cause of her misery.

Some years before she had come under the spell of a sailor whose ship was in port for only a few days. He, too, loved the sea and seemed to be part of it. Indeed, he and Ellida seemed to be animals or birds of the sea, so closely did they identify themselves with the vast waters. When the sailor murdered his captain, he was forced to flee. Before he left, he took a ring from his hand and one from hers, joined them together, and threw them into the sea. He told her that this act joined them in marriage and that she was to wait for him.

At the time, she seemed to have no will of her own and to be completely under his spell. Later, she regained her senses and wrote to tell him that she did not consider the joining of the rings a lasting bond. He ignored her letters, however, and continued to tell her that he would come back to her.

Ellida told her husband that she had forgotten the sailor until three years ago, when she was carrying the doctor's child. Then, suddenly, the sailor seemed very close to her. Her child, who lived only a few months, was born—or so she believed—with the eyes of the Stranger. She had felt such guilt that from that time on she had not lived with her husband as his wife. The anguish she had suffered was affecting her mind, and she feared that she would go mad. She loved her husband, but she was drawn to the man of the sea whom she had not seen in ten years.

Doctor Wangel tried to comfort his wife, but he was also worried about her sanity. One day, a Stranger appeared in their garden. He was the sailor, come to claim Ellida. He told her that he had come to hold her to the vow she had taken years before. Ellida said that she could never leave her husband, but the Stranger would not listen. The doctor told the Stranger that he would never allow his wife to leave him and that the Stranger could not force her to go against her will. The Stranger responded that he would never force her but that she would come to him of her own free will. Those words, of her own free will, seemed to fascinate Ellida. She repeated them over and over and gained strength from them. The Stranger left, saying that he would return for her answer the next night; if she refused to join him, she would never see him again.

Ellida begged her husband to save her from the Stranger. He tried to persuade her that her mind had been conditioned by Lyngstrand's story of the sailor and his unfaithful wife, and he also reminded her that the sailor did not even look as she had remembered him. Ellida would not be comforted. She decided that there was only one way she could make the right decision and save her sanity: The doctor must release her from her marriage vows, not by divorce but verbally. Then she would be free to choose between her husband and the Stranger. She said that she had never been free, for first she had been under the will of the Stranger and then under the will of her husband.

The doctor refused her request because he thought he must save her from the Stranger and from herself. He felt that the Stranger exerted an evil influence over her, and he wanted to save her from disaster. He promised her, however, that after the Stranger left, he would release her from her vow to him and give her the freedom she wished.

The next night, the Stranger came again, as he had promised, and Ellida and her husband met him in the garden. When the Stranger asked Ellida to come with him of her own free will, the doctor ordered the Stranger to leave the country or be exposed as a murderer. The Stranger showed them a pistol that he said he would use to take his own life rather than give up his freedom.

Ellida again told her husband that he must release her from her marriage vows; although he could keep her body tied down he could not fetter her soul and her desires. Seeing that she was right and that his refusal would drive his wife out of her mind, the doctor told her that he would release her from her commitment to him. When she saw that he loved her enough to put her happiness above his own, she turned to the Stranger, who was pleading with her to leave with him on the ship standing offshore, and told him that now she could never go with him. The Stranger, realizing that there was something between these two that was stronger than his will, left them, promising never to return again.

Ellida assured her husband that her mind was whole once more and that she would never again long for the Stranger or the sea. The unknown no longer had a power over her, for at last she had made a decision of her own free will. Because she had been free to choose or reject the Stranger, his fascination was gone. Now she could go with her husband and live again as his wife. She knew too that she could win his daughters to her and think of them as her own. Ellida would never again feel like the wild, eager birds of the sea. In binding herself forever to the land, she would find freedom.

Critical Evaluation:

In the last phase of his career, Henrik Ibsen turned from the realistic social plays of his middle period toward a more psychological and, eventually, symbolic drama. He also shifted his emphasis from characters who were "normal," if extreme, to those more obviously "abnormal." He became fascinated by what he called the "trolls" or "demons" present in the back of the mind, that is, the irrational, subconscious side of the human personality that could erupt and dominate the actions of the most apparently stable individuals. Although there are important aspects of this transition in such earlier plays as *The Wild Duck* (1884) and *Rosmersholm* (1886), it was in *The Lady from the Sea* that he first overtly dramatized this new preoccupation with the "demonic." *The Lady from the Sea* may lack the stature of Ibsen's major plays, both in the level of its craftsmanship and in the depth of its perceptions, but it remains a pivotal play in his development, as well as offering one of Ibsen's most fascinating female characters.

Ellida Wangel, "the lady from the sea," is an intelligent, sensitive, vivacious, sensuous woman. She is also, clearly, on the edge of an emotional breakdown. She feels oppressed by her domestic routine and alienated from her immediate surroundings. Her husband, Dr. Wangel, loves her but is unable either to understand her or communicate with her. Ellida respects and feels gratitude toward him, but, because she feels her marriage to have been a "business arrangement," she is unable to confide in him or respond to him emotionally. She is even more isolated from his daughters, Boletta and Hilda, who treat Ellida as an intruder. They make this evident to her by celebrating their dead mother's birthday behind her back.

Such a stifling environment is, of course, common to many of Ibsen's great heroines—among them, Nora Helmer, Mrs. Alving, Gina Ekdal, Hedda Gabler—but only in *The Lady from the Sea* does it actually threaten to drive a woman to madness. Ellida's grasp on reality is precarious. She cannot forget that her own mother died in an asylum, and she is irrationally drawn to the sea; she is obsessed by the memory of her dead son, whose eyes, she believes, "changed with the seas." Her mood shifts are abrupt and erratic; she cannot even remember what people look like when they are out of her sight.

The focus of her obsession is, of course, the mysterious sailor whom she met before meeting Wangel. Although the vow she made to him was unsanctioned by law, Ellida cannot disregard it. She has felt his presence ever since her marriage to Wangel, and especially since the death of her son. The final crisis is provoked by his return to claim her as his "bride."

When he does appear, however, Ellida's reaction is a curious one, for she does not recognize him until she looks him directly in the eyes. It is not the Stranger for whom Ellida longs, but what he has come to represent to her. The sea, not the sailor, is the primary symbol, and it suggests the life of the imagination, of daring (he once killed a man), of experience, and of total personal and spiritual fulfillment. The risk, however, is self-destruction. The real contest, all three participants realize, lies not in any contention over the physical possession of Ellida, but within the mind and heart of the woman herself. "The root of that fascination lies in my own mind," she tells Wangel, "what can you do against that?"

Wangel finally realizes that, even if he forces her to remain with him, he will lose her to insanity. As a trained and sensitive doctor, he also sees that she will be destroyed if she goes with the Stranger. Caught on the horns of this dilemma, he makes a desperate and, for him, soul-wrenching decision: He gives her the absolute freedom to make her own choice and be responsible for the consequences of it.

Those two words, "freedom" and "responsibility," give Ellida power over herself, and they resolve the play. Three factors free her from the Stranger's power. Hilda's emotional reaction to the news that she will be going away suggests to Ellida the real possibility of a relationship with the girls; Wangel's obvious agonizing over his decision proves the depths of his devotion; and her own restored responsibility has given her the strength to look directly at the Stranger. Once she sees things clearly, the choice is not difficult. Because Ellida has been allowed, indeed, forced, to take control of her own life, she does so, thus not only resolving her marital difficulties but, more importantly, regaining her mental and emotional stability.

Bibliography:
Durbach, Errol. *"Ibsen the Romantic": Analogues of Paradise in the Later Plays*. Athens: University of Georgia Press, 1982. Durbach argues that the marriage depicted in *The Lady from the Sea* is a positive counterpart to those of *A Doll's House* (1879) and *Hedda Gabler* (1890).

Haugen, Einar. *Ibsen's Drama: Author to Audience*. Minneapolis: University of Minnesota Press, 1979. Written by a master teacher and scholar, this is a superb general introduction to Ibsen's works and their place in European cultural history. Comments on *The Lady from the Sea* are found throughout the book.

Holtan, Orley I. *Mythic Patterns in Ibsen's Last Plays*. Minneapolis: University of Minnesota Press, 1970. An overview of the mythic content in Ibsen's later plays. Presents a thorough discussion of the psychological, philosophical, and mythic aspects of the drama, which Holtan argues ought to be regarded from the perspective of myth or allegory.

Jacobsen, Per Schelde, and Barbara Fass Leavy. *Ibsen's Forsaken Merman: Folklore in the Late Plays*. New York: New York University Press, 1988. An overview of Ibsen's use of folklore motifs. Discusses the similarities between Ellida and such mythological creatures as mermaids and seal maidens.

Weigand, Herman J. *The Modern Ibsen: A Reconsideration*. New York: Holt, 1925. An excellent introduction to Ibsen's later plays. Contains a good discussion of *The Lady from the Sea*. Praises the subtlety of the psychological portrayal of the main character, but he lacks understanding of the importance of the subplots.

THE LADY OF THE LAKE

Type of work: Poetry
Author: Sir Walter Scott (1771-1832)
Type of plot: Historical
Time of plot: Sixteenth century
Locale: Scottish Highlands
First published: 1810

Principal characters:
JAMES OF DOUGLAS, a banished nobleman
ELLEN DOUGLAS, his daughter
MALCOLM GRAEME, loved by Ellen
RODERICK DHU, a rebel Highland chief
JAMES FITZ-JAMES, a nobleman of royal birth
ALLAN-BANE, a minstrel

The Story:

As he followed a stag during a hunt, James Fitz-James became lost in the Highlands. He wandered around until he came to Loch Katrine, a beautiful lake surrounded by steep mountains. There he met the lovely Ellen, who told him that his coming had been foretold by Allan-Bane, an ancient minstrel who served her father. When she offered the hunter food and shelter for the night, Ellen did not volunteer to tell him her name or anything of her family history, and out of courtesy he did not ask questions. Fitz-James was disturbed, however, because she bore such a marked resemblance to members of the Douglas clan, a family banished by the king. When he departed the next morning, he still knew nothing about the young woman whose beauty and grace had deeply touched his heart.

Fitz-James was correct in his fear that Ellen was of the Douglas clan. Her father was James of Douglas, once a powerful friend of the king but now hunted and with a price on his head. He and Ellen and his sister were protected by Roderick Dhu, a rebel against the king and the leader of a large and powerful Highland clan. Roderick Dhu wanted Ellen's hand in marriage, but although she honored him for the aid he gave her father she detested him for his many cruel and merciless deeds. He killed and plundered at will, trying to avenge himself on the king and the Lowlanders, who he felt had robbed him and his people of their land and wealth. Among the men he hated was Malcolm Graeme, a young nobleman, Ellen's former suitor, whom she loved. After Ellen's refusal of his proposal, Roderick Dhu called his clan together to fight Malcolm and the other supporters of the king. His excuse was that he feared Malcolm would lead the king to the hiding place of Douglas.

Like lightning, burning beacons and swift-riding messengers carried through the Highlands word that the clan was gathering. Young men left their brides at the church door and boys replaced fathers who had died since the last gathering. The women and children were placed on a lonely and protected island for safety, for a fierce and dangerous battle was to be fought. A hermit monk prophesied that the party who spilled the first foe's blood would be the victor. The prophecy suited Roderick Dhu, whose men had seen a spy lurking in the mountains and even now had lured the stranger into paths that would lead him into a trap. He would be killed by Roderick Dhu's men and thus the Highlanders would be assured of victory.

James of Douglas left Ellen. Although he did not tell her his destination, she knew that he had gone to give himself up to the king in order to prevent the bloodshed of a great battle.

Allan-Bane tried to cheer Ellen by telling her that his harp sang of glad tidings, but she would not hear him. As she sat grieving, Fitz-James appeared again. Ellen knew that he had been tricked by Roderick Dhu's men, for no one could gain entrance to a place so hidden and secret without their knowledge. Fitz-James, refusing to heed her warning, asked her to return to the court with him. She refused, telling him of her love for Malcolm Graeme. Then Fitz-James gave her his ring, which had been given to him by the king. He said the king owed him a favor and would grant any request made by the bearer of the ring. It would also promise a safe journey through the Lowlands to anyone wearing it. Fitz-James placed the ring on Ellen's finger and then departed quickly.

His guide led him through the mountain paths until they came upon a crazed woman who sang a warning song to Fitz-James. The guide thrust his sword into her. Fitz-James then killed the guide and returned to the side of the crazed woman who, before she died, told him that Roderick Dhu had killed her lover and caused her to lose her sanity. Fitz-James vowed that he would meet Roderick Dhu and avenge the woman. Having been warned by her as well as by Ellen, he was traveling cautiously when he stumbled on a guard stationed by a watch fire. The sentry called him a spy, wanted by Roderick Dhu, but offered him rest and safety, for the laws of the clansmen demanded courtesy even to one's enemy. The guard, after promising to lead Fitz-James safely through Roderick Dhu's lines, kept his word, even though Fitz-James called Roderick Dhu a coward and a murderer. When they reached a place of safety, the sentry revealed himself as Roderick Dhu. His promise fulfilled, he then challenged Fitz-James to a duel. In personal combat Roderick Dhu proved the stronger, but Fitz-James, who was more skilled, overcame the rebel. Then Fitz-James blew his horn and called his men to carry Roderick Dhu to a prison cell.

In the meantime, James of Douglas went to the court to give himself up. First, however, he took part in some games being staged that day and won every event he entered. The whisper went through the crowds that only a Douglas could possess such skill and strength. Then Douglas offered himself to the king as a ransom for his friends and clansmen. When the king ordered him thrown into prison, the people sided with Douglas and would have risen against the king. Douglas quieted them, for he would not act against his monarch, and allowed himself to be taken. The king sent messengers to the Highlanders with word that there was no need to fight; Douglas had surrendered and Roderick Dhu was a prisoner.

Ellen and Allan-Bane went to the court to seek the release of her father. The ring given her by Fitz-James afforded her safety along the way. Before news came that a truce had been arranged, Allan-Bane went to Roderick Dhu's cell and sang to him of a fierce battle that had been fought. Roderick Dhu died with a smile, for he believed that his clansmen had fought bravely.

Ellen prepared for her audience with the king. Fitz-James went to her quarters to conduct her to the court, but when they arrived she noted that everyone bowed before Fitz-James. It was not until then that she knew Fitz-James was in reality the king. He told her to claim the favor promised by the ring, but there was nothing she could ask. The king had already restored her father to favor and Roderick Dhu was dead, so that she could not plead mercy for him. She tried to stammer something about Malcolm Graeme, but the king read her heart and called Malcolm to her side. He forgave Malcolm for trying to aid the rebels and redeemed the ring Ellen wore by joining her with her beloved.

Critical Evaluation:
  After the unexpected popularity of *The Lay of the Last Minstrel* (1805), Walter Scott began *The Lady of the Lake* but laid it aside in favor of *Marmion* (1809), which was again a success

with his readers. *The Lady of the Lake* is now regarded as a better poem than either *The Lay of the Last Minstrel* or *Marmion* and is probably read more often. After writing it, Scott created several other long poems of the same kind. His next, *The Vision of Don Roderick* (1811), failed to satisfy the expectations raised by his former efforts and was made to look all the worse when a previously little-known poet named George Gordon, Lord Byron came out in 1812 with the first half of his electrifying *Childe Harold's Pilgrimage*, which dealt not with the Scottish past but with the English present.

Unwilling as yet to be shunted aside, Scott persevered with *Rokeby* (1813), a poem set in Yorkshire. He had little firsthand knowledge of that area and lacked the intuitive understanding of its people that had make his Scottish poems so popular. *Rokeby*, therefore, is the worst of his failures. *The Bridal of Triermain* (1813) is the first of many nineteenth century poems with an Arthurian theme. *The Lord of the Isles* (1815) and *Harold the Dauntless* (1817) have Scottish themes and each has some fine elements, but neither equals *The Lady of the Lake*. By the time they appeared, Scott had lost confidence in his abilities as a poet and was instead committed to a series of influential but anonymous historical novels, of which the first is *Waverley* (1814; begun in 1805). It is his novels for which Scott is best known in the twentieth century.

Scott's poems were written at a time when poetry was still a more prestigious literary form than prose. At the time of his birth, in 1771, there were few good poets in English literature, and none of them were Scots. Robert Burns, whom Scott met as a boy, became famous for his short poems, called lyrics, which were often set to music. Burns and other poets of his time turned away from the impersonal moralizing and philosophical reflection previously typical of literary practice and emphasized the pleasure or pain of intense but momentary emotions. This same concentration on the inner states of the poet himself proved increasingly more congenial to readers during the stressful years of the Napoleonic Wars than did Scott's restraint.

The Lady of the Lake was published in 1810, while the conflict with Napoleon was at its height. As a result of the war, British tourists could not visit France and Italy on the extended jaunts that previously had been popular. In prewar times, few Englishmen had thought of Scotland as a scenic destination. Once trapped at home by international strife, however, British readers were attracted to literature that enhanced the scenic and historic value of their own island. After 1815, when the Battle of Waterloo had been fought and Napoleon subdued for the final time, there was a great rush by the English to revisit places in other European countries that they had been unable to reach since the beginning of the troubles with France in 1789. The popularity of Scotland therefore fell off to a considerable extent, and Scott's popularity as a poet fell with it.

Although Scott is known for re-creating actual great events, *The Lady of the Lake* is only marginally historical. Unlike other of Scott's poems and novels, it lacks a fierce concluding battle. The most historical character is the disguised hunter at the beginning of the poem, James Fitz-James. In canto 6, stanza 26, it is revealed that he is actually James V (1512-1542), king of Scotland. The reign of James V, begun in 1524, was notable for his oppression of the Douglas clan, for his defense of the Catholic faith in opposition to that of newly arisen Protestantism, and for his popularity with the Scottish people. James's daughter and successor was Mary, Queen of Scots, who was held prisoner for years by Elizabeth I of England and eventually executed by her. None of the other characters in *The Lady of the Lake* has a historical identity.

James of Douglas, Malcolm Graeme, Roderick Dhu, and Allan-Bane are plausible but fictitious creations of Scott's imagination. One has only to compare them with similar characters in Scott's two earlier poems to discover how much his ability to create characters improved. Ellen Douglas is an attractive heroine and the title character (see 1, 17). The lake of the title is

Loch Katrine, a beautiful spot in the Trossachs northwest of Sterling. Although it had been previously ignored, Loch Katrine achieved great fame through the publication of Scott's poem and its continuing renown is still in evidence. Perhaps no other poem in the English language has immortalized a scene so effectively.

Not surprisingly, *The Lady of the Lake* is particularly noted for its descriptive passages, but one should not overlook the quality of its interpolated lyrics, including "Hail to the Chief" (2, 19-20), "Coronach" (3, 16), and "Hymn to the Virgin" (3, 29), among others. The last (based in part on Luke 1:28) has been set to music as "Ave Maria."

"Critical Evaluation" by Dennis R. Dean

Bibliography:
Cockshut, A. O. J. *The Achievement of Walter Scott.* London: Collins, 1969. A widely available introduction to the man and his work—reasonable, centrist, and modern. Chapters on Scott's major poems precede those dealing with his novels and other works.
Daiches, David. *Sir Walter Scott and His World.* London: Thames and Hudson, 1971. Competently written, well-illustrated introduction to Scott. Includes good views of the landscapes and other settings that *The Lady of the Lake* made famous.
Goslee, Nancy Moore. *Scott the Rhymer.* Lexington: University Press of Kentucky, 1988. Includes separate chapters on *The Lay of the Last Minstrel, Marmion,* and *The Lady of the Lake.* Almost the only serious critique of Scott's long poems as wholes since modern techniques of analysis were developed, the work of Goslee deserves to be read in full.
Johnson, Edgar. *Sir Walter Scott: The Great Unknown.* 2 vols. New York: Macmillan, 1970. Intended to commemorate the two hundredth anniversary of Scott's birth, Johnson's critical biography is the most important modern book on Scott. Contains unsurpassed discussions of his major poems, including *The Lay of the Last Minstrel, Marmion,* and *The Lady of the Lake.*
Nielsen, Jorgen E. "Scott's Use of Two Danish Ballads in *The Lady of the Lake.* In *Scott in Carnival,* edited by J. H. Alexander and David Hewett. Aberdeen, Scotland: Association for Scottish Literary Studies, 1993. Stresses Scott's indebtedness to Danish literature.

LADY WINDERMERE'S FAN

Type of work: Drama
Author: Oscar Wilde (1854-1900)
Type of plot: Comedy of manners
Time of plot: Nineteenth century
Locale: London
First performed: 1892; first published, 1893

> *Principal characters:*
> LADY WINDERMERE, a proper woman
> LORD WINDERMERE, her husband
> LORD DARLINGTON, a man about town
> MRS. ERLYNNE, an adventuress
> LORD AUGUSTUS LORTON, Mrs. Erlynne's fiancé

The Story:

On his wife's birthday, Lord Windermere presented her with a beautiful, delicately wrought fan with her name, Margaret, engraved upon it. She intended to carry the fan at a ball she was giving that evening, a ball to which everyone of importance in London had been invited. That afternoon, the Duchess of Berwick called on Lady Windermere, to tell her friend of a rumored affair between Lord Windermere and Mrs. Erlynne, a fascinating but notorious woman not received in the best houses. According to the duchess' story, Lord Windermere had for some months been supplying Mrs. Erlynne with funds for her support. The old dowager suggested that Lady Windermere take immediate steps to learn the relationship between the two.

Lady Windermere was upset. Determined to find out if there were any truth to the gossip, she opened her husband's desk. In a locked bank book, which she ripped open, she found evidence of her husband's duplicity, a record of checks issued to Mrs. Erlynne over a long period of time. Angry and hurt at Lord Windermere's apparent failure to appreciate love and virtue, she turned on him the moment he appeared. His main concern was annoyance that his wife had dared tamper with his property behind his back. He informed her that his relations with Mrs. Erlynne were perfectly honorable, that she was a fine but unfortunate woman who wished to win the regard of society once more. Moreover, Lord Windermere explicitly ordered his wife to send Mrs. Erlynne an invitation to the ball. When Lady Windermere refused, her husband wrote an invitation. Angered at his act, Lady Windermere threatened to strike Mrs. Erlynne with the fan if she dared cross the threshold of Windermere House.

When Mrs. Erlynne appeared at the ball, Lady Windermere lost her resolution and let the fan drop to the floor. The guests, believing that Mrs. Erlynne had been invited by Lady Windermere herself, accepted her. She was lionized by all the men, and the women, curious because of the many stories they had heard, wanted to see at first hand what she was really like. Among her special admirers was Lord Augustus Lorton, the Duchess of Berwick's disreputable brother, to whom she had just become engaged to be married.

Mrs. Erlynne was not the only woman greatly admired that evening. Lord Darlington was persistently attentive to Lady Windermere. Having sharply turned Lord Darlington's advances down, Lady Windermere became despondent when she unexpectedly caught sight of her husband and Mrs. Erlynne in rapt conversation.

Without waiting to see her guests out, Lady Windermere wrote a letter informing Lord Windermere that she was leaving his house forever. She gave the letter to a servant to deliver and left for Lord Darlington's apartments.

Mrs. Erlynne, who with Lord Augustus had remained behind to talk with Lord Windermere, discovered the letter Lady Windermere had written, and the thought of that lady's rash act brought back old memories. Twenty years before, Mrs. Erlynne had written a similar letter to her husband, and had left him and their child for a lover who had deserted her. Her years of social ostracism had made her a stranger to her own daughter. Perhaps, however, she could keep her daughter from making the same mistake. Lady Windermere should never feel the remorse that her mother, Mrs. Erlynne, had known.

Mrs. Erlynne took Lady Windermere's letter and hurried to Lord Darlington's apartments, first persuading Lord Augustus to take Lord Windermere to his club and keep him there for the rest of the night. In Lord Darlington's rooms, without revealing her identity, Mrs. Erlynne managed to persuade Lady Windermere to think of her child and go back to her husband. Out of the depths of her own bitter experience, Mrs. Erlynne insisted that Lady Windermere's first duty was not to her husband but to her child.

As Lady Windermere was leaving, Lord Darlington returned, accompanied by Lord Windermere, Lord Augustus, and several cohorts. Ready to face the men, Mrs. Erlynne counseled Lady Windermere to slip behind a curtain to await a fortuitous moment for escape. Upon learning of Lord Augustus' presence, Mrs. Erlynne went into the next room, hoping to avoid detection. Lord Windermere soon discovered his wife's fan and faced Lord Darlington with it. Giving Lady Windermere the opportunity to exit, Mrs. Erlynne appeared suddenly from the adjoining room, with the explanation that she had taken the fan, mistaking it for her own, when she left Windermere House. Her explanation saved Lady Windermere at the cost of her own reputation. Lord Windermere was furious, for he felt that he had in good faith befriended and helped a woman who was beneath contempt, and Lord Augustus turned away.

The next morning, having realized that, by some strange irony, the "bad" woman had accepted public disgrace in order to save the "good" one, Lady Windermere defended Mrs. Erlynne to her husband, who persisted in disparaging the adventuress. Frustrated by Windermere's demand that she not see Mrs. Erlynne again, Lady Windermere poised herself to explain all. Then Mrs. Erlynne arrived to return the fan, but refused to reveal herself to her daughter, not wanting to shatter Lady Windermere's illusions. Taking advantage of the simultaneous arrival of Lord Augustus and her coach, Mrs. Erlynne asked her now-cold suitor to escort her out, where he accepted her explanation that his own interests had taken her to Lord Darlington's rooms. When he returned to the Windermeres to share his good news, Lord Windermere told him that he was marrying a very clever woman. Lady Windermere insisted that he was marrying someone rarer, a good woman.

Critical Evaluation:

Oscar Wilde, the celebrated dandy of the Victorian *fin de siècle*, described *Lady Windermere's Fan*, his first financially successful theater piece, as "one of those modern drawing-room plays with pink lampshades." Although such a classification might initially appear to be frivolous, when this remark is placed in the context of Mrs. Erlynne's statement, "I have never admitted that I am more than twenty-nine, or thirty at the most. Twenty-nine when there are pink shades, thirty when there are not," it can be seen that Wilde saw his play as generously contributing to society's ability to pose as what the careful observer might call an illusion. Wilde's own description demonstrates how his play will marshal witty epigrams to dismiss itself as fluff, foster society's illusions about itself, and reveal—to those careful about construing his meaning—how what is seen is pure fabrication. With or without pink lampshades, Mrs. Erlynne nears forty, but given her society's values, to present herself as forty would severely limit her options.

Mrs. Erlynne will hardly limit her options unnecessarily, since Wilde wishes her—as a fallen woman and beautiful adventuress—to represent the role he would have art play in the world. For the timid, such as Lord and Lady Windermere, who can only function adequately in a world of illusion, art hides the truths that would ravage their lives, while saving them from ruinous mistakes by living those mistakes for them. For those reckless enough to know more, art can help them to understand and find peace with the complexities and compromises necessary to achieve wider vision and greater—as Wilde would put it—individualism.

Mrs. Erlynne sees and understands more than any of the other characters in *Lady Windermere's Fan*, which she can do because she has fallen. She has seen and embraced the other side of life, so she can face the reality of both good and evil, dealing with each appropriately without letting society's definitions rule her. She can cross the line because she has already crossed the line and survived. She can blackmail Windermere and bamboozle Lord Augustus because she does not fear falling anymore. She can get what she wants from those who have the power to refuse her—although they choose not to—in contrast to the Duchess of Berwick, who, tied up in society's knots, must get what she wants by dominating her powerless daughter and devastating other inexperienced women through gossip and cynical sexism.

This contrast between Mrs. Erlynne and the duchess reveals the beauty of the freedom Mrs. Erlynne has. She can live her own life while allowing others to live theirs. If, in Lord Darlington's apartment, she decides Lady Windermere's fate for her, she does so with the understanding of the fate Lady Windermere would prefer for herself but thinks she has lost. If she decides Lord Augustus' fate, she does so knowing that he believes, "She is just the woman for me. Suits me down to the ground." When she gets each of them what they want, she does so fully aware that she is compromising some of her own needs but meeting others. So she can sacrifice without eliciting from them a guilty sense of debt: "Then pay your debt by silence. That is the only way in which it can be paid."

Because she can compromise, she can find a certain contentment in a future abroad, which Lord Darlington, who gives up and leaves the country in a fit of romantic torpor, lacks the maturity to understand. She can take pleasure in a man who loves her. In contrast, when Lord Darlington is rejected by Lady Windermere, "all other women in the world become absolutely meaningless" to him. The dandy's delights, which Lord Darlington had previously avowed, disintegrate in the face of defeat. Lord Darlington has only assumed the dandy's pose, not learned to live it. Mrs. Erlynne, on the other hand, knowing full well that life consists of nothing but poses, can deftly lie to snatch victory from the reversals that structure the play as a whole.

Mrs. Erlynne's consummate gift for lying with total awareness and fully conscious control not only distinguishes her from the rest of her society, but also most clearly identifies her with Wilde's realm of art. Wilde had courage enough to break free from earlier theorists who sought to validate art on the basis of its access to fictional truth, to a truth that goes beneath and beyond ordinary perceptions of reality. Wilde was not afraid to face the truth that all societies base themselves on an ideology of lies, and that cultures cannot be preserved and purified through truth—which is seldom conclusively definable and often downright harmful—but only through lies, though not typical, everyday, vapid lies, such as the exchanges among the guests when they first arrive at the ball, although those have their place. What are needed are artful, daring, perceptive lies that create new possibilities for a social order that allows as many people as possible the chance to live more happily than before.

Wilde recognizes that lies will always rule the world. So instead of attempting to conquer self-serving and decayed lies with an unconvincing "truth," he proposes surpassing them with better and more beautiful lies that would lead to a more general good. To believe, as Lady Windermere does at the end of the play, that Mrs. Erlynne is a very good woman remains debatable as truth. Wilde takes great care to show Mrs. Erlynne's rejecting her newly discovered maternal instincts and threatening Lord Windermere that she will "mar every moment of [Lady Windermere's] life" should he divulge Mrs. Erlynne's identity. Such a scene helps the audience to resist sentimentalizing Mrs. Erlynne as Lady Windermere does. Nevertheless, one must question whether Mrs. Erlynne really meant her threat, or whether this was just another pose to accomplish a goal. If she really meant it, then she might be considered truly bad, but if she were lying, then she is really very good.

Lady Windermere's Fan forces the audience to recognize the logical impossibility of clearly separating good from evil and offers a marvelous illustration of what Wilde proposes as the ideological role of art.

"Critical Evaluation" by David B. Arnett

Bibliography:

Brooks, Cleanth, and Robert B. Heilman. *Understanding Drama: Twelve Plays.* New York: Holt, 1945. An indispensable act-by-act analysis that points to problems in characterization and motivation, and measures *Lady Windermere's Fan* against defined genres. Eloquently establishes the myopia of bringing predetermined standards to art.

Cohen, Philip K. *The Moral Vision of Oscar Wilde.* Rutherford, N.J.: Fairleigh Dickinson University Press, 1978. The chapter on the comedies includes ten pages that read *Lady Windermere's Fan* in terms of the shift from Old Testament to New Testament values.

Davidson, David. "The Importance of Being Ernst: Lubitsch and *Lady Windermere's Fan.*" *Literature/Film Quarterly* 11, no. 2 (1983): 120-131. Highlights the unique potentialities and limitations of film in handling *Lady Windermere's Fan.*

Powell, Kerry. *Oscar Wilde and the Theater of the 1890's.* Cambridge, England: Cambridge University Press, 1990. Sets Wilde's work within its theatrical and social contexts. The chapter devoted to *Lady Windermere's Fan* provides the basis for comparisons made throughout the book.

Small, Ian, ed. Introduction to *Lady Windermere's Fan,* by Oscar Wilde. New York: Norton, 1980. Explicates the differences in existing versions of the text. Discusses the role of deceit in both play and culture, drawing on contemporary etiquette handbooks to illustrate the protocols of London society.

THE LADY'S NOT FOR BURNING

Type of work: Drama
Author: Christopher Fry (1907-   )
Type of plot: Comedy
Time of plot: c. 1400
Locale: The small market town of Cool Clary
First performed: 1948; first published, 1949

Principal characters:
RICHARD, an orphaned clerk
THOMAS MENDIP, a discharged soldier
HEBBLE TYSON, mayor of Cool Clary
MARGARET DEVIZE, his sister
NICHOLAS and
HUMPHREY, her sons
ALIZON ELIOT, betrothed to Humphrey
JENNET JOURDEMAYNE, an alleged witch

The Story:

Thomas Mendip wanted to be hanged, but he could get no one to take an interest in his case because everyone in Cool Clary was interested in a woman accused of witchcraft, specifically, of having turned old Skipps, the rag and bone man, into a dog. Thomas begged the mayor's clerk, Richard, to get him an audience with the mayor so that he could confess his crime. Richard had other things on his mind. The mayor's nephew, Humphrey Devize, had been betrothed to Alizon Eliot, and the girl was due to arrive any minute. No one had time for a fool who wanted to be hanged.

Alizon was one of six daughters whose father feared he had too many girls to marry off. He had placed Alizon in a convent, but after he had married off his other daughters easily enough, he changed his mind about her and promised her to Humphrey. Humphrey's brother Nicholas had read in the stars that Alizon belonged to him, however, and so he knocked his brother down, hoping to kill him and take Alizon for himself. Humphrey, although he was not dead, lay still. He had not knocked himself down, so he would not pick himself up. Their mother, Margaret Devize, sister of the mayor, sometimes thought motherhood was too much for any woman. Since the boys had become untidy from lying in the rain and mud, she feared Humphrey's appearance might discourage Alizon, which it did.

When Mayor Hebble Tyson found Thomas waiting to be hanged, he was very much upset. Hebble was tired of strangers dropping into town with such ridiculous requests. It was all very irregular. Suspecting that someone was making a mockery of his authority, he threatened to have Thomas tortured if he did not go away and stop his bother. Thomas, however, held out for hanging. He confessed to killing old Skipps and a worthless pander. He did not expect to get the favor of hanging for nothing; he knew the rules, all right.

Thomas' interview with Hebble was interrupted by the announcement from Nicholas that a witch was waiting to see the mayor. Poor Hebble, upset at that news, insisted that he would not have his dignity mocked. The witch was young and beautiful. Her name was Jennet Jourdemayne, a wealthy young orphan whose property would be confiscated if she were condemned for witchcraft. Jennet thought the accusations a joke; she had been accused of turning old Skipps into a dog and of doing other evil deeds. She had come to Hebble for the protection of his laughter at the crimes of which the mob outside accused her. Hebble, not amused, sent for the constable to arrest her. Thomas tried to divert attention from her to himself by insisting that he had murdered Skipps and the pander, but no one paid attention to him; he was poor, and decidedly strange. He even told all assembled that the end of the world would come that night. All he got for his pains was to be thrown into the cellar with Jennet, to await her burning on the morrow.

Hebble and his associates had a problem on their hands. Jennet would admit nothing, and Thomas would not stop confessing. Thomas was a poor former soldier, and Jennet had property; she had to be the guilty one. At last Hebble had an idea. Hebble and his associates would leave Jennet and Thomas alone together while Hebble and the others listened at an open door. Hebble expected that, thinking themselves alone, the unfortunate pair would confess—she to witchcraft and he to innocence. The two were brought forth from the cellar, Thomas still wearing thumb screws that had been used to try to make him stop confessing. Jennet told Thomas of her father, a scientist who had given his life to his dreams. She would have no such nonsense. Facts and facts alone would rule her life—until tomorrow, when she would be burned. Fancy and imagination, she said, had caused her present trouble. Overhearing this conversation, Hebble was convinced that Jennet was a witch. At any rate she was wealthy, and her property would go to the city when she was burned.

From the conversation Hebble also learned that Thomas wanted to be hanged because he found life mean and dull. Therefore his punishment was to spend the night in joy and revelry at the party celebrating the betrothal of Humphrey and Alizon. Thomas would not agree to attend until Jennet was allowed to go to the party with him. Dressed in one of Margaret's old gowns, she was sent to the party, where Humphrey, the bridegroom-to-be, no longer wanted Alizon. Since Humphrey would not claim her, neither would Nicholas. Unknown to them, Alizon had found that she loved Richard and that Richard returned her love. They slipped away and were married by the priest who had found Richard in the poor box when he was just a tiny baby.

Unhappily for Thomas, he had fallen in love with Jennet and she with him. He had no wish to be in love; life was miserable enough. Jennet, on the other hand, did not want to renounce her factual world for one of love and fancy. Jennet knew that Thomas had not committed murder, that he had heard the mobs accusing her of turning Skipps into a dog and said he murdered the ragman only to divert suspicion from her. Then Humphrey went to Jennet and offered to get her free from the charge of witchery if she would entertain him in her cell that night. Although her body loved the thought of living, her mind and heart rebelled, and she turned down his offer. She loved Thomas too much to take life at such a price.

Fortunately for all, old Skipps was found alive. Hebble, still coveting Jennet's property, would not be satisfied, but a soft-hearted justice allowed Thomas and Jennet to slip out of town in the dark. Thomas hated to face living again, but he decided to forgo the pleasure of dying for another fifty years and spend his time of waiting with Jennet.

Critical Evaluation:

The English dramatist Christopher Fry restored poetry and humor to the modern stage. From 1948 to 1970, Fry wrote a quartet of comedies, *The Lady's Not for Burning, A Yard of Sun* (1970), *Venus Observed* (1950), and *The Dark Is Light Enough* (1954), each related to a season of the year. The first written and probably the most successful of the quartet is *The Lady's Not for Burning*, the play associated with springtime. The simple mention of a particular season carries with it the burden of traditional connotation. Spring suggests fertility, rebirth, new love, and the giddiness of spring fever. Summer suggests growth, heat, and languidness; autumn, ripeness, harvest, maturity. Winter is inevitably associated with coldness and death. Fry uses this imagery in traditional contexts, but also plays with the seasonal references in ironic contexts.

The Lady's Not for Burning is set in April, and the characters frequently remark upon the weather and how it affects their states of mind. The play begins in a fit of spring fever with all the characters' actions seeming quite mad. Alizon quizzes Richard as to the nature of males, whom she finds so strange that she is surprised when they actually speak English. Richard blames the madness of men on the "machinations of nature;/ As April does to the earth." Alizon is delighted with the analogy: "I wish it were true/ Show me daffodils happening to a man!" Precisely at this point Nicholas enters to claim Alizon as his bride, declaring that he has killed his twin brother and rival, Humphrey, in a bed of daffodils. Not surprisingly, Humphrey is not dead in the least and is found lying on his back picking daffodils. As the action becomes more complicated, Margaret Devize, in motherly fashion, finally declares to her brother that the younger generation is all "in the same April fit of exasperating nonsense." The silly but mostly harmless spring fever of the younger generation contrasts with the absurd and dangerous behavior of the elders.

The Lady's Not for Burning teeters between rebirth and stagnation. The year of the play, "1400 either more or less exactly," traditionally marks the end of the Middle Ages and the beginning of the modern world in England. The elders of the town of Cool Clary are stuck in a medieval worldview in which the unusual is dangerous, and the status quo must be preserved.

The Lady's Not for Burning is a quixotic comedy, one in which the comic heroes, as does Don Quixote of Miguel de Cervantes' famous novel, flee into "madness" in order to escape the madness of an authoritarian society. The youthful lovers—Jennet and Thomas, Richard and Alizon—cannot transform the ludicrous society of Hebble Tyson and the Devizes, a society in which material gain is the predominant virtue, so they must escape from it. The escape in this play resembles the severance from parental authority that youth must accomplish before reaching maturity. The younger characters are in tune with the mad delight and love of an "April anarchy," so they must flee from those who are out of tune and who cannot recognize the rebirth that spring brings.

Margaret and Hebble declare their distaste for spring quite emphatically, and they cannot see the possibility for redemption in their midst. The redeemers are outsiders and will remain so: Alizon, the child of nature who "appeared overnight/ As mushrooms do" and was given to God; Richard, no one's child, who was not born but "was come across"; Jennet, the alchemist's daughter, who is called a witch because she speaks French to her poodle and dines with a peacock; and Thomas Mendip, the disillusioned soldier, who wants to be hanged because "each time I thought I was on the way/ To a faintly festive hiccup/ The sight of the damned world sobered me up again." Humor is not tolerated in this most rigid of societies; it is seen as tiresome and incompatible with good citizenship.

Laughter, however, is what Jennet seeks, and it is laughter, "the surest touch of genius in creation," with which Thomas Mendip cheers her when things look bleakest. Only in each other can the lovers create a festive society. The world, however, does not change because of their love, as Thomas declares to Jennet. Although their festive society does not triumph, the play ends on a wish: "Good morning. —And God have mercy on our souls." The ironic absurdity of the existing society does not destroy the idealism and desire of the protagonists for harmony. *The Lady's Not for Burning* is a youthful comedy—one that looks forward with hope.

Christopher Fry wrote *The Lady's Not for Burning* shortly after the end of World War II, when the austerities of wartime were still very much a part of English life. The lushness of the play's poetic language and the fancy of its romantic setting were fashioned to appeal to the audience's longing for relief from drab reality. The war-weariness of Thomas Mendip is a reminder of the harshness of what was, when the play was first performed, recent history. The verbal wit and sensuous imagery of Fry's language satisfied a hunger for sophisticated drama in the generation coming home from World War II. *The Lady's Not for Burning*, first produced in a regional theater in 1948, was transferred to the West End in 1949 in a highly successful production directed by and starring John Gielgud. The play was subsequently produced on Broadway. Fry's poetic drama was eclipsed in the 1960's with the revival of the harsh naturalism of Britain's "angry young men" and the experimentation of the absurdists. Revivals of *The Lady's Not for Burning* were televised in the 1970's (starring Richard Chamberlain and Eileen Atkins) and in 1987 with Kenneth Branagh. While perhaps not as poetically impressive as T. S. Eliot's dramas, Fry's seasonal comedies have a much stronger theatrical appeal, undoubtedly drawn from the playwright's long association with the theater as actor, director, and dramatist. *The Lady's Not for Burning* helped to define the theatrical accomplishment of the mid-twentieth century of the English-speaking world.

"Critical Evaluation" by Jane Anderson Jones

Bibliography:

Donoghue, Denis. "Christopher Fry's Theatre of Words." In *The Third Voice: Modern British and American Verse Drama*. Princeton, N.J.: Princeton University Press, 1959. Deplores the eccentricity of Fry's language in the early plays, including *The Lady's Not for Burning*.

Leeming, Glenda. "Christopher Fry: Poetic Drama in Conventional Setting." In *Poetic Drama*. New York: St. Martin's Press, 1989. Traces the development of twentieth century verse drama from William Butler Yeats and T. S. Eliot to W. H. Auden, Christopher Isherwood, and Christopher Fry. Emphasizes how the imagery in *The Lady's Not for Burning* evokes and insists upon the beauty of the natural world.

_____. "Condoning Creation in *The Lady's Not for Burning*." In *Christopher Fry*. Boston: Twayne, 1990. Reveals the source for the play and focuses discussion on the characters and the imagery of the play.

Roy, Emil. *Christopher Fry*. Carbondale: Southern Illinois University Press, 1968. Contains a chapter on each of Fry's plays until 1968 and chapters on Fry's "Outlook and Ideas," his "Imagery" and an "Overview." Discusses the literary influences on *The Lady's Not for Burning*, its themes and plot structure, Fry's language, and the motifs of alchemy, martyrdom, and seduction.

Stanford, Derek. *Christopher Fry*. Rev. ed. London: Longmans, Green, 1962. Includes a brief biographical sketch and a discussion of each of the plays written before 1962. Emphasizes Fry's intuition of the presence of the mystery that informs mortality.

THE LAIS OF MARIE DE FRANCE

Type of work: Poetry
Author: Marie de France (c. 1150-c. 1190)
First transcribed: c. 1167 (English translation, 1911)

The Story:

The Lay of Guigemar. In the days of King Arthur, Guigemar, a knight who loved no lady, was injured by an arrow with which he had shot a white doe. In human speech, the doe told Guigemar that he would have no relief from his hurt until he found a woman who would suffer as never woman did before and for whom he would suffer as well. Binding his wound with the hem of his shirt, Guigemar boarded an empty ship he came across in the harbor. He fell asleep and awakened in another land, where he was discovered by the queen, a young woman whom her old lord kept as a prisoner. The queen took him home, concealed him, and healed him; the two became lovers. They lived happily for a year and a half. As tokens of their love, the queen tied a knot in the hem of Guigemar's shirt that only she could untie and Guigemar fastened a girdle about the queen's waist that only he could unbuckle. They pledged that they would never take another love who was unable to unfasten the knot or buckle.

When the king discovered Guigemar, he allowed him to leave on the ship in the hope that it would perish at sea. He threw the queen in a tower where she stayed for two years. One day, finding the door unlocked, she went to the harbor and boarded an empty vessel, which carried her to the shore of a warlike prince, Meriadus, who lodged her with his unmarried sister and tried to win her love. Because he could not loosen the buckle, he brought to her a knight who had a mysterious knot tied in his shirt. The knight was Guigemar. After the knot and buckle had been loosed, Guigemar wanted to take the queen away, but Meriadus would not let her go. Guigemar joined forces with Meriadus' enemy. They laid siege to the castle, captured it when its defenders became weak with hunger, burned the fortress, and killed Meriadus. The lovers then departed in triumph.

The Lay of Chaitivel. In Nantes in Brittany, a beautiful lady who was loved by four knights but undecided which knight she liked best, sent presents and messages to all. Each carried her favor and cried her name in the lists. During an Easter tournament, three of the knights were slain and the fourth was severely wounded. All four of the knights were brought on their shields to the lady. Distressed, she had the three slain knights buried in an abbey and nursed the wounded knight back to health. Mourning for the three dead knights, she told the fourth knight that she was going to make a lay about their deaths and his terrible wounds and call it "The Lay of the Four Sorrows." The knight suggested that she call it "The Lay of the Dolorous Knight." His three comrades were past suffering, he declared, but he received every day only a few courteous, empty words from the lady but no love. The lady agreed that this was a good title. However, some still call it "The Lay of the Four Sorrows."

The Lay of Eliduc. In Brittany, Eliduc, having lost favor with the king because of false rumors, was forced to leave the country. After he and Guideluec, his wife, had pledged their faith to each other, Eliduc took a ship to Totenois. There, he helped an aged king defeat a prince who wanted to marry his daughter, Guilliadun. The king gave Eliduc reward and honor, and the princess gave him her love. Although Eliduc reminded himself of his wife at home, he neglected to mention his wife to the princess. His own king, needing his help against an enemy, sent for his return. At home, Eliduc's wife was delighted to see him, but Eliduc was sad. He returned to the country of Totenois and sent word to the princess to meet him. They left secretly on a ship.

During a heavy storm, one of the men cried that the princess was the cause of the storm because Eliduc had deserted his wife at home. When the man wanted to throw the princess overboard, Eliduc hit him with an oar and cast him into the sea. The princess fainted when she heard that Eliduc was married, and all believed her to be dead. Going ashore, they carried her to a chapel, intending to give her burial rites. Eliduc left her at the altar and went home in such a downcast mood that his wife decided to learn the cause. When she found the princess, she was overcome at the sadness of her death, even though she realized that Eliduc loved the maiden. When she saw a weasel revive its dead mate by putting a red flower in his mouth, she took the flower, revived the girl, and told her that she would release Eliduc from his marriage vows. She took the princess to her home, released Eliduc, and became an abbess. Eliduc and the princess married and lived happily for a time. Then they parted and took holy orders. The princess went to the abbess, who received her as a sister. Eliduc and the princess sent messages back and forth between the convent and the monastery, each encouraging the other in the holy life. Their repentance was lasting.

The Lay of Laüstic. In the town of Saint Malo, in Brittany, a bachelor knight fell in love with his friend's wife. Although they seldom met, the two at last became lovers. Because their houses stood side by side, they were able to pass messages and gifts through the casements and gaze at each other. When the husband asked the wife why she spent her nights watching at the casement, she said that she was listening to the nightingale. He had servants trap the bird; then he wrung its neck and threw it in her lap. The wife, sad because she could not use the bird as an excuse to see her lover, embroidered the story of the nightingale's fate on white samite, wrapped the bird in the cloth, and sent it to her lover. The doleful knight had a little chest made of gold and precious stones for the body of the bird and carried it everywhere with him.

The Lay of Sir Lanval. Because of trouble with the Picts and Scots, King Arthur was lodging at Caerleon-on-Usk in Wales. There, at Pentecost, he bestowed honors and lands on all except Sir Lanval, the son of a king in a distant country, whom he despised. Too proud to ask his lord for his due, Lanval remained poor.

Riding unattended in a meadow near a stream, Lanval dismounted because his horse was trembling. He let the horse graze while he tried to sleep. Two maidens wearing purple mantles appeared and told him that their mistress had summoned him. He found a beautiful maiden lying on a richly covered bed in a silken pavilion with a golden eagle on top. She was dressed in white linen with a mantle of ermine trimmed in purple. When she offered Lanval her love, provided that he tell no one of her existence, he accepted. She gave him rich clothing and a purse that was never empty. Now wealthy, Lanval redeemed captives, clothed the minstrels, comforted strangers, and was completely happy. The beautiful maiden appeared whenever he called her.

At a party in the royal orchard, Lanval ignored the queen and thirty of her most beautiful maidens because they looked like kitchen wenches to him. Calling Lanval to her, the queen offered him her love. Lanval refused, saying that he would not betray his lord. Angrily, the queen retorted that Lanval must despise women, but Lanval told her that his love was richer than any there and that the meanest of her maidens excelled the queen in goodness and beauty. The queen fled weeping to her chamber.

When Arthur returned, she told him that Lanval had sought her love and that she had refused him. At her refusal, she declared, Lanval had reviled her and said that his love was set on a lady whose meanest wench was fairer than the queen. Arthur swore that he would burn or hang Lanval if he could not deny his boast before his peers.

Because he had revealed her existence, Lanval lost contact with his lady. He wanted to die; instead he was compelled to appear before the court of barons. The barons said that they would look at Lanval's lady and decide if she was more beautiful than the queen. If so, there would be no trial. Because Lanval could not produce her, the barons prepared to pass judgment upon him. At that moment, two beautiful maidens, followed by two even more beautiful maidens, appeared and announced that their lady was approaching. They were so beautiful that many said the queen had already lost. Soon Lanval's lady appeared, riding a white horse and wearing white with a purple mantle. Every man marveled at her beauty and cared no more for mortal women. She said that Lanval had never craved the love of the queen but that he had spoken hastily. The barons were overcome by her beauty, and Arthur suggested that she stay a while at court. She declined and together with Lanval she rode away forever, perhaps to Avalon.

The Lay of the Two Lovers. A king in Normandy had a fair daughter whom he did not wish to give in marriage, and he proclaimed that no one should wed her except he who carried her to the pinnacle of a great and perilous mountain. Many tried and failed. The girl fell in love with a slender young man and obtained from her aunt a magic potion that would enable him to reach the mountaintop. Armed with this herbal, the youth asked and received the king's permission to carry the girl to the pinnacle. To lighten his load, the maiden fasted for several days and wore only her smock. The youth set out bravely but refused the potion in the presence of the watchers. As he went higher, the maiden urged him to take the potion; he refused and finally fell dead of exhaustion. Flinging away the flask of potion, the girl died of grief holding her lover in her arms. A search party led by the king found them dead. The king was distraught. They buried the lovers in a marble coffin on the mountain where they had died. Wherever the magic potion touched the barren ground, saving herbs sprang up.

The Lay of Bisclavret. At the insistence of his wife, who demanded an explanation of his absence from home three nights a week, Bisclavret, a baron in Brittany, revealed that he was a werewolf. He told her that he hid his clothing in a hollow stone near a chapel and that if he were to lose his clothing he would not be able to return to man's shape. The wife, who was afraid of her husband, sent for a knight who had long loved her unrewarded. She told him that her husband was a werewolf and asked him to steal her husband's clothing from his hiding place. He did so and married the wife. Bisclavret seemed lost forever from the world of men.

More than a year later, the king, hunting in the woods, was surprised by a wolf that fawned on him, and he took the animal home as a pet. Bisclavret made an admirable pet until his wife's second husband came to court, when he sprang for his rival's throat. The king called him off, but when Bisclavret's wife came to court, he bit off her nose. Although men beat the wolf, they did not kill him, for a wise counselor pointed out that the wolf's malice was directed at only the woman and her husband. Questioned by the king, the woman revealed the truth. He made her return her first husband's clothing, but Bisclavret ignored the garments. The counselor then suggested putting the wolf and the clothing alone in a room. Bisclavret returned to his human form. The king, delighted, restored his fief. The wife and her second husband left the country.

The Lay of Le Fresne. When the wife of a knight in Brittany bore twin sons, the wife of another knight spread the story that twin children always had two fathers. A year later, that woman had twin girls. Since she had spread the word about the double paternity, she was afraid to reveal that she had given birth to twins. At first, she considered killing one. Later, a serving maid took the child, wrapped in sanguine silk and with a rich ring tied to her wrist, and left her in an ash tree near a church. She was found and reared by an abbess, who called her Le Fresne, which means ash.

When the beautiful Le Fresne was grown, a knight, Gurun, loved her and persuaded her to run away with him to his castle. There, they lived happily until the knights of the realm persuaded Gurun to put Le Fresne away and take a wife. At last he agreed to marry another beautiful girl named La Codre, which means hazel. Although the servants were angry with Gurun, Le Fresne accepted this development with grace and decked her lord's bed with the sanguine silk in which she had been found. After the wedding, La Codre's mother brought her daughter to the bridal bed and recognized the silk as that in which she had wrapped her twin daughter when she sent her away. She questioned Le Fresne, who showed her the ring. The mother obtained her husband's forgiveness and the archbishop dissolved the marriage between Gurun and La Codre. Le Fresne married her lord, and La Codre soon found another husband.

The Lay of the Honeysuckle. King Marc banished his nephew Tristan for having fallen in love with the queen. Tristan went to his native South Wales but before long he returned to Cornwall to be near the queen. Living in the forest, he sought shelter from friendly peasants. Hearing that King Marc planned to keep high court at Tintagel, Tristan entered a wood through which he knew Isolde would pass. He cut a wand from a hazel tree, peeled it, carved his name on it, and set it in the road where the queen found it. To her alone, it was a message that Tristan was waiting and that, like the honeysuckle and the hazel tree, they were eternally inseparable. She sent her knights aside, entered the wood with her maiden, Brangwaine, found Tristan, and spent a joyful hour with him. She told him that she was trying to reconcile Marc to him. After they parted, Tristan returned to Wales, where he made a new lay.

The Lay of Equitan. King Equitan, a great but not wise lover, decided to win the love of his seneschal's wife. Although she refused at first, Equitan finally won her and they exchanged rings. When Equitan's people urged him to marry, the wife heard the news and came to him in tears. Equitan assured her that he would never marry unless her husband were to die and he might marry her. This declaration quickly brought a plan to mind. The wife asked Equitan to be bled with her husband at their castle; she would prepare a bath for both and make her husband's so hot that he would die. The king agreed and rode to the chase with the seneschal, after which the surgeon bled them. Beside each bed, the wife placed a bath, her husband's boiling. When the husband delayed his appearance, the wife and Equitan looked tenderly at each other while they sat waiting on the seneschal's bed by the steaming bath. The husband returned, brushed aside the maiden guarding the door, and found his wife and the king in each other's arms. The king, jumping up, sprang into the fatally hot bath. Enraged, the seneschal threw his wife into the same bath, where they both died.

The Lay of Milun. Milun, a famous knight in South Wales, received word from an unknown maiden that she would give him her love. Milun accepted, and she bore him a son. Fearing her father, the girl kept the birth secret, and Milun's servants carried the baby to his mother's sister, who was married to a lord in Northumberland. With the child went letters and his father's signet ring to be given him when he came of age. Then Milun went in search of reward in a foreign country, and the girl was given in marriage to an old lord.

Returning to South Wales, Milun was sad to learn that his love was married, but he was happy to know that they were not far apart. He sent to her a swan with a letter concealed in a feather. She was instructed to answer the letter but to keep the bird unfed for three days before she wanted the letter returned. She did as he asked, although she was compelled to wait a month before she could get parchment and ink. The swan then flew home to be fed and delivered her letter. For twenty years, the swan served as messenger between the lovers, who never saw each other during that time.

In Northumberland, the son, now grown, was known as the Knight Peerless. His aunt told him of his origin and gave him the signet ring. His fame spread to Brittany, where Milun heard of the unknown young knight and determined to joust with him to preserve his own fame. Milun crossed the sea and met the youth in tournament, where the boy unhorsed him. When Milun's helmet was knocked off, his white hair and beard were revealed. The Knight Peerless dismounted and apologized to his elder. When Milun asked him his name, the boy told his story and showed Milun the ring. Father and son were joyfully united, and the son promised to kill his mother's husband. They set forth for Brittany, but when they landed a messenger met Milun with the happy news that his love's husband was dead. Milun and his son went to the mother, and the youth had the joy of seeing his parents wed.

The Lay of Yonec. In Britain, a rich old man married a beautiful young girl whom he guarded for seven years in a castle. One day, she cried out in despair that old tales about young wives married to old lords finding lovers could not be true. In a few minutes, a falcon alighted on her window, entered the room, and turned into a handsome knight. He said that his name was Eudemarec and that he had come at her call. The two immediately became lovers. The husband became suspicious because his wife suddenly appeared to be so happy. He pretended to leave and set his older sister to watch. When she learned the secret and told her brother, the husband set sharp blades in the window to kill the hawk. When Eudemarec alighted there next, he received his death wound. He fluttered, bleeding, to his love's bed, told her that he would die, and promised that she would bear a son, Yonec, who would avenge both his death and her suffering. The wife followed the hawk out the window and tracked him by the trail of blood until she found him dying in a royal bed. He gave her a ring that he said would cause her husband to leave her alone. He also gave her a sword as a gift to his son. When the proper time came, she was to go with her husband and son to an abbey where they would see a tomb. There she was to tell her son of his father and give him the sword.

These events came to be. At the tomb, the wife told Yonec of his father and gave him the sword before she fell dead on Eudamarec's tomb. The son then took the sword and cut off the old man's head. Because Eudamarec was king of the land, the people proclaimed Yonec their lord as he left the church.

Critical Evaluation:

Probably connected with the court of the Anglo-Norman King Henry II of England, Marie de France is credited with the creation of the *lai* as a literary genre. The lais are Celtic stories she had heard recounted and sung in the Breton language and which she chose to preserve in written verse form in the Anglo-Norman dialect of Old French. They are narratives with frequent lyrical and moral overtones and occasional brief intrusions by the author to express her own opinions. Their popular appeal to readers, both in Marie's time and today, has gained for her recognition as the first important female literary figure of the Western world.

Familiar with the classical and vernacular literature circulating in Britain and Western Europe during the second half of the twelfth century, Marie de France synthesizes in her verse tales the narrative tradition of northern France and the courtly love lyrics of the southern troubadours. Knightly activities and adventures such as hunting parties, tournament jousts, mercenary military engagements, and the wielding of weapons, which were the essence of Old French *chansons de geste* and the medieval *romances*, figure prominently in the *lais*. These events are never gratuitous, but occur rather because they have a direct effect on the central love relationship, for each of Marie's *lais* is, above all, a love story. Each *lai* presents a different scenario, which presents a new perspective on the subject.

In her depiction of love and its intricacies, Marie uses a number of literary themes. One of the most popular motifs is that of the *mal mariée* (mismatched wife). In the first story, Guigemar's lover is married to a wealthy old man who, because of jealousy, has locked her away. The reader is not surprised that the wife falls instantly in love with the handsome, wounded knight. Similarly, Yonec's mother is married to an old man who had taken her as his wife for the purposes of begetting an heir. The reader, medieval or modern, is sympathetic to her illicit affair with the bird/man. A mismarriage is also implied in the *lais* of Laüstic and Milun, although a mismarriage is not essential to the plot. Reversal of this theme, the mismatched husband, appears in *The Lay of Equitan* and *The Lay of Bisclavret*.

Lack of self-control is illustrated in several of the stories. In *The Lay of the Two Lovers*, the young lover, overconfident of his strength, will not stop to drink his energizing potion when making the mandatory ascent of the mountain with his bride-to-be in his arms, and he dies of the physical strain. In three of the tales, overindulgence in sexual pleasure on the part of adulterous lovers results in detection of the affairs by the cuckolded husbands. The result is separation or even death of the lovers. On the other hand, the patience and composure of Le Fresne, Milun, and Eliduc's first wife bring about happiness of all concerned.

All twelve stories rest on the premise that love brings with it suffering in the form of physical and emotional distress. In *The Lay of Guigemar*, Marie de France declares, "Love is an invisible wound within the body, and, since it has its source in nature, it is a long-lasting ill." In the first story, love is symbolized by the rebounding arrow that strikes Guigemar in the thigh. By contrast, it is the lack of love that keeps the young wife in *The Lay of Yonec* awake. Separation from the beloved is the worst of all the woes sustained by the lovers in *The Lais of Marie de France*. Their anguished longing is portrayed with poignancy and delicate lyricism. Several of the estranged couples are reunited, but some must endure permanent despair.

Supernatural elements, particularly those characteristic of Celtic legend, are present in several of the *lais*. Since much of the natural world was as yet unexplained in the twelfth century, the medieval mind easily accepted the possibility of human transformation into wolves or birds, visits from otherworldly beings, animals that talk, magic potions, and magic boats that sail without a crew. Whenever it occurs, paranormal activity in the *lais* always moves the story forward; the activity is not intended to dismay the reader.

The author of the twelve *lais* presents a composite picture of love that is strikingly more modern than the concept of courtly love established by the Provençal troubadours. For Marie de France, true love can exist only between equals—persons of the same age, social status, and education. Moreover, people must possess the same courtly qualities as each other, and they must be completely loyal to each other. Although never overtly expressed, it is implicit in the stories that God condones such love, even when, through circumstances, the love is necessarily illicit or adulterous. As in the well-known legend of Tristan and Isolde, true love in the *lais* is a product of destiny, and the love is eternal.

Symmetry and balance are evident in the structure and style of the *lais*. In the only manuscript containing all twelve stories, long tales are followed by short ones; the opening and closing tales, both extended ones, end with the triumph of love in this life, whereas the two middle tales end with the union of the lovers in death. In one story a lonely knight is loved by an otherworldly female; in another story, an imprisoned lady is visited by a supernatural bird/man/lover. The *lais* are replete with polarities of vices and virtues: cupidity and charity, deceit and loyalty, generosity and greed, excess and moderation, egotism and altruism.

Obviously, moral lessons can be inferred from such narratives. In her prologue to the tales, Marie discusses ancient texts which, on close scrutiny, reveal subtle truths. However, it is clear in the prologue that the author's primary purpose is to relate interesting stories and, by doing so, preserve them and her own name for posterity. She insists that her tales are not fictitious, and she frequently lends them veracity by including precise geographical locations and by associating events with specific dates in the Church calendar. Her concise writing is occasionally punctuated with analytical or descriptive passages vital to proper comprehension of the narrative. Unlike many medieval texts, there are no obscurities in her plots. The *lais* are the product of a gifted young writer and consummate storyteller; they will doubtless continue to delight readers everywhere, just as they did in the twelfth century.

"Critical Evaluation" by Judith L. Barban

Bibliography:

Bruckner, Matilda Tomaryn. "Marie de France." In *French Women Writers*, edited by Eva Sartori and Dorothy Zimmerman. Westport, Conn.: Greenwood Press, 1991. Discussions of the chronology and themes of the *lais* and a concise survey of critical writings, including the importance of the *lais* in feminist studies.

Burgess, Glyn S., and Keith Busby. Introduction to *The Lais of Marie de France*. London: Penguin Books, 1986. Overview of the extant manuscripts, composition of *The Lais of Marie de France*, and the major themes and impact of the work. Includes a comparison of the *lais* with other medieval genres.

Chamberlain, David. "Marie de France's Arthurian Lai: Subtle and Political." In *Culture and the King: The Social Implications of the Arthurian Legend*, edited by Martin Shichtman and James Carley. Albany: State University of New York Press, 1994. An interpretation of the story of Lanval. Points out the importance of irony, iconography, and humor.

Clifford, Paula. *Marie de France: Lais*. London: Grant & Cutler, 1982. A succinct study of love and destiny in the *lais*, with background information on Marie de France and her contribution to twelfth century literature.

Ferrante, Joan M. "The French Courtly Poet: Marie de France." In *Medieval Women Writers*, edited by Katharina M. Wilson. Athens: University of Georgia Press, 1984. Contains a brief résumé and an analysis of the stories from the perspective of love and personal relations. Provides information on Marie's other works and includes Ferrante's own English translation of the Yonec tale.

Rothschild, Judith Rice. "Sin, Charity and Punishment in Marie de France's *Lais*." *Medieval Perspectives* 2, no. 1 (Spring, 1987): 91-103. An examination of nontraditional morality expressed in the *lais*.

LALLA ROOKH
An Oriental Romance

Type of work: Poetry
Author: Thomas Moore (1779-1852)
Type of plot: Love
Time of plot: c. 1700
Locale: India
First published: 1817

Principal characters:
> AURUNGZEBE, the emperor of Delhi
> LALLA ROOKH, Aurungzebe's daughter
> FERAMORZ, a young poet of Cashmere
> ABDALLA, the king of Lesser Bucharia
> ALIRIS, the young king of Bucharia and Abdalla's son
>   disguised as Feramorz
> FADLADEEN, a chamberlain of the harem

The Story:

Aurungzebe, the emperor of Delhi, entertained Abdalla, who had recently abdicated his throne to his son Aliris and was on a pilgrimage to the Shrine of the Prophet. Aurungzebe had promised his daughter Lalla Rookh (Tulip Cheek) in marriage to Aliris. The lonely princess was to journey to Cashmere, where she and Aliris would meet and be married.

Lalla Rookh's caravan, of the finest and most comfortable equipment, was manned by the most loyal and efficient of servants, the entire cavalcade having been sent by Aliris to conduct his bride to him. Among the servants sent by Aliris was a young poet of Cashmere, Feramorz. Feramorz captivated all the women with his beauty and charming musical ability as he sang and recited to the accompaniment of his kitar. Lalla Rookh, not immune, became enamored of the young poet.

Fadladeen, the chamberlain traveling as Lalla Rookh's protector, was a bumptious, all-knowing, perspicacious authority on any subject: food, science, religion, and literature. His criticisms were so detailed and harsh that the person being assessed was reduced to feeling like a virtual ignoramus. He criticized Feramorz's tale of "The Veiled Prophet of Khorassan."

In this story, Azim and Zelica were young lovers who lived in the province of Khorassan. After Azim went off to fight in the wars in Greece, Zelica was enticed into the harem of Mokanna, the "veiled prophet of Khorassan," in the belief that she would gain admission into Paradise; there she would be reunited with Azim, whom she believed killed in the Greek wars. Mokanna was a dastardly, cruel ruler, who had gained the throne through his magic. When Azim learned, in a dream, of Zelica's plight, he returned to his country to join the army of the veiled prophet. Discovering that his vision of Zelica's unhappy state was true, he joined the troops of an enemy caliph and fought against Mokanna.

Mokanna, defeated, committed suicide by plunging into a vat of corrosive poison. Zelica, feeling remorse for having become Mokanna's wife and sadness at seeing her young lover but not being able to be his, put on the veil of Mokanna and confronted the caliph's army, with the intention of being mistaken for Mokanna and being killed. Azim, mistaking her for Mokanna, killed her. The lovers exchanged vows of devotion and forgiveness as Zelica died. Azim grew old grieving by Zelica's grave, where he finally died after another vision in which Zelica appeared and told him she was blessed.

Feramorz, unaccustomed to criticism, was taken aback by Fadladeen's reactions to this beautiful love poem. Fadladeen was caustic. He belabored the subject of long speeches by the characters in the story; he contrasted Feramorz's poem with the fluency and tone of poems of other writers of the day; he analyzed the meter of specific lines in the poem. Feramorz did not attempt another story for some days.

Encouraged to sing by Lalla Rookh, he began his second poem only after an appealing look at Fadladeen as he explained that this tale, "Paradise and the Peri," was in a lighter and humbler vein than the first. The Peri, wishing to be admitted to Paradise, was told to bring as her passport the gift most treasured by heaven. Her first offering was a drop of blood from a dying Indian patriot; this unacceptable gift was followed by the last sigh of an Egyptian maiden as she died of grief at the loss of the lover whom she had nursed through the plague. Rejected for this gift, the Peri was finally admitted to Paradise when she presented the penitential tear of a hardened criminal of Balbec. The criminal's tear had been shed as he heard a child's prayer. Fadladeen was even more outspoken in his criticism of Feramorz's second story. He refused to be halted in his critical onslaught by Lalla Rookh.

By the time the party had arrived in Lahore, Lalla Rookh realized not only that she was in love with Feramorz but also that the handsome singer was in love with her, and she resolved that he should not be admitted to her presence again. Although the heart she was to give to her bridegroom would be cold and broken, it must be pure.

As they journeyed on, the travelers came upon the ruins of an ancient tower, a structure that aroused the curiosity of the entire group. Fadladeen, who had never before been outside Delhi, proceeded learnedly to show that he knew nothing whatever about the building. Despite Lalla Rookh's admonition that Feramorz not be called to identify the ruins for them, he was brought before her.

The tower, he said, was the remains of an ancient Fire-Temple, built by Ghebers, or Zoroastrian Persians, who had fled to the site from their Arab conquerors in order to have liberty in a foreign country rather than persecution in their own land. This historical detail gave rise to Feramorz's third song, "The Fire-Worshippers." In this story, Hafed, the leader of the resisting Gheber forces in the mountains, fell in love with Hinda, the daughter of the Arabian emir who had come to rout out the insurrectionists. Hafed, his identity concealed, gained access to Hinda's quarters and won her love before he was captured by the Ghebers.

The Arabs defeated the Ghebers in a sudden attack, and Hafed sacrificed himself on a funeral pyre. As Hinda watched from a distance, she plunged into a lake and was drowned. On this occasion Fadladeen decided to forgo criticism of Feramorz's tale. Rather, Fadladeen decided to report this profane story to Aliris. Fadladeen hoped in this manner to bring about punishment for Feramorz and to secure for himself a place in Aliris' court.

In the tranquil, beautiful valley of Hussun Abdaul, Feramorz sang his last song, "The Light of the Haram." This song was an account of married love reconciled after a misunderstanding between husband and wife. The "Light of the Haram" was Sultana Nourmahal, the favorite wife of the Emperor Selim, son of the great Acbar. During the celebration of the Feast of Roses, Nourmahal quarreled with Selim. The couple's period of sadness and remorse because of their harsh words to each other ended when Nourmahal learned a magic song from an enchantress, Namouna. Masked, Nourmahal sang the song to Selim at the emperor's banquet, and they were reunited in undying love for each other.

After considerable hardship the party crossed the mountains that separate Cashmere (Kashmir) from the rest of India. At a temple where they rested, the young king came to welcome his bride into his kingdom. Lalla Rookh, seeing his face full view for the first time, fainted. The king was the young singer, Feramorz. The young king had traveled disguised as a poet. He had wished to win Lalla Rookh's love.

Learning the identity of the man whose songs he had criticized so caustically, Fadladeen recanted immediately and declared that Aliris was the greatest poet of all time. In his new position of prestige, bestowed on him by Aliris, Fadladeen recommended the whip for anyone who questioned Aliris' poetic ability. It was reported that to her dying day, Lalla Rookh never called the king by any name other than Feramorz.

Critical Evaluation:

Lalla Rookh, one of Romantic Great Britain's literary sensations, is a prose narrative that frames four successive episodes. The setting is Lalla Rookh's journey from Delhi to Cashmere. The irony of her story is her love for Feramorz, the young and handsome poet who tells the verse tales to entertain the entourage sent by her bridegroom Aliris; only after much agitation of spirit does she find that Aliris is Feramorz in disguise.

The frame of the journey and the storytelling places *Lalla Rookh* structurally in the tradition of *The Canterbury Tales* (c. 1387) by Geoffrey Chaucer. In the four poems, Thomas Moore's musical gifts tap a rich vein of lyricism in the English language, revivifying the aural qualities of written verse. The first tale, "The Veiled Prophet of Khorassan," told in heroic couplets, combines the Romantic era's fascination with the gothic and the Oriental. Moore transformed history to tell the story of two ill-fated lovers destroyed by the evil magician Mokanna, a gothic villain who entraps a pure and virtuous heroine. The veiled prophet was the historical figure of al-Mukanna, who led a revolt against the Abbasid caliphs between 775 and 780 C.E. in the mountains of Usbekistan. The tragedy of Zelica and her nightmarish sufferings drew upon a familiar theme of death by mistaken identity, not unlike the melodrama found in contemporary opera. The ending, with Azim praying by Zelica's grave, must have appealed to the sentimental literary tastes of the time.

The second tale, "Paradise and the Peri," is written in a very different vein and displays Moore's gift for song. Like the *Songs of Innocence and of Experience* (1794) by William Blake, easy elegant tone and accessible language of "The Veiled Prophet" disguise the seriousness of a moral theme. The piece looks forward to the sentimental Victorian ideal of the purity of children.

By Moore's time, the English in India had become acquainted with the Parsis, descendants of those who had escaped to India during the Arab conquest of Zoroastrian Persia in the seventh century. Moore takes another turn in tone and execution when he takes this as his grim subject in "The Fire-Worshippers," in which there are no happy endings. The star-crossed lovers are parted forever, and warring nations will never make peace. For contemporaneous readers, this tragic drama evoked a sense of remote history and satisfied their pleasure in weeping copious tears at inexorable twists of fate.

The fourth poem deals with the doting love of the Mughal emperor for his wife, Nur Mahal (later Nur Jahan). With this tale of Aurungzebe's grandfather, the reader is returned to Mughal India, where the work began with Aurungzebe receiving Abdalla at his court. Reflecting contemporary British familiarity with India and Persia, Moore's stories are drawn from either Persian literature and tradition or from the Persianized court culture of Mughal India.

The whimsical Moore introduces a satirical note into an otherwise serious text. Critical of

Feramorz's poetry as melodramatic and exaggerated, the pedantic Fadladeen brings the fanciful and exotic storytelling heavily down to earth. He dismisses the ghastly Mokanna as "an ill-favoured gentleman, with a veil over his face." A charlatan who knows little about poetry or religion, he thinks himself qualified to pronounce upon both. In this character, Moore, who had suffered personally from the vituperative literary criticism of Sir Francis Jeffrey (1773-1850) in the *Edinburgh Review*, may have seized the opportunity to retaliate by pricking the bubble of critical pretentiousness.

The most fruitful way for readers to evaluate *Lalla Rookh* is to see it as Moore's contemporaries saw it. The reading public had anticipated its publication for six years. When the first readers of *Lalla Rookh* opened their copies in May, 1817, they found that Moore had not disappointed them in satisfying their voracious taste for all things Oriental. They had just learned of places like Bukhara, to which no European had been since the time of Queen Elizabeth I; the name of Cashmere (Kashmir) evoked images of incomparable natural beauty, of perfumed gardens and limpid lakes. New scholarship had revealed the Orient for the first time to British readers; travelers had been writing exotic accounts; and poets knew the great theme of the time was the mysterious, remote, and opulent Orient. When the conquering British reached Delhi in 1803, the Taj Mahal in Agra and other fascinating examples of Indo-Islamic architecture became known to the West through paintings and engravings. Moore's readers had already heard of Mughal India and the splendor of its Persianized culture. They had read William Beckford's *Vathek* (1786) and countless gothic novels set in the Orient, as well as the translations by Sir William Jones of the Persian poetry of Hafez. Literary Britain was eager for more, in such a book as *Lalla Rookh*.

Moore's readers reveled in the evocative power of the Oriental names and the images of wealth, power, and exotic beauty that Moore conjured up. Since the time of the heroic drama *Aureng-Zebe* (1675) by John Dryden, they would have known about the sixth and last of the great Mughal emperors, Aurungzebe. Moore's readers were aware of the story of the love of Jahangir, the fourth great Mughal emperor, for Nur Mahal; they had recently been introduced to Persian folklore' and the history of the conflicts between the Arabs and the pre-Islamic Persians. Moore's detailed footnotes from respected authorities authenticated for his readers the images of the remote Orient, of "all Bocára's vaunted gold" and of "all the gems of Samarcand," of which they had read in Jones's translations. Just as the prince regent indulged himself by building his Royal Pavillion at Brighton—a Taj Mahal on the English Channel coast—Moore indulged his readers by bringing them the quintessential Romantic poem about the sumptuous East, replete with sensuous images of nightingales, roses, perfumed fountains, and shimmering gossamer veils. Moore's readers could learn of the world of the remote Orient through the enchanted verses of *Lalla Rookh* and enjoy the love story of concealed identity in which all is well that ends well.

"Critical Evaluation" by Donna Berliner

Bibliography:
Birley, Robert. "Thomas Moore: *Lalla Rookh*. In *Sunk Without Trace: Some Forgotten Masterpieces Reconsidered*. London: Rupert Hart-Davis, 1962. Discusses the reputation of *Lalla Rookh*, both in and since its own time.
Heseltine, J. E. "The Royame of Perse." In *The Legacy of Persia*, edited by Arthur J. Arberry. Oxford, England: Clarendon Press, 1953. Positions *Lalla Rookh* in a survey of English writing on Persia in the Oriental tradition.

Jones, Howard Mumford. *The Harp That Once—A Chronicle of the Life of Thomas Moore*. New York: Henry Holt, 1937. Points out some aesthetic successes of *Lalla Rookh*, especially in the context of other Romantic works.

Mack, Robert L. Introduction to *Oriental Tales*. Oxford, England: Oxford University Press, 1992. Discusses the tradition of Orientalism in British literature.

Schwab, Raymond. *Oriental Renaissance: Europe's Rediscovery of India and the East, 1680-1880*. Translated by Gene Patterson-Black and Victor Reinking. New York: Columbia University Press, 1984. Discusses development of British interest in things Oriental.

Strong, L. A. G. *The Minstrel Boy: A Portrait of Tom Moore*. New York: Alfred A. Knopf, 1937. Advocates a reevaluation of Moore's poetry as music.

Tidrick, Kathryn. *Heart-Beguiling Araby*. Cambridge, England: Cambridge University Press, 1981. Follows the interest in Orientalism in the nineteenth century.

Wickens, G. M. "*Lalla Rookh* and the Romantic Tradition of Islamic Literature in English." *Yearbook of Comparative and General Literature* 20 (1971): 61-66. Discusses Moore's effect on English translations of Islamic literature. Shows Moore to be very much at the heart of the Romantic movement, but suggests ways in which translators might revise their methods to render more faithfully the originals.

LANCELOT
Or, The Knight of the Cart

Type of work: Poetry
Author: Chrétien de Troyes (c. 1150-c. 1190)
Type of plot: Romance
Time of plot: Sixth century
Locale: Britain
First transcribed: Lancelot: Ou, Le Chevalier à la charrette, c. 1168 (English translation, 1913)

> *Principal characters:*
> ARTHUR, the king of Britain
> LANCELOT, King Arthur's greatest knight
> GUENEVERE, the wife of King Arthur
> GAWAIN, the nephew of King Arthur
> MELEAGANT, a treacherous knight
> BADEMAGU, the father of Meleagant

The Story:

On Ascension Day, as usual, King Arthur held a splendid feast; but when this particular feast was over and when Arthur's knights were still gathered, a knight entered the hall with an unusual challenge. He held, he claimed, many of Arthur's knights in prison, and he defied Arthur to rescue them. He also cast aspersions upon Arthur's knights, doubting if they were able to defend the queen from him. He stated that if there were any knight that Arthur trusted, he should allow him to escort the queen into the forest, and, if he could defend her successfully, the strange knight would return the prisoners.

King Arthur agreed to the terms, and Kay, his foster brother, asked for permission to escort the queen. Arthur agreed, reluctantly, and Kay led her into the forest. Gawain admonished his uncle for his foolishness, for it was well known that Kay was a poor knight; so, together with other knights of the Round Table, he rode into the forest to help Kay. Before long, they came upon what was obviously the scene of a recent combat, but there was no sign of Kay, the queen, or the knight, only a riderless horse.

At this point, a knight, who had evidently been riding hard, approached Gawain and asked if he could borrow one of his horses. Gawain agreed, and the knight charged off into the forest, Gawain in hot pursuit. Before very long, Gawain came upon the knight, now on foot once more. He had overtaken a cart, of the kind used to take criminals to the place of execution. It was being driven by a dwarf. The knight, who was known as Lancelot, asked the dwarf if he knew what had become of the queen, and the dwarf told him that, if he cared to climb aboard the cart, he would soon know of her fate. Since it was a great dishonor, the knight hesitated three steps before leaping on board.

Gawain and the unknown knight stayed the evening in a castle. Setting out again the following morning, the two knights soon came to a fork in the road. They asked a damsel where the queen was. The damsel replied that she had been taken to the land of Gorre by Meleagant, the son of the king. Both roads led to Gorre, one by the perilous Underwater Bridge, and the other by the even more perilous Sword Bridge. Gawain chose the Underwater Bridge, Lancelot the Sword Bridge.

Lancelot faced many dangers on his way to Gorre, but his love for Guenevere sustained him throughout. Once, he was so wrapped in thoughts of love that he failed to hear the challenge of another knight until that knight knocked him from his horse; on another occasion, the sight of Guenevere's golden hair, left in a comb he found beside the road, caused him to swoon and nearly fall from his horse. Knights challenged him, maidens tempted him, and perilous cemeteries barred his way, but he overcame them all, arriving finally at the Sword Bridge.

The Sword Bridge was made of a single blade of shining steel, stretching from one side of a roaring river to the other. At the far end were two hungry lions. The knight took off his armor, so that he might grip the blade more firmly, and set off at once. Though the blade cut his hands and knees, he struggled on until he came to the other side. When he finally reached the far bank, the lions, which were merely illusions, disappeared. Meleagant rode out immediately and challenged him to fight. The knight was unable to gain the upper hand, until he caught a glimpse of Guenevere. The sight of his beloved enabled the knight to overcome Meleagant. Seeing his son in peril, King Bademagu besought the queen to spare his life. Guenevere agreed, and Lancelot spared him. Meleagant was not satisfied, and only agreed to hand over the queen if Lancelot would fight him a year hence. Lancelot agreed, and went immediately to find Guenevere; she, however, behaved coldly toward him and, disconsolately, Lancelot left the castle to find Gawain.

Rumors began to circulate that Lancelot and Guenevere were both dead, and when Lancelot heard them, he rushed back to Gorre. He and the queen were reconciled, and she revealed to him that she had been offended by his hesitation before entering the cart. He should not have put honor before love. They agreed that he would come to her chamber that night. When he did climb to her window, however, he had to pry open the bars on her window and, in doing so, cut his hand so that he unwittingly bled all over the sheets of her bed. Seeing the sheets the following morning, Meleagant accused her of sleeping with the wounded Kay, who had been sleeping in the antechamber. Lancelot offered to fight to defend her honor, but Meleagant had him slung into prison as soon as the queen had left.

It seemed, at first, that the queen would have no champion on the appointed day at Camelot. Indeed, Gawain had already agreed to defend her, and was armed, when Lancelot sped toward them on his horse. He had managed to persuade his jailer to release him, and at last was able to defeat and kill Meleagant.

Critical Evaluation:

In his *Lancelot: Or, The Knight of the Cart*, Chrétien de Troyes explored the theme of what scholars have since called courtly love. This involved a new emphasis on love in poetry. The knight idolized his lady and would do anything for her. When at a tournament Guenevere commands Lancelot to lose, he obediently does so; when she commands him to win, he likewise does so. Since marriages were usually political in the twelfth century, they were also often loveless, and this meant that true love had to be adulterous, almost by definition, and this is why the love affair explored here is between Lancelot and the wife of King Arthur.

However, there are some indications that suggest that Chrétien was not altogether happy with the theme. He says in the prologue to the poem that the "sense and subject matter" were given to him by Marie de Champagne, his patroness. This in itself is unusual, but scholars have occasionally seen his words as a kind of disclaimer. This idea gains some force when we realize that he never actually finished it, but left it to a clerk named Godefroy de Leigny to complete. It is the only poem other than *Perceval: Ou, Le Conte du Graal* (c. 1180) that he did not complete. *Perceval* was his last work, and it seems likely that death cut him short, but that cannot be urged for *Lancelot*. It seems more likely that he was dissatisfied with it for some reason. Finally, his other works stress the importance of love within marriage. *Cligés* (c. 1164), Chrétien's second extant romance, goes out of its way to establish the fact that the love of the hero and his lady is not in fact legally adulterous, and it is possible that Perceval is chaste. If this were the case, *Lancelot* would be the only poem in which adulterous love were praised, an interpretation that might suggest that he wrote it reluctantly.

One of the oddest moments in the poem is when Guenevere reveals to Lancelot that she has been cold toward him because he hesitated before leaping into the cart. Since she was not present, she could hardly have found out about this. Gawain had not yet reached Gorre, and the only other person present was the dwarf driving the cart. If he told her, it implies that the whole business with the cart was designed to test Lancelot's devotion. If that is the case, then the very abduction itself seems geared toward proving Lancelot's love. Another thorny problem is the fortuitous arrival of Lancelot on the scene. There is no indication of how he heard of her abduction. The adventures he goes through on his way to rescue her seem odd and somewhat disconnected. There is no causal relationship between them, and, in fact, they could be reordered more or less freely without any interruption of the poem's logic.

This is what Chrétien does best. The episodes that seem odd to the reader are almost certainly deliberately so. There is, in all likelihood, no rational explanation for the supernatural knowledge Guenevere and Lancelot have; it simply emphasizes the strangeness of Arthur's realm. This is important to our appreciation of Chrétien. He based most of his poems on old Breton stories of King Arthur and his knights, and there is a distinctly otherworldly mood to most of these. The earliest stories of Arthur are mythical and almost always involve the descent of the king to the underworld to rescue various treasures or kill various magical beasts. Chrétien used these otherworldly elements to create atmosphere, the feeling that the world in which the knights move is unpredictable. The relationships between the weird episodes are what, in Chrétien's best poems, create meaning. Here, the oddness serves to emphasize the closeness of the lovers and their mutual devotion. The quest is a test of Lancelot's devotion, and possibly nothing more than that. The magic enables the poet to explore the psychology of love, and his conclusion is to regard the lovers with a satirical, but somewhat affectionate eye. He sees the extremities to which Lancelot will go for love, the swooning and the contemplative rather than active nature of his knighthood, as being rather comical. At the same time, Guenevere is somewhat inhuman in her treatment of Lancelot, whether she is giving him the cold shoulder in Gorre or urging him to lose a tournament for her love elsewhere. Nowhere, however, do we get the impression that Chrétien disliked her.

C. M. Adderley

Bibliography:
Brewer, Derek. "The Presentation of the Character of Lancelot: Chrétien to Malory." In *Arthurian Literature*, edited by Richard Barber. Vol. 4. Totowa, N.J.: D. S. Brewer, 1984. This article discusses the character of Lancelot in relation to his portrayal in other medieval works.
Frappier, Jean. "Chrétien de Troyes." In *Arthurian Literature in the Middle Ages*, edited by R. S. Loomis. Oxford, England: Clarendon Press, 1959. This is a good starting point for a study of Chrétien and deals mainly with sources and characterization.
Kelly, Douglas. *Sens and Conjointure in the "Chevalier de la Charrette."* The Hague: Mouton, 1966. Kelly's argument is that Chrétien was really in favor of adulterous courtly love and that Godefroy de Leigny finished the poem under his supervision.

Lacy, Norris J. *The Craft of Chrétien de Troyes: An Essay on Narrative Art*. Leiden, The Netherlands: E. J. Brill, 1980. Lacy observes that *Lancelot* is composed from a number of similar episodes, and he notes that the meaning can be found by a comparison of those episodes.

Loomis, Roger Sherman. *Arthurian Tradition and Chrétien de Troyes*. New York: Columbia University Press, 1949. Loomis shows how Chrétien's romances were influenced by Celtic mythology. Although his conclusions have been challenged, his work is very stimulating, especially when he deals with the Sword Bridge.

Rougement, Denis de. *Love in the Western World*. Translated by Montgomery Belgion. New York: Harcourt, Brace, 1940. Rougement describes courtly love and argues that it is self-defeating and even masks a death wish.

LARGO DESOLATO

Type of work: Drama
Author: Václav Havel (1936-   )
Type of plot: Absurdist
Time of plot: Late 1970's or early 1980's
Locale: Prague, Czechoslovakia
First performed: 1985; first published, 1985 (English translation, 1987)

Principal characters:
PROFESSOR LEOPOLD NETTLES, a philosopher
EDWARD, his friend and his wife's companion
SUZANA, Leopold's wife
FIRST SIDNEY, a mill worker
SECOND SIDNEY, a mill worker
LUCY, Leopold's lover
BERTRAM, a friend
FIRST CHAP, a government agent
SECOND CHAP, a government agent
FIRST MAN, the agents' assistant
SECOND MAN, the agents' assistant
MARGUERITE, a student

The Story:

At the beginning of scene i Professor Leopold Nettles sat on the living room couch watching the front door. After a while he walked to the door, peered through the peephole, and listened at the door as if expecting someone; he appeared tense. After a long pause, the curtain dropped.

Scene ii repeated scene i exactly. Scene iii began in the same way and continued until the doorbell rang and Nettles jumped. After he recognized the man at the door, he opened the door and Edward, his friend and his wife's companion, entered. The two engaged in small talk, mostly about Leopold's digestion and nerves; Edward expressed concern that Leopold was drinking too much and that he had not gone outside in some time. Suzana, Leopold's wife, returned from shopping and asked Leopold about his activities of the day. He detailed his morning's tidying and fixing of breakfast. Suzana chastised him for eating his eggs with a silver teaspoon. Suzana left and Leopold and Edward resumed their conversation. Leopold appeared very anxious and concerned that he would soon be arrested, although he did not reveal where he would be taken or by whom.

The doorbell rang again, startling Leopold. Two workers from a paper mill, First Sidney and Second Sidney, whom Nettles had met two years ago but had forgotten, came to request that Leopold take some sort of action, described only in the vaguest of terms. The two Sidneys declared themselves fans of Leopold and claimed that many people were looking to him for direction. The doorbell rang again, and Lucy, Leopold's mistress, entered; the conversation repeated much of what had already been said. The two Sidneys, having overstayed their welcome, eventually left, promising to return with writing paper and imploring Leopold to maintain his courage. When Leopold and Lucy were finally alone, Lucy also encouraged Leopold to resume his writing and suggested that her love should be an inspiration. Leopold remained unresponsive, and the curtain fell.

When scene iv began, it was night. Leopold's friend Bertram was sitting on the sofa. Like Edward in scene iii, he asked Leopold about his drinking and his nerves and alluded to Leopold's inactivity. He repeated that many people were concerned about Leopold, and, like the two Sidneys, presented himself as an emissary representing Leopold's supporters. Bertram referred to uncertainties and possible danger, suggesting that Leopold's anxieties were related to past actions and future consequences. Lucy emerged from Leopold's bedroom, causing Bertram some embarrassment. After Bertram left, Lucy insisted on talking about their affair, which Leopold refused to acknowledge. Lucy asserted that she had entered the relationship in order to stimulate him to some sort of intellectual activity but now felt used; Leopold claimed he was incapable of love. Their discussion was interrupted by the doorbell and the appearance of First Chap and Second Chap, government agents representing the source of Leopold's fears. The Chaps had Lucy removed by the First Man and the Second Man; they then inquired about Leopold's activities.

The Chaps had come to offer a resolution to Leopold's difficulties, which were revealed to have come about because of an essay he had published called *Ontology of the Human Self*. If Leopold would sign a statement saying that he was not the same Professor Nettles who wrote the paper, the matter would be dropped, and he would be exonerated. The Chaps assured Leopold that many others in similar predicaments had accepted similar offers. However, Leopold was visibly disturbed and requested time to consider his decision. The scene ended with Leopold sitting on the couch, wrapped in a blanket.

Leopold was alone at the beginning of scene v. He alternately paced, checked the peephole, took vitamins from a collection of vials on the table, and retired to the bathroom to wash his face. Suzana entered with shopping bags, and their conversation paralleled that of the third scene. Leopold explained the visit of the previous night and the Chaps' offer. Suzana was angered that Leopold would even consider accepting and exited to her room. Leopold repeated the actions of the opening of the scene.

Next, Edward arrived and questioned Leopold about his digestion, his drinking, and the events of the previous night. Leopold continued to pace, took vitamins, and left the room to wash his face. The two Sidneys arrived with writing paper and suitcases full of documents from the mill. They repeated their encouragement and support. Bertram arrived and he, the two Sidneys, Suzana, and Edward repeated lines from earlier scenes, all calling upon Leopold to act. Leopold ordered them out, and, as the curtain fell, he could be heard running water in the bathroom. The doorbell rang again.

Scene vi continued where scene v ended. Leopold emerged from the shower to answer the door. The caller, Marguerite, was a philosophy student who admired his work; like Lucy, she offered her love as an inspiration to Leopold, and it appeared that Leopold had decided to replace Lucy with Marguerite. They were interrupted by the doorbell and the reappearance of the two Chaps. Leopold announced that they might arrest him, for he refused to sign their paper and relinquish his identity; however, the Chaps replied that they had not come to arrest him or to require his signature, but to inform him that his case has been postponed indefinitely. Leopold begged to be arrested rather than to continue in limbo with an uncertain future. As the curtain fell, he had collapsed on the floor. Scene vii repeated the opening scene.

Critical Evaluation:

Largo Desolato, whose title is taken from a string quartet by Alban Berg, is the most autobiographical of Václav Havel's dramatic works. Havel, a playwright, philosopher, and political activist who later served as president of Czechoslovakia, was imprisoned in 1979 by the Communist regime in Czechoslovakia (which took control of the country in 1968) for his opposition to totalitarianism and his leadership of the dissident group Charter 77. Havel was released in 1983, without having served his entire sentence, but remained under police surveillance and the constant threat of reincarceration. He composed *Largo Desolato* in 1984. It is an absurdist drama that draws on repetition of action and dialogue to produce an unsettling and sometimes humorous effect.

The character Leopold Nettles, a philosopher who has published a controversial essay, *Ontology of the Human Self*, appears to have undergone an imprisonment and release similar to Havel's, and lives in fear of future punishment. Although much is left open to interpretation, one can conclude from the title of the essay that Leopold's crime is to have insisted on individuality in a world that demands its sacrifice. The destruction of individual identity is apparent from the names of several characters: First Sidney, Second Sidney, First Chap, Second Chap, First Man, and Second Man. The workers and the government agents are interchangeable cogs in the mechanism of bureaucracy and totalitarianism. In fact, what the state requests of Nettles is self-annihilation, a denial of authorship that entails the creation of a fictitious Nettles-the-author-and-public-enemy and that would rob Leopold of his sense of identity.

The theme of the individual in conflict with the system, which occurs throughout Havel's plays, has its antecedents in the works of two earlier Prague writers, Franz Kafka and Jaroslav Hašek. In Kafka's novels, the protagonists find themselves both alienated from and manipulated by impenetrable bureaucracies; any effort to retain a sense of self and survive within the system results in failure and destruction of self. In Hašek's classic Czech novel, *The Good Soldier Švejk* (1921-1923), the title character repeatedly undermines the system by carrying its false logic to an extreme. In *Largo Desolato*, Havel's protagonist exists within a similarly oppressive system that would destroy his identity, but Leopold recognizes the flaw in the logic of oppression: to imprison him would only increase his reputation and sphere of influence. Once Leopold has decided against recanting his work, he has achieved a personal victory, yet one which is undermined by the system's retraction of its offer, rendering his decision meaningless and leaving him in the same position as when the play began.

The ambiguous conclusion and the circular structure of the play are characteristic of absurdist drama, particularly the work of Samuel Beckett, and Beckett and Havel are frequently compared. Both rely on repetition of action and dialogue, yet to different effects. While Beckett places his characters in incomprehensible settings, outside recognizable time and place, Havel situates his drama in realism. Leopold's apartment is a typical apartment; his daily routines are quite ordinary. This normality, however, is mere illusion, and that is Havel's point. For the home is no safe haven from the oppression of the totalitarian state, and the appearance of order, characterized through mundane activities like preparing meals, tidying rooms, and grooming, only camouflages the ubiquity of government control over individual lives. Even more than the action, the dialogue reinforces this theme. Characters speak in stock phrases and clichés whether they are discussing daily routine, emotional intimacy, or politics. Havel heightens the effect through a technique called "time slips," in which different characters repeat the lines or actions of other characters. For example, the two Chaps begin their apparent interrogation by asking exactly the same questions of Leopold as does his friend Bertram; Leopold's conversation with Lucy, which marks the decline in their relationship, is repeated almost verbatim with Marguerite, suggesting the beginning of an affair. At the end of scene v, the words of the two Sidneys, Edward, Bertram, Suzana, and Lucy form a chorus as each remarks "some hero." Thus, speech and action become nonsensical; relationships appear superficial; barriers between the external world and the internal world disintegrate. In Beckett's plays, characters create their own realities through language. In Havel's work, language threatens to imprison the characters in a reality that has slipped from their control. The clichés, circular reasoning, and bureaucratic language employed by all of the characters represent the extent to which the control of the state has infiltrated their daily lives.

Largo Desolato lends itself to several interpretive approaches. It can be viewed as autobiographical, as a political work critical of Communism, or as an absurdist play. Its appeal to Western scholars derives from its thematic universality and its reflection of late twentieth century concerns with the interrelationship of language, self, and truth. Of his own work, Havel has stated, "Drama's success in transcending the limits of its age and country depends entirely on how far it succeeds in finding a way to its own place and time." Regarded by many as his most successful play, *Largo Desolato* depicts life in Communist Czechoslovakia in a manner that allows those who enjoy democracy to recognize themselves and the problems of their own society.

K Edgington

Bibliography:

Goetz-Stankiewicz, Marketa. *The Silenced Theatre: Czech Playwrights Without a Stage.* Toronto: University of Toronto Press, 1979. A comprehensive study that locates the Czech theater of the absurd in a Czech rather than a Western European literary tradition. See chapter 2 for a discussion of Havel's early plays, *The Garden Party* (1963) and *The Memorandum* (1965), which introduce themes also evident in *Largo Desolato*.

Havel, Václav. *Open Letters: Selected Writings 1965-1990.* Translated and edited by Paul Wilson. New York: Alfred A. Knopf, 1991. See "Stories and Totalitarianism" for a discussion of the relationship between literature and politics.

Kriseova, Eda. *Václav Havel: The Authorized Biography.* Translated by Caleb Crain. New York: St. Martin's Press, 1993. A biography that explores Havel's development as a writer in conjunction with his political activism. The brief chapter on *Largo Desolato* details the autobiographical elements of the play.

Skloot, Robert. "Václav Havel: The Once and Future Playwright." *The Kenyon Review* 15, no. 2 (Spring, 1993): 223-231. An article critical of Havel's later plays, including *Largo Desolato*, valuable in presenting a dissenting voice in a field of largely adulatory response.

Vladislav, Jan, ed. *Václav Havel or Living in Truth: Twenty-two Essays Published on the Occasion of the Award of the Erasmus Prize to Václav Havel.* London: Faber and Faber, 1987. A rich collection of essays by sixteen of Havel's contemporaries that provides a variety of insights into influences on Havel as a dramatist and the significance of his work artistically, philosophically, and politically.

THE LAST CHRONICLE OF BARSET

Type of work: Novel
Author: Anthony Trollope (1815-1882)
Type of plot: Domestic realism
Time of plot: Mid-nineteenth century
Locale: Barsetshire, England
First published: 1867

Principal characters:
MR. CRAWLEY, the curate of Hogglestock
MRS. CRAWLEY, his wife
GRACE CRAWLEY, their daughter
MR. PROUDIE, Bishop of Barchester
MRS. PROUDIE, his wife
HENRY GRANTLY, Grace's suitor
LILY DALE, Grace's friend
JOHN EAMES, Lily's suitor

The Story:

The citizens in the community of Hogglestock were upset because Mr. Crawley, the curate, had been accused of stealing a check for twenty pounds. In Archdeacon Grantly's home, where there was concern that Henry Grantly might marry Grace Crawley, the curate's schoolteacher daughter, feeling was high.

Bishop Proudie and his wife were set against the unfortunate Crawley. Mrs. Proudie, who exerted great power over her husband, persuaded the bishop to write a letter forbidding Mr. Crawley to preach in his church until the case should have been settled one way or another. Mr. Crawley refused the injunction. Mr. and Mrs. Proudie quarreled over the answer, and Mr. Proudie sent for Mr. Crawley to attend him in the bishop's palace at once. When Mr. Crawley arrived, he was hot and tired from walking. He repeated what he had stated in his letter and left the bishop and his wife amazed at his boldness.

Mr. Crawley was not kept from performing his duties on Christmas morning. Since he could not recall how he had come into possession of the money in question, he informed his wife that he had but two choices—either to go to jail or to bedlam. At last, Henry Grantly decided to ask Grace Crawley to marry him, even though he would be going against his parents' wishes. At the same time Lily Dale, Grace Crawley's friend, was being wooed by young John Eames, a clerk in the Income Tax Office in London and a suitor, once rejected, whom Lily's mother favored. Eames was the friend of a London artist named Conway Dalrymple, who was painting a portrait of Miss Clara Van Siever, a mutual friend, in the sitting room of Mrs. Dobbs Broughton. Meanwhile, the aged Mrs. Van Siever was engaged in forcing Dobbs Broughton to pay money he owed to her.

Not long afterward, John Eames met Henry Grantly. Neither liked the other at first. John met Lily in Lady Julia de Guest's home, where Grace was also a guest. He discussed his unfavorable meeting with Henry Grantly in front of Grace. When Henry proposed to Grace, she refused him and returned home to be with her father during his trial. Lily told John that she planned to die an old maid, her heart having been broken by Adolphus Crosbie, a former suitor.

Mr. Toogood, a distant relative, was to defend Mr. Crawley. John Eames was brought into the Crawley case by Mr. Toogood, who wanted John to go to Florence and attempt to persuade Mr. Arabin, an influential clergyman, to come to Mr. Crawley's rescue. There was another reason why Arabin should return to England: Mrs. Arabin's father, Mr. Harding, was ailing and growing weaker each day.

Conway Dalrymple worked on Miss Van Siever's picture, which was still a secret from Dobbs Broughton, in whose house it was being painted. Although Broughton had ordered the artist out of his house, Mrs. Broughton wanted the picture painted, regardless of her jealous husband's reactions.

The clerical commission summoned by Bishop Proudie reached no decision concerning Mr. Crawley. It was resolved that nothing should be done until the civil courts had decided his case.

Archdeacon Grantly tried to engage the help of Lady Lufton to prevent the marriage of his son to Grace Crawley, but Lady Lufton refused. The archdeacon finally promised that he would no longer oppose the marriage if Mr. Crawley was found innocent of any crime.

Dobbs Broughton was being pressured for money by old Mrs. Van Siever. Clara Van Siever was to marry Musselboro, Broughton's former partner. Still hoping to marry Clara, Dalrymple was putting the last touches to the canvas when Mrs. Van Siever entered the Broughton house. At her word, he destroyed the portrait. Over Clara's objections, Mrs. Van Siever announced that her daughter was to marry Musselboro. After the Van Sievers left, Musselboro arrived with news that Dobbs Broughton had killed himself that morning. Clara and Dalrymple resolved to face Mrs. Van Siever's wrath together.

Mrs. Proudie continued her fight to have Mr. Crawley removed. After a quarrel between the bishop and Mrs. Proudie, she retired to her room and died there of a heart attack. True to the resolution imposed upon him by Mrs. Proudie before her death, Mr. Crawley preached a final sermon in his church and never again entered it as the curate.

On the Continent, John Eames learned from Mrs. Arabin the cause of Mr. Crawley's troubles. Mrs. Arabin, who had received the check from a tenant, had turned it over to Mr. Crawley without telling her husband, the dean, of the transaction. She had only recently heard of the charges, and she was hurrying home to England to do what could be done to straighten out the matter. In the meantime, Mr. Toogood traced the theft of the check to the tenant who had forwarded it to Mrs. Arabin.

Mr. Toogood and Henry Grantly took the good news to Mr. and Mrs. Crawley. When she heard their story, Mrs. Crawley, who had defended her husband from the beginning, broke into tears. The messengers had to explain the situation carefully to Mr. Crawley, who could not at first believe that his innocence was about to be proved. Then Mr. Harding, the aged incumbent in St. Ewold's, died. Archdeacon Grantly offered the living to Mr. Crawley as a recompense for all he had suffered. In midsummer, Grace Crawley became Mrs. Henry Grantly.

John Eames did not marry Lily Dale after all, for Lily was unable to make her decision; Dalrymple, however, married Clara Van Siever as he had planned. Musselboro, who had lost Clara, proceeded to marry the widow of his old partner, and Mrs. Broughton's sorrows were thus brought to an end.

Critical Evaluation:

This is the last of a series of novels about the ecclesiastical community of Barsetshire, based upon the Anglican church life in and around Salisbury in southwestern England in the mid-nineteenth century. It was preceded by *The Warden* (1855), *Barchester Towers* (1857), *Doctor*

Thorne (1858), *Framley Parsonage* (1861), and *The Small House at Allington* (1864). Many of the characters appear in all six novels, so the ideal way to read this novel is as the conclusion of the accumulated tale of nineteenth century social and professional life, particularly among the churchmen and their families in Barsetshire.

Anthony Trollope is aware of the possibility of the novel being read outside that context, and he provides sufficient information as the book progresses for it to be read alone. Repetition of incidents from previous novels is a common practice for Trollope, but one that can be irritating at times for readers who are not accustomed to detailed repetitions of matters long since settled. This is part of a more serious difficulty that is common to nineteenth century novels in general: They tend to be very long; narrative alone was not considered to be adequate for the experience of reading novels. There was a taste for novels of extraordinary length in a society that had plenty of time for reading, given its lack of other forms of entertainment. Many novels, including this one, were originally published in magazines in serial form, a few thousand words at a time. Trollope knew that details may be forgotten between readings. He provides comment on the narrative as it takes its leisurely time to unfold. It is not solely a matter of an interesting story, but a story told with considerable detail and much measured, sophisticated, philosophic rumination by a wise narrator. The novel is also a contemplation of ethical and social insight, and an opportunity for witty, sometimes satirical, comment on the eccentricities, and sometime cruelties, of supposedly civilized characters. Trollope does not attack the structures of British society or of the Anglican church, which follows similar patterns of privilege. What he is against is the way in which power often falls into the hands of ambitious, thrusting careerists who are more interested in exercising power for personal gain and satisfaction than for the benefit of the church or its parishioners. It can be argued that *The Last Chronicle of Barset* is as pertinent as ever, given its exploration of the ways in which power often is grasped by the least capable members of society.

Mrs. Proudie is the most blatant example of this misplaced power. Mrs. Proudie's power comes not from any official position that she possesses, but from her influence over her husband, who has, despite his intellectual and personal limitations, managed to become the bishop of Barset. The earlier novels had much to say about the politics of his appointment and his malpractice of the office under the malign influence of his wife. Mrs. Proudie exercises the same irresponsible conduct in this novel, as she attempts to drive Mr. Crawley from his pulpit long before his guilt can be determined.

The Last Chronicle of Barset is less concerned with the internal politics of ecclesiastical life than were the previous works, and concentrates on two further themes that interest Trollope: character and the eccentric nature of human conduct. The plot is dependent upon the slight fact of the Arabins' absence on the Continent, and their misunderstanding of what Crawley's problem is. Once they know the facts of the matter, the mystery is solved. The novel's real theme is how Crawley, those around him, and those with power over him cope with the idea that this penurious cleric would steal money, however small the sum might be. The matter is complicated by Crawley's intransigently honest character and his financial and personal situation. Prone to depression, worn out by years of poverty and despair, he is fragile, emotionally and intellectu-ally. A brilliant ecclesiastical scholar, but lacking in the political and social skills to make his way in the church, he has wound up at the bottom of the institution, working hard and constantly with his poor parishioners, but with a fixed sense of outrage at the lack of recognition and his inability to provide for his family. He is a man difficult to patronize, given his high skills and intelligence, and he is prideful in his righteousness. For all his pride, however, he is also a man of considerable humility, which is to do him great harm when Arabin denies the check. Crawley gives up, presuming that it must be true, since his friend's word must, necessarily, be better than his own. He must be wrong, must have somehow taken the check improperly, although he has no memory of doing so.

A variation on this battle of personal honor is shown in Crawley's daughter's determination to refuse the man she loves if her father is legally proven to be a thief. The ramifications of that decision move through the community as the love affair impinges upon the family relations of her prospective in-laws, themselves prominent members of the ecclesiastical society. Not the least interesting is the way in which the entire society, so closely connected by professional power and intermarriage, reacts to and is affected by Crawley's plight. He is a man whom they have, in the main, conveniently patronized and attempted to ignore in his serious financial struggles, but whom they feel inclined to judge, for good or ill. *The Last Chronicle of Barset* is a close study of a good man who is his own worst enemy, but it is also an involved exploration of the problem of how people live together in close-knit social structures, and how, sometimes, they simply make a muddle of life, given the inclinations of human nature. It is also a charming love story and a tale of family affections, in sorrow and pleasure—an example of how Trollope generously cultivates a multiplicity of themes into his novels.

"Critical Evaluation" by Charles Pullen

Bibliography:
apRoberts, Ruth. *The Moral Trollope.* Athens: Ohio University Press, 1971. Discusses Trollope's efforts as a moralist; helpful in thinking about this particular novel.

Booth, Bradford A. *Anthony Trollope: Aspects of His Life and Art.* Bloomington: Indiana University Press, 1958. Discusses how Trollope's view of the world, particularly the religious and political world, affected his fiction thematically and aesthetically.

Cockshut, A. O. J. *Anthony Trollope: A Critical Study.* London: Collins, 1955. Trollope's entire career, with substantial discussion of the Barsetshire series and this novel in particular.

Davies, Hugh Sykes. *Trollope.* London: Published for the British Council by Longmans, Green, 1960. Short pamphlet that provides an accurate, succinct introduction to a long, complicated career.

Edwards, P. D. *Anthony Trollope.* London: Routledge & Kegan Paul, 1968. Short study of Trollope's work with a section on *The Last Chronicle of Barset.* Uses extracts from the novels to discuss specific topics. A good starting place.

Gill, Stephen. Introduction to *The Last Chronicle of Barset.* Oxford, England: Oxford University Press, 1980. Attractive, short introduction to the novel and its relation to the other works in the Barsetshire series.

THE LAST DAYS OF POMPEII

Type of work: Novel
Author: Edward Bulwer-Lytton (1803-1873)
Type of plot: Historical
Time of plot: 79 C.E.
Locale: Pompeii
First published: 1834

> *Principal characters:*
> GLAUCUS, a wealthy young Greek
> ARBACES, the Egyptian priest of Isis
> IONE, his Greek ward
> APAECIDES, her brother
> NYDIA, a blind flower seller

The Story:

Late one afternoon in the ancient city of Pompeii, the fashionable rich young men were congregating for the daily rite of the public baths. Among them were Clodius, a foppish Roman, and Glaucus, a popular young Greek. Together the two strolled toward the baths, mingling with slaves bearing bronze buckets and idlers gowned in purple robes. Along the way, they saw the beautiful blind flower seller, Nydia. She, too, was from Greece and for that reason Glaucus took an interest in her. It was still too early for the baths, and the two friends walked along the seafront as Glaucus described a Neapolitan woman of Greek birth with whom he had fallen in love. Unfortunately, he had lost contact with the woman and was now morose. While they talked, Arbaces, the evil-looking Egyptian priest of Isis, intercepted them. The two young men were barely able to conceal their dislike for the Egyptian.

Arbaces secretly defied the Romans and the Greeks and prayed for the day when Egypt would once again be powerful. He revealed to a lesser priest his interest in the brother and sister, Apaecides and Ione, his wards. He hoped to make a priest of Apaecides, and he planned to marry Ione. They had been in Naples, but recently he had brought them to Pompeii, where he could influence them.

Glaucus met Ione at a party. She was the one he had seen and lost in Naples. At the same time, Arbaces developed his hold over Apaecides, who was growing more and more confused after coming in contact with the sophistries of the corrupt priest of Isis. Meanwhile, the blind flower seller, Nydia, was falling hopelessly in love with Glaucus.

It happened that Glaucus and Clodius were loitering in the establishment of Burbo, the wine seller, when the innkeeper and his wife were beating Nydia, their slave. Glaucus, hearing the woman's cries, bought her; he planned to give her to Ione. Nydia realized Glaucus could never love her after he gave her a letter to deliver to Ione. In this letter, he accused Arbaces of false imputations. On reading his letter, Ione decided to go at once to Arbaces' palace and to face him with Glaucus' charges.

Knowing the danger to Ione at Arbaces' palace, Nydia warned both Ione's brother and Glaucus. Glaucus hurried to the palace to confront the priest. An earthquake interrupted the quarrel between the two men. When a statue of the goddess Isis fell from a pedestal, striking Arbaces, Glaucus and Ione ran from the building to join the throng in the street. Alone and deserted, the blind slave wept bitterly.

The earthquake left little damage, and the people of Pompeii took up again the threads of their lives. Apaecides became a convert to Christianity. Glaucus and Ione remained together.

Julia, daughter of a wealthy freedman named Diomed, was also in love with Glaucus and sought to interfere between him and Ione. She went to the house of Arbaces, where the two plotted together. Arbaces had a drug prepared that was administered to Glaucus. The drug drove him into a demented stupor so that he ran from his house into a cemetery. Apaecides and Arbaces then came to this cemetery. They quarreled, and Arbaces stabbed Apaecides, killing him. Then, hoping to kill Glaucus indirectly, the priest summoned the crowd and declared that Glaucus in his drunken rage had killed Apaecides. Glaucus and a Christian who attempted to defend him were arrested. They were condemned to be given to wild beasts at the public games.

After the funeral of her brother, Ione resolved to declare her belief in the innocence of Glaucus. Before she could carry out her plan, however, Arbaces had seized her and carried her off to his palace. The only one who knew of Arbaces' guilt was a priest who was also his prisoner, but Arbaces reckoned without Nydia, who as a dancing woman at his palace had learned most of his secrets. Nydia contacted the priest imprisoned by Arbaces and agreed to carry his story to the authorities. Unfortunately, she too was captured. She persuaded a slave to carry the message to Sallust, a friend of Glaucus. The message, however, was delivered while Sallust was drunk, and he refused to read it.

The last day of Pompeii arrived. It was also a day of celebration in the arena, for which the populace had been waiting. The games began with gladiatorial combat, which the audience watched listlessly; they were bored because the deaths did not come fast enough or with enough suffering. After one combat, an unpopular gladiator was condemned to death by the crowd. His body was dragged before the arena and placed on the heap with those previously slain. Unfortunately for the crowd's amusement, the lion that had been turned loose in the arena with Glaucus now crept with a moan back into its cage. Before the lion could be prodded into action, Sallust appeared and demanded the arrest of Arbaces. A slave had called his attention to Nydia's letter, which he had thrown aside the night before. Reading it, he had hurried to lay his information before the praetor. The mob, not to be cheated after Glaucus had been set free, demanded that Arbaces be thrown to the lion.

Then the famous fatal eruption began. The whole gladiatorial scene became chaos as terrified thousands poured out of the doomed amphitheater, crushing the weakest in their hurry to escape. Looting began in the temples. Nydia reached Glaucus. Together, they hurried to the house of Arbaces to discover and save Ione. It was too dark to see, but Nydia, accustomed to darkness, was able to lead Ione and Glaucus through the streets. Arbaces was killed in the earthquake. At last Glaucus, Ione, and Nydia gained the safety of the seaside and put out to sea in a small ship. They slept all night in the boat. In the morning, Glaucus and Ione discovered that before they had awakened, the heartbroken Nydia had cast herself into the sea.

Critical Evaluation:

The Last Days of Pompeii was written before Edward Bulwer-Lytton inherited his family estate, in the days when he was forced to make his living as a hack writer. His mother, who disapproved of his marriage, refused to support him in the manner to which he had hoped to become accustomed. He had made his name with mildly scandalous novels of high society and with crime thrillers. *The Last Days of Pompeii* was a calculated move upmarket, into the genre of historical romance, which had proved not only popular but also respectable, thanks to the endeavors of Sir Walter Scott.

Bulwer-Lytton began to write *The Last Days of Pompeii* in a more conscientious spirit than he had applied to his earlier works, and he put a great deal of effort into the background research. He paid a lengthy visit to the partly excavated city, which had by then become a popular stopping-off point for the early generations of European tourists. Although subsequent research has provided much more information about the era in which the novel is set, and about Pompeii itself, the lavishly footnoted reconstruction of everyday life in the city that Bulwer-Lytton provides in the early chapters of his novel are as good and as full as could have been expected at the time.

Bulwer-Lytton presumably thought this research work was justified, because he had great hopes for the novel. The idea was full of potential; in setting out to write it he was forearmed with a ready-made climax far more spectacular than any that had recommended itself to Scott: the eruption of Vesuvius and the devastation of Pompeii. Regardless of whether he chose to represent this event as an act of God, punishing the wickedness of the decadent Romans, it was there to be invoked as a *deus ex machina* whose fallout could destroy the villainous characters and provide the virtuous with a magnificently narrow escape.

The book became one of the best-sellers of the Victorian era, obtaining a new lease of life when it was reprinted in a cheap format in mid-century as one of the earliest "railway novels." It cannot be said, however, that Bulwer-Lytton exploited the story's melodramatic potential to the full. The story seems to lose its way toward the end, and the volcanic eruption—when it arrives—is described in a cursory and distinctly halfhearted fashion. It may be that the pressure of financial necessity made the author determined to get the final part of the text over and done with. It is also possible that Bulwer-Lytton found his story an increasingly uncomfortable straitjacket and hurried through the final chapters.

The most interesting aspect of the text is the role played by Arbaces. He is cast as the villain and is duly destroyed in the climax, but the author seems far more interested in Arbaces' cynical view of the world than in the careful piety of the Christian characters. Beneath his hypocritical pose as a priest of Isis, Arbaces' true faith substitutes the "Necessity of Nature" for the gods and includes an occult "secret wisdom." This places him within a long tradition of Bulwerian mystics, which also included the enigmatic Volktman in *Godolphin* (1833) and the central characters of *Zanoni* (1842) and *A Strange Story* (1861).

Bulwer-Lytton remained uneasily skeptical about the occult, but it always fascinated him, and the rejection implied by his allocation of villainous roles to these charismatic magicians rings false. His endeavors in this regard were much appreciated by some, including the Theosophist Helena Blavatsky, who borrowed heavily from Bulwer-Lytton's occult fiction in compiling her "secret wisdom." Bulwer-Lytton was equally skeptical about orthodox religion and Victorian morality. This skepticism is also evident in *The Last Days of Pompeii*, most obviously in the priggish fashion in which Glaucus announces his eventual conversion to Christianity.

This ambivalent quality is all the more interesting by virtue of its being somewhat hidden. Victorian puritanism ruthlessly repressed the fascination that English writers might otherwise have found in contemplation of pagan antiquity; Bulwer-Lytton's description of the orgies that take place in the secret chambers of the temple of Isis is very carefully censored. The author's fascinations, some incorrect for his time, always seem to be seething beneath the surface of the narrative, rather like the pent-up fires of the volcano. Some of this impatience is revealed in what looks suspiciously like an act of wanton cruelty, when the author flings the unfortunate Nydia into the sea to die a suicide, simply because there is no clear happy ending ready to receive her.

The "confused and perplexed" character of Arbaces, formed by the "spirit of discontented pride" is a far closer reflection of Bulwer-Lytton's own personality (and his fierce resentment of his temporary disinheritance) than anything to be found in the character of the hero, Glaucus, or in that of the ascetic Apaecides. Bulwer-Lytton was not in the least attracted to the kind of Christianity that could rejoice in humility, and he despised those who could take comfort from the belief that the end of the world might arrive at any moment in a flurry of fire and brimstone. In order to secure publication and an adequate measure of popularity, however, he had no alternative but to meet the expectations of his audience by bringing Glaucus into the Christian fold.

As a depiction of the classical world, *The Last Days of Pompeii* has been superseded by more recent research, and its melodramatic potential is at best half-fulfilled. As a specimen of the way in which one era's contemplation of another can reveal all kinds of insights and prejudices, however, it remains an interesting and valuable work.

"Critical Evaluation" by Brian Stableford

Bibliography:
Campbell, James L., Sr. *Edward Bulwer-Lytton*. Boston: Twayne, 1986. Surveys Bulwer-Lytton's career, the influences on his work, and his fictional output. Analyzes the elements that contributed to the writing of the novel, judging it to be a sensationalistic costume romance rather than a serious exploration of Roman history.
Fleishman, Avrom. *The English Historical Novel: Walter Scott to Virginia Woolf*. Baltimore: The Johns Hopkins University Press, 1971. A study of the English tradition of historical fiction from its beginnings to the start of World War II, when, Fleishman contends, the tradition ended. Praises the novel's depiction of Roman society and the novel's use of Roman history in terms of nineteenth century political controversy.
Ford, George H., ed. *Victorian Fiction: A Second Guide to Research*. New York: Modern Language Association of America, 1978. One essay on Bulwer-Lytton discusses bibliography and criticism for each of the novels, and observes that the success of *The Last Days of Pompeii* is explained in part because its publication coincided with an eruption of Vesuvius.
Sutherland, J. A. *Victorian Novelists and Publishers*. Chicago: University of Chicago Press, 1976. Examines how business relationships between novelists and publishers affected novels. It describes the negotiations between Bulwer-Lytton and his publishers that preceded the novel's writing, and explains how the finished product differed from the author's expectations.

THE LAST OF THE MOHICANS
A Narrative of 1757

Type of work: Novel
Author: James Fenimore Cooper (1789-1851)
Type of plot: Adventure
Time of plot: 1757
Locale: Northern New York State
First published: 1826

Principal characters:
NATTY BUMPPO, a frontier scout known as Hawkeye
CHINGACHGOOK, Hawkeye's friend
UNCAS, Chingachgook's son
MAJOR DUNCAN HEYWARD, an English soldier and Hawkeye's friend
MAGUA, a renegade Huron
CORA MUNRO, the daughter of the commander of Fort William Henry
ALICE MUNRO, her sister

The Story:

Major Duncan Heyward had been ordered to escort Cora and Alice Munro from Fort Edward to Fort William Henry, where the girls' father, Colonel Munro, was commandant. Also in the party was David Gamut, a Connecticut singing master. On their way to Fort William Henry, they did not follow the military road through the wilderness. Instead, they placed themselves in the hands of a renegade Huron known as Magua, who claimed that he could lead them to their destination by a shorter trail.

It was afternoon when the little party met the woodsman Hawkeye and his Delaware Mohican friends, Chingachgook and his son Uncas. To their dismay, they learned that they were but an hour's distance from their starting point. Hawkeye deduced that Magua had been planning to lead the party into a trap. His Mohican comrades tried to capture the renegade, but Magua took alarm and fled into the woods. At Heyward's urging, the hunter agreed to guide the travelers to their destination. The horses were tied and hidden among rocks along a river. Hawkeye produced a hidden canoe from among the bushes and paddled the party to a rock at the foot of Glenn's Falls. There they prepared to spend the night in a cave.

That night, the party was surprised by a band of Iroquois led by Magua. They might have been victorious but unfortunately their ammunition, which had been left in the canoe, was stolen by one of the enemy. The only hope then lay in the possibility of future rescue, for the capture of the rock and the little group was a certainty. Hawkeye, Chingachgook, and Uncas escaped by floating downstream, leaving the girls and Major Heyward to meet the savages.

Captured, Cora and Alice were allowed to ride their horses, but their captors forced Heyward and David to walk. Although they took a road paralleling that to Fort William Henry, Heyward could not determine the destination the Indians had in mind. Drawing close to Magua, he tried to persuade him to betray his companions and deliver the party safely to Colonel Munro. The Huron agreed on the condition that Cora be given to him to live with him among his tribe as his wife. When she refused, the enraged Magua had everyone bound. He was threatening Alice with his tomahawk when Hawkeye and his friends crept silently upon the band and attacked. The Iroquois fled, leaving several of their dead behind. The party, under David's guidance, sang a hymn of thanksgiving and then pushed onward.

Toward evening, they stopped at a deserted blockhouse to rest. Many years before, it had been the scene of a fight between the Mohicans and the Mohawks, and a mound still showed where bodies lay buried. While Chingachgook watched, the others slept. At moonrise, they continued on their way. It was dawn when Hawkeye and his charges drew near Fort William Henry. They were intercepted and challenged by a sentinel of the French under Montcalm, who was about to lay siege to the fort. Heyward was able to answer him in French, and they were allowed to proceed. Chingachgook killed and scalped the French sentinel. Then, through the fog that had risen from Lake George and through the enemy forces that thronged the plain before the fort, Hawkeye led the way to the gates of the fort.

On the fifth day of the siege, Hawkeye, who had been sent to Fort Edward to seek help, was intercepted on his way back, and a letter he carried was captured. Webb, the commander of Fort Edward, had refused to come to Munro's aid. Under a flag of truce, Montcalm and Munro held a parley. Montcalm showed Webb's letter to Munro and offered honorable terms of surrender. Colonel Munro and his men would be allowed to keep their colors, their arms, and their baggage, if they vacated the fort the next morning. Helpless to do otherwise, Munro accepted these terms. During one of the parleys, Heyward was surprised to see Magua in the camp of the French. He had not been killed during the earlier skirmish.

The following day, the vanquished English started their trip back to Fort Edward. Under the eyes of the French and their Indian allies, they passed across the plain and entered the forest. Suddenly an Indian grabbed at a brightly colored shawl worn by one of the women. Terrified, she wrapped her child in it. The Indian darted to her, grabbed the child from her arms, and dashed out its brains on the ground. Then under the eyes of Montcalm, who did nothing to hold back his savage allies, a monstrous slaughter began.

Cora and Alice, entrusted to David Gamut's protection, were in the midst of the killing when Magua swooped down upon them and carried Alice away. Cora ran after her sister, and faithful David followed her. They were soon atop a hill, from which they watched the slaughter of the garrison. Three days later, Hawkeye, leading Heyward, Munro, and his Indian comrades, traced the girls and David with the help of Cora's veil, which had caught on a tree. Heyward was concerned above all for the safety of Alice. The day before the massacre, he had been given her father's permission to court her.

Hawkeye, knowing that hostile Indians were on their trail, decided to save time by traveling across the lake in a canoe that he discovered in its hiding place nearby. He was certain that Magua had taken the girls north, where he planned to rejoin his own people. Heading their canoe in that direction, the five men paddled all day, at one point having a close escape from some of their enemies. They spent that night in the woods and next day turned west in an effort to find Magua's trail.

After much searching, Uncas found the trail of the captives. That evening, as the party drew near the Huron camp, they met David Gamut wandering about. He told his friends that the Indians thought him crazy because of his habit of breaking into song, and they allowed him to roam the woods unguarded. Alice, he said, was being held at the Huron camp. Cora had been entrusted to the care of a tribe of peaceful Delawares a short distance away.

Heyward, disguising his face with paint, went to the Huron camp in an attempt to rescue Alice, while the others set about to help Cora. Heyward had been in the camp but a short time, posing as a French doctor, when Uncas was brought in, a captive. Called to treat a sick Indian woman, Heyward found Alice in the cave with his patient. He was able to rescue the girl by wrapping her in a blanket and declaring to the Hurons that she was his patient, whom he was carrying off to the woods for treatment. Hawkeye, attempting to rescue Uncas, entered the camp disguised in a medicine man's bearskin he had stolen. Uncas was cut loose and given the disguise, while the woodsman borrowed David Gamut's clothes. The singer was left to take Uncas' place while the others escaped, for Hawkeye was certain that the Indians would not harm David because of his supposed mental condition. Uncas and Hawkeye fled to the Delaware camp.

The following day, Magua and a group of his warriors visited the Delawares in search of their prisoners. The chief of that tribe decided the Hurons had a just claim to Cora because Magua wished to make her his wife. Under inviolable Indian custom, the Huron was permitted to leave the camp unmolested, but Uncas warned him that in a few hours he and the Delawares would follow his trail.

During a bloody battle, Magua fled with Cora to the top of a cliff. There, pursued by Uncas, he stabbed and killed the young Mohican, and was, in turn, sent to his death by a bullet from Hawkeye's long rifle. Cora, too, was killed by a Huron. Amid deep mourning by the Delawares, she and Uncas were laid in their graves in the forest. Colonel Munro and Heyward conducted Alice to English territory and safety. Hawkeye returned to the forest. He had promised to remain with his sorrowing friend Chingachgook forever.

Critical Evaluation:

The Last of the Mohicans is the second title published in what was to become a series of five entitled collectively The Leatherstocking Tales. When James Fenimore Cooper published the first of these "romances," as he called them to distinguish them from the somewhat more realistic contemporary novels, he had no plan for a series with a hero whose life would be shown from youth to old age and death. In *The Pioneers* (1823), Natty Bumppo, or Leatherstocking, is in his early seventies. Responding to a suggestion from his wife, Cooper in *The Last of the Mohicans* went back to Natty's early thirties, when he was called Hawkeye. The great popularity of *The Last of the Mohicans* led Cooper then to move chronologically beyond *The Pioneers* and to picture in *The Prairie* (1827) the last of Natty's life when he was in his eighties, living as a trapper and finally dying on the Great Plains far from his early home. At the time, Cooper did not intend to revive Natty in further books. One minor romance of the forest, *The Wept of Wish-ton-Wish* (1829), was followed by a stream of nautical novels, sociopolitical novels, and nonfictional works of social and political criticism. In 1840, Cooper finally answered the pleas of literary critics and readers and revived the hero whose death he had so touchingly portrayed at the end of *The Prairie*. In *The Pathfinder* (1840), Natty Bumppo is called Pathfinder, and the action shifts from land to the waters of Lake Ontario and back again. Pleased by the resounding praise he gained for having brought back his famed hero, Cooper then decided to write one final romance about him. In *The Deerslayer* (1841), Natty is in his early twenties and goes by the nickname Deerslayer. In 1850, Cooper brought out a new edition of all five Leatherstocking Tales arranged according to the order of events in Natty Bumppo's life: *The Deerslayer, The Last of the Mohicans, The Pathfinder, The Pioneers, The Prairie*. For this edition, he wrote a preface in which he remarked (prophetically, as it turned out): "If anything from the pen of the writer of these romances is at all to outlive himself, it is, unquestionably, the series of *The Leatherstocking Tales*." Despite the many complaints, particularly from Mark Twain and later critics, about Cooper's style, plots, structure, characterization, and dialogue, the Leatherstocking Tales continue to be read, both in the United States and in many foreign countries, and they seem assured of a long life to come.

In Cooper's day, *The Last of the Mohicans* was the most popular of the five tales, and it has continued to be so. Structurally, the novel is superior to the other tales, with three major plot actions and a transitional though bloody interlude (the massacre after the surrender of Fort

William Henry). Cooper depicted romantic love conventionally. His portrayal of Duncan Heyward and the Munro sisters, Cora and Alice—who carry most of the love interest in *The Last of the Mohicans*—shows little originality. They are all genteel characters, and they speak in a stiff, formalized manner. Duncan is gentlemanly, and the two "females" (as Cooper repeatedly refers to them) are ladylike. Cooper contrasts Cora and Alice as he does the pairs of women who keep turning up in his books. Cora, the dark one, is passionate, independent, unafraid, even defiant; blond Alice is timid and easily frightened into faints—she resembles the sentimentalized helpless girls of popular early nineteenth century fiction.

Cooper does much better with his forest characters. Hawkeye is talkative, boastful, superstitious, scornful of the book learning he does not possess, and inclined to be sententious at times. Yet he is brave, resourceful, and loyal to his two Indian friends. His French nickname, La Longue Carabine, attests to his shooting skill. He is religious but sometimes seems more pantheistic than Christian in any formal sense. Hawkeye's arguments with David Gamut contrast his generalized beliefs and Gamut's narrow Calvinism. With his dual background of white birth and early education by Moravian missionaries on the one side and his long experience of living with the Indians on the other, he is, as Honoré de Balzac called him, "a moral hermaphrodite, a child of savagery and civilization."

Chingachgook and Uncas are idealized representatives of their race. As "good" Indians, they are dignified, taciturn, even noble despite their savage ways, which Hawkeye excuses as being simply their native "gifts." Uncas is lithe, strong, handsome, and he reminds the Munro sisters of a Greek statue. Magua is the "bad" Indian, sullen, fierce, cunning, and treacherous. His desire for Cora as his squaw is motivated by his wish to avenge a whipping once inflicted on him by Colonel Munro's order.

In addition to the love story that leads to the marriage of Heyward and Alice, the book contains an interesting relationship between Cora and Uncas, who wants to marry her. Cooper has been accused of evading the theme of miscegenation by killing off both Cora, who is part black, and Uncas. Another important theme in the book is suggested by the title. Chingachgook is left mourning for his son, the last of the Mohican sagamores. He grieves also because he foresees the eventual vanishing of his race. Both he and Hawkeye despair as they envision the end of their way of life in the American wilderness. Implicit in much of the novel is the opposition of savagism and civilization, with Hawkeye realizing that civilization will triumph.

It is easy to complain of Cooper's faulty style, his verbosity, his heavy-handed humor, his improbable actions, the insufficient motivation of his characters, and the inconsistency and inaccuracy of his dialogue. Yet many readers willingly suspend their disbelief or modify their critical objections in order to enjoy the rush of action that makes up so much of *The Last of the Mohicans*. They sorrow over the deaths of Cora and Uncas, and their sympathies go out to Chingachgook and Hawkeye for the loss of what had meant so much in their lives. Moreover, readers continue to enjoy Cooper's descriptions of the natural beauties of the northeastern wilderness as it was in the eighteenth century.

"Critical Evaluation" by Henderson Kincheloe

Bibliography:
Cooper, James Fenimore. *The Last of the Mohicans: A Narrative of 1757*. Albany: State University of New York Press, 1983. A beautiful edition that includes the definitive text, a historical introduction, sixteen illustrations, commentary from the early nineteenth century, and explanatory notes and textual commentary. Exhaustive.

McWilliams, John. *"The Last of the Mohicans": Civil Savagery and Savage Civility*. New York: Twayne, 1995. An excellent starting place. Provides literary and historical contexts, as well as a reading of the novel that focuses on style and genre, race and gender, and the use of history. Four illustrations, a chronology of Cooper's life and works, and a bibliography.

Martin, Terence. "From the Ruins of History: *The Last of the Mohicans*." In *James Fenimore Cooper: A Collection of Critical Essays*, edited by Wayne Fields. Englewood Cliffs, N.J.: Prentice-Hall, 1979. An exploration of the strategies Cooper employs to make actual historical events serve the thematic concerns of his novel.

Peck, H. Daniel, ed. *New Essays on "The Last of the Mohicans."* Cambridge, England: Cambridge University Press, 1992. An introductory critical guide with six social, historical, feminist, and psychological reassessments, all written at the end of the twentieth century. The introduction provides information on the novel's composition and critical reception. Bibliography.

Rans, Geoffrey. *Cooper's Leather-Stocking Novels: A Secular Reading*. Chapel Hill: University of North Carolina Press, 1991. In the introduction, Rans discusses why interest in Cooper has lasted so long. The chapter on *The Last of the Mohicans*, "The Death of a Nation, the Denial of a Genre," focuses on the fact that the Indians' superiority does not protect them from annihilation.

THE LAST OF THE WINE

Type of work: Novel
Author: Mary Renault (Mary Challans, 1905-1983)
Type of plot: Historical
Time of plot: 430-402 B.C.E.
Locale: Athens and the Aegean Sea
First published: 1956

Principal characters:
ALEXIAS, a young Athenian
MYRON, his father
LYSIS, his mentor and lover
XENOPHON, Alexias' friend and later Athenian leader
SOKRATES, a famous philosopher
PLATO, nickname of Aristokles, disciple of Sokrates
PHAEDO, another disciple of Sokrates
KRITIAS, family acquaintance, orator, politician, and member of the
    Thirty Tyrants
ALKIBIADES, controversial politician and military leader

The Story:

Alexias was born prematurely at a most unpropitious time: Pericles had died, the Athenians were embroiled in skirmishes with the Spartans, and a plague threatened the city-state. When Alexias' father was called to military duty, he ordered the death of the puny baby, but the household, distracted by the death of Myron's brother, also named Alexias, and Alexias' lover, spared the child.

Alexias grew into childhood and adolescence as a typical Athenian boy of a good family; he attended school accompanied by his tutor, made friends such as his schoolmate Xenophon, developed strength as a runner, and bloomed into a beautiful youth. His fifteenth year witnessed the desecration of the Herms (square pillars of stone topped by busts of Hermes), a portent of disaster. On the evening of this sacrilege, Myron hosted his club. Serving wine at the feast, Alexias observed guests such as Theramenes and Kritias, later to play significant roles in Athenian politics, and Kritias spilled wine on the boy to mask fondling him. Alexias also overheard a discussion of Alkibiades, a charismatic orator, Athenian leader, and Myron's treasured friend. Myron cherished Alkibiades' gift of a winecup, which was later destroyed when Alkibiades was disgraced. Alkibiades may have been responsible for the desecration of the Herms. Alexias' beauty attracted suitors, but, with Sokrates' help, Alexias committed himself of Lysis, a handsome athlete and another disciple of Sokrates.

Myron was supposedly killed in the catastrophic Sicilian campaign. When Sparta broke a truce with Athens, Alexias served in the military guard under Lysis' command. War did not interrupt the Isthmian Games; Alexias was able to win his race, but his hopes for competing in the Olympics were destroyed when his heart was damaged because of the exertion. His weakened and demoralized father, having escaped slavery, returned to a depleted estate. The Council of 400 was established. Alexias and Lysis joined the Athenian navy and, while in Samos, participated in the navel coup against the oligarchs. The once-exiled Alkibiades returned triumphantly to Athens and was made supreme leader. Alexias served under his command in the war against Sparta, whose general was Lysander. In 405 B.C.E., the Athenians were slaughtered in the battle of Aegospotami; Athens suffered under a Spartan siege. Myron returned with the other negotiators for peace with Sparta. Athens surrendered, its defenses were destroyed, and it had to endure occupation by Spartan troops. When Myron, a moderate, was killed by Kritias to help establish the Thirty Tyrants, Alexias killed Kritias in revenge and escaped with Lysis to Thebes. Allied with the Thebans, Athenians gained control of the city, but Lysis was killed. A year later, Alexias watched the torchlit race, symbolizing the passing of the sacred fire, a symbol of Athenian civilization, heard Amytos attack Sokrates, and saw Sokrates among the spectators, drinking wine with friends and disciples.

Critical Evaluation:

Although *The Last of the Wine* is a historical novel, its literary importance as a *Bildungsroman* (developmental novel) is not to be underrated. Mary Renault focuses on a fictional character, Alexias, as a plot device and as a model of the ideal Athenian, the character in search of excellence, living during the waning years of Athenian dominance, the second Peloponnesian War.

The historical background of Alexias' story is impeccable—accurate, detailed, and absorbing. Although Mary Renault uses sources such as Thucydides and Xenophon, she enlivens them through detail and description, as in the gripping scene, taken from Thucydides, in which the Athenians sail to attack Sicily. Alexias watches the ships leave with pride and ruefully remarks that he wishes his tears of patriotic fervor were the only ones Athenians had to shed. Renault is familiar with Greek warfare, its men, armament, and strategies, as is evidenced by her description of the Spartans' ramming of Alexias' ship, the *Siren*, the ensuing battle, and the sinking of the ship. Renault traveled in the area to confirm details, but her powerful imagination enlivens the factual accounts and the anecdotal suggestions of her sources.

Presenting the novel as a memoir enabled Renault to lend immediacy and authenticity by providing a witness to events. The first-person narrative excludes any authorial comment, but an ironic perspective is provided by foreshadowing as the fictional Alexias writes his memoir in retrospect. Alexias can examine his friend Xenophon in the light of future events and can foresee Sokrates' fate as he watches the philosopher drinking wine during the last scene of the novel. The use of irony reminds the reader that the writer of the memoir is a mature Alexias whose search for excellence has been tempered by time and experience.

The novel is consciously written in a simple, classless language, deliberately eschewing polysyllabic Latinized words, but the prose achieves a poetic richness in its use of image and symbol, such as the leaves that crown victorious athletes, the torch-lit races, and, most important, the wine. Dregs of wine are spilled to write lovers' initials; wine is drunk in celebration by newly pledged lovers; wine commemorates past joys and new losses, death and change, the condemnation of Athens' most civilized citizen and the end of Athenian supremacy and culture. Alexias' loss is not only of friends such as Lysis and Sokrates, but also of the end of the Athens that nurtured him. Renault's style, choice of narration, and sense of history have captured a moment in time and made it significant for generations.

Elizabeth R. Nelson

Bibliography:
Burns, Landon C., Jr. "Men Are Only Men: The Novels of Mary Renault." *Critique* 6 (1963-1964): 102-121. Evaluates Renault's early historical novels, defending them as fiction mer-

iting critical approbation. Commends Renault's reconstruction of the period, her development of the theme of growth and maturity, and her style, particularly her use of imagery and symbol in *The Last of the Wine*.

Dick, Bernard F. *The Hellenism of Mary Renault*. Carbondale: Southern Illinois University Press, 1972. Essential study of Renault's work; his comments received her personal approbation. Discusses her use of language, the authenticity of historical background, the novel as *Bildungsroman*, and the novel's themes and symbols.

McEwan, Neil. *Perspective in British Historical Fiction Today*. Wolfeboro, N.H.: Longwood Academic, 1987. A chapter on Renault's fiction interprets her earlier novels and emphasizes historical accuracy, immediacy of first-person narrative, and writing style as features contributing to the success of *The Last of the Wine*.

Sweetman, David. *Mary Renault: A Biography*. 1st U.S. ed. New York: Harcourt Brace Jovanovich, 1993. Detailed biography with strong personal references. Provides illuminating commentary on the novels and clarifies the introduction of homosexual love in the novel as both historically and thematically correct.

Wolfe, Peter. *Mary Renault*. New York: Twayne, 1969. Useful insights, such as viewing the book as an epic in reverse and focusing on its historical authenticity, but too wedded to reading historical parallels, especially of the literary 1930's, into the novel.

THE LAST PURITAN
A Memoir in the Form of a Novel

Type of work: Novel
Author: George Santayana (1863-1952)
Type of plot: Social realism
Time of plot: Early twentieth century
Locale: Connecticut, Massachusetts, and England
First published: 1935

> *Principal characters:*
> OLIVER ALDEN, the last Puritan
> PETER ALDEN, his father
> HARRIET ALDEN, his mother
> FRAULEIN IRMA SCHLOTE, Oliver's governess
> JIM DARNLEY, Oliver's friend
> ROSE DARNLEY, Jim's sister
> MARIO VAN DE WEYER, Oliver's cousin
> EDITH VAN DE WEYER, another cousin
> BOBBY, Jim's illegitimate son

The Story:

Young Peter Alden was educated in America but left Harvard before he had completed his studies and went abroad with a tutor. After he had come of age and had inherited his money, he wandered aimlessly about the world, studying occasionally. He was in his early middle years before he completed any one course. Licensed to practice medicine, his practice was limited to himself, for he had burdened himself with many ills, some real but most of them imaginary. Once he consulted Dr. Bumstead, a psychiatrist whose main concern was Peter's money. Dr. Bumstead convinced Peter that a home and a wife would be the best treatment possible and, as a consequence, Peter married the doctor's daughter Harriet. Oliver was their only child.

Little Oliver was a Puritan from the beginning. He accepted things as they were, never complaining, never wondering why. There were no other children with whom he could play because his mother feared that other children might be dirty or vulgar. Furthermore, there were no stories, songs, or prayers for the boy, as Mrs. Alden would not have him filled with nonsensical ideas. Oliver's father, who spent most of his time traveling, was no more than a polite stranger.

Fraulein Irma Schlote, a German, became Oliver's governess, and from her he had what little brightness there was in his childhood. On their long walks together, Irma instilled in Oliver his first love of nature and a love for the German language. Yet even with Irma, Oliver remained a stoical little Puritan. If he were tired or his foot hurt, there was no use to complain. They had come for a walk, and they must finish that walk. One must do his duty, even an unpleasant one. As he grew older, Oliver hated human weakness with the hatred of a true Puritan.

When Oliver was fifteen, he went to high school, where he excelled in scholarship and in athletics because it was his duty to do everything that the school demanded. During one holiday season, Oliver joined his father on his yacht. There he met Jim Darnley, the captain, who had been a British sailor before he became involved in a scandal. Jim was an entirely new type of person in Oliver's world. Oliver knew that the sailor was worldly and had no sense of duty, but strangely enough, Oliver was always to consider Jim his dearest friend.

After his graduation from high school, Oliver joined his father and Jim in England. There, while visiting Jim's family, he learned to respect Jim's minister father and to enjoy the company of Rose, Jim's young sister. He learned also that Jim had an illegitimate child, Bobby, who lived with Mrs. Bowler, his tavern-keeping mother.

While in England, Oliver also met his distant cousin, Mario Van de Weyer, a worldly young man dependent upon his rich relatives for his education and livelihood. Mario also puzzled Oliver. Mario had nothing, not even much real intelligence, yet he was happy. Oliver, who had everything, was not consciously happy; he merely lived as he felt it his duty to live.

Before they left England, Oliver's father committed suicide. He felt that Oliver needed to be free of him and as much as possible of his own mother. Rather than see the boy torn between his conflicting duties to both parents, Peter took his life. Back in America, Oliver entered Williams College. While playing football, he broke his leg. In the infirmary, he was visited by his cousin Mario and another cousin, Edith Van de Weyer. Mario attended Harvard on Oliver's money, but he seemed to feel no reluctance about living extravagantly on his cousin's bounty. Oliver began to think of Edith as a possible wife. Like his father, he did not consider love an important element in marriage, but he felt it his duty to marry and have children.

In his last year of college, Oliver transferred to Harvard University. There he spent much time with Mario, until that young man was forced to leave college because he had been found in his room with a young woman. When he went to Edith's home to tell her about Mario, Oliver found that Edith's family had already heard the story from Mario and had forgiven him. Oliver also learned that Edith had great affection for Mario. Yet because he thought a match between himself and Edith a sensible one, he proposed to her anyway, forgetting to mention love. Edith refused him. She knew that marriage with Oliver would be a dutiful experience only, and she wanted more than duty.

When he had finished college, Oliver took a cruise around the world. Then he settled in England and lived for a time near Jim Darnley's family. War was coming closer, but Oliver felt no duty toward either side. Mario enlisted at once, for Mario was a romantic. The war became more personal for Oliver when he learned that Jim had been killed. Jim's death seemed proof of war's useless waste. More practically, Jim's death meant that Bobby and Rose were Oliver's responsibility.

When the United States entered the war, Oliver felt that it was his duty to go home and join the army. After his training, he was sent to France. Before he went to the front, he wrote to Rose Darnley, asking her to marry him at once, so that she would be his wife and would be cared for if he were killed. Rose, like Edith, wanted love, and she refused to marry him. She knew, too, that Oliver should never marry, because love should be unreasoning and illogical at times, conditions that Oliver could never accept.

After Rose's refusal, Oliver seemed free for the first time. No one needed him any longer. Jim was dead. Mario was in the army and provided for in case of Oliver's death. Bobby had been made secure financially. Edith was engaged to be married. Rose was provided for in Oliver's will. All of his life he had acted in accordance with duty—in his parental relations, in school, and in the army. At least he would not be a dutiful husband. Now he need be true only to himself. That night he slept peacefully.

Oliver was killed, but not in battle. He was a post-Armistice casualty, the victim of a motorcycle accident. His will told the story of his life. He had left adequate, but not extravagant, provisions for Mario, Rose, Mrs. Darnley, Fraulein Irma, and Bobby. He left the bulk of his fortune to his mother because he had believed it his duty to provide for her.

Oliver Alden lived his life as a true Puritan, doing what must be done without flinching, taking little pleasure in worldly things, yet not withdrawing from the world. He did not believe in Puritanism, for he knew that those who lived selfishly were often more happy than he. He was not a prig. He had been a Puritan in spite of himself, and for that reason, perhaps, the last true Puritan.

Critical Evaluation:

George Santayana's *The Last Puritan* offers a probing critique of the romantic philosophy of Ralph Waldo Emerson and Arthur Schopenhauer, as well as a caustic treatment of what Santayana identifies as the Puritan strain in pre-World War I American upper-class society. Santayana's only novel shows the influence of at least three major sources: first, the insightful but somewhat cynical philosophical treatment of religion by William James; second, the novels of Henry James, with their probing explorations of American and European society; third, the biting social satire of Samuel Butler's *The Way of All Flesh* (1903). Although Santayana gradually grew toward affirming the Roman Catholic faith, he spent most of his life denouncing religious sentiments and championing a materialistic view of life, a view rooted in what people can experience here and now in life. *The Last Puritan* reflects a tension between Santayana's loathing of religion and his fascination for principles of spirituality and beauty.

The Last Puritan begins with a description of a Boston resident named Mr. Nathaniel Alden, a half brother of Peter Alden, who later becomes the father of Oliver Alden, the central figure of the novel. While Nathaniel and Oliver never meet, Nathaniel's rigid, stingy, coldhearted ways seem to foreshadow all that will prove debilitating in Oliver. The Alden family has descended from a line of Puritans turned Unitarians, a group determined to maintain a high moral tone even though they have abandoned any sense of a personal God and prefer a vague philosophical view of deity. They accept all religions, provided they are not taken too seriously. Like his father, who was murdered for his ruthless treatment of his tenants, Nathaniel loathes human weaknesses and upon discovering moral shortcomings in his ward, Peter, sends him away, never to see his face again. Nathaniel is the epitome of religious façade and pretense, of a lifestyle lacking all sense of feeling, especially human compassion.

Although Peter Alden, Oliver's father, proves to be a womanizer and a drug addict, Oliver turns out to be quite free of these tendencies. As the narrator notes, "All sensation in Oliver was, as it were, retarded; it hardly became conscious until it became moral." This tendency in Oliver so stifles his life that he finds himself incapable of relating to a potential wife, such as his cousin Edith Van de Weyer and his best friend's sister, Rose Darnley, both of whom reject Oliver because they know he is incapable of loving. That Oliver should die not in the battles of World War I, but in his effort to avoid a motorcycle driver speeding on the wrong side of the road, symbolizes how much of his life is spent in avoiding possible problems, only to encounter a worse one—the wasting of his own life. As the narrator notes, living longer would have been useless to Oliver Alden because he lacked the capacity to enjoy life. As a young man with all of the advantages of wealth and education and culture at his disposal, Oliver was incapable of experiencing life as more than a duty, a moral obligation to be endured with stoic discipline.

While George Santayana seems to have aimed much of his criticism at the Puritan pseudore-ligious work ethic, he also seems to have taken special pleasure in debunking the Romantic philosophy of Ralph Waldo Emerson and Arthur Schopenhauer. These two Romantic philoso-phers were much more reserved than some of their contemporaries such as Walt Whitman, Friedrich von Schiller, and Johann Wolfgang von Goethe, whose writings Oliver Alden does not like. While preparing to attend Harvard, Oliver stops at Concord to admire the landmarks associated with his hero Emerson, and later stays in a room thought to have once been used by that philosopher. Like Emerson, Oliver admires nature and looks to it as the ultimate source of revelation and beauty. Like Emerson, Oliver fails to see that the best part of life cannot be actualized without commitment to choices. Oliver drifts through life in a theoretical mode that rarely touches the world in which most people live. He is not unconcerned about others, nor is he consciously arrogant or selfish, but he fails to discover how to move beyond his own little sphere of sensibility. Oliver's life has great capacity for good, as his cousin Caleb Wetherbee indicates when he prophesies that Oliver may soon feel a call into ministry. Much later in the novel, Rose Darnley also notes Oliver's capacity for a religious vocation, but she does so in a context that underscores his unsuitability for normal, domestic life in marriage. As the novel emphasizes, Oliver lacks the boldness and commitment necessary to make himself more than an idealistic young man with high expectations that the world will never meet.

The strength of *The Last Puritan* lies in its insightful exploration of human failings and disappointments. At times the style of the book is almost poetic. Many of Santayana's characters in this novel are capable of surprising action, intriguing, and memorable. Although not as stylistically fluid as the works of Henry James, Santayana's *The Last Puritan* is at least as rich in insights into human personalities as James's works are. The primary weakness of the novel lies in its blatant dismissal of religious ideals as being of any worth, and in the novel's presentation of irresponsible and selfish people as offering a higher standard than the Puritans offered. This latter problem is caused primarily by the author's limited point of view. The novel itself, as a work of art, is certainly one of the most memorable American novels of the 1930's.

"Critical Evaluation" by Daven M. Kari

Bibliography:
Lachs, John. *George Santayana*. Boston: Twayne, 1988. Does not treat *The Last Puritan* but does provide a useful framework for interpreting Santayana's life and philosophical works. Helpful chronology and bibliography.
Levinson, Henry Samuel. *Santayana, Pragmatism, and the Spiritual Life*. Chapel Hill: University of North Carolina Press, 1992. Discusses philosophical issues at the core of *The Last Puritan*. Sees the novel as an exploration of the failure of romantic, Emersonian philosophy to teach action as the basis for enlightenment.
McCormick, John. *George Santayana: A Biography*. New York: Alfred A. Knopf, 1987. Detailed, readable biography surveying the author's life and writings. Contains several sections and many useful references to *The Last Puritan*, especially pages 323-339.
Price, Kenneth M., and Robert C. Leitz III, eds. *Critical Essays on George Santayana*. Boston: G. K. Hall, 1991. Includes nine essays about *The Last Puritan*. Useful for serious students of Santayana's works.
Santayana, George. *Persons and Places*. 3 vols. New York: Charles Scribner's Sons, 1944-1953. A colorful and philosophical interpretation of the author's life and the aesthetic significance he discovered in living. Since *The Last Puritan* is semiautobiographical and these memoirs are semiliterary, they complement each other nicely.

THE LAST TEMPTATION OF CHRIST

Type of work: Novel
Author: Nikos Kazantzakis (1883-1957)
Type of plot: Psychological realism
Time of plot: First century C.E.
Locale: Israel
First published: Ho teleutaios peirasmos, 1955 (English translation, 1960)

> *Principal characters:*
> JESUS, a carpenter of Nazareth
> SIMEON, his uncle, a rabbi
> BARABBAS, a bandit
> MARY MAGDALENE, a prostitute
> SIMON PETER,
> ANDREW,
> JAMES,
> JOHN,
> PHILIP,
> JUDAS ISCARIOT,
> THOMAS, and
> MATTHEW, Jesus' disciples

The Story:

Israel was occupied by the forces of the Roman Empire. In his village of Nazareth in Galilee, Jesus had just finished building a cross ordered by the Romans when Judas Iscariot, a member of the rebel group called the Zealots, came to ask his help. Judas' leader, known simply as the Zealot, had been sentenced to be crucified that same day. Judas believed that the Zealot was the Messiah promised to the Jews by the ancient prophets, the man who would save Israel, and that if the people rose up against the Romans to prevent his execution, the Zealot would reveal himself as the Messiah and cast the Romans out of Israel.

Jesus refused to take part in the rebellion, which he knew the Romans would crush. He had long suspected that he himself was the Messiah, but he was terrified of crucifixion, and he was angry that the role God had chosen for him would deny him the earthly joys beloved by all men in ancient Israel: a hearth, a home, a loving wife, and children. As a young man he had loved Mary Magdalene, but the hand of God had kept them apart, and Jesus blamed himself for Mary's descent into sin. His fear and anger led Jesus to rebel against God.

As part of that rebellion he had built the cross for the execution of the Zealot. He delivered the cross to the Romans and helped to set it in place. The people of Nazareth were stunned, and the planned rebellion never occurred. After the crucifixion, the people called Jesus a traitor, and Jesus, ashamed, set out for a distant monastery, where he stayed for some months. There he gave himself to God and began his ministry.

For some months, Jesus wandered Galilee and Judea, preaching the gospel. At Capernaum he saved Mary Magdalene from a mob under the sway of Barabbas, the bandit and Zealot. He was baptized by John the Baptist, then he went into the desert and wrestled with Satan, who appeared to him as a serpent with the eyes and breasts of a woman. Satan offered Jesus the world, and in particular, Mary Magdalene, whom Jesus, the man, still loved. Jesus resisted, hoping that he had conquered temptation, but Satan promised to see him again at Passover.

Jesus continued preaching, performing miracles, and gathering followers. In Cana he cured the daughter of Rufus, the Roman centurion of Nazareth, of a mysterious disease. In Bethany, he raised Lazarus from the dead. In Jerusalem, he turned the money changers out of the temple. There, on his own orders, Judas betrayed him to the hypocritical Pharisees, who arrested him for blasphemy. Lacking the legal authority to punish prisoners, the Pharisees turned Jesus over to the Roman ruler of Judea, Pontius Pilate, and they demanded that Jesus be crucified. Pilate, no stranger to the ruthless suppression of troublemakers, complied.

On the cross, Jesus experienced his last temptation. In agony, his head swimming, he shouted "My God, my God!" but he fainted before he could finish. While he was unconscious, an angel came to him and explained that his crucifixion had been a dream, a test of his resolve. The angel explained that the disciples had all run away, and that Jesus' reward for his suffering was to be the earthly joys that had for so long been denied him. The angel led him to Mary Magdalene and her servant. Jesus and Mary made love, but a short time later Mary was stoned to death by an angry mob. Jesus returned to Bethany, where he married Lazarus' sister, Mary. He later entered into a bigamous relationship with Mary and her sister, Martha.

The years passed, and Jesus prospered. Mary and Martha gave him many children. As an old man, near death, Jesus was visited by his aged disciples, including Judas, who reviled him as a traitor. Jesus realized that the angel who had led him down from the cross was really Satan in disguise, and that all of his years of happiness with Mary and Martha were an illusion conjured up by Satan to sway Jesus from his divine purpose. In an instant he finished his cry: "My God, my God, why hast thou forsaken me?" and was transported back onto the cross, thereby completing his divine mission.

Critical Evaluation:

Born in 1883, on the Greek island of Crete, then a possession of Turkey, Nikos Kazantzakis was sent to a monastery on nearby Naxos at the age of four when his home island was torn by armed rebellion against the Turks. Franciscan monks introduced him to Western thought and to the spiritual heroism personified by Christ. He began a quest for spiritual perfection that led Kazantzakis to reject Christianity for a series of saviors. He became a follower first of the German philosopher Friedrich Nietzsche (1844-1900), then of the Indian philosopher and founder of Buddhism, Siddhārtha Guatama (563-483 B.C.E.), then of the Russian revolutionary leader, Vladimir Ilich Lenin (1870-1924), and, finally, of the ancient Greek hero, Odysseus, before returning to Catholicism in late middle age. The dominant theme of his major works—all published after Kazantzakis' fifty-eighth birthday—was the necessity of struggling against the temptations of the flesh in order to achieve spiritual enlightenment. From his personal struggles sprang his questions about Christ; these questions are explored in *The Last Temptation of Christ.*

From its first publication, *The Last Temptation of Christ* has been a highly controversial novel; the German edition was placed on the Vatican's Index of Forbidden Books in 1954, and an English-language film version, released in 1988, scandalized Christians around the world. Kazantzakis saw Christ, like the other heroes in his life, as engaged in the struggle for freedom—freedom from limitations imposed by family, freedom from the pleasures of the flesh, freedom from political entities, and freedom from the fear of death. He came to believe that Christ, given human flesh and human experiences, removed from his heavenly home by three decades of life on earth, must have felt the same doubts and desires that other people feel, and he must have struggled to overcome these doubts and desires. In orthodox Christian terms, this position is heretical, but like the Puritan poet John Milton, Kazantzakis believed that choice is essential to virtue. For Kazantzakis, the wonder of Christ's sacrifice lies less in his divinity than in his humanity; the stronger Christ's attraction to temptation, the more meaningful is his ultimate choice to reject it.

The result of Kazantzakis' exploration is a moving portrait of Christ as a man struggling toward union with God. Kazantzakis filled in from his own imagination the human details typically missing from sacred texts. The novel begins, for example, with Jesus' tortured dreams, his subconscious and human struggles between flesh and spirit, and it ends with his agonized fantasies on the cross. Unlike the Gospel, which mentions only one incident in which the twelve-year-old Jesus amazed the elders in the Temple of Jerusalem with his wisdom, the novel describes Jesus' early life in detail. Kazantzakis gives Jesus a father struck by lightning and completely disabled. The Gospel does not mention Joseph after the incident in the Temple. Kazantzakis gives Jesus a domineering mother desperate for grandchildren. Once Jesus' ministry had begun, his disciples, all save Judas, who is weak and vacillating, bicker among themselves incessantly and achieve only a shallow, worldly understanding of Jesus' divine message. Judas himself becomes not the archetypical traitor vilified throughout Christian history, but, instead, a great patriot who saves Jesus from the wrath of Barabbas, who stays with him even while the others deny him, and who is chosen to betray Jesus because he alone can be trusted to follow orders and because he alone has the strength and courage to perform such a dangerous—but necessary—mission. Kazantzakis tightens the familiar plot of the Passion, bringing causal relations to events left disconnected in the Gospel; when word reaches Jerusalem that Jesus has raised Lazarus from the dead, Caiaphas, the high priest of the Pharisees, plots with Barabbas to murder Lazarus, thereby destroying evidence of Jesus' divinity. It is for this crime that Barabbas is accused when the mob chooses him, instead of Jesus, to be spared from the cross.

Aside from the final chapters, in which Christ experiences his last temptation, Kazantzakis' most interesting additions appear in the parables. Kazantzakis believes that Christianity is the religion of divine love; therefore, he writes new endings for several parables—endings more in keeping with his own vision of a forgiving, all-inclusive Christ. In his new version of the parable of the wise and foolish virgins, both the wise and foolish are invited to the wedding feast; none are excluded. In the parable of the rich man, Dives, and the beggar, Lazarus, God allows Dives into heaven at the request of the forgiving Lazarus. Kazantzakis' Christ tempers justice with mercy throughout the novel.

In a 1954 letter to a friend, Kazantzakis insisted that the novel was a "laborious, sacred, creative endeavor to reincarnate the essence of Christ, setting aside the dross—falsehoods and pettiness which all the Churches and all the cassocked representatives of Christianity have heaped upon His figure, thereby distorting it." The Christ portrayed by Kazantzakis in *The Last Temptation of Christ* is a highly personal vision; it is nonetheless a compelling one.

Craig A. Milliman

Bibliography:
Bien, Peter. *Nikos Kazantzakis*. New York: Columbia University Press, 1972. An excellent starting point. Contains limited commentary on *The Last Temptation of Christ*.
_____. *Nikos Kazantzakis, Novelist*. Bristol: Bristol Classical Press, 1989. An excellent introduction to Kazantzakis. Includes an appraisal of Kazantzakis' importance as a novelist and his worldview, plus an analysis of *The Last Temptation of Christ* and other major novels.

Friar, Kimon. *The Spiritual Odyssey of Nikos Kazantzakis: A Talk*. Edited with an introduction by Theofanis G. Stavrou. St. Paul, Minn.: North Central Publishing, 1979. Explains Kazantzakis' return to Catholicism, an essential point in understanding *The Last Temptation of Christ*.

Kazantzakis, Helen. *Nikos Kazantzakis: A Biography Based on His Letters*. Translated by Amy Mims. New York: Simon & Schuster, 1968. A loving portrait of the author by his second wife. Provides insights into Kazantzakis' often turbulent mind during the writing of his greatest works.

Levitt, Morton P. *The Cretan Glance: The World and Art of Nikos Kazantzakis*. Columbus: Ohio State University Press, 1980. Beginning with *Freedom or Death*, one of Kazantzakis' few novels set on his home island of Crete, Levitt discusses the development of Crete as metaphor in the major novels, including *The Last Temptation of Christ* and the great epic poem, *The Odyssey: A Modern Sequel*.

THE LAST TYCOON

Type of work: Novel
Author: F. Scott Fitzgerald (1896-1940)
Type of plot: Social realism
Time of plot: 1930's
Locale: Hollywood
First published: 1941

> *Principal characters:*
> MONROE STAHR, a film producer
> KATHLEEN MOORE, his mistress
> PAT BRADY, Stahr's partner
> CECILIA BRADY, his daughter

The Story:

Cecilia Brady was flying to California for a summer vacation from college. On the plane she met Wylie White, an alcoholic screenwriter, and Schwartz, a ruined producer. Monroe Stahr, the partner of Cecilia's father, was also aboard, though traveling as Mr. Smith. When the plane was grounded at Nashville, Schwartz sent a note to Stahr, warning him about Pat Brady, Cecilia's father. When the plane took off again, Schwartz stayed behind and committed suicide.

Stahr had been the boy wonder of the film industry. He had been in charge of the studio in his twenties, almost dead from overwork at thirty-five. Indeed, he was half in love with death for the sake of his dead wife, Minna Davis, a great star with whom he had been deeply in love. Since her death, he had worked harder than ever, often remaining in his office around the clock. In contrast to Stahr, Brady was mean and selfish. Lacking taste and understanding little of the technical end of the industry, Brady had acquired his share of the studio through luck and had retained it through shrewdness.

One night, while Cecilia was visiting the studio, there was an earthquake. Stahr, working with his troubleshooter, Robinson, to clear away the mess, saw a sightseer perched on top of a floating idol. The girl reminded him of his dead wife, and he tried to discover her identity. That night, Cecilia fell in love with Stahr, but she felt that her attachment was hopeless.

A self-made, paternalistic employer, Stahr personally managed almost every detail at the studio. Though he was not an educated man, he had raised the artistic level of motion pictures and did not hesitate to make good pictures that might lose money. As a result, he had incurred the distrust of the stockholders, who saw filmmaking only as a business. Their distrust of the producer was, however, mixed with a genuine respect for his many abilities. In addition to the opposition of the stockholders, Stahr was concerned because Communists were trying to organize the writers; he worked closely with his writers and wanted them to trust him. Wylie White, in particular, enjoyed his favor, although White resented him. At this time, White hoped to marry Cecilia for the sake of her father's influence. Typical of Stahr's interest in his employees was his investigation of the attempted suicide of a cameraman, Pete Zavras. Stahr learned that Zavras had been unable to find work because of a rumor that he was going blind. Stahr was able to scotch the rumor by providing Zavras with a statement from an oculist.

By this time, Stahr had succeeded in locating the young woman who resembled his wife. She was Kathleen Moore, and though she was at first reluctant to meet him, they later had a brief, passionate affair. Stahr learned that she had been the mistress of a deposed monarch who had undergone a personality deterioration and that she was about to marry an American who had rescued her from that situation. Stahr realized that marriage to Kathleen could give him the will to go on living. While he hesitated, her fiancé arrived ahead of schedule, and she went through with the marriage from a sense of obligation. Cecilia, knowing nothing of these matters, was still desperately hoping to attract Stahr's attention, all the more so after she discovered her father with his nude secretary. At Stahr's request, she arranged a meeting with a Communist organizer. Stahr got drunk, however, and tried to beat him up.

At this point, F. Scott Fitzgerald's manuscript ends, but the rest of the story may be pieced together from the author's notes.

Because the studio was in financial difficulties, Brady had tried to push through a wage cut. Stahr, opposing this plan, had gone East to convince the other stockholders to postpone the wage slash. Brady cut the salaries and betrayed the writers while Stahr was ill in Washington. Although he broke with Brady after that, Stahr agreed to go along with Brady's plan for a company union, chiefly because Stahr felt personally responsible for the welfare of his employees. Wylie White had also turned on Stahr.

Kathleen and Stahr resumed their relationship. When Brady tried to blackmail Stahr, the producer threatened him with information about the death of Brady's wife. At one time, the author considered having Brady persuade Robinson to undertake Stahr's murder; however, Fitzgerald rejected this idea in favor of having Brady inform Kathleen's husband, a film technician involved with the union organizers, of Kathleen's affair with Stahr. That led to an alienation-of-affection suit, but Stahr was somehow saved by Zavras, the cameraman.

Stahr became alienated from Kathleen and was no longer able to dominate his associates at the studio. Nevertheless, he continued to oppose Brady. Finally, Stahr felt that he had to eliminate Brady before Brady had him killed. After hiring gangsters to murder Brady, Stahr flew East to provide himself with an alibi; he changed his mind on the plane, however, and decided to call off the killers at the next airport. The plane crashed before he could carry out his intention.

Fitzgerald was uncertain about including an episode in which the plane's wreckage was plundered by three children who discovered it, the idea being that each child's personality was reflected by the items he stole. Stahr's funeral would have been a powerful, detailed, ironic arraignment of Hollywood sham. It would have included the incident of a has-been cowboy actor who was invited to be a pallbearer by mistake and consequently enjoyed a return of good fortune. Cecilia later had an affair, probably with Wylie White, and then suffered a complete breakdown. At the end of the novel, the reader was to learn that she was telling the story while a patient in a tuberculosis sanatorium.

Critical Evaluation:

After the overwhelming success of his autobiographical novel, *This Side of Paradise* (1920), and *Tender Is the Night* (1934), describing the precipitation of what he later termed "emotional bankruptcy," F. Scott Fitzgerald settled in Hollywood. There, he died while pursuing a fruitless career as a screenwriter. *The Last Tycoon*, Fitzgerald's last and unfinished novel, is a sobering picture of society written by a man who had experienced both ends of prosperity's spectrum.

Although Fitzgerald intended this novel to be "an escape into a lavish, romantic past that perhaps will not come again in our time," the fragmentary novel has at least two qualities that transcend its nostalgia: the manner in which the narrative is handled and the characters' views of society. Cecilia Brady functions as both narrator and character and is able to piece the story together by collecting fragments from people involved in various incidents. By means of a retrospective device revealed in the novel's projected outline, however, she is shown to be as limited in her view of American society as anyone else in the novel connected with the motion-picture industry. It is this limited viewpoint that gives unity between plot and theme to the novel as well as credibility to the characters.

Fitzgerald's decision to use Cecilia Brady instead of a detached narrator allows him to reveal only those elements of reality that he deems thematically essential. Reality is filtered through life in Hollywood; Hollywood, in turn, is revealed only in relation to Stahr; and Cecilia reveals only the aspects of Stahr's life that she finds interesting. The narrator functions as a personification of the illnesses of Hollywood life; the illnesses physically manifest themselves in the form of her tuberculosis.

The major significance of this unfinished novel is the evidence in its stylistic daring and social criticism that Fitzgerald was far from through as a novelist. The moral subtleties of Stahr's characterization recall Fitzgerald's greatest achievement: *The Great Gatsby* (1925). Like the hero of that novel, Stahr becomes involved with the underworld to preserve a dream. The difference between Gatsby's illusion of Daisy and Stahr's professional integrity is the measure of Fitzgerald's own hard-won maturity as a writer and man.

Bibliography:

Bloom, Harold, ed. *F. Scott Fitzgerald.* New York: Chelsea House, 1985. A well-indexed collection of contemporary criticism on Fitzgerald. Includes an article that focuses on social statement and technique in *The Last Tycoon*. The novel is also discussed in considerable detail in other articles.

Ebel, Kenneth. *F. Scott Fitzgerald.* 1968. Rev. ed. Boston: Twayne, 1977. A good introductory reference, which includes biographical information; readings of novels, stories, and articles; and critical responses. *The Last Tycoon* is referred to throughout. Includes bibliography, chronology, and index.

Hook, Andrew. *F. Scott Fitzgerald.* London: Edward Arnold, 1992. An accessible reading of Fitzgerald and his work that refers to criticism and to scholarship. The chapter on *The Last Tycoon* draws from Fitzgerald's letters, in which he discusses his intentions and plans for the novel. Includes a chronology, bibliography, and index.

Lee, A. Robert, ed. *Scott Fitzgerald: The Promises of Life.* London: Vision, 1989. The article on *The Last Tycoon* argues that the novel is memorable not because it is a faithful portrait of the motion-picture industry at a particular time, but because of the way Fitzgerald uses this material to explore relationships among creative individuals, industry, and society.

Seiters, Dan. *Image Patterns in the Novels of F. Scott Fitzgerald.* Ann Arbor, Mich.: UMI Research Press, 1986. In his discussion of *The Last Tycoon*, Seiters offers a detailed analysis of such images as water, decay, transportation, communication, and the contrast between light and dark.

THE LATE GEORGE APLEY
A Novel in the Form of a Memoir

Type of work: Novel
Author: John Phillips Marquand (1893-1960)
Type of plot: Naturalism
Time of plot: Late nineteenth and early twentieth centuries
Locale: Boston
First published: 1937

Principal characters:
GEORGE APLEY, a proper Bostonian
JOHN, his son
ELEANOR, his daughter
CATHARINE, his wife
MR. WILLING, George Apley's biographer

The Story:

George William Apley was born on Beacon Hill, on January 25, 1866. The Apleys were an old family in Massachusetts. Thomas, known in the old records as Goodman Apley, had emigrated from England to America and settled in Roxbury in 1636. Goodman Apley's son, John, had been graduated from Harvard in 1662. From his time, there had been an Apley in Harvard in each succeeding generation. John Apley's son, Nathaniel, established himself in Boston. A later Apley, Moses, became a shipping master and laid the foundation of the Apley fortune. Moses Apley was George Apley's grandfather.

George Apley grew up in a quiet atmosphere of wealth and social position. He learned his parents' way of living calmly and with fortitude. In an orderly way, he was introduced to the polite world, at first through visits to relatives; later, through study at Harvard.

His Harvard days were probably the high point of his life. He was sent to Harvard to weld those qualities of gentlemanly behavior that private grammar school and parents together had tried to encourage. His parents were anxious that he should make friends with the right people. George was carefully instructed in the ways of high-minded gentlemen. His training was indicated by a theme in which he wrote a description of a Boston brothel in terms expressing his repulsion and shock. In the gymnasium, George won distinction as a boxer. Moreover, he became a member of the board of the Harvard Lampoon. He was taken into the Club, an honor his father appreciated greatly. In his junior and senior years, he took part in the musical extravaganzas of the Hasty Pudding Club. In spite of these activities, he never neglected his studies, and he was known as a respectable student with grades placing him in the middle of his class at graduation.

While in college, he fell in love with an impossible woman, Mary Monahan. The affair was cut short by the Apleys and never referred to publicly. Shortly thereafter, his family prescribed a sea voyage for him. When he returned home, he took up the study of law and became a member of the board for the Boston Waifs' Society. George was instructed in the shrewd businesslike manners and knowledge of the Apleys. He was sent to work with his Uncle William for one summer. William sensed that his nephew would never make a good businessman and advised that George should be put into law or made a trustee of other peoples' money, not his own. As a result George, like many of his friends, never went actively into business but spent his lifetime clipping coupons.

3540

In February, 1890, George followed his parents' wishes and suitably became engaged to Catharine Bosworth. His father-in-law and his own father saw to it that the young couple had a summer cottage and a house for the winter. The two mothers were equally solicitous. George discovered that he had married not only Catharine but also her family.

As the years passed, George devoted his time to charitable groups, to learned societies, and to writing for his clubs. One of his papers, "Jonas Good and Cow Corner," was said to be among the best papers read before the Browsers in fifty years. His first child's name was a subject for debate in his own and Catharine's family. The name John, common to both families, was finally chosen. His second child was a daughter, Eleanor.

Shortly after his sister Amelia's marriage, George's father died of a stroke. He left a million dollars to Harvard, other large sums to his charities, and the remainder of his fortune in trust for his family. George had to pay a sum of money to a woman who claimed she had borne a son to his father. Although he did not believe the charge, he paid rather than cause scandal in the family.

George invested in a place known as Pequod Island, and he took his friends there when he wanted to get away from Boston. On the island, he and his friends condescended to share the campfire with their guides. Planned as a male retreat, the island was soon overrun with literary lights of the times invited by George's wife and sister.

As his son grew up, George noted an increasing desire on the part of the younger generation to be wild and careless with money. Later, George began to realize that he and his generation had let much slip and that Boston was going to the Irish. He gave his name to the "Save Boston Association" as he considered his membership an Apley duty. He also interested himself in bird lore and philosophy and took as much personal concern as possible in the affairs of his children. When his mother died in 1908, George counted her death as one of his most poignant tragedies.

When George's son entered Harvard, George took a new interest in the university and noted many changes he did not like. Old Uncle William, now more than eighty years old, still controlled the Apley mills and held out successfully against the new labor unions. One day, the old man shocked his family by marrying his nurse, Miss Prentiss.

Eleanor's marriage was completely unsatisfactory to George because she did not induce her husband to give up his job for a position in the Apley mills and to take up residence near her family. George, however, was proud of his son John for his service at the front. George himself belonged to the Home Guards. When John married a girl of good connections after the war, George was doubly pleased.

At last, George came into opposition with a man named O'Reilly, whom George planned to have brought before criminal court on charges of extortion. O'Reilly, however, tricked George into a scandal. George intended to have the whole case cleared in court, but before the trial, he received a note from his onetime sweetheart, Mary Monahan. After an interview with her, he settled the case quietly and bought off his opponents. In 1928, he became a grandfather. As soon as the baby had been born, George telegraphed Groton to include his grandson's name among the entrance applicants.

In his last years, George took interest in the new novels, condemning those too blatant in their description of sex and fighting against the inclusion of some of them in the Boston libraries. He hid his own copy of *Lady Chatterley's Lover* (1928) in the silver safe to keep his daughter from seeing it. He defied Prohibition as an abuse of his rights and kept a private bootlegger on principle because he thought it important to help break the prohibition law.

He thought, too, that the colossal fortunes being gathered by the uneducated should be handed over to the government. In the autumn of 1929, he and his wife made a trip to Rome, where they visited Horatio Apley, recently appointed to a diplomatic post there. George was absent from America when the stock market crash came. His financial affairs did not suffer greatly, but, his health breaking, he began to plan his will and his funeral. George Apley died in December, 1933.

Critical Evaluation:

The Late George Apley, considered by many to be the best of John P. Marquand's novels, was a turning point in its author's career. For fifteen years prior to its publication, Marquand had, as a "slick" popular writer, enjoyed considerable commercial success but no critical recognition. *The Late George Apley,* however, was immediately recognized as an important book, and its author was promoted by the critics from "popular" to "serious" writer. This elevation was certified when the novel earned for Marquand the Pulitzer Prize in 1938. Throughout the remaining years of his writing career, he confirmed and further consolidated his reputation, although never completely abandoning the commercial marketplace.

The Late George Apley is the first of a trilogy of novels in which Marquand minutely describes and analyzes the social patterns, behaviors, mores, and conflicts in upper-class Boston society during the rapidly changing 1880-1920 period. This novel pictures that part of old Boston society with Puritanical antecedents and commercial traditions; the second of the books, *Wickford Point* (1939), shows the decline of Bostonians with Transcendentalist ancestors and artistic pretensions; while the last, *H. M. Pulham, Esquire* (1941), examines the Boston businessman as he tries to accommodate his geographical and class inheritances to the pressures of the contemporary world.

In each of these books, Marquand explores the ways in which social forms and cultural assumptions left over from the past bind those in the present and how, in short, those environments that evolved to assure familial and social protection, identity, and continuity become prisons for the individuals who inherit them. This is most obvious in *The Late George Apley.* George's father, Thomas, represents the old nineteenth century individualistic businessman. He is highly intelligent, austere, rigid, hardworking, and uncompromising. His relationship with his son is reserved and formal, almost institutionalized, although he shows concern and, on occasion, affection for the boy. The doubts that are to plague his son are foreign to Thomas. He knows who he is and what his roles are as father, as businessman, as member of the community, and as an Apley. When he and George have their only real public disagreement, the older man emphatically quashes George's fuzzy democratic ideas: "You and I do not stand for the common good. We stand for a small class; but you don't see it. . . . Nobody sees it but me and my contemporaries." Thomas, however, is saved from robber baron status by a sincere Puritan "stewardship" ethic; he truly believes that the Apley position and fortune are signs of Godly favor and that the money must be conserved and shared with the community—but only on terms dictated by that "small class" of superior people at the top of the social pyramid.

George Apley envies his father's certainty and strength but cannot emulate him personally. Early in his life, he accepts the verdict of his Uncle William, and subsequently Thomas, that he is "not a businessman," that he is "too easy going" and "erratic" and so accepts permanent placement as an investment counselor (of other people's money), lawyer, and civic leader. George assumes from the beginning that his environment is the only one he "could have survived in," but neither he nor the reader can ever be sure. He is never able to test his well-meaning mediocrity; he is given the opportunity neither to succeed nor to fail but only to fit into a predetermined groove.

In his youth, George makes a few feeble attempts at nonconformity; he chooses some dubious friends, questions a few Apley dogmas, and, most important, has a brief, intense love affair with a middle-class Irish Catholic girl. It is squelched, of course; George is sent on a grand tour, and Mary Monahan becomes a sad memory (until the end of the book). Throughout his life, George is plagued by the sense that he is trapped and is living a life filled with activity but devoid of action or meaning. The most important events of his life are family disputes: what to name the baby, how to prevent cousin John from divorcing his wife, where to bury cousin Hattie, whether or not to move the rosebushes.

George's few attempts to find even momentary respite from his milieu fail before they begin. He travels abroad but carries Boston with him. "I am a raisin," he says, "in a slice of pie which has been conveyed from one plate to another." He buys an island as a masculine retreat from Bostonian formality and its guardians, the womenfolk, and before he knows it, the ladies arrive and "Boston has come to Pequod Island." Throughout his life, he suspects that he cannot escape the "net" (young John's phrase) of an environment that stifles more than it supports, and shortly before his death, he acknowledges it. Worst of all, he realizes that it has cost him the one important thing that he might have had from his life: happiness.

As his father before him, George tries to pass the Apley ethic down to his own son. John rebels more directly and emphatically than his father did. His social and political views baffle and alarm George. John pushes the rebellion further by refusing to join his father's firm, by going to New York City, and by marrying a divorcée. He is much more attuned to the modern world than his father, and his World War I experiences at the front have matured and sophisticated him. In the end, however, John proves to be his father's son; he returns to Boston and sets up housekeeping at Hillcrest, the family estate. George dies secure in the knowledge that the Apley niche in Boston remains filled; the cycle continues.

The Late George Apley is more than a sad story of the environment's tyranny over individuals. For all of the bleakness of its conclusions, the novel is most entertaining and amusing. The comedic and satiric center of the novel lies in its narrator, Mr. Willing. Marquand decided to tell the story as "a novel in the form of a memoir" for two reasons: first, to parody the then-common subliterary genre of the "collected papers" and, more important, to filter the information about the Apleys through the mind and language of a character even more dogmatically committed to the proper Bostonian vision of life.

Willing understands none of George Apley's incipient rebellions and his son's more blatant social improprieties. Much of the novel's rich humor and gentle satire comes from his fussy, polite, pseudoliterary apologies and rationalizations for the errant Apley behavior. In the end, in spite of Willing's stuffy shortsightedness, the reader gets to know and understand the subject very well, is amused and saddened by his weaknesses and narrowness, but is finally tolerant of, and sympathetic toward, the late George Apley.

"Critical Evaluation" by Keith Neilson

Bibliography:
Bell, Millicent. *Marquand: An American Life*. Boston: Little, Brown, 1979. Analyzes *The Late George Apley* as an accurate depiction and study of the Bostonian world its author loved and resented. Summarizes the mainly hostile reviews in Boston periodicals.
Gross, John J. *John P. Marquand*. New York: Twayne, 1963. Sees the novel as concerned with the increasing atomization of contemporary society and as depicting old New England values, including frugality and charity, taken too far. Commends Marquand for having an insensitive narrator.

Kazin, Alfred. "John P. Marquand and the American Failure." *Atlantic Monthly* 202 (November, 1958): 152-154, 156. Sees Marquand, a genteel satirist, ideally positioned in *The Late George Apley* as an observer. Regards Apley's abandoning his Irish girlfriend as representing the dilemma of many Americans—wishing to defy conventions but finding it difficult to do.

Marquand, John P. "Apley, Wickford Point, and Pulham: My Early Struggles." *Atlantic Monthly* 198 (September, 1956): 71-74. Comments on his decision to parody the epistolary novel by having a preposterous, pompous, obtuse, conceited biographer as narrator.

Tuttleton, James W. *The Novel of Manners in America.* Chapel Hill: University of North Carolina Press, 1972. Shows in a thumbnail biography of Marquand the importance of social influences on his writings. Sees *The Late George Apley* as an exposure of the Boston Brahman caste system and the tragedy of its perpetuation.

LAUGHTER
An Essay on the Meaning of the Comic

Type of work: Philosophical
Author: Henri Bergson (1859-1941)
First published: Le Rire: Essai sur la signification du comique, 1900 (English translation, 1911)

Laughter, Henri Bergson's profound essay on the nature and source of laughter, grows out of his concern with nineteenth century mechanization of life. For Bergson life is ever in flux through time and space, and any divergence from this principle of flux, any attempt to fix or concretize life, is removed from life. Bergson's famous principle of *élan vital*, the vital life force that underlies all living things, leads to the central motif of his theory of comedy, that "the mechanical encrusted upon the living" promotes laughter. Any time a living thing takes on attributes of death or mechanization or rigid automatism, it ceases to be wholly alive and inspires social laughter. Comedy, in Bergson's view, is a social gesture designed to promote organic health in the social body. Laughter, by ridiculing social outsiders, effects in those at whom others laugh a desire to purge themselves of unsocial traits. Comedy attempts to return to life those half-alive people on society's fringes whose failure to adapt themselves impairs social well-being.

Bergson opens chapter 1, a general discussion of comedy, with three fundamental observations on the nature of the comic spirit: "the comic does not exist outside the pale of what is strictly human"; an "absence of feeling . . . usually accompanies laughter"; and laughter's "natural environment . . . is society." Laughter's function is social: It "must have social signification." People only laugh, Bergson asserts, at things that in some way they have stamped as theirs. People do not laugh at landscapes, for instance, but at humans or at animals in which people see human elements. Nor can people laugh at things without putting aside their emotions. People may laugh at one they pity, but their pity must first be silenced. Emotion stifles laughter; intellect kindles it. Viewing life disinterestedly, people can disengage their emotions, permitting life to impress them as comic. Finally, laughter occurs in company with others; one does not often laugh in isolation.

A man who stumbles and falls as he runs along the street becomes an object of people's laughter because of his "rigidity" or "momentum," his clumsiness, or as Bergson terms it, "lack of elasticity through absentmindedness and a kind of physical obstinacy." This involuntary comic movement caused by mechanical inelasticity is a failure to adapt oneself to circumstance, an inability to be flexible and responsive to change. It may be external, as when people fail to notice a chair being pulled away from behind, or internal, as with the absentminded individual whose mind is so engaged with things other than the present place and time that he or she cannot function. In either case, the more natural the cause of inelasticity the more comic the effect will be. In the instance of Don Quixote, whose absentmindedness is largely due to his belief in an imaginary world, we have the whimsical madman with a systematic absentmindedness "organized around one central idea." It is therefore doubly comic when he falls into a well while gazing at a star.

Vice may so affect comic characters that the rigidity of a fixed idea of, for example, avarice or jealousy infects their personalities to the extent that they personify avarice or jealousy. The vice exists rather than the person, who becomes an automaton, and the character is comic "in proportion to his ignorance of himself." Awareness of others' laughter corrects people's manners, compelling people to try to appear less ridiculous, but self-correction cannot occur when ignorance of one's absurdity remains.

Laughter has a social function and results from one's inelasticity or rigidity. Society imposes on its members the necessity to adapt to circumstance. Life offers two forces, tension and elasticity, that enable people to avoid routine or empty habit and to encourage a constant effort toward "reciprocal adaptation." Society fears eccentricity, which presupposes a separatist tendency in the individual, and endeavors to harmonize individual wills. No cut-and-dried harmony may exist, however, so society demands a continual readjustment of individual egos. Society therefore must prod the slumbering individual, who respects the group but lets his or her adjustment drift into dead conformity, as well as guide the eccentric, who gravitates toward nonsocietal values. Laughter is the social gesture by which society imposes its lessons upon the eccentric or the conformist; laughter satisfies aesthetic and utilitarian aims.

Having outlined this formula for the comic spirit, Bergson then proceeds to detail the sequence of comic forms, from a clown's horseplay to the most refined effects of comedy. The comic element resident in forms derives from the opposition of soul, supple and in perpetual motion, to matter, inertly resistant to movement. When matter or body succeeds, for example, in capturing fleeting states of being of the face, it petrifies the "outward life of the soul" in a material, "mechanical operation" and achieves a comic effect.

It is this admixture of the human and the mechanical that accounts for the comic element of gesture and movement. The more the "attitudes, gestures and movements of the human body" remind one of a machine the more they are laughable. Whenever mechanism appears in the human body, as in the gestures of a public speaker, the repetition elicits the comic response. When attention focuses on form instead of matter, on body instead of soul, comic response occurs. Physical comedy, then, is a parody of the mechanization of human life.

In chapter 2, Bergson turns to the comic element in situations and in words. He again finds the comic residing in the dualism of the mechanical and the human. Acts or events that give, in a single combination, the "illusion of life and the distinct impression of a mechanical arrangement" produce comedy. The ultimate formulas for the comic state are repetition, inversion, and reciprocal interference of series. Repetition reflects a mathematical or symmetrical ordering of life. Inversion is simply the reversal of roles, as when a prisoner lectures the judge. Reciprocal interference describes a situation, belonging simultaneously to different series of events, yet capable of two entirely different interpretations. The classic "Who's on first?" dialogue is an example. The laughter of words also falls under the same three headings. Again, whenever the living quality, the suppleness, of language is contrasted to the rigid mechanism of language, laughter searches out this automatism and corrects it.

Chapter 3 examines the comic element of character. Bergson asserts that laughter has a social meaning, expresses a special lack of adaptation to society, and cannot exist apart from humanity. Characters who remove themselves from society are fundamentally comic; such characters illustrate the basis of comedy, which begins with a "growing callousness to social life." Comedy does not necessarily direct itself at moral faults; rather it usually aims to correct social aloofness.

Bergson places comedy midway between life and art. Art expresses true reality. Society constructs its values on the superficial perceptions of ordinary people, but art deals with deeper realities. Comedy, because it accepts a social, utilitarian goal—correction of the social outsider—lies close to life. Comedy also aims to please, however, and may require more accurate perception than that available to everyone; therefore, comedy belongs to art. Comedy differs from tragedy in that the latter seeks the individual, the unique, while comedy presents the general, the type. Comedy depicts general characters, universals of humanity, categorizing people by surface distinctions and by the roles of everyday life. The comic poet observes inductively and surveys people for external, general eccentricities. Such a writer never endeavors to portray alienation for fear of engaging the emotions, hence endangering the comic element. Comedy tries to isolate the superficial, telling facet of character, the mechanical, and creates types. Tragedy examines the depths of the individual, gives an impression of life, and develops out of the emotions. The tragic poet's characters are in a sense extensions of his or her own personality—in contrast to the comic character, the tragic character arises deductively, from within, rather than from without.

Comedy therefore is not disinterested as genuine art is. Comedy accepts social life as a natural environment; it even obeys an impulse of social life. In this respect it rejects art, which is a reaction against society.

Bibliography:
Bergson, Henri. *The Creative Mind.* Translated by Mabelle L. Andison. New York: Philosophical Library, 1946. Gives Bergson's views on metaphysics and science, relative to comedy; on the role of the mechanical (especially in gestures) as a device for humor; and on intuition, absolutes, language, and logic relative to humor. This work postdates *Laughter.* See Introduction (part 1) and chapters 3, 4, and 5.
Carr, H. Wildon. *Henri Bergson: The Philosophy of Change.* London: T. C. & E. C. Jack, 1912. Brief presentation of Bergson's philosophic views on life, intellect and matter, instinct and intelligence, intuition, freedom, mind and body, and creative evolution. Those unacquainted with Bergson's work should read this before reading *Laughter.* Short annotated bibliography.
Sypher, Wylie. Introduction to *Laughter: An Essaye on Comedy,* by George Meredith. Garden City, N.Y.: Doubleday, 1956. Offers an extensive, readable, and interesting comparative analysis of George Meredith's essay on comedy and Bergson's *Laughter.* Reviews the foundations of Bergson's complicated notions on comedy and the mechanical.
_____. "The Meanings of Comedy." *Laughter, Essays on Comedy.* Garden City, N.Y.: Doubleday, 1956. Brings Bergson's and George Meredith's nineteenth century notions of laughter and the comedic in art alongside late twentieth century views. Notes and a bibliographical note of chief secondary sources. Readable and interesting.
Taylor, Mark C. *Erring: A Postmodern A/theology.* Chicago: University of Chicago Press, 1984. Discussion of comedy, language, and laughter—particularly in chapter 7—is an excellent analogy to Bergson's philosophy on these elements. Comparison of Bergson's philosophy of laughter to that of Taylor reveals astonishing similarities.

LAVENGRO
The Scholar—The Gypsy—The Priest

Type of work: Novel
Author: George Henry Borrow (1803-1881)
Type of plot: Autobiographical
Time of plot: Nineteenth century
Locale: England, Scotland, and Ireland
First published: 1851

Principal characters:
LAVENGRO, a scholar, journalist, and tinker
JOHN, his brother
JASPER PETULENGRO, his gypsy friend
MRS. HERNE, an old crone
THE FLAMING TINMAN, a bully of the roads
ISOPEL BERNERS, Lavengro's companion
PETER WILLIAMS, an evangelist
WINIFRED, his wife

The Story:

Lavengro was the son of an army officer who had fought against Napoleon, and the boy spent his early years at army garrisons in various parts of England, Scotland, Ireland, and Wales. When he was six years old, Lavengro discovered Daniel Defoe's *Robinson Crusoe* (1719), a book that stimulated his imagination and aroused in him a desire to read and to study languages. One day while wandering on the outskirts of a garrison town, he met a group of gypsies who threatened to do him harm. They drew back, however, when he showed them a tame snake that he was carrying. The gypsies, becoming friendly, nicknamed him Sapengro, or snake tamer. A young gypsy named Jasper declared that they would always be brothers. He also met a Romany at the gypsy camp whom he saw hanged fifteen years later at Newgate.

A few years later, he began the study of Latin. About the same time, his father was ordered to Edinburgh. In Scotland, Lavengro took part in several bickers, or fights, with his school-mates. Lavengro also learned mountain climbing. Then in 1815, his father was ordered to Ireland. Lavengro went to a seminary at Clonmel and studied more Latin and Greek; in an incidental fashion, he also learned to speak Irish. His brother John was made an ensign and transferred to a post a few miles away. After peace was signed with the French, opportunities for military employment were few. John had always wanted to paint; therefore, his father allowed him to go to London to study art.

Lavengro again met Jasper, his gypsy friend, and discovered that Jasper's last name was Petulengro. Jasper was now a Romany Kral—or gypsy king—a horseshoer, pugilist, jockey, and soothsayer. Through Jasper, Lavengro made the acquaintance of a malignant old crone named Herne, who hated him because she believed that he was stealing the Romany tongue. It was Jasper who had named him Lavengro, which means "word-master," because he learned the gypsy language so rapidly. All the gypsies departed for London, except Mrs. Herne, who went to Yorkshire. Lavengro remained at home with his parents while his father tried to decide what to do with him. It was finally agreed that Lavengro would enter a solicitor's office to study law. Lavengro, however, neglected his law studies while he learned Welsh and translated the poetry of Ab Gwilym. About the same time Lavengro obtained a Danish book and learned to read it by first studying the Danish Bible. One day, Lavengro was sent to deliver a thousand pounds to a magistrate with whom he had a very entertaining conversation concerning the art of self-defense. In spite of the magistrate's fondness for boxing, however, he refused a match.

Lavengro met Jasper again and put on the gloves with him for a friendly bout. Later, he returned home and discovered that his father was seriously ill. His brother John also arrived home just before his father died. Shortly afterward, Lavengro went to London to seek his fortune as a writer, taking with him a letter of introduction to a noted publisher. The publisher seemed delighted to be able to employ him but was not interested in such things as Lavengro's translations of the songs of Ab Gwilym and his translations of Danish songs. Lavengro was informed that the reading public scoffed at works such as those. Instead, the publisher recommended a story modeled after a work that had sold well.

While walking through Cheapside one day, Lavengro climbed upon the balustrade of a bridge in order to see something below. An old woman selling apples nearby thought he was trying to commit suicide and begged him not to fling himself over. The old lady had a partiality for a book about the "blessed" Mary Flanders. Lavengro returned from time to time to see her and to talk with her.

Lavengro was invited to dinner at the publisher's house one Sunday and discovered that the publisher did not believe in eating meat or drinking wine. After dinner, Lavengro heard what was to be his new assignment. He was to prepare a collection of the stories of the lives and trials of famous criminals incarcerated at Newgate. In addition, he was to translate the publisher's book of philosophy into German and to write an article about it for the *Review*.

In the company of an acquaintance named Francis Ardry, Lavengro visited many of the underworld spots of London. This experience, together with the series on criminals which he was preparing, gave him a wide and practical knowledge of the underworld. Then Lavengro's brother came to London and introduced him to a painter of the heroic. The peculiar thing about this painter's pictures was the short legs of the people in his paintings. When Lavengro's stories of crime were finished, he took them to the publisher. The publisher, however, was displeased because Lavengro had omitted several of the publisher's favorite criminal histories.

Lavengro went to visit the apple-woman again, and his despondent appearance led her to think that he had been caught stealing. The apple-woman never became aware of Lavengro's profession. He talked her into letting him read her cherished copy of the life of Mary Flanders.

The publisher's speculations failed and left Lavengro without money, but Lavengro finally obtained all the wages that were due him. Taggart, the publisher's assistant, told Lavengro that Glorious John, another printer, would publish his ballads and the songs of Ab Gwilym, but Lavengro never offered his ballads to Glorious John. In midwinter, he went again to visit the apple-woman and found that she had moved her stall to the other side of the bridge. He promised to take her book and trade it in for a Bible; however, he lost the book and had nothing to trade. He decided to purchase a Bible and never let her know about his negligence.

About this time, Lavengro saved an Armenian from pickpockets. The Armenian wished him to translate some Armenian fables into English, but Lavengro refused. The Armenian, who had inherited a hundred thousand pounds from his father, was intent upon doubling the amount through speculation. The Armenian ran into a bit of luck and came into possession of two hundred thousand pounds. Lavengro's advice to the Armenian was to take his fortune and fight the Persians.

When his money ran short, Lavengro decided to do the translations for the Armenian, but the man had already departed to invest his money in a war against the Persians. Lavengro left

London after having some small success writing fiction. He met and talked with many and various people on his travels about England. On his rambles, he heard the stories concerning the Flaming Tinman, who held a great repute as a fighter and who had forced Jack Slingsby, another tinker, out of business on threats of death. Lavengro met Slingsby and bought him out. He decided to become a tinker himself in the hope of meeting the Flaming Tinman.

One day while he was mending pots and pans, he encountered Mrs. Herne and Leonora, a thirteen-year-old girl who was traveling with the old woman. Leonora brought him cakes made by Mrs. Herne. He ate one of them and that night became seriously ill. When the evil old crone came to gloat over him, he realized that the cakes had been poisoned. Then the sound of wheels frightened the old woman away, and Lavengro was saved by the timely arrival of Peter Williams, a traveling Welsh preacher, and Winifred, his wife. Peter Williams told Lavengro the sad story of his life and related how he had been led to commit a sin against the Holy Ghost, a sin for which there was no redemption. Peter had become a preacher to warn other people against the unforgivable sin. Lavengro journeyed with Peter and his wife as far as the Welsh border, where he left them to join Jasper Petulengro and his band of gypsies.

Jasper told Lavengro how Mrs. Herne had hanged herself because of her failure to poison him. Since Jasper was a blood kinsman of Mrs. Herne, it was required by Romany law that he obtain revenge from Lavengro. Lavengro, however, was really only indirectly responsible for the old woman's death, a fact of which Jasper was well aware. They retired to a place where they could fight, and there Jasper received full satisfaction when he made Lavengro's nose bleed.

Soon after his friendly tussle with Jasper, Lavengro met the Flaming Tinman, Moll, his wife, and Isopel Berners, child of a gypsy mother and a noble father and now a free woman of the roads. Isopel was responsible for Lavengro's victory in a brawl with the Flaming Tinman, for she had told him to use his right hand and to strike at the bully's face. The Flaming Tinman and Moll departed, leaving the territory to Lavengro the tinker, but Isopel remained behind with her belongings. The story of the Flaming Tinman's defeat was soon known throughout the neighborhood, and Lavengro became a hero of the roads. At a public house, he met a priest whom he called the Man in Black. He and Lavengro had many conversations concerning religion and the attempt to establish Catholicism in England.

On a wild stormy night, Isopel and Lavengro helped a coachman right his coach, which had overturned. Later, the coachman told them the story of his life; his tale was proof that in those days romance journeyed on the highways and adventure waited around the turn of any English lane.

Critical Evaluation:

Lavengro may or may not be an autobiographical novel. George Henry Borrow was trained in law and traveled widely. His primary interest, however, was literature. How much of himself he put into that literature—and how much he fantasized—is irrelevant, because the writing itself stands on its own merits. Although he contributed to the Newgate Calendar—a compilation of infamous crimes—Borrow is best known for the novels about gypsy life: *The Zincali* (1841), *Lavengro*, and *The Romany Rye* (1857). The fact that Borrow was well traveled and proficient in languages may account for some of his knowledge of and easy entrée into non-Anglo cultures, hence his familiarity with esoteric customs.

As Borrow depicts it, Romany life certainly differs from Western European life. *Lavengro*, in the Romany tongue, means "philologist"—a student of languages. In Borrow's novel, the lust for language amounts to a lust for life—a theme carried more or less explicitly through his other novels. Knowledge of languages is the key to a gypsy's survival, since the gypsy is by definition a nomad and must adapt to differing linguistic circumstances upon a moment's notice. Linguistic facility is thus at a premium; therefore, Borrow's novel is aptly titled to suggest the central ingredient in a gypsy's life.

One consequence of the peripatetic Romany life, however, is a selective skepticism toward political and religious institutions. Here, *Lavengro* delivers the message clearly: Popery, radicalism, and anything inimical to the Church of England were abhorrent, Romany customs notwithstanding. Gypsies can adapt to and live within a system while still maintaining their own customs and integrity; yet because their way of life is dissident, they cannot tolerate dissidents from their own ranks, as these individuals endanger the safety of the gypsy community. Borrow has not been given proper credit for this astute political insight, for he demonstrates it rather than preaches it.

To nineteenth century readers, Borrow's *Lavengro* was at least a curiosity and at most a perplexity. It depicted a totally foreign way of life—something exotic and appealing yet simultaneously repugnant for its unconventional ways. The Western reader, even today, may be caught in such a dilemma. Although *Lavengro* possesses a compelling fascination, the novel nevertheless depicts an experience largely alien to the Western reader because gypsies are essentially private people, with their own customs and values. Assimilation with the dominant culture is incompatible with Romany life. From this novel, the Western reader can understand the features that human beings hold in common as well as appreciate differences that may seem anomalous.

Bibliography:

Hollingsworth, Keith. *The Newgate Novel, 1830-1847: Bulwer, Ainsworth, Dickens, and Thackeray.* Detroit: Wayne State University Press, 1963. The best study of the English tradition of stories about criminals. Discusses the references in *Lavengro* to John Thurtell, a childhood acquaintance of Borrow, whose sensational murder trial and execution in 1823 left many traces in literature.

Knapp, William I. *Life, Writings, and Correspondence of George Borrow, Based on Official and Other Authentic Sources.* 2 vols. London: John Murray, 1899. The best study of Borrow's life. Relates the narrative of *Lavengro* to verifiable events in Borrow's early life.

Meyers, Robert R. *George Borrow.* New York: Twayne, 1966. Provides an objective and realistic assessment of *Lavengro* as an account of Gypsy culture, description of the Gypsy language, and autobiography. It emphasizes Borrow's indebtedness to the Bible, to *Robinson Crusoe*, and to the eighteenth century picaresque tradition of Henry Fielding, Tobias Smollett, and Laurence Sterne.

Shorter, Clement. *The Life of George Borrow.* New York: E. P. Dutton, 1928. Uses unpublished documents to form this enthusiastic account of Borrow's work. Emphasizes the way that the novel reflects Borrow's linguistic abilities. A good starting point.

Stonyk, Margaret. *Nineteenth-Century English Literature.* New York: Schocken Books, 1984. Includes an excellent discussion of the novel. Shows how *Lavengro* uses dialogue to reveal hypocrisy, describes its outrageous characters, and comments on how its seemingly random organization repelled its audience.

THE LAY OF IGOR'S CAMPAIGN

Type of work: Poetry
Author: Unknown
Type of plot: Romance
Time of plot: Late twelfth century
Locale: The Russian steppes
First transcribed: Slovo o polku Igoreve, c. 1187 (English translation, 1919)

Principal characters:
IGOR, the prince of Novgorod-Seversk
PRINCE VSEVOLOD, his brother
PRINCE VLADIMIR, his son
PRINCE SVATOSLAV, his nephew
THE GREAT PRINCE OF KIEV

The Lay of Igor's Campaign, a heroic romance, is the earliest great work of Russian literature. Moreover, it is the only surviving heroic poem of the Russian Middle Ages, and it is one of the few pieces of literature known to have appeared in Russia before the nineteenth century. The poem, of which the author is unknown, is admired by most educated Russians both for its place in the Russian tradition and for its literary excellence. Although it is relatively unknown outside of Russia, it has been widely translated.

The subject matter of *The Lay of Igor's Campaign* is typically medieval: the expedition, defeat, capture, and escape of a knightly warrior—Prince Igor of Novgorod-Seversk (not to be confused with Novgorod the great, a much more famous and important city of old Kievian Russia). Igor's antagonists were the Kumans, a race of pagan nomads who inhabited the southern steppes around the Don River. Three other princes and their troops accompanied Igor's contingent: Igor's brother, Prince Vsevolod; Igor's son, Prince Vladimir; and Igor's nephew, Prince Svatoslav. However, while it is an early work, and while it did not appear in a culture notable for its literary and artistic achievements, and while it is a heroic tale of warriors and battle, the poem is far from being a primitive and unsophisticated work. Like the other medieval national epics to which it is sometimes compared, the poem is the product of a very skillful artist whose insight and poetic skill is of the highest order. In fact, the art of this Russian poem strikes one as being in some respects subtler than that of the nations' romantic epics; it has been said with some justice that the sophisticated, symbolic technique of the lay has a striking kinship with modern poetic techniques.

The history of the poem is somewhat obscure. While it was probably written about 1187, memory of it was soon lost and it remained unknown until 1795, when Count Alexei Wanovich Musin-Pushkin, a distinguished literary amateur, discovered a manuscript copy of the poem. He purchased what was probably a sixteenth century codex from a former official of a recently dissolved monastery. The codex had been in the monastery library. *The Lay of Igor's Campaign* was one of several manuscript items included in it. The text was published in 1800, but little was known at that time about interpreting and editing early Russian texts, and the edition was marred by errors and misinterpretations. Moreover, the sixteenth century scribe who had copied the text into the codex was himself unfamiliar with the twelfth century Russian language, and thus the manuscript itself was far from accurate. Before a second edition of the poem could be prepared for the printer, the manuscript was burned when Napoleon burned Moscow in 1812. Modern scholars have succeeded in repairing much of the damage of time, but nevertheless certain brief passages in the poem remain obscure. It should be noted also that it was for a time assumed by some that the story of the discovery of the poem in 1795 was a hoax and that the poem was a modern forgery. However, a portion of the poem has been found quoted verbatim in a manuscript made in 1307, and thus it has been certified that the poem is genuine.

The unknown author of the lay composed his masterpiece late in the twelfth century, about one or two years after the events of which he writes had occurred. This date can be determined by certain matters that are mentioned in the text. It is known that the characters and the events of the narrative are historical, for the story can be checked in certain surviving medieval chronicles. So far as can be determined from the poem, the author was a layman, very likely a soldier, who was the companion of some prince of Kievian Russia, perhaps of Igor himself. The poet was a city dweller but was familiar with the life of the steppes. He was also familiar with the literature and oral traditions, such as they were, of his times. One can tell from references in the text that there was a tradition of heroic oral poetry in the generations before the author of *The Lay of Igor's Campaign* wrote. The author refers to and quotes one of those older poets, one Bayan the Bard.

However, the poem was not written by a professional singer. That is, although the author did not hesitate to use the techniques of oral poetry to achieve many of his poetic effects, the lay is a purely literary work, and is written to be read. The spirit of the poem, it should be noted, is secular, heroic, and, crucially, patriotic. Russia as much as Igor is the hero of the piece. While the poem is nominally a Christian work, Christianity is only an incidental element in it. The older pagan nature worship of pre-Christian Russia has a much more integral place in the imagery and the tone of the poem.

Although often called a heroic poem, in fact *The Lay of Igor's Campaign* is not a heroic tale per se. It is really quite difficult to classify. For while a heroic narrative is the foundation of the piece, much of it is a lyric lament for the feudal discord that characterized the poet's age; moreover, much of the time the author's objective seems to admonish the princes responsible for the feuds and troubles of Kievian Russia, and to that extent the lay is an inspired piece of political oratory. One must conclude that the work is a blend of the narrative, the lyric, and the hortatory. Further, it is not a poem in the strict sense, but a prose poem. The rhythm of the language is not that of verse, and the work is not composed in lines, but in the rhythmical prose typical of the old Russian liturgy. Although it may be sung, *The Lay of Igor's Campaign* is not composed in verse. Nevertheless, it is emphatically poetic in its complex and vivid use of imagery, metaphor, and simile; and the total effect of the work can only be described as powerfully poetic.

Structurally, the poem falls into eight sections. The first is the poet's prologue, in which the author comments on the literary usage of the past and the departures he will make to achieve his own literary ends. The second deals with the determination of Igor and his brother to make their expedition. The third describes the advance across the steppes and Igor's initial success. The fourth is about the defeat and capture of the Russian forces. At this point the scope of the poem expands dramatically. The poet begins to dramatize the meaning of Igor's defeat to the Russian people. In the fifth section, the poet begins a lyrical-oratorical digression, first in his own voice and then in the voice of the Great Prince of Kiev. The prince, not yet aware of the disaster of Igor, has had a prophetic and symbolic dream of ill omen. Next, in the sixth section, the poet apostrophizes to nine other princes, asking them to end their quarrels and to join together to save Igor and Russia. This section is followed, in section seven, by a lyric lament by Igor's wife on the walls of her city. The poem ends (section eight) with a brief account of Igor's escape from the Kumans and a closing apostrophe by the poet.

3553

This structure is supported by a pattern of metaphor, symbol, and imagery based primarily on nature: the sun, light and darkness, the land, the rivers, plants, winds, and the ancient nature gods. The men of the poem, their actions, their emotions, and the political, military, and social forces in the world of the poem, are all perceived and expressed in terms of this nature imagery and symbolism. In the end, the picture that *The Lay of Igor's Campaign* presents is one of a totally integrated world in which there is no distinct line of separation between the world of people and the world of nature. For example, the expedition begins amid ominous eclipses of the sun—the light-darkness idea is complicated throughout the narrative until, at the end, Igor escapes his captors under cover of darkness. Also, at the sight of Igor's defeat, the trees bow down in grief. Throughout the poem the foreboding and anxious voices of nature can be heard moving in the wind and the rivers; and as Igor escapes, he holds a thankful dialogue with the pro-Russian river Donets while he sneeringly mocks the anti-Russian river Stugna. For all the lay's complexity of parts, when it is seen as a whole, it has, as do all great works of art, an overall simplicity and power that no serious reader can miss.

Bibliography:
Gudzii, N. K. *History of Early Russian Literature.* 2d ed. Translated by Susan Wilbur Jones. New York: Macmillan, 1949. Reviews the textual history of the work and comments on the issue of its authenticity. Examines the tale in its historical context with respect to the Old Russian chronicles. Reflects on references to nature, pagan gods, and folk elements.
Howes, Robert C. Introduction to *The Tale of the Campaign of Igor.* New York: W. W. Norton, 1973. Probably the most thorough and readily accessible treatment of the work in English, providing solid historical background, examination of the poem, and commentary on nature, religion, and the role of the hero. The translation includes very useful footnotes.
Muchnic, Helen. *An Introduction to Russian Literature.* New York: Doubleday, 1947. The dozen pages on *The Lay of Igor's Campaign* reflect especially on the presumed character of the anonymous poet as well as the nature of the poetry itself.
Pronin, Alexander. *History of Old Russian Literature.* Frankfurt, Germany: Posev, 1968. Three discussions include brief historical context and a genealogical chart of the major characters. Provides a simple section-by-section analysis.
Tschizewskij, Dmitrij. *History of Russian Literature from the Eleventh Century to the End of the Baroque.* The Hague: Mouton, 1960. The section on *The Lay of Igor's Campaign,* about a dozen pages, focuses on the poetic elements (metaphors, imagery, sounds). Notes the predominance of auditory and color images.

THE LAY OF THE LAST MINSTREL

Type of work: Poetry
Author: Sir Walter Scott (1771-1832)
Type of plot: Historical
Time of plot: Mid-sixteenth century
Locale: The Scottish border
First published: 1805

> *Principal characters:*
> LADY BUCCLEUCH, the widow of the lord of Branksome
> MARGARET, her daughter
> THE MASTER OF BUCCLEUCH, her son
> LORD CRANSTOUN, Margaret's lover
> SIR WILLIAM OF DELORAINE, a knight in Lady Buccleuch's service
> THE DWARF, an evil magician
> THE GHOST OF MICHAEL SCOTT, a wizard

The Story:

As an old minstrel, the last of his kind, wandered through the country, he was treated kindly by a duchess at whose mansion he asked food and shelter. Later he rewarded her by singing a song of days gone by. What follows is the story contained in the song he sang.

Bold Lord Buccleuch had been killed in battle with the English, but his widow and children were well protected in their castle at Branksome by a group of brave knights who had followed their dead leader. Although a truce had been declared, there were skirmishes between the English and the Scots throughout the border country.

The widow, Lady Buccleuch, was the daughter of a magician; before he died he had taught her to talk with the spirits. One night she heard the spirits predicting that the stars would show no favor to Branksome castle until pride should die and make love free. Lady Buccleuch knew this omen was meant for her, for her daughter Margaret loved the young Lord Cranstoun, who had fought against Lord Buccleuch. Lady Buccleuch nevertheless swore that Margaret should never wed a foe of the family, no matter what the spirits might say. She sent William of Deloraine to Melrose Abbey, there to secure the mystic book of Michael Scott, a wizard long dead and buried in the abbey crypt. She ordered William of Deloraine not to look into the book on peril of his life.

The monk at the abbey, although he quavered at the request made by Deloraine, obeyed without question Lady Buccleuch's command. Leading him deep into the vaults, he took the knight to the wizard's tomb. Deloraine, bravest of knights in battle, shivered with dread as he looked at the body of the magician. The man lay as if he had not been dead a day, and when the knight took the book from his hand, he seemed to frown. As Deloraine left the vault, he heard noises like the laughter and sobbing of friends.

On the same day, while Deloraine went to the abbey, Margaret slipped out of the castle to meet her lover, Lord Cranstoun. Cranstoun was accompanied by a Dwarf, who had some time before attached himself to Cranstoun and now would not leave his side. Since the Dwarf served him well, Cranstoun had ceased his efforts to rid himself of the little page. The Dwarf warned the lovers of the approach of a horseman. The traveler was Deloraine, returning from his mission, and while Margaret fled, the two knights battled. Deloraine was seriously wounded. Cranstoun ordered the Dwarf to take Deloraine to Branksome Hall so that his wounds could be properly tended. The Dwarf found the book but could not open it until after he had smeared the cover with the blood of Deloraine, who was almost an infidel. While he was reading one of the spells described in the book, an unseen hand struck him on the cheek and knocked him to the ground. The book snapped shut and could not be opened again. The Dwarf, hiding it under his cloak, proceeded to Branksome Hall with the wounded Deloraine.

At the castle the Dwarf spied the young Master of Buccleuch. Changing himself and the boy into dogs, he led the child into the woods. There, after they had resumed their real shapes, the child was captured by the English soldiers patrolling the border. At the castle his absence was not known, for the Dwarf returned there and, taking the child's shape, made mischief for everyone. Lady Buccleuch, busy tending the wounds of her faithful Deloraine, failed to notice the child's strange behavior.

Suddenly watchers in the castle sighted signal fires. Their meaning was clear; the English were gathering to attack the Scots. From the castle, messengers were sent hurriedly to summon friendly clans of the border to the defense of Branksome Hall. In the confusion the Dwarf, still in the form of the Master of Buccleuch, escaped from the knight assigned to watch him.

The English, arriving before the castle, made their demands. They wanted Deloraine turned over to them, for they accused him of murdering the brother of one of their group. They also demanded that two hundred English knights be quartered in Branksome, to prevent the Scotsmen from making raids on the English side of the border. If these demands were not met, they declared, the castle would be stormed and the young heir of Buccleuch, who was held by the English, would be sent to the English court to serve as a page.

Lady Buccleuch would not meet the demands. She could not send her faithful knight to his doom, though her deed might cost her her son, her castle, and perhaps her life. She proposed that Deloraine meet the brother of the slain man in combat and settle the dispute in that knightly fashion. The English leaders, refusing to accept these terms, were preparing to attack the castle when one of their number brought word that strong Scottish clans were approaching the castle. Fearful of a trap, the English agreed to accept the proposal for a settlement by mortal combat between the two knights concerned, or by the wronged man and a substitute for Deloraine should his wounds not be healed by the next day. Then English and Scots joined together in feasting and revelry until the time appointed for the combat.

As the time approached, other knights argued over the right to represent Deloraine, who was still weak from his wounds. At the last minute Deloraine appeared in full armor, ready to defend himself. The fighting was long and fierce, and both knights lost much blood before the Englishman fell wounded. Deloraine, standing triumphantly over his victim, did not remove his visor. Then the spectators saw with amazement that Deloraine was approaching from the castle. Quickly the supposed Deloraine was uncovered. In his place stood young Lord Cranstoun. He had stolen Deloraine's armor so that he might defend the home and save the brother of Margaret. At first Lady Buccleuch would not greet him, but at last she thought of the prophecy of the spirits and knew that she must forget pride and allow love to prevail. Yielding, she gave her daughter to the knight who had been her husband's enemy. She also swore to herself that she would return the book to Michael Scott's tomb.

At the wedding feast the Dwarf continued to make trouble. In order to undo the mischief he caused, all the minstrels sang songs of days gone past. As the last song died away, the banquet hall grew suddenly dark. A great flash of lightning streaked through the room and struck the Dwarf. The evil page was seen no more. Deloraine was terrified, for in the unearthly light he had seen the shape of the dead wizard. Lady Buccleuch renounced forever the magic of her father, and all the knights made pilgrimages to pray for peace and rest for Michael Scott's soul.

Critical Evaluation:

Sir Walter Scott's explicit purpose in *The Lay of the Last Minstrel* is to describe the manners and the scenery of the Scottish border country during the middle of the sixteenth century. He is concerned more with these than he is with the story and often leaves the narrative for several stanzas in order to portray customs of the Scottish clans. Scott's ability to tell a picturesque, rousing story in verse is almost as great as his achievement in the novel.

A minstrel is a musical entertainer and traveling poet of the later Middle Ages in Europe. Especially in the thirteenth and fourteenth centuries, minstrels wandered from town to town, castle to castle, bringing news. Accompanying himself on a harp or drum, the minstrel would also sing, recite, and otherwise perform ballads, legends, and romances that belonged equally to music, literature, and history. In an age when most people could not read and had no access to what few hand-written books there were, minstrels fulfilled an important cultural function. They began to decline in popularity after the invention of printing in the middle of the fifteenth century and eventually were superseded by increasing literacy.

The ballad is a form of poetry adapted for singing or recitation; primarily narrative, it usually recalls some particularly dramatic or exciting episode, such as a battle, and might well appear in several versions, there being no written text to stabilize its form. Legend is past history in any form, embellished by the teller perhaps, but still held to be true. "Romance" is a still more general term, which could refer to any literary work written in medieval French. Most of the stories celebrated in the romances concern knights and their deeds, however, so the term often applies specifically to ballads or narrative poems on chivalric subjects. In later developments, the term "romance" referred to tales of wonder in general or the increasingly favored love interest within such fantasies.

The lay, yet another literary type, originated in France during the Middle Ages as an elaboration upon earlier songs and verse tales sung by Breton minstrels. These French poems were imitated by contemporaneous English writers, including Geoffrey Chaucer. A lay is usually written in lines of eight syllables, each arranged in rhyming couplets.

After a long period of neglect, minstrels and their works became popular again in the eighteenth century. In rural parts of Great Britain, especially just north of the border with Scotland, it was possible to hear some of the old ballads, which had been preserved in oral tradition from one generation to another over the years. A few of them had also been written down. In 1765, Bishop Thomas Percy published a collection of these ballads as *Reliques of Ancient English Poetry*. This influential book called attention to the patriotic tradition of lyric and dramatic poetry that soon became unusually fashionable. Further collections of old ballads then appeared, together with modern imitations.

Among those prominent in these endeavors was an Edinburgh lawyer named Walter Scott. Stimulated by his own explorations of the border country, by Percy's *Reliques of Ancient English Poetry*, and by the old romances, in 1802 and 1803 Scott published *Border Minstrelsy*. This three-volume collection contained authentic ballads and, in a separate section, Scott's imitations of the form. Two years later, he offered the first of his major original poems, *The Lay of the Last Minstrel*.

Like many in the tradition it attempts to recall, *The Lay of the Last Minstrel* is a primarily narrative poem with interspersed lyrics or ballads. It is divided into cantos and stanzas. Although written more often than not in octosyllabic couplets, individual stanzas feature a variety of poetical forms. These can be discovered by counting the number of syllables in each line and the number of lines in each stanza, then determining the rhyme scheme of each stanza. A couplet consists of two successive lines that rhyme. Scott also uses triplets (three consecutive lines with the same rhyme) and alternating rhymes (for example, lines one and three, two and four). The rhymes sometimes help the reader to pronounce names within the poem (try "Buccleuch" in canto 3, stanza 19). Like his medieval predecessors, Scott adds filler phrases such as "I ween" or "I say" (both 1, 29) for the sake of the rhymes, which generally are pedestrian.

The plot of *The Lay of the Last Minstrel* is fairly complicated; the poem is written deliberately in archaic language, and the plot depends at several turns on magic. Michael Scott (1175?-1234?), whose ghost is one of the characters, was a real person, renowned for his knowledge of astrology and alchemy. There are few extant facts regarding Michael Scott but many legends, including tales that can be true only if one believes in the supernatural. As Walter Scott was well aware, supernaturalist beliefs once were prominent in Scotland. In Walter Scott's *Guy Mannering* (1815), the title character is an astrologer. There had been a long and hideous tradition of prosecuting witches in Scotland that endured into the eighteenth century. Reginald Scott (1538-1599) protested against witchcraft trials as early as 1584, in a book that influenced William Shakespeare's play *Macbeth* (1605-1606), but his humanitarian appeal to reason would not prevail for centuries.

Walter Scott believed himself related to both Michael and Reginald Scott. He also was related to the dukes of Buccleuch, including Henry Scott, the first earl of Deloraine (1676-1730). It was supposedly the Duchess of Buccleuch in his own time who suggested to Walter Scott that he write a ballad on the border legend of Gilpin Horner (the Dwarf). The resulting poem lengthened, changed direction, and became *The Lay of the Last Minstrel*, which is dedicated to the duchess' husband. Its main story takes place a little after 1552 (see Scott's note 5) and is retold more than a century later by a minstrel who has been displaced from his earlier career by the events of 1689, when there was a period of armed rebellion in Scotland opposing the deposition of King James II in favor of William and Mary. Scott then offers a further retelling for his own generation, which was at war with France and in danger of imminent invasion by Napoleon's forces.

Although *The Lay of the Last Minstrel* includes the traditional ballad themes of love, war, and fame, it emphasizes the importance of patriotism (the famous "Breathes there the man" passage of canto 6, stanza 1 is the most stirring in the poem). In canto 5, the power and importance of poetry are stressed. Both themes were of central importance to Scott. The unexpected popularity of *The Lay of the Last Minstrel* encouraged Scott to spend the rest of his life working to be one of Scotland's greatest and most influential writers.

"Critical Evaluation" by Dennis R. Dean

Bibliography:
Cockshut, A. O. J. *The Achievement of Walter Scott*. London: Collins, 1969. A widely available introduction to the man and his work—reasonable, centrist, and modern. Chapters on Scott's major poems precede those dealing with his novels and other works.
Davis, Lloyd. "The Story in History: Time and Truth in Scott's *The Lay of the Last Minstrel*." *Clio* 18, no. 3 (1989): 221-238. Assesses the validity of the poem as history.
Elton, Oliver. "Scott's Verse." In *A Survey of English Literature, 1780-1830*. 2 vols. London: Edward Arnold, 1948. Originally published in 1912, when Scott's poetry was more often read than now. Elton is particularly good on the transition between Scott's *Border Minstrelsy*, which was mostly a collection of other people's poems, and *The Lay of the Last Minstrel*, which was his own poem.

Goslee, Nancy Moore. *Scott the Rhymer*. Lexington: University Press of Kentucky, 1988. Includes separate chapters on *The Lay of the Last Minstrel, Marmion,* and *The Lady of the Lake*. Almost the only serious criticism of Scott's long poems as wholes since modern techniques of analysis were developed, it deserves to be read in full.

Scott, Sir Walter. *Poems*. Edinburgh, Scotland: Ballantyne, 1830. For this collected edition of his verse, Scott wrote chatty and sometimes helpful prefaces to each of his major poems. The original is hard to find, but these same prefaces reappear in many later editions.

LAZARILLO DE TORMES

Type of work: Novel
Author: Unknown
Type of plot: Picaresque
Time of plot: Sixteenth century
Locale: Spain
First published: La vida de Lazarillo de Tormes y de sus fortunas y adversidades, 1553
  (English translation, 1576)

Principal character:
LAZARILLO DE TORMES, a picaro

The Story:

Lazarillo's surname came from the peculiar circumstance of his birth. His mother happened to stay the night at the mill where his father was employed. Lazarillo was born on the mill floor just over the river Tormes, after which he was named.

He had reached his ninth year when his father was caught taking flour from customers' sacks. After being soundly punished, the father joined an army that was preparing to move against the Moors. He became a mule driver for a gentleman soldier and was killed in action. Lazarillo's mother opened an eating house near a nobleman's estate. The widow soon made the acquaintance of Zayde, a black groom who frequently visited them. At first Lazarillo was afraid of the black man, but he quickly learned that Zayde's visits meant food and firewood. One consequence was a bit displeasing: Lazarillo acquired a small, dark brother to look after.

The nobleman's steward began to miss horseshoes and brushes as well as other supplies. When he was asked directly about the thefts, Lazarillo told all that he knew of Zayde's peccadillos. Zayde was soundly flogged, and boiling fat was poured on his ribs. To avoid further scandal, Lazarillo's mother set up a new eating house in a different neighborhood.

When Lazarillo was fairly well grown, his mother apprenticed him to a blind man who wanted a boy to lead him about. Although old, the blind man was shrewd and tough. As they were leaving the city, they passed by a stone bull. When the blind man told the boy to put his ear to the statue and listen for a peculiar noise, Lazarillo obeyed. Then the old man knocked the boy's head sharply against the stone, hard enough so his ears rang for three days. Lazarillo was forced to learn a few tricks for himself in order to survive.

The blind man, when they squatted over a fire to cook a meal, kept his hand over the mouth of his wine jug. Lazarillo bored a tiny hole in the jug, and, lying down, let the liquid trickle into his mouth. Then he stopped up the hole with beeswax. When the suspicious old man felt the jug, the wax had melted and he found the hole. Giving no sign, the next night he again put the jug in front of him and Lazarillo again lay down expecting to guzzle wine once more. Suddenly the blind man raised the jug and brought it down with great force in Lazarillo's face. All the boy's teeth were loosened.

On another occasion, Lazarillo seized a roasting sausage from the spit and substituted a rotten turnip. When the blind man bit into his supposed sausage, he roared with rage and scratched the boy severely with his long nails. Resolved to leave his master, Lazarillo guided him to the shores of a brook. Telling the blind man he must run and leap, he placed his master behind a stone pillar. The old man gave a mighty jump, cracked his head on the stone, and fell down senseless. Lazarillo left town quickly.

His next master was a penurious priest who engaged him to assist at mass. Unfortunately, the priest watched the collection box like a hawk, and Lazarillo had no chance to filch a single coin. For food, the priest allowed him an onion every fourth day. If it had not been for an occasional funeral feast, the boy would have starved to death.

The priest kept his fine bread securely locked in a chest. Luckily, Lazarillo met a strolling tinker who made him a key. Then to avoid suspicion, he gnawed each loaf to make it look as if rats had gotten into the chest. The alarmed priest nailed up the holes securely, but Lazarillo made new holes. Then the priest set numerous traps from which Lazarillo ate the cheese. The puzzled priest was forced to conclude that a snake was stealing his bread.

Fearing a search while he was asleep, Lazarillo kept his key in his mouth while he was in bed. One night the key shifted so that he was blowing through the keyhole. The resulting whistle awoke the priest. Seizing a club, he broke it over Lazarillo's head. After his head had been bandaged by a kind neighbor, Lazarillo was dismissed. Hoping to find employment in a larger city, he sought further fortune in Toledo.

One night while his pockets were full of crusts he had begged on the city streets, a careless young dandy, a real esquire, engaged Lazarillo as a servant. Thinking himself lucky to have a wealthy master, Lazarillo followed him to a bare, mean house with scarcely a stick of furniture. After waiting a long time for a meal, the boy began to eat his crusts. To his surprise, his master joined him. The days went by, both of them living on what Lazarillo could beg.

At last the esquire procured a little money and sent Lazarillo out for bread and wine. On the way he met a funeral procession. The weeping widow loudly lamented her husband and cried out that the dead man was going to an inhospitable house where there was no food or furniture. Thinking they were going to bring the corpse to his esquire's house, Lazarillo ran home in fear. His master disabused him of his fear and sent him back on his errand.

At last the master left town. Lazarillo was forced to meet the bailiffs and the wrathful landlord. After some difficulty, he persuaded the bailiffs of his innocence and was allowed to go free.

His next master was a *bulero*, a dealer in papal indulgences, who was an accomplished rogue. Rumors began to spread that his indulgences were forged, and even the bailiff accused him publicly of fraud. The wily *bulero* prayed openly for his accuser to be confounded, and forthwith the bailiff, falling down in a fit, foamed at the mouth and grew rigid. The prayers and forgiveness of the *bulero* were effective, however, and little by little the bailiff recovered. From that time on the *bulero* earned a rich harvest selling his papal indulgences. Lazarillo, wise in roguery, wondered how the *bulero* had worked the trick; but he never found out.

Four years of service with a chaplain who sold water enabled Lazarillo to save a little money and buy respectable clothes. At last he was on his way to some standing in the community. On the strength of his new clothes, he was appointed to a government post that would furnish him an income for life. All business matters of the town passed through his hands.

The archpriest of Salvador, seeing how affluent Lazarillo had become, gave him a wife from his own household. The woman made a useful wife, for the archpriest frequently gave them substantial presents. Lazarillo's wife repaid the holy man by taking care of his wardrobe; but evil tongues wagged, and the archpriest asked Lazarillo if he had heard stories about his wife. Lazarillo disclosed that he had been told that his wife had borne three of the archpriest's children. The archpriest advised him sagely to think of his profit more and his honor less. Lazarillo was content, for surely the archpriest was an honorable man.

Lazarillo had become so influential that it was said that he could commit any crime with impunity. His happiness increased when his wife presented him with a baby daughter. The good lady swore that it was truly Lazarillo's child.

Critical Evaluation:

In the fifteenth and sixteenth centuries, the Spanish novel began to develop into a modern form. This early novel form—particularly during the sixteenth century, the Spanish Golden Age of literature—evolved into four types. The earliest was the novel of chivalry. *Amadís de Gaul*, written in about the mid-fourteenth century but not published until 1508, is one of the best known of this type. Next in chronological order was the dramatic novel—a novel in dialogue—of which *La Celestina* (1499) is the prime example. The other two types appeared at approximately the same time, the mid-sixteenth century. One was the pastoral novel, the first and greatest being Jorge de Montemayor's *La Diana* (1559; *Diana*, 1596). The other was the picaresque novel, exemplified by *Lazarillo de Tormes*.

The anonymous *Lazarillo de Tormes* is generally conceded to be the earliest and the best of the picaresque novels. Episodic in form, the picaresque novel's narrative is usually told in the first person, the story dealing with the life of a picaro, or rogue, who is narrator and protagonist. In spite of much scholarly investigation, the origin of the terms picaresque and picaro is still doubtful, and etymological research has so far proved fruitless. Picaro, however, is understood to designate a wandering knave, a poor adventurer, who lives by his wits on the fringes of a class-conscious society and who must subordinate the luxury of ethics to the necessities of survival. Since the picaro typically serves several masters sequentially and in the course of his service observes their weaknesses and those of others, the picaresque novel becomes an ideal vehicle for depicting a wide cross section of society and, with its satirical tone, manages to attack broad segments of that society in the process. Yet these picaresque elements of satire, parody, caricature, and the like were not unique to picaresque novels. These traits also existed in earlier literature—such as Juan Ruiz, the Archpriest of Hita's *El libro de buen amor* (1330) and Fernando de Rojas' *La Celestina*—which influenced the development of the picaresque novel. Still, it was in the picaresque novel that society was held up to most careful scrutiny and given the most scathing denunciation.

In addition, *Lazarillo de Tormes* is often thought, by virtue of its form, to be autobiographical. The likelihood of such an eventuality, however, is slim. The anonymous author refers to Latin authors—improbable for a real-life Lazarillo—and reveals a distinct influence of the philosopher Erasmus—equally improbable for Lazarillo, whose formal education might charitably be described as lacking. The intrinsically fascinating adventures of Lazarillo need no autobiographical buttress. The instant and enduring popularity of the novel—three editions from 1554 alone are extant—is testimony to its compelling qualities as literature. So, too, is the number of translations: French, English, Dutch, German, and Italian versions appeared within less than seventy years of *Lazarillo de Tormes'* first publication; others followed. Imitation is another gauge of the novel's popularity and influence: In addition to Alain-René Lesage's *Gil Blas* (1715-1735), among many others, there were even two sequels to *Lazarillo de Tormes* written. Perhaps the ultimate accolade, however, was that the novel was placed on the *Index librorum prohibitorum* for its anticlericalism. This anticlericalism is routinely attributed to the influence of Erasmus.

As a character, Lazarillo is not original, cut from the whole cloth of the author's imagination. Before becoming the novel's protagonist, he was a character in folklore, with his name appearing in early proverbs and anecdotes. In fact, a quarter century before *Lazarillo de Tormes* was published, Lazarillo had a cameo role in Francisco Delicado's novel *La Lozana Andaluza* (1528), which features a *pícara*, a female rogue after the *La Celestina* model. Following *Lazarillo de Tormes*, however, Lazarillo himself became such a staple that the name itself became a generic term for those who guide the blind.

The most important aspect of *Lazarillo de Tormes*, however, is satiric, and the targets of this satire are lined up like ducks in a shooting gallery. All in all, Lazarillo serves seven masters before becoming his own master, so to speak. The story is thus divided into seven *tratados* (treatises or chapters), each dealing with a particular employer. The first is the blind beggar; the next, a priest; the third, a nobleman; the fourth, a friar; the fifth, a seller of indulgences; the sixth, a chaplain; the last, a constable. After narrating his unconventional background, Lazarillo launches his attack on social stratification, beginning with the blind man and continuing through the penniless nobleman and the constable; his harshest commentary, however, is reserved for the clergy—priest, friar, seller of indulgences, and chaplain—whose duplicity and venality are a constant source of amazement and embarrassment to him. Lazarillo's implicit and explicit criticism of the clergy constitutes the preponderant thrust of the novel. Yet Lazarillo's observations are astute, and the account accurately reflects contemporary conditions. Nevertheless, in such perceptivity lies a challenge to the status quo, a challenge which those in power were obliged to suppress, as they did by banning the novel.

Above all, *Lazarillo de Tormes* conveys a mood, a temper, a tenor: a cynical antidote to the idealistic worldviews, secular or religious, that characterized the medieval age of faith. In this sense, the novel is refreshing, breathing clear air into a musty, closed era. It wafts a clarity that should, but does not, make the blind man see, the exploiter turn philanthropist, the self-seeking cleric become true shepherd, and so on. The unalloyed power of this novel in fact stems from its lack of malice: It deplores corruption, but it does not hate.

Although it focuses on the lower levels of society, the novel is not intended to reform. Although it attacks clerical depredations, it is not sacrilegious. Still, *Lazarillo de Tormes* is, in the last analysis, more than a bitter tale of personal privation. It is a realistic commentary—a foil to the competing idealism of chivalric romances—on life as it is actually lived by common people who have neither privilege nor power. Beyond cynicism and despair, the novel offers hope for better things to come, since Lazarillo ultimately gets his foot on the bottom rung of the ladder to respectable success. As town crier, he has a steady, assured income, even if his wife is a hand-me-down mistress of the archpriest of Salvador. Lazarillo is willing thus to compromise. The reader is inclined to respect Lazarillo's judgment in this and other matters of the art of survival.

"Critical Evaluation" by Joanne G. Kashdan

Bibliography:
Alter, Robert. *Rogue's Progress: Studies in the Picaresque Novel.* Cambridge, Mass.: Harvard University Press, 1965. Discusses several picaresque novels, beginning with *Lazarillo de Tormes*, and (by stretching the meaning of "picaresque") traces the form's survival into the twentieth century.
Bjornson, Richard. *The Picaresque Hero in European Fiction.* Madison: University of Wisconsin Press, 1977. An expansive survey of picaresque literature in Spain, Germany, England, and France. Declares that *Lazarillo de Tormes'* author was among the first to realize "the novel's potential as a serious form of literary expression."
Deyermond, A. D. *"Lazarillo de Tormes": A Critical Guide.* London: Grant & Cutler in association with Tamesis Books, 1975. Discusses the novel in its social and religious context, and analyzes the novel's structure, style, and imagery. Indispensable. Annotated bibliography.
Dunn, Peter N. *The Spanish Picaresque Novel.* Boston: Twayne, 1979. Surveys the birth of the

form with *Lazarillo de Tormes* and its growth in Spain until the first half of the seventeenth century. Also discusses the many sequels to the short novel that appeared after its publication.

Fiore, Robert L. *Lazarillo de Tormes*. Boston: Twayne, 1984. A starting point for the general reader. Devotes a chapter to the novel's disputed authorship and concludes by praising the novel as being "universal in scope." Chronology, annotated bibliography.

LEAVES OF GRASS

Type of work: Poetry
Author: Walt Whitman (1819-1892)
First published: 1855

"America" is the first word of Walt Whitman's 1855 preface to *Leaves of Grass*, but this most American of poetic achievements is also the most universal. "The United States themselves are essentially the greatest poem," Whitman says, a belief that informs *Leaves of Grass* and led Whitman to redefine "poem" in such a way as to change forever the face of poetry.

Whitman paid for the publication of the first version of *Leaves of Grass* and even set some of the type himself. It was a slim volume, containing a preface and twelve poems, each several pages in length, sprawling across the pages, and looking quite unlike the neatly rhymed and metered poems then popular with readers. Whitman revised and expanded the book six times and reprinted it twice more. The final and most complete version of *Leaves of Grass*, published while Whitman was on his deathbed (1891-1892), included hundreds of pages and dozens of poems. Through its various versions, *Leaves of Grass* always remained a unified whole, and several themes and stylistic innovations remained constant.

Whitman believed that his lyrical epic poem about a new land required a new voice. *Leaves of Grass* represents a major innovation in poetic form. It is the first great nineteenth century work in English in what has come to be called free verse, poetry without obvious rhyme or meter. Whitman drew on other poets' experiments with unrhymed, nonmetrical poetry and on the sonorous rhythms of the King James version of the Bible, but he developed the form in volume and expressive power. Free verse—long lines and loose rhythmic structure—became the perfect vehicle for poems with themes of identity, nationality, and transcendence.

At best, the poems of *Leaves of Grass* are brilliantly rhythmic, with an eloquent use of the American language to describe ordinary experience. In "The blab of the pave, tires of carts, sluff of boot-soles," for example, colloquial diction and onomatopoeia re-create the sights and sounds of the streets. Whitman took risks by presenting himself as a typical American working man, "one of the roughs" and a democratic Everyman, but also as a poet of frank sexuality. This image of the poet as sensuous Everyman represents the masterly centerpiece of all the versions of *Leaves of Grass*, that long poem that Whitman did not title in 1855 but that he eventually called "Song of Myself." In the 1855 edition, Whitman's name did not appear on the title page but popped up in that poem: "Walt Whitman, an American, one of the roughs, a kosmos,/ Disorderly fleshy and sensual . . . eating drinking and breeding."

"Myself" in the poem is and is not Walt Whitman, for the poem is at once personal and an elevation of the individual to the mythic. A central idea of "Song of Myself" is that the cycle of life constantly renews itself and so triumphs over death: "The smallest sprout shows there really is no death."

Whitman is preeminently a poet of joy and of the intersection of body and soul: "I and this mystery here we stand." Individual identity therefore becomes at once fragile and transcendent. The individual dies and "life" goes on. By recognizing and absorbing this knowledge, Whitman says, all may feel unity with life and so triumph over death.

Early in "Song of Myself," Whitman introduces leaves as a metaphor, likening the grass to a flag, a handkerchief, a child, a hieroglyphic, "the beautiful uncut hair of graves," and "so many uttering tongues." By using metaphor, Whitman helps the reader see grass differently. Like the speaker, who is an ordinary man, grass represents an ordinary creation so plentiful it is likely to go unnoticed. Yet just as in a democracy every voice is important, in *Leaves of Grass* every leaf is a reminder of the beauty and transcendence of life.

Like *Leaves of Grass* as a whole, "Song of Myself" progresses toward its climax by dilating and contracting on a number of themes and images. Section by section, this poem includes many subtle and not-so-subtle modulations in tone. Sometimes these shifts occur from one section to the next, from, for example, "twenty-eight young men bathe by the shore" (section 11) to "the butcher-boy puts off his killing-clothes" (section 12). Over the larger structure of the poem, Whitman's expression ranges from passages of personal emotion such as "To touch my person to some one else's is about as much as I can stand" (section 27) to descriptive passages that, while also intensely emotional, find their focus outside the speaker's consciousness, as in "The spotted hawk swoops by" (section 89).

The sections of the poem shuttle constantly between general and specific, between description and emotion, and between the body and the soul. These shifts are appropriate to the theme of endless renewal, but "Song of Myself" also moves toward a conclusion in which the poet disappears into the cycle of life, and readers are left to find their own way.

The roughness and sensuality of *Leaves of Grass* offended and frightened many of Whitman's early readers. "Song of Myself" in particular still has the power to surprise and even shock, as when Whitman says in section 24, "The scent of these arm-pits aroma finer than prayer," words that still dismay some readers. Sexuality is the common denominator of human beings, and Whitman wants to strip away pretense (represented by clothing) to reveal the naked body, which is also the naked soul, for soul and body are one: "Behold," he says in "Starting from Paumanok," "the body includes and is . . . the soul."

In addition to long poems such as "Song of Myself," the smaller poems in *Leaves of Grass* also contribute to the book's unity. Many readers have found homoerotic imagery in Whitman's celebration of "adhesiveness" and "manly love," though Whitman himself denied that connection. In "I Saw in Louisiana a Live Oak Growing," which first appeared in *Leaves of Grass* in 1860, Whitman uses the live oak tree as an image of solitary strength; unlike the tree, the speaker says he could not live "without a friend or lover near." In another major poem that appears in every version of *Leaves of Grass*, "The Sleepers," Whitman provides counterpoint to the joyous optimism of "Song of Myself" when he describes the narrator going from bedside to bedside like an angel overseeing suffering humanity. The imagery of "The Sleepers" takes on a special poignancy from the fact that, long after he wrote this poem, Whitman cared for hospitalized soldiers during the Civil War. When his brother George was listed among those wounded at the Battle of Fredericksburg, he headed south to look for him; George's wound was slight, but Whitman stayed on in Washington, D.C., to visit the sick and wounded soldiers in the military hospitals.

Whitman's charitable work in the hospitals allowed him to participate in the war without fighting and to express his complex amorous and charitable feelings toward men. These feelings surface in *Leaves of Grass*:

> I stand in the dark with drooping eyes by the worst-suffering and most restless,
> I pass my hands soothingly to and fro a few inches from them,
> The restless sink in their beds, they fitfully sleep.

"The Sleepers" is a difficult, visionary poem, full of troubled and troubling imagery, as in the line "The wretched features of the ennuyés, the white features of corpses." The poem has the quality of a nightmare but might more accurately be characterized—as it was by Whitman's friend and first biographer, Richard M. Bucke—as "a representation of the mind during sleep" moving rapidly over loosely connected images. The central metaphors are darkness and sleep, which stand for confusion and death. In the end, however, just as night disappears into sunrise, death must disappear into life and the poem returns to the affirmative voice of "Song of Myself."

"Crossing Brooklyn Ferry," added to *Leaves of Grass* in 1856, describes the immortality of the individual across the sweep of time. As the speaker rides a ferryboat across the East River, he contemplates the crowd on the boat, the flow of the water, and the motion of the boat, finding in them a transcendent continuity: "It avails not, time nor place—distance avails not,/ I am with you, you men and women of a generation, of ever so many generations hence." When he is gone, other people will look at the crowd and think the same thoughts he is thinking. These others will in that sense become him. By accepting one's own identity, by trusting life and the soul's natural impulses, one can be happy and recognize the interrelationship with all of life, past, present, and future.

"Out of the Cradle Endlessly Rocking," published first in 1871 in a separate volume of poems entitled *Passage to India*, and later incorporated into the expanded 1881 edition of *Leaves of Grass*, is a poem of reminiscence. The speaker looks back on his boyhood to a time when, near the ocean, he was awakened from innocence to an empathetic experience of a male mockingbird's loss of his mate. This empathy leads him directly to an enlightened state that gives him sense of his identity and vocation as a poet, or a bard. By revising "Out of the Cradle Endlessly Rocking," Whitman brought the italicized sections representing the mockingbird's song to an increasingly subtle onomatopoeia, which united the bird's song and the poet's words just as the poet's empathy for the bird's loss had united them through the bird's song. "My own songs awaked from that hour," the speaker says.

"When Lilacs Last in the Dooryard Bloom'd," Whitman's great elegy for Lincoln, also first appeared in *Passage to India*, before becoming part of *Leaves of Grass* in 1881. Just as "Out of the Cradle Endlessly Rocking" weaves together a bird's song, ocean, beach, and memory, "When Lilacs Last in the Dooryard Bloom'd" uses three key symbols—the blooming lilac, the "western fallen star," and the warbling of a thrush in a swamp—to mourn the death of Abraham Lincoln: "Lilac and star and bird twined with the chant of my soul." Whitman adored Lincoln as the preserver of the Union, and in this poem he was able to pay homage to Lincoln's greatness and come to terms with his tragic death.

In "A Passage to India," the title poem of the 1871 collection of that name, Whitman celebrates the great breakthroughs in communication during his lifetime: the Suez Canal, which opened up access to the Orient; the transcontinental railroad, which made travel across America easier; and the laying of telegraph cables across the Atlantic and Pacific oceans, which made virtually instantaneous international communication possible. Whitman himself described that the poem concerned the way evolution unfolds "cosmic purposes."

Leaves of Grass is a work of integration and wholeness. Through its dozens of poems and many revisions, the central themes of the work—the transcendence of the individual through knowledge of the wholeness and continuity of life, the naturalness of death, and the beauty of the living world—serve to describe the joy Whitman took in his own American century.

Thomas Lisk

Bibliography:
Allen, Gay Wilson. *A Reader's Guide to Walt Whitman.* New York: Farrar, Straus & Giroux,

1970. A succinct survey intended to be an introductory work for readers and students of Whitman. A good place to start the study of Whitman.

_____. *The Solitary Singer: A Critical Biography of Walt Whitman*. Chicago: University of Chicago Press, 1985. First published in 1955, this is still one of the best "life-and-works" sources available on Whitman.

Folsom, Ed, ed. *Walt Whitman: The Centennial Essays*. Iowa City: University of Iowa Press, 1994. A collection of essays in honor of the centennial of Whitman's death. Provides a good overview of trends in literary criticism of *Leaves of Grass*.

Kaplan, Justin. *Walt Whitman: A Life*. New York: Simon & Schuster, 1980. An elegant, deeply imagined biography that focuses on Whitman and his times.

Miller, James E. *Leaves of Grass: America's Lyric-Epic of Self and Democracy*. New York: Twayne, 1992. An excellent introduction to the background, themes, and style of *Leaves of Grass*; especially helpful on the work's structure.

Pearce, Roy Harvey, ed. *Whitman: A Collection of Critical Essays*. Englewood Cliffs, N.J.: Prentice-Hall, 1962. A collection of articles gathered primarily for use by students. Contains interesting material, including William Carlos Williams' "An Essay on *Leaves of Grass*."

Zweig, Paul. *Walt Whitman: The Making of a Poet*. New York: Basic Books, 1984. Not a chronological biography but a very interesting biographical/critical meditation on Whitman's development.

THE LEFT HAND OF DARKNESS

Type of work: Novel
Author: Ursula K. Le Guin (1929-   )
Type of plot: Science fiction
Time of plot: Hainish Cycle 93, Ekumenical year 1490-1497
Locale: The planet Gethen/Winter
First published: 1969

Principal characters:
GENLY AI, the envoy from Ekumen to Gethen
THEREM HARTH REM IR ESTRAVEN, a Karhidish noble and official
KING ARGAVEN XV, ruler of the country of Karhide on Gethen
THE COMMENSALS, top officials of Orgota, a country on Gethen

The Story:

Genly Ai, the Ekumen's envoy to the planet Gethen/Winter, was dealt a setback in his mission to recruit Gethen to the Ekumen when Therem Harth rem ir Estraven, formerly Ai's ally, withdrew support. Estraven had fallen from favor with Karhide's King Argaven XV, because his efforts to avoid a war between his country and the neighboring nation of Orgoreyn caused the king to lose *shifgrethor*, a complex Karhidish version of honor. Estraven tried to explain to Ai that his new coolness to the Ekumen was a ploy to keep his dishonor from infecting the Ekumen's mission, but Ai, a stranger to the intricate subtleties of *shifgrethor* and still unused to Gethen's politics, failed to see anything but betrayal in Estraven's actions.

Ai's alien nature haunted his mission. He was unused to the planet's intense cold, its complex cultural codes, and, most of all, its unique form of human sexuality. Gethenians were ambisexual, uninterested four-fifths of the time, then intensely sexual during "kemmer," when they might manifest as male for a kemmer or two, then female during the next cycle. Ai persisted in trying to interpret Gethenians as men or women, even though intellectually he knew differently. The Gethenians faced a similar problem with Ai, and viewed his persistent maleness as a perversion.

Ai met with the king on the day Estraven was banished from the country. Argaven, although suspicious of the Ekumen and Ai, nevertheless gave the envoy freedom to travel throughout Karhide. Ai used his freedom to explore, and met with the Handdara Foretellers, who practiced a meditative religion based on unlearning what culture had taught them. For the price of two rubies, Ai's question, Would Gethen join the Ekumen within five years?, was undertaken by the Foretellers. Their answer, after a harrowing ceremony, came back as a single word—yes.

Ai applied for admission to the neighboring country of Orgoreyn, where Estraven had fled after his banishment. Estraven's influence gained him swift entry. Ai immediately noticed differences between the nations: Karhide was feudal and anarchic, Orgoreyn was socialistic and totalitarian.

Ai's first night in Orgoreyn was disrupted by raiders from Karhide, involved in the same Sinoth valley land dispute that had cost Estraven his position. Ai's escape from the raiders put him in contact with the Orgota, who struck him as excessively passive people, in contrast to the highly individualistic and passionate Karhiders. He spent a night locked in a grain bin with others displaced by the raid, then was recognized by officialdom and given a vehicle and a pass to take him to the capital city, Mishnory, where he was welcomed by Commissioner Shusgis.

For a while, Ai was feted by the Commensals who ruled Orgota, but then subtle changes

3569

occurred. Estraven, living in that city, recognized that no news of Ai's presence had been communicated to the rest of the country. His diplomatic experience had taught him that, in this country ruled by secret police, this was a bad sign, and he hurried to warn Ai. The envoy distrusted him too much to take immediate action, so when government agents came to arrest him in the night, they faced no opposition.

Ai went first to Kunderer Prison, where he was drugged and questioned for days on end. Then officials loaded him onto a truck with dozens of other prisoners and sent him on a nightmarish journey to a voluntary farm. The envoy nearly died on the journey—the truck was unheated, the prisoners were not fed, and, at the standard rate of twenty-five miles per hour, not including long, inexplicable stops, the trip took many days to accomplish.

Once at the farm, Ai was fed inadequately, worked moderately, and again subjected to repeated drugged inquisitions. The drugs proved toxic to his alien system; soon he lay comatose for days after each interrogation.

Estraven followed him through Orgota, using falsified papers. Despite his seeming treachery, Estraven believed entirely in Ai's mission, and, in the underground ways of Gethen, had been working ceaselessly for Ai's benefit. He bought provisions for a long winter journey and, posing as a guard, carried the unconscious Ai out of Pulefen Farm.

To escape, the two faced an almost impossible journey across the Gobrin Ice in the winter. They had enough food for seventy-eight days, and approximately eight hundred miles to cover. During the journey, which threw Ai and Estraven into extremely close contact and taxed both to their physical limits, Estraven went into kemmer, his sexual phase. It was this that finally brought the two together, as Ai realized the sexual prejudice that had kept him from seeing Estraven as fully human.

The journey did not end until the food had been gone for three days. When they finally reached Karhide, Estraven sent Ai to sell their valuable Chabe stove and buy transmission time from a local radio station to call his ship out of orbit. While Ai was doing this, Estraven was betrayed by an old acquaintance. He fled for the border, was shot by the guards, and died in Ai's arms.

Saddened, but determined not to let his friend's death destroy their mutual goal, Ai approached King Argaven once more and secured Karhide's decision to enter the Ekumen. After the Ekumen ship landed and final details had been settled, Ai journeyed to Estraven's home, where he met his friend's child, and told him of "other worlds out among the stars—the other kinds of men, the other lives."

Critical Evaluation:

Ursula K. Le Guin has described *The Left Hand of Darkness* as a thought experiment, a place where she changed the world in her imagination, then observed how this change affected her understanding of human nature. The book was written in 1969, at the start of the late twentieth century women's movement, when women were struggling to discover what was essential about their gender, and what seemingly gender-driven behavior was the result of cultural adaptation. The novel won two prestigious awards, the Hugo and the Nebula, both given for excellence in the genre of science fiction.

Drawing on her background in mythology and anthropology, Le Guin incorporates several different points of view, in chapters that retell the mythical tales of the planet and other chapters written as scientific reports from the Ekumen's first, anonymous corps of observers. All deal with the concepts of duality and unity, and seek to explain how the Gethenians' unique sexual nature has influenced their civilization and worldview.

Some critics, including science fiction writer Stanisław Lem, have taken Le Guin to task for creating androgynous beings who seem more male than female. She has challenged these critics to show her a single action performed by a character in the novel that had to be performed by a specifically male or female character. At the same time, she notes that she did not show many characters engaging in activities that are currently regarded as feminine, such as child rearing. She also laments the lack of a genderless pronoun in the English language that would have allowed her to avoid calling the Gethenians "he."

Without a male-female split to suggest an intrinsically dualistic worldview to the Gethenians, they have created a society that, in many ways, seeks to see all in one. Genly Ai at one moment muses, "Perhaps you are as obsessed with wholeness as we are with dualism." Because this world is seen through Genly Ai's eyes, the reader can perceive how different it is from human experience. Ai cannot shake his desire to see Gethenians as male or female, nor can he feel comfortable with someone who does not give him some sexual regard. He continually describes Estraven using feminine qualities as the basis for his dislike, calling the other "womanly, all charm and tact and lack of substance."

This shifts during their flight across the Gobrin Ice, when Estraven enters kemmer. He asks Ai about women, bringing the envoy to realize that gender is "the heaviest single factor in one's life," and that he knows nothing of a woman's life, that women are, in fact, "more alien to me than you are."

While Le Guin exposes disturbing trends in the ways culture shapes gendered behavior, she does not advocate life without duality. As Ai and Estraven realize, even in the absence of a second gender, humans will always face the gap between self and other. Le Guin insists, however, that humans seek the creative tension between opposites that comes when both sides of a duality are honored. She shows the importance of this as she compares the two religions of Gethen, the Handdara, which actively explores the dark unknowns of human existence, and the Yomeshta, which insists that light is the only truth. The Handdara religion has made Karhide anarchic and individualistic, but essentially human. The Yomeshta, worshiping Orgota, have created a socialistic bureaucracy in which the individual is completely subordinated to the public good. As a result, the Orgota commit acts of great barbarity without any thought of conscience.

The shadow as metaphor for other also surfaces as Ai and Estraven labor across the Gobrin Ice. The weather changes to a white mist, the shadows disappear, and Ai realizes that, without the shadows, he cannot see the dangers that lie in his path: the crevasses, the rotten ice, the cracks. He draws the Taoist yin-yang symbol for Estraven, finally understanding in a deep way the need for duality in the world, and the ability of one human being to contain both light and shadow, working in creative harmony.

Le Guin's depiction of the world of Gethen in minute and realistic detail further adds to the thematic material of the novel. Winter is both a cruel reality of the planet and a mythological setting for the journey Gethenians make from an isolated and relatively static planet to a planet preparing to join an alliance of similarly human, yet largely alien, brethren. Genly Ai's journey, beginning and ending in spring, takes both him and Gethen from a flowering abundance, to near destruction, and back into a springtime of regeneration and re-creation.

Susan E. Keegan

Bibliography:
Ketterer, David. "*The Left Hand of Darkness*: Ursula Le Guin's Archetypal Winter Journey." In

New Worlds for Old: The Apocalyptic Imagination, Science Fiction, and American Literature. Garden City, N.Y.: Anchor, 1974. Looks at Le Guin's use of myth in the novel, especially as it concerns her depictions of duality and mystical unity. Ketterer was the first to expose the mythology of winter as contained in the book.

Le Guin, Ursula. "Is Gender Necessary?" In *The Language of the Night*, edited by Susan Wood. New York: G. P. Putnam's Sons, 1979. Le Guin looks back on the artistic choices she made in the novel, and comments on her motives in conducting this "thought experiment."

Sargent, Pamela. "Introduction: Women and Science Fiction." In *Women of Wonder*, edited by Pamela Sargent. New York: Vintage Books, 1975. Places Le Guin's work in the context of feminist trends in science fiction. Textual notes recount discussion by writer Stanisław Lem and Le Guin of Le Guin's success in portraying Gethenian sexuality.

Slusser, George Edgar. *The Farthest Shores of Ursula K. Le Guin*. San Bernardino, Calif.: Borgo Press, 1976. This pamphlet discusses most of Le Guin's earlier writings, and sees in *The Left Hand of Darkness* the workings of paradoxes that defy simple moral interpretation.

Spivack, Charlotte. *"The Left Hand of Darkness."* In *Ursula K. Le Guin*. Boston: Twayne, 1984. A thorough discussion of all of Le Guin's works. Includes sections on narrative structure, use of mythology, political and religious themes, and critical reception.

THE LEGEND OF GOOD WOMEN

Type of work: Poetry
Author: Geoffrey Chaucer (c. 1343-1400)
First transcribed: 1380-1386

Principal characters:
CHAUCER, the dreamer
CUPID, the god of love
ALCESTE, the wife of Admetus, the king of Pherae
CLEOPATRA, the queen of Egypt
THISBE, the beloved of Pyramus
DIDO, the queen of Carthage
HYPSIPYLE, the queen of Lemnos, who is betrayed by Jason
MEDEA, the princess of Colchis, who is betrayed by Jason
LUCRETIA, a Roman matron ravished by Tarquin
ARIADNE, a Cretan princess betrayed by Theseus
PHILOMELA, an Athenian princess ravished by Tereus
PHYLLIS, a Greek maiden betrayed by Demophon
HYPERMNESTRA, the daughter of Danaüs, the king of Egypt

The Legend of Good Women, a poem recounting the stories of women from history and myth who were martyrs to love, is written in the tradition of medieval love poetry. Unlike Geoffrey Chaucer's masterpieces, *Troilus and Criseyde* (1382) and *The Canterbury Tales* (1387-1400), this work only occasionally rises above the limitations imposed by the artificial conventions of the times and is, therefore, somewhat inferior to these other works. Chaucer's greatness as a poet resulted not so much from his ability to perfect the current modes of writing as from his capacity to transcend them. Although his debt to contemporary thought and literary practice was considerable, his lasting position among English writers depends largely on his gift for bringing reality to a literature that was customarily unrealistic. Yet in *The Legend of Good Women*, he constructed a framework so restrictive as to prevent his being able to infuse it with the richness and subtle shadings of human existence.

The most engaging part of the poem is the prologue, in which Chaucer expresses his elation at the arrival of spring. He delighted in roaming through the meadows, listening to the small birds, and gazing at the flowers. He was especially attracted to the daisy, which he could observe for hours without becoming bored. One spring day, after a walk in the fields, he fell asleep and had a vision in which the god of love and the beautiful Alceste, dressed in the colors of the daisy, appeared before him. Cupid denounced the dreamer for having committed heresy against the laws of love in writing of Criseyde's infidelity and translating *The Romance of the Rose* (c. 1370) with its disparaging remarks about womankind. Yet Cupid's companion (the same Alceste whom Hercules rescued from Hades after she had given her life to redeem her husband from death) rose to the poet's defense by contending that he, having appropriated his plots from other writers, acted out of ignorance, not malice. She concluded that he might gain Cupid's forgiveness by writing a legendary of wives and maidens who had been faithful in love all of their lives.

The prologue is filled with literary devices popular in the fourteenth century. The religion of love—which had its sins, penances, self-abnegation, and sanctity, as well as the figures of Cupid and Alceste, somewhat analogous to God and the Virgin Mary—closely paralleled the Christian religion. The daisy, having recently replaced the rose, was the symbol of love. Chaucer touches on the question whether the flower or the leaf is superior, apparently a hotly debated issue in courtly circles, but the poet does not commit himself. The dream-vision used here had been a very popular device ever since the appearance of *The Romance of the Rose*, and Chaucer himself employed it in several works. Despite this elaborate machinery, which today is mainly of historic interest, the prologue has about it a universal appeal; cheerfulness, humor, and a tinge of ironic detachment preserve it from mediocrity. Also delightful is Chaucer's expression of delight in nature.

According to the prologue, Chaucer planned to write twenty tales about good women. He finished eight and left a ninth just short of completion. The theme of all the legends is the fidelity of women in love. All the heroines suffer for, and the majority die for, their love. All are treated as wholly admirable, even saintly, without regard to the illicit nature of some of the relationships presented. Events in their lives not concerned with their fidelity are omitted or hastily summarized. With the exception of the first two legends, the women suffer as the result of the treachery of men, who are generally thoroughgoing villains.

The longest and one of the best of the legends retells the story of Dido's love for Aeneas. After Aeneas landed on the Libyan coast, he had met Venus, his mother, who instructed him to go to the court of Dido, the queen of Carthage. Dido greeted him cordially and, knowing his flight from Troy, felt great pity for the disinherited hero. With her pity, came love. To comfort and entertain him during his visit, she provided everything riches could command.

One day, when Aeneas, Dido, and her retinue were hunting, a thunderstorm burst upon them. Everyone rushed for shelter, and Dido and Aeneas found themselves together in a cave. There the perfidious Aeneas protested his love for her, and she, after much importuning, had pity and yielded herself to him. For a time, Aeneas did everything a courtly lover should, but finally, becoming weary, he made plans to leave. When Dido noted his lessened ardor and asked what was wrong, he told her of a vision (a pure fabrication, Chaucer implied) in which his father had reminded him of his destiny to conquer Italy. Ignoring her pleas, Aeneas stole away to his ships without her. As soon as she discovered his absence, she had her sister build a funeral pyre upon which, using Aeneas' sword, she stabbed herself.

Chaucer's principal source for this tale was Vergil's *Aeneid* (c. 29-19 B.C.E.). Chaucer made only slight modifications in the plot but substantial changes in characterization. Dido, who in Vergil's telling had not escaped censure, was made blameless by Chaucer, mainly by his elaboration of the scene in the cave. By minimizing the intervention of the gods and degrading his motives, Chaucer turned Vergil's pious Aeneas into a mere seducer. Thus a story of tragic struggle between love and duty was transformed into one of man's treachery and woman's loyalty.

Chaucer's source for "The Legend of Lucretia" was Ovid's *Fasti* (before 8 C.E.), which he followed quite closely. To prove the virtues of his wife Lucretia, Collatinus offered to accompany Tarquin, the king's son, to Rome to see her. Secreted outside her chamber door, they found her spinning among her servants and expressing concern for her husband's safety. Tarquin, observing her beauty, conceived a great desire for her. The next day, his lust increasing, he determined to return to Collatinus' house and seduce Lucretia. Stealing into her room at night, he threatened her at sword's point and, while she lay in a swoon, ravished her. After he left, Lucretia dressed in mourning, called her friends about her, and told them what had happened. Declaring that her husband should not gain a foul name from her guilt, she stabbed herself.

"The Legend of Hypsipyle and Medea" recounts Jason's double treachery, who, on his expedition to recover the Golden Fleece, stopped at the island of Lemnos. Here he and Hercules met Queen Hypsipyle and conspired to win her for Jason. While Jason counterfeited modesty, Hercules extolled his virtues, thus ensnaring Hypsipyle, who consented to marry him. After using her wealth and begetting two children with her, he left. He ignored her letter imploring him to return, but she remained true to him and died of a broken heart.

After arriving at Colchis, where Jason was entertained by King Aeetes, Medea, the king's daughter, became enamored of him and told him that the Golden Fleece could be secured only with her help. They agreed to marry, and Jason made a solemn promise never to be untrue. Later, after the expedition was successful, Jason again proved false, leaving her to marry Creusa.

Toward the end of *The Legend of Good Women*, Chaucer indicated a definite weariness with his subject. By adhering to his original plan, he had written tales with a tiresome sameness about them. Committed to depicting perfect women and, in most instances, evil men, he found it difficult to develop his characters. A further deterrent to good characterization was his effort to keep the tales brief; as a result, some are little more than plot summaries. Because he lavished more attention on Dido than on his other heroines, hers is the most lifelike portrait. There are, however, good touches in the other female characters, including, for example, the pathos of Lucretia in her death scene and the mingled fear and courage of Thisbe. Chaucer's men are, however, little more than abstractions.

These tales mark a step toward Chaucer's later work. In *The Legend of Good Women*, he first used the decasyllabic couplet that he afterward employed so successfully in *The Canterbury Tales*. Moreover, juxtaposing of *The Legend of Good Women* with *Troilus and Criseyde* was good preparation for the subtler contrasts of the Marriage Group. It is possible that Chaucer abandoned the work because of growing absorption with *The Canterbury Tales*. Whatever the case, *The Legend of Good Women* is an interesting transitional work with merits of its own.

Bibliography:
Chaucer, Geoffrey. *The Legend of Good Women*. Translated by Ann McMillan. Houston, Tex.: Rice University Press, 1987. Provides a literal modern English translation of Chaucer's Middle English verse. Includes a sixty-page general introduction and useful "Suggestions for Further Reading" on the subject of medieval women.

Frank, Robert Worth, Jr. *Chaucer and "The Legend of Good Women."* Cambridge, Mass.: Harvard University Press, 1972. The first full-length study of the poem and probably the best source for the general reader. Focuses on narrative technique and finds the work to represent a stylistic turning point in Chaucer's development.

Fyler, John M. *Chaucer and Ovid*. New Haven, Conn.: Yale University Press, 1979. Chapter 4, "The *Legend of Good Women*: Palinode and Procrustean Bed," offers a clearly written, concise reading of the poem as a comic exercise.

Kiser, Lisa J. *Telling Classical Tales: Chaucer and "The Legend of Good Women."* Ithaca, N.Y.: Cornell University Press, 1983. Argues that the work is really more about Chaucer's basic views of literature than about his views of love. Includes discussions of medieval theories of literature and an analysis of Chaucer's use of sources.

Rowe, Donald W. *Through Nature to Eternity: Chaucer's "The Legend of Good Women."* Lincoln: University of Nebraska Press, 1988. Surveys relevant contexts and earlier criticism and argues that the poem has a circular or cyclical structure rather than being merely a series of loosely related portraits. Interprets the nine legends as a complete, coherent, and artistically successful whole.

THE LEGEND OF SLEEPY HOLLOW

Type of work: Short fiction
Author: Washington Irving (1783-1859)
Type of plot: Tall tale
Time of plot: Eighteenth century
Locale: New York State
First published: 1820

Principal characters:
ICHABOD CRANE, a schoolteacher
KATRINA VAN TASSEL, a rustic heiress
ABRAHAM VAN BRUNT, a young squire known as Brom Bones

The Story:

Near Tarrytown on the Hudson River is a little valley which, years ago, was the quietest place in the world. A drowsy influence hung over the place and people so that the region was known as Sleepy Hollow, and the lads were called Sleepy Hollow boys. Some said that the valley was bewitched. It was true that marvelous stories were told there.

The main figure to haunt the valley was one on horseback, without a head. Some said the specter was the apparition of a Hessian horseman who had lost his head to a cannonball, but, whatever it was, it was often seen in the valley and adjacent countryside in the gloom of winter nights. The specter was known to all as the Headless Horseman of Sleepy Hollow.

In the valley, years ago, there lived a schoolteacher named Ichabod Crane. He looked like a scarecrow because of his long, skinny frame and his snipelike nose. As was the custom in that fertile Dutch countryside, he boarded with the parents of his pupils a week at a time. Fortunately for him, the Dutch larders were full and the tables groaning with food, for the schoolmaster had a wonderful appetite. He was always welcome in the country homes because, in small ways, he made himself useful to the farmers. He was patient with the children, and he loved to spend the long winter nights with the families of his pupils, exchanging tales of ghosts and haunted places, while ruddy apples roasted on the hearths.

Ichabod believed heartily in ghosts, and his walks home after an evening of storytelling were often filled with fear. His only source of courage at those times was his voice, loud and nasal as it made the night resound with many a psalm tune.

The schoolteacher picked up a little extra money by holding singing classes. In one of his classes, he first became aware of a plump and rosy-cheeked girl named Katrina Van Tassel. She was the only child of a very substantial farmer, and that fact added to her charms for the ever-hungry Ichabod. Since she was not only beautiful but also lively, she was a great favorite among the lads in the neighborhood.

Abraham Van Brunt was Katrina's favorite squire. The Dutch first shortened his name to Brom and then called him Brom Bones when he became known for the tall and powerful frame of his body. He was a lively lad with a fine sense of humor and a tremendous amount of energy. When other suitors saw his horse hitched outside Katrina's house on a Sunday night, they went on their way. Brom Bones was a formidable rival for the gaunt and shaggy Ichabod. Brom would have liked to carry the battle into the open, but the schoolteacher knew better than to tangle with him physically. Brom Bones could do little but play practical jokes on lanky Ichabod.

The whole countryside was invited one fall evening to a quilting frolic at Mynheer Van Tassel's. For the occasion, Ichabod borrowed a horse from the farmer with whom he was then living. The horse, called Gunpowder, was as gaunt as Ichabod himself, but the steed still had a fair amount of spirit. The two of them were a sight as they jogged happily along to the party.

Ichabod was well pleased by every prospect he saw on the Van Tassel farm, the most prosperous holding for miles around. Perhaps Ichabod might be able to sell it and, with the proceeds, go farther west. It was a pretty picture he saw as he passed fields full of shocks of corn and pumpkins, granaries stuffed with grain, and meadows and barnlots filled with sleek cattle and plump fowls.

The party was a merry one with many lively dances. Ichabod was at his best when he danced with Katrina. After a time, he went out on the dark porch with the men and exchanged more Sleepy Hollow ghost stories—but the food was best of all. Ichabod did credit to all the cakes and pies, meats and tea.

After the others left, he tarried to pay court to Katrina, but it was not long before he started home crestfallen on the gaunt Gunpowder. All the stories he had heard came back to him, and as he rode along in the darkness, he became more dismal. He heard groans as the branches of the famed Major Andre tree rubbed against one another. He even thought he saw something moving beneath it.

When he came to the bridge over Wiley's Swamp, Gunpowder balked. The harder Ichabod urged him, the more the horse bucked. Then, on the other side of the marsh, Ichabod saw something huge and misshapen.

The figure refused to answer him when he called. Ichabod's hair stood straight on end. Because it was too late to turn back, however, the schoolmaster kept to the road. The stranger—it looked like a headless horseman holding its head on the pommel of the saddle—kept pace with him, fast or slow. Ichabod could not stand going slowly, and he whipped Gunpowder to a gallop. As his saddle loosened, he nearly lost his grip, but he hugged the horse around the neck. He could not even sing a psalm tune.

When he reached the church bridge, where by tradition the headless specter would disappear in a flash of fire and brimstone, Ichabod heard the horseman close in on him. As he turned to look, the spirit threw his head at him. Ichabod tried to dodge, but the head tumbled him into the dust.

In the morning, a shattered pumpkin was found near the bridge. Gunpowder was grazing at the farmer's gate nearby. Ichabod, however, was never seen in Sleepy Hollow again. In the valley, they say that Brom Bones, long after he had married the buxom Katrina, laughed heartily whenever the story was told of the horseman who had thrown his head at the schoolteacher during that ghostly midnight pursuit.

Critical Evaluation:

Washington Irving, the first professional writer in America, was by inclination an amused observer of people and customs. By birth, he was in a position to be that observer. The son of a New York merchant in good financial standing, he was the youngest of eleven children, several of whom helped him to take prolonged trips to Europe for his health and fancy. He was responsible for two trends in American literature: the regional, legendary tale and the historical novel. "The Legend of Sleepy Hollow" belongs to the first trend.

The two best-known of Irving's stories are "Rip Van Winkle" and "The Legend of Sleepy Hollow," both of which appeared originally in *The Sketch Book of Geoffrey Crayon, Gent.*, a collection of tales and familiar essays. Both stories are based on German folklore which Irving adapted to a lower New York State setting and peopled with Dutch farmers.

In "The Legend of Sleepy Hollow," the Dutch farmers make up most of the folkloric elements, for Ichabod Crane is an outsider, a Yankee schoolmaster among the canny Dutch settlers. As an outsider, and a peculiar-looking one at that, Ichabod Crane becomes the butt of local humor and the natural victim for Brom Bones's practical jokes. Most of the humorous sallies of the Sleepy Hollow boys are in the vein of good-natured ribbing. Yet Brom Bones's practical jokes were somewhat more serious because of the rather unequal rivalry between Brom and Ichabod for the hand of Katrina Van Tassel. It is in the relationship between Brom and Ichabod that the common folk theme of the scapegoat is most clearly seen.

Other folk themes appear in the story as well. Among them is the belief that one can ward off evil spirits with religious symbols; thus, Ichabod sings psalms on his fear-filled homeward treks after evenings of storytelling. The distinction of having a special ghost—one with a definite identity—to haunt a specific locality is a matter of honor and prestige, highly respected as a folkloric theme. Here, the putative Hessian, the Headless Horseman of Sleepy Hollow, fills the role with grace, wit, and style. The character of the comely wench, over whose favors men wrangle, dispute, and plot, is as common a catalyst in folklore as in life; hence, Katrina Van Tassel functions as fulcrum and folk theme in the story.

These and other themes from folklore and legend appear in "The Legend of Sleepy Hollow" as well as in other tales by Washington Irving, for folk and legendary material was one of Irving's two major interests, the other being history, a closely related field. As far as Irving's work is concerned, the two interests seem to feed upon each other to the mutual benefit of both. Irving's historical writings are thus enlivened by his cultural perceptions, and his stories are made more vivid by his knowledge of history. This symbolic relationship between Irving's interests has generally been neglected, and, as a result, his other writings have generally been underrated. Although he was a prolific author, most people know him only for "Rip Van Winkle" and "The Legend of Sleepy Hollow." Yet the First American Man of Letters, the Ambassador of the New World to the Old, and the Father of American Literature are all titles that have deservedly been accorded him by both popular and critical acclaim.

Bibliography:
Bowden, Mary Weatherspoon. *Washington Irving*. Boston: Twayne, 1981. Good introduction to Irving's work. Bowden examines the first edition of "The Legend of Sleepy Hollow" within the context of its place and importance in *The Sketch Book of Geoffrey Crayon, Gent.*
Hedges, William L. *Washington Irving: An American Study, 1802-1832*. Westport, Conn.: Greenwood Press, 1980. Hedges seeks to substantiate Irving's relevance as a writer, define his major contributions, and detail aspects of his intellectual environment. The work presents "The Legend of Sleepy Hollow" as proof that Irving was a pioneer in the renaissance of American prose fiction.
Roth, Martin. *Comedy and America: The Lost World of Washington Irving*. Port Washington, N.Y.: Kennikat Press, 1976. This study surveys Irving's American period of creativity, including "The Legend of Sleepy Hollow," demonstrating that his last experiment creates a comic vision of America.
Rubin-Dorsky, Jeffrey. *Adrift in the Old World: The Psychological Pilgrimage of Washington Irving*. Chicago: University of Chicago Press, 1988. Critical revisionist view of Irving and his work primarily seen in psychological terms. It dissects Irving's personal problems and political orientation as reflected in his writings, particularly in a substantive chapter discussing "The Legend of Sleepy Hollow."

Tuttleton, James W., ed. *Washington Irving: The Critical Reaction.* New York: AMS Press, 1993. Solid collection of sixteen essays that survey the breadth of Irving's work from early sketches to his final biographies. Two essays, Terence Martin's "Rip and Ichabod" and Daniel Hoffman's "The Legend of Sleepy Hollow," scrutinize the story in depth and view it as a unique creation.

THE LEOPARD

Type of work: Novel
Author: Giuseppe Tomasi di Lampedusa (1896-1957)
Type of plot: Historical
Time of plot: 1860-1910
Locale: Sicily
First published: Il gattopardo, 1958 (English translation, 1960)

Principal characters:

DON FABRIZIO CORBERA, the prince of Salina
TANCREDI FALCONERI, his nephew and ward, an opportunist
PRINCESS MARIA STELLA, Don Fabrizio's wife
PAOLO,
FRANCESCO PAOLO,
CAROLINA,
CONCETTA, and
CATERINA, five of their seven children
DON CALOGERO SEDÀRA, a provincial mayor
ANGELICA, his daughter
COUNT CARLO CAVRIAGHI, Concetta's suitor
FATHER PIRRONE, a chaplain in the Salina household
THE CAVALIERE AIMONE CHEVALLEY DI MONTERZUOLO, a Piedmontese
    politician

The Story:

In 1860, Sicily, a land reduced to political apathy by centuries of conquest and foreign rule, was being invaded by Giuseppe Garibaldi's red-shirted volunteers. Don Fabrizio, prince of the ancient feudal house of Salina, waited to see whether Garibaldi was only another upstart adventurer or a patriot dedicated to the unification of Italy under *il galantuomo*, the Piedmontese king Victor Emmanuel. A tawny-haired man of passive disposition, great physical energy in the hunting field, strong sensual appetites, and some reputation as an amateur astronomer, the prince ruled his family and the peasants on his estates with unconscious arrogance. Although his allegiance was to King Francis II, his common sense told him that the Bourbon regime in Naples was tottering and would soon fall. At the same time, he was too shrewd and worldly-wise to expect that the Risorgimento would greatly transform a way of life that had been molded by Byzantine tax collectors, Berber emirs, Spanish viceroys, the Church, and the Bourbons. Faced with the necessity of choosing a side, he hesitated and, in the end, did nothing. For him, while all Italy was being shaken, life went on very much as before. He ignored his pious wife, disliked his heir, kept a mistress close at hand for his bodily needs and a browbeaten chaplain for his soul's salvation, and watched the stars.

The only person for whom he had any real affection was his penniless, scapegrace nephew Tancredi, Prince of Falconeri, in whom he found a reflection of his own restless youth. Ironically, his fondness for the boy turned out to be his salvation. When Tancredi went off to join Garibaldi in the hills, Don Fabrizio gave him a roll of gold pieces. This act of love and family feeling had political consequences, for when the Garibaldists triumphed, Don Fabrizio found himself regarded as a supporter of the cause.

As for Tancredi, he bobbed like a cork on the wave of the future. His philosophy, as he explained it to his uncle, was simple: If they were not with the cause, the rebels would form a republic, and if they did not want change, the rebels would make changes. He fought with Garibaldi in the hills, took a commission in the Piedmontese army before Garibaldi and his ragged followers were defeated by *il galantuomo*'s troops at Aspromonti, and, to recoup his family fortunes, courted and married the beautiful daughter of a rich, vulgar provincial upstart.

Don Fabrizio met the future three times. The first time was in the person of Don Calogero Sedàra, the mayor of Donnafugata, who in the time of the Risorgimento bought, traded, and sold so shrewdly that before long his revenues almost matched those of the Salina estates. The second occasion was the time of the plebiscite for unification. Don Fabrizio, knowing that there could be no return to the old ways, advised those who asked his opinion to vote Yes. Secretly he knew that a number had voted against unification, but when the votes were counted in Donnafugata, out of 515 who voted, 512 voted Yes. The wily mayor had stuffed the ballot box. The third time was again in the person of Don Calogero when Don Fabrizio had to eat his pride and go to the town hall formally to ask the mayor for the hand of his daughter Angelica in the name of his nephew, Tancredi Falconeri. In earlier times, the Salinas had exercised *droit de seigneur* over handsome girls like Angelica; in the new Italy, spendthrift young noblemen tried to marry them. He was made no happier by the knowledge that his daughter Concetta also loved Tancredi and had now lost him to the daughter of a grasping, ambitious peasant father and a mother who had once tended pigs.

When the Cavaliere Aimone Chevalley di Monterzuolo asked Don Fabrizio to accept a post as senator in the new kingdom, the prince, being what he was, felt this to be no particular honor and pretended not to understand whether or not being senator was a title of honor or a decoration. Chevalley was sincerely disturbed, whereupon the prince undertook to explain his attitude, the one occasion Don Fabrizio allowed himself to speak openly and bitterly about the history of Sicily and the character of Sicilians, who never want to improve because they think themselves already perfect and whose vanity was greater than their misery. He explained that he was caught between the old world and the new and felt ill at ease in both. Moreover, he was without illusions and lacked the talent for self-deception, a necessary quality for guiding others. He was unable to blend personal interest with vague public aims and ideals. Don Fabrizio ended his remarkable discourse on time, mutability, and knowledge of tragic destiny enclosed in the ambiguities of the past by suggesting that Don Calogero Sedàra, a man for the future, be named to the new senate.

In 1888, Don Fabrizio died, the survivor of a way of life that was feudal and despotic but in many ways fruitful and good; he had lived to see the new class of money and bourgeois power exercising its authority with brutal realism.

By 1910, Tancredi was dead and Angelica a dashing widow. Don Fabrizio's spinster daughters, Carolina, Concetta, and Caterina, lived in pious seclusion amid religious relics and souvenirs of the past. Concetta realized too late that she had lost Tancredi to Angelica because of her own pride and folly, and that it had been a futile love that had caused her to reject Tancredi's friend Count Carlo Cavriaghi when he wooed her. In a final gesture, she threw out on a rubbish heap the moth-eaten pelt of Bendico, her father's favorite dog. As it fell from the open window into the courtyard, it assumed for a moment the appearance of a dancing quadruped with long whiskers and one foreleg raised as if in imprecation—a ghastly travesty of the Salina crest.

Critical Evaluation:
The fundamental theme of Giuseppe Tomasi di Lampedusa's *The Leopard* is death—the

death of a civilization, of an era, and, eventually, of the hero of the novel. From the novel's opening line, taken from the traditional "Ave Maria" prayer, the narrative moves through a series of passages that describe various declines. The novel's first scene begins with *Nunc et in hora mortis nostrae* (Now and in the hour of our death) and takes place in the hero's palace near Palermo. The drawing room's decor, a mélange of rococo style and Roman mythology, offers an odd backdrop for a Christian service, but the contradictions inherent in this scene set the tone for the narrative's basic themes.

The novel's story encompasses some twenty-eight years in the lives of Sicily, the new united Italy, and Prince Don Fabrizio Corbera, who is a transitional figure himself, a symbol of the old order's reaction to the new world.

Don Fabrizio, like Sicily and Italy, is a tangle of paradoxes. He is proud, conscious of his aristocratic heritage, a cultivated, sensitive, and sensuous man who regrets seeing the past give way to the future. At the same time, he realizes that change and death are inevitable and inescapable; if he is unable to summon great enthusiasm for the new Italy, he nevertheless accepts the transformations that are taking place in the country, in his family, and in himself as he ages.

Don Fabrizio finds comfort in his sons, in his nephew Tancredi, and in the stars. As an amateur astronomer, Don Fabrizio has gained a certain amount of notoriety; moreover, his research satisfies his need for stability amid the flux he sees around him on earth. Beyond his interest in his sons, nephew, and the stars, he finds little of interest or fulfillment. His onetime passion for his wife—ironically named Maria Stella (Mary Star)—has long since faded into quiet affection and occasional mild contempt. Much of the novel, therefore, concerns how Don Fabrizio reacts to the changes in Sicily and the ways in which Tancredi adapts to the new society and its conditions.

Early in the novel's first chapter, there appears a symbol that establishes the tone of what is taking place in Sicily and foreshadows some of the tragedy that befalls Don Fabrizio. He and his villa caretakers discover the body of a young soldier, wounded in a skirmish with Garibaldi's rebels, in a grove of trees on Don Fabrizio's estate. In its state of ugly decomposition, the corpse brings home the cruel reality of war as well as the unpleasant death of the old Bourbon monarchy for which the soldier died.

The image of the dead soldier reappears, directly or somewhat transformed, later in the novel. Don Fabrizio recalls the corpse when his tenant farmers present him with some newly slaughtered lambs; when he is hunting, he sees the lacerated corpse of a rabbit, which inspires him to ponder the similar futility of human life and death; near the end of the story, Don Fabrizio's obsession with the dead soldier's body resurfaces as he thinks about his son Paolo's fatal equestrian accident, his own forthcoming death, and how everyone faces the same fate.

In a discussion with the Cavaliere Aimone Chevalley di Monterzuolo, a representative of the Piedmontese government of unification, Don Fabrizio declines to serve as a senator, citing Sicily's fundamental collective death wish. Instead, in a gesture of enlightened resignation, he recommends Don Calogero Sedàra, an ambitious provincial mayor of peasant stock, for the senate post.

To a great extent, *The Leopard* focuses on coming to terms with life and the disappointment it brings, and with death. For Don Fabrizio, there is considerable regret. In the novel's penultimate chapter, just before Don Fabrizio expires, he calculates that very little of his seventy-three years has been real living; most of it has been pain and boredom. His final moments contain a certain logic, however: Death appears to the sensuous prince as a beautiful woman whom he has long courted and with whom he has been long familiar. Death comes to

Don Fabrizio in the guise of his love of beauty and sensuality, but also as something and someone he has seen in the stars.

Ironically, some of Don Fabrizio's fondest memories are of Tancredi, the nephew who, by marrying Angelica Sedàra, has compromised with modern Italy. Tancredi (ironically named for a legendary hero of the Crusades) understands that the old order is passing and that survival is better than complete extinction. His marriage is of the kind familiar to European aristocracy since the Renaissance, when hereditary nobility began to see the necessity of union with the more prosperous emerging middle classes. Tancredi's marriage, like that of his uncle, begins in passion, but also in Tancredi's consciousness of the need to accept the fact that the bourgeoisie and the people inevitably will have roles in modern society. The former two Sicilies will be united as one with the new Italian monarchy; Don Fabrizio understands that he is the last of his line and that Garibaldi and those like him—the new revolutionaries—have won the struggle for change.

The Leopard's last chapter is a lugubrious epilogue, a coda that takes place in 1910, twenty-two years after the death of the novel's hero. The focus of this chapter is demythologization on two levels: First, many of the Christian relics that Don Fabrizio's daughters have collected in the family chapel are judged by the Church to be profane. Then, in the novel's final image, one of the daughters at last throws the mummified Bendico, what is left of the prince's faithful dog, on the trash heap. Thus the image of the Leopard, the symbol of the Salina line, disintegrates into the pitiful bits of what was Bendico, whose final gesture, as the carcass flies from a villa window, is a curse.

"Critical Evaluation" by Gordon Walters

Bibliography:

Butcher, Danny. Review of *The Leopard*, by Giuseppe Tomasi di Lampedusa. *The Chicago Sunday Tribune*, May 1, 1960, p. 1. A sensitive review, humanistic in scope, focusing on characters and scene instead of careful literary analysis.

Forster, E. M. Review of *The Leopard*, by Giuseppe Tomasi di Lampedusa. *The Spectator*, May 13, 1960, p. 702. A review by one of the masters of twentieth century fiction. Forster considers the Archibal Colquohon translation of the novel, and, like other critics, finds the translation somewhat lacking.

Hollander, John. "Plain and Fancy: Notes on Four Novels." *The Yale Review* 50, no. 1 (September, 1960): 149-156. Calls attention to *The Leopard*'s stature as a *Bildungsroman*, a poetic novel similar to the work of Jean Giraudoux, and a monument of European literature.

Pritchett, V. S. "A Sicilian Novel." *The New Statesman* 59, no. 1522 (May 14, 1960): 721-722. High praise of Lampedusa's lyricism; contrasts the obvious similarity with Stendhal, noting that Lampedusa's style lacks the coldness of the French writer.

Slonim, Marc. Review of *The Leopard*, by Giuseppe Tomasi di Lampedusa. *The New York Times Book Review*, May 1, 1960, 1, p. 24. Places *The Leopard* in its historical and literary context, and deals with some of the novel's primary symbols.

LET US NOW PRAISE FAMOUS MEN

Type of work: Journalism
Author: James Agee (1909-1955); Walker Evans (1903-   ), photographer
First published: 1941

In 1936, James Agee, a writer, and Walker Evans, a photographer on leave from the Farm Security Administration, were commissioned by the staff of a magazine to do an article on cotton tenantry that would be a photographic and verbal record of the daily lives of the average white sharecropper. As the two men carried out their assignment, they found it developing into a much larger project than that originally conceived. Ultimately, they were forced to return to their jobs much sooner than they wished and the work that they had done and assembled was refused publication by those who had commissioned it. Eventually it found publication on condition that certain words be deleted that were illegal in Massachusetts. By that time, 1941, Agee and Evans envisioned *Let Us Now Praise Famous Men*, complete in itself, as part of a larger whole to be called *Three Tenant Families*. The other part was never done. In its present form the book consists of sixty-two photographs followed by a lengthy text, partly factual, partly imaginative, all extremely detailed. A narrative of fact, a regional study, a moving moral document, a lyric meditation on life and art, an exercise in style, it is one of the most remarkable books of the century.

First, as in a play script, the members of the three families are listed, their ages, relationships, and their farms. In this list Agee casts himself as a spy, traveling as a journalist, and Evans as a counterspy, traveling as a photographer. Listed also are William Blake, Louis-Ferdinand Céline, Ring Lardner, Jesus Christ, and Sigmund Freud, as unpaid agitators.

Many critics considered the book a structural failure. It has no apparent pattern of development. Agee begins by explaining that the project was corrupt, obscene, terrifying, and mysterious. He realized painfully that he was spying into the private misery of these people, that their lives would thus be exposed as passing entertainment to the curious and casual reader, and that he was being paid for doing this. Determined to show the sacredness and dignity of each life down to the smallest detail, he approached his subjects with boundless love and humility.

He records three incidents, called "Late Sunday Morning," "At the Forks," and "Near a Church," so moving to him as to render him almost inarticulate at the time of the event, but about which he writes simply and vividly. In the first, a white foreman intrudes into the black community and forces three African Americans to sing for Agee and Evans. At the forks, Agee asks directions of a sick young man, his worn wife, and a mentally retarded older man. Near a church which Evans wished to enter in order to take photographs, Agee frightened a young black couple by running up behind them. In each case he empathized so strongly with each individual that he felt sympathy and understanding for the foreman even though he humiliated the black singers; he felt sick with joy and gratitude when the wife at the forks showed sufficient confidence in him to smile slightly; he felt the fear of the young couple and the utter impossibility of ever communicating clearly to them his intentions.

A Country Letter, which begins part 1, and which Agee wrote while sitting up late at night, contains some of the most beautiful lyric prose of the entire book. It is unified, developed, and complete in itself. Agee speaks of his tenants specifically, but he places them and their flimsy homes against a backdrop of the earth and the universe so that they and their problems, their joys and sorrows, become representative of all; and the theme running through the piece is of aspirations and ideals dulled and lost, worn down by the hard necessities of living, of the flame of life that sinks down almost to an ember as they ask themselves how they were thus caught.

Parts 1 and 2 are primarily factual. The people are introduced and their complex family relationships are clarified. The order of their rising and getting breakfast are described in detail. Agee explains simply the attempts of the men to find other work during slack times on the farm and the kinds of jobs available to them. The chapter on money is an objective and devastating account of the tenant farmers' financial situation. The section on shelter is almost a hundred pages long. He details the setting of one tenant home, the surrounding fields, the spring, the garden, and the outbuildings, including the contour and quality of the soil, the angle of the path, the flavor of the water, the shape and size of the building, the boards and nails holding them together, and the odds and ends found inside them. Systematically he examines, as with a microscope, the house itself, its outside structure and materials, the space underneath the house including the dampness, insects living there, the odors; then, inside, the front bedroom, where he slept, the rear bedroom, where the family slept, the kitchen and storeroom, and the space beneath the roof. For each room he describes the walls, floor, placement of furniture, the furniture itself and the contents of each drawer down to bits of dust, the items on the furniture and pinned to the walls, the insects inhabiting the bed, the wasps in the beams of the roof, the textures and odors, and the imagined hopes and feelings of the people whose home it is. His description of the house is of a living thing, flimsy and inadequate, but alive and placed, like the people, against the curve of the earth and sky. He describes the homes of the other two families also, but chiefly to point out their differences from the first. The final part of this section is devoted to the life present other than human: the dogs, cats, cows, mules, pigs, snakes, insects, birds, and trees. These lives too are described with respect and consideration, with humor, and with an appreciation of the beauty to be found in them.

Part 2 is devoted to sections on clothing, education, and work. Agee lists the items of clothing worn by the men and women on Sundays, Saturdays, and workdays. He describes in particular detail a suit of overalls and the shirt worn with them, their cut, pockets, stitching, straps, color, and texture when new, when partly worn out, and when completely worn out, differentiating carefully between the three stages; and again he makes the clothes almost alive, an outer skin, part of the man who wears them.

The section on education, termed brilliant by some critics, is an angry analysis of the failure of schools and teachers not only in the South but everywhere to educate the young properly, and of society's forcing on them work which has no bearing on their lives and values which are meaningless and harmful.

In "Work" Agee gives a step-by-step description of the raising of cotton, from the preparation of the soil through the sowing, cultivating, and harvesting of the crop. This work is extremely laborious and is done with primitive, inadequate tools. The entire family participates in the labor and in the anxious waiting for harvest, which will determine the meager incomes of the sharecroppers. The next part of the book, called "Intermission," is illustrative of the confused structure of the book. It deals with a questionnaire sent to writers by *The Partisan Review* and Agee's answer to it.

Part 3, "Inductions," goes back in point of time to the first meetings between Agee and Evans and the three families involved in their work. In particular, the section describes Agee's first night in the Gudgers' home, how he came to be there, what they said and ate, and how they all reacted to the situation.

From that point on the book consists of short pieces: descriptions of a graveyard, of Squinchy Gudger and his mother, of Ellen Woods; a poem, the first line of which gives the book its title;

and a section entitled "Notes and Appendices" containing various notes, chiefly on American photographer Margaret Bourke-White, and a listing of Anglo-Saxon monosyllables.

The concluding piece describes a call, possibly of a small furbearing animal, probably a fox, heard one night from the Gudgers' front porch. The call was answered by another animal, and as the two continued to call back and forth Agee and his friend speculated on the animals and their locations. Finally, within himself, Agee experienced the joy of hearing the world talk, of nature talking, as well as the grief that comes from the inability to communicate.

The faults of the book arise from its very virtues: Agee's love and compassion for people result not only in vivid, lyric prose but also in verbosity and repetition. When it first appeared, some critics thought Agee's prose arrogant, mannered, precious, nonsensical; others found it confused and adolescent. Obsessed though the author was with his own complex reactions to his subjects and the rest of the world, and his failure to convey all that he felt, he nevertheless gave a picture of himself and of the tenants and their lives in a way that is vivid and overwhelming. At times the writer's sensibility would be almost unbearable if it were not of a high moral order. *Let Us Now Praise Famous Men* breaks through the limits of reality to convey meanings and insights that are rich and strange. Its personal revelations are of great moral significance.

Bibliography:

Chesnick, Eugene. "The Plot Against Fiction: *Let Us Now Praise Famous Men*." *Southern Literary Journal* 4 (1971): 48-67. Examines the relationship between art and life in Agee's work and Agee's uncertainty about the falsifying effects which his writing inevitably forced on his subjects.

Holder, Alan. "Encounter in Alabama: Agee and the Tenant Farmer." *Virginia Quarterly Review* 42 (1966): 189-206. Examines the antibook that Agee produced out of his desire to accurately portray his subjects. Agee's sensitivity to the plight of the tenant farmer sometimes led him to sneer at his readers—and at himself as well.

Seib, Kenneth. *James Agee: Promise and Fulfillment*. Pittsburgh: University of Pittsburgh Press, 1968. The third chapter, "The Failure of Reality," notes the linguistic power and epic scale of Agee's essays. Views the work in the tradition of literary social protest and analyzes its structure.

Tindall, George Brown. "The Lost World of Agee's *Let Us Now Praise Famous Men*." In *James Agee: Reconsiderations*, edited by Michael A. Lofaro. Knoxville: University of Tennessee Press, 1992. Examines the literary and sociological interest of the 1930's in the Southern rural poor, a trend which fostered Agee's work.

Wagner-Martin, Linda. "*Let Us Now Praise Famous Men*—and Women: Agee's Absorption in the Sexual." In *James Agee: Reconsiderations*, edited by Michael A. Lofaro. Knoxville: University of Tennessee Press, 1992. Views the emphasis Agee placed on the Gudger women and his awareness of their sexuality as well as his own role as voyeur.

LETTERS FROM AN AMERICAN FARMER

Type of work: Essays
Author: J. Hector St. John (Michel-Guillaume-Jean de Crèvecœur, 1735-1813)
First published: 1782

When, in 1759, Voltaire published his *Candide*, Crèvecœur was already planning to cultivate his garden, hewn out of the Pennsylvania frontier. Like Voltaire's naïve hero, he had seen too much of the horrors of the civilized world and was more than ready to retire to his bucolic paradise, where for nineteen years he lived in peace and happiness until the civilized world intruded upon him and his family with the outbreak of the American Revolution. The twelve essays that make up his *Letters from an American Farmer* are, ostensibly at least, the product of a hand unfamiliar with the pen. The opening letter presents the central theme quite clearly: The decadence of European civilization makes the American frontier one of the great hopes for a regeneration of humanity. Crèvecœur wonders why people travel to Italy to "amuse themselves in viewing the ruins of temples . . . half-ruined amphitheatres and the putrid fevers of the Campania must fill the mind with most melancholy reflections." By contrast, Crèvecœur delights in the humble rudiments of societies spreading everywhere in the colonies, people converting large forests into pleasing fields and creating thirteen provinces of easy subsistence and political harmony. He has his interlocutor say of him, "Your mind is . . . a Tabula rasa where spontaneous and strong impressions are delineated with felicity." Similarly, he sees the American continent as a clean slate on which people can inscribe a new society and the good life. It may be said that Crèvecœur is a Lockean gone romantic, but retaining just enough practical good sense to see that reality is not rosy. The book is the crude, occasionally eloquent, testimony of a man trying desperately to convince himself and his readers that it was possible to live the idealized life advocated by Jean-Jacques Rousseau.

With a becoming modesty, appropriate to a man who had learned English at sixteen, Crèvecœur begins with a confession of his literary inadequacy and decides simply to write down what he would say. His style, however, is not smoothly colloquial. Except in a few passages, in which conviction generates enthusiasm, one senses the strain of the unlettered man writing with feeling but not cunning.

The first image Crèvecœur presents is perhaps a bit too idyllic for modern taste. He dandles his little boy on the plow as his wife sits at the edge of the field knitting and praising the straightness of the furrows, while birds fill the air with summer melodies. "Who can listen unmoved to the sweet love tales of our robins told from tree to tree?" This is, nevertheless, the testimony of a man who for nineteen years actually lived at the edge of the wilderness, three hundred miles from the Atlantic. He was no Henry David Thoreau at Walden Pond, within easy walking distance of friends, family, and a highly developed New England culture at Concord. He was, instead, a responsible man, who cleared 371 acres of virgin land and raised enough crops and animals to provide for his family, black workers, and all peaceful strangers who chanced to appear at his door. Also unlike Thoreau (with whom he inevitably invites comparison), Crèvecœur was acutely aware of his social responsibilities and enormously proud of the way in that they could be fulfilled in the new world. It was the third epistle, "What Is an American?" that caught the attention of Benjamin Franklin and the Europeans of the Age of Enlightenment:

[America] is not composed, as in Europe, of great lords who possess everything, and of a herd of people who have nothing. Here are no aristocratical families, no courts, no kings, no bishops, no ecclesiastical dominion, no invisible power giving to a few a very visible one; no great manufacturers employing thousands, no great refinements of luxury. The rich and the poor are not so far removed from each other as they are in Europe. . . . We are the most perfect society now existing in the world.

Enthusiastic as this description is, it is not as extravagant as it might seem; Crèvecœur does not claim that the Colonies had founded the best of all possible worlds. He is, for example, acutely aware that religious influence gradually declines as one goes west, and that, instead of liberating, this decline reduces humanity to a perfect state of war, each against each. Yet Crèvecœur rejoices that there are almost no concentrated religious sects preying upon each other: "Zeal in Europe is confined . . . a grain of powder enclosed; here it burns away in the open air, and consumes without effect."

Furthermore, not every man succeeds after arriving in the New World—only the sober, the honest, the industrious. In his "History of Andrew, the Hebridean," Crèvecœur presents a case history of the Horatio Alger hero in primitive America, the story of a simple illiterate Scot who, after four years of sweat and toil became a prospering freeholder. Franklin had occasion to caution his friends in France that Crèvecœur's was a highly colored account.

Part of the coloring is contributed by the pervasive nature imagery. The freedom and beauty of birds seem to symbolize the condition Europeans might achieve when immersing themselves in nature. Crèvecœur describes hours spent in quiet admiration of the hummingbirds, tells regretfully of shooting a kingbird to rescue bees, describes the feeding and care of quail in the winter. Insects, too, fascinated him; he kept a hornet's nest in the house. The letter on rattlers and copperheads is horrendous and awesome. Crèvecœur tells of copperheads enticing birds by the power of their eyes, of a defanged rattler trained as a pet, of a pair of snakes in mortal combat. Most curious of all is the account of a farmer who kicked away a snake that had thrust its fangs into his boot. After pulling off his boots that night, he suddenly became violently ill, writhed horribly, and died. His son, inheriting the boots, suffered the same fate. A neighbor, next in succession, almost died, too, but was saved when a shrewd doctor located the poison-filled fangs stuck in the boot. Crèvecœur in these passages reveals an exciting narrative power.

Apart from the agricultural life inland, Crèvecœur praises most the industry and sobriety of the coastal fishing communities at Nantucket and Martha's Vineyard, where "perfect equanimity prevails." At Nantucket, five thousand prosperous people inhabited a place which in Europe would have housed a few simple fishermen. Their Yankee ingenuity and sound business sense had enabled them to build—beginning with one whale boat—a whaling fleet that ranged even to the South Seas. Martha's Vineyard was already the "nursery" of seamen for the entire East Coast. So detailed is Crèvecœur's description of the chase, the ferocity of the whale's struggle, the dangers from sharks and thrasher whales, the processing of blubber into whale oil—in short, the entire experience—that one wonders how Herman Melville could have overlooked it in compiling the extracts in *Moby Dick* (1851).

Crèvecœur found Nantucket a model community in that it contained only one minister (a Presbyterian—the Quakers, much to Crèvecœur's delight, do not have special ministers), two doctors, one lawyer (seldom employed), no soldiers, and no governors. "Happy the people who are subject to so mild a government; happy the government which has to rule over such harmless and such industrious subjects! . . . I wish I had it in my power to send the most persecuting bigot I could find in ―― to the whale fisheries; in three or four years you would find him a much more tractable man and therefore a better Christian." Colonial Nantucket was apparently not perfect; the Quakers persisted in their ungrammatical English, did not tolerate any deviation from their sober customs and homespun dress, sternly prohibited music, singing, and dancing. "Such an island . . . is not the place where gay travellers should resort in order to enjoy the variety of pleasures the more splendid towns of this continent afford." Crèvecœur also reports, obviously misled by some notorious gossip, that the women were addicted to opium. "But," he philosophizes, "where is the society perfectly free from error and folly?"

Crèvecœur's criticism is reserved for the most European of American cities, which he called Charles-Town, "gayest in America . . . centre of our beau monde." Lawyers, planters, and merchants make up the population, all addicted to dangerous excesses of all kinds. At the heart of this social corruption, Crèvecœur finds the brutal institution of slavery. He tells the horrifying tale of his chance encounter with a slave who had been driven to kill an overseer. The slave's punishment was to be suspended from a tree in a cage for two days. Vicious birds had already plucked out his eyes and bared his cheekbones. No sooner were the birds dispersed than swarms of insects covered him. The miserable man begged for water and hoped it was poisoned. "Gracious God!" cries Crèvecœur, "to what end is the introduction of so many beings into [such] a mode of existence! . . . Is there then no superintending power who conducts the moral operations of the world?"

Some of Crèvecœur's faith is restored by the spectacle of the humble, kind, and generous aspect of William Bartram, a Quaker botanist, who employed black men as salaried, free men, workers on his plantation, companions at his table, and worshipers at the Friends' meeting-house.

Letters from an American Farmer ends in ominous tones of impending tragedy. Unwilling to commit his allegiance to either the British or the colonists, Crèvecœur finds it necessary to flee: "Must I in order to be called a faithful subject, coolly and philosophically say it is necessary for the good of Britain that my children's brains should be dashed against the walls of the house in which they were reared; that my wife should be stabbed and scalped before my face; that I should be either murdered or captivated?" To escape such a fate, Crèvecœur develops an intricate plan to take his family to join an American Indian settlement in the uncultivated wilderness (a plan which he never actually carried out). It is tragically ironic that this mild Frenchman's absolute certainty of the blessings of life in the colonies should be so violently shattered after nineteen years of expending all his energies to make a decent life possible. It is appropriate that his final impulse is to immerse himself deeper into nature by joining the Indians. Whatever flaws it may have, *Letters from an American Farmer* is the most sympathetic and thoughtful of all eighteenth century analyses of frontier life and its shaping influence on the emerging American character.

Bibliography:

Arch, Stephen Carl. "The 'Progressive Steps' of the Narrator in Crèvecœur's *Letters from an American Farmer*." *Studies in American Fiction* 18 (Autumn, 1990): 145-158. Separates Crèvecœur from the character of James and traces James's progression through the work as closely related to the "epistolary form" and the "dialogic structure." James is not the main character in an American Dream, but a character threatened by the dangers of revolution.

Grabo, Norman S. "Crèvecœur's American: Beginning the World Anew." *The William and Mary Quarterly: A Magazine of Early American History and Culture* 48, no. 2 (1991): 159-172. Identifies the biographical, political, and cultural contexts of the work and argues that the seeming discontinuity of the letters reflects Crèvecœur's recognition of the variety and diversity of America.

Philbrick, Thomas. *St. John de Crèvecœur*. Boston: Twayne, 1970. A general and comprehensive introduction to Crèvecœur's life and work, including two major sections on *Letters from an American Farmer*. Argues for Crèvecœur's "complex artistry."

Winston, Robert P. "'Strange Order of Things!' The Journey to Chaos in *Letters from an American Farmer*." *Early American Literature* 19, no. 3 (Winter, 1984/1985): 249-267. Examines the structure of *Letters from an American Farmer* and finds elements of romance that anticipate James Fenimore Cooper, Nathaniel Hawthorne, and Herman Melville. Crèvecœur identifies an idyllic world and a demoniac one and struggles to find a compromise between the two.

Ziff, Larzer. *Writing in the New Nation: Prose, Print, and Politics in the Early United States.* New Haven, Conn.: Yale University Press, 1991. Chapter 2 explores Crèvecœur's life, the epistolary nature of the *Letters from an American Farmer*, and Crèvecœur's attempts to find a middle ground between the old and the new cultures.

LETTERS FROM THE UNDERWORLD

Type of work: Novel
Author: Fyodor Dostoevski (1821-1881)
Type of plot: Impressionistic realism
Time of plot: Mid-nineteenth century
Locale: St. Petersburg, Russia
First published: Zapiski iz podpolya, 1864 (English translation, 1913)

> *Principal characters:*
> THE NARRATOR
> SIMONOV, his acquaintance from school days
> ZVERKOV, a young Russian officer
> LIZA, a prostitute

The Story:

The narrator, addressing an imaginary group of acquaintances, declared that after many years of life as a rude and spiteful government official, and after many years as a recluse, he was not really bitter in his heart. Something perverse in him, his acute consciousness, had led him to find pleasure in the pain of humiliating experiences. From experience, he advised against intellectual acuteness. The intellectual, when faced with revenge, surrounds himself with a legion of doubts; then he would crawl into his self-imposed rat's nest and torture himself with petty spite. The direct man, in wreaking revenge, might with dispatch hit his head against a wall, but he would accept the wall. The intellectual, however, would not accept the wall. Indeed, he would feel responsibility for the presence of the wall. The narrator declared that he had always had to feign taking offense and that he had had, in the face of life's transiency, to pretend to love. Life to him was a colossal bore. He could never avenge wrongs done him because the culprit, the culprit's motives, and the very misdeed itself were all subject to overanalysis in his doubting intellect.

Given another chance at life, he would have chosen a career of complete laziness, one in which he might have reveled among good and beautiful things. He declared that even if a man were to know absolutely what things in life were to his best advantage, he would perversely avoid these things. The narrator advanced the idea that people may be destined for creativeness, and for this reason, conscious of their fate, they perversely practiced destruction to individuate themselves. Perhaps people were fearful of completion, of perfection; perhaps they found final attainment distasteful: Life consisted in the attaining, not in the attainment. The narrator concluded his philosophical soliloquy by pointing out that conscious inertia was the ideal state. He provocatively insisted that he did not believe a word he had written, that he had written only because the written word seemed imposing and dignified. He was oppressed by memories that were evoked by the fall of snow outside.

At the age of twenty-four, the narrator had an inchoate character. He talked to no one. His intense self-consciousness caused him to be vain at one moment and self-loathing the next. He tried to look intelligent and feared any eccentricity in himself. This acute awareness of self made him lonely, yet he felt superior to others. He became a recluse. He read voraciously and began to walk the streets at night.

One night he saw a man thrown out of the window of a billiard parlor. In envy, he went into the parlor in the hope that he, too, might be thrown out. He was humiliated when an officer shoved him aside without noticing him. He returned the next night, but, morally fearful that all the fools in the parlor would jeer at his being thrown out, he did not enter. Dedicated to revenge, he followed the officer about for months. He learned the officer's name and wrote a satirical novel in which the officer was the principal character. The novel was rejected; its style was out of date.

Two years passed. He wrote a letter challenging the officer to a duel, but he did not mail the letter. Instead, he began to take regular walks along the river promenade, where he reveled in his resentment. One Sunday he was rudely pushed aside by the officer. Maddened at his weakness, he conceived the idea of not giving way next time. He gloated over his idea. He practiced pushing aside an imaginary officer. His courage had failed him once, but he finally stood his ground when the officer tried again to push him aside. Actually, the officer did not notice him at all, but he was delirious with happiness in having gained back his self-respect.

The narrator began to daydream. In his fantasies, he brought beauty and good to the world. During the fever pitch of his dream life, feeling the need of companionship, he visited his immediate superior, Anton, and sat in silence with Anton's family for hours.

He called on an old schoolmate, Simonov, and found Simonov planning, with two other old schoolmates, a farewell dinner for Zverkov, a fellow student of the direct, not too acutely conscious type, whom he hated. Zverkov, a wealthy man, was successful in the army. The narrator, greeted coldly by his boyhood acquaintances, invited himself to the dinner party. The other young men agreed reluctantly; he was obviously not a favorite with them. Later the narrator detested himself for consciously having opened himself up to humiliation, but secretly he rather enjoyed having discomfited his companions.

The next day, as he dressed for the dinner, he felt doubt and misgiving. He wanted to make a great impression; he wanted to eclipse the popular Zverkov. Yet he knew that he really did not want to do this either. He arrived too early and was humiliated by his wait. During the dinner he antagonized everyone and drank incontinently. Having thoroughly degraded himself, he offered conciliation and sought the love of his companions. When he apologized to Zverkov for insulting him, Zverkov humiliated him by saying that such as he could not possibly insult him. Filled with a wild, unreasonable intention of slapping Zverkov and fighting a duel with him, he followed the others to a brothel.

A young girl was brought into the parlor to him; he was pleased with the prospect of being repulsive to her. He slept off his drunkenness, awoke, and delivered a bookish, insincere sermon to Liza, the prostitute, on the hazards of her profession. He was grandstanding, and he knew it to his shame. He told her of the importance of human love, something about which he actually knew nothing. Liza, to prove to him that she was not entirely lost, showed him a love letter that she had received from a young gentleman. He gave her his address and left her. The next day, he regretted having given Liza his address. He hated himself for his insincerity with her, and he feared her coming, but she did not come. He imagined an idyllic relationship between himself and Liza. He would be her tutor and would mold her into a perfect creature.

When Liza finally came, she was confused by the wretched conditions in the poor narrator's rooms. She said that she had left the brothel. Alarmed, he confessed his insincerity and declared that he had sought power over someone because he himself had been humiliated. Liza understood his inner turmoil and took him in her arms.

Liza's intuition soon told her, however, that he was despicable and that he was incapable of love. After she left his rooms, he ran after her to seek her forgiveness, but he never saw her again. He derived some consolation from the thought that her resentment of him would give her pleasure for the rest of her life.

Critical Evaluation:

In *Letters from the Underworld*, Fyodor Dostoevski creates a character—the "underground Man"—who is crucial not only to Dostoevski's own best fiction but also to the whole of nineteenth and twentieth century literature. Indeed, some critics even date the beginning of modern literature from the publication of this short novel and identify the underground man as the archetypal modern antihero. At the very least, *Letters from the Underworld* can be seen as the prologue to the five great novels that climaxed Dostoevski's career: *Crime and Punishment* (1866), *The Idiot* (1868-1869), *The Possessed* (1871-1872), *A Raw Youth* (1875), and *The Brothers Karamazov* (1879-1880).

On the other hand, however, it is sometimes denied that *Letters from the Underworld* is actually a novel at all: The first part is too fragmentary and incoherent, the second too short and arbitrary, and the relationship between them too unclear to allow it that formal designation. In fact, the form and style of *Letters from the Underworld* are as radical as its content and fuse perfectly into an organic, if unorthodox, work of art.

The first part (subtitled "Underground") presents the underground man's philosophy; the second part ("Apropos of Wet Snow") recounts a series of early experiences that explain the origins of that worldview, while suggesting a possible alternative to it. Without part 2, part 1 is little more than the bitter rantings of a semihysterical social misfit; without part 1, the second part is only the pathetic narrative of a petty, self-destructive neurotic; but, together, they combine into a powerful statement about the nature and situation of humanity in the nineteenth century and after.

In the first sentence of the book, the underground man states that he is sick but later defines that sickness as "acute consciousness"—a malady characteristic of the sensitive modern individual. This consciousness has made the narrator aware of the contradictions in his own behavior and the consequent impossibility of acting forcefully and meaningfully in his society. He feels superior to his fellows, yet knows he is incapable of dealing with them. He despises them, yet obsessively wants their acceptance and approval. He acts spitefully toward them yet feels personally insulted when they ignore or berate him. He asserts his need for dignity and then forces himself into situations that can only end in humiliation. The narrator is not the first Dostoevskian character to have such contradictory, self-defeating qualities, but he is the first to be aware of them and their sources and so he represents a significant development in the novelist's career.

Even the underground man's attitude toward his own pain and humiliation is ambivalent. He does not actually enjoy his sufferings, and yet he takes satisfaction in them because they make him conscious of himself and give him a feeling of power over his own actions. The narrator claims to admire the man of action, who does things and has experiences unfettered by the doubts, hesitations, and defeats that plague the narrator. He sees a profound contradiction, however, in the very notion of a man of action; although such a person acts, he does so not of his own volition but as the end result of a long cause-and-effect sequence. The man of action does not think, so his ability to act is not so laudable.

The basic reason for the underground man's rebellion is a reaction against the deterministic, scientific view of humanity that was prevalent in the late nineteenth century. If all human activity is regulated by environmental and hereditary factors, of which the individual is unconscious, then a person is reduced to the status of a piano key. The underground man denies that conception of himself, even while conceding that it is probably true.

This posture explains Dostoevski's apparently ambiguous attitude toward his fictional creation. While the author obviously despises the underground man's pettiness, nastiness, cruelty, vanity, and spite, he clearly admires the man, because the narrator possesses the one basic virtue: He asserts his freedom in the face of logic, self-interest, and nature itself; he insists on his "fatal fantastic element."

Dostoevski's real targets in writing *Letters from the Underworld* are the social theorists and human engineers who would rationally create the perfect society—symbolized by the "Crystal Palace"—in which human happiness and fulfillment would be "scientifically" designed and implemented. The underground man rejects this view of human nature. He insists on using his free choice to assert his individuality, but the actions he takes to demonstrate this freedom are, he admits, meaningless. Thus, the dilemma of the sensitive insightful modern man: If he accepts a logical, well-ordered, "scientific" society, he gains happiness, but he gives up free will; but, if he rejects such a rational society and insists on expressing his individuality, he can do so only with impulsive, arbitrary gestures that have neither real meaning nor lasting effect. Is there any way out of this apparent impasse?

Dostoevski suggests an answer, or at least an approach to one, in part 2, although the fact that the underground man is incapable of seizing upon it underscores the difficulty of the solution. Readers also come to understand how he became the way he is. The action takes place sixteen years earlier and shows his contradictory attitudes in practice. He alienates those he would cultivate, plots revenge against "enemies" who are unaware of his existence, and creates situations that guarantee the humiliations and frustrations he fears.

After a number of minor skirmishes, he gives his theories a final test in two important human activities—friendship and love. Having forced himself on some old school acquaintants, he gets drunk and nearly provokes them to violence. Then, his attempt at friendship a failure, the underground man pursues the role of lover. He follows the others to a brothel where he purchases the favors of a prostitute named Liza. Upon awakening the next morning, he berates her for her profession, describes her inevitable and appalling future, and urges her to change her life. She responds with contrition and deep emotion.

When she comes to him the next day, however, the underground man is in the midst of a vicious, demeaning argument with his manservant. Humiliated, he feels the need for revenge on her for witnessing his degradation. He realizes that it was a desire for power over another human being, not sincerity or compassion, that accounted for his moral strictures of the previous night. That power gone and his true pettiness revealed, he reacts brutally; she offers him love and he turns on her, rebukes her, mocks his earlier statements, and finally drives her off by paying for her services. Sensing his pain and desperation, however, she demonstrates her moral superiority in her response to his tirade. Thus, the underground man is denied even the satisfaction of bringing another human being down to his own level—a fact he realizes immediately after she leaves.

The underground man, therefore, is given a chance to escape from his self-imposed exile, and he rejects it, dooming himself to psychological fragmentation and social isolation. Had he been able to accept and respond to Liza's love, he might have transcended the narrow confines of his narcissistic world and become a whole, purposeful human being.

This last positive possibility, however, is a very muted one. *Letters from the Underworld* leaves the reader with feelings of depression and frustration. Although he espouses the saving capacities of spontaneous love, Dostoevski does not explicitly tie that love to the Christian vision which was to become central in his last great works. Thus, *Letters from the Underworld* remains Dostoevski's great transitional work, not only for his own writing but also for Western literature in general.

"Critical Evaluation" by Keith Neilson

Bibliography:

Holquist, Michael. *Dostoevsky and the Novel*. Princeton, N.J.: Princeton University Press, 1977. Detailed readings of several works, including *Letters from the Underworld*. An introductory text contains information on Dostoevski's Russia.

Jackson, Robert Louis. *The Art of Dostoevsky: Deliriums and Nocturnes*. Princeton, N.J.: Princeton University Press, 1981. An authority on Dostoevski examines the novels written in Dostoevski's last twenty years. Links the themes of these most important novels and considers *Letters from the Underworld*.

Jones, Malcolm V. *Dostoyevsky: The Novel of Discord*. London: Elek Books Limited, 1976. Gives an overview of the complexity, chaos, and discord that are to be expected in Dostoevski. Extended section on *Letters from the Underworld*, and concludes with extensive notes. A serious study of Dostoevski.

Leatherbarrow, William J. *Fedor Dostoevsky*. Boston: Twayne, 1981. Includes a biographical sketch and chronology of Dostoevski. Has commentary on *Letters from the Underworld* (also known as *Notes from Underground*) and his four major novels. Extended bibliography and an index.

Mackiewicz, Stanislaw. *Dostoyevsky*. Maryknoll, N.Y.: Orbis Books, 1947. Good companion to other, more critical evaluations of Dostoevski. Examines the women characters of the novels with relevance to the loves of Dostoevski's life.

LETTERS TO HIS SON

Type of work: Epistolary
Author: Lord Chesterfield (Philip Dormer Stanhope, 1694-1773)
First published: 1774

On the periphery of literature exists a valuable and fascinating genre, the personal letter. This, like the private diary, reveals an individual and an age far more intimately than any other form of writing. Probably no era practiced the epistolary art more widely than the eighteenth century and no man more skillfully than the fourth earl of Chesterfield. Although the earl had served his country unimpeachably as a member of Parliament, lord lieutenant of Ireland, and ambassador to Holland, and although his name came to designate an overcoat and a couch, it is generally conceded that Lord Chesterfield would have remained an inconspicuous figure in the eighteenth century historical scene had it not been for the unintended publication of some four hundred letters to his illegitimate son, Philip Stanhope. No doubt the very fact that these letters were private, intended to develop the education and manners of a young man who was expected to take a significant place in government and cultivated society, endows them with a frankness and honesty that betrays the cultivated self-seeking and the hypocritical morality of the upper-class society of the time. Eugenia Stanhope, whose secret marriage with young Philip was only one of the many disappointments Lord Chesterfield suffered at the hands of his intractable son, was so incensed at being excluded from the earl's will that, against the family's wishes, she sold the letters for L1,575, thus infuriating English society and securing for Lord Chesterfield minor but recognized importance in the history of English prose.

The early letters are charmingly didactic essays addressed to a preadolescent boy whom the writer hoped would become "not only the best scholar but the best bred boy in England of your age." "Dear boy," they all begin, and then proceed to shape little lessons on language, literature, geography, history, and good manners. They conclude with admonitions to obey his seventy-year-old tutor Maittaire and with promises of "very pretty things" to reward him for industrious study. There is irony in Lord Chesterfield's explanation of irony—"Suppose that I were to commend you for your great attention to your book, and for your retaining and remembering what you have once learned; would you not plainly perceive the irony, and see that I laughed at you?" Reasons for such laughter were to come, but it was never bitter or audible ("there is nothing so illiberal, and so ill-bred as audible laughter"). Lord Chesterfield's optimism and faith in rationalism may have diminished somewhat, but it was never extinguished completely. After his failure in making an outstanding figure of young Philip, he began the whole process over again in 1761 with his godson, to whom he wrote almost three hundred letters in one decade, published posthumously as *Letters to His Godson* (1890).

It is not the early letters to his son but the later ones—addressed to "My Dear Friend"—that have aroused controversy. A strong believer in John Locke's educational theory that a mind is wax to be molded into shape by environmental influences, Lord Chesterfield sent his son at the age of fourteen not to a university but on the grand tour accompanied by a new tutor, the Reverend Walter Harte. The boy was supplied with letters of introduction into the highest social circles of great European cities, and he was spied upon by the earl's agents and pursued by the affectionate but earnest epistles from an anxious father. How earnest they were can be gauged from this excerpt written to Lausanne in 1746: "I do not so much as hint to you how absolutely dependent you are on me; and that, as I have no womanish weakness for your person, your merit must and will be the only measure of my kindness." It would nevertheless be unfair to charge that even if the father had never displayed warmth, love, or understanding, his kindness far exceeded the boy's merit.

The controversy concerns Lord Chesterfield's realistic observations on those aspects of life that he constantly urges his son to explore:

> Search, therefore, with the greatest care, into the characters of those whom you converse with; endeavor to discover their predominant passions, their prevailing weaknesses, their vanities, their follies, and their humours, with all the right and wrong, wise and silly springs of human actions, which make such inconsistent and whimsical beings of us rational creatures. . . . This is the true knowledge of the world; and the world is a country which nobody ever yet knew by description; one must travel through it oneself to be acquainted with it.

Having traveled that country well himself, Lord Chesterfield could advise his son with cynical sophistication. A man who never knew love and who married for a dowry to repair his fortunes, he wrote: "Women are merely children of a larger growth. . . . A man of sense only trifles with them. . . . They will greedily swallow the highest [flattery], and gratefully accept the lowest . . . [but] They have, from the weakness of men, more or less influence in all courts. It is therefore necessary to manage, please and flatter them." It is this worldly self-interest that constitutes the dominant tone of the letters; as he declares, "without some dissimulation no business can be carried on at all." There was no trace of mysticism or sentimentality about him: "Religion must still be allowed to be a collateral security, at least, to Virtue." Yet virtue, apparently, was not an end in itself. Rather, it was a means to worldly success, a dependable means, if Lord Chesterfield's own career based on honesty and integrity is any measure. Worldly success was the goal, and though "learning, honour, and virtue are absolutely necessary to gain you the esteem and admiration of mankind, politeness and good breeding are equally necessary to make you welcome and agreeable in conversation and common life." Elsewhere, Lord Chesterfield urges his son to be neat and clean, to avoid obesity, to care for his teeth, and never under any circumstances to stick his finger into his nose. The ultimate purpose was that young Stanhope should become—at the very least—a successful diplomat; but the principal objective of that occupation was "to get into the secrets of the court at which he resides" through any means including flattery or intimacy with a king's or minister's mistresses.

On the Continent, publication of *Letters to His Son* was met with acclaim, their greatest admirer probably being Lord Chesterfield's old friend Voltaire: "I am not certain that it is not the best book on education which has ever been written." In England, however, the reaction was sternly condemnatory, even virulent. One periodical declared that as a man, he was "certainly solely actuated by pride, vanity, and ambition," and in her own letters Mrs. Montagu expressed her belief that "tho' many admired, no one ever esteem'd Lord Chesterfield."

Bibliography:
Franklin, Colin. *Lord Chesterfield: His Character and Characters.* Aldershot, England: Scolar Press, 1993. Presents Lord Chesterfield's other writings, pieces on contemporary people and events, which were never published or meant to be published. Includes commentary and annotations.
Shellabarger, Samuel. *Lord Chesterfield and His World.* 2d ed. Boston: Little, Brown, 1951. Emphasizes the intimate connection between Lord Chesterfield's conduct and teaching, and the rationalism of his time. Offers an enjoyable and illuminating picture of a life whose primary motivation was worldly ambition.

LEVIATHAN
Or, The Matter, Form, and Power of a Commonwealth
Ecclesiastical and Civil

Type of work: Politics
Author: Thomas Hobbes (1588-1679)
First published: 1651

In considering the "matter, form, and power" of the commonwealth, or state, Thomas Hobbes does far more than describe governments as he finds them. His goal is to explain the origin of political institutions and to define their powers and right limits. To this end he draws an analogy between the art of nature, which produces humanity, and the art of humanity, productive of the commonwealth. In drawing the analogy he first explains humanity, giving to the description a thoroughly mechanistic bias. He then proceeds to explain the state as humanity's artful creation, designed to put an end to the war of all against all.

The state, "that great Leviathan," is but an "Artificial Man," writes Hobbes. The sovereign is an artificial soul, the officers of the state are artificial joints, reward and punishment are nerves, wealth and riches are strength. The people's safety is the business of the artificial man; the laws are its reason and will; concord, its health; sedition, its sickness; and civil war, its death.

All human ideas originate in sense, according to Hobbes—that is, they are derived from sense impressions. All sensation is a result of external bodies pressing upon the sense organs. Imagination is "nothing but decaying sense," the effect of sense impressions after the external body has ceased to press upon the organs. If one wants to emphasize the past cause of the impression, one calls the fading image a "memory" image. If one wants to emphasize the image as one not now related to any present cause, one calls it "fancy" or "imagination."

Hobbes was led by his mechanistic psychology to deny content to such a term as "infinite." He argued that when one says something is infinite one merely shows that one cannot conceive its boundaries. Consequently, such a term as "God" is used not to conceive any being, but only to honor something incomprehensible.

Common names, such as "man," "horse," and "tree," may be applied to a number of individual things, yet there is nothing universal but names. In making this claim Hobbes was denying the Platonic belief that individual objects share a certain common character, or universal, in virtue of which they are similar. According to Hobbes, then, reasoning is simply the manipulation—the addition and subtraction—of names.

The passions are the "interior beginnings of voluntary motions," writes Hobbes. Given that Hobbes argues that everything can be understood in terms of bodies in motion, it is not surprising that even the emotions are, to him, simply motions inside the body. Motion toward something is desire; motion away, aversion. In terms of these two basic motions Hobbes defines the other passions.

After considering the intellectual virtues and defects, the two kinds of knowledge (knowledge of observed fact, and the conditional knowledge of science), and the powers and manners of people, Hobbes turns his analytical mind to religion. Religion, he writes, is a human invention, the result of ignorance and fear. Religious power and dogma are used to serve the interests of the priests. It is not surprising that, with these views, Hobbes was constantly in trouble at home and abroad, and was attacked from the pulpit for generations.

When Hobbes declares that people are by nature equal, he does so with no tone of ringing idealism. He means only that the differences among people are not so marked as the similarities, and he means also that there is no natural sanction for one person's assuming authority over another. People are similar, so they sometimes come to desire the same thing; and if they cannot both enjoy the object of their desire, they become enemies and war over the object. There are three principal causes of fights: competition, diffidence, and glory. While people have no common power over them to keep them all in check, they are in "that condition which is called Warre; and such a warre, as is of every man, against every man." There are many inconveniences to war, and the fact that in a state of war there is no injustice (since there is no natural law governing action) in no way makes that state of affairs satisfactory. In order to secure peace, people enter upon certain agreements by which the people bring about a transferring of rights. It is possible for people to make such agreements, or contracts, because they have certain natural rights to use their power however they choose in order to preserve themselves.

Having discussed people, their nature, and their rights, Hobbes argues, in the second part of *Leviathan*, that the commonwealth is brought into being in order to enable people to escape from the state of war. Loving liberty and dominion over others, humans agree to make some person sovereign over them all to work for their peace and benefit. The sovereign is not bound by the contract or covenant; the contract is among those who are to be ruled. If the ruler turns out to be a despot, it must be remembered that it is better to be ruled in a commonwealth than to be in a state of nature and, consequently, a continual state of war.

Hobbes considers three kinds of commonwealth: monarchy, democracy, and aristocracy, the latter being ruled by an assembly of part of the commonwealth. There are certain advantages to the monarchal form of government, according to Hobbes: A monarch combines the private and public interest. A monarch is better able to consult with those whose knowledge the monarch needs. The only inconstancy with which monarchs have to live is their own. Monarchs cannot disagree with themselves; and although it is sometimes inconvenient to have power vested in one person, particularly when the monarch may be an infant because of succession, the disadvantages are no greater than they are in other forms of government.

The subjects in a commonwealth are not entirely subject to the sovereign. The basic principle is that they cannot be compelled to act against that natural inclination toward self-preservation which the commonwealth is supposed to serve. They cannot be bound to injure themselves or to wage war—although this is a dubious right since the sovereign is free to imprison or execute them for disobedience. If the sovereign is not able to protect the sovereign's subjects, the subjects are absolved of obedience to the sovereign.

The civil law of a commonwealth is made up of all those rules that prescribe what is right and wrong for the subjects; since the commonwealth itself is no lawmaker, the sovereign must be the legislator. The sovereign is not subject to civil law, and only the sovereign can abrogate the law. Since an undeclared law is no law at all, and since law is not binding unless it is clearly commanded by the sovereign, the sovereign must make the law known and understood, and the sovereign must see to it that it be known as the law. The only laws that need not be published are laws of nature, and they can be contained in one sentence: "Do not that to another, which thou thinkest unreasonable to be done by another to thy selfe."

Hobbes regarded crime as resulting from some defect of the understanding, or from some error of reasoning, or from some force of the passions. He declares that "No law, made after a Fact done, can make it a Crime," and that although ignorance of natural law is no excuse, ignorance of civil law may excuse one provided one has not had the opportunity to hear the law declared. Punishment is not fundamentally retributive in Hobbes's scheme: "A Punishment, is an Evill inflicted by publique Authority, on him that hath done, or omitted that which is Judged by the same Authority, to be a Transgression of the Law; to the end that the will of men may thereby the better be disposed to obedience."

Like anything made by people, a commonwealth can perish. Its infirmities result from what Hobbes calls an "Imperfect Institution"—errors in the creation of the commonwealth. Perhaps the sovereign is not given enough power, or everyone is allowed to be a judge, or conscience is authoritative in moral judgment, or supernatural inspiration is given precedence over reason, or the sovereign is held to be subject to civil law, or it is supposed that everyone has some absolute property that the sovereign cannot touch, or it is supposed that sovereign power can be divided. Other difficulties, such as the lack of money, the presence of monopolies and corrupt politicians, the popularity of certain subjects, the greatness of a town, or the invasion by a foreign power, can lead to the dissolution of the commonwealth.

Part 3 of *Leviathan* is concerned with showing the relations between a Christian commonwealth and commonwealths in general. Hobbes uses hundreds of biblical references, as interpreted by him, to support his conclusion that it is possible to reconcile obedience to God with our obedience to a civil sovereign, for the sovereign is either a Christian or is not. If the sovereign is a Christian, then, even if the sovereign may sometimes err in supposing that some act is God's will, the proper thing for the subject, who has no right to judge, is to obey. If the sovereign is an infidel, then the subject must obey because the law of nature justifies the sovereign's power in a commonwealth, and to disobey would be to disobey the laws of nature which are the laws of God. No church leader, even a pope, can rule the sovereign; and this situation is not contrary to God's law, for the church works through civil government.

The concluding section, "Of the Kingdome of Darknesse," argues that spiritual darkness has not been completely eliminated from the church—by which Hobbes means the Roman Catholic church. His principal attack on the church of Rome is based on his claim that the Scripture is misinterpreted in order to justify the assumption of temporal power by the popes.

Although Hobbes maintains that his entire argument is based upon a study of nature and of humanity's natural inclinations, it is clear that a large part of his discourse is an expression of his own preference for absolute monarchy. On this account he tends to overlook the possibility of restraining the power of a sovereign by democratic procedures. Nevertheless, *Leviathan* is a remarkable attempt to explain and justify the institution of government, and it remains one of the masterpieces of political thought.

Bibliography:
Baumrin, Bernard H., ed. *Hobbes's "Leviathan": Interpretation and Criticism.* Belmont, Calif.: Wadsworth, 1969. An interesting and varied collection of essays, ranging from Richard Cumberland's attack on Hobbes (1727) to essays from the 1960's. Useful bibliographical suggestions for further reading.
Dietz, Mary G., ed. *Thomas Hobbes and Political Theory.* Lawrence: University Press of Kansas, 1990. Nine contemporary papers covering the implications of Hobbes's political thought; refers to *Leviathan* throughout. For the more advanced student.
Gauthier, David P. *The Logic of "Leviathan": The Moral and Political Theory of Thomas Hobbes.* Oxford, England: Clarendon Press, 1969. A careful analysis, showing the dependency of Hobbes's political theory on his theories of human nature and morality. Uses a unique critical method of alternating formal and material definitions of categories under discussion.
McNeilly, F. S. *The Anatomy of "Leviathan."* London: Macmillan, 1968. Divided into four parts: an introduction that discusses approaches to the work; "Method"; "Man," discussing

Hobbes's views on human nature; and "Society," which covers natural law and political science. Excellent bibliography. Recommended for all levels.

Martinich, A. P. *The Two Gods of "Leviathan": Thomas Hobbes on Religion and Politics.* Cambridge, England: Cambridge University Press, 1992. Reassessment of Hobbes's reputation as a purely secular thinker, arguing that religious concerns provide the foundation for the political theories of *Leviathan*. Covers the religious background to Hobbes's work and its relationship to Christian doctrine.

THE LIAR

Type of work: Drama
Author: Pierre Corneille (1606-1684)
Type of plot: Farce
Time of plot: Seventeenth century
Locale: Paris
First performed: Le Menteur, 1643; first published, 1644 (English translation, 1671)

> *Principal characters:*
> DORANTE, a student newly arrived in Paris
> GERONTE, his father
> CLITON, his valet and confidant
> ALCIPPE, his friend, engaged secretly to Clarice
> PHILISTE, a friend to both Alcippe and Dorante
> CLARICE, a young précieuse, betrothed to Alcippe
> LUCRECE, her friend and fellow conspirator
> SABINE, the maid and confidante of Lucrece

The Story:

Dorante, a young gallant who had come to Paris in order to get his social education and not to take a wife as his father Geronte wished, hired Cliton, a valet who had military and amatory connections, as his mentor. The young man wished to be schooled in the ways of the world, though the only advice he ever took from his man was to spend freely. Quite by planned accident Clarice, tired of waiting for her lethargic lover Alcippe to conclude their secret arrangements to marry, tripped onto the waiting arm of the newly arrived student. Although a rustic, Dorante immediately accommodated himself to the situation and exchanged euphemistic compliments with the young coquette, much to his valet's despair. The brazen liar captivated not only Clarice but her companions, especially Lucrece, who was silent throughout, by his false accounts of the wars he had fought in and the deeds he had accomplished in Germany during the last four years.

The arrival of Alcippe put the girls to flight, but not before Alcippe saw Clarice talking to his old friend Dorante—who quite ecstatically informed his companions that he had had amazing amatory adventures during his month's stay in Paris. Last night, for example, he had entertained a beautiful lady and five companions on five boats with four choirs of instruments playing all night and with dancing until dawn after a sumptuous repast of six courses, and so on. Cliton attempted to break into this mad monologue, but with no result, for Dorante's philosophy was to tell the big lie of wars and adventures in order to be believed. His stories were so plausible and his manner so persuasive that the two young ladies fell in love with him. His friend Alcippe burned with jealousy because he thought his fiancée had been on the barge, and his friend Philiste was completely mystified when he tried to reconcile the tales with what he later found to be the unvarnished and unromantic truth. The one flaw in the liar's plans was that in his conversation with Cliton, who had gained information about the young women from a coachman, Dorante had confused Clarice with Lucrece.

Into this confused web of mendacity and misplaced affections came the good-natured Geronte, who without his son's knowledge pressed the young man's suit for marriage with the daughter of an old friend. The girl was Clarice, ready and willing to be wooed after all the time she had spent waiting for Alcippe's advances. The old man and the young girl contrived a meeting that evening under her balcony and incognito, though she doubted that she could judge her suitor's character from such a distance and under such unintimate circumstances. A friend then suggested that she receive him at Lucrece's house and as Lucrece.

Alcippe, consumed with jealousy, angrily accused Clarice of infidelity. Although she denied his charges, she refused to seal their engagement with two kisses, her hand, and her faith. Alcippe, thinking himself the injured party, swore revenge.

Meanwhile, the tolerant father retracted his offer of his son's hand in marriage to Clarice because the young scoundrel had invented a touching story to escape the wedding planned for him. The story, a cape-and-sword melodrama, concerned his marriage to a poor girl whose father found them alone; in his anxiety to disguise their presence his gun went off, his sword was broken, his barricade smashed, and her reputation threatened—what could he do but marry sweet Orphise? Cliton's despair changed to admiration, now that he realized how useful his master's ability at lying could be. Although Cliton tried to acquaint Dorante with his mistake about the shy, virtuous, and quiet Lucrece, with whom Dorante had not spoken, the bewitched swain swore he would keep his appointment under the balcony. Alcippe wrote a letter breaking off his friendship with Dorante and demanding satisfaction. In one short day, his second in the big city, the provincial student had quarreled, made love, and reported a marriage. To lie effectively, Cliton observed, one must have a good memory.

Confronted by his accuser, Dorante told Alcippe and Philiste that he had known Clarice for several years but was not interested in her; he had, he said, taken a beautiful married woman with him on the barge, a woman whom Alcippe could not possibly know. He cautioned Alcippe not to believe all he heard and not to be led by the green-eyed monster. When Philiste revealed to Alcippe that the young dandy had only yesterday arrived from the college at Poitiers—proof that while he might be valorous, his deeds were imaginary—Alcippe asked the innocent scoundrel's pardon.

Clarice, by the time she had exchanged places on the balcony with Lucrece, also knew about the lies Dorante had told. Lucrece thought his actions a sign of love. Confronted, Dorante denied all accusations save one; he declared that he had pretended marriage in order to wed his Lucrece—at this point there was consternation on the balcony—whom he would marry that next day as proof of his sincerity. By group action he was ordered hence, so shocked were the young ladies at his effrontery—or naïveté.

Dorante now promised Cliton not to lie any more, or at least to give a signal when he did. He immediately lied by saying that the rumor of his fight with Alcippe was true and that the unfortunate challenger had been left for dead. He lied again when he claimed that the secret of Alcippe's recovery lay in the magic of a Hebrew word. Hebrew, he claimed, was one of his ten languages. He lied also to Sabine, the servant, in order to get back in Lucrece's good graces, and he invented new names so that his father could send his daughter-in-law his good wishes; the duped father was pleased to learn a grandchild was even now six months along. His lies were met by counter-lies told by the clever Sabine, who lied for money and kept herself in constant employment by delivering letters and arranging assignations.

By now neither Dorante, Lucrece, nor Clarice knew whom they loved. Clarice declared herself in favor of Alcippe, whose father finally settled the marriage arrangements. Dorante then observed that she had only been flirtatious and curious, while the real Lucrece—he declared that he had fallen in love with a name and henceforth changed the face to fit it—was much deeper. The father, declaring as he did so that he would never again help his scoundrel of a son, arranged quite docilely for his marriage. Lucrece, who swore she would love the liar when she could believe him, was suddenly converted to belief when she saw that his avowals were true in spirit. Cliton knew as much all along.

Critical Evaluation:

Pierre Corneille composed works for the aristocratic ladies and gentlemen of the seventeenth century. Acclaimed by many critics to have brought new levels of psychological realism and elegance of language into French comedy, he rejected, for example, the pastoral tradition of disguising noble or gentle characters in shepherds' clothing in *Mélite: Ou, Les Fausses Lettres* (1630), which portrays gentle people of the gallant world of the 1620's and 1630's. The lively dialogue that characterizes Corneille's comedies especially dazzled his audience in *The Liar*. His penchant for creating verse was manifested before he began composing the French neoclassical twelve-syllable Alexandrine lines that were so sparkling in *The Liar*; Corneille won prizes in Latin versification in both 1618 and 1620.

The Liar played a significant role in the development of French comedy because it moves away from the farcical techniques and the obscenities of earlier comedies. In accordance with the French classical style, emphasizing reason, order, and clarity, *The Liar* portrays life and manners in Paris. In the first scene of Act I, Dorante's valet Cliton gives a realistic account of the Parisian manner of living. By pointing out that all types of people inhabit Paris, Cliton presents the central theme of reality versus appearances; the valet's idea that appearances are often deceptive because people enjoy pretending to be what they are not shows his keen perception about people.

The Liar, based on Juan Ruiz de Alarcón's *La verdad sospechosa* (1630), contained elements that showed the influence of Spain, with Spanish drama's emphasis on the themes of instability, confusion, misunderstandings, and the comic relationship of valet and master. Corneille presented the theme of instability as the falseness of appearances. For example, Clarice wants to discern between appearance and reality in Act II, scene ii, when she speaks to Isabelle about Dorante, whose father had just proposed her marriage to his son. While wondering if Dorante's gracious appearance could possibly mask vices, she realizes that the eyes can deceive the lover, since many handsome lovers possess a vile heart.

Another variation of the theme of instability is deception. Dorante practices deception when he invents stories about his being a soldier and about his marriage to a well-bred lady carrying an unborn child. The protagonist tells the first story in order to gain favor with the beautiful Clarice, who he thinks is Lucrece. He relates the second story because his father proposes Dorante's marriage to Clarice to Clarice's father, who reacts favorably to the proposal. This pattern of deception becomes so familiar to Dorante that distinction between truth and deception seems impossible. The theme of instability is also manifested in the conflict of illusion and reality. This conflict is especially significant to *The Liar* because the play has considerable confusion of identity. Dorante's valet Cliton informs his master that Lucrece is the more beautiful of the two young women he has met. However, the interpretation of the word "beautiful" causes confusion, since the coachman who is the source of Cliton's information designates Lucrece as the more beautiful. The confusion of identity produces jealousy between Dorante and Alcippe, who are both attracted to Clarice; this rivalry is accentuated because Dorante believes that his beloved is named Lucrece. Although Dorante is unaffected by Alcippe's declaration of love for Clarice, Dorante's creation of a fictitious background to impress his beloved causes Alcippe to become jealous. Since Alcippe acts on the assumption that the reputation Dorante has created for himself is accurate, Alcippe is a comic character; his jealousy gives rise to various ridiculous rages directed toward Philiste and Clarice. The fact that Clarice, who does not give credence to Alcippe's rages, remains calm underlines his comic role. This manner of underscoring Alcippe's ridiculous role enables Corneille to make the audience more aware of the comic nature of the irony of the situation: Alcippe and Dorante really do love the same woman. The rivals' jealousy is dramatically effective. Although Alcippe's jealousy is based on illusion, this emotion illustrates the playwright's use of dramatic irony, in which the truth is hidden from the character but clear to the audience. The rival's jealousy, presented in the form of comic irony, is characteristic of Corneille's work, combining in a refined manner truth and deception, reality and illusion.

The irony produced by the confusion of identity is further developed when Dorante's father Geronte suggests to his son that Dorante become engaged to Clarice, a suggestion that causes the protagonist, unaware that Clarice is his beloved, to invent the lie that he is already married. Alcippe then challenges his rival to a duel. Dorante, still unaware of his rivalry with Alcippe, relates to Cliton that he has killed a man in a duel. This confession leads to comic tension when Dorante learns of Alcippe's previous betrothal to Clarice. Pointing out that he has already successfully courted Clarice, Alcippe unknowingly promotes the rivalry between himself and Dorante; the presentation of Dorante's imagined victory in a duel over his real rival gains comic authenticity. Dorante's illusionary role of rival thus becomes his comic misunderstanding of the truth.

Although Corneille's play reflects the influence of its Spanish origins, the French version's accent on the comic elements rather than on the moral aspects is reflected in the relationship between the master and his valet. Corneille converted the Spanish valet, whose role was to judge his master's behavior, into a witty person capable of astute observation and helpful advice. For example, Cliton's reaction to his master's untruthfulness is considerably less emphatic than that of his Spanish counterpart. Corneille gives Cliton his own identity, as distinct as his master's. Corneille's adaptation of the baroque theme of instability to the orderly French classical style is especially evident in the conclusion. Instead of being a victim forced into marrying someone he does not love, Dorante logically fulfills his "false" reputation, triumphantly transforming himself into the role of lover.

"Critical Evaluation" by Linda Prewett Davis

Bibliography:
Abraham, Claude. *Pierre Corneille*. Boston: Twayne, 1972. Aimed at the English-speaking nonspecialist. All quotations are translated into English. A short biographical sketch helps explain the evolution of the playwright's works. Bibliography suggests background material for the general reader.
Adam, Antoine. *Grandeur and Illusion: French Literature and Society 1600-1715*. Translated by Herbert Tint. New York: Basic Books, 1972. Shows the relationship between French society in the seventeenth century and its literature. Relates the history of the theater.
Brereton, Geoffrey. *French Comic Drama: From the Sixteenth to the Eighteenth Century*. New York: Methuen, 1977. Discusses the relationship of a comedy with its epoch. Spans three centuries but contains a meaningful history of the comic genre and has an explanation of *The Liar*.
Mallinson, G. J. *The Comedies of Corneille: Experiments in the Comic*. Manchester, England: Manchester University Press, 1984. Gives a thorough analysis of Corneille's comic plays in terms of composition and style. Shows how in *The Liar* Corneille shifts the emphasis from the original source, creating the neoclassical French version.
Rutherford, Malcolm. "Corneille and Comedy." *Encounter* 74, no. 4 (May, 1990): 74-75. A short analysis that points out some interesting facts about theater companies. Discusses the names of the characters in *The Liar*.

LIBER AMORIS
Or, The New Pygmalion

Type of work: Autobiography
Author: William Hazlitt (1778-1830)
First published: 1823

Because William Hazlitt was a writer, it was not enough that he found himself passionately attracted to his landlord's daughter; he had to write about it. *Liber Amoris: Or, The New Pygmalion* appeared in 1823, slightly disguised by initials in place of names, as the anonymous account of a writer's foolish passion, but it was not long before the secret was out. A reviewer for *John Bull*, claiming that the review in the *Times,* which was favorable, had been written by Hazlitt himself, attempted to picture the young woman in the book as a young, innocent child and Hazlitt as an "impotent sensualist."

Hazlitt quite properly gave his work a subtitle, for his passion led him into flights of creative imagination whereby he sought to give his beloved traits of character and depth of feeling to match her physical charms. His conversations with the landlord's daughter, delightfully transcribed at the beginning of the work, show Hazlitt to have been as much dazzled by his own literary facility in describing her charms as he was with the charmer herself when she was seated on his lap returning his kisses. By the time the affair ended—after he had discovered that she was no more than a flirt, and not an innocent one at that—what impressed him most was that she was not what she had seemed. What she had seemed to be is what, in his writer's imagination, he had made her; what he discovered, when he realized her true nature, was that reality does not copy the images of poets, even when they write a *Liber Amoris*.

The Pygmalion theme is never explicitly developed in the book, but Hazlitt speaks of Sarah as "the statue." In the first of his letters to C. P., Esq., written from Scotland, Hazlitt wrote in a footnote, "I have begun a book of our conversations (I mean mine and the statue's) which I call *Liber Amoris*." Later, in letter 13, the penultimate letter of part 2, he wrote to Peter George Patmore again about Sarah: "Since I wrote to you about making a formal proposal, I have had her face constantly before me, looking so like some faultless marble statue, as cold, as fixed and graceful as ever statue did."

Liber Amoris begins with a series of conversations, apparently the result of Hazlitt's attempt to re-create the substance and feeling of amatory moments spent with Sarah. After that, a series of letters to Patmore carries the narrative forward as it tells of Hazlitt's hopes and doubts while in Scotland awaiting a divorce from his wife. The book closes with some letters to J. S. K., which, unlike the letters to Patmore, were never actually sent but composed solely to complete the book.

Hazlitt became acquainted with Sarah Walker after his separation from his wife. Sarah, the second daughter of his landlord, Micaiah Walker, a tailor, was then in her late teens, and according to the account in *Liber Amoris*, Sarah let him kiss her the first time they met. During the first week of their acquaintance, she sat upon his knee, and, as he wrote, "twined your arms round me, caressed me with every mark of tenderness consistent with modesty."

Later, Hazlitt was to tell Sarah's father that she had made a habit of sitting on his knee and kissing him. The father had supposed that the occasion upon which he had surprised the two lovers together was the only time such a thing occurred, but Hazlitt, trying to win sympathy for himself when he could not convince Sarah to marry him, assured Walker that "it was a constant habit; it has happened a hundred times since, and a thousand before. I lived on her caresses as my daily food, nor can I live without them."

The conversations are convincing and lively, more self-revealing than Hazlitt probably supposed. They show a man convinced of his ability to charm with language one whom he had so often kept busy with embraces. By the brief answers that Sarah gives it is clear that she found Hazlitt something of a chatterbox and wished that he would pay more attention to the physical side of love and less to the spiritual and literary aspects of the experience.

For Hazlitt the overwhelming problem of his affair with Sarah was how to reconcile their hours of intimacy with her refusal to marry him or, at least, to live with him "in friendship." He asks her for an answer; he asks his friends; he asks her mother and father. Sarah had given him the answer all along, but he lacked the ability to recognize its truth: "I told you my regard could amount to no more than friendship." Sarah's friendship was that of a healthy young woman who enjoyed being fondled by the lodgers in her father's house, whereas Hazlitt had the conventional notion that a young woman who seems innocent and demure makes love only because she wishes to accept a proposal of marriage.

The course of the affair is simply told. Hazlitt met the tailor's daughter, kissed her on their first meeting, and held her on his lap. The entertainment continued for hundreds of performances. Hazlitt spent a good part of the time expressing his love in elaborate, literary ways which, for the most part, Sarah failed to appreciate. He repeatedly tried to win from her a declaration of love to match his own, but she insisted that he could never be more than a friend to her. He gave her various books, including several he had written—and a small bronze figure of Napoleon, which she treasured because it reminded her of a man she had cared for, a nobleman who considered the social distance between himself and Sarah too great to be bridged.

After Hazlitt went to Scotland to await a divorce from his wife, he wrote entreating letters to Sarah, which were either not answered or answered perfunctorily. Hazlitt expressed his doubts and hopes at great length in letters to his friend Patmore.

Upon returning to London, after having obtained the divorce, Hazlitt again tried to persuade Sarah to marry him; but on the pretext that he had insulted her in a quarrel before his journey, when he had suggested vaguely that she was easy in her favors, she not only refused to marry him but returned the books and the statuette, which he promptly smashed. He finally discovered that she was playing the same game with another gentleman, C——, and that she had been doing so during the very period when he thought he had her embraces to himself alone. His final opinion of her, contrasting with his first image of her, was that she was "a practiced, callous jilt, a regular lodging-house decoy, played off by her mother upon the lodgers, one after another, applying them to her different purposes, laughing at them in turns, and herself the probable dupe and victim of some gallant in the end."

Despite Hazlitt's literary flights shown in both the conversations and the letters, *Liber Amoris* is a convincing and compelling account of an ordinary love affair. The style is mannered, in the fashion of a time when literary elaboration of ordinary passion was as much a sport as holding the landlord's daughter on one's knee. Yet beneath the poetry and the banter there is something of the English spirit and attitude, which gives a dignity to what would otherwise be too trivial to warrant description, whatever the joys and pains of the participants. Hazlitt shows himself to be a divided man, worldly enough to realize that Sarah, for all her demureness, allowed him liberties that she could not have allowed were she all she seemed to be, yet romantic enough and idealistic enough to suppose that somehow the fault was in himself and that all he had to do was to make himself worthy of her love and esteem. In this division of self Hazlitt shows himself to be the romantic Englishman, at once cynical and hopeful.

It is not enough to say that the portrait of Hazlitt and his "statue" is convincing and typical. Considered as a piece of literary work, *Liber Amoris* is remarkable because it sustains interest with such slight material. What accounts for Hazlitt's success is the spirit of the piece, for it is amusing, lively, sophisticated, and revealing of human foibles. It is a minor piece, and perhaps it is better to remember Hazlitt as a critical essayist; yet it is from such minor pieces that English literature acquires its distinctive flavor and enduring charm.

Bibliography:
Beaty, Frederick L. *Light from Heaven: Love in British Romantic Literature.* DeKalb: Northern Illinois University Press, 1971. Describes *Liber Amoris* as the author's attempt to punish and purge himself. He develops the romantic notion of love as a hallucination.
Butler, Marilyn. "Satire and the Images of Self in the Romantic Period: The Long Tradition of Hazlitt's *Liber Amoris.*" In *English Satire and the Satiric Tradition*, edited by Claude Rawson and Jenny Mezciems. Oxford, England: Blackwell, 1984. Also in *Spirits of Fire: English Romantic Writers and Contemporary Historical Methods*, edited by G. A. Rosso and Daniel P. Watkins. Rutherford, N.J.: Fairleigh Dickinson University Press, 1990. Discusses the fact that *Liber Amoris*, the agonized record of a man in the grip of a sexual obsession, has been regarded as an artless Romantic autobiography, but argues that its satirical elements reveal themselves if it is read alongside Thomas De Quincey's *The Confessions of an English Opium Eater* (1821).
Friedman, Martin B. "Hazlitt, Jerrold, and Horne: *Liber Amoris* Twenty Years After." *Review of English Studies* 22, no. 88 (November, 1971): 455-462. An account of Douglas William Jerrold's short story, which parodied *Liber Amoris* and the scandalous publicity the book elicited. Friedman discusses Richard Henry Horne's accusation that Jerrold was impolite.
Priestley, J. B. *William Hazlitt.* London: Longmans, 1960. Interprets *Liber Amoris* from a Jungian perspective, noting how the book exemplifies Hazlitt's characteristically personal obsession in his writing.
Wardle, Ralph M. *Hazlitt.* Lincoln: University of Nebraska Press, 1971. Uses Hazlitt's letters to his friend Patmore during the *Liber Amoris* affair to show his development as a writer.

LIE DOWN IN DARKNESS

Type of work: Novel
Author: William Styron (1925-   )
Type of plot: Psychological realism
Time of plot: Mid-twentieth century
Locale: Virginia
First published: 1951

Principal characters:
  PEYTON LOFTIS, deceased young woman
  MILTON LOFTIS, her father
  HELEN LOFTIS, her mother
  HARRY MILLER, Peyton's husband
  DOLLY BONNER, Milton's mistress
  CAREY CARR, Helen's minister

The Story:

Young Peyton Loftis, daughter of a Virginia family, had committed suicide in New York City. Her body had been barely rescued from Potter's Field, and it had been transported by train to Port Warwick, Virginia. Her father, Milton, and his mistress, Dolly Bonner, arrived in one car to meet the body, and her mother, Helen, and Helen's minister, Carey Carr, arrived in another car.

Only the two cars followed the hearse on the trip to the cemetery on a hot August afternoon. Several incidents of car trouble delayed the trip, and during the trip and the funeral service, the characters took turns remembering all of the events that had led to Peyton's death. Even Peyton's memories were recalled.

Milton, an alcoholic father, remembered incidents from his youth, his wartime marriage to Helen, the birth of Maudie, their older daughter, retarded and crippled, and then the birth of Peyton, perfect and beautiful. Helen, the disturbed mother, also remembered, but from a different perspective. Helen had devoted all of her attention and love to the deficient Maudie, while Milton had doted on and spoiled Peyton with obsessive love.

They both remembered that Helen had blamed both Milton and Peyton for Maudie's death. Helen, unable to love either Milton or Peyton, had turned to religion and her minister, Carey Carr, and, ultimately, to mental illness. Milton had become an alcoholic, and, after rejection by Helen, had begun an affair with Dolly Bonner on the night of Peyton's sixteenth birthday. Peyton lost her innocence shortly thereafter, and she had followed in her father's pattern of alcoholism and sexual promiscuity. At her wedding to Harry, a Jewish New York artist, Milton was very drunk and made sexual advances to Peyton. Peyton moved to New York with Harry but separated from him because of her affairs with other men. She killed herself by leaping off a building in New York City.

After the funeral, Helen and Milton had a violent confrontation at the cemetery, then Milton tried to choke Helen. They left the cemetery separately. The novel concludes with an African American religious revival service.

Critical Evaluation:

The title of William Styron's *Lie Down in Darkness* comes from Sir Thomas Browne's *Urn Burial*, published in 1658 ("it cannot be long before we lie down in darkness and have our light in ashes"). The overall theme is similar to most Southern fiction, the decadence of the family. Styron's novel is most often compared to William Faulkner's *As I Lay Dying* (1930) in both theme and technique.

The last section, Peyton's soliloquy, is most often compared to Molly Bloom's soliloquy in James Joyce's final section of *Ulysses* (1922) or to Quentin Compson's narrative section in Faulkner's *The Sound and the Fury* (1929).

Although post World War II concerns—the bomb, apathy, drugs, ecology—are evident in *Lie Down in Darkness*, Styron, like his predecessors in stream-of-consciousness fiction, is more concerned with alienation, lack of communication, and loss of self in the twentieth century. *Lie Down in Darkness*, like Faulkner's *The Sound and the Fury*, is strongly Freudian with mythical overtones, does not proceed in chronological order, uses multiple points of view, is poetic in diction and imagery, and emphasizes internal portrayal of characters. There are also differences in Styron's contributions to this particular style of modern fiction.

Styron's two greatest strengths in *Lie Down in Darkness* are his skill in scene construction and the sustained power of his poetic imagery in Peyton Loftis' internal monologue of memories—a monologue which continues for fifty-one pages near the conclusion of the novel.

Most of Styron's novel is a series of flashbacks, moving back and forth in time, with each scene skillfully constructed to present an increasingly climactic effect. Styron begins with an omniscient narrator and then achieves multiple points of view by moving into several minds: those of Milton Loftis, Dolly Bonner, Helen Loftis, Reverend Carey Carr, and, ultimately, that of Peyton Loftis.

Peyton, like Addie Bundren in Faulkner's *As I Lay Dying*, is the catalyst for the action of the novel; each of the dramatic scenes occurs at different points in her life—all family occasions, such as birthday parties, that disintegrate into chaos. Styron, in using this dramatic structure of increasing intensity, occasionally slips into melodrama; that is, there are too many scenes with too much tension. The result is anticlimactic rather than climactic by the time the macabre wedding scene of Peyton and Harry is related. Critic Marc Ratner calls these scenes "bomb-flashes of recollection," but with the characters not reflecting or evaluating their lives.

This inability to reflect on their lives is a clear departure from the characters of the stream-of-consciousness novels of James Joyce, Virginia Woolf, and William Faulkner. Even Peyton's long monologue, that portion of the novel most clearly stream of consciousness in technique, does not include any real self-awareness. It includes recognition at the conscious level of her forbidden love for her father just before she leaps to her death, but most of the monologue is at a level near the subconscious, marked by strong imagery and fragmentation, with no clear pattern of association.

In stream-of-consciousness writing, imagery is generally recognized as the means to present the subconscious thought process of the character. The character's thoughts reflect needs and desires that the character represses from conscious thought. The governing principle behind the monologue of Peyton Loftis is, therefore, her repressed sexual love for her father. Styron uses three distinct controlling metaphors or clusters of images to present that passion: the clock into which Peyton and Harry (always a surrogate father because she cannot say Milton, even to herself) can retreat—a symbolic return to the womb and childhood where it is not a sin to love one's father; the flightless birds which "suffer without soaring"—the projection of her nympho-mania; and "drowning," which reflects her increasing disorientation and retreat into mental illness. The clock and the drowning are both symbolic of withdrawal, and the birds are symbolic of her double-edged guilt (for both loving and rejecting her father), frustration, and pain.

Thematically, Peyton's monologue reminds readers of Quentin Compson in Faulkner's *The*

Sound and the Fury; Compson is also drawn toward suicide. Peyton is destroyed and does in fact kill herself in order to escape from life. Critics generally agree that her monologue is the most powerful piece of writing in Styron's novel; without Peyton's monologue, the novel would be incomplete. Without her perspective, the novel would present a spoiled, beautiful, and intelligent brat, instead of a tortured girl destroyed by her parents—a mother who cannot love her and a father who loves too much—and by her own inability to love or to take responsibility for her actions. All three members of the Loftis family, especially after the death of the retarded older sister Maudie, are emotional children who live in fantasy worlds of their own design. Helen retreats into madness and religion, Milton into drunkenness and adultery, and Peyton, ultimately, into death.

Peyton Loftis, in her monologue, is alternately childlike and adult. The organizational structure of the monologue, in spite of the illusion which Styron carefully creates of no structure, has three unifying elements: the chronology of the last day of her life in her desperate search for her father, her relationships with men, and the three controlling metaphors (clock, drowning, birds). The recurring image of Peyton's grandmother, the mother that Peyton never had, is also in the monologue. The pace of the monologue is frantic, both physically and emotionally.

Peyton's monologue follows her through a day, in a pattern similar to that of *Ulysses* as well as *The Sound and the Fury*. The time references are chronological and give a narrative skeleton to the retelling of Peyton's activities from the time she awakens from sleep to the moment of her death. The clock as a symbol, however, functions quite apart from chronological time. It is used as a reference to Peyton's continued state of withdrawal. The clock, the traditional "womb of time," provides a clean, cold, emotionless peace of nonexistence for Peyton. Living for her means pain, and Peyton withdraws from the pain of living.

Part of Peyton's withdrawal is her nymphomania. Through her nymphomania, she does not have to feel or to take responsibility. Love and sexual relations with her husband Harry are not possible because she has married him as a surrogate father; therefore, she must reject him as she has rejected Milton's advances, and she must punish Harry for any attention he gives to other women, no matter how trivial. Whenever Peyton commits adultery, she is reenacting the punishment of her father for his transgressions with Dolly Bonner on the night of Peyton's sixteenth birthday. Following that episode, Peyton had allowed herself to be seduced, beginning what was to become a familiar pattern.

Throughout the monologue, Peyton associates images of drowning and flightless birds with those sexual experiences. As the birds become further visualized in Peyton's mind, they become specific and exotic, but also landbound and impotent, dirtied by their own excrement and dust. The bird image culminates in Peyton's mind just before she leaps to her death, associating the birds as suffering without soaring, but now ascending through the night, "toward paradise."

The birds are symptomatic of the guilt from which she is able to free herself (and her flightless birds) only by plunging to her own destruction. Having faced the unalterable fact of her sexual love for her father and having rejected her surrogate father (her husband Harry), she kills herself.

The monologue concludes on this downward plunge into chaos, and Styron ends his "landscape of nightmare" with violence between the parents and then a parody of a religious service which only reinforces the fragmentation and destruction. Styron offers no affirmation of life at the conclusion of the novel.

Betty Alldredge

Bibliography:

Baumbach, Jonathan. "Paradise Lost: *Lie Down in Darkness* by William Styron." In *The Landscape of Nightmare: Studies in the Contemporary Novel*. New York: New York University Press, 1965. Places novel in the context of Southern gothic literature. Useful for comparisons with Faulkner and other writers of the genre.

Casciato, Arthur D., and James L. W. West III, eds. *Critical Essays on William Styron*. Boston: G. K. Hall, 1982. The most comprehensive collection of criticism available on Styron. Good basic resource for scholars and students, making available some of the more useful work published on Styron.

Crane, John Kenny. *The Root of All Evil: The Thematic Unity of William Styron's Fiction*. Columbia: University of South Carolina Press, 1984. Organized around the themes in Styron's *Sophie's Choice* and traces the themes through his earlier works including *Lie Down in Darkness*.

Pearce, Richard. *William Styron*. University of Minnesota Pamphlets on American Writers, No. 98. Minneapolis: University of Minnesota Press, 1971. Traces Styron's development as a writer in his four novels. Examines the tensions between Styron's belief in the traditional form of the novel and the nontraditional techniques he uses.

Ratner, Marc L. *William Styron*. New York: Twayne, 1972. Deals with Styron's main techniques and ideas inherent in his characters' struggles as "rebellious children." Sees Styron as apart from the Southern tradition of literature.

THE LIFE AND OPINIONS OF TRISTRAM SHANDY, GENT.

Type of work: Novel
Author: Laurence Sterne (1713-1768)
Type of plot: Satire
Time of plot: 1718-1766
Locale: Shandy Hall in England
First published: 1759-1767

> *Principal characters:*
> TRISTRAM SHANDY, the narrator
> MR. WALTER SHANDY, his father
> MR. TOBY SHANDY, his uncle and an old soldier
> CORPORAL TRIM, Uncle Toby's servant
> MR. YORICK, a parson
> DR. SLOP, a medical quack
> WIDOW WADMAN, a romantic widow

The Story:

Tristram Shandy, in telling the story of his earliest years, always believed that most of the problems of his life were brought about by the fact that the moment of his conception was interrupted when his mother asked his father whether he had remembered to wind the clock. Tristram knew the exact date of his conception, the night between the first Sunday and the first Monday of March, 1718. He was certain of this because Mr. Shandy's notebook indicated that before that Monday he had been seriously inconvenienced by an attack of sciatica, but immediately afterward he had set out for London.

Another complication of Tristram's birth was the marriage settlement of his parents. According to this settlement, which Tristram quotes in full, Mrs. Shandy had the privilege of going to London in preparation for childbirth. If Mrs. Shandy were to put Mr. Shandy to the expense of a trip to London on false pretenses, however, then the next child was to be born at Shandy Hall. The circumstance of a needless trip to London had occurred some time before, and Mr. Shandy stoutly insisted that Tristram should be born at Shandy Hall; the birth would be in the hands of a country midwife rather than in those of a London doctor.

On the night of Tristram's birth, his father and his Uncle Toby were sitting in the living room engaged in one of their interminable debates. Informed by Susannah, the maid, that Mrs. Shandy was about to deliver a child, they sent for the midwife. As an extra measure of safety, they also sent for Dr. Slop, a bungling country practitioner whom Mr. Shandy admired because he had written a five-shilling book on the history of midwifery. While the midwife attended Mrs. Shandy, the doctor, for a fee of five guineas, drank a bottle of wine in the back parlor with Mr. Shandy and his brother, Toby.

Uncle Toby, who had been called the highest compliment ever paid human nature, had been a soldier until he was wounded during the siege of Namur in 1695. The wound, the exact position of which was to play such a large part in Tristram's story later on, forced him to retire to the country. At the suggestion of his faithful servant, Corporal Trim, he had built a large and complicated series of model fortifications and military emplacements on a bowling green behind Shandy Hall. Uncle Toby's entire time was spent playing soldier and thinking about this miniature battlefield. Mr. Shandy was not impressed with his brother's hobby and kept him from discussing it by violent interruptions, so that he could continue, or start, one of his own long and detailed digressions on obscure information.

As the two brothers sat awaiting the arrival of the midwife and her rival, Dr. Slop, Mr. Shandy made a rhetorical question of the subject of Mrs. Shandy's preference for a midwife rather than a male doctor. When Uncle Toby suggested naïvely that modesty might explain her choice, Mr. Shandy launched into a long discussion of the nature of women and of the fact that everything has two handles. Given his naïveté, it was impossible for Uncle Toby to understand such affairs.

Dr. Slop finally arrived with his bag of tools. The midwife was already in attendance when he went up to see about the birth of the child. Corporal Trim read a sermon aloud to pass the time. In attending Mrs. Shandy, Dr. Slop unfortunately mistook Tristram's hip for his head. In probing with his large forceps, he flattened what Tristram always referred to as his nose. Tristram essentially blamed this mistake on the affair of the winding of the clock mentioned earlier. This, and a later incident concerning the falling of a window sash when Tristram, still a little boy, was relieving himself through a window, brought about a problem in his anatomy which he mentioned often.

Between Tristram's birth and almost immediate baptism, Mr. Shandy entertained the company with a long story he had translated from the Latin of the ancient German writer Slawkenbergius, a story telling of the adventures of a man with an especially long nose. When Mr. Shandy had recovered from hearing the bad news about the accident with the forceps, he was told that his child was very sickly and weak; consequently, he summoned Mr. Yorick, the curate, to baptize the child immediately. While rushing to get dressed to attend the ceremony, Mr. Shandy sent word to the parson by the maid, Susannah, to name the child Trismegistus, after an ancient philosopher who was one of his favorites. Susannah forgot the name, however, and told Mr. Yorick to name the child Tristram. This name pleased the old man because it happened to be his own as well. When Mr. Shandy, still half unbuttoned, reached the scene, the evil had been done. Despite the fact that Mr. Shandy thought correct naming most important, his child was Tristram, a name Mr. Shandy believed the worst in the world. He lamented that he had lost three-fourths of his son in his unfortunate geniture, nose, and name. There remained only one fourth—Tristram's education.

Tristram managed to give a partial account of his topsy-turvy boyhood between many digressions on the other members of his family. Uncle Toby continued to answer most of his brother's arguments by softly whistling Lillibullero, his favorite tune, and by going out to the little battlefield to wage small wars with Corporal Trim. The next important event in the family was the death of Master Bobby, Tristram's older brother, who had been away at Westminster school. Mr. Shandy reacted to this event in his usual way by calling up all the philosophic ideas of the past on death and discoursing on them until he had adjusted himself to the new situation. The tragic news was carried to the kitchen staff. Susannah, despite a desire to show grief, could think of nothing but the wonderful wardrobe of dresses she would inherit when her mistress went into mourning. Corporal Trim well demonstrated the transitory nature of life by dropping his hat, as if it had suddenly died; then he made an extemporaneous funeral oration.

After many more digressions on war, health, the fashions of ancient Roman dress, his father's doubts as to whether to get Tristram a tutor and whether to put him into long trousers, Tristram proceeded to tell the history of his Uncle Toby, both in war and in love. Near Shandy Hall lived the Widow Wadman, who, after laying siege to Uncle Toby's affections for a long time, almost got him to propose marriage to her. The gentle former soldier, who literally would not kill a fly, finally learned the widow's purpose when she began pointedly to inquire into the extent and position of his wound. First, he promised the widow that he would allow her to put her finger on the very spot where he was wounded, and then he brought her a map of Namur to touch. Uncle Toby's innocence protected him until Corporal Trim finally told his master that the Widow Wadman was interested in the spot on his body, not the spot on the surface of the world where the accident took place. This realization so embarrassed the old man that the idea of marriage disappeared from his mind forever. Tristram concluded his story with Parson Yorick's statement that the book had been one of the cock and bull variety: The reader had been led on a mad but merry chase through the satirical and witty mind of the author.

Critical Evaluation:

This masterpiece of eighteenth century narrative, *The Life and Opinions of Tristram Shandy, Gent.*, was written by a man who never reconciled his sentimental nature with his roguish tendencies and who never tried to reconcile them. Laurence Sterne was educated at Jesus College, Cambridge, where he met John Hall-Stevenson, a young aristocrat who shared and encouraged his taste for erotic subjects and exaggeration. After taking holy orders, Sterne received an ecclesiastical appointment in Sutton through family connections, but he was temperamentally completely unsuited for the clerical life. In fact, the only part of religion he mastered was sermon-writing, but at that he excelled. Eventually, he turned his pen to miscellaneous journalism in York periodicals. In 1759, *A Political Romance* appeared, which included many elements that would characterize his masterpiece: allegory, levels of meaning, verbal fanfare, whimsical use of scholastic learning, profanity, and great stylistic versatility.

Nevertheless, it was the appearance of the first two volumes of *The Life and Opinions of Tristram Shandy, Gent.* (commonly known simply as *Tristram Shandy*) that made Sterne an instant celebrity, despite the immediate denunciation of Samuel Johnson, Samuel Richardson, Horace Walpole, Oliver Goldsmith, and other literary establishment figures who condemned Sterne's iconoclastic style and frankly mercenary attitude for both ethical and artistic reasons. Sterne characterized the first part of his life's work as "taking on, not only the weak part of the sciences in which the true part of Ridicule lies, but everything else which I find laugh-at-able." The reader soon discovers that Sterne finds everything laughable, his comic vision as universal and as detailed as that of François Rabelais and Miguel de Cervantes, whose works strongly influenced Sterne. Like Rabelais' *Gargantua and Pantagruel* (1653-1694), moreover, Sterne's is a work held together only by the unswerving and exuberant force of the author's own personality. "'Tis a picture of myself," he admitted; indeed, it is impossible to distinguish the profane minister from the alleged narrator, young Tristram—just as Rabelais makes his narrator Alcofibras tangible only when it suits him.

Tristram Shandy also has been called "a prolonged conversation" between Sterne and his reader, a conversation in which acquaintance becomes familiarity and, then, an enduring friendship. For this friendship to occur, however, readers must accept certain ground rules and must be willing to adapt to conventions rarely embraced willingly. In his endless comments to the reader (who is sometimes addressed in the plural, sometimes in the singular, sometimes as "your worship," sometimes as "Madam"), Sterne scolds readers for wanting to know everything at once (book 1, chapter 4), asks readers to help him sell his "dedication," assures readers that their company will swell to include all the world and all time, and dismisses any objections with a mad swirl of his pen. He tells readers that he is quite aware that some will understand and others will not; indeed, the varying forms of address to the reader indicate his astute consciousness of the variety of his audience. He says the "cholerick" reader will toss the book away, the "mercurial will laugh most heartily at it," and the "saturnine" will condemn it as fanciful and extravagant. Like Cervantes, he is not interested (or so he claims) in apologizing for his work or for himself. Readers either take him or leave him. At the very beginning, as he begins one of his great digressions, he warns readers that to continue may annoy them—only the curious need pass through the narrative line into this first of many excursions with him. "Shut the door," he directs the first kind of reader; if readers pass through it with him, they realize the door is never opened again. Only the reader who is willing to let "anything go" will remain on speaking terms with this most quixotic, irrepressible author.

The work itself, alternately characterized by Tristram as "vile" and as "rhapsodic," defies structural analysis. Sterne makes his formal principles clear from the beginning: "not to be in a hurry" but to follow every new thought in whatever direction it may beckon until he loses track of his starting point and has to flip back the pages to find his place; "to spend two years discussing one," just as Tristram's mental and emotional autobiography reflects his father's *Tristrapaedia* (the gargantuan work of pedagogy that takes so long in the writing that Tristram grows up before he can start following its directives); and "in writing what I have set about, shall confine myself neither to his [Horace's] rules, nor to any man's rules that ever lived." Sterne would have understood T. S. Eliot's dictum, "Immature poets borrow, mature poets steal." He not only steals—whether it is the actual music of Uncle Toby's "Lillibullero" or a medieval French theological tract on baptism—but also openly admits and boasts of his thefts. The boast, however, is itself misleading since, as William Shakespeare did with North's Plutarch, Sterne subtly but most effectively alters his thieveries to fit the chaotic image of his own work. At one point, in discussing the nature of digressions, Sterne characterizes that work as "digressive, and . . . progressive too—and at the same time." Digressions, he continues, are "the sunshine" of a writer's art, the very stuff of literary and fictional vitality. Life itself, in the ultimate reading, is nothing but a diverting digression for Sterne; the role of the author, as he embraces it, is to make that essential human digression as diverting, as complicated, and as emotionally and intellectually rich as possible.

The greatness of Sterne's comic wit lies in its indefatigable mastery of making one detail relevant to another, a detail from Tristram's unfortunate life immediately provoking in his father a pointed consideration of Saxo Grammaticus' Danish history or causing Uncle Toby to expound its relationship to the siege of Navarre. Reading *Tristram Shandy* is an education in the esoteric and picayune minutiae of forgotten scholarship at the same time that it is a parody of the irrelevance of scholarship (also following closely in the spirit of Rabelais). By the time readers close even the first volume, they are convinced of the validity of Sterne's point of departure: Epictetus' statement that "Not actions but opinions of actions are the concern of men." In other words, it is not what happens to the reader that matters but what the reader thinks of what happens to him. The relationship between the Shandean world and the real world is a very close, in fact a promiscuous, one; it is defined by Sterne's deliberate blurring of the line between fictional and real events and by his thematic insistence on the interdependence of thought, feeling, and action. Thought without emotion, he would say, is futile; but feeling without reason is equally sterile. All the elements in human life, love, war, business, theology, religion, science, trade, and medicine are treated in an epic comprehensiveness, and everything is shown to be related to everything else. The texture of the style, however, is not the reassuring predictability of epic; instead, it is a formal collage of typographical caprice, gestures, dramatic devices, soliloquies, offhand obscenity, and serious and mock-serious treatises—all mixed together extemporaneously and punctuated orally. Sterne is like a magician juggling more balls than anyone can see, but he never loses control because his magic is as unflagging as it is electric. More than any other work of his century, Sterne's *Tristram Shandy* is a monument to the complexity, vitality, and *sprezzatura* of the mind.

"Critical Evaluation" by Kenneth John Atchity

Bibliography:
Booth, Wayne. "Did Sterne Complete *Tristram Shandy?*" *Modern Philology* 48, no. 3 (February, 1951): 172-183. Draws on extensive biographical and textual evidence to dispel the notion that *Tristram Shandy* is a careless, haphazard book without logical structure. Claims that Sterne intended to end with Uncle Toby's story from the novel's inception.

Jefferson, D. W. "*Tristram Shandy* and the Tradition of Learned Wit." In *Laurence Sterne: A Collection of Critical Essays*, edited by John Traugott. Englewood Cliffs, N.J.: Prentice-Hall, 1968. Locates *Tristram Shandy* in the satirical tradition of François Rabelais and Jonathan Swift. Studies how Sterne juxtaposes the discourses of medieval cosmology, medicine, physiology, law, religion, and military science with human folly.

New, Melvyn. *"Tristram Shandy": A Book for Free Spirits*. New York: Twayne, 1994. A helpful introduction designed for students. A discussion of the historical milieu, literary importance, and critical reception of *Tristram Shandy* precedes five different, often contradictory, readings of the novel. Includes a brief annotated bibliography.

Traugott, John. *Tristram Shandy's World: Sterne's Philosophical Rhetoric*. Berkeley: University of California Press, 1954. Asserts that Sterne's rhetorical project subverts John Locke's rationalist doctrine of the association of ideas by positing the moral value of wit and human feeling. A valuable treatment of Sterne's philosophy.

Zimmerman, Everett. "*Tristram Shandy* and Narrative Representation." *The Eighteenth Century: Theory and Interpretation* 28, no. 2 (Spring, 1987): 127-147. Engages eighteenth century historical scholarship to balance Sterne's moral vision and the limitations of viewpoint, narrative, and representation as they are reflected in *Tristram Shandy*.

LIFE IS A DREAM

Type of work: Drama
Author: Pedro Calderón de la Barca (1600-1681)
Type of plot: Melodrama
Time of plot: Sixteenth century
Locale: Poland
First performed: La vida es sueño, 1635; first published, 1636 (English translation, 1830)

Principal characters:
BASILIO, king of Poland
SEGISMUNDO, his son
ASTOLFO, Basilio's nephew and a duke of Muscovy
ESTRELLA, the infanta, Basilio's niece
CLOTALDO, a Polish general
ROSAURA, a Russian noblewoman disguised as a man
FIFE, her servant

The Story:

One night, in the wild, mountainous country between Poland and Russia, a Russian noblewoman, Rosaura, and her servant, Fife, found themselves in distress. Their horses had bolted, and they feared that they would have to make on foot the remainder of their journey to the royal court of Poland. Rosaura, for protection through that barbarous frontier country, was disguised as a man. Their weary way brought them at last to a forbidding fortress. There they overheard a young man, chained to the doorway of the castle, deliver a heart-rending soliloquy in which he lamented the harshness of his life. Rosaura approached the youth, who greeted her eagerly, with the excitement of one who had known little of sympathy or kindness during his brief span of years. At the same time he warned her to beware of violence. No sooner had he spoken these words than a shrill trumpet blast filled the night. Rosaura tossed her sword to the captive before she and Fife hid themselves among the rocks.

Clotaldo, a Polish general and the keeper of the youth, galloped up to the young man. Seeing the sword in his prisoner's hand, he ordered his men to seek the stranger who must be lurking nearby. Apprehended, Rosaura explained that she and Fife were Russian travelers on their way to the Polish court and that they were in distress because of the loss of their horses. Fife inadvertently hinted that Rosaura was really a woman. Yet the sword interested Clotaldo most of all, for he recognized the weapon as one which he had owned years before and which he had left in the keeping of a young noblewoman with whom he had been deeply in love. He decided that Rosaura must be his own son, but, torn between his sworn duty to his king and his paternal obligation toward his supposed son, he decided at last to say nothing for the time being. The fact that Rosaura possessed the sword obligated him to protect the travelers and to escort them safely through the mountains.

Meanwhile, in King Basilio's royal castle, the problem of succession to the Polish throne was to be decided. To this purpose, the king welcomed his nephew Astolfo and his niece Estrella. The problem of the succession existed because it was generally believed that the true heir, King Basilio's son, had died with his mother in childbirth many years before. The need for a decision was pressing; both Astolfo and Estrella were supported by strong rival factions which, in their impatience, were threatening the peace of the realm.

King Basilio greeted his niece and nephew with regal ceremony and then startled them with the news that his son Segismundo was not really dead. The readings of learned astrologers and horrible portents which had accompanied Segismundo's birth had led the superstitious king to imprison the child in a mountain fortress for fear that otherwise the boy might grow up to be a monster who would destroy Poland. Now, years later, King Basilio was not sure that he had done right. He proposed that Segismundo be brought to the court in a drug-induced sleep, awakened after being dressed in attire befitting a prince, and observed carefully for evidence of his worthiness to wear his father's crown. Astolfo and Estrella agreed to that proposal.

In accordance with the plan, Segismundo, who dressed in rough wolfskins in his captivity, was drugged, taken to the royal castle, and dressed in rich attire. Awaking, he was disturbed to find himself suddenly the center of attention among obsequious strangers. Force of habit caused him to recall sentimentally his chains, the wild mountains, and his former isolation. Convinced that he was dreaming, he sat on the throne while his father's officers and the noble courtiers treated him with the respect due his rank. When they told him that he was the heir to the throne, he was mystified and somewhat apprehensive, but before long he began to enjoy his new feeling of power.

Clotaldo, his former guard and tutor, appeared to confirm the fact that Segismundo was really the prince. The young man then demanded an explanation of his lifelong imprisonment. Clotaldo patiently explained King Basilio's actions in terms that Segismundo might understand, but the youth, blinded by the sudden change in his fortunes, could see only that he had been grievously mistreated by his father. Declaring that he would have revenge for his unwarranted imprisonment, he seized Clotaldo's sword, but before he could strike the old general, Rosaura appeared out of the crowd, took the weapon from him, and reproved him for his rashness.

Segismundo, in a calmer mood, was introduced to Astolfo, whose courtly bearing and formal speech the prince could not bear. Sick of the whole aspect of the court, he ordered the guards to clear the audience hall. Again, however, he was mollified, this time by the appearance of Estrella and her ladies-in-waiting. Unaccustomed to feminine society, he behaved in a boorish manner, even attempting to embrace Estrella. The courtiers advised him to behave in a manner befitting a prince, and Astolfo, who hoped to marry his beautiful cousin, cautioned Segismundo about his behavior toward the princess. Unfamiliar with the formalities of court life, Segismundo lost all patience. Holding all present responsible for his long exile, he reminded them of his exalted position and defied anyone to touch Estrella. When Astolfo did not hesitate to take her by the hand, Segismundo seized Astolfo by the throat.

At this crucial moment in Segismundo's test, King Basilio entered the throne room and saw his son behaving like a wild beast. Crushed, he feared that the forecast had been true after all. Segismundo faced his father with shocking disrespect. Pressed for an explanation of his son's imprisonment, the king tried to prove that it had been written in the stars. Segismundo scoffed at the folly of man in putting responsibility for his actions on the disinterested heavens. Then he cursed his father and called the guards to seize the king and Clotaldo. At a trumpet blast, however, the soldiers quickly surrounded Segismundo himself and took him prisoner.

Having failed the test of princehood, Segismundo was drugged and returned in chains to the mountain fortress. In his familiar surroundings once more, he had full opportunity to reflect on his late experiences. When he spoke to Clotaldo about them, the old general assured him that all had been a dream. Since the prince had been drugged before he left the fortress and before he returned, he was quite convinced that he had suffered an unpleasant dream. Clotaldo assured him that dreams reveal the true character of the dreamer. Because Segismundo had conducted himself with violence in his dream, there was great need for the young man to bridle his fierce passions.

Meanwhile Rosaura, aware of Segismundo's plight and anxious to thwart the ambitions of Astolfo, who had once promised to marry her, stirred up a faction to demand the prince's release. The rebels invaded the mountains and seized the fortress; they failed, however, to seize Clotaldo, who had already returned to the royal castle to report to King Basilio. When the rebel army carried the sleeping Segismundo out of the fortress and awakened him with trumpet blasts, the unhappy prince would not be persuaded that his new experience was real, and he doubted the assurance that he had been rescued from his imprisonment. The rebel leader finally convinced him that it would be well for him to join the dream soldiers and fight with them against King Basilio's very real army, which was approaching.

Clotaldo was taken prisoner by Segismundo's forces, but the young prince, remembering the advice to curb his passions, ordered the old general's release. A great battle then took place, in which Segismundo proved his princely valor and chivalric bearing. King Basilio, defeated but refusing Clotaldo's and Astolfo's pleas to flee to safety, in admiration surrendered his crown to his son.

King of Poland in his own right, Segismundo ordered the marriage of Astolfo to Rosaura, who had, in the meantime, been revealed as Clotaldo's daughter. Estrella became Segismundo's queen. The young king made Clotaldo his trusted adviser.

Critical Evaluation:

Before Pedro Calderón de la Barca's *La vida es sueño* was freely adapted by Edward Fitzgerald in 1853, it had been known to most English and European readers through the medium of French translations from the original Spanish. In spite of their richness of imagination, however, Calderón's plays are still little known outside the Spanish-speaking world. All of this playwright's work has vigor and brilliance; in *Life Is a Dream*, for example, he used his Polish setting and period as freely as William Shakespeare used the seacoast of Bohemia or the forest of Arden. There is also a gothic quality in the mountain scenes which suggests the popular atmosphere of much eighteenth-century fiction, and there is considerable psychological insight into character as well. This play reveals admirably the personality of its writer, who was a soldier, an ardent patriot, an artist, and a devout son of the Church. It has also been translated as *Such Stuff as Dreams Are Made Of*.

Life Is a Dream is one of the masterpieces of world literature. Its power, along with the sheer beauty of its verse, lies in the questions it asks but never answers. It is as relevant today as when it was first performed in 1635. Its richness of meaning can be inferred from the various categorizations that have been applied to it; it has been called Christian, romantic, philosophical, existentialist, absurdist, and tragic theater.

The drama is organized around three great soliloquies by Segismundo that not only further the action but exemplify the dominant themes of the play. The first, spoken by Segismundo while he is still in chains, imprisoned in his tower, centers on his lack of freedom as compared to that of other creatures of the earth; the second is the famous "life is a dream" speech, in which Segismundo can no longer distinguish between reality and dream; the third focuses on Segismundo's decision to act and act well, no matter whether he is awake or asleep.

The imagery reflects his confusion between reality and dream. *Life Is a Dream* is magnificent in its dramatic interplay of light and shadow. For example, the abrupt change from the perpetual twilight of Segismundo's tower to the hurtful brilliance of the court is the stuff of nightmares.

Ironically, the court's light should symbolize knowledge and wisdom, but in the play its harshness, which blinds Segismundo, represents the cruelty of a king who is blinded in turn by his self-image and mistaken beliefs. Segismundo, on the other hand, finds the light of truth in his dark tower.

The paradoxes of the imagery mirror the ambiguities of the themes. What is the principal theme of *Life Is a Dream*? Is it the triumph of free will? Out of fear, Basilio rejects the concept of free will and robs his son of his freedom, but Segismundo finds that only by controlling his will can he achieve the freedom he seeks. Segismundo, at the end of the work, has triumphed over his baser nature, but has had to give up the woman he loves. The denouement, although it ties up the loose ends of the plot, is far from being that of a typical romance. It is not a happy one, and when the final action of Segismundo is to imprison in his tower for rebellion a soldier who helped to set him free, an ironic cycle is completed. The richness of the text can be seen in its artful weaving of other, perhaps secondary themes, such as love, loyalty, honor, education, ambition, and power. Much has been written of the metaphysical nature of the work. Calderón has always been considered the foremost idea-oriented dramatist of the Spanish language. Many critics label him as one of the first existentialists. *Life Is a Dream* takes place in no particular time, and therefore in every time, and Segismundo can be seen to represent every human being forced to find the right way in a shadow world, imprisoned and oppressed by forces unknowable and uncontrollable, and fettered by ignorance and base instincts. No matter how strong the philosophical underpinnings of the work, it should not be forgotten that Segismundo is also strong as a dramatic character. He is very much a flesh and blood person and loves Rosaura. This makes his giving her up a greater sacrifice, not just the politic and dutiful gesture of some hypothetical model of the good ruler.

A sense of personal loss is evident in this play. Segismundo has lost his childhood and adolescence. He also recovers what was lost: his identity. All the other major characters' lives are colored by the question of what might have been. Such melancholy explains their unwillingness to act in an uncertain world. This fear is given beautiful poetic expression in Segismundo's comparison of life to a flowering almond tree whose blooms, appearing too soon, wither and die at the first slightly cold wind.

There is one character who does not fit in this mold of passivity before loss; she is Rosaura. She has lost her lover Astolfo, but she decides to seek, not accept, her fate and go after him. Defying convention, disguised as a man, she travels to Poland and ends up serving in Segismundo's army. She is an elemental force whose actions turn Segismundo's, Clotaldo's, Astolfo's, and Estrella's lives upside down. Her determination and will are juxtaposed, on a higher level, to the cowardice of Basilio. Basilio has spent his whole life, and ruined his son's, trying to flee his supposed preordained fate. He realizes his error when, on fleeing the battlefield, he stumbles across a dead body. Rosaura's servant, thinking to avoid death on the battlefield, had run straight into it.

Philosophy, characterization, emotions, and action are all realized in a masterful poetic tapestry. The Romantics considered Calderón to be the greatest of all lyrical dramatists. Selections from his plays, especially the sonnets, are always included in Spanish poetry anthologies. The 3,315 verses of *Life Is a Dream* could be used as a textbook on how to write verse drama. Evaluation of Spanish Golden Age drama has gone through many changes depending on prevailing literary and political winds, but not the appreciation of *Life Is a Dream*. It is a complex, intricate work which cannot be pigeonholed into any comfortable critical niche.

"Critical Evaluation" by Charlene E. Suscavage

Bibliography:

Honig, Edwin. *Calderón and the Seizures of Honor*. Cambridge, Mass.: Harvard University Press, 1972. A good discussion of one of the dominant issues of Calderónian theater. Compares the treatment of the concept of honor in *The Mayor of Zalamea* (1643) with that of other plays in which the protagonist is an aristocrat.

Maraniss, James. *On Calderón*. Columbia: University of Missouri Press, 1978. One of the starting points in the discussion of the new interpretations of Calderónian drama.

Parker, A. A. *The Mind and Art of Calderón: Essays on the Comedia*. Cambridge, England: Cambridge University Press, 1989. A discussion of Calderónian theater from one of the critics responsible for renewed interest in and new interpretations of Golden Age theater.

Sloman, Albert. *The Dramatic Craftsmanship of Calderón*. Oxford, England: Dolfin Book Company, 1958. A good analysis of structure and dramatic technique; insists on close reading of text.

Wilson, Margaret. *Spanish Drama of the Golden Age*. Elmsford, N.Y.: Pergammon Press, 1967. A basic introduction to Spanish Golden Age drama. Calderón's plays are compared to those of his contemporaries. Wilson comes to different conclusions than those of many critics.

THE LIFE OF MARIANNE

Type of work: Novel
Author: Marivaux (Pierre Carlet de Chamblain Marivaux, 1688-1763), completed by Marie-
  Jeanne Riccoboni
Type of plot: Psychological realism
Time of plot: Late seventeenth century
Locale: France
First published: La Vie de Marianne, 1731-1741 (English translation, 1736-1742)

> *Principal characters:*
> MARIANNE, COUNTESS OF ——, a virtuous orphan
> MONSIEUR DE CLIMAL, Marianne's benefactor and Madame de Valville's
>   brother
> MONSIEUR DE VALVILLE, affianced to Marianne
> MADAME DE VALVILLE, his mother
> MADEMOISELLE VARTHON, loved by Valville
> MADEMOISELLE DE TERVIRE, now a nun

The Story:

Shortly after he rented a country house near Rennes, the narrator came upon several
notebooks containing the story of a lady, presented in her own handwriting. At the request of
his friends, he agreed to edit and publish her account. Marianne, the name the lady in the
autobiography gave herself, was a countess, about fifty years of age at the time she was writing.
She explained that she was describing her past because her dear friend had entreated her to tell
the full story of her life.

While still an infant, Marianne had been orphaned in an attack by brigands on the coach in
which she and her parents were traveling. She was the only survivor of this brutal encounter,
and as a result her identity was unknown. Passersby rescued the child and put her in the care of
the sister of the local priest. Marianne remained the ward of that kind person until she was
fifteen years of age. At that time, she accompanied her foster mother on a visit to Paris.

Misfortune came to her almost immediately. An epidemic broke out, and all of those
intimately concerned with Marianne's welfare were fatally stricken. Soon another benefactor
appeared, Monsieur de Climal, who offered to aid her out of charitable piety. By this time,
Marianne was a beautiful young woman, and Climal showed his fondness by buying her
expensive clothing and arranging for her lodging with a widowed shopkeeper, Madame Dutour.
Marianne objected strongly to the bourgeois atmosphere of her new home, but her circumstances gave her no other choice. For a religious holiday, she dressed in her finery and strolled
about the city after church. The young men ogled her; one, in particular, was especially attracted
to her and she to him, although no words passed between them. Bemused by the encounter,
Marianne stepped into the path of a moving carriage and was knocked down.

Her unknown admirer, Monsieur de Valville, came immediately to her aid. At the time,
neither learned the other's identity, for Monsieur de Climal arrived and jealously insisted on
taking his charge home. Beside himself, Climal declared his undying love and offered to set
Marianne up in an apartment. Proudly refusing this hypocritical proposal and also his protection, she went to a nearby convent to live. Meanwhile, Valville set about to learn her name and
whereabouts. Successful in his search, he arrived at the convent soon after Marianne had

acquired a loving benefactress, who turned out to be his mother. When Madame de Valville learned of the mutual attraction between her son and Marianne, she agreed that they could well be in love, but she counseled delay in the affair. In the meantime, Climal had succumbed to a fatal illness; as an act of repentance, he bequeathed one-third of his estate to Marianne. The remainder was to go to his nephew, Valville.

As soon as Valville's noble and influential relatives found out about Marianne's dubious parentage and her brief stay with a shopkeeper, they took steps to stop the marriage. In an elaborate abduction scheme, they succeeded in luring Marianne away from the convent. Then she was told that she had two choices: to become a nun or to marry a young man they had provided. In the hope of gaining time, she agreed to talk with the prospective bridegroom, but informed her captors that she would wed no one but Valville. At that moment, Madame de Valville and her son caught up with the plot and arrived to defend Marianne. At last the relatives, convinced of Marianne's strength of character, nobility, and worthiness, withdrew their objections to the marriage, and plans for the wedding were made. Within a few weeks, Marianne was to leave the convent and become a bride.

A chance call upon friends brought Mademoiselle Varthon to the attention of Valville. During a brief illness when Marianne was confined, Valville became infatuated with Mlle Varthon, who promptly told Marianne of her love for the young man. Deeply grieved by her son's infidelity, Madame de Valville assured Marianne of her own love and affection, which she continued to shower upon the unfortunate young woman until death ended Madame de Valville's acts of kindness a short time later. Once more, Marianne was alone in the world.

To take Marianne's mind off her misfortunes and to give her a perspective on the curious happenings that befall human beings, a nun who had become very friendly with her suggested that Marianne should hear the story of her own life. Depressed and lonely, Marianne agreed to listen to the nun's account.

The nun, the daughter of Monsieur de Tervire and Mademoiselle de Tresle, had learned early in life that her father was dead. Sometime later, her mother married a grand seigneur of the court, and the young girl was left to the care of a farmer. Although her mother sent money for her support and promised again and again to bring her daughter to live with her in Paris, the invitation was constantly delayed. When Mlle de Tervire was seventeen years of age, Baron de Sercour sought her hand in marriage. An unscrupulous trick by the baron's heir disgraced the bride-to-be, however, and the marriage never took place. Madame de Dursan then became the young woman's foster mother. She willed her estate to Mlle de Tervire, but an estranged son turned up as Madame de Dursan was dying and the will was changed. When Madame de Dursan's relatives refused to give Mlle de Tervire one-third of the property, as had been promised, she decided to go to Paris. On the stagecoach, she met a Madame Darcire. Ultimately, Mlle de Tervire discovered that Madame Darcire knew her mother well. From a lawyer, they learned that Madame la Marquise, the young woman's mother, had been persuaded to turn her estates over to her son. He then took all the property and abandoned his mother to poverty. Furious at this turn of events, Mlle de Tervire went to her sister-in-law and demanded that her half brother take proper care of their parent. The nun's story was terminated with the recounting of a disastrous love affair and her ultimate decision to take the veil. Marianne finally married Valville after years of tribulation and also learned that she was of noble birth.

Critical Evaluation:

Marivaux's eleven-volume tale about the vicissitudes of a young woman thrust upon the world with no clear-cut social identity ranks with Samuel Richardson's *Pamela: Or, Virtue*

Rewarded (1740) and *Clarissa* (1747-1748) as one of the first modern psychological novels. It is a pity that Marivaux did not finish the novel; it was completed by Marie-Jeanne Riccoboni. The unfinished novel stops before the nun finishes her story and before Marianne is jilted, suffers various tribulations, and at last marries Valville.

Writing in the early decades of the eighteenth century, Marivaux used a variety of devices already common in the fiction of the day to give his work an air of verisimilitude. Using the device of the memoir and telling the story in the epistolary form were both well-tried techniques that helped readers accept the story as plausible and the behavior of the characters as realistic.

Marivaux is successful in creating lifelike characters because, unlike many of his predecessors and contemporaries, he concentrates on the exploration of emotion rather than on development of action. He goes beyond a number of novelists of his time to achieve a sense of realism by including language spoken by commoners, a device scorned by earlier writers who attempted to maintain standards of decorum prescribed by neoclassical theories of literature in vogue at the time. He often uses the language of the streets when appropriate for the scene and situation he is depicting. As a result, a number of his characters become individualized through their language, an accomplishment that links Marivaux with the realistic tradition.

The writer's major success in *The Life of Marianne* is his creation of a heroine whose behavior seems psychologically sound. Marianne is a complex character who succeeds by her wits and charm rather than by social position. Throughout the story, she struggles to find her rightful place in society. She is unable simply to claim that right because her origins are unknown, so she must earn her social rewards by acting in such a way that the upper classes of society will accept her. Her efforts are not always successful, and often she stumbles because she makes poor decisions. She is not always a sound judge of character, nor does she always make the right choices, but she is resilient and resourceful. As she admits, she is often blessed by good fortune; circumstance and coincidence play no small role in extricating her from potentially devastating situations. She is not presented as perfect, however; Marivaux and his eighteenth century contemporaries make that distinction between their heroines and those of earlier ages, whose virtues are often so great that they become mere pasteboard figures rather than believable human beings. Marianne has her faults, but she also has a certain inner strength that allows her to appreciate her triumphs without becoming too elated, and to deal realistically with her tragedies. This is especially true when she loses Valville to the vapid Mlle Varthon.

Although there is no evidence that Marivaux modeled his work on any of the English writers, clear parallels exist between Marianne and that paragon of resourcefulness, Daniel Defoe's Moll Flanders. Like Defoe, Marivaux structures his tale so that the elder Marianne tells readers of her life as a younger woman. Doing so allows her to serve, in the same fashion as Moll Flanders did, as commentator and judge of her own past behavior. Unlike Moll, Marianne has not been forced to resort to a life of crime to preserve herself; however, both women share a certain quality of self-awareness and an understanding that being true to oneself is often more critical to one's psychological health than being accepted in the eyes of society.

Marivaux did not finish *The Life of Marianne*, so it is impossible to know exactly what he had planned for his heroine in her struggle to retrieve her good name and her heritage. Hints in the novelist's writings suggest that eventually she would have discovered the identity of her parents and been restored to her rightful place in society. Nevertheless, the materials available indicate that Marivaux is more interested in character development than in knitting together the disparate strands of plot; action, for him, seems simply an excuse for character revelation.

Perhaps the most significant contribution Marivaux makes to French literature stems from his decision to concentrate not on the nobility but on the middle classes. No writer before him had chosen as the subject for such an extended romantic tale a woman whose claim to nobility could be disputed. His focus throughout the eleven volumes is on the lower classes of society. He paints meticulous, favorable portraits of characters such as Mme Dutour, the simple shopkeeper with whom Marianne lives for a time. His interest in the common people of France precedes the work of the greatest of all French chroniclers of everyday life, the nineteenth century novelist Honoré de Balzac. So accurate and detailed are Marivaux's descriptions that one critic has asserted about *The Life of Marianne* that even Balzac "has done nothing better than this realistic study of a little bourgeois milieu."

"Critical Evaluation" by Laurence W. Mazzeno

Bibliography:
Greene, E. J. H. *Marivaux*. Toronto: University of Toronto Press, 1965. Detailed, sensitive reading of *The Life of Marianne*, examining Marivaux's artistic intentions, his handling of characterization, his adroit use of sentimentalism, and his hardheaded analysis of a corrupt society. Speculates on reasons the novel was never finished.

Haac, Oscar A. *Marivaux*. New York: Twayne, 1974. General survey of the writer's achievements. Discusses *The Life of Marianne* as an early example of the psychological novel. Pays special attention to Marivaux's development of major characters in the work.

Jamieson, Ruth Kirby. *Marivaux: A Study in Sensibility*. New York: Octagon Books, 1969. Examines *The Life of Marianne* as one of the works that reveals Marivaux's contributions to the "novel of sensibility"; contrasts it with the extremely sentimental works of some of his contemporaries. Asserts that Marivaux balances reason and emotion in telling his story.

Laden, Marie-Paule. *Self-Imitation in the Eighteenth-Century Novel*. Princeton, N.J.: Princeton University Press, 1987. Extended analysis of *The Life of Marianne* focuses on Marivaux's handling of narrative voice. Explains how he gives emotional and moral perspective to Marianne's adventures by having the heroine serve as both protagonist and commentator, since she writes as an older woman about her life as a younger ingenue.

Rosbottom, Ronald C. *Marivaux's Novels: Theme and Function in European Eighteenth Century Narrative*. Rutherford, N.J.: Fairleigh Dickinson University Press, 1974. Devotes two chapters to an analysis of *The Life of Marianne*. Focuses on the accommodations Marianne must make to succeed in society and the limits beyond which she cannot compromise her principles.

THE LIFE OF SAMUEL JOHNSON, LL.D.

Type of work: Biography
Author: James Boswell (1740-1795)
First published: 1791

> *Principal personages:*
> SAMUEL JOHNSON, author, critic, and lexicographer
> JAMES BOSWELL, the biographer, Johnson's friend
> DAVID GARRICK,
> SIR JOSHUA REYNOLDS,
> MR. and MRS. THRALE,
> DAVID HUME, and
> OLIVER GOLDSMITH, members of the Johnson circle

James Boswell's life of Samuel Johnson has often been considered the greatest biography produced in the English language, and it has probably had more readers than any other biography written in English. Among the works published during Boswell's lifetime *The Life of Samuel Johnson, LL.D.* stood out as the greatest for almost a century and a half. A new estimate of James Boswell's work has had to be taken since 1950, however, for much of Boswell's writing was lost in manuscript until the 1920's. During the period between 1927 and 1949 Colonel Isham, a collector, brought together the papers that had been stored at Malahide Castle, near Dublin, Ireland, and the Forbes collection, which had accidentally passed into the hands of one of Boswell's executors and descended to the latter's heirs. Some of the papers were published by Isham, who sold the entire collection to Yale University in 1949 and 1950. The university has published several volumes of the papers under the general title of *The Yale Editions of the Private Papers of James Boswell.* Through such volumes of Boswell's writing as *Boswell's London Journal, 1762-1763* (1950), *Boswell in Holland, 1763-1764* (1952), and *Boswell on the Grand Tour: Germany and Switzerland, 1764* (1953), Boswell has emerged as a splendid writer of journals. This fact, however, does not detract from his stature as the author of the biography of Johnson, nor will these newer works replace the biography as the most important of Boswell's books, although critical opinion may be modified to grant him greater stature in literature than he once had.

Readers now know that *The Life of Samuel Johnson, LL.D.* was based upon what Boswell had recorded in copious journals that he kept during the greater part of his adult life. This is not to say, however, that the biography was merely a transcription of materials from those journals. From present knowledge of the papers it can be seen that Boswell was an artist in biography, choosing carefully what suited his needs and goals. Even those who feel that Boswell intruded too much into the biography must now recognize that Boswell was at some pains to omit much material about Johnson in which Boswell figured. Those who felt that Boswell intruded too much into the work possibly overlooked the fact that during Johnson's life, Boswell was Johnson's friend and spent from four hundred to five hundred days with his subject, thus becoming himself a part of Johnson's life and the Johnsonian environment.

Boswell's method was to record materials about Johnson in his journals. Sometimes the material was recorded daily, but on occasion Boswell fell behind and had to rely upon his memory—a phenomenal one—to recall materials he had garnered in a period of four or five days and evenings. It is notable, too, that Boswell was careful to prompt Johnson into conversation, often asking what seem to be obvious or absurd questions in order to goad Johnson into making remarks worthy of record. One such question noted by critics is that in which Boswell asked Johnson what he would do if given the solitary care of a small infant; the question, seemingly absurd, led Johnson to reply in such fashion as to comment on rearing and educating children and to set forth a philosophy of education. The more readers learn about Boswell and his work, the more they understand that he was not a mere transcriber, as critical legend held for some time, but that he was a skillful writer who shaped his materials with great care. The casual reader may even miss some of the more obvious points of artistry, such as notations on how Johnson looked and spoke when delivering comments and opinions.

Johnson was a man of many achievements. He single-handedly brought forth the first recognized dictionary of the English language. He also made himself famous as a writer by means of his writings for *The Rambler* (1750-1752), his drama *Irène: A Tragedy* (1749), his poetry, and his essays. As a moralist Johnson also won fame as the author of the didactic novel, *Rasselas, a Prince of Abyssinia: A Tale by S. Johnson* (1759). As a critic he was famous for his *The Lives of the Poets* (1779-1781) and his preface to an edition of William Shakespeare's plays. People great and small admired Johnson, including many of the famous and remarkable Englishmen of his time, men like David Hume, Sir Joshua Reynolds, Oliver Goldsmith, and David Garrick. In addition, he was a picturesque, at times even ludicrous, figure, and this fact Boswell did not attempt to hide, taking to himself the task of writing "not his panegyrick, which must be all praise, but his Life; which great and good as he was, must not be supposed to be perfect." In further defense of his way of writing biography, Boswell wrote near the beginning of the biography:

I am fully aware of the objections which may be made to the minuteness on some occasions of my detail of Johnson's conversation, and how happily it is adapted for the petty exercise of ridicule by men of superficial understanding, and ludicrous fancy; but I remain firm and confident in my opinion, that minute particulars are frequently characteristick, and always amusing, when they relate to a distinguished man. I am therefore exceedingly unwilling that anything, however slight, which my illustrious friend thought it worth his while to express, with any degree of point, should perish.

Boswell realized, as readers know from what he said and wrote, that the function and art of biography is to focus on the subject and keep that person constantly before the reader. This Boswell did in his biography of Johnson. To do so he carefully gathered together more than what he knew firsthand of the man who was his friend and subject. He exercised diligence and care in collecting letters written by Johnson, including the text of the famous letter to Lord Chesterfield. He collected, too, letters written about Johnson, as well as anecdotes about his subject's life, trying at the same time to establish the authenticity of these reports he had of Johnson. These materials are presented in the biography in chronological order. If the results have some defects, the defects are more or less forgivable in view of their sparseness. Seldom did Boswell record facts that later biographers needed to correct.

The account of Johnson's life before meeting Boswell is relatively short. This fact may be excused on the ground that Boswell used only the information about Johnson's early life that he could gather and trust. Naturally, he had a much larger fund of materials from the period during which he knew Johnson personally. Some critics have noted Boswell's reluctance to interpret. Of this reluctance, it must be said that interpretation was not Boswell's way. Upon occasion he generalized upon Johnson perceptively, but he preferred, as he carefully stated, to present the particulars, rather than the generalizations. The result is that Johnson is "alive" in

The Life of Samuel Johnson, LL.D. as few biographical subjects are, with his personality and character borne out by his own spoken and written words. On occasion the reader may feel that Johnson's written words, usually letters, have been inserted where they fit none too well, seeming to interfere with the flow of the book. They are nevertheless a part of the scheme Boswell worked out and put together.

Samuel Johnson has been the subject of many biographies; five, for example, appeared after Johnson's death and before Boswell's work. Others have been written since, but none has ever equaled Boswell's *The Life of Samuel Johnson, LL.D.*

Bibliography:
Bronson, Bertrand H. "Samuel Johnson and James Boswell." In *Facets of the Enlightenment*. Berkeley: University of California Press, 1968. A negative review of Boswell's literary artistry, arguing against his dramatic abilities. Implies that Boswell's perspective was narrow, his style mechanical, and his great success accidental.
Clingham, Greg, ed. *New Light on Boswell: Critical and Historical Essays on the Occasion of the Bicentenary of "The Life of Johnson."* Cambridge, England: Cambridge University Press, 1991. A collection of essays that explore Boswell's literary and personal achievements and limitations. Noteworthy for the investigation of the critical and theoretical questions surrounding the notion of biographical representation.
Delaney, Frank. *A Walk to the Western Isles: After Boswell and Johnson*. New York: Harper-Collins, 1993. A chronicle of Delaney's journey that retraced the 1773 Scotland trip taken by James Boswell and Samuel Johnson. Beautiful photographs and illustrations. Re-creates the time, place, and intellectual environment where the two scholars cemented their friendship.
Siebenschuh, William R. "The Life of Johnson." In *Form and Purpose in Boswell's Biographical Works*. Berkeley: University of California Press, 1972. A critical study of James Boswell's methods for dramatizing the primary factual materials in his biographical work, with particular emphasis on his gift for characterization, structure, and style.

LIFE ON THE MISSISSIPPI

Type of work: Fictionalized autobiography
Author: Mark Twain (Samuel Langhorne Clemens, 1835-1910)
First published: 1883

Principal characters:
THE NARRATOR, a former steamboat pilot
MR. BIXBY, the master pilot who trains him
HENRY, the narrator's brother, a clerk on the *Pennsylvania*
MR. BROWN, an unpleasant pilot on the *Pennsylvania*
THOMPSON (the poet) and
ROGERS (the stenographer), the narrator's travel companions in 1882
"UNCLE" MUMFORD, a mate on the *Gold Dust*
ROBERT STYLES, a pilot on the *Gold Dust*
KARL RITTER, a German whom the narrator meets in Munich

The Story:

As a boy growing up in a Mississippi River town, the narrator shared the common ambition of becoming a steamboatman. He especially wanted to be a pilot. Later, while living in Cincinnati, he decided to make his fortune in the Amazon and bought passage on the steamboat *Paul Jones* to New Orleans, from where he intended to sail to the Amazon. After arriving there, however, he discovered he would not be able to continue his journey, so he looked for a new career. He laid siege to Mr. Bixby, pilot of the *Paul Jones*, and persuaded him to accept him as a cub pilot on the return voyage upriver.

The new pilot began his education under Bixby's tutelage by steering the *Paul Jones* out of New Orleans and listening to Bixby call attention to monotonously nondescript points along the way. At midnight of his first day, he was rudely turned out of his bed to stand watch—his first intimation that piloting might not be quite as romantic as he had imagined. His second such intimation came when he learned that Bixby expected him to remember everything he had been told. As the boat continued upriver, the narrator's new notebook filled with information, but his head remained empty.

After switching boats at St. Louis for the return trip, the cub discovered that downstream navigation differed greatly from upstream navigation. In fact, each time he thought he was mastering his new trade, Bixby piled on more facts for him to learn. He was expected to memorize the river's features and its shape, then he had to learn the river's depths and how to "read" it as a book. Eventually, the narrator thought his education was complete, only to be told that he now had to learn how to read the river's fluctuating depths from its banks. His education thereupon began anew.

The narrator explained the minutiae of piloting because he loved the profession more than any other. In the early days, a steamboat pilot had been the only completely unfettered human being on earth. That situation had begun changing before the Civil War, when the rapid increase in licensed pilots started cutting into wages. A handful of bold veterans reversed the trend by forming a professional association that forced the steamboat companies to restore their former wages. Shortly after, however, the war halted commercial steamboat traffic, and it never recovered because of postwar competition from railroads and tow barges.

A prime example of a master pilot with an exceptional memory, Bixby proved his skill by switching to the more difficult Missouri River, where he quickly earned a new license. Meanwhile, the young cub stayed on the Mississippi and apprenticed himself on the *Pennsylvania* under the despotic tutelage of Mr. Brown. His younger brother Henry had joined the *Pennsylvania* as a lowly clerk. One day, Brown assaulted Henry, which provoked the narrator to beat him up. The narrator thought that his career was ruined, but kindly Captain Klinefelter approved of his action and even offered to put Brown ashore in New Orleans. Not feeling up to assuming Brown's piloting responsibilities, the cub himself stayed ashore and followed the *Pennsylvania* upriver on another boat. Near Memphis, Tennessee, he learned that the *Pennsylvania*'s boilers had exploded, killing 150 people. His own brother was fatally injured, and Brown disappeared.

Eventually the narrator earned his license and became steadily employed as a pilot. Soon, however, the Civil War intervened and brought his occupation to an end. Twenty-one years later—after going through a succession of careers—he decided to return to the Mississippi, and he enlisted a poet named Thompson and a stenographer named Rogers to accompany him. At St. Louis, they boarded the *Gold Dust*, on which the narrator quickly began discovering how much steamboating had changed. Traveling under a pseudonym, he sat quietly in the pilothouse and listened while the pilot, Robert Styles—who had once been his fellow cub—tried to impress him with outrageous lies before revealing that he had recognized him immediately.

As the *Gold Dust* went south, the mate, "Uncle" Mumford, and other crew members recounted the river's recent history and the impact of the Civil War on Southern towns. The narrator observed how much navigational techniques had been modernized, which he felt had destroyed the river's romance.

When the boat neared Napoleon, Arkansas, the narrator told his companions an amazing story about a German named Ritter whose last wish he had promised to fulfill by retrieving $10,000 that Ritter had hidden in Napoleon and sending it to the son of a man whom Ritter had wronged. The story aroused avarice among the narrator's companions until they learned that the entire town of Napoleon had been washed away by a flood.

At Vicksburg, Mississippi, the travelers switched to another steamboat that took them to Baton Rouge, where they entered the "absolute South," where romantic influences in architecture reminded the narrator of the debilitating influence that Sir Walter Scott's Romanticism had had on the South. In New Orleans, the narrator spent much of his visit with George Washington Cable and Joel Chandler Harris. He also met Horace Bixby, who was now captain of the *City of Baton Rouge*. He, Bixby, and other old-time pilots swapped stories about former rivermen, including Captain Isaiah Sellers, from whom the narrator had appropriated his pen name, "Mark Twain." After returning to St. Louis on Bixby's boat, the narrator continued upriver to Hannibal, Missouri—his boyhood home. There he recalled poignant memories from his youth. He then went north to St. Paul, Minnesota, from where he returned home by land.

Critical Evaluation:

Though usually classified among Mark Twain's five travel books, *Life on the Mississippi* defies neat categorization. Like much of his work, it is structurally flawed and uneven in tone; indeed, it even resists simple synopsis. Nevertheless, the book is generally recognized as one of Twain's finest works, a true classic about the great Mississippi River. It is, moreover, the immediate predecessor to his masterpiece, *Adventures of Huckleberry Finn* (1884).

The book's structural problems arise from its author's conflicting goals. A decade before Twain began the book, he entertained the idea of writing a standard work on the Mississippi

River. The germ of this idea can be seen in the book's first three chapters, which describe the river's history and geographical peculiarities. As early as chapter 3, however, Twain's resolve to continue along these lines began wavering, and he shifted directions by introducing an extract from a novel on which he had worked for several years. Taken from what became chapter 16 of *Adventures of Huckleberry Finn*, this passage introduces Huck and Jim and depicts life on a great commercial river raft. A beautifully realized passage, it evokes the power and romance of the Mississippi and links the book directly to the novel.

Chapter 4 of *Life on the Mississippi* opens what is generally acknowledged to be one of Twain's finest pieces of writing: an almost lyrical account of his two years as an apprentice steamboat pilot on the lower Mississippi. He originally composed most of those seventeen chapters for magazine serialization. With the encouragement of his friends Joseph Twichell and W. D. Howells, the editor of the *Atlantic Monthly*, he wrote these articles in order to re-create the great age of steamboating. After they appeared in the *Atlantic Monthly* in 1876 as "Old Times on the Mississippi," he put aside his idea of writing a book on the Mississippi until six years later, when he succumbed to the itch to return to the river.

In early 1882, Twain spent just over a month on the Mississippi with his book publisher, James R. Osgood ("Thompson" in the narrative), and a Hartford, Connecticut, stenographer named Roswell Phelps ("Rogers"). Afterward, he returned home to Hartford and threw himself into writing what he believed must be a large book. After completing the introductory chapters, he naturally returned to his "Old Times" articles. These he lightly revised and supplemented with several new chapters—including those recounting his troubles with Mr. Brown.

Although chapters 4 through 20 of *Life on the Mississippi* are based on Twain's own experiences as a cub pilot from early 1858 through early 1859, they cannot strictly be regarded as autobiography. Twain's narrator writes in the first person, but the cub whom he depicts as his youthful self appears to be a much younger and more naïve person than the twenty-one-year-old Sam Clemens, who had become an apprentice pilot. Twain's interest in writing these chapters was to describe the marvelous art of piloting and the wonders of the Mississippi River, not to recount his own life. Once he achieved these objectives, he dismissed the two years that he spent as a licensed pilot in one brief paragraph (chapter 21).

The balance of the sixty-chapter book recounts Twain's return to the Mississippi in 1882. Much of this section is straightforward travel narrative, but even it cannot be read as unadulterated autobiography. As with Twain's other travel books, much of this section is embroidered for entertainment and literary effect. More even than in the earlier chapters, the narrator speaks with the voice of Twain, but here, too, he never openly identifies himself as Mark Twain (or as Sam Clemens), although he twice alludes to his famous pen name. Keeping the identity of his narrator vague—a technique that typifies most of Twain's travel writing—leaves him free to invent and embroider without the strictures of nonfiction.

Readers unaware of the extent to which Twain freed himself to invent may become confused in reading *Life on the Mississippi*. The second part of the book contains several frame-stories that are pure fiction, but the author gives no hint of their nature. A prime example is the Karl Ritter episode, which blends so seamlessly into chapters 31 and 32 that one might mistakenly read the story as authentic. Another example occurs in chapter 52—"The Burning Brand"—to which Twain adds a realistic note by working in the name of his literary friend Charles Dudley Warner.

Although *Life on the Mississippi* should not be read as authentic autobiography, the book is filled with autobiographical interest. Its cub-piloting chapters help illuminate an important phase of Twain's early life, just as the book's later narrative at least approximates Twain's 1882 experiences. Of perhaps greater autobiographical significance, and of often superior literary interest, are the chapters concerning his return visit to Hannibal, Missouri. Chapters 53-56 take Twain deeper into his youth than anything he wrote until he seriously undertook his autobiography a quarter century later.

R. Kent Rasmussen

Bibliography:
Cox, James M. *"Life on the Mississippi* Revisited." In *The Mythologizing of Mark Twain*, edited by Sara deSaussure Davis and Phillip D. Beidler. Tuscaloosa: University of Alabama Press, 1984. Presents a persuasive argument that *Life on the Mississippi* converts the life of Samuel L. Clemens into the "myth" of Mark Twain.
Emerson, Everett. *The Authentic Mark Twain: A Literary Biography of Samuel L. Clemens.* Philadelphia: University of Pennsylvania Press, 1985. Contains a useful summary of Twain's composition of *Life on the Mississippi*, concluding that the "real" Mark Twain disappears from the last part of his book. Emerson also wrote on this book for *The Mark Twain Encyclopedia*, edited by J. R. LeMaster and James D. Wilson (New York: Garland, 1993).
Kruse, Horst H. *Mark Twain and "Life on the Mississippi."* Amherst: University of Massachusetts Press, 1981. Much the fullest study of its subject, this book focuses on Twain's composition of *Life on the Mississippi*. Kruse concludes that one of Twain's intentions was to help redeem the South from the Romanticism that brought on the Civil War. Includes an extensive bibliography.
Rasmussen, R. Kent. *Mark Twain A to Z.* New York: Facts On File, 1995. This comprehensive reference work has a long analytical synopsis of *Life on the Mississippi* which is cross-referenced to essays on individual characters, places, and other topics. It also has extended essays on such related topics as piloting, steamboats, and the Mississippi River.
Twain, Mark. *Life on the Mississippi.* New York: Limited Editions Club, 1944. A full edition of the work with an authoritative introduction by Edward Wagenknecht and an appendix that restores fifteen thousand words cut from the original text. Also published in a Heritage Press edition.

LIGEIA

Type of work: Short fiction
Author: Edgar Allan Poe (1809-1849)
Type of plot: Gothic
Time of plot: Early nineteenth century
Locale: Germany and England
First published: 1838

> *Principal characters:*
> THE NARRATOR
> LIGEIA, his first wife
> LADY ROWENA TREVANION, his second wife

The Story:

He could not remember when he had first met Ligeia, and he knew nothing of her family except that it was old. Ligeia herself, once his wife, he could remember in every detail. She was tall and slender. Ethereal as a shadow, her face was faultless in its beauty, her skin like ivory, her features classic. Crowning the perfect face and body was raven-black, luxuriant hair. Her eyes, above all else, held the key to Ligeia's mystery. Larger than most, those black eyes held an expression unfathomable even to her husband. It became his all-consuming passion to unravel the secret of that expression.

In character, Ligeia possessed a stern will that never failed to astound him. Outwardly she was placid and calm, but she habitually uttered words that stunned him with their intensity. Her learning was immense. She spoke many tongues, and in metaphysical investigations she was never wrong. Her husband was engrossed in a study of metaphysics, but it was she who guided him and unraveled the secrets of his research. With Ligeia to assist him, he knew that he would one day reach a goal of wisdom undreamed of by others.

Then Ligeia fell ill. Her skin became transparent and waxen, her eyes wild, and he knew that she must die. The passion of her struggles against death was frightening. He had always known that she loved him, but in those last days she abandoned herself completely to love. From her heart, she poured forth phrases of idolatry, and on what was to be the last day of her life, she bade him repeat to her a poem she had composed not long before. It was a morbid thing about death, about the conquering of Man by the Worm. As he finished repeating the melancholy lines, Ligeia leaped to her feet with a shriek, then fell back on her deathbed. In a scarcely audible whisper, she repeated a proverb that had haunted her: that human beings did not yield to death save through the weakness of their own will. So Ligeia died.

Crushed with sorrow, her husband left his desolate home by the Rhine and retired to an old and decayed abbey in a deserted region in England. He left the exterior of the building in its sagging state, but inside he furnished the rooms lavishly and strangely. He had become the slave of opium, and the furnishings took on the shapes and colors of his fantastic dreams. One bedchamber received the most bizarre treatment of all, and it was to this chamber that he led his new bride, the blue-eyed Lady Rowena Trevanion, of Tremaine.

The room was in a high turret of the abbey. It was of immense proportions, lighted by a single huge window. The pane had a leaden hue, giving a ghastly luster to all objects within. The walls, floors, and furniture were all covered with a heavy, arabesque tapestry showing black figures on pure gold. The figures changed as one looked at them from different angles, their appearance being changed by an artificial current of air that constantly stirred the draperies.

In rooms such as this, he spent a bridal month with Lady Rowena. It was easy to perceive that she loved him but little, and he hated her with a passion more demoniac than human. In his opium dreams, he called aloud for Ligeia, as if he could restore her to the earthly life she had abandoned. He reveled in memories of her purity and her love.

In the second month of her marriage, Rowena grew ill, and in her fever she spoke of sounds and movements in the chamber, fantasies unheard and unseen by her husband. Although she recovered, she had recurring attacks of the fever, and it became evident that she would soon succumb. Her imaginings became stronger, and she grew more insistent about the sounds and movements in the tapestries.

One night in September, she became visibly weaker and unusually agitated. Seeking to calm her, her husband stepped across the room to get some wine, but he was arrested midway by the sense of something passing lightly by him. Then he was startled to see on the gold carpet a shadow of angelic aspect. Saying nothing to Rowena, he poured the wine into a goblet. As she took the vessel, he distinctly heard a light footstep upon the carpet and saw, or thought he saw, three or four drops of a ruby-colored liquid fall into the goblet from an invisible source.

Immediately Rowena grew worse, and on the third night, she died. As he sat by her shrouded body in that bridal chamber, he thought of his lost Ligeia. Suddenly, he heard a sound from the bed upon which the corpse of his wife lay. Going closer, he perceived that Rowena had a faint color. It was unmistakable; Rowena lived. Unable to summon aid, he watched her with mounting terror. Then a relapse came, and she subsided into a death pallor more rigid than before. All night this phenomenon recurred. Rowena returned briefly from the dead, only to sink once more into oblivion. Each time he saw again a vision of Ligeia.

Toward morning of that fearful night, the enshrouded figure rose from the bed and tottered to the center of the chamber. Terrified, he fell at her feet. She unwound the burial cerements from her head and there streamed down raven-black hair that did not belong to the living Rowena. Then the spectral figure slowly opened her eyes. He could not be mistaken. Staring at him were the full black eyes of his lost love, Ligeia.

Critical Evaluation:

First published in *The Baltimore American Museum* in September, 1838, "Ligeia" was included in Edgar Allan Poe's *Tales of the Grotesque and Arabesque* (1839-1840). The final text appeared in *The Broadway Journal* in 1845. One of Poe's most famous tales, "Ligeia" is also among his most brilliantly written, and he himself once declared it his best. He considered it an "arabesque," a term he used to refer to tales that, while scarcely credible as a realistic occurrence, are told seriously, without the tone of mockery or satire that he used in his so-called grotesques. Examples of the latter include "King Pest," with its fantastic group of characters, "every one of whom seemed to possess a monopoly of some particular portion of physiognomy," and "A Predicament," in which a lady writer tells in shuddering detail how she felt when the minute hand of a giant clock cut off her head. Later critics have called "Ligeia" a tale of terror, since the narrator is frightened and horrified by what he sees, or thinks he sees, at the story's end. Similar terror is experienced by Roderick Usher in "The Fall of the House of Usher," and by a number of Poe's other narrators who undergo harrowing experiences.

The narrator of "Ligeia," who should not in any way be autobiographically identified with the author, never tells his name, a device Poe employed often, as in "The Pit and the Pendulum," "The Tell-Tale Heart," "The Black Cat," and many other tales. Telling the story from a first-person point of view increases the final dramatic effect, a predetermined element that, as Poe said in his famous review of Nathaniel Hawthorne's *Twice-Told Tales* (1837), should always be the aim of a serious artist in short fiction.

Two themes in "Ligeia" appear elsewhere in Poe's tales. Psychic survival through reincarnation is the theme in an early tale, "Morella," in which a bereaved husband learns that his dead wife has taken over the body and the character of the daughter who was born just before the mother died. In the climactic closing scene of "Ligeia," the supposedly dead first wife, Ligeia, has (or seems to have) appropriated the body of the second wife, Rowena. A second theme, that of premature burial, appears in the early tale, "Berenice," and in such later tales as "The Fall of the House of Usher" and "The Premature Burial."

"Ligeia" illustrates Poe's skill in achieving that unity of impression that, like his "predetermined effect," he considered of primary importance in telling a tale. Throughout, the tone of the narrator is intensely serious as he relates the story of his two marriages. He dwells on his love for and passionate adoration of the beautiful, mysterious, intellectual Ligeia. There is foreshadowing when he speaks of his suffering and of the loss "of her who is no more." The final scene is anticipated in several ways. The description of Ligeia at the beginning emphasizes "the raven-black, the glossy, the luxuriant, and naturally-curling tresses," and her eyes are repeatedly mentioned: "Those eyes! those large, those shining, those divine orbs!" The brief, hectic excitement of the second marriage, to the "fair-haired and blue-eyed Lady Rowena Trevanion, of Tremaine," is quickly followed by the husband's obsessed memories of "the beloved, the august, the beautiful, the entombed" Ligeia. In the second paragraph of the tale, Ligeia's beauty of face is described as "the radiance of an opium dream." This anticipates the actual opium dreams that result from the husband's addiction following his loss of Ligeia. Those dreams, which accompany his loathing and hatred of Rowena, are filled with Ligeia, and the intensity of the husband's longing for his lost love climaxes with her return at the story's end. When she opens her eyes, he is sure of her identity, and he shrieks "these are the full, and the black, and the wild eyes—of my lost love— . . . of the LADY Ligeia."

The theme of psychic survival is suggested first in the epigraph from Joseph Glanvill, with its final sentence, "Man doth not yield himself to the angels, nor unto death utterly, save only through the weakness of his feeble will." This theme first appears in the story when the narrator recalls having read the passage from Glanvill, which he quotes. He connects Glanvill's words with Ligeia when he speaks of her "intensity in thought, action, or speech" as "a result, or at least an index" of her "gigantic volition." After she fell ill, he was struck by "the fierceness of resistance with which she wrestled with the Shadow." He recalls that just before she died, she asked him to repeat a poem she had written some days before, a symbolic poem portraying life as a tragic drama with "its hero, the conqueror Worm," which finally devours each actor. As he concluded the poem, Ligeia shrieked and pleaded, "O God! O Divine Father! . . . shall this conqueror be not once conquered?" Her last murmured words were Glanvill's: "Man doth not yield him to the angels, nor unto death utterly, save only through the weakness of his feeble will." Yet her own fierce will to live did not save her from death—or so her husband thought. He left Germany, moved to England, purchased a decaying abbey, extravagantly refurnished its interior, and led his new bride to the bedroom in the high turret. Though entombed, Ligeia continued to "wrestle with the Shadow." She filled her husband's memories, and in final triumph she replaced her blonde successor. Or did she?

"Ligeia" has achieved considerable fame as the subject of many widely divergent interpretations. It has been argued that Ligeia is not a real woman but symbolically "the very incarnation of German idealism, German transcendentalism provided with an allegorical form." One critic has suggested that Ligeia never existed at all but was merely imagined by a madman. Another has called her a witch, and still another a "revenant—a spirit who has spent immemorial lifetimes on earth." As for the husband, he has been termed a liar and even a murderer who killed Rowena, his second wife, by poisoning her with the "ruby drops" that fall into her wine glass.

Perhaps the most acceptable interpretation of the story is a literal one. The narrator marries the beautiful, brilliant Ligeia, and they live happily in Germany until she dies of a mysterious disease. He then marries Rowena in England but soon turns against her. Rowena suffers spells of illness, and her husband endlessly dreams of his lost Ligeia, for whom he longs deeply. His increasing use of opium causes his dreams to become so confused with reality that in a final frightening hallucination, he believes he sees standing before him the beloved dark-haired and large-eyed Ligeia, who has taken over the body of her fair-haired successor. By the strength of her intense will, Ligeia would thus have defeated Death, the Conquering Worm.

Dramatically, the scene achieves the effect for which the Glanvill quotation prepared readers. That the return of Ligeia is only imagined is also prepared for by the narrator's repeated references to his drug addiction:

> I had become a bounden slave in the trammels of opium. . . . I was habitually fettered in the shackles of the drug. . . . I was wild with the excitement of an immoderate dose of opium. . . . Wild visions, opium-engendered, flitted, shadow-like, before me . . . passionate waking visions of Ligeia . . . a crowd of unutterable fancies . . . had chilled me into stone.

In his numbed state he has regained his intensely desired Ligeia, but surely it is a drug-induced fancy that shocks him into shrieking the words that end the story.

"Critical Evaluation" by Henderson Kincheloe

Bibliography:
Basler, Roy P. "The Interpretation of 'Ligeia.'" In *Poe: A Collection of Critical Essays*, edited by Robert Regan. Englewood Cliffs, N.J.: Prentice-Hall, 1967. A psychological study of "Ligeia" that interprets the work as an exploration of the narrator's rational and nonrational obsession and madness.

Jones, Daryl E. "Poe's Siren: Character and Meaning in 'Ligeia.'" *Studies in Short Fiction* 20, no. 1 (Winter, 1983): 33-37. Dismisses critics who interpret "Ligeia" as a straightforward gothic tale or a tale of psychological realism. Instead, explores the title character as a siren, which justifies her strength as well as the narrator's weakness of will.

Levine, Stuart. "'Ligeia': Multiple Intention, Unified Effect." In *Edgar Poe: Seer and Craftsman*. DeLand, Fla.: Everett/Edwards, 1972. Argues that Poe uses Ligeia's beauty to establish an explicitly romantic aesthetic. Explores several reasons why the story is difficult to interpret.

Matheson, Terence J. "The Multiple Murders in 'Ligeia': A New Look at Poe's Narrator." *Canadian Review of American Studies* 13, no. 3 (Winter, 1982): 279-289. Sees the story as flawed and tries to reason through Poe's own contention that "Ligeia" was his best tale.

Saliba, David R. "Formulaic Achievement: 'Ligeia.'" In *A Psychology of Fear: The Nightmare Formula of Edgar Allan Poe*. Lanham, Md.: University Press of America, 1980. Explores "Ligeia" as one of Poe's most successful nightmare pieces. Accepts the premise that the title character is a dream figure.

LIGHT IN AUGUST

Type of work: Novel
Author: William Faulkner (1897-1962)
Type of plot: Psychological realism
Time of plot: 1930
Locale: Mississippi
First published: 1932

> *Principal characters:*
> JOE CHRISTMAS, a light-skinned African American man
> DOC HINES, his grandfather
> MR. MCEACHERN, his foster father
> JOANNA BURDEN, his benefactress and mistress
> JOE BROWN, alias Lucas Burch, his partner
> LENA GROVE, the mother of Brown's child
> BYRON BUNCH, a man in love with Lena

The Story:

Joe Christmas was the illegitimate son of a dark-skinned circus trouper who was thought to be of African American descent and a white girl named Milly Hines. Joe's grandfather, old Doc Hines, killed the circus man, let Milly die in childbirth, and put Joe—at Christmas time, hence his last name—into an orphanage, where the children learned to call him "Nigger." Doc Hines then arranged to have Joe adopted by a religious and heartless farmer named McEachern, whose cruelties to Joe were met with a matching stubbornness that turned the boy into an almost subhuman being.

One day in town, McEachern took Joe to a disreputable restaurant, where he talked to the waitress, Bobbie Allen. McEachern told the adolescent never to patronize the place alone. Joe went back, however, where he met Bobbie at night and became her lover. Night after night, while the McEacherns were asleep, he would creep out of the house and hurry to meet her in town.

One night, McEachern followed Joe to a country dance and ordered him home. Joe reached for a chair, knocked McEachern unconscious, whispered to Bobbie that he would meet her soon, and raced McEachern's mule home. There he gathered up all the money he could lay his hands on and went into town. At the house where Bobbie stayed, he encountered the restaurant proprietor, his wife, and another man. The two men beat up Joe, took his money, and left for Memphis with the two women.

Joe moved on. Sometimes he worked, but more often he simply lived off the money women would give him. He slept with many women and nearly always told them he was African American. At last, he went to Jefferson, a small town in Mississippi, where he got work shoveling sawdust in a lumber mill. He found lodging in a long-deserted cabin near the country home of Miss Joanna Burden, a spinster of Yankee origin who had few associates in Jefferson because of her zeal for bettering the lot of African Americans. She fed Joe and planned to send him to a school for African Americans. Joe was her lover for three years. Her reactions ranged from sheer animalism to evangelism, in which she tried to make Joe repent his sins and become a Christian.

A young man who called himself Joe Brown came to work at the sawmill, and Joe Christmas invited Brown to share his cabin with him. The two began to sell bootleg whiskey. After a while, Joe told Brown that he was African American; before long, Brown discovered the relationship of Joe and Miss Burden. When their bootlegging prospered, they bought a car and gave up their jobs at the lumber mill.

One night, Joe went to Miss Burden's room half-determined to kill her. She attempted to shoot him with an antiquated pistol that did not fire. Joe cut her throat with his razor and ran out of the house. Later in the evening, a fire was discovered in Miss Burden's house. When the townspeople started to go upstairs in the burning house, Brown tried to stop them. They brushed him aside. They found Miss Burden's body in the bedroom and carried it outside before the house burned to the ground.

Through a letter in the Jefferson bank, the authorities learned of Miss Burden's New Hampshire relatives, whom they notified. Almost at once, word came back offering a thousand-dollar reward for the capture of the murderer. Brown tried to tell the story as he knew it, putting the blame on Joe Christmas, so that he could collect the money. Few believed his story, but he was held in custody until Joe Christmas could be found.

Joe Christmas remained at large for several days, but at last, with the help of bloodhounds, he was found. Meanwhile, old Doc Hines had learned of his grandson's crime, and he came with his wife to Jefferson. He urged the white people to lynch Joe, but his rantings went unheeded.

On the way to face indictment by the grand jury in the courthouse, Joe, handcuffed but not manacled to the deputy, managed to escape. He ran to a cabin and found a gun. Some volunteer guards from the American Legion gave chase, and finally found him in the kitchen of the Reverend Gail Hightower, a former Presbyterian minister who was now an outcast because he had driven his wife into dementia by his obsession with the gallant death of his grandfather in the Civil War. Joe had gone to Hightower at the suggestion of his grandmother, Mrs. Hines, who had had a conference with him in his cell just before he escaped. She had been advised of this possible way of escape by Byron Bunch, Hightower's only friend in Jefferson. The Legionnaires shot Joe; then their leader mutilated him with a knife.

Brown now claimed his reward. A deputy took him out to the cabin where he had lived with Joe Christmas. On entering the cabin, he saw Mrs. Hines holding a newborn baby. In the bed was a girl, Lena Grove, with whom he had slept in a town in Alabama. Lena had started out to find Brown when she knew she was going to have a baby. Traveling most of the way on foot, she had arrived in Jefferson on the day of the murder and the fire. Directed to the sawmill, she had at once seen that Byron Bunch, to whom she had been sent, was not the same man as Lucas Burch, which was Brown's real name. Byron, a kindly soul, had fallen in love with her. Having identified Brown from Byron's description, Lena was sure that, in spite of his new name, Brown was the father of her child. She gave birth to the baby in Brown's cabin, where Byron had made her as comfortable as he could, with the aid of Mrs. Hines.

Brown jumped from a back window and escaped. Byron, torn between a desire to marry Lena and the wish to give her baby its rightful father, tracked Brown to the railroad grade outside town and fought with him. Brown escaped aboard a freight train.

Three weeks later, Lena and Byron took to the road with the baby, Lena still searching for Brown. A truck driver gave them a lift. Byron was patient, but one night, he tried to sleep with her. When she repulsed him, he left the little camp where the truck was parked. The next morning, however, he was waiting at the bend of the road, and he climbed up on the truck as it made its way toward Tennessee.

Critical Evaluation:

William Faulkner was thirty-five when he wrote *Light in August* as the final explosive creation of the richest part of his artistic career, the time that saw the production of *Sartoris* (1929), *The Sound and the Fury* (1929), *As I Lay Dying* (1930), and *Sanctuary* (1931). Only *Absalom, Absalom!* (1936) would approach again the intensity and splendid richness of this, his tenth book published and the seventh in the series about Yoknapatawpha County. Armstid, who appears in the novel's first chapter, is the same farmer of *As I Lay Dying*; and Joanna Burden mentions Colonel Sartoris in her account of her own family's blood-spattered history. *Light in August* is Faulkner's longest work and his most varied "in mood and character" (as noted by critic Richard H. Rovere). It is perhaps equaled only by *The Sound and the Fury* as a penetrating and compelling analysis of Southern society.

The style of this novel has often been criticized for its inconsistency, often presented as an example of Faulkner's "undisciplined genius." Indeed, its stylistic characteristics are manifold and complex. He incorporates sudden changes of narrative tense, from present to past and back again and abrupt shifts in point of view, ranging from the viewpoints of the major characters to viewpoints of characters who apparently have no part in the main action at all. Faulkner also utilizes stream-of-consciousness techniques similar to the emphasis on key images found in the works of Marcel Proust or on what James Joyce termed "radiating imagery," while creating long compound words, also a Joycean technique, such as "womanpinksmelling," "Augusttremulous," "stillwinged," and "womanshenegro." Epiphanies similar to those found in the works of Joyce also appear in the novel, as when Joe Christmas is caught in the glare of headlights after the murder of Joanna Burden. Faulkner places emphasis on all the senses, similar to T. S. Eliot, while utilizing a simplicity of imagery, evocative of the works of Robert Frost. He mixes this with a flamboyant poetic diction that is characteristic of the works of Wallace Stevens and includes the repetition of implicit interrogatives and phrases such as "grown heroic at the instant of vanishment" and the "two inescapable horizons of the implacable earth." There is, in fact, awkwardly repetitious use of manneristic expressions such as "by ordinary," "terrific," and the adverb "quite" that seems to support the argument that the composition of this admitted masterpiece was at times hurried and even heedless.

The last two chapters of the novel—Hightower's rambling retrogression into Civil War history and the resumption of Lena's travels (this time with Byron)—achieve a sense of open-ended comprehensiveness that does indicate Faulkner's epic concept of his novel. Furthermore, it is the universality of the epic genre that may account for the apparently arbitrary grouping of stylistic elements. Every angle of insight, every avenue of perspective, every mode of entry is used by the author to compel the reader into the world of the novel—a world complete with its own dimensions: of time and space, of emotions, and of events. As an epic, *Light in August* falls into the genre of "search epics." Joe is searching for a light that will give meaning to his existence, exploring, in turn, the light of McEachern's "home," the light of his adolescent town, the lamp of Bobbie Allen's room, the inordinate streetlights of nameless ghettos, the light of Joanna's candle and, finally, the light of the flames of Joanna's burning house—the "light in August" around whose central, sinister radiance all the main characters' lives revolve. That burning light brings their identities into momentary and terrible focus, disillusioning Lena of her dreams of trust and security, forcing Lucas Burch and Gail Hightower to confront their cowardice, coercing Byron Bunch to throw in his lot irrevocably with his love, ending Joanna's ambiguously introverted life in perverted horror and, with supreme irony, ultimately identifying Christmas through the reaction of the outraged town and, through this identification, ending his search in death.

The novel is also epic in its thematic scope, a scope embodied in the ambivalence of Christmas himself who, through no fault of his own, is tragically made to straddle two worlds—neither of which will accept him because of his relation to the other, neither of which he will accept because of his inherent inability to be singularly defined. The two worlds, as Faulkner steeps them through the very fiber of his novel, may be described as a kind of movable equation—an equation generally defined by the racial distinction between black and white. On one side, Christmas confronts his African American identity, death (as stasis), darkness or artificial light, evil, fire, the female, sleeping, insanity, sin, savageness, violence, secrecy, cunning and deceit, softness, the fugitive state, belief, and passivity. Opposed to these elements, but also mingling and combining with them in unpredictable and unmanageable patterns, are his white identity, life (as kinesis and fluid movement), light, good, the sun, the male, being awake and aware, control, righteousness, calm, openness, durability and determination, domestic security, knowing, and activity. "He never acted like either a nigger or a white man," one of his murderers comments at the end. Because Christmas could not find himself on either side of the equation, because his entire life was a confusion between the two sides, his epic quest ends in his own individual death and in the symbolic death of the community of Jefferson.

It is because Faulkner envisioned Christmas as an epic hero that he identified him with Christ, not only in name but also in his peculiar silences, his master-disciple relationship with Brown, his capture on a Friday, Joanna's resemblance to both Mary Magdalene and the Virgin Mary, his thirty years of private life (about which the narrator reveals nothing specific), his refusal to complain when beaten at the end, and the town's final comment that "it was as though he had set out and made his plans to passively commit suicide." *Light In August*, however, is christological only in the sense that it draws upon Christian ideas to complicate and deepen the essentially secular, sociological myth Faulkner constructs consistently in all the saga of Yoknapatawpha County. *Light in August* professes only the religion of humanity, a religion that must function in a world "peopled principally by the dead," as Hightower, the rejected minister, remarks. This is a novel of "mighty compassion."

"Critical Evaluation" by Kenneth John Atchity

Bibliography:
Inge, M. Thomas, ed. *The Merrill Studies in "Light in August."* Columbus, Ohio: Charles E. Merrill, 1971. Good collection of articles on Christ imagery and symbolism, myth and ritual, and the "Frozen Moment," which clarifies Faulkner's use of contradictions like movement and motionlessness. Also includes reprints of contemporary reviews.
Karl, Frederick R. *William Faulkner, American Writer: A Biography.* New York: Ballantine Books, 1989. An interpretation of Faulkner's life revealed with psychological, emotional, and literary precision. Focuses on the strengths on which Faulkner relied in his growth as a great American writer of the twentieth century. Includes an excellent bibliography, chronology, and notes.
Lewis, Wyndham. "William Faulkner (the Moralist with a Corn Cob)." In *Men Without Art.* New York: Russell & Russell, 1964. Analyzes Faulkner's fatalism and melodrama in major novels. Uniquely argues that Faulkner is not a good or acceptable writer, but that, instead, he is just a flash in the pan. Accuses Faulkner of being old-fashioned, too romantic, and one of the "psychological" school.
Millgate, Michael, ed. *New Essays on "Light in August."* New York: Cambridge University Press, 1987. Includes a very good introduction, a clarification of the structure of the novel,

an analysis of women, sexism, and racism in *Light in August*, and an exploration of "the difference between enduring and prevailing," an analysis of Faulkner's Nobel Prize speech about humanity's endurance as it is revealed in *Light in August*.

Pitavy, François L., ed. *William Faulkner's "Light in August": A Critical Casebook*. New York: Garland, 1982. A critical collection of the best available scholarship on Faulkner's novel and a discussion of the genesis of the book as well as a superb annotated bibliography. Includes analysis of themes such as "God the Father and Motherless Children," "Other Competitors for the Cross," and various symbols, myths, voices, and style.

LIGHTNING

Type of work: Novel
Author: Santō Kyōden (1761-1816)
Type of plot: Romance
Time of plot: Fifteenth century
Locale: Japan
First published: Mukashigatari inazuma-byōshi, 1806 (English translation, 1986)

Principal characters:
    SASAKI SADAKUNI, the feudal lord of Yamato Province
    SASAKI KATSURA, his firstborn son, by his deceased first wife
    SASAKI HANAGATA, his second son, by his present wife
    KUMODE NO KATA or LADY SPIDER, Sadakuni's present wife and
        Hanagata's mother
    ICHŌ NO MAE or LADY GINKGO, Katsura's wife
    TSUKIWAKA or YOUNG-MOON, the son of Katsura and Lady Ginkgo
    FUWA DŌKEN or ROAD-DOG, a steward to the House of Sasaki
    FUWA BANZAEMON, Dōken's son
    HASEBE UNROKU, a disloyal retainer
    NAGOYA SABUROZAEMON, a loyal retainer
    NAGOYA SANSABURŌ, his son
    FUJINAMI or WISTERIA-WAVE, a dancer
    SASARA SAMPACHIRŌ, a loyal retainer, also known as Namuemon
    KURITARO or CHESTNUT-SON, Namuemon's son
    KAEDE or MAPLE, Namuemon's daughter
    YUASA MATAHEI, Fujinami's brother
    UMEZU KAMON or GOOD-GATE, a recluse
    SARUJIRO or MONKEY-SON, Sampachirō's servant
    SHIKAZŌ or DEER, Sansaburō's servant

The Story:
    During the mid-fifteenth century, under the shogunate of Ashikaga Yoshimasa, there lived a warrior lord by the name of Sasaki Sadakuni, lord of the Province of Yamato. He had two sons. One, twenty-five years old and named Katsura, was the son of Sadakuni's first wife; the other, twelve-year-old Hanagata, was the son of Sadakuni's second and present wife, Lady Spider. Katsura, a handsome young man, was taken into the luxurious and self-indulgent service of the shogun at Kyoto. There, at the instigation of one of Katsura's retainers, Fuwa Banzaemon, Katsura fell in love with a dancer, Wisteria-wave, and he began to lead a life of pleasure.
    A retainer of the House of Sasaki, Nagoya Sansaburō, was sent to Kyoto to present a treasured painting to the shogun. Learning how matters stood with Katsura, he did his best to make the young lord mend his ways, but to no avail. Meanwhile, Banzaemon himself had been discovered to be in love with Wisteria-wave, and he was discharged from feudal service. Sansaburō was sent back to the Sasaki provincial headquarters. At the same time, a loyal retainer, Sasara Sampachirō, killed Wisteria-wave and went into hiding. On the same night, a disloyal retainer, Hasebe Unroku, stole the treasured painting and disappeared.

The next day Banzaemon's father, Road-dog, steward to the House of Sasaki, arrived as Sadakuni's emissary, severely reprimanded Katsura for his dissolute ways, and discharged Katsura's retinue as being disloyal. Behind Road-dog's outwardly righteous actions lay a deeper plan, a plot to take over his lord's domain with the connivance of Governor General Hamana. Knowing Lady Spider's hope that her own son Hanagata would succeed to the lordship of Sasaki, Road-dog had joined forces with her. With the backing of an evil sorcerer, the two attempted to do away with Katsura's wife, Lady Ginkgo, and her son Young-moon, who were living in the Sasaki villa in Heguri, guarded by Sansaburō and his father, Nagoya Saburozaemon. Although their plot failed, Sadakuni was deceived, and troops were dispatched against Lady Ginkgo and her young son.

In the meantime Banzaemon, who held a grudge against Sansaburō, killed Saburozaemon. Sansaburō placed Young-moon in the care of Young-moon's elderly nurse and helped them escape; he fought valiantly in defense of Lady Ginkgo, but in spite of his courage and efforts his lord's lady was abducted. He escaped into Kawachi Province.

The old woman in charge of Young-moon had met with difficulty in escaping with her charge. Young-moon was saved, however, by Sasara Sampachirō, who meanwhile had changed his name to Namuemon, and was hidden in Tamba Province.

Namuemon was still haunted by the spirit of the dead Wisteria-wave, whom he had killed for the sake of his lord; his son, Chestnut-son, became blind, and his daughter Maple was haunted by a serpent. When it was known that Namuemon was secretly watching Road-dog's movements with the idea of killing him, warriors were sent against Namuemon, who beheaded his own son and then, in order that Young-moon's life might be spared, identified the head as Young-moon's. Namuemon's daughter Maple sold herself for the painting. Namuemon, with his wife and Young-moon, sought refuge in Kawachi Province. Leaving the two in a place of safety, Namuemon set out to find his master Katsura and Katsura's wife, Lady Ginkgo.

Meanwhile, Lady Ginkgo, who had fallen into Road-dog's hands, was about to be murdered, but she was saved by a hero-recluse by the name of Umezu (Good-gate). Katsura, who had become an itinerant Buddhist priest, was about to meet his death at a temple festival in Omi Province, when his life was saved by Monkey-son, Sansaburō's son who had become a street preacher. After his delivery, Katsura was hidden in the home of Yuasa Matahei, Wisteria-wave's older brother and a painter living in Otsu. By chance, Namuemon was also staying there. Matahei, becoming aware that Namuemon was his own sister's murderer, was at the same time deeply impressed by the quality of Namuemon's loyalty. Matahei's wife confessed that six years ago she had attempted to hang herself because a ruffian had robbed her of twenty pieces of gold. At the time, Namuemon had not only saved her from death but had also given her twenty gold pieces to make up for her loss. Torn between revenge and gratitude, Matahei drew his sword, cut Namuemon's traveling hat in place of Namuemon's head, and offered the sundered hat to Wisteria-wave's departed but still vengeful spirit. With past wrongs thus redressed, Matahei repaid his gratitude by bringing Namuemon to Katsura. At that point Hasebe Unroku appeared on the scene and was recognized by Matahei's wife as the man who had robbed her six years before. Namuemon forced Unroku to commit suicide to expiate his sins.

Meanwhile, Maple had joined a traveling theatrical troupe that had come to those parts. Namuemon, now revealed as Sampachirō, met his daughter, whose affliction from serpents that always accompanied her had been healed by the painting she had so dearly bought. Matahei, for the first time, realized that he had attained the inner secret that he had striven for in his art—its magical power.

On the following day, Katsura and his party left Otsu for Kawachi Province. He acquired a book on military strategy and tactics belonging to Good-gate, who had saved Lady Ginkgo's life. Intending to seek the assistance of the new governor general, Katsumoto, the party arrived at Good-gate's secluded abode on Diamond Mountain to find that Katsumoto was already there in an attempt to persuade Good-gate to accept the position of chief of military strategy. It was also revealed that Good-gate was related to Katsura by marriage. Katsura was reunited with Lady Ginkgo, who had been staying there under Good-gate's protection. With the backing of the governor general and Good-gate, Katsura prepared to return to his home province of Yamato.

Meanwhile, in Kyoto, Sansaburō, accompanied by his faithful servant Deer, had been searching for Fuwa Banzaemon and his gang in the brothels of that city. Finally he found them and with the assistance of a courtesan and Good-gate, who had been a friend of his slain father, Saburozaemon, Sansaburō achieved his revenge. Good-gate, appointed the governor general's deputy, received orders to go to the headquarters of the House of Sasaki. Requesting the attendance of Sadakuni's wife, Lady Spider, and his steward, Road-dog, as well, Good-gate told Lord Sasaki Sadakuni that Katsura had not only mended his former ways but also had displayed great military valor. He requested Sadakuni to pardon his son and to name Katsura his heir and successor; Sadakuni would then retire in Katsura's favor as head of the clan. Good-gate also revealed Lady Spider's and Road-dog's plot to take over the House of Sasaki by conniving for the succession of the second-born, Lady Spider's son Hanagata. With Road-dog under arrest in a caged carriage, and his mission accomplished, Good-gate took his leave amid the low and reverent bows of the House of Sasaki.

Critical Evaluation:

Santō Kyōden, also known in the West by his artist's name of Kitao Masanobu, followed his early successes in print-designing and fiction by concentrating his attention on the latter. He was the most versatile and gifted of the popular Edo (modern Tokyo) writers. Besides the picture books and fanciful didactic *yomihon* reading books to which he turned under the pressure of Tokugawa censorship, he wrote many excellent *sharebon* ("books of wit"), sophisticated sketches of manners in the Yoshiwara and other pleasure quarters. Though these were limited in subject matter, their realistic dialogue technique greatly influenced the two leading kinds of realistic Edo fiction of the nineteenth century. This tendency toward realism is evident in *Lightning*.

Using the central theme of rivalry for succession to a great feudal house, and the triumph of good over evil, right over wrong, Kyōden took his materials from traditional Kabuki plays and wrote *Lightning* with stage production in mind. The scenes change rapidly, and the plot is complicated by the appearance of a large number of secondary characters who disrupt the unity of the story. Thus, the principal theme tends to move away from the succession intrigues to a depiction of the feudal loyalty of a secondary character, Sasara Sampachirō. That this novel was soon produced on the Kabuki stage was a matter of course, and it was staged under various titles. The first was in Osaka in 1808, and then in Edo in 1809. As a novel, the work comprised a unit in itself, but Kyōden wrote a sequel, the *Honchō suibodai*, which was published in 1806. This later work, making greater use of syllabic meter, has little in connection with the original and is thin in plot, but it carries the reader on through the author's sheer writing ability.

Like many of Kyōden's works, this novel is written in a vigorous, popular style, simple and direct, and often melodramatic in plot. Because of the skillful handling of action and the true-to-life emotions of the characters, the novel was very widely read in Japan. A somber history of vengeance, the novel abounds in violence, suicides, torture, combat, and rapid shifts of plot. It reads often like an early nineteenth century European romantic novel, filled with Gothic horrors and boiling emotions, but, at the same time, a lusty quality and a certain vigorous humor raises the book to a greater level of realism. Kyōden was considered one of the leaders in Japan in the development of the realistic school of fiction.

Although the plot at times is confusing, owing partly to the large number of characters, a vigor of style and narrative drive carries the action steadily forward. The minor characters tend to be stylized, boldly sketched figures, but the principal characters are much more realistically portrayed. *Lightning* possesses an almost cinematic sweep and power of movement, and the Western reader should not become sidetracked by attempting to follow every minute plot thread; the novel's romantic vision of feudal life in Japan is rendered in an exciting, enjoyable style.

Bibliography:

Devitt, Jane. "Santō Kyōden and the Yomihon." *Harvard Journal of Asiatic Studies* 39, no. 2 (1979): 253-274. Discusses the life and the works of Santō Kyōden. Discusses Kyōden's central themes: the samurai class and its values.

Korniki, Peter F. "*Nishiki no ura*: An Instance of Censorship and the Structure of a *Sharebon*." *Monumenta Nipponica* 32, no. 2 (1977): 153-188. Discusses the historical context of the work, the censorship of *sharebon*, or comic books, and Kyōden's success with the genre.

LILIOM
A Legend in Seven Scenes

Type of work: Drama
Author: Ferenc Molnár (1878-1952)
Type of plot: Fantasy
Time of plot: Early twentieth century
Locale: Budapest
First performed: 1909; first published, 1909 (English translation, 1921)

Principal characters:
LILIOM, a merry-go-round barker
MRS. MUSKAT, his employer
JULIE, his wife
MARIE, her friend
WOLF, Marie's husband
MRS. HOLLUNDER, Julie's aunt
FICSUR, Liliom's friend
LINZMAN, the cashier whom Ficsur suggests robbing
LOUISE, daughter of Julie and Liliom

The Story:

Liliom was a barker for Mrs. Muskat's merry-go-round at an amusement park on the edge of Budapest. As a barker he was a great success, for he had a stock of funny jokes that kept the customers laughing, and he had a playful way with young women.

One day two young servants, Marie and Julie, came to the merry-go-round. To Mrs. Muskat's indignation, Liliom followed Julie onto the merry-go-round and put his arm around her. Mrs. Muskat warned Julie that if she ever came near the merry-go-round again, she would be thrown out, as she did not wish to lose her license because of questionable behavior in the park. Liliom, however, told Julie to come back any time and she would be welcome. Although Mrs. Muskat was reluctant to let Liliom go, she could not ignore his insolence, and she dismissed him.

Liliom, to show his independence, announced that he was going to get some beer. While he was collecting his belongings, Marie disclosed to Julie that she was in love with a man in a uniform—a porter, however, not a soldier. When Liliom returned, he turned Marie away and began to discuss love with Julie, bragging and bullying all the while. Julie showed that she was deeply in love, because she had forfeited her job by staying out late with him. Two policemen looking for vagrants interrupted their conversation. After asking routine questions and warning Julie that Liliom was a notorious ne'er-do-well, the policemen continued on their rounds. Although Julie protested that she did not love Liliom, it was obvious that she did.

They were married and moved into a run-down photographer's shop, operated by Mrs. Hollunder and her son, at the edge of the park. Mrs. Hollunder, Julie's aunt, provided them not only with shelter but also with food and fuel. She grumbled all the time, but she was good-hearted beneath her gruffness. Marie, meanwhile, was falling more deeply in love with Wolf, the porter. One day, while the two women were exchanging confidences, Mrs. Hollunder came in and said that Julie's other suitor, a widowed carpenter with two children and a respectable income, still

3647

wanted to take her out of the poverty in which she lived. Julie preferred to stay where she was. Mrs. Muskat came and offered to take Liliom back, but he refused. He and a friend named Ficsur had a scheme for getting a great deal of money; he was no longer interested in his old job at the merry-go-round.

Ficsur was planning a robbery. Each Saturday a cashier for a leather factory passed a nearby railway embankment, with the workmen's wages in a leather bag. Liliom was to accost the man and ask him what time it was, while Ficsur was to come up from behind and stab the man. Ficsur encouraged Liliom to steal a knife from Mrs. Hollunder's kitchen. Julie, knowing that the two men were up to no good, begged Liliom not to go out with Ficsur, for she had arranged to have the carpenter come that evening and offer Liliom work. After Liliom had gone, Mrs. Hollunder missed her knife and suspected Liliom of taking it. Julie lied, saying that she had gone through Liliom's pockets and had found only a pack of cards.

Liliom and Ficsur arrived at the embankment just as the six o'clock train passed. Being early, they started a game of twenty-one, and Ficsur won from Liliom his share in the loot they hoped to take from the cashier. Liliom accused Ficsur of cheating. Then their victim appeared, and Liliom accosted him. As Ficsur was about to strike, however, the cashier seized Ficsur's arm. He pointed a pistol at Liliom's breast. Ironically, he had come from the factory, where he had just finished paying off the workers; if Ficsur had killed him, the robbers would have gotten no money. As the cashier called out to two policemen in the distance, Liliom broke away and stabbed himself with the kitchen knife. The policemen attempted to take him to a hospital, but his condition was too critical. They took him back to the photographer's studio, where he died with Julie by his side holding his hand.

Dying, Liliom had a vision. Two heavenly policemen came to him and told him to follow them. They reminded him that death was not the end, that he was not through with earth until his memory had also passed away. Then they led him to the heavenly court assigned to suicide cases. There he learned that, after a period of purification by fire, suicides were sent back to earth for one day to see whether they had profited by their purification. Liliom was sentenced to sixteen years in the fires.

At the end of that time, Liliom returned to earth to find his wife and sixteen-year-old daughter, Louise, about to lunch in the garden of their dilapidated little house. Liliom was unrecognized. Julie gave him some food. He learned from Louise that her father, a handsome man, had gone to the United States before she was born and had died there. When Liliom accused her husband of having struck her, Julie denied that he had ever mistreated her, and she dismissed Liliom as an ungrateful wretch. Liliom tried to please his daughter with card tricks and with a beautiful star that he had stolen from heaven, but Louise would have nothing more to do with him. As he left, he struck her hard on the hand, but the blow felt as tender as a caress to her. Her mother told her that there had been times when she, too, had experienced that sort of reaction from a blow. So Liliom left in the company of the two policemen, who shook their heads in profound regret at Liliom's failure.

Critical Evaluation:

Known primarily as a playwright outside his native Hungary, Ferenc Molnár was the most prolific and versatile Hungarian writer of the first half of the twentieth century. Educated in Budapest and Geneva, Molnár early deserted the study of law for journalism and, in a short time, was publishing novels, essays, poetry, and short stories. His first play, *The Devil* (1905), was a great success, launching him on a theatrical and dramatic career that lasted almost forty years and brought him international recognition as a master of ingenious light comedy. His penchant for juxtaposing realistic, often urban and lower-class, characters and situations with the fantastic placed him at the cutting edge of avant-garde theater in the 1920's and 1930's, and his admirers saw in him a genuine, if quixotic, champion of the common person. Although he continued to write until his death in 1952, his reputation suffered a rapid decline in the 1940's, from which it has not recovered. Critics generally agree that most of his plays exhibit a flair for comic dialogue and dazzling theatrical technique but lack substance, all too often substituting cleverness and the shock of the unexpected for a serious engagement with social and moral issues.

A product of the earliest period of Molnár's career, *Liliom* has long been regarded as his finest work. Not only does it showcase his gift for developing comic situations, it also makes startlingly effective use of his characteristic and innovative blend of realism and fantasy. In these respects, it strongly resembles many of his less well regarded dramas. Although the writing here may be a bit finer, Molnár is often funnier and wittier elsewhere. What sets *Liliom* apart is a seriousness of purpose that is lacking in almost all of his other dramas. It is not merely an exercise in cleverness or an excuse for light entertainment, but a sincere attempt to grapple with difficult moral and ethical questions without settling for an easy answer—a point that is emphasized by its ambiguous ending. Nowhere else in his oeuvre is Molnár so nearly serious, so seriously in earnest, as he is in *Liliom*.

Subtitled *A Legend in Seven Scenes*, the play proceeds according to the intuitive logic of an Eastern European folktale. By turns whimsical and violent, realistic and fanciful, dramatic and sentimental, its brilliant use of sudden and increasingly shocking reversals of expectation to move the action forward attests Molnár's mastery of dramatic technique.

The play dramatizes twin themes: the inability of accepted Judeo-Christian standards of morality to accord with human nature; and the fact that the ruling classes use those standards to control—to police—the masses of working men and women. This theme is initially expressed in the contrast between the deep and true love of Liliom and Julie, and that of Wolf and Marie. Julie somehow can withstand Liliom's verbal and physical abuse, as well as the sixteen years of widowhood and poverty his criminal lack of judgment and impulsive suicide force upon her and his daughter. In contrast, the love Wolf and Marie share is portrayed as emotionally shallow. They begin by holding hands and sitting silently on park benches together and end by formally calling each other "Mr. Beifeld" and "Mrs. Beifeld" to keep from quarreling so they can "get along with society folk." By conforming to the moral guidelines laid down by society, Wolf and Marie are socially and economically successful, but they cannot experience life or love fully, as Liliom and Julie do. This double theme is extended through the pervasive presence of the police—in both its earthly and heavenly forms—who observe and regulate the morality of the actions and activities of the characters of the play from beginning to end.

Within the framework provided by the opposition of Liliom and Julie's relationship to Wolf and Marie's, and by the parallel of earthly and heavenly police, the play moves ahead swiftly through a series of increasingly severe reversals. The unexpected marriage of Liliom and Julie solves the problems created by being in love, but that solution creates a new problem: It leaves them both unemployed. Mrs. Muskat's offer to hire Liliom convinces him to abandon Julie for his old life until Julie's news that she is pregnant catalyzes both Liliom's rejection of Mrs. Muskat's offer and his ill-fated try at thievery, which in turn leads to suicide and then to a heavenly court that duplicates the order of the world below. In contrast to expressionist drama, the fusion of realism and the fantastic that dominates the play from this point forward does not externalize interior, psychological, or emotional states. Rather, it is a metaphysical extension of the real world, a kind of transcendent realism, presenting the afterlife in a simple, matter-of-fact manner, rather than by means of distortion or exaggeration. The rules, the moral guidelines, and the power to punish those who flout them are symbolized here, as in life, by the courts and the police.

Despite *Liliom*'s undeniable effectiveness in the theater and the brilliance of its dramatic technique and the craftsmanship of its design, the play's greatest achievement is the character of Liliom himself. Unpredictable, brash, rough, funny, proud, tender, stubborn, violent, unhappy—he transcends the ordinary limits of theatrical characters. His personality is so complex and contradictory, so true to the inconsistency of judgment and impulse that mark all human beings and their actions, that, like Hamlet and King Lear, he cannot be reduced to a symbol. The difference between William Shakespeare's great theatrical characters and Molnár's, however, is that Hamlet and King Lear can live outside the plays that bear their names, while Liliom cannot. Hamlet and Lear simply exist, contradictions and all, without enduring any authorial attempt at shaping our opinion of them, whereas Molnár tries to justify Liliom's moral ambivalence and to "damn the police," thereby confining his greatest character to the limits of the argument he makes in his play.

"Critical Evaluation" by R. A. Martin

Bibliography:
Clark, Barrett H., and George Freedley, eds. *A History of Modern Drama.* New York: Appleton-Century-Crofts, 1947. Molnár is considered in a section on Central European playwrights.
Gassner, John. *Masters of the Drama.* New York: Random House, 1940. An excellent chapter on the German dramatist Gerhart Hauptmann and his followers offers an account of Molnár's dramatic art, linking the fantastic and expressionist elements to the unusual blend of realism and romanticism pioneered by Hauptmann.
Gergely, Emro Joseph. *Hungarian Drama in New York: American Adaptations 1908-1940.* Philadelphia: University of Pennsylvania Press, 1947. A balanced, perceptive, highly informed account of Hungarian dramas adapted for the U.S. stage. Features substantial and penetrating analyses of all of Molnár's major plays, and discusses a number of his lesser works.
Remenyi, Joseph. *Hungarian Writers and Literature: Modern Novelists, Critics, and Poets.* Edited and with an introduction by August J. Molnar. New Brunswick, N.J.: Rutgers University Press, 1964. The essay on Molnár assesses his plays in a literary rather than a dramatic context, examining them in terms of the seriousness and complexity of their themes, the deployment and use of symbols and imagery, and the adequacy of his style to his subject matter.
Varkonyi, Istvan. *Ferenc Molnár and the Austro-Hungarian "Fin de Siècle."* New York: Peter Lang, 1992. This book-length study of the playwright in English focuses on the work he produced before 1920. Argues that Molnár forged a new literary style, based in realism, that enabled him to deal more effectively with the complex issues of social transformation, industrialization, and urbanization than could be done in the fundamentally Romantic style favored by other writers of the period.

THE LITTLE CLAY CART

Type of work: Drama
Author: Unknown, attributed to Sudraka (fl. 100 B.C.E.)
Type of plot: Tragicomedy
Time of plot: Fifth century B.C.E.
Locale: Ancient city of Ujjayini
First performed: Mrcchakatika, between second century B.C.E. and sixth century C.E.
   (English translation, 1905)

> *Principal characters:*
> CHĀRUDATTA, an impoverished young Brāhmana
> VASANTASENĀ, a courtesan in love with Chārudatta
> MAITREYA, a poor Brāhmana, Chārudatta's friend
> SAMSTHĀNAKA, King Pālaka's brother-in-law
> ĀRYAKA, an exiled prince
> SARVILAKA, a Brāhmana and a thief
> MADANIKĀ, Vasantasenā's slave and confidante

The Story:

Chārudatta was a Brāhmana who had impoverished himself by spending his substance on the public welfare and in helping those individuals who sought his aid. Although dwelling in poverty in a broken-down house, he still enjoyed a fine reputation in Ujjayini as an honest and upright man of rare wisdom. This reputation eased somewhat the fact that he had been deserted by most of his friends and was embarrassed by his lack of wealth.

Although married happily and the proud father of a small son, Rohasena, Chārudatta was enamored of Vasantasenā, a courtesan of great wealth and reputation who, having seen him at a temple, was also in love with him. One evening as Chārudatta and his friend Maitreya sat discussing Chārudatta's misfortunes and the efficacy of devotion to the gods, Vasantasenā found herself pursued by Samsthānaka, a half-mad brother-in-law of King Pālaka, and one of his henchmen. The men threatened to do violence to Vasantasenā, but she escaped from them in the darkness and found safety in the house of Chārudatta, where a meeting between the two increased the love they already felt for each other. The courtesan, before she left to return to her own palace, entrusted a casket of jewelry to Chārudatta, as an excuse to see him again.

During the night a thief, Sarvilaka, entered Chārudatta's house and stole the jewelry to buy his love, Madanikā, who was Vasantasenā's slave and confidante. The courtesan accepted the jewels and freed Madanikā to marry Sarvilaka, intending to see that Chārudatta should learn that the jewels had been recovered. In the meantime, Chārudatta sent a rare pearl necklace of his wife's to Vasantasenā to recompense the courtesan for the loss of the less valuable jewels. His friend Maitreya, fearing that Vasantasenā's attentions could bring only bad luck and disaster, cautioned Chārudatta against doing so. Maitreya, knowing courtesans, believed that Vasantasenā was merely scheming to take from Chārudatta the few possessions he still had.

After leaving Vasantasenā's palace with his newly freed bride, Sarvilaka learned that his friend, Prince Āryaka, had been arrested by King Pālaka and placed in a dungeon. The king, neither a popular nor a just monarch, feared that the people might rise up, as a soothsayer had predicted, to place Prince Āryaka on the throne. After Sarvilaka succeeded in freeing the prince from prison, Āryaka sought help from Chārudatta, who aided him in escaping the pursuing guards.

Vasantasenā, having become Chārudatta's mistress, met his small son and gave him some jewels with which to purchase a golden toy cart to replace the unsatisfactory clay cart Chārudatta had been able to afford. She made arrangements to meet Chārudatta in Pushpakaran-daka Park, outside the city, for a day's outing, but by mistake she entered the wrong vehicle and found herself in the gharri belonging to Samsthānaka, who still pursued her and was madly jealous of the love and favors she bestowed freely upon Chārudatta. When Vasantasenā arrived at the park, she was discovered in the gharri by Samsthānaka, who at first was overjoyed at seeing her because he thought she had come to him voluntarily. When she spurned him and declared her love for Chārudatta, Samsthānaka tried to make his henchmen kill her, but they refused. Samsthānaka sent his followers away and choked her himself. Believing her dead, he hid the body under a pile of leaves. Then, hoping to escape the penalty for his crime, Samsthānaka decided to go to a court and accuse Chārudatta of murdering Vasantasenā.

When Samsthānaka first appeared at court, the judges, who knew him to be somewhat mad, refused to see him or take him seriously; but when he threatened to go to King Pālaka, the judges became frightened and sent for Chārudatta. Falsely accused, Chārudatta proclaimed his innocence, but circumstances were against him. He admitted having been in the park, and the jewels of Vasantasenā were found at his home, offering a motive for the poverty-stricken man to have killed her. The judges, in spite of his previous reputation, found Chārudatta guilty. Although Chārudatta's status as a Brāhmana exempted him from the death penalty for any crime, King Pālaka ordered Chārudatta put to death. No one knew that the body identified as Vasantasenā's was that of another woman or that Vasantasenā, befriended by a Buddhist monk, was recovering near the park from Samsthānaka's attack.

Chārudatta was taken through the city by two executioners, who stopped several times to announce the name of the condemned man and the nature of his crime. Although the people of the city loved Chārudatta, they dared not intervene on his behalf, even though he steadfastly maintained his innocence. Samsthānaka's slave tried to tell that his master had really committed the crime, but no one believed him, and so Chārudatta and his executioners, accompanied by a crowd, continued on their way to the place of execution, a cemetery south of the city.

The executioners, thinking to be merciful, offered to decapitate Chārudatta, but a miracle prevented their sword from touching him, and so they prepared the victim for the slow, agonizing death by impalement upon a pike. Fortunately, Vasantasenā, seeing the excited crowd as she made her way back to the city, intervened in time. When she told who had really attacked her, Samsthānaka was arrested. The excitement was not ended, however, for word came that Chārudatta's wife, believing herself a widow, was about to cast herself upon a funeral pyre. Chārudatta reached her in time to prevent her death, and she and Vasantasenā met and accepted each other. Word came, too, that Prince Āryaka had deposed King Pālaka and was now king. One of his first deeds was to restore Chārudatta's fortune and make him an important official of the court. Chārudatta, still a man of conscience and charity, forgave Samsthānaka's villainy and caused him to be set free.

Critical Evaluation:

Many critics have pointed out that *The Little Clay Cart* is more like Western drama than any other Sanskrit play, in structure, characterization, and tone. This may account for the fact that its Indian critics have been less enthusiastic than those of the Western world. *The Little Clay*

Cart is noteworthy for being the only known Sanskrit play to show a courtesan in love with a Brāhmana, as it is also the only known one to contain important characters from various strata of Hindu society, rather than from the upper castes only. It is the realistic and vivid presentation of these characters that probably has appealed most to Western readers.

In Hindu philosophy, there is less emphasis than there is in Western, Christian philosophy on one's power to alter one's life or one's destiny. Throughout the drama, nearly all the characters speak of destiny and fate. Hindu thought also tends toward seeing life and history as circular, moving in cycles of such opposites as destruction and creation, growth and decay, and the like, rather than the Western view, which tends toward a linear interpretation.

The title is a summation of this wheel-of-fortune concept, although the section of the drama dealing with the cart is extremely short. Chārudatta's young son had been playing with a gold cart belonging to a friend. The friend then wants it back. Chārudatta, an impoverished Brāhmana, can afford only to have his servant make a clay cart for the boy. When the courtesan Vasantasenā, of whom Chārudatta is enamored, sees the boy crying for the gold cart, she gives him jewels with which to buy one for himself. Thus the circle is complete.

Many other circles complete the plot. Āryaka, an exiled prince, is imprisoned but escapes. The mad king is killed and Āryaka becomes king. A gambler who has lost his money and owes much, is rescued and becomes a friar. As all turns out well in the end, he is asked what ambition he might have. He replies that having watched the instability of human fortune, he prefers to remain a friar.

The overall circle that encloses all the rest is the story of Chārudatta and his lover, Vasantasenā. The Brāhmana has become poor because he has given away his fortune to help others in need. To add to his troubles, he is accused of the murder of Vasantasenā, whom he loves, and actually has his head on the chopping block with the axe raised above his head before Vasantasenā appears and points out the attempted murderer, Samsthānaka, who is arrested while Chārudatta is freed. Āryaka, the king, whom Chārudatta had protected when he escaped from prison, names him viceroy of the city of Kusavati.

The opening and closing dialogues by Chārudatta bring the total drama to its complete circle. In the beginning dialogue he is scattering grain for the birds and notes that when he was wealthy his offerings were of better quality; swans and cranes fed upon his terrace. Now the poor seed is thrown into the tangled grass where even wrens shun it. In the ending dialogue he remarks that "Destiny, as it plays with us, teaches us that the world is a union of opposites, an alternate recurrence of fortune and misfortune."

The drama is acted out in mime with no setting. A minimum of properties is used, and each may represent a number of things, from an altar to a tree or a carriage. The tempo is rapid, with one scene following the next so quickly that illusions created by the actions, gestures, and dialogues of the players are of prime importance. The actions are carried out like a ritualized dance. Emotional reactions are played down so that viewer or reader has a continuous feeling of repose and enjoyment at the finale. There is no catharsis as in Western drama.

Readers learn about the characters through what they say and what is said about them. No physical descriptions are given; one knows only that the courtesan is beautiful. In *The Little Clay Cart* the characters are from all walks of life, and their dialogues are apropos of their station. Vasantasenā comes through as the strongest and most astute character; Samsthānaka is the most pompous and ridiculous. The play has much wit, humor, and buffoonery, as well as wisdom, which appears in similes and metaphors, aphorisms and maxims. When presented properly, *The Little Clay Cart* is a delight.

Bibliography:

Buitenen, J. A. B. van, trans. *Two Plays of Ancient India: The Little Clay Cart, The Minister's Seal*. New York: Columbia University Press, 1968. Buitenen's introduction describes how the purported author, Sudraka, employed what may, in the context of ancient Sanskrit literature, be called "borrowing" privileges in the creation of the play, which is a completion of an earlier, incomplete work. Offers a synopsis of the play.

Keith, Arthur Berriedale. *The Sanskrit Drama in Its Origin, Development, Theory, and Practice*. New York: Oxford University Press, 1964. Accessible and well-indexed guide to Sanskrit drama. Somewhat dated but still a good starting place for further study.

Ryder, Arthur William, trans. *The Little Clay Cart (Mrcchakatika): A Hindu Drama Attributed to King Shudraka*. Cambridge, Mass.: Harvard University Press, 1905. Ryder's introduction discusses authorship, the method of translation, and an outline of the plot.

LITTLE DORRIT

Type of work: Novel
Author: Charles Dickens (1812-1870)
Type of plot: Social realism
Time of plot: 1820's
Locale: England
First published: 1855-1857

Principal characters:
> LITTLE DORRIT, a young woman who was born and reared in a
> debtors' prison
> WILLIAM DORRIT, her father
> FANNY, her older sister
> ARTHUR CLENNAM, Little Dorrit's friend
> MRS. CLENNAM, Arthur's mother and Little Dorrit's employer
> MONSIEUR BLANDOIS, a blackmailer
> MR. MERDLE, a banker and Fanny Dorrit's father-in-law

The Story:

Amy Dorrit, who was better known as Little Dorrit, had been born in Marshalsea debtors' prison. Although her mother died soon after, the little girl, along with her older brother and sister, continued to live in the prison with their bankrupt father; he was the only member of the family not permitted to leave the prison. As she became older, Little Dorrit worked as a seamstress. One of her clients was Mrs. Clennam, a widow who was also a businesswoman, although she had been confined to her room by illness for fifteen years. Mrs. Clennam's forty-year-old son had gone to the Orient twenty years earlier to join his father, who looked after the company's business in the East. After his father's death, Arthur Clennam returned. He told his mother that he would take his part of the inheritance and fend for himself; he did not want to remain in the business with his miserly, grasping, and rather inhuman mother. Mrs. Clennam thereupon took her old clerk, Flintwich, into partnership with her.

While he was staying at his mother's house, Arthur noticed Little Dorrit and was struck by her retiring disposition and sweet appearance. He went to Marshalsea prison and tried to help the Dorrit family. When he raised the possibility of getting Mr. Dorrit out of prison, everyone thought it would be impossible, for Mr. Dorrit's affairs were in hopeless confusion; some of his debts were owed to the crown through the Circumlocution Office, a place of endless red tape.

Arthur found that he had a confederate in his endeavor to help Mr. Dorrit in a clerk named Pancks, an odd creature who collected rents for the father of Arthur's former fiancée, Flora. Pancks was aided in turn by John Chivery, the son of a turnkey, who was in love with Little Dorrit, and by Mr. Rugg, an elderly lawyer. In addition to helping Little Dorrit by trying to help her father and getting her brother out of trouble, Arthur helped her get more sewing clients and provided small amounts of money to the Dorrit household in the prison.

When Pancks discovered that Mr. Dorrit was the only surviving heir to a large fortune that had gone unclaimed for years, Little Dorrit's father, who had been in prison more than twenty years, was finally released. He immediately set himself up as a man of fortune, and he and his two oldest children were determined to live up to their new social position and try to forget the past. They decided that Arthur Clennam had insulted them by having acted condescendingly toward them, and they refused to have anything more to do with him. Only Little Dorrit remained unspoiled.

The Dorrit family went to the Continent, where they could successfully carry out the fiction that they had never seen a debtor's prison and where they were admitted to the society of expatriate Britons. Fanny Dorrit, the older of the two daughters, was pursued by Mr. Sparkle, the stepson of Mr. Merdle, who was reputed to be the richest and most influential banker in England. Although not in love with Sparkle, Fanny liked the prospect of marrying into a wealthy family. The Merdles, who saw only that the Dorrits had a fortune, agreed to the match, even though Mrs. Merdle was well aware of the fact that her son had fallen in love with Fanny when she was only an impecunious dancer in London.

After the marriage, Fanny and her husband went to live in London. Mr. Dorrit visited them there and became a close friend of Mr. Merdle. The banker even proposed to help Mr. Dorrit increase his already large fortune through shrewd and well-paying investments. Mr. Dorrit, the former debtor, was elated by his new prospects.

Little Dorrit wondered at the change in her family but remained her old self. She wrote to Arthur at intervals, for she not only continued to be grateful for all he had done to help her but was in love with him.

Arthur had remained in London, where he tried to discover the identity of the mysterious people who visited his mother. At the same time, he was trying to keep his own business solvent. Neither task was easy. On two occasions, Mrs. Clennam was visited by a Monsieur Blandois, whom Arthur knew to be a knave and possibly a murderer. He wondered what business his mother could have with such a person. He also distrusted Flintwich, a grubbing miserly fellow who mistreated his wife and had taken a great dislike to Arthur.

While trying to unravel the mystery, Arthur became bankrupt. Like many others, he had invested all of his and his company's money in Mr. Merdle's business ventures, believing them a safe and quick way to make a fortune. When Merdle and his bank failed, Arthur was sent to the Marshalsea debtors' prison, where he was assigned to Mr. Dorrit's old quarters. Mr. Rugg and Pancks did their best to make Arthur's imprisonment a short one, but he seemed to have lost all desire to live. Only after Little Dorrit returned to England and took up residence within the prison to comfort him as she had comforted her father did Arthur begin to recover.

Learning that Monsieur Blandois had disappeared from Mrs. Clennam's house, Pancks tracked the man down and brought him back to London. Mrs. Clennam realized at that point that she had to reveal the truth unless she resigned herself to paying blackmail to Blandois. Rising from her wheelchair and leaving her house for the first time in almost twenty years, she went to the prison to tell Arthur that he was not her child and that she had for many years been keeping money from him and from Little Dorrit. Once restitution had been made, Arthur was released from prison. Shortly afterward, he and Little Dorrit were married.

Critical Evaluation:

Little Dorrit has been hailed as one of Charles Dickens' greatest novels and one of the major novels of the nineteenth century. Despite its prevailingly somber and gloomy character, the book was among the most popular of Dickens' novels during his lifetime.

The structure of the novel is rather complex, consisting as it does of two books, "Poverty" and "Riches." The first book is determined by Mr. Dorrit's imprisonment for debt, "Riches" by his sudden inheritance of a fortune. Interwoven through both parts are the romantic story of the gradually awakening love between Clennam and Amy Dorrit (which Clennam does not realize until near the end of the novel) and biting social criticism, as in the descriptions of the Circumlocution Office, its officials, and its obstructionism. Dickens originally intended to call the novel "Nobody's Fault," with the thesis that social decay, rather than the actions of individuals,was responsible for the misfortunes of the various characters.

Little Dorrit is, next to *David Copperfield* (1849-1859), the most autobiographical of Dickens' novels. The author's father was imprisoned for debt in the Marshalsea prison in 1823 and 1834, and during his first term the boy Dickens stayed there on weekends while working in a blacking factory during the week, a routine he vividly describes in *David Copperfield*. Although the Marshalsea prison had been closed and torn down by the time Dickens wrote *Little Dorrit*, its memory and geography remained searingly vivid to him.

The metaphor of prison dominates the entire novel, not only as represented by the Marshalsea but in many other incidents and objects. The novel opens with descriptions of the swindler Blandois in prison in Marseilles; a group of English citizens, including Clennam, the Meagles family, and Miss Wade, in quarantine; the miserable Sunday in London preceding Clennam's reunion with his mother, which reminds him of his rigid Calvinist upbringing and unhappy childhood. These small prisons all precede the reader's introduction to the Marshalsea and the Dorrit family.

One of the more striking of the many prison images throughout the novel occurs at the opening of book 2, where the convent of St. Bernard in the Swiss Alps is compared to a prison. The expatriate English colonies in Italian cities are in their own kind of prison. When old Mr. Dorrit has a stroke at Mrs. Merdle's banquet, he imagines himself back at the Marshalsea. The world of social climbing and assumed gentility is a prison, which Dickens uses to create one of his most comic characters, Mrs. General, a warden of social climbing who is brought into the Dorrit entourage to teach the young ladies proper manners. Mrs. Clennam and Miss Wade are among those characters who live in prisons of their own making; Tattycoram, for example, in a fit of temper, exchanges the easy life as a servant to the Meagles family for the undisclosed bondage of life with Miss Wade. Both comic and pathetic at the same time is Flora Finching (based on Dickens' own first love, whom he later met again), whose engagement to Clennam was broken off at his mother's insistence before his departure for the Orient, and who has now become fat and almost incoherently talkative.

By far the greatest prison, and the cause of so many of the smaller ones, is the Circumlocution Office, a mysterious branch of government where nothing gets done, everything is obstructed, and the officeholders receive their positions through family connections. The topicality of the description stems from investigations into the conduct of the Crimean War; about the time Dickens began *Little Dorrit* knowledge of the incompetence with which the war was directed had become common and was shown to have stemmed in large part from the tradition of staffing government bureaus and the higher positions in the military through family connections. Dickens includes a scathing exposé of such connections in his description of one of Merdle's dinner parties, where Lord Barnacle (supposedly a portrait of Lord Palmerston, Britain's prime minister at the time) makes arrangements for Merdle's stepson (who marries Fanny Dorrit) to get a position with the Circumlocution Office. Those most victimized by this office are Clennam's business partner Doyce, whose invention is swallowed up by this immense and mysterious bureaucracy; Clennam, who is abused by the office when he tries to find out why Mr. Dorrit has been imprisoned; and Dorrit himself, who has fallen between the cracks of the system. The exact duties of the Circumlocution Office are never described. Here Dickens can be considered to anticipate Franz Kafka's device of depicting an isolated individual at the mercy of an unfeeling and mysterious bureaucracy.

Social climbing is another prison in which many of the characters are trapped: Fanny Dorrit when she makes an advantageous match with Merdle's stepson; Pet Meagles when she marries the well-connected Henry Gowan, a dilettante artist who regards it as a matter of course that his in-laws pay his debts; and above all Mr. Dorrit, who is both comic and tragic in his attempts to put a veneer of distinction on his position as "Father of the Marshalsea" and later when he assumes the airs of an English lord. Clennam and Little Dorrit are exempt from this climbing, Clennam perhaps more because he does not care to take the trouble, but Little Dorrit because of her innate goodness and nobility.

Although this novel contains a wealth of memorable characters, Dickens portrays all of his principal ones obliquely. The villain, the blackmailing swindler Blandois, has two other disguises as Rigaud and Lagnier, for example, and in many cases it takes the reader a while to guess the identities of characters. In the opening of book 2, for example, a group of travelers in the Alps is only gradually revealed to be the Dorrit entourage. Merdle's suicide, which marks the crash of his financial empire and the ruin of its investors (including Clennam and the Dorrit heirs), is treated with similar obliqueness. The various mysteries are only explicitly clarified in the three final chapters.

"Critical Evaluation" by R. M. Longyear

Bibliography:

Grant, Allan. *A Preface to Dickens*. London: Longman, 1984. An excellent introduction to Dickens' life and times, with especially good descriptions of the author's London, which forms the background to so many of his novels.

Lund, Roger. "Genteel Fictions: Caricature and Satirical Design in *Little Dorrit*." *Dickens Studies Annual* 10 (1982): 45-66. An excellent overview of the characters in the novel with society as the backdrop. Also contains Barbara Weiss' study "Secret Pockets and Secret Breasts," which gives the background for the commercial scandals of the 1850's on which Dickens based his portrait of Mr. Merdle.

Shelston, Alan, ed. *Charles Dickens: "Dombey and Son" and "Little Dorrit," A Casebook.* London: Macmillan, 1985. A collection of essays and observations. Concerning *Little Dorrit*, the volume includes T. A. Jackson's Marxist interpretation, Edmund Wilson's psychological explanation, Hillis Miller's close reading of the text, and Lionel Trilling's classic appreciation.

Sucksmith, Harvey. Preface to *Little Dorrit*, by Charles Dickens. Oxford, England: Clarendon Press, 1979. The standard text of Dickens' novel, which includes variant readings and the author's preliminary notes and outline. The excellent preface traces the background and the compositional history of the novel.

THE LITTLE FOXES

Type of work: Drama
Author: Lillian Hellman (1905-1984)
Type of plot: Social realism
Time of plot: 1900
Locale: The Deep South
First performed: 1939; first published, 1939

Principal characters:
REGINA GIDDENS, a predatory woman
BENJAMIN HUBBARD and
OSCAR HUBBARD, her brothers
HORACE GIDDENS, her husband
ALEXANDRA, daughter of Regina and Horace
BIRDIE HUBBARD, Oscar's wife

The Story:

William Marshall, a Chicago businessman, came South to negotiate with Benjamin and Oscar Hubbard and their sister, the striking Regina Giddens, over matters concerning the construction of a cotton mill. The Hubbard brothers and Regina foresaw a glittering future for them all. No longer would the cotton have to come to the machines; instead, at long last, it would be the other way around. They firmly believed that millions awaited them: The Hubbards would be the richest family in the South. Ben foresaw a stable of race horses, Oscar speculated on a new home, and the hapless Birdie, whom Oscar had married for her father's cotton fields, longed to see Lionnet, her old family home, restored to its former grace and beauty. Birdie continually sought a return to the genteel, refined behavior of earlier days, before the rise of materialistic ruthlessness.

Later, certain difficulties arose. The brothers lacked seventy-five thousand dollars, Regina's third of the sum which the Hubbards were to put up. Presumably this amount would come from Horace, Regina's husband, who lay in a Baltimore hospital with a fatal heart ailment. Though Regina had given Ben and Oscar her promise that Horace would put up the money, no word had yet reached them. Horace, away five months, had failed to acknowledge Regina's demands for his return. Regina suggested, however, that he was possibly holding out for a larger share of the profits; when one's money was badly needed, one should be entitled to a bigger share of the eventual returns. After crafty manipulation, Regina extracted from Ben a promise of a greater share of the profits if she could get Horace home within two weeks. Regina immediately dispatched Alexandra, her daughter, to Baltimore.

When Horace arrived a week later, in response to his daughter's summons, the Hubbards and Regina descended on him. No one in his right mind, the argument ran, would refuse a seventy-five thousand dollar investment that would garner a million. Ben explained how water power would be cheap and how the men of the mountains and small towns would be happy to work for low wages. Thus the profits would be tremendous. Horace, however—though sourly admitting that the venture was a good deal for the Hubbards—stated that he and Regina had enough money already. The truth was that Horace had had enough of his scheming wife and her equally conniving family, who, having made a sizable sum already through their exploitation of the poor, were now on their way to greater fortune in identical fashion.

Regina protested furiously, but to no avail. However, Ben and Oscar were not too upset. Oscar's son Leo, through a young banking employee, had discovered that Horace had eighty-eight thousand dollars in bonds in his safe deposit box, securities which he checked only once in six months. Assuming that Horace would never miss them for a few months, Ben had Oscar seize the bonds—more than enough to meet the sum required by Marshall—and leave for Chicago to complete negotiations. Regina, after a fierce argument with Horace, learned that Oscar had gone. Ben now held the upper hand; he simply told Regina that everything had been settled. Horace, an onlooker, was quietly amused. Now, he thought, he would not be a party to the wrecking of the town. He would at least die honestly. To the watching Alexandra's horror, Regina calmly informed him that she hoped he would indeed die as quickly as possible.

Two weeks later, Horace went to his now estranged wife's part of the house. Knowing that he was to be short-lived, he had had his deposit box brought to him and had discovered the theft. This he told Regina, along with his accurate suspicions as to the thieves' identity. To Regina's surprise, however, he stated that he intended to say nothing unless forced to, and then he would simply call the theft a loan. Horace planned to make a new will, leaving Regina eighty-eight thousand dollars in bonds. Thus she would eventually inherit his bonds, but she would not receive a single cent of the millions Ben and Oscar prophesied for the Hubbard family. For once Horace had tied the hands of his cunning wife.

Recalling their unhappy married life, Regina shrewishly revealed her contempt for Horace from the start. Horace, feeling an attack coming on, broke his bottle of medicine. Regina, hoping that his efforts to climb the stairs would prove fatal, cruelly refused to go upstairs for his second bottle. Horace staggered from his wheelchair and collapsed on the stair landing.

In an interview with her brothers after Horace was carried to his room, Regina revealed what she had learned from her husband. Should he die, she would blackmail them for a seventy-five percent share of the profits in exchange for the bonds. Soon word came, in the person of the silent Alexandra, that Regina's plan had worked. Horace was dead. Regina then announced her plans for seeing the judge the next day. Any jury would be swayed by a woman whose brothers had stolen from her. Regina also declared that there were not twelve men in the state whom the brothers had not cheated. A philosophical Ben gave in to Regina's demands, but as he left he was wondering what Horace, who had been in a wheelchair, was doing on the landing. Perhaps in the future he might find out, and when he did, he would let Regina know.

Realizing that Alexandra loved her father very much, Regina tried to be sympathetic. However, her saddened, sickened daughter defied her plans for their future in Chicago. Alexandra announced her final departure from Regina and the Hubbards because she believed that her father would have wanted it that way.

Critical Evaluation:

Lillian Hellman wrote or adapted twelve plays during a writing career that spanned more than four decades and earned her many honors, including two New York Drama Critics Circle Awards, one in 1941 and one in 1960. Hellman was prolific in other literary areas as well, with numerous screenplays, articles, and memoirs to her credit. The controversial *Scoundrel Time* (1976) excoriated the House Committee on Un-American Activities, which had subjected her, in 1952, to interrogations. Four years earlier the outspoken writer had been blacklisted by the Hollywood film industry. Eighteen months after her death in 1984, a one-woman show, *Lillian*, by William Luce, based on Hellman's colorful and contentious career, opened on Broadway—an honor very few writers have achieved.

The Little Foxes remains Hellman's most popular play. It ran for 410 performances in its

Broadway premiere. Not only is it her most frequently performed work, including two success-ful Broadway revivals, but it also has received the highest critical praise. Curiously, the playwright was less than enthusiastic about the play and its initial reception. She states in her memoir *Pentimento* (1973) that writing it was very difficult because of its autobiographical ties to her mother's family. The dramatist was puzzled by the first reviews which called the play morbid in spirit because she viewed it an ironic comedy.

It is difficult to categorize *The Little Foxes*, which may be the key to its continued success. Reviews of the original Broadway production, for example, often described it as grim, as a well-made play, as melodramatic, and as a dark comedy, but later critics understood the play was all of the above. It is suffused with an ironic detachment that each new generation of audiences finds refreshing.

In *The Little Foxes*, Hellman has created a taut and spellbinding tale revolving around sex, power, and greed. It is set in the New South, sloughing off the devastating effects of Recon-struction. The playwright has created strongly etched characters who may be greedy and avaricious, but they are charming. They largely succeed in winning the audiences' favor. Regina Giddens, for example, may be a larger-than-life embodiment of evil, yet she is also totally believable. About to lose everything she has struggled for, Regina is saved by Horace's heart attack. The heroine does not help him, but neither does she plan his death. The same amoral quality can also be seen in Regina's two brothers and in Leo. They may be hateful, but they are always strong, alert, and patient in plotting Regina's downfall. The play's ambiguous ending suggests they may not have to wait too long. In *The Little Foxes* Hellman has created a polished piece of Americana and an American classic.

"Critical Evaluation" by Terry Theodore

Bibliography:
Falk, Doris V. *Lillian Hellman*. New York: Frederick Ungar, 1978. Introduction to Hellman's overall literary career. Chapter on *The Little Foxes* reveals Hellman's use of research material, creation of nine drafts, and inclusion of her own family background into several of the characters.
Lederer, Katherine. *Lillian Hellman*. Boston: Twayne, 1979. Solid survey of Hellman, the writer and the individual. Attempts to correct misinterpretations of Hellman's Southern background and political philosophy. Analysis of *The Little Foxes* is thoughtful.
Moody, Richard. *Lillian Hellman: Playwright*. New York: Pegasus, 1972. First important book-length examination of Hellman's work. Readable, by important American theater scholar. Long chapter on *The Little Foxes* scrutinizes play itself as well as circumstances surrounding first Broadway production.
Rollyson, Carl. *Lillian Hellman: Her Legend and Her Legacy*. New York: St. Martin's Press, 1988. Sympathetic portrayal of Hellman's life. Features a cast of characters who played important roles in Hellman's life Chapter on *The Little Foxes* examines the writing of the play and its first Broadway production. Lengthy bibliography.
Wright, William. *Lillian Hellman: The Image, the Woman*. New York: Simon & Schuster, 1986. Biographical investigation that attempts to bring disparate elements of Hellman's life and literary work into resolution. Survey of *The Little Foxes* focuses on its initial New York City production and an analysis of play.

LITTLE WOMEN

Type of work: Novel
Author: Louisa May Alcott (1832-1888)
Type of plot: Didactic
Time of plot: Nineteenth century
Locale: A New England village, New York City, and Italy
First published: 1868-1869

Principal characters:
MEG,
JO,
BETH, and
AMY, the March sisters
MRS. MARCH or "MARMEE," their mother
MR. MARCH, their father
THEODORE LAWRENCE or LAURIE, a young neighbor
PROFESSOR BHAER, a tutor, in love with Jo

The Story:

The March family lived in a small house next door to the Lawrence mansion, where young Theodore Lawrence and his aged grandfather had only each other for company. Old Mr. Lawrence was wealthy, and he indulged every wish of his grandson, but often Laurie was lonely. When the lamp was lit and the shades were up in the March house, he could see the four March girls, with their mother in the center, seated around a cheerful fire. He learned to know them by name before he met them, and in his imagination, he almost felt himself a member of the family.

The oldest was plump Meg, who had to earn her living as the governess of a group of unruly youngsters in the neighborhood. Next was Jo, tall, awkward, and tomboyish, who liked to write, and who spent all her spare time devising plays and entertainments for her sisters. Then there was gentle Beth, the homebody, content to sit knitting by the fire, or to help her mother take care of the house. The youngest was curly-haired Amy, a schoolgirl who dreamed of someday becoming a famous artist like Michelangelo or Leonardo da Vinci.

At Christmastime, the girls were confronted with the problem of what to do with the dollar Marmee, as they called their mother, had said they might spend. At first, each thought only of her own pleasure, but all ended by buying a gift for Marmee instead. On Christmas morning, they insisted on sharing their breakfast with the Hummels, a poor family in the neighborhood, and for this unselfishness, they were rewarded when rich Mr. Lawrence sent over a surprise Christmas feast consisting of ice cream, bonbons, and four bouquets of flowers for the table.

Many happy days followed, with Laurie, who had met Jo at a fashionable New Year's Eve dance, becoming a part of the March family circle. In November, however, a telegram brought a message that the girls' father, an army chaplain in the Civil War, was critically ill. Mrs. March did not know what to do. She felt that she should go to her husband at once, but she had barely five dollars in her purse. She was hesitant about going to wealthy, irascible Aunt March for help. Jo solved the problem by selling her beautiful, long, chestnut hair, which was her only vanity, for twenty-five dollars. She made the sacrifice willingly, but that night, after the others had gone to bed, Meg, who thought Jo was asleep, heard her weeping softly. Gently, Meg asked if Jo were crying over her father's illness, and Jo sobbed that it was not her father she was crying for now, but for her hair.

During Marmee's absence, dark days fell upon the little women. Beth, who had never been strong, contracted scarlet fever, and for a time it looked as if Jo were going to lose her dearest sister. Marmee was sent for, but by the time she arrived, the crisis had passed and her little daughter was better. By the next Christmas, Beth was her old contented self again. Mr. March surprised them all when he returned home from the front well and happy. The little family was together once more.

Then John Brooke, Laurie's tutor, fell in love with Meg. This fact was disclosed when Mr. Brooke surreptitiously stole one of Meg's gloves and kept it in his pocket as a memento. Laurie discovered the glove and informed Jo. To his great surprise, she was infuriated at the idea that the family circle might be disturbed. Yet she was quite reconciled when, three years later, Meg became Mrs. Brooke.

Jo herself had grown up. She began to take her writing seriously and even sold a few stories, which helped with the family budget. Her greatest disappointment came when Aunt Carrol, a relative of the Marches, decided she needed a companion on a European trip, and asked the more ladylike Amy to accompany her, rather than Jo. Then Jo, with Marmee's permission, decided to go to New York. She took a job as governess for a Mrs. Kirke, who ran a large boardinghouse. There she met Professor Bhaer, a lovable and eccentric German tutor, who proved to be a good friend and companion.

When Jo returned home, Laurie, who had always loved her, asked her to marry him. Jo, who imagined that she would always remain unmarried, devoting herself exclusively to her writing, tried to convince Laurie that they were not made for each other. He persisted, pointing out that his grandfather and her family both expected them to marry. When she made him realize that her refusal was final, he stomped off, and shortly afterward went to Europe with his grandfather. In Europe, he saw a great deal of Amy, and the two became close friends, so that Laurie was able to transfer to her younger sister a great deal of the feeling he previously had had for Jo.

Jo was now at home caring for Beth, who had never fully recovered from her earlier illness. In the spring, Beth died, practically in Jo's arms, and after the loss of her gentle sister, Jo was lonely indeed. She tried to comfort herself with her writing and with Meg's two babies, Daisy and Demi, but not until the return of Amy, now married to Laurie, did she begin to feel her old self again. When Professor Bhaer stopped off on his way to a university appointment in the Midwest, Jo was delighted. One day, under an umbrella he had supplied to shield her from a pouring rain, he asked her to marry him, and Jo accepted. Within a year, old Aunt March died and willed her home, Plumfield, to Jo. Jo decided to open a boys' school, where she and her professor could devote their lives to instructing the young.

So the little women reached maturity, and on their mother's sixtieth birthday, they all had a great celebration at Plumfield. Around the table, at which there was but one empty chair, sat Marmee, her children, and her grandchildren. When Laurie proposed a toast to her, she replied by stretching out her arms to them all and saying that she could wish nothing better for them than this present happiness for the rest of their lives.

Critical Evaluation:

Little Women has been condemned by critics as being little more than a moral battering ram aimed at nineteenth century adolescent girls. Louisa May Alcott, however, produced a work much larger in scope and more complex in feeling. On the surface, it is a series of episodes depicting each of the four March girls' private battles with the moral conduct befitting a good

Christian girl. If the story of the Marches were merely that, it would not have sparked so much controversy and analysis, nor would it have remained a children's book so popular that libraries find it hard to keep copies on the shelves more than a hundred years after its publication.

Although it was Alcott's intention to demonstrate right behavior, her method of presenting a problem for each sister to solve without much adult influence makes the characters real and the situations believable. The sisters all harbor a weakness lovingly noted by Marmee, their conscience and gentle guide. Meg is vain and wishes to live in luxury; Jo is spontaneous, direct, and temperamental; Beth is a timid, gentle homebody who wishes for a piano; and Amy is artistic and mannerly, with a tendency to be pretentious. These character flaws may seem mild by the standards of the 1990's, but they are timeless benchmarks of youth from which Alcott draws out and measures each girl's growth. However predictable the outcome, their journeys to womanhood involve pain and hardship, humiliation, and even danger in the midst of the protective family nest.

The process of individual growth within the family is Alcott's focus. Alcott was a realist, so she does not develop any progressive notions that were impossible to pursue in Victorian-era America. Jo will not marry Laurie, because their bold, adventuresome natures simply do not apply to the marriage conventions of the mid-nineteenth century. Alcott was a feminist, however, and she depicts the relentless self-denial of Victorian women as it was. Her purpose is echoed in Marmee's wish for her daughters to become happy, loved, dutiful wives and mothers. To accomplish this, they must sacrifice independence of thought and action, and that is what each girl does. Alcott does not gloss over the price they pay, nor does she neglect to show the personal rewards of happy married life and motherhood, self-discipline, and altruism.

The focus on these qualities makes the work timeless. The story opens in the early years of the Civil War, but little is said about Mr. March and his experiences as a chaplain at the front lines. Slavery is never mentioned, nor is Lincoln's assassination. It would be wrong to assume that Alcott neglected these happenings out of disinterest, or an assumed disinterest on the part of her readers. She served as a nurse during the war and knew intimately the suffering and tragedy that befell young men. Her father, Bronson Alcott, was a progressive educator, and Louisa was raised with an awareness of politics and social problems. She smartly focused the story on the family, the center toward which the March girls are drawn time and again for moral support and rejuvenation.

The story opens at Christmas, when the girls are sad and disappointed about their father's absence and their own poverty. Marmee gently reminds them that others suffer more, and the women troop to the poor Hummel household laden with their own Christmas breakfast. Their selflessness is rewarded with a sumptuous dinner courtesy of neighbor Lawrence. When Jo nearly lets Amy drown in the river after she destroys Jo's precious manuscript, Jo appeals to Marmee to help control her anger. Marmee reveals her own struggle with rage and frustration, and from that point on, the two share a special bond. Jo has learned to separate her feelings from her actions. After Meg spends a week with wealthy friends whose lifestyle she envies, she returns home grateful for the simplicity and authentic love and comfort of her humble home. Meg has learned the high price of vanity. Amy, the baby of the family, does some rather extreme things to win the approval of her affluent schoolmates. A comic episode concerning pickled limes and public humiliation prompts her to realize the consequences of climbing the social ladder. Amy has learned that it is better to stand on the lower rungs in safety than to make it to the top and fall flat on her face. Beth's character is virtually undeveloped, and she changes the least. She is a touching reminder that some delicate souls are simply too vulnerable to remain for very long on this planet. Her death leaves its mark on the March family, particularly Jo.

Jo is the most challenged to change, because she is the most tenacious and free-spirited character. Her tempestuous behavior and childlike joy for living are appealing to readers. She chafes at the expectations of women in her day and vows to remain unmarried and fulfilled by her work as a writer. Neighbor Laurie, her charming and rebellious kindred spirit, grows to love her, and it seems that the two will end up together. Jo's vow is half fulfilled as she turns her back on the radical choice to marry her best friend and embark on a life of self-absorbed adventure. Instead, she marries Professor Bhaer and engages herself in work more suitable to women of the day, by opening a school for boys. This choice may disappoint readers, but she and her sisters have fulfilled their mother's wish that they be married, loved, and valued by others, a theme that constantly resonates throughout the story.

However idealistic and dependent the relationships may seem between the daughters and their parents and husbands, the family represents an unchanging core around which world events and personal calamity spiral. This family portrait contains both real life conflicts with which any reader can sympathize, and a model for the kind of family most readers privately long for. The result is irresistible.

"Critical Evaluation" by Kim Dolce

Bibliography:
Delamar, Gloria T. *Louisa May Alcott and "Little Women": Biography, Critique, Publications, Poems, Songs, and Contemporary Relevance.* Jefferson, N.C.: McFarland, 1990. Goes beyond a biography of Alcott to include a comprehensive bibliography of Alcott's works and analyses of her work. Includes critical analysis of *Little Women* and selections from letters by Alcott and her close associates.
Keyser, Elizabeth Lennox. *Whispers in the Dark: The Fiction of Louisa May Alcott.* Knoxville: University of Tennessee Press, 1993. Intriguing analysis of Jo and Laurie's relationship as the Sleeping Beauty tale with gender roles reversed. Suggests that Alcott depicted them as androgynous characters who together made a whole person, but whose wholeness could not exist in the Victorian era.
Showalter, Elaine. *Sister's Choice: Tradition and Change in American Women's Writing.* New York: Oxford University Press, 1991. Discusses American women writers and the diversity of their language and literary vision in the context of race, ethnicity, and class. Influential analysis of *Little Women.*
Stern, Madeleine, ed. *Critical Essays on Louisa May Alcott.* Boston: G. K. Hall, 1984. A collection of essays on Alcott's body of work, from nineteenth century reviews to late twentieth century criticism and interpretation.
Strickland, Charles. *Victorian Domesticity: Families in the Life and Art of Louisa May Alcott.* Tuscaloosa: University of Alabama Press, 1985. A thoughtful exploration of the sentimental and its implications in Alcott's work. Suggests that her juvenile fiction offers the most radical departure from Victorian conventions. Connects to Alcott's own struggle with the sentimental ideals of child and parent in her own family.

LIVES OF THE POETS

Type of work: Biography and literary criticism
Author: Samuel Johnson (1709-1784)
First published: Prefaces, Biographical and Critical, to the Works of the English Poets,
1779-1781; revised edition, 1781 as *The Lives of the Most Eminent English Poets*

The essays contained in Samuel Johnson's *Lives of the Poets* were composed as prefaces to a large collection of the works of English writers of the seventeenth and eighteenth centuries, and they are therefore primarily critical rather than biographical. Johnson related the known information about the lives of his subjects, but he was content to rely upon facts gathered by earlier biographers, reserving his original thoughts for his critical commentary.

The more than fifty essays vary greatly in both length and detail. Johnson wrote extensive studies of men such as John Dryden, Alexander Pope, John Milton, and Jonathan Swift, whereas he only briefly summarized the achievements of minor figures whose names subsequently vanished from all but the pages of detailed literary histories. It is a tribute to the soundness of Johnson's judgment that the writers whom he considered important are those whose works continue to be highly regarded.

The collection belongs to Johnson's best, most readable works. His language is characteristically stately, but his style is less formal than in some of his earlier writing. He occasionally departs from the easy narrative flow to write a striking rhetorical passage in which balanced phrases and carefully constructed comparisons make his critical judgments memorable. One of his most famous "set pieces" is his contrast of the writings of Dryden and Pope.

> The style of Dryden is capricious and varied, that of Pope is cautious and uniform; Dryden obeys the motions of his own mind, Pope constrains his mind to his own rules of composition. Dryden is sometimes vehement and rapid; Pope is always smooth, uniform, and gentle. Dryden's page is a natural field, rising into inequalities, and diversified by the varied exuberance of abundant vegetation; Pope's is a velvet lawn, shaven by the scythe, and levelled by the roller.

Most of the *Lives of the Poets* follows the same structural pattern. Johnson begins with an account of his subject's family and education, then summarizes the main events of his life and gives brief notes on the time and circumstances of the composition and publication of his major works. The biographies conclude with critical commentary on specific poems and a final assessment of the poet's literary talents and faults.

Johnson's moral and literary standards formed a strong foundation for all his writings, and both the biographical and critical portions of *Lives of the Poets* reveal their author's characteristic points of view. The biographical sketch of a popular Restoration dramatist, for example, begins with the statement: "Of Thomas Otway, one of the first names in the English drama, little is known; nor is there any part of that little which his biographer can take pleasure in relating."

The character and personality of his poets were far more interesting to Johnson than facts and dates. He had begun his career as a biographer with a searching study of the motives that shaped the life of his friend Richard Savage, and he often manages to convey the essential qualities of his subject in a few words. Writing of the charming, somewhat irresponsible, author of *The Beggar's Opera* (1728), he notes: "[John] Gay is represented as a man easily incited to hope, and deeply depressed when his hopes were disappointed. This is not the character of a hero, but it may naturally imply something more generally welcome, a soft and civil companion."

Johnson's insights into the human personality are shown especially clearly in his life of Pope.

He brings the brilliant, ambitious, often ailing and bad-tempered poet vividly before the reader, chiding the excessive sensitivity that made Pope viciously attack critics of his writing in satirical works such as *The Dunciad* (1728-1743) and led him to hold grudges against his "enemies" far longer than most people thought reasonable. He also comments on one of Pope's rather amusing foibles: "In all his intercourse with mankind he had great delight in artifice, and endeavored to attain all his purposes by indirect and unsuspected methods. He practised his arts on such small occasions that Lady Bolingbroke used to say, in a French phrase, that 'he plaid the politician about cabbages and turnips.'" Johnson points out Pope's more appealing characteristics as well, noting his loyalty to his friends and his respect and tenderness for his elderly parents, and he tries to suggest something of the state of mind brought about by Pope's physical disabilities, his small stature, his weakness, and his almost constant pain.

Although *Lives of the Poets* reveals Johnson as a skillful analyst of the human personality, the book is still more interesting as a work of theoretical and practical criticism. The life of Cowley contains a famous discussion of metaphysical poetry, in which Johnson defines the wit that was the essence of the technique of John Donne and his followers: "Wit, abstracted from its effects upon the hearer, may be more rigorously and philosophically considered as a kind of discordia concors; a combination of dissimilar images, or discovery of occult resemblances in things apparently unlike."

Johnson, who believed that great poetry should deal with universal thoughts in general terms, felt that the achievement of the metaphysical poets was a minor one, and he quotes many lines to illustrate the absurdities often produced by their quest for novelty. He does, however, show appreciation of their intellectual efforts and grants that they occasionally succeeded: "Yet great labor directed by great ability is never wholly lost: if they frequently threw away their wit upon false conceits, they likewise sometimes struck out unexpected truth: if their conceits were far-fetched, they were often worth the carriage."

The life of Milton shows Johnson at once at his worst and at his best. His natural antipathy for allegory in general and pastoral allegory in particular led him scornfully to dismiss "Lycidas," the elegy that many consider one of the finest English lyrics:

> In this poem there is no nature, for there is no truth; there is no art, for there is nothing new. Its form
> is that of a pastoral, easy, vulgar, and therefore disgusting; whatever images it can supply are long
> ago exhausted; and its inherent improbability always forces dissatisfaction on the mind.

Johnson's succinct praise of *L'Allegro* and *Il Penseroso* (both 1631) conforms more closely to later views, however: "Every man that reads them, reads them with pleasure." His extensive remarks on *Paradise Lost* (1667) are undeniably illuminating, for he recognizes and pays tribute to the epic's greatness, majesty, unity, and powerful theological foundation; however, he also examines closely what he feels to be a major flaw. All the characters except Adam and Eve are supernatural beings, and even these two are in a situation different from that of all other men and women: "The reader finds no transaction in which he can be engaged, beholds no condition in which he can, by any effort of the imagination place himself; he has, therefore, little natural curiosity or sympathy."

This comment shows clearly Johnson's conviction that literature should be, as Aristotle had declared, an imitation of life and a reflection of the real emotions of men. This viewpoint led Johnson to conclude, a little reluctantly:

> The want of human interest is always felt. *Paradise Lost* is one of the books which the reader ad-
> mires and lays down, and forgets to take up again. None ever wished it longer than it is. Its perusal

is a duty rather than a pleasure. We read Milton for instruction, retire harassed and overburdened, and look elsewhere for recreation; we desert our master and seek for companions.

Although Johnson's general statements are the passages from the *Lives of the Poets* most often quoted, he actually devoted much of his attention to commentary on specific lines. He gives, for example, a detailed discussion of the individual stanzas of Thomas Gray's ode "The Bard," criticizing the poet's excessive alliteration, his use of "the puerilities of obsolete mythology," and the many clichés among his images.

Quotation of brief passages is especially effective in the life of Dryden, where Johnson cites many lines to illustrate both the elegance and majesty as well as the pedantry and carelessness of the poet. He finds that Dryden "delighted to tread upon the brink of meaning, where light and darkness begin to mingle; to approach the precipice of absurdity, and hover over the abyss of unideal vacancy." Close examination of many passages leads Johnson to lament Dryden's carelessness, although he admires his great talent:

> Such is the unevenness of his composition that ten lines are seldom found together without something of which the reader is ashamed. Dryden was no rigid judge of his own pages; he seldom struggled after supreme excellence, but snatched in haste what was within his reach; and when he could content others, was himself contented.

A reading of *Lives of the Poets* indicates why Johnson has become increasingly famous not only as the colorful personage immortalized by James Boswell but also as one of the best prose writers and ablest critics in English literary history. Although his many prejudices occasionally brought forth declarations that later opinion considers absurd, his personal standards generally contributed to the lasting worth of his criticism. He evaluated literature on the basis of its truth to life, and, since he understood better than most men what human beings think and feel, his judgments for the most part remain valid. He appreciated the appeal of the new and the unusual, but he reserved his highest praise for what he considered lastingly true and moving.

Bibliography:
Burke, John J., Jr., and Donald Kay. *The Unknown Samuel Johnson.* Madison: University of Wisconsin Press, 1983. An overview of Johnson's method and style of writing. Makes a distinction between professional writing and academic critique, and declares *Lives of the Poets* to be an instance of the former.
Damrosch, Leopold, Jr. *The Uses of Johnson's Criticism.* Charlottesville: University Press of Virginia, 1976. A detailed look at what Johnson had to say about the poets featured in *Lives of the Poets* and the application of his critiques to subsequent literary studies.
Hardy, J. P. *Samuel Johnson: A Critical Study.* London: Routledge & Kegan Paul, 1979. An examination of Johnson's critical abilities. Focuses on his artistry in the critical genre rather than on the historical value of his work.
Nath, Prem, ed. *Fresh Reflections on Samuel Johnson: Essays in Criticism.* Troy, N.Y.: Whitston, 1987. A broad range of critical essays dealing with Johnson's writings, with particular emphasis on his critical style in *Lives of the Poets.*
Wain, John, ed. *Johnson as Critic.* London: Routledge & Kegan Paul, 1973. Concerned primarily with the factual accuracy of *Lives of the Poets.* Explores Johnson's critical expectations, his idealism, and the assumptions about poetry that he shared with his contemporaries.

LOLITA

Type of work: Novel
Author: Vladimir Nabokov (1899-1977)
Type of plot: Satire
Time of plot: 1910-1952
Locale: France and numerous small American towns
First published: 1955

Principal characters:
HUMBERT HUMBERT, an intellectual from France
DOLORES HAZE, his stepdaughter
CHARLOTTE BECKER HAZE HUMBERT, her mother, Humbert's second wife
CLARE QUILTY, a playwright
RITA, Humbert's traveling companion
MISS PRATT, a girls' school headmistress
RICHARD F. SCHILLER, Dolly's husband
ANNABEL LEIGH, Humbert's first love
VALERIA HUMBERT, Humbert's first wife
JOHN RAY, JR., an academic and editor

The Story:

After the death by heart attack of Humbert Humbert, before his trial for murder, his lawyer asked John Ray, Jr., Ph.D., to edit the accused murderer's last manuscript. It is entitled "Lolita, or the Confession of a White Widowed Male." Dolores Schiller, the girl Humbert called Lolita, died giving birth to a stillborn daughter a few weeks after Humbert's fatal heart attack. Ray defended the manuscript against charges of pornography and claimed it would become a classic in psychiatric circles. Humbert's confession begins with a summary of his life from his birth in 1910 until his discovery of Lolita in 1947. He was born in Paris to an English mother and Swiss father, who ran a luxurious hotel on the Riviera. At thirteen, he fell in love with Annabel Leigh, who was close to his age, and experienced unfulfilled lust. Four months later, Annabel died of typhus. He had been haunted by her memory until he found her essence reincarnated in Lolita. After studying English literature in Paris, Humbert became a teacher, discovering himself drawn to certain girls between nine and fourteen, whom he called nymphets. Trying to lead a conventional existence, he was married to Valeria from 1935 until 1939, when she left him for a White Russian taxi driver, only to die in childbirth. At the start of World War II, Humbert came to America.

After his second stay in a mental institution, Humbert sought refuge in the small New England town of Ramsdale, where he rented a room from Charlotte Haze, a widow, after seeing her twelve-year-old daughter, Dolores, known as Lo to her mother and Dolly to her friends. The darkly handsome Humbert soon discovered that he resembled some singer or actor on whom Lolita had a schoolgirl crush. When the girl went away to summer camp, Humbert decided he could not live without her. Then Charlotte left a note confessing her love for Humbert and ordering him either to leave or marry her. After they were married, he hinted to her friends that he and she had had an affair thirteen years previously, and he began to regard Lolita as his child. Humbert decided he must somehow get rid of her mother, his wife, but he could not bring himself to kill her.

Humbert's problem was solved when Charlotte broke into his locked desk to read his journal and discovered his disdain for her and his lust for Lolita. Crossing the street, in an emotional turmoil, to mail some letters incriminating him (for protection, having read of his desire for her death), she was struck and killed by a car. Humbert recovered the letters, played the role of a grieving widower, continued planting suggestions that he was Dolly's real father, and announced plans to take his stepdaughter on a trip west. Humbert retrieved Lolita from Camp Q on the pretext that her mother was ill and took her to the Enchanted Hunters, a hotel in Briceland. As Humbert relates it, before he could break the news of Lolita's mother's death to the girl, and comfort her, Lolita seduced him and afterward revealed she had lost her virginity to the son of the camp director. Humbert was immediately consumed by guilt but continued to have sexual relations with her. When Lolita demanded to call her mother, Humbert admitted that Charlotte was dead. The couple began traveling from motel to motel across the United States. Seeing how other adult men were attracted to little Dolly, Humbert was constantly on his guard. He was also aware of the repercussions that awaited him if his criminal treatment of Lolita were discovered.

After a year and 27,000 miles on the road, they returned east to Beardsley, where Lolita attended the private girls' school. Miss Pratt, the headmistress, convinced him to let Dolly play the lead in the school's production of a new play, *The Enchanted Hunters*. Just before it opened, Lolita announced that she hated school and the play and wanted to travel again. Humbert was told that the playwright, identified by Dolly as "Some old woman. Clare Something," had been raving about the young actress. Humbert took with him a gun once owned by Harold Haze, Dolly's father. He felt he might need it after seeing they were being followed by an Aztec red convertible and discovering Lolita talking to a stranger resembling Gustave Trapp, Humbert's cousin.

In Elphinstone, Lolita developed a high fever. While Humbert was incapacitated by the same fever, she was checked out of the hospital by "her uncle, Mr. Gustave." Humbert spent the next four months searching for her and her abductor, tormented by the taunting clues left by his nemesis. In a Northeastern bar, he met Rita, an alcoholic, suicidal young woman who traveled with him for two years. After a letter arrived from Lolita, then Mrs. Richard F. Schiller, Humbert found her pregnant and married to a young Korean War veteran in dismal Coalmont. He was surprised how much he still loved the haggard, seventeen-year-old housewife. After she identified her abductor, who had wanted her to perform in pornographic home movies and had thrown her out when she had refused, Humbert gave her and Dick $4,000 so that they could move to Alaska. Humbert then set out to find Clare Quilty. After returning to Ramsdale to sign over all his money and possessions to Lolita, Humbert tracked Quilty down in Parkington and, after a lengthy confrontation, shot and killed him.

Critical Evaluation:

Before the publication of *Lolita*, the Russian-born Vladimir Nabokov was not widely known in English-speaking literary circles; most of his early work had not yet been translated from Russian. After *Lolita* was rejected by four American publishers, Nabokov's French agent sent it to Olympia Press in Paris, which quickly published it. Although Olympia published many controversial works by writers such as Jean Genet, it was notorious for cheap editions of pornographic books, a fact of which Nabokov was ignorant at the time. The novel went virtually unnoticed until novelist Graham Greene praised it in London's *Daily Express*. When Putnam published the first American edition in 1958, it became a best-seller. Many readers, expecting salacious fun, were disappointed by the lack of overt sexual content and dismayed by the demanding style. Still others attacked the book as immoral. Nabokov is not for passive readers who resist being drawn into his linguistic games. *Lolita* is considered one of this highly acclaimed writer's two greatest novels—*Pale Fire* (1962) is the other—and a masterpiece of American comic fiction.

Lolita is a highly literary work, filled with allusions to famous and little-known novels, poems, and plays. The highest number of allusions are to Edgar Allan Poe who, at twenty-seven, married his thirteen-year-old cousin. Poe wrote "Annabel Lee" (1849), a poem about a child love dead by the seaside. He also wrote "William Wilson," a tale of a psychological double, and invented the detective story. Nabokov works these and other allusions to Poe into his novel. There are also many references to *Carmen* (1845), not the Georges Bizet opera but the Prosper Mérimée novella about love, loss, and revenge and an imprisoned narrator. Another strong influence is James Joyce, whose ornate, self-aware, stylistic whimsy is reflected in *Lolita*. Joyce pioneered heavily allusive fiction, full of word games, and *Lolita* is full of puns, coinages ("nymphet"), neologisms, and foreign, archaic, and unusual words. There are also jokes such as the appearance of Vivian Darkbloom, the letters of whose name may be rearranged, changing one *o* to an *a*, to spell Vladimir Nabokov. *Lolita* is drunk on language; a typical sentence reads: "I spend my doleful days in dumps and dolors." In his afterword, Nabokov says the novel is about his love affair with the English language.

Lolita can be seen as a parody of such literary forms as autobiography, the confessional tale, the Romantic novel, the tale of the *Doppelgänger* or double, and the detective story. As for the latter, the reader knows from the beginning that Humbert has murdered someone but does not know more. Hints of the victim's identity are scattered throughout the novel, and Humbert even warns his readers to keep their eyes on the clues. Nabokov has fun with the detective element by having Quilty appear to Humbert in a Dick Tracy mask.

The *Doppelgänger* device is central to the novel. Humbert Humbert sees the old lecher Clare Quilty as his evil double. Lolita has her double in Annabel Leigh (herself a reference to another, and a joke about the youth of Edgar Allan Poe's wife). Humbert Humbert has two wives, both, in his eyes, contemptible. One dies in childbirth, as does Lolita. The three main characters have a multitude of names. Humbert thinks of the mysterious stranger as Trapp and McFate, Quilty's friends call him Cue, Humbert calls him Punch, as in Punch and Judy, and Lolita tries to convince Humbert that the playwright is a woman. Dolores Haze is Lo, Dolly, Lolita, Lola, and Mrs. Richard F. Schiller. She is a girl and a woman, a victim and a manipulator. Humbert's name is a double; he uses it for wordplay. It is mispronounced numerous ways by those he encounters (and once by him), and he is frequently called "Mr. Haze." His calling himself Edgar H. Humbert is typical of Nabokov's jokes within jokes. Humbert's editor is another double: The initials of John Ray, Jr., are JR, Jr. Beyond the gamesmanship, however, the novel conveys the pain the protagonists suffer.

One of the main targets of Nabokov's satire is Freudian psychology. Humbert admits, but glosses over, his mental instability and refuses to see himself as a stereotype or a case study. *Lolita* is thus a parody of the psychiatric simplicity of a case study, with Humbert sneering at those who would see his affair with Lolita as an attempt to rid himself of his obsession with Annabel, laughing at those who interpret the incestuous relationship in Oedipal terms. Humbert's attacks on Sigmund Freud can be taken seriously, for he is not just a comic figure but a tormented, guilt-ridden soul.

Humbert is a complex figure because he changes from a self-centered sexual pervert to something of a caring father. Even as Lolita loses her nymphet charms, he falls more deeply in love with her. Pregnant by another and worn out by poverty, she remains his ideal. His moral growth is shown by his lament at robbing Dolly Haze of the stable family life to which every child is entitled and at stealing her childhood for his selfish pleasures. He must kill Quilty, his double, to destroy the evil side of his nature. His confession, far from being pornography, is an attempt at a moral cleansing and illustrates the healing power of art.

This double-edged approach can also be seen in Nabokov's treatment of his adopted country. He satirizes the vulgar, commercialized side of American life through Lolita's love of junk food, trashy movies, and bland popular singers. Humbert writes of Lolita, "She it was to whom ads were dedicated: the ideal consumer, the subject and object of every foul poster." Nabokov makes fun of such topics as American progressive education: "What we are concerned with is the adjustment of the child to group life," says Miss Pratt. Humbert is more amused at than appalled by these excesses and sincerely loves the American landscape, the West in particular. *Lolita* was partially inspired by the summer trips Nabokov and his wife took over several years to forty-six of the states in pursuit of rare butterflies. (The writer was also a prominent lepidopterist.) His novel is a comic valentine to "the lovely, trustful, dreamy, enormous country."

Michael Adams

Bibliography:
Bloom, Harold, ed. *Lolita*. Edgemont, Pa.: Chelsea House, 1993. Contains nine essays on such topics as the effect of America on Humbert, necrophilia, the attacks on Freud, the parodic elements, the treatment of women, and Humbert as a writer.
Field, Andrew. *Nabokov: His Life in Art*. Boston: Little, Brown, 1967. Explains how *Lolita* grew out of an unsuccessful short story Nabokov wrote in 1939. Also finds similarities to other Nabokov works in Russian. Excellent analysis of how Humbert and Quilty are psychological doubles.
Maddox, Lucy. *Nabokov's Novels in English*. Athens: University of Georgia Press, 1983. Interprets the novel as an anatomy of an obsession, with Humbert romanticizing Lolita and America and discovering that both are flawed yet still endearing.
Nabokov, Vladimir. *The Annotated Lolita*. Edited by Alfred Appel, Jr. New York: McGraw-Hill, 1970. The text of the novel, followed by notes explaining the allusions and translating the French passages, with occasional comments by Nabokov.
Proffer, Carl. *Keys to Lolita*. Bloomington: Indiana University Press, 1968. Argues that Nabokov's works require especially close readings because of the elaborate linguistic and literary games. Identifies allusions and stylistic devices, such as alliteration, rhyme, puns, and image patterns.

A LONG AND HAPPY LIFE

Type of work: Novel
Author: Reynolds Price (1933-   )
Type of plot: Domestic realism
Time of plot: 1957
Locale: Rural North Carolina
First published: 1962

Principal characters:

ROSACOKE MUSTIAN, a young woman and protagonist
WESLEY BEAVERS, the object of her love
EMMA MUSTIAN, Rosacoke's mother
MILO, her older brother
RATO, her younger brother
BABY SISTER, her younger sister
SISSIE, Milo's wife
MILDRED SUTTON, a young black woman who has just died
WILLIE DUKE AYCOCK, Rosacoke's rival
DR. SLEDGE, medical doctor
HEYWOOD BETTS, Willie Duke's boy friend

The Story:

Mildred Sutton, a black woman and friend of Rosacoke Mustian, had just died while giving birth to a son. She had not been married and the father was not known. Rosacoke was on her way to the funeral in the local black church in a rural part of North Carolina. On her way there she saw Wesley Beavers, who had been her erstwhile boyfriend for some six years. Wesley, too, was on his way to the funeral.

At the funeral, Rosacoke was entirely preoccupied with Wesley. As Mildred's friend, it was expected that Rosacoke would give a few words of "testimony" (that is, eulogy), at the service. When Wesley left the church early, however, Rosacoke decided to follow him into the woods (after attending a Sunday afternoon picnic and social event at the white church), where he tried to seduce her. Rosacoke did not give in to his wishes, but she did learn that Wesley, who now lived in a nearby city and worked in a motorcycle shop, was undeniably experienced in such matters. Wesley had brought condoms with him.

Back at home, Rosacoke engaged in small chat with her family members. She awaited more attention from Wesley; however, he returned to the city without coming to her house. She wrote him one of many letters, inquiring about whether or not and how much he truly loved her. A few weeks later a short postcard of a reply, ambiguously written, arrived in response.

Rosacoke continued to pine away, wanting only a profession of love from Wesley, but he stayed gone and did not return home for a visit for many weeks. He eventually arrived one morning in an airplane, accompanying Willie Duke Aycock and her boyfriend Heywood Betts. Rosacoke waited for him to visit, anxiously and impatiently, but for three days he did not appear. Nor did he show up at church for the service. When the airplane flew away, Rosacoke saw it in the sky and gave in to her obsession to know if Wesley had gone back to town without seeing her, after three days.

Rosacoke manufactured an excuse to find out. She ostensibly claimed that she had promised to take a picture of Mildred Sutton's baby for relatives in the North. The Suttons' home was near that of the Beavers. Rosacoke found an excuse for stopping at the Beavers' home, and she was greatly pleased to learn that Wesley was yet there. He lied to her, saying that he had not been to see her because the airplane ride had made him sick. He offered to give Rosacoke a ride home on his motorcycle.

On the way, the two stopped in the woods, where they had sex. At the very moment of consummation, Wesley moaned, "I thank you, Mae." Rosacoke was overcome with the fact of her own stupidity—no part of her name is Mae. Shattered, Rosacoke was returned home by Wesley, and she became absolutely determined to have nothing else to do with him.

A very short letter arrived from Wesley, who invited her to come to town and spend a holiday, clearly for the purpose of having sex. Rosacoke did not immediately answer the letter; or, rather, she wrote an answer that told him good-bye but did not mail it.

Milo's wife Sissie, overdue with her pregnancy, went into labor. The child died, and Rosacoke was so distracted by the event that she was no longer concerned about her own problems with Wesley. She wrote to him a detailed letter about the baby's death. After the funeral, Milo was distraught and had to get away from the home for a period of time. He invited Rosacoke to go with him to town. She agreed, but on the way realized that she herself was pregnant. She insisted upon returning home at once, whereupon she wrote a letter to Wesley informing him.

The Christmas holidays were now approaching. Wesley came home to visit. Immediately, this time, he went to visit Rosacoke. He announced that the two would elope to South Carolina. Rosacoke refused, unable to get around the clear evidence that Wesley did not love her—he called her "Mae" at the most important moment of her life, making it clear that he did not even care enough about her to know who she was.

At the Delight Baptist Church, the annual Christmas pageant of the Bethlehem story was to be reenacted. Willie Duke had been chosen to play the part of the Virgin Mary, but she un-expectedly left home and returned to town. In the confusion, it fell to the pregnant Rosacoke to play the part. She could not get out of it. Wesley Beavers also had a role in the reenactment of the Christmas birth.

The pageant ended, after which Wesley and Rosacoke discussed what they were going to do. Rosacoke insistently refused to elope with him. Wesley, in the fashion of a Southern "good ol' boy," insisted repeatedly. Finally, Rosacoke acknowledged to herself that marriage was what she had wanted all along. She realized that she had done what she had done in order "to hold him." They decided to marry.

Critical Evaluation:

Every Southerner writing fiction about the American South since William Faulkner has been inevitably compared to Faulkner. Since the publication of Reynolds Price's *A Long and Happy Life* in 1962, which won the Faulkner Foundation Award for a first novel, the author has, perhaps more than any other writer, been compared to Faulkner. Price's delicate diction and word choice, his elongated syntax, his attention to psychological imagery and symbolism have assured him this distinction. Price also writes of families in history and crisis in the vein of Faulkner. It is easy, for example, to compare Rosacoke Mustian to Lena Grove of Faulkner's *Light in August* (1932).

The subtlety of theme and message is surely another matter which brings to mind Faulkner's canon. Rosacoke Mustian knows from the offset what she wants, and she has known this for over six years: Wesley Beavers. Toward this end it becomes clear that she will do anything, as eventually she does, in order to secure him for a husband.

Rosacoke Mustian is innocent only in the sense that she has not yet sinned. Repeatedly, she seeks out Wesley Beavers, chasing him, but does not offer sex to him. Rather, she resists his blatant advances so as to preserve a guise and aura of this innocence. It is not innocence, however, but merely inexperience and the absence of matrimony that keeps her (until it appears nothing else will work) from violating the social norms of family and the Delight Baptist Church.

The central event of the novel, of course, is the seduction. It is not clear, however, who seduces whom. In one view, Rosacoke follows Wesley to the woods where she woos and pretentiously gives in. In another, Wesley has been playing the part by making it clear what she will have to do in order to get him and keep him. Two fools meet.

One of the most memorable lines of modern American fiction, surely, is: "I thank you, Mae." Uttered by Wesley at the moment of sexual climax, he mistakenly thinks he is with another woman. At this moment, of course, Rosacoke realizes that she has given that most valuable part of herself to someone who does not care about her beyond gratification of his own physical desires. She now has her proof that he does not love her and that he is interested in her only for sex.

The moral question then becomes whether or not she will marry him. Both do the "honorable" things in terms of social conventions and dictates. Wesley insists that they marry; Rosacoke realizes that she is responsible for her pregnancy and determines not to marry him, no matter what.

In a masterful stroke of humor and symbolism, events of the plot unfold so as to assure that both Rosacoke and Wesley (his first name refers to Methodist preacher John Wesley) will have roles in the Christmas pageant at the rural church. In a matter of irony, humor, and regret Rosacoke must play the Virgin Mary while pregnant. Price provides readers with something of an inversion of the grotesque in Southern literature.

Rosacoke's decision to marry Wesley brings the novel to an end but not to much of a conclusion. She realizes that she will have a limited life living with him in town eating pork chops and grits, as she says, and living in some rented room upstairs. At the same time, he is what she wanted. She is honest enough to herself to admit that she did what she had to do to keep him. There is little hope for happiness for these two characters.

Price interweaves other themes throughout the novel, particularly matters of family history, race, religion, and setting. All of these are accomplished in manners reminiscent of Faulkner. Price succeeds, however, in establishing an authentic voice of his own. He is never an imitator of Faulkner.

Carl Singleton

Bibliography:

Hoffman, Frederick J. *The Art of Southern Fiction.* Carbondale: Southern Illinois University Press, 1967. Hoffman was the first noteworthy critic to announce that Reynolds Price's work was an important event in Southern fiction. Hoffman defends Price's work against charges that the author is imitating William Faulkner.

Holman, David Marion. "Reynolds Price." *Fifty Southern Writers After 1900.* Edited by Joseph M. Flora and Robert Bain. Westport, Conn.: Greenwood Press, 1987. Holman provides the best overall discussion of *A Long and Happy Life* within the context of the novelist's career and of Southern fiction. With a select bibliography and survey of major criticism.

Rooke, Constance. *Reynolds Price.* Boston: Twayne, 1983. One chapter of this text is given to Price's first novel, *A Long and Happy Life*. Rooke does a thorough investigation and criticism of the novel. The novel's connections to Price's later works are delineated.

Shepherd, Allen. "Love (and Marriage) in *A Long and Happy Life*." *Twentieth Century Literature* 17 (January, 1971): 20-35. Addresses the clichés of the situation (for example, of a "barefoot and pregnant" Southern belle) in order to point out its possible humor.

Vauthier, Simone. "The 'Circle in the Forest': Fictional Space in Reynolds Price's *A Long and Happy Life*." *Mississippi Quarterly* 28 (Spring, 1975): 123-146. Discussion of the connection between environment and psychological and emotional backgrounds.

LONG DAY'S JOURNEY INTO NIGHT

Type of work: Drama
Author: Eugene O'Neill (1888-1953)
Type of plot: Psychological realism
Time of plot: August, 1912
Locale: The Tyrones' summer house, New London, Connecticut
First performed: 1956; first published, 1956

Principal characters:
    JAMES TYRONE, an aging actor
    MARY TYRONE, his wife
    JAMIE TYRONE, their elder son
    EDMUND TYRONE, their younger son
    CATHLEEN, their housemaid

The Story:

After breakfast on a warm summer day in August, 1912, as brothers Jamie and Edmund Tyrone joked in the dining room, their mother Mary teased husband James Tyrone about his real estate bargains and expressed concern about Edmund's illness. Tyrone reassured her about Edmund's health and complimented her upon her healthy appearance. When the sons joined their parents in the living room, the lighthearted family conversation turned increasingly critical among them until Edmund repeated a humorous story told him by their farm tenant Shaughnessy, who had managed to get the best of Harker, the Standard Oil millionaire, and the tension was broken.

With Edmund upstairs, the others discussed his illness. Mary claimed it was only a cold, but Tyrone admitted privately to Jamie that the doctor suspected tuberculosis. Jamie responded by accusing his father of not sending Edmund to a real doctor but to a quack. The conversation escalated into an argument, which ended with both ashamed and guilty, and Jamie's revealing his suspicion that Mary had relapsed in her drug addiction. Tyrone and Jamie decided to clip the hedge. When Edmund tried to express to Mary his concern about her health, she accused him of not trusting her and spying on her, and declared that she was going to lie down before lunch.

At twelve forty-five, restless with hedge-clipping, Jamie joined Edmund for a clandestine drink and reprimanded him for leaving his mother alone so long. When Mary entered, Jamie could tell with certainty that she had been unable to resist her need for drugs. Her excited and nervous ramblings led first Edmund and then Tyrone, as he arrived inside for lunch, to the same sad conclusion.

About a half hour later the family emerged from the dining room, Tyrone's face showing weary resignation, Jamie's cynicism, and Edmund's illness. Mary was extremely nervous. The men prepared to go into town. Edmund had an appointment with Doctor Hardy (who had already informed Tyrone that Edmund had consumption and would need to go to a sanatorium). Mary insisted that Edmund had only a cold, but after a brief respite upstairs, she became more remote, scolding and complaining, revealing her morphine addiction with each guilty speech. Edmund pleaded with Mary not to talk any more; she continued to deny her problem and Edmund's illness.

The men escaped into town, leaving Mary alone. While the servant Cathleen imbibed Tyrone's liquor freely, Mary recalled her dreams of becoming a nun or a concert pianist, and her first meeting with James Tyrone. Home again, Edmund and Tyrone responded differently to Mary's reminiscences. While Tyrone sought another bottle of whiskey, Edmund desperately attempted to communicate once again with his mother about his illness. She refused to listen, and angrily cried: "I hate you when you become gloomy and morbid." Edmund retorted bitterly: "It's pretty hard to take at times, having a dope fiend for a mother." Discouraged, he left the house, Mary went upstairs, and Tyrone alone remained for dinner.

When Edmund returned from a walk on the beach, colliding with the furniture in the darkened hall because Tyrone would not waste money on electricity, he and his father began to argue about Tyrone's miserliness and about Jamie's profligacy. By midnight they were drunk. They drank deliberately, seeking oblivion, avoiding mentioning Mary upstairs or Edmund's tuberculosis. The movements they heard above triggered comments about her condition, followed by accusations and recriminations, then a moment of affection until the accusations began again. After Edmund labeled his father "a stinking old miser" who planned to save money on medical treatment because he thought that Edmund would die, Tyrone related his life's story: a childhood in dire poverty, and the concern for money that had wasted his talent as an actor. In response, Edmund described his love of the sea, where he felt a wild joy, and where, he said, "there is meaning." Jamie returned, more drunk than usual, thus annoying Tyrone, and entertained his brother with his adventure with the prostitute Fat Violet, until his cynical question, "Where's the hophead?" brought a punch from Edmund and immediate remorse. Another moment of affection occurred before Jamie confessed his ambivalence toward Edmund and fell into a drunken stupor, rousing himself to fight only when Tyrone returned.

With the foghorn sounding in the background, Mary descended the stairs, dragging her wedding dress, a precious object from the past. Jamie sneered: "The Mad Scene: Enter Ophelia." Tyrone and Edmund turned on him, as Jamie broke down in heartbroken sobs. Mary, completely detached, had regressed totally into the past, murmuring about something she had lost and could not remember. Frozen with the pain of their family situation, the three men stared at her in misery.

Critical Evaluation:

Written "with deep pity and understanding and forgiveness for all the four haunted Tyrones," *Long Day's Journey into Night* may be the greatest American play of the twentieth century. After a career of many dramatic experiments, some successful, some failures, in the last years of his life Eugene O'Neill found his most truthful and artistic voice in an autobiographical work detailing the torment of his own family. It earned him a fourth Pulitzer Prize, awarded posthumously in 1957. In O'Neill's Tyrone family, James Tyrone resembles his father James O'Neill, a famous actor known for his role as the Count of Monte Cristo. Mary Tyrone is a thinly disguised portrait of his mother Ella Quinlan O'Neill. The two sons, Jamie and Edmund, are pictures of Eugene's older brother and the playwright himself.

The play is classically structured, the title appropriate. The events of this four-hour drama are compressed into one day, with the first act occurring at eight-thirty in the morning, the two scenes of the second act before and after lunch, the third act at six-thirty in the evening, and the final act at midnight. It tells of the journey shared by the four principal characters through one particular day, but the past is always with them. Like Sophocles' *Oedipus Tyrannus*, it is a play of revelation rather than action.

The Tyrone family is like a single living organism; what affects one affects them all. Each person may be in conflict over his or her role, but they are inextricably bound by love and hate. Hostility is never far from the surface. The Tyrones are well aware of each others' vulnerabilities and are skilled in attacking them. Like musical motifs, each person's flaws are played again and again: Tyrone's miserliness, Jamie's profligacy, Edmund's illness, and, most important, Mary's dependence upon morphine. The drinking problem of the three men is ignored and excused, for the most part, because they share it. At the beginning of the play, Mary is supposedly cured after a stay in a sanatorium. The three men hope for a period of normal life, suppressing their fears for her continued health. Concern over Edmund's illness provides Mary with an excuse to resume her habit, and, as though afflicted with a growing cancer, the family organism quickly deteriorates.

Also just below the surface is the guilt accompanying the question of responsibility for Mary's addiction. At one time or another Mary accuses each of the men: Tyrone because he hired a quack doctor (that is, cheaper), who prescribed morphine when she was ill after the birth of Edmund; Jamie, because he infected her second baby with measles, and when the baby died, she felt obligated to produce another child; Edmund, because his was the difficult birth (her third) that required the medication. Unwilling consciously to accept the burden of blame, the men nevertheless are never free of the guilty roles imposed upon them. Mary appears to be a helpless victim, overwhelmed by the vicissitudes of life and the insensitivity of the men around her.

From another perspective, Mary is a self-involved child, infusing her husband and sons with guilt, demanding sympathy and consideration, avoiding reality and the responsibility for her own plight. From either point of view, Mary Tyrone is the catalyst for the family's long journey into a night of sorrow.

The style of *Long Day's Journey into Night* is realistic; the set described by O'Neill is an exact replica of the O'Neill summer home in New London, Connecticut, with its living room and dining room behind, a front porch overlooking the river, and the Connecticut Sound at the end of the road. The fog of the play has a basis in reality, and its increasing presence, as it rolls in from the Sound throughout the day, threatening to envelop the house, achieves a symbolic dimension. Edmund enjoys the fog because in it "life can hide from itself." Mary, too, loves the fog because "it hides you from the world." The fog is the void beyond the family, linked with the mystery of life and death, representing escape and oblivion. The foghorn is an irritation, as Mary says, "calling you back," back to reality, back to the world.

Another contribution to the realism of the play is the subtext, the means by which the actors physically convey the feelings of the characters that are not revealed in dialogue. As did Henrik Ibsen and August Strindberg, to whom he acknowledged a debt, O'Neill wrote scenes in which the characters do not speak what they feel; only at moments of high emotion does the truth emerge. The result is that a reading does not convey the full impact of this play; it must be experienced in performance.

The family unit is a favorite subject in American literature. Themes of alienation, isolation, and the inability to communicate with those closest to one have preoccupied novelists and playwrights alike. Eugene O'Neill's *Long Day's Journey into Night* is a masterpiece of this genre.

Joyce E. Henry

Bibliography:

Bloom, Harold, ed. *Eugene O'Neill's "Long Day's Journey into Night."* New York: Chelsea House, 1987. A collection of ten essays by O'Neill's major critics arranged in the chronological order of their publication, examining such topics as the monologues, the characters, the form, and the language. A helpful guide to the play.

Gelb, Arthur, and Barbara Gelb. *O'Neill*. Enlarged ed. New York: Harper & Row, 1973. A monumental one-volume biography. Invaluable to the serious student of the playwright and his work.

Hinden, Michael. *"Long Day's Journey into Night": Native Eloquence*. Boston: Twayne, 1990. An excellent introduction to the play and its history. Two admirable chapters are devoted to a close analysis of the major characters and their motivations. Extensive bibliography.

Manheim, Michael. *Eugene O'Neill's New Language of Kinship*. Syracuse, N.Y.: Syracuse University Press, 1982. Argues that the early plays contain the same autobiographical characters and situations as *Long Day's Journey into Night*. An interesting list of motifs for each character in the play is included.

Porter, Laurin. *The Banished Prince: Time, Memory, and Ritual in the Late Plays of Eugene O'Neill*. Ann Arbor, Mich.: Research Press, 1988. Analyzes the futile attempts of characters in the last plays, including *Long Day's Journey into Night*, to reclaim the past through memory and the ritual of confession.

THE LONG JOURNEY

Type of work: Novel
Author: Johannes V. Jensen (1873-1950)
Type of plot: Epic
Time of plot: Prehistoric to historic
Locale: Northern Europe
First published: Den lange rejse, 1908-1922, 6 volumes (English translations, 1922-1924,
 3 volumes: *Fire and Ice,* 1922; *The Cimbrians,* 1923; *Christopher Columbus,* 1924)

Principal characters:
 FYR, typical of the earliest users of fire
 CARL, typical of the early Stone Age man in the glacial period
 WHITE BEAR, typical of the later Stone Age man
 WOLF, typical of the horse-riding and horse-breeding man
 NORNA GEST, typical of the man who entered the Iron Age and lingered
  to the fall of the Roman Empire
 CHRISTOPHER COLUMBUS, typical of the Renaissance man
 CHARLES DARWIN, typical of modern man

The Story:
 In the north of what is now Europe, in the prehistoric days before the glaciers came from the North, humans lived in fear and trembling—in fear of the elements, the beasts of the jungles, and their own primitive leaders. Into one of those herdlike groups was born a boy who was named Fyr. As the child grew older, he was seized with a desire to climb to the top of Gunung Api, a vast volcano, quiet but not extinct. There on the slopes of the volcano, wandering by himself, Fyr learned to make use of the flames and their heat to keep himself warm, to cook his meat, to provide himself with a deity, and to enhance his own importance.
 Attracted first by his songs and then by his person, women joined Fyr, until he, like other leaders, was the head of a primitive family group. After the women came children and, finally, other men who made themselves subservient to Fyr. Under his leadership, the tribe became a band of hunters, using the pits, spears, and bows that Fyr devised for them. Wherever they went, they took with them burning wood to re-create their god and household symbol: the fire. Soon all the forest folk bowed to the authority of Fyr, bound to him by his fire and by the tools of wood and stone that he created to make their lives more bearable. One day, however, the god seemed to demand a sacrifice, and the people, making Fyr their scapegoat, placed him in the fire he had brought them. Although he was roasted and eaten, he lived on, a representative of human ingenuity that they could not understand.
 As ages passed, Gunung Api became extinct. Still later, the northern ice cap, beginning to move over the land, brought cold to the tropic jungles. After other ages had passed, a small band of hunters lay crouched in the same forest. The seasons were much colder, and the tribe and most of the animals had moved to the South, until a hunting expedition had brought them back to the old territory. One of their number, Carl, was the tender of the fire. He was thrown out of the band, an outcast, when he let the fire die.
 Carl fled to the North, somehow keeping himself alive in the winter by wrapping himself in skins and burrowing into the ground or building rude huts of stone. High on the extinct volcanic cone he traveled. Everywhere he saw only desolation and ice. He sought the enemy of his tribe,

the cold, but he did not find it. He was joined in his wandering by a dog; the animal slowly joined into a comradeship with the man, although not without some trembling and hesitancy on the part of each. As the winters passed, Carl learned to prepare for them by laying in a supply of food and building a shelter. He even learned to foretell when the great cold was coming and where he would find food and shelter as its ice and snows moved gradually to the South. When he did find an occasional human being, the encounter served only as an opportunity for Carl to eat a different kind of meat. One day, he gave chase to a human being who turned out to be a woman. He captured her by the sea, and the lure of the sea was to call him again.

Carl's wife was Mam. She brought new habits of gathering and storing, as well as children. She added vegetables to Carl's diet, and their home became a permanent one. Carl was still aware of fire, a possession that he had lost and not regained. Gathering many stones, he chipped them against one another in his efforts to strike fire from them. At last, he was successful and bequeathed fire to his children.

The children of Carl and their wives added pottery work to their skills; with ceramics came boiling, a new way of cooking. Among the descendants of Carl there arose a group of priests, against whom rebels were sometimes pitted. Such a rebel was White Bear. Denied a certain woman for his wife, he killed the leader of the priestly clan. Like Carl before him, White Bear became an outcast, taking May, his woman, with him. White Bear became a seaman, building small boats and sailing them, in company with his sons, while May and the daughters remained at home to farm and care for the cattle.

White Bear began to use horses. He built a chariot, with horses to draw it. His sons, more adventurous, learned to ride. One of the sons, Wolf, became so enamored of the horses that he rode them away to become a nomad, forerunner of the Golden Horde of Genghis Khan.

Ages later, a new man appeared. He was Norna Gest, son of the matriarch Gro. While he was still a young boy, dwelling at the edge of the sea on an island, he built himself a dugout canoe and sailed away, carrying with him a girl who was, after a time, to become his mate. They and their child explored a new land to the north, now Sweden, but returned to the home island in later years. Gest himself was not an ordinary mortal; he was to live as long as he kept a partially burned candle. After his return to his original home, he and his companions went on many voyages and made use of sails as well as paddles.

As years passed, Gest found he had outlived his companions. He awoke one day to find himself in a changed Sealand, a place where people were either thralls or nobles. Disturbed at the changes and despised because he had taken as his new wife a milkmaid, one of the thralls, he wandered sadly about the land.

Unhappy in the changed Sealand, Gest and his wife sailed to Sweden to found a new colony in which they were to be the leaders. They took with them new techniques of smelting and forging metals. They gradually acquired domestic animals—horses, sheep, and cattle. Their sons and daughters married, and the colony grew. The mother died, and one day Gest disappeared, to wander again over the globe. Unnoticed but noticing, he traveled through central Europe and floated down the Danube. He traversed the Mediterranean lands, where his life began in the early Stone Age. Finding something wanting in the lands of the South, Gest turned his face once again toward his homeland, where he became a wandering skald.

Arriving in Jutland, he was welcomed by Tole, a leader who was guardian of the ancient god of the Jutlanders. This was a wooden idol that Tole wished to enclose in a great bronze bull. Tole welcomed Gest as the bringer of skills with metals and as a man of great wisdom. The two men made plans to cast the bronze bull at the time of the great spring festivals, before the flocks and herds were taken up to the summer pastures. The bull was successfully cast, and the festivities ended with human sacrifices of slaves and thralls. Gest wandered off afoot after the festival.

In later years, floods rose up in the seas about Jutland, and the younger men wished to leave the country to search for a homeland safe from the ever-encroaching sea. The entire tribe left, except for elderly Tole. With the tribe went the bronze bull, destined now to long journeys across the face of central and southern Europe.

Back and forth across the lands went the Cimbrians, enlisting other tribes in their search for better lands. At last, they traveled far enough to come to the notice of the Romans. Failing to obey the warning of the Romans to remain out of their dominions, the Cimbrians and their allies of the North became enemies of the empire. They decided to strike at Rome itself. Victorious at first, they became proud and reckoned not at all on the strategy of the Roman generals, strategy that defeated them. In their defeat, the Cimbrians and their allies were ruined. Those who were not killed or did not commit suicide were sold into bondage to the Romans, to live miserably as captives in the South, where eventually their blood blended with the blood of their conquerors.

Norna Gest saw these things happening. Finally, knowing that his time was at an end, he left Rome in his boat and glided slowly toward the sea, there to burn his candle to its end. After the fall of the Roman Empire, barbarians from the North were gradually assimilated into the Christian religion. The ancient ship of the North, inverted on land, became the Gothic cathedral, a compound of the mariner's vessel and the stately forests through which humans had roamed earlier. Among the descendants of the barbaric tribes of the North were the Langobards. One of the descendants of the latter group was a man named Christopher Columbus, who was to lead humankind farther on its journey of discovery across the seas and into a whole new hemisphere then undreamed of, or at least forgotten by the descendants of the early Northmen who had once visited it.

Columbus saw himself as a veritable Christopher, one who carried the Christ into the world. While others caroused before setting out across the ocean with him, he prepared himself by attending masses in the cathedral. He had faith in divine help and a divine purpose. When the qualities that his faith gave him proved insufficient to meet the demands of leadership, he could also call upon an amazing strength of body that his northern forebears had bequeathed him.

Although he reached the islands of the West Indies, others carried the long journey into the New World; Columbus was doomed to be only a leader pointing the way. To later conquistadors, men like Hernán Cortés and Francisco Pizarro, went the credit for gaining the mainland for European culture. They faced the odds of sheer numbers when they met the strength of the late Stone Age people, the followers of Montezuma and the Incas, who still existed in America, caught in the lag where European culture had left them many ages before. In Mexico, for example, Cortés was to find human sacrifices and worship of volcanic spirits, examples of cultural practices that had long since ceased to exist in the Old World. The light that Columbus saw from his ship at night was a symbol of the fire worship that existed throughout the New World.

The Indians believed that the coming of the white men marked the return of their great sun god, Quetzalcoatl. Perhaps the god might have been Norna Gest, visiting the New World during his travels. The natives, however, soon lost their superstitious awe of men with fair skins and hair, and many Europeans were sacrificed on the altars of Mexico and other southern countries.

The great battle of the New World was fought in Mexico. There the journey of the European culture was most seriously threatened. In the north, the Indians seemed to fade away before the white culture; in the West Indies, disease had killed them like summer flies at the first autumn frost. In Mexico, however, there was warfare between the eagle and the serpent, symbols of the migrations and conflicting cultures of humankind. Cortés and his soldiers were like eagles swooping down on the snake, insignia of the Aztecs.

Although Cortés was temporarily successful, with the help of a woman who turned against her own people, and although he was able to send the idol of Huitzilopochtli toppling down the long flights of stairs which led to its temple, the Spaniards were doomed to temporary defeat. Cortés had to hack his way out of Tenochtitlán while the screams of Spaniards who were being sacrificed echoed in his ears.

Years later, a young man named Charles Darwin, a naturalist on H.M.S. *Beagle*, was to become a new symbol in humanity's journey from the past, through the present, into the future. Those on the *Beagle* thought they saw the Flying Dutchman. Perhaps that dread captain, doomed to sail forever, will become the symbol of humanity's long journey as it continues. Perhaps the long journey is now almost ended. No one knows.

Critical Evaluation:

Although a winner of the Nobel Prize in Literature in 1944, the Danish writer Johannes V. Jensen has been little known in the United States—a remarkable oversight in view of the fact that for almost fifty years after his first visit to this country in 1897, Jensen was a major interpreter of U.S. life and letters for Scandinavian readers. This preoccupation with the United States was only part of a larger interest in and frank acceptance of the modern age in all its nervous variety. Jensen's probing curiosity and rich imagination ranged over the whole of the modern world and found expression in a large published body of novels, verse, essays, short stories, and travel impressions.

The author was born in that section of Northern Jutland that is known as Himmerland, a region characterized by large tracts of somber landscapes broken only by a few sparse settlements and an occasional farm. His descent from peasant stock and a boyhood spent in play among the burial mounds of Jutland left a distinct mark on Jensen's writings. It shows up not only in a dry and often mordant humor, but also in the fact that, throughout his career, Jensen kept his origin and the distant past that lies behind his people as constant points of reference. He was a prolific writer. Besides the monumental *The Long Journey*, he published several other books on a variety of subjects, often with his own interpretations of Darwinism. Few writers have done so much to interpret in creative terms the past of their own race and to point to the interdependence of past, present, and future; and perhaps no writer has caught the intimate charm of Danish nature quite as has Jensen.

The Long Journey, the author's most ambitious work, is a long cyclic novel of three volumes: *Fire and Ice*, *The Cimbrians*, and *Christopher Columbus*. The epic traces the long journey of the people of the North from the forest, through the rigors of the Ice Age, and out on many journeys in search of the "lost land" that, in the author's mind, is represented symbolically by the warm tropical forest of the race's infancy. Its aim is to show the development of humankind from primeval chaos to modern civilization. The narrative is in story form, showing how the actual stages of the ascent of humankind and of the climactic conditions of the earth's surface have left their traces in mythology and religion. On a symbolic level, the work shows how the forest became a ship and the ship became a church, until people like Christopher Columbus changed the church back into a ship in their quest for the New World. With the discovery of the New World and its natives, the ship reverts to the forest and the cycle is complete.

The Long Journey should not be taken seriously as anthropology, yet to refer to it simply as a novel falls short of an accurate appraisal of its merit. It is a work of mythology that, in the boldness of its conception, deserves a place among the finest works of fiction of the modern era. To a reader who is of the firm conviction that the account of the world related in the first five books of the Bible is literally true, *The Long Journey* would be heresy. Jensen is convinced that the world, as it stands, is open to various explanations. Although he makes no direct statements about evolution, Jensen regards this theory as another indication of the advance of humankind. Few readers will contend, however, that Jensen wrote this novel as a conscious and scientific attempt to refute biblical interpretation, or that he has unconsciously refuted it. Evolution, according to Jensen, is a strong proof for the existence of a supernatural deity and is probably the one principle of life that makes homage to God obligatory. He implies that the world would be found lacking as a piece of divine handiwork if there had been no progress, no evolution within the most recent thousands of years.

In many respects, *The Long Journey* is similar to Knut Hamsun's *Growth of the Soil* (1917), in that both novels go back to a primitive state of the world, both deal with elemental traits in man, and both rise, in some instances, to great heights as truly epic portrayals of the workings of the human heart—but here the similarities stop. When Hamsun's novel concludes, the sons of Isak and Inger have grown up, and even Barbro, the once citified lady, has married and settled down. Hamsun covers the period from about 1916 to roughly 1950. In contrast, when Jensen's Gunung Api stands in airy solitude in the third paragraph of *The Long Journey*, chewing the fire within him, there was no fire, no ice; there was nothing but unmeasured time, millions of years before the modern era. When Jensen is through, Christopher Columbus has discovered America. Jensen does not note time except by its passing.

Jensen's work necessitates a familiarity with archaeology, geology, ethnology, and mythology, for *The Long Journey* deals with the unfolding of a particular idea and the delineation of that theory of origin, growth, and development through a long period of time. Parts of the novel are ostensibly irrelevant, in that they apply neither to science nor literature. On the whole, however, *The Long Journey* is a unique and epic treatment of the genesis of humanity and the world.

"Critical Evaluation" by Stephen Hanson

Bibliography:
Bredsdorff, Elias, Brita Mortensen, and Ronald Popperwell. *An Introduction to Scandinavian Literature.* Cambridge, England: Cambridge University Press, 1951. Surveys Jensen's achievements as a novelist and poet. Calls *The Long Journey* the novelist's most important fictional work; comments on Jensen's reliance on Darwinian theory as the basis for his assessment of human nature.
Mitchell, P. M. *A History of Danish Literature.* Copenhagen: Gyldendal, 1957. Summarizes Jensen's career and influence. Describes *The Long Journey* as a work heavily influenced by Darwinism; claims characters serve as types symbolizing the cultural and technical progress of humankind.
Rossel, Sven H. *A History of Scandinavian Literature, 1870-1980.* Translated by Anne Ulmer. Minneapolis: University of Minnesota Press, 1982. Describes Jensen as a literary pathfinder for twentieth century Scandinavian writing. Explains how his early prose essays form the ideological basis for the plot and theme of *The Long Journey*.
_____. *Johannes V. Jensen.* Boston: Twayne, 1984. Introductory study containing a chapter on the novelist's handling of mythic themes in his novels, including *The Long Journey*; claims the work vivifies a central theme in Jensen's work, the longing for the lost

land of Paradise. Explains how the author viewed the novel as a kind of Bible for modern times.

Topsöe-Jensen, H. G. *Scandinavian Literature: From Brandes to Our Day*. Translated by Isaac Anderson. New York: W. W. Norton, 1929. Reviews the literary achievement of a writer considered the central figure in Danish literature in the early decades of the century. Considers *The Long Journey* to be one of several works in which Jensen dramatizes humankind's evolutionary progress.

THE LONGEST JOURNEY

Type of work: Novel
Author: E. M. Forster (1879-1970)
Type of plot: Social realism
Time of plot: Early twentieth century
Locale: England
First published: 1907

> *Principal characters:*
> RICKIE ELLIOT, a student at Cambridge
> AGNES PEMBROKE, an old friend
> HERBERT PEMBROKE, her brother
> STEWART ANSELL, a friend of Rickie at Cambridge
> MRS. EMILY FAILING, Rickie's aunt
> STEPHEN WONHAM, his half-brother

The Story:

Frederick Elliot was a student at Cambridge and almost alone in the world. He had finally attained some degree of contentment in his life after a rather unhappy childhood. Born with a lame left foot that kept him from most of the normal activities of children, he had grown up virtually without friends. Early in his life, his father had begun to call him Rickie because of its close similarity to rickety, and the name had stayed with him. Besides his deformity there was another, more serious difficulty. He found out quite early that his father and mother did not love each other and that he was not loved at all by his father and only a little by his mother. Both his parents died when he was fifteen years old, leaving him comfortably well off so far as finances were concerned but without anyone who wanted to give him a home.

At Cambridge, he had shown himself to be a capable student but one without any scholarly pretensions. He had made several friends among the nonathletic groups and spent much of his time in long discussions on topics of literary or philosophical interest. During such a discussion one day, he was interrupted by the arrival of his old friends, Agnes and Herbert Pembroke, whom he had invited for the weekend. In the meantime, he had completely forgotten about them. Because these two people were part of that very small group which took an interest in Rickie's career, they spent a great part of their time at Cambridge encouraging him to decide on a particular course for his life, even if he did nothing more than write, the only thing he admitted having an interest in. They pointed out that money was not important as long as he met a certain standard of ideals.

At Christmas of the same year, Rickie saw his friends again. He had stayed several days with Stewart Ansell, a friend from Cambridge, but he felt that it was necessary to spend a part of his vacation with the Pembrokes as well. He dreaded this part of his vacation because Agnes' fiancé, a man whom Rickie had known at public school, was to be there. Rickie not only disliked Gerald Dawes but also hated to witness the happiness of the lovers; he felt that such happiness was forever denied him because of his lame foot, which he considered a hereditary disorder. During this time, Gerald was killed while playing football, and it was Rickie who was able to offer the most comfort to Agnes by convincing her that she should suffer since her love for Gerald had been the greatest thing she could ever experience.

Two years later, when she came again to visit him at Cambridge, Rickie realized that he was in love with Agnes, although he still felt that he could never marry because of his deformity. She convinced him, however, that they should be married. Rickie was about to finish his work at Cambridge, but they felt a long engagement was necessary for him to settle himself. Ansell immediately opposed the marriage because he sensed that Agnes was not a sincere person. She laid constant claim to honesty and forthrightness, but Ansell could not be convinced that these qualities revealed the true Agnes. He knew immediately that she would force Rickie into a dull and conventional life, convincing him at the same time that he was taking the proper step.

Soon after their engagement, Rickie and Agnes visited his aunt, Mrs. Emily Failing, at her country home. Rickie had never particularly liked his aunt, but since she was his only known relative, he and Agnes felt that they should go to see her. Mrs. Failing was a woman who liked to have people do what she wanted, and she was never happier than when they were obviously uncomfortable while carrying out her desires. While Rickie and Agnes were visiting her, they also saw Stephen Wonham, a young man whom Rickie had met before but whose relation to Mrs. Failing had never been clear. After Rickie engaged in an argument with his aunt, she informed him that Stephen was actually his brother. It was not until later that Rickie found out that Stephen was the son of his mother, not of his father. Stephen himself did not know who he was, but the matter had never greatly concerned him.

After their marriage, Rickie and Agnes went to live with Herbert at Sawston School. The arrangement had been worked out between Herbert and Agnes because Herbert needed help in his duties as a housemaster. Although Rickie soon realized that Herbert was basically stupid and that they disagreed on many points, he adapted himself to whatever course Herbert and Agnes chose. His marriage, in which he had hoped to find certain spiritual ideals, never reached a very intimate level; before long, his life became a shell. Ansell would have no more to do with him, and he was cut off from the one intellect at the school because of Herbert's feelings and aspirations.

Two years later after Rickie had apparently succumbed completely to the forces playing on him, Stephen Wonham again entered his life. It became apparent immediately that Agnes, who had kept up a connection with Mrs. Failing and who wished to inherit the money from the estate, had been instrumental in having Stephen thrown out of her house. Rickie was furious but again submitted. Stephen, who had finally been told the truth about himself, came to Sawston expecting to find the kind of love that he had never known before; but when Rickie refused to see him and Agnes offered him money never to say anything about his parentage, he left immediately.

Stephen wandered around London for several days doing odd jobs and supporting himself as best he could. Before long, he had saved enough money for a drunken spree. During his drunkenness, he intended to wreck Rickie's house and returned to Sawston, but he might have killed himself if Rickie had not saved him. By this time, Rickie was under the influence of Ansell again and had begun to see how foolish he had been. He decided to give Stephen a home, but Stephen, who rejected this idea, managed to convince Rickie that they should go away together.

With that, the regeneration of Rickie's soul began, but it was of short duration. On a subsequent visit to his aunt, at which time Stephen insisted on accompanying him, he again saved Stephen's life but lost his own. Stephen, who had promised not to drink, got drunk and collapsed on the railroad crossing. Rickie managed to get him off but was himself killed. Just before he died, he realized that he had been betrayed a second time by his belief in the individual.

Critical Evaluation:

Best known for his haunting novel *A Passage to India* (1924), E. M. Forster in *The Longest Journey* created a less exotic setting but an equally powerful delineation of character and exploration of humanist values. The primary theme of *The Longest Journey* is Rickie Elliot's progression from an unloved child to a responsible brother, a lengthy progression of his own soul epitomized by the novel's very title. Unlike Rickie, Forster had a close attachment to his mother, but like his character, Forster had a very lonely childhood that did not end until he entered King's College, Cambridge, in 1897. As an undergraduate there, he studied classics and history and joined a circle of intellectuals—the so-called Cambridge Apostles—who met regularly to discuss aesthetics and art. It was the sort of life that Forster thoroughly enjoyed, and he was sorry to see it end upon his graduation in 1901. After he had established himself as an important writer with the publication of *A Passage to India*, Cambridge invited him to deliver a series of lectures about the art of fiction; these lectures were revised and published as *Aspects of the Novel* (1927). He later became an honorary Fellow at King's College and continued to visit and lecture at Cambridge until his death on June 7, 1970.

To understand the primary theme of *The Longest Journey*—Rickie's gradual acceptance of responsibility for his half brother Stephen Wonham—a reader should consider the characters symbolically. Forster conceived Rickie as an Everyman, a person intended to set an example for the reader. After a life of frustrations, Rickie thinks he finally understands the nature of things and, more important, of himself. As it turns out, all of his hard-earned knowledge is irrelevant when he is confronted by a person who is anti-intellectual and continually acts from impulse. This person is Rickie's own half brother, who symbolizes passion. At first, Rickie denies the importance of his half brother and rejects the notion of any relationship between them. Symbolically, he thereby rejects the idea that impulse, or passion, is necessary for life.

The necessity of passion in life is a major theme in nearly all of Forster's early novels and short stories, as, for example, in "The Road from Colonus" (1903), "The Story of a Panic" (1904), and *A Room with a View* (1908). Essentially, Forster argues in these works that English men and women are so preoccupied with material society that they neglect their inner selves. This neglect, though, may be rectified with a trip to Southern Europe—specifically, Greece or Italy—where the people have not lost their passion for life. Indeed, in each of these works the central character travels to Greece or Italy and there experiences a revelation about how to live. In *A Room with a View*, for instance, Lucy Honeychurch, who is somewhat similar in nature to Rickie, travels to Florence and learns the value of passionate love. Rickie, however, never travels to Italy, although he longs to do so throughout the novel. Consequently, he is left unfulfilled and dies without ever learning about the human need for passion. Certainly, he gains a measure of self-knowledge when he saves his drunken brother from the train, but it comes too late for him to change his life for the better, as Lucy Honeychurch changes hers in *A Room with a View*. Thus, while Lucy's novel ends happily with her new insight into human nature, Rickie's ends tragically just as he begins to attain a glimpse into human nature.

A secondary theme of *The Longest Journey* attempts to answer the question: What is a proper education? The Sawston School, where Rickie teaches, is modeled after the public school in Tonbridge that Forster attended from 1893 to 1897. Forster, however, loathed the educational system of Tonbridge and often said that his four years there were the worst of his life. He particularly despised the bullying inflicted upon him by the older boys, although he found some solace in being one of the better scholars of his class. Contrasting the harshness of Sawston School with the freedom of Cambridge (as he does so dramatically in *The Longest Journey*), Forster makes clear his belief in the importance of a liberal, humanist education that allows a mind to roam freely through the arts and sciences. Forster intends that his readers see Cambridge as the ideal environment in which young people should be educated.

The Longest Journey remained Forster's own favorite novel throughout his life. It was the only one of his works that had practically written itself. Upon its publication on April 16, 1907, the novel received favorable reviews from most critics, although some of Forster's closest friends felt that the characters were poorly developed. Their objections to it did not, however, discourage Forster from resuming work on his next novel, *A Room with a View*, which he had begun to write in 1902, or from planning another novel that eventually became *Howards End* (1910). *The Longest Journey* is certainly not the best novel by Forster, but it is the one that helped to establish him as a leading novelist in Edwardian England.

"Critical Evaluation" by Jim McWilliams

Bibliography:
Beauman, Nicola. *E. M. Forster: A Biography*. New York: Alfred A. Knopf, 1994. Shows clearly the autobiographical elements of *The Longest Journey*, including how Forster's relationship with a close friend at Tonbridge School parallels the Rickie-Stewart relationship. Argues that the novel was influenced by Forster's reading of Edward Carpenter, an English philosopher and social critic.
Furbank. P. N. *E. M. Foster: A Life*. New York: Harcourt Brace Jovanovich, 1978. Comprehensive biography with many details about Forster's life and ideas. Provides details of his schooling and how he used his own public school, Tonbridge, as a model for Sawston School in the novel. Includes a good discussion of Forster's residency at Cambridge.
Godfrey, Denis. *E. M. Forster's Other Kingdom*. New York: Barnes & Noble, 1968. Focuses on Rickie's unconscious search for salvation and sees his acknowledgement of Stephen as a sort of acceptance of nature, which is always in conflict with the modern world. Argues that until Rickie accepts his half brother, he cannot understand himself.
Land, Stephen K. *Challenge and Conventionality in the Fiction of E. M. Forster*. New York; AMS Press, 1990. Finds *The Longest Journey* interesting because of the depth of the evolution of Rickie. Argues that Forster's primary theme is the conflict between conventional and liberal worlds as symbolized by the characters in the novel.
Rosecrance, Barbara. *Forster's Narrative Vision*. Ithaca, N.Y.: Cornell University Press, 1982. Points out that while *The Longest Journey* ends tragically with Rickie's death, it also concludes on an affirmative note of hope for the future. Demonstrates how Forster's second novel is markedly better than his first, *Where Angels Fear to Tread* (1905).

A LONGING FOR THE LIGHT
Selected Poems of Vicente Aleixandre

Type of work: Poetry
Author: Vicente Aleixandre (1898-1984)
First published: 1979

The poetry of Vicente Aleixandre, who won the Nobel Prize in Literature in 1977, became more accessible to the English-speaking readership with the publication of *A Longing for the Light*, a collection of translations from the Spanish by editor Lewis Hyde and fourteen other hands. Most of the poems in the English-language collection were initially selected by Aleixandre, and they exemplify some of the best and most representative works of Aleixandre's career to 1979. The title is a translation of a phrase that Aleixandre used to characterize his poetry. Aleixandre used the metaphor of differing lights to describe his belief that poetry is both composed and read in differing circumstances. He advised his readers that his poems may be read in terms of "rainbow light," understanding that he may have composed them in other lights such as the "black light" with which he says he wrote his very early poems. In a sense, then, *A Longing for the Light* traces Aleixandre's journey through various densities of light, exploring the relative solitude and connectedness possible to the human condition as well as the possibilities of the artistic vision and artistic creation to communicate.

His first published work, *Ámbito* (1928), shows the influence of Juan Ramón Jiménez and displays Aleixandre's affinities with other members of the Generation of '27, such as Jorge Guillén. Unlike Guillén, who believed that the poetic experience is a heightening of reality, Aleixandre believed that it is a means of tapping into the subconscious mind at the level where people are connected to the universe. Selections from *Ámbito* in *A Longing for the Light* are "Closed," "Sea and Sunrise," and "Sea and Night." In these, as in the rest of the collection, night is a major player, "famous" and "quiet": "Mouth—sea—all of it pleads for night." It is an essentially sensual collection: "Either flesh or the light of flesh,/ deep," he writes. In *Ámbito*, Aleixandre begins to develop a view of the universe that would unfold in his poetic career: The sea and the sun and the night all exist in a cycle of absorption, destruction, and rebirth.

His critics generally divide his work into three major groups, the first of which, his surrealist group, includes *Espadas como labios* (swords like lips, 1932), *La destrucción o el amor* (1935; *Destruction or Love*, 1976), *Pasión de la tierra* (the earth's passion, 1935), *Sombra del paraíso* (1944, written earlier; *Shadow of Paradise*, 1987), and *Mundo a solas* (1950, written earlier; *World Alone*, 1982). He described his work beginning in 1928 as "a gradual emergence into light." It seems that his way into the light was a path through the darkness of the subconscious, for in 1928, he read and became profoundly influenced by the psychoanalytic work of Sigmund Freud. His poetry thereafter self-consciously deals with many issues raised by Freud, most especially that of the existence of a subconscious mind, of dreams, of the ground of consciousness, of the libido, of the tension between love and death. Aleixandre stated that his themes of his first period concerned creation and the possibility of the poet losing his own identity and fusing with the cosmos through an escape from the bounds of rational consciousness. Works of this phase explore the themes of love and death; the ability of the mind as well as of the universe to create and to destroy; and the power of the mind to connect with cosmic forces. His work is well-characterized by a statement of his translator, Lewis Hyde, that it represents "the reflective mind trying to think its way out of coherence and precision."

Pasión de la tierra, included in *A Longing for the Light*, explores the poetic possibilities of

Freudian dream imagery. Much of his work relies upon the kind of associative movement that one finds in dreams; most of his poems ought to be read for their connections in this manner; coherence comes through associative links rather than through linear narrative progression. The prose-poems of *Pasión de la tierra* represent Aleixandre's poetic compositions most closely associated with the Surrealist movement. This collection is characterized by the erratic and the irrational images of turbulence and upheaval, of "torrential silence and lava," of a speaker who is often threatened by death when isolated from love. It displays his penchant for the macabre and even the gothic as it translates into a twentieth century idiom, to be further developed in *Espadas como labios*. This collection, represented by "Death or the Waiting Room," "Silence," and "Flying Fugue on a Horse," has been called one of the most unfathomable works of twentieth century Spanish poetry. The prose-poems express what Aleixandre termed the *conciencia sin funda*, or "consciousness without limitations": He remarked that this is his most difficult book. His declared aesthetic intent was to utilize all of language, even the ugly and inharmonious, to reach that profound plane of consciousness. He wrote: "I shall not avoid even one word."

Included in the second major group of *A Longing for the Light*, "Poems with Red Light," are selections dealing with love and the physical world. In these poems, human sexual interaction may be viewed as emblematic of the nature of a universe that destroys and re-creates itself.

In *Espadas como labios*, Aleixandre returns from the prose-poems of *Pasión de la tierra* to verse, or more specifically free verse characterized by his evolving and idiosyncratic style. He maintains the surreal idiom. Aleixandre challenges the reader to make the leaps in comparison and in irrational logic with him, like those in "At the Bottom of the Well (The Buried Man)," when "in the ear the echo was already solid," and in "The Waltz," when things clash together: "seashells, heels, foam and false teeth," a kiss turns into a deadly "fishbone." His poetry is of the realm of heightened senses, in which moments of transformation follow one after another with lightning rapidity. Accustomed to working through only one poetic experience in a lyric poem, the reader is challenged by Aleixandre's demand to move with him through series after series of rapid succession of transformative images. In this volume, Aleixandre is already using one of his characteristic poetic devices (one that will appear again in the title of his next volume), that of juxtaposing with the word "or" two elements that may be set in contrast or that may be intended as comparisons or that may even be meant to represent the same thing.

Destruction or Love and *Shadow of Paradise* have been said to form the cornerstones of Aleixandre's work. *Destruction or Love* is a very complex work, produced in return to health after a serious illness. Aleixandre described the volume's theme as "the poet's vision of the world," the "amorous unity of the universe" in which a poet's vision of a whole cosmos becomes coherent within this world of change through love. He turns from the spiritual to the physical, and to that kind of consuming love that allows the individual, through his or her own destruction, to become one with the cosmic forces in a mystical union.

Images of the elemental forces of the universe and processions of living things on earth flicker in a panoply as parts of a woman's body transform into emblems of the universe. In "The Jungle and the Sea," wild animals "draw their swords or teeth/ like blood" out of an innocent and loving heart. Tigers' claws sink into the earth like love into a heart. Above them flies a "bird of happiness" toward "the distant sea that recedes like the light." One's actual ability to fuse with the cosmos is questionable, for solitude informs the mortal state, and one's finitude prevents one from being other than what one is, a physical being of the material world. The sexual act, then, becomes the sole means of becoming one with the universe, for in it, the individual and the light of individual consciousness emblematically die, permitting oceanic darkness to overwhelm the psyche. In "The Wholeness Within Her," the speaker longs for "love or death," knowing he is threatened by "light or fatal sword" which "could never break up the wholeness of this world."

World Alone reflects Aleixandre's plunge into postwar depression. Sadness and a return to hope mark the third group of poems. The speaker of "Under the Ground," for example, becomes the serpentine "dark shadow coiled among tree roots" as he contrasts life above and below ground, life and death. The poem ends, as Aleixandre's poems often do, with a paradox that sends the reader back into the poem to make it divulge its meaning. In this volume, he writes, "man doesn't exist."

In *Shadow of Paradise*, published after the Spanish Civil War, he revises his most dismal vision of *World Alone* and returns to the pristine world of Málaga and the Mediterranean of his childhood, although such hopeful works as "the Hands" are set in contrast to those like "What Happens to All Flesh." Aleixandre believed that *World Alone* was the transition point between his earlier, more surrealistic phase and his work to come. In it, he fuses his dream style with one more accessible to waking consciousness, more "coherent." Many of its poems look forward to the shift in subject matter that occurs in *Historia del corazón* (history of the heart, 1954). In *Shadow of Paradise* he begins his turning away from the completely interior world to the waking world of living humanity, envisioning the possibilities of compassion in daily life. The physical body and the soul are blended and separated as are the metaphysical circumstances of each. As with much in Aleixandre, the cognizance of the human being's ultimate isolation colors everything, so that paradise here must remain only a shadow, as his title indicates.

Works published in the aftermath of the Spanish Civil War are respresented in the section "Poems with White Light." This section includes poems from his books *Nacimiento último* (final birth, 1953), *Historia del corazón*, *En un vasto dominio* (in a vast dominion, 1962), and *Retratos con nombre* (portraits with names, 1965). Fundamentally a pessimist, Aleixandre made a breakthrough with *Historia del corazón*. Prior to this volume, he explored the depths of human solitude, but in *Historia del corazón*, he writes: "This now is the opposite of human loneliness. No, we aren't alone." Here, the sky shines "with mercy." The volume marks the change in his poetic world from the surreal to the real and which adulates the possibilities of communication, of friendship, brotherhood, and other ties of the human heart that occur within the cycle of life. The images and style are as accessible as those of *Sombra del paraíso*. Critics have praised several of the love poems in this collection, wherein, possibly for the first time in Spanish poetry, the love relationship becomes conscious of its own myths and illusions. The human condition Aleixandre describes as "A lightning flash between two darknesses." The "dream or its shadow" is that on which we "feed," and, Aleixandre writes, "Its name is Love!" Although Aleixandre's thematic focus has, in these postwar, more accessible, more hopeful poems, shifted in many ways, the problem of solitude remains.

En un vasto dominio opens in a most physical way, with poems that deal with bodily parts, in order to minutely examine the functioning of humanity. It is the story of humanity evolving. The poet then shifts his focus to a rich stream of Spanish life, from town square to cemetery, from local history to a young couple who have between them the capacity to ensure the continuation of life. In "Human Matter," for example, the entire city is described as "one substance" in which every action affects everyone and everything.

Poemas de la consumación (poems of ripeness, 1968) and *Diálogos del conocimiento* (dialogues of knowledge, 1974) are grouped together as "Recent Poems." These books are represented by several poems, one of the most compelling of which is "The Old Man Is Like Moses": "not with the useless tablets and the chisel and the lightning in the mountains/ but with words broken on the ground, his hair/ on fire, his ears singed by the terrifying words." In *Poemas de la consumación*, old age is portrayed as a time in which the possibilities of love are past. The *Diálogos del conocimiento* universalizes the intensely personal vision of *Poemas de la consumación*. In *Diálogos del conocimiento*, fifteen dialogues are actually juxtaposed monologues, reflecting the failure of spoken language to reach another individual, as well as the necessity of artistic expression to verbalize the significant. Aleixandre's intent is to show that any situation can be perceived differently by everyone. As the title indicates, he examines the various ways in which life experience teaches one to know and to understand. "To know by experience is to love," he writes, "To know intellectually is to die." He introduces the distinction between knowing with the mind and knowing with the body. For example, in "Sound of the War," the voices of a soldier, a sorcerer, a bird, and a lark talk—but not to each other—about war. Aleixandre's groundbreaking prosody in the *Diálogos de conocimiento* is of an unforgettable and majestic slowness.

Donna Berliner

Bibliography:
Aleixandre, Vicente. *A Longing for the Light: Selected Poems of Vicente Aleixandre*. Edited and translated by Lewis Hyde. New York: Harper & Row, 1979. Contains a descriptive bibliography with brief critical summaries of individual books by Aleixandre.
Cabrera, Vicente, and Harriet Boyer, eds. *Critical Views on Vicente Aleixandre's Poetry*. Lincoln, Nebr.: Society of Spanish and Spanish-American Studies, 1979. A collection of articles in English.
Cobb, Carl W. "Poets Uprooted and Revellious: Lorca, Alberti, Aleixandre, Cernuda." In *Contemporary Spanish Poetry 1898-1963*, edited by Carl W. Cobb. Boston: Twayne, 1976. Discusses the significant characteristics of work by the Generation of '27. The section on Aleixandre is coherent and accessible, explaining the aesthetic and thematic significance of each of his works.
Daydi-Tolson, Santiago, ed. *Vicente Aleixandre: A Critical Appraisal*. Ypsilanti, Mich.: Bilingual Press, 1981. Contains several chapters in English on Aleixandre as well as the poet's Nobel Prize lecture and an English translation of an article by Carlos Bousoño. Bibliography.
Morris, C. B. *A Generation of Spanish Poets, 1920-1936*. Cambridge, England: Cambridge University Press, 1969. Places Aleixandre with his contemporaries, showing generational affinities, and examines them as links in the greater Spanish literary tradition.
Schwartz, Kessel. *Vicente Aleixandre*. New York: Twayne, 1970. An accessible introduction by a Freudian critic.

LOOK BACK IN ANGER

Type of work: Drama
Author: John Osborne (1929-1994)
Type of plot: Protest drama
Time of plot: 1950's
Locale: A city in the English Midlands
First performed: 1956; first published, 1957

> *Principal characters:*
> JIMMY PORTER, a young man
> ALISON PORTER, his wife
> CLIFF LEWIS, their friend
> HELENA CHARLES, a friend of Alison and later Jimmy's mistress
> COLONEL REDFERN, Alison's father

The Story:

On a Sunday evening in April, Jimmy Porter and Cliff Lewis, both working-class men, and Jimmy's upper-class wife, Alison, were in the attic flat they shared. While Alison ironed, Jimmy and Cliff read the newspapers. From time to time, Jimmy made acid comments on what he read, ordered the other two to minister to his needs, or pointed out Cliff's defects, in particular his ignorance and his ineffectuality. Jimmy's worst venom was reserved for his wife, who he said was as vacuous as her mother and father, and like them, incapable of thought. Cliff defended Alison, and she treated him with sisterly affection, pressing his trousers and giving him cigarettes, despite the fact that the doctor and Jimmy had forbidden him to smoke. Furious because Cliff and Alison refused to fight with him, Jimmy contrasted their lethargy with the energy of his former mistress, Madeline, and of Webster, a gay friend of Alison. He then returned to his verbal attacks on Alison, her family, and her gender, claiming that women's worst vice was that they were noisy. Increasingly annoyed with both Alison and Cliff, Jimmy turned off the radio, contending that when Alison ironed and Cliff turned the pages of his newspaper, it was impossible to hear the music.

Cliff finally insisted that Jimmy apologize to them both, and in the resulting scuffle, the ironing board was knocked down and Alison was burned. Angry at last, she told Jimmy to leave. While Cliff was treating her injury, she confided in him. She was miserable, she said, and even though she was pregnant, she was seriously considering leaving Jimmy. When Jimmy came back into the room, he apologized to Alison and attempted to explain his behavior as a reaction against his feeling that he was trapped by his love for her; he also acknowledged an abiding anger because Alison had never felt pain and could not understand him. Alison was called to the telephone. She returned to report that she had invited an actress friend, Helena Charles, who had just come to town, to stay with them for a few days until she found a place to live.

Two weeks later, Helena had established herself in the household, and, as Cliff commented, the tension had mounted. It was true that by doing most of the cooking Helena was a great help to Alison; however, she made no secret of her dislike for Jimmy. She pressured Alison to take immediate action about her situation, either by telling Jimmy about her pregnancy and demanding that he become a responsible member of society or by leaving him and returning to her parents. Jimmy made no secret of his hatred for Helena, and after Alison announced that she was going to church with her friend, Jimmy drew the battle lines. Helena and he were fighting for Alison, he said, and he was determined to win. Without Alison's knowledge, Helena had, however, already sent Colonel Redfern a telegram, telling him that his daughter needed him. Somewhat uncertainly, Alison said that she would go home with her father. She did not tell Jimmy of her plans, but when he was summoned to the deathbed of his best friend's mother and begged Alison to accompany him, she coldly refused and walked out, followed by Helena, who was accompanying her to church.

When Colonel Redfern appeared at the Porter apartment the next afternoon, Jimmy had not returned. In his conversation with Alison, her father showed considerable sympathy for Jimmy, even commenting that Alison seemed to have learned a lot from him. He also suggested that Alison's mother had wronged Jimmy by hiring detectives to find some way to discredit or destroy him. Alison had made her decision, however. In response to Cliff's question as to who would break the news of her departure to her husband, she handed him a letter for Jimmy. Indicating that he did not like to see anyone suffer, Cliff went out to get something to eat and, he said, probably to have a few drinks. The colonel had assumed that Helena would be leaving along with Alison, but, as Cliff had predicted, Helena made her excuses and remained. When Jimmy appeared, he was so furious because Alison had slighted the dying woman that he did not seem to care much about her having walked out on him. He was not even particularly affected by Helena's revelation that Alison was pregnant. Helena slapped him, but when Jimmy collapsed with grief, she kissed him and pulled him into an embrace.

Several months later, Helena was doing the ironing, sweetly approving of everything Jimmy did or said. Helena told Jimmy that she did not intend to go to church, and Jimmy exulted at having led her into a state of sin. Cliff, who did not like Helena and obviously missed Alison, was planning to move out. Cliff and Jimmy, both in a good humor, made up a vaudeville skit, which, as usual, ended in a tussle. Helena told Jimmy that she loved him, and, although he did not respond in kind, he was tender and affectionate toward her, even offering to take her out on the town. Unexpectedly, Alison arrived, looking extremely unwell. Jimmy refused to speak to his wife and left the room. When they were alone, the women confided in each other. Helena told Alison that her affair with Jimmy was finished and that she intended to leave him. Alison told Helena that she had lost the baby and could not have another. Concerned about Jimmy, Alison urged Helena to remain with him, but Helena reiterated her opinion that all was over between the two of them, in part because they were so different, in part because she could not overcome her feeling of guilt. The women argued as to which of them, if either, Jimmy really needed. When Jimmy came back into the room, Helena told him of her decision. Angrily, he swept her possessions off the dresser and thrust them into her arms, and she went downstairs to pack.

Still angry about Alison's indifference to the death of his friend's mother, Jimmy told Alison how disappointed he had been in her, and she collapsed on the floor, begging his forgiveness. By losing the baby, she said, she had at last experienced the pain of living and so could be what he wanted her to be. Tenderly, Jimmy comforted her, and, clinging together, the two promised from that time on to protect each other in a world that was inimical to love.

Critical Evaluation:

Look Back in Anger established John Osborne as the leader and prototype of the so-called Angry Young Men, a group of British playwrights and novelists of the 1950's who shared leftist or even anarchic political views and wrote to express their disillusionment with the status quo. Although *Look Back in Anger* is not as unconventional or original as it initially appeared to be—its popular and critical success must in part be attributed to the fact that it appeared after one of the dullest decades in British theater—it is nevertheless of more than merely historical importance.

Osborne's greatest strengths are in dialogue and characterization. Except for entrances, exits, and an occasional kiss, slap, or scuffle, there is little physical action in *Look Back in Anger*. Instead, the real drama is found in the verbal interplay between the characters. It is also interesting that in this play, as is generally true of Osborne's works, there is only one character with a real gift for language. Cliff and Alison, who are both at the mercy of Jimmy's sharper wit, feel they can fight back only by refusing to respond to his insults. Helena at first exhibits some cleverness, but once Jimmy has chained her to the bed and the ironing board, she simply works at being a good audience for him.

It has been noted that the most dramatic, and indeed the most hilarious, segments of *Look Back in Anger* are Jimmy's monologues. This is, of course, consistent with the fact that *Look Back in Anger* is essentially a one-character play—something that is also true of Osborne's best-known later works, *The Entertainer* (1957) and *Luther* (1961). Osborne himself had not intended *Look Back in Anger* to be centered only on Jimmy. Colonel Redfern is a complex character, not nearly as obtuse as Jimmy suggests, and Helena, who at first appears to be the villain of the piece, develops into a rather fascinating individual by the end of the play. Interestingly, it is not Jimmy but Alison who, according to Osborne's stage directions, is the most complicated of the three characters onstage at the beginning of the play. Yet the fact remains that, because of his verbal brilliance, Jimmy upstages everyone else.

Osborne's theory and his practice are at odds in *Look Back in Anger*. The play is generally classified as a protest play, one that voices the anger of the working class at having willingly fought Great Britain's wars only to return to a caste-conscious society that denied them opportunity, advancement, and even an acknowledgment of their dignity. Although the classless society that Osborne advocated could easily find room for weaker souls like Cliff or the suggestible Alison, it would have no place, however, for a Jimmy Porter who would refuse or be unable to suppress his insistent self for the common good.

Moreover, the play does not end with the triumph of the revolution or even with a useful martyrdom. If Jimmy Porter has succeeded in bringing his wife into the working-class camp, that was accomplished not by him but by life; only because life brought Alison pain, loss, and the experience of death did it become possible for her to empathize with her husband and, by implication, to surrender to his enormous ego. When the two are reconciled, they return to the fantasy world of their honeymoon; playing bear and squirrel, they retreat from the world. This is a far cry from the joint plans for social action that could be expected from a protest playwright.

Whatever its deficiencies or its inconsistencies, however, *Look Back in Anger* delighted contemporary audiences, who, like the playwright himself, saw the play as a comedy. If Osborne is to be faulted for writing a play with much talk and little commitment, one must applaud him for creating at least one unforgettable character and for bringing new energy to the British theater.

Rosemary M. Canfield Reisman

Bibliography:

Carter, Alan. *John Osborne*. Edinburgh: Oliver & Boyd, 1969. The chapter on *Look Back in Anger* is a good starting point for study of the play. Discusses critical and popular reception and explains its importance in theatrical history.

Elsom, John. *Post-War British Theatre*. London: Routledge & Kegan Paul, 1976. Compares Osborne with other writers of the period. Affirms that, though hardly the proletarian war cry some have supposed, *Look Back in Anger* inspired other dramatists, particularly through its vivid characterization and riveting dialogue.

Hayman, Ronald. *John Osborne*. London: Heinemann, 1968. Argues that Osborne's characters are not in fact representatives of a class or a point of view, but rebels dominated by their own egomania. A readable and persuasive analysis.

Hinchliffe, Arnold P. *John Osborne*. Boston: Twayne, 1984. A balanced and detailed work, tracing the action of Osborne's plays in each scene and suggesting various interpretations. Also contains an extended and thoughtful discussion of Osborne's politics.

LOOK HOMEWARD, ANGEL
A Story of the Buried Life

Type of work: Novel
Author: Thomas Wolfe (1900-1938)
Type of plot: Impressionistic realism
Time of plot: 1900 to early 1920's
Locale: North Carolina
First published: 1929

Principal characters:
EUGENE GANT
ELIZA GANT, his mother
OLIVER GANT, his father
BEN GANT, his brother
MARGARET LEONARD, his teacher
LAURA JAMES, his first sweetheart

The Story:

Eugene, the youngest child in the Gant family, came into the world when Eliza Gant was forty-two years old. His father went on periodic drinking sprees to forget his unfulfilled ambitions and the unsatisfied wanderlust that had brought him to Altamont in the hills of Old Catawba. When Eugene was born, his father was asleep in a drunken stupor.

Eliza disapproved of her husband's debauches, but she lacked the imagination to understand their cause. Oliver, who had been raised amid the plenty of a Pennsylvania farm, had no comprehension of the privation and suffering that had existed in the South after the Civil War, the cause of the hoarding and acquisitiveness of his wife and her Pentland relations in the Old Catawba hill country.

Eliza bore the burden of Oliver's drinking and promiscuousness until Eugene was four years old. Then she departed for St. Louis, taking all the children but the oldest daughter, Daisy, with her. It was 1904, the year of the great St. Louis Fair, and Eliza had gone to open a boardinghouse for her visiting fellow townspeople. The idea was abhorrent to Oliver. He stayed in Altamont. Eliza's sojourn in St. Louis ended abruptly when twelve-year-old Grover fell ill of typhoid and died. Stunned, she gathered her remaining children to her and went home.

Young Eugene was a shy, awkward boy with dark, brooding eyes. He was, like his ranting, histrionic father, a dreamer. He was not popular with his schoolmates, who sensed instinctively that he was different and made him pay the price; at home, he was the victim of his sisters' and brothers' taunts and torments. His one champion was his brother Ben, though even he had been conditioned by the Gants' unemotional family life to give his caresses as cuffs.

There was little time, however, for Eugene's childish daydreaming. Eliza believed early jobs taught her boys manliness and self-reliance. Ben got up at three o'clock every morning to deliver papers. Luke had been a *Saturday Evening Post* agent since he was twelve. Eugene was put under his wing. Although the boy loathed the work, he was forced every Thursday to corner customers and keep up a continuous line of chatter until he broke down their sales resistance.

Eugene was not yet eight when his parents separated. Eliza had bought the Dixieland boardinghouse as a good investment. Helen remained at the old house with her father. Daisy married and left town. Mrs. Gant took Eugene with her. Ben and Luke were left to shift for themselves, to shuttle back and forth between the two houses. Eugene grew to detest his new home. When the Dixieland was crowded, there was no privacy, and Eliza advertised the Dixieland on printed cards which Eugene had to distribute to customers on his magazine route and to travelers arriving at the Altamont station.

Although life at the boardinghouse was drab, the next four years were the golden days of Eugene's youth, for he was allowed to go to the Leonards' private school. Margaret Leonard, the tubercular wife of the schoolmaster, recognized Eugene's hunger for beauty and love and was able to find in literature the words that she herself had not the power to utter. By the time he was fifteen, Eugene knew the best and the greatest lyrics almost line for line.

Eugene was also about to encounter other changes in his life. Oliver Gant, who had been fifty when his youngest son was born, was beginning to feel his years. Although he was never told, he was slowly dying of cancer. Eugene was fourteen when World War I began, and Ben, who wanted to join the Canadian Army, was warned by his doctor that he would be refused because he had weak lungs.

At age fifteen, Eugene was sent to the university at Pulpit Hill. It was his father's plan that Eugene should be well on his way toward being a great statesman before the time came for old Oliver to die. Eugene's youth and tremendous height made him a natural target for dormitory horseplay, and his shy, awkward manners were intensified by his ignorance of the school's traditions and rituals. He roomed alone. His only friends were four wastrels, one of whom contributed to his social education by introducing him to a brothel.

That summer, back at the Dixieland, Eugene met Laura James. Sitting with her on the front porch at night, he was taken in by her quiet smile and clear, candid eyes. He became her lover on a summer afternoon of sunlit green and gold. Yet Laura went home to visit her parents and wrote Eugene that she was about to marry a boy to whom she had been engaged for nearly a year.

Eugene went back to Pulpit Hill that fall, still determined to go his way alone. Although he had no intimate friends, he gradually became a campus leader. The commonplace good fellows of his world tolerantly made room for the one who was not like them.

In October of the following year, Eugene received an urgent summons to come home. Ben was finally paying the price of his parents' neglect and the drudgery of his life. He was dying of pneumonia. Eliza had neglected to call a competent doctor until it was too late, and Oliver, as he sat at the foot of the dying boy's bed, could think only of the burial expenses. As the family kept their vigil through Ben's last night, they were touched with the realization of the greatness of the boy's generous soul. Ben was given, a final irony, the best funeral money could buy.

With Ben went the family's last pretenses. When Eugene came back to the Dixieland after graduation, Eliza was in control of Oliver's property and selling it as quickly as she could in order to use the money for further land speculations. She had disposed of their old home. Oliver lived in a back room of the boardinghouse. His children watched one another suspiciously as he wasted away, each concerned for his or her own inheritance. Eugene managed to remain unembroiled in their growing hatred of one another, but he could not avoid being a target for that hatred. Helen, Luke, and Steve had always resented his schooling. In September, before he left for Harvard to begin graduate work, Luke asked Eugene to sign a release saying that he had received his inheritance as tuition and school expenses. Though his father had promised him an education when he was still a child and Eliza was to pay for his first year in the North, Eugene was glad to sign. He was free, and he was never coming back to Altamont.

On his last night at home, he had a vision of his dead brother Ben in the moonlit square at midnight: Ben, the unloved of the Gants, and the most lovable. It was for Eugene as well a vision of old, unhappy, unforgotten years, and in his restless imagination, he dreamed of the hidden door through which he would escape forever the mountain-rimmed world of his boyhood.

Critical Evaluation:

An alert reader of *Look Homeward, Angel* does not have to go very far into this long book before realizing that it is largely autobiographical. Though many details are imaginatively transformed, the hero, Eugene Gant, is Thomas Wolfe himself. The Gant family is Wolfe's family, and Altamont is Asheville, North Carolina, through the first two decades of the twentieth century. When the story concludes with Eugene's preparations to leave home for graduate study at Harvard, it has in effect come to a transitional moment in Wolfe's life. Wolfe finished at the University of North Carolina with the desire to become a playwright, and he went to Harvard primarily to study playwriting under George Pierce Baker.

All of this background is useful to know because it helps to explain the inception of *Look Homeward, Angel* and the curiosity of its form. After Wolfe completed a master's degree at Harvard he went to New York to live, teaching composition at New York University while attempting to launch the career on which he was intent: playwriting. Success did not come quickly; readers of Wolfe should be able to see without difficulty that his peculiar gift was not one to fit easily with the tight discipline of the stage. He began to write the prose narrative that was published as *Look Homeward, Angel* in 1929.

Publication of Wolfe's manuscript followed substantial revision under the tutelage of Maxwell Perkins, a remarkable editor who saw in Wolfe an enormous but undisciplined talent. With the almost fatherly guidance of Perkins, Wolfe was able to bring a measure of order out of the sometimes brilliant chaos that frequently attended his writing. Upon the publication of *Look Homeward, Angel*, Wolfe more or less forsook playwriting to become a novelist and continued on this track until his early death in 1938.

This brings us back to the form of *Look Homeward, Angel*, which is called a novel because that seems to be the most convenient term, even if it is only approximate. The book is a prose narrative, and it is too imaginative to be called an autobiography. It is too enthusiastic to be called a meditation, too unsentimental, for all of its emotion, to be called a reminiscence. It has sometimes been called a *Bildungsroman*, a German term for novels which give an account of the education of someone, usually a young man or woman. For lack of a better term to describe its form, Wolfe's book is simply regarded as a novel, which has put it at somewhat of a disadvantage because it does not measure up very well in relation to other novels that can be admired for their formal artistry.

Wolfe's problem was that he undertook to do two things that do not especially fit with each other. First, and perhaps foremost, he wanted to express, in lyric prose, the complexity and wonder of American provincial life. In this artistic goal he might be seen as a kind of Walt Whitman of twentieth century America, and indeed his best prose is little different from Whitman's free verse expression of America in the previous century. This intent, however, if it can be seen as such, does not fit very well with Wolfe's other goal, which might be expressed as a portrait of the artist as a growing boy. *Look Homeward, Angel* has for its subtitle *A Story of the Buried Life*. Eugene Gant, its hero, is seen from his infancy to a few months before his twentieth birthday (Wolfe was precocious and finished college himself at that early age). Eugene's life is "buried" because he has little outlet at home for the energy, emotional and intellectual and creative, with which he has been gifted. His closest ally is his older brother Ben, who has died before the novel concludes. Eugene Gant is essentially alone. Loneliness is frequently the artist's lot; not only is there the problem of the artistic sensibility, but there is the further need for the artist to accept the measure of self-isolation necessary for the mastery of a creative discipline.

Thomas Wolfe's enthusiasm, personal and artistic, is largely evident in *Look Homeward, Angel*. It is his lyrical expression of an abundance of characters and dramatic moments that captured a reading audience from the time of his first novel's publication and held it for many years thereafter. His other theme, the isolation of the artistic sensibility, is occasionally striking and once in a while a trifle embarrassing as a barely concealed confessional. If, however, the artist, in Wolfe or in his character Eugene Gant, must choose isolation or be chosen for it, the enthusiast of American experience must be hugely involved. In *Look Homeward, Angel*, Wolfe seems to have tried to have it both ways, and he was successful only in part. This may finally be the reason for the criticism to which he has been subjected. He didn't understand that he could write one kind of book, or he could write the other, but if he tried to do both at the same time, he was going to have trouble with his form.

Look Homeward, Angel is a book that is best read in parts. After it has been read through once, a second reading will not produce the rewards that come from repeated engagements with selected parts, for example, W. O. Gant's stream of consciousness as he rides a trolley home on his return from California, or the gathering of town characters at Uneeda Lunch, or the chapter wherein W. O. Gant sells the sculpted stone angel on the porch of his business to the town madam, who needs it for one of her girls, who has died. Wolfe's readers tend to select their own favorite passages, which can sometimes be justified on critical grounds, but not always. This is the virtue of a large book about ordinary American experience. What is perceived as extraordinary will vary with its readers.

"Critical Evaluation" by John Higby

Bibliography:
Bloom, Harold, ed. *Thomas Wolfe*. New York: Chelsea House, 1987. Bloom, himself a distinguished critic, gathers in his book eight essays by seven different writers, suggesting that the collection is what he considers "the most useful criticism of Thomas Wolfe's fiction." A bibliography of critical pieces on Wolfe is included.

Donald, David Herbert. *Look Homeward: A Life of Thomas Wolfe*. Boston: Little, Brown, 1987. Donald prepared this admired biography of Wolfe with the aid of the novelist's voluminous papers, lodged at Harvard University. The preface announces that, in addition to Wolfe's biography, an attempt is made to offer "a group photograph . . . of what can properly be called the Great Generation in American literature."

Idol, John Lane, Jr. *A Thomas Wolfe Companion*. New York: Greenwood Press, 1987. A very useful handbook for the study of Wolfe. It includes a selected bibliography of Wolfe publications, an annotated bibliography of criticism, and a short list of information sources. A helpful glossary of characters and places identifies many characters and places fictionalized by Wolfe.

Rubin, Louis D., Jr. *Thomas Wolfe: The Weather of His Youth*. Baton Rouge: Louisiana State University Press, 1955. Rubin considers Wolfe's first novel as autobiographical fiction and then moves on to examine "the meaning of the time structure" in Wolfe's fiction.

Wolfe, Thomas. *The Notebooks of Thomas Wolfe*. 2 vols. Edited by Richard S. Kennedy and Paschal Reeves. Chapel Hill: University of North Carolina Press, 1970. The first in this two-volume set includes the entire period when Wolfe was at work on *Look Homeward, Angel*. Editors' notes help relate Wolfe's various jottings to incidents in his book.

LOOKING BACKWARD
2000-1887

Type of work: Novel
Author: Edward Bellamy (1850-1898)
Type of plot: Utopian
Time of plot: 1887 and 2000
Locale: Boston, Massachusetts
First published: 1888

Principal characters:
JULIAN WEST, a traveler in time
EDITH BARTLETT, his nineteenth century fiancée
DR. LEETE, a twentieth century citizen
EDITH, his daughter

The Story:

Julian West had had difficulty sleeping. In order to have complete quiet, he had built a soundproof room with thick cement walls in the cellar of his house. He was also in the habit of having a mesmerist named Dr. Pillsbury put him to sleep by hypnosis. On May 30, 1887, he went to dinner at the home of his fiancée and spent an enjoyable evening with Edith and her father, Mr. Bartlett. He went home, had the doctor give him a treatment, and went to sleep. He awoke to find strange people in the room. They asked him who he was and when he had gone to sleep. Julian was amazed when he realized that he had been asleep 113 years, 3 months, and 11 days.

In the course of lengthy questioning, Julian learned that during the night he last remembered, his house had burned down except for the sealed room in which he slept. Not knowing about that room, everyone assumed that he had died in the fire. Because of his hypnotic state, his body had remained the same, and he was still a young man of thirty when he was discovered by Dr. Leete in the year 2000. Dr. Leete and his daughter, Edith, were very kind to their guest from the past and tried to explain the changes in the world since he had last seen it.

Boston was a beautiful, new city; only the bay and the inlets were as he remembered them, and the city now had attractive buildings and spacious parks. The strikes and labor troubles of the nineteenth century had resulted in a bloodless revolution, and now a socialized government controlled all business. There was no smoke or pollution because heating was done by electricity. All the people were healthy and happy.

Dr. Leete tried to explain the world of 2000. There was no money. The state gave everyone, regardless of position, a debit card of equal value to cover all annual expenses. If people proved incapable of handling the debit card intelligently, the government provided supervision to enhance their understanding of the system and how it worked. Julian was taken to one of the big distribution centers to see how goods were sold. The store had nothing but samples, representing every type of material made in or imported by the United States. The buyer picked out the desired items, called a clerk and placed the order, whereupon the clerk relayed the order to the central warehouse that delivered the items to the buyer's home before the buyer had even returned from the store. Julian was much impressed with this system.

Everyone was given a full education until the age of twenty-one. A broad cultural course was taught so that there was no intellectual snobbery among the people. At age twenty-one, students went into menial service for three years, performing simple tasks like waiting on tables in large public eating houses. After that, they were given an examination to qualify them for one of the government professional schools. If they failed, they were helped in finding the job for which they were best suited and that they would most enjoy. If their first jobs proved to be wrong for them, they could try another kind of work. In order that there would be sufficient staff for all the essential jobs, positions were structured so as to be equally attractive. If a particular job was so boring or arduous that few people would want to choose it, the hours were shortened so as to attract enough applicants. Whether citizens were doctors or bricklayers, they were given the same amount of credit for their work.

Crime was treated as a mental disease; criminals were put in hospitals and treated as patients. Julian learned that crime had been cut down amazingly as soon as money was abolished. Theft became silly when everyone had the right and power to own the same things. At the head of the government was the president, who was controlled by Congress. Education and medicine were controlled by boards made up of older professional advisers to the president. A woman chosen by the women of the country had the power to veto any bill concerning the rights of the female population. There was no public discontent with government, and there was international cooperation.

Julian asked Dr. Leete what he had done in life and learned that the doctor had practiced medicine until he was forty-five years old. At that time, he had retired. Now he studied and enjoyed various kinds of recreation.

Edith Leete took great pleasure in showing Julian the various advances the world had made in culture since his day. She showed him how music was carried into all the homes in the country by telephone. She showed him the public libraries in which Julian learned that his old favorites were still read. Dickens was especially popular, as the new world thought him one of the wisest men in judging the sadness of the old capitalistic system. Books were published by the government at the authors' expense; if a book proved a popular success, the author received royalties in additional credit. Works of art were voted on by the public in the same way. When Julian commented that this plan would not have worked in his day because of the lack of public taste, Edith told him that with general education the taste of the people had developed greatly. Julian became very fond of Edith and thought how strange it was that she should have the same name as his long-dead fiancée.

When Julian became worried about a means of support, Dr. Leete told him that he had arranged for him to take a college lectureship in history, as Julian knew much about the past which historians would be delighted to learn. Knowing that he was secure in this new world, Julian asked Edith to marry him. She told him that she had always loved him. She explained that she was the great-granddaughter of Edith Bartlett. She had found some of Julian's old love letters to the other Edith and had been charmed by them. She had always told her parents that she would marry only a man like the lover who had written them. Julian was pleased at this unexpected turn of affairs, and the two planned to marry and live happily in the wonderful world of the twenty-first century.

Critical Evaluation:

Considered one of the most influential nineteenth century American novels and surely the most enduring of the American utopian stories, *Looking Backward* was ideally suited to appeal to middle-class readers. The book endorsed a socialist future while at the same time denying the inevitability of class warfare and portraying a world in which individuals were given carte blanche as long as they did not dominate or exploit others.

Throughout the novel, Edward Bellamy contrasts the domestic and international strife of the nineteenth century with the harmonious relationships of his utopian late twentieth and early twenty-first centuries. Gone are the social and economic conditions that separated people into antagonistic groups and compelled them to attempt to advance at the expense of others. Gone, too, are the structural limitations that forced some to remain forever subservient to those who, either through hard work or through the benefit of birth, had attained economic security.

To underscore the absurdity of distributing rewards on the basis of social position, Bellamy uses the analogy of a prodigious coach carrying those seeking to avoid contact with the seamier side of life; the coach's course roughly parallels the economic fluctuations that made life inherently unstable and unsafe. Bellamy reinforces the alienation implicit in such an arrangement by depicting Julian as a member of the moneyed elite who felt compelled further to insulate himself by constructing a hermetically sealed sleeping chamber. In Bellamy's view, the attempt of the wealthy to protect themselves through the construction of artificial barriers merely increased their vulnerability.

To eliminate such barriers, the new society provides everyone with a solid education and access to cultural refinements once reserved for the elite. In this way, the level of appreciation of life is raised, as is the quality of life. Though seen by many as a sign of Bellamy's elitism, his emphasis on education and culture reflects his belief that nurture, rather than nature, determines social outcomes. Bellamy believed that a humane society could only be created by reconstructing social institutions in such a way as to change the objective circumstances of people's lives. He argues that an individual, much like a rose, will flourish if transplanted to a more hospitable environment and that individuals who once felt excluded will identify with the common good and be motivated to contribute to the fullest extent of their abilities. With money and material goods devalued and the issues of security and safety resolved, selfishness could, he believed, be eliminated, and no one would want to manipulate the system to gain a valueless advantage.

To demonstrate the feasibility of his arguments, Bellamy uses the military analogy of conscripts unselfishly defending their country in times of war. The motivations, in times of war as in times of peace, he argues, could be very similar: patriotism and the gratitude of their fellow citizens.

Because their incomes are equal and they gain nothing by attempting to upstage others, Bellamy's citizens of the twenty-first century select occupations that are ideally suited to their talents and temperaments; as a result, society is able to make the best use of individual and collective resources. Even those who are relegated to the more trivial tasks have no reason to feel envy or remorse because they know that their services will be more than repaid. While coordinating such a system might promise to be a bureaucratic nightmare, Bellamy argues that such a government, though more encompassing, is simpler and more benign. It blends the principles of meritocracy and Jeffersonian democracy and is staffed by those who have proven their commitment to the general well-being and have been "mustered" into retirement. To guard against influence-peddling among those who select the leaders, Bellamy excludes members of the active work force from taking part in elections; voting is left to those who are retired. He justifies this suspension of the popular vote by arguing that government as an institution is only needed in the most extraordinary of circumstances. Its sole function seems to be maintaining a set of conditions that make most legislative activities passé. To authenticate his point, Bellamy notes that much of the legislation that was thought necessary in the past was actually the result of the inherent instability of a society that rewarded the few at the expense of the many.

Despite the sanguine portrait that Bellamy paints, the question arises as to the quality of individual human life and whether there is any provision to ensure that innovators have a means of influencing the society at large. Perhaps most important, Bellamy's future vision fails to include legitimate channels for dissent. Notwithstanding his claim that a change in objective circumstances will result in a change in subjective responses, in his utopia those who defy authority or refuse to work are placed in solitary confinement.

Women, too, get short shrift. Although they are allowed to work and receive individual stipends, their career choices are strictly limited. It is also curious that while women are supposed to be full participants in the society, the twenty-first century Edith does not appear to attend school or work for a living and is, instead, described by her father as a consummate shopper.

This portrayal may very well result from the fact that Bellamy is far more interested in advancing his arguments than in developing his characters. Even Julian and Dr. Leete remain two-dimensional mouthpieces for particular points of view. It is not, therefore, surprising that Edith's main function in the novel is not as a representative woman, but as a tool that allows him to incorporate some of the elements of the standard romance into his novel.

Bellamy's use of the dream vision, however, is anything but standard. Rather than using the dream as a convenient travel mode, Bellamy allows the dream to become the reality. When Julian is returned to the nineteenth century, it is as if he were going through an expiation for his past indifference and self-absorption. He is, as the title suggests, looking backward and realizing the limitations inherent in outmoded social and economic arrangements.

"Critical Evaluation" by C. Lynn Munro

Bibliography:
Aaron, Daniel. "Edward Bellamy: Village Utopian." In *Men of Good Hope*. New York: Oxford University Press, 1951. Discusses *Looking Backward* as part of the progressive reform movement. Provides insights into Bellamy's military model and transcendental religious perspective and highlights the safeguards Bellamy includes to guard against authoritarian and bureaucratic domination.

Berneri, Marie Louise. "Edward Bellamy: Looking Backward." In *Journey Through Utopia*. London: Routledge & Kegan Paul, 1950. Contends that Bellamy's utopia is based on a naïve faith in experts and technological progress. Berneri is troubled by the inherent regimentation and argues that the need for compulsion and the prohibition of dissent belie the supposed happiness within the industrial republic.

Bowman, Sylvia E. *Edward Bellamy*. Boston: Twayne, 1986. Offers an interdisciplinary analysis of Bellamy's intellectual development and considers *Looking Backward* within the context of his other writings. Chapter 5 focuses on the book's influence on sociopolitical developments and major nineteenth and twentieth century thinkers.

Parrington, Vernon L. "The Quest of Utopia." In *Main Currents in American Thought*. Vol. 3. New York: Harcourt, Brace, 1930. Following a brief contextual summary, Parrington describes *Looking Backward* as a book about democratic political economy that revolves around the moral questions of right and justice. Links Bellamy's nationalism to trustee theory, which gives the government responsibility for equitable resource allocation.

Patai, Daphne, ed. *Looking Backward, 1988-1888*. Amherst: University of Massachusetts Press, 1988. Contains eight retrospective essays that assess *Looking Backward* in view of twentieth century developments. Some contributors view Bellamy as a proponent of a dated, patriarchal world; others praise his integration of contradictory principles. Includes a useful annotated bibliography.

LORD JIM

Type of work: Novel
Author: Joseph Conrad (Jósef Teodor Konrad Nałęcz Korzeniowski, 1857-1924)
Type of plot: Psychological realism
Time of plot: Late nineteenth century
Locale: Ports and islands of the East
First published: 1900

Principal characters:
LORD JIM, a British sailor
MARLOW, his friend
STEIN, a trader
DAIN WARIS, a native

The Story:

Jim was an outcast and a wanderer. He worked as a water clerk in seaports throughout the East but would keep his job only until his identity became known. Then he would move on. The story of Lord Jim began when he determined to leave home to go to sea. His father obtained a berth for him as an officer candidate, and he began his service. Although he loved the sea, his beginning was not heroic, for almost at once he was injured and had to be left behind in an Eastern port. When he recovered, he accepted a berth as chief mate aboard an ancient steamer, the *Patna*, which was carrying Muslim pilgrims on their way to Mecca. The steamer was unseaworthy, her German captain a gross coward, and her chief engineer liquor-soaked. One sultry night in the Red Sea, the ship struck a floating object. The captain sent Jim to investigate.

One month later, Jim testified in court that when he went to investigate, he found the forward hold rapidly filling with seawater. Hearing his report, the captain, declaring that the *Patna* would sink quickly, gave orders for the crew to abandon ship. At first, Jim was determined to stand by his post. At the last minute, on sudden impulse, he jumped to join the other white men in the lifeboat they had launched. The pilgrims were left aboard the sinking vessel. The *Patna* did not sink, however. A French gunboat overtook the vessel and towed it and the abandoned passengers into port without its chief officers aboard.

Marlow, a white man, sat at the inquiry. There was something about Jim that became unforgettable to Marlow, and he was forced to recall the event and to tell the story to friends as long as he lived; it became a part of his own life.

Marlow's story had begun with a cable from Aden announcing that the *Patna*, abandoned by its officers, had been towed into port. Two weeks later, the captain, the two engineers, and Jim had come ashore. Their boat had been picked up by a steamer of the Dale Line, and they were immediately whisked into court for the investigation. The captain lost his papers for deserting his ship, and he stormed away declaring that his disgrace did not matter; he would become an American citizen. The chief engineer went to a hospital. Raving in delirium tremens, he declared that he had seen the *Patna* go down and that the vessel was full of reptiles when she sank. He also stated that the space under his bed was crammed with pink toads. The second engineer had a broken arm and was also in the hospital. Neither was called to testify.

Jim, wrestling with the thoughts of his upbringing and his father's teaching as well as his own deeply established sense of honor, was a marked man for the rest of his life. Marlow told how during the trial he had dinner with the young man, who seemed of a different stamp from the other officers of the *Patna*. Marlow was determined to fathom the boy's spirit, just as Jim was determined to regain his lost moral identity.

Jim told Marlow how the disgraceful affair had happened. After he had investigated the damage, he had felt that the ship could not remain afloat, for her plates were rust-eaten and unable to stand much strain. There were eight hundred passengers and seven boats, but there did not seem to be enough time to get a few passengers into the boats. Shortly afterward, he discovered the captain and the engineers preparing to desert the ship. They insisted that he join them; the passengers were doomed anyway. The acting third engineer had a heart attack in the excitement and died. Jim never knew when—or why—he had jumped into the lifeboat the other officers had launched. Jim told Marlow how they had agreed to tell the same story. Actually, he and his companions thought that the *Patna* had gone down. Jim said that he had felt relief when he learned that the passengers were safe. The whole story made sailor-talk in all ports where seamen met and talked. After the inquiry, Marlow offered to help Jim, but the young man was determined to become a wanderer, to find out by himself what had happened to his soul.

In his wanderings, Jim went to Bombay, Calcutta, Penang, Batavia, and the islands of the East. For a time, he found work with an acquaintance of Marlow, but he gave up his job when the second engineer of the *Patna* turned up unexpectedly. Afterward, he became a runner for ship chandlers, but he left them when he heard one of the owners discussing the case of the *Patna*. He moved on, always toward the East, from job to job.

Marlow continued his efforts to help Jim. He sought out Stein, a trader who owned a number of trading posts on the smaller islands of the East Indies. Stein made Jim his agent at Patusan, an out-of-the-way settlement where he was sure Jim might recover his balance. In that remote place, Jim tried to find an answer to his self-hatred. Determined never to leave Patusan, he associated with the natives, and by his gentleness and consideration he became their leader. They called him Tuan Jim—Lord Jim. Dain Waris, the son of Doramin, the old native chief, was his friend. In the ports, rumors spread that Jim had discovered a valuable emerald and had presented it to a native woman. There was a story about a native girl who loved him and who had given him warning when some jealous natives came to murder him.

Marlow followed Jim to Patusan. When Marlow prepared to leave, Jim accompanied him part of the way. He explained to Marlow that at last he felt as though his way had been justified. Somehow, because the simple natives trusted him, he felt linked again to the ideals of his youth. Marlow felt there was a kind of desperation to his declaration.

The end came when Gentleman Brown, a roving cutthroat, determined to loot Lord Jim's stronghold. He arrived while Jim was away. Led by Dain Waris, the natives isolated Brown and his marauders on a hilltop but were unable to capture them. When Jim returned, he had a long talk with Brown and became convinced that Brown would leave peaceably if the siege were lifted. He persuaded the reluctant natives to withdraw. The vicious Brown repaid Jim's magnanimity by vengefully murdering Dain Waris. Lord Jim went unflinchingly to face native justice when he offered himself to the stern old chieftain as the cause of Dain Waris' death. Doramin shot Jim through the breast. Marlow, who had watched Jim's life so closely, felt that Jim had at last won back his lost honor.

Critical Evaluation:

Born in the Polish Ukraine in 1857, Joseph Conrad was the son of a political exile who championed Poland's resistance to Russian rule and was consequently forced to leave his native land. Conrad lost both parents before he was ten years old, and he was reared by an uncle. In 1874, he went to sea; by 1886, he had earned his master mariner's certificate and had become a naturalized British citizen. Working in the merchant service, Conrad served mostly in eastern waters with the exception of one trip to the Congo. His first novel, *Almayer's Folly*, was written in 1895; in 1896, he married Jessie George and settled down to write. During his last years he suffered from rheumatic gout and worried about his work and finances.

Some critics have said that *Lord Jim*, which began as a short story and was first published as a magazine serial, became a novel because its author lost control of his material. They also point out how unlikely it is that Jim's long, tragic story would be told on one occasion among a group of men sitting on a veranda. Conrad claimed that men do sit up for hours at night exchanging stories, and he declared that Jim's story is interesting enough to hold the attention of listeners and readers, for, as suggested by the motif of the novel, "He is one of us." Because Jim, like every man, is an enigmatic paradox of strength and weakness, Conrad allows the reader to judge Jim's actions but reminds him that often there is "not the thickness of a sheet of paper between the right and wrong" of something.

The novel is often confusing, and shifts in point of view and a seeming disregard for a logical time sequence give the novel a meditative style. Narrating the first four chapters himself, Conrad shifts in chapter 5 to Marlow's oral narration and then in chapter 36 to a letter written by Marlow. As Jim's story unfolds, however, Conrad also allows other reliable characters to comment on Jim and his actions: the French lieutenant, who saves the *Patna* after Jim deserts it; Stein, who gives Jim another chance to prove himself; and Jewel, the native girl who loves him. Conrad thus gives his readers the pieces to a gigantic puzzle—the connection between human motivation and human character—but he himself admitted that much in the novel would remain inscrutable.

Conrad said that the central theme of *Lord Jim* is the "acute consciousness of lost honour." Jim may be uncommonly idealistic, but Conrad claimed to have seen Jim's "form" in the Eastern port. To help clarify Jim's desperate preoccupation with his dreams of himself, Conrad describes Jim as having in his youth spent his time reading "light holiday literature" and having imagined himself "always an example of devotion to duty, and as unflinching as a hero in a book." In addition, Jim had been brought up by a father who was a minister and who held absolute ideas of right and wrong. He had written Jim just before he joined the *Patna* as chief mate that one who "gives way to temptation . . . hazards his total depravity and everlasting ruin." Jim is a dreamer who becomes lost in his own imagination; this aspect of his character is revealed by the training ship incident in which he fails to respond to a cry for help from a wrecked schooner because he was reveling in his dreams of heroism. His inability to face the reality of his failure is seen when he blames nature for catching him off guard and when he rationalizes that he is saving himself for bigger emergencies. When the crucial emergency comes—that of the *Patna*'s crisis—he again fails to act because he imagines the chaos and the screaming desperation of eight hundred pilgrims fighting for seven lifeboats; he stands frozen while the other members of the crew lower their lifeboat and prepare to jump. Jim wants to make it clear that he did not plan to jump, nor did he help to lower the boat. He interprets his having jumped as a subconscious but understandable urge for survival. He tells Marlow: "I had jumped . . . It seems."

The French lieutenant does not condemn Jim's actions. He blames Jim's youth and natural fear. He believes that "Man is born a coward" but that he does brave deeds to make others believe he is heroic. Jim, he notes, faced a situation in which he thought no one would ever know that he had acted cowardly: During the crisis it was dark, and Jim thought all the passengers would die. The lieutenant recognizes Jim's self-condemnation: "the honour . . . that is real . . . and what life may be worth when . . . the honour is gone" is the real question of *Lord Jim*.

Stein also diagnoses Jim's problem: "He is romantic. . . . And that is very bad. . . . Very good, too." He sees in Jim the potential tragic hero who has high ideals but fails as the result of a tragic flaw. Jim's flaw is his excessive imagination and his inability to face the reality of his weakness and his guilt. Not until the end of the novel, when he knows his limitations and accepts his guilt for Dain Waris' death, does he redeem his lost honor by giving his own life unflinchingly in atonement for his error in misjudging Gentleman Brown. It is Brown who makes Jim see the depravity and ugliness of reality; yet in his death, Jim remains true to his concept of the hero. He has transcended his guilt and declares that "Nothing can touch me now." Earlier, when Jewel expresses to Marlow her fear that Jim will leave her, Marlow assures her that Jim will not go back to his world because "he is not good enough." In the end, however, Marlow seems to believe in Jim's final heroism and sees him as an "extraordinary success."

Whose evaluation of Jim is accurate? Jim's own evaluation comes when he feels that he has finally found himself and thus dies willingly, with "a proud and unflinching glance." Marlow sees Jim as a fallible creature who looks trustworthy but fails when an emergency arises. Stein says that a romantic like Jim has no choice but to follow his dream, even if it costs him his life. The French lieutenant refuses to judge Jim but shows, by his own heroic example, Jim's weakness. Jewel ultimately calls Jim a traitor and refuses to forgive or understand him. The novel is puzzling, and Jim remains "inscrutable at heart," but he also remains "one of us."

"Critical Evaluation" by Janet Wester

Bibliography:
Cox, C. B. *Joseph Conrad: The Modern Imagination.* London: J. M. Dent, 1974. Maintains that the novel reveals the meaninglessness of the modern age. Marlow and Jim cannot find the language to reveal the truth of Jim's actions. No words can be found; meaning can only be apprehended through glimpses and hints.
Guerard, Albert J. *Conrad the Novelist.* Cambridge, Mass.: Harvard University Press, 1966. Includes two extended chapters on *Lord Jim*, the first of which explores the work as impressionistic rather than realistic, which requires the reader to reflect morally and emotionally on the central character. The second examines Marlow's role and character as narrator.
Karl, Frederick R. *A Reader's Guide to Joseph Conrad.* New York: Farrar, Straus & Giroux, 1969. An excellent beginner's source on Conrad's works. Provides analyses of major works, characters, and themes. Especially helpful is the explanation of Conrad's time shifts and use of the Marlow narrator figure in *Lord Jim.*
Kuehn, Robert E., ed. *Twentieth Century Interpretations of "Lord Jim": A Collection of Critical Essays.* Englewood Cliffs, N.J.: Prentice-Hall, 1969. Fourteen essays covering the novel's composition and its themes and symbolism. Chapters discuss guilt and redemption, the loss of innocence, and Marlow's judgment of Jim. Helpful chronology and selected bibliography.
Watt, Ian. *Conrad in the Nineteenth Century.* Berkeley: University of California Press, 1979. Provides a history of the book's composition and includes sources for the plot and main character. Covers such topics as the development and method of the narrative, Marlow's use of symbols, Conrad's structure of time, Jim's sojourn in Patusan as romantic escapism, the relationship between Jim and Marlow, and the significance of the ending.

LORD OF THE FLIES

Type of work: Novel
Author: William Golding (1911-1993)
Type of plot: Fable
Time of plot: The future, during a nuclear war
Locale: An uninhabited tropical island
First published: 1954

Principal characters:
RALPH, a British schoolboy
PIGGY, another schoolboy, overweight, nearsighted, and afflicted
with asthma
SAM and
ERIC, twins
JACK MERRIDEW, choir leader and head boy
SIMON, a quiet, introspective boy

The Story:

An airplane evacuating a group of British schoolboys from a war zone crashed on a Pacific island, killing all the adults aboard. Two of the boys, Ralph and "Piggy," found a conch shell and used it as a horn to summon the other survivors, including a boys' choir headed by Jack Merridew. An election was held. Jack had the choir's grudging support, but Ralph possessed the conch and was elected chief. Jack and his choir became hunters.

Later, Ralph called an assembly to set rules. The first rule was that holding the conch gave one the right to speak. A young boy about six years old asked what would be done about the "snake-thing" he had seen. Ralph insisted that no such thing existed and changed the subject to the possibility of rescue. He ordered the boys to make a fire atop the mountain to signal rescuers. Jack volunteered his choir to keep the fire going. Using Piggy's glasses to focus the sunlight on some fuel, they lit the fire. It leaped out of control, and in the confusion the boy who had asked about the "snake-thing" disappeared. He would not be seen again.

Jack, obsessed with the desire to kill a wild pig, and Ralph, who wanted to erect shelters, were often at odds, dividing the boys' allegiance. One day, Ralph spotted smoke from a ship. Looking up at the mountaintop, he discovered that the fire had gone out. Desperately, he and Simon clawed their way up the mountainside, but they were too late. Below, they saw Jack and his hunters (who should have been tending the fire) carrying the carcass of a pig.

Jack was ecstatic, exclaiming over the spilled blood. When Ralph admonished him for letting the fire die, Jack lashed out, breaking a lens of Piggy's glasses.

Meanwhile, a veiled fear had begun to spread, especially among the "littluns," of something that haunted the night. At an assembly, Ralph tried to insist that the rules be followed and the fire kept burning, but discussion turned to the "beast," and the assembly soon degenerated into chaos, with Jack refusing to abide by Ralph's rules.

One day, a victim of the air war being fought overhead fell from the sky in a parachute. He lay against the rocks, dead, buffeted by the wind. Sam and Eric (twins later dubbed "Samneric") were tending the signal fire when they saw the corpse and ran back to camp, screaming that they had seen the beast. Leaving Piggy to watch the littluns, Jack and Ralph went to search the far end of the island, thinking the beast might live there, but found nothing.

Night fell, and Jack challenged Ralph to accompany him up the mountain in the darkness to seek the beast. At the top of the mountain, near the place where the fire was built, they saw a dark shape and, when the wind blew, a skeletal face. They fled in terror.

Back at the base camp, Jack seized the conch and spoke out against Ralph, asking the boys, by a show of hands, to reject him as chief. When the boys refused, Jack went off by himself.

With the beast guarding the mountain, Piggy suggested that they build their signal fire on the rocks near their bathing pool. As they worked, however, several of the older boys slipped off to follow Jack.

With his new band of hunters, Jack pursued a sow caught feeding her litter. Running the sow down, the boys fell on her in a frenzy and killed her. Then, as an offering to the beast, they mounted the pig's severed head on a stake. Unbeknown to Jack and his band, Simon had hidden himself away beneath some vines and witnessed their ritual. When they left, he had a silent conversation with the pig—"the Lord of the Flies"—during which it seemed to reveal to him that the beast was actually something within them. Jack and his followers, smeared with body paint, burst into Ralph's camp, and Jack invited everyone to join his band and feast on roast pig.

Meanwhile, Simon inched his way to the mountaintop, where he discovered the dead parachutist. All the boys, including Ralph and Piggy, had gone to Jack's camp to eat the pig. Under the threat of a downpour, they began to dance and chant, miming the killing of the sow. Suddenly, Simon burst into their circle, trying to tell them of his discovery. The boys, maddened by the chanting, attacked and killed him, thinking him the beast.

Ralph and Piggy returned to their camp. Only Sam and Eric and the littluns remained with them, and all denied—to themselves, as well as to one another—any responsibility for the killing of Simon.

Later, Jack and two of his hunters attacked them. Ralph and Eric fought viciously, but in the end, Jack's party made off with Piggy's glasses, which they needed to light a fire of their own.

Ralph, Piggy, and Samneric went to Jack's lair to demand the return of the glasses. Jack's followers seized Samneric, and Ralph and Jack fought until Piggy, holding the conch, demanded a chance to speak. As Piggy spoke, drawing a line between savagery and order, Roger, standing watch on a cliff overhead, set loose a boulder that crashed down on the boys, smashed the conch, and crushed Piggy's skull. Alone now, Ralph ran, pursued by Jack and his followers hurling spears.

Later, Ralph crept back to the encampment and discovered that Samneric, threatened with torture or worse, had become part of the tribe. They told him that Jack had sharpened a stick at both ends and would hunt him down.

In the morning, Ralph was discovered and forced out of his hiding place. Pursued, he managed to wound two of the boys, but when he attempted to hide again, the hunters lit a fire to smoke him out. The chase became a frantic fight for life that ended when Ralph suddenly came upon a uniformed naval officer whose cutter was moored on the beach. "We saw your smoke," the officer said, grinning at what he presumed to be a boys' game of war.

Critical Evaluation:

William Golding's work has always been somewhat controversial, with many critics hailing him as a literary giant and others decrying what they see as a tendency to create contrived, manipulative works laden with heavy-handed symbolism. His reputation grew slowly. In 1955, when *Lord of the Flies* was first published in the United States, few readers had ever heard of him, and the book (which had been rejected by twenty-one publishers) sold only a handful of copies. Four years later, however, when a paperback edition appeared, Golding's sales, promoted by word of mouth, began to increase. Not long afterward, *Lord of the Flies* became required reading in many secondary schools and colleges, prompting interest in his subsequent work. In 1983, Golding received the Nobel Prize in Literature.

Born in Cornwall, England, in 1911, Golding attended Oxford University, changing his major from science to literature halfway through, and then, after publishing a book of poetry, became caught up in World War II. He spent five years serving with the Royal Navy, emerging as a lieutenant and embarking on a teaching and writing career. During his lifetime, he wrote novels, novellas, poetry, plays, essays, and travel articles.

Lord of the Flies remains his best-known work. It is a superficially simple but densely layered tale that has been labeled, among other things, a fable, a myth, an allegory, and a parable. On the surface, it is an adventure story. A group of schoolboys await rescue on a deserted island, meanwhile exploring, hunting, and finally warring with one another. In Golding's hands, the story becomes a parable that probes the nature and origin of evil.

The point of departure for *Lord of the Flies* is a nineteenth century boys' novel titled *The Coral Island* (1858), by R. M. Ballantyne. In Ballantyne's story, a group of shipwrecked British schoolboys (two of whom share their names with Golding's main characters) manage to create on their deserted island a fair replica of British civilization. Golding's view of human nature is less sanguine. His is a view that accepts the doctrine of original sin but without the accompanying doctrine of redemption. People, in a state of nature, quickly revert to evil, but even in a so-called civilized state, people simply mask their evil beneath a veneer of order. After all, while the boys on the island are sinking into a state of anarchy and blood lust, their civilized parents and teachers are waging nuclear war in the skies overhead.

The novel's central symbol, the pig's head around which buzz flies, which the boys dub the Lord of the Flies, is an allusion to Beelzebub, one of the most loathsome and repulsive of the false gods assailed in the Old Testament. Here, Beelzebub is represented by the rotting head of the sow killed by Jack Merridew and his hunters (choir members) in a frenzy of bloodletting that, in the language used to describe it, has sexual overtones. As Simon realizes, however, the beast, the Lord of the Flies, represents something anarchic and evil in the very core of human nature, not—as in the Bible and religious folklore—a demon separate from humanity but capable of taking possession of one's soul. Although human beings are gifted with at least a glimmer of intelligence and reason—represented in the novel by Piggy and Ralph, respectively—the power of evil is sufficient to overwhelm any opposition.

Lord of the Flies bears a close resemblance to Joseph Conrad's *Heart of Darkness* (1902); each involves a journey by representatives of one of the supposedly most civilized nations of the world into a darkness that lies at the very core of the human self. The irony in *Lord of the Flies* is even more pointed, however, in that Golding's entire cast of characters consists of children—traditional symbols of innocence ("trailing clouds of glory" from their heavenly home, William Wordsworth claims). That they are British public schoolboys only adds to the irony in that perhaps the chief goal of the British public school is to instill in its charges a sense of honor and civil behavior. Indeed, the boys' first impulse is toward order: Jack Merridew, later to become the most barbarous of them all, enters the novel marching his choir members along in two parallel lines.

Golding's story unfolds amid a dense web of symbols, including the conch shell, which represents the fragile hold of rule and order and which is finally smashed to bits when Piggy is killed. Piggy's spectacles, too, symbolize the weakness of intellect and (as a tool for making fire) the loss to humanity when intellect is quashed by superstition and irrationality. The Beast, the parachutist, the fire, the killing of the sow—all assume symbolic significance in the novel, justifying the label of allegory that is often applied to this work.

Ron Carter

Bibliography:
Baker, James, ed. *Critical Essays on William Golding*. Boston: G. K. Hall, 1988. Twelve wide-ranging essays by critics and part of Baker's interview with Golding. Includes Golding's Nobel Prize address.
Dick, Bernard F. *William Golding*. Rev. ed. Boston: Twayne, 1987. Contains a chronology of Golding's literary career.
Friedman, Lawrence S. *William Golding*. New York: Continuum, 1993. Sets *Lord of the Flies* in the context of Golding's entire body of work. The philosophical first chapter is especially useful in focusing on significant themes and concerns.
Gindin, James. *William Golding*. New York: St. Martin's Press, 1988. A biography and survey of Golding's literary career. Includes an enlightening comparison of *Lord of the Flies* with R. M. Ballantyne's nineteenth century novel, *The Coral Island*.
Reilly, Patrick. *"Lord of the Flies": Fathers and Sons*. Boston: Twayne, 1992. Defends the novel from charges of unrelieved despair.

LORNA DOONE
A Romance of Exmoor

Type of work: Novel
Author: R. D. Blackmore (1825-1900)
Type of plot: Adventure
Time of plot: Late seventeenth century
Locale: England
First published: 1869

> *Principal characters:*
> JOHN RIDD, the yeoman of the parish of Oare in Somerset
> SIR ENSOR DOONE, the head of the outlaw Doone clan
> LORNA DOONE, his ward
> CARVER DOONE, his son
> TOM FAGGUS, a highwayman
> JEREMY STICKLES, the king's messenger
> REUBEN HUCKABACK, John Ridd's great-uncle

The Story:

John Ridd was engaged in a schoolboy fight in the yard of Blundell's school when John Fry, employed by Ridd's father, came to take the boy home. Before the two left, however, young John completed his fight by knocking out his opponent. On their way home through the moorlands, they were nearly captured by members of the outlaw Doone band, who had been ravaging the countryside by stealing and killing. When John Ridd reached his father's farm, he learned that the Doones had attacked and murdered his father only a few days previously. This incident stimulated the desire for revenge in all the residents of the parish of Oare, for the murdered man had been greatly respected.

John settled down to the responsibilities that the death of his father had thrust upon him. At first, his time was greatly consumed by farm work as he grew into the largest and strongest man in the Exmoor country. As he matured, John learned much about the wild Doone clan. There was one Doone, however, for whom he felt no animosity. This was the beautiful daughter of the man supposed to be the murderer of John's father. At first sight, John had been stirred by the beauty of Lorna Doone. Thereafter, he was in great conflict when he understood that his passion was directed toward the girl whom he ought to hate for his father's sake. When John's great-uncle, Master Reuben Huckaback, was attacked and robbed by the Doones, he went with John to swear out a warrant for their arrest, but he had no luck because the magistrates were unwilling to incur the enmity of the Doones.

John was drawn deeper into his relationship with Lorna Doone. At their secret meetings in Doone Valley, she told him the story of her life with the outlaws. She always had loved her grandfather, Sir Ensor Doone, but had feared and had come to hate the rough, savage sons, nephews, and grandsons of Sir Ensor. This hatred was increased when Carver Doone cold-bloodedly murdered Lord Alan Brandir, a distant relative who had come to take her away from the Doones.

About this time, John was called to London to serve the cause of James II's tottering throne. There he disclosed all he knew of the Doones's activities and of the false magistrates who seemed to be in league with them. He was warned that Tom Faggus, a highwayman who was John's own cousin, might go to the gallows soon. Because of his refusal to accept bribes or to become the dupe of sly lawyers in the city, he returned to his mother and his farm, not a penny richer or poorer than when he left.

In the meantime, John's concern over Lorna, who had two suitors among the Doones themselves, had almost unhinged his mind. He was delighted to discover that Lorna, still only seventeen years old, had refused both her suitors. At the same time, he feared more than ever losing his chance of winning the ward of the outlaws he was pledged to help the king destroy. He at last, however, won Lorna's agreement, and, with her support, felt that nothing could stop him.

At home, the love of his sister Annie for her cousin, Tom Faggus, reminded John of his duties as his father's son and plunged him into the worries over his mother and Annie and the farm. John's mother had other plans for his marriage, but when he revealed the only course his love must take, he changed her mind. In the meantime, Master Jeremy Stickles brought news of the rising of the Duke of Monmouth and of troubles brewing for the king.

Suddenly, Lorna's signals stopped. John made his will and descended into the Doone hideout. There, he discovered at great risk that Lorna had been kept in her rooms because she would not marry Carver Doone. John managed to talk to her, and she pledged never to give in to her family. He narrowly escaped capture, and, at the same time, managed to save the life of Jeremy Stickles, the king's messenger, by overhearing the outlaws as they plotted to kill Jeremy when he crossed the valley bridge. The Doones's plot to kill Stickles brought further plans for retaliation from the king's men.

Old Sir Ensor Doone was close to death. Before he died, he gave John Ridd and Lorna Doone his blessing, and he presented to Lorna the glass necklace he had kept for her since childhood. Then John took Lorna home with him to his mother's farm. Jeremy Stickles went south to muster forces for the destruction of the Doone clan. The counselor of the Doones took advantage of his absence to visit the Ridd farm in order to make a truce with John. His offer was rejected, but he threw trouble into the paths of the lovers by telling them that Lorna's father had murdered John's father and that his own father was the murderer of Lorna's father. Moreover, he tricked them out of Lorna's necklace, which by now, through the word of Tom Faggus, they knew to be made of diamonds.

Uncle Ruben Huckaback grew interested in having John marry his granddaughter Ruth, and he took John to see the gold mine he had just bought. Upon his return, John learned that Lorna had disappeared. She had been taken away by the Dugals, who claimed her as their missing heiress.

When Tom Faggus joined the rebels against the king, John, at his sister Annie's request, went to find him and to bring him back to safety. John discovered Tom almost dead. John was taken prisoner and was nearly executed. He was saved only by the arrival of his friend, Jeremy Stickles.

John went to London and saw Lorna there. By good chance and virtue of his great strength, he overcame two villains who were attempting to rob and kill a nobleman. The man happened to be Lorna's relative. In return for this deed, the king gave John the title of knight. Moreover, he had the court of heralds design a coat of arms for John's family. The coat of arms was soundly made. When the king declined, the queen herself paid for it.

When John returned from London, covered with honors, he discovered the Doones had been raiding once more. Then came the long awaited revenge. The Doones were routed, their houses were burned, and their stolen booty was divided among those who put in claims for redress.

Lorna's necklace was also recovered. The Doones's counselor revealed that it was Carver Doone who had killed John's father.

Arrangements for the wedding of John and Lorna were made. At the end of the ceremony in the church, Carver Doone, out of great jealousy, shot Lorna. Without a weapon in his hand, John rushed out in pursuit of Carver and found him at Barrow Down. The greatest battle between two men ever told of in books took place there. It was a fight of giants. As John felt his ribs cracking in Carver's tremendous hug, he fastened his own iron grip upon his enemy's arm and ripped it loose. Then he threw his crushed and bleeding enemy into the bog and saw Carver Doone sucked down into its black depths. The greatest enemy of John Ridd was at last destroyed. John returned to his bride to find that she might live. She did survive, and, in peace and plenty, John Ridd lived among his friends to a hearty old age.

Critical Evaluation:

R. D. Blackmore, in his preface to *Lorna Doone: A Romance of Exmoor*, was content to call his work a "romance," because the historical element was only incidental to the work as a whole. Secret agents, highwaymen, clannish marauders, and provincial farmers figure against a background of wild moor country. A feeling for the old times, for great, courageous people, and for love in danger made the novel popular with Victorian readers. People who have read it in their youth remember it with nostalgia, for the book has a penetrating simplicity. Told in the first person by John Ridd, the main character in the novel, it has an authentic ring, the sound of a garrulous man relating the adventures of his youth.

The most memorable features of this novel, which is often reputed to be Blackmore's best, are its characterizations and its setting. The characters are drawn in the dramatic and often exaggerated fashion of the Romantic tradition, with its larger-than-life heroes, heroines, and villains. John Ridd, who narrates the story, is a powerful figure, a giant of a man whose honesty, virtue, patience, and steadfastness match his great size and towering strength. His true love, Lorna Doone, is the epitome of the Romantic heroine; she is mysterious and enchanting but entirely unrealistic. Lorna grows up pure, shy, and virtuous—a priceless pearl of femininity by Victorian standards—in the coarse and isolated environment of a robbers' den, surrounded by a clan of thieves and ruthless cutthroats. Perhaps of necessity, Blackmore paints his heroine in wispy, shimmering terminology; at the close of the novel, the reader still has no clear idea of her actual features. At the other end of the spectrum is the villainous Carver Doone, an unforgettably cruel, almost satanic, figure. The most vital force in *Lorna Doone*, however, is the Exmoor landscape. In soulful descriptions, Blackmore brings to life the wild moors, with their violent, stormy climate and harsh, forbidding countryside as well as their magnificent awesome beauty and loneliness.

The plot of *Lorna Doone* has its weak spots, such as the unnecessary and unconvincing conferral of knighthood upon John Ridd, for whose impressive nature such an honor is trivial and extraneous, or the mediocre description of the Battle of Sedgemoor, which Blackmore borrowed from Thomas Macaulay. Overall, however, the narrative is filled with gripping excitement and told in a rugged, simple, and often lyrical prose. Some scenes in particular are unsurpassed, such as the wonderfully taut and realistic one in which John pits his strength and stubbornness against the fury of Tom Faggus' mare. In a different vein, but equally skillful, is John's description of his sorrow at Lorna's unexplained absence from their secret meeting place, a sorrow that spoils the natural beauty of the place in his eyes.

Ironically, *Lorna Doone* first became popular by accident; people bought the novel on the mistaken assumption—owing to a journalist's blunder—that it was about the Marquis of

Lorna's marriage, which had captured public interest at the time. It was a propitious error, however, creating as it did the novel's first devoted reading audience, which has had its descendants in every succeeding generation.

Bibliography:
Budd, Kenneth George. *The Last Victorian: R. D. Blackmore and His Novels*. London: Centaur Press, 1960. A good introduction, connecting the plot to legend and to children's nursery tales. Analyzes Blackmore's style and lyricism, rebutting accusations of wordiness and lack of realism. Favorably compares Blackmore to other Victorian rural novelists.

Burris, Quincy Guy. *Richard Doddridge Blackmore: His Life and Novels*. Westport, Conn.: Greenwood Press, 1973. Discusses Blackmore's attitudes about nature and civilization, analyzing plot, character, and theme. Compares *Lorna Doone* with other Blackmore novels, tracing symbol and imagery, recurring ideas, and character types.

Dunn, Waldo Hilary. *R. D. Blackmore*. New York: Longmans, Green, 1956. Although marred by some inaccuracies about Blackmore's father, provides the best introduction to his life and work. Discusses details of various editions and Blackmore's changing views about *Lorna Doone* by comparing the prefaces to various editions of the novel.

Elwin, Malcolm. *Victorian Wallflowers*. Port Washington, N.Y.: Kennikat Press, 1966. Presents Blackmore as an unjustly neglected author by providing a literary history of the period, comparing Blackmore's works with Anthony Trollope's and Thomas Hardy's. Asserts Blackmore's portrayal of rural England ranks with Dickens' portraits of cockney London.

Sutton, Max Keith. *R. D. Blackmore*. Boston: Twayne, 1979. Provides an excellent beginning source, the most detailed critical study of *Lorna Doone*. Short biography provides updated information about Blackmore's life. Extensive discussion of the novel's mythic nature, both as an initiation rite and as a re-creation of the story of Persephone and Demeter. Analyzes character, theme, symbol, and language.

LOST HORIZON

Type of work: Novel
Author: James Hilton (1900-1954)
Type of plot: Adventure
Time of plot: 1931
Locale: Tibet
First published: 1933

> *Principal characters:*
> HUGH CONWAY, a British consul
> RUTHERFORD, his friend
> HENRY BARNARD, an American embezzler
> MISS BRINKLOW, a missionary
> CAPTAIN MALLINSON, another British consul
> CHANG, a Chinese lama
> FATHER PERRAULT, the High Lama

The Story:

When Rutherford found Hugh Conway, a former schoolmate, suffering from fatigue and amnesia in a mission hospital, Conway related a weird and almost unbelievable story concerning his disappearance many months before.

Conway was a member of the consulate at Baskul when trouble broke out there in May, 1931, and he was considered a hero because of the efficiency and coolness he displayed while white civilians were being evacuated. When it was his turn to leave, he boarded a plane in the company of Miss Roberta Brinklow, a missionary, Henry Barnard, an American, and Captain Charles Mallinson, another member of the consulate. The plane was a special high-altitude cabin aircraft provided by the Maharajah of Chandapore. Conway was thirty-seven years old and had been in the consular service for ten years. His work had not been spectacular, and he was expecting to rest in England before being assigned to another undistinguished post.

After the plane had been in the air about two hours, Mallinson noticed that their pilot was the wrong man and that they were not headed toward Peshawur, the first scheduled stop. Conway was undisturbed until he realized they were flying over strange mountain ranges. When the pilot landed and armed tribesmen refueled the plane before it took off again, Conway began to agree with Mallinson and Barnard, who thought they had been kidnapped and would be held for ransom.

When Conway tried to question the pilot, the man pointed a revolver at him. A little after midnight, the pilot landed again, this time narrowly averting a crackup. The passengers climbed out of the plane and found the pilot badly injured. Conway believed that they were high on the Tibetan plateau, far beyond the western range of the Himalaya Mountains. The air was bitterly cold, with no signs of human habitation in this region of sheer-walled mountains. The pilot died before morning, murmuring something about a lamasery called Shangri-La. As the little group started in search of the lamasery, they saw a group of men coming toward them.

When the men reached them, one introduced himself in perfect English; he was a Chinese named Chang. Following the men, Conway and his friends arrived at the lamasery of Shangri-La that evening. There they found central heat, plumbing, and many other luxuries more commonly found only in the West. They were given fine rooms and excellent food. They learned that there was a High Lama whom they would not be privileged to meet. Although Chang told them porters would arrive in a few weeks to lead them back to the outer world, Conway had the strange feeling that their coming had not been an accident and that they were not destined to leave soon.

Presently, Chang told them that Conway was to be honored by an interview with the High Lama. Mallinson begged him to force the High Lama to provide guides for them, for Mallinson had learned that Barnard was wanted for fraud and embezzlement in the United States and was anxious to turn Barnard over to the British authorities. Conway, however, did not discuss their departure with the High Lama, whom he found a very intelligent and very old man. Instead, he listened to the lama's remarkable story of Father Perrault, a Capuchin friar lost in the mountains in 1734, when he was fifty-three years old. Father Perrault had found sanctuary in a lamasery and had stayed there after adopting the Buddhist faith. In 1789, the old man lay dying, but the miraculous power of some drugs he had perfected, coupled with the marvelous air on the plateau, prolonged his life. Later, tribesmen from the valley helped him build the lamasery of Shangri-La, where he lived the life of a scholar. In 1804, another European came to the lamasery; then others came from Europe and from Asia. No guest was ever allowed to leave.

Conway learned then that the kidnapping of their plane had been deliberate. More important, he learned that the High Lama was Father Perrault and that he was two hundred and fifty years old. The old man told Conway that all who lived at Shangri-La had the secret of long life. He had sent the pilot for new people because he believed a war was coming that would destroy all known civilization; Shangri-La would then be the nucleus of a new world. His picture of life in the lamasery pleased Conway. He was content to stay.

Conway knew that the others would find it hard to accept the news and did not tell them that they could never leave. Mallinson continued to talk of the coming of the porters, but Barnard and Miss Brinklow announced that they intended to pass up the first opportunity to leave Shangri-La and wait for a later chance. Barnard faced jail if he returned, and Miss Brinklow thought she should not miss the opportunity to convert the lamas and the tribesmen in the valley.

The weeks passed pleasantly for Conway. He met a Frenchman called Briac, who had been Chopin's pupil. He also met Lo-Tsen, a Chinese woman who seemed quite young, but Chang told him she was really sixty-five years old. Conway had more meetings with the High Lama; at one of the meetings, the old man told Conway that he knew he was going to die at last and that he wanted Conway to take his place as ruler of the lamasery and the valley and to act wisely so that all culture would not be lost after war had destroyed Western civilization.

While he was explaining these matters, the old lama lay back in his chair, and Conway knew the lama was dead. Conway wandered out into the garden, too moved to talk to anyone. He was interrupted by Mallinson, with the news that the porters had arrived. Although Barnard and Miss Brinklow would not leave, Mallinson had paid the porters to wait for him and Conway. Mallinson said that the Chinese woman was going with them, that he had made love to her and that she wanted to stay with him. Conway tried to tell Mallinson that the woman was really an old woman who would die if she left the valley, but Mallinson refused to listen. At first, Conway also refused to leave Shangri-La, but after Mallinson and the woman started and then came back because they were afraid to go on alone, Conway felt responsible for them as well and left the lamasery with them. He felt that he was fleeing from the place where he would be happy for the rest of his life.

Rutherford ended his story at that point, for Conway had slipped away and disappeared. Later, Rutherford met a doctor who told him that Conway had been brought to the mission by a woman, a bent, withered, old Chinese woman. Perhaps, then, the story was true. Convinced that Conway had headed for the hidden lamasery, Rutherford hoped that his journey had been successful, that Conway had reached Shangri-La.

Critical Evaluation:

In *Lost Horizon*, James Hilton combines disillusioned pessimism with romantic escapism. It is significant that the novel begins in Berlin, where two terrible specters of the period, the Great Depression and Adolf Hitler, loom in the reader's mind. Given the apparent collapse of "rational" Western civilization, it is not surprising that a fiction writer should look to the East for an idealized and exotic sanctuary.

It is also important that the hero of this quest, Hugh Conway, although jaded by his experiences, still embodies basic Western virtues—a strong sense of purpose, personal loyalty, a rigid ethic, and efficiency, especially during moments of crisis. Hilton gives readers the best of both worlds. On the intellectual level, he postulates a synthesis of Eastern moderation and Western activism; on the emotional level, he confronts the complexities and tensions of the times with a hopeful vision that shows the best in the Western tradition surviving, even if the worst destroys itself.

Hilton's small group of involuntary explorers is well chosen, if not deeply characterized. They are all characteristic Western types, and the qualities they represent can, to a considerable extent, account for the state of the modern world.

Miss Brinklow symbolizes Western missionary zeal, in a rather benign and comical form. Of the four, she is the most easily recognized stereotype—the righteous, moralistic, spinster lady who, having no personal life of her own, tries to interfere with everyone else's. Hilton's treatment of the type, however, is gently ironical rather than sharply satirical; Miss Brinklow is likable, sincere, and feisty, rather than priggish and icy. Her plans to convert and animate the Tibetan peasants are taken seriously by no one but herself. The implications of her actions, however, are not so amusing; such missionary fervor in souls less benevolent than Miss Brinklow's leads to violence and oppression.

Henry Barnard, the American financier, suggests the pragmatic, greedy, opportunistic side of Western culture. Personally, he is a most engaging character—affable, entertaining, adaptable, easygoing, and levelheaded. He is also a wanted criminal. He insists that circumstances and bad luck caught up with him and forced him into defensive monetary manipulations, that he is a fugitive by accident and a victim himself—the classic rationalization of the white-collar criminal.

Miss Brinklow and Barnard, however, are easily distracted in Shangri-La, and their vices are indulged harmlessly. Presumably they will eventually outgrow their particular Western preoccupations and achieve that detached serenity characteristic in the Valley of the Blue Moon. The third member of the party, Captain Mallinson, is another matter.

Mallinson is young, passionate, idealistic, and loyal. He is, perhaps, even more admirable as an individual and more dangerous as a character type. A product of an upper-class British gentleman's education, Mallinson firmly believes in all the ideals of his country and class: honor, common sense, patriotism, and a hard distinction between right and wrong—with rightness residing in the upper-class English view of life. Mallinson saw Conway acting with heroism in the Baskul evacuation, so Mallison idealizes Conway. As Conway adjusts to Shangri-La, Mallinson berates him for not living up to that idealization. Mallinson is the one member of the party who is so Westernized that he cannot adapt to Shangri-La for even a short time. To him, life in the lamasery is "unhealthy and unclean . . . hateful . . . filthy." Mallinson feels that anything he cannot understand or relate to is wrong and deserves destruction. "God," he tells Conway, "I'd give a good deal to fly over with a load of bombs!" Mallinson's idealism and passion, coupled with his narrowness of vision, make him the most dangerous of the group.

Therefore, all three characters are people who are personally likable and admirable but who embody qualities that, if pursued to their logical and probable conclusions, would bring devastation upon themselves and the civilization they so admire and seek to serve.

Conway also represents a characteristic failing in Western society. Although he is not destructive, he contributes nothing toward averting the impending chaos. He clearly embodies the best qualities of the cultivated Westerner. He is intelligent, sensitive, tolerant, sympathetic, courageous when he has to be, and resourceful. To his detriment and the detriment of his culture, he is also without any direction or purpose. He is not able to avert the destruction brought on by the zealot, the criminal, or the idealist. For all of his knowledge and talent, he has wandered aimlessly from one minor diplomatic post to another, never much caring where he has been or where he is headed, only hoping for a few incidental pleasures along the way. "Label me '1914-18,'" he tells the High Lama, "I used up most of my passion and energies during the years I've mentioned . . . the chief thing I've asked from the world since then is to leave me alone." Therefore, Conway represents the potential leader who understands the world and has the capacities at least to attempt to deal with it but whose will has been stultified by the traumas and complexities of the times. The underlying question of the book is whether or not Conway will find the will and purpose that he needs in Shangri-La.

The answer to that question and the center of the novel lies in the series of interviews between Conway and the High Lama, Father Perrault. In these scenes, the history and nature of Shangri-La are explored, and its mission is presented to Conway. For his part, he must measure his own values, experiences, and apathy against the doctrines presented by the High Lama.

Despite the Tibetan trappings, Shangri-La is a very Western establishment. All the high officials and prime movers have been transplanted Europeans, especially Father Perrault, once a Capuchin friar, and his practical right-hand man, Henschell, an Austrian soldier. The central philosophy is the Aristotelian golden mean, and the underlying assumption is that if human life can be extended long enough, people will outlive the passions and extremes that lead to destruction. The purpose of Shangri-La, therefore, is survival: "We may pray to outlive the doom that gathers around on every side," Perrault tells Conway. "Then, my son, when the strong have devoured each other, the Christian ethic may at last be fulfilled, and the meek shall inherit the earth."

Conway apparently has already achieved a state of passionlessness and possesses the Western capacities of practicality, rationalism, and efficiency. He is the logical choice as Perrault's successor. The old man tells Conway so and then promptly dies. Almost immediately thereafter, Mallinson proposes an escape back to civilization, and Conway is forced to the climactic decision of the novel.

Despite Mallison's irritating behavior, Conway likes Mallinson, to some extent identifies with him, and, because of Mallinson's idealization, feels responsibility toward the younger man. When Conway learns that Lo-Tsen will accompany them and that she and Mallinson are romantically attracted, his feelings and ideas about Shangri-La are shaken. He respects honest, youthful passion and is not too old to feel some of it himself—especially with regard to Lo-Tsen. At the logical level, Mallinson has doubts about the High Lama's story. He dismisses Conway's references to the woman's age as absurd, and Lo-Tsen's willingness to leave the valley supports the young man's analysis. In summary, all Conway "felt was that he liked Mallinson and must help him; he was doomed, like millions, to flee wisdom and be a hero."

Therefore, the rational hero acts, finally, on impulse; the passionless spectator acts out of feeling. Such reversals are not unusual in the best of writing and may be a sign of complexity and stature in a character, or they may represent an easy way to solve a difficult plot dilemma. Whether or not the reader can accept such a facile resolution is a matter of individual taste and judgment. What is most important about *Lost Horizon*, however, is that in it James Hilton creates a new mythical kingdom, an exotic retreat to serenity and moderation, perfectly suited to the frenzied and bombarded sensibilities of the Westerner.

Bibliography:

Crawford, John W. "The Utopian Dream: Alive and Well." *Cuyahoga Review*, Spring/Summer, 1984, 27-33. Compares *Lost Horizon* and Aldous Huxley's 1962 novel *Island*, citing them as two rare examples of utopias appearing in a century of dystopias.

_____. "Utopian Eden of *Lost Horizon*." *Extrapolation* 22 (Summer, 1981): 186-190. Places *Lost Horizon* in the utopian tradition of such writers as John Milton, Samuel Johnson, and H. G. Wells, and likens its appeal to that enjoyed by such popular authors as Rudyard Kipling and H. Rider Haggard.

Heck, Francis S. "The Domain as a Symbol of a Paradise Lost: *Lost Horizon* and *Brideshead Revisited*." *The Nassau Review: The Journal of Nassau Community College Devoted to Arts, Letters, and Sciences* 4, no. 3 (1982): 24-29. Discusses significant parallels between *Lost Horizon* and Evelyn Waugh's 1945 novel, *Brideshead Revisited*. Heck and Crawford (above) are notable for comparing Hilton to other, more critically accepted writers.

"Utopia in Tibet." Review of *Lost Horizon*, by James Hilton. *The New York Times Book Review*, October 15, 1933, 8-9. One of the first U.S. reviews of *Lost Horizon*. The anonymous writer finds the characters and their problems too unrealized to make an impression, but calls the picture of the lamasery in Shangri-La memorable.

Whissen, Thomas R. *Classic Cult Fiction: A Companion to Popular Cult Literature*. Westport, Conn.: Greenwood Press, 1992. The chapter on *Lost Horizon* points out that Shangri-La has become part of our vocabulary and treats its popularity in terms of the myths it utilizes. The best single investigation of the book's perennial appeal.

LOST ILLUSIONS

Type of work: Novel
Author: Honoré de Balzac (1799-1850)
Type of plot: Naturalism
Time of plot: Early nineteenth century
Locale: Angoulême, France
First published: Illusions perdues, 1837-1843 (English translation, 1893)

Principal characters:
DAVID SÉCHARD, a printer
EVE, his wife
LUCIEN CHARDON, his brother-in-law
MADAME DE BARGETON, a woman loved by Lucien

The Story:

Angoulême was divided into two classes: the aristocrats of fashionable society and the bourgeois. David Séchard and Lucien Chardon were scarcely aware that they belonged to the less privileged class. Lucien was the brilliant, handsome, unstable son of a chemist. David was the sober, kind son of a printer.

David's father sent him to Paris to learn all the latest innovations in the printing trade. The illiterate father, avaricious and mean, hoped that David would learn how to extract more money from the old-fashioned print shop of Séchard and Son. When David returned from Paris, his father quickly sold him the business at a high price and retired to his vineyard.

Partly because of his friendship with poetic Lucien and partly because of his temperament, David did not prosper. He was always discussing a grand project with Lucien or dreaming of Eve, Lucien's beautiful sister. Lucien wrote some verses that attracted attention. Even the aristocrats of the town heard of him, and Madame de Bargeton, a thirty-six-year-old woman married to an old husband, invited him to one of her famous evening gatherings. Eve scrimped to buy Lucien the proper clothes for the occasion. The evening was not an entire success. Few except Madame de Bargeton listened to Lucien's poetry, but he made a real conquest of his hostess.

While Lucien did his best to break into society and win the heart of Madame de Bargeton, David and Eve were quietly falling in love. David strained his resources to the utmost to furnish rooms over the print shop for his wife-to-be, a room at the rear for his mother-in-law, and a comfortable room on the street for Lucien. David had determined to promote Lucien's literary talent by supporting him. Two days before the wedding, Lucien was surprised in Madame de Bargeton's boudoir. Her husband, old as he was, fought a duel with a man who had gossiped about Madame de Bargeton. Not wishing to face the scandal, Madame de Bargeton decided to go to Paris, and Lucien was to follow her. With a heavy heart, for he knew Lucien's weaknesses, David drove his friend at night along the Paris road. Safely away from Angoulême, Lucien joined his mistress.

David and Eve married and settled into their new rooms. Eve was a devoted wife, although foolishly fond of her scapegrace brother. Before her child was born, she began to grow uneasy. Lucien wrote very seldom, and David paid little attention to his business. He was too busy working on an experiment to find a new way to make paper without rags. If he could invent a new process, they would all be rich. Meanwhile the family was desperately in need, for Lucien's demands for money kept them poor. At last Eve herself took charge of the print shop.

She had her first small success when she thought of the idea of printing a *Shepherd's Calendar*, a cheap almanac to peddle to farmers, but the firm of Cointet Brothers, rivals in the printing trade, gave her so much unfair competition that she made only a small profit from her printing venture. After her baby came, she had to give up her efforts for a while. David was more than ever wrapped up in his attempts to find a new process for making paper.

Meanwhile, Lucien had failed completely to make his way in Paris. He had quarreled with his rich mistress, and they had parted. He could find only odd jobs as a journalist. He borrowed continually from David to lead the dissolute life of a man-about-town. Finally, when he went to live openly with Coralie, an actress, he lost all chances for any real success.

Pressed for money, Lucien forged David's name to notes for three thousand francs. When the firm of Cointet Brothers, acting as bankers, presented the notes to David for payment, he was unable to raise the money. The lawsuit that followed disturbed Eve so much that she had to hire a wet nurse for her baby; in the eyes of the people of her small French town, she was disgraced. Cointet Brothers promised a profitable marriage to Petit-Claud, David's lawyer, if he would prolong the suit, increase the costs to David, and eventually force him into debtor's prison. During the delays, Eve and David both appealed to his father for help, but the old miser refused aid to his son. He was mainly interested in collecting rent for the building in which David had his shop. With all help denied, David went into hiding and worked feverishly on his paper process.

In Paris, Coralie died, leaving Lucien without a place to live. Having no money, he began the long walk home. One night he caught a ride among the trunks of a carriage and went to sleep on his precarious perch. When he awoke the carriage had stopped. As he got off he saw that he had been riding with his former mistress, Madame de Bargeton, now Madame la Comtesse Châtelet, wife of the new prefect of the district. She and her husband laughed openly as the disheveled Lucien stalked away.

A few miles from Angoulême, Lucien became ill and sought refuge with a miller. Thinking Lucien was near death, the miller sent for a priest. When Lucien begged for news of his family, the priest told him of David's troubles. Lucien hurried to town to see what he could do for the brother-in-law he had helped to ruin. In Angoulême, Lucien was sorrowfully received by his sister. To add to the distress of David and his family, Cointet Brothers published in the paper a glowing account of Lucien's successes in Paris. There was a parade in Lucien's honor, and the Châtelets even invited him to dinner.

Realizing that he still had a hold over Madame de Châtelet, Lucien tried to get David released from his debts through her influence. Meanwhile, after seeing some samples of David's work, the Cointets offered to pay off his debts, buy his print shop, and develop his invention for him. The offer, however, was intended to bring David out of hiding. Then a letter from Lucien to his friend was intercepted and a forged note substituted, appointing a place of meeting. On the way to the meeting, David was arrested and thrown into prison. Lucien, after a despairing farewell to his sister, left Angoulême. He intended to kill himself, but on the road he was picked up by a Spanish priest, an emissary traveling between Madrid and Paris. The envoy saw promise in Lucien and offered him fifteen thousand francs in return for Lucien's promise to do as the priest wished. The Spaniard meant to acquire power through Lucien's attraction for women and his poetic fervor. The bargain sealed, Lucien sent the fifteen thousand francs to David.

The money arrived just after David had signed away his shop and his papermaking process to the Cointets. David and Eve retired to the country and in due time inherited money and a vineyard from his father. Petit-Claud, the double-crossing lawyer, became a famous prosecutor. The Cointets made a great fortune from David's process, and one of them became a deputy and a peer.

Critical Evaluation:

Honoré de Balzac wrote *Lost Illusions* after he had finally succeeded in conceiving of his life's work as a large, comprehensive, and accurate portrayal of contemporary French society. Almost every novel he would write or had written was to become a part of this larger entity, which he called *The Human Comedy*, in reference to the Italian epic poem *The Divine Comedy* (c. 1320) by Dante Alighieri. When *Lost Illusions* began appearing in serial form in 1837, Balzac's conception of the narrative framework for his life's work was taking shape as well. Balzac's famous introduction to the first edition of *The Human Comedy*, in which he provides the theoretical basis for his enterprise, appeared in 1842, which is roughly when the three narratives that make up *Lost Illusions* were completed.

Lost Illusions concerns itself with the indissoluble relationship between art and money, a recurring obsession throughout Balzac's work. The experiences of the two main characters, Lucien and David, illustrate the difficulty of escaping from the corrupting power of society, represented by market forces. At first readers see the two men as close friends, although physical and psychological opposites. David is the conscientious, unassuming, and quietly proud craftsman who hopes to become rich by marketing a new process for making paper. Lucien desires immortality as an author. David's ambitions are to be useful to society while remaining in the provinces. Lucien is self-interested and sees his destiny in Paris.

When Lucien leaves in order to make a name for himself, however, he gradually comes to view his art as a business rather than a vocation. As he squanders David's money in the attempt to reach his goal, he justifies his actions as an investment in himself, which would pay off in the form of literary fame and material wealth. The reader begins to realize that the two men's fates are not only linked, but also very similar, and that David's print business and Lucien's writing are simply two aspects of the same industry. Another apparent difference is undermined when it becomes clear that Paris, rather than being the opposite of the provinces, is in truth simply the distillation of the corrupt way of life that exists everywhere.

Lucien's downfall begins as soon as he arrives in Paris from Angoulême. Its causes reach back to the beginning of the novel when he tries his best to shine in the literary salon of Madame de Bargeton. His good looks and charm seduce her at least as much as his poetry. Hoping to make an impression in the big city, the first thing he does is buy the best clothes, boots, and accessories he can find. When he shows them off at the opera that same evening, however, he realizes that his flashy, off-the-rack wardrobe identifies him as a vulgar provincial. His quest for artistic success immediately becomes subordinate to the desire to appear successful, which he is never able to satisfy. Every time he feels he has achieved a goal, he learns that it is still beyond his grasp. From the beginning, therefore, the aspiring artist deviates from his proper path as a result of the corrupting forces that he is too weak to control.

Balzac's pessimism about the fate of the individual in society is a constant in this novel and in most of his work. True feeling also is in doubt, since Lucien does not let the reader or himself know whether his love for Madame de Bargeton is genuine or whether he merely uses her as an instrument for the fulfillment of his ambitions. Noble principles and abstractions repeatedly turn into their mundane counterparts: Love becomes prostitution; literature becomes journalism; greatness becomes material wealth. At the end of Lucien's Parisian adventures, the mysterious Spanish priest who once saved him from suicide gives him a lesson in life that provides a summary of all his experiences in Paris, as well as a blueprint for the future. Armed with this new pragmatism, the aspiring artist may, perhaps, conquer the world, which Lucien sets out to do in the sequel to *Lost Illusions*.

Only through reading the novels that come before and after *Lost Illusions* does one fully realize the identity of the Spanish priest: He is Vautrin, a master criminal who escapes from the prison where he had been sent in Balzac's earlier novel, *Père Goriot* (1834-1835). This revelation points out one of the most effective techniques of Balzac's writing, the use of recurring characters throughout *The Human Comedy*. Alluding to characters and events from other novels, and using the same characters from one novel to another, Balzac reinforces the impression that his great work constitutes a unified world, rather than a series of discrete narratives. A character—Eugène de Rastignac—in *Père Goriot*, for example, makes an appearance in *Lost Illusions*. Several other characters appear in the sequel to *Lost Illusions* and in other works, making the novel a meeting place not only of major Balzac themes but also of characters and plots.

Not all is bleak in *Lost Illusions*. While in Paris, Lucien belongs to a group of young artists known as the Cenacle, led by the passionate Daniel d'Arthez. They are devoted to literature in its purest form. Lucien betrays the Cenacle (whose name alludes to Jesus and his disciples), and d'Arthez and the other members are not immune to corruption themselves, but the group nevertheless stands as a reminder of artistic achievement outside the marketplace. David's process for manufacturing paper proves to be a success, confirming his genius as an inventor. His bankruptcy, caused by Lucien, may be considered a blessing in disguise, since it forces him away from a corrupt society in which an honest man such as he cannot succeed. Eve remains steadfastly devoted as a wife to David and a sister to Lucien, symbolizing the disinterested side of human nature and presenting a type of feminine ideal to which Balzac often returns. Such sentimental, transcendent values are common in Balzac.

With *Lost Illusions*, Balzac creates a new variation on the genre of the *Bildungsroman*, or novel of formation. According to tradition, the hero of such a novel finds a place and achieves individual fulfillment when the institutions of society are in harmony with the individual's ambitions. In Balzac, the opposite occurs: The hero succeeds when he gives up his individuality and idealism. By recognizing the alienation resulting from such a process, Balzac was a precursor to modern novelists. His characterization of art as a hostage to crass commercialism is an uncanny prefiguration of some of the concerns of artists of the twentieth century.

"Critical Evaluation" by M. Martin Guiney

Bibliography:

Adamson, Donald. *Balzac: Illusions Perdues*. London: Grant and Cutler, 1981. A comprehensive, step-by-step guide that greatly facilitates the student's task. The best introduction available in English.

Festa-McCormick, Diana. *Honoré de Balzac*. Boston: Twayne, 1979. Contains a chapter on *Lost Illusions* and its sequel, pointing out certain faults in each work, such as excessive length and detail, but also explaining why the books are among Balzac's best novels. Draws interesting parallels to other novels by Balzac.

Marceau, Félicien. *Balzac and His World*. Translated by Derek Coltman. New York: Orion Press, 1966. Provides the best available overview of the complex fictional world Balzac created. Contains an index of the characters in the *Human Comedy*. Marceau looks for the recurring characters and themes in Balzac's novels.

Maurois, André. *Prometheus: The Life of Balzac*. Translated by Norman Denny. London: Bodley Head, 1965. An accessible introduction to Balzac's life. Describes the circumstances of the creation of his major works in fascinating detail.

Schilling, Bernard N. *The Hero as Failure: Balzac and the Rubempré Cycle*. Chicago: University of Chicago Press, 1968. A scholarly, accessible study that situates the novel within the various contexts of French history, Balzac's work, works by other authors that deal with similar themes, and the French society of the nineteenth century.

A LOST LADY

Type of work: Novel
Author: Willa Cather (1873-1947)
Type of plot: Domestic realism
Time of plot: Late nineteenth century
Locale: Nebraska
First published: 1923

> *Principal characters:*
> CAPTAIN FORRESTER, a railroad constructor
> MRS. FORRESTER, his wife
> JUDGE POMMEROY, his friend and legal adviser
> NIEL HERBERT, the judge's nephew
> IVY PETERS, a shyster lawyer

The Story:

The Forrester home at Sweet Water was a stopping-off place for railroad magnates riding through the prairie states along the Burlington line. Old Captain Forrester liked to drive his guests from the station and watch them as they approached his estate. He enjoyed their praise of his stock farm and their delight when his charming wife met them at the front door. Everyone from railroad presidents to the village butcher boy and the kitchen maids liked Mrs. Forrester; her manner was always one of friendliness and respect.

Niel Herbert's acquaintance with Mrs. Forrester began when he fell from a tree while playing with some village boys on the Captain's property, and Mrs. Forrester summoned a doctor. He did not know it at the time, but Mrs. Forrester had already singled him out from the others because he was Judge Pommeroy's nephew. After his recovery, he was often invited to the Forrester home with his uncle.

The boy who had caused Niel's fall was Ivy Peters. He had winged a woodpecker and then had slit its eyes. The bird had fumbled back into its hole, and Niel was trying to reach the creature to put it out of its misery when he lost his balance and fell.

During a period of hard times, Niel's father went out of business and left Sweet Water. Niel stayed on to read law in his uncle's office. A few days before Christmas, Mrs. Forrester invited Niel to her home to help entertain Constance Ogden, the daughter of one of the Captain's friends, who was coming to spend the holidays with the Forresters. Also included in the party was Frank Ellinger, a bachelor of forty. The dinner was a festive one. Niel decided that Constance was neither pretty nor pleasant. It was evident that she had designs on Frank Ellinger.

The following day, Niel was asked to stay with Constance during the afternoon, while Mrs. Forrester and Frank took the small cutter and went after cedar for the Christmas decorations. The Blum boy, out hunting, saw Mrs. Forrester and Frank after he came upon the deserted cutter beside a thicket, but he did not give away their secret. The doings of the rich were not his concern, and Mrs. Forrester had been kind to him on many occasions.

During that winter, Judge Pommeroy and his nephew often went to play cards with the Forresters. One night, during a snowstorm, Mrs. Forrester revealed to Niel how much she missed the excitement and glamour of former winters at fashionable resorts. She mocked the life of quiet domesticity which she and the Captain were living.

In the spring, the Captain went to Denver on business, and while he was gone, Frank Ellinger arrived for a visit. One morning, Niel cut a bouquet of wild roses to leave outside the windows of Mrs. Forrester's bedroom. Suddenly he heard from the bedroom the voices of Mrs. Forrester and Frank Ellinger. The first illusion of his life was shattered by a man's yawn and a woman's laugh.

When the Captain came home from Denver, he announced that he was a poor man. Having satisfied his creditors, he had only his pension from the Civil War and the income from his farm left. Shortly afterward, the Captain had a stroke.

Niel continued to visit the sick man and his wife. He realized that Mrs. Forrester was facing her new life with terror, which she tried to hide for her husband's sake. Niel, having decided to become an architect, left Sweet Water to spend two years at school in the East. When he returned, he learned that Ivy Peters, shrewd and grasping, had become an important person in the town. Niel, who despised Peters, was disappointed to learn that Peters, now the Captain's tenant, had drained the marsh where the boys had gone fishing years before. The Captain himself had become wasted and old. Most of the time, he sat in his garden staring at a strange sundial he had made.

Niel learned that Mrs. Forrester, who seemed little older, was still writing to Frank Ellinger. He observed, too, that Mrs. Forrester treated Peters with easy familiarity, and he wondered how she could be on friendly terms with the pushy young lawyer.

That summer, a storm flooded the fields along the creek. Niel went to Judge Pommeroy's office to read. He thought of an item he had seen in the Denver paper earlier in the day: Frank Ellinger had finally married Constance Ogden. Close to midnight, Mrs. Forrester, drenched to the skin, appeared at the office. At her demand, Niel made the telephone connection with Ellinger in Colorado Springs. Mrs. Forrester began to talk politely, as though complimenting Ellinger on his marriage. Then she became hysterical. When she began to scream reproaches, Niel cut the wires. Mrs. Forrester recovered after her collapse, but the gossipy town telephone operator pieced together a village scandal from what she had overheard. Captain Forrester died in December. None of his wealthy friends attended the funeral, but old settlers and former employees came to do honor to the railroad pioneer who had been one of the heroes of the early West.

One day, Mr. Ogden stopped in Sweet Water. He thought that Judge Pommeroy ought to send a claim to Washington to have Mrs. Forrester's pension increased. Niel was forced to explain that Mrs. Forrester had turned her affairs over to Ivy Peters.

After her husband's death, Mrs. Forrester began to entertain Ivy Peters and other young men of the village. At her urging, Niel went to one party, but he was disgusted with the cheap manners of both hostess and guests. He could not bear to see the old Captain's home thus abused.

Niel felt that an era was ending. The great old people who had built the railroads and towns, such as the Judge and the Captain and their friends, were passing. The old men of gallant manners and their lovely ladies had gone forever. In their place was a new type of man, the shrewd opportunist, like Ivy Peters. On the day Niel saw Peters putting his arms around Mrs. Forrester, he decided to leave Sweet Water.

As long as his uncle lived, however, he had news of Mrs. Forrester. The Judge wrote that she was sadly broken. Then his uncle died, and Niel heard no more for many years.

A long time afterward, a mutual friend told him what had happened to his lost lady. She had gone to California. Later, she had married a rich Englishman and had gone with him to South America. She had dyed her hair and had dressed expensively in an effort to keep her youth.

Finally, one year, came a letter from Mrs. Forrester's English husband. It enclosed money for the continued care of Captain Forrester's grave. His gift was a memorial to his late wife, Marian Forrester Collins.

Critical Evaluation:

Willa Cather was of a generation of writers who lived through the passing of the old frontier, who saw the region of the homesteader transformed into a countryside of tidy farms and small towns. She found in the primitive virtues of the pioneer experience her values as an artist. The West is the setting of her best work, and the past is its spiritual home.

A Lost Lady is the first example in Cather's writing of what she called the novel *démeublé*, or fiction stripped of all "furnishings." Her method is well illustrated in the scene in which young Niel suffers his disillusionment in Marian Forrester. The whole passage is built upon the symbol of the wild roses that Niel picks early in the morning to place on Marian's windowsill so that she will find them when she opens the blinds of her bedroom. As he bends to place the flowers, he hears beyond the closed blinds a woman's laugh: "impatient, indulgent, teasing, eager," and then a man's "like a yawn." Niel flees and throws the roses in the mud where cattle can trample them. The brief bloom of his worship of Mrs. Forrester is gone like the transient beauty of the flowers. *A Lost Lady* is short, a reflection of Cather's philosophy of the novel *démeublé*. Its prose is stripped of unnecessary adjectives; circumstantial details are taken away.

Niel Herbert initially looks upon Marian Forrester as an idol. Niel sees her as a woman of Old World charm who is gracious and can do no wrong. The novel is the story of how Marian changes. Many critics have seen *A Lost Lady* as a study in the degeneration of the title character as well as society. Cather wrote *A Lost Lady* during the Depression, a time of little hope. The Forresters originally represented gentility and the code of the pioneers. When the Captain's bank failed, he lived by the code and repaid the bank's investors from his personal fortune until he was bankrupt. He wanted to be an honorable man even though it meant personal sacrifice for him and his wife. Cather, like Niel, admired the old values and the pioneer spirit. She wrote: "The Old West had been settled by dreamers, great-hearted adventurers who were practical to the point of magnificence; a courteous brotherhood, strong in attack but weak in defence, who could conquer but could not hold." For the cunning and the self-interested, who can hold, the novel has little respect. The Forresters are symbolic of the declining spirit of the West. As Niel matures, he not only sees a change in Marian as she adopts the habits and philosophies of the new era and rejects the values of her husband and the pioneers but also sadly observes the change in the values of his society in general. The pioneer spirit had given way to the values incarnated in the amoral Ivy Peters.

Cather based *A Lost Lady* on a true story. In her childhood, Cather had liked a woman named Mrs. Lyra Garber. Cather's goal in writing *A Lost Lady* was to recapture the feelings that Mrs. Garber invoked in her. Cather did little to conceal that Marian is Mrs. Lyra Garber. Garber's husband Silas was a Nebraskan builder and a captain in the Union army. Marian's husband likewise was a captain who lived in Nebraska. Silas Garber founded Red Cloud, Cather's hometown. As the town became more settled, Garber became wealthy from the banking business and eventually, in 1873, became governor of Nebraska. Garber, a widower, visited California to meet his brother and sister-in-law. He was also introduced to his sister-in-law's sister, Lyra Wheeler. He fell in love and married her. They settled in Lincoln, Nebraska, at the governor's mansion, and later they came to live in Red Cloud. Garber's bank failed, and he lost his fortune as well as his health. Garber fell from a carriage and was injured. After Captain Garber died, Lyra moved away from Red Cloud, returning to California and remarrying. There are many parallels between the life of Lyra Garber and that of Marian Forrester.

"Critical Evaluation" by Mary C. Bagley

Bibliography:

Dollar, J. Gerard. "Community and Connectedness in *A Lost Lady*." In *Willa Cather: Family, Community and History*, edited by John J. Murphy et al. Provo, Utah: Brigham Young University Humanities Publications Center, 1990. Sees *A Lost Lady* in relation to Cather's statement that 1922 was the year "the world broke in two." Claims the novel is about connectedness and disconnectedness, with the latter as predominant.

Harris, Richard C. "First Loves: Willa Cather's Niel Herbert and Ivan Turgenev's Vladimir Petrovich." *Studies in American Fiction* 17 (Spring, 1989): 81-91. Relates how Cather received the idea to write *A Lost Lady* from knowing Mrs. Lyra Garber. Finds similarities between Ivan Turgenev's "First Love" and Cather's novel.

Helmick, Evelyn Thomas. "The Broken World: Medievalism in *A Lost Lady*." *Renascence* 28 (Autumn, 1975): 39-46. When Cather visited France, she made a remark that she wanted to live in the Middle Ages. Claims Captain Forrester is symbolic of a medieval king, and the railroad builders are symbolic of knights. Marks the transition of the age of heroes to lesser people.

Murphy, John J. "Euripides' *Hippolytus* and Cather's *A Lost Lady*." *American Literature* 53 (March, 1981): 72-86. Emphasizes Cather's classical education. Compares Hippolytus with Niel Herbert, in that they had the same temperament, and Phaedra, Hippolytus' wife, with Marian Forrester.

Rosowski, Susan J. "Willa Cather's *A Lost Lady:* The Paradoxes of Change." *Novel* 11, no. 1 (Fall, 1977): 51-62. Cather's later novels are the opposite of the earlier ones: The first ones emphasize the pioneer spirit and are positive; the latter ones show the decline of the pioneer spirit and a negative outlook on life.